Bill James presents . . .

STATS™ 1994
Major League
Handbook

STATS, Inc. • Bill James

STATS
PUBLISHING

Published by STATS Publishing
A division of Sports Team Analysis & Tracking Systems, Inc.
Dr. Richard Cramer, Chairman • John Dewan, President

Cover by John Grimwade, New York, NY

Photo by Tony Inzerillo, Bensenville, IL

First Edition: November, 1993

Printed in the United States of America

ISBN 1-8840-6400-0

This book is dedicated to

Dan Burton, Eric Faubert, Brian Gross, Sue Gripp, Kurt Hoyt, Mark Hughes, John Ricci, and Jim Warnock.

MVR's (Most Valuable Reporters) in 1993.

Acknowledgments

Hi. I'm not Bill James. I'm Steve Moyer. (I've wanted to see that in print for so long.) I've put in an inhuman amount of my time the last three Octobers getting this and our other two November books ready and, therefore, have been given the honor of writing these "Acknowledgments by Sue Dewan." The other eleven months of the year, I'm Director of Sports Operations here at STATS, making sure all our data gets here, and once it's here, making sure it's correct. (If you think I'm obnoxious and self-serving for mentioning myself first, Sue made me do it . . . not that you're totally inaccurate though.)

As STATS, Inc. continues to grow and produce new editions of our Reference Library, two somewhat pleasant problems have arisen: we are always pressed for page space due to the addition of new sections each year, and, for that reason, detailed acknowledgments for every STATS employee in each book are not possible. But we still do that in this book, the fifth edition of the old standby **Major League Handbook**. So, enjoy, STATS employees, because as a young friend of Chuck Miller's once said, "No one reads the acknowledgments."

Dr. Richard Cramer, Chairman of STATS, still keeps a watchful eye over his creation, logging onto the STATS system daily from his St. Louis area home and making semi-frequent trips to the STATS office. STATS customers who like STATS football On-Line or enjoyed our new In-Progress On-Line boxscores can thank Dick. Surely, he was rewarded in part this season by the success of his beloved Philadelphia Phillies. He also plays a mean BJFB "Winter Game."

John Dewan, President and CEO, continues to guide STATS' transition from a three-man operation to a thirty-employee growing business. It's not easy to hob-nob with top executives in the world of sports and still find 25 hours a day to produce three books in a two-week period. I don't think he takes Geritol yet, either.

Sue Dewan, Vice President, faces more challenges in the coming year. She will be taking back the reigns of the Computer Systems department in 1994, no small feat for a mother of two. If she can keep three-year-old Jason Dewan clear of the main on-off switch, surely her life will be easier.

Arthur Ashley, Vice President, serves as both software and hardware expert extraordinare. He knows much too much about many too many things, an unfortunate side effect of having been at STATS since 1988. Art enjoys the finer things in life, but can be found amidst the crowded Wrigley Field pressbox, PR'ing PR directors at least a few times a year.

Bob Mecca, Associate - Systems, will be heading for New England, while continuing as a STATS' full-timer from his new home. Bob will still be the main man when it comes to managing our immense baseball database. When working in his pajamas at three in the afternoon with the phone off the hook, I'm sure Bob will be a happy man.

Ross Schaufelberger, Director of Marketing, is highly regarded at STATS due to his prowess in marketing, client services, and general business savvy. Ross manages many of STATS' biggest accounts and STATS' continuous aggressive expansion can be attributed in large part to Ross' contributions.

David Pinto, Senior Associate - Systems, is our baseball/computer genius who works full-time at ESPN. During the off-baseball-season, David also works in New England in his pajamas. Say hi to Bob for us this winter, David.

Don Zminda, Director of Publications, joined the STATS staff full-time last Fall. Don's work can be enjoyed now in our brand new **1993-1994 Basketball Scoreboard** and later this Spring in our more traditional **Scouting Report:1994** and **1994 Baseball Scoreboard**. Karl Malone still refers to Don as "The Mailman."

Michael Coulter, Kevin Davis, Alissa Hudson, and Allan Spear work for me, and since my staff is the best, they'll get first mention. Kevin slayed the "GDIFF monster" (our enormous triple-check of every detail of every 1993 baseball game) practically by himself. Kevin will surely tell his children grisly tales of Friday nights during the summer of '93. Mike and Allan were this year's primary day and night editor, respectively, and now are spending most of their time keeping our football operations gaining yardage. Allan takes lots of abuse about his favorite baseball player (I'll spare his mention) and Mike about his preseason "sleeper" football team, the Atlanta Falcons. Needless to say, I respect their work even as I scoff at their preferences. Alissa has assumed our shipping responsibilities, which keeps her even more in touch with the customer service issues she loves and cares so much about. If you didn't get this book yet, be sure to call Alissa.

Jules Aquino, Jason Gumbs, Mike Hammer, Shawna Hawkins, Chuck Miller, Jim Musso, and Kenn Ruby work for Ross. Chuck works hard on advertising, graphic design, and basketball innovation. He'll also be happily married (for the first time, unbelievably) by the 1994 All-Star break. Congrats, Chuck! Jim Musso has, for the most part, taken over as Fantasy Game Guru. He wrestles each summer night about whether to allow Sue Dewan to trade all her good players to John for bums. Jules Aquino is known as "the nicest phone guy" and has also begun his climb up the ladder by assuming some important corporate responsibilites this year. Jules will be happily married barely two weeks into next season. Congrats Jules! Mike Hammer and Kenn Ruby moved from part to full-time status in 1993 and dissolve yards and yards of faxed football play-by-play into a neat, clean database between Sunday night and Wednesday each week. Mike is already happily married (sticking to the subject), while Kenn has no time for love. He needs to think about football. Shawna and Jason are new at STATS. Shawna will soon become very tired of looking at Ken Griffey, Jr. finishing his swing as she survives her first book season. Jason will find that his increased involvement in marketing and advertising will make taking advantage of Friday night Happy Hour drink specials more and more difficult.

Michael Canter, Stefan Kretchmann, Rob McQuown, Jeff Schinski, and Debbi Spence round out the systems staff. Michael's 1993 season was as effective as Willie Hernandez's 1984 and Michael will be trying his hand at management in 1994. Too bad Willie can't say the same. Rob churns out Player Profiles, Kickoff disks (our football reporter entry program), and football On-Line updates with equal ease. Rob also knows exactly how to throw the dice to avoid all the homers on Ben McDonald's 1992 Strato card. Stefan, Jeff, and Debbi are three more new STATS' employees, who will make an impact in 1994. Stefan already is the king of hockey programming, Jeff programmed the first ever minor league lefty/righty stats in the **Minor League Handbook** and also helped with the football On-Line. Debbi is settling in as head receptionist.

Stephanie Armstrong is John's new executive secretary and has already made a significant impact at STATS. And to conclude the subject, she'll be married by the time the six division races are winding down. Congrats, Stephanie! Marge Morra is always extremely pleasant and always willing to listen, while keeping on top of financial matters. Pat Quinn lends his desktop publishing and financial expertise to the cause when he's not Mr. Mom. Matt Greenberger does freelancing for us and stole my Al Simmons League crown away. Tom Hilgendorf takes time to creatively sell orphaned fantasy teams during his evenings.

Steve Heinecke works as a consultant to STATS in the promotion, design, and marketing of all titles in the STATS Publishing library. His efforts have been a boon to the growing popularity of our products.

And, finally, as always, a great big thanks to Bill James. If someone would have told me five years ago I'd be signing a card congratulating he and his wife on their new baby, I'd have fallen on the floor.

— *Steve Moyer*

Table of Contents

Introduction

Welcome back everyone. You're holding the biggest **Major League Handbook** ever published! In fact, it's so big this year that we were worried that our pre-printed covers wouldn't fit. If the cover looks a little off-center, you know why. There are two more teams this year and that's the main reason the book is bigger. But we've also added some new features, like additional minor league stats, a brand new Manager Tendencies section, and hitters pitching (so that our book is absolutely complete).

I hope you enjoy the book once again.

A Labor of Love

I have to tell you how this book gets done each year. There are three of us. Steve Moyer, Bob Mecca and me, John Dewan. From the last day of the regular baseball season until about two weeks later, the only things we do in life are eat, sleep and work on our three November 1 books. We get plenty of help from the rest of the STATS crew, but it's the three of us who are in the office until midnight or past almost every night.

Let me have Steve, who joined STATS two-and-a-half years ago, tell you why these books are so special to him and why he works so hard on them:

"This is a landmark edition for the **Major League Handbook**, this being the fifth year of its existence. Yes, a half-decade of **Major League Handbooks** have come to pass. Just to refresh my memory how far the book has come, I decided to take a look at the first edition of the book, the **STATS 1990 Major League Handbook**. I have fond memories of this book. I remember seeing it at the Willow Grove Mall in suburban Philadelphia, about an hour away from my old home. Even though the book sat on the shelf shrink-wrapped, Bill James' name on the cover prompted me to plunk down my $17.95 without any second thought. On the way home, I didn't open the wrap, but instead savored thoughts of what might be inside. Would it be stories? Predictions? Historical info? Well, it wasn't exactly any of those, and really didn't have a whole lot of Bill James in it at all."

"But it was far from a disappointment. I joined a Rotisserie League before the 1988 season and was used to the usual conglomeration of reference materials. This book had it all. I can picture all the guys asking to see my book while considering trades at our monthly meetings. And what did that magic book consist of? It had a cute little clip-art batter on the front, career major league stats for everyone who played in 1989, lefty-righty data, eight pages of leader boards, a bunch of in-depth player profiles, and projections. That's it. A total of 285 pages from cover to cover. (It's no wonder we're eating our shoes, with the size of this book now!) So what made this book so great? It was the concepts. So much of what was "cutting edge" about that book is now second nature. Just the fact that each player's age was in gigantic print next to his name was revolutionary. We don't need to be hit over the head with that information now, but we did then. (I recall 38-year-old Mike Schmidt going about fifth in our league-opening draft.) Does **anyone** under the age of 30 not realize the value of platooning in this day and age? Believe it or not, Earl Weaver's ideas were very radical in the early 1970's. I really believe our book has helped open baseball experts and fans up to these new ideas and I'm proud of that. You've come a long way, little clip-art man."

— *Steve Moyer*

What's Official and What's Not

The statistics in this book are technically unofficial. The Official Major League Baseball Averages are not released until December. But as usual, we (and our readers) can't wait that long. We've found in the past that if you compare these stats with the official version that comes out in December, you'll find no major differences. We take extraordinary efforts to insure accuracy.

Career Stats

Be sure to save this book. It should be the last one for George Brett, Carlton Fisk and Nolan Ryan. But just think of the space we gain for new blood next season. We get a quarter of a page for Brett, over a third for Fisk and almost an entire half page for Ryan. With that trio's exit, this is the last Handbook where you'll find any player who played Major League ball in the 1960's. In an office in which most of us began following baseball in that era, the thought seems kind of sad. Time marches on.

By the way, we once again added our most-suggested feature to this section. Every player's 1993 minor league data is now included, regardless of when he debuted or whether or not he was a rookie. (Any player with an asterisk on his 1993 minor player is a player for whom only 1993 minor league data is shown.) No more missing out on rehab assignments or how that minor league vet did last season. Check out Roger Clemens' outing at Pawtucket. Awesome.

As always:

- **Age** is seasonal age based on July 1, 1994. This means our age is the player's age as of July 1. By choosing this particular date, almost exactly mid-season, we get the age at which each player will play during most of the 1994 season.

- **Hm** and **Rd** in the batters' tables stand for home runs hit at home and home runs hit on the road, respectively.

- **TBB** and **IBB** are Total Bases on Balls and Intentional Bases on Balls.

- **SB%** is Stolen Base Percentage (stolen bases divided by attempts). **OBP** and **SLG** are On-Base Percentage and Slugging Percentage.

- **BFP**, **Bk**, and **ShO** are Batters Faced Pitcher, Balks, and Shutouts.

- For pitchers, thirds of an inning were not officially kept prior to 1982. Therefore, there are no thirds of an inning for 1981 and before for older pitchers.

- For players who played for more than one major league team in a season, stats for each team are shown just above the bottom line career totals.

Jim Abbott

Pitches: Left Bats: Left Pos: SP   Ht: 6' 3" Wt: 210 Born: 09/19/67 Age: 26

Year Team	Lg	G	GS	CG	GF	IP	BFP	H	R	ER	HR	SH	SF	HB	TBB	IBB	SO	WP	Bk	W	L	Pct.	ShO	Sv	ERA
1989 California	AL	29	29	4	0	181.1	788	190	95	79	13	11	5	4	74	3	115	8	2	12	12	.500	2	0	3.92
1990 California	AL	33	33	4	0	211.2	925	**246**	116	106	16	9	6	5	72	6	105	4	3	10	14	.417	1	0	4.51
1991 California	AL	34	34	5	0	243	1002	222	85	78	14	7	7	5	73	6	158	1	**4**	18	11	.621	1	0	2.89
1992 California	AL	29	29	7	0	211	874	208	73	65	12	8	4	4	68	3	130	2	0	7	15	.318	0	0	2.77
1993 New York	AL	32	32	4	0	214	906	221	115	104	22	12	4	3	73	4	95	9	0	11	14	.440	1	0	4.37
5 ML YEARS		157	157	24	0	1061	4495	1087	484	432	77	47	26	21	360	22	603	24	9	58	66	.468	5	0	3.66

Kurt Abbott

Bats: Right Throws: Right Pos: LF   Ht: 6' 0" Wt: 170 Born: 06/02/69 Age: 25

Year Team	Lg	G	AB	H	2B	3B	HR	(Hm	Rd)	TB	R	RBI	TBB	IBB	SO	HBP	SH	SF	SB	CS	SB%	GDP	Avg	OBP	SLG
1989 Sou Oregon	A	5	10	1	0	0	0	--	--	1	2	1	0	0	3	0	0	1	1	0	1.00	0	.100	.091	.100
Athletics	R	36	155	42	5	3	0	--	--	53	27	25	8	2	40	2	0	4	0	1	.00	2	.271	.308	.342
1990 Madison	A	104	362	84	18	0	0	--	--	102	38	28	47	1	74	5	5	4	21	9	.70	10	.232	.325	.282
1991 Modesto	A	58	216	55	8	2	3	--	--	76	36	25	29	0	55	1	2	4	6	3	.67	2	.255	.340	.352
Huntsville	AA	53	182	45	6	1	0	--	--	53	18	11	17	0	39	1	1	1	6	3	.67	4	.247	.313	.291
1992 Tacoma	AAA	11	39	6	1	0	0	--	--	7	2	1	4	0	9	1	2	0	1	0	1.00	0	.154	.250	.179
Huntsville	AA	124	452	115	14	5	9	--	--	166	64	52	31	0	75	3	4	3	16	5	.76	5	.254	.305	.367
1993 Tacoma	AAA	133	480	153	36	11	12	--	--	247	75	79	33	4	123	2	4	3	19	9	68	8	.319	.363	.515
1993 Oakland	AL	20	61	15	1	0	3	(0	3)	25	11	9	3	0	20	0	3	0	2	0	1.00	3	.246	.281	.410

Paul Abbott

Pitches: Right Bats: Right Pos: SP   Ht: 6' 3" Wt: 194 Born: 09/15/67 Age: 26

Year Team	Lg	G	GS	CG	GF	IP	BFP	H	R	ER	HR	SH	SF	HB	TBB	IBB	SO	WP	Bk	W	L	Pct.	ShO	Sv	ERA
1993 Charlotte *	AAA	4	4	0	0	19	91	25	16	14	4	3	1	0	7	0	12	3	0	0	1	.000	0	0	6.63
Canton-Akrn *	AA	13	12	1	0	75.1	315	71	34	34	4	1	0	1	28	2	86	6	0	4	5	.444	0	0	4.06
1990 Minnesota	AL	7	7	0	0	34.2	162	37	24	23	0	1	1	1	28	0	25	1	0	0	5	.000	0	0	5.97
1991 Minnesota	AL	15	3	0	1	47.1	210	38	27	25	5	7	3	0	36	1	43	5	0	3	1	.750	0	0	4.75
1992 Minnesota	AL	6	0	0	5	11	50	12	4	4	1	0	1	1	5	0	13	1	0	0	0	.000	0	0	3.27
1993 Cleveland	AL	5	5	0	0	18.1	84	19	15	13	5	0	0	0	11	1	7	1	0	0	1	.000	0	0	6.38
4 ML YEARS		33	15	0	6	111.1	506	106	70	65	11	8	5	2	80	2	88	8	0	3	7	.300	0	0	5.25

Juan Agosto

Pitches: Left Bats: Left Pos: RP   Ht: 6' 2" Wt: 190 Born: 02/23/58 Age: 36

Year Team	Lg	G	GS	CG	GF	IP	BFP	H	R	ER	HR	SH	SF	HB	TBB	IBB	SO	WP	Bk	W	L	Pct.	ShO	Sv	ERA
1993 Las Vegas *	AAA	19	0	0	5	18	78	21	8	8	2	0	0	1	5	2	15	1	0	2	0	1.000	0	0	4.00
Tucson *	AAA	32	0	0	13	33	168	45	24	22	2	3	5	2	24	3	18	5	0	5	3	.625	0	3	6.00
1981 Chicago	AL	2	0	0	1	6	22	5	3	3	1	0	0	1	0	0	3	0	0	0	0	.000	0	0	4.50
1982 Chicago	AL	1	0	0	1	2	13	7	4	4	0	0	0	0	0	0	1	0	0	0	0	.000	0	0	18.00
1983 Chicago	AL	39	0	0	13	41.2	166	41	20	19	2	5	4	1	11	1	29	2	0	2	2	.500	0	7	4.10
1984 Chicago	AL	49	0	0	18	55.1	243	54	20	19	2	5	1	3	34	7	26	1	0	2	1	.667	0	7	3.09
1985 Chicago	AL	54	0	0	21	60.1	246	45	27	24	3	3	3	3	23	1	39	0	0	4	3	.571	0	1	3.58
1986 2 ML Teams		26	1	0	4	25	139	49	30	24	1	2	0	2	18	0	12	1	0	1	4	.200	0	1	8.64
1987 Houston	NL	27	0	0	13	27.1	118	26	12	8	1	3	0	0	10	1	6	1	0	1	1	.500	0	2	2.63
1988 Houston	NL	75	0	0	33	91.2	371	74	27	23	6	9	5	0	30	13	33	3	5	10	2	.833	0	4	2.26
1989 Houston	NL	71	0	0	28	83	361	81	32	27	3	5	6	2	32	10	46	4	1	4	5	.444	0	1	2.93
1990 Houston	NL	**82**	0	0	29	92.1	404	91	46	44	4	7	2	7	39	8	50	1	0	9	8	.529	0	4	4.29
1991 St. Louis	NL	72	0	0	22	86	377	92	52	46	4	11	3	8	39	4	34	6	0	5	3	.625	0	2	4.81
1992 2 ML Teams		39	1	0	12	50	227	66	36	34	2	5	4	3	12	2	25	2	0	2	4	.333	0	0	6.12
1993 Houston	NL	6	0	0	3	6	26	8	4	4	1	0	0	0	0	0	3	0	1	0	0	.000	0	0	6.00
1986 Chicago	AL	9	0	0	1	4.2	24	6	5	4	0	0	0	0	4	0	3	0	0	0	2	.000	0	0	7.71
Minnesota		17	1	0	3	20.1	115	43	25	20	1	2	0	2	14	0	9	1	0	1	2	.333	0	1	8.85
1992 St. Louis	AL	22	0	0	10	31.2	143	39	24	22	2	3	3	3	9	2	13	2	0	2	4	.333	0	0	6.25
Seattle	AL	17	1	0	2	18.1	84	27	12	12	0	2	1	0	3	0	12	0	0	0	0	.000	0	0	5.89
13 ML YEARS		543	2	0	198	626.2	2713	639	313	279	30	55	28	30	248	47	307	21	7	40	33	.548	0	29	4.01

Rick Aguilera

Pitches: Right Bats: Right Pos: RP   Ht: 6' 5" Wt: 205 Born: 12/31/61 Age: 32

Year Team	Lg	G	GS	CG	GF	IP	BFP	H	R	ER	HR	SH	SF	HB	TBB	IBB	SO	WP	Bk	W	L	Pct.	ShO	Sv	ERA
1985 New York	NL	21	19	2	1	122.1	507	118	49	44	8	7	4	2	37	2	74	5	2	10	7	.588	0	0	3.24
1986 New York	NL	28	20	2	2	141.2	605	145	70	61	15	6	5	7	36	1	104	5	3	10	7	.588	0	0	3.88

Year	Team	Lg	G	GS	CG	GF	IP	BFP	H	R	ER	HR	SH	SF	HB	TBB	IBB	SO	WP	Bk	W	L	Pct.	ShO	Sv	ERA
1987	New York	NL	18	17	1	0	115	494	124	53	46	12	7	2	3	33	2	77	9	0	11	3	.786	0	0	3.60
1988	New York	NL	11	3	0	2	24.2	111	29	20	19	2	2	0	1	10	2	16	1	1	0	4	.000	0	0	6.93
1989	2 ML Teams		47	11	3	19	145	594	130	51	45	8	7	1	3	38	4	137	4	3	9	11	.450	0	7	2.79
1990	Minnesota	AL	56	0	0	54	65.1	268	55	27	20	5	0	0	4	19	6	61	3	0	5	3	.625	0	32	2.76
1991	Minnesota	AL	63	0	0	60	69	275	44	20	18	3	1	3	1	30	6	61	3	0	4	5	.444	0	42	2.35
1992	Minnesota	AL	64	0	0	61	66.2	273	60	28	21	7	1	2	1	17	4	52	5	0	2	6	.250	0	41	2.84
1993	Minnesota	AL	65	0	0	61	72.1	287	60	25	25	9	2	1	1	14	3	59	1	0	4	3	.571	0	34	3.11
1989	New York	NL	36	0	0	19	69.1	284	59	19	18	3	5	1	2	21	3	80	3	3	6	6	.500	0	7	2.34
	Minnesota	AL	11	11	3	0	75.2	310	71	32	27	5	2	0	1	17	1	57	1	0	3	5	.375	0	0	3.21
	9 ML YEARS		373	70	8	260	822	3414	765	343	299	69	33	18	23	234	30	641	36	9	55	49	.529	0	156	3.27

Scott Aldred

Pitches: Left **Bats:** Left **Pos:** RP **Ht:** 6' 4" **Wt:** 215 **Born:** 06/12/68 **Age:** 26

| | | | HOW MUCH HE PITCHED | | | | | | WHAT HE GAVE UP | | | | | | | | | | | | THE RESULTS | | | | | |
Year	Team	Lg	G	GS	CG	GF	IP	BFP	H	R	ER	HR	SH	SF	HB	TBB	IBB	SO	WP	Bk	W	L	Pct.	ShO	Sv	ERA
1990	Detroit	AL	4	3	0	0	14.1	63	13	6	6	0	2	1	1	10	1	7	0	0	1	2	.333	0	0	3.77
1991	Detroit	AL	11	11	1	0	57.1	253	58	37	33	9	3	2	0	30	2	35	3	1	2	4	.333	0	0	5.18
1992	Detroit	AL	16	13	0	0	65	304	80	51	49	12	4	3	3	33	4	34	1	0	3	8	.273	0	0	6.78
1993	2 ML Teams		8	0	0	2	12	65	19	14	12	2	2	0	1	10	1	9	2	0	1	0	1.000	0	0	9.00
1993	Colorado	NL	5	0	0	1	6.2	40	10	10	8	1	2	0	1	9	1	5	1	0	0	0	.000	0	0	10.80
	Montreal	NL	3	0	0	1	5.1	25	9	4	4	1	0	0	0	1	0	4	1	0	1	0	1.000	0	0	6.75
	4 ML YEARS		39	27	1	2	148.2	685	170	108	100	23	11	6	5	83	8	85	6	1	7	14	.333	0	0	6.05

Mike Aldrete

Bats: Left **Throws:** Left **Pos:** 1B/LF **Ht:** 5'11" **Wt:** 185 **Born:** 01/29/61 **Age:** 33

| | | | BATTING | | | | | | | | | BASERUNNING | | | | PERCENTAGES | | | | | | | | |
Year	Team	Lg	G	AB	H	2B	3B	HR	(Hm	Rd)	TB	R	RBI	TBB	IBB	SO	HBP	SH	SF	SB	CS	SB%	GDP	Avg	OBP	SLG
1993	Tacoma *	AAA	37	122	39	11	2	7	--	--	75	20	21	26	5	22	0	1	0	2	2	.50	6	.320	.439	.615
1986	San Francisco	NL	84	216	54	18	3	2	(1	1)	84	27	25	33	4	34	2	4	1	1	3	.25	3	.250	.353	.389
1987	San Francisco	NL	126	357	116	18	2	9	(7	2)	165	50	51	43	5	50	0	4	2	6	0	1.00	6	.325	.396	.462
1988	San Francisco	NL	139	389	104	15	0	3	(3	0)	128	44	50	56	13	65	0	1	3	6	5	.55	10	.267	.357	.329
1989	Montreal	NL	76	136	30	8	1	1	(0	1)	43	12	12	19	0	30	1	1	2	1	3	.25	4	.221	.316	.316
1990	Montreal	NL	96	161	39	7	1	1	(0	1)	51	22	18	37	2	31	1	0	1	1	2	.33	2	.242	.385	.317
1991	2 ML Teams		97	198	48	6	1	1	(0	1)	59	24	20	39	1	41	0	1	2	1	3	.25	1	.242	.364	.298
1993	Oakland	AL	95	255	68	13	1	10	(5	5)	113	40	33	34	2	45	0	3	0	1	1	.50	7	.267	.353	.443
1991	San Diego	NL	12	15	0	0	0	0	(0	0)	0	1	2	3	0	4	0	0	0	0	1	.00	1	.000	.167	.000
	Cleveland	AL	85	183	48	6	1	1	(0	1)	59	22	19	36	1	37	0	1	2	1	2	.33	0	.262	.380	.322
	7 ML YEARS		713	1712	459	85	9	27	(16	11)	643	219	209	261	27	296	4	14	11	17	17	.50	33	.268	.364	.376

Manny Alexander

Bats: Right **Throws:** Right **Pos:** SS **Ht:** 5'10" **Wt:** 150 **Born:** 03/20/71 **Age:** 23

| | | | BATTING | | | | | | | | | BASERUNNING | | | | PERCENTAGES | | | | | | | | |
Year	Team	Lg	G	AB	H	2B	3B	HR	(Hm	Rd)	TB	R	RBI	TBB	IBB	SO	HBP	SH	SF	SB	CS	SB%	GDP	Avg	OBP	SLG
1989	Bluefield	R	65	274	85	13	2	2	--	--	108	49	34	20	1	49	3	0	2	19	8	.70	2	.310	.361	.394
1990	Wausau	A	44	152	27	3	1	0	--	--	32	16	11	12	1	41	1	1	3	8	3	.73	2	.178	.238	.211
1991	Frederick	A	134	548	143	17	3	3	--	--	175	81	42	44	0	68	2	3	1	47	14	.77	4	.261	.318	.319
	Hagerstown	AA	3	9	3	1	0	0	--	--	4	3	2	1	0	3	1	0	1	0	0	.00	0	.333	.417	.444
1992	Hagerstown	AA	127	499	129	23	8	2	--	--	174	69	41	25	0	62	6	4	4	43	12	.78	10	.259	.300	.349
	Rochester	AAA	6	24	7	1	0	0	--	--	8	3	3	1	0	3	0	1	0	2	2	.50	0	.292	.320	.333
1993	Rochester	AAA	120	471	115	23	8	6	--	--	172	55	51	22	0	60	4	2	1	19	7	.73	11	.244	.283	.365
1992	Baltimore	AL	4	5	1	0	0	0	(0	0)	1	1	0	0	0	3	0	0	0	0	0	.00	0	.200	.200	.200
1993	Baltimore	AL	3	0	0	0	0	0	(0	0)	0	0	0	0	0	0	0	0	0	0	0	.00	0	.000	.000	.000
	2 ML YEARS		7	5	1	0	0	0	(0	0)	1	1	0	0	0	3	0	0	0	0	0	.00	0	.200	.200	.200

Luis Alicea

Bats: Both **Throws:** Right **Pos:** 2B **Ht:** 5' 9" **Wt:** 177 **Born:** 07/29/65 **Age:** 28

| | | | BATTING | | | | | | | | | BASERUNNING | | | | PERCENTAGES | | | | | | | | |
Year	Team	Lg	G	AB	H	2B	3B	HR	(Hm	Rd)	TB	R	RBI	TBB	IBB	SO	HBP	SH	SF	SB	CS	SB%	GDP	Avg	OBP	SLG
1988	St. Louis	NL	93	297	63	10	4	1	(1	0)	84	20	24	25	4	32	2	4	2	1	1	.50	12	.212	.276	.283
1991	St. Louis	NL	56	68	13	3	0	0	(0	0)	16	5	0	8	0	19	0	0	0	0	1	.00	0	.191	.276	.235
1992	St. Louis	NL	85	265	65	9	11	2	(2	0)	102	26	32	27	1	40	4	2	4	2	5	.29	5	.245	.320	.385
1993	St. Louis	NL	115	362	101	19	3	3	(2	1)	135	50	46	47	2	54	4	1	7	11	1	.92	10	.279	.362	.373
	4 ML YEARS		349	992	242	41	18	6	(5	1)	337	101	102	107	7	145	10	7	13	14	8	.64	27	.244	.320	.340

Andy Allanson

Bats: Right **Throws:** Right **Pos:** C **Ht:** 6' 5" **Wt:** 225 **Born:** 12/22/61 **Age:** 32

Year Team	Lg	G	AB	H	2B	3B	HR	(Hm	Rd)	TB	R	RBI	TBB	IBB	SO	HBP	SH	SF	SB	CS	SB%	GDP	Avg	OBP	SLG
1993 Phoenix *	AAA	50	161	57	15	2	6	--	--	94	31	23	10	1	18	1	1	2	7	4	.64	4	.354	.391	.584
1986 Cleveland	AL	101	293	66	7	3	1	0	1	82	30	29	14	0	36	1	11	4	10	1	.91	7	.225	.260	.280
1987 Cleveland	AL	50	154	41	6	0	3	2	1	56	17	16	9	0	30	0	4	5	1	1	.50	2	.266	.298	.364
1988 Cleveland	AL	133	434	114	11	0	5	4	1	140	44	50	25	2	63	3	8	4	5	9	.36	6	.263	.305	.323
1989 Cleveland	AL	111	323	75	9	1	3	1	2	95	30	17	23	2	47	4	6	3	4	4	.50	7	.232	.289	.294
1991 Detroit	AL	60	151	35	10	0	1	0	1	48	10	16	7	0	31	0	2	0	0	1	.00	3	.232	.266	.318
1992 Milwaukee	AL	9	25	8	1	0	0	0	0	9	6	0	1	0	2	0	2	0	3	1	.75	1	.320	.346	.360
1993 San Francisco	NL	13	24	4	1	0	0	0	0	5	3	2	1	0	2	0	1	0	0	0	.00	1	.167	.200	.208
7 ML YEARS		477	1404	343	45	4	13	7	6	435	140	130	80	4	211	8	34	16	23	17	.58	27	.244	.286	.310

Roberto Alomar

Bats: Both **Throws:** Right **Pos:** 2B **Ht:** 6' 0" **Wt:** 185 **Born:** 02/05/68 **Age:** 26

Year Team	Lg	G	AB	H	2B	3B	HR	(Hm	Rd)	TB	R	RBI	TBB	IBB	SO	HBP	SH	SF	SB	CS	SB%	GDP	Avg	OBP	SLG
1988 San Diego	NL	143	545	145	24	6	9	5	4	208	84	41	47	5	83	3	16	0	24	6	.80	15	.266	.328	.382
1989 San Diego	NL	158	623	184	27	1	7	3	4	234	82	56	53	4	76	1	17	8	42	17	.71	10	.295	.347	.376
1990 San Diego	NL	147	586	168	27	5	6	4	2	223	80	60	48	1	72	2	5	5	24	7	.77	16	.287	.340	.381
1991 Toronto	AL	161	637	188	41	11	9	6	3	278	88	69	57	3	86	4	16	5	53	11	.83	5	.295	.354	.436
1992 Toronto	AL	152	571	177	27	8	8	5	3	244	105	76	87	5	52	5	6	2	49	9	.84	8	.310	.405	.427
1993 Toronto	AL	153	589	192	35	6	17	8	9	290	109	93	80	5	67	5	4	5	55	15	.79	13	.326	.408	.492
6 ML YEARS		914	3551	1054	181	37	56	31	25	1477	548	395	372	23	436	20	64	25	247	65	.79	67	.297	.364	.416

Sandy Alomar Jr

Bats: Right **Throws:** Right **Pos:** C **Ht:** 6' 5" **Wt:** 215 **Born:** 06/18/66 **Age:** 28

Year Team	Lg	G	AB	H	2B	3B	HR	(Hm	Rd)	TB	R	RBI	TBB	IBB	SO	HBP	SH	SF	SB	CS	SB%	GDP	Avg	OBP	SLG
1993 Charlotte *	AAA	12	44	16	5	0	1	--	--	24	8	8	5	1	8	1	0	0	0	0	.00	1	.364	.440	.545
1988 San Diego	NL	1	1	0	0	0	0	0	0	0	0	0	0	0	1	0	0	0	0	0	.00	0	.000	.000	.000
1989 San Diego	NL	7	19	4	1	0	1	1	0	8	1	6	3	1	3	0	0	0	0	0	.00	1	.211	.318	.421
1990 Cleveland	AL	132	445	129	26	2	9	5	4	186	60	66	25	2	46	2	5	6	4	1	.80	10	.290	.326	.418
1991 Cleveland	AL	51	184	40	9	0	0	0	0	49	10	7	8	1	24	4	2	1	0	4	.00	4	.217	.264	.266
1992 Cleveland	AL	89	299	75	16	0	2	1	1	97	22	26	13	3	32	5	3	0	3	3	.50	7	.251	.293	.324
1993 Cleveland	AL	64	215	58	7	1	6	3	3	85	24	32	11	0	28	6	1	4	3	1	.75	3	.270	.318	.395
6 ML YEARS		344	1163	306	59	3	18	10	8	425	117	137	60	7	134	17	11	11	10	9	.53	25	.263	.306	.365

Moises Alou

Bats: Right **Throws:** Right **Pos:** LF/CF/RF **Ht:** 6' 3" **Wt:** 190 **Born:** 07/03/66 **Age:** 27

Year Team	Lg	G	AB	H	2B	3B	HR	(Hm	Rd)	TB	R	RBI	TBB	IBB	SO	HBP	SH	SF	SB	CS	SB%	GDP	Avg	OBP	SLG
1990 2 ML Teams		16	20	4	0	1	0	0	0	6	4	0	0	0	3	0	1	0	0	0	.00	1	.200	.200	.300
1992 Montreal	NL	115	341	96	28	2	9	6	3	155	53	56	25	0	46	1	5	5	16	2	.89	5	.282	.328	.455
1993 Montreal	NL	136	482	138	29	6	18	10	8	233	70	85	38	9	53	5	3	7	17	6	.74	9	.286	.340	.483
1990 Pittsburgh	NL	2	5	1	0	0	0	0	0	1	0	0	0	0	0	0	0	0	0	0	.00	1	.200	.200	.200
Montreal	NL	14	15	3	0	1	0	0	0	5	4	0	0	0	3	0	1	0	0	0	.00	0	.200	.200	.333
3 ML YEARS		267	843	238	57	9	27	16	11	394	127	141	63	9	102	6	9	12	33	8	.80	15	.282	.332	.467

Wilson Alvarez

Pitches: Left **Bats:** Left **Pos:** SP **Ht:** 6' 1" **Wt:** 235 **Born:** 03/24/70 **Age:** 24

Year Team	Lg	G	GS	CG	GF	IP	BFP	H	R	ER	HR	SH	SF	HB	TBB	IBB	SO	WP	Bk	W	L	Pct.	ShO	Sv	ERA
1993 Nashville *	AAA	1	1	0	0	6.1	31	7	7	2	0	0	0	0	2	0	8	0	0	0	1	.000	0	0	2.84
1989 Texas	AL	1	1	0	0	0	5	3	3	3	2	0	0	0	2	0	0	0	0	0	1	.000	0	0	0.00
1991 Chicago	AL	10	9	2	0	56.1	237	47	26	22	9	3	1	0	29	0	32	2	0	3	2	.600	1	0	3.51
1992 Chicago	AL	34	9	0	4	100.1	455	103	64	58	12	3	4	4	65	2	66	2	0	5	3	.625	0	1	5.20
1993 Chicago	AL	31	31	1	0	207.2	877	168	78	68	14	13	6	7	122	8	155	2	1	15	8	.652	1	0	2.95
4 ML YEARS		76	50	3	4	364.1	1574	321	171	151	37	19	11	11	218	10	253	6	1	23	14	.622	2	1	3.73

Rich Amaral

Bats: Right **Throws:** Right **Pos:** 2B/3B/SS **Ht:** 6' 0" **Wt:** 175 **Born:** 04/01/62 **Age:** 32

Year Team	Lg	G	AB	H	2B	3B	HR	(Hm	Rd)	TB	R	RBI	TBB	IBB	SO	HBP	SH	SF	SB	CS	SB%	GDP	Avg	OBP	SLG
1984 Quad City	A	34	119	25	1	0	0	--	--	26	21	7	24	0	29	0	1	0	12	0	1.00	0	.210	.343	.218

Year	Team	Lg	G	AB	H	2B	3B	HR	(Hm	Rd)	TB	R	RBI	TBB	IBB	SO	HBP	SH	SF	SB	CS	SB%	GDP	Avg	OBP	SLG
1985	Winston-Sal	A	124	428	116	15	5	3	--	--	150	62	36	59	1	68	2	5	1	26	7	.79	11	.271	.361	.350
1986	Pittsfield	AA	114	355	89	12	0	0	--	--	101	43	24	39	1	65	4	5	2	25	8	.76	5	.251	.330	.285
1987	Pittsfield	AA	104	315	80	8	5	0	--	--	98	45	28	43	2	50	3	6	1	28	6	.82	1	.254	.348	.311
1988	Pittsfield	AA	122	422	117	15	4	4	--	--	152	66	47	56	1	53	1	5	5	54	5	.92	2	.277	.360	.360
1989	Birmingham	AA	122	432	123	15	6	4	--	--	162	90	48	88	2	66	2	7	4	57	14	.80	6	.285	.405	.375
1990	Vancouver	AAA	130	462	139	39	5	4	--	--	200	87	56	88	3	68	4	9	4	20	14	.59	4	.301	.414	.433
1991	Calgary	AAA	86	347	120	26	2	3	--	--	159	79	36	53	0	37	3	3	3	30	8	.79	6	.346	.433	.458
1992	Calgary	AAA	106	403	128	21	8	0	--	--	165	79	21	67	1	69	1	2	2	53	16	.77	7	.318	.414	.409
1991	Seattle	AL	14	16	1	0	0	0	(0	0)	1	2	0	1	0	5	1	0	0	0	0	.00	1	.063	.167	.063
1992	Seattle	AL	35	100	24	3	0	1	(0	1)	30	9	7	5	0	16	0	4	0	4	2	.67	4	.240	.276	.300
1993	Seattle	AL	110	373	108	24	1	1	(0	1)	137	53	44	33	0	54	3	7	5	19	11	.63	5	.290	.348	.367
	3 ML YEARS		159	489	133	27	1	2	(0	2)	168	64	51	39	0	75	4	11	5	23	13	.64	10	.272	.328	.344

Ruben Amaro

Bats: Both   **Throws:** Right   **Pos:** CF   **Ht:** 5'10"   **Wt:** 170   **Born:** 02/12/65   **Age:** 29

						BATTING													BASERUNNING				PERCENTAGES		
Year	Team	Lg	G	AB	H	2B	3B	HR	(Hm	Rd)	TB	R	RBI	TBB	IBB	SO	HBP	SH	SF	SB	CS	SB%	GDP	Avg	OBP	SLG
1993	Scranton/wb *	AAA	101	412	120	30	5	9	--	--	187	76	37	31	2	44	5	3	3	25	4	.86	5	.291	.346	.454
1991	California	AL	10	23	5	1	0	0	(0	0)	6	0	2	3	1	3	0	0	0	0	0	.00	1	.217	.308	.261
1992	Philadelphia	NL	126	374	82	15	6	7	(5	2)	130	43	34	37	1	54	9	4	2	11	5	.69	11	.219	.303	.348
1993	Philadelphia	NL	25	48	16	2	2	1	(0	1)	25	7	6	6	0	5	0	3	1	0	0	.00	1	.333	.400	.521
	3 ML YEARS		161	445	103	18	8	8	(5	3)	161	50	42	46	2	62	9	7	3	11	5	.69	13	.231	.314	.362

Larry Andersen

Pitches: Right   **Bats:** Right   **Pos:** RP   **Ht:** 6' 3"   **Wt:** 205   **Born:** 05/06/53   **Age:** 41

			HOW MUCH HE PITCHED						WHAT HE GAVE UP											THE RESULTS					
Year	Team	Lg	G	GS	CG	GF	IP	BFP	H	R	ER	HR	SH	SF	HB	TBB	IBB	SO	WP	Bk	W	L	Pct.	ShO	Sv	ERA
1975	Cleveland	AL	3	0	0	1	6	23	4	3	3	0	0	1	0	2	0	4	2	0	0	0	.000	0	0	4.50
1977	Cleveland	AL	11	0	0	7	14	62	10	7	5	1	3	0	0	9	3	8	1	0	0	1	.000	0	0	3.21
1979	Cleveland	AL	8	0	0	4	17	77	25	14	14	3	1	2	0	4	0	7	0	0	0	0	.000	0	0	7.41
1981	Seattle	AL	41	0	0	23	68	273	57	27	20	4	0	3	2	18	2	40	0	0	3	3	.500	0	5	2.65
1982	Seattle	AL	40	1	0	14	79.2	354	100	56	53	16	2	3	4	23	1	32	2	0	0	0	.000	0	1	5.99
1983	Philadelphia	NL	17	0	0	8	26.1	106	19	7	7	0	1	1	0	9	1	14	1	1	1	0	1.000	0	0	2.39
1984	Philadelphia	NL	64	0	0	25	90.2	376	85	32	24	5	4	4	0	25	6	54	2	1	3	7	.300	0	4	2.38
1985	Philadelphia	NL	57	0	0	19	73	318	78	41	35	5	3	1	3	26	4	50	1	1	3	3	.500	0	1	4.32
1986	2 ML Teams		48	0	0	8	77.1	323	83	30	26	2	10	5	1	26	10	42	1	0	2	1	.667	0	1	3.03
1987	Houston	NL	67	0	0	31	101.2	440	95	46	39	7	7	4	2	41	10	94	1	0	9	5	.643	0	5	3.45
1988	Houston	NL	53	0	0	25	82.2	350	82	29	27	3	3	3	1	20	8	66	1	2	2	4	.333	0	5	2.94
1989	Houston	NL	60	0	0	21	87.2	351	63	19	15	2	4	5	0	24	4	85	2	1	4	4	.500	0	3	1.54
1990	2 ML Teams		65	0	0	24	95.2	387	79	22	19	2	5	5	2	27	5	93	4	0	5	2	.714	0	7	1.79
1991	San Diego	NL	38	0	0	24	47	188	39	13	12	0	4	2	0	13	3	40	1	0	3	4	.429	0	13	2.30
1992	San Diego	NL	34	0	0	13	35	140	26	14	13	2	1	1	1	8	2	35	0	0	1	1	.500	0	2	3.34
1993	Philadelphia	NL	64	0	0	13	61.2	256	54	22	20	4	2	0	1	21	2	67	2	1	3	2	.600	0	0	2.92
1986	Philadelphia	NL	10	0	0	1	12.2	55	19	8	6	0	2	1	0	3	0	9	0	0	0	0	.000	0	0	4.26
	Houston	NL	38	0	0	7	64.2	268	64	22	20	2	8	4	1	23	10	33	1	0	2	1	.667	0	1	2.78
1990	Houston	NL	50	0	0	20	73.2	301	61	19	16	2	5	5	1	24	5	68	2	0	5	2	.714	0	6	1.95
	Boston	AL	15	0	0	4	22	86	18	3	3	0	0	0	1	3	0	25	2	0	0	0	.000	0	1	1.23
	16 ML YEARS		670	1	0	256	963.1	4024	899	382	332	56	50	40	17	296	61	731	21	7	39	37	.513	0	49	3.10

Brady Anderson

Bats: Left   **Throws:** Left   **Pos:** LF/CF   **Ht:** 6' 1"   **Wt:** 190   **Born:** 01/18/64   **Age:** 30

						BATTING													BASERUNNING				PERCENTAGES		
Year	Team	Lg	G	AB	H	2B	3B	HR	(Hm	Rd)	TB	R	RBI	TBB	IBB	SO	HBP	SH	SF	SB	CS	SB%	GDP	Avg	OBP	SLG
1988	2 ML Teams		94	325	69	13	4	1	(1	0)	93	31	21	23	0	75	4	11	1	10	6	.63	3	.212	.272	.286
1989	Baltimore	AL	94	266	55	12	2	4	(2	2)	83	44	16	43	6	45	3	5	0	16	4	.80	4	.207	.324	.312
1990	Baltimore	AL	89	234	54	5	2	3	(1	2)	72	24	24	31	2	46	5	4	5	15	2	.88	4	.231	.327	.308
1991	Baltimore	AL	113	256	59	12	3	2	(1	1)	83	40	27	38	0	44	5	11	3	12	5	.71	1	.230	.338	.324
1992	Baltimore	AL	159	623	169	28	10	21	(15	6)	280	100	80	98	14	98	9	10	9	53	16	.77	2	.271	.373	.449
1993	Baltimore	AL	142	560	147	36	8	13	(2	11)	238	87	66	82	4	99	10	6	6	24	12	.67	4	.263	.363	.425
1988	Boston	AL	41	148	34	5	3	0	(0	0)	45	14	12	15	0	35	4	4	1	4	2	.67	2	.230	.315	.304
	Baltimore	AL	53	177	35	8	1	1	(1	0)	48	17	9	8	0	40	0	7	0	6	4	.60	1	.198	.232	.271
	6 ML YEARS		691	2264	553	106	29	44	(22	22)	849	326	234	315	26	407	36	47	24	130	45	.74	18	.244	.343	.375

Brian Anderson

Pitches: Left **Bats:** Both **Pos:** RP   **Ht:** 6' 1" **Wt:** 195 **Born:** 04/26/72 **Age:** 22

Year Team	Lg	G	GS	CG	GF	IP	BFP	H	R	ER	HR	SH	SF	HB	TBB	IBB	SO	WP	Bk	W	L	Pct.	ShO	Sv	ERA
1993 Midland	AA	2	2	0	0	10.2	47	16	5	4	2	0	0	0	0	0	9	0	0	0	1	.000	0	0	3.38
Vancouver	AAA	2	2	0	0	8	42	13	12	11	3	0	2	1	6	0	2	1	1	0	0	.000	0	0	12.38
1993 California	AL	4	1	0	3	11.1	45	11	5	5	1	0	0	0	2	0	4	0	0	0	0	.000	0	0	3.97

Mike Anderson

Pitches: Right **Bats:** Right **Pos:** RP   **Ht:** 6' 3" **Wt:** 200 **Born:** 07/30/66 **Age:** 27

Year Team	Lg	G	GS	CG	GF	IP	BFP	H	R	ER	HR	SH	SF	HB	TBB	IBB	SO	WP	Bk	W	L	Pct.	ShO	Sv	ERA
1988 Reds	R	2	2	0	0	7.1	34	6	7	4	0	0	0	0	5	0	11	3	4	0	1	.000	0	0	4.91
Billings	R	17	4	0	12	44.1	192	36	17	16	1	0	4	2	21	1	52	4	0	3	1	.750	0	2	3.25
1989 Greensboro	A	25	25	4	0	154.1	647	117	64	49	7	2	3	8	72	0	154	9	2	11	6	.647	2	0	2.86
1990 Cedar Rapds	A	23	23	2	0	138.1	613	134	67	52	6	8	7	5	62	0	101	10	0	10	5	.667	0	0	3.38
1991 Chattanooga	AA	28	26	3	1	155.1	698	142	94	76	8	4	4	8	93	2	115	17	1	10	9	.526	3	0	4.40
1992 Chattanooga	AA	28	26	4	1	171.2	716	155	59	48	4	0	3	7	61	1	149	15	3	13	7	.650	4	0	2.52
1993 Chattanooga	AA	2	2	1	0	15	54	10	3	2	0	1	1	0	1	0	14	0	0	1	1	.500	0	0	1.20
Indianapols	AAA	23	23	2	0	151	647	150	73	63	10	7	7	4	56	5	111	8	0	10	6	.625	1	0	3.75
1993 Cincinnati	NL	3	0	0	0	5.1	30	12	11	11	3	0	0	0	3	0	4	0	0	0	0	.000	0	0	18.56

Eric Anthony

Bats: Left **Throws:** Left **Pos:** RF/CF   **Ht:** 6' 2" **Wt:** 195 **Born:** 11/08/67 **Age:** 26

Year Team	Lg	G	AB	H	2B	3B	HR	(Hm	Rd)	TB	R	RBI	TBB	IBB	SO	HBP	SH	SF	SB	CS	SB%	GDP	Avg	OBP	SLG
1989 Houston	NL	25	61	11	2	0	4	(2	2)	25	7	7	9	2	16	0	0	0	0	0	.00	1	.180	.286	.410
1990 Houston	NL	84	239	46	8	0	10	(5	5)	84	26	29	29	3	78	2	1	6	5	0	1.00	4	.192	.279	.351
1991 Houston	NL	39	118	18	6	0	1	(0	1)	27	11	7	12	1	41	0	0	2	1	0	1.00	2	.153	.227	.229
1992 Houston	NL	137	440	105	15	1	19	(9	10)	179	45	80	38	5	98	1	0	4	5	4	.56	7	.239	.298	.407
1993 Houston	NL	145	486	121	19	4	15	(5	10)	193	70	66	49	2	88	2	0	2	3	5	.38	9	.249	.319	.397
5 ML YEARS		430	1344	301	50	5	49	(21	28)	508	159	189	137	13	321	5	1	14	14	9	.61	23	.224	.295	.378

Kevin Appier

Pitches: Right **Bats:** Right **Pos:** SP   **Ht:** 6' 2" **Wt:** 195 **Born:** 12/06/67 **Age:** 26

Year Team	Lg	G	GS	CG	GF	IP	BFP	H	R	ER	HR	SH	SF	HB	TBB	IBB	SO	WP	Bk	W	L	Pct.	ShO	Sv	ERA
1989 Kansas City	AL	6	5	0	0	21.2	106	34	22	22	3	0	3	0	12	1	10	0	0	1	4	.200	0	0	9.14
1990 Kansas City	AL	32	24	3	1	185.2	784	179	67	57	13	5	9	6	54	2	127	6	1	12	8	.600	3	0	2.76
1991 Kansas City	AL	34	31	6	1	207.2	881	205	97	79	13	8	6	2	61	3	158	7	1	13	10	.565	3	0	3.42
1992 Kansas City	AL	30	30	3	0	208.1	852	167	59	57	10	8	3	2	68	5	150	4	0	15	8	.652	0	0	2.46
1993 Kansas City	AL	34	34	5	0	238.2	953	183	74	68	8	3	5	1	81	3	186	5	0	18	8	.692	1	0	2.56
5 ML YEARS		136	124	17	2	862	3576	768	319	283	47	24	26	11	276	14	631	22	2	59	38	.608	7	0	2.95

Luis Aquino

Pitches: Right **Bats:** Right **Pos:** RP/SP   **Ht:** 6' 1" **Wt:** 195 **Born:** 05/19/65 **Age:** 29

Year Team	Lg	G	GS	CG	GF	IP	BFP	H	R	ER	HR	SH	SF	HB	TBB	IBB	SO	WP	Bk	W	L	Pct.	ShO	Sv	ERA
1986 Toronto	AL	7	0	0	3	11.1	50	14	8	8	2	0	1	0	3	1	5	1	0	1	1	.500	0	0	6.35
1988 Kansas City	AL	7	5	1	0	29	136	33	15	9	1	0	1	1	17	0	11	1	1	1	0	1.000	1	0	2.79
1989 Kansas City	AL	34	16	2	7	141.1	591	148	62	55	6	2	4	4	35	4	68	4	0	6	8	.429	1	0	3.50
1990 Kansas City	AL	20	3	1	3	68.1	287	59	25	24	6	5	2	4	27	6	28	3	1	4	1	.800	0	0	3.16
1991 Kansas City	AL	38	18	1	9	157	661	152	67	60	10	2	7	4	47	5	80	1	0	8	4	.667	1	3	3.44
1992 Kansas City	AL	15	13	0	1	67.2	293	81	35	34	5	2	3	1	20	1	11	1	1	3	6	.333	0	0	4.52
1993 Florida	NL	38	13	0	5	110.2	471	115	43	42	6	7	2	5	40	1	67	4	0	6	8	.429	0	0	3.42
7 ML YEARS		159	68	5	28	585.1	2489	602	255	232	36	18	20	19	189	18	270	15	3	29	28	.509	3	3	3.57

Alex Arias

Bats: Right **Throws:** Right **Pos:** 2B/3B/SS   **Ht:** 6' 3" **Wt:** 185 **Born:** 11/20/67 **Age:** 26

Year Team	Lg	G	AB	H	2B	3B	HR	(Hm	Rd)	TB	R	RBI	TBB	IBB	SO	HBP	SH	SF	SB	CS	SB%	GDP	Avg	OBP	SLG
1987 Wytheville	R	61	233	69	7	0	0	--	--	76	41	24	27	0	29	1	0	1	16	6	.73	2	.296	.370	.326
1988 Chston-Wv	A	127	472	122	12	1	0	--	--	136	57	33	54	3	44	3	10	3	41	12	.77	9	.258	.336	.288
1989 Peoria	A	136	506	140	10	11	2	--	--	178	74	64	49	3	67	7	9	2	31	6	.84	11	.277	.348	.352
1990 Charlotte	AA	119	419	103	16	3	4	--	--	137	55	38	42	0	52	2	9	3	11	5	.69	11	.246	.315	.327
1991 Charlotte	AA	134	488	134	26	0	4	--	--	172	69	47	47	2	41	3	3	3	22	9	.71	9	.275	.340	.352
1992 Iowa	AAA	106	409	114	23	3	5	--	--	158	52	40	44	1	27	6	7	0	14	3	.82	4	.279	.357	.386

8

Year Team	Lg	G	AB	H	2B	3B	HR	(Hm	Rd)	TB	R	RBI	TBB	IBB	SO	HBP	SH	SF	SB	CS	SB%	GDP	Avg	OBP	SLG
1992 Chicago	NL	32	99	29	6	0	0	(0	0)	35	14	7	11	0	13	2	1	0	0	0	.00	4	.293	.375	.354
1993 Florida	NL	96	249	67	5	1	2	(1	1)	80	27	20	27	0	18	3	1	3	1	1	.50	5	.269	.344	.321
2 ML YEARS		128	348	96	11	1	2	(1	1)	115	41	27	38	0	31	5	2	3	1	1	.50	9	.276	.353	.330

Marcos Armas

Bats: Right **Throws:** Right **Pos:** 1B **Ht:** 6' 5" **Wt:** 195 **Born:** 08/05/69 **Age:** 24

Year Team	Lg	G	AB	H	2B	3B	HR	(Hm	Rd)	TB	R	RBI	TBB	IBB	SO	HBP	SH	SF	SB	CS	SB%	GDP	Avg	OBP	SLG
1988 Athletics	R	17	58	17	2	1	0	--	--	21	14	10	5	0	17	0	0	0	0	0	.00	2	.293	.349	.362
1989 Sou Oregon	A	36	136	43	5	2	3	--	--	61	18	22	6	0	42	0	1	1	1	0	1.00	6	.316	.343	.449
1990 Madison	A	75	260	62	13	0	7	--	--	96	32	33	10	0	80	2	1	3	3	5	.38	11	.238	.269	.369
1991 Modesto	A	36	140	39	7	0	8	--	--	70	21	33	10	0	41	2	1	5	0	0	.00	5	.279	.325	.500
Huntsville	AA	81	305	69	16	1	8	--	--	111	40	53	18	1	89	0	2	4	2	1	.67	11	.226	.266	.364
1992 Huntsville	AA	132	509	144	30	6	17	--	--	237	83	84	41	4	133	3	0	6	9	1	.90	11	.283	.336	.466
1993 Tacoma	AAA	117	434	126	27	8	15	--	--	214	69	89	35	1	113	3	1	6	4	0	1.00	7	.290	.343	.493
1993 Oakland	AL	15	31	6	2	0	1	(1	0)	11	7	1	1	0	12	1	0	0	0	0	1.00	0	.194	.242	.355

Jack Armstrong

Pitches: Right **Bats:** Right **Pos:** SP **Ht:** 6' 5" **Wt:** 220 **Born:** 03/07/65 **Age:** 29

Year Team	Lg	G	GS	CG	GF	IP	BFP	H	R	ER	HR	SH	SF	HB	TBB	IBB	SO	WP	Bk	W	L	Pct.	ShO	Sv	ERA
1988 Cincinnati	NL	14	13	0	0	65.1	293	63	44	42	8	4	5	0	38	2	45	3	2	4	7	.364	0	0	5.79
1989 Cincinnati	NL	9	8	0	1	42.2	187	40	24	22	5	2	1	0	21	4	23	0	0	2	3	.400	0	0	4.64
1990 Cincinnati	NL	29	27	2	1	166	704	151	72	63	9	8	5	6	59	7	110	7	5	12	9	.571	1	0	3.42
1991 Cincinnati	NL	27	24	1	1	139.2	611	158	90	85	25	6	9	2	54	2	93	2	1	7	13	.350	0	0	5.48
1992 Cleveland	AL	35	23	1	5	166.2	735	176	100	86	23	6	5	3	67	0	114	6	3	6	15	.286	0	0	4.64
1993 Florida	NL	36	33	0	2	196.1	879	210	105	98	29	8	10	7	78	6	118	7	2	9	17	.346	0	0	4.49
6 ML YEARS		150	128	4	10	776.2	3409	798	435	396	99	34	35	18	317	21	503	25	13	40	64	.385	1	0	4.59

Rene Arocha

Pitches: Right **Bats:** Right **Pos:** SP **Ht:** 6' 0" **Wt:** 180 **Born:** 02/24/66 **Age:** 28

Year Team	Lg	G	GS	CG	GF	IP	BFP	H	R	ER	HR	SH	SF	HB	TBB	IBB	SO	WP	Bk	W	L	Pct.	ShO	Sv	ERA
1992 Louisville	AAA	25	25	3	0	166.2	705	145	59	50	8	9	4	6	65	0	128	3	2	12	7	.632	1	0	2.70
1993 St. Louis	NL	32	29	1	0	188	774	197	89	79	20	8	5	3	31	2	96	3	1	11	8	.579	0	0	3.78

Andy Ashby

Pitches: Right **Bats:** Right **Pos:** SP/RP **Ht:** 6' 5" **Wt:** 180 **Born:** 07/11/67 **Age:** 26

Year Team	Lg	G	GS	CG	GF	IP	BFP	H	R	ER	HR	SH	SF	HB	TBB	IBB	SO	WP	Bk	W	L	Pct.	ShO	Sv	ERA
1993 Colo Sprngs *	AAA	7	6	1	0	41.2	181	45	25	19	2	2	1	3	12	0	35	3	2	4	2	.667	0	0	4.10
1991 Philadelphia	NL	8	8	0	0	42	186	41	28	28	5	1	3	3	19	0	26	6	0	1	5	.167	0	0	6.00
1992 Philadelphia	NL	10	8	0	0	37	171	42	31	31	6	2	2	1	21	0	24	2	0	1	3	.250	0	0	7.54
1993 2 ML Teams		32	21	0	3	123	577	168	100	93	19	6	7	4	56	5	77	6	3	3	10	.231	0	1	6.80
1993 Colorado	NL	20	9	0	3	54	277	89	54	51	5	3	3	3	32	4	33	2	3	0	4	.000	0	1	8.50
San Diego	NL	12	12	0	0	69	300	79	46	42	14	3	4	1	24	1	44	4	0	3	6	.333	0	0	5.48
3 ML YEARS		50	37	0	3	202	934	251	159	152	30	9	12	8	96	5	127	14	3	5	18	.217	0	1	6.77

Billy Ashley

Bats: Right **Throws:** Right **Pos:** LF **Ht:** 6' 7" **Wt:** 220 **Born:** 07/11/70 **Age:** 23

Year Team	Lg	G	AB	H	2B	3B	HR	(Hm	Rd)	TB	R	RBI	TBB	IBB	SO	HBP	SH	SF	SB	CS	SB%	GDP	Avg	OBP	SLG
1988 Dodgers	R	9	26	4	0	0	0	--	--	4	3	0	1	0	9	0	0	0	1	0	1.00	0	.154	.185	.154
1989 Dodgers	R	48	160	38	6	2	1	--	--	51	23	19	19	1	42	2	0	3	9	1	.90	4	.238	.321	.319
1990 Bakersfield	A	99	331	72	13	1	9	--	--	114	48	40	25	1	135	3	3	1	17	3	.85	4	.218	.278	.344
1991 Vero Beach	A	60	206	52	11	2	7	--	--	88	18	42	7	0	69	0	0	1	9	2	.82	4	.252	.276	.427
1992 Albuquerque	AAA	25	95	20	7	0	2	--	--	33	11	10	6	0	42	0	0	0	1	0	1.00	2	.211	.257	.347
San Antonio	AA	101	380	106	23	1	24	--	--	203	60	66	16	3	111	6	0	2	13	7	.65	9	.279	.317	.534
1993 Albuquerque	AAA	125	482	143	31	4	26	--	--	260	88	100	35	1	143	2	0	5	6	4	.60	16	.297	.344	.539
1992 Los Angeles	NL	29	95	21	5	0	2	(2	0)	32	6	6	5	0	34	0	0	0	0	0	.00	2	.221	.260	.337
1993 Los Angeles	NL	14	37	9	0	0	0	(0	0)	9	0	0	2	0	11	0	0	0	0	0	.00	0	.243	.282	.243
2 ML YEARS		43	132	30	5	0	2	(2	0)	41	6	6	7	0	45	0	0	0	0	0	.00	2	.227	.266	.311

9

Paul Assenmacher

Pitches: Left **Bats:** Left **Pos:** RP   **Ht:** 6' 3" **Wt:** 210 **Born:** 12/10/60 **Age:** 33

Year Team	Lg	G	GS	CG	GF	IP	BFP	H	R	ER	HR	SH	SF	HB	TBB	IBB	SO	WP	Bk	W	L	Pct.	ShO	Sv	ERA
1986 Atlanta	NL	61	0	0	27	68.1	287	61	23	19	5	7	1	0	26	4	56	2	3	7	3	.700	0	7	2.50
1987 Atlanta	NL	52	0	0	10	54.2	251	58	41	31	8	2	1	1	24	4	39	0	0	1	1	.500	0	2	5.10
1988 Atlanta	NL	64	0	0	32	79.1	329	72	28	27	4	8	1	1	32	11	71	7	0	8	7	.533	0	5	3.06
1989 2 ML Teams		63	0	0	17	76.2	331	74	37	34	3	9	3	1	28	8	79	3	1	3	4	.429	0	0	3.99
1990 Chicago	NL	74	1	0	21	103	426	90	33	32	10	10	3	1	36	8	95	2	0	7	2	.778	0	10	2.80
1991 Chicago	NL	75	0	0	31	102.2	427	85	41	37	10	8	4	3	31	6	117	4	0	7	8	.467	0	15	3.24
1992 Chicago	NL	70	0	0	23	68	298	72	32	31	6	1	2	3	26	5	67	4	0	4	4	.500	0	8	4.10
1993 2 ML Teams		72	0	0	21	56	237	54	21	21	5	4	0	1	22	6	45	0	0	4	3	.571	0	0	3.38
1989 Atlanta	NL	49	0	0	14	57.2	247	55	26	23	2	7	2	1	16	7	64	3	1	1	3	.250	0	0	3.59
Chicago	NL	14	0	0	3	19	84	19	11	11	1	2	1	0	12	1	15	0	0	2	1	.667	0	0	5.21
1993 Chicago	NL	46	0	0	15	38.2	166	44	15	15	5	0	0	0	13	3	34	0	0	2	1	.667	0	0	3.49
New York	AL	26	0	0	6	17.1	71	10	6	6	0	4	0	1	9	3	11	0	0	2	2	.500	0	0	3.12
8 ML YEARS		531	1	0	182	608.2	2586	566	256	232	51	49	15	11	225	52	569	22	4	41	32	.562	0	47	3.43

Pedro Astacio

Pitches: Right **Bats:** Right **Pos:** SP   **Ht:** 6' 2" **Wt:** 190 **Born:** 11/28/69 **Age:** 24

Year Team	Lg	G	GS	CG	GF	IP	BFP	H	R	ER	HR	SH	SF	HB	TBB	IBB	SO	WP	Bk	W	L	Pct.	ShO	Sv	ERA
1989 Dodgers	R	12	12	1	0	76.2	321	77	30	27	3	4	2	4	12	0	52	4	2	7	3	.700	1	0	3.17
1990 Vero Beach	A	8	8	0	0	47	215	54	39	33	3	1	1	1	23	0	41	4	5	1	5	.167	0	0	6.32
Yakima	A	3	3	0	0	20.2	79	9	8	4	0	0	0	2	4	0	22	3	0	2	0	1.000	0	0	1.74
Bakersfield	A	10	7	1	0	52	213	46	22	16	3	1	1	3	15	1	34	2	1	5	2	.714	0	0	2.77
1991 Vero Beach	A	9	9	3	0	59.1	223	44	19	11	0	2	1	1	8	0	45	2	0	5	3	.625	1	0	1.67
San Antonio	AA	19	19	2	0	113	497	142	67	60	9	5	3	3	39	3	62	4	2	4	11	.267	1	0	4.78
1992 Albuquerque	AAA	24	15	1	4	98.2	442	115	68	60	8	3	1	2	44	1	66	6	1	6	6	.500	0	0	5.47
1992 Los Angeles	NL	11	11	4	0	82	341	80	23	18	1	3	2	2	20	4	43	1	0	5	5	.500	4	0	1.98
1993 Los Angeles	NL	31	31	3	0	186.1	777	165	80	74	14	7	8	5	68	5	122	8	9	14	9	.609	2	0	3.57
2 ML YEARS		42	42	7	0	268.1	1118	245	103	92	15	10	10	7	88	9	165	9	9	19	14	.576	6	0	3.09

Rich Aude

Bats: Right **Throws:** Right **Pos:** 1B   **Ht:** 6' 5" **Wt:** 180 **Born:** 07/13/71 **Age:** 22

Year Team	Lg	G	AB	H	2B	3B	HR	(Hm	Rd)	TB	R	RBI	TBB	IBB	SO	HBP	SH	SF	SB	CS	SB%	GDP	Avg	OBP	SLG
1989 Pirates	R	24	88	19	3	0	0	--	--	22	13	7	5	0	17	3	0	1	2	0	1.00	1	.216	.278	.250
1990 Augusta	A	128	475	111	23	1	6	--	--	154	48	61	41	1	133	7	0	4	3	1	.75	11	.234	.302	.324
1991 Salem	A	103	366	97	12	2	3	--	--	122	45	43	27	5	72	9	0	0	3	0	1.00	7	.265	.331	.333
1992 Salem	A	122	447	128	26	4	9	--	--	189	63	60	50	2	79	8	0	1	11	2	.85	10	.286	.368	.423
Carolina	AA	6	20	4	1	0	2	--	--	11	4	3	1	0	3	0	0	0	0	0	.00	0	.200	.238	.550
1993 Buffalo	AAA	21	64	24	9	0	4	--	--	45	17	16	10	0	15	1	0	1	0	0	.00	1	.375	.461	.703
Carolina	AA	120	422	122	25	3	18	--	--	207	66	73	50	7	79	12	1	6	8	4	.67	6	.289	.376	.491
1993 Pittsburgh	NL	13	26	3	1	0	0	(0	0)	4	1	4	1	0	7	0	0	0	0	0	.00	0	.115	.148	.154

Brad Ausmus

Bats: Right **Throws:** Right **Pos:** C   **Ht:** 5'11" **Wt:** 185 **Born:** 04/14/69 **Age:** 25

Year Team	Lg	G	AB	H	2B	3B	HR	(Hm	Rd)	TB	R	RBI	TBB	IBB	SO	HBP	SH	SF	SB	CS	SB%	GDP	Avg	OBP	SLG
1988 Oneonta	A	2	4	1	0	0	0	--	--	1	0	0	0	0	2	0	0	0	0	0	.00	0	.250	.250	.250
Yankees	R	43	133	34	2	0	0	--	--	36	22	15	11	1	25	2	4	1	5	2	.71	4	.256	.320	.271
1989 Oneonta	A	52	165	43	6	0	1	--	--	52	29	18	22	0	28	0	2	0	6	4	.60	2	.261	.348	.315
1990 Pr William	A	107	364	86	12	2	0	--	--	102	46	27	32	0	73	3	3	0	2	8	.20	7	.236	.303	.280
1991 Pr William	A	63	230	70	14	3	2	--	--	96	28	30	24	3	37	0	1	3	17	6	.74	2	.304	.366	.417
Albany	AA	67	229	61	9	2	1	--	--	77	36	29	27	1	36	1	3	1	14	3	.82	8	.266	.345	.336
1992 Albany	AA	5	18	3	0	1	0	--	--	5	0	1	2	0	3	0	0	0	2	1	.67	1	.167	.250	.278
Columbus	AAA	111	364	88	14	3	2	--	--	114	48	35	40	0	56	1	2	2	19	5	.79	14	.242	.317	.313
1993 Colo Sprngs	AAA	76	241	65	10	4	2	--	--	89	31	33	27	1	41	1	2	3	10	6	.63	6	.270	.342	.369
1993 San Diego	NL	49	160	41	8	1	5	(4	1)	66	18	12	6	0	28	0	0	0	2	1	1.00	2	.256	.283	.413

James Austin

Pitches: Right **Bats:** Right **Pos:** RP   **Ht:** 6' 2" **Wt:** 200 **Born:** 12/07/63 **Age:** 30

Year Team	Lg	G	GS	CG	GF	IP	BFP	H	R	ER	HR	SH	SF	HB	TBB	IBB	SO	WP	Bk	W	L	Pct.	ShO	Sv	ERA
1993 New Orleans *	AAA	8	3	0	0	16	72	17	11	9	3	0	1	0	7	0	7	4	1	1	2	.333	0	0	5.06
1991 Milwaukee	AL	5	0	0	1	8.2	46	8	8	8	1	2	1	3	11	1	3	1	0	0	0	.000	0	0	8.31

Year Team	Lg	G	GS	CG	GF	IP	BFP	H	R	ER	HR	SH	SF	HB	TBB	IBB	SO	WP	Bk	W	L	Pct.	ShO	Sv	ERA
1992 Milwaukee	AL	47	0	0	12	58.1	235	38	13	12	2	1	1	2	32	6	30	1	0	5	2	.714	0	0	1.85
1993 Milwaukee	AL	31	0	0	8	33	137	28	15	14	3	1	0	1	13	1	15	4	0	1	2	.333	0	0	3.82
3 ML YEARS		83	0	0	21	100	418	74	36	34	6	4	2	6	56	8	48	6	0	6	4	.600	0	0	3.06

Steve Avery

Pitches: Left   **Bats:** Left   **Pos:** SP   **Ht:** 6' 4"   **Wt:** 190   **Born:** 04/14/70   **Age:** 24

		HOW MUCH HE PITCHED						WHAT HE GAVE UP												THE RESULTS					
Year Team	Lg	G	GS	CG	GF	IP	BFP	H	R	ER	HR	SH	SF	HB	TBB	IBB	SO	WP	Bk	W	L	Pct.	ShO	Sv	ERA
1990 Atlanta	NL	21	20	1	1	99	466	121	79	62	7	14	4	2	45	2	75	5	1	3	11	.214	1	0	5.64
1991 Atlanta	NL	35	35	3	0	210.1	868	189	89	79	21	8	4	3	65	0	137	4	1	18	8	.692	1	0	3.38
1992 Atlanta	NL	35	35	2	0	233.2	969	216	95	83	14	12	8	0	71	3	129	7	3	11	11	.500	2	0	3.20
1993 Atlanta	NL	35	35	3	0	223.1	891	216	81	73	14	12	8	0	43	5	125	3	1	18	6	.750	1	0	2.94
4 ML YEARS		126	125	9	1	766.1	3194	742	344	297	56	46	24	5	224	10	466	19	6	50	36	.581	5	0	3.49

Bobby Ayala

Pitches: Right   **Bats:** Right   **Pos:** RP/SP   **Ht:** 6' 2"   **Wt:** 190   **Born:** 07/08/69   **Age:** 24

		HOW MUCH HE PITCHED						WHAT HE GAVE UP												THE RESULTS					
Year Team	Lg	G	GS	CG	GF	IP	BFP	H	R	ER	HR	SH	SF	HB	TBB	IBB	SO	WP	Bk	W	L	Pct.	ShO	Sv	ERA
1988 Reds	R	20	0	0	15	33	153	34	23	14	0	3	3	3	12	0	24	1	0	0	4	.000	0	3	3.82
1989 Greensboro	A	22	19	1	1	105.1	467	97	73	48	7	2	3	4	50	0	70	10	2	5	8	.385	0	0	4.10
1990 Cedar Rapds	A	18	7	3	3	53.1	215	40	24	20	6	2	1	4	18	0	59	6	0	3	2	.600	1	0	3.38
Chston-Wv	A	21	4	2	8	74	287	48	23	20	2	2	1	3	21	1	73	0	0	6	1	.857	1	2	2.43
1991 Chattanooga	AA	39	8	1	16	90.2	404	79	52	47	10	4	3	4	58	4	92	10	1	3	1	.750	0	4	4.67
1992 Chattanooga	AA	27	27	3	0	162.2	690	152	75	64	14	8	2	11	58	0	154	9	0	12	6	.667	3	0	3.54
1993 Indianapols	AAA	5	5	0	0	27	123	36	19	17	1	3	0	1	12	1	19	1	0	0	2	.000	0	0	5.67
1992 Cincinnati	NL	5	5	0	0	29	127	33	15	14	1	2	0	1	13	2	23	0	0	2	1	.667	0	0	4.34
1993 Cincinnati	NL	43	9	0	8	98	450	106	72	61	16	9	2	7	45	4	65	5	0	7	10	.412	0	3	5.60
2 ML YEARS		48	14	0	8	127	577	139	87	75	17	11	2	8	58	6	88	5	0	9	11	.450	0	3	5.31

Bob Ayrault

Pitches: Right   **Bats:** Right   **Pos:** RP   **Ht:** 6' 4"   **Wt:** 235   **Born:** 04/27/66   **Age:** 28

		HOW MUCH HE PITCHED						WHAT HE GAVE UP												THE RESULTS					
Year Team	Lg	G	GS	CG	GF	IP	BFP	H	R	ER	HR	SH	SF	HB	TBB	IBB	SO	WP	Bk	W	L	Pct.	ShO	Sv	ERA
1989 Reno	A	24	14	3	5	109.2	478	104	56	46	7	3	4	11	57	3	91	3	3	7	4	.636	1	0	3.78
Batavia	A	4	3	2	1	26	93	13	5	4	2	1	0	2	7	0	20	0	0	2	1	.667	1	0	1.38
Reading	AA	2	1	0	0	8.2	33	3	1	1	0	0	0	0	4	0	8	0	0	0	0	.000	0	1	1.04
1990 Reading	AA	44	9	0	29	109.1	432	77	33	28	4	3	5	2	34	1	84	2	2	4	6	.400	0	10	2.30
1991 Scranton-Wb	AAA	68	0	0	21	98.2	433	91	58	53	11	6	5	5	47	4	103	4	1	8	5	.615	0	3	4.83
1992 Scranton/wb	AAA	20	0	0	14	25.1	110	19	15	14	4	3	2	1	15	3	30	0	0	5	1	.833	0	6	4.97
1993 Scranton/wb	AAA	5	1	0	3	7.1	33	8	2	1	0	0	0	0	3	1	9	0	0	0	1	.000	0	0	1.23
Calgary	AAA	3	0	0	2	4.1	22	8	5	5	0	0	0	0	2	0	3	0	0	0	0	.000	0	1	10.38
Albuquerque	AAA	11	0	0	1	14.2	74	21	10	10	2	1	0	2	7	3	13	0	0	2	2	.500	0	0	6.14
1992 Philadelphia	NL	30	0	0	7	43.1	178	32	16	15	0	4	3	1	17	1	27	0	0	2	2	.500	0	0	3.12
1993 2 ML Teams		24	0	0	9	30	139	36	19	18	2	1	2	1	16	2	15	1	0	3	1	.750	0	0	5.40
1993 Philadelphia	NL	10	0	0	3	10.1	59	18	11	11	1	0	0	1	10	1	8	1	0	2	0	1.000	0	0	9.58
Seattle	AL	14	0	0	6	19.2	80	18	8	7	1	1	2	0	6	1	7	0	0	1	1	.500	0	0	3.20
2 ML YEARS		54	0	0	16	73.1	317	68	35	33	2	5	5	2	33	3	42	1	0	5	3	.625	0	0	4.05

Wally Backman

Bats: Left   **Throws:** Right   **Pos:** 3B   **Ht:** 5' 9"   **Wt:** 168   **Born:** 09/22/59   **Age:** 34

		BATTING																BASERUNNING				PERCENTAGES		
Year Team	Lg	G	AB	H	2B	3B	HR	(Hm	Rd)	TB	R	RBI	TBB	IBB	SO	HBP	SH	SF	SB	CS	SB%	GDP	Avg	OBP	SLG
1980 New York	NL	27	93	30	1	1	0	(0	0)	33	12	9	11	1	14	1	4	1	2	3	.40	3	.323	.396	.355
1981 New York	NL	26	36	10	2	0	0	(0	0)	12	5	0	4	0	7	0	2	0	1	0	1.00	1	.278	.350	.333
1982 New York	NL	96	261	71	13	2	3	(1	2)	97	37	22	49	1	47	0	2	0	8	7	.53	6	.272	.387	.372
1983 New York	NL	26	42	7	0	1	0	(0	0)	9	6	3	2	0	8	0	1	0	0	0	.00	2	.167	.205	.214
1984 New York	NL	128	436	122	19	2	1	(0	1)	148	68	26	56	2	63	0	5	2	32	9	.78	13	.280	.360	.339
1985 New York	NL	145	520	142	24	5	1	(0	1)	179	77	38	36	1	72	1	14	3	30	12	.71	3	.273	.320	.344
1986 New York	NL	124	387	124	18	2	1	(1	0)	149	67	27	36	1	32	0	14	3	13	7	.65	3	.320	.376	.385
1987 New York	NL	94	300	75	6	1	1	(0	1)	86	43	23	25	0	43	0	9	1	11	3	.79	5	.250	.307	.287
1988 New York	NL	99	294	89	12	0	0	(0	0)	101	44	17	41	1	49	1	9	2	9	5	.64	6	.303	.388	.344
1989 Minnesota	AL	87	299	69	9	2	1	(0	1)	85	33	26	32	0	45	1	4	1	1	1	.50	4	.231	.306	.284
1990 Pittsburgh	NL	104	315	92	21	3	2	(0	2)	125	62	28	42	1	53	1	0	3	6	3	.67	5	.292	.374	.397
1991 Philadelphia	NL	94	185	45	12	0	0	(0	0)	57	20	15	30	0	30	0	2	3	3	2	.60	2	.243	.344	.308
1992 Philadelphia	NL	42	48	13	1	0	0	(0	0)	14	6	6	6	1	9	0	1	0	1	0	1.00	3	.271	.352	.292
1993 Seattle	AL	10	29	4	0	0	0	(0	0)	4	2	0	1	0	8	0	1	0	0	0	.00	0	.138	.167	.138
14 ML YEARS		1102	3245	893	138	19	10	(2	8)	1099	482	240	371	9	480	5	68	19	117	52	.69	55	.275	.349	.339

Carlos Baerga

Bats: Both **Throws:** Right **Pos:** 2B **Ht:** 5'11" **Wt:** 200 **Born:** 11/04/68 **Age:** 25

Year Team	Lg	G	AB	H	2B	3B	HR	(Hm	Rd)	TB	R	RBI	TBB	IBB	SO	HBP	SH	SF	SB	CS	SB%	GDP	Avg	OBP	SLG
1990 Cleveland	AL	108	312	81	17	2	7	(3	4)	123	46	47	16	2	57	4	1	5	0	2	.00	4	.260	.300	.394
1991 Cleveland	AL	158	593	171	28	2	11	(2	9)	236	80	69	48	5	74	6	4	3	3	2	.60	12	.288	.346	.398
1992 Cleveland	AL	161	657	205	32	1	20	(9	11)	299	92	105	35	10	76	13	2	9	10	2	.83	15	.312	.354	.455
1993 Cleveland	AL	154	624	200	28	6	21	(8	13)	303	105	114	34	7	68	6	3	13	15	4	.79	17	.321	.355	.486
4 ML YEARS		581	2186	657	105	11	59	(22	37)	961	323	335	133	24	275	29	10	30	28	10	.74	48	.301	.344	.440

Kevin Baez

Bats: Right **Throws:** Right **Pos:** SS **Ht:** 6' 0" **Wt:** 170 **Born:** 01/10/67 **Age:** 27

Year Team	Lg	G	AB	H	2B	3B	HR	(Hm	Rd)	TB	R	RBI	TBB	IBB	SO	HBP	SH	SF	SB	CS	SB%	GDP	Avg	OBP	SLG
1988 Little Fls	A	70	218	58	7	1	1	--	--	70	23	19	32	1	30	2	2	3	7	3	.70	3	.266	.361	.321
1989 Columbia	A	123	426	108	25	1	5	--	--	150	59	44	58	3	53	6	9	3	11	9	.55	5	.254	.349	.352
1990 Jackson	AA	106	327	76	11	0	2	--	--	93	29	29	37	4	44	2	11	2	3	4	.43	7	.232	.313	.284
1991 Tidewater	AAA	65	210	36	8	0	0	--	--	44	18	13	12	1	32	4	5	4	0	1	.00	5	.171	.226	.210
1992 Tidewater	AAA	109	352	83	16	1	2	--	--	107	30	33	13	1	57	4	5	5	1	1	.50	9	.236	.267	.304
1993 Norfolk	AAA	63	209	54	11	1	2	--	--	73	23	21	20	1	29	1	2	1	0	2	.00	3	.258	.325	.349
1990 New York	NL	5	12	2	1	0	0	(0	0)	3	0	0	0	0	0	0	0	0	0	0	.00	2	.167	.167	.250
1992 New York	NL	6	13	2	0	0	0	(0	0)	2	0	0	0	0	0	0	0	0	0	0	.00	0	.154	.154	.154
1993 New York	NL	52	126	23	9	0	0	(0	0)	32	10	7	13	1	17	0	4	0	0	0	.00	1	.183	.259	.254
3 ML YEARS		63	151	27	10	0	0	(0	0)	37	10	7	13	1	17	0	4	0	0	0	.00	4	.179	.244	.245

Jeff Bagwell

Bats: Right **Throws:** Right **Pos:** 1B **Ht:** 6' 0" **Wt:** 195 **Born:** 05/27/68 **Age:** 26

Year Team	Lg	G	AB	H	2B	3B	HR	(Hm	Rd)	TB	R	RBI	TBB	IBB	SO	HBP	SH	SF	SB	CS	SB%	GDP	Avg	OBP	SLG
1991 Houston	NL	156	554	163	26	4	15	(6	9)	242	79	82	75	5	116	13	1	7	7	4	.64	12	.294	.387	.437
1992 Houston	NL	162	586	160	34	6	18	(8	10)	260	87	96	84	13	97	12	2	13	10	6	.63	17	.273	.368	.444
1993 Houston	NL	142	535	171	37	4	20	(9	11)	276	76	88	62	6	73	3	0	9	13	4	.76	21	.320	.388	.516
3 ML YEARS		460	1675	494	97	14	53	(23	30)	778	242	266	221	24	286	28	3	29	30	14	.68	50	.295	.380	.464

Cory Bailey

Pitches: Right **Bats:** Right **Pos:** RP **Ht:** 6' 1" **Wt:** 210 **Born:** 01/24/71 **Age:** 23

Year Team	Lg																						

Year Team	Lg	G	GS	CG	GF	IP	BFP	H	R	ER	HR	SH	SF	HB	TBB	IBB	SO	WP	Bk	W	L	Pct.	ShO	Sv	ERA
1991 Red Sox	R	1	0	0	1	2	9	2	1	0	0	0	0	0	1	0	1	0	0	0	0	.000	0	1	0.00
Elmira	A	28	0	0	25	39	151	19	10	8	2	1	0	3	12	0	54	2	0	2	4	.333	0	15	1.85
1992 Lynchburg	A	49	0	0	43	66.1	272	43	20	18	3	6	2	2	30	2	87	5	0	5	7	.417	0	23	2.44
1993 Pawtucket	AAA	52	0	0	40	65.2	264	48	21	21	1	2	2	1	31	5	59	5	1	4	5	.444	0	20	2.88
1993 Boston	AL	11	0	0	5	15.2	66	12	7	6	0	1	1	0	12	3	11	2	1	0	1	.000	0	0	3.45

Harold Baines

Bats: Left **Throws:** Left **Pos:** DH **Ht:** 6' 2" **Wt:** 195 **Born:** 03/15/59 **Age:** 35

Year Team	Lg	G	AB	H	2B	3B	HR	(Hm	Rd)	TB	R	RBI	TBB	IBB	SO	HBP	SH	SF	SB	CS	SB%	GDP	Avg	OBP	SLG
1993 Bowie *	AA	2	6	0	0	0	0	--	--	0	0	1	1	0	1	0	0	0	0	0	.00	0	.000	.143	.000
1980 Chicago	AL	141	491	125	23	6	13	(3	10)	199	55	49	19	7	65	1	2	5	2	4	.33	15	.255	.281	.405
1981 Chicago	AL	82	280	80	11	7	10	(3	7)	135	42	41	12	4	41	2	0	2	6	2	.75	6	.286	.318	.482
1982 Chicago	AL	161	608	165	29	8	25	(11	14)	285	89	105	49	10	95	0	2	9	10	3	.77	12	.271	.321	.469
1983 Chicago	AL	156	596	167	33	2	20	(8	12)	264	76	99	49	13	85	1	3	6	7	5	.58	15	.280	.333	.443
1984 Chicago	AL	147	569	173	28	10	29	(16	13)	308	72	94	54	9	75	0	1	5	1	2	.33	12	.304	.361	.541
1985 Chicago	AL	160	640	198	29	3	22	(13	9)	299	86	113	42	8	89	1	0	10	1	1	.50	23	.309	.348	.467
1986 Chicago	AL	145	570	169	29	2	21	(8	13)	265	72	88	38	9	89	2	0	8	2	1	.67	14	.296	.338	.465
1987 Chicago	AL	132	505	148	26	4	20	(12	8)	242	59	93	46	2	82	1	0	2	0	0	.00	12	.293	.352	.479
1988 Chicago	AL	158	599	166	39	1	13	(5	8)	246	55	81	67	14	109	1	0	7	0	0	.00	21	.277	.347	.411
1989 2 ML Teams		146	505	156	29	1	16	(5	11)	235	73	72	73	13	79	1	0	4	0	3	.00	15	.309	.395	.465
1990 2 ML Teams		135	415	118	15	1	16	(9	7)	183	52	65	67	10	80	0	0	7	0	3	.00	17	.284	.378	.441
1991 Oakland	AL	141	488	144	25	1	20	(11	9)	231	76	90	72	22	67	1	0	5	0	1	.00	12	.295	.383	.473
1992 Oakland	AL	140	478	121	18	0	16	(10	6)	187	58	76	59	6	61	0	0	6	1	3	.25	11	.253	.331	.391
1993 Baltimore	AL	118	416	130	22	0	20	(12	8)	212	64	78	57	9	52	0	0	6	0	0	.00	14	.313	.390	.510
1989 Chicago	AL	96	333	107	20	1	13	(4	9)	168	55	56	60	13	52	1	0	3	0	1	.00	11	.321	.423	.505
Texas	AL	50	172	49	9	0	3	(1	2)	67	18	16	13	0	27	0	0	1	0	2	.00	4	.285	.333	.390
1990 Texas	AL	103	321	93	10	1	13	(6	7)	144	41	44	47	9	63	0	0	3	0	1	.00	13	.290	.377	.449
Oakland	AL	32	94	25	5	0	3	(3	0)	39	11	21	20	1	17	0	0	4	0	2	.00	4	.266	.381	.415
14 ML YEARS		1962	7160	2060	356	46	261	(130	131)	3291	929	1144	704	136	1069	11	9	82	30	28	.52	199	.288	.349	.460

12

Steve Balboni

Bats: Right **Throws:** Right **Pos:** DH   **Ht:** 6' 3" **Wt:** 252 **Born:** 01/16/57 **Age:** 37

									BATTING											BASERUNNING				PERCENTAGES		
Year	Team	Lg	G	AB	H	2B	3B	HR	(Hm	Rd)	TB	R	RBI	TBB	IBB	SO	HBP	SH	SF	SB	CS	SB%	GDP	Avg	OBP	SLG
1993	Okla City *	AAA	126	471	115	22	0	36	--	--	245	67	108	51	4	98	6	0	7	0	1	.00	16	.244	.321	.520
1981	New York	AL	4	7	2	1	1	0	(0	0)	5	2	2	1	0	4	0	0	0	0	0	.00	0	.286	.375	.714
1982	New York	AL	33	107	20	2	1	2	(0	2)	30	8	4	6	0	34	0	0	1	0	0	.00	1	.187	.228	.280
1983	New York	AL	32	86	20	2	0	5	(0	5)	37	8	17	8	0	23	0	0	1	0	0	.00	2	.233	.295	.430
1984	Kansas City	AL	126	438	107	23	2	28	(10	18)	218	58	77	45	5	139	4	0	1	0	0	.00	9	.244	.320	.498
1985	Kansas City	AL	160	600	146	28	2	36	(17	19)	286	74	88	52	4	166	5	0	5	1	1	.50	14	.243	.307	.477
1986	Kansas City	AL	138	512	117	25	1	29	(10	19)	231	54	88	43	2	146	1	0	6	0	0	.00	8	.229	.286	.451
1987	Kansas City	AL	121	386	80	11	1	24	(8	16)	165	44	60	34	1	97	2	0	3	0	1	.00	11	.207	.273	.427
1988	2 ML Teams		118	413	97	17	1	23	(15	8)	185	46	66	24	2	87	1	0	2	0	0	.00	8	.235	.277	.448
1989	New York	AL	110	300	71	12	2	17	(7	10)	138	33	59	25	5	91	3	0	6	0	0	.00	10	.237	.296	.460
1990	New York	AL	116	266	51	6	0	17	(8	9)	108	24	34	35	2	91	3	1	2	0	0	.00	4	.192	.291	.406
1993	Texas	AL	2	5	3	0	0	0	(0	0)	3	0	0	0	0	2	0	0	0	0	0	.00	0	.600	.600	.600
1988	Kansas City	AL	21	63	9	2	0	2	(1	1)	17	2	5	1	0	20	0	0	0	0	0	.00	0	.143	.156	.270
	Seattle	AL	97	350	88	15	1	21	(14	7)	168	44	61	23	2	67	1	0	2	0	1	.00	8	.251	.298	.480
	11 ML YEARS		960	3120	714	127	11	181	(75	106)	1406	351	495	273	21	856	19	1	27	1	2	.33	67	.229	.293	.451

Jeff Ballard

Pitches: Left **Bats:** Left **Pos:** RP/SP   **Ht:** 6' 2" **Wt:** 203 **Born:** 08/13/63 **Age:** 30

			HOW MUCH HE PITCHED						WHAT HE GAVE UP										THE RESULTS					
Year	Team	Lg	G	GS	CG	GF	IP	BFP	H	R	ER	HR	SH	SF	HB	TBB	IBB	SO	WP	Bk	W	L	Pct.	ShO	Sv	ERA
1993	Buffalo *	AAA	12	12	1	0	74.2	311	79	22	19	4	3	3	2	17	0	40	0	0	6	1	.857	0	0	2.29
1987	Baltimore	AL	14	14	0	0	69.2	327	100	60	51	15	0	1	0	35	1	27	0	1	2	8	.200	0	0	6.59
1988	Baltimore	AL	25	25	6	0	153.1	654	167	83	75	15	3	3	6	42	2	41	2	2	8	12	.400	1	0	4.40
1989	Baltimore	AL	35	35	4	0	215.1	912	240	95	82	16	10	5	4	57	5	62	3	0	18	8	.692	1	0	3.43
1990	Baltimore	AL	44	17	0	6	133.1	578	152	79	73	22	5	2	3	42	6	50	2	1	2	11	.154	0	0	4.93
1991	Baltimore	AL	26	22	0	1	123.2	540	153	91	77	16	1	3	2	28	2	37	3	1	6	12	.333	0	0	5.60
1993	Pittsburgh	NL	25	5	0	4	53.2	234	70	31	29	3	5	1	2	15	3	16	2	0	4	1	.800	0	0	4.86
	6 ML YEARS		169	118	10	11	749	3245	882	439	387	87	24	15	17	219	19	233	12	5	40	52	.435	2	0	4.65

Scott Bankhead

Pitches: Right **Bats:** Right **Pos:** RP   **Ht:** 5'10" **Wt:** 185 **Born:** 07/31/63 **Age:** 30

			HOW MUCH HE PITCHED						WHAT HE GAVE UP										THE RESULTS					
Year	Team	Lg	G	GS	CG	GF	IP	BFP	H	R	ER	HR	SH	SF	HB	TBB	IBB	SO	WP	Bk	W	L	Pct.	ShO	Sv	ERA
1986	Kansas City	AL	24	17	0	2	121	517	121	66	62	14	5	5	3	37	7	94	1	0	8	9	.471	0	0	4.61
1987	Seattle	AL	27	25	2	1	149.1	642	168	96	90	35	3	6	3	37	0	95	2	2	9	8	.529	0	0	5.42
1988	Seattle	AL	21	21	2	0	135	557	115	53	46	8	3	1	1	38	5	102	3	1	7	9	.438	1	0	3.07
1989	Seattle	AL	33	33	3	0	210.1	862	187	84	78	19	4	8	3	63	1	140	2	0	14	6	.700	2	0	3.34
1990	Seattle	AL	4	4	0	0	13	63	18	16	16	2	0	2	0	7	0	10	1	0	0	2	.000	0	0	11.08
1991	Seattle	AL	17	9	0	2	60.2	271	73	35	33	8	0	2	2	21	2	28	0	0	3	6	.333	0	0	4.90
1992	Cincinnati	NL	54	0	0	10	70.2	299	57	26	23	4	3	3	3	29	5	53	6	0	10	4	.714	0	1	2.93
1993	Boston	AL	40	0	0	4	64.1	272	59	28	25	7	3	4	0	29	3	47	1	0	2	1	.667	0	0	3.50
	8 ML YEARS		220	109	7	19	824.1	3483	798	404	373	97	21	31	15	261	23	569	16	3	53	45	.541	3	1	4.07

Willie Banks

Pitches: Right **Bats:** Right **Pos:** SP   **Ht:** 6' 1" **Wt:** 202 **Born:** 02/27/69 **Age:** 25

			HOW MUCH HE PITCHED						WHAT HE GAVE UP										THE RESULTS					
Year	Team	Lg	G	GS	CG	GF	IP	BFP	H	R	ER	HR	SH	SF	HB	TBB	IBB	SO	WP	Bk	W	L	Pct.	ShO	Sv	ERA
1991	Minnesota	AL	5	3	0	2	17.1	85	21	15	11	1	0	0	0	12	0	16	3	0	1	1	.500	0	0	5.71
1992	Minnesota	AL	16	12	0	2	71	324	80	46	45	6	2	5	2	37	0	37	5	1	4	4	.500	0	0	5.70
1993	Minnesota	AL	31	30	0	1	171.1	754	186	91	77	17	4	4	3	78	2	138	9	5	11	12	.478	0	0	4.04
	3 ML YEARS		52	45	0	5	259.2	1163	287	152	133	24	6	9	5	127	2	191	17	6	16	17	.485	0	0	4.61

Bret Barberie

Bats: Both **Throws:** Right **Pos:** 2B   **Ht:** 5'11" **Wt:** 180 **Born:** 08/16/67 **Age:** 26

									BATTING											BASERUNNING				PERCENTAGES		
Year	Team	Lg	G	AB	H	2B	3B	HR	(Hm	Rd)	TB	R	RBI	TBB	IBB	SO	HBP	SH	SF	SB	CS	SB%	GDP	Avg	OBP	SLG
1993	Edmonton *	AAA	4	19	8	2	0	1	--	--	13	3	8	0	0	2	1	0	0	0	0	.00	0	.421	.450	.684
	Marlins *	R	2	8	2	0	0	0	--	--	2	0	1	1	0	1	0	0	0	0	0	.00	0	.250	.333	.250
1991	Montreal	NL	57	136	48	12	2	2	(2	0)	70	16	18	20	2	22	2	1	3	0	0	.00	4	.353	.435	.515
1992	Montreal	NL	111	285	66	11	0	1	(0	1)	80	26	24	47	3	62	8	1	2	9	5	.64	3	.232	.354	.281
1993	Florida	NL	99	375	104	16	2	5	(2	3)	139	45	33	33	2	58	7	5	3	2	4	.33	7	.277	.344	.371
	3 ML YEARS		267	796	218	39	4	8	(4	4)	289	87	75	100	7	142	17	7	8	11	9	.55	15	.274	.364	.363

Brian Barnes

Pitches: Left **Bats:** Left **Pos:** RP/SP **Ht:** 5' 9" **Wt:** 170 **Born:** 03/25/67 **Age:** 27

			HOW MUCH HE PITCHED						WHAT HE GAVE UP									THE RESULTS					
Year Team	Lg	G	GS	CG	GF	IP	BFP	H	R	ER	HR	SH	SF	HB	TBB	IBB	SO	WP	Bk	W	L	Pct.	ShO	Sv	ERA
1990 Montreal	NL	4	4	1	0	28	115	25	10	9	2	2	0	0	7	0	23	2	0	1	1	.500	0	0	2.89
1991 Montreal	NL	28	27	1	0	160	684	135	82	75	16	9	5	6	84	2	117	5	1	5	8	.385	0	0	4.22
1992 Montreal	NL	21	17	0	2	100	417	77	34	33	9	5	1	3	46	1	65	1	2	6	6	.500	0	0	2.97
1993 Montreal	NL	52	8	0	8	100	442	105	53	49	9	8	3	0	48	2	60	5	1	2	6	.250	0	3	4.41
4 ML YEARS		105	56	2	10	388	1658	342	179	166	36	24	9	9	185	5	265	13	4	14	21	.400	0	3	3.85

Skeeter Barnes

Bats: Right **Throws:** Right **Pos:** 1B/3B/LF/DH **Ht:** 5'10" **Wt:** 180 **Born:** 03/07/57 **Age:** 37

							BATTING												BASERUNNING				PERCENTAGES		
Year Team	Lg	G	AB	H	2B	3B	HR	(Hm	Rd)	TB	R	RBI	TBB	IBB	SO	HBP	SH	SF	SB	CS	SB%	GDP	Avg	OBP	SLG
1983 Cincinnati	NL	15	34	7	0	0	1	(1	0)	10	5	4	7	0	3	2	0	0	2	2	.50	0	.206	.372	.294
1984 Cincinnati	NL	32	42	5	0	0	1	(1	0)	8	5	3	4	1	6	0	0	0	0	0	.00	1	.119	.196	.190
1985 Montreal	NL	19	26	4	1	0	0	(0	0)	5	0	0	0	0	2	0	0	0	0	1	.00	1	.154	.154	.192
1987 St. Louis	NL	4	4	1	0	0	1	(0	1)	4	1	3	0	0	0	0	0	0	0	0	.00	0	.250	.250	1.000
1989 Cincinnati	NL	5	3	0	0	0	0	(0	0)	0	1	0	0	0	0	0	0	0	0	1	.00	0	.000	.000	.000
1991 Detroit	AL	75	159	46	13	2	5	(1	4)	78	28	17	9	1	24	0	2	1	10	7	.59	1	.289	.325	.491
1992 Detroit	AL	95	165	45	8	1	3	(3	0)	64	27	25	10	1	18	2	2	2	3	1	.75	4	.273	.318	.388
1993 Detroit	AL	84	160	45	8	1	2	(2	0)	61	24	27	11	0	19	0	4	5	5	5	.50	2	.281	.318	.381
8 ML YEARS		329	593	153	30	4	13	(8	5)	230	91	79	41	3	72	4	8	8	20	17	.54	9	.258	.307	.388

Kevin Bass

Bats: Both **Throws:** Right **Pos:** RF/LF **Ht:** 6' 0" **Wt:** 190 **Born:** 05/12/59 **Age:** 35

							BATTING												BASERUNNING				PERCENTAGES		
Year Team	Lg	G	AB	H	2B	3B	HR	(Hm	Rd)	TB	R	RBI	TBB	IBB	SO	HBP	SH	SF	SB	CS	SB%	GDP	Avg	OBP	SLG
1982 2 ML Teams		30	33	1	0	0	0	(0	0)	1	6	1	1	0	9	0	1	0	0	0	.00	1	.030	.059	.030
1983 Houston	NL	88	195	46	7	3	2	(2	0)	65	25	18	6	1	27	0	4	1	2	2	.50	2	.236	.257	.333
1984 Houston	NL	121	331	86	17	5	2	(1	1)	119	33	29	6	1	57	3	2	0	5	5	.50	2	.260	.279	.360
1985 Houston	NL	150	539	145	27	5	16	(9	7)	230	72	68	31	4	63	6	4	2	19	8	.70	10	.269	.315	.427
1986 Houston	NL	157	591	184	33	5	20	(5	15)	287	83	79	38	11	72	6	1	4	22	13	.63	15	.311	.357	.486
1987 Houston	NL	157	592	168	31	5	19	(10	9)	266	83	85	53	13	77	4	0	5	21	8	.72	15	.284	.344	.449
1988 Houston	NL	157	541	138	27	2	14	(5	9)	211	57	72	42	10	65	6	3	3	31	6	.84	16	.255	.314	.390
1989 Houston	NL	87	313	94	19	4	5	(2	3)	136	42	44	29	3	44	1	1	4	11	4	.73	2	.300	.357	.435
1990 San Francisco	NL	61	214	54	9	1	7	(3	4)	86	25	32	14	3	26	2	2	1	2	2	.50	5	.252	.303	.402
1991 San Francisco	NL	124	361	84	10	4	10	(5	5)	132	43	40	36	8	56	4	2	3	7	4	.64	12	.233	.307	.366
1992 2 ML Teams		135	402	108	23	5	9	(7	2)	168	40	39	23	3	70	1	1	3	14	9	.61	8	.269	.308	.418
1993 Houston	NL	111	229	65	18	0	3	(2	1)	92	31	37	26	3	31	1	2	0	7	1	.88	4	.284	.359	.402
1982 Milwaukee	AL	18	9	0	0	0	0	(0	0)	0	4	0	1	0	1	0	1	0	0	0	.00	0	.000	.100	.000
Houston	NL	12	24	1	0	0	0	(0	0)	1	2	1	0	0	8	0	0	0	0	0	.00	1	.042	.042	.042
1992 San Francisco	NL	89	265	71	11	3	7	(5	2)	109	25	30	16	1	53	1	1	2	7	7	.50	6	.268	.310	.411
New York	NL	46	137	37	12	2	2	(2	0)	59	15	9	7	2	17	0	0	1	7	2	.78	2	.270	.303	.431
12 ML YEARS		1378	4341	1173	221	39	107	(51	56)	1793	540	544	305	57	597	34	23	26	141	62	.69	92	.270	.321	.413

Richard Batchelor

Pitches: Right **Bats:** Right **Pos:** RP **Ht:** 6' 1" **Wt:** 195 **Born:** 04/08/67 **Age:** 27

					HOW MUCH HE PITCHED						WHAT HE GAVE UP								THE RESULTS				
Year Team	Lg	G	GS	CG	GF	IP	BFP	H	R	ER	HR	SH	SF	HB	TBB	IBB	SO	WP	Bk	W	L	Pct.	ShO	Sv	ERA
1990 Greensboro	A	27	0	0	18	51.1	200	39	15	9	1	0	2	0	14	1	38	2	0	2	2	.500	0	8	1.58
1991 Ft.Laudrdle	A	50	0	0	41	62	269	55	28	19	1	6	1	1	22	5	58	4	0	4	7	.364	0	25	2.76
Albany	AA	1	0	0	1	1	9	5	5	5	0	1	0	0	1	0	0	0	0	0	0	.000	0	0	45.00
1992 Albany	AA	58	0	0	34	70.2	320	79	40	33	5	1	2	6	34	3	45	4	0	4	5	.444	0	7	4.20
1993 Albany	AA	36	0	0	32	40.1	162	27	9	4	1	1	0	1	12	0	40	3	0	1	3	.250	0	19	0.89
Columbus	AAA	15	0	0	14	16.1	74	14	5	5	0	0	0	0	8	1	17	3	0	1	1	.500	0	6	2.76
1993 St. Louis	NL	9	0	0	2	10	45	14	12	9	1	1	2	0	3	1	4	0	0	0	0	.000	0	0	8.10

Kim Batiste

Bats: Right **Throws:** Right **Pos:** 3B/SS **Ht:** 6' 0" **Wt:** 193 **Born:** 03/15/68 **Age:** 26

							BATTING												BASERUNNING				PERCENTAGES		
Year Team	Lg	G	AB	H	2B	3B	HR	(Hm	Rd)	TB	R	RBI	TBB	IBB	SO	HBP	SH	SF	SB	CS	SB%	GDP	Avg	OBP	SLG
1991 Philadelphia	NL	10	27	6	0	0	0	(0	0)	6	2	1	1	1	8	0	0	0	0	1	.00	0	.222	.250	.222
1992 Philadelphia	NL	44	136	28	4	0	1	(0	1)	35	9	10	4	1	18	0	2	3	0	0	.00	7	.206	.224	.257
1993 Philadelphia	NL	79	156	44	7	1	5	(1	4)	68	14	29	3	2	29	1	0	1	0	1	.00	3	.282	.298	.436
3 ML YEARS		133	319	78	11	1	6	(1	5)	109	25	40	8	4	55	1	2	4	0	2	.00	10	.245	.262	.342

14

Danny Bautista

Bats: Right **Throws:** Right **Pos:** CF **Ht:** 5'11" **Wt:** 170 **Born:** 05/24/72 **Age:** 22

						BATTING												BASERUNNING				PERCENTAGES		
Year	Team	Lg	G	AB	H	2B	3B	HR	(Hm	Rd)	TB	R	RBI	TBB	IBB	SO	HBP	SH	SF	SB	CS	SB%	GDP	Avg	OBP	SLG
1990	Bristol	R	27	95	26	3	0	2	--	--	35	9	11	8	1	21	0	1	0	2	3	.40	1	.274	.330	.368
1991	Fayetteville	A	69	234	45	6	4	1	--	--	62	21	30	21	1	64	1	4	3	6	7	.46	8	.192	.259	.265
1992	Fayetteville	A	121	453	122	22	0	5	--	--	159	59	52	29	0	76	5	4	2	18	20	.47	9	.269	.319	.351
1993	London	AA	117	424	121	21	1	6	--	--	162	55	48	32	1	69	2	4	8	28	12	.70	8	.285	.334	.382
1993	Detroit	AL	17	61	19	3	0	1	(0	1)	25	6	9	1	0	10	0	0	1	3	1	.75	1	.311	.317	.410

Jose Bautista

Pitches: Right **Bats:** Right **Pos:** RP/SP **Ht:** 6' 2" **Wt:** 205 **Born:** 07/25/64 **Age:** 29

			HOW MUCH HE PITCHED					WHAT HE GAVE UP									THE RESULTS					
Year	Team	Lg	G	GS	CG	GF	IP	BFP	H	R	ER	HR	SH	SF	HB	TBB	IBB	SO	WP	Bk	W	L	Pct.	ShO	Sv	ERA
1988	Baltimore	AL	33	25	3	5	171.2	721	171	86	82	21	2	3	7	45	3	76	4	5	6	15	.286	0	0	4.30
1989	Baltimore	AL	15	10	0	4	78	325	84	46	46	17	1	1	1	15	0	30	0	0	3	4	.429	0	0	5.31
1990	Baltimore	AL	22	0	0	9	26.2	112	28	15	12	4	1	1	0	7	3	15	2	0	1	0	1.000	0	0	4.05
1991	Baltimore	AL	5	0	0	3	5.1	34	13	10	10	1	0	0	1	5	0	3	1	0	0	1	.000	0	0	16.88
1993	Chicago	NL	58	7	1	14	111.2	459	105	38	35	11	4	3	5	27	3	63	4	1	10	3	.769	0	2	2.82
	5 ML YEARS		133	42	4	35	393.1	1651	401	195	185	54	8	8	14	99	9	187	11	6	20	23	.465	0	2	4.23

Billy Bean

Bats: Left **Throws:** Left **Pos:** RF/1B/LF/CF **Ht:** 6' 1" **Wt:** 185 **Born:** 05/11/64 **Age:** 30

						BATTING												BASERUNNING				PERCENTAGES		
Year	Team	Lg	G	AB	H	2B	3B	HR	(Hm	Rd)	TB	R	RBI	TBB	IBB	SO	HBP	SH	SF	SB	CS	SB%	GDP	Avg	OBP	SLG
1993	Las Vegas *	AAA	53	167	59	11	2	7	--	--	95	31	40	32	3	14	2	0	4	3	1	.75	2	.353	.454	.569
1987	Detroit	AL	26	66	17	2	0	0	(0	0)	19	6	4	5	0	11	0	0	1	1	1	.50	1	.258	.310	.288
1988	Detroit	AL	10	11	2	0	1	0	(0	0)	4	2	0	0	0	2	0	1	0	0	0	.00	0	.182	.182	.364
1989	2 ML Teams		60	82	14	4	0	0	(0	0)	18	7	3	6	0	13	2	0	0	0	2	.00	0	.171	.244	.220
1993	San Diego	NL	88	177	46	9	0	5	(4	1)	70	19	32	6	1	29	2	2	5	2	4	.33	4	.260	.284	.395
1989	Detroit	AL	9	11	0	0	0	0	(0	0)	0	0	0	2	0	3	1	0	0	0	0	.00	0	.000	.214	.000
	Los Angeles	NL	51	71	14	4	0	0	(0	0)	18	7	3	4	0	10	1	0	0	0	2	.00	0	.197	.250	.254
	4 ML YEARS		184	336	79	15	1	5	(4	1)	111	34	39	17	1	55	4	3	5	3	7	.30	5	.235	.276	.330

Rod Beck

Pitches: Right **Bats:** Right **Pos:** RP **Ht:** 6' 1" **Wt:** 236 **Born:** 08/03/68 **Age:** 25

			HOW MUCH HE PITCHED					WHAT HE GAVE UP									THE RESULTS					
Year	Team	Lg	G	GS	CG	GF	IP	BFP	H	R	ER	HR	SH	SF	HB	TBB	IBB	SO	WP	Bk	W	L	Pct.	ShO	Sv	ERA
1991	San Francisco	NL	31	0	0	10	52.1	214	53	22	22	4	4	2	1	13	2	38	0	0	1	1	.500	0	1	3.78
1992	San Francisco	NL	65	0	0	42	92	352	62	20	18	4	6	2	2	15	2	87	5	2	3	3	.500	0	17	1.76
1993	San Francisco	NL	76	0	0	71	79.1	309	57	20	19	11	6	3	3	13	4	86	4	0	3	1	.750	0	48	2.16
	3 ML YEARS		172	0	0	123	223.2	875	172	62	59	19	16	7	6	41	8	211	9	2	7	5	.583	0	66	2.37

Rich Becker

Bats: Both **Throws:** Left **Pos:** CF **Ht:** 5'10" **Wt:** 180 **Born:** 02/01/72 **Age:** 22

						BATTING												BASERUNNING				PERCENTAGES		
Year	Team	Lg	G	AB	H	2B	3B	HR	(Hm	Rd)	TB	R	RBI	TBB	IBB	SO	HBP	SH	SF	SB	CS	SB%	GDP	Avg	OBP	SLG
1990	Elizabethtn	R	56	194	56	5	1	6	--	--	81	54	24	53	0	54	3	5	0	16	2	.89	3	.289	.448	.418
1991	Kenosha	A	130	494	132	38	3	13	--	--	215	100	53	72	3	108	2	1	4	19	4	.83	7	.267	.360	.435
1992	Visalia	A	136	506	160	37	2	15	--	--	246	118	82	114	2	122	4	1	6	29	13	.69	5	.316	.441	.486
1993	Nashville	AA	138	516	148	25	7	15	--	--	232	93	66	94	5	117	3	2	3	29	7	.81	10	.287	.398	.450
1993	Minnesota	AL	3	7	2	2	0	0	(0	0)	4	3	0	5	0	4	0	0	0	1	1	.50	0	.286	.583	.571

Steve Bedrosian

Pitches: Right **Bats:** Right **Pos:** RP **Ht:** 6' 3" **Wt:** 205 **Born:** 12/06/57 **Age:** 36

			HOW MUCH HE PITCHED					WHAT HE GAVE UP									THE RESULTS					
Year	Team	Lg	G	GS	CG	GF	IP	BFP	H	R	ER	HR	SH	SF	HB	TBB	IBB	SO	WP	Bk	W	L	Pct.	ShO	Sv	ERA
1981	Atlanta	NL	15	1	0	5	24	106	15	14	12	2	0	1	1	15	2	9	0	0	1	2	.333	0	0	4.50
1982	Atlanta	NL	64	3	0	30	137.2	567	102	39	37	7	9	2	4	57	5	123	6	0	8	6	.571	0	11	2.42
1983	Atlanta	NL	70	1	0	52	120	500	100	50	48	11	8	4	4	51	8	114	2	0	9	10	.474	0	19	3.60
1984	Atlanta	NL	40	4	0	28	83.2	345	65	23	22	5	1	1	1	33	5	81	4	0	9	6	.600	0	11	2.37
1985	Atlanta	NL	37	37	0	0	206.2	907	198	101	88	17	6	7	5	111	6	134	6	0	7	15	.318	0	0	3.83
1986	Philadelphia	NL	68	0	0	56	90.1	381	79	39	34	12	3	3	0	34	10	82	5	2	8	6	.571	0	29	3.39
1987	Philadelphia	NL	65	0	0	56	89	366	79	31	28	11	2	1	1	28	5	74	3	1	5	3	.625	0	40	2.83
1988	Philadelphia	NL	57	0	0	49	74.1	322	75	34	31	6	6	0	3	27	5	61	0	0	6	6	.500	0	28	3.75
1989	2 ML Teams		68	0	0	60	84.2	342	56	31	27	12	1	4	1	39	5	58	2	0	3	7	.300	0	23	2.87
1990	San Francisco	NL	68	0	0	53	79.1	349	72	40	37	6	3	1	2	44	9	43	1	0	9	9	.500	0	17	4.20
1991	Minnesota	AL	56	0	0	22	77.1	332	70	42	38	11	4	6	4	35	6	44	1	0	5	3	.625	0	6	4.42

1993 Atlanta	NL	49	0	0	12	49.2	198	34	11	9	4	3	4	2	14	2	33	5	1	5	2	.714	0	0	1.63
1989 Philadelphia	NL	28	0	0	27	33.2	135	21	13	12	7	0	2	1	17	1	24	0	0	2	3	.400	0	6	3.21
San Francisco	NL	40	0	0	33	51	207	35	18	15	5	1	2	0	22	4	34	2	0	1	4	.200	0	17	2.65
12 ML YEARS		657	46	0	423	1116.2	4719	945	455	411	104	38	35	24	488	68	856	32	4	75	75	.500	0	184	3.31

Tim Belcher

Pitches: Right **Bats:** Right **Pos:** SP   **Ht:** 6' 3" **Wt:** 220 **Born:** 10/19/61 **Age:** 32

		HOW MUCH HE PITCHED						WHAT HE GAVE UP												THE RESULTS					
Year Team	Lg	G	GS	CG	GF	IP	BFP	H	R	ER	HR	SH	SF	HB	TBB	IBB	SO	WP	Bk	W	L	Pct.	ShO	Sv	ERA
1987 Los Angeles	NL	6	5	0	1	34	135	30	11	9	2	2	1	0	7	0	23	0	1	4	2	.667	0	0	2.38
1988 Los Angeles	NL	36	27	4	5	179.2	719	143	65	58	8	6	1	2	51	7	152	4	0	12	6	.667	1	4	2.91
1989 Los Angeles	NL	39	30	10	6	230	937	182	81	72	20	6	6	7	80	5	200	7	2	15	12	.556	8	1	2.82
1990 Los Angeles	NL	24	24	5	0	153	627	136	76	68	17	5	6	2	48	0	102	6	1	9	9	.500	2	0	4.00
1991 Los Angeles	NL	33	33	2	0	209.1	880	189	76	61	10	11	3	2	75	3	156	7	0	10	9	.526	1	0	2.62
1992 Cincinnati	NL	35	34	2	1	227.2	949	201	104	99	17	12	11	3	80	2	149	3	1	15	14	.517	1	0	3.91
1993 2 ML Teams		34	33	5	0	208.2	886	198	108	103	19	8	4	8	74	4	135	6	0	12	11	.522	3	0	4.44
1993 Cincinnati	NL	22	22	4	0	137	590	134	72	68	11	6	3	7	47	4	101	6	0	9	6	.600	2	0	4.47
Chicago	AL	12	11	1	0	71.2	296	64	36	35	8	2	1	1	27	0	34	0	0	3	5	.375	1	0	4.40
7 ML YEARS		207	186	28	13	1242.1	5133	1079	521	470	93	50	32	24	415	21	917	33	5	77	63	.550	16	5	3.40

Stan Belinda

Pitches: Right **Bats:** Right **Pos:** RP   **Ht:** 6' 3" **Wt:** 187 **Born:** 08/06/66 **Age:** 27

		HOW MUCH HE PITCHED						WHAT HE GAVE UP												THE RESULTS					
Year Team	Lg	G	GS	CG	GF	IP	BFP	H	R	ER	HR	SH	SF	HB	TBB	IBB	SO	WP	Bk	W	L	Pct.	ShO	Sv	ERA
1989 Pittsburgh	NL	8	0	0	2	10.1	46	13	8	7	0	0	0	0	2	0	10	1	0	0	1	.000	0	0	6.10
1990 Pittsburgh	NL	55	0	0	17	58.1	245	48	23	23	4	2	2	1	29	3	55	1	0	3	4	.429	0	8	3.55
1991 Pittsburgh	NL	60	0	0	37	78.1	318	50	30	30	10	4	3	4	35	4	71	2	0	7	5	.583	0	16	3.45
1992 Pittsburgh	NL	59	0	0	42	71.1	299	58	26	25	8	4	6	0	29	5	57	1	0	6	4	.600	0	18	3.15
1993 2 ML Teams		63	0	0	44	69.2	287	65	31	30	6	3	2	2	17	4	55	2	0	4	2	.667	0	19	3.88
1993 Pittsburgh	NL	40	0	0	37	42.1	171	35	18	17	4	1	2	1	11	4	30	0	0	3	1	.750	0	19	3.61
Kansas City	AL	23	0	0	7	27.1	116	30	13	13	2	2	0	1	6	0	25	2	0	1	1	.500	0	0	4.28
5 ML YEARS		245	0	0	142	288	1195	234	118	115	28	13	13	7	112	16	248	7	0	20	16	.556	0	61	3.59

Derek Bell

Bats: Right **Throws:** Right **Pos:** CF/3B   **Ht:** 6' 2" **Wt:** 200 **Born:** 12/11/68 **Age:** 25

		BATTING																BASERUNNING				PERCENTAGES		
Year Team	Lg	G	AB	H	2B	3B	HR	(Hm | Rd)	TB	R	RBI	TBB	IBB	SO	HBP	SH	SF	SB	CS	SB%	GDP	Avg	OBP	SLG
1991 Toronto	AL	18	28	4	0	0	0	(0 | 0)	4	5	1	6	0	5	1	0	0	3	2	.60	0	.143	.314	.143
1992 Toronto	AL	61	161	39	6	3	2	(2 | 0)	57	23	15	15	1	34	5	2	1	7	2	.78	6	.242	.324	.354
1993 San Diego	NL	150	542	142	19	1	21	(12 | 9)	226	73	72	23	5	122	12	0	8	26	5	.84	7	.262	.303	.417
3 ML YEARS		229	731	185	25	4	23	(14 | 9)	287	101	88	44	6	161	18	2	9	36	9	.80	13	.253	.308	.393

Eric Bell

Pitches: Left **Bats:** Left **Pos:** RP   **Ht:** 6' 0" **Wt:** 165 **Born:** 10/27/63 **Age:** 30

		HOW MUCH HE PITCHED						WHAT HE GAVE UP												THE RESULTS					
Year Team	Lg	G	GS	CG	GF	IP	BFP	H	R	ER	HR	SH	SF	HB	TBB	IBB	SO	WP	Bk	W	L	Pct.	ShO	Sv	ERA
1993 Tucson *	AAA	22	16	3	1	106.2	474	131	59	48	8	7	4	1	39	0	53	5	0	4	6	.400	1	0	4.05
1985 Baltimore	AL	4	0	0	3	5.2	24	4	3	3	1	0	0	0	4	0	4	0	0	0	0	.000	0	0	4.76
1986 Baltimore	AL	4	4	0	0	23.1	105	23	14	13	4	1	1	0	14	0	18	0	0	1	2	.333	0	0	5.01
1987 Baltimore	AL	33	29	2	1	165	729	174	113	100	32	4	2	2	78	0	111	11	1	10	13	.435	0	0	5.45
1991 Cleveland	AL	10	0	0	3	18	61	5	2	1	0	0	0	1	5	0	7	0	0	4	0	1.000	0	0	0.50
1992 Cleveland	AL	7	1	0	2	15.1	75	22	13	13	1	1	1	1	9	0	10	1	0	0	2	.000	0	0	7.63
1993 Houston	NL	10	0	0	2	7.1	34	10	5	5	0	0	0	0	2	0	2	0	0	0	1	.000	0	0	6.14
6 ML YEARS		68	34	2	11	234.2	1028	238	150	135	38	6	4	4	112	0	152	12	1	15	18	.455	0	0	5.18

George Bell

Bats: Right **Throws:** Right **Pos:** DH   **Ht:** 6' 1" **Wt:** 210 **Born:** 10/21/59 **Age:** 34

		BATTING																BASERUNNING				PERCENTAGES		
Year Team	Lg	G	AB	H	2B	3B	HR	(Hm | Rd)	TB	R	RBI	TBB	IBB	SO	HBP	SH	SF	SB	CS	SB%	GDP	Avg	OBP	SLG
1993 South Bend *	A	2	8	1	0	0	0	--	--	1	1	0	1	0	0	0	0	0	0	0	.00	2	.125	.222	.125
1981 Toronto	AL	60	163	38	2	1	5	(3 | 2)	57	19	12	5	1	27	0	0	0	3	2	.60	1	.233	.256	.350
1983 Toronto	AL	39	112	30	5	4	2	(1 | 1)	49	5	17	4	1	17	2	0	0	1	1	.50	4	.268	.305	.438
1984 Toronto	AL	159	606	177	39	4	26	(12 | 14)	302	85	87	24	2	86	8	0	3	11	2	.85	14	.292	.326	.498
1985 Toronto	AL	157	607	167	28	6	28	(10 | 18)	291	87	95	43	6	62	8	0	8	21	6	.78	8	.275	.327	.479
1986 Toronto	AL	159	641	198	38	6	31	(15 | 16)	341	101	108	41	3	62	2	0	6	7	8	.47	15	.309	.349	.532
1987 Toronto	AL	156	610	188	32	4	47	(19 | 28)	369	111	134	39	9	75	7	0	9	5	1	.83	17	.308	.352	.605
1988 Toronto	AL	156	614	165	27	5	24	(9 | 15)	274	78	97	34	5	66	1	0	8	4	2	.67	21	.269	.304	.446

16

1989	Toronto	AL	153	613	182	41	2	18	(8	10)	281	88	104	33	3	60	4	0	14	4	3	.57	18	.297	.330	.458
1990	Toronto	AL	142	562	149	25	0	21	(11	10)	237	67	86	32	7	80	3	0	11	3	2	.60	14	.265	.303	.422
1991	Chicago	NL	149	558	159	27	0	25	(9	16)	261	63	86	32	6	62	4	0	9	2	6	.25	10	.285	.323	.468
1992	Chicago	AL	155	627	160	27	0	25	(16	9)	262	74	112	31	8	97	6	0	6	5	2	.71	29	.255	.294	.418
1993	Chicago	AL	102	410	89	17	2	13	(7	6)	149	36	64	13	2	49	4	0	9	1	1	.50	14	.217	.243	.363
12 ML YEARS			1587	6123	1702	308	34	265	(120	145)	2873	814	1002	331	53	771	49	0	83	67	36	.65	165	.278	.316	.469

Jay Bell

Bats: Right **Throws:** Right **Pos:** SS **Ht:** 6' 0" **Wt:** 185 **Born:** 12/11/65 **Age:** 28

								BATTING												BASERUNNING				PERCENTAGES		
Year	Team	Lg	G	AB	H	2B	3B	HR	(Hm	Rd)	TB	R	RBI	TBB	IBB	SO	HBP	SH	SF	SB	CS	SB%	GDP	Avg	OBP	SLG
1986	Cleveland	AL	5	14	5	2	0	1	(0	1)	10	3	4	2	0	3	0	0	0	0	0	.00	0	.357	.438	.714
1987	Cleveland	AL	38	125	27	9	1	2	(1	1)	44	14	13	8	0	31	1	3	0	2	0	1.00	0	.216	.269	.352
1988	Cleveland	AL	73	211	46	5	1	2	(2	0)	59	23	21	21	0	53	1	1	2	4	2	.67	3	.218	.289	.280
1989	Pittsburgh	NL	78	271	70	13	3	2	(1	1)	95	33	27	19	0	47	1	10	2	5	3	.63	9	.258	.307	.351
1990	Pittsburgh	NL	159	583	148	28	7	7	(1	6)	211	93	52	65	0	109	3	39	6	10	6	.63	14	.254	.329	.362
1991	Pittsburgh	NL	157	608	164	32	8	16	(7	9)	260	96	67	52	1	99	4	30	3	10	6	.63	15	.270	.330	.428
1992	Pittsburgh	NL	159	632	167	36	6	9	(5	4)	242	87	55	55	0	103	4	19	2	7	5	.58	12	.264	.326	.383
1993	Pittsburgh	NL	154	604	187	32	9	9	(3	6)	264	102	51	77	6	122	6	13	1	16	10	.62	16	.310	.392	.437
8 ML YEARS			823	3048	814	157	35	48	(20	28)	1185	451	290	299	7	567	20	115	16	54	32	.63	69	.267	.335	.389

Juan Bell

Bats: Both **Throws:** Right **Pos:** SS/2B **Ht:** 5'11" **Wt:** 170 **Born:** 03/29/68 **Age:** 26

								BATTING												BASERUNNING				PERCENTAGES		
Year	Team	Lg	G	AB	H	2B	3B	HR	(Hm	Rd)	TB	R	RBI	TBB	IBB	SO	HBP	SH	SF	SB	CS	SB%	GDP	Avg	OBP	SLG
1989	Baltimore	AL	8	4	0	0	0	0	(0	0)	0	2	0	0	0	1	0	0	0	1	0	1.00	0	.000	.000	.000
1990	Baltimore	AL	5	2	0	0	0	0	(0	0)	0	1	0	0	0	1	0	0	0	0	0	.00	0	.000	.000	.000
1991	Baltimore	AL	100	209	36	9	2	1	(0	1)	52	26	15	8	0	51	0	4	2	0	0	.00	1	.172	.201	.249
1992	Philadelphia	NL	46	147	30	3	1	1	(0	1)	38	12	8	18	5	29	1	0	2	5	0	1.00	1	.204	.292	.259
1993	2 ML Teams		115	351	80	12	3	5	(2	3)	113	47	36	41	0	76	2	5	1	6	7	.46	4	.228	.311	.322
1993	Philadelphia	NL	24	65	13	6	1	0	(0	0)	21	5	7	5	0	12	1	2	0	0	1	.00	0	.200	.268	.323
	Milwaukee	AL	91	286	67	6	2	5	(2	3)	92	42	29	36	0	64	1	3	1	6	6	.50	4	.234	.321	.322
5 ML YEARS			274	713	146	24	6	7	(3	4)	203	88	59	67	5	158	3	9	5	12	7	.63	6	.205	.274	.285

Albert Belle

Bats: Right **Throws:** Right **Pos:** LF **Ht:** 6' 2" **Wt:** 210 **Born:** 08/25/66 **Age:** 27

								BATTING												BASERUNNING				PERCENTAGES		
Year	Team	Lg	G	AB	H	2B	3B	HR	(Hm	Rd)	TB	R	RBI	TBB	IBB	SO	HBP	SH	SF	SB	CS	SB%	GDP	Avg	OBP	SLG
1989	Cleveland	AL	62	218	49	8	4	7	(3	4)	86	22	37	12	0	55	2	0	2	2	2	.50	4	.225	.269	.394
1990	Cleveland	AL	9	23	4	0	0	1	(1	0)	7	1	3	1	0	6	0	1	0	0	0	.00	1	.174	.208	.304
1991	Cleveland	AL	123	461	130	31	2	28	(8	20)	249	60	95	25	2	99	5	0	5	3	1	.75	24	.282	.323	.540
1992	Cleveland	AL	153	585	152	23	1	34	(15	19)	279	81	112	52	5	128	4	1	8	8	2	.80	18	.260	.320	.477
1993	Cleveland	AL	159	594	172	36	4	38	(20	18)	328	93	129	76	13	96	8	0	14	23	12	.66	18	.290	.370	.552
5 ML YEARS			506	1881	507	98	10	108	(47	61)	949	257	376	166	20	384	19	3	29	36	17	.68	65	.270	.330	.505

Rafael Belliard

Bats: Right **Throws:** Right **Pos:** SS/2B **Ht:** 5' 6" **Wt:** 160 **Born:** 10/24/61 **Age:** 32

								BATTING												BASERUNNING				PERCENTAGES		
Year	Team	Lg	G	AB	H	2B	3B	HR	(Hm	Rd)	TB	R	RBI	TBB	IBB	SO	HBP	SH	SF	SB	CS	SB%	GDP	Avg	OBP	SLG
1982	Pittsburgh	NL	9	2	1	0	0	0	(0	0)	1	3	0	0	0	0	0	0	0	1	0	1.00	0	.500	.500	.500
1983	Pittsburgh	NL	4	1	0	0	0	0	(0	0)	0	1	0	0	0	1	0	0	0	0	0	.00	0	.000	.000	.000
1984	Pittsburgh	NL	20	22	5	0	0	0	(0	0)	5	3	0	0	0	1	0	0	0	4	1	.80	0	.227	.227	.227
1985	Pittsburgh	NL	17	20	4	0	0	0	(0	0)	4	1	1	0	0	5	0	0	0	0	0	.00	0	.200	.200	.200
1986	Pittsburgh	NL	117	309	72	5	2	0	(0	0)	81	33	31	26	6	54	3	11	1	12	2	.86	8	.233	.298	.262
1987	Pittsburgh	NL	81	203	42	4	3	1	(0	1)	55	26	15	20	6	25	3	2	1	5	1	.83	4	.207	.286	.271
1988	Pittsburgh	NL	122	286	61	0	4	0	(0	0)	69	28	11	26	3	47	4	5	0	7	1	.88	10	.213	.288	.241
1989	Pittsburgh	NL	67	154	33	4	0	0	(0	0)	37	10	8	8	2	22	0	3	0	5	2	.71	1	.214	.253	.240
1990	Pittsburgh	NL	47	54	11	3	0	0	(0	0)	14	10	6	5	0	13	1	1	0	1	2	.33	2	.204	.283	.259
1991	Atlanta	NL	149	353	88	9	2	0	(0	0)	101	36	27	22	2	63	2	7	1	3	1	.75	4	.249	.296	.286
1992	Atlanta	NL	144	285	60	6	1	0	(0	0)	68	20	14	14	4	43	3	13	0	0	1	.00	6	.211	.255	.239
1993	Atlanta	NL	91	79	18	5	0	0	(0	0)	23	6	6	4	0	13	3	3	0	0	0	.00	1	.228	.291	.291
12 ML YEARS			868	1768	395	36	12	1	(0	1)	458	177	119	125	23	287	19	45	3	38	11	.78	36	.223	.281	.259

Freddie Benavides

Bats: Right **Throws:** Right **Pos:** SS/2B   **Ht:** 6' 2" **Wt:** 185 **Born:** 04/07/66 **Age:** 28

								BATTING										BASERUNNING				PERCENTAGES		
Year	Team	Lg	G	AB	H	2B	3B	HR	(Hm	Rd)	TB	R	RBI	TBB	IBB	SO	HBP	SH	SF	SB	CS	SB%	GDP	Avg	OBP	SLG
1993	Colo Sprngs *	AAA	5	16	7	1	0	0	--	--	8	3	2	1	0	0	0	0	0	0	0	.00	0	.438	.471	.500
1991	Cincinnati	NL	24	63	18	1	0	0	(0	0)	19	11	3	1	1	15	1	1	1	1	0	1.00	1	.286	.303	.302
1992	Cincinnati	NL	74	173	40	10	1	1	(1	0)	55	14	17	10	4	34	1	2	0	0	1	.00	3	.231	.277	.318
1993	Colorado	NL	74	213	61	10	3	3	(3	0)	86	20	26	6	1	27	0	3	1	3	2	.60	4	.286	.305	.404
	3 ML YEARS		172	449	119	21	4	4	(4	0)	160	45	46	17	6	76	2	6	2	4	3	.57	8	.265	.294	.356

Andy Benes

Pitches: Right **Bats:** Right **Pos:** SP   **Ht:** 6' 6" **Wt:** 240 **Born:** 08/20/67 **Age:** 26

			HOW MUCH HE PITCHED						WHAT HE GAVE UP										THE RESULTS					
Year	Team	Lg	G	GS	CG	GF	IP	BFP	H	R	ER	HR	SH	SF	HB	TBB	IBB	SO	WP	Bk	W	L	Pct.	ShO	Sv	ERA
1989	San Diego	NL	10	10	0	0	66.2	280	51	28	26	7	6	2	1	31	0	66	0	3	6	3	.667	0	0	3.51
1990	San Diego	NL	32	31	2	1	192.1	811	177	87	77	18	5	6	1	69	5	140	2	5	10	11	.476	0	0	3.60
1991	San Diego	NL	33	33	4	0	223	908	194	76	75	23	5	4	4	59	7	167	3	4	15	11	.577	1	0	3.03
1992	San Diego	NL	34	34	2	0	231.1	961	230	90	86	14	19	6	5	61	6	169	1	1	13	14	.481	2	0	3.35
1993	San Diego	NL	34	34	4	0	230.2	968	200	111	97	23	10	6	4	86	7	179	14	2	15	15	.500	2	0	3.78
	5 ML YEARS		143	142	12	1	944	3928	852	392	361	85	45	24	15	306	25	721	20	15	59	54	.522	5	0	3.44

Mike Benjamin

Bats: Right **Throws:** Right **Pos:** 2B/3B/SS   **Ht:** 6' 0" **Wt:** 169 **Born:** 11/22/65 **Age:** 28

								BATTING										BASERUNNING				PERCENTAGES		
Year	Team	Lg	G	AB	H	2B	3B	HR	(Hm	Rd)	TB	R	RBI	TBB	IBB	SO	HBP	SH	SF	SB	CS	SB%	GDP	Avg	OBP	SLG
1993	San Jose *	A	2	8	0	0	0	0	--	--	0	1	0	1	0	0	1	0	0	0	0	.00	0	.000	.200	.000
1989	San Francisco	NL	14	6	1	0	0	0	(0	0)	1	6	0	0	0	1	0	0	0	0	0	.00	0	.167	.167	.167
1990	San Francisco	NL	22	56	12	3	1	2	(2	0)	23	7	3	3	1	10	0	0	0	1	0	1.00	2	.214	.254	.411
1991	San Francisco	NL	54	106	13	3	0	2	(0	2)	22	12	8	7	2	26	2	3	2	3	0	1.00	3	.123	.188	.208
1992	San Francisco	NL	40	75	13	2	1	1	(0	1)	20	4	3	4	1	15	0	3	0	1	0	1.00	1	.173	.215	.267
1993	San Francisco	NL	63	146	29	7	0	4	(3	1)	48	22	16	9	2	23	4	6	0	3	1	.00	3	.199	.264	.329
	5 ML YEARS		193	389	68	15	2	9	(5	4)	114	51	30	23	6	75	6	12	2	5	0	1.00	7	.175	.231	.293

Todd Benzinger

Bats: Both **Throws:** Right **Pos:** 1B   **Ht:** 6' 1" **Wt:** 195 **Born:** 02/11/63 **Age:** 31

								BATTING										BASERUNNING				PERCENTAGES		
Year	Team	Lg	G	AB	H	2B	3B	HR	(Hm | Rd)	TB	R	RBI	TBB	IBB	SO	HBP	SH	SF	SB	CS	SB%	GDP	Avg	OBP	SLG
1987	Boston	AL	73	223	62	11	1	8	(5 | 3)	99	36	43	22	3	41	2	3	3	5	4	.56	5	.278	.344	.444
1988	Boston	AL	120	405	103	28	1	13	(6 | 7)	172	47	70	22	4	80	1	6	2	2	3	.40	8	.254	.293	.425
1989	Cincinnati	NL	161	628	154	28	3	17	(6 | 11)	239	79	76	44	13	120	2	4	8	3	7	.30	5	.245	.293	.381
1990	Cincinnati	NL	118	376	95	14	2	5	(4 | 1)	128	35	46	19	4	69	4	2	7	3	4	.43	3	.253	.291	.340
1991	2 ML Teams		129	416	109	18	5	3	(2 | 1)	146	36	51	27	4	66	3	2	3	4	6	.40	7	.262	.310	.351
1992	Los Angeles	NL	121	293	70	16	2	4	(1 | 3)	102	24	31	15	1	54	0	0	5	2	4	.33	6	.239	.272	.348
1993	San Francisco	NL	86	177	51	7	2	6	(0 | 6)	80	25	26	13	1	35	0	1	3	0	0	.00	2	.288	.332	.452
1991	Cincinnati	NL	51	123	23	3	2	1	(1 | 0)	33	7	11	10	2	20	0	1	2	2	0	1.00	2	.187	.244	.268
	Kansas City	AL	78	293	86	15	3	2	(1 | 1)	113	29	40	17	2	46	3	1	1	2	6	.25	5	.294	.338	.386
	7 ML YEARS		808	2518	644	122	16	56	(24 | 32)	966	282	343	162	30	465	12	18	31	19	28	.40	36	.256	.300	.384

Jason Bere

Pitches: Right **Bats:** Right **Pos:** SP   **Ht:** 6' 3" **Wt:** 185 **Born:** 05/26/71 **Age:** 23

			HOW MUCH HE PITCHED						WHAT HE GAVE UP										THE RESULTS					
Year	Team	Lg	G	GS	CG	GF	IP	BFP	H	R	ER	HR	SH	SF	HB	TBB	IBB	SO	WP	Bk	W	L	Pct.	ShO	Sv	ERA
1990	White Sox	R	15	2	0	6	36	156	25	19	10	1	1	2	1	19	0	38	1	0	0	4	.000	0	1	2.50
1991	South Bend	A	27	27	2	0	163	686	116	66	52	8	7	4	5	100	0	158	11	1	9	12	.429	1	0	2.87
1992	Sarasota	A	18	18	1	0	116	458	84	35	31	3	4	3	1	34	3	106	6	0	7	2	.778	1	0	2.41
	Birmingham	AA	8	8	4	0	54	216	44	22	18	1	1	2	1	20	1	45	1	0	4	4	.500	2	0	3.00
	Vancouver	AAA	1	0	0	0	1	6	2	0	0	0	1	0	1	0	0	2	0	0	0	0	.000	0	0	0.00
1993	Nashville	AAA	8	8	0	0	49.1	206	36	19	13	1	3	2	1	25	1	52	2	0	5	1	.833	0	0	2.37
1993	Chicago	AL	24	24	1	0	142.2	610	109	60	55	12	4	2	5	81	0	129	8	0	12	5	.706	0	0	3.47

Sean Bergman

Pitches: Right **Bats:** Right **Pos:** SP   **Ht:** 6' 4" **Wt:** 205 **Born:** 04/11/70 **Age:** 24

			HOW MUCH HE PITCHED						WHAT HE GAVE UP										THE RESULTS					
Year	Team	Lg	G	GS	CG	GF	IP	BFP	H	R	ER	HR	SH	SF	HB	TBB	IBB	SO	WP	Bk	W	L	Pct.	ShO	Sv	ERA
1991	Niagara Fls	A	15	15	0	0	84.2	384	88	57	42	1	1	4	2	42	0	77	5	7	5	7	.417	0	0	4.46
1992	Lakeland	A	13	13	0	0	83	320	61	28	23	2	3	0	2	14	0	67	2	2	5	2	.714	0	0	2.49
	London	AA	14	14	1	0	88.1	390	85	52	42	2	6	1	6	45	2	59	4	0	4	7	.364	0	0	4.28

Year Team	Lg	G	GS	CG	GF	IP	BFP	H	R	ER	HR	SH	SF	HB	TBB	IBB	SO	WP	Bk	W	L	Pct.	ShO	Sv	ERA
1993 Toledo	AAA	19	19	3	0	117	503	124	62	57	9	6	3	8	53	0	91	6	2	8	9	471	0	0	4.38
1993 Detroit	AL	9	6	1	1	39.2	189	47	29	25	6	3	2	1	23	3	19	3	1	1	4	.200	0	0	5.67

Geronimo Berroa

Bats: Right **Throws:** Right **Pos:** RF   **Ht:** 6' 0" **Wt:** 165 **Born:** 03/18/65 **Age:** 29

Year Team	Lg	G	AB	H	2B	3B	HR	(Hm	Rd)	TB	R	RBI	TBB	IBB	SO	HBP	SH	SF	SB	CS	SB%	GDP	Avg	OBP	SLG
1993 Edmonton *	AAA	90	327	107	33	4	16	--	--	196	64	68	36	3	71	4	0	3	1	2	.33	6	.327	.397	.599
1989 Atlanta	NL	81	136	36	4	0	2	(1	1)	46	7	9	7	1	32	0	0	0	0	1	.00	2	.265	.301	.338
1990 Atlanta	NL	7	4	0	0	0	0	(0	0)	0	0	0	1	1	1	0	0	0	0	0	.00	0	.000	.200	.000
1992 Cincinnati	NL	13	15	4	1	0	0	(0	0)	5	2	0	2	0	1	1	0	0	0	1	.00	1	.267	.389	.333
1993 Florida	NL	14	34	4	1	0	0	(0	0)	5	3	0	2	0	7	0	0	0	0	0	.00	2	.118	.167	.147
4 ML YEARS		115	189	44	6	0	2	(1	1)	56	12	9	12	2	41	1	0	0	0	2	.00	5	.233	.282	.296

Sean Berry

Bats: Right **Throws:** Right **Pos:** 3B   **Ht:** 5'11" **Wt:** 205 **Born:** 03/22/66 **Age:** 28

Year Team	Lg	G	AB	H	2B	3B	HR	(Hm	Rd)	TB	R	RBI	TBB	IBB	SO	HBP	SH	SF	SB	CS	SB%	GDP	Avg	OBP	SLG
1990 Kansas City	AL	8	23	5	1	1	0	(0	0)	8	2	4	2	0	5	0	0	0	0	0	.00	0	.217	.280	.348
1991 Kansas City	AL	31	60	8	3	0	0	(0	0)	11	5	1	5	0	23	1	0	0	0	0	.00	1	.133	.212	.183
1992 Montreal	NL	24	57	19	1	0	1	(0	1)	23	5	4	1	0	11	0	0	0	2	1	.67	1	.333	.345	.404
1993 Montreal	NL	122	299	78	15	2	14	(5	9)	139	50	49	41	6	70	2	3	6	12	2	.86	4	.261	.348	.465
4 ML YEARS		185	439	110	20	3	15	(5	10)	181	62	58	49	6	109	3	3	6	14	3	.82	6	.251	.326	.412

Damon Berryhill

Bats: Both **Throws:** Right **Pos:** C   **Ht:** 6' 0" **Wt:** 205 **Born:** 12/03/63 **Age:** 30

Year Team	Lg	G	AB	H	2B	3B	HR	(Hm	Rd)	TB	R	RBI	TBB	IBB	SO	HBP	SH	SF	SB	CS	SB%	GDP	Avg	OBP	SLG
1987 Chicago	NL	12	28	5	1	0	0	(0	0)	6	2	1	3	0	5	0	0	0	0	1	.00	1	.179	.258	.214
1988 Chicago	NL	95	309	80	19	1	7	(5	2)	122	19	38	17	5	56	0	0	3	1	1	1.00	11	.259	.295	.395
1989 Chicago	NL	91	334	86	13	0	5	(2	3)	114	37	41	16	4	54	2	4	5	1	0	1.00	13	.257	.291	.341
1990 Chicago	NL	17	53	10	4	0	1	(1	0)	17	6	9	5	1	14	0	0	1	0	0	.00	3	.189	.254	.321
1991 2 ML Teams		63	160	30	7	0	5	(3	2)	52	13	14	11	1	42	1	0	1	1	2	.33	2	.188	.243	.325
1992 Atlanta	NL	101	307	70	16	1	10	(6	4)	118	21	43	17	4	67	1	0	3	0	2	.00	4	.228	.268	.384
1993 Atlanta	NL	115	335	82	18	2	8	(6	2)	128	24	43	21	1	64	2	2	3	0	0	.00	7	.245	.291	.382
1991 Chicago	NL	62	159	30	7	0	5	(3	2)	52	13	14	11	1	41	1	0	1	1	2	.33	2	.189	.244	.327
Atlanta	NL	1	1	0	0	0	0	(0	0)	0	0	0	0	0	1	0	0	0	0	0	.00	0	.000	.000	.000
7 ML YEARS		494	1526	363	78	4	36	(23	13)	557	122	189	90	16	302	6	9	16	3	5	.38	41	.238	.280	.365

Dante Bichette

Bats: Right **Throws:** Right **Pos:** RF   **Ht:** 6' 3" **Wt:** 225 **Born:** 11/18/63 **Age:** 30

Year Team	Lg	G	AB	H	2B	3B	HR	(Hm	Rd)	TB	R	RBI	TBB	IBB	SO	HBP	SH	SF	SB	CS	SB%	GDP	Avg	OBP	SLG
1988 California	AL	21	46	12	2	0	0	(0	0)	14	1	8	0	0	7	0	0	4	0	0	.00	0	.261	.240	.304
1989 California	AL	48	138	29	7	0	3	(2	1)	45	13	15	6	0	24	0	0	2	3	0	1.00	3	.210	.240	.326
1990 California	AL	109	349	89	15	1	15	(8	7)	151	40	53	16	1	79	3	1	2	5	2	.71	9	.255	.292	.433
1991 Milwaukee	AL	134	445	106	18	3	15	(6	9)	175	53	59	22	4	107	1	1	6	14	8	.64	9	.238	.272	.393
1992 Milwaukee	AL	112	387	111	27	2	5	(3	2)	157	37	41	16	3	74	3	2	3	18	7	.72	13	.287	.318	.406
1993 Colorado	NL	141	538	167	43	5	21	(11	10)	283	93	89	28	2	99	7	0	8	14	8	.64	7	.310	.348	.526
6 ML YEARS		565	1903	514	112	11	59	(30	29)	825	237	265	88	10	390	14	4	25	54	25	.68	41	.270	.303	.434

Mike Bielecki

Pitches: Right **Bats:** Right **Pos:** SP   **Ht:** 6' 3" **Wt:** 195 **Born:** 07/31/59 **Age:** 34

Year Team	Lg	G	GS	CG	GF	IP	BFP	H	R	ER	HR	SH	SF	HB	TBB	IBB	SO	WP	Bk	W	L	Pct.	ShO	Sv	ERA
1993 Rochester *	AAA	9	9	0	0	48.1	215	56	33	27	4	2	2	1	16	1	31	6	0	5	3	.625	0	0	5.03
1984 Pittsburgh	NL	4	0	0	1	4.1	17	4	0	0	0	1	0	0	0	0	1	0	1	0	0	.000	0	0	0.00
1985 Pittsburgh	NL	12	7	0	1	45.2	211	45	26	23	5	4	0	1	31	1	22	1	1	2	3	.400	0	0	4.53
1986 Pittsburgh	NL	31	27	0	0	148.2	667	149	87	77	10	7	6	2	83	3	83	7	5	6	11	.353	0	0	4.66
1987 Pittsburgh	NL	8	8	2	0	45.2	192	43	25	24	6	5	2	1	12	0	25	3	0	2	3	.400	0	0	4.73
1988 Chicago	NL	19	5	0	7	48.1	215	55	22	18	4	1	4	0	16	1	33	3	3	2	2	.500	0	0	3.35
1989 Chicago	NL	33	33	4	0	212.1	882	187	82	74	16	9	3	0	81	8	147	9	4	18	7	.720	3	0	3.14
1990 Chicago	NL	36	29	0	6	168	749	188	101	92	13	16	4	5	70	11	103	11	0	8	11	.421	0	1	4.93
1991 2 ML Teams		41	25	0	9	173.2	727	171	91	86	18	10	6	2	56	6	75	6	0	13	11	.542	0	0	4.46
1992 Atlanta	NL	19	14	1	0	80.2	336	77	27	23	2	3	2	1	27	1	62	4	0	2	4	.333	1	0	2.57
1993 Cleveland	AL	13	13	0	0	68.2	317	90	47	45	8	0	2	2	23	3	38	1	0	4	5	.444	0	0	5.90
1991 Chicago	NL	39	25	0	8	172	718	169	91	86	18	10	6	2	54	6	72	6	0	13	11	.542	0	0	4.50

Atlanta	NL	2	0	0	1	12	9	2	0	0	0	0	0	0	2	0	3	0	0	0	0	.000	0	0	0.00
10 ML YEARS		216	161	7	24	996	4313	1009	508	462	82	56	29	14	399	34	589	45	14	57	57	.500	4	1	4.17

Craig Biggio

Bats: Right **Throws:** Right **Pos:** 2B   **Ht:** 5'11" **Wt:** 180 **Born:** 12/14/65 **Age:** 28

		BATTING																BASERUNNING				PERCENTAGES		
Year Team	Lg	G	AB	H	2B	3B	HR	(Hm | Rd)	TB	R	RBI	TBB	IBB	SO	HBP	SH	SF	SB	CS	SB%	GDP	Avg	OBP	SLG
1988 Houston	NL	50	123	26	6	1	3	(1 | 2)	43	14	5	7	2	29	0	1	0	6	1	.86	1	.211	.254	.350
1989 Houston	NL	134	443	114	21	2	13	(6 | 7)	178	64	60	49	8	64	6	6	5	21	3	.88	7	.257	.336	.402
1990 Houston	NL	150	555	153	24	2	4	(2 | 2)	193	53	42	53	1	79	3	9	1	25	11	.69	11	.276	.342	.348
1991 Houston	NL	149	546	161	23	4	4	(0 | 4)	204	79	46	53	3	71	2	5	3	19	6	.76	2	.295	.358	.374
1992 Houston	NL	162	613	170	32	3	6	(3 | 3)	226	96	39	94	9	95	7	5	2	38	15	.72	5	.277	.378	.369
1993 Houston	NL	155	610	175	41	5	21	(8 | 13)	289	98	64	77	7	93	10	4	15	15	17	.47	10	.287	.373	.474
6 ML YEARS		800	2890	799	147	17	51	(20 | 31)	1133	404	256	333	30	431	28	30	16	124	53	.70	36	.276	.355	.392

Bud Black

Pitches: Left **Bats:** Left **Pos:** SP   **Ht:** 6'2" **Wt:** 188 **Born:** 06/30/57 **Age:** 37

		HOW MUCH HE PITCHED						WHAT HE GAVE UP										THE RESULTS					
Year Team	Lg	G	GS	CG	GF	IP	BFP	H	R	ER	HR	SH	SF	HB	TBB	IBB	SO	WP	Bk	W	L	Pct.	ShO	Sv	ERA
1993 San Jose *	A	1	1	0	0	1	4	2	1	1	0	0	0	0	0	0	2	0	0	0	0	.000	0	0	9.00
1981 Seattle	AL	2	0	0	0	1	7	2	0	0	0	0	0	0	3	1	0	1	0	0	0	.000	0	0	0.00
1982 Kansas City	AL	22	14	0	2	88.1	386	92	48	45	10	4	3	3	34	6	40	4	7	4	6	.400	0	0	4.58
1983 Kansas City	AL	24	24	3	0	161.1	672	159	75	68	19	4	5	2	43	1	58	4	0	10	7	.588	0	0	3.79
1984 Kansas City	AL	35	35	8	0	257	1045	226	99	89	22	6	1	4	64	2	140	2	2	17	12	.586	1	0	3.12
1985 Kansas City	AL	33	33	5	0	205.2	885	216	111	99	17	8	4	8	59	4	122	9	1	10	15	.400	2	0	4.33
1986 Kansas City	AL	56	4	0	26	121	503	100	49	43	14	4	4	7	43	5	68	2	2	5	10	.333	0	9	3.20
1987 Kansas City	AL	29	18	0	4	122.1	520	126	63	49	16	1	3	5	35	2	61	6	0	8	6	.571	0	1	3.60
1988 2 ML Teams		33	7	0	9	81	358	82	47	45	8	6	3	4	34	3	63	5	6	4	4	.500	0	1	5.00
1989 Cleveland	AL	33	32	6	0	222.1	912	213	95	83	14	9	5	1	52	0	88	13	5	12	11	.522	3	0	3.36
1990 2 ML Teams		32	31	5	1	206.2	857	181	86	82	19	6	7	5	61	1	106	6	1	13	11	.542	2	0	3.57
1991 San Francisco	NL	34	34	3	0	214.1	893	201	104	95	25	11	7	4	71	8	104	6	6	12	16	.429	3	0	3.99
1992 San Francisco	NL	28	28	2	0	177	749	178	88	78	23	8	4	1	59	11	82	3	7	10	12	.455	1	0	3.97
1993 San Francisco	NL	16	16	0	0	93.2	394	89	44	37	13	8	4	2	33	2	45	0	4	8	2	.800	0	0	3.56
1988 Kansas City	AL	17	0	0	5	22	98	23	12	12	2	1	0	0	11	2	19	0	2	2	1	.667	0	0	4.91
Cleveland	AL	16	7	0	4	59	260	59	35	33	6	5	3	4	23	1	44	5	4	2	3	.400	0	1	5.03
1990 Cleveland	AL	29	29	5	0	191	796	171	79	75	17	4	5	4	58	1	103	6	1	11	10	.524	2	0	3.53
Toronto	AL	3	2	0	1	15.2	61	10	7	7	2	2	2	1	3	0	3	0	0	2	1	.667	0	0	4.02
13 ML YEARS		377	276	32	42	1951.2	8181	1865	909	813	200	75	50	46	591	46	977	61	41	113	112	.502	12	11	3.75

Willie Blair

Pitches: Right **Bats:** Right **Pos:** RP/SP   **Ht:** 6'1" **Wt:** 185 **Born:** 12/18/65 **Age:** 28

		HOW MUCH HE PITCHED						WHAT HE GAVE UP										THE RESULTS					
Year Team	Lg	G	GS	CG	GF	IP	BFP	H	R	ER	HR	SH	SF	HB	TBB	IBB	SO	WP	Bk	W	L	Pct.	ShO	Sv	ERA
1990 Toronto	AL	27	6	0	8	68.2	297	66	33	31	4	0	4	1	28	4	43	3	0	3	5	.375	0	0	4.06
1991 Cleveland	AL	11	5	0	1	36	168	58	27	27	7	1	2	1	10	0	13	1	0	2	3	.400	0	0	6.75
1992 Houston	NL	29	4	0	1	78.2	331	74	47	35	5	4	3	2	25	2	48	2	0	5	7	.417	0	0	4.00
1993 Colorado	NL	46	18	1	5	146	664	184	90	77	20	10	8	3	42	4	84	6	1	6	10	.375	0	0	4.75
4 ML YEARS		113	37	1	15	329.1	1460	382	197	170	36	15	17	7	105	10	188	12	1	16	25	.390	0	0	4.65

Lance Blankenship

Bats: Right **Throws:** Right **Pos:** CF/2B/LF   **Ht:** 6'0" **Wt:** 185 **Born:** 12/06/63 **Age:** 30

		BATTING																BASERUNNING				PERCENTAGES		
Year Team	Lg	G	AB	H	2B	3B	HR	(Hm | Rd)	TB	R	RBI	TBB	IBB	SO	HBP	SH	SF	SB	CS	SB%	GDP	Avg	OBP	SLG
1988 Oakland	AL	10	3	0	0	0	0	(0 | 0)	0	1	0	0	0	1	0	0	0	0	1	.00	0	.000	.000	.000
1989 Oakland	AL	58	125	29	5	1	1	(1 | 0)	39	22	4	8	0	31	0	3	1	5	1	.83	0	.232	.276	.312
1990 Oakland	AL	86	136	26	3	0	0	(0 | 0)	29	18	10	20	0	23	0	6	0	3	1	.75	6	.191	.295	.213
1991 Oakland	AL	90	185	46	8	0	3	(0 | 3)	63	33	21	23	0	42	3	2	3	12	3	.80	2	.249	.336	.341
1992 Oakland	AL	123	349	84	24	1	3	(1 | 2)	119	59	34	82	2	57	6	8	1	21	7	.75	10	.241	.393	.341
1993 Oakland	AL	94	252	48	8	1	2	(2 | 0)	64	43	23	67	0	64	2	6	1	13	5	.72	9	.190	.363	.254
6 ML YEARS		461	1050	233	48	3	9	(4 | 5)	314	176	92	200	2	218	11	25	6	54	18	.75	27	.222	.350	.299

Jeff Blauser

Bats: Right **Throws:** Right **Pos:** SS   **Ht:** 6'0" **Wt:** 170 **Born:** 11/08/65 **Age:** 28

		BATTING																BASERUNNING				PERCENTAGES		
Year Team	Lg	G	AB	H	2B	3B	HR	(Hm | Rd)	TB	R	RBI	TBB	IBB	SO	HBP	SH	SF	SB	CS	SB%	GDP	Avg	OBP	SLG
1987 Atlanta	NL	51	165	40	6	3	2	(1 | 1)	58	11	15	18	1	34	3	1	0	7	3	.70	4	.242	.328	.352

20

Year Team	Lg	G	AB	H	2B	3B	HR	(Hm	Rd)	TB	R	RBI	TBB	IBB	SO	HBP	SH	SF	SB	CS	SB%	GDP	Avg	OBP	SLG
1988 Atlanta	NL	18	67	16	3	1	2	(2	0)	27	7	7	2	0	11	1	3	1	0	1	.00	1	.239	.268	.403
1989 Atlanta	NL	142	456	123	24	2	12	(5	7)	187	63	46	38	2	101	1	8	4	5	2	.71	7	.270	.325	.410
1990 Atlanta	NL	115	386	104	24	3	8	(3	5)	158	46	39	35	1	70	5	3	0	3	5	.38	4	.269	.338	.409
1991 Atlanta	NL	129	352	91	14	3	11	(7	4)	144	49	54	54	4	59	2	4	3	5	6	.45	4	.259	.358	.409
1992 Atlanta	NL	123	343	90	19	3	14	(5	9)	157	61	46	46	2	82	4	7	3	5	5	.50	2	.262	.354	.458
1993 Atlanta	NL	161	597	182	29	2	15	(4	11)	260	110	73	85	0	109	16	5	7	16	6	.73	13	.305	.401	.436
7 ML YEARS		739	2366	646	119	17	64	(27	37)	991	347	280	278	10	466	32	31	18	41	28	.59	35	.273	.355	.419

Greg Blosser

Bats: Left **Throws:** Left **Pos:** LF **Ht:** 6' 3" **Wt:** 200 **Born:** 06/26/71 **Age:** 23

						BATTING														BASERUNNING				PERCENTAGES		
Year Team	Lg	G	AB	H	2B	3B	HR	(Hm	Rd)	TB	R	RBI	TBB	IBB	SO	HBP	SH	SF	SB	CS	SB%	GDP	Avg	OBP	SLG
1989 Red Sox	R	40	146	42	7	3	2	--	--	61	17	20	25	1	19	1	0	2	3	0	1.00	7	.288	.391	.418
Winter Havn	A	28	94	24	1	1	2	--	--	33	6	14	8	0	14	1	0	1	1	0	1.00	1	.255	.317	.351
1990 Lynchburg	A	119	447	126	23	1	18	--	--	205	63	62	55	3	99	1	0	1	5	4	.56	13	.282	.361	.459
1991 New Britain	AA	134	452	98	21	3	8	--	--	149	48	46	63	0	114	1	0	4	9	4	.69	16	.217	.312	.330
1992 New Britain	AA	129	434	105	23	4	22	--	--	202	59	71	64	9	122	1	0	3	0	2	.00	7	.242	.339	.465
Pawtucket	AAA	1	0	0	0	0	0	--	--	0	1	0	1	0	0	0	0	0	0	0	.00	0	.000	1.000	.000
1993 Pawtucket	AAA	130	478	109	22	2	23	--	--	204	66	66	58	5	139	2	1	4	3	3	.50	4	.228	.312	.427
1993 Boston	AL	17	28	2	1	0	0	(0	0)	3	1	1	2	0	7	0	0	0	1	0	1.00	0	.071	.133	.107

Mike Blowers

Bats: Right **Throws:** Right **Pos:** 3B **Ht:** 6' 2" **Wt:** 210 **Born:** 04/24/65 **Age:** 29

						BATTING														BASERUNNING				PERCENTAGES		
Year Team	Lg	G	AB	H	2B	3B	HR	(Hm	Rd)	TB	R	RBI	TBB	IBB	SO	HBP	SH	SF	SB	CS	SB%	GDP	Avg	OBP	SLG
1989 New York	AL	13	38	10	0	0	0	(0	0)	10	2	3	3	0	13	0	0	0	1	0	.00	1	.263	.317	.263
1990 New York	AL	48	144	27	4	0	5	(1	4)	46	16	21	12	1	50	1	0	1	1	0	1.00	3	.188	.255	.319
1991 New York	AL	15	35	7	0	0	1	(0	1)	10	3	1	4	0	3	0	1	0	0	0	.00	1	.200	.282	.286
1992 Seattle	AL	31	73	14	3	0	1	(0	1)	20	7	2	6	0	20	0	1	0	0	0	.00	3	.192	.253	.274
1993 Seattle	AL	127	379	106	23	3	15	(8	7)	180	55	57	44	3	98	2	3	1	1	5	.17	12	.280	.357	.475
5 ML YEARS		234	669	164	30	3	22	(9	13)	266	83	84	69	4	184	3	5	1	2	5	.29	20	.245	.318	.398

Mike Boddicker

Pitches: Right **Bats:** Right **Pos:** SP **Ht:** 5'11" **Wt:** 190 **Born:** 08/23/57 **Age:** 36

				HOW MUCH HE PITCHED					WHAT HE GAVE UP										THE RESULTS				
Year Team	Lg	G	GS	CG	GF	IP	BFP	H	R	ER	HR	SH	SF	HB	TBB	IBB	SO	WP	Bk	W	L	Pct.	ShO	Sv	ERA
1993 Omaha *	AAA	3	3	0	0	15.2	66	18	9	8	3	0	0	0	4	0	12	0	0	0	2	.000	0	0	4.60
Beloit *	A	1	1	0	0	4	16	3	1	1	0	0	0	0	1	0	4	1	0	0	0	.000	0	0	2.25
1980 Baltimore	AL	1	1	0	0	7.1	34	6	6	5	1	0	0	0	5	0	4	0	0	0	1	.000	0	0	6.14
1981 Baltimore	AL	2	0	0	1	5.2	25	6	4	3	1	0	0	0	2	0	2	2	0	0	0	.000	0	0	4.76
1982 Baltimore	AL	7	0	0	4	25.2	110	25	10	10	2	1	0	0	12	2	20	0	0	1	0	1.000	0	0	3.51
1983 Baltimore	AL	27	26	10	1	179	711	141	65	55	13	4	3	0	52	1	120	5	0	16	8	.667	5	0	2.77
1984 Baltimore	AL	34	34	16	0	261.1	1051	218	95	81	23	2	7	5	81	1	128	6	1	20	11	.645	4	0	2.79
1985 Baltimore	AL	32	32	9	0	203.1	899	227	104	92	13	9	2	5	89	7	135	5	0	12	17	.414	2	0	4.07
1986 Baltimore	AL	33	33	7	0	218.1	934	214	125	114	30	3	6	11	74	4	175	7	0	14	12	.538	0	0	4.70
1987 Baltimore	AL	33	33	7	0	226	950	212	114	105	29	7	4	7	78	4	152	10	0	10	12	.455	2	0	4.18
1988 2 ML Teams		36	35	5	0	236	1001	234	102	89	17	4	12	14	77	6	156	6	4	13	15	.464	1	0	3.39
1989 Boston	AL	34	34	3	0	211.2	912	217	101	94	19	8	10	10	71	4	145	4	1	15	11	.577	2	0	4.00
1990 Boston	AL	34	34	4	0	228	956	225	92	85	16	3	1	10	69	6	143	10	0	17	8	.680	0	0	3.36
1991 Kansas City	AL	30	29	1	1	180.2	775	188	89	82	13	10	1	13	59	0	79	3	2	12	12	.500	0	0	4.08
1992 Kansas City	AL	29	8	0	8	86.2	392	92	50	48	5	2	3	8	37	3	47	2	0	1	4	.200	0	3	4.98
1993 Milwaukee	AL	10	10	1	0	54	249	77	35	34	6	1	1	4	15	1	24	0	0	3	5	.375	0	0	5.67
1988	AL	21	21	4	0	147	636	149	72	63	14	3	8	11	51	5	100	3	4	6	12	.333	1	0	3.86
Boston		15	14	1	0	89	365	85	30	26	3	1	4	3	26	1	56	3	0	7	3	.700	1	0	2.63
14 ML YEARS		342	309	63	15	2123.2	8999	2082	992	897	188	54	50	87	721	39	1330	60	8	134	116	.536	16	3	3.80

Joe Boever

Pitches: Right **Bats:** Right **Pos:** RP **Ht:** 6' 1" **Wt:** 200 **Born:** 10/04/60 **Age:** 33

				HOW MUCH HE PITCHED					WHAT HE GAVE UP										THE RESULTS				
Year Team	Lg	G	GS	CG	GF	IP	BFP	H	R	ER	HR	SH	SF	HB	TBB	IBB	SO	WP	Bk	W	L	Pct.	ShO	Sv	ERA
1985 St. Louis	NL	13	0	0	5	16.1	69	17	8	8	3	1	1	0	4	1	20	1	0	0	0	.000	0	0	4.41
1986 St. Louis	NL	11	0	0	4	21.2	93	19	5	4	2	0	0	0	11	0	8	1	0	0	1	.000	0	0	1.66
1987 Atlanta	NL	14	0	0	10	18.1	93	29	15	15	4	1	1	0	12	1	18	1	0	1	0	1.000	0	0	7.36
1988 Atlanta	NL	16	0	0	13	20.1	70	12	4	4	1	2	0	1	9	1	7	0	0	0	2	.000	0	1	1.77
1989 Atlanta	NL	66	0	0	53	82.1	349	78	37	36	6	5	0	1	34	5	68	5	0	4	11	.267	0	21	3.94
1990 2 ML Teams		67	0	0	34	88.1	388	77	35	33	6	4	2	0	51	12	75	3	2	3	6	.333	0	14	3.36
1991 Philadelphia	NL	68	0	0	27	98.1	431	90	45	42	10	3	6	0	54	11	89	6	1	3	5	.375	0	0	3.84

Year	Team	Lg	G	GS	CG	GF	IP	BFP	H	R	ER	HR	SH	SF	HB	TBB	IBB	SO	WP	Bk	W	L	Pct.	ShO	Sv	ERA
1992	Houston	NL	**81**	0	0	26	111.1	479	103	38	31	3	10	4	4	45	9	67	4	0	3	6	.333	0	2	2.51
1993	2 ML Teams		61	0	0	22	102.1	449	101	50	41	9	5	7	4	44	7	63	1	0	6	3	.667	0	3	3.61
1990	Atlanta	NL	33	0	0	21	42.1	198	40	23	22	6	2	2	0	35	10	35	2	0	1	3	.250	0	8	4.68
	Philadelphia	NL	34	0	0	13	46	190	37	12	11	0	2	0	0	16	2	40	1	2	2	3	.400	0	6	2.15
1993	Oakland	AL	42	0	0	19	79.1	353	87	40	34	8	2	3	4	33	4	49	1	0	4	2	.667	0	6	3.86
	Detroit	AL	19	0	0	3	23	96	14	10	7	1	3	4	0	11	3	14	0	0	2	1	.667	0	3	2.74
	9 ML YEARS		397	0	0	194	559.1	2421	526	237	214	44	31	21	10	256	46	415	22	3	20	34	.370	0	41	3.44

Tim Bogar

Bats: Right **Throws:** Right **Pos:** SS   **Ht:** 6' 1" **Wt:** 190 **Born:** 10/28/66 **Age:** 27

							BATTING										BASERUNNING				PERCENTAGES		
Year	Team	Lg	G	AB	H	2B	3B	HR	(Hm	Rd)	TB	R	RBI	TBB	IBB	SO	HBP	SH	SF	SB	CS	SB%	GDP	Avg	OBP	SLG
1987	Little Fls	A	58	205	48	9	0	0	--	--	57	31	23	18	0	39	3	0	2	2	2	.50	3	.234	.303	.278
1988	Columbia	A	45	142	40	4	2	3	--	--	57	19	21	22	0	29	3	1	2	5	3	.63	6	.282	.385	.401
	St. Lucie	A	76	236	65	7	1	2	--	--	80	34	30	34	0	57	2	4	1	9	7	.56	4	.275	.370	.339
1989	Jackson	AA	112	406	108	13	5	4	--	--	143	44	45	41	4	57	7	3	5	8	3	.73	15	.266	.340	.352
1990	Tidewater	AAA	33	117	19	2	0	0	--	--	21	10	4	8	0	22	1	4	0	1	1	.50	4	.162	.222	.179
1991	Williamsprt	AA	63	243	61	12	2	2	--	--	83	33	25	20	0	44	2	2	4	13	8	.62	5	.251	.309	.342
	Tidewater	AAA	65	218	56	11	0	1	--	--	70	23	23	20	2	35	1	4	2	1	0	1.00	8	.257	.320	.321
1992	Tidewater	AAA	129	481	134	32	1	5	--	--	183	54	38	14	1	65	3	5	0	7	7	.50	15	.279	.303	.380
1993	New York	NL	78	205	50	13	0	3	(1	2)	72	19	25	14	2	29	3	1	1	0	1	.00	2	.244	.300	.351

Wade Boggs

Bats: Left **Throws:** Right **Pos:** 3B   **Ht:** 6' 2" **Wt:** 197 **Born:** 06/15/58 **Age:** 36

							BATTING										BASERUNNING				PERCENTAGES		
Year	Team	Lg	G	AB	H	2B	3B	HR	(Hm | Rd)	TB	R	RBI	TBB	IBB	SO	HBP	SH	SF	SB	CS	SB%	GDP	Avg	OBP	SLG
1982	Boston	AL	104	338	118	14	1	5	(4 | 1)	149	51	44	35	4	21	0	4	4	1	0	1.00	9	.349	.406	.441
1983	Boston	AL	153	582	210	44	7	5	(2 | 3)	283	100	74	92	2	36	1	3	7	3	3	.50	15	**.361**	**.444**	.486
1984	Boston	AL	158	625	203	31	4	6	(5 | 1)	260	109	55	89	6	44	0	8	4	3	2	.60	13	.325	.407	.416
1985	Boston	AL	161	653	**240**	42	3	8	(6 | 2)	312	107	78	96	5	61	4	3	2	2	1	.67	20	**.368**	**.450**	.478
1986	Boston	AL	149	580	207	47	2	8	(3 | 5)	282	107	71	**105**	14	44	0	4	4	0	4	.00	11	.357	.453	.486
1987	Boston	AL	147	551	200	40	6	24	(10 | 14)	324	108	89	105	**19**	48	2	1	8	1	3	.25	13	**.363**	**.461**	.588
1988	Boston	AL	155	584	214	**45**	6	5	(4 | 1)	286	**128**	58	**125**	**18**	34	3	0	7	2	3	.40	**23**	.366	**.476**	.490
1989	Boston	AL	156	621	205	**51**	7	3	(2 | 1)	279	**113**	54	107	19	51	7	0	7	2	6	.25	19	.330	**.430**	.449
1990	Boston	AL	155	619	187	44	5	6	(3 | 3)	259	89	63	87	**19**	68	1	0	6	0	0	.00	14	.302	.386	.418
1991	Boston	AL	144	546	181	42	2	8	(6 | 2)	251	93	51	89	**25**	32	0	0	6	1	2	.33	16	.332	.421	.460
1992	Boston	AL	143	514	133	22	4	7	(4 | 3)	184	62	50	74	**19**	31	4	0	6	1	3	.25	10	.259	.353	.358
1993	New York	AL	143	560	169	26	1	2	(1 | 1)	203	83	59	74	4	49	0	1	9	0	1	.00	10	.302	.378	.363
	12 ML YEARS		1768	6773	2267	448	48	87	(50 | 37)	3072	1150	746	1078	154	519	22	24	70	16	28	.36	173	.335	.424	.454

Brian Bohanon

Pitches: Left **Bats:** Left **Pos:** RP/SP   **Ht:** 6' 2" **Wt:** 220 **Born:** 08/01/68 **Age:** 25

			HOW MUCH HE PITCHED					WHAT HE GAVE UP										THE RESULTS					
Year	Team	Lg	G	GS	CG	GF	IP	BFP	H	R	ER	HR	SH	SF	HB	TBB	IBB	SO	WP	Bk	W	L	Pct.	ShO	Sv	ERA
1993	Okla City *	AAA	2	2	0	0	7	31	7	6	5	1	0	0	1	3	0	7	1	0	0	1	.000	0	0	6.43
1990	Texas	AL	11	6	0	1	34	158	40	30	25	6	0	3	2	18	0	15	1	0	0	3	.000	0	0	6.62
1991	Texas	AL	11	11	1	0	61.1	273	66	35	33	4	2	5	2	23	0	34	3	1	4	3	.571	0	0	4.84
1992	Texas	AL	18	7	0	3	45.2	220	57	38	32	7	0	2	1	25	0	29	2	0	1	1	.500	0	0	6.31
1993	Texas	AL	36	8	0	4	92.2	418	107	54	49	8	2	5	4	46	3	45	10	0	4	4	.500	0	0	4.76
	4 ML YEARS		76	32	1	8	233.2	1069	270	157	139	25	4	15	9	112	3	123	16	1	9	11	.450	0	0	5.35

Frank Bolick

Bats: Both **Throws:** Right **Pos:** 1B/3B   **Ht:** 5'10" **Wt:** 180 **Born:** 06/28/66 **Age:** 28

							BATTING										BASERUNNING				PERCENTAGES		
Year	Team	Lg	G	AB	H	2B	3B	HR	(Hm	Rd)	TB	R	RBI	TBB	IBB	SO	HBP	SH	SF	SB	CS	SB%	GDP	Avg	OBP	SLG
1987	Helena	R	52	156	39	8	1	10	--	--	79	41	28	41	1	44	3	1	0	4	0	1.00	3	.250	.415	.506
1988	Beloit	A	55	180	41	14	1	2	--	--	63	28	16	43	0	49	1	1	0	3	3	.50	3	.228	.379	.350
	Brewers	R	23	80	30	9	3	1	--	--	48	20	20	22	0	8	0	0	3	1	0	1.00	0	.375	.495	.600
	Helena	R	40	131	39	10	1	10	--	--	81	35	28	32	2	31	1	1	2	5	1	.83	2	.298	.434	.618
1989	Beloit	A	88	299	90	23	0	9	--	--	140	44	41	47	5	52	6	0	2	9	6	.60	3	.301	.404	.468
1990	Stockton	A	50	164	51	9	1	8	--	--	86	39	36	38	1	33	2	0	5	5	3	.63	0	.311	.435	.524
	San Berndno	A	78	277	92	24	4	10	--	--	154	61	66	53	6	53	2	0	8	3	6	.33	2	.332	.432	.556
1991	Jacksnville	AA	136	468	119	19	0	16	--	--	186	69	73	84	3	115	5	2	7	5	4	.56	7	.254	.369	.397
1992	Jacksnville	AA	63	226	60	9	0	13	--	--	108	32	42	42	1	38	1	0	4	1	4	.20	3	.268	.380	.482
	Calgary	AAA	78	274	79	18	6	14	--	--	151	35	54	39	2	52	1	1	4	4	4	.50	4	.288	.374	.551
1993	Ottawa	AAA	2	8	1	0	0	0	--	--	1	0	0	0	0	0	0	0	0	0	0	.00	0	.125	.125	.125
1993	Montreal	NL	95	213	45	13	0	4	(2	2)	70	25	24	23	2	37	4	0	2	1	0	1.00	4	.211	.298	.329

Rodney Bolton

Pitches: Right **Bats:** Right **Pos:** SP   **Ht:** 6' 2" **Wt:** 190 **Born:** 09/23/68 **Age:** 25

			HOW	MUCH	HE	PITCHED			WHAT	HE	GAVE	UP									THE	RESULTS			
Year Team	Lg	G	GS	CG	GF	IP	BFP	H	R	ER	HR	SH	SF	HB	TBB	IBB	SO	WP	Bk	W	L	Pct.	ShO	Sv	ERA
1990 Utica	A	6	6	1	0	44	168	27	4	2	0	1	0	3	11	0	45	0	0	5	1	.833	1	0	0.41
South Bend	A	7	7	3	0	51	196	34	14	11	0	1	1	1	12	1	50	1	1	5	1	.833	1	0	1.94
1991 Sarasota	A	15	15	5	0	103.2	412	81	29	22	2	5	1	2	23	0	77	3	1	7	6	.538	2	0	1.91
Birmingham	AA	12	12	3	0	89	360	73	26	16	3	0	2	8	21	1	57	3	0	8	4	.667	2	0	1.62
1992 Vancouver	AAA	27	27	3	0	187.1	781	174	72	61	9	9	4	1	59	2	111	9	2	11	9	.550	2	0	2.93
1993 Nashville	AAA	18	16	1	1	115.2	486	108	40	37	10	2	3	3	37	2	75	11	0	10	1	.909	0	1	2.88
1993 Chicago	AL	9	8	0	0	42.1	197	55	40	35	4	1	4	1	16	0	17	4	0	2	6	.250	0	0	7.44

Tom Bolton

Pitches: Left **Bats:** Left **Pos:** RP/SP   **Ht:** 6' 3" **Wt:** 185 **Born:** 05/06/62 **Age:** 32

			HOW	MUCH	HE	PITCHED			WHAT	HE	GAVE	UP									THE	RESULTS			
Year Team	Lg	G	GS	CG	GF	IP	BFP	H	R	ER	HR	SH	SF	HB	TBB	IBB	SO	WP	Bk	W	L	Pct.	ShO	Sv	ERA
1987 Boston	AL	29	0	0	5	61.2	287	83	33	30	5	3	3	2	27	2	49	3	0	1	0	1.000	0	0	4.38
1988 Boston	AL	28	0	0	8	30.1	140	35	17	16	1	2	1	0	14	1	21	2	1	1	3	.250	0	1	4.75
1989 Boston	AL	4	4	0	0	17.1	83	21	18	16	1	1	0	0	10	1	9	1	0	0	4	.000	0	0	8.31
1990 Boston	AL	21	16	3	2	119.2	501	111	46	45	6	3	5	3	47	3	65	1	1	10	5	.667	0	0	3.38
1991 Boston	AL	25	19	0	4	110	499	136	72	64	16	2	4	1	51	2	64	3	0	8	9	.471	0	0	5.24
1992 2 ML Teams		37	9	0	9	75.1	345	86	39	38	9	1	1	4	37	3	50	5	2	4	5	.444	0	0	4.54
1993 Detroit	AL	43	8	0	9	102.2	462	113	57	51	5	7	2	7	45	10	66	5	1	6	6	.500	0	0	4.47
1992 Boston	AL	21	1	0	6	29	135	34	11	11	0	0	0	2	14	1	23	2	1	1	2	.333	0	0	3.41
Cincinnati	NL	16	8	0	3	46.1	210	52	28	27	9	1	1	2	23	2	27	3	1	3	3	.500	0	0	5.24
7 ML YEARS		187	56	3	37	517	2317	585	282	260	43	18	17	17	231	22	324	20	5	30	32	.484	0	1	4.53

Barry Bonds

Bats: Left **Throws:** Left **Pos:** LF   **Ht:** 6' 1" **Wt:** 185 **Born:** 07/24/64 **Age:** 29

							BATTING												BASERUNNING				PERCENTAGES		
Year Team	Lg	G	AB	H	2B	3B	HR	(Hm	Rd)	TB	R	RBI	TBB	IBB	SO	HBP	SH	SF	SB	CS	SB%	GDP	Avg	OBP	SLG
1986 Pittsburgh	NL	113	413	92	26	3	16	(9	7)	172	72	48	65	2	102	2	2	2	36	7	.84	4	.223	.330	.416
1987 Pittsburgh	NL	150	551	144	34	9	25	(12	13)	271	99	59	54	3	88	3	0	3	32	10	.76	4	.261	.329	.492
1988 Pittsburgh	NL	144	538	152	30	5	24	(14	10)	264	97	58	72	14	82	2	0	2	17	11	.61	3	.283	.368	.491
1989 Pittsburgh	NL	159	580	144	34	6	19	(7	12)	247	96	58	93	22	93	1	1	4	32	10	.76	9	.248	.351	.426
1990 Pittsburgh	NL	151	519	156	32	3	33	(14	19)	293	104	114	93	15	83	3	0	6	52	13	.80	6	.301	.406	**.565**
1991 Pittsburgh	NL	153	510	149	28	5	25	(12	13)	262	95	116	107	25	73	4	0	13	43	13	.77	8	.292	**.410**	.514
1992 Pittsburgh	NL	140	473	147	36	5	34	(15	**19**)	295	**109**	103	**127**	**32**	69	5	0	7	39	8	.83	9	.311	**.456**	**.624**
1993 San Francisco	NL	159	539	181	38	4	**46**	(21	**25**)	**365**	129	**123**	126	**43**	79	2	0	7	29	12	.71	11	**.336**	**.458**	**.677**
8 ML YEARS		1169	4123	1165	258	40	222	(104	118)	2169	801	679	737	156	669	22	3	44	280	84	.77	56	.283	.391	.526

Ricky Bones

Pitches: Right **Bats:** Right **Pos:** SP   **Ht:** 6' 0" **Wt:** 190 **Born:** 04/07/69 **Age:** 25

			HOW	MUCH	HE	PITCHED			WHAT	HE	GAVE	UP									THE	RESULTS			
Year Team	Lg	G	GS	CG	GF	IP	BFP	H	R	ER	HR	SH	SF	HB	TBB	IBB	SO	WP	Bk	W	L	Pct.	ShO	Sv	ERA
1991 San Diego	NL	11	11	0	0	54	234	57	33	29	3	0	4	0	18	0	31	4	0	4	6	.400	0	0	4.83
1992 Milwaukee	AL	31	28	0	0	163.1	705	169	90	83	27	2	5	9	48	0	65	3	2	9	10	.474	0	0	4.57
1993 Milwaukee	AL	32	31	3	1	203.2	883	222	122	110	28	5	7	8	63	3	63	6	1	11	11	.500	0	0	4.86
3 ML YEARS		74	70	3	1	421	1822	448	245	222	58	7	16	17	129	3	159	13	3	24	27	.471	0	0	4.75

Bobby Bonilla

Bats: Both **Throws:** Right **Pos:** RF/3B   **Ht:** 6' 3" **Wt:** 240 **Born:** 02/23/63 **Age:** 31

							BATTING												BASERUNNING				PERCENTAGES		
Year Team	Lg	G	AB	H	2B	3B	HR	(Hm	Rd)	TB	R	RBI	TBB	IBB	SO	HBP	SH	SF	SB	CS	SB%	GDP	Avg	OBP	SLG
1986 2 ML Teams		138	426	109	16	4	3	(2	1)	142	55	43	62	3	88	2	5	1	8	5	.62	9	.256	.330	.333
1987 Pittsburgh	NL	141	466	140	33	3	15	(7	8)	224	58	77	39	4	64	2	0	8	3	5	.38	8	.300	.351	.481
1988 Pittsburgh	NL	159	584	160	32	7	24	(9	15)	278	87	100	85	19	82	4	0	8	3	5	.38	4	.274	.366	.476
1989 Pittsburgh	NL	**163**	616	173	37	10	24	(13	11)	302	96	86	76	20	93	1	0	5	8	8	.50	10	.281	.358	.490
1990 Pittsburgh	NL	160	625	175	39	7	32	(13	19)	324	112	120	45	9	103	1	0	**15**	4	3	.57	11	.280	.322	.518
1991 Pittsburgh	NL	157	577	174	**44**	6	18	(9	9)	284	102	100	90	8	67	2	0	11	2	4	.33	14	.302	.391	.492
1992 New York	NL	128	438	109	23	0	19	(5	14)	189	62	70	66	10	73	1	0	1	4	3	.57	11	.249	.348	.432
1993 New York	NL	139	502	133	21	3	34	(18	16)	262	81	87	72	11	96	0	0	8	3	3	.50	12	.265	.352	.522
1986 Chicago	AL	75	234	63	10	2	2	(2	0)	83	27	26	33	2	49	1	2	1	4	1	.80	4	.269	.361	.355
Pittsburgh	NL	63	192	46	6	2	1	(0	1)	59	28	17	29	1	39	1	3	0	4	4	.50	5	.240	.342	.307
8 ML YEARS		1185	4234	1173	245	40	169	(76	93)	2005	653	683	535	84	666	13	5	57	35	36	.49	79	.277	.356	.474

Bret Boone

Bats: Right **Throws:** Right **Pos:** 2B **Ht:** 5'10" **Wt:** 175 **Born:** 04/06/69 **Age:** 25

								BATTING										BASERUNNING				PERCENTAGES		
Year Team	Lg	G	AB	H	2B	3B	HR	(Hm | Rd)	TB	R	RBI	TBB	IBB	SO	HBP	SH	SF	SB	CS	SB%	GDP	Avg	OBP	SLG
1990 Peninsula	A	74	255	68	13	2	8	--	--	109	42	38	47	0	57	1	0	0	5	2	.71	1	.267	.383	.427
1991 Jacksnville	AA	139	475	121	18	1	19	--	--	198	64	75	72	2	123	5	1	3	9	9	.50	21	.255	.357	.417
1992 Calgary	AAA	118	439	138	26	5	13	--	--	213	73	73	60	7	88	5	1	6	17	12	.59	12	.314	.398	.485
1993 Calgary	AAA	71	274	91	18	3	8	--	--	139	48	56	28	0	58	1	0	6	3	8	.27	7	.332	.388	.507
1992 Seattle	AL	33	129	25	4	0	4	(2 | 2)	41	15	15	4	0	34	1	1	0	1	1	.50	4	.194	.224	.318
1993 Seattle	AL	76	271	68	12	2	12	(7 | 5)	120	31	38	17	1	52	4	6	4	2	3	.40	6	.251	.301	.443
2 ML YEARS		109	400	93	16	2	16	(9 | 7)	161	46	53	21	1	86	5	7	4	3	4	.43	10	.233	.277	.403

Pedro Borbon

Pitches: Left **Bats:** Left **Pos:** RP **Ht:** 6' 1" **Wt:** 205 **Born:** 11/15/67 **Age:** 26

			HOW MUCH HE PITCHED					WHAT HE GAVE UP										THE RESULTS					
Year Team	Lg	G	GS	CG	GF	IP	BFP	H	R	ER	HR	SH	SF	HB	TBB	IBB	SO	WP	Bk	W	L	Pct.	ShO	Sv	ERA
1988 White Sox	R	16	11	1	2	74.2	299	52	28	20	1	3	3	2	17	0	67	5	14	5	3	.625	1	1	2.41
1990 Burlington	A	14	14	6	0	97.2	381	73	25	16	3	0	0	3	23	0	76	4	1	11	3	.786	2	0	1.47
Durham	A	11	11	0	0	61.1	266	73	40	37	8	2	2	2	16	0	37	2	1	4	5	.444	0	0	5.43
1991 Durham	A	37	6	1	21	90.2	388	85	40	23	2	5	4	2	35	2	79	4	2	4	3	.571	0	5	2.28
Greenville	AA	4	4	0	0	29	120	23	12	9	1	1	0	3	10	0	22	2	0	0	1	.000	0	0	2.79
1992 Greenville	AA	39	10	0	14	94	384	73	36	32	6	1	3	3	42	1	79	2	0	8	2	.800	0	3	3.06
1993 Richmond	AAA	52	0	0	15	76.2	344	71	40	36	7	10	3	2	42	9	95	3	1	5	5	.500	0	1	4.23
1992 Atlanta	NL	2	0	0	2	1.1	7	2	1	1	0	0	0	0	1	1	1	0	0	0	1	.000	0	0	6.75
1993 Atlanta	NL	3	0	0	0	1.2	11	3	4	4	0	0	0	0	3	0	2	0	0	0	0	.000	0	0	21.60
2 ML YEARS		5	0	0	2	3	18	5	5	5	0	0	0	0	4	1	3	0	0	0	1	.000	0	0	15.00

Pat Borders

Bats: Right **Throws:** Right **Pos:** C **Ht:** 6' 2" **Wt:** 200 **Born:** 05/14/63 **Age:** 31

								BATTING										BASERUNNING				PERCENTAGES		
Year Team	Lg	G	AB	H	2B	3B	HR	(Hm	Rd)	TB	R	RBI	TBB	IBB	SO	HBP	SH	SF	SB	CS	SB%	GDP	Avg	OBP	SLG
1988 Toronto	AL	56	154	42	6	3	5	(2	3)	69	15	21	3	0	24	0	2	1	0	0	.00	5	.273	.285	.448
1989 Toronto	AL	94	241	62	11	1	3	(1	2)	84	22	29	11	2	45	1	1	2	2	1	.67	7	.257	.290	.349
1990 Toronto	AL	125	346	99	24	2	15	(10	5)	172	36	49	18	2	57	0	1	3	0	1	.00	17	.286	.319	.497
1991 Toronto	AL	105	291	71	17	0	5	(2	3)	103	22	36	11	1	45	1	6	3	0	0	.00	8	.244	.271	.354
1992 Toronto	AL	138	480	116	26	2	13	(7	6)	185	47	53	33	3	75	2	1	5	1	1	.50	11	.242	.290	.385
1993 Toronto	AL	138	488	124	30	0	9	(6	3)	181	38	55	20	2	66	2	7	3	2	2	.50	18	.254	.285	.371
6 ML YEARS		656	2000	514	114	8	50	(28	22)	794	180	243	96	10	312	6	18	17	5	5	.50	66	.257	.291	.397

Mike Bordick

Bats: Right **Throws:** Right **Pos:** SS **Ht:** 5'11" **Wt:** 175 **Born:** 07/21/65 **Age:** 28

								BATTING										BASERUNNING				PERCENTAGES		
Year Team	Lg	G	AB	H	2B	3B	HR	(Hm	Rd)	TB	R	RBI	TBB	IBB	SO	HBP	SH	SF	SB	CS	SB%	GDP	Avg	OBP	SLG
1990 Oakland	AL	25	14	1	0	0	0	(0	0)	1	0	0	1	0	4	0	0	0	0	0	.00	0	.071	.133	.071
1991 Oakland	AL	90	235	56	5	1	0	(0	0)	63	21	21	14	0	37	3	12	1	3	4	.43	3	.238	.289	.268
1992 Oakland	AL	154	504	151	19	4	3	(3	0)	187	62	48	40	2	59	4	14	5	12	6	.67	10	.300	.358	.371
1993 Oakland	AL	159	546	136	21	2	3	(2	1)	170	60	48	60	2	58	11	10	6	10	10	.50	9	.249	.332	.311
4 ML YEARS		428	1299	344	45	7	6	(5	1)	421	143	117	115	4	158	23	36	12	25	20	.56	22	.265	.333	.324

Chris Bosio

Pitches: Right **Bats:** Right **Pos:** SP/RP **Ht:** 6' 3" **Wt:** 225 **Born:** 04/03/63 **Age:** 31

			HOW MUCH HE PITCHED					WHAT HE GAVE UP										THE RESULTS					
Year Team	Lg	G	GS	CG	GF	IP	BFP	H	R	ER	HR	SH	SF	HB	TBB	IBB	SO	WP	Bk	W	L	Pct.	ShO	Sv	ERA
1986 Milwaukee	AL	10	4	0	3	34.2	154	41	27	27	9	1	0	0	13	0	29	2	1	0	4	.000	0	0	7.01
1987 Milwaukee	AL	46	19	2	8	170	734	187	102	99	18	3	3	1	50	3	150	14	2	11	8	.579	1	2	5.24
1988 Milwaukee	AL	38	22	9	15	182	766	190	80	68	13	7	9	2	38	6	84	1	2	7	15	.318	1	6	3.36
1989 Milwaukee	AL	33	33	8	0	234.2	969	225	90	77	16	5	5	6	48	1	173	4	2	15	10	.600	2	0	2.95
1990 Milwaukee	AL	20	20	4	0	132.2	557	131	67	59	15	4	4	3	38	1	76	7	0	4	9	.308	1	0	4.00
1991 Milwaukee	AL	32	32	5	0	204.2	840	187	80	74	15	2	6	8	58	0	117	5	0	14	10	.583	1	0	3.25
1992 Milwaukee	AL	33	33	4	0	231.1	937	223	100	93	21	6	5	4	44	1	120	8	2	16	6	.727	2	0	3.62
1993 Seattle	AL	29	24	3	2	164.1	678	138	75	63	14	7	4	6	59	3	119	5	0	9	9	.500	1	1	3.45
8 ML YEARS		241	187	35	28	1354.1	5635	1322	621	560	121	35	36	30	348	15	868	46	9	76	71	.517	9	9	3.72

Shawn Boskie

Pitches: Right **Bats:** Right **Pos:** RP   **Ht:** 6' 3" **Wt:** 200 **Born:** 03/28/67 **Age:** 27

			HOW MUCH HE PITCHED						WHAT HE GAVE UP										THE RESULTS				
Year Team	Lg	G	GS	CG	GF	IP	BFP	H	R	ER	HR	SH	SF	HB	TBB	IBB	SO	WP	Bk	W	L	Pct.	ShO	Sv	ERA
1993 Iowa *	AAA	11	11	1	0	71.2	300	70	35	34	4	2	1	7	21	0	35	1	0	6	1	.857	0	0	4.27
1990 Chicago	NL	15	15	1	0	97.2	415	99	42	40	8	8	2	1	31	3	49	3	2	5	6	.455	0	0	3.69
1991 Chicago	NL	28	20	0	2	129	582	150	78	75	14	8	6	5	52	4	62	1	1	4	9	.308	0	0	5.23
1992 Chicago	NL	23	18	0	2	91.2	393	96	55	51	14	9	6	4	36	3	39	5	1	5	11	.313	0	0	5.01
1993 Chicago	NL	39	2	0	10	65.2	277	63	30	25	7	4	1	7	21	2	39	5	0	5	3	.625	0	0	3.43
4 ML YEARS		105	55	1	14	384	1667	408	205	191	43	29	15	17	140	12	189	14	4	19	29	.396	0	0	4.48

Daryl Boston

Bats: Left **Throws:** Left **Pos:** LF/CF   **Ht:** 6' 3" **Wt:** 210 **Born:** 01/04/63 **Age:** 31

								BATTING											BASERUNNING				PERCENTAGES		
Year Team	Lg	G	AB	H	2B	3B	HR	(Hm	Rd)	TB	R	RBI	TBB	IBB	SO	HBP	SH	SF	SB	CS	SB%	GDP	Avg	OBP	SLG
1984 Chicago	AL	35	83	14	3	1	0	(0	0)	19	8	3	4	0	20	0	0	0	6	0	1.00	0	.169	.207	.229
1985 Chicago	AL	95	232	53	13	1	3	(1	2)	77	20	15	14	1	44	0	1	1	8	6	.57	3	.228	.271	.332
1986 Chicago	AL	56	199	53	11	3	5	(1	4)	85	29	22	21	3	33	0	3	1	9	5	.64	4	.266	.335	.427
1987 Chicago	AL	103	337	87	21	2	10	(5	5)	142	51	29	25	2	68	0	4	3	12	6	.67	5	.258	.307	.421
1988 Chicago	AL	105	281	61	12	2	15	(6	9)	122	37	31	21	5	44	0	2	1	9	3	.75	5	.217	.271	.434
1989 Chicago	AL	101	218	55	3	4	5	(3	2)	81	34	23	24	3	31	0	4	1	7	2	.78	1	.252	.325	.372
1990 2 ML Teams		120	367	100	21	2	12	(4	8)	161	65	45	28	2	50	2	0	0	19	7	.73	7	.272	.327	.439
1991 New York	NL	137	255	70	16	4	4	(2	2)	106	40	21	30	0	42	0	0	1	15	8	.65	2	.275	.350	.416
1992 New York	NL	130	289	72	14	2	11	(5	6)	123	37	35	38	6	60	3	0	4	12	6	.67	5	.249	.338	.426
1993 Colorado	NL	124	291	76	15	4	14	(3	11)	135	46	40	26	1	57	2	0	1	1	6	.14	5	.261	.325	.464
1990 Chicago	AL	5	1	0	0	0	0	(0	0)	0	0	0	0	0	0	0	0	0	1	0	1.00	0	.000	.000	.000
New York	NL	115	366	100	21	2	12	(4	8)	161	65	45	28	2	50	2	0	0	18	7	.72	7	.273	.328	.440
10 ML YEARS		1006	2552	641	129	22	79	(30	49)	1051	367	264	231	23	449	7	14	13	98	49	.67	37	.251	.314	.412

Kent Bottenfield

Pitches: Right **Bats:** Both **Pos:** SP/RP   **Ht:** 6' 3" **Wt:** 225 **Born:** 11/14/68 **Age:** 25

			HOW MUCH HE PITCHED						WHAT HE GAVE UP										THE RESULTS				
Year Team	Lg	G	GS	CG	GF	IP	BFP	H	R	ER	HR	SH	SF	HB	TBB	IBB	SO	WP	Bk	W	L	Pct.	ShO	Sv	ERA
1986 Expos	R	13	13	2	0	74.1	323	73	42	27	2	2	6	3	30	0	41	0	1	5	6	.455	0	0	3.27
1987 Burlington	A	27	27	6	0	161	706	175	98	81	12	3	3	2	42	0	103	9	2	9	13	.409	3	0	4.53
1988 Wst Plm Bch	A	27	27	9	0	181	745	165	80	67	10	3	5	5	47	0	120	4	3	10	8	.556	4	0	3.33
1989 Jacksnville	AA	25	25	1	0	138.2	625	137	101	81	13	6	9	9	73	2	91	6	2	3	17	.150	0	0	5.26
1990 Jacksnville	AA	29	28	2	0	169	718	158	72	64	14	7	4	11	67	1	121	9	2	12	10	.545	1	0	3.41
1991 Indianaplis	AAA	29	27	5	0	166.1	712	155	97	75	15	11	5	4	61	7	108	5	1	8	15	.348	2	0	4.06
1992 Indianaplis	AAA	25	23	3	1	152.1	629	139	64	58	12	6	4	2	58	1	111	2	0	12	8	.600	1	0	3.43
1992 Montreal	NL	10	4	0	2	32.1	135	26	9	8	1	1	2	1	11	1	14	0	0	1	2	.333	0	1	2.23
1993 2 ML Teams		37	25	1	2	159.2	710	179	102	90	24	21	4	6	71	3	63	4	1	5	10	.333	0	0	5.07
1993 Montreal	NL	23	11	0	2	83	373	93	49	38	11	11	1	5	33	2	33	4	1	2	5	.286	0	0	4.12
Colorado	NL	14	14	1	0	76.2	337	86	53	52	13	10	3	1	38	1	30	0	0	3	5	.375	0	0	6.10
2 ML YEARS		47	29	1	4	192	845	205	111	98	25	22	6	7	82	4	77	4	1	6	12	.333	0	1	4.59

Denis Boucher

Pitches: Left **Bats:** Right **Pos:** SP   **Ht:** 6' 1" **Wt:** 195 **Born:** 03/07/68 **Age:** 26

			HOW MUCH HE PITCHED						WHAT HE GAVE UP										THE RESULTS				
Year Team	Lg	G	GS	CG	GF	IP	BFP	H	R	ER	HR	SH	SF	HB	TBB	IBB	SO	WP	Bk	W	L	Pct.	ShO	Sv	ERA
1993 Las Vegas *	AAA	24	7	1	2	70	331	101	59	50	12	4	1	6	27	3	46	4	1	4	7	.364	0	1	6.43
Ottawa *	AAA	11	6	0	1	43	169	36	13	13	0	2	0	1	11	0	22	3	0	6	0	1.000	0	0	2.72
1991 2 ML Teams		12	12	0	0	58	270	74	41	39	12	3	1	2	24	1	29	1	4	1	7	.125	0	0	6.05
1992 Cleveland	AL	8	7	0	0	41	184	48	29	29	9	1	3	1	20	0	17	1	0	2	2	.500	0	0	6.37
1993 Montreal	NL	5	5	0	0	28.1	111	24	7	6	1	0	3	0	3	1	14	0	0	3	1	.750	0	0	1.91
1991 Toronto	AL	7	7	0	0	35.1	162	39	20	18	6	3	1	2	16	1	16	0	4	0	3	.000	0	0	4.58
Cleveland	AL	5	5	0	0	22.2	108	35	21	21	6	0	0	0	8	0	13	1	0	1	4	.200	0	0	8.34
3 ML YEARS		25	24	0	0	127.1	565	146	77	74	22	4	7	3	47	2	60	2	6	6	10	.375	0	0	5.23

Rafael Bournigal

Bats: Right **Throws:** Right **Pos:** 2B   **Ht:** 5'11" **Wt:** 160 **Born:** 05/12/66 **Age:** 28

								BATTING											BASERUNNING				PERCENTAGES		
Year Team	Lg	G	AB	H	2B	3B	HR	(Hm	Rd)	TB	R	RBI	TBB	IBB	SO	HBP	SH	SF	SB	CS	SB%	GDP	Avg	OBP	SLG
1987 Great Falls	R	30	82	12	4	0	0	--	--	16	5	4	3	0	7	1	1	0	0	1	.00	1	.146	.186	.195
1988 Salem	A	70	275	86	10	1	0	--	--	98	54	25	38	0	32	0	6	2	11	6	.65	5	.313	.394	.356
1989 Vero Beach	A	132	484	128	11	1	1	--	--	144	74	37	33	0	21	3	5	3	18	13	.58	19	.264	.314	.298
1990 San Antonio	AA	69	194	41	4	2	0	--	--	49	20	14	8	0	24	0	7	2	2	1	.67	9	.211	.240	.253
1991 Vero Beach	A	20	66	16	2	0	0	--	--	18	6	3	1	0	3	0	1	1	2	1	.67	1	.242	.250	.273
San Antonio	AA	16	65	21	2	0	0	--	--	23	6	9	2	0	7	1	1	1	2	3	.40	2	.323	.338	.354

Year Team	Lg	G	AB	H	2B	3B	HR	(Hm	Rd)	TB	R	RBI	TBB	IBB	SO	HBP	SH	SF	SB	CS	SB%	GDP	Avg	OBP	SLG
Albuquerque AAA		66	215	63	5	5	0	--	--	78	34	29	14	1	13	0	8	4	4	1	.80	3	.293	.330	.363
1992 Albuquerque AAA		122	395	128	18	1	0	--	--	148	47	34	22	5	7	5	10	4	5	3	.63	17	.324	.364	.375
1993 Albuquerque AAA		134	465	129	25	0	4	--	--	166	75	55	29	1	18	3	8	5	3	5	.38	11	.277	.321	.357
1992 Los Angeles NL		10	20	3	1	0	0	(0	0)	4	1	0	1	0	2	1	0	0	0	0	.00	0	.150	.227	.200
1993 Los Angeles NL		8	18	9	1	0	0	(0	0)	10	0	3	0	0	2	0	0	0	0	0	.00	0	.500	.500	.556
2 ML YEARS		18	38	12	2	0	0	(0	0)	14	1	3	1	0	4	1	0	0	0	0	.00	0	.316	.350	.368

Ryan Bowen

Pitches: Right **Bats:** Right **Pos:** SP   **Ht:** 6' 0" **Wt:** 185 **Born:** 02/10/68 **Age:** 26

		HOW MUCH HE PITCHED						WHAT HE GAVE UP												THE RESULTS					
Year Team	Lg	G	GS	CG	GF	IP	BFP	H	R	ER	HR	SH	SF	HB	TBB	IBB	SO	WP	Bk	W	L	Pct.	ShO	Sv	ERA
1991 Houston	NL	14	13	0	0	71.2	319	73	43	41	4	2	6	3	36	1	49	8	1	6	4	.600	0	0	5.15
1992 Houston	NL	11	9	0	2	33.2	179	48	43	41	8	3	0	2	30	3	22	5	0	0	7	.000	0	0	10.96
1993 Florida	NL	27	27	2	0	156.2	693	156	83	77	11	5	4	3	87	7	98	10	4	8	12	.400	1	0	4.42
3 ML YEARS		52	49	2	2	262	1191	277	169	159	23	10	10	8	153	11	169	23	5	14	23	.378	1	0	5.46

Jeff Branson

Bats: Left **Throws:** Right **Pos:** SS/2B/3B   **Ht:** 6' 0" **Wt:** 180 **Born:** 01/26/67 **Age:** 27

		BATTING																	BASERUNNING				PERCENTAGES		
Year Team	Lg	G	AB	H	2B	3B	HR	(Hm	Rd)	TB	R	RBI	TBB	IBB	SO	HBP	SH	SF	SB	CS	SB%	GDP	Avg	OBP	SLG
1989 Cedar Rapds A		127	469	132	28	1	10	--	--	192	70	68	41	3	90	2	4	4	5	6	.45	10	.281	.339	.409
1990 Chattanooga AA		63	233	49	9	1	2	--	--	66	19	29	13	2	48	0	1	2	3	1	.75	4	.210	.250	.283
Cedar Rapds A		62	239	60	13	4	6	--	--	99	37	24	24	3	45	0	0	2	11	3	.79	6	.251	.317	.414
1991 Chattanooga AA		88	304	80	13	3	2	--	--	105	35	28	31	2	51	1	2	5	3	7	.30	4	.263	.328	.345
Nashville AAA		43	145	35	4	1	0	--	--	41	10	11	8	2	31	0	1	0	5	4	.56	1	.241	.281	.283
1992 Nashville AAA		36	123	40	6	3	4	--	--	64	18	12	9	1	19	0	1	0	3	0	.00	1	.325	.371	.520
1992 Cincinnati	NL	72	115	34	7	1	0	(0	0)	43	12	15	5	2	16	0	2	1	0	1	.00	4	.296	.322	.374
1993 Cincinnati	NL	125	381	92	15	1	3	(2	1)	118	40	22	19	2	73	0	8	4	4	1	.80	4	.241	.275	.310
2 ML YEARS		197	496	126	22	2	3	(2	1)	161	52	37	24	4	89	0	10	5	4	2	.67	8	.254	.286	.325

Jeff Brantley

Pitches: Right **Bats:** Right **Pos:** RP/SP   **Ht:** 5'10" **Wt:** 189 **Born:** 09/05/63 **Age:** 30

		HOW MUCH HE PITCHED						WHAT HE GAVE UP												THE RESULTS					
Year Team	Lg	G	GS	CG	GF	IP	BFP	H	R	ER	HR	SH	SF	HB	TBB	IBB	SO	WP	Bk	W	L	Pct.	ShO	Sv	ERA
1988 San Francisco	NL	9	1	0	2	20.2	88	22	13	13	2	1	0	1	6	1	11	0	1	0	1	.000	0	1	5.66
1989 San Francisco	NL	59	1	0	15	97.1	422	101	50	44	10	7	3	2	37	8	69	3	2	7	1	.875	0	4	4.07
1990 San Francisco	NL	55	0	0	32	86.2	361	77	18	15	3	2	2	3	33	6	61	0	3	5	3	.625	0	19	1.56
1991 San Francisco	NL	67	0	0	39	95.1	411	78	27	26	8	4	4	5	52	10	81	6	0	5	2	.714	0	15	2.45
1992 San Francisco	NL	56	4	0	32	91.2	381	67	32	30	8	7	3	4	45	5	86	3	1	7	7	.500	0	7	2.95
1993 San Francisco	NL	53	12	0	9	113.2	496	112	60	54	19	5	5	7	46	2	76	3	4	5	6	.455	0	0	4.28
6 ML YEARS		299	18	0	129	505.1	2159	457	200	182	50	26	17	21	219	32	384	15	11	29	20	.592	0	42	3.24

Sid Bream

Bats: Left **Throws:** Left **Pos:** 1B   **Ht:** 6' 4" **Wt:** 220 **Born:** 08/03/60 **Age:** 33

		BATTING																	BASERUNNING				PERCENTAGES		
Year Team	Lg	G	AB	H	2B	3B	HR	(Hm	Rd)	TB	R	RBI	TBB	IBB	SO	HBP	SH	SF	SB	CS	SB%	GDP	Avg	OBP	SLG
1983 Los Angeles	NL	15	11	2	0	0	0	(0	0)	2	0	2	2	0	2	0	0	0	0	0	.00	1	.182	.308	.182
1984 Los Angeles	NL	27	49	9	3	0	0	(0	0)	12	2	6	6	2	9	0	1	2	1	0	1.00	1	.184	.263	.245
1985 2 ML Teams		50	148	34	7	0	6	(2	4)	59	18	21	18	5	24	0	3	2	0	2	.00	4	.230	.310	.399
1986 Pittsburgh	NL	154	522	140	37	5	16	(5	11)	235	73	77	60	5	73	1	1	7	13	7	.65	14	.268	.341	.450
1987 Pittsburgh	NL	149	516	142	25	3	13	(10	3)	212	64	65	49	11	69	0	3	4	9	8	.53	19	.275	.336	.411
1988 Pittsburgh	NL	148	462	122	37	0	10	(6	4)	189	50	65	47	6	64	1	4	8	9	9	.50	11	.264	.328	.409
1989 Pittsburgh	NL	19	36	8	3	0	0	(0	0)	11	3	4	12	0	10	0	2	0	0	4	.00	0	.222	.417	.306
1990 Pittsburgh	NL	147	389	105	23	2	15	(8	7)	177	39	67	48	5	65	2	4	6	8	4	.67	6	.270	.349	.455
1991 Atlanta	NL	91	265	67	12	0	11	(3	8)	112	32	45	25	5	31	0	4	4	0	3	.00	8	.253	.313	.423
1992 Atlanta	NL	125	372	97	25	1	10	(4	6)	154	30	61	46	2	51	1	3	4	6	0	1.00	3	.261	.340	.414
1993 Atlanta	NL	117	277	72	14	1	9	(5	4)	115	33	35	31	3	43	0	1	2	4	2	.67	6	.260	.332	.415
1985 Los Angeles	NL	24	53	7	0	0	3	(2	1)	16	4	6	7	3	10	0	2	1	0	0	.00	0	.132	.230	.302
Pittsburgh	NL	26	95	27	7	0	3	(0	3)	43	14	15	11	2	14	0	1	1	0	2	.00	4	.284	.355	.453
11 ML YEARS		1042	3047	798	186	12	90	(43	47)	1278	344	448	344	44	441	5	26	38	50	39	.56	73	.262	.334	.419

Bill Brennan

Pitches: Right **Bats:** Right **Pos:** RP   **Ht:** 6' 3" **Wt:** 185 **Born:** 01/15/63 **Age:** 31

		HOW MUCH HE PITCHED						WHAT HE GAVE UP												THE RESULTS					
Year Team	Lg	G	GS	CG	GF	IP	BFP	H	R	ER	HR	SH	SF	HB	TBB	IBB	SO	WP	Bk	W	L	Pct.	ShO	Sv	ERA
1985 Vero Beach	A	22	21	5	0	142	616	121	64	45	1	8	6	5	59	1	74	11	2	10	9	.526	1	0	2.85

Year	Team	Lg	G	GS	CG	GF	IP	BFP	H	R	ER	HR	SH	SF	HB	TBB	IBB	SO	WP	Bk	W	L	Pct.	ShO	Sv	ERA
1986	San Antonio	AA	26	21	3	2	146.2	642	149	75	63	11	2	5	2	61	7	83	7	0	7	9	.438	0	0	3.87
1987	Albuquerque	AAA	28	28	4	0	171.1	747	188	95	82	9	9	3	7	67	0	95	20	0	10	9	.526	1	0	4.31
1988	Albuquerque	AAA	29	28	5	0	167.1	719	177	85	71	15	4	2	5	51	0	83	3	4	14	8	.636	2	0	3.82
1989	Albuquerque	AAA	34	17	2	2	129	573	149	87	75	7	3	3	1	57	0	104	15	1	6	9	.400	0	0	5.23
1990	Tucson	AAA	41	8	2	5	110.1	521	104	68	58	5	5	3	10	89	3	88	10	1	8	7	.533	0	0	4.73
1991	Harrisburg	AA	21	0	0	6	34.2	162	35	21	12	1	2	1	4	30	1	33	9	0	3	2	.600	0	1	3.12
1992	Toledo	AAA	12	3	0	4	26.2	130	29	29	24	1	0	0	2	23	0	28	8	0	0	4	.000	0	1	8.10
	Iowa	AAA	19	1	0	9	29.2	147	43	27	21	4	0	0	2	12	1	34	3	0	1	4	.200	0	0	6.37
1993	Iowa	AAA	28	28	2	0	179	773	180	96	88	13	7	4	15	64	0	143	23	0	10	7	.588	1	0	4.42
1988	Los Angeles	NL	4	2	0	2	9.1	44	13	7	7	0	0	0	0	6	1	7	2	1	0	1	.000	0	0	6.75
1993	Chicago	NL	8	1	0	0	15	65	16	8	7	2	0	1	1	8	1	11	0	0	2	1	.667	0	0	4.20
	2 ML YEARS		12	3	0	2	24.1	109	29	15	14	2	0	1	1	14	2	18	2	1	2	2	.500	0	0	5.18

George Brett

Bats: Left Throws: Right Pos: DH Ht: 6' 0" Wt: 205 Born: 05/15/53 Age: 41

Year	Team	Lg	G	AB	H	2B	3B	HR	(Hm	Rd)	TB	R	RBI	TBB	IBB	SO	HBP	SH	SF	SB	CS	SB%	GDP	Avg	OBP	SLG
1973	Kansas City	AL	13	40	5	2	0	0	(0	0)	7	2	0	0	0	5	0	1	0	0	0	.00	0	.125	.125	.175
1974	Kansas City	AL	133	457	129	21	5	2	(0	2)	166	49	47	21	3	38	0	6	2	8	5	.62	9	.282	.313	.363
1975	Kansas City	AL	159	634	195	35	13	11	(2	9)	289	84	89	46	6	49	2	9	6	13	10	.57	8	.308	.353	.456
1976	Kansas City	AL	159	645	215	34	14	7	(6	1)	298	94	67	49	4	36	1	2	8	21	11	.66	8	.333	.377	.462
1977	Kansas City	AL	139	564	176	32	13	22	(9	13)	300	105	88	55	9	24	2	3	3	14	12	.54	12	.312	.373	.532
1978	Kansas City	AL	128	510	150	45	8	9	(4	5)	238	79	62	39	6	35	1	3	5	23	7	.77	9	.294	.342	.467
1979	Kansas City	AL	154	645	212	42	20	23	(11	12)	363	119	107	51	14	36	0	1	4	17	10	.63	8	.329	.376	.563
1980	Kansas City	AL	117	449	175	33	9	24	(13	11)	298	87	118	58	16	22	1	0	7	15	6	.71	11	.390	.454	.664
1981	Kansas City	AL	89	347	109	27	7	6	(2	4)	168	42	43	27	7	23	1	0	4	14	6	.70	7	.314	.361	.484
1982	Kansas City	AL	144	552	166	32	9	21	(9	12)	279	101	82	71	14	51	1	0	5	6	1	.86	12	.301	.378	.505
1983	Kansas City	AL	123	464	144	38	2	25	(7	18)	261	90	93	57	13	39	1	0	3	0	1	.00	9	.310	.385	.563
1984	Kansas City	AL	104	377	107	21	3	13	(6	7)	173	42	69	38	6	37	0	0	7	0	2	.00	11	.284	.344	.459
1985	Kansas City	AL	155	550	184	38	5	30	(15	15)	322	108	112	103	31	49	3	0	9	9	1	.90	12	.335	.436	.585
1986	Kansas City	AL	124	441	128	28	4	16	(8	8)	212	70	73	80	18	45	4	0	4	1	2	.33	6	.290	.401	.481
1987	Kansas City	AL	115	427	124	18	2	22	(14	8)	212	71	78	72	14	47	1	0	8	6	3	.67	10	.290	.388	.496
1988	Kansas City	AL	157	589	180	42	3	24	(13	11)	300	90	103	82	15	51	3	0	7	14	3	.82	15	.306	.389	.509
1989	Kansas City	AL	124	457	129	26	3	12	(3	9)	197	67	80	59	14	47	3	0	9	14	4	.78	18	.282	.362	.431
1990	Kansas City	AL	142	544	179	45	7	14	(3	11)	280	82	87	56	14	63	0	0	7	9	2	.82	18	.329	.387	.515
1991	Kansas City	AL	131	505	129	40	2	10	(3	7)	203	77	61	58	10	75	0	1	8	2	0	1.00	20	.255	.327	.402
1992	Kansas City	AL	152	592	169	35	5	7	(1	6)	235	55	61	35	6	69	6	0	4	8	6	.57	15	.285	.330	.397
1993	Kansas City	AL	145	560	149	31	3	19	(7	12)	243	69	75	39	9	67	3	0	10	7	5	.58	20	.266	.312	.434
	21 ML YEARS		2707	10349	3154	665	137	317	(136	181)	5044	1583	1595	1096	229	908	33	26	120	201	97	.67	235	.305	.369	.487

Billy Brewer

Pitches: Left Bats: Left Pos: RP Ht: 6' 1" Wt: 175 Born: 04/15/68 Age: 26

Year	Team	Lg	G	GS	CG	GF	IP	BFP	H	R	ER	HR	SH	SF	HB	TBB	IBB	SO	WP	Bk	W	L	Pct.	ShO	Sv	ERA
1990	Jamestown	A	11	2	0	4	27.2	115	23	10	10	0	1	0	0	13	0	37	2	1	2	3	.400	0	1	2.93
1991	Rockford	A	29	0	0	16	41	176	32	12	9	1	2	1	1	25	0	43	6	0	3	3	.500	0	1	1.98
1992	Wst Plm Bch	A	28	0	0	20	36.1	144	27	10	7	0	1	0	2	14	1	37	2	0	2	2	.500	0	8	1.73
	Harrisburg	AA	20	0	0	4	23.1	114	25	15	13	1	0	1	1	18	1	18	5	0	2	1	1.000	0	0	5.01
1993	Kansas City	AL	46	0	0	14	39	157	31	16	15	6	1	1	0	20	4	28	2	1	2	2	.500	0	0	3.46

Rod Brewer

Bats: Left Throws: Left Pos: 1B/LF/RF Ht: 6' 3" Wt: 218 Born: 02/24/66 Age: 28

Year	Team	Lg	G	AB	H	2B	3B	HR	(Hm	Rd)	TB	R	RBI	TBB	IBB	SO	HBP	SH	SF	SB	CS	SB%	GDP	Avg	OBP	SLG
1990	St. Louis	NL	14	25	6	1	0	0	(0	0)	7	4	2	0	0	4	0	0	0	0	0	.00	1	.240	.240	.280
1991	St. Louis	NL	19	13	1	0	0	0	(0	0)	1	0	1	0	0	5	0	0	0	0	0	.00	0	.077	.077	.077
1992	St. Louis	NL	29	103	31	6	0	0	(0	0)	37	11	10	8	0	12	1	0	1	0	0	.00	1	.301	.354	.359
1993	St. Louis	NL	110	147	42	8	0	2	(0	2)	56	15	20	17	5	26	1	2	2	1	0	1.00	5	.286	.359	.381
	4 ML YEARS		172	288	80	15	0	2	(0	2)	101	30	33	25	5	47	2	2	3	1	1	.50	7	.278	.336	.351

Greg Briley

Bats: Left Throws: Right Pos: RF/LF Ht: 5' 9" Wt: 170 Born: 05/24/65 Age: 29

Year	Team	Lg	G	AB	H	2B	3B	HR	(Hm	Rd)	TB	R	RBI	TBB	IBB	SO	HBP	SH	SF	SB	CS	SB%	GDP	Avg	OBP	SLG
1988	Seattle	AL	13	36	9	2	0	1	(0	1)	14	6	4	5	1	6	0	0	1	0	1	.00	0	.250	.333	.389
1989	Seattle	AL	115	394	105	22	4	13	(5	8)	174	52	52	39	1	82	5	1	5	11	5	.69	9	.266	.336	.442

Year Team	Lg	G	AB	H	2B	3B	HR	(Hm	Rd)	TB	R	RBI	TBB	IBB	SO	HBP	SH	SF	SB	CS	SB%	GDP	Avg	OBP	SLG
1990 Seattle	AL	125	337	83	18	2	5	(4	1)	120	40	29	37	0	48	1	1	4	16	4	.80	6	.246	.319	.356
1991 Seattle	AL	139	381	99	17	3	2	(2	0)	128	39	26	27	0	51	0	1	3	23	11	.68	7	.260	.307	.336
1992 Seattle	AL	86	200	55	10	0	5	(1	4)	80	18	12	4	0	31	1	0	2	9	2	.82	4	.275	.290	.400
1993 Florida	NL	120	170	33	6	0	3	(2	1)	48	17	12	12	0	42	1	1	1	6	2	.75	4	.194	.250	.282
6 ML YEARS		598	1518	384	75	9	29	(14	15)	564	172	135	124	2	260	8	4	16	65	25	.72	30	.253	.310	.372

Brad Brink

Pitches: Right **Bats:** Right **Pos:** RP **Ht:** 6' 2" **Wt:** 195 **Born:** 01/20/65 **Age:** 29

		HOW MUCH HE PITCHED						WHAT HE GAVE UP												THE RESULTS				
Year Team	Lg	G	GS	CG	GF	IP	BFP	H	R	ER	HR	SH	SF	HB	TBB	IBB	SO	WP	Bk	W	L	Pct.	ShO	Sv	ERA
1986 Reading	AA	5	4	0	0	23.2	107	22	12	10	2	3	1	1	20	2	8	0	0	0	4	.000	0	0	3.80
1987 Clearwater	A	17	17	2	0	94.1	418	99	50	40	5	4	5	2	39	0	64	1	0	4	7	.364	1	0	3.82
Reading	AA	12	11	1	0	72	308	76	42	40	7	2	4	5	23	2	50	3	2	3	2	.600	1	0	5.00
1988 Maine	AAA	17	17	3	0	86	375	100	43	41	8	2	3	4	21	0	58	4	2	5	5	.500	1	0	4.29
1989 Scr Wil-Bar	AAA	3	3	0	0	11	49	11	7	5	0	1	1	0	6	0	3	0	0	0	1	.000	0	0	4.09
1991 Spartanburg	A	3	3	1	0	16.1	68	15	3	3	1	0	0	0	5	0	16	1	1	2	1	.667	0	0	1.65
Clearwater	A	2	2	0	0	13	46	6	1	1	1	1	0	0	3	0	10	0	1	2	0	1.000	0	0	0.69
Reading	AA	5	5	0	0	34	138	32	14	14	3	2	2	1	6	0	27	1	0	2	2	.500	0	0	3.71
1992 Reading	AA	3	3	0	0	13.2	59	14	6	5	0	1	0	0	3	0	12	0	0	1	1	.500	0	0	3.29
Scranton/wb	AA	17	17	5	0	111.1	454	100	47	43	15	0	1	2	34	0	92	3	0	8	2	.800	2	0	3.48
1993 Scranton/wb	AAA	18	18	2	0	106.2	445	104	53	50	10	6	0	5	27	1	89	0	0	7	7	.500	2	0	4.22
1992 Philadelphia	NL	8	7	0	0	41.1	187	53	27	19	2	1	0	1	13	2	16	0	0	0	4	.000	0	0	4.14
1993 Philadelphia	NL	2	0	0	1	6	24	3	2	2	1	0	0	0	3	0	8	1	0	0	0	.000	0	0	3.00
2 ML YEARS		10	7	0	1	47.1	211	56	29	21	3	1	0	1	16	2	24	1	0	0	4	.000	0	0	3.99

John Briscoe

Pitches: Right **Bats:** Right **Pos:** RP **Ht:** 6' 3" **Wt:** 185 **Born:** 09/22/67 **Age:** 26

		HOW MUCH HE PITCHED						WHAT HE GAVE UP												THE RESULTS				
Year Team	Lg	G	GS	CG	GF	IP	BFP	H	R	ER	HR	SH	SF	HB	TBB	IBB	SO	WP	Bk	W	L	Pct.	ShO	Sv	ERA
1988 Athletics	R	7	6	0	0	25.2	105	26	14	10	1	0	1	1	6	0	23	3	3	1	1	.500	0	0	3.51
1989 Madison	A	21	20	1	1	117.2	524	121	66	55	7	10	9	9	57	0	69	11	1	7	5	.583	0	0	4.21
1990 Modesto	A	29	12	1	12	86.1	373	72	50	44	12	4	1	2	52	0	66	6	0	3	6	.333	0	4	4.59
Huntsville	AA	3	0	0	0	4.2	30	9	7	7	1	0	0	0	7	0	7	1	0	0	0	.000	0	0	13.50
1991 Huntsville	AA	2	0	0	2	4.1	19	1	2	0	0	0	0	0	2	0	6	0	0	2	0	1.000	0	0	0.00
Tacoma	AAA	22	9	0	6	76.1	342	73	35	31	7	2	2	5	44	1	66	3	0	3	5	.375	0	1	3.66
1992 Tacoma	AAA	33	6	0	11	78	368	78	62	51	7	5	2	1	68	5	66	6	0	2	5	.286	0	0	5.88
1993 Huntsville	AA	30	0	0	28	38.2	158	28	14	13	3	3	0	1	16	1	62	0	0	4	0	1.000	0	16	3.03
Tacoma	AAA	9	0	0	8	12.1	59	13	5	4	1	2	0	0	9	3	16	1	0	1	1	.500	0	6	2.92
1991 Oakland	AL	11	0	0	9	14	62	12	11	11	3	0	1	0	10	0	9	3	0	0	0	.000	0	0	7.07
1992 Oakland	AL	2	2	0	0	7	40	12	6	5	0	1	0	0	9	0	4	2	0	0	1	.000	0	0	6.43
1993 Oakland	AL	17	0	0	6	24.2	122	26	25	22	2	0	2	0	26	3	24	5	0	1	0	1.000	0	0	8.03
3 ML YEARS		30	2	0	15	45.2	224	50	42	38	5	1	3	0	45	3	37	10	0	1	1	.500	0	0	7.49

Bernardo Brito

Bats: Right **Throws:** Right **Pos:** LF **Ht:** 6' 1" **Wt:** 190 **Born:** 12/04/63 **Age:** 30

		BATTING																	BASERUNNING			PERCENTAGES		
Year Team	Lg	G	AB	H	2B	3B	HR	(Hm	Rd)	TB	R	RBI	TBB	IBB	SO	HBP	SH	SF	SB	CS	SB%	GDP	Avg	OBP	SLG
1984 Batavia	A	76	297	89	19	3	19	--	--	171	41	57	14	1	67	1	2	0	3	4	.43	7	.300	.333	.576
1985 Waterloo	A	135	498	128	27	1	29	--	--	244	66	78	24	1	133	4	0	3	1	4	.20	15	.257	.295	.490
1986 Waterbury	AA	129	479	118	17	1	18	--	--	191	61	75	22	0	127	3	3	3	0	1	.00	10	.246	.282	.399
1987 Williamsprt	AA	124	452	125	20	4	24	--	--	225	64	79	24	2	121	5	0	6	2	6	.25	15	.277	.316	.498
1988 Orlando	AA	135	508	122	20	4	24	--	--	222	55	76	20	2	138	1	0	9	2	2	.50	12	.240	.266	.437
1989 Portland	AAA	111	355	90	12	7	22	--	--	182	51	74	31	4	111	4	2	2	1	3	.25	7	.254	.319	.513
1990 Portland	AAA	113	376	106	26	3	25	--	--	213	48	79	27	3	102	2	2	4	1	4	.20	13	.282	.330	.566
1991 Portland	AAA	115	428	111	17	2	27	--	--	213	65	83	28	2	110	7	0	7	1	0	1.00	9	.259	.311	.498
1992 Portland	AAA	140	564	152	27	7	26	--	--	271	80	96	32	6	124	6	0	5	0	1	.00	19	.270	.313	.480
1993 Portland	AAA	85	319	108	18	3	20	--	--	192	64	72	26	5	65	4	0	6	0	2	.00	8	.339	.389	.602
1992 Minnesota	AL	8	14	2	1	0	0	(0	0)	3	1	2	0	0	4	0	0	1	0	1	.00	1	.143	.133	.214
1993 Minnesota	AL	27	54	13	2	0	4	(0	4)	27	8	9	1	0	20	0	0	0	0	0	.00	1	.241	.255	.500
2 ML YEARS		35	68	15	3	0	4	(0	4)	30	9	11	1	0	24	0	0	1	0	1	.00	1	.221	.229	.441

Doug Brocail

Pitches: Right **Bats:** Left **Pos:** SP **Ht:** 6' 5" **Wt:** 190 **Born:** 05/16/67 **Age:** 27

		HOW MUCH HE PITCHED						WHAT HE GAVE UP												THE RESULTS				
Year Team	Lg	G	GS	CG	GF	IP	BFP	H	R	ER	HR	SH	SF	HB	TBB	IBB	SO	WP	Bk	W	L	Pct.	ShO	Sv	ERA
1986 Spokane	A	16	15	0	0	85	0	85	52	36	4	0	0	6	53	1	77	10	1	5	4	.556	0	0	3.81
1987 Chston-Sc	A	19	18	0	0	92.1	393	94	51	42	6	3	3	1	28	0	68	4	0	2	6	.250	0	0	4.09

Year	Team	Lg	G	GS	CG	GF	IP	BFP	H	R	ER	HR	SH	SF	HB	TBB	IBB	SO	WP	Bk	W	L	Pct.	ShO	Sv	ERA
1988	Chston-Sc	A	22	13	5	7	107	447	107	40	32	3	4	2	0	25	0	107	4	3	8	6	.571	0	2	2.69
1989	Wichita	AA	23	22	1	0	134.2	603	158	88	78	11	5	5	1	50	4	95	9	4	5	9	.357	1	0	5.21
1990	Wichita	AA	12	9	0	1	52	227	53	30	25	7	1	0	2	24	0	27	4	0	2	2	.500	0	0	4.33
1991	Wichita	AA	34	16	3	11	146.1	625	147	77	63	15	7	3	4	43	3	108	13	0	10	7	.588	3	6	3.87
1992	Las Vegas	AAA	29	25	4	2	172.1	733	187	82	76	7	6	1	6	63	5	103	6	0	10	10	.500	0	0	3.97
1993	Las Vegas	AAA	10	8	0	1	51.1	219	51	26	21	4	2	1	1	14	0	32	2	0	4	2	.667	0	1	3.68
1992	San Diego	NL	3	3	0	0	14	64	17	10	10	2	2	0	0	5	0	15	0	0	0	0	.000	0	0	6.43
1993	San Diego	NL	24	24	0	0	128.1	571	143	75	65	16	10	8	4	42	4	70	4	1	4	13	.235	0	0	4.56
2 ML YEARS			27	27	0	0	142.1	635	160	85	75	18	12	8	4	47	4	85	4	1	4	13	.235	0	0	4.74

Jeff Bronkey

Pitches: Right **Bats:** Right **Pos:** RP **Ht:** 6' 3" **Wt:** 210 **Born:** 09/18/65 **Age:** 28

			HOW MUCH HE PITCHED						WHAT HE GAVE UP											THE RESULTS				
Year	Team	Lg	G	GS	CG	GF	IP	BFP	H	R	ER	HR	SH	SF	HB	TBB	IBB	SO	WP	Bk	W	L	Pct.	ShO	Sv	ERA
1986	Kenosha	A	14	6	1	5	49.1	221	41	24	21	5	4	2	4	30	3	25	5	0	4	6	.400	0	0	3.83
1987	Orlando	AA	24	4	1	16	48.2	239	70	40	34	5	1	5	4	28	1	23	0	0	1	6	.143	0	7	6.29
	Visalia	A	27	0	0	20	35.1	175	26	21	15	2	3	1	6	32	6	31	5	0	2	5	.286	0	5	3.82
1988	Visalia	A	43	6	1	27	85.1	382	66	44	32	0	2	1	11	67	1	58	14	1	4	6	.400	1	9	3.38
1989	Orlando	AA	16	13	0	1	61.2	294	74	53	37	2	1	3	6	35	1	47	7	3	1	2	.333	0	0	5.40
1990	Okla City	AAA	28	0	0	7	51.2	237	58	28	25	3	1	3	6	28	1	18	6	0	2	0	1.000	0	0	4.35
1991	Okla City	AAA	7	0	0	1	10	52	16	13	12	2	0	1	1	4	0	7	2	0	1	0	1.000	0	0	10.80
	Tulsa	AA	4	0	0	3	7.2	39	11	9	8	0	0	0	2	5	0	5	1	0	0	0	.000	0	0	9.39
1992	Tulsa	AA	45	0	0	34	70.2	286	51	27	20	0	6	2	3	25	4	58	6	4	2	7	.222	0	13	2.55
	Okla City	AAA	13	0	0	8	15.2	78	26	13	13	1	0	0	2	7	0	10	1	0	0	1	.000	0	3	7.47
1993	Okla City	AAA	29	0	0	26	37.1	144	29	11	11	2	0	4	0	7	2	19	2	0	2	2	.500	0	14	2.65
1993	Texas	AL	21	0	0	6	36	152	39	20	16	4	1	2	1	11	4	18	2	0	1	1	.500	0	1	4.00

Hubie Brooks

Bats: Right **Throws:** Right **Pos:** RF **Ht:** 6' 0" **Wt:** 205 **Born:** 09/24/56 **Age:** 37

						BATTING													BASERUNNING				PERCENTAGES		
Year	Team	Lg	G	AB	H	2B	3B	HR	(Hm	Rd)	TB	R	RBI	TBB	IBB	SO	HBP	SH	SF	SB	CS	SB%	GDP	Avg	OBP	SLG
1980	New York	NL	24	81	25	2	1	1	(0	1)	32	8	10	5	0	9	2	1	0	1	1	.50	1	.309	.364	.395
1981	New York	NL	98	358	110	21	2	4	(2	2)	147	34	38	23	2	65	1	1	6	9	5	.64	9	.307	.345	.411
1982	New York	NL	126	457	114	21	2	2	(1	1)	145	40	40	28	5	76	5	3	5	6	3	.67	11	.249	.297	.317
1983	New York	NL	150	586	147	18	4	5	(4	1)	188	53	58	24	2	96	4	7	3	6	4	.60	14	.251	.284	.321
1984	New York	NL	153	561	159	23	2	16	(12	4)	234	61	73	48	15	79	2	0	2	6	5	.55	17	.283	.341	.417
1985	Montreal	NL	156	605	163	34	7	13	(4	9)	250	67	100	34	6	79	5	0	8	6	9	.40	20	.269	.310	.413
1986	Montreal	NL	80	306	104	18	5	14	(3	11)	174	50	58	25	3	60	2	0	5	4	2	.67	11	.340	.388	.569
1987	Montreal	NL	112	430	113	22	3	14	(9	5)	183	57	72	24	2	72	1	0	4	4	3	.57	7	.263	.301	.426
1988	Montreal	NL	151	588	164	35	2	20	(9	11)	263	61	90	35	3	108	1	0	4	7	3	.70	21	.279	.318	.447
1989	Montreal	NL	148	542	145	30	1	14	(7	7)	219	56	70	39	2	108	4	0	8	6	11	.35	15	.268	.317	.404
1990	Los Angeles	NL	153	568	151	28	1	20	(9	11)	241	74	91	33	10	108	6	0	11	2	5	.29	13	.266	.307	.424
1991	New York	NL	103	357	85	11	1	16	(4	12)	146	48	50	44	8	62	3	0	3	3	1	.75	7	.238	.324	.409
1992	California	AL	82	306	66	13	0	8	(2	6)	103	28	36	12	3	46	1	0	1	3	3	.50	10	.216	.247	.337
1993	Kansas City	AL	75	168	48	12	0	1	(0	1)	63	14	24	11	1	27	1	0	1	0	1	.00	5	.286	.331	.375
14 ML YEARS			1611	5913	1594	288	31	148	(66	82)	2388	651	810	385	62	995	38	12	61	63	56	.53	161	.270	.315	.404

Jerry Brooks

Bats: Right **Throws:** Right **Pos:** RF **Ht:** 6' 0" **Wt:** 195 **Born:** 03/23/67 **Age:** 27

						BATTING													BASERUNNING				PERCENTAGES		
Year	Team	Lg	G	AB	H	2B	3B	HR	(Hm	Rd)	TB	R	RBI	TBB	IBB	SO	HBP	SH	SF	SB	CS	SB%	GDP	Avg	OBP	SLG
1988	Great Falls	R	68	285	99	21	3	8	--	--	150	63	60	24	0	25	4	0	9	7	4	.64	9	.347	.394	.526
1989	Bakersfield	A	141	565	164	39	1	16	--	--	253	70	87	25	0	79	6	0	8	9	6	.60	10	.290	.323	.448
1990	San Antonio	AA	106	391	118	19	0	9	--	--	164	52	58	26	4	39	4	1	5	5	8	.38	7	.302	.347	.419
1991	Albuquerque	AAA	125	429	126	20	7	13	--	--	199	64	82	29	5	49	6	1	4	4	3	.57	14	.294	.344	.464
1992	Albuquerque	AAA	129	467	124	36	1	14	--	--	204	77	78	39	1	68	4	0	7	3	2	.60	9	.266	.323	.437
1993	Albuquerque	AAA	116	421	145	28	4	11	--	--	214	67	71	21	2	44	2	3	7	3	4	.43	11	.344	.373	.508
1993	Los Angeles	NL	9	9	2	1	0	1	(0	1)	6	2	1	0	0	2	0	0	0	0	0	.00	0	.222	.222	.667

Scott Brosius

Bats: Right **Throws:** Right **Pos:** CF/1B **Ht:** 6' 1" **Wt:** 185 **Born:** 08/15/66 **Age:** 27

						BATTING													BASERUNNING				PERCENTAGES		
Year	Team	Lg	G	AB	H	2B	3B	HR	(Hm	Rd)	TB	R	RBI	TBB	IBB	SO	HBP	SH	SF	SB	CS	SB%	GDP	Avg	OBP	SLG
1993	Tacoma *	AAA	56	209	62	13	2	8	--	--	103	38	41	26	4	50	2	2	3	8	5	.62	5	.297	.367	.493
1991	Oakland	AL	36	68	16	5	0	2	(1	1)	27	9	4	3	0	11	0	1	0	3	1	.75	2	.235	.268	.397
1992	Oakland	AL	38	87	19	2	0	4	(1	3)	33	13	13	3	1	13	2	0	1	3	0	1.00	0	.218	.258	.379

29

		G	AB	H	2B	3B	HR	(Hm	Rd)	TB	R	RBI	TBB	IBB	SO	HBP	SH	SF	SB	CS	SB%	GDP	Avg	OBP	SLG
1993 Oakland	AL	70	213	53	10	1	6	(3	3)	83	26	25	14	0	37	1	3	2	6	0	1.00	6	.249	.296	.390
3 ML YEARS		144	368	88	17	1	12	(5	7)	143	48	42	20	1	61	3	4	3	12	1	.92	8	.239	.282	.389

Terry Bross

Pitches: Right **Bats:** Right **Pos:** RP **Ht:** 6' 9" **Wt:** 230 **Born:** 03/30/66 **Age:** 28

		HOW MUCH HE PITCHED						WHAT HE GAVE UP										THE RESULTS					
Year Team	Lg	G	GS	CG	GF	IP	BFP	H	R	ER	HR	SH	SF	HB	TBB	IBB	SO	WP	Bk	W	L	Pct.	ShO	Sv	ERA
1987 Little Fls	A	10	3	0	1	28	129	22	23	12	3	2	1	0	20	0	21	1	1	2	0	1.000	0	0	3.86
1988 Little Fls	A	20	6	0	8	55.1	248	43	25	19	2	1	2	1	38	0	59	2	2	2	1	.667	0	1	3.09
1989 St.Lucie	A	35	0	0	26	58	234	39	21	18	1	0	4	1	26	3	47	3	1	8	2	.800	0	11	2.79
1990 Jackson	AA	58	0	0	48	71.2	289	46	21	21	4	5	3	2	40	5	51	4	4	3	4	.429	0	28	2.64
1991 Tidewater	AAA	27	0	0	10	33	159	31	21	16	0	1	1	1	32	2	23	3	2	2	0	1.000	0	2	4.36
Williamsprt	AA	20	0	0	16	25.1	98	13	12	7	1	2	1	0	11	0	28	1	1	2	0	1.000	0	5	2.49
1992 Las Vegas	AAA	49	0	0	12	85.2	356	83	36	31	4	5	6	0	30	3	42	5	1	7	3	.700	0	0	3.26
1993 Phoenix	AAA	54	0	0	28	79.1	343	76	37	35	4	1	5	1	37	1	69	3	2	4	4	.500	0	5	3.97
1991 New York	NL	8	0	0	4	10	39	7	2	2	1	1	0	0	3	0	5	0	0	0	0	.000	0	0	1.80
1993 San Francisco	NL	2	0	0	1	2	10	3	2	2	1	0	0	0	1	0	1	0	0	0	0	.000	0	0	9.00
2 ML YEARS		10	0	0	5	12	49	10	4	4	2	1	0	0	4	0	6	0	0	0	0	.000	0	0	3.00

Scott Brow

Pitches: Right **Bats:** Right **Pos:** SP **Ht:** 6' 3" **Wt:** 190 **Born:** 03/17/69 **Age:** 25

		HOW MUCH HE PITCHED						WHAT HE GAVE UP										THE RESULTS					
Year Team	Lg	G	GS	CG	GF	IP	BFP	H	R	ER	HR	SH	SF	HB	TBB	IBB	SO	WP	Bk	W	L	Pct.	ShO	Sv	ERA
1990 St. Cath	A	9	7	0	0	39.2	165	34	18	10	2	2	0	2	11	0	39	4	0	3	1	.750	0	0	2.27
1991 Dunedin	A	15	12	0	1	69.2	306	73	50	37	5	3	3	2	28	1	31	2	5	3	7	.300	0	0	4.78
1992 Dunedin	A	25	25	3	0	170.2	690	143	53	46	8	4	5	7	44	2	107	3	3	14	2	.875	1	0	2.43
1993 Knoxville	AA	3	3	1	0	19	74	13	8	7	3	1	1	0	9	0	12	2	0	1	2	.333	0	0	3.32
Syracuse	AAA	20	19	2	0	121.1	510	119	63	59	8	3	8	6	37	1	64	4	2	6	8	.429	0	0	4.38
1993 Toronto	AL	6	3	0	1	18	83	19	15	12	2	1	2	1	10	1	7	0	0	1	1	.500	0	0	6.00

Jarvis Brown

Bats: Right **Throws:** Right **Pos:** CF **Ht:** 5' 7" **Wt:** 170 **Born:** 03/26/67 **Age:** 27

		BATTING																	BASERUNNING				PERCENTAGES		
Year Team	Lg	G	AB	H	2B	3B	HR	(Hm	Rd)	TB	R	RBI	TBB	IBB	SO	HBP	SH	SF	SB	CS	SB%	GDP	Avg	OBP	SLG
1986 Elizabethtn	R	49	180	41	4	0	3	--	--	54	28	23	18	0	41	4	5	1	15	3	.83	3	.228	.310	.300
1987 Elizabethtn	R	67	258	63	9	1	1	--	--	77	52	15	48	1	50	5	3	0	30	2	.94	3	.244	.373	.298
Kenosha	A	43	117	22	4	1	3	--	--	37	17	16	19	0	24	2	1	2	6	2	.75	2	.188	.307	.316
1988 Kenosha	A	138	531	156	25	7	7	--	--	216	108	45	71	0	89	10	7	5	72	15	.83	10	.294	.384	.407
1989 Visalia	A	141	545	131	21	6	4	--	--	176	95	46	73	0	112	13	4	4	49	13	.79	12	.240	.342	.323
1990 Orlando	AA	135	527	137	22	7	14	--	--	215	104	57	80	1	79	9	5	2	33	19	.63	13	.260	.366	.408
1991 Portland	AAA	108	436	126	5	8	3	--	--	156	62	37	36	1	66	6	3	1	26	12	.68	6	.289	.351	.358
1992 Portland	AAA	62	224	56	8	2	2	--	--	74	25	16	20	0	37	5	1	1	17	1	.94	2	.250	.324	.330
1993 Las Vegas	AAA	100	402	124	27	9	3	--	--	178	74	47	41	1	55	5	5	2	22	5	.81	10	.308	.378	.443
1991 Minnesota	AL	38	37	8	0	0	0	(0	0)	8	10	0	2	0	8	0	1	0	7	1	.88	0	.216	.256	.216
1992 Minnesota	AL	35	15	1	0	0	0	(0	0)	1	8	0	2	0	4	1	0	0	2	2	.50	0	.067	.222	.067
1993 San Diego	NL	47	133	31	9	2	0	(0	0)	44	21	8	15	0	26	6	2	1	3	3	.50	4	.233	.335	.331
3 ML YEARS		120	185	40	9	2	0	(0	0)	53	39	8	19	0	38	7	3	1	12	6	.67	4	.216	.311	.286

Kevin Brown

Pitches: Right **Bats:** Right **Pos:** SP **Ht:** 6' 4" **Wt:** 195 **Born:** 03/14/65 **Age:** 29

		HOW MUCH HE PITCHED						WHAT HE GAVE UP										THE RESULTS					
Year Team	Lg	G	GS	CG	GF	IP	BFP	H	R	ER	HR	SH	SF	HB	TBB	IBB	SO	WP	Bk	W	L	Pct.	ShO	Sv	ERA
1986 Texas	AL	1	1	0	0	5	19	6	2	2	0	0	0	0	0	0	4	0	0	1	0	1.000	0	0	3.60
1988 Texas	AL	4	4	1	0	23.1	110	33	15	11	2	1	0	1	8	0	12	1	0	1	1	.500	0	0	4.24
1989 Texas	AL	28	28	7	0	191	798	167	81	71	10	3	6	4	70	2	104	7	2	12	9	.571	0	0	3.35
1990 Texas	AL	26	26	6	0	180	757	175	84	72	13	2	7	3	60	3	88	9	2	12	10	.545	2	0	3.60
1991 Texas	AL	33	33	0	0	210.2	934	233	116	103	17	6	4	13	90	5	96	12	3	9	12	.429	0	0	4.40
1992 Texas	AL	35	35	11	0	265.2	1108	262	117	98	11	7	8	10	76	2	173	8	2	21	11	.656	1	0	3.32
1993 Texas	AL	34	34	12	0	233	1001	228	105	93	14	5	3	15	74	5	142	8	1	15	12	.556	3	0	3.59
7 ML YEARS		161	161	37	0	1108.2	4727	1104	520	450	67	24	28	46	378	17	619	45	10	71	55	.563	6	0	3.65

Jerry Browne

Bats: Both **Throws:** Right **Pos:** LF/3B/CF **Ht:** 5'10" **Wt:** 170 **Born:** 02/03/66 **Age:** 28

		BATTING																	BASERUNNING				PERCENTAGES		
Year Team	Lg	G	AB	H	2B	3B	HR	(Hm	Rd)	TB	R	RBI	TBB	IBB	SO	HBP	SH	SF	SB	CS	SB%	GDP	Avg	OBP	SLG
1993 Tacoma *	AAA	6	25	6	0	0	0	--	--	6	3	2	0	0	4	0	0	0	1	0	1.00	1	.240	.240	.240
1986 Texas	AL	12	24	10	2	0	0	(0	0)	12	6	3	1	0	4	0	0	0	0	2	.00	0	.417	.440	.500

Year	Team	Lg	G	AB	H	2B	3B	HR	(Hm	Rd)	TB	R	RBI	TBB	IBB	SO	HBP	SH	SF	SB	CS	SB%	GDP	Avg	OBP	SLG
1987	Texas	AL	132	454	123	16	6	1	(1	0)	154	63	38	61	0	50	2	7	2	27	17	.61	6	.271	.358	.339
1988	Texas	AL	73	214	49	9	2	1	(1	0)	65	26	17	25	0	32	0	3	1	7	5	.58	5	.229	.308	.304
1989	Cleveland	AL	153	598	179	31	4	5	(1	4)	233	83	45	68	10	64	1	14	4	14	6	.70	9	.299	.370	.390
1990	Cleveland	AL	140	513	137	26	5	6	(2	4)	191	92	50	72	1	46	2	12	11	12	7	.63	12	.267	.353	.372
1991	Cleveland	AL	107	290	66	5	2	1	(1	0)	78	28	29	27	0	29	1	12	4	2	4	.33	5	.228	.292	.269
1992	Oakland	AL	111	324	93	12	2	3	(1	2)	118	43	40	40	0	40	4	16	6	3	3	.50	7	.287	.366	.364
1993	Oakland	AL	76	260	65	13	0	2	(1	1)	84	27	19	22	0	17	0	2	2	4	0	1.00	9	.250	.306	.323
	8 ML YEARS		804	2677	722	114	21	19	(8	11)	935	368	241	316	11	282	10	66	30	69	44	.61	53	.270	.346	.349

Tom Browning

Pitches: Left   **Bats:** Left   **Pos:** SP   **Ht:** 6' 1" **Wt:** 195 **Born:** 04/28/60 **Age:** 34

			HOW MUCH HE PITCHED						WHAT HE GAVE UP									THE RESULTS					
Year	Team	Lg	G	GS	CG	GF	IP	BFP	H	R	ER	HR	SH	SF	HB	TBB	IBB	SO	WP	Bk	W	L	Pct.	ShO	Sv	ERA
1984	Cincinnati	NL	3	3	0	0	23.1	95	27	4	4	0	1	0	0	5	0	14	1	0	1	0	1.000	0	0	1.54
1985	Cincinnati	NL	38	38	6	0	261.1	1083	242	111	103	29	13	7	3	73	8	155	2	0	20	9	.690	4	0	3.55
1986	Cincinnati	NL	39	39	4	0	243.1	1016	225	123	103	26	14	12	1	70	6	147	3	0	14	13	.519	2	0	3.81
1987	Cincinnati	NL	32	31	2	1	183	791	201	107	102	27	10	7	5	61	7	117	2	4	10	13	.435	0	0	5.02
1988	Cincinnati	NL	36	36	5	0	250.2	1001	205	98	95	36	6	8	7	64	3	124	2	4	18	5	.783	2	0	3.41
1989	Cincinnati	NL	37	37	9	0	249.2	1031	241	109	94	31	12	6	3	64	10	118	2	1	15	12	.556	2	0	3.39
1990	Cincinnati	NL	35	35	2	0	227.2	957	235	98	96	24	13	5	5	52	13	99	5	1	15	9	.625	1	0	3.80
1991	Cincinnati	NL	36	36	1	0	230.1	983	241	124	107	32	8	9	4	56	4	115	3	1	14	14	.500	0	0	4.18
1992	Cincinnati	NL	16	16	0	0	87	386	108	49	49	6	5	4	2	28	7	33	3	1	6	5	.545	0	0	5.07
1993	Cincinnati	NL	21	20	0	0	114	505	159	61	60	15	4	2	1	20	2	53	1	1	7	7	.500	0	0	4.74
	10 ML YEARS		293	291	29	1	1870.1	7848	1884	884	813	226	86	60	31	493	60	975	24	13	120	87	.580	11	0	3.91

J.T. Bruett

Bats: Left   **Throws:** Left   **Pos:** RF   **Ht:** 5'11" **Wt:** 175 **Born:** 10/08/67 **Age:** 26

									BATTING									BASERUNNING				PERCENTAGES		
Year	Team	Lg	G	AB	H	2B	3B	HR	(Hm | Rd)	TB	R	RBI	TBB	IBB	SO	HBP	SH	SF	SB	CS	SB%	GDP	Avg	OBP	SLG
1988	Elizabethtn	R	28	91	27	3	0	0	--	--	30	23	3	19	0	15	0	0	0	17	4	.81	3	.297	.418	.330
	Kenosha	A	3	10	2	0	0	0	--	--	2	2	0	3	0	0	0	0	0	1	1	.50	0	.200	.385	.200
1989	Kenosha	A	120	445	119	9	1	3	--	--	139	82	29	89	2	64	0	2	1	61	27	.69	6	.267	.389	.312
1990	Portland	AAA	10	34	8	2	0	0	--	--	10	8	3	11	0	4	0	0	1	2	1	.67	0	.235	.413	.294
	Visalia	A	123	437	134	15	3	1	--	--	158	86	33	101	4	60	4	8	3	50	21	.70	8	.307	.439	.362
1991	Portland	AAA	99	345	98	6	3	0	--	--	110	51	35	40	1	41	3	9	0	21	9	.70	10	.284	.363	.319
1992	Portland	AAA	77	280	70	10	3	0	--	--	86	41	17	60	3	27	1	3	3	29	12	.71	5	.250	.381	.307
1993	Portland	AAA	90	320	103	17	6	2	--	--	138	70	40	55	3	38	3	10	3	12	11	.52	7	.322	.423	.431
1992	Minnesota	AL	56	76	19	4	0	0	(0 | 0)	23	7	2	6	1	12	1	1	0	6	3	.67	0	.250	.313	.303
1993	Minnesota	AL	17	20	5	2	0	0	(0 | 0)	7	2	1	1	0	4	1	0	0	0	0	.00	0	.250	.318	.350
	2 ML YEARS		73	96	24	6	0	0	(0 | 0)	30	9	3	7	1	16	2	1	0	6	3	.67	0	.250	.314	.313

Jacob Brumfield

Bats: Right   **Throws:** Right   **Pos:** CF/LF   **Ht:** 6' 0" **Wt:** 180 **Born:** 05/27/65 **Age:** 29

									BATTING									BASERUNNING				PERCENTAGES		
Year	Team	Lg	G	AB	H	2B	3B	HR	(Hm | Rd)	TB	R	RBI	TBB	IBB	SO	HBP	SH	SF	SB	CS	SB%	GDP	Avg	OBP	SLG
1986	Ft. Myers	A	12	41	13	3	1	1	--	--	21	3	5	2	0	11	0	0	0	0	1	.00	0	.317	.349	.512
1987	Memphis	AA	9	39	13	3	2	1	--	--	23	7	6	3	0	8	0	1	0	2	1	.67	0	.333	.381	.590
	Ft. Myers	A	114	379	93	14	10	6	--	--	145	56	34	45	2	78	0	1	0	43	14	.75	12	.245	.325	.383
1988	Memphis	AA	128	433	98	15	5	6	--	--	141	70	28	52	0	104	1	8	5	47	7	.87	2	.226	.308	.326
1989	Memphis	AA	104	346	79	14	2	1	--	--	100	43	25	53	0	74	3	5	0	28	12	.70	1	.228	.336	.289
1990	Baseball Cy	A	109	372	125	24	3	0	--	--	155	66	40	60	6	44	2	2	2	47	10	.82	7	.336	.429	.417
	Omaha	AAA	24	77	25	6	1	2	--	--	39	10	11	7	0	14	0	1	2	10	3	.77	2	.325	.372	.506
1991	Omaha	AAA	111	397	106	14	7	3	--	--	143	62	43	33	0	64	1	2	3	36	17	.68	9	.267	.323	.360
1992	Nashville	AAA	56	208	59	10	3	5	--	--	90	32	19	26	0	35	2	3	0	22	11	.67	1	.284	.369	.433
1993	Indianapols	AAA	33	144	45	14	1	4	--	--	69	23	19	6	0	14	1	2	1	11	0	1.00	4	.325	.358	.548
1992	Cincinnati	NL	24	30	4	0	0	0	(0 | 0)	4	6	2	1	0	4	1	0	0	6	0	1.00	0	.133	.212	.133
1993	Cincinnati	NL	103	272	73	17	3	6	(1 | 5)	114	40	23	21	4	47	1	3	2	20	8	.71	4	.268	.321	.419
	2 ML YEARS		127	302	77	17	3	6	(1 | 5)	118	46	25	23	5	51	2	3	2	26	8	.76	4	.255	.310	.391

Mike Brumley

Bats: Both   **Throws:** Right   **Pos:** 3B   **Ht:** 5'10" **Wt:** 175 **Born:** 04/09/63 **Age:** 31

									BATTING									BASERUNNING				PERCENTAGES		
Year	Team	Lg	G	AB	H	2B	3B	HR	(Hm | Rd)	TB	R	RBI	TBB	IBB	SO	HBP	SH	SF	SB	CS	SB%	GDP	Avg	OBP	SLG
1993	Tucson *	AAA	93	346	122	25	8	0	--	--	163	65	46	44	6	71	0	0	6	24	11	.69	4	.353	.419	.471
1987	Chicago	NL	39	104	21	2	2	1	(0 | 1)	30	8	9	10	1	30	1	1	1	7	1	.88	2	.202	.276	.288
1989	Detroit	AL	92	212	42	5	2	1	(1 | 0)	54	33	11	14	0	45	1	3	0	8	4	.67	4	.198	.251	.255
1990	Seattle	AL	62	147	33	5	4	0	(0 | 0)	46	19	7	10	0	22	0	4	1	2	0	1.00	5	.224	.272	.313
1991	Boston	AL	63	118	25	5	0	0	(0 | 0)	30	15	5	10	0	22	0	0	0	2	0	1.00	0	.212	.273	.254

Year	Team	Lg																								Pct.		Sv		Avg	OBP	SLG
1992	Boston	AL	2	1	0	0	0	0	(0	0)	0	0	0	0	0	0	0	0	0	0	0	.00	0							.000	.000	.000
1993	Houston	NL	8	10	3	0	0	0	(0	0)	3	1	2	1	0	3	0	0	0	1	.00	0								.300	.364	.300
	6 ML YEARS		266	592	124	17	8	2	(1	1)	163	77	34	45	1	122	2	12	2	19	6	.76	11							.209	.267	.275

Greg Brummett

Pitches: Right **Bats:** Right **Pos:** SP **Ht:** 6' 0" **Wt:** 180 **Born:** 04/20/67 **Age:** 27

			HOW MUCH HE PITCHED						WHAT HE GAVE UP												THE RESULTS					
Year	Team	Lg	G	GS	CG	GF	IP	BFP	H	R	ER	HR	SH	SF	HB	TBB	IBB	SO	WP	Bk	W	L	Pct.	ShO	Sv	ERA
1989	San Jose	A	2	2	0	0	9.2	49	15	7	6	2	0	1	1	8	0	3	0	0	0	1	.000	0	0	5.59
	Everett	A	14	10	1	2	72	311	63	34	23	1	0	3	6	24	0	76	6	4	4	2	.667	0	0	2.88
1990	Clinton	A	6	4	0	0	25.2	107	18	14	10	0	1	0	3	9	0	22	1	3	2	2	.500	0	0	3.51
1991	Clinton	A	16	16	5	0	112.1	445	91	39	34	2	2	2	3	32	2	74	5	1	10	5	.667	2	0	2.72
1992	San Jose	A	19	13	2	1	100	379	74	32	29	2	6	1	4	21	0	68	1	0	10	4	.714	2	0	2.61
	Phoenix	AAA	3	1	0	2	4.2	21	8	4	4	0	0	0	0	1	0	2	1	0	0	1	.000	0	0	7.71
1993	Phoenix	AAA	18	18	1	0	107	454	114	56	44	3	1	2	2	27	3	84	3	3	7	7	.500	0	0	3.70
1993	2 ML Teams		13	13	0	0	72.2	311	82	42	41	12	1	5	0	28	2	30	2	2	4	4	.500	0	0	5.08
1993	San Francisco	NL	8	8	0	0	46	196	53	25	24	9	1	2	0	13	1	20	2	2	2	3	.400	0	0	4.70
	Minnesota	AL	5	5	0	0	26.2	115	29	17	17	3	0	3	0	15	1	10	0	0	2	1	.667	0	0	5.74

Tom Brunansky

Bats: Right **Throws:** Right **Pos:** RF **Ht:** 6' 4" **Wt:** 220 **Born:** 08/20/60 **Age:** 33

							BATTING												BASERUNNING				PERCENTAGES		
Year	Team	Lg	G	AB	H	2B	3B	HR	(Hm	Rd)	TB	R	RBI	TBB	IBB	SO	HBP	SH	SF	SB	CS	SB%	GDP	Avg	OBP	SLG
1981	California	AL	11	33	5	0	0	3	(1	2)	14	7	6	8	0	10	0	0	0	1	0	1.00	0	.152	.317	.424
1982	Minnesota	AL	127	463	126	30	1	20	(10	10)	218	77	46	71	0	101	8	1	2	1	2	.33	12	.272	.377	.471
1983	Minnesota	AL	151	542	123	24	5	28	(8	20)	241	70	82	61	4	95	4	1	3	2	5	.29	13	.227	.308	.445
1984	Minnesota	AL	155	567	144	21	0	32	(14	18)	261	75	85	57	2	94	0	0	4	4	5	.44	15	.254	.320	.460
1985	Minnesota	AL	157	567	137	28	4	27	(12	15)	254	71	90	71	7	86	0	0	13	5	3	.63	12	.242	.320	.448
1986	Minnesota	AL	157	593	152	28	1	23	(15	8)	251	69	75	53	4	98	1	1	7	12	4	.75	15	.256	.315	.423
1987	Minnesota	AL	155	532	138	22	2	32	(19	13)	260	83	85	74	5	104	4	0	4	11	11	.50	12	.259	.352	.489
1988	2 ML Teams		157	572	137	23	4	23	(7	16)	237	74	85	86	6	93	4	1	6	17	8	.68	17	.240	.340	.414
1989	St. Louis	NL	158	556	133	29	3	20	(4	16)	228	67	85	59	3	107	2	0	5	5	9	.36	10	.239	.312	.410
1990	2 ML Teams		148	518	132	27	5	16	(13	3)	217	66	73	66	7	115	4	0	9	5	10	.33	13	.255	.338	.419
1991	Boston	AL	142	459	105	24	1	16	(10	6)	179	54	70	49	2	72	3	0	8	1	2	.33	8	.229	.303	.390
1992	Boston	AL	138	458	122	31	3	15	(10	5)	204	47	74	66	2	96	0	2	7	2	5	.29	11	.266	.354	.445
1993	Milwaukee	AL	80	224	41	7	3	6	(2	4)	72	20	29	25	0	59	0	2	0	3	4	.43	6	.183	.265	.321
1988	Minnesota	AL	14	49	9	1	0	1	(0	1)	13	5	6	7	0	11	0	0	0	1	2	.33	0	.184	.286	.265
	St. Louis	NL	143	523	128	22	4	22	(7	15)	224	69	79	79	6	82	4	1	6	16	6	.73	17	.245	.345	.428
1990	St. Louis	NL	19	57	9	3	0	1	(0	1)	15	5	2	12	0	10	1	0	1	0	0	.00	1	.158	.310	.263
	Boston	AL	129	461	123	24	5	15	(13	2)	202	61	71	54	7	105	3	0	8	5	10	.33	12	.267	.342	.438
	13 ML YEARS		1736	6084	1495	294	32	261	(125	136)	2636	780	885	746	42	1130	30	8	68	69	68	.50	144	.246	.328	.433

Steve Buechele

Bats: Right **Throws:** Right **Pos:** 3B **Ht:** 6' 2" **Wt:** 200 **Born:** 09/26/61 **Age:** 32

							BATTING												BASERUNNING				PERCENTAGES		
Year	Team	Lg	G	AB	H	2B	3B	HR	(Hm	Rd)	TB	R	RBI	TBB	IBB	SO	HBP	SH	SF	SB	CS	SB%	GDP	Avg	OBP	SLG
1985	Texas	AL	69	219	48	6	3	6	(5	1)	78	22	21	14	2	38	2	0	1	3	2	.60	11	.219	.271	.356
1986	Texas	AL	153	461	112	19	2	18	(6	12)	189	54	54	35	1	98	5	9	3	5	8	.38	10	.243	.302	.410
1987	Texas	AL	136	363	86	20	0	13	(6	7)	145	45	50	28	3	66	1	4	4	2	2	.50	7	.237	.290	.399
1988	Texas	AL	155	503	126	21	4	16	(8	8)	203	68	58	65	6	79	5	6	0	2	4	.33	8	.250	.342	.404
1989	Texas	AL	155	486	114	22	2	16	(7	9)	188	60	59	36	0	107	5	2	1	1	3	.25	21	.235	.294	.387
1990	Texas	AL	91	251	54	10	0	7	(5	2)	85	30	30	27	1	63	2	7	2	1	0	1.00	5	.215	.294	.339
1991	2 ML Teams		152	530	139	22	3	22	(9	13)	233	74	85	49	4	97	7	11	3	0	5	.00	14	.262	.331	.440
1992	2 ML Teams		145	524	137	23	4	9	(4	5)	195	52	64	52	6	105	7	4	3	1	3	.25	10	.261	.334	.372
1993	Chicago	NL	133	460	125	27	2	15	(8	7)	201	53	65	48	5	87	5	4	3	1	1	.50	12	.272	.345	.437
1991	Texas	AL	121	416	111	17	2	18	(7	11)	186	58	66	39	4	69	5	10	2	0	4	.00	11	.267	.335	.447
	Pittsburgh	NL	31	114	28	5	1	4	(2	2)	47	16	19	10	0	28	2	1	1	0	1	.00	3	.246	.315	.412
1992	Pittsburgh	NL	80	285	71	14	1	8	(3	5)	111	27	43	34	4	61	2	2	2	0	2	.00	5	.249	.331	.389
	Chicago	NL	65	239	66	9	3	1	(1	0)	84	25	21	18	2	44	5	2	1	1	1	.50	5	.276	.338	.351
	9 ML YEARS		1189	3797	941	170	20	122	(58	64)	1517	458	486	354	28	740	39	47	20	16	28	.36	98	.248	.317	.400

Damon Buford

Bats: Right **Throws:** Right **Pos:** CF/DH **Ht:** 5'11" **Wt:** 170 **Born:** 06/12/70 **Age:** 24

							BATTING												BASERUNNING				PERCENTAGES		
Year	Team	Lg	G	AB	H	2B	3B	HR	(Hm	Rd)	TB	R	RBI	TBB	IBB	SO	HBP	SH	SF	SB	CS	SB%	GDP	Avg	OBP	SLG
1990	Wausau	A	41	160	48	7	2	1	--	--	62	31	14	21	1	32	4	1	2	15	4	.79	1	.300	.390	.388
1991	Frederick	A	133	505	138	25	6	8	--	--	199	71	54	51	1	92	10	7	2	50	14	.78	1	.273	.350	.394

Year	Team	Lg	G	AB	H	2B	3B	HR	(Hm	Rd)	TB	R	RBI	TBB	IBB	SO	HBP	SH	SF	SB	CS	SB%	GDP	Avg	OBP	SLG
1992	Hagerstown	AA	101	373	89	17	3	1	--	--	115	53	30	42	0	62	1	7	3	41	12	.77	3	.239	.315	.308
	Rochester	AAA	45	155	44	10	2	1	--	--	61	29	12	14	0	23	1	2	1	23	4	.85	5	.284	.345	.394
1993	Rochester	AAA	27	116	33	6	1	1	--	--	44	24	4	7	0	16	0	1	0	10	2	.83	0	.284	.325	.379
1993	Baltimore	AL	53	79	18	5	0	2	(0	2)	29	18	9	9	0	19	1	1	0	2	2	.50	1	.228	.315	.367

Jay Buhner

Bats: Right **Throws:** Right **Pos:** RF **Ht:** 6' 3" **Wt:** 210 **Born:** 08/13/64 **Age:** 29

				BATTING																BASERUNNING			PERCENTAGES		
Year	Team	Lg	G	AB	H	2B	3B	HR	(Hm	Rd)	TB	R	RBI	TBB	IBB	SO	HBP	SH	SF	SB	CS	SB%	GDP	Avg	OBP	SLG
1987	New York	AL	7	22	5	2	0	0	(0	0)	7	0	1	1	0	6	0	0	0	0	0	.00	1	.227	.261	.318
1988	2 ML Teams		85	261	56	13	1	13	(8	5)	110	36	38	28	1	93	6	1	3	1	1	.50	5	.215	.302	.421
1989	Seattle	AL	58	204	56	15	1	9	(7	2)	100	27	33	19	0	55	2	0	1	1	4	.20	0	.275	.341	.490
1990	Seattle	AL	51	163	45	12	0	7	(2	5)	78	16	33	17	1	50	4	0	1	2	2	.50	6	.276	.357	.479
1991	Seattle	AL	137	406	99	14	4	27	(14	13)	202	64	77	53	5	117	6	2	4	0	1	.00	10	.244	.337	.498
1992	Seattle	AL	152	543	132	16	3	25	(9	16)	229	69	79	71	2	146	6	1	8	0	6	.00	12	.243	.333	.422
1993	Seattle	AL	158	563	153	28	3	27	(13	14)	268	91	98	100	11	144	2	2	8	2	5	.29	12	.272	.379	.476
1988	New York	AL	25	69	13	0	0	3	(1	2)	22	8	13	3	0	25	3	0	1	0	0	.00	1	.188	.250	.319
	Seattle	AL	60	192	43	13	1	10	(7	3)	88	28	25	25	1	68	3	1	2	1	1	.50	4	.224	.320	.458
	7 ML YEARS		648	2162	546	100	12	108	(53	55)	994	303	359	289	20	611	26	6	25	6	19	.24	46	.253	.344	.460

Scott Bullett

Bats: Left **Throws:** Left **Pos:** CF **Ht:** 6' 2" **Wt:** 200 **Born:** 12/25/68 **Age:** 25

				BATTING																BASERUNNING			PERCENTAGES		
Year	Team	Lg	G	AB	H	2B	3B	HR	(Hm	Rd)	TB	R	RBI	TBB	IBB	SO	HBP	SH	SF	SB	CS	SB%	GDP	Avg	OBP	SLG
1988	Pirates	R	21	61	11	1	0	0	--	--	12	6	8	7	1	9	0	1	1	2	5	.29	2	.180	.261	.197
1989	Pirates	R	46	165	42	7	3	1	--	--	58	24	16	12	2	31	5	1	0	15	5	.75	2	.255	.324	.352
1990	Welland	A	74	256	77	11	4	3	--	--	105	46	33	13	2	50	2	1	0	30	6	.83	7	.301	.339	.410
1991	Augusta	A	95	384	109	21	6	1	--	--	145	61	36	27	2	79	2	1	1	48	17	.74	1	.284	.333	.378
	Salem	A	39	156	52	7	5	2	--	--	75	22	15	8	1	29	0	0	0	15	7	.68	0	.333	.366	.481
1992	Carolina	AA	132	518	140	20	5	8	--	--	194	59	45	28	5	98	10	2	7	29	21	.58	7	.270	.316	.375
	Buffalo	AAA	3	10	4	0	2	0	--	--	8	1	0	0	0	2	0	0	0	0	0	.00	0	.400	.400	.800
1993	Buffalo	AAA	110	408	117	13	6	1	--	--	145	62	30	39	0	67	1	8	0	28	17	.62	5	.287	.350	.355
1991	Pittsburgh	NL	11	4	0	0	0	0	(0	0)	0	2	0	0	0	3	1	0	0	1	1	.50	0	.000	.200	.000
1993	Pittsburgh	NL	23	55	11	0	2	0	(0	0)	15	2	4	3	0	15	0	0	1	3	2	.60	1	.200	.237	.273
	2 ML YEARS		34	59	11	0	2	0	(0	0)	15	4	4	3	0	18	1	0	1	4	3	.57	1	.186	.234	.254

Jim Bullinger

Pitches: Right **Bats:** Right **Pos:** RP **Ht:** 6' 2" **Wt:** 185 **Born:** 08/21/65 **Age:** 28

			HOW MUCH HE PITCHED					WHAT HE GAVE UP									THE RESULTS				
Year	Team	Lg	G	GS	CG	GF	IP	BFP	H	R	ER	HR	SH	SF	HB	TBB	IBB	SO	WP	Bk	W	L	Pct.	ShO	Sv	ERA
1989	Charlotte	AA	2	0	0	2	3	14	2	0	0	0	0	0	0	3	0	5	1	0	0	0	.000	0	0	0.00
1990	Winston-Sal	A	14	13	3	0	90	392	81	43	37	5	3	2	7	46	0	85	6	1	7	6	.538	0	0	3.70
	Charlotte	AA	9	9	0	0	44	194	42	30	25	7	1	1	3	18	0	33	3	1	3	4	.429	0	0	5.11
1991	Charlotte	AA	20	20	8	0	142.2	595	132	62	56	5	5	1	6	61	2	128	5	3	9	9	.500	0	0	3.53
	Iowa	AAA	8	8	0	0	46.2	203	47	32	28	6	1	1	0	23	0	30	7	0	3	4	.429	0	0	5.40
1992	Iowa	AAA	20	0	0	20	22	91	17	6	6	0	1	1	0	12	3	15	2	1	1	2	.333	0	14	2.45
1993	Iowa	AAA	49	3	0	37	73.2	326	64	29	28	3	2	3	4	43	5	74	13	0	4	6	.400	0	20	3.42
1992	Chicago	NL	39	9	1	15	85	380	72	49	44	9	9	4	4	54	6	36	4	0	2	8	.200	0	7	4.66
1993	Chicago	NL	15	0	0	6	16.2	75	18	9	8	1	0	1	0	9	0	10	0	0	1	0	1.000	0	1	4.32
	2 ML YEARS		54	9	1	21	101.2	455	90	58	52	10	9	5	4	63	6	46	4	0	3	8	.273	0	8	4.60

Dave Burba

Pitches: Right **Bats:** Right **Pos:** RP/SP **Ht:** 6' 4" **Wt:** 240 **Born:** 07/07/66 **Age:** 27

			HOW MUCH HE PITCHED					WHAT HE GAVE UP									THE RESULTS				
Year	Team	Lg	G	GS	CG	GF	IP	BFP	H	R	ER	HR	SH	SF	HB	TBB	IBB	SO	WP	Bk	W	L	Pct.	ShO	Sv	ERA
1990	Seattle	AL	6	0	0	2	8	35	8	6	4	0	2	0	1	2	0	4	0	0	0	0	.000	0	0	4.50
1991	Seattle	AL	22	2	0	11	36.2	153	34	16	15	6	0	0	0	14	3	16	1	0	2	2	.500	0	1	3.68
1992	San Francisco	NL	23	11	0	4	70.2	318	80	43	39	4	2	4	2	31	2	47	1	1	2	7	.222	0	0	4.97
1993	San Francisco	NL	54	5	0	9	95.1	408	95	49	45	14	6	3	3	37	5	88	4	0	10	3	.769	0	0	4.25
	4 ML YEARS		105	18	0	26	210.2	914	217	114	103	24	10	7	6	84	10	155	6	1	14	12	.538	0	1	4.40

Enrique Burgos

Pitches: Left **Bats:** Left **Pos:** RP **Ht:** 6' 4" **Wt:** 195 **Born:** 10/07/65 **Age:** 28

			HOW MUCH HE PITCHED					WHAT HE GAVE UP									THE RESULTS				
Year	Team	Lg	G	GS	CG	GF	IP	BFP	H	R	ER	HR	SH	SF	HB	TBB	IBB	SO	WP	Bk	W	L	Pct.	ShO	Sv	ERA
1993	Omaha	AAA	48	0	0	26	62.2	263	36	26	22	4	2	3	1	37	0	91	9	0	2	4	.333	0	9	3.16
1993	Kansas City	AL	5	0	0	3	5	28	5	5	5	0	0	0	1	6	1	6	3	0	0	1	.000	0	0	9.00

John Burkett

Pitches: Right **Bats:** Right **Pos:** SP **Ht:** 6' 2" **Wt:** 211 **Born:** 11/28/64 **Age:** 29

			HOW MUCH HE PITCHED						WHAT HE GAVE UP												THE RESULTS					
Year	Team	Lg	G	GS	CG	GF	IP	BFP	H	R	ER	HR	SH	SF	HB	TBB	IBB	SO	WP	Bk	W	L	Pct.	ShO	Sv	ERA
1987	San Francisco	NL	3	0	0	1	6	28	7	4	3	2	1	0	1	3	0	5	0	0	0	0	.000	0	0	4.50
1990	San Francisco	NL	33	32	2	1	204	857	201	92	86	18	6	5	4	61	7	118	3	3	14	7	.667	0	1	3.79
1991	San Francisco	NL	36	34	3	0	206.2	890	223	103	96	19	8	8	10	60	2	131	5	1	12	11	.522	1	0	4.18
1992	San Francisco	NL	32	32	3	0	189.2	799	194	96	81	13	11	4	4	45	6	107	0	0	13	9	.591	1	0	3.84
1993	San Francisco	NL	34	34	2	0	231.2	942	224	100	94	18	8	4	11	40	4	145	1	2	22	7	.759	1	0	3.65
	5 ML YEARS		138	132	10	2	838	3516	849	395	360	70	34	21	30	209	19	506	9	5	61	34	.642	3	1	3.87

Ellis Burks

Bats: Right **Throws:** Right **Pos:** RF/CF **Ht:** 6' 2" **Wt:** 205 **Born:** 09/11/64 **Age:** 29

						BATTING														BASERUNNING				PERCENTAGES		
Year	Team	Lg	G	AB	H	2B	3B	HR	(Hm	Rd)	TB	R	RBI	TBB	IBB	SO	HBP	SH	SF	SB	CS	SB%	GDP	Avg	OBP	SLG
1987	Boston	AL	133	558	152	30	2	20	(11	9)	246	94	59	41	0	98	2	4	1	27	6	.82	1	.272	.324	.441
1988	Boston	AL	144	540	159	37	5	18	(8	10)	260	93	92	62	1	89	3	4	6	25	9	.74	8	.294	.367	.481
1989	Boston	AL	97	399	121	19	6	12	(6	6)	188	73	61	36	2	52	5	2	4	21	5	.81	8	.303	.365	.471
1990	Boston	AL	152	588	174	33	8	21	(10	11)	286	89	89	48	4	82	1	2	2	9	11	.45	18	.296	.349	.486
1991	Boston	AL	130	474	119	33	3	14	(8	6)	200	56	56	39	2	81	6	2	3	6	11	.35	7	.251	.314	.422
1992	Boston	AL	66	235	60	8	3	8	(4	4)	98	35	30	25	2	48	1	0	2	5	2	.71	5	.255	.327	.417
1993	Chicago	AL	146	499	137	24	4	17	(7	10)	220	75	74	60	2	97	4	3	8	6	9	.40	11	.275	.352	.441
	7 ML YEARS		868	3293	922	184	31	110	(54	56)	1498	515	461	311	13	547	22	17	26	99	53	.65	58	.280	.344	.455

Jeromy Burnitz

Bats: Left **Throws:** Right **Pos:** RF/CF **Ht:** 6' 0" **Wt:** 190 **Born:** 04/15/69 **Age:** 25

						BATTING														BASERUNNING				PERCENTAGES		
Year	Team	Lg	G	AB	H	2B	3B	HR	(Hm	Rd)	TB	R	RBI	TBB	IBB	SO	HBP	SH	SF	SB	CS	SB%	GDP	Avg	OBP	SLG
1990	Pittsfield	A	51	173	52	6	5	6	--	--	86	37	22	45	5	39	3	0	4	12	5	.71	3	.301	.444	.497
	St. Lucie	A	11	32	5	1	0	0	--	--	6	6	3	7	0	12	4	0	0	1	0	1.00	0	.156	.372	.188
1991	Williamsprt	AA	135	457	103	16	10	31	--	--	232	80	85	104	4	127	4	0	8	31	13	.70	7	.225	.368	.508
1992	Tidewater	AAA	121	445	108	21	3	8	--	--	159	56	40	33	2	84	3	2	3	30	7	.81	7	.243	.298	.357
1993	Norfolk	AAA	65	255	58	15	3	8	--	--	103	33	44	25	2	53	2	0	3	10	7	.59	6	.227	.298	.404
1993	New York	NL	86	263	64	10	6	13	(6	7)	125	49	38	38	4	66	1	2	2	3	6	.33	2	.243	.339	.475

Todd Burns

Pitches: Right **Bats:** Right **Pos:** RP/SP **Ht:** 6' 2" **Wt:** 195 **Born:** 07/06/63 **Age:** 30

						HOW MUCH HE PITCHED						WHAT HE GAVE UP										THE RESULTS					
Year	Team	Lg	G	GS	CG	GF	IP	BFP	H	R	ER	HR	SH	SF	HB	TBB	IBB	SO	WP	Bk	W	L	Pct.	ShO	Sv	ERA
1988	Oakland	AL	17	14	2	3	102.2	425	93	38	36	8	2	1	1	34	1	57	3	6	8	2	.800	0	1	3.16
1989	Oakland	AL	50	2	0	22	96.1	374	66	27	24	3	7	1	1	28	5	49	4	0	6	5	.545	0	8	2.24
1990	Oakland	AL	43	2	0	9	78.2	337	78	28	26	8	5	3	0	32	4	43	5	0	3	3	.500	0	3	2.97
1991	Oakland	AL	9	0	0	5	13.1	57	10	5	5	2	1	2	0	8	1	3	1	0	1	0	1.000	0	0	3.38
1992	Texas	AL	35	10	0	9	103	433	97	54	44	8	2	4	4	32	1	55	5	0	3	5	.375	0	1	3.84
1993	2 ML Teams		49	5	0	13	95.2	419	95	57	54	14	5	5	2	41	9	45	3	3	0	8	.000	0	0	5.08
1993	Texas	AL	25	5	0	8	65	288	63	36	33	6	2	3	2	32	3	35	3	2	0	4	.000	0	0	4.57
	St. Louis	NL	24	0	0	5	30.2	131	32	21	21	8	3	2	0	9	6	10	0	1	0	4	.000	0	0	6.16
	6 ML YEARS		203	33	2	61	489.2	2045	439	209	189	43	22	17	8	175	21	252	21	9	21	23	.477	0	13	3.47

Randy Bush

Bats: Left **Throws:** Left **Pos:** DH **Ht:** 6' 1" **Wt:** 190 **Born:** 10/05/58 **Age:** 35

						BATTING														BASERUNNING				PERCENTAGES		
Year	Team	Lg	G	AB	H	2B	3B	HR	(Hm	Rd)	TB	R	RBI	TBB	IBB	SO	HBP	SH	SF	SB	CS	SB%	GDP	Avg	OBP	SLG
1982	Minnesota	AL	55	119	29	6	1	4	(2	2)	49	13	13	8	0	28	3	0	1	0	0	.00	1	.244	.305	.412
1983	Minnesota	AL	124	373	93	24	3	11	(4	7)	156	43	56	34	8	51	7	0	1	0	1	.00	7	.249	.323	.418
1984	Minnesota	AL	113	311	69	17	1	11	(8	3)	121	46	43	31	6	60	4	0	10	1	2	.33	1	.222	.292	.389
1985	Minnesota	AL	97	234	56	13	3	10	(5	5)	105	26	35	24	1	30	5	0	2	3	0	1.00	3	.239	.321	.449
1986	Minnesota	AL	130	357	96	19	7	7	(6	1)	150	50	45	39	2	63	4	1	1	5	3	.63	7	.269	.347	.420
1987	Minnesota	AL	122	293	74	10	2	11	(3	8)	121	46	46	43	5	49	3	5	5	10	3	.77	6	.253	.349	.413
1988	Minnesota	AL	136	394	103	20	3	14	(10	4)	171	51	51	58	14	49	9	0	5	8	6	.57	8	.261	.365	.434
1989	Minnesota	AL	141	391	103	17	4	14	(6	8)	170	60	54	48	6	73	3	0	2	5	8	.38	16	.263	.347	.435
1990	Minnesota	AL	73	181	44	8	0	6	(4	2)	70	17	18	21	2	27	6	0	2	0	3	.00	2	.243	.338	.387
1991	Minnesota	AL	93	165	50	10	1	6	(2	4)	80	21	23	24	3	25	3	0	0	0	2	.00	5	.303	.401	.485
1992	Minnesota	AL	100	182	39	8	1	2	(0	2)	55	14	22	11	3	37	2	0	3	1	1	.50	5	.214	.263	.302
1993	Minnesota	AL	35	45	7	2	0	0	(0	0)	9	1	3	7	1	13	0	0	0	0	0	.00	3	.156	.269	.200
	12 ML YEARS		1219	3045	763	154	26	96	(50	46)	1257	388	409	348	51	505	49	6	32	33	29	.53	64	.251	.334	.413

Chris Bushing

Pitches: Right **Bats:** Right **Pos:** RP **Ht:** 6' 0" **Wt:** 183 **Born:** 11/04/67 **Age:** 26

			HOW MUCH HE PITCHED						WHAT HE GAVE UP												THE RESULTS					
Year	Team	Lg	G	GS	CG	GF	IP	BFP	H	R	ER	HR	SH	SF	HB	TBB	IBB	SO	WP	Bk	W	L	Pct.	ShO	Sv	ERA
1986	Bluefield	R	13	1	0	7	26.1	104	14	5	4	1	0	2	0	12	0	30	4	0	2	0	1.000	0	2	1.37
1987	Bluefield	R	20	0	0	11	37	157	27	20	15	2	1	0	1	18	0	51	1	1	2	0	1.000	0	6	3.65
1989	Peninsula	A	35	14	1	13	99.2	472	96	64	48	4	3	5	6	79	0	99	10	5	2	7	.222	1	3	4.33
1990	Rockford	A	46	0	0	32	79.2	344	62	38	29	5	8	2	2	38	6	99	3	0	3	6	.333	0	12	3.28
1991	Wst Plm Bch	A	46	0	0	26	65	274	41	15	14	1	6	1	1	41	3	68	4	7	2	1	.667	0	9	1.94
	Harrisburg	AA	3	1	0	0	8.2	37	3	2	1	0	0	0	1	8	0	8	2	0	1	0	1.000	0	1	1.04
1992	Reading	AA	22	8	0	2	70.1	305	68	38	34	9	2	3	2	30	0	72	4	0	3	6	.333	0	1	4.35
	Nashville	AAA	5	0	0	1	10.1	42	8	4	4	1	1	1	0	6	0	6	0	0	1	0	1.000	0	0	3.48
1993	Chattanooga	AA	61	0	0	50	70	279	50	20	18	7	2	2	2	23	3	84	2	1	6	1	.857	0	29	2.31
1993	Cincinnati	NL	6	0	0	2	4.1	25	9	7	6	1	0	1	0	4	0	3	2	0	0	0	.000	0	0	12.46

Mike Butcher

Pitches: Right **Bats:** Right **Pos:** RP **Ht:** 6' 1" **Wt:** 200 **Born:** 05/10/65 **Age:** 29

			HOW MUCH HE PITCHED						WHAT HE GAVE UP												THE RESULTS					
Year	Team	Lg	G	GS	CG	GF	IP	BFP	H	R	ER	HR	SH	SF	HB	TBB	IBB	SO	WP	Bk	W	L	Pct.	ShO	Sv	ERA
1986	Eugene	A	14	14	1	0	72.1	0	51	39	31	2	0	0	7	49	0	68	5	1	5	4	.556	0	0	3.86
1987	Ft. Myers	A	5	5	1	0	31.1	133	33	20	19	3	0	0	1	8	0	17	0	0	2	2	.500	0	0	5.46
	Appleton	A	20	19	3	0	121.1	525	101	50	36	4	5	5	5	56	5	89	9	2	10	4	.714	1	0	2.67
1988	Baseball Cy	A	6	6	0	0	32.2	143	32	19	14	2	1	4	2	10	1	20	1	0	1	4	.200	0	0	3.86
	Appleton	A	4	4	0	0	18	73	17	7	6	0	1	1	2	5	0	7	3	0	0	1	.000	0	0	3.00
	Quad City	A	3	0	0	0	6	28	6	3	3	0	1	0	2	4	0	7	1	0	0	0	.000	0	0	4.50
	Palm Sprngs	A	7	7	0	0	42.2	199	57	33	27	3	0	1	4	19	0	37	6	0	3	2	.600	0	0	5.70
1989	Midland	AA	15	15	0	0	68.2	331	92	54	50	6	2	4	3	41	1	49	7	2	2	6	.250	0	0	6.55
1990	Midland	AA	35	8	0	6	87	413	109	68	60	8	6	9	3	55	2	84	3	1	3	7	.300	0	0	6.21
1991	Midland	AA	41	6	0	13	88	394	93	54	51	6	2	7	8	46	0	70	3	0	9	6	.600	0	3	5.22
1992	Edmonton	AAA	26	0	0	16	29.1	130	24	12	10	2	5	1	2	18	2	32	1	0	5	2	.714	0	4	3.07
1993	Vancouver	AAA	14	1	0	5	24.1	108	21	16	12	3	2	1	1	12	0	12	3	2	2	3	.400	0	3	4.44
1992	California	AL	19	0	0	6	27.2	125	29	11	10	3	0	1	2	13	1	24	0	0	2	2	.500	0	0	3.25
1993	California	AL	23	0	0	11	28.1	124	21	12	9	2	1	3	2	15	1	24	0	0	1	0	1.000	0	8	2.86
	2 ML YEARS		42	0	0	17	56	249	50	23	19	5	1	4	4	28	2	48	0	0	3	2	.600	0	8	3.05

Brett Butler

Bats: Left **Throws:** Left **Pos:** CF **Ht:** 5'10" **Wt:** 161 **Born:** 06/15/57 **Age:** 37

			BATTING																BASERUNNING				PERCENTAGES		
Year	Team	Lg	G	AB	H	2B	3B	HR	(Hm | Rd)	TB	R	RBI	TBB	IBB	SO	HBP	SH	SF	SB	CS	SB%	GDP	Avg	OBP	SLG
1981	Atlanta	NL	40	126	32	2	3	0	(0 | 0)	40	17	4	19	0	17	0	0	0	9	1	.90	0	.254	.352	.317
1982	Atlanta	NL	89	240	52	2	0	0	(0 | 0)	54	35	7	25	0	35	0	3	0	21	8	.72	1	.217	.291	.225
1983	Atlanta	NL	151	549	154	21	13	5	(4 | 1)	216	84	37	54	3	56	2	3	5	39	23	.63	5	.281	.344	.393
1984	Cleveland	AL	159	602	162	25	9	3	(1 | 2)	214	108	49	86	1	62	4	11	6	52	22	.70	6	.269	.361	.355
1985	Cleveland	AL	152	591	184	28	14	5	(1 | 4)	255	106	50	63	2	42	1	8	3	47	20	.70	8	.311	.377	.431
1986	Cleveland	AL	161	587	163	17	14	4	(0 | 4)	220	92	51	70	1	65	4	17	5	32	15	.68	8	.278	.356	.375
1987	Cleveland	AL	137	522	154	25	8	9	(4 | 5)	222	91	41	91	0	55	1	2	2	33	16	.67	3	.295	.399	.425
1988	San Francisco	NL	157	568	163	27	9	6	(1 | 5)	226	109	43	97	4	64	4	8	2	43	20	.68	2	.287	.393	.398
1989	San Francisco	NL	154	594	168	22	4	4	(2 | 2)	210	100	36	59	2	69	3	13	3	31	16	.66	4	.283	.349	.354
1990	San Francisco	NL	160	622	192	20	9	3	(3 | 0)	239	108	44	90	1	62	6	7	7	51	19	.73	3	.309	.397	.384
1991	Los Angeles	NL	161	615	182	13	5	2	(2 | 0)	211	112	38	108	4	79	1	4	2	38	28	.58	3	.296	.401	.343
1992	Los Angeles	NL	157	553	171	14	11	3	(1 | 2)	216	86	39	95	2	67	3	24	1	41	21	.66	4	.309	.413	.391
1993	Los Angeles	NL	156	607	181	21	10	1	(0 | 1)	225	80	42	86	1	69	5	14	4	39	19	.67	6	.298	.387	.371
	13 ML YEARS		1834	6776	1958	237	109	45	(19 | 26)	2548	1128	481	943	21	742	34	114	40	476	228	.68	53	.289	.377	.376

Rob Butler

Bats: Left **Throws:** Left **Pos:** LF **Ht:** 5'11" **Wt:** 185 **Born:** 04/10/70 **Age:** 24

			BATTING																BASERUNNING				PERCENTAGES		
Year	Team	Lg	G	AB	H	2B	3B	HR	(Hm | Rd)	TB	R	RBI	TBB	IBB	SO	HBP	SH	SF	SB	CS	SB%	GDP	Avg	OBP	SLG
1991	St.Cathrnes	A	76	311	105	16	5	7	--	--	152	71	45	20	5	21	2	6	3	31	15	.67	2	.338	.378	.489
1992	Dunedin	A	92	391	140	13	7	4	--	--	179	67	41	22	2	36	2	2	5	19	14	.58	7	.358	.394	.458
1993	Syracuse	AAA	55	208	59	11	2	1	--	--	77	30	14	15	2	29	3	3	2	7	5	.58	6	.284	.338	.370
1993	Toronto	AL	17	48	13	4	0	0	(0 | 0)	17	8	2	7	0	12	1	0	0	2	2	.50	0	.271	.375	.354

Jim Byrd

Bats: Right **Throws:** Right **Pos:** SS   **Ht:** 6' 1" **Wt:** 186 **Born:** 10/03/68 **Age:** 25

								BATTING												BASERUNNING				PERCENTAGES		
Year Team	Lg	G	AB	H	2B	3B	HR	(Hm	Rd)	TB	R	RBI	TBB	IBB	SO	HBP	SH	SF	SB	CS	SB%	GDP	Avg	OBP	SLG
1988 R.S./mamrs	R	33	121	36	7	2	2	--	--	53	18	13	6	0	19	2	0	1	7	1	.88	3	.298	.338	.438
1989 Winter Havn	A	126	447	88	17	2	3	--	--	118	42	25	25	0	104	4	11	0	22	10	.69	13	.197	.246	.264
1990 Lynchburg	A	131	511	115	20	1	8	--	--	161	59	45	38	0	139	15	1	4	24	11	.69	14	.225	.296	.315
New Britain	AA	2	5	1	1	0	0	--	--	2	1	0	0	0	1	0	0	0	0	0	.00	1	.200	.200	.400
1991 Lynchburg	A	52	206	49	10	0	1	--	--	62	29	18	13	0	50	3	0	1	9	3	.75	6	.238	.291	.301
New Britain	AA	79	292	70	9	1	0	--	--	81	28	15	28	1	53	1	5	2	14	10	.58	12	.240	.307	.277
1992 Winter Havn	A	18	71	19	2	1	0	--	--	23	12	1	5	0	7	0	1	0	4	0	1.00	3	.268	.316	.324
New Britain	AA	20	63	14	1	2	0	--	--	19	5	6	3	0	13	1	0	0	2	3	.40	1	.222	.269	.302
Pawtucket	AAA	72	246	55	5	1	2	--	--	68	27	18	7	0	48	4	4	0	2	3	.40	5	.224	.257	.276
1993 Pawtucket	AAA	117	378	67	12	4	3	--	--	96	33	26	18	1	111	9	5	0	10	9	.53	5	.177	.232	.254
1993 Boston	AL	2	0	0	0	0	0	(0	0)	0	0	0	0	0	0	0	0	0	0	0	.00	0	.000	.000	.000

Francisco Cabrera

Bats: Right **Throws:** Right **Pos:** 1B   **Ht:** 6' 4" **Wt:** 193 **Born:** 10/10/66 **Age:** 27

								BATTING												BASERUNNING				PERCENTAGES		
Year Team	Lg	G	AB	H	2B	3B	HR	(Hm	Rd)	TB	R	RBI	TBB	IBB	SO	HBP	SH	SF	SB	CS	SB%	GDP	Avg	OBP	SLG
1989 2 ML Teams		7	26	5	3	0	0			8	1	0	1	0	6	0	0	0	0	0	.00	0	.192	.192	.308
1990 Atlanta	NL	63	137	38	5	1	7	(4	3)	66	14	25	5	0	21	0	0	1	1	0	1.00	4	.277	.301	.482
1991 Atlanta	NL	44	95	23	6	0	4	(2	2)	41	7	23	6	0	20	0	0	1	1	1	.50	5	.242	.284	.432
1992 Atlanta	NL	12	10	3	0	0	2	(0	2)	9	2	3	1	0	1	0	0	0	0	0	.00	0	.300	.364	.900
1993 Atlanta	NL	70	83	20	3	0	4	(1	3)	35	8	11	8	1	21	0	0	2	0	0	.00	2	.241	.308	.422
1989 Toronto	AL	3	12	2	1	0	0	(0	0)	3	1	0	1	0	3	0	0	0	0	0	.00	0	.167	.231	.250
Atlanta	NL	4	14	3	2	0	0	(0	0)	5	0	0	0	0	3	0	0	0	0	0	.00	0	.214	.214	.357
5 ML YEARS		196	351	89	17	1	17	(7	10)	159	32	62	21	1	69	0	0	2	2	1	.67	11	.254	.294	.453

Greg Cadaret

Pitches: Left **Bats:** Left **Pos:** RP   **Ht:** 6' 3" **Wt:** 215 **Born:** 02/27/62 **Age:** 32

				HOW MUCH HE PITCHED				WHAT HE GAVE UP												THE RESULTS					
Year Team	Lg	G	GS	CG	GF	IP	BFP	H	R	ER	HR	SH	SF	HB	TBB	IBB	SO	WP	Bk	W	L	Pct.	ShO	Sv	ERA
1987 Oakland	AL	29	0	0	7	39.2	176	37	22	20	6	2	2	1	24	1	30	1	0	6	2	.750	0	0	4.54
1988 Oakland	AL	58	0	0	16	71.2	311	60	26	23	2	5	3	1	36	1	64	5	3	5	2	.714	0	3	2.89
1989 2 ML Teams	AL	46	13	3	7	120	531	130	62	54	7	3	5	2	57	4	80	6	2	5	5	.500	1	0	4.05
1990 New York	AL	54	6	0	9	121.1	525	120	62	56	8	9	4	1	64	5	80	14	0	5	4	.556	0	3	4.15
1991 New York	AL	68	5	0	17	121.2	517	110	52	49	8	6	3	2	59	6	105	3	1	8	6	.571	0	3	3.62
1992 New York	AL	46	11	1	9	103.2	471	104	53	49	12	3	3	2	74	7	73	5	1	4	8	.333	1	1	4.25
1993 2 ML Teams	AL	47	0	0	18	48	220	54	24	23	3	4	0	2	30	5	25	2	0	3	2	.600	0	2	4.31
1989 Oakland	AL	26	0	0	6	27.2	119	21	9	7	0	0	2	0	19	3	14	0	0	0	0	.000	0	0	2.28
New York	AL	20	13	3	1	92.1	412	109	53	47	7	3	3	2	38	1	66	6	2	5	5	.500	1	0	4.58
1993 Cincinnati	NL	34	0	0	15	32.2	158	40	19	18	3	3	0	1	23	5	23	2	0	2	1	.667	0	1	4.96
Kansas City	AL	13	0	0	3	15.1	62	14	5	5	0	1	0	1	7	0	2	0	0	1	1	.500	0	0	2.93
7 ML YEARS		348	35	4	83	626	2751	615	301	274	46	32	20	11	344	29	457	36	7	36	29	.554	2	11	3.94

Ivan Calderon

Bats: Right **Throws:** Right **Pos:** RF/DH   **Ht:** 6' 1" **Wt:** 221 **Born:** 03/19/62 **Age:** 32

								BATTING												BASERUNNING				PERCENTAGES		
Year Team	Lg	G	AB	H	2B	3B	HR	(Hm	Rd)	TB	R	RBI	TBB	IBB	SO	HBP	SH	SF	SB	CS	SB%	GDP	Avg	OBP	SLG
1984 Seattle	AL	11	24	5	1	0	1	(0	1)	9	2	1	2	0	5	0	0	0	1	0	1.00	3	.208	.269	.375
1985 Seattle	AL	67	210	60	16	4	8	(6	2)	108	37	28	19	1	45	2	1	1	4	2	.67	10	.286	.349	.514
1986 2 ML Teams		50	164	41	7	1	2	(1	1)	56	16	15	9	1	39	1	0	0	3	1	.75	1	.250	.293	.341
1987 Chicago	AL	144	542	159	38	2	28	(15	13)	285	93	83	60	6	109	1	0	4	10	5	.67	13	.293	.362	.526
1988 Chicago	AL	73	264	56	14	0	14	(6	8)	112	40	35	34	2	66	0	0	3	4	4	.50	6	.212	.299	.424
1989 Chicago	AL	157	622	178	34	9	14	(2	12)	272	83	87	43	7	94	3	2	6	7	1	.88	20	.286	.332	.437
1990 Chicago	AL	158	607	166	44	2	14	(6	8)	256	85	74	51	7	79	1	0	8	32	16	.67	26	.273	.327	.422
1991 Montreal	NL	134	470	141	22	3	19	(7	12)	226	69	75	53	4	64	3	1	10	31	16	.66	7	.300	.368	.481
1992 Montreal	NL	48	170	45	14	2	3	(2	1)	72	19	24	14	1	22	1	0	1	1	2	.33	4	.265	.323	.424
1993 2 ML Teams		82	239	50	10	2	1	(0	1)	67	26	22	21	1	33	1	2	2	4	2	.67	13	.209	.274	.280
1986 Seattle	AL	37	131	31	5	0	2	(1	1)	42	13	13	6	0	33	1	0	0	3	1	.75	1	.237	.275	.321
Chicago	AL	13	33	10	2	1	0	(0	0)	14	3	2	3	1	6	0	0	0	0	0	.00	0	.303	.361	.424
1993 Boston	AL	73	213	47	8	2	1	(0	1)	62	25	19	21	1	28	1	2	2	4	2	.67	13	.221	.291	.291
Chicago	AL	9	26	3	2	0	0	(0	0)	5	1	3	0	0	5	0	0	0	0	0	.00	2	.115	.115	.192
10 ML YEARS		924	3312	901	200	25	104	(45	59)	1463	470	444	306	30	556	13	6	35	97	49	.66	103	.272	.333	.442

Ken Caminiti

Bats: Both   **Throws:** Right   **Pos:** 3B   **Ht:** 6' 0"   **Wt:** 200   **Born:** 04/21/63   **Age:** 31

						BATTING														BASERUNNING				PERCENTAGES		
Year Team	Lg	G	AB	H	2B	3B	HR	(Hm	Rd)	TB	R	RBI	TBB	IBB	SO	HBP	SH	SF		SB	CS	SB%	GDP	Avg	OBP	SLG
1987 Houston	NL	63	203	50	7	1	3	(2	1)	68	10	23	12	1	44	0	2	1		0	0	.00	6	.246	.287	.335
1988 Houston	NL	30	83	15	2	0	1	(0	1)	20	5	7	5	0	18	0	0	1		0	0	.00	3	.181	.225	.241
1989 Houston	NL	161	585	149	31	3	10	(3	7)	216	71	72	51	9	93	3	3	4		4	1	.80	8	.255	.316	.369
1990 Houston	NL	153	541	131	20	2	4	(2	2)	167	52	51	48	7	97	0	3	4		9	4	.69	15	.242	.302	.309
1991 Houston	NL	152	574	145	30	3	13	(9	4)	220	65	80	46	7	85	5	3	4		4	5	.44	18	.253	.312	.383
1992 Houston	NL	135	506	149	31	2	13	(7	6)	223	68	62	44	13	68	1	2	4		10	4	.71	14	.294	.350	.441
1993 Houston	NL	143	543	142	31	0	13	(5	8)	212	75	75	49	10	88	0	1	3		8	5	.62	15	.262	.321	.390
7 ML YEARS		837	3035	781	152	11	57	(28	29)	1126	346	370	255	47	493	9	14	21		35	19	.65	79	.257	.315	.371

Kevin Campbell

Pitches: Right   **Bats:** Right   **Pos:** RP   **Ht:** 6' 2"   **Wt:** 225   **Born:** 12/06/64   **Age:** 29

			HOW MUCH HE PITCHED					WHAT HE GAVE UP										THE RESULTS					
Year Team	Lg	G	GS	CG	GF	IP	BFP	H	R	ER	HR	SH	SF	HB	TBB	IBB	SO	WP	Bk	W	L	Pct.	ShO	Sv	ERA
1993 Tacoma *	AAA	40	0	0	28	55.2	230	42	19	17	5	3	2	2	19	6	46	4	0	3	5	.375	0	12	2.75
1991 Oakland	AL	14	0	0	2	23	94	13	7	7	4	1	0	1	14	0	16	0	0	1	0	1.000	0	0	2.74
1992 Oakland	AL	32	5	0	6	65	297	66	39	37	4	3	2	0	45	3	38	2	0	2	3	.400	0	1	5.12
1993 Oakland	AL	11	0	0	4	16	77	20	13	13	1	0	1	1	11	1	9	0	0	0	0	.000	0	0	7.31
3 ML YEARS		57	5	0	12	104	468	99	59	57	9	4	3	2	70	4	63	2	0	3	3	.500	0	1	4.93

Willie Canate

Bats: Right   **Throws:** Right   **Pos:** LF   **Ht:** 6' 0"   **Wt:** 170   **Born:** 12/11/71   **Age:** 22

						BATTING														BASERUNNING				PERCENTAGES		
Year Team	Lg	G	AB	H	2B	3B	HR	(Hm	Rd)	TB	R	RBI	TBB	IBB	SO	HBP	SH	SF		SB	CS	SB%	GDP	Avg	OBP	SLG
1989 Indians	R	11	24	5	2	0	0	--	--	7	4	0	0	0	8	0	0	0		0	0	.00	0	.208	.208	.292
1990 Watertown	A	57	199	52	6	2	2	--	--	68	28	15	10	0	43	3	1	0		9	4	.69	6	.261	.307	.342
1991 Kinston	A	51	189	41	3	1	1	--	--	49	28	12	14	0	29	3	5	0		4	2	.67	5	.217	.282	.259
Columbus	A	62	204	49	13	2	4	--	--	78	32	20	25	0	32	4	7	3		14	5	.74	10	.240	.331	.382
1992 Columbus	A	133	528	167	37	8	5	--	--	235	110	63	56	3	66	10	3	6		25	9	.74	3	.316	.388	.445
1993 Indianapolis	AAA	3	5	0	0	0	0	--	--	0	0	0	0	0	1	0	0	0		0	0	.00	0	.000	.000	.000
Knoxville	AA	9	37	10	2	0	1	--	--	15	8	4	5	0	2	0	0	0		2	1	.67	1	.270	.357	.405
Syracuse	AAA	7	24	6	0	0	2	--	--	12	3	5	5	0	3	0	0	0		0	2	.00	1	.250	.379	.500
1993 Toronto	AL	38	47	10	0	0	1	(1	0)	13	12	3	6	0	15	1	1	2		1	1	.50	2	.213	.309	.277

Casey Candaele

Bats: Both   **Throws:** Right   **Pos:** 2B/SS/CF   **Ht:** 5' 9"   **Wt:** 165   **Born:** 01/12/61   **Age:** 33

						BATTING														BASERUNNING				PERCENTAGES		
Year Team	Lg	G	AB	H	2B	3B	HR	(Hm	Rd)	TB	R	RBI	TBB	IBB	SO	HBP	SH	SF		SB	CS	SB%	GDP	Avg	OBP	SLG
1993 Tucson *	AAA	6	27	8	1	0	0	--	--	9	4	4	3	1	2	0	0	0		1	2	.33	2	.296	.367	.333
1986 Montreal	NL	30	104	24	4	1	0	(0	0)	30	9	6	5	0	15	0	0	1		3	5	.38	3	.231	.264	.288
1987 Montreal	NL	138	449	122	23	4	1	(1	0)	156	62	23	38	3	28	2	4	2		7	10	.41	5	.272	.330	.347
1988 2 ML Teams		57	147	25	8	1	0	(0	0)	35	11	5	11	1	17	0	3	0		1	1	.50	7	.170	.228	.238
1990 Houston	NL	130	262	75	8	6	3	(1	2)	104	30	22	31	5	42	1	4	0		7	5	.58	4	.286	.364	.397
1991 Houston	NL	151	461	121	20	7	4	(1	3)	167	44	50	40	7	49	0	1	3		9	3	.75	5	.262	.319	.362
1992 Houston	NL	135	320	68	12	1	1	(1	0)	85	19	18	24	3	36	3	7	6		7	1	.88	5	.213	.269	.266
1993 Houston	NL	75	121	29	8	0	1	(0	1)	40	18	7	10	0	14	0	0	0		2	3	.40	0	.240	.298	.331
1988 Montreal	NL	36	116	20	5	1	0	(0	0)	27	9	4	10	1	11	0	2	0		1	0	1.00	7	.172	.238	.233
Houston	NL	21	31	5	3	0	0	(0	0)	8	2	1	1	0	6	0	1	0		0	1	.00	0	.161	.188	.258
7 ML YEARS		716	1864	464	83	20	10	(4	6)	617	193	131	159	19	201	6	19	12		36	28	.56	29	.249	.308	.331

John Candelaria

Pitches: Left   **Bats:** Right   **Pos:** RP   **Ht:** 6' 6"   **Wt:** 225   **Born:** 11/06/53   **Age:** 40

			HOW MUCH HE PITCHED					WHAT HE GAVE UP										THE RESULTS					
Year Team	Lg	G	GS	CG	GF	IP	BFP	H	R	ER	HR	SH	SF	HB	TBB	IBB	SO	WP	Bk	W	L	Pct.	ShO	Sv	ERA
1975 Pittsburgh	NL	18	18	4	0	121	497	95	47	37	8	6	4	2	36	9	95	1	0	8	6	.571	1	0	2.75
1976 Pittsburgh	NL	32	31	11	1	220	881	173	87	77	22	13	6	2	60	5	138	0	0	16	7	.696	4	1	3.15
1977 Pittsburgh	NL	33	33	6	0	231	917	197	64	60	29	9	6	2	50	2	133	1	2	20	5	.800	1	0	2.34
1978 Pittsburgh	NL	30	29	3	1	189	796	191	73	68	15	8	2	5	49	6	94	3	3	12	11	.522	1	1	3.24
1979 Pittsburgh	NL	33	30	8	2	207	850	201	83	74	25	4	7	3	41	6	101	2	0	14	9	.609	0	0	3.22
1980 Pittsburgh	NL	35	34	7	1	233	969	246	114	104	14	14	12	3	50	4	97	0	2	11	14	.440	0	1	4.02
1981 Pittsburgh	NL	6	6	0	0	41	168	42	17	16	3	1	1	0	11	1	14	0	0	2	2	.500	0	0	3.51
1982 Pittsburgh	NL	31	30	1	1	174.2	704	166	62	57	13	5	6	4	37	3	133	1	0	12	7	.632	1	0	2.94
1983 Pittsburgh	NL	33	32	2	0	197.2	797	191	73	71	15	4	4	2	45	3	157	3	2	15	8	.652	0	0	3.23
1984 Pittsburgh	NL	33	28	3	4	185.1	751	179	69	56	19	10	6	1	34	3	133	1	1	12	11	.522	1	2	2.72

Year	Team	Lg	G	GS	CG	GF	IP	BFP	H	R	ER	HR	SH	SF	HB	TBB	IBB	SO	WP	Bk	W	L	Pct.	ShO	Sv	ERA
1985	2 ML Teams		50	13	1	26	125.1	530	127	56	52	14	7	7	4	38	3	100	2	0	9	7	.563	1	9	3.73
1986	California	AL	16	16	1	0	91.2	365	68	30	26	4	3	3	3	26	2	81	2	1	10	2	.833	1	0	2.55
1987	2 ML Teams		23	23	0	0	129	544	144	78	69	18	8	6	1	23	0	84	0	1	10	6	.625	0	0	4.81
1988	New York	AL	25	24	6	1	157	640	150	69	59	18	4	6	2	23	2	121	2	12	13	7	.650	2	1	3.38
1989	2 ML Teams		22	6	1	3	65.1	274	66	36	34	11	3	5	0	16	3	51	2	1	3	5	.375	0	0	4.68
1990	2 ML Teams		47	3	0	15	79.2	345	87	36	35	11	2	6	2	20	5	63	5	0	7	6	.538	0	5	3.95
1991	Los Angeles	NL	59	0	0	10	33.2	138	31	16	14	3	1	3	0	11	2	38	1	1	1	1	.500	0	2	3.74
1992	Los Angeles	NL	50	0	0	11	25.1	108	20	9	8	1	2	2	0	13	3	23	1	0	2	5	.286	0	5	2.84
1993	Pittsburgh	NL	24	0	0	6	19.2	92	25	19	18	2	1	1	1	9	1	17	1	0	0	3	.000	0	1	8.24
1985	Pittsburgh	NL	37	0	0	26	54.1	229	57	23	22	7	3	4	1	14	2	47	0	0	2	4	.333	0	9	3.64
	California	AL	13	13	1	0	71	301	70	33	30	7	4	3	3	24	1	53	2	0	7	3	.700	1	0	3.80
1987	California	AL	20	20	0	0	116.2	487	127	70	61	17	6	5	1	20	0	74	0	0	8	6	.571	0	0	4.71
	New York	NL	3	3	0	0	12.1	57	17	8	8	1	2	1	0	3	0	10	0	1	2	0	1.000	0	0	5.84
1989	New York	AL	10	6	1	1	49	206	49	28	28	8	2	2	0	12	1	37	2	1	3	3	.500	0	0	5.14
	Montreal	NL	12	0	0	2	16.1	68	17	8	6	3	1	3	0	4	2	14	0	0	0	2	.000	0	0	3.31
1990	Minnesota	AL	34	1	0	10	58.1	239	55	23	22	9	2	3	0	9	2	44	3	0	7	3	.700	0	4	3.39
	Toronto	AL	13	2	0	5	21.1	106	32	13	13	2	0	3	2	11	3	19	2	0	0	1	.000	0	1	5.48
	19 ML YEARS		600	356	54	82	2526.1	10366	2399	1038	935	245	105	93	37	592	63	1673	28	26	177	122	.592	13	29	3.33

Tom Candiotti

Pitches: Right **Bats:** Right **Pos:** SP **Ht:** 6' 2" **Wt:** 215 **Born:** 08/31/57 **Age:** 36

			HOW MUCH HE PITCHED						WHAT HE GAVE UP												THE RESULTS				
Year	Team	Lg	G	GS	CG	GF	IP	BFP	H	R	ER	HR	SH	SF	HB	TBB	IBB	SO	WP	Bk	W	L	Pct.	ShO	Sv	ERA
1983	Milwaukee	AL	10	8	2	1	55.2	233	62	21	20	4	0	2	2	16	0	21	0	0	4	4	.500	1	0	3.23
1984	Milwaukee	AL	8	6	0	0	32.1	147	38	21	19	5	0	0	0	10	0	23	1	0	2	2	.500	0	0	5.29
1986	Cleveland	AL	36	34	17	1	252.1	1078	234	112	100	18	3	9	8	106	0	167	12	4	16	12	.571	3	0	3.57
1987	Cleveland	AL	32	32	7	0	201.2	888	193	132	107	28	8	10	4	93	2	111	13	2	7	18	.280	2	0	4.78
1988	Cleveland	AL	31	31	11	0	216.2	903	225	86	79	15	12	5	6	53	3	137	5	7	14	8	.636	1	0	3.28
1989	Cleveland	AL	31	31	4	0	206	847	188	80	71	10	6	4	4	55	5	124	4	8	13	10	.565	0	0	3.10
1990	Cleveland	AL	31	29	3	1	202	856	207	92	82	23	4	3	6	55	1	128	9	3	15	11	.577	1	0	3.65
1991	2 ML Teams		34	34	6	0	238	981	202	82	70	12	4	11	6	73	1	167	11	0	13	13	.500	2	0	2.65
1992	Los Angeles	NL	32	30	6	1	203.2	839	177	78	68	13	20	6	3	63	5	152	9	2	11	15	.423	2	0	3.00
1993	Los Angeles	NL	33	32	2	0	213.2	898	192	86	74	12	15	9	6	71	1	155	6	0	8	10	.444	0	0	3.12
1991	Cleveland	AL	15	15	3	0	108.1	442	88	35	27	6	1	7	2	28	0	86	6	0	7	6	.538	0	0	2.24
	Toronto	AL	19	19	3	0	129.2	539	114	47	43	6	3	4	4	45	1	81	5	0	6	7	.462	2	0	2.98
	10 ML YEARS		278	267	58	4	1822	7670	1718	790	690	140	72	59	45	595	18	1185	70	26	103	103	.500	10	0	3.41

Jose Canseco

Bats: Right **Throws:** Right **Pos:** RF **Ht:** 6' 4" **Wt:** 240 **Born:** 07/02/64 **Age:** 29

			BATTING																BASERUNNING				PERCENTAGES		
Year	Team	Lg	G	AB	H	2B	3B	HR	(Hm | Rd)	TB	R	RBI	TBB	IBB	SO	HBP	SH	SF	SB	CS	SB%	GDP	Avg	OBP	SLG
1985	Oakland	AL	29	96	29	3	0	5	(4 | 1)	47	16	13	4	0	31	0	0	0	1	1	.50	1	.302	.330	.490
1986	Oakland	AL	157	600	144	29	1	33	(14 | 19)	274	85	117	65	1	175	8	0	9	15	7	.68	12	.240	.318	.457
1987	Oakland	AL	159	630	162	35	3	31	(16 | 15)	296	81	113	50	2	157	2	0	9	15	3	.83	16	.257	.310	.470
1988	Oakland	AL	158	610	187	34	0	42	(16 | 26)	347	120	124	78	10	128	10	1	6	40	16	.71	15	.307	.391	.569
1989	Oakland	AL	65	227	61	9	1	17	(8 | 9)	123	40	57	23	4	69	2	0	6	6	3	.67	4	.269	.333	.542
1990	Oakland	AL	131	481	132	14	2	37	(18 | 19)	261	83	101	72	8	158	9	0	5	19	10	.66	9	.274	.371	.543
1991	Oakland	AL	154	572	152	32	1	44	(16 | 28)	318	115	122	78	8	152	9	0	6	26	6	.81	16	.266	.359	.556
1992	2 ML Teams		119	439	107	15	0	26	(15 | 11)	200	74	87	63	2	128	6	0	4	6	7	.46	16	.244	.344	.456
1993	Texas	AL	60	231	59	14	1	10	(6 | 4)	105	30	46	16	2	62	3	0	3	6	6	.50	6	.255	.308	.455
1992	Oakland	AL	97	366	90	11	0	22	(12 | 10)	167	66	72	48	1	104	3	0	4	5	7	.42	15	.246	.335	.456
	Texas	AL	22	73	17	4	0	4	(3 | 1)	33	8	15	15	1	24	3	0	0	1	0	1.00	1	.233	.385	.452
	9 ML YEARS		1032	3886	1033	185	9	245	(113 | 132)	1971	644	780	449	37	1060	45	1	48	134	59	.69	95	.266	.345	.507

Ozzie Canseco

Bats: Right **Throws:** Right **Pos:** LF **Ht:** 6' 3" **Wt:** 220 **Born:** 07/02/64 **Age:** 29

			BATTING																BASERUNNING				PERCENTAGES		
Year	Team	Lg	G	AB	H	2B	3B	HR	(Hm | Rd)	TB	R	RBI	TBB	IBB	SO	HBP	SH	SF	SB	CS	SB%	GDP	Avg	OBP	SLG
1993	Louisville *	AAA	44	154	37	6	1	13	--	--	84	20	33	15	4	59	0	0	1	2	1	.33	3	.240	.306	.545
1990	Oakland	AL	9	19	2	1	0	0	(0 | 0)	3	1	1	1	0	10	0	0	0	0	0	.00	0	.105	.150	.158
1992	St. Louis	NL	9	29	8	5	0	0	(0 | 0)	13	7	3	7	0	4	0	0	0	0	0	.00	1	.276	.417	.448
1993	St. Louis	NL	6	17	3	0	0	0	(0 | 0)	3	0	0	1	0	3	0	0	0	0	0	.00	0	.176	.222	.176
	3 ML YEARS		24	65	13	6	0	0	(0 | 0)	19	8	4	9	0	17	0	0	0	0	0	.00	1	.200	.297	.292

Ramon Caraballo

Bats: Both **Throws:** Right **Pos:** 2B **Ht:** 5' 7" **Wt:** 150 **Born:** 05/23/69 **Age:** 25

Year	Team	Lg	G	AB	H	2B	3B	HR	(Hm	Rd)	TB	R	RBI	TBB	IBB	SO	HBP	SH	SF	SB	CS	SB%	GDP	Avg	OBP	SLG
1989	Braves	R	20	77	19	3	1	1	--	--	27	9	10	10	0	14	0	1	1	5	4	.56	0	.247	.330	.351
	Sumter	A	45	171	45	10	5	1	--	--	68	22	32	16	0	38	2	1	3	9	4	.69	5	.263	.328	.398
1990	Burlington	A	102	390	113	18	14	7	--	--	180	84	54	49	2	69	7	2	2	41	20	.67	9	.290	.377	.462
1991	Durham	A	120	444	111	13	8	6	--	--	158	73	52	38	1	91	3	3	2	53	23	.70	5	.250	.312	.356
1992	Greenville	AA	24	93	29	4	4	1	--	--	44	15	8	14	0	13	0	0	1	10	6	.63	1	.312	.398	.473
	Richmond	AAA	101	405	114	20	3	2	--	--	146	42	40	22	1	60	3	7	1	19	16	.54	6	.281	.323	.360
1993	Richmond	AAA	126	470	128	25	9	3	--	--	180	73	41	30	3	81	7	7	5	20	14	.59	3	.272	.322	.383
1993	Atlanta	NL	6	0	0	0	0	0	(0	0)	0	0	0	0	0	0	0	0	0	0	0	.00	0	.000	.000	.000

Paul Carey

Bats: Right **Throws:** Left **Pos:** 1B **Ht:** 6' 4" **Wt:** 215 **Born:** 01/08/68 **Age:** 26

Year	Team	Lg	G	AB	H	2B	3B	HR	(Hm	Rd)	TB	R	RBI	TBB	IBB	SO	HBP	SH	SF	SB	CS	SB%	GDP	Avg	OBP	SLG
1990	Miami	A	49	153	50	5	3	4	--	--	73	23	20	43	1	39	2	0	1	4	3	.57	2	.327	.477	.477
1991	Hagerstown	AA	114	373	94	29	1	12	--	--	161	63	65	68	8	109	4	2	5	5	4	.56	11	.252	.369	.432
1992	Frederick	A	41	136	41	6	0	9	--	--	74	24	26	28	5	22	2	0	1	0	1	.00	2	.301	.425	.544
	Rochester	AAA	30	87	20	4	1	1	--	--	29	9	7	6	0	16	2	0	1	0	0	.00	2	.230	.292	.333
	Hagerstown	AA	48	163	44	8	0	4	--	--	64	17	18	15	5	37	2	0	1	3	2	.60	4	.270	.337	.393
1993	Rochester	AAA	96	325	101	20	4	12	--	--	165	63	50	65	11	92	5	1	2	0	0	.00	10	.311	.431	.508
1993	Baltimore	AL	18	47	10	1	0	0	(0	0)	11	1	3	5	0	14	0	0	0	0	0	.00	4	.213	.288	.234

Cris Carpenter

Pitches: Right **Bats:** Right **Pos:** RP **Ht:** 6' 1" **Wt:** 185 **Born:** 04/05/65 **Age:** 29

			HOW MUCH HE PITCHED						WHAT HE GAVE UP											THE RESULTS					
Year	Team	Lg	G	GS	CG	GF	IP	BFP	H	R	ER	HR	SH	SF	HB	TBB	IBB	SO	WP	Bk	W	L	Pct.	ShO	Sv	ERA
1988	St. Louis	NL	8	8	1	0	47.2	203	56	27	25	3	1	4	1	9	2	24	1	0	2	3	.400	0	0	4.72
1989	St. Louis	NL	36	5	0	10	68	303	70	30	24	4	4	4	2	26	9	35	1	0	4	4	.500	0	0	3.18
1990	St. Louis	NL	4	0	0	1	8	32	5	4	4	2	0	0	0	2	1	6	0	0	0	0	.000	0	0	4.50
1991	St. Louis	NL	59	0	0	19	66	266	53	31	31	6	3	2	0	20	9	47	1	0	10	4	.714	0	0	4.23
1992	St. Louis	NL	73	0	0	21	88	355	69	29	29	10	8	3	4	27	8	46	5	0	5	4	.556	0	1	2.97
1993	2 ML Teams		56	0	0	17	69.1	293	64	30	27	5	2	4	4	25	3	53	7	0	4	2	.667	0	1	3.50
1993	Florida	NL	29	0	0	9	37.1	154	29	15	12	1	1	1	2	13	2	26	5	0	0	1	.000	0	1	2.89
	Texas	AL	27	0	0	8	32	139	35	15	15	4	1	3	2	12	1	27	2	0	4	1	.800	0	1	4.22
	6 ML YEARS		236	13	1	68	347	1452	317	151	140	30	18	17	11	109	32	211	15	0	25	17	.595	0	2	3.63

Chuck Carr

Bats: Both **Throws:** Right **Pos:** CF **Ht:** 5'10" **Wt:** 165 **Born:** 08/10/68 **Age:** 25

Year	Team	Lg	G	AB	H	2B	3B	HR	(Hm	Rd)	TB	R	RBI	TBB	IBB	SO	HBP	SH	SF	SB	CS	SB%	GDP	Avg	OBP	SLG
1986	Reds	R	44	123	21	5	0	0	--	--	26	13	10	10	0	27	0	5	2	9	1	.90	2	.171	.230	.211
1987	Bellingham	A	44	165	40	1	1	1	--	--	46	31	11	12	0	38	1	3	0	20	1	.95	2	.242	.298	.279
1988	Wausau	A	82	304	91	14	2	6	--	--	127	58	30	14	0	49	1	3	5	41	11	.79	3	.299	.327	.418
	Vermont	AA	41	159	39	4	2	1	--	--	50	26	13	8	0	33	0	3	1	21	9	.70	1	.245	.280	.314
1989	Jackson	AA	116	444	107	13	1	0	--	--	122	45	22	27	2	66	1	7	2	47	20	.70	3	.241	.285	.275
1990	Tidewater	AAA	20	81	21	5	1	0	--	--	28	13	8	4	0	12	0	0	2	6	4	.60	0	.259	.287	.346
	Jackson	AA	93	360	93	20	9	3	--	--	140	60	24	44	2	77	2	3	2	47	15	.76	2	.258	.341	.389
1991	Tidewater	AAA	64	246	48	6	1	1	--	--	59	34	11	18	0	37	1	1	0	27	8	.77	3	.195	.253	.240
1992	Arkansas	AA	28	111	29	5	1	1	--	--	39	17	6	8	1	23	0	0	0	8	2	.80	2	.261	.311	.351
	Louisville	AAA	96	377	116	11	9	3	--	--	154	68	29	31	0	60	3	0	0	53	10	.84	4	.308	.365	.408
1993	Marlins	R	3	12	5	1	0	0	--	--	9	4	3	0	0	2	0	0	0	3	0	1.00	0	.417	.417	.750
1990	New York	NL	4	2	0	0	0	0	(0	0)	0	0	0	0	0	2	0	0	0	1	0	1.00	0	.000	.000	.000
1991	New York	NL	12	11	2	0	0	0	(0	0)	2	1	1	0	0	2	0	0	0	1	0	1.00	0	.182	.182	.182
1992	St. Louis	NL	22	64	14	3	0	0	(0	0)	17	8	3	9	0	6	0	3	0	10	2	.83	0	.219	.315	.266
1993	Florida	NL	142	551	147	19	2	4	(3	1)	182	75	41	49	0	74	2	7	4	58	22	.73	6	.267	.327	.330
	4 ML YEARS		180	628	163	22	2	4	(3	1)	201	84	45	58	0	84	2	10	4	70	24	.74	6	.260	.322	.320

Mark Carreon

Bats: Right **Throws:** Left **Pos:** RF **Ht:** 6' 0" **Wt:** 195 **Born:** 07/09/63 **Age:** 30

Year	Team	Lg	G	AB	H	2B	3B	HR	(Hm	Rd)	TB	R	RBI	TBB	IBB	SO	HBP	SH	SF	SB	CS	SB%	GDP	Avg	OBP	SLG
1987	New York	NL	9	12	3	0	0	0	(0	0)	3	0	1	1	0	1	0	0	0	0	1	.00	0	.250	.308	.250
1988	New York	NL	7	9	5	2	0	1	(0	0)	10	5	2	0	0	1	0	0	0	0	0	.00	0	.556	.636	1.111

39

Year	Team	Lg	G	AB	H	2B	3B	HR	(Hm	Rd)	TB	R	RBI	TBB	IBB	SO	HBP	SH	SF	SB	CS	SB%	GDP	Avg	OBP	SLG
1989	New York	NL	68	133	41	6	0	6	(4	2)	65	20	16	12	0	17	1	0	0	2	3	.40	1	.308	.370	.489
1990	New York	NL	82	188	47	12	0	10	(1	9)	89	30	26	15	0	29	2	0	0	1	0	1.00	1	.250	.312	.473
1991	New York	NL	106	254	66	6	0	4	(3	1)	84	18	21	12	2	26	2	1	1	2	1	.67	13	.260	.297	.331
1992	Detroit	AL	101	336	78	11	1	10	(5	5)	121	34	41	22	2	57	1	1	4	3	1	.75	12	.232	.278	.360
1993	San Francisco	NL	78	150	49	9	1	7	(2	5)	81	22	33	13	2	16	1	0	5	1	0	1.00	8	.327	.373	.540
7 ML YEARS			451	1082	289	46	2	38	(15	23)	453	129	139	77	6	147	7	2	10	9	6	.60	35	.267	.317	.419

Matias Carrillo

Bats: Left   **Throws: Left**   **Pos: RF**   **Ht: 5'11"**   **Wt: 190**   **Born: 02/24/63**   **Age: 31**

								BATTING												BASERUNNING				PERCENTAGES		
Year	Team	Lg	G	AB	H	2B	3B	HR	(Hm	Rd)	TB	R	RBI	TBB	IBB	SO	HBP	SH	SF	SB	CS	SB%	GDP	Avg	OBP	SLG
1990	Denver	AAA	21	75	20	6	2	2	--	--	36	15	10	2	0	16	0	0	1	0	2	.00	2	.267	.282	.480
1991	Denver	AAA	120	421	116	18	5	8	--	--	168	56	56	32	2	84	0	5	3	11	13	.46	11	.276	.325	.399
1991	Milwaukee	AL	3	0	0	0	0	0	(0	0)	0	0	0	0	0	0	0	0	0	0	0	.00	0	.000	.000	.000
1993	Florida	NL	24	55	14	6	0	0	(0	0)	20	4	3	1	0	7	1	1	0	0	0	.00	5	.255	.281	.364
2 ML YEARS			27	55	14	6	0	0	(0	0)	20	4	3	1	0	7	1	1	0	0	0	.00	5	.255	.281	.364

Joe Carter

Bats: Right   **Throws: Right**   **Pos: RF/LF**   **Ht: 6'3"**   **Wt: 225**   **Born: 03/07/60**   **Age: 34**

								BATTING												BASERUNNING				PERCENTAGES		
Year	Team	Lg	G	AB	H	2B	3B	HR	(Hm	Rd)	TB	R	RBI	TBB	IBB	SO	HBP	SH	SF	SB	CS	SB%	GDP	Avg	OBP	SLG
1983	Chicago	NL	23	51	9	1	1	0	(0	0)	12	6	1	0	0	21	0	1	0	1	0	1.00	1	.176	.176	.235
1984	Cleveland	AL	66	244	67	6	1	13	(9	4)	114	32	41	11	0	48	1	0	1	2	4	.33	2	.275	.307	.467
1985	Cleveland	AL	143	489	128	27	0	15	(5	10)	200	64	59	25	2	74	2	3	4	24	6	.80	9	.262	.298	.409
1986	Cleveland	AL	162	663	200	36	9	29	(14	15)	341	108	121	32	3	95	5	1	8	29	7	.81	6	.302	.335	.514
1987	Cleveland	AL	149	588	155	27	2	32	(9	23)	282	83	106	27	6	105	9	1	4	31	6	.84	8	.264	.304	.480
1988	Cleveland	AL	157	621	168	36	6	27	(16	11)	297	85	98	35	6	82	7	1	6	27	5	.84	6	.271	.314	.478
1989	Cleveland	AL	162	651	158	32	4	35	(16	19)	303	84	105	39	8	112	8	2	5	13	5	.72	6	.243	.292	.465
1990	San Diego	NL	162	634	147	27	1	24	(12	12)	248	79	115	48	18	93	7	0	8	22	6	.79	12	.232	.290	.391
1991	Toronto	AL	162	638	174	42	3	33	(23	10)	321	89	108	49	12	112	10	0	9	20	9	.69	6	.273	.330	.503
1992	Toronto	AL	158	622	164	30	7	34	(21	13)	310	97	119	36	4	109	11	1	13	12	5	.71	14	.264	.309	.498
1993	Toronto	AL	155	603	153	33	5	33	(21	12)	295	92	121	47	5	113	9	0	10	8	3	.73	10	.254	.312	.489
11 ML YEARS			1499	5804	1523	297	39	275	(146	129)	2723	819	994	349	64	964	69	10	68	189	56	.77	82	.262	.309	.469

Chuck Cary

Pitches: Left   **Bats: Left**   **Pos: RP**   **Ht: 6'4"**   **Wt: 216**   **Born: 03/03/60**   **Age: 34**

					HOW MUCH HE PITCHED				WHAT HE GAVE UP										THE RESULTS					
Year	Team	Lg	G	GS	CG	GF	IP	BFP	H	R	ER	HR	SH	SF	HB	TBB	IBB	SO	WP	Bk	W	L	Pct.	ShO	Sv	ERA
1993	Nashville *	AAA	1	0	0	0	2	10	4	2	2	0	0	0	0	2	0	1	0	0	0	1	.000	0	0	9.00
	South Bend *	A	8	3	0	4	18	69	13	4	4	0	0	0	2	1	0	28	4	0	1	1	.500	0	1	2.00
1985	Detroit	AL	16	0	0	6	23.2	95	16	9	9	2	0	1	2	8	1	22	0	0	0	1	.000	0	2	3.42
1986	Detroit	AL	22	0	0	6	31.2	140	33	18	12	3	2	2	0	15	4	21	1	1	1	2	.333	0	0	3.41
1987	Atlanta	NL	13	0	0	6	16.2	70	17	7	7	3	1	0	1	4	3	15	1	0	1	1	.500	0	1	3.78
1988	Atlanta	NL	7	0	0	1	8.1	39	8	6	6	1	2	0	1	4	0	7	1	0	0	0	.000	0	0	6.48
1989	New York	AL	22	11	2	4	99.1	404	78	42	36	13	1	1	0	29	6	79	6	1	4	4	.500	0	0	3.26
1990	New York	AL	28	27	2	1	156.2	661	155	77	73	21	3	5	1	55	1	134	11	2	6	12	.333	0	0	4.19
1991	New York	AL	10	9	0	0	53.1	247	61	35	35	6	1	0	0	32	2	34	2	1	1	6	.143	0	0	5.91
1993	Chicago	AL	16	0	0	4	20.2	96	22	12	12	1	1	4	3	11	0	10	4	0	1	0	1.000	0	0	5.23
8 ML YEARS			134	47	4	28	410.1	1752	390	206	190	50	11	13	8	158	17	322	26	5	14	26	.350	0	3	4.17

Larry Casian

Pitches: Left   **Bats: Right**   **Pos: RP**   **Ht: 6'0"**   **Wt: 170**   **Born: 10/28/65**   **Age: 28**

					HOW MUCH HE PITCHED				WHAT HE GAVE UP										THE RESULTS					
Year	Team	Lg	G	GS	CG	GF	IP	BFP	H	R	ER	HR	SH	SF	HB	TBB	IBB	SO	WP	Bk	W	L	Pct.	ShO	Sv	ERA
1993	Portland *	AAA	7	0	0	5	7.2	31	9	0	0	0	0	0	0	2	1	2	0	0	1	0	1.000	0	2	0.00
1990	Minnesota	AL	5	3	0	1	22.1	90	26	9	8	2	0	1	0	4	0	11	0	0	2	1	.667	0	0	3.22
1991	Minnesota	AL	15	0	0	4	18.1	87	28	16	15	4	0	0	1	7	2	6	2	0	0	0	.000	0	0	7.36
1992	Minnesota	AL	6	0	0	1	6.2	28	7	2	2	0	0	0	0	1	0	2	0	0	1	0	1.000	0	0	2.70
1993	Minnesota	AL	54	0	0	8	56.2	241	59	23	19	1	3	3	1	14	2	31	2	0	5	3	.625	0	1	3.02
4 ML YEARS			80	3	0	14	104	446	120	50	44	7	3	4	2	26	4	50	4	0	8	4	.667	0	1	3.81

Pedro Castellano

Bats: Right   **Throws: Right**   **Pos: 3B**   **Ht: 6'1"**   **Wt: 175**   **Born: 03/11/70**   **Age: 24**

								BATTING												BASERUNNING				PERCENTAGES		
Year	Team	Lg	G	AB	H	2B	3B	HR	(Hm	Rd)	TB	R	RBI	TBB	IBB	SO	HBP	SH	SF	SB	CS	SB%	GDP	Avg	OBP	SLG
1989	Wytheville	R	66	244	76	17	4	9	--	--	128	55	42	46	2	44	3	1	3	5	2	.71	9	.311	.422	.525

Year	Team	Lg	G	AB	H	2B	3B	HR	(Hm	Rd)	TB	R	RBI	TBB	IBB	SO	HBP	SH	SF	SB	CS	SB%	GDP	Avg	OBP	SLG
1990	Peoria	A	117	417	115	27	4	2	--	--	156	61	44	63	2	72	3	3	4	7	1	.88	9	.276	.372	.374
	Winston-Sal	A	19	66	13	0	0	1	--	--	16	6	8	10	0	11	2	2	0	1	0	1.00	3	.197	.321	.242
1991	Winston-Sal	A	129	459	139	25	3	10	--	--	200	59	88	72	4	97	3	2	5	11	10	.52	13	.303	.397	.436
	Charlotte	AA	7	19	8	0	0	0	--	--	8	2	2	1	0	6	1	0	1	0	0	.00	1	.421	.455	.421
1992	Iowa	AAA	74	238	59	14	4	2	--	--	87	25	20	32	0	42	1	8	1	2	2	.50	6	.248	.338	.366
	Charlotte	AA	45	147	33	3	0	1	--	--	39	16	15	19	0	21	4	3	2	0	1	.00	2	.224	.326	.265
1993	Colo Sprngs	AAA	90	304	95	21	2	12	--	--	156	61	60	36	0	63	6	1	8	3	5	.38	8	.313	.387	.513
1993	Colorado	NL	34	71	13	2	0	3	(1	2)	24	12	7	8	0	16	0	0	0	1	1	.50	1	.183	.266	.338

Vinny Castilla

Bats: Right **Throws:** Right **Pos:** SS **Ht:** 6' 1" **Wt:** 175 **Born:** 07/04/67 **Age:** 26

									BATTING											BASERUNNING				PERCENTAGES		
Year	Team	Lg	G	AB	H	2B	3B	HR	(Hm	Rd)	TB	R	RBI	TBB	IBB	SO	HBP	SH	SF	SB	CS	SB%	GDP	Avg	OBP	SLG
1990	Sumter	A	93	339	91	15	2	9	--	--	137	47	53	28	1	54	8	1	5	2	5	.29	8	.268	.334	.404
	Greenville	AA	46	170	40	5	1	4	--	--	59	20	16	13	3	23	2	0	1	4	4	.50	7	.235	.296	.347
1991	Greenville	AA	66	259	70	17	3	7	--	--	114	34	44	9	1	35	2	2	4	0	1	.00	4	.270	.296	.440
	Richmond	AAA	67	240	54	7	4	7	--	--	90	25	36	14	2	31	3	0	5	1	1	.50	4	.225	.271	.375
1992	Richmond	AAA	127	449	113	29	1	7	--	--	165	49	44	21	1	68	4	3	6	1	2	.33	19	.252	.288	.367
1991	Atlanta	NL	12	5	1	0	0	0	(0	0)	1	0	0	0	0	2	0	1	0	0	0	.00	0	.200	.200	.200
1992	Atlanta	NL	9	16	4	1	0	0	(0	0)	5	1	1	1	1	4	1	0	0	0	0	.00	0	.250	.333	.313
1993	Colorado	NL	105	337	86	9	7	9	(5	4)	136	36	30	13	4	45	2	0	5	2	5	.29	10	.255	.283	.404
	3 ML YEARS		126	358	91	10	7	9	(5	4)	142	38	31	14	5	51	3	1	5	2	5	.29	10	.254	.284	.397

Frank Castillo

Pitches: Right **Bats:** Right **Pos:** SP **Ht:** 6' 1" **Wt:** 195 **Born:** 04/01/69 **Age:** 25

			HOW MUCH HE PITCHED						WHAT HE GAVE UP										THE RESULTS					
Year	Team	Lg	G	GS	CG	GF	IP	BFP	H	R	ER	HR	SH	SF	HB	TBB	IBB	SO	WP	Bk	W	L	Pct.	ShO	Sv	ERA
1991	Chicago	NL	18	18	4	0	111.2	467	107	56	54	5	6	3	0	33	2	73	5	1	6	7	.462	0	0	4.35
1992	Chicago	NL	33	33	0	0	205.1	856	179	91	79	19	11	5	6	63	6	135	11	0	10	11	.476	0	0	3.46
1993	Chicago	NL	29	25	2	0	141.1	614	162	83	76	20	10	3	9	39	4	84	5	3	5	8	.385	0	0	4.84
	3 ML YEARS		80	76	6	0	458.1	1937	448	230	209	44	27	11	15	135	12	292	21	4	21	26	.447	0	0	4.10

Tony Castillo

Pitches: Left **Bats:** Left **Pos:** RP **Ht:** 5'10" **Wt:** 188 **Born:** 03/01/63 **Age:** 31

			HOW MUCH HE PITCHED						WHAT HE GAVE UP										THE RESULTS					
Year	Team	Lg	G	GS	CG	GF	IP	BFP	H	R	ER	HR	SH	SF	HB	TBB	IBB	SO	WP	Bk	W	L	Pct.	ShO	Sv	ERA
1993	Syracuse *	AAA	1	1	0	0	6	22	4	2	0	0	0	0	0	0	0	2	0	0	0	0	.000	0	0	0.00
1988	Toronto	AL	14	0	0	6	15	54	10	5	5	2	0	2	0	2	0	14	0	0	1	0	1.000	0	0	3.00
1989	2 ML Teams		29	0	0	9	27	127	31	19	17	0	3	4	1	14	6	15	3	0	1	2	.333	0	1	5.67
1990	Atlanta	NL	52	3	0	7	76.2	337	93	41	36	5	4	4	1	20	3	64	2	2	5	1	.833	0	1	4.23
1991	2 ML Teams		17	3	0	6	32.1	148	40	16	12	4	2	1	0	11	1	18	0	0	2	1	.667	0	0	3.34
1993	Toronto	AL	51	0	0	10	50.2	211	44	19	19	4	5	2	0	22	5	28	1	0	3	2	.600	0	1	3.38
1989	Toronto	AL	17	0	0	8	17.2	86	23	14	12	0	2	4	1	10	5	10	3	0	1	1	.500	0	1	6.11
	Atlanta	NL	12	0	0	1	9.1	41	8	5	5	0	1	0	0	4	1	5	0	0	0	1	.000	0	0	4.82
1991	Atlanta	NL	7	0	0	5	8.2	44	13	9	7	3	1	0	0	5	0	8	0	0	1	1	.500	0	0	7.27
	New York	NL	10	3	0	1	23.2	104	27	7	5	1	1	1	0	6	1	10	0	0	1	0	1.000	0	0	1.90
	5 ML YEARS		163	6	0	38	201.2	877	218	100	89	15	14	13	2	69	15	139	6	2	12	6	.667	0	2	3.97

Andujar Cedeno

Bats: Right **Throws:** Right **Pos:** SS **Ht:** 6' 1" **Wt:** 168 **Born:** 08/21/69 **Age:** 24

									BATTING											BASERUNNING				PERCENTAGES		
Year	Team	Lg	G	AB	H	2B	3B	HR	(Hm	Rd)	TB	R	RBI	TBB	IBB	SO	HBP	SH	SF	SB	CS	SB%	GDP	Avg	OBP	SLG
1990	Houston	NL	7	8	0	0	0	0	(0	0)	0	0	0	0	0	5	0	0	0	0	0	.00	0	.000	.000	.000
1991	Houston	NL	67	251	61	13	2	9	(4	5)	105	27	36	9	1	74	1	1	2	4	3	.57	3	.243	.270	.418
1992	Houston	NL	71	220	38	13	2	2	(2	0)	61	15	13	14	2	71	3	0	0	2	0	1.00	1	.173	.232	.277
1993	Houston	NL	149	505	143	24	4	11	(6	5)	208	69	56	48	9	97	3	4	5	9	7	.56	17	.283	.346	.412
	4 ML YEARS		294	984	242	50	8	22	(12	10)	374	111	105	71	12	247	7	5	7	15	10	.60	21	.246	.299	.380

Domingo Cedeno

Bats: Both **Throws:** Right **Pos:** SS **Ht:** 6' 1" **Wt:** 170 **Born:** 11/04/68 **Age:** 25

									BATTING											BASERUNNING				PERCENTAGES		
Year	Team	Lg	G	AB	H	2B	3B	HR	(Hm	Rd)	TB	R	RBI	TBB	IBB	SO	HBP	SH	SF	SB	CS	SB%	GDP	Avg	OBP	SLG
1989	Myrtle Bch	A	9	35	7	0	0	0	--	--	7	4	2	3	0	12	0	1	0	1	1	.50	0	.200	.263	.200
	Dunedin	A	9	28	6	0	1	0	--	--	8	3	1	3	0	10	0	0	0	1	0	1.00	1	.214	.290	.286
	Medicne Hat	R	53	194	45	6	4	1	--	--	62	28	20	23	0	65	3	3	1	6	6	.50	0	.232	.321	.320
1990	Dunedin	A	124	493	109	12	10	7	--	--	162	64	61	48	2	127	2	4	8	10	6	.63	4	.221	.289	.329
1991	Knoxville	AA	100	336	75	7	6	1	--	--	97	39	26	29	1	78	1	12	1	11	6	.65	2	.223	.286	.289
1992	Knoxville	AA	106	337	76	7	7	2	--	--	103	31	21	18	0	88	4	7	0	8	9	.47	6	.226	.273	.306

41

			G	AB	H	2B	3B	HR	(Hm	Rd)	TB	R	RBI	TBB	IBB	SO	HBP	SH	SF	SB	CS	SB%	GDP	Avg	OBP	SLG
	Syracuse	AAA	18	57	11	4	0	0	--	--	15	4	5	3	0	14	0	2	0	0	0	.00	1	.193	.233	.263
1993	Syracuse	AAA	103	382	104	16	10	2	--	--	146	58	28	33	2	67	1	8	2	15	10	.60	6	.272	.330	.382
1993	Toronto	AL	15	46	8	0	0	0	(0	0)	8	5	7	1	0	10	0	2	1	1	0	1.00	2	.174	.188	.174

Wes Chamberlain

Bats: Right **Throws:** Right **Pos:** RF   **Ht:** 6' 2" **Wt:** 219 **Born:** 04/13/66 **Age:** 28

							BATTING													BASERUNNING				PERCENTAGES		
Year	Team	Lg	G	AB	H	2B	3B	HR	(Hm	Rd)	TB	R	RBI	TBB	IBB	SO	HBP	SH	SF	SB	CS	SB%	GDP	Avg	OBP	SLG
1990	Philadelphia	NL	18	46	13	3	0	2	(0	2)	22	9	4	1	0	9	0	0	0	4	0	1.00	0	.283	.298	.478
1991	Philadelphia	NL	101	383	92	16	3	13	(9	4)	153	51	50	31	0	73	2	1	0	9	4	.69	8	.240	.300	.399
1992	Philadelphia	NL	76	275	71	18	0	9	(3	6)	116	26	41	10	2	55	1	1	2	4	0	1.00	7	.258	.285	.422
1993	Philadelphia	NL	96	284	80	20	2	12	(5	7)	140	34	45	17	3	51	1	0	4	2	1	.67	7	.282	.320	.493
	4 ML YEARS		291	988	256	57	5	36	(17	19)	431	120	140	59	5	188	4	2	6	19	5	.79	22	.259	.302	.436

Norm Charlton

Pitches: Left **Bats:** Both **Pos:** RP   **Ht:** 6' 3" **Wt:** 205 **Born:** 01/06/63 **Age:** 31

			HOW MUCH HE PITCHED						WHAT HE GAVE UP									THE RESULTS					
Year	Team	Lg	G	GS	CG	GF	IP	BFP	H	R	ER	HR	SH	SF	HB	TBB	IBB	SO	WP	Bk	W	L	Pct.	ShO	Sv	ERA
1988	Cincinnati	NL	10	10	0	0	61.1	259	60	27	27	6	1	2	2	20	2	39	3	2	4	5	.444	0	0	3.96
1989	Cincinnati	NL	69	0	0	27	95.1	393	67	38	31	5	9	2	2	40	7	98	2	4	8	3	.727	0	0	2.93
1990	Cincinnati	NL	56	16	1	13	154.1	650	131	53	47	10	7	2	4	70	4	117	9	1	12	9	.571	1	2	2.74
1991	Cincinnati	NL	39	11	0	10	108.1	438	92	37	35	6	7	1	6	34	4	77	11	0	3	5	.375	0	1	2.91
1992	Cincinnati	NL	64	0	0	46	81.1	341	79	39	27	7	7	3	3	26	4	90	8	0	4	2	.667	0	26	2.99
1993	Seattle	AL	34	0	0	29	34.2	141	22	12	9	4	0	1	0	17	0	48	6	0	1	3	.250	0	18	2.34
	6 ML YEARS		272	37	1	125	535.1	2222	451	206	176	38	31	11	17	207	21	469	39	7	32	27	.542	1	47	2.96

Mike Christopher

Pitches: Right **Bats:** Right **Pos:** RP   **Ht:** 6' 5" **Wt:** 205 **Born:** 11/03/63 **Age:** 30

			HOW MUCH HE PITCHED						WHAT HE GAVE UP									THE RESULTS					
Year	Team	Lg	G	GS	CG	GF	IP	BFP	H	R	ER	HR	SH	SF	HB	TBB	IBB	SO	WP	Bk	W	L	Pct.	ShO	Sv	ERA
1985	Oneonta	A	15	9	2	3	80.1	317	58	21	13	2	1	2	3	22	0	84	3	0	8	1	.889	2	0	1.46
1986	Albany	AA	11	11	2	0	60.2	273	75	48	34	6	2	4	3	12	1	34	3	0	3	5	.375	0	0	5.04
	Ft.Laudrdle	A	15	14	3	0	102.2	421	92	37	30	2	4	2	1	36	0	56	1	1	7	3	.700	1	0	2.63
1987	Ft.Laudrdle	A	24	24	9	0	169.1	694	183	63	46	5	6	4	0	28	1	81	4	0	13	8	.619	4	0	2.44
1988	Albany	AA	24	24	5	0	152.2	648	166	75	65	7	4	5	6	44	3	67	2	4	13	7	.650	1	0	3.83
1989	Columbus	AAA	13	11	1	0	73	331	95	45	39	6	6	5	3	21	3	42	1	0	5	6	.455	0	0	4.81
	Albany	AA	8	8	3	0	53.2	213	48	17	15	1	0	1	1	7	0	33	0	0	6	1	.857	0	0	2.52
1990	Albuquerque	AAA	54	0	0	25	68.2	287	62	20	15	3	5	4	2	23	3	47	0	0	6	1	.857	0	8	1.97
1991	Albuquerque	AAA	63	0	0	34	77.1	334	73	25	21	2	4	1	3	30	5	67	7	1	7	2	.778	0	16	2.44
1992	Colo Sprngs	AAA	49	0	0	45	58.2	240	59	21	19	2	5	4	0	13	6	39	3	0	4	4	.500	0	26	2.91
1993	Charlotte	AAA	50	0	0	46	50.1	204	51	21	18	2	3	2	0	6	4	36	2	0	3	6	.333	0	22	3.22
1991	Los Angeles	NL	3	0	0	2	4	15	2	0	0	0	0	0	0	3	0	2	0	0	0	0	.000	0	0	0.00
1992	Cleveland	AL	10	0	0	4	18	79	17	8	6	2	1	1	0	10	1	13	2	0	0	0	.000	0	0	3.00
1993	Cleveland	AL	9	0	0	3	11.2	51	14	6	5	3	0	0	0	2	1	8	0	0	0	0	.000	0	0	3.86
	3 ML YEARS		22	0	0	9	33.2	145	33	14	11	5	1	1	0	15	2	23	2	0	0	0	.000	0	0	2.94

Archi Cianfrocco

Bats: Right **Throws:** Right **Pos:** 3B/1B   **Ht:** 6' 5" **Wt:** 205 **Born:** 10/06/66 **Age:** 27

							BATTING													BASERUNNING				PERCENTAGES		
Year	Team	Lg	G	AB	H	2B	3B	HR	(Hm	Rd)	TB	R	RBI	TBB	IBB	SO	HBP	SH	SF	SB	CS	SB%	GDP	Avg	OBP	SLG
1987	Jamestown	A	70	251	62	8	4	2	--	--	84	28	27	9	2	59	1	4	4	2	0	1.00	2	.247	.272	.335
1988	Rockford	A	126	455	115	34	0	15	--	--	194	54	65	26	0	99	6	2	5	6	1	.86	8	.253	.299	.426
1989	Jacksnville	AA	132	429	105	22	7	7	--	--	162	46	50	37	1	126	1	0	5	3	7	.30	8	.245	.303	.378
1990	Jacksnville	AA	62	196	43	10	0	5	--	--	68	18	29	12	1	45	2	0	3	0	1	.00	4	.219	.268	.347
1991	Harrisburg	AA	124	456	144	21	10	9	--	--	212	71	77	38	2	112	9	2	2	11	3	.79	11	.316	.378	.465
1992	Indianapols	AAA	15	59	18	3	0	4	--	--	33	12	16	5	0	15	2	0	1	1	0	1.00	0	.305	.373	.559
1993	Ottawa	AAA	50	188	56	14	2	4	--	--	86	21	27	7	0	33	2	0	4	4	2	.67	5	.298	.323	.457
1992	Montreal	NL	86	232	56	5	2	6	(3	3)	83	25	30	11	1	66	1	1	2	3	0	1.00	0	.241	.276	.358
1993	2 ML Teams		96	296	72	11	2	12	(6	6)	123	30	48	17	1	69	3	2	5	2	0	1.00	9	.243	.287	.416
1993	Montreal	NL	12	17	4	1	0	1	(0	1)	8	3	1	0	0	5	0	0	0	0	0	.00	0	.235	.235	.471
	San Diego	NL	84	279	68	10	2	11	(6	5)	115	27	47	17	1	64	3	2	5	2	0	1.00	9	.244	.289	.412
	2 ML YEARS		182	528	128	16	4	18	(9	9)	206	55	78	28	2	135	4	3	7	5	0	1.00	11	.242	.282	.390

Dave Clark

Bats: Left **Throws:** Right **Pos:** RF/LF **Ht:** 6' 2" **Wt:** 210 **Born:** 09/03/62 **Age:** 31

Year Team	Lg	G	AB	H	2B	3B	HR	(Hm	Rd)	TB	R	RBI	TBB	IBB	SO	HBP	SH	SF	SB	CS	SB%	GDP	Avg	OBP	SLG
1986 Cleveland	AL	18	58	16	1	0	3	(1	2)	26	10	9	7	0	11	0	2	1	1	0	1.00	1	.276	.348	.448
1987 Cleveland	AL	29	87	18	5	0	3	(1	2)	32	11	12	2	0	24	0	0	0	1	0	1.00	4	.207	.225	.368
1988 Cleveland	AL	63	156	41	4	1	3	(2	1)	56	11	18	17	2	28	0	0	1	0	2	.00	8	.263	.333	.359
1989 Cleveland	AL	102	253	60	12	0	8	(4	4)	96	21	29	30	5	63	0	1	1	0	2	.00	7	.237	.317	.379
1990 Chicago	NL	84	171	47	4	2	5	(3	2)	70	22	20	8	1	40	0	0	2	7	1	.88	4	.275	.304	.409
1991 Kansas City	AL	11	10	2	0	0	0	(0	0)	2	1	1	1	0	1	0	0	0	0	0	.00	0	.200	.273	.200
1992 Pittsburgh	NL	23	33	7	0	0	2	(2	0)	13	3	7	6	0	8	0	0	1	0	0	.00	0	.212	.325	.394
1993 Pittsburgh	NL	110	277	75	11	2	11	(8	3)	123	43	46	38	5	58	1	0	2	1	0	1.00	10	.271	.358	.444
8 ML YEARS		440	1045	266	37	5	35	(21	14)	418	122	142	109	13	233	1	3	8	10	5	.67	34	.255	.323	.400

Jerald Clark

Bats: Right **Throws:** Right **Pos:** LF/1B/RF **Ht:** 6' 4" **Wt:** 205 **Born:** 08/10/63 **Age:** 30

Year Team	Lg	G	AB	H	2B	3B	HR	(Hm	Rd)	TB	R	RBI	TBB	IBB	SO	HBP	SH	SF	SB	CS	SB%	GDP	Avg	OBP	SLG
1988 San Diego	NL	6	15	3	1	0	0	(0	0)	4	0	3	0	0	4	0	0	0	0	0	.00	0	.200	.200	.267
1989 San Diego	NL	17	41	8	2	0	1	(1	0)	13	5	7	3	0	9	0	0	0	1	0	.00	0	.195	.250	.317
1990 San Diego	NL	52	101	27	4	1	5	(2	3)	48	12	11	5	0	24	0	0	1	0	0	.00	3	.267	.299	.475
1991 San Diego	NL	118	369	84	16	0	10	(8	2)	130	26	47	31	2	90	6	1	4	2	1	.67	10	.228	.295	.352
1992 San Diego	NL	146	496	120	22	6	12	(9	3)	190	45	58	22	3	97	4	1	3	3	0	1.00	7	.242	.278	.383
1993 Colorado	NL	140	478	135	26	6	13	(8	5)	212	65	67	20	2	60	10	3	1	9	6	.60	12	.282	.324	.444
6 ML YEARS		479	1500	377	71	13	41	(28	13)	597	153	193	81	7	284	20	5	9	14	8	.64	32	.251	.297	.398

Mark Clark

Pitches: Right **Bats:** Right **Pos:** SP/RP **Ht:** 6' 5" **Wt:** 225 **Born:** 05/12/68 **Age:** 26

Year Team	Lg	G	GS	CG	GF	IP	BFP	H	R	ER	HR	SH	SF	HB	TBB	IBB	SO	WP	Bk	W	L	Pct.	ShO	Sv	ERA
1993 Charlotte *	AAA	2	2	0	0	13	52	9	5	3	0	0	1	0	2	0	12	0	0	1	0	1.000	0	0	2.08
1991 St. Louis	NL	7	2	0	0	22.1	93	17	10	10	3	0	3	0	11	0	13	2	0	1	1	.500	0	0	4.03
1992 St. Louis	NL	20	20	1	0	113.1	488	117	59	56	12	7	4	0	36	2	44	4	0	3	10	.231	1	0	4.45
1993 Cleveland	AL	26	15	1	1	109.1	454	119	55	52	18	1	1	1	25	1	57	1	0	7	5	.583	0	0	4.28
3 ML YEARS		53	37	2	2	245	1035	253	124	118	33	8	8	1	72	3	114	7	0	11	16	.407	1	0	4.33

Phil Clark

Bats: Right **Throws:** Right **Pos:** 1B/C/LF/RF **Ht:** 6' 0" **Wt:** 180 **Born:** 05/06/68 **Age:** 26

Year Team	Lg	G	AB	H	2B	3B	HR	(Hm	Rd)	TB	R	RBI	TBB	IBB	SO	HBP	SH	SF	SB	CS	SB%	GDP	Avg	OBP	SLG
1986 Bristol	R	66	247	82	4	2	4	--	--	102	40	36	19	2	42	6	1	4	12	1	.92	3	.332	.388	.413
1987 Fayetteville	A	135	542	160	26	9	8	--	--	228	83	79	25	0	43	6	1	8	25	9	.74	16	.295	.329	.421
1988 Lakeland	A	109	403	120	17	4	9	--	--	172	60	66	15	2	43	10	2	7	16	7	.70	9	.298	.333	.427
1989 London	AA	104	373	108	15	4	8	--	--	155	43	42	31	1	49	8	2	1	2	2	.50	16	.290	.356	.416
1990 Toledo	AAA	75	207	47	14	1	2	--	--	69	15	22	14	0	35	4	6	2	1	1	.50	6	.227	.286	.333
1991 Toledo	AAA	110	362	92	13	4	4	--	--	125	47	45	21	0	49	5	3	2	6	6	.50	10	.254	.303	.345
1992 Toledo	AAA	79	271	76	20	0	10	--	--	126	29	39	16	0	35	2	1	2	4	2	.67	8	.280	.323	.465
1992 Detroit	AL	23	54	22	4	0	1	(0	1)	29	3	5	6	1	9	0	1	0	1	0	1.00	2	.407	.467	.537
1993 San Diego	NL	102	240	75	17	0	9	(6	3)	119	33	33	8	2	31	5	1	2	2	0	1.00	2	.313	.345	.496
2 ML YEARS		125	294	97	21	0	10	(6	4)	148	36	38	14	3	40	5	2	2	3	0	1.00	4	.330	.368	.503

Will Clark

Bats: Left **Throws:** Left **Pos:** 1B **Ht:** 6' 1" **Wt:** 196 **Born:** 03/13/64 **Age:** 30

Year Team	Lg	G	AB	H	2B	3B	HR	(Hm	Rd)	TB	R	RBI	TBB	IBB	SO	HBP	SH	SF	SB	CS	SB%	GDP	Avg	OBP	SLG
1986 San Francisco	NL	111	408	117	27	2	11	(7	4)	181	66	41	34	10	76	3	9	4	4	7	.36	3	.287	.343	.444
1987 San Francisco	NL	150	529	163	29	5	35	(22	13)	307	89	91	49	11	98	5	3	2	5	17	.23	9	.308	.371	.580
1988 San Francisco	NL	162	575	162	31	6	29	(14	15)	292	102	109	100	27	129	4	0	10	9	1	.90	9	.282	.386	.508
1989 San Francisco	NL	159	588	196	38	9	23	(9	14)	321	104	111	74	14	103	5	0	8	8	3	.73	6	.333	.407	.546
1990 San Francisco	NL	154	600	177	25	5	19	(8	11)	269	91	95	62	9	97	3	0	13	8	2	.80	7	.295	.357	.448
1991 San Francisco	NL	148	565	170	32	7	29	(17	12)	303	84	116	51	12	91	2	0	4	4	2	.67	5	.301	.359	.536
1992 San Francisco	NL	144	513	154	40	1	16	(11	5)	244	69	73	73	23	82	4	0	11	12	7	.63	5	.300	.384	.476
1993 San Francisco	NL	132	491	139	27	2	14	(5	9)	212	82	73	63	6	68	6	1	6	2	2	.50	10	.283	.367	.432
8 ML YEARS		1160	4269	1278	249	37	176	(93	83)	2129	687	709	506	112	744	32	13	58	52	41	.56	47	.299	.373	.499

Royce Clayton

Bats: Right   **Throws:** Right   **Pos:** SS   **Ht:** 6' 0"   **Wt:** 183   **Born:** 01/02/70   **Age:** 24

					BATTING														BASERUNNING				PERCENTAGES		
Year	Team	Lg	G	AB	H	2B	3B	HR	(Hm	Rd)	TB	R	RBI	TBB	IBB	SO	HBP	SH	SF	SB	CS	SB%	GDP	Avg	OBP	SLG
1991	San Francisco	NL	9	26	3	1	0	0	(0	0)	4	0	2	1	0	6	0	0	0	0	0	.00	1	.115	.148	.154
1992	San Francisco	NL	98	321	72	7	4	4	(3	1)	99	31	24	26	3	63	0	3	2	8	4	.67	11	.224	.281	.308
1993	San Francisco	NL	153	549	155	21	5	6	(5	1)	204	54	70	38	2	91	5	8	7	11	10	.52	16	.282	.331	.372
	3 ML YEARS		260	896	230	29	9	10	(8	2)	307	85	96	65	5	160	5	11	9	19	14	.58	28	.257	.308	.343

Roger Clemens

Pitches: Right   **Bats:** Right   **Pos:** SP   **Ht:** 6' 4"   **Wt:** 220   **Born:** 08/04/62   **Age:** 31

				HOW MUCH HE PITCHED					WHAT HE GAVE UP									THE RESULTS					
Year	Team	Lg	G	GS	CG	GF	IP	BFP	H	R	ER	HR	SH	SF	HB	TBB	IBB	SO	WP	Bk	W	L	Pct.	ShO	Sv	ERA
1993	Pawtucket *	AAA	1	1	0	0	3.2	16	1	0	0	0	0	0	1	4	0	8	0	0	0	0	.000	0	0	0.00
1984	Boston	AL	21	20	5	0	133.1	575	146	67	64	13	2	3	2	29	3	126	4	0	9	4	.692	1	0	4.32
1985	Boston	AL	15	15	3	0	98.1	407	83	38	36	5	1	2	3	37	0	74	1	3	7	5	.583	1	0	3.29
1986	Boston	AL	33	33	10	0	254	997	179	77	70	21	4	6	4	67	0	238	11	3	24	4	.857	1	0	2.48
1987	Boston	AL	36	36	18	0	281.2	1157	248	100	93	19	6	4	9	83	4	256	4	3	20	9	.690	7	0	2.97
1988	Boston	AL	35	35	14	0	264	1063	217	93	86	17	6	3	6	62	4	291	4	7	18	12	.600	8	0	2.93
1989	Boston	AL	35	35	8	0	253.1	1044	215	101	88	20	9	5	8	93	5	230	7	0	17	11	.607	3	0	3.13
1990	Boston	AL	31	31	7	0	228.1	920	193	59	49	7	7	5	7	54	3	209	8	0	21	6	.778	4	0	1.93
1991	Boston	AL	35	35	13	0	271.1	1077	219	93	79	15	6	8	5	65	12	241	6	0	18	10	.643	4	0	2.62
1992	Boston	AL	32	32	11	0	246.2	989	203	80	66	11	5	5	9	62	5	208	3	0	18	11	.621	5	0	2.41
1993	Boston	AL	29	29	2	0	191.2	808	175	99	95	17	5	7	11	67	4	160	3	1	11	14	.440	1	0	4.46
	10 ML YEARS		302	301	91	0	2222.2	9037	1878	807	726	145	51	48	64	619	40	2033	51	17	163	86	.655	35	0	2.94

Craig Colbert

Bats: Right   **Throws:** Right   **Pos:** C   **Ht:** 6' 0"   **Wt:** 214   **Born:** 02/13/65   **Age:** 29

					BATTING														BASERUNNING				PERCENTAGES		
Year	Team	Lg	G	AB	H	2B	3B	HR	(Hm	Rd)	TB	R	RBI	TBB	IBB	SO	HBP	SH	SF	SB	CS	SB%	GDP	Avg	OBP	SLG
1986	Clinton	A	72	263	60	12	0	1	--	--	75	26	17	23	1	53	3	0	1	4	1	.80	7	.228	.297	.285
1987	Fresno	A	115	388	95	12	4	6	--	--	133	41	51	22	2	89	4	3	5	5	5	.50	11	.245	.289	.343
1988	Clinton	A	124	455	106	19	2	11	--	--	162	56	64	41	0	100	1	2	2	8	9	.47	4	.233	.297	.356
1989	Shreveport	AA	106	363	94	19	3	7	--	--	140	47	34	23	5	67	0	4	2	3	7	.30	11	.259	.302	.386
1990	Phoenix	AAA	111	400	112	22	2	8	--	--	162	41	47	31	3	80	3	1	2	4	5	.44	8	.280	.335	.405
1991	Phoenix	AAA	42	142	35	6	2	2	--	--	51	9	13	11	2	38	0	0	1	0	1	.00	7	.246	.299	.359
1992	Phoenix	AAA	36	140	45	8	1	1	--	--	58	16	12	3	0	16	1	2	2	0	1	.00	4	.321	.336	.414
1993	Phoenix	AAA	13	45	10	2	1	1	--	--	17	5	7	0	0	11	1	0	1	0	0	.00	1	.222	.234	.378
1992	San Francisco	NL	49	126	29	5	2	1	(0	1)	41	10	16	9	0	22	0	2	2	1	0	1.00	8	.230	.277	.325
1993	San Francisco	NL	23	37	6	2	0	1	(1	0)	11	2	5	3	1	13	0	0	0	0	0	.00	0	.162	.225	.297
	2 ML YEARS		72	163	35	7	2	2	(1	1)	52	12	21	12	1	35	0	2	2	1	0	1.00	8	.215	.266	.319

Greg Colbrunn

Bats: Right   **Throws:** Right   **Pos:** 1B   **Ht:** 6' 0"   **Wt:** 205   **Born:** 07/26/69   **Age:** 24

					BATTING														BASERUNNING				PERCENTAGES		
Year	Team	Lg	G	AB	H	2B	3B	HR	(Hm	Rd)	TB	R	RBI	TBB	IBB	SO	HBP	SH	SF	SB	CS	SB%	GDP	Avg	OBP	SLG
1988	Rockford	A	115	417	111	18	2	7	--	--	154	55	46	22	2	60	11	2	3	5	3	.63	5	.266	.318	.369
1989	Wst Plm Bch	A	59	228	54	8	0	0	--	--	62	20	25	6	1	29	2	0	2	3	1	.75	5	.237	.261	.272
	Jacksonville	AA	55	178	49	11	1	3	--	--	71	21	18	13	0	33	2	0	1	1	0	1.00	9	.275	.330	.399
1990	Jacksnville	AA	125	458	138	29	1	13	--	--	208	57	76	38	4	78	6	3	6	1	2	.33	8	.301	.358	.454
1992	Indianapols	AAA	57	216	66	19	1	11	--	--	120	32	48	7	2	41	3	0	1	1	0	1.00	7	.306	.333	.556
1993	Wst Plm Bch	A	8	31	12	2	1	0	--	--	19	6	5	4	0	1	0	0	0	0	0	.00	2	.387	.457	.613
	Ottawa	AAA	6	22	6	1	0	0	--	--	7	4	8	1	0	2	0	0	1	1	0	1.00	1	.273	.292	.318
1992	Montreal	NL	52	168	45	8	0	2	(1	1)	59	12	18	6	1	34	2	0	4	3	2	.60	1	.268	.294	.351
1993	Montreal	NL	70	153	39	9	0	4	(2	2)	60	15	23	6	1	33	1	1	3	4	2	.67	1	.255	.282	.392
	2 ML YEARS		122	321	84	17	0	6	(3	3)	119	27	41	12	2	67	3	1	7	7	4	.64	2	.262	.289	.371

Alex Cole

Bats: Left   **Throws:** Left   **Pos:** CF   **Ht:** 6' 0"   **Wt:** 170   **Born:** 08/17/65   **Age:** 28

					BATTING														BASERUNNING				PERCENTAGES		
Year	Team	Lg	G	AB	H	2B	3B	HR	(Hm	Rd)	TB	R	RBI	TBB	IBB	SO	HBP	SH	SF	SB	CS	SB%	GDP	Avg	OBP	SLG
1990	Cleveland	AL	63	227	68	5	4	0	(0	0)	81	43	13	28	0	38	1	0	0	40	9	.82	2	.300	.379	.357
1991	Cleveland	AL	122	387	114	17	3	0	(0	0)	137	58	21	58	2	47	1	4	5	27	17	.61	8	.295	.386	.354
1992	2 ML Teams		105	302	77	4	7	0	(0	0)	95	44	15	28	1	67	1	1	2	16	6	.73	4	.255	.318	.315
1993	Colorado	NL	126	348	89	9	4	0	(0	0)	106	50	24	43	3	58	2	4	2	30	13	.70	6	.256	.339	.305
1992	Cleveland	AL	41	97	20	1	0	0	(0	0)	21	11	5	10	0	21	1	0	1	9	2	.82	2	.206	.284	.216
	Pittsburgh	NL	64	205	57	3	7	0	(0	0)	74	33	10	18	1	46	0	1	1	7	4	.64	2	.278	.335	.361
	4 ML YEARS		416	1264	348	35	18	0	(0	0)	419	195	73	157	6	210	5	9	9	113	45	.72	20	.275	.356	.331

Vince Coleman

Bats: Both **Throws:** Right **Pos:** LF **Ht:** 6' 1" **Wt:** 185 **Born:** 09/22/61 **Age:** 32

								BATTING										BASERUNNING				PERCENTAGES		
Year	Team	Lg	G	AB	H	2B	3B	HR	(Hm | Rd)	TB	R	RBI	TBB	IBB	SO	HBP	SH	SF	SB	CS	SB%	GDP	Avg	OBP	SLG
1985	St. Louis	NL	151	636	170	20	10	1	(1 | 0)	213	107	40	50	1	115	0	5	1	110	25	.81	3	.267	.320	.335
1986	St. Louis	NL	154	600	139	13	8	0	(0 | 0)	168	94	29	60	0	98	2	3	5	107	14	.88	4	.232	.301	.280
1987	St. Louis	NL	151	623	180	14	10	3	(3 | 0)	223	121	43	70	0	126	3	5	1	109	22	.83	7	.289	.363	.358
1988	St. Louis	NL	153	616	160	20	10	3	(2 | 1)	209	77	38	49	4	111	1	8	5	81	27	.75	4	.260	.313	.339
1989	St. Louis	NL	145	563	143	21	9	2	(1 | 1)	188	94	28	50	0	90	2	7	2	65	10	.87	4	.254	.316	.334
1990	St. Louis	NL	124	497	145	18	9	6	(5 | 1)	199	73	39	35	1	88	2	4	1	77	17	.82	6	.292	.340	.400
1991	New York	NL	72	278	71	7	5	1	(0 | 1)	91	45	17	39	0	47	0	1	0	37	14	.73	3	.255	.347	.327
1992	New York	NL	71	229	63	11	1	2	(2 | 0)	82	37	21	27	3	41	2	2	1	24	9	.73	1	.275	.355	.358
1993	New York	NL	92	373	104	14	8	2	(2 | 0)	140	64	25	21	1	58	0	3	2	38	13	.75	2	.279	.316	.375
	9 ML YEARS		1113	4415	1175	138	70	20	(16 | 4)	1513	712	280	401	10	774	12	38	18	648	151	.81	34	.266	.328	.343

Darnell Coles

Bats: Right **Throws:** Right **Pos:** LF/3B/RF **Ht:** 6' 1" **Wt:** 185 **Born:** 06/02/62 **Age:** 32

								BATTING										BASERUNNING				PERCENTAGES		
Year	Team	Lg	G	AB	H	2B	3B	HR	(Hm | Rd)	TB	R	RBI	TBB	IBB	SO	HBP	SH	SF	SB	CS	SB%	GDP	Avg	OBP	SLG
1983	Seattle	AL	27	92	26	7	0	1	(0 | 1)	36	9	6	7	0	12	0	1	0	0	3	.00	8	.283	.333	.391
1984	Seattle	AL	48	143	23	3	1	0	(0 | 0)	28	15	6	17	0	26	2	3	0	2	1	.67	5	.161	.259	.196
1985	Seattle	AL	27	59	14	4	0	1	(0 | 1)	21	8	5	9	0	17	1	0	2	0	1	.00	0	.237	.338	.356
1986	Detroit	AL	142	521	142	30	2	20	(12 | 8)	236	67	86	45	3	84	6	7	8	6	2	.75	8	.273	.333	.453
1987	2 ML Teams		93	268	54	13	1	10	(8 | 2)	99	34	39	34	3	43	3	5	3	1	4	.20	4	.201	.295	.369
1988	2 ML Teams		123	406	106	23	2	15	(10 | 5)	178	52	70	37	1	67	7	2	10	4	3	.57	8	.261	.326	.438
1989	Seattle	AL	146	535	135	21	3	10	(4 | 6)	192	54	59	27	1	61	6	2	3	5	4	.56	13	.252	.294	.359
1990	2 ML Teams		89	215	45	7	1	3	(3 | 0)	63	22	20	16	2	38	1	1	2	0	4	.00	4	.209	.265	.293
1991	San Francisco	NL	11	14	3	0	0	0	(0 | 0)	3	1	0	0	0	2	0	0	0	0	0	.00	1	.214	.214	.214
1992	Cincinnati	NL	55	141	44	11	2	3	(1 | 2)	68	16	18	3	0	15	0	3	2	1	0	1.00	1	.312	.322	.482
1993	Toronto	AL	64	194	49	9	1	4	(3 | 1)	72	26	26	16	1	29	4	1	2	1	1	.50	3	.253	.319	.371
1987	Detroit	AL	53	149	27	5	1	4	(3 | 1)	46	14	15	15	1	23	2	2	1	0	1	.00	1	.181	.263	.309
	Pittsburgh	NL	40	119	27	8	0	6	(5 | 1)	53	20	24	19	2	20	1	3	2	1	3	.25	3	.227	.333	.445
1988	Pittsburgh	NL	68	211	49	13	1	5	(1 | 4)	79	20	36	20	1	41	3	0	7	1	1	.50	3	.232	.299	.374
	Seattle	AL	55	195	57	10	1	10	(9 | 1)	99	32	34	17	0	26	4	2	3	3	2	.60	5	.292	.356	.508
1990	Seattle	AL	37	107	23	5	1	2	(2 | 0)	36	9	16	4	1	17	1	0	1	0	0	.00	1	.215	.248	.336
	Detroit	AL	52	108	22	2	0	1	(1 | 0)	27	13	4	12	1	21	0	1	1	0	4	.00	3	.204	.281	.250
	11 ML YEARS		825	2588	641	128	13	67	(41 | 26)	996	304	335	211	11	394	30	25	32	20	23	.47	55	.248	.308	.385

David Cone

Pitches: Right **Bats:** Left **Pos:** SP **Ht:** 6' 1" **Wt:** 190 **Born:** 01/02/63 **Age:** 31

			HOW MUCH HE PITCHED						WHAT HE GAVE UP											THE RESULTS					
Year	Team	Lg	G	GS	CG	GF	IP	BFP	H	R	ER	HR	SH	SF	HB	TBB	IBB	SO	WP	Bk	W	L	Pct.	ShO	Sv	ERA
1986	Kansas City	AL	11	0	0	5	22.2	108	29	14	14	2	0	0	1	13	1	21	3	0	0	0	.000	0	0	5.56
1987	New York	NL	21	13	1	3	99.1	420	87	46	41	11	4	3	5	44	1	68	2	4	5	6	.455	0	1	3.71
1988	New York	NL	35	28	8	0	231.1	936	178	67	57	10	11	5	4	80	7	213	10	10	20	3	.870	4	0	2.22
1989	New York	NL	34	33	7	0	219.2	910	183	92	86	20	6	4	4	74	6	190	14	4	14	8	.636	2	0	3.52
1990	New York	NL	31	30	6	1	211.2	860	177	84	76	21	4	6	1	65	7	233	10	4	14	10	.583	2	0	3.23
1991	New York	NL	34	34	5	0	232.2	966	204	95	85	13	13	7	5	73	2	241	17	1	14	14	.500	2	0	3.29
1992	2 ML Teams		35	34	7	0	249.2	1055	201	91	78	15	6	9	12	111	7	261	12	1	17	10	.630	5	0	2.81
1993	Kansas City	AL	34	34	6	0	254	1060	205	102	94	20	7	9	10	114	2	191	14	2	11	14	.440	1	0	3.33
1992	New York	NL	27	27	7	0	196.2	831	162	75	63	12	6	6	9	82	5	214	9	1	13	7	.650	5	0	2.88
	Toronto	AL	8	7	0	0	53	224	39	16	15	3	0	3	3	29	2	47	3	0	4	3	.571	0	0	2.55
	8 ML YEARS		235	206	40	9	1521	6315	1264	591	531	112	51	43	42	574	27	1418	82	26	95	65	.594	16	1	3.14

Jeff Conine

Bats: Right **Throws:** Right **Pos:** LF/1B **Ht:** 6' 1" **Wt:** 220 **Born:** 06/27/66 **Age:** 28

								BATTING										BASERUNNING				PERCENTAGES		
Year	Team	Lg	G	AB	H	2B	3B	HR	(Hm	Rd)	TB	R	RBI	TBB	IBB	SO	HBP	SH	SF	SB	CS	SB%	GDP	Avg	OBP	SLG
1988	Baseball Cy	A	118	415	113	23	9	10	--	--	184	63	59	46	1	77	0	5	4	26	12	.68	6	.272	.342	.443
1989	Baseball Cy	A	113	425	116	12	7	14	--	--	184	68	60	40	2	91	3	0	3	32	13	.71	14	.273	.338	.433
1990	Memphis	AA	137	487	156	37	8	15	--	--	254	89	95	94	6	88	1	0	8	21	6	.78	10	.320	.425	.522
1991	Omaha	AAA	51	171	44	9	1	3	--	--	64	23	15	26	2	39	1	0	0	0	6	.00	3	.257	.359	.374
1992	Omaha	AAA	110	397	120	24	5	20	--	--	214	69	72	54	5	67	2	2	6	4	5	.44	6	.302	.383	.539
1990	Kansas City	AL	9	20	5	2	0	0	(0	0)	7	3	2	2	0	5	0	0	0	0	0	.00	0	.250	.318	.350
1992	Kansas City	AL	28	91	23	5	2	0	(0	0)	32	10	9	8	1	23	0	0	0	0	0	.00	1	.253	.313	.352
1993	Florida	NL	162	595	174	24	3	12	(5	7)	240	75	79	52	0	135	5	0	6	2	2	.50	14	.292	.351	.403
	3 ML YEARS		199	706	202	31	5	12	(5	7)	279	88	90	62	3	163	5	0	6	2	2	.50	16	.286	.345	.395

45

Jim Converse

Pitches: Right **Bats:** Left **Pos:** SP **Ht:** 5' 9" **Wt:** 180 **Born:** 08/17/71 **Age:** 22

			HOW MUCH HE PITCHED						WHAT HE GAVE UP												THE RESULTS					
Year	Team	Lg	G	GS	CG	GF	IP	BFP	H	R	ER	HR	SH	SF	HB	TBB	IBB	SO	WP	Bk	W	L	Pct.	ShO	Sv	ERA
1990	Bellingham	A	12	12	0	0	66.2	281	50	31	29	1	0	1	2	32	0	75	2	9	2	4	.333	0	0	3.92
1991	Peninsula	A	26	26	1	0	137.2	643	143	90	76	12	3	4	2	97	2	137	9	2	6	15	.286	0	0	4.97
1992	Jacksonville	AA	27	26	2	0	159	677	134	61	47	9	3	4	5	82	1	157	8	1	12	7	.632	0	0	2.66
1993	Calgary	AAA	23	22	4	0	121.2	565	144	86	73	6	2	7	3	64	1	78	8	0	7	8	.467	0	0	5.40
1993	Seattle	AL	4	4	0	0	20.1	93	23	12	12	0	0	1	0	14	2	10	0	0	1	3	.250	0	0	5.31

Andy Cook

Pitches: Right **Bats:** Right **Pos:** RP **Ht:** 6' 5" **Wt:** 205 **Born:** 08/30/67 **Age:** 26

			HOW MUCH HE PITCHED						WHAT HE GAVE UP												THE RESULTS					
Year	Team	Lg	G	GS	CG	GF	IP	BFP	H	R	ER	HR	SH	SF	HB	TBB	IBB	SO	WP	Bk	W	L	Pct.	ShO	Sv	ERA
1988	Oneonta	A	16	16	2	0	102	444	116	50	41	2	2	1	4	21	0	65	2	3	4	6	.667	0	0	3.62
1989	Pr William	A	25	24	5	0	153	621	123	68	56	7	4	2	6	49	0	83	6	7	8	12	.400	1	0	3.29
1990	Albany	AA	24	24	5	0	156.2	648	146	69	60	12	4	5	4	52	2	53	5	4	12	8	.600	0	0	3.45
1991	Albany	AA	14	14	1	0	82	360	94	46	36	2	0	3	0	27	0	46	1	0	6	3	.667	0	0	3.95
	Columbus	AAA	13	13	2	0	79.1	338	63	34	31	0	5	3	4	38	1	40	1	1	5	5	.500	0	0	3.52
1992	Columbus	AAA	32	9	0	7	99.2	411	85	41	35	8	5	1	3	36	0	58	3	0	7	5	.583	0	2	3.16
1993	Columbus	AAA	21	20	0	0	118.1	543	149	91	86	14	6	5	7	49	3	47	4	3	6	7	.462	0	0	6.54
1993	New York	AL	4	0	0	3	5.1	28	4	3	3	1	1	0	0	7	0	4	2	0	0	1	.000	0	0	5.06

Dennis Cook

Pitches: Left **Bats:** Left **Pos:** RP/SP **Ht:** 6' 3" **Wt:** 190 **Born:** 10/04/62 **Age:** 31

			HOW MUCH HE PITCHED						WHAT HE GAVE UP												THE RESULTS					
Year	Team	Lg	G	GS	CG	GF	IP	BFP	H	R	ER	HR	SH	SF	HB	TBB	IBB	SO	WP	Bk	W	L	Pct.	ShO	Sv	ERA
1993	Charlotte *	AAA	12	6	0	3	42.2	179	46	26	24	6	0	0	2	6	1	40	1	2	3	2	.600	0	0	5.06
1988	San Francisco	NL	4	4	1	0	22	86	9	8	7	1	0	3	0	11	1	13	1	0	2	1	.667	1	0	2.86
1989	2 ML Teams		23	18	2	1	121	499	110	59	50	18	5	2	2	38	6	67	4	2	7	8	.467	1	0	3.72
1990	2 ML Teams		47	16	2	4	156	663	155	74	68	20	7	7	2	56	9	64	6	3	9	4	.692	1	1	3.92
1991	Los Angeles	NL	20	1	0	5	17.2	69	12	3	1	0	1	2	0	7	1	8	0	0	1	0	1.000	0	0	0.51
1992	Cleveland	AL	32	25	1	1	158	669	156	79	67	29	3	3	2	50	2	96	4	5	5	7	.417	0	0	3.82
1993	Cleveland	AL	25	6	0	2	54	233	62	36	34	9	3	2	2	16	1	34	0	1	5	5	.500	0	0	5.67
1989	San Francisco	NL	2	2	1	0	15	58	13	3	3	1	0	0	0	5	0	9	1	0	1	0	1.000	0	0	1.80
	Philadelphia	NL	21	16	1	1	106	441	97	56	47	17	5	2	2	33	6	58	3	2	6	8	.429	1	0	3.99
1990	Philadelphia	NL	42	13	2	4	141.2	594	132	61	56	13	5	5	2	54	9	58	6	3	8	3	.727	1	1	3.56
	Los Angeles	NL	5	3	0	0	14.1	69	23	13	12	7	2	2	0	2	0	6	0	0	1	1	.500	0	0	7.53
	6 ML YEARS		151	70	6	13	528.2	2219	504	259	227	77	19	19	8	178	20	282	15	11	29	25	.537	3	1	3.86

Mike Cook

Pitches: Right **Bats:** Right **Pos:** RP **Ht:** 6' 3" **Wt:** 215 **Born:** 08/14/63 **Age:** 30

			HOW MUCH HE PITCHED						WHAT HE GAVE UP												THE RESULTS					
Year	Team	Lg	G	GS	CG	GF	IP	BFP	H	R	ER	HR	SH	SF	HB	TBB	IBB	SO	WP	Bk	W	L	Pct.	ShO	Sv	ERA
1993	Rochester *	AAA	57	0	0	38	81.1	373	77	39	28	3	7	1	5	48	9	74	11	0	6	7	.462	0	13	3.10
1986	California	AL	5	1	0	1	9	46	13	12	9	3	0	0	0	7	1	6	0	0	0	2	.000	0	0	9.00
1987	California	AL	16	1	0	6	34.1	148	34	21	21	7	1	0	0	18	0	27	3	1	1	2	.333	0	0	5.50
1988	California	AL	3	0	0	1	3.2	15	4	2	2	0	0	0	1	1	0	2	1	0	0	1	.000	0	0	4.91
1989	Minnesota	AL	15	0	0	5	21.1	102	22	12	12	1	0	2	1	17	1	15	0	0	0	1	.000	0	0	5.06
1993	Baltimore	AL	2	0	0	0	3	13	1	0	0	0	0	0	0	2	1	3	1	0	0	0	.000	0	0	0.00
	5 ML YEARS		41	2	0	13	71.1	324	74	47	44	11	1	2	2	45	3	53	5	1	1	6	.143	0	0	5.55

Steve Cooke

Pitches: Left **Bats:** Right **Pos:** SP **Ht:** 6' 6" **Wt:** 220 **Born:** 01/14/70 **Age:** 24

			HOW MUCH HE PITCHED						WHAT HE GAVE UP												THE RESULTS					
Year	Team	Lg	G	GS	CG	GF	IP	BFP	H	R	ER	HR	SH	SF	HB	TBB	IBB	SO	WP	Bk	W	L	Pct.	ShO	Sv	ERA
1990	Welland	A	11	11	0	0	46	188	36	21	18	2	1	1	2	17	0	43	6	1	2	3	.400	0	0	3.52
1991	Augusta	A	11	11	1	0	60.2	269	50	28	19	0	3	1	5	35	1	52	3	0	5	4	.556	0	0	2.82
	Salem	A	2	2	0	0	13	57	14	8	7	0	0	0	0	2	0	5	4	1	1	0	1.000	0	0	4.85
	Carolina	AA	9	9	1	0	55.2	223	39	21	14	2	1	1	4	19	0	46	5	0	3	3	.500	1	0	2.26
1992	Carolina	AA	6	6	0	0	36	143	31	13	12	1	0	1	3	12	1	38	1	0	2	2	.500	0	0	3.00
	Buffalo	AAA	13	13	0	0	74.1	325	71	35	31	2	5	3	4	36	2	52	5	1	6	3	.667	0	0	3.75
1992	Pittsburgh	NL	11	0	0	8	23	91	22	9	9	2	0	0	4	4	1	10	0	0	2	0	1.000	0	1	3.52
1993	Pittsburgh	NL	32	32	3	0	210.2	882	207	101	91	22	13	6	3	59	4	132	3	3	10	10	.500	1	0	3.89
	2 ML YEARS		43	32	3	8	233.2	973	229	110	100	24	13	6	3	63	5	142	3	3	12	10	.545	1	1	3.85

Scott Cooper

Bats: Left **Throws:** Right **Pos:** 3B **Ht:** 6' 3" **Wt:** 205 **Born:** 10/13/67 **Age:** 26

Year Team	Lg	G	AB	H	2B	3B	HR	(Hm	Rd)	TB	R	RBI	TBB	IBB	SO	HBP	SH	SF	SB	CS	SB%	GDP	Avg	OBP	SLG
1990 Boston	AL	2	1	0	0	0	0	(0	0)	0	0	0	0	0	1	0	0	0	0	0	.00	0	.000	.000	.000
1991 Boston	AL	14	35	16	4	2	0	(0	0)	24	6	7	2	0	2	0	0	0	0	0	.00	0	.457	.486	.686
1992 Boston	AL	123	337	93	21	0	5	(2	3)	129	34	33	37	0	33	0	2	2	1	1	.50	5	.276	.346	.383
1993 Boston	AL	156	526	147	29	3	9	(3	6)	209	67	63	58	15	81	5	4	3	5	2	.71	8	.279	.355	.397
4 ML YEARS		295	899	256	54	5	14	(5	9)	362	107	103	97	15	117	5	6	5	6	3	.67	13	.285	.356	.403

Joey Cora

Bats: Both **Throws:** Right **Pos:** 2B **Ht:** 5' 8" **Wt:** 155 **Born:** 05/14/65 **Age:** 29

Year Team	Lg	G	AB	H	2B	3B	HR	(Hm	Rd)	TB	R	RBI	TBB	IBB	SO	HBP	SH	SF	SB	CS	SB%	GDP	Avg	OBP	SLG
1987 San Diego	NL	77	241	57	7	2	0	(0	0)	68	23	13	28	1	26	1	5	1	15	11	.58	4	.237	.317	.282
1989 San Diego	NL	12	19	6	1	0	0	(0	0)	7	5	1	1	0	0	0	0	0	1	0	1.00	0	.316	.350	.368
1990 San Diego	NL	51	100	27	3	0	0	(0	0)	30	12	2	6	1	9	0	0	0	8	3	.73	1	.270	.311	.300
1991 Chicago	AL	100	228	55	2	3	0	(0	0)	63	37	18	20	0	21	5	8	3	11	6	.65	1	.241	.313	.276
1992 Chicago	AL	68	122	30	7	1	0	(0	0)	39	27	9	22	1	13	4	2	3	10	3	.77	2	.246	.371	.320
1993 Chicago	AL	153	579	155	15	13	2	(0	2)	202	95	51	67	0	63	9	19	4	20	8	.71	14	.268	.351	.349
6 ML YEARS		461	1289	330	35	19	2	(0	2)	409	199	94	144	3	132	19	34	11	65	31	.68	22	.256	.337	.317

Wil Cordero

Bats: Right **Throws:** Right **Pos:** SS **Ht:** 6' 2" **Wt:** 185 **Born:** 10/03/71 **Age:** 22

Year Team	Lg	G	AB	H	2B	3B	HR	(Hm	Rd)	TB	R	RBI	TBB	IBB	SO	HBP	SH	SF	SB	CS	SB%	GDP	Avg	OBP	SLG
1988 Jamestown	A	52	190	49	3	0	2	--	--	58	18	22	15	0	44	4	0	2	3	3	.50	2	.258	.322	.305
1989 Wst Plm Bch	A	78	289	80	12	2	6	--	--	114	37	29	33	2	58	3	1	2	2	5	.29	6	.277	.355	.394
Jacksnville	AA	39	121	26	6	1	3	--	--	43	9	17	12	0	33	0	3	1	1	2	.33	3	.215	.284	.355
1990 Jacksnville	AA	131	444	104	18	4	7	--	--	151	63	40	56	0	122	5	3	1	9	4	.69	5	.234	.326	.340
1991 Indianapols	AAA	98	360	94	16	4	11	--	--	151	48	52	26	2	89	3	0	2	8	3	.73	4	.261	.315	.419
1992 Indianapols	AAA	52	204	64	11	1	6	--	--	95	32	27	24	2	54	0	1	1	6	7	.46	7	.314	.384	.466
1992 Montreal	NL	45	126	38	4	1	2	(1	1)	50	17	8	9	0	31	1	1	0	0	0	.00	3	.302	.353	.397
1993 Montreal	NL	138	475	118	32	2	10	(8	2)	184	56	58	34	8	60	7	4	1	12	3	.80	12	.248	.308	.387
2 ML YEARS		183	601	156	36	3	12	(9	3)	234	73	66	43	8	91	8	5	1	12	3	.80	15	.260	.317	.389

Rheal Cormier

Pitches: Left **Bats:** Left **Pos:** SP/RP **Ht:** 5'10" **Wt:** 185 **Born:** 04/23/67 **Age:** 27

Year Team	Lg	G	GS	CG	GF	IP	BFP	H	R	ER	HR	SH	SF	HB	TBB	IBB	SO	WP	Bk	W	L	Pct.	ShO	Sv	ERA
1991 St. Louis	NL	11	10	2	1	67.2	281	74	35	31	5	1	3	2	8	1	38	2	1	4	5	.444	0	0	4.12
1992 St. Louis	NL	31	30	3	1	186	772	194	83	76	15	11	3	5	33	2	117	4	2	10	10	.500	0	0	3.68
1993 St. Louis	NL	38	21	1	4	145.1	619	163	80	70	18	10	4	4	27	3	75	6	0	7	6	.538	0	0	4.33
3 ML YEARS		80	61	6	6	399	1672	431	198	177	38	22	10	11	68	6	230	12	3	21	21	.500	0	0	3.99

Rod Correia

Bats: Right **Throws:** Right **Pos:** SS/2B **Ht:** 5'11" **Wt:** 180 **Born:** 09/13/67 **Age:** 26

Year Team	Lg	G	AB	H	2B	3B	HR	(Hm	Rd)	TB	R	RBI	TBB	IBB	SO	HBP	SH	SF	SB	CS	SB%	GDP	Avg	OBP	SLG
1988 Sou Oregon	A	56	207	52	7	3	1	--	--	68	23	19	18	0	42	3	1	1	6	1	.86	9	.251	.319	.329
1989 Modesto	A	107	339	71	9	3	0	--	--	86	31	26	34	0	64	12	4	1	7	7	.50	10	.209	.303	.254
1990 Modesto	A	87	246	60	6	3	0	--	--	72	27	16	22	0	41	4	5	1	4	6	.40	6	.244	.315	.293
1991 Modesto	A	5	19	5	0	0	0	--	--	5	8	3	2	0	1	0	1	0	1	0	1.00	1	.263	.333	.263
Tacoma	AAA	17	56	14	0	0	1	--	--	17	9	7	4	0	6	1	3	0	0	0	.00	1	.250	.311	.304
Huntsville	AA	87	290	64	10	1	1	--	--	79	25	22	31	0	50	6	8	1	2	4	.33	11	.221	.308	.272
1992 Midland	AA	123	482	140	23	1	6	--	--	183	73	56	28	2	72	8	5	6	20	11	.65	14	.290	.336	.380
1993 Vancouver	AAA	60	207	56	10	4	4	--	--	86	43	28	15	1	25	1	3	5	11	4	.73	5	.271	.316	.415
1993 California	AL	64	128	34	5	0	0	(0	0)	39	12	9	20	1	20	4	5	0	2	4	.33	1	.266	.319	.305

Jim Corsi

Pitches: Right **Bats:** Right **Pos:** RP **Ht:** 6' 1" **Wt:** 220 **Born:** 09/09/61 **Age:** 32

Year Team	Lg	G	GS	CG	GF	IP	BFP	H	R	ER	HR	SH	SF	HB	TBB	IBB	SO	WP	Bk	W	L	Pct.	ShO	Sv	ERA
1993 High Desert *	A	3	3	0	0	9	38	11	3	3	1	0	0	0	2	0	6	0	0	0	1	.000	0	0	3.00
1988 Oakland	AL	11	1	0	7	21.1	89	20	10	9	1	3	3	0	6	1	10	1	1	0	1	.000	0	0	3.80
1989 Oakland	AL	22	0	0	14	38.1	149	26	8	8	2	2	1	0	10	0	21	0	0	1	2	.333	0	0	1.88

Year	Team	Lg	G	GS	CG	GF	IP	BFP	H	R	ER	HR	SH	SF	HB	TBB	IBB	SO	WP	Bk	W	L	Pct.	ShO	Sv	ERA
1991	Houston	NL	47	0	0	15	77.2	322	76	37	32	6	3	2	0	23	5	53	1	1	0	5	.000	0	0	3.71
1992	Oakland	AL	32	0	0	16	44	185	44	12	7	2	4	2	0	18	2	19	0	0	4	2	.667	0	0	1.43
1993	Florida	NL	15	0	0	6	20.1	97	28	15	15	1	3	1	0	10	3	7	0	0	0	2	.000	0	0	6.64
5 ML YEARS			127	1	0	58	201.2	842	194	82	71	12	15	10	1	67	11	110	2	2	5	12	.294	0	0	3.17

Tim Costo

Bats: Right **Throws:** Right **Pos:** RF/LF   **Ht:** 6' 5" **Wt:** 230 **Born:** 02/16/69 **Age:** 25

						BATTING													BASERUNNING				PERCENTAGES		
Year	Team	Lg	G	AB	H	2B	3B	HR	(Hm | Rd)	TB	R	RBI	TBB	IBB	SO	HBP	SH	SF	SB	CS	SB%	GDP	Avg	OBP	SLG
1990	Kinston	A	56	206	65	13	1	4	--	--	92	34	42	23	0	47	6	0	8	4	0	1.00	3	.316	.387	.447
1991	Canton-Akrn	AA	52	192	52	10	3	1	--	--	71	28	24	15	0	44	0	0	6	2	1	.67	10	.271	.315	.370
	Chattanooga	AA	85	293	82	19	3	5	--	--	122	31	29	20	0	65	4	0	2	11	4	.73	5	.280	.332	.416
1992	Chattanooga	AA	121	424	102	18	2	28	--	--	208	63	71	48	1	128	11	1	2	4	5	.44	10	.241	.332	.491
1993	Indianapols	AAA	106	362	118	30	2	11	--	--	185	49	57	22	1	60	5	1	1	3	2	.60	5	.326	.372	.511
1992	Cincinnati	NL	12	36	8	2	0	0	(0 | 0)	10	3	2	5	0	6	0	0	1	0	0	.00	4	.222	.310	.278
1993	Cincinnati	NL	31	98	22	5	0	3	(0 | 3)	36	13	12	4	0	17	0	0	2	0	0	.00	1	.224	.250	.367
2 ML YEARS			43	134	30	7	0	3	(0 | 3)	46	16	14	9	0	23	0	0	3	0	0	.00	5	.224	.267	.343

Henry Cotto

Bats: Right **Throws:** Right **Pos:** LF/CF/RF/DH   **Ht:** 6' 2" **Wt:** 180 **Born:** 01/05/61 **Age:** 33

						BATTING													BASERUNNING				PERCENTAGES		
Year	Team	Lg	G	AB	H	2B	3B	HR	(Hm | Rd)	TB	R	RBI	TBB	IBB	SO	HBP	SH	SF	SB	CS	SB%	GDP	Avg	OBP	SLG
1984	Chicago	NL	105	146	40	5	0	0	(0 | 0)	45	24	8	10	2	23	1	3	0	9	3	.75	1	.274	.325	.308
1985	New York	AL	34	56	17	1	0	1	(0 | 1)	21	4	6	3	0	12	0	1	0	1	1	.50	1	.304	.339	.375
1986	New York	AL	35	80	17	3	0	1	(0 | 1)	23	11	6	2	0	17	0	0	1	3	0	1.00	3	.213	.229	.288
1987	New York	AL	68	149	35	10	0	5	(5 | 0)	60	21	20	6	0	35	1	0	0	4	2	.67	7	.235	.269	.403
1988	Seattle	AL	133	386	100	18	1	8	(5 | 3)	144	50	33	23	0	53	2	4	3	27	3	.90	8	.259	.302	.373
1989	Seattle	AL	100	295	78	11	2	9	(5 | 4)	120	44	33	12	3	44	3	0	0	10	4	.71	4	.264	.300	.407
1990	Seattle	AL	127	355	92	14	3	4	(2 | 2)	124	40	33	22	2	52	4	6	3	21	3	.88	13	.259	.307	.349
1991	Seattle	AL	66	177	54	6	2	6	(2 | 4)	82	35	23	10	0	27	2	2	1	16	3	.84	7	.305	.347	.463
1992	Seattle	AL	108	294	76	11	1	5	(2 | 3)	104	42	27	14	3	49	1	3	1	23	2	.92	2	.259	.294	.354
1993	2 ML Teams		108	240	60	8	0	5	(1 | 4)	83	25	21	5	0	40	2	2	2	16	5	.76	3	.250	.269	.346
1993	Seattle	AL	54	105	20	1	0	2	(0 | 2)	27	10	7	2	0	22	1	1	0	5	4	.56	0	.190	.213	.257
	Florida	NL	54	135	40	7	0	3	(1 | 2)	56	15	14	3	0	18	1	1	2	11	1	.92	3	.296	.312	.415
10 ML YEARS			884	2178	569	87	9	44	(22 | 22)	806	296	210	107	10	352	16	21	11	130	26	.83	49	.261	.299	.370

Danny Cox

Pitches: Right **Bats:** Right **Pos:** RP   **Ht:** 6' 4" **Wt:** 225 **Born:** 09/21/59 **Age:** 34

			HOW MUCH HE PITCHED						WHAT HE GAVE UP											THE RESULTS					
Year	Team	Lg	G	GS	CG	GF	IP	BFP	H	R	ER	HR	SH	SF	HB	TBB	IBB	SO	WP	Bk	W	L	Pct.	ShO	Sv	ERA
1983	St. Louis	NL	12	12	0	0	83	352	92	38	30	6	6	1	0	23	2	36	2	0	3	6	.333	0	0	3.25
1984	St. Louis	NL	29	27	1	0	156.1	668	171	81	70	9	10	5	7	54	6	70	2	4	9	11	.450	1	0	4.03
1985	St. Louis	NL	35	35	10	0	241	989	226	91	77	19	12	9	3	64	5	131	3	1	18	9	.667	4	0	2.88
1986	St. Louis	NL	32	32	8	0	220	881	189	85	71	14	8	3	2	60	6	108	3	4	12	13	.480	0	0	2.90
1987	St. Louis	NL	31	31	2	0	199.1	864	224	99	86	17	14	4	3	71	6	101	5	1	11	9	.550	0	0	3.88
1988	St. Louis	NL	13	13	0	0	86	361	89	40	38	6	5	3	1	25	7	47	4	3	3	8	.273	0	0	3.98
1991	Philadelphia	NL	23	17	0	2	102.1	433	98	57	52	14	6	7	1	39	2	46	7	1	4	6	.400	0	0	4.57
1992	2 ML Teams		25	7	0	8	62.2	278	66	37	32	5	5	3	0	27	2	48	1	0	5	3	.625	0	3	4.60
1993	Toronto	AL	44	0	0	13	83.2	348	73	31	29	8	0	1	0	29	5	84	5	0	7	6	.538	0	2	3.12
1992	Philadelphia	NL	9	7	0	0	38.1	178	46	28	23	3	3	2	0	19	1	30	0	0	2	2	.500	0	0	5.40
	Pittsburgh	NL	16	0	0	8	24.1	100	20	9	9	2	2	1	0	8	1	18	1	0	3	1	.750	0	3	3.33
9 ML YEARS			244	174	21	23	1234.1	5174	1228	559	485	98	66	36	17	392	41	671	32	14	72	71	.503	5	5	3.54

Chuck Crim

Pitches: Right **Bats:** Right **Pos:** RP   **Ht:** 6' 0" **Wt:** 185 **Born:** 07/23/61 **Age:** 32

			HOW MUCH HE PITCHED						WHAT HE GAVE UP											THE RESULTS					
Year	Team	Lg	G	GS	CG	GF	IP	BFP	H	R	ER	HR	SH	SF	HB	TBB	IBB	SO	WP	Bk	W	L	Pct.	ShO	Sv	ERA
1987	Milwaukee	AL	53	5	0	18	130	549	133	60	53	15	6	1	3	39	5	56	2	1	6	8	.429	0	12	3.67
1988	Milwaukee	AL	70	0	0	25	105	425	95	38	34	11	5	6	2	28	3	58	9	2	7	6	.538	0	9	2.91
1989	Milwaukee	AL	76	0	0	31	117.2	487	114	42	37	7	3	6	2	36	9	59	5	0	9	7	.563	0	7	2.83
1990	Milwaukee	AL	67	0	0	25	85.2	367	88	39	33	7	1	4	2	23	4	39	0	1	3	5	.375	0	11	3.47
1991	Milwaukee	AL	66	0	0	29	91.1	408	115	52	47	9	3	1	2	25	9	39	3	3	8	5	.615	0	3	4.63
1992	California	AL	57	0	0	16	87	383	100	56	50	11	3	4	6	29	6	30	4	0	7	6	.538	0	1	5.17
1993	California	AL	11	0	0	3	15.1	67	17	11	10	2	2	1	2	5	1	10	0	0	2	2	.500	0	0	5.87
7 ML YEARS			400	5	0	147	632	2686	662	298	264	62	23	23	19	185	37	291	23	7	42	39	.519	0	43	3.76

Tripp Cromer

Bats: Right **Throws:** Right **Pos:** SS 　　　　　　　**Ht:** 6' 2" **Wt:** 165 **Born:** 11/21/67 **Age:** 26

Year	Team	Lg	G	AB	H	2B	3B	HR	(Hm	Rd)	TB	R	RBI	TBB	IBB	SO	HBP	SH	SF	SB	CS	SB%	GDP	Avg	OBP	SLG
1989	Hamilton	A	35	137	36	6	3	0	--	--	48	18	6	17	0	30	1	2	1	4	4	.50	5	.263	.346	.350
1990	St. Pete	A	121	408	88	12	5	5	--	--	125	53	38	46	0	79	5	3	5	7	12	.37	11	.216	.300	.306
1991	St. Pete	A	43	137	28	3	1	0	--	--	33	11	10	9	0	17	1	3	1	0	0	.00	8	.204	.257	.241
	Arkansas	AA	73	227	52	12	1	1	--	--	69	28	18	15	1	37	3	2	3	0	1	.00	7	.229	.282	.304
1992	Arkansas	AA	110	339	81	16	6	7	--	--	130	30	29	22	1	82	4	4	2	4	6	.40	9	.239	.292	.383
	Louisville	AAA	6	25	5	1	1	1	--	--	11	5	7	1	0	6	0	0	1	0	0	.00	0	.200	.222	.440
1993	Louisville	AAA	86	309	85	8	4	11	--	--	134	39	33	15	3	60	2	2	0	1	3	.25	10	.275	.313	.434
1993	St. Louis	NL	10	23	2	0	0	0	(0	0)	2	1	0	1	0	6	0	0	0	0	0	.00	0	.087	.125	.087

John Cummings

Pitches: Left **Bats:** Left **Pos:** SP 　　　　　　　**Ht:** 6' 3" **Wt:** 200 **Born:** 05/10/69 **Age:** 25

Year	Team	Lg	G	GS	CG	GF	IP	BFP	H	R	ER	HR	SH	SF	HB	TBB	IBB	SO	WP	Bk	W	L	Pct.	ShO	Sv	ERA
1990	Bellingham	A	6	6	0	0	34	129	25	11	8	1	1	1	0	8	0	39	2	3	1	1	.500	0	0	2.12
	San Berndno	A	7	7	1	0	40.2	186	47	27	19	3	0	1	0	20	0	30	3	0	2	4	.333	0	0	4.20
1991	San Berndno	A	29	20	0	2	124	567	129	79	56	7	1	6	3	61	1	120	15	4	4	10	.286	0	1	4.06
1992	Peninsula	A	27	27	4	0	168.1	712	149	71	48	11	7	5	10	63	6	144	4	1	16	6	.727	1	0	2.57
1993	Jacksnville	AA	7	7	1	0	45.2	194	50	24	16	1	2	0	1	9	0	35	1	2	2	2	.500	0	0	3.15
	Calgary	AAA	11	10	0	0	65.1	280	69	40	30	6	0	1	2	28	2	42	7	0	3	4	.429	0	0	4.13
1993	Seattle	AL	10	8	1	0	46.1	207	59	34	31	6	0	2	2	16	2	19	1	1	0	6	.000	0	0	6.02

Midre Cummings

Bats: Left **Throws:** Right **Pos:** LF 　　　　　　　**Ht:** 6' 1" **Wt:** 190 **Born:** 10/14/71 **Age:** 22

Year	Team	Lg	G	AB	H	2B	3B	HR	(Hm	Rd)	TB	R	RBI	TBB	IBB	SO	HBP	SH	SF	SB	CS	SB%	GDP	Avg	OBP	SLG
1990	Twins	R	47	177	56	3	4	5	--	--	82	28	28	13	1	32	2	0	4	13	9	.59	1	.316	.362	.463
1991	Kenosha	A	106	382	123	20	4	4	--	--	163	59	54	22	2	66	6	4	2	28	10	.74	7	.322	.367	.427
1992	Salem	A	113	420	128	20	5	14	--	--	200	55	75	35	2	67	4	0	3	23	9	.72	2	.305	.361	.476
1993	Carolina	AA	63	237	70	17	2	6	--	--	109	33	26	14	1	23	1	2	0	5	3	.63	3	.295	.337	.460
	Buffalo	AAA	60	232	64	12	1	9	--	--	105	36	21	22	4	45	0	0	2	5	1	.83	4	.276	.336	.453
1993	Pittsburgh	NL	13	36	4	1	0	0	(0	0)	5	5	3	4	0	9	0	0	1	0	0	.00	1	.111	.195	.139

Chad Curtis

Bats: Right **Throws:** Right **Pos:** CF 　　　　　　　**Ht:** 5'10" **Wt:** 175 **Born:** 11/06/68 **Age:** 25

Year	Team	Lg	G	AB	H	2B	3B	HR	(Hm	Rd)	TB	R	RBI	TBB	IBB	SO	HBP	SH	SF	SB	CS	SB%	GDP	Avg	OBP	SLG
1989	Angels	R	32	122	37	4	4	3	--	--	58	30	20	14	2	20	2	1	2	17	2	.89	3	.303	.379	.475
	Quad City	A	23	78	19	3	0	2	--	--	28	7	11	6	0	17	0	1	1	7	5	.58	1	.244	.294	.359
1990	Quad City	A	135	492	151	28	1	14	--	--	223	87	65	57	3	76	12	4	3	63	21	.75	8	.307	.390	.453
1991	Edmonton	AAA	115	431	136	28	7	9	--	--	205	81	61	51	1	58	3	4	4	46	11	.81	10	.316	.389	.476
1992	California	AL	139	441	114	16	2	10	(5	5)	164	59	46	51	2	71	6	5	4	43	18	.70	10	.259	.341	.372
1993	California	AL	152	583	166	25	3	6	(3	3)	215	94	59	70	2	89	4	7	7	48	24	.67	16	.285	.361	.369
	2 ML YEARS		291	1024	280	41	5	16	(8	8)	379	153	105	121	4	160	10	12	11	91	42	.68	26	.273	.352	.370

Milt Cuyler

Bats: Both **Throws:** Right **Pos:** CF 　　　　　　　**Ht:** 5'10" **Wt:** 185 **Born:** 10/07/68 **Age:** 25

Year	Team	Lg	G	AB	H	2B	3B	HR	(Hm	Rd)	TB	R	RBI	TBB	IBB	SO	HBP	SH	SF	SB	CS	SB%	GDP	Avg	OBP	SLG
1990	Detroit	AL	19	51	13	3	1	0	(0	0)	18	8	8	5	0	10	0	2	1	1	2	.33	1	.255	.316	.353
1991	Detroit	AL	154	475	122	15	7	3	(1	2)	160	77	33	52	0	92	5	12	2	41	10	.80	4	.257	.335	.337
1992	Detroit	AL	89	291	70	11	1	3	(1	2)	92	39	28	10	0	62	4	8	0	8	5	.62	4	.241	.275	.316
1993	Detroit	AL	82	249	53	11	4	0	(0	0)	78	46	19	19	0	53	3	4	1	13	2	.87	2	.213	.276	.313
	4 ML YEARS		344	1066	258	40	16	6	(2	4)	348	170	88	86	0	217	12	26	4	63	19	.77	11	.242	.305	.326

Omar Daal

Pitches: Left **Bats:** Left **Pos:** RP 　　　　　　　**Ht:** 6' 3" **Wt:** 160 **Born:** 03/01/72 **Age:** 22

Year	Team	Lg	G	GS	CG	GF	IP	BFP	H	R	ER	HR	SH	SF	HB	TBB	IBB	SO	WP	Bk	W	L	Pct.	ShO	Sv	ERA
1992	Albuquerque	AAA	12	0	0	4	10.1	54	14	9	9	1	2	0	0	11	1	9	0	2	0	2	.000	0	0	7.84
	San Antonio	AA	35	5	0	16	57.1	257	60	39	32	3	6	2	4	33	1	52	7	3	2	6	.250	0	5	5.02
1993	Albuquerque	AAA	6	0	0	4	5.1	23	5	2	2	1	0	0	0	3	1	2	0	0	1	1	.500	0	0	3.38
1993	Los Angeles	NL	47	0	0	12	35.1	155	36	20	20	5	2	2	0	21	3	19	1	2	2	3	.400	0	0	5.09

Ron Darling

Pitches: Right **Bats:** Right **Pos:** SP   **Ht:** 6' 3" **Wt:** 195 **Born:** 08/19/60 **Age:** 33

Year Team	Lg	G	GS	CG	GF	IP	BFP	H	R	ER	HR	SH	SF	HB	TBB	IBB	SO	WP	Bk	W	L	Pct.	ShO	Sv	ERA
1983 New York	NL	5	5	1	0	35.1	148	31	11	11	0	3	0	3	17	1	23	3	2	1	3	.250	0	0	2.80
1984 New York	NL	33	33	2	0	205.2	884	179	97	87	17	7	6	5	104	2	136	7	1	12	9	.571	2	0	3.81
1985 New York	NL	36	35	4	1	248	1043	214	93	80	21	13	4	3	114	1	167	7	1	16	6	.727	2	0	2.90
1986 New York	NL	34	34	4	0	237	967	203	84	74	21	10	6	3	81	2	184	7	3	15	6	.714	2	0	2.81
1987 New York	NL	32	32	2	0	207.2	891	183	111	99	24	5	3	3	96	3	167	6	3	12	8	.600	0	0	4.29
1988 New York	NL	34	34	7	0	240.2	971	218	97	87	24	10	8	5	60	2	161	7	2	17	9	.654	4	0	3.25
1989 New York	NL	33	33	4	0	217.1	922	214	100	85	19	7	13	3	70	7	153	12	4	14	14	.500	0	0	3.52
1990 New York	NL	33	18	1	3	126	554	135	73	63	20	7	3	5	44	4	99	5	1	7	9	.438	0	0	4.50
1991 3 ML Teams		32	32	0	0	194.1	827	185	100	92	22	12	8	9	71	3	129	16	5	8	15	.348	0	0	4.26
1992 Oakland	AL	33	33	4	0	206.1	866	198	98	84	15	4	3	4	72	5	99	13	0	15	10	.600	3	0	3.66
1993 Oakland	AL	31	29	3	1	178	793	198	107	102	22	5	6	5	72	5	95	3	1	5	9	.357	0	0	5.16
1991 New York	NL	17	17	0	0	102.1	427	96	50	44	9	7	4	6	28	1	58	9	4	5	6	.455	0	0	3.87
Montreal	NL	3	3	0	0	17	81	25	16	14	6	0	0	1	5	0	11	4	0	0	2	.000	0	0	7.41
Oakland	AL	12	12	0	0	75	319	64	34	34	7	5	4	2	38	2	60	3	1	3	7	.300	0	0	4.08
11 ML YEARS		336	318	32	5	2096.1	8866	1958	971	864	205	83	60	48	801	35	1413	86	23	122	98	.555	13	0	3.71

Danny Darwin

Pitches: Right **Bats:** Right **Pos:** SP   **Ht:** 6' 3" **Wt:** 195 **Born:** 10/25/55 **Age:** 38

Year Team	Lg	G	GS	CG	GF	IP	BFP	H	R	ER	HR	SH	SF	HB	TBB	IBB	SO	WP	Bk	W	L	Pct.	ShO	Sv	ERA
1978 Texas	AL	3	1	0	2	9	36	11	4	4	0	0	1	0	1	0	8	0	0	1	0	1.000	0	0	4.00
1979 Texas	AL	20	6	1	4	78	313	50	36	35	5	3	6	5	30	2	58	0	1	4	4	.500	0	0	4.04
1980 Texas	AL	53	2	0	35	110	468	98	37	32	4	5	7	2	50	7	104	3	0	13	4	.765	0	8	2.62
1981 Texas	AL	22	22	6	0	146	601	115	67	59	12	8	3	6	57	5	98	1	0	9	9	.500	2	0	3.64
1982 Texas	AL	56	1	0	41	89	394	95	38	34	6	10	5	2	37	8	61	2	1	10	8	.556	0	7	3.44
1983 Texas	AL	28	26	9	0	183	780	175	86	71	9	7	7	3	62	3	92	2	0	8	13	.381	2	0	3.49
1984 Texas	AL	35	32	5	2	223.2	955	249	110	98	19	3	3	4	54	2	123	3	0	8	12	.400	1	0	3.94
1985 Milwaukee	AL	39	29	11	8	217.2	919	212	112	92	34	7	9	4	65	4	125	6	0	8	18	.308	1	2	3.80
1986 2 ML Teams		39	22	6	6	184.2	759	170	81	65	16	6	9	3	44	1	120	7	1	11	10	.524	1	0	3.17
1987 Houston	NL	33	30	3	0	195.2	833	184	87	78	17	8	3	5	69	12	134	3	1	9	10	.474	1	0	3.59
1988 Houston	NL	44	20	3	9	192	804	189	86	82	20	10	9	7	48	9	129	1	2	8	13	.381	0	3	3.84
1989 Houston	NL	68	0	0	26	122	482	92	34	32	8	8	5	2	33	9	104	2	3	11	4	.733	0	7	2.36
1990 Houston	NL	48	17	3	14	162.2	646	136	42	40	11	4	2	4	31	4	109	0	2	11	4	.733	0	2	2.21
1991 Boston	AL	12	12	0	0	68	292	71	39	39	15	1	2	4	15	1	42	2	0	3	6	.333	0	0	5.16
1992 Boston	AL	51	15	2	21	161.1	688	159	76	71	11	7	5	5	53	9	124	5	0	9	9	.500	0	3	3.96
1993 Boston	AL	34	34	2	0	229.1	919	196	93	83	31	6	9	3	49	8	130	5	1	15	11	.577	1	0	3.26
1986 Milwaukee	AL	27	14	5	4	130.1	537	120	62	51	13	5	6	3	35	1	80	5	0	6	8	.429	1	0	3.52
Houston	NL	12	8	1	2	54.1	222	50	19	14	3	1	3	0	9	0	40	2	1	5	2	.714	0	0	2.32
16 ML YEARS		585	269	51	168	2372	9889	2202	1028	915	218	93	85	59	698	84	1561	42	12	138	135	.505	9	32	3.47

Doug Dascenzo

Bats: Both **Throws:** Left **Pos:** CF/LF/RF   **Ht:** 5' 8" **Wt:** 160 **Born:** 06/30/64 **Age:** 30

Year Team	Lg	G	AB	H	2B	3B	HR	(Hm	Rd)	TB	R	RBI	TBB	IBB	SO	HBP	SH	SF	SB	CS	SB%	GDP	Avg	OBP	SLG
1993 Okla City *	AAA	38	157	39	8	2	1	(--	--)	54	21	13	16	0	16	0	2	1	6	5	.55	7	.248	.316	.344
1988 Chicago	NL	26	75	16	3	0	0	(0	0)	19	9	4	9	1	4	0	1	0	6	1	.86	2	.213	.298	.253
1989 Chicago	NL	47	139	23	1	0	0	(0	1)	27	20	12	13	0	13	0	3	2	6	3	.67	2	.165	.234	.194
1990 Chicago	NL	113	241	61	9	5	1	(1	0)	83	27	26	21	2	18	1	5	3	15	6	.71	3	.253	.312	.344
1991 Chicago	NL	118	239	61	11	0	1	(0	1)	75	40	18	24	2	26	2	6	1	14	7	.67	3	.255	.327	.314
1992 Chicago	NL	139	376	96	13	4	0	(0	0)	117	37	20	27	2	32	0	4	2	6	8	.43	3	.255	.304	.311
1993 Texas	AL	76	146	29	5	1	2	(0	2)	42	20	10	8	0	22	0	3	1	2	0	1.00	1	.199	.239	.288
6 ML YEARS		519	1216	286	42	10	5	(1	4)	363	153	90	102	7	115	3	22	9	49	25	.66	14	.235	.294	.299

Jack Daugherty

Bats: Both **Throws:** Left **Pos:** LF   **Ht:** 6' 0" **Wt:** 190 **Born:** 07/03/60 **Age:** 33

Year Team	Lg	G	AB	H	2B	3B	HR	(Hm	Rd)	TB	R	RBI	TBB	IBB	SO	HBP	SH	SF	SB	CS	SB%	GDP	Avg	OBP	SLG
1993 Tucson *	AAA	42	141	55	9	2	2	(--	--)	74	23	29	26	2	12	3	0	1	1	0	1.00		.390	.488	.525
1987 Montreal	NL	11	10	1	1	0	0	(0	0)	2	1	1	0	0	3	0	2	0	0	0	.00	0	.100	.100	.200
1989 Texas	AL	52	106	32	4	2	1	(1	0)	43	15	10	11	0	21	1	0	0	2	1	.67		.302	.364	.406
1990 Texas	AL	125	310	93	20	2	6	(5	1)	135	36	47	22	0	49	2	2	3	0	0	.00	4	.300	.347	.435
1991 Texas	AL	58	144	28	3	2	1	(0	1)	38	8	11	16	1	23	0	4	3	1	0	1.00	2	.194	.270	.264

								(Hm	Rd)																
1992 Texas	AL	59	127	26	9	0	0	(0	0)	35	13	9	16	1	21	1	0	2	2	1	.67	3	.205	.295	.276
1993 2 ML Teams		50	62	14	2	0	2	(2	0)	22	7	9	11	0	15	0	0	1	0	0	.00	0	.226	.338	.355
1993 Houston	NL	4	3	1	0	0	0	(0	0)	1	0	0	0	0	0	0	0	0	0	0	.00	0	.333	.333	.333
Cincinnati	NL	46	59	13	2	0	2	(2	0)	21	7	9	11	0	15	0	0	1	0	0	.00	0	.220	.338	.356
6 ML YEARS		355	759	194	39	6	10	(8	2)	275	80	87	76	2	132	4	8	12	5	2	.71	10	.256	.322	.362

Darren Daulton

Bats: Left   **Throws:** Right   **Pos:** C   **Ht:** 6' 2"   **Wt:** 201   **Born:** 01/03/62   **Age:** 32

		BATTING																	BASERUNNING				PERCENTAGES		
Year Team	Lg	G	AB	H	2B	3B	HR	(Hm	Rd)	TB	R	RBI	TBB	IBB	SO	HBP	SH	SF	SB	CS	SB%	GDP	Avg	OBP	SLG
1983 Philadelphia	NL	2	3	1	0	0	0	(0	0)	1	1	0	1	0	1	0	0	0	0	0	.00	0	.333	.500	.333
1985 Philadelphia	NL	36	103	21	3	1	4	(0	4)	38	14	11	16	0	37	0	0	0	3	0	1.00	1	.204	.311	.369
1986 Philadelphia	NL	49	138	31	4	0	8	(4	4)	59	18	21	38	3	41	1	2	2	2	3	.40	1	.225	.391	.428
1987 Philadelphia	NL	53	129	25	6	0	3	(1	2)	40	10	13	16	1	37	0	4	1	0	0	.00	0	.194	.281	.310
1988 Philadelphia	NL	58	144	30	6	0	1	(0	1)	39	13	12	17	1	26	0	0	2	2	1	.67	2	.208	.288	.271
1989 Philadelphia	NL	131	368	74	12	2	8	(2	6)	114	29	44	52	8	58	2	1	1	2	1	.67	4	.201	.303	.310
1990 Philadelphia	NL	143	459	123	30	1	12	(5	7)	191	62	57	72	9	72	2	3	4	7	1	.88	6	.268	.367	.416
1991 Philadelphia	NL	89	285	56	12	0	12	(8	4)	104	36	42	41	4	66	2	2	5	5	0	1.00	4	.196	.297	.365
1992 Philadelphia	NL	145	485	131	32	5	27	(17	10)	254	80	**109**	88	11	103	6	0	6	11	2	.85	3	.270	.385	.524
1993 Philadelphia	NL	147	510	131	35	4	24	(10	14)	246	90	105	117	12	111	2	0	8	5	0	1.00	2	.257	.392	.482
10 ML YEARS		853	2624	623	140	13	99	(47	52)	1086	353	414	458	49	552	15	12	29	37	8	.82	23	.237	.351	.414

Butch Davis

Bats: Right   **Throws:** Right   **Pos:** LF/RF   **Ht:** 6' 0"   **Wt:** 193   **Born:** 06/19/58   **Age:** 36

		BATTING																	BASERUNNING				PERCENTAGES		
Year Team	Lg	G	AB	H	2B	3B	HR	(Hm	Rd)	TB	R	RBI	TBB	IBB	SO	HBP	SH	SF	SB	CS	SB%	GDP	Avg	OBP	SLG
1983 Kansas City	AL	33	122	42	2	6	2	(0	2)	62	13	18	4	0	19	0	2	2	4	3	.57	3	.344	.359	.508
1984 Kansas City	AL	41	116	17	3	0	2	(1	1)	26	11	12	10	0	19	0	0	2	4	3	.57	2	.147	.211	.224
1987 Pittsburgh	NL	7	7	1	1	0	0	(0	0)	2	3	0	1	0	3	0	0	0	0	0	.00	0	.143	.250	.286
1988 Baltimore	AL	13	25	6	1	0	0	(0	0)	7	2	0	0	0	8	0	0	0	1	0	1.00	0	.240	.240	.280
1989 Baltimore	AL	5	6	1	1	0	0	(0	0)	2	1	0	0	0	3	0	0	0	0	0	.00	0	.167	.167	.333
1991 Los Angeles	NL	1	1	0	0	0	0	(0	0)	0	0	0	0	0	0	0	0	0	0	0	.00	0	.000	.000	.000
1993 Texas	AL	62	159	39	10	4	3	(0	3)	66	24	20	5	1	28	1	5	0	3	1	.75	0	.245	.273	.415
7 ML YEARS		162	436	106	18	10	7	(1	6)	165	54	50	20	1	80	1	7	4	12	7	.63	7	.243	.275	.378

Chili Davis

Bats: Both   **Throws:** Right   **Pos:** DH   **Ht:** 6' 3"   **Wt:** 217   **Born:** 01/17/60   **Age:** 34

		BATTING																	BASERUNNING				PERCENTAGES		
Year Team	Lg	G	AB	H	2B	3B	HR	(Hm	Rd)	TB	R	RBI	TBB	IBB	SO	HBP	SH	SF	SB	CS	SB%	GDP	Avg	OBP	SLG
1981 San Francisco	NL	8	15	2	0	0	0	(0	0)	2	1	0	1	0	2	0	0	0	2	0	1.00	1	.133	.188	.133
1982 San Francisco	NL	154	641	167	27	6	19	(6	13)	263	86	76	45	2	115	2	7	6	24	13	.65	13	.261	.308	.410
1983 San Francisco	NL	137	486	113	21	2	11	(7	4)	171	54	59	55	6	108	0	3	9	10	12	.45	9	.233	.305	.352
1984 San Francisco	NL	137	499	157	21	6	21	(7	14)	253	87	81	42	6	74	1	2	2	12	8	.60	13	.315	.368	.507
1985 San Francisco	NL	136	481	130	25	2	13	(7	6)	198	53	56	62	12	74	0	1	7	15	7	.68	16	.270	.349	.412
1986 San Francisco	NL	153	526	146	28	3	13	(7	6)	219	71	70	84	23	96	1	2	5	16	13	.55	11	.278	.375	.416
1987 San Francisco	NL	149	500	125	22	1	24	(9	15)	221	80	76	72	15	109	2	0	4	16	9	.64	8	.250	.344	.442
1988 California	AL	158	600	161	29	3	21	(11	10)	259	81	93	56	14	118	0	1	**10**	9	10	.47	13	.268	.326	.432
1989 California	AL	154	560	152	24	1	22	(6	16)	244	81	90	61	12	109	0	3	6	3	0	1.00	21	.271	.340	.436
1990 California	AL	113	412	109	17	1	12	(10	2)	164	58	58	61	4	89	0	0	3	1	2	.33	14	.265	.357	.398
1991 Minnesota	AL	153	534	148	34	1	29	(14	15)	271	84	93	95	13	117	1	0	4	5	6	.45	9	.277	.385	.507
1992 Minnesota	AL	138	444	128	27	2	12	(6	6)	195	63	66	73	11	76	3	0	5	4	5	.44	11	.288	.386	.439
1993 California	AL	152	573	139	32	0	27	(13	14)	252	74	112	71	12	135	1	0	4	4	1	.80	18	.243	.327	.440
13 ML YEARS		1742	6271	1677	307	28	224	(103	121)	2712	873	930	778	130	1222	11	19	65	121	86	.58	157	.267	.346	.432

Eric Davis

Bats: Right   **Throws:** Right   **Pos:** LF/CF   **Ht:** 6' 3"   **Wt:** 185   **Born:** 05/29/62   **Age:** 32

		BATTING																	BASERUNNING				PERCENTAGES		
Year Team	Lg	G	AB	H	2B	3B	HR	(Hm	Rd)	TB	R	RBI	TBB	IBB	SO	HBP	SH	SF	SB	CS	SB%	GDP	Avg	OBP	SLG
1984 Cincinnati	NL	57	174	39	10	1	10	(3	7)	81	33	30	24	0	48	1	0	1	10	2	.83	1	.224	.320	.466
1985 Cincinnati	NL	56	122	30	3	3	8	(1	7)	63	26	18	7	0	39	0	2	0	16	3	.84	1	.246	.287	.516
1986 Cincinnati	NL	132	415	115	15	3	27	(12	15)	217	97	71	68	5	100	1	0	3	80	11	.88	6	.277	.378	.523
1987 Cincinnati	NL	129	474	139	23	4	37	(17	20)	281	120	100	84	8	134	1	0	3	50	6	.89	6	.293	.399	.593
1988 Cincinnati	NL	135	472	129	18	3	26	(14	12)	231	81	93	65	10	124	3	0	3	35	3	.92	11	.273	.363	.489
1989 Cincinnati	NL	131	462	130	14	2	34	(15	19)	250	74	101	68	12	116	1	0	11	21	7	.75	16	.281	.367	.541
1990 Cincinnati	NL	127	453	118	26	2	24	(13	11)	220	84	86	60	6	100	2	0	3	21	3	.88	7	.260	.347	.486
1991 Cincinnati	NL	89	285	67	10	0	11	(5	6)	110	39	33	48	5	92	5	0	2	14	2	.88	4	.235	.353	.386

1992 Los Angeles	NL	76	267	61	8	1	5	(1	4)	86	21	32	36	2	71	3	0	2	19	1	.95	9	.228	.325	.322
1993 2 ML Teams		131	451	107	18	1	20	(10	10)	187	71	68	55	7	106	1	0	4	35	7	.83	12	.237	.319	.415
1993 Los Angeles	NL	108	376	88	17	0	14	(7	7)	147	57	53	41	6	88	1	0	4	33	5	.87	8	.234	.308	.391
Detroit	AL	23	75	19	1	1	6	(3	3)	40	14	15	14	1	18	0	0	0	2	2	.50	4	.253	.371	.533
10 ML YEARS		1063	3575	935	145	20	202	(91	111)	1726	646	632	515	55	930	18	2	32	301	45	.87	73	.262	.355	.483

Glenn Davis

Bats: Right **Throws:** Right **Pos:** 1B   **Ht:** 6' 3" **Wt:** 212 **Born:** 03/28/61 **Age:** 33

								BATTING											BASERUNNING				PERCENTAGES		
Year Team	Lg	G	AB	H	2B	3B	HR	(Hm	Rd)	TB	R	RBI	TBB	IBB	SO	HBP	SH	SF	SB	CS	SB%	GDP	Avg	OBP	SLG
1993 Frederick *	A	3	11	3	1	0	0	--	--	4	1	2	1	0	3	0	0	0	0	0	.00	0	.273	.333	.364
Rochester *	AAA	7	24	6	1	1	0	--	--	9	2	3	2	0	8	0	0	0	0	0	.00	0	.250	.308	.375
Bowie *	AA	2	6	2	1	0	1	--	--	6	2	1	0	0	1	0	0	0	0	0	.00	0	.333	.429	1.000
1984 Houston	NL	18	61	13	5	0	2	(1	1)	24	6	8	4	0	12	0	2	1	0	0	.00	0	.213	.258	.393
1985 Houston	NL	100	350	95	11	0	20	(8	12)	166	51	64	27	6	68	7	2	4	0	0	.00	12	.271	.332	.474
1986 Houston	NL	158	574	152	32	3	31	(17	14)	283	91	101	64	6	72	9	0	7	3	1	.75	11	.265	.344	.493
1987 Houston	NL	151	578	145	35	2	27	(12	15)	265	70	93	47	10	84	5	0	5	4	1	.80	16	.251	.310	.458
1988 Houston	NL	152	561	152	26	0	30	(15	15)	268	78	99	53	20	77	11	0	9	4	3	.57	11	.271	.341	.478
1989 Houston	NL	158	581	156	26	1	34	(15	19)	286	87	89	69	17	123	7	0	6	4	2	.67	9	.269	.350	.492
1990 Houston	NL	93	327	82	15	4	22	(4	18)	171	44	64	46	17	54	8	0	0	8	3	.73	5	.251	.357	.523
1991 Baltimore	AL	49	176	40	9	1	10	(3	7)	81	29	28	16	0	29	5	0	2	4	0	1.00	2	.227	.307	.460
1992 Baltimore	AL	106	398	110	15	2	13	(5	8)	168	46	48	37	2	65	2	1	4	1	0	1.00	12	.276	.338	.422
1993 Baltimore	AL	30	113	20	3	0	1	(1	0)	26	8	9	7	0	29	1	1	1	0	1	.00	2	.177	.230	.230
10 ML YEARS		1015	3719	965	177	13	190	(81	109)	1738	510	603	370	78	613	55	6	39	28	11	.72	80	.259	.332	.467

Mark Davis

Pitches: Left **Bats:** Left **Pos:** RP   **Ht:** 6' 4" **Wt:** 210 **Born:** 10/19/60 **Age:** 33

		HOW MUCH HE PITCHED						WHAT HE GAVE UP											THE RESULTS				
Year Team	Lg	G	GS	CG	GF	IP	BFP	H	R	ER	HR	SH	SF	HB	TBB	IBB	SO	WP	Bk	W	L	Pct.	ShO	Sv	ERA
1980 Philadelphia	NL	2	1	0	0	7	30	4	2	2	0	0	0	0	5	0	5	0	0	0	0	.000	0	0	2.57
1981 Philadelphia	NL	9	9	0	0	43	194	49	37	37	7	2	4	0	24	0	29	1	1	1	4	.200	0	0	7.74
1983 San Francisco	NL	20	20	2	0	111	469	93	51	43	14	4	3	3	50	4	83	8	1	6	4	.600	2	0	3.49
1984 San Francisco	NL	46	27	1	6	174.2	766	201	113	104	25	10	10	5	54	12	124	8	4	5	17	.227	0	0	5.36
1985 San Francisco	NL	77	1	0	38	114.1	465	89	49	45	13	13	1	3	41	7	131	6	1	5	12	.294	0	7	3.54
1986 San Francisco	NL	67	2	0	20	84.1	342	63	33	28	6	5	5	1	34	7	90	3	0	5	7	.417	0	4	2.99
1987 2 ML Teams		63	11	1	18	133	566	123	64	59	14	7	2	6	59	8	98	6	2	9	8	.529	0	2	3.99
1988 San Diego	NL	62	0	0	52	98.1	402	70	24	22	2	7	1	0	42	11	102	9	1	5	10	.333	0	28	2.01
1989 San Diego	NL	70	0	0	65	92.2	370	66	21	19	6	3	4	2	31	1	92	8	0	4	3	.571	0	44	1.85
1990 Kansas City	AL	53	3	0	28	68.2	334	71	43	39	9	2	2	4	52	3	73	6	0	2	7	.222	0	6	5.11
1991 Kansas City	AL	29	5	0	8	62.2	276	55	36	31	6	2	5	1	39	0	47	1	0	6	3	.667	0	1	4.45
1992 2 ML Teams		27	6	0	11	53	261	64	44	42	9	1	5	4	41	2	34	5	1	2	3	.400	0	0	7.13
1993 2 ML Teams		60	0	0	13	69.2	327	79	37	33	10	4	1	1	44	7	70	2	1	1	5	.167	0	4	4.26
1987 San Francisco	NL	20	11	1	1	70.2	301	72	38	37	9	3	2	4	28	1	51	4	2	4	5	.444	0	0	4.71
San Diego	NL	43	0	0	17	62.1	265	51	26	22	5	4	0	2	31	7	47	2	0	5	3	.625	0	2	3.18
1992 Kansas City	AL	13	6	0	4	36.1	176	42	31	29	6	1	4	0	28	0	19	1	0	1	3	.250	0	0	7.18
Atlanta	NL	14	0	0	7	16.2	85	22	13	13	3	0	1	1	13	2	15	4	1	1	0	1.000	0	0	7.02
1993 Philadelphia	NL	25	0	0	4	31.1	154	35	22	18	4	1	0	1	24	1	28	1	0	1	2	.333	0	1	5.17
San Diego	NL	35	0	0	9	38.1	173	44	15	15	6	3	1	0	20	6	42	1	1	0	3	.000	0	4	3.52
13 ML YEARS		585	85	4	259	1112.1	4802	1027	554	504	121	58	44	27	516	62	978	63	12	51	83	.381	2	96	4.08

Storm Davis

Pitches: Right **Bats:** Right **Pos:** RP/SP   **Ht:** 6' 4" **Wt:** 225 **Born:** 12/26/61 **Age:** 32

		HOW MUCH HE PITCHED						WHAT HE GAVE UP											THE RESULTS				
Year Team	Lg	G	GS	CG	GF	IP	BFP	H	R	ER	HR	SH	SF	HB	TBB	IBB	SO	WP	Bk	W	L	Pct.	ShO	Sv	ERA
1982 Baltimore	AL	29	8	1	9	100.2	412	96	40	39	8	4	6	0	28	4	67	2	1	8	4	.667	0	0	3.49
1983 Baltimore	AL	34	29	6	0	200.1	831	180	90	80	14	5	4	2	64	4	125	7	2	13	7	.650	1	0	3.59
1984 Baltimore	AL	35	31	10	3	225	923	205	86	78	7	7	9	5	71	6	105	6	1	14	9	.609	2	1	3.12
1985 Baltimore	AL	31	28	8	0	175	750	172	92	88	11	3	3	1	70	5	93	2	1	10	8	.556	1	0	4.53
1986 Baltimore	AL	25	25	2	0	154	657	166	70	62	16	3	2	0	49	2	96	5	0	9	12	.429	0	0	3.62
1987 2 ML Teams		26	15	0	5	93	420	98	61	64	8	2	3	2	47	6	65	9	1	3	8	.273	0	0	5.23
1988 Oakland	AL	33	33	1	0	201.2	872	211	86	83	16	3	8	1	91	2	127	16	2	16	7	.696	0	0	3.70
1989 Oakland	AL	31	31	1	0	169.1	733	187	91	82	19	5	7	3	68	1	91	8	1	19	7	.731	0	0	4.36
1990 Kansas City	AL	21	20	0	0	112	498	129	66	59	9	1	3	0	35	1	62	8	1	7	10	.412	0	0	4.74
1991 Kansas City	AL	51	9	1	22	114.1	515	140	69	63	11	6	4	1	46	9	53	1	0	3	9	.250	1	2	4.96
1992 Baltimore	AL	48	2	0	24	89.1	372	79	35	34	5	6	4	2	36	6	53	4	0	7	3	.700	0	4	3.43
1993 2 ML Teams		43	8	0	12	98	428	93	57	55	9	2	3	3	48	6	73	3	0	2	8	.200	0	4	5.05
1987 San Diego	NL	21	10	0	5	62.2	292	70	48	43	5	2	2	2	36	6	37	7	1	2	7	.222	0	0	6.18
Oakland	AL	5	5	0	0	30.1	128	28	13	11	3	0	1	0	11	0	28	2	0	1	1	.500	0	0	3.26
1993 Oakland	AL	19	8	0	2	62.2	284	68	45	43	5	1	2	2	33	2	37	2	0	2	6	.250	0	0	6.18

Detroit	AL	24	0	0	10	35.1	144	25	12	12	4	1	1	1	15	4	36	1	0	0	2	.000	0	4	3.06
12 ML YEARS		407	239	30	75	1732.2	7411	1756	843	777	133	47	56	20	653	52	1010	71	10	111	92	.547	5	11	4.04

Andre Dawson

Bats: Right **Throws:** Right **Pos:** DH/RF   **Ht:** 6' 3" **Wt:** 197 **Born:** 07/10/54 **Age:** 39

							BATTING												BASERUNNING				PERCENTAGES		
Year Team	Lg	G	AB	H	2B	3B	HR	(Hm	Rd)	TB	R	RBI	TBB	IBB	SO	HBP	SH	SF	SB	CS	SB%	GDP	Avg	OBP	SLG
1976 Montreal	NL	24	85	20	4	1	0	(0	0)	26	9	7	5	1	13	0	2	0	1	2	.33	0	.235	.278	.306
1977 Montreal	NL	139	525	148	26	9	19	(7	12)	249	64	65	34	4	93	2	1	4	21	7	.75	6	.282	.326	.474
1978 Montreal	NL	157	609	154	24	8	25	(12	13)	269	84	72	30	3	128	12	4	5	28	11	.72	7	.253	.299	.442
1979 Montreal	NL	155	639	176	24	12	25	(13	12)	299	90	92	27	5	115	6	8	4	35	10	.78	10	.275	.309	.468
1980 Montreal	NL	151	577	178	41	7	17	(7	10)	284	96	87	44	7	69	6	1	10	34	9	.79	9	.308	.358	.492
1981 Montreal	NL	103	394	119	21	3	24	(9	15)	218	71	64	35	14	50	7	0	5	26	4	.87	6	.302	.365	.553
1982 Montreal	NL	148	608	183	37	7	23	(9	14)	303	107	83	34	4	96	8	4	6	39	10	.80	8	.301	.343	.498
1983 Montreal	NL	159	633	189	36	10	32	(10	22)	341	104	113	38	12	81	9	0	18	25	11	.69	14	.299	.338	.539
1984 Montreal	NL	138	533	132	23	6	17	(6	11)	218	73	86	41	2	80	2	1	6	13	5	.72	12	.248	.301	.409
1985 Montreal	NL	139	529	135	27	2	23	(11	12)	235	65	91	29	8	92	4	1	7	13	4	.76	12	.255	.295	.444
1986 Montreal	NL	130	496	141	32	2	20	(11	9)	237	65	78	37	11	79	6	1	6	18	12	.60	13	.284	.338	.478
1987 Chicago	NL	153	621	178	24	2	49	(27	22)	353	90	137	32	7	103	7	0	2	11	3	.79	15	.287	.328	.568
1988 Chicago	NL	157	591	179	31	8	24	(12	12)	298	78	79	37	12	73	4	1	7	12	4	.75	13	.303	.344	.504
1989 Chicago	NL	118	416	105	18	6	21	(6	15)	198	62	77	35	13	62	1	0	7	8	5	.62	16	.252	.307	.476
1990 Chicago	NL	147	529	164	28	5	27	(14	13)	283	72	100	42	21	65	2	0	8	16	2	.89	12	.310	.358	.535
1991 Chicago	NL	149	563	153	21	4	31	(22	9)	275	69	104	22	3	80	5	0	6	4	5	.44	10	.272	.302	.488
1992 Chicago	NL	143	542	150	27	2	22	(13	9)	247	60	90	30	8	70	4	0	6	6	2	.75	13	.277	.316	.456
1993 Boston	AL	121	461	126	29	1	13	(8	5)	196	44	67	17	4	49	13	0	7	2	1	.67	18	.273	.313	.425
18 ML YEARS		2431	9351	2630	473	95	412	(197	215)	4529	1303	1492	569	139	1398	98	24	114	312	107	.74	194	.281	.325	.484

Ken Dayley

Pitches: Left **Bats:** Left **Pos:** RP   **Ht:** 6' 0" **Wt:** 180 **Born:** 02/25/59 **Age:** 35

		HOW MUCH HE PITCHED						WHAT HE GAVE UP												THE RESULTS					
Year Team	Lg	G	GS	CG	GF	IP	BFP	H	R	ER	HR	SH	SF	HB	TBB	IBB	SO	WP	Bk	W	L	Pct.	ShO	Sv	ERA
1993 Albuquerque*	AAA	9	1	0	3	10.1	55	14	15	14	1	1	0	0	12	1	9	5	1	0	0	.000	0	0	12.19
1982 Atlanta	NL	20	11	0	3	71.1	313	79	39	36	9	7	5	0	25	2	34	2	0	5	6	.455	0	0	4.54
1983 Atlanta	NL	24	16	0	1	104.2	436	100	59	50	12	3	3	2	39	2	70	3	0	5	8	.385	0	0	4.30
1984 2 ML Teams		7	6	0	1	23.2	124	44	28	21	6	4	0	1	11	1	10	0	0	0	5	.000	0	0	7.99
1985 St. Louis	NL	57	0	0	27	65.1	271	65	24	20	2	4	2	0	18	9	62	4	0	4	4	.500	0	11	2.76
1986 St. Louis	NL	31	0	0	13	38.2	170	42	19	14	1	1	1	1	11	3	33	0	0	3	3	.000	0	5	3.26
1987 St. Louis	NL	53	0	0	29	61	260	52	21	18	2	2	1	2	33	8	63	5	0	9	5	.643	0	4	2.66
1988 St. Louis	NL	54	0	0	21	55.1	226	48	20	17	2	4	1	1	19	7	38	2	0	2	7	.222	0	5	2.77
1989 St. Louis	NL	71	0	0	28	75.1	310	63	26	24	3	3	1	0	30	10	40	2	1	4	3	.571	0	12	2.87
1990 St. Louis	NL	58	0	0	17	73.1	307	63	32	29	5	2	5	0	30	7	51	6	0	4	4	.500	0	2	3.56
1991 Toronto	AL	8	0	0	3	4.1	26	7	3	3	0	0	1	1	5	0	3	2	0	0	0	.000	0	0	6.23
1993 Toronto	AL	2	0	0	0	0.2	7	1	2	0	0	0	0	0	4	0	2	0	0	0	0	.000	0	0	0.00
1984 Atlanta	NL	4	4	0	0	18.2	92	28	18	11	5	3	0	1	6	1	10	0	0	0	3	.000	0	0	5.30
St. Louis	NL	3	2	0	1	5	32	16	10	10	1	1	0	0	5	0	0	0	0	0	2	.000	0	0	18.00
11 ML YEARS		385	33	0	145	573.2	2450	564	273	232	42	33	20	8	225	49	406	26	1	33	45	.423	0	39	3.64

Steve Decker

Bats: Right **Throws:** Right **Pos:** C   **Ht:** 6' 3" **Wt:** 205 **Born:** 10/25/65 **Age:** 28

							BATTING												BASERUNNING				PERCENTAGES		
Year Team	Lg	G	AB	H	2B	3B	HR	(Hm	Rd)	TB	R	RBI	TBB	IBB	SO	HBP	SH	SF	SB	CS	SB%	GDP	Avg	OBP	SLG
1990 San Francisco	NL	15	54	16	4	0	3	(2	1)	27	5	8	1	0	10	0	1	0	0	0	.00	0	.296	.309	.500
1991 San Francisco	NL	79	233	48	7	1	5	(4	1)	72	11	24	16	1	44	3	2	4	0	1	.00	7	.206	.262	.309
1992 San Francisco	NL	15	43	7	1	0	0	(0	0)	8	3	1	6	0	7	1	0	0	0	0	.00	0	.163	.280	.186
1993 Florida	NL	8	15	0	0	0	0	(0	0)	0	0	1	3	0	3	0	0	0	0	0	.00	2	.000	.158	.000
4 ML YEARS		117	345	71	10	1	8	(5	3)	107	19	34	26	1	64	4	3	5	0	1	.00	10	.206	.266	.310

Rob Deer

Bats: Right **Throws:** Right **Pos:** RF   **Ht:** 6' 3" **Wt:** 225 **Born:** 09/29/60 **Age:** 33

							BATTING												BASERUNNING				PERCENTAGES		
Year Team	Lg	G	AB	H	2B	3B	HR	(Hm	Rd)	TB	R	RBI	TBB	IBB	SO	HBP	SH	SF	SB	CS	SB%	GDP	Avg	OBP	SLG
1984 San Francisco	NL	13	24	4	0	0	3	(2	1)	13	5	3	7	0	10	1	0	0	1	1	.50	0	.167	.375	.542
1985 San Francisco	NL	78	162	30	5	1	8	(5	3)	61	22	20	23	0	71	0	0	2	0	1	.00	0	.185	.283	.377
1986 Milwaukee	AL	134	466	108	17	3	33	(19	14)	230	75	86	72	3	179	3	2	3	5	2	.71	4	.232	.336	.494
1987 Milwaukee	AL	134	474	113	15	2	28	(11	17)	216	71	80	86	6	186	5	0	1	12	4	.75	4	.238	.360	.456
1988 Milwaukee	AL	135	492	124	24	0	23	(12	11)	217	71	85	51	4	153	7	0	5	9	5	.64	4	.252	.328	.441
1989 Milwaukee	AL	130	466	98	18	2	26	(15	11)	198	72	65	60	5	158	4	0	2	4	8	.33	8	.210	.305	.425

Year	Team	Lg	G	AB	H	2B	3B	HR	(Hm	Rd)	TB	R	RBI	TBB	IBB	SO	HBP	SH	SF	SB	CS	SB%	GDP	Avg	OBP	SLG
1990	Milwaukee	AL	134	440	92	15	1	27	(11	16)	190	57	69	64	6	147	4	0	3	2	3	.40	0	.209	.313	.432
1991	Detroit	AL	134	448	80	14	2	25	(12	13)	173	64	64	89	1	**175**	0	0	2	1	3	.25	3	.179	.314	.386
1992	Detroit	AL	110	393	97	20	1	32	(13	19)	215	66	64	51	1	131	3	0	1	4	2	.67	8	.247	.337	.547
1993	2 ML Teams		128	466	98	17	1	21	(12	9)	180	66	55	58	1	169	5	0	3	5	2	.71	6	.210	.303	.386
1993	Detroit	AL	90	323	70	11	0	14	(9	5)	123	48	39	38	1	120	3	0	3	3	2	.60	4	.217	.302	.381
	Boston	AL	38	143	28	6	1	7	(3	4)	57	18	16	20	0	49	2	0	0	2	0	1.00	2	.196	.303	.399
	10 ML YEARS		1130	3831	844	145	13	226	(112	114)	1693	569	591	561	27	1379	32	2	22	43	31	.58	37	.220	.323	.442

Jose DeLeon

Pitches: Right **Bats:** Right **Pos:** RP/SP   **Ht:** 6' 3" **Wt:** 226 **Born:** 12/20/60 **Age:** 33

| | | | HOW MUCH HE PITCHED | | | | | | WHAT HE GAVE UP | | | | | | | | | | THE RESULTS | | | | | |
Year	Team	Lg	G	GS	CG	GF	IP	BFP	H	R	ER	HR	SH	SF	HB	TBB	IBB	SO	WP	Bk	W	L	Pct.	ShO	Sv	ERA
1983	Pittsburgh	NL	15	15	3	0	108	438	75	36	34	5	4	3	1	47	2	118	5	2	7	3	.700	2	0	2.83
1984	Pittsburgh	NL	30	28	5	0	192.1	795	147	86	80	10	7	7	3	92	5	153	6	2	7	13	.350	1	0	3.74
1985	Pittsburgh	NL	31	25	1	5	162.2	700	138	93	85	15	7	4	3	89	3	149	7	1	2	**19**	.095	0	3	4.70
1986	2 ML Teams		22	14	1	5	95.1	408	66	46	41	9	5	1	5	59	3	79	7	0	5	8	.385	0	1	3.87
1987	Chicago	AL	33	31	2	0	206	889	177	106	92	24	6	6	10	97	4	153	6	1	11	12	.478	0	0	4.02
1988	St. Louis	NL	34	34	3	0	225.1	940	198	95	92	13	10	7	2	86	7	208	10	0	13	10	.565	1	0	3.67
1989	St. Louis	NL	36	36	5	0	244.2	972	173	96	83	16	5	3	6	80	5	**201**	2	0	16	12	.571	3	0	3.05
1990	St. Louis	NL	32	32	0	0	182.2	793	168	96	90	15	11	8	5	86	9	164	5	0	7	**19**	.269	0	0	4.43
1991	St. Louis	NL	28	28	1	0	162.2	679	144	57	49	15	5	4	6	61	1	118	1	1	5	9	.357	0	0	2.71
1992	2 ML Teams		32	18	0	3	117.1	506	111	63	57	7	6	6	2	48	1	79	3	0	2	8	.200	0	0	4.37
1993	2 ML Teams		35	3	0	7	57.1	244	44	27	19	7	3	2	6	30	3	40	5	0	3	0	1.000	0	0	2.98
1986	Pittsburgh	NL	9	1	0	5	16.1	83	17	16	15	2	1	0	1	17	3	11	1	0	1	3	.250	0	1	8.27
	Chicago	AL	13	13	1	0	79	325	49	30	26	7	4	1	4	42	0	68	6	0	4	5	.444	0	0	2.96
1992	St. Louis	NL	29	15	0	3	102.1	443	95	56	52	7	5	6	2	43	1	72	3	0	2	7	.222	0	0	4.57
	Philadelphia	NL	3	3	0	0	15	63	16	7	5	0	1	0	0	5	0	7	0	0	0	1	.000	0	0	3.00
1993	Philadelphia	NL	24	3	0	6	47	207	39	25	17	5	3	2	5	27	3	34	5	0	3	0	1.000	0	0	3.26
	Chicago	AL	11	0	0	1	10.1	37	5	2	2	2	0	0	1	3	0	6	0	0	0	0	.000	0	0	1.74
	11 ML YEARS		328	264	21	20	1754.1	7364	1441	801	722	136	69	51	49	775	43	1462	57	7	78	113	.408	7	4	3.70

Carlos Delgado

Bats: Left **Throws:** Right **Pos:** C   **Ht:** 6' 3" **Wt:** 206 **Born:** 06/25/72 **Age:** 22

| | | | BATTING | | | | | | | | | | | | | | | | BASERUNNING | | | | PERCENTAGES | | |
Year	Team	Lg	G	AB	H	2B	3B	HR	(Hm	Rd)	TB	R	RBI	TBB	IBB	SO	HBP	SH	SF	SB	CS	SB%	GDP	Avg	OBP	SLG
1989	St.Cathmes	A	31	89	16	5	0	0	--	--	21	9	11	23	1	39	0	0	1	0	0	.00	4	.180	.345	.236
1990	St. Cath	A	67	226	64	13	0	6	--	--	95	29	39	35	2	65	5	1	4	2	7	.22	2	.283	.385	.420
1991	Myrtle Bch	A	132	441	126	18	2	18	--	--	202	72	71	74	2	97	8	1	4	9	10	.47	7	.286	.395	.458
	Syracuse	AAA	1	3	0	0	0	0	--	--	0	0	0	0	0	2	0	0	0	0	0	.00	0	.000	.000	.000
1992	Dunedin	A	133	485	157	30	2	30	--	--	281	83	100	59	11	91	6	0	2	2	5	.29	8	.324	.402	.579
1993	Knoxville	AA	140	468	142	28	0	25	--	--	245	91	102	102	18	98	6	0	5	10	3	.77	11	.303	.430	.524
1993	Toronto	AL	2	1	0	0	0	0	(0	0)	0	0	0	1	0	0	0	0	0	0	0	.00	0	.000	.500	.000

Rich DeLucia

Pitches: Right **Bats:** Right **Pos:** RP   **Ht:** 6' 0" **Wt:** 185 **Born:** 10/07/64 **Age:** 29

| | | | HOW MUCH HE PITCHED | | | | | | WHAT HE GAVE UP | | | | | | | | | | THE RESULTS | | | | | |
Year	Team	Lg	G	GS	CG	GF	IP	BFP	H	R	ER	HR	SH	SF	HB	TBB	IBB	SO	WP	Bk	W	L	Pct.	ShO	Sv	ERA
1993	Calgary *	AAA	8	7	0	1	44	192	45	30	28	6	0	3	0	20	1	38	4	0	1	5	.167	0	0	5.73
1990	Seattle	AL	5	5	1	0	36	144	30	9	8	2	2	0	0	9	0	20	0	0	1	2	.333	0	0	2.00
1991	Seattle	AL	32	31	0	0	182	779	176	107	103	31	5	14	4	78	4	98	10	0	12	13	.480	0	0	5.09
1992	Seattle	AL	30	11	0	6	83.2	382	100	55	51	13	2	2	2	35	1	66	1	0	3	6	.333	0	1	5.49
1993	Seattle	AL	30	1	0	11	42.2	195	46	24	22	5	1	1	1	23	3	48	4	0	3	6	.333	0	0	4.64
	4 ML YEARS		97	48	1	17	344.1	1500	352	195	184	51	10	17	7	145	8	232	15	0	19	27	.413	0	1	4.81

Drew Denson

Bats: Right **Throws:** Right **Pos:** 1B   **Ht:** 6' 5" **Wt:** 220 **Born:** 11/16/65 **Age:** 28

| | | | BATTING | | | | | | | | | | | | | | | | BASERUNNING | | | | PERCENTAGES | | |
Year	Team	Lg	G	AB	H	2B	3B	HR	(Hm	Rd)	TB	R	RBI	TBB	IBB	SO	HBP	SH	SF	SB	CS	SB%	GDP	Avg	OBP	SLG
1984	Braves	R	62	239	77	20	3	10	--	--	133	43	45	17	0	41	3	0	1	5	2	.71	8	.322	.373	.556
1985	Sumter	A	111	383	115	18	4	14	--	--	183	59	74	53	3	76	4	0	4	5	3	.63	16	.300	.387	.478
1986	Durham	A	72	231	54	6	3	4	--	--	78	31	23	25	0	46	2	1	0	6	1	.86	10	.234	.314	.338
1987	Greenville	AA	128	447	98	23	1	14	--	--	165	54	55	33	1	95	11	1	2	1	2	.33	15	.219	.288	.369
1988	Greenville	AA	140	507	136	26	4	13	--	--	209	85	78	44	1	116	14	3	4	11	9	.55	11	.268	.341	.412
1989	Richmond	AAA	138	463	118	32	0	9	--	--	177	50	59	42	2	116	12	1	5	0	1	.00	4	.255	.330	.382
1990	Richmond	AAA	90	295	68	4	1	7	--	--	95	25	29	26	2	57	9	0	3	0	0	.00	9	.231	.309	.322
1992	Vancouver	AAA	105	440	94	7	3	13	--	--	146	43	70	36	3	58	7	0	0	1	0	1.00	12	.276	.358	.429
1993	Nashville	AAA	136	513	144	36	0	24	--	--	252	82	103	46	7	98	23	0	8	0	0	.00	22	.281	.361	.491
1989	Atlanta	NL	12	36	9	1	0	0	(0	0)	10	1	5	3	0	9	0	0	0	1	0	1.00	0	.250	.308	.278

Year	Team	Lg	G	GS	CG	GF	IP	BFP	H	R	ER	HR	SH	SF	HB	TBB	IBB	SO	WP	Bk	W	L	Pct.	ShO	Sv	ERA
1993	Chicago	AL	4	5	1	0	0	0	(0	0)	1	0	0	0	0	2	0	0	0	0	0	0	.00	0	.200	.200 .200
	2 ML YEARS		16	41	10	1	0	0	(0	0)	11	1	5	3	0	11	0	0	0	1	0	1.00	0	.244	.295 .268

Jim Deshaies

Pitches: Left   **Bats:** Left   **Pos:** SP   **Ht:** 6' 5"   **Wt:** 220   **Born:** 06/23/60   **Age:** 34

			HOW MUCH HE PITCHED						WHAT HE GAVE UP												THE RESULTS					
Year	Team	Lg	G	GS	CG	GF	IP	BFP	H	R	ER	HR	SH	SF	HB	TBB	IBB	SO	WP	Bk	W	L	Pct.	ShO	Sv	ERA
1984	New York	AL	2	2	0	0	7	40	14	9	9	1	0	1	0	7	0	5	0	0	0	1	.000	0	0	11.57
1985	Houston	NL	2	0	0	0	3	10	1	0	0	0	0	0	0	0	0	2	0	0	0	0	.000	0	0	0.00
1986	Houston	NL	26	26	1	0	144	599	124	58	52	16	4	3	2	59	2	128	0	7	12	5	.706	1	0	3.25
1987	Houston	NL	26	25	1	0	152	648	149	81	78	22	9	3	0	57	7	104	4	5	11	6	.647	0	0	4.62
1988	Houston	NL	31	31	3	0	207	847	164	77	69	20	8	13	2	72	5	127	1	6	11	14	.440	2	0	3.00
1989	Houston	NL	34	34	6	0	225.2	928	180	80	73	15	11	5	4	79	8	153	8	1	15	10	.600	3	0	2.91
1990	Houston	NL	34	34	2	0	209.1	881	186	93	88	21	17	12	8	84	9	119	3	3	7	12	.368	0	0	3.78
1991	Houston	NL	28	28	1	0	161	686	156	90	89	19	4	7	1	72	5	98	0	5	5	12	.294	0	0	4.98
1992	San Diego	NL	15	15	0	0	96	395	92	40	35	6	3	2	1	33	2	46	1	2	4	7	.364	0	0	3.28
1993	2 ML Teams		32	31	1	1	184.1	770	183	94	90	26	5	7	7	57	1	85	1	4	13	15	.464	0	0	4.39
1993	Minnesota	AL	27	27	1	0	167.1	693	159	85	82	24	4	7	6	51	1	80	0	4	11	13	.458	0	0	4.41
	San Francisco	NL	5	4	0	1	17	77	24	9	8	2	1	0	1	6	0	5	1	0	2	2	.500	0	0	4.24
	10 ML YEARS		230	226	15	1	1389.1	5804	1249	622	583	146	61	53	25	520	39	867	18	33	78	82	.488	6	0	3.78

Delino DeShields

Bats: Left   **Throws:** Right   **Pos:** 2B   **Ht:** 6' 1"   **Wt:** 170   **Born:** 01/15/69   **Age:** 25

								BATTING											BASERUNNING				PERCENTAGES		
Year	Team	Lg	G	AB	H	2B	3B	HR	(Hm | Rd)	TB	R	RBI	TBB	IBB	SO	HBP	SH	SF	SB	CS	SB%	GDP	Avg	OBP	SLG
1990	Montreal	NL	129	499	144	28	6	4	(3 | 1)	196	69	45	66	3	96	4	1	2	42	22	.66	10	.289	.375	.393
1991	Montreal	NL	151	563	134	15	4	10	(3 | 7)	187	83	51	95	2	151	2	8	5	56	23	.71	6	.238	.347	.332
1992	Montreal	NL	135	530	155	19	8	7	(1 | 6)	211	82	56	54	4	108	3	9	3	46	15	.75	10	.292	.359	.398
1993	Montreal	NL	123	481	142	17	7	2	(2 | 0)	179	75	29	72	3	64	3	4	2	43	10	.81	5	.295	.389	.372
	4 ML YEARS		538	2073	575	79	25	23	(9 | 14)	773	309	181	287	12	419	12	22	12	187	70	.73	31	.277	.367	.373

John DeSilva

Pitches: Right   **Bats:** Right   **Pos:** RP   **Ht:** 6' 0"   **Wt:** 193   **Born:** 09/30/67   **Age:** 26

			HOW MUCH HE PITCHED						WHAT HE GAVE UP												THE RESULTS					
Year	Team	Lg	G	GS	CG	GF	IP	BFP	H	R	ER	HR	SH	SF	HB	TBB	IBB	SO	WP	Bk	W	L	Pct.	ShO	Sv	ERA
1989	Niagara Fls	A	4	4	0	0	24	95	15	5	5	0	1	0	2	8	0	24	3	1	3	0	1.000	0	0	1.88
	Fayetteville	A	9	9	0	0	52.2	215	40	23	16	4	1	2	0	21	0	54	2	3	2	2	.500	0	0	2.73
1990	Lakeland	A	14	14	0	0	91	349	54	18	15	4	1	2	4	25	0	113	3	1	8	1	.889	0	0	1.48
	London	AA	14	14	1	0	89	372	87	47	37	4	1	4	2	27	0	76	3	0	5	6	.455	1	0	3.74
1991	London	AA	11	11	2	0	73.2	294	51	24	23	4	2	2	0	24	0	80	1	0	5	4	.556	1	0	2.81
	Toledo	AAA	11	11	1	0	58.2	254	62	33	30	10	0	1	1	21	0	56	1	0	5	4	.556	0	0	4.60
1992	Toledo	AAA	7	2	0	3	19	89	26	18	18	5	1	0	0	8	0	21	0	0	0	3	.000	0	0	8.53
	London	AA	9	9	1	0	52.1	216	51	24	24	4	1	2	1	13	0	53	2	1	2	4	.333	1	0	4.13
1993	Toledo	AAA	25	24	1	0	161	675	145	73	66	13	2	5	0	60	2	136	3	1	7	10	.412	0	0	3.69
1993	2 ML Teams		4	0	0	3	6.1	27	8	5	5	0	0	1	0	1	0	6	0	0	0	0	.000	0	0	7.11
1993	Detroit	AL	1	0	0	1	1	4	2	1	1	0	0	0	0	0	0	0	0	0	0	0	.000	0	0	9.00
	Los Angeles	NL	3	0	0	2	5.1	23	6	4	4	0	0	0	0	1	0	6	0	0	0	0	.000	0	0	6.75

Orestes Destrade

Bats: Both   **Throws:** Right   **Pos:** 1B   **Ht:** 6' 4"   **Wt:** 230   **Born:** 05/08/62   **Age:** 32

								BATTING											BASERUNNING				PERCENTAGES		
Year	Team	Lg	G	AB	H	2B	3B	HR	(Hm | Rd)	TB	R	RBI	TBB	IBB	SO	HBP	SH	SF	SB	CS	SB%	GDP	Avg	OBP	SLG
1987	New York	AL	9	19	5	0	0	0	(0 | 0)	5	5	1	5	0	5	0	0	0	0	0	.00	1	.263	.417	.263
1988	Pittsburgh	NL	36	47	7	1	0	1	(1 | 0)	11	2	3	5	0	17	0	0	1	0	0	.00	0	.149	.226	.234
1993	Florida	NL	153	569	145	20	3	20	(9 | 11)	231	61	87	58	8	130	3	1	6	0	2	.00	17	.255	.324	.406
	3 ML YEARS		198	635	157	21	3	21	(10 | 11)	247	68	91	68	8	152	3	1	7	0	2	.00	18	.247	.320	.389

Mike Devereaux

Bats: Right   **Throws:** Right   **Pos:** CF   **Ht:** 6' 0"   **Wt:** 195   **Born:** 04/10/63   **Age:** 31

								BATTING											BASERUNNING				PERCENTAGES		
Year	Team	Lg	G	AB	H	2B	3B	HR	(Hm | Rd)	TB	R	RBI	TBB	IBB	SO	HBP	SH	SF	SB	CS	SB%	GDP	Avg	OBP	SLG
1993	Bowie *	AA	2	7	2	1	0	0	--	--	3	1	2	0	0	2	0	0	0	0	0	.00	1	.286	.286	.429
1987	Los Angeles	NL	19	54	12	3	0	0	(0 | 0)	15	7	4	3	0	10	0	1	0	3	1	.75	0	.222	.263	.278
1988	Los Angeles	NL	30	43	5	1	0	0	(0 | 0)	6	4	2	2	0	10	0	0	0	0	1	.00	0	.116	.156	.140
1989	Baltimore	AL	122	391	104	14	3	8	(4 | 4)	148	55	46	36	0	60	2	2	3	22	11	.67	7	.266	.329	.379
1990	Baltimore	AL	108	367	88	18	1	12	(6 | 6)	144	48	49	28	0	48	4	4	4	13	12	.52	10	.240	.291	.392
1991	Baltimore	AL	149	608	158	27	10	19	(10 | 9)	262	82	59	47	2	115	2	7	4	16	9	.64	13	.260	.313	.431
1992	Baltimore	AL	156	653	180	29	11	24	(14 | 10)	303	76	107	44	1	94	4	0	9	10	8	.56	14	.276	.321	.464

Year Team	Lg	G	AB	H	2B	3B	HR	(Hm	Rd)	TB	R	RBI	TBB	IBB	SO	HBP	SH	SF	SB	CS	SB%	GDP	Avg	OBP	SLG
1993 Baltimore	AL	131	527	132	31	3	14	(8	6)	211	72	75	43	0	99	1	2	4	3	3	.50	13	.250	.306	.400
7 ML YEARS		715	2643	679	123	28	77	(42	35)	1089	344	342	203	3	436	9	16	24	67	45	.60	57	.257	.309	.412

Mark Dewey

Pitches: Right **Bats:** Right **Pos:** RP　　　　　**Ht:** 6' 0" **Wt:** 207 **Born:** 01/03/65 **Age:** 29

		HOW MUCH HE PITCHED						WHAT HE GAVE UP									THE RESULTS					
Year Team	Lg	G	GS	CG	GF	IP	BFP	H	R	ER	HR	SH	SF	HB	TBB	IBB	SO	WP	Bk	W	L	Pct.	ShO	Sv	ERA
1993 Buffalo *	AAA	22	0	0	11	29.1	114	21	9	4	2	0	0	3	5	0	17	0	0	2	0	1.000	0	6	1.23
1990 San Francisco	NL	14	0	0	5	22.2	92	22	7	7	1	2	0	0	5	1	11	0	1	1	1	.500	0	0	2.78
1992 New York	NL	20	0	0	6	33.1	143	37	16	16	2	1	0	0	10	2	24	0	1	1	0	1.000	0	0	4.32
1993 Pittsburgh	NL	21	0	0	17	26.2	108	14	8	7	0	3	3	3	10	1	14	0	0	1	2	.333	0	7	2.36
3 ML YEARS		55	0	0	28	82.2	343	73	31	30	3	6	3	3	25	4	49	0	2	3	3	.500	0	7	3.27

Alex Diaz

Bats: Both **Throws:** Right **Pos:** RF/CF　　　　　**Ht:** 5'11" **Wt:** 175 **Born:** 10/05/68 **Age:** 25

		BATTING																	BASERUNNING				PERCENTAGES		
Year Team	Lg	G	AB	H	2B	3B	HR	(Hm	Rd)	TB	R	RBI	TBB	IBB	SO	HBP	SH	SF	SB	CS	SB%	GDP	Avg	OBP	SLG
1987 Kingsport	R	54	212	56	9	1	0	--	--	67	29	13	16	0	31	1	4	1	34	9	.79	4	.264	.317	.316
Little Fls	A	12	47	16	4	1	0	--	--	22	7	8	2	0	3	0	0	0	2	2	.50	1	.340	.367	.468
1988 Columbia	A	123	481	126	14	11	0	--	--	162	82	37	21	3	49	2	9	2	28	8	.78	4	.262	.294	.337
St. Lucie	A	3	6	0	0	0	0	--	--	0	2	1	0	0	4	2	0	0	0	0	.00	1	.000	.250	.000
1989 St.Lucie	A	102	416	106	11	10	1	--	--	140	54	33	20	3	38	3	5	3	43	16	.73	8	.255	.292	.337
Jackson	AA	23	95	26	5	1	2	--	--	39	11	9	3	0	11	0	0	0	3	4	.43	1	.274	.296	.411
1990 Tidewater	AAA	124	437	112	15	2	1	--	--	134	55	36	30	4	39	1	7	4	23	13	.64	7	.256	.303	.307
1991 Indianapols	AAA	108	370	90	14	4	1	--	--	115	48	21	27	2	46	1	3	2	16	3	.84	6	.243	.295	.311
1992 Denver	AAA	106	455	122	17	4	1	--	--	150	67	41	24	0	36	5	5	5	42	12	.78	12	.268	.309	.330
1993 New Orleans	AAA	16	55	16	2	0	0	--	--	18	8	5	3	1	6	0	1	0	7	0	1.00	1	.291	.328	.327
1992 Milwaukee	AL	22	9	1	0	0	0	(0	0)	1	5	1	0	0	0	0	0	0	3	2	.60	0	.111	.111	.111
1993 Milwaukee	AL	32	69	22	2	0	0	(0	0)	24	9	1	0	0	12	0	0	0	5	3	.63	3	.319	.319	.348
2 ML YEARS		54	78	23	2	0	0	(0	0)	25	14	2	0	0	12	0	0	0	8	5	.62	3	.295	.295	.321

Mario Diaz

Bats: Right **Throws:** Right **Pos:** SS/3B　　　　　**Ht:** 5'10" **Wt:** 160 **Born:** 01/10/62 **Age:** 32

		BATTING																	BASERUNNING				PERCENTAGES		
Year Team	Lg	G	AB	H	2B	3B	HR	(Hm	Rd)	TB	R	RBI	TBB	IBB	SO	HBP	SH	SF	SB	CS	SB%	GDP	Avg	OBP	SLG
1993 Okla City *	AAA	48	177	58	12	2	3	--	--	83	24	20	7	0	15	1	1	2	3	1	.75	7	.328	.353	.469
1987 Seattle	AL	11	23	7	0	1	0	(0	0)	9	4	3	0	0	4	0	0	0	0	0	.00	0	.304	.304	.391
1988 Seattle	AL	28	72	22	5	0	0	(0	0)	27	6	9	3	0	5	0	0	1	0	0	.00	0	.306	.329	.375
1989 Seattle	AL	52	74	10	0	0	1	(0	1)	13	9	7	7	0	7	0	5	0	0	0	.00	2	.135	.210	.176
1990 New York	NL	16	22	3	1	0	0	(0	0)	4	0	1	0	0	3	0	0	1	0	0	.00	0	.136	.130	.182
1991 Texas	AL	96	182	48	7	0	1	(1	0)	58	24	22	15	0	18	0	4	1	0	1	.00	5	.264	.318	.319
1992 Texas	AL	19	31	7	1	0	0	(0	0)	8	2	1	1	1	2	0	1	0	0	1	.00	2	.226	.250	.258
1993 Texas	AL	71	205	56	10	1	2	(1	1)	74	24	24	8	0	13	1	7	5	1	0	1.00	6	.273	.297	.361
7 ML YEARS		293	609	153	24	2	4	(2	2)	193	69	67	34	1	52	1	17	8	1	2	.33	18	.251	.288	.317

Rob Dibble

Pitches: Right **Bats:** Left **Pos:** RP　　　　　**Ht:** 6' 4" **Wt:** 230 **Born:** 01/24/64 **Age:** 30

		HOW MUCH HE PITCHED						WHAT HE GAVE UP									THE RESULTS					
Year Team	Lg	G	GS	CG	GF	IP	BFP	H	R	ER	HR	SH	SF	HB	TBB	IBB	SO	WP	Bk	W	L	Pct.	ShO	Sv	ERA
1988 Cincinnati	NL	37	0	0	6	59.1	235	43	12	12	2	2	3	1	21	5	59	3	2	1	1	.500	0	0	1.82
1989 Cincinnati	NL	74	0	0	18	99	401	62	23	23	4	3	4	3	39	11	141	7	0	10	5	.667	0	2	2.09
1990 Cincinnati	NL	68	0	0	29	98	384	62	22	19	3	4	6	1	34	3	136	3	1	8	3	.727	0	11	1.74
1991 Cincinnati	NL	67	0	0	57	82.1	334	67	32	29	5	5	3	0	25	2	124	5	0	3	5	.375	0	31	3.17
1992 Cincinnati	NL	63	0	0	49	70.1	286	48	26	24	3	2	2	2	31	2	110	6	0	3	5	.375	0	25	3.07
1993 Cincinnati	NL	45	0	0	37	41.2	196	34	33	30	8	1	0	2	42	0	49	4	0	1	4	.200	0	19	6.48
6 ML YEARS		354	0	0	196	450.2	1836	316	148	137	25	17	18	9	192	23	619	28	3	26	23	.531	0	88	2.74

Frank DiPino

Pitches: Left **Bats:** Left **Pos:** RP　　　　　**Ht:** 6' 0" **Wt:** 195 **Born:** 10/22/56 **Age:** 37

		HOW MUCH HE PITCHED						WHAT HE GAVE UP									THE RESULTS					
Year Team	Lg	G	GS	CG	GF	IP	BFP	H	R	ER	HR	SH	SF	HB	TBB	IBB	SO	WP	Bk	W	L	Pct.	ShO	Sv	ERA
1993 Omaha *	AAA	15	0	0	8	22.2	90	21	9	7	3	1	0	2	4	1	9	0	0	1	2	.333	0	1	2.78
1981 Milwaukee	AL	2	0	0	2	2	10	0	0	0	0	0	0	0	3	0	3	0	0	0	0	.000	0	1	0.00
1982 Houston	NL	6	6	0	0	28.1	122	32	20	19	1	3	2	0	11	1	25	0	0	2	2	.500	0	0	6.04
1983 Houston	NL	53	0	0	32	71.1	279	52	21	21	2	1	3	1	20	5	67	3	0	3	4	.429	0	20	2.65
1984 Houston	NL	57	0	0	44	75.1	329	74	32	28	3	5	2	1	36	11	65	3	1	4	9	.308	0	14	3.35
1985 Houston	NL	54	0	0	29	76	329	69	44	34	7	3	2	1	43	6	49	0	0	3	7	.300	0	6	4.03

Year	Team	Lg	G	GS	CG	GF	IP	BFP	H	R	ER	HR	SH	SF	HB	TBB	IBB	SO	WP	Bk	W	L	Pct.	ShO	Sv	ERA
1986	2 ML Teams		61	0	0	26	80.1	345	74	45	39	11	9	3	2	30	6	70	3	0	3	7	.300	0	3	4.37
1987	Chicago	NL	69	0	0	20	80	343	75	31	28	7	6	4	1	34	2	61	5	0	3	3	.500	0	4	3.15
1988	Chicago	NL	63	0	0	23	90.1	398	102	54	50	6	2	6	0	32	7	69	6	1	2	3	.400	0	6	4.98
1989	St. Louis	NL	67	0	0	8	88.1	347	73	26	24	6	1	5	0	20	7	44	2	0	9	0	1.000	0	0	2.45
1990	St. Louis	NL	62	0	0	24	81	360	92	45	41	8	8	7	1	31	12	49	2	1	5	2	.714	0	3	4.56
1992	St. Louis	NL	9	0	0	3	11	45	9	2	2	0	1	0	0	3	0	8	0	0	0	0	.000	0	0	1.64
1993	Kansas City	AL	11	0	0	5	15.2	74	21	12	12	2	0	2	2	6	0	5	0	0	1	1	.500	0	0	6.89
1986	Houston	NL	31	0	0	14	40.1	167	27	18	16	5	5	1	2	16	1	27	0	0	1	3	.250	0	3	3.57
	Chicago	NL	30	0	0	12	40	178	47	27	23	6	4	2	0	14	5	43	3	0	2	4	.333	0	0	5.18
	12 ML YEARS		514	6	0	216	699.2	2981	673	332	298	53	39	37	10	269	57	515	28	4	35	38	.479	0	56	3.83

Jerry DiPoto

Pitches: Right Bats: Right Pos: RP **Ht: 6' 2" Wt: 200 Born: 05/24/68 Age: 26**

			HOW MUCH HE PITCHED						WHAT HE GAVE UP												THE RESULTS					
Year	Team	Lg	G	GS	CG	GF	IP	BFP	H	R	ER	HR	SH	SF	HB	TBB	IBB	SO	WP	Bk	W	L	Pct.	ShO	Sv	ERA
1989	Watertown	A	14	14	1	0	87.1	373	75	42	35	3	4	2	4	39	0	98	10	4	6	5	.545	0	0	3.61
1990	Kinston	A	24	24	1	0	145.1	636	129	75	61	6	5	4	10	77	1	143	12	3	11	4	.733	0	0	3.78
	Canton-Akrn	AA	3	2	0	0	14	59	11	5	4	0	0	0	2	4	0	12	1	0	1	0	1.000	0	0	2.57
1991	Canton-Akrn	AA	28	26	2	0	156	670	143	83	66	10	1	9	2	74	2	97	15	3	6	11	.353	0	0	3.81
1992	Colo Sprngs	AAA	50	9	0	21	122	568	148	78	67	6	9	2	6	66	3	62	9	6	9	9	.500	0	2	4.94
1993	Charlotte	AAA	34	0	0	27	46.2	177	34	10	10	2	1	1	1	13	2	44	4	0	6	3	.667	0	12	1.93
1993	Cleveland	AL	46	0	0	26	56.1	247	57	21	15	0	3	2	1	30	7	41	0	0	4	4	.500	0	11	2.40

Gary DiSarcina

Bats: Right Throws: Right Pos: SS **Ht: 6' 1" Wt: 178 Born: 11/19/67 Age: 26**

							BATTING												BASERUNNING				PERCENTAGES		
Year	Team	Lg	G	AB	H	2B	3B	HR	(Hm | Rd)	TB	R	RBI	TBB	IBB	SO	HBP	SH	SF	SB	CS	SB%	GDP	Avg	OBP	SLG
1989	California	AL	2	0	0	0	0	0	(0 | 0)	0	0	0	0	0	0	0	0	0	0	0	.00	0	.000	.000	.000
1990	California	AL	18	57	8	1	1	0	(0 | 0)	11	8	0	3	0	10	0	1	0	1	0	1.00	3	.140	.183	.193
1991	California	AL	18	57	12	2	0	0	(0 | 0)	14	5	3	3	0	4	2	2	0	0	0	.00	0	.211	.274	.246
1992	California	AL	157	518	128	19	0	3	(2 | 1)	156	48	42	20	0	50	7	5	3	9	7	.56	15	.247	.283	.301
1993	California	AL	126	416	99	20	1	3	(2 | 1)	130	44	45	15	0	38	6	5	3	5	7	.42	13	.238	.273	.313
	5 ML YEARS		321	1048	247	42	2	6	(4 | 2)	311	105	90	41	0	102	15	13	6	15	14	.52	31	.236	.273	.297

Steve Dixon

Pitches: Left Bats: Left Pos: RP **Ht: 6' 0" Wt: 190 Born: 08/03/69 Age: 24**

			HOW MUCH HE PITCHED						WHAT HE GAVE UP												THE RESULTS					
Year	Team	Lg	G	GS	CG	GF	IP	BFP	H	R	ER	HR	SH	SF	HB	TBB	IBB	SO	WP	Bk	W	L	Pct.	ShO	Sv	ERA
1989	Johnson Cty	R	18	3	0	5	43.1	200	50	34	29	1	4	3	2	23	2	29	4	2	1	3	.250	0	0	6.02
1990	Savannah	A	64	0	0	21	83.2	355	59	34	18	1	8	0	4	38	5	92	4	0	7	3	.700	0	8	1.94
1991	St. Pete	A	53	0	0	23	64.1	269	54	32	27	3	7	4	0	24	1	54	2	2	5	4	.556	0	1	3.78
1992	Arkansas	AA	40	0	0	20	49	192	34	11	10	2	3	2	0	15	4	65	2	0	2	1	.667	0	2	1.84
	Louisville	AAA	18	0	0	8	19.2	94	20	12	11	0	0	0	1	19	2	16	0	1	1	2	.333	0	2	5.03
1993	Louisville	AAA	57	0	0	41	67.2	292	57	38	37	4	3	3	3	33	7	61	2	0	5	7	.417	0	20	4.92
1993	St. Louis	NL	4	0	0	0	2.2	20	7	10	10	1	2	0	0	5	0	2	1	0	0	0	.000	0	0	33.75

John Doherty

Pitches: Right Bats: Right Pos: SP **Ht: 6' 4" Wt: 210 Born: 06/11/67 Age: 27**

			HOW MUCH HE PITCHED						WHAT HE GAVE UP												THE RESULTS					
Year	Team	Lg	G	GS	CG	GF	IP	BFP	H	R	ER	HR	SH	SF	HB	TBB	IBB	SO	WP	Bk	W	L	Pct.	ShO	Sv	ERA
1989	Niagara Fls	A	26	1	0	25	47.1	177	30	7	5	1	1	1	0	3	6	2	45	2	2	1	1	.500	0	14	0.95
1990	Fayettevile	A	7	0	0	2	9.1	50	17	12	6	1	0	1	0	1	0	6	1	2	1	0	1.000	0	5	5.79
	Lakeland	A	30	0	0	20	41	153	33	7	5	1	2	1	1	5	2	23	0	4	5	1	.833	0	10	1.10
1991	London	AA	53	0	0	44	65	281	62	29	16	2	2	2	2	21	0	42	1	1	3	3	.500	0	15	2.22
1992	Detroit	AL	47	11	0	9	116	491	131	61	50	4	3	2	4	25	5	37	5	0	7	4	.636	0	3	3.88
1993	Detroit	AL	32	31	3	1	184.2	780	205	104	91	19	5	4	5	48	7	63	4	1	14	11	.560	2	0	4.44
	2 ML YEARS		79	42	3	10	300.2	1271	336	165	141	23	8	6	9	73	12	100	9	1	21	15	.583	2	3	4.22

Chris Donnels

Bats: Left Throws: Right Pos: 3B/1B **Ht: 6' 0" Wt: 185 Born: 04/21/66 Age: 28**

							BATTING												BASERUNNING				PERCENTAGES		
Year	Team	Lg	G	AB	H	2B	3B	HR	(Hm | Rd)	TB	R	RBI	TBB	IBB	SO	HBP	SH	SF	SB	CS	SB%	GDP	Avg	OBP	SLG
1991	New York	NL	37	89	20	2	0	0	(0 | 0)	22	7	5	14	1	19	0	1	0	1	1	.50	0	.225	.330	.247
1992	New York	NL	45	121	21	4	0	0	(0 | 0)	25	8	6	17	0	25	0	1	0	1	0	1.00	1	.174	.275	.207
1993	Houston	NL	88	179	46	14	2	2	(0 | 2)	70	18	24	19	0	33	0	0	1	2	0	1.00	6	.257	.327	.391
	3 ML YEARS		170	389	87	20	2	2	(0 | 2)	117	33	35	50	1	77	0	2	1	4	1	.80	7	.224	.311	.301

57

John Dopson

Pitches: Right **Bats:** Left **Pos:** SP/RP **Ht:** 6' 4" **Wt:** 230 **Born:** 07/14/63 **Age:** 30

			HOW MUCH HE PITCHED						WHAT HE GAVE UP										THE RESULTS					
Year	Team	Lg	G	GS	CG	GF	IP	BFP	H	R	ER	HR	SH	SF	HB	TBB	IBB	SO	WP	Bk	W	L	Pct.	ShO	Sv	ERA
1985	Montreal	NL	4	3	0	0	13	70	25	17	16	4	0	0	0	4	0	4	2	0	0	2	.000	0	0	11.08
1988	Montreal	NL	26	26	1	0	168.2	704	150	69	57	15	5	2	1	58	3	101	3	1	3	11	.214	0	0	3.04
1989	Boston	AL	29	28	2	0	169.1	727	166	84	75	14	5	4	2	69	0	95	7	15	12	8	.600	0	0	3.99
1990	Boston	AL	4	4	0	0	17.2	75	13	7	4	2	0	1	0	9	0	9	0	0	0	0	.000	0	0	2.04
1991	Boston	AL	1	0	0	1	1	6	2	2	2	0	0	1	0	1	0	0	0	0	0	0	.000	0	0	18.00
1992	Boston	AL	25	25	0	0	141.1	598	159	78	64	17	2	2	2	38	2	55	3	3	7	11	.389	0	0	4.08
1993	Boston	AL	34	28	1	3	155.2	681	170	93	86	16	8	8	2	59	12	89	1	3	7	11	.389	1	0	4.97
	7 ML YEARS		123	114	4	4	666.2	2861	685	350	304	68	20	18	7	238	17	353	16	22	29	43	.403	1	0	4.10

Billy Doran

Bats: Both **Throws:** Right **Pos:** 2B **Ht:** 6' 0" **Wt:** 180 **Born:** 05/28/58 **Age:** 36

						BATTING														BASERUNNING				PERCENTAGES		
Year	Team	Lg	G	AB	H	2B	3B	HR	(Hm	Rd)	TB	R	RBI	TBB	IBB	SO	HBP	SH	SF	SB	CS	SB%	GDP	Avg	OBP	SLG
1993	Stockton *	A	1	2	1	0	0	0	--	--	1	0	0	1	0	1	0	0	0	0	1	.00	0	.500	.667	.500
	El Paso *	AA	5	11	4	1	0	0	--	--	5	3	0	3	1	2	0	0	0	0	0	.00	0	.364	.500	.455
1982	Houston	NL	26	97	27	3	0	0	(0	0)	30	11	6	4	0	11	0	0	1	5	0	1.00	0	.278	.304	.309
1983	Houston	NL	154	535	145	12	7	8	(1	7)	195	70	39	86	11	67	0	7	1	12	12	.50	6	.271	.371	.364
1984	Houston	NL	147	548	143	18	11	4	(2	2)	195	92	41	66	7	69	2	7	3	21	12	.64	6	.261	.341	.356
1985	Houston	NL	148	578	166	31	6	14	(5	9)	251	84	59	71	6	69	0	3	5	23	15	.61	10	.287	.362	.434
1986	Houston	NL	145	550	152	29	3	6	(3	3)	205	92	37	81	7	57	2	4	5	42	19	.69	10	.276	.368	.373
1987	Houston	NL	162	625	177	23	3	16	(7	9)	254	82	79	82	3	64	3	2	7	31	11	.74	11	.283	.365	.406
1988	Houston	NL	132	480	119	18	1	7	(2	5)	160	66	53	65	3	60	1	4	2	17	4	.81	7	.248	.338	.333
1989	Houston	NL	142	507	111	25	2	8	(3	5)	164	65	58	59	2	63	2	3	3	22	3	.88	8	.219	.301	.323
1990	2 ML Teams		126	403	121	29	2	7	(4	3)	175	59	37	79	2	58	0	1	5	23	9	.72	3	.300	.411	.434
1991	Cincinnati	NL	111	361	101	12	2	6	(3	3)	135	51	35	46	1	39	0	0	0	5	4	.56	4	.280	.359	.374
1992	Cincinnati	NL	132	387	91	16	2	8	(6	2)	135	48	47	64	9	40	0	3	2	7	4	.64	11	.235	.342	.349
1993	Milwaukee	AL	28	60	13	4	0	0	(0	0)	17	7	6	6	1	3	0	0	1	1	0	1.00	3	.217	.284	.283
1990	Houston	NL	109	344	99	21	2	6	(3	3)	142	49	32	71	1	53	0	1	5	18	9	.67	2	.288	.405	.413
	Cincinnati	NL	17	59	22	8	0	1	(1	0)	33	10	5	8	1	5	0	0	0	5	0	1.00	1	.373	.448	.559
	12 ML YEARS		1453	5131	1366	220	39	84	(36	48)	1916	727	497	709	52	600	10	34	38	209	93	.69	79	.266	.354	.373

Brian Dorsett

Bats: Right **Throws:** Right **Pos:** C **Ht:** 6' 3" **Wt:** 215 **Born:** 04/09/61 **Age:** 33

						BATTING														BASERUNNING				PERCENTAGES		
Year	Team	Lg	G	AB	H	2B	3B	HR	(Hm	Rd)	TB	R	RBI	TBB	IBB	SO	HBP	SH	SF	SB	CS	SB%	GDP	Avg	OBP	SLG
1993	Indianapolis *	AAA	77	278	83	27	0	18	--	--	164	38	57	28	2	53	3	0	5	2	0	1.00	4	.299	.363	.590
1987	Cleveland	AL	5	11	3	0	0	1	(1	0)	6	2	3	0	0	3	1	0	0	0	0	.00	0	.273	.333	.545
1988	California	AL	7	11	1	0	0	0	(0	0)	1	0	2	1	0	5	0	0	0	0	0	.00	0	.091	.167	.091
1989	New York	AL	8	22	8	1	0	0	(0	0)	9	3	4	1	0	3	0	0	0	0	0	.00	0	.364	.391	.409
1990	New York	AL	14	35	5	2	0	0	(0	0)	7	2	0	2	0	4	0	0	0	0	0	.00	2	.143	.189	.200
1991	San Diego	NL	11	12	1	0	0	0	(0	0)	1	0	1	0	0	3	0	0	0	0	0	.00	0	.083	.083	.083
1993	Cincinnati	NL	25	63	16	4	0	2	(2	0)	26	7	12	3	0	14	0	0	0	0	0	.00	1	.254	.288	.413
	6 ML YEARS		70	154	34	7	0	3	(3	0)	50	14	22	7	0	32	1	0	0	0	0	.00	3	.221	.259	.325

Kelly Downs

Pitches: Right **Bats:** Right **Pos:** RP/SP **Ht:** 6' 4" **Wt:** 200 **Born:** 10/25/60 **Age:** 33

			HOW MUCH HE PITCHED						WHAT HE GAVE UP											THE RESULTS					
Year	Team	Lg	G	GS	CG	GF	IP	BFP	H	R	ER	HR	SH	SF	HB	TBB	IBB	SO	WP	Bk	W	L	Pct.	ShO	Sv	ERA
1986	San Francisco	NL	14	14	1	0	88.1	372	78	29	27	5	4	4	3	30	7	64	3	2	4	4	.500	0	0	2.75
1987	San Francisco	NL	41	28	4	6	186	797	185	83	75	14	7	1	4	67	11	137	12	4	12	9	.571	3	1	3.63
1988	San Francisco	NL	27	26	6	0	168	685	140	67	62	11	4	9	3	47	8	118	7	4	13	9	.591	3	0	3.32
1989	San Francisco	NL	18	15	0	1	82.2	349	82	47	44	7	4	4	1	26	4	49	3	3	4	8	.333	0	0	4.79
1990	San Francisco	NL	13	9	0	1	63	265	56	26	24	2	2	1	2	20	4	31	2	1	3	2	.600	0	0	3.43
1991	San Francisco	NL	45	11	0	4	111.2	479	99	59	52	12	4	4	3	53	9	62	4	1	10	4	.714	0	0	4.19
1992	2 ML Teams		37	20	0	7	144.1	636	137	63	54	8	13	6	7	70	3	71	7	1	6	7	.462	0	0	3.37
1993	Oakland	AL	42	12	0	12	119.2	539	135	80	75	14	3	4	2	60	8	66	4	1	5	10	.333	0	0	5.64
1992	2 ML Teams		19	7	0	5	62.1	272	65	27	24	4	7	2	3	24	0	33	4	0	1	2	.333	0	0	3.47
	Oakland	AL	18	13	0	2	82	364	72	36	30	4	6	4	4	46	3	38	3	1	5	5	.500	0	0	3.29
	8 ML YEARS		237	135	11	29	963.2	4122	912	454	413	73	41	33	25	373	54	598	42	17	57	53	.518	6	1	3.86

Doug Drabek

Pitches: Right **Bats:** Right **Pos:** SP   **Ht:** 6' 1" **Wt:** 185 **Born:** 07/25/62 **Age:** 31

Year	Team	Lg	G	GS	CG	GF	IP	BFP	H	R	ER	HR	SH	SF	HB	TBB	IBB	SO	WP	Bk	W	L	Pct.	ShO	Sv	ERA
1986	New York	AL	27	21	0	2	131.2	561	126	64	60	13	5	2	3	50	1	76	2	0	7	8	.467	0	0	4.10
1987	Pittsburgh	NL	29	28	1	0	176.1	721	165	86	76	22	3	4	0	46	2	120	5	1	11	12	.478	1	0	3.88
1988	Pittsburgh	NL	33	32	3	0	219.1	880	194	83	75	21	7	5	6	50	4	127	4	1	15	7	.682	1	0	3.08
1989	Pittsburgh	NL	35	34	8	1	244.1	994	215	83	76	21	13	7	3	69	3	123	3	0	14	12	.538	5	0	2.80
1990	Pittsburgh	NL	33	33	9	0	231.1	918	190	78	71	15	10	3	3	56	2	131	6	0	**22**	6	**.786**	3	0	2.76
1991	Pittsburgh	NL	35	35	5	0	234.2	977	245	92	80	16	12	6	3	62	6	142	5	0	15	14	.517	2	0	3.07
1992	Pittsburgh	NL	34	34	10	0	256.2	1021	218	84	79	17	8	8	6	54	8	177	11	1	15	11	.577	4	0	2.77
1993	Houston	NL	34	34	7	0	237.2	991	242	108	100	18	14	8	3	60	12	157	12	0	9	**18**	.333	2	0	3.79
	8 ML YEARS		260	251	43	3	1732	7063	1595	678	617	143	72	43	27	447	38	1053	48	3	108	88	.551	18	0	3.21

Brian Drahman

Pitches: Right **Bats:** Right **Pos:** RP   **Ht:** 6' 3" **Wt:** 205 **Born:** 11/07/66 **Age:** 27

Year	Team	Lg	G	GS	CG	GF	IP	BFP	H	R	ER	HR	SH	SF	HB	TBB	IBB	SO	WP	Bk	W	L	Pct.	ShO	Sv	ERA
1993	Nashville *	AAA	54	0	0	50	55.2	249	59	29	18	3	3	4	2	19	8	49	6	0	9	4	.692	0	20	2.91
1991	Chicago	AL	28	0	0	8	30.2	125	21	12	11	4	2	1	0	13	1	18	0	0	3	2	.600	0	0	3.23
1992	Chicago	AL	5	0	0	2	7	29	6	3	2	0	0	0	0	2	0	1	1	0	0	0	.000	0	0	2.57
1993	Chicago	AL	5	0	0	4	5.1	23	7	0	0	0	0	0	0	2	0	3	0	0	0	0	.000	0	1	0.00
	3 ML YEARS		38	0	0	14	43	177	34	15	13	4	2	1	0	17	1	22	1	0	3	2	.600	0	1	2.72

Mike Draper

Pitches: Right **Bats:** Right **Pos:** RP   **Ht:** 6' 2" **Wt:** 175 **Born:** 09/14/66 **Age:** 27

Year	Team	Lg	G	GS	CG	GF	IP	BFP	H	R	ER	HR	SH	SF	HB	TBB	IBB	SO	WP	Bk	W	L	Pct.	ShO	Sv	ERA
1988	Oneonta	A	8	0	0	8	10.2	46	10	4	1	0	0	0	0	3	0	16	1	0	2	1	.667	0	3	0.84
	Pr William	A	9	5	1	1	35.1	155	37	22	13	1	1	3	4	4	1	20	4	2	2	3	.400	0	0	3.31
1989	Pr William	A	25	24	6	0	153.1	646	147	66	53	7	3	4	6	42	4	84	12	1	14	8	.636	1	0	3.11
1990	Albany	AA	8	8	0	0	43.1	196	51	34	31	4	0	1	2	19	0	15	0	1	2	2	.500	0	0	6.44
	Ft.Laudrdle	A	14	14	1	0	96	389	80	30	24	1	5	3	3	22	0	52	5	4	9	1	.900	1	0	2.25
	Pr William	A	5	4	1	0	22.2	107	31	20	16	2	1	1	2	9	0	8	4	0	0	2	.000	0	0	6.35
1991	Albany	AA	36	14	1	6	131.1	555	125	58	48	6	5	3	6	47	3	71	10	1	10	6	.625	1	2	3.29
	Columbus	AAA	4	4	2	0	28.2	132	36	21	12	1	0	1	0	5	0	13	0	0	1	3	.250	0	0	3.77
1992	Columbus	AAA	57	3	0	50	80	332	70	36	32	3	2	5	0	28	2	42	3	0	5	6	.455	0	37	3.60
1993	New York	NL	29	1	0	11	42.1	184	53	22	20	2	3	5	0	14	3	16	0	1	1	1	.500	0	0	4.25

Steve Dreyer

Pitches: Right **Bats:** Right **Pos:** SP   **Ht:** 6' 3" **Wt:** 180 **Born:** 11/19/69 **Age:** 24

Year	Team	Lg	G	GS	CG	GF	IP	BFP	H	R	ER	HR	SH	SF	HB	TBB	IBB	SO	WP	Bk	W	L	Pct.	ShO	Sv	ERA
1990	Butte	R	8	8	0	0	35.2	146	32	21	18	2	0	0	0	10	0	29	1	0	1	1	.500	0	0	4.54
1991	Gastonia	A	25	25	3	0	162	661	137	51	43	5	5	4	5	62	1	122	4	0	7	10	.412	1	0	2.39
1992	Charlotte	A	26	26	4	0	168.2	675	164	54	45	8	10	0	6	37	2	111	4	0	11	7	.611	3	0	2.40
1993	Tulsa	AA	5	5	1	0	31.1	128	26	13	13	4	0	1	0	8	1	27	0	0	2	2	.500	1	0	3.73
	Okla City	AAA	16	16	1	0	107	445	108	39	36	5	4	3	2	31	1	59	4	0	4	6	.400	0	0	3.03
1993	Texas	AL	10	6	0	1	41	186	48	26	26	7	0	0	1	20	0	23	0	0	3	3	.500	0	0	5.71

Rob Ducey

Bats: Left **Throws:** Right **Pos:** CF/RF   **Ht:** 6' 2" **Wt:** 180 **Born:** 05/24/65 **Age:** 29

Year	Team	Lg	G	AB	H	2B	3B	HR	(Hm	Rd)	TB	R	RBI	TBB	IBB	SO	HBP	SH	SF	SB	CS	SB%	GDP	Avg	OBP	SLG
1993	Okla City *	AAA	105	389	118	17	10	17	--	--	206	68	56	46	2	97	1	0	4	17	9	.65	5	.303	.375	.530
1987	Toronto	AL	34	48	9	1	0	1	(1	0)	13	12	6	8	0	10	0	0	1	2	0	1.00	0	.188	.298	.271
1988	Toronto	AL	27	54	17	4	1	0	(0	0)	23	15	6	5	0	7	0	2	2	1	0	1.00	1	.315	.361	.426
1989	Toronto	AL	41	76	16	4	0	0	(0	0)	20	5	7	9	1	25	0	1	0	2	1	.67	2	.211	.294	.263
1990	Toronto	AL	19	53	16	5	0	0	(0	0)	21	7	7	7	0	15	1	0	1	2	1	1.00	1	.302	.387	.396
1991	Toronto	AL	39	68	16	2	2	1	(0	1)	25	8	4	6	0	26	0	1	0	2	0	1.00	1	.235	.297	.368
1992	2 ML Teams		54	80	15	4	0	0	(0	0)	19	7	2	5	0	22	0	0	1	2	4	.33	1	.188	.233	.238
1993	Texas	AL	27	85	24	6	3	2	(2	0)	42	15	9	10	2	17	0	2	2	2	3	.40	1	.282	.351	.494
1992	Toronto	AL	23	21	1	1	0	0	(0	0)	2	3	1	0	0	10	0	0	0	0	1	.00	0	.048	.048	.095
	California	AL	31	59	14	3	0	0	(0	0)	17	4	2	5	0	12	0	0	1	2	3	.40	1	.237	.292	.288
	7 ML YEARS		241	464	113	26	6	4	(3	1)	163	69	41	50	3	122	1	6	7	12	9	.57	6	.244	.314	.351

Mariano Duncan

Bats: Right **Throws:** Right **Pos:** 2B/SS **Ht:** 6' 0" **Wt:** 191 **Born:** 03/13/63 **Age:** 31

Year	Team	Lg	G	AB	H	2B	3B	HR	(Hm	Rd)	TB	R	RBI	TBB	IBB	SO	HBP	SH	SF	SB	CS	SB%	GDP	Avg	OBP	SLG
1985	Los Angeles	NL	142	562	137	24	6	6	(1	5)	191	74	39	38	4	113	3	13	4	38	8	.83	9	.244	.293	.340
1986	Los Angeles	NL	109	407	93	7	0	8	(2	6)	124	47	30	30	1	78	2	5	1	48	13	.79	6	.229	.284	.305
1987	Los Angeles	NL	76	261	56	8	1	6	(3	3)	84	31	18	17	1	62	2	6	1	11	1	.92	4	.215	.267	.322
1989	2 ML Teams		94	258	64	15	2	3	(2	1)	92	32	21	8	0	51	5	2	0	9	5	.64	3	.248	.284	.357
1990	Cincinnati	NL	125	435	133	22	11	10	(5	5)	207	67	55	24	4	67	4	4	4	13	7	.65	10	.306	.345	.476
1991	Cincinnati	NL	100	333	86	7	4	12	(10	2)	137	46	40	12	0	57	3	5	3	5	4	.56	0	.258	.288	.411
1992	Philadelphia	NL	142	574	153	40	3	8	(3	5)	223	71	50	17	0	108	5	5	4	23	3	.88	15	.267	.292	.389
1993	Philadelphia	NL	124	496	140	26	4	11	(5	6)	207	68	73	12	0	88	4	4	2	6	5	.55	13	.282	.304	.417
1989	Los Angeles	NL	49	84	21	5	1	0	(0	0)	28	9	8	0	0	15	2	1	0	3	3	.50	1	.250	.267	.333
	Cincinnati	NL	45	174	43	10	1	3	(2	1)	64	23	13	8	0	36	3	1	0	6	2	.75	2	.247	.292	.368
	8 ML YEARS		912	3326	862	149	31	64	(31	33)	1265	436	326	158	10	624	28	44	19	153	46	.77	60	.259	.297	.380

Shawon Dunston

Bats: Right **Throws:** Right **Pos:** SS **Ht:** 6' 1" **Wt:** 175 **Born:** 03/21/63 **Age:** 31

Year	Team	Lg	G	AB	H	2B	3B	HR	(Hm	Rd)	TB	R	RBI	TBB	IBB	SO	HBP	SH	SF	SB	CS	SB%	GDP	Avg	OBP	SLG
1985	Chicago	NL	74	250	65	12	4	4	(3	1)	97	40	18	19	3	42	0	1	2	11	3	.79	3	.260	.310	.388
1986	Chicago	NL	150	581	145	37	3	17	(10	7)	239	66	68	21	5	114	3	4	2	13	11	.54	5	.250	.278	.411
1987	Chicago	NL	95	346	85	18	3	5	(3	2)	124	40	22	10	1	68	1	0	2	12	3	.80	6	.246	.267	.358
1988	Chicago	NL	155	575	143	23	6	9	(5	4)	205	69	56	16	8	108	2	4	2	30	9	.77	6	.249	.271	.357
1989	Chicago	NL	138	471	131	20	6	9	(3	6)	190	52	60	30	15	86	1	6	4	19	11	.63	7	.278	.320	.403
1990	Chicago	NL	146	545	143	22	8	17	(7	10)	232	73	66	15	1	87	3	4	6	25	5	.83	9	.262	.283	.426
1991	Chicago	NL	142	492	128	22	7	12	(7	5)	200	59	50	23	5	64	4	4	11	21	6	.78	9	.260	.292	.407
1992	Chicago	NL	18	73	23	3	1	0	(0	0)	28	8	2	3	0	13	0	0	0	2	3	.40	1	.315	.342	.384
1993	Chicago	NL	7	10	4	2	0	0	(0	0)	6	3	2	0	0	1	0	0	0	0	0	.00	0	.400	.400	.600
	9 ML YEARS		925	3343	867	159	38	73	(38	35)	1321	410	344	137	38	583	14	23	29	133	51	.72	45	.259	.289	.395

Lenny Dykstra

Bats: Left **Throws:** Left **Pos:** CF **Ht:** 5'10" **Wt:** 193 **Born:** 02/10/63 **Age:** 31

Year	Team	Lg	G	AB	H	2B	3B	HR	(Hm	Rd)	TB	R	RBI	TBB	IBB	SO	HBP	SH	SF	SB	CS	SB%	GDP	Avg	OBP	SLG
1985	New York	NL	83	236	60	9	3	1	(0	1)	78	40	19	30	0	24	1	4	2	15	2	.88	4	.254	.338	.331
1986	New York	NL	147	431	127	27	7	8	(4	4)	192	77	45	58	1	55	0	7	2	31	7	.82	4	.295	.377	.445
1987	New York	NL	132	431	123	37	3	10	(7	3)	196	86	43	40	3	67	4	4	0	27	7	.79	1	.285	.352	.455
1988	New York	NL	126	429	116	19	3	8	(3	5)	165	57	33	30	2	43	3	2	2	30	8	.79	3	.270	.321	.385
1989	2 ML Teams		146	511	121	32	4	7	(5	2)	182	66	32	60	1	53	3	5	5	30	12	.71	7	.237	.318	.356
1990	Philadelphia	NL	149	590	192	35	3	9	(6	3)	260	106	60	89	14	48	7	2	3	33	5	.87	5	.325	.418	.441
1991	Philadelphia	NL	63	246	73	13	5	3	(3	0)	105	48	12	37	1	20	1	0	0	24	4	.86	1	.297	.391	.427
1992	Philadelphia	NL	85	345	104	18	0	6	(5	1)	140	53	39	40	3	32	3	0	4	30	5	.86	1	.301	.375	.406
1993	Philadelphia	NL	161	637	194	44	6	19	(12	7)	307	143	66	129	9	64	2	0	5	37	12	.76	8	.305	.420	.482
1989	New York	NL	56	159	43	12	1	3	(2	1)	66	27	13	23	0	15	2	4	4	13	1	.93	2	.270	.362	.415
	Philadelphia	NL	90	352	78	20	3	4	(3	1)	116	39	19	37	1	38	1	1	1	17	11	.61	5	.222	.297	.330
	9 ML YEARS		1092	3856	1110	234	34	71	(45	26)	1625	676	349	513	35	406	24	24	23	257	62	.81	34	.288	.373	.421

Damion Easley

Bats: Right **Throws:** Right **Pos:** 2B/3B **Ht:** 5'11" **Wt:** 185 **Born:** 11/11/69 **Age:** 24

Year	Team	Lg	G	AB	H	2B	3B	HR	(Hm	Rd)	TB	R	RBI	TBB	IBB	SO	HBP	SH	SF	SB	CS	SB%	GDP	Avg	OBP	SLG
1989	Bend	A	36	131	39	5	1	4	--	--	58	34	21	25	0	21	4	0	0	9	4	.69	1	.298	.425	.443
1990	Quad City	A	103	365	100	19	3	10	--	--	155	59	56	41	0	60	8	1	2	24	8	.75	8	.274	.358	.425
1991	Midland	AA	127	452	115	24	4	6	--	--	165	73	57	58	2	67	7	6	2	22	9	.71	12	.254	.347	.365
1992	Edmonton	AAA	108	429	124	18	3	3	--	--	157	61	44	31	0	44	5	3	6	26	10	.72	13	.289	.340	.366
1992	California	AL	47	151	39	5	0	1	(1	0)	47	14	12	8	0	26	3	2	1	9	5	.64	2	.258	.307	.311
1993	California	AL	73	230	72	13	2	2	(0	2)	95	33	22	28	2	35	3	1	2	6	6	.50	5	.313	.392	.413
	2 ML YEARS		120	381	111	18	2	3	(1	2)	142	47	34	36	2	61	6	3	3	15	11	.58	7	.291	.359	.373

Dennis Eckersley

Pitches: Right **Bats:** Right **Pos:** RP **Ht:** 6' 2" **Wt:** 195 **Born:** 10/03/54 **Age:** 39

Year	Team	Lg	G	GS	CG	GF	IP	BFP	H	R	ER	HR	SH	SF	HB	TBB	IBB	SO	WP	Bk	W	L	Pct.	ShO	Sv	ERA
1975	Cleveland	AL	34	24	6	5	187	794	147	61	54	16	6	7	7	90	8	152	4	2	13	7	.650	2	2	2.60
1976	Cleveland	AL	36	30	9	3	199	821	155	82	76	13	10	4	5	78	2	200	6	1	13	12	.520	3	1	3.44
1977	Cleveland	AL	33	33	12	0	247	1006	214	100	97	31	11	6	7	54	11	191	3	0	14	13	.519	3	0	3.53
1978	Boston	AL	35	35	16	0	268	1121	258	99	89	30	7	8	7	71	8	162	3	0	20	8	.714	3	0	2.99

Year Team	Lg	G	GS	CG	GF	IP	BFP	H	R	ER	HR	SH	SF	HB	TBB	IBB	SO	WP	Bk	W	L	Pct.	ShO	Sv	ERA
1979 Boston	AL	33	33	17	0	247	1018	234	89	82	29	10	6	6	59	4	150	1	1	17	10	.630	2	0	2.99
1980 Boston	AL	30	30	8	0	198	818	188	101	94	25	7	8	2	44	7	121	0	0	12	14	.462	0	0	4.27
1981 Boston	AL	23	23	8	0	154	649	160	82	73	9	6	5	3	35	2	79	0	0	9	8	.529	2	0	4.27
1982 Boston	AL	33	33	11	0	224.1	926	228	101	93	31	4	4	2	43	3	127	1	0	13	13	.500	3	0	3.73
1983 Boston	AL	28	28	2	0	176.1	787	223	119	110	27	1	5	6	39	4	77	1	0	9	13	.409	0	0	5.61
1984 2 ML Teams		33	33	4	0	225	932	223	97	90	21	11	9	5	49	9	114	3	2	14	12	.538	0	0	3.60
1985 Chicago	NL	25	25	6	0	169.1	664	145	61	58	15	6	2	3	19	4	117	0	3	11	7	.611	2	0	3.08
1986 Chicago	NL	33	32	1	0	201	862	226	109	102	21	13	10	3	43	3	137	2	5	6	11	.353	0	0	4.57
1987 Oakland	AL	54	2	0	33	115.2	460	99	41	39	11	3	3	3	17	3	113	1	0	6	8	.429	0	16	3.03
1988 Oakland	AL	60	0	0	53	72.2	279	52	20	19	5	1	3	1	11	2	70	0	2	4	2	.667	0	45	2.35
1989 Oakland	AL	51	0	0	46	57.2	206	32	10	10	5	0	4	1	3	0	55	0	0	4	0	1.000	0	33	1.56
1990 Oakland	AL	63	0	0	61	73.1	262	41	9	5	2	0	1	0	4	1	73	0	0	4	2	.667	0	48	0.61
1991 Oakland	AL	67	0	0	59	76	299	60	26	25	11	1	0	1	9	3	87	1	0	5	4	.556	0	43	2.96
1992 Oakland	AL	69	0	0	65	80	309	62	17	17	5	3	0	1	11	6	93	0	0	7	1	.875	0	51	1.91
1993 Oakland	AL	64	0	0	52	67	276	67	32	31	7	2	2	2	13	4	80	0	0	2	4	.333	0	36	4.16
1984 Boston	AL	9	9	2	0	64.2	270	71	38	36	10	3	3	1	13	2	33	2	0	4	4	.500	0	0	5.01
Chicago	NL	24	24	2	0	160.1	662	152	59	54	11	8	6	4	36	7	81	1	2	10	8	.556	0	0	3.03
19 ML YEARS		804	361	100	377	3038.1	12489	2814	1256	1164	314	102	87	65	692	84	2198	26	16	183	149	.551	20	275	3.45

Tom Edens

Pitches: Right   Bats: Left   Pos: RP   Ht: 6' 2"   Wt: 188   Born: 06/09/61   Age: 33

Year Team	Lg	G	GS	CG	GF	IP	BFP	H	R	ER	HR	SH	SF	HB	TBB	IBB	SO	WP	Bk	W	L	Pct.	ShO	Sv	ERA
1993 Osceola *	A	3	1	0	0	4	17	5	0	0	0	0	0	1	1	0	4	0	0	1	0	1.000	0	0	0.00
Tucson *	AAA	5	0	0	1	7.1	34	9	5	5	0	0	0	1	3	0	6	0	0	1	0	1.000	0	0	6.14
1987 New York	NL	2	2	0	0	8	42	15	6	6	2	2	0	0	4	0	4	2	0	0	0	.000	0	0	6.75
1990 Milwaukee	AL	35	6	0	9	89	387	89	52	44	8	6	4	4	33	3	40	1	0	4	5	.444	0	2	4.45
1991 Minnesota	AL	8	6	0	0	33	143	34	15	15	2	0	0	0	10	1	19	1	0	2	2	.500	0	0	4.09
1992 Minnesota	AL	52	0	0	14	76.1	317	65	26	24	1	4	0	2	36	3	57	5	0	6	3	.667	0	3	2.83
1993 Houston	NL	38	0	0	20	49	203	47	17	17	4	4	1	0	19	7	21	3	0	1	1	.500	0	3	3.12
5 ML YEARS		135	14	0	43	255.1	1092	250	116	106	17	16	5	6	102	14	141	12	0	13	11	.542	0	5	3.74

Jim Edmonds

Bats: Left   Throws: Left   Pos: RF   Ht: 6' 1"   Wt: 200   Born: 06/27/70   Age: 24

Year Team	Lg	G	AB	H	2B	3B	HR	(Hm	Rd)	TB	R	RBI	TBB	IBB	SO	HBP	SH	SF	SB	CS	SB%	GDP	Avg	OBP	SLG
1988 Bend	A	35	122	27	4	0	0	--	--	31	23	13	20	0	44	0	0	1	4	0	1.00	2	.221	.329	.254
1989 Quad City	A	31	92	24	4	0	1	--	--	31	11	4	7	0	34	0	0	0	1	0	1.00	3	.261	.313	.337
1990 Palm Sprngs	A	91	314	92	18	6	3	--	--	131	36	56	27	3	75	2	1	2	5	2	.71	10	.293	.351	.417
1991 Palm Sprngs	A	60	187	55	15	1	2	--	--	78	28	27	40	3	57	0	3	1	2	2	.50	2	.294	.417	.417
1992 Midland	AA	70	246	77	15	2	8	--	--	120	42	32	41	1	83	1	1	0	3	4	.43	8	.313	.413	.488
Edmonton	AAA	50	194	58	15	2	6	--	--	95	37	36	14	2	55	0	2	2	3	1	.75	2	.299	.343	.490
1993 Vancouver	AAA	95	356	112	28	4	9	--	--	175	59	74	41	4	81	0	2	4	6	8	.43	5	.315	.382	.492
1993 California	AL	18	61	15	4	1	0	(0	0)	21	5	4	2	1	16	0	0	0	0	2	.00	1	.246	.270	.344

Mark Eichhorn

Pitches: Right   Bats: Right   Pos: RP   Ht: 6' 3"   Wt: 210   Born: 11/21/60   Age: 33

Year Team	Lg	G	GS	CG	GF	IP	BFP	H	R	ER	HR	SH	SF	HB	TBB	IBB	SO	WP	Bk	W	L	Pct.	ShO	Sv	ERA
1982 Toronto	AL	7	7	0	0	38	171	40	28	23	4	1	2	0	14	1	16	3	0	0	3	.000	0	0	5.45
1986 Toronto	AL	69	0	0	38	157	612	105	32	30	8	9	2	7	45	14	166	2	1	14	6	.700	0	10	1.72
1987 Toronto	AL	89	0	0	27	127.2	540	110	47	45	14	7	4	6	52	13	96	3	1	10	6	.625	0	4	3.17
1988 Toronto	AL	37	0	0	17	66.2	302	79	32	31	3	8	1	6	27	4	28	3	6	0	3	.000	0	1	4.18
1989 Atlanta	NL	45	0	0	13	68.1	286	70	36	33	6	7	4	1	19	8	49	0	1	5	5	.500	0	0	4.35
1990 California	AL	60	0	0	40	84.2	374	98	36	29	2	2	4	6	23	0	69	2	0	2	5	.286	0	13	3.08
1991 California	AL	70	0	0	23	81.2	311	63	21	18	2	5	3	2	13	1	49	0	0	3	3	.500	0	1	1.98
1992 2 ML Teams		65	0	0	26	87.2	372	86	34	30	3	3	5	2	25	8	61	9	1	4	4	.500	0	2	3.08
1993 Toronto	AL	54	0	0	16	72.2	309	76	26	22	3	3	2	2	22	7	47	2	0	3	1	.750	0	0	2.72
1992 California	AL	42	0	0	19	56.2	237	51	19	15	2	2	3	0	18	8	42	3	1	2	4	.333	0	2	2.38
Toronto	AL	23	0	0	7	31	135	35	15	15	1	1	2	2	7	0	19	6	0	2	0	1.000	0	0	4.35
9 ML YEARS		496	7	0	200	784.1	3277	727	292	261	45	45	27	33	240	56	581	24	10	41	36	.532	0	31	2.99

Dave Eiland

Pitches: Right   Bats: Right   Pos: SP   Ht: 6' 3"   Wt: 210   Born: 07/05/66   Age: 27

Year Team	Lg	G	GS	CG	GF	IP	BFP	H	R	ER	HR	SH	SF	HB	TBB	IBB	SO	WP	Bk	W	L	Pct.	ShO	Sv	ERA
1993 Charlotte *	AAA	8	8	0	0	35.2	154	42	22	21	8	1	0	1	12	0	13	0	0	1	3	.250	0	0	5.30

							IP	BFP	H	R	ER										W	L	Pct.	ShO	Sv	ERA
Okla City *	AAA	7	7	1	0		35.2	155	39	18	17	1	1	1	1	9	0	15	0	0	3	1	.750	0	0	4.29
1988 New York	AL	3	3	0	0		12.2	57	15	9	9	6	0	0	2	4	0	7	0	0	0	0	.000	0	0	6.39
1989 New York	AL	6	6	0	0		34.1	152	44	25	22	5	1	2	2	13	3	11	0	0	1	3	.250	0	0	5.77
1990 New York	AL	5	5	0	0		30.1	127	31	14	12	2	0	0	0	5	0	16	0	0	2	1	.667	0	0	3.56
1991 New York	AL	18	13	0	4		72.2	317	87	51	43	10	0	3	3	23	1	18	0	0	2	5	.286	0	0	5.33
1992 San Diego	NL	7	7	0	0		27	120	33	21	17	1	0	0	0	5	0	10	0	1	0	2	.000	0	0	5.67
1993 San Diego	NL	10	9	0	0		48.1	217	58	33	28	5	2	2	1	17	1	14	1	0	0	3	.000	0	0	5.21
6 ML YEARS		49	43	0	4		225.1	990	268	153	131	29	3	7	8	67	5	76	1	1	5	14	.263	0	0	5.23

Jim Eisenreich

Bats: Left   **Throws:** Left   **Pos:** RF   **Ht:** 5'11"   **Wt:** 200   **Born:** 04/18/59   **Age:** 35

								BATTING											BASERUNNING				PERCENTAGES		
Year Team	Lg	G	AB	H	2B	3B	HR	(Hm Rd)	TB	R	RBI	TBB	IBB	SO	HBP	SH	SF	SB	CS	SB%	GDP	Avg	OBP	SLG
1982 Minnesota	AL	34	99	30	6	0	2	(1 1)	42	10	9	11	0	13	1	0	0	0	0	.00	1	.303	.378	.424
1983 Minnesota	AL	2	7	2	1	0	0	(0 0)	3	1	0	1	0	1	0	0	0	0	0	.00	0	.286	.375	.429
1984 Minnesota	AL	12	32	7	1	0	0	(0 0)	8	1	3	2	1	4	0	0	0	2	0	1.00	0	.219	.250	.250
1987 Kansas City	AL	44	105	25	8	2	4	(3 1)	49	10	21	7	2	13	0	0	3	1	1	.50	2	.238	.278	.467
1988 Kansas City	AL	82	202	44	8	1	1	(0 1)	57	26	19	6	1	31	0	2	4	9	3	.75	2	.218	.236	.282
1989 Kansas City	AL	134	475	139	33	7	9	(4 5)	213	64	59	37	9	44	0	3	4	27	8	.77	8	.293	.341	.448
1990 Kansas City	AL	142	496	139	29	7	5	(2 3)	197	61	51	42	2	51	1	2	4	12	14	.46	7	.280	.335	.397
1991 Kansas City	AL	135	375	113	22	3	2	(2 0)	147	47	47	20	1	35	1	3	6	5	3	.63	10	.301	.333	.392
1992 Kansas City	AL	113	353	95	13	3	2	(1 1)	120	31	28	24	4	36	0	0	3	11	6	.65	6	.269	.313	.340
1993 Philadelphia	NL	153	362	113	17	4	7	(3 4)	161	51	54	26	5	36	1	3	2	5	0	1.00	6	.318	.363	.445
10 ML YEARS		851	2506	709	138	27	32	(16 16)	997	302	291	176	25	264	4	13	28	72	35	.67	43	.283	.328	.398

Cal Eldred

Pitches: Right   **Bats:** Right   **Pos:** SP   **Ht:** 6' 4"   **Wt:** 215   **Born:** 11/24/67   **Age:** 26

			HOW MUCH HE PITCHED					WHAT HE GAVE UP										THE RESULTS				
Year Team	Lg	G	GS	CG	GF	IP	BFP	H	R	ER	HR	SH	SF	HB	TBB	IBB	SO	WP	Bk	W	L	Pct.	ShO	Sv	ERA
1991 Milwaukee	AL	3	3	0	0	16	73	20	9	8	2	0	0	0	6	0	10	0	0	2	0	1.000	0	0	4.50
1992 Milwaukee	AL	14	14	2	0	100.1	394	76	21	20	4	1	0	2	23	0	62	3	0	11	2	.846	1	0	1.79
1993 Milwaukee	AL	36	36	8	0	258	1087	232	120	115	32	5	12	10	91	5	180	2	0	16	16	.500	1	0	4.01
3 ML YEARS		53	53	10	0	374.1	1554	328	150	143	38	6	12	12	120	5	252	5	0	29	18	.617	2	0	3.44

Scott Erickson

Pitches: Right   **Bats:** Right   **Pos:** SP   **Ht:** 6' 4"   **Wt:** 224   **Born:** 02/02/68   **Age:** 26

			HOW MUCH HE PITCHED					WHAT HE GAVE UP										THE RESULTS				
Year Team	Lg	G	GS	CG	GF	IP	BFP	H	R	ER	HR	SH	SF	HB	TBB	IBB	SO	WP	Bk	W	L	Pct.	ShO	Sv	ERA
1990 Minnesota	AL	19	17	1	1	113	485	108	49	36	9	5	2	5	51	4	53	3	0	8	4	.667	0	0	2.87
1991 Minnesota	AL	32	32	5	0	204	851	189	80	72	13	5	7	6	71	3	108	4	0	20	8	.714	3	0	3.18
1992 Minnesota	AL	32	32	5	0	212	888	197	86	80	18	9	7	8	83	3	101	6	1	13	12	.520	3	0	3.40
1993 Minnesota	AL	34	34	1	0	218.2	976	266	138	126	17	10	13	10	71	1	116	5	0	8	19	.296	0	0	5.19
4 ML YEARS		117	115	12	1	747.2	3200	760	353	314	57	29	29	29	276	11	378	18	1	49	43	.533	6	0	3.78

Alvaro Espinoza

Bats: Right   **Throws:** Right   **Pos:** 3B/SS   **Ht:** 6' 0"   **Wt:** 190   **Born:** 02/19/62   **Age:** 32

								BATTING											BASERUNNING				PERCENTAGES		
Year Team	Lg	G	AB	H	2B	3B	HR	(Hm Rd)	TB	R	RBI	TBB	IBB	SO	HBP	SH	SF	SB	CS	SB%	GDP	Avg	OBP	SLG
1984 Minnesota	AL	1	0	0	0	0	0	(0 0)	0	0	0	0	0	0	0	0	0	0	0	.00	0	.000	.000	.000
1985 Minnesota	AL	32	57	15	2	0	0	(0 0)	17	5	9	1	0	9	1	3	0	0	1	.00	0	.263	.288	.298
1986 Minnesota	AL	37	42	9	1	0	0	(0 0)	10	4	1	1	0	10	0	2	0	0	1	.00	2	.214	.233	.238
1988 New York	AL	3	3	0	0	0	0	(0 0)	0	0	0	0	0	0	0	0	0	0	0	.00	0	.000	.000	.000
1989 New York	AL	146	503	142	23	1	0	(0 0)	167	51	41	14	1	60	1	23	3	3	3	.50	14	.282	.301	.332
1990 New York	AL	150	438	98	12	2	2	(0 2)	120	31	20	16	0	54	5	11	2	1	2	.33	13	.224	.258	.274
1991 New York	AL	148	480	123	23	2	5	(2 3)	165	51	33	16	0	57	2	9	2	4	1	.80	10	.256	.282	.344
1993 Cleveland	AL	129	263	73	15	0	4	(3 1)	100	34	27	8	0	36	1	8	3	2	2	.50	7	.278	.298	.380
8 ML YEARS		646	1786	460	76	5	11	(5 6)	579	176	131	56	1	226	10	56	10	10	10	.50	46	.258	.282	.324

Cecil Espy

Bats: Both   **Throws:** Right   **Pos:** LF   **Ht:** 6' 3"   **Wt:** 195   **Born:** 01/20/63   **Age:** 31

								BATTING											BASERUNNING				PERCENTAGES		
Year Team	Lg	G	AB	H	2B	3B	HR	(Hm Rd)	TB	R	RBI	TBB	IBB	SO	HBP	SH	SF	SB	CS	SB%	GDP	Avg	OBP	SLG
1993 Indianapols *	AAA	25	83	19	3	0	0	(-- --)	22	10	7	6	0	16	0	0	0	2	0	1.00	2	.229	.281	.265
1983 Los Angeles	NL	20	11	3	1	0	0	(0 0)	4	4	1	1	0	2	0	0	0	2	0	1.00	1	.273	.333	.364
1987 Texas	AL	8	0	0	0	0	0	(0 0)	0	1	0	1	0	3	0	0	0	2	0	1.00	0	.000	.111	.000
1988 Texas	AL	123	347	86	17	6	2	(2 0)	121	46	39	20	1	83	1	5	3	33	10	.77	2	.248	.288	.349
1989 Texas	AL	142	475	122	12	7	3	(2 1)	157	65	31	38	2	99	2	10	2	45	20	.69	6	.257	.313	.331

Year	Team	Lg	G	AB	H	2B	3B	HR	(Hm	Rd)	TB	R	RBI	TBB	IBB	SO	HBP	SH	SF	SB	CS	SB%	GDP	Avg	OBP	SLG
1990	Texas	AL	52	71	9	0	0	0	(0	0)	9	10	1	10	0	20	0	1	0	11	5	.69	1	.127	.235	.127
1991	Pittsburgh	NL	43	82	20	4	0	1	(1	0)	27	7	11	5	0	17	0	3	2	4	0	1.00	0	.244	.281	.329
1992	Pittsburgh	NL	112	194	50	7	3	1	(0	1)	66	21	20	15	2	40	0	1	1	6	3	.67	3	.258	.310	.340
1993	Cincinnati	NL	40	60	14	2	0	0	(0	0)	16	6	5	14	0	13	0	0	2	2	2	.50	2	.233	.368	.267
8	ML YEARS		546	1248	304	43	16	7	(5	2)	400	160	108	104	5	277	3	20	10	103	40	.72	11	.244	.301	.321

Mark Ettles

Pitches: Right **Bats:** Right **Pos:** RP **Ht:** 6' 0" **Wt:** 185 **Born:** 10/30/66 **Age:** 27

			HOW MUCH HE PITCHED						WHAT HE GAVE UP												THE RESULTS					
Year	Team	Lg	G	GS	CG	GF	IP	BFP	H	R	ER	HR	SH	SF	HB	TBB	IBB	SO	WP	Bk	W	L	Pct.	ShO	Sv	ERA
1989	Niagara Fls	A	5	0	0	3	17.2	66	12	3	2	0	0	0	0	2	0	21	1	1	3	0	1.000	0	1	1.02
	Fayetteville	A	19	0	0	11	27.2	120	28	9	7	1	2	0	1	9	2	34	1	2	2	2	.500	0	4	2.28
1990	Lakeland	A	45	0	0	21	68	295	63	34	25	1	4	2	6	16	1	62	4	2	5	5	.500	0	3	3.31
1991	Lakeland	A	8	1	0	0	17	74	19	11	9	2	0	0	1	6	0	14	1	1	2	1	.667	0	0	4.76
	Chston-Sc	A	29	0	0	23	45.2	193	36	15	12	2	5	2	2	12	2	57	2	0	2	1	.667	0	12	2.36
	Waterloo	A	14	0	0	14	16	60	6	5	4	2	4	0	0	6	2	24	2	0	1	2	.333	0	8	2.25
1992	Wichita	AA	54	0	0	43	68.1	283	54	23	21	6	4	1	4	23	6	86	8	1	3	8	.273	0	22	2.77
1993	Las Vegas	AAA	47	0	0	41	49.2	224	58	28	26	2	3	1	2	22	6	29	13	0	6	3	.333	0	15	4.71
1993	San Diego	NL	14	0	0	5	18	81	23	16	13	4	0	2	0	4	1	9	3	0	1	0	1.000	0	0	6.50

Carl Everett

Bats: Both **Throws:** Right **Pos:** CF **Ht:** 6' 0" **Wt:** 190 **Born:** 06/03/70 **Age:** 24

			BATTING																	BASERUNNING				PERCENTAGES		
Year	Team	Lg	G	AB	H	2B	3B	HR	(Hm	Rd)	TB	R	RBI	TBB	IBB	SO	HBP	SH	SF	SB	CS	SB%	GDP	Avg	OBP	SLG
1990	Yankees	R	48	185	48	8	5	1	--	--	69	28	14	15	0	38	6	2	1	15	2	.88	1	.259	.333	.373
1991	Greensboro	A	123	468	127	18	0	4	--	--	157	97	40	57	2	122	23	2	3	28	19	.60	1	.271	.376	.335
1992	Ft. Laud	A	46	183	42	8	2	2	--	--	60	30	9	12	1	40	4	4	0	11	3	.79	1	.230	.291	.328
	Pr William	A	6	22	7	0	0	4	--	--	19	7	9	5	0	7	0	0	0	1	0	1.00	0	.318	.444	.864
1993	High Desert	A	59	253	73	12	6	10	--	--	127	48	52	22	0	73	6	0	1	24	9	.73	3	.289	.358	.502
	Edmonton	AAA	35	136	42	13	4	6	--	--	81	28	16	19	0	45	2	1	0	12	1	.92	1	.309	.401	.596
1993	Florida	NL	11	19	2	0	0	0	(0	0)	2	2	0	2	0	9	0	0	0	1	0	1.00	0	.105	.150	.105

Hector Fajardo

Pitches: Right **Bats:** Right **Pos:** RP **Ht:** 6' 4" **Wt:** 200 **Born:** 11/06/70 **Age:** 23

			HOW MUCH HE PITCHED						WHAT HE GAVE UP												THE RESULTS					
Year	Team	Lg	G	GS	CG	GF	IP	BFP	H	R	ER	HR	SH	SF	HB	TBB	IBB	SO	WP	Bk	W	L	Pct.	ShO	Sv	ERA
1989	Pirates	R	10	6	0	0	34.2	154	38	24	23	0	0	1	0	20	0	19	1	0	0	5	.000	0	0	5.97
1990	Pirates	R	5	4	0	0	21	92	23	10	9	0	0	1	3	8	0	17	1	1	1	1	.500	0	0	3.86
	Augusta	A	7	7	0	0	39.2	173	41	18	17	1	1	0	2	15	0	28	0	1	2	2	.500	0	0	3.86
1991	Augusta	A	11	11	1	0	60.1	250	44	26	18	1	1	2	2	24	0	79	3	1	4	3	.571	1	0	2.69
	Salem	A	1	1	1	0	7.2	30	4	3	2	1	1	0	0	1	1	7	0	0	0	1	.000	0	0	2.35
	Carolina	AA	10	10	1	0	61	258	55	32	28	4	2	3	0	24	0	53	3	2	3	4	.429	0	0	4.13
	Buffalo	AAA	8	0	0	4	9.1	36	6	1	1	0	0	0	0	3	0	12	0	0	1	0	1.000	0	1	0.96
1992	Rangers	R	1	1	0	0	6.1	27	5	4	4	0	0	0	0	2	0	9	1	0	0	1	.000	0	0	5.68
	Charlotte	A	4	4	0	0	22.2	95	22	9	7	0	2	1	1	8	0	12	0	0	2	2	.500	0	0	2.78
	Tulsa	AA	5	4	0	0	25	99	19	6	6	2	0	1	0	7	0	26	1	0	2	1	.667	0	0	2.16
	Okla City	AAA	1	1	0	0	7	30	8	0	0	0	0	0	0	2	0	6	0	0	1	0	1.000	0	0	0.00
1993	Rangers	R	6	6	0	0	30	114	21	8	6	0	1	0	0	5	0	27	0	0	3	1	.750	0	0	1.80
	Charlotte	A	2	1	0	0	5	21	5	1	1	0	0	0	0	1	0	3	0	0	0	0	.000	0	0	1.80
1991	2 ML Teams		6	5	0	1	25.1	119	35	20	19	2	0	3	1	11	0	23	3	0	0	2	.000	0	0	6.75
1993	Texas	AL	1	0	0	1	0.2	9	0	0	0	0	0	0	0	1	0	0	0	0	0	0	.000	0	0	0.00
1991	Pittsburgh	NL	2	2	0	0	6.1	35	10	7	7	0	0	0	0	7	0	8	3	0	0	0	.000	0	0	9.95
	Texas	AL	4	3	0	1	19	84	25	13	12	2	0	3	1	4	0	15	0	0	0	2	.000	0	0	5.68
	2 ML YEARS		7	5	0	2	26	121	35	20	19	2	0	3	1	11	0	24	3	0	0	2	.000	0	0	6.58

Rikkert Faneyte

Bats: Right **Throws:** Right **Pos:** CF **Ht:** 6' 1" **Wt:** 170 **Born:** 05/31/69 **Age:** 25

			BATTING																	BASERUNNING				PERCENTAGES		
Year	Team	Lg	G	AB	H	2B	3B	HR	(Hm	Rd)	TB	R	RBI	TBB	IBB	SO	HBP	SH	SF	SB	CS	SB%	GDP	Avg	OBP	SLG
1991	Clinton	A	107	384	98	14	7	6	--	--	144	73	52	61	1	106	9	3	4	18	11	.62	8	.255	.367	.375
1992	San Jose	A	94	342	90	13	2	9	--	--	134	69	43	73	3	65	6	4	3	17	9	.65	7	.263	.399	.392
1993	Phoenix	AAA	115	426	133	23	2	11	--	--	193	71	71	40	1	72	8	2	3	15	9	.63	8	.312	.379	.453
1993	San Francisco	NL	7	15	2	0	0	0	(0	0)	2	2	0	2	0	4	0	0	0	0	0	.00	0	.133	.235	.133

Paul Faries

Bats: Right **Throws:** Right **Pos:** 2B   **Ht:** 5'10" **Wt:** 170 **Born:** 02/20/65 **Age:** 29

Year Team	Lg	G	AB	H	2B	3B	HR	(Hm	Rd)	TB	R	RBI	TBB	IBB	SO	HBP	SH	SF	SB	CS	SB%	GDP	Avg	OBP	SLG
1993 Phoenix *	AAA	78	327	99	14	5	2	--	--	129	56	32	22	1	30	3	1		18	11	.62	8	.303	.348	.394
1990 San Diego	NL	14	37	7	1	0	0	(0	0)	8	4	2	4	0	7	1	2	1	0	1	.00	0	.189	.279	.216
1991 San Diego	NL	57	130	23	3	1	0	(0	0)	28	13	7	14	0	21	1	4	0	3	1	.75	5	.177	.262	.215
1992 San Diego	NL	10	11	5	1	0	0	(0	0)	6	3	1	1	0	2	0	0	0	0	0	.00	0	.455	.500	.545
1993 San Francisco	NL	15	36	8	2	1	0	(0	0)	12	6	4	1	0	4	0	1	1	2	0	1.00	0	.222	.237	.333
4 ML YEARS		96	214	43	7	2	0	(0	0)	54	26	14	20	0	34	2	7	2	5	2	.71	6	.201	.273	.252

Monty Fariss

Bats: Right **Throws:** Right **Pos:** RF   **Ht:** 6' 4" **Wt:** 205 **Born:** 10/13/67 **Age:** 26

Year Team	Lg	G	AB	H	2B	3B	HR	(Hm	Rd)	TB	R	RBI	TBB	IBB	SO	HBP	SH	SF	SB	CS	SB%	GDP	Avg	OBP	SLG
1993 Edmonton *	AAA	74	254	65	11	4	6	--	--	102	32	37	43	0	74	2	1	2	1	5	.17	3	.256	.365	.402
1991 Texas	AL	19	31	8	1	0	1	(1	0)	12	6	6	7	0	11	0	0	0	0	0	.00	0	.258	.395	.387
1992 Texas	AL	67	166	36	7	1	3	(0	3)	54	13	21	17	0	51	2	2	0	0	2	.00	3	.217	.297	.325
1993 Florida	NL	18	29	5	2	1	0	(0	0)	9	3	2	5	0	13	0	0	0	0	0	.00	2	.172	.294	.310
3 ML YEARS		104	226	49	10	2	4	(1	3)	75	22	29	29	0	75	2	2	0	0	2	.00	5	.217	.311	.332

Steve Farr

Pitches: Right **Bats:** Right **Pos:** RP   **Ht:** 5'11" **Wt:** 204 **Born:** 12/12/56 **Age:** 37

Year Team	Lg	G	GS	CG	GF	IP	BFP	H	R	ER	HR	SH	SF	HB	TBB	IBB	SO	WP	Bk	W	L	Pct.	ShO	Sv	ERA
1984 Cleveland	AL	31	16	0	4	116	488	106	61	59	14	3	3	5	46	3	83	2	2	3	11	.214	0	1	4.58
1985 Kansas City	AL	16	3	0	5	37.2	164	34	15	13	2	1	2	2	20	4	36	3	0	2	1	.667	0	1	3.11
1986 Kansas City	AL	56	0	0	33	109.1	443	90	39	38	10	3	2	4	39	8	83	4	1	8	4	.667	0	8	3.13
1987 Kansas City	AL	47	0	0	19	91	408	97	47	42	9	0	3	2	44	4	88	2	0	4	3	.571	0	1	4.15
1988 Kansas City	AL	62	1	0	49	82.2	344	74	25	23	5	1	3	2	30	6	72	4	2	5	4	.556	0	20	2.50
1989 Kansas City	AL	51	2	0	40	63.1	279	75	35	29	5	0	3	1	22	5	56	2	0	2	5	.286	0	18	4.12
1990 Kansas City	AL	57	6	1	20	127	515	99	32	28	6	10	1	5	48	9	94	2	0	13	7	.650	1	1	1.98
1991 New York	AL	60	0	0	48	70	285	57	19	17	4	0	0	5	20	3	60	2	0	5	5	.500	0	23	2.19
1992 New York	AL	50	0	0	42	52	207	34	10	9	2	1	2	2	19	0	37	0	0	2	2	.500	0	30	1.56
1993 New York	AL	49	0	0	37	47	211	44	22	22	8	3	4	2	28	4	39	2	0	2	2	.500	0	25	4.21
10 ML YEARS		479	28	1	297	796	3344	710	305	280	65	21	23	30	316	46	648	23	5	46	44	.511	1	128	3.17

John Farrell

Pitches: Right **Bats:** Right **Pos:** SP   **Ht:** 6' 4" **Wt:** 210 **Born:** 08/04/62 **Age:** 31

Year Team	Lg	G	GS	CG	GF	IP	BFP	H	R	ER	HR	SH	SF	HB	TBB	IBB	SO	WP	Bk	W	L	Pct.	ShO	Sv	ERA
1993 Vancouver *	AAA	12	12	2	0	85.2	363	83	44	38	7	2	2	8	28	1	71	4	0	4	5	.444	0	0	3.99
1987 Cleveland	AL	10	9	1	1	69	297	68	29	26	7	3	1	5	22	1	28	1	1	5	1	.833	0	0	3.39
1988 Cleveland	AL	31	30	4	0	210.1	895	216	106	99	15	9	6	9	67	3	92	2	3	14	10	.583	0	4	4.24
1989 Cleveland	AL	31	31	7	0	208	895	196	97	84	14	8	6	7	71	4	132	4	0	9	14	.391	2	0	3.63
1990 Cleveland	AL	17	17	1	0	96.2	418	108	49	46	10	5	2	1	33	1	44	1	0	4	5	.444	0	0	4.28
1993 California	AL	21	17	0	1	90.2	420	110	74	74	22	2	2	7	44	3	45	3	0	3	12	.200	0	0	7.35
5 ML YEARS		110	104	13	2	674.2	2925	698	355	329	68	27	17	29	237	12	341	11	4	35	42	.455	2	0	4.39

Jeff Fassero

Pitches: Left **Bats:** Left **Pos:** RP/SP   **Ht:** 6' 1" **Wt:** 195 **Born:** 01/05/63 **Age:** 31

Year Team	Lg	G	GS	CG	GF	IP	BFP	H	R	ER	HR	SH	SF	HB	TBB	IBB	SO	WP	Bk	W	L	Pct.	ShO	Sv	ERA
1991 Montreal	NL	51	0	0	30	55.1	223	39	17	15	1	6	0	1	17	1	42	4	0	2	5	.286	0	8	2.44
1992 Montreal	NL	70	0	0	22	85.2	368	81	35	27	1	5	2	2	34	6	63	7	1	8	7	.533	0	1	2.84
1993 Montreal	NL	56	15	1	10	149.2	616	119	50	38	7	7	4	0	54	0	140	5	0	12	5	.706	0	2	2.29
3 ML YEARS		177	15	1	62	290.2	1207	239	102	80	9	18	6	3	105	7	245	16	1	22	17	.564	0	10	2.48

Mike Felder

Bats: Both **Throws:** Right **Pos:** LF   **Ht:** 5' 9" **Wt:** 175 **Born:** 11/18/62 **Age:** 31

Year Team	Lg	G	AB	H	2B	3B	HR	(Hm	Rd)	TB	R	RBI	TBB	IBB	SO	HBP	SH	SF	SB	CS	SB%	GDP	Avg	OBP	SLG
1985 Milwaukee	AL	15	56	11	1	0	0	(0	0)	12	8	0	5	0	6	0	1	0	4	1	.80	2	.196	.262	.214
1986 Milwaukee	AL	44	155	37	2	4	1	(1	0)	50	24	13	13	1	16	0	1	5	16	2	.89	2	.239	.289	.323
1987 Milwaukee	AL	108	289	77	5	7	2	(1	1)	102	48	31	28	0	23	0	9	2	34	8	.81	3	.266	.329	.353
1988 Milwaukee	AL	50	81	14	1	0	0	(0	0)	15	14	5	0	0	11	1	3	0	8	2	.80	1	.173	.183	.185
1989 Milwaukee	AL	117	315	76	11	3	3	(1	2)	102	50	23	23	2	38	0	7	0	26	5	.84	4	.241	.293	.324
1990 Milwaukee	AL	121	237	65	7	2	3	(1	2)	85	38	27	22	0	17	0	4	5	20	9	.69	0	.274	.330	.359

Year	Team	Lg	G	AB	H	2B	3B	HR	(Hm	Rd)	TB	R	RBI	TBB	IBB	SO	HBP	SH	SF	SB	CS	SB%	GDP	Avg	OBP	SLG
1991	San Francisco	NL	132	348	92	10	6	0	(0	0)	114	51	18	30	2	31	1	4	0	21	6	.78	1	.264	.325	.328
1992	San Francisco	NL	145	322	92	13	3	4	(1	3)	123	44	23	21	1	29	2	3	3	14	4	.78	3	.286	.330	.382
1993	Seattle	AL	109	342	72	7	5	1	(0	1)	92	31	20	22	2	34	2	7	1	15	9	.63	2	.211	.262	.269
	9 ML YEARS		841	2145	536	57	30	14	(5	9)	695	308	160	164	8	205	6	43	16	158	46	.77	18	.250	.303	.324

Junior Felix

Bats: Both   **Throws:** Right   **Pos:** RF   **Ht:** 5'11"   **Wt:** 165   **Born:** 10/03/67   **Age:** 26

			BATTING																BASERUNNING				PERCENTAGES		
Year	Team	Lg	G	AB	H	2B	3B	HR	(Hm	Rd)	TB	R	RBI	TBB	IBB	SO	HBP	SH	SF	SB	CS	SB%	GDP	Avg	OBP	SLG
1993	Edmonton *	AAA	7	31	11	2	0	0	--	--	13	7	5	4	0	8	0	0	0	0	0	.00	1	.355	.429	.419
1989	Toronto	AL	110	415	107	14	8	9	(4	5)	164	62	46	33	2	101	3	0	3	18	12	.60	5	.258	.315	.395
1990	Toronto	AL	127	463	122	23	7	15	(7	8)	204	73	65	45	0	99	2	2	5	13	8	.62	4	.263	.328	.441
1991	California	AL	66	230	65	10	2	2	(2	0)	85	32	26	11	0	55	3	0	2	7	5	.58	5	.283	.321	.370
1992	California	AL	139	509	125	22	5	9	(5	4)	184	63	72	33	5	128	2	5	9	8	8	.50	9	.246	.289	.361
1993	Florida	NL	57	214	51	11	1	7	(3	4)	85	25	22	10	1	50	1	0	0	2	1	.67	6	.238	.276	.397
	5 ML YEARS		499	1831	470	80	23	42	(21	21)	722	255	231	132	8	433	11	7	19	48	34	.59	29	.257	.308	.394

Felix Fermin

Bats: Right   **Throws:** Right   **Pos:** SS   **Ht:** 5'11"   **Wt:** 170   **Born:** 10/09/63   **Age:** 30

			BATTING																BASERUNNING				PERCENTAGES		
Year	Team	Lg	G	AB	H	2B	3B	HR	(Hm	Rd)	TB	R	RBI	TBB	IBB	SO	HBP	SH	SF	SB	CS	SB%	GDP	Avg	OBP	SLG
1987	Pittsburgh	NL	23	68	17	0	0	0	(0	0)	17	6	4	4	1	9	1	2	0	0	0	.00	3	.250	.301	.250
1988	Pittsburgh	NL	43	87	24	0	2	0	(0	0)	28	9	2	8	1	10	3	1	1	3	1	.75	3	.276	.354	.322
1989	Cleveland	AL	156	484	115	9	1	0	(0	0)	126	50	21	41	0	27	4	32	1	6	4	.60	15	.238	.302	.260
1990	Cleveland	AL	148	414	106	13	2	1	(1	0)	126	47	40	26	0	22	0	13	5	3	3	.50	13	.256	.297	.304
1991	Cleveland	AL	129	424	111	13	2	0	(0	0)	128	30	31	26	0	27	3	13	3	5	4	.56	17	.262	.307	.302
1992	Cleveland	AL	79	215	58	7	2	0	(0	0)	69	27	13	18	1	10	1	9	2	0	0	.00	7	.270	.326	.321
1993	Cleveland	AL	140	480	126	16	2	2	(0	2)	152	48	45	24	1	14	4	5	1	4	5	.44	12	.263	.303	.317
	7 ML YEARS		718	2172	557	58	11	3	(1	2)	646	217	156	147	4	119	16	75	13	21	17	.55	70	.256	.307	.297

Alex Fernandez

Pitches: Right   **Bats:** Right   **Pos:** SP   **Ht:** 6' 1"   **Wt:** 215   **Born:** 08/13/69   **Age:** 24

			HOW MUCH HE PITCHED					WHAT HE GAVE UP										THE RESULTS					
Year	Team	Lg	G	GS	CG	GF	IP	BFP	H	R	ER	HR	SH	SF	HB	TBB	IBB	SO	WP	Bk	W	L	Pct.	ShO	Sv	ERA
1990	Chicago	AL	13	13	3	0	87.2	378	89	40	37	6	5	0	3	34	0	61	1	0	5	5	.500	0	0	3.80
1991	Chicago	AL	34	32	2	1	191.2	827	186	100	96	16	7	11	2	88	2	145	4	1	9	13	.409	0	0	4.51
1992	Chicago	AL	29	29	4	0	187.2	804	199	100	89	21	6	4	8	50	3	95	3	0	8	11	.421	2	0	4.27
1993	Chicago	AL	34	34	3	0	247.1	1004	221	95	86	27	9	3	6	67	5	169	8	0	18	9	.667	1	0	3.13
	4 ML YEARS		110	108	12	1	714.1	3013	695	335	308	70	27	18	19	239	10	470	16	1	40	38	.513	3	0	3.88

Sid Fernandez

Pitches: Left   **Bats:** Left   **Pos:** SP   **Ht:** 6' 1"   **Wt:** 225   **Born:** 10/12/62   **Age:** 31

			HOW MUCH HE PITCHED					WHAT HE GAVE UP										THE RESULTS					
Year	Team	Lg	G	GS	CG	GF	IP	BFP	H	R	ER	HR	SH	SF	HB	TBB	IBB	SO	WP	Bk	W	L	Pct.	ShO	Sv	ERA
1993	St.Lucie *	A	1	1	0	0	4	16	3	2	2	1	0	0	0	1	0	7	0	0	0	0	.000	0	0	4.50
	Binghamton *	AA	2	2	0	0	10	36	6	2	2	0	0	0	0	3	0	11	0	0	0	1	.000	0	0	1.80
1983	Los Angeles	NL	2	1	0	0	6	33	7	4	4	0	0	0	1	7	0	9	0	0	0	1	.000	0	0	6.00
1984	New York	NL	15	15	0	0	90	371	74	40	35	8	5	5	0	34	3	62	1	4	6	6	.500	0	0	3.50
1985	New York	NL	26	26	3	0	170.1	685	108	56	53	14	4	3	2	80	3	180	3	2	9	9	.500	0	0	2.80
1986	New York	NL	32	31	2	1	204.1	855	161	82	80	13	9	7	2	91	1	200	6	0	16	6	.727	1	1	3.52
1987	New York	NL	28	27	3	0	156	665	130	75	66	16	3	6	8	67	8	134	2	0	12	8	.600	1	0	3.81
1988	New York	NL	31	31	1	0	187	751	127	69	63	15	2	7	6	70	1	189	4	9	12	10	.545	1	0	3.03
1989	New York	NL	35	32	6	0	219.1	883	157	73	69	21	4	4	6	75	3	198	1	3	14	5	.737	2	0	2.83
1990	New York	NL	30	30	2	0	179.1	735	130	79	69	18	7	6	5	67	4	181	1	0	9	14	.391	1	0	3.46
1991	New York	NL	8	8	0	0	44	177	36	18	14	4	5	1	0	9	0	31	0	0	1	3	.250	0	0	2.86
1992	New York	NL	32	32	5	0	214.2	865	162	67	65	12	12	11	4	67	4	193	0	0	14	11	.560	2	0	2.73
1993	New York	NL	18	18	1	0	119.2	469	82	42	39	17	3	1	3	36	0	81	2	0	5	6	.455	1	0	2.93
	11 ML YEARS		257	251	23	1	1590.2	6489	1174	605	557	138	54	51	37	603	27	1458	20	18	98	79	.554	9	1	3.15

Tony Fernandez

Bats: Both   **Throws:** Right   **Pos:** SS   **Ht:** 6' 2"   **Wt:** 175   **Born:** 06/30/62   **Age:** 32

			BATTING																BASERUNNING				PERCENTAGES		
Year	Team	Lg	G	AB	H	2B	3B	HR	(Hm	Rd)	TB	R	RBI	TBB	IBB	SO	HBP	SH	SF	SB	CS	SB%	GDP	Avg	OBP	SLG
1983	Toronto	AL	15	34	9	1	1	0	(0	0)	12	5	2	2	0	2	1	1	0	0	1	.00	1	.265	.324	.353
1984	Toronto	AL	88	233	63	5	3	3	(1	2)	83	29	19	17	0	15	0	2	3	5	7	.42	3	.270	.317	.356
1985	Toronto	AL	161	564	163	31	10	2	(1	1)	220	71	51	43	2	41	2	7	2	13	6	.68	12	.289	.340	.390
1986	Toronto	AL	163	687	213	33	9	10	(4	6)	294	91	65	27	0	52	4	5	4	25	12	.68	8	.310	.338	.428

1987 Toronto	AL	146	578	186	29	8	5	(1	4)	246	90	67	51	3	48	5	4	4	32	12	.73	14	.322	.379	.426
1988 Toronto	AL	154	648	186	41	4	5	(3	2)	250	76	70	45	3	65	4	3	4	15	5	.75	9	.287	.335	.386
1989 Toronto	AL	140	573	147	25	9	11	(2	9)	223	64	64	29	1	51	3	2	10	22	6	.79	9	.257	.291	.389
1990 Toronto	AL	161	635	175	27	17	4	(2	2)	248	84	66	71	4	70	7	2	6	26	13	.67	17	.276	.352	.391
1991 San Diego	NL	145	558	152	27	5	4	(1	3)	201	81	38	55	0	74	0	7	1	23	9	.72	12	.272	.337	.360
1992 San Diego	NL	155	622	171	32	4	4	(3	1)	223	84	37	56	4	62	4	9	3	20	20	.50	6	.275	.337	.359
1993 2 ML Teams		142	526	147	23	11	5	(1	4)	207	65	64	56	3	45	1	8	3	21	10	.68	17	.279	.348	.394
1993 New York	NL	48	173	39	5	2	1	(0	1)	51	20	14	25	0	19	1	3	2	6	2	.75	4	.225	.323	.295
Toronto	AL	94	353	108	18	9	4	(1	3)	156	45	50	31	3	26	0	5	1	15	8	.65	13	.306	.361	.442
11 ML YEARS		1470	5658	1612	274	81	53	(19	34)	2207	740	543	452	20	525	31	50	39	202	101	.67	108	.285	.339	.390

Mike Fetters

Pitches: Right **Bats:** Right **Pos:** RP   **Ht:** 6' 4" **Wt:** 212 **Born:** 12/19/64 **Age:** 29

		HOW MUCH HE PITCHED						WHAT HE GAVE UP										THE RESULTS					
Year Team	Lg	G	GS	CG	GF	IP	BFP	H	R	ER	HR	SH	SF	HB	TBB	IBB	SO	WP	Bk	W	L	Pct.	ShO	Sv	ERA
1989 California	AL	1	0	0	0	3.1	16	5	4	3	1	0	0	0	1	0	4	2	0	0	0	.000	0	0	8.10
1990 California	AL	26	2	0	10	67.2	291	77	33	31	9	1	0	2	20	0	35	3	0	1	1	.500	0	1	4.12
1991 California	AL	19	4	0	8	44.2	206	53	29	24	4	1	0	3	28	2	24	4	0	2	5	.286	0	0	4.84
1992 Milwaukee	AL	50	0	0	11	62.2	243	38	15	13	3	5	2	7	24	2	43	4	1	5	1	.833	0	2	1.87
1993 Milwaukee	AL	45	0	0	14	59.1	246	59	29	22	4	5	5	2	22	4	23	0	0	3	3	.500	0	0	3.34
5 ML YEARS		141	6	0	43	237.2	1002	232	110	93	21	12	7	14	95	8	129	13	1	11	10	.524	0	3	3.52

Cecil Fielder

Bats: Right **Throws:** Right **Pos:** 1B/DH   **Ht:** 6' 3" **Wt:** 250 **Born:** 09/21/63 **Age:** 30

							BATTING												BASERUNNING				PERCENTAGES		
Year Team	Lg	G	AB	H	2B	3B	HR	(Hm	Rd)	TB	R	RBI	TBB	IBB	SO	HBP	SH	SF	SB	CS	SB%	GDP	Avg	OBP	SLG
1985 Toronto	AL	30	74	23	4	0	4	(2	2)	39	6	16	6	0	16	0	0	1	0	0	.00	2	.311	.358	.527
1986 Toronto	AL	34	83	13	2	0	4	(0	4)	27	7	13	6	0	27	1	0	0	0	0	.00	3	.157	.222	.325
1987 Toronto	AL	82	175	47	7	1	14	(10	4)	98	30	32	20	2	48	1	0	1	0	1	.00	6	.269	.345	.560
1988 Toronto	AL	74	174	40	6	1	9	(6	3)	75	24	23	14	0	53	1	0	1	0	1	.00	6	.230	.289	.431
1990 Detroit	AL	159	573	159	25	1	51	(25	26)	339	104	132	90	11	182	5	0	5	0	1	.00	15	.277	.377	.592
1991 Detroit	AL	162	624	163	25	0	44	(27	17)	320	102	133	78	12	151	6	0	4	0	0	.00	17	.261	.347	.513
1992 Detroit	AL	155	594	145	22	0	35	(18	17)	272	80	124	73	8	151	2	0	7	0	0	.00	14	.244	.325	.458
1993 Detroit	AL	154	573	153	23	0	30	(20	10)	266	80	117	90	15	125	4	0	5	0	1	.00	22	.267	.368	.464
8 ML YEARS		850	2870	743	114	3	191	(108	83)	1436	433	590	377	48	753	20	0	24	0	4	.00	85	.259	.346	.500

Chuck Finley

Pitches: Left **Bats:** Left **Pos:** SP   **Ht:** 6' 6" **Wt:** 214 **Born:** 11/26/62 **Age:** 31

		HOW MUCH HE PITCHED						WHAT HE GAVE UP										THE RESULTS					
Year Team	Lg	G	GS	CG	GF	IP	BFP	H	R	ER	HR	SH	SF	HB	TBB	IBB	SO	WP	Bk	W	L	Pct.	ShO	Sv	ERA
1986 California	AL	25	0	0	7	46.1	198	40	17	17	2	4	0	1	23	1	37	2	0	3	1	.750	0	0	3.30
1987 California	AL	35	3	0	17	90.2	405	102	54	47	7	2	2	3	43	3	63	4	3	2	7	.222	0	0	4.67
1988 California	AL	31	31	2	0	194.1	831	191	95	90	15	7	10	6	82	7	111	5	8	9	15	.375	0	0	4.17
1989 California	AL	29	29	9	0	199.2	827	171	64	57	13	7	3	2	82	0	156	4	2	16	9	.640	1	0	2.57
1990 California	AL	32	32	7	0	236	962	210	77	63	17	12	3	2	81	3	177	9	0	18	9	.667	2	0	2.40
1991 California	AL	34	34	4	0	227.1	955	205	102	96	23	4	3	8	101	1	171	6	3	18	9	.667	2	0	3.80
1992 California	AL	31	31	4	0	204.1	885	212	99	90	24	10	10	3	98	2	124	6	0	7	12	.368	1	0	3.96
1993 California	AL	35	35	13	0	251.1	1065	243	108	88	22	11	7	6	82	1	187	8	1	16	14	.533	2	0	3.15
8 ML YEARS		252	195	39	24	1450	6128	1374	616	548	121	57	38	31	592	18	1026	44	17	89	76	.539	8	0	3.40

Steve Finley

Bats: Left **Throws:** Left **Pos:** CF   **Ht:** 6' 2" **Wt:** 180 **Born:** 03/12/65 **Age:** 29

							BATTING												BASERUNNING				PERCENTAGES		
Year Team	Lg	G	AB	H	2B	3B	HR	(Hm	Rd)	TB	R	RBI	TBB	IBB	SO	HBP	SH	SF	SB	CS	SB%	GDP	Avg	OBP	SLG
1989 Baltimore	AL	81	217	54	5	2	2	(0	2)	69	35	25	15	1	30	1	6	2	17	3	.85	3	.249	.298	.318
1990 Baltimore	AL	142	464	119	16	4	3	(1	2)	152	46	37	32	3	53	2	10	5	22	9	.71	8	.256	.304	.328
1991 Houston	NL	159	596	170	28	10	8	(0	8)	242	84	54	42	5	65	2	10	6	34	18	.65	8	.285	.331	.406
1992 Houston	NL	162	607	177	29	13	5	(5	0)	247	84	55	58	6	63	3	16	2	44	9	.83	10	.292	.355	.407
1993 Houston	NL	142	545	145	15	13	8	(1	7)	210	69	44	28	1	65	3	6	3	19	6	.76	8	.266	.304	.385
5 ML YEARS		686	2429	665	93	42	26	(7	19)	920	318	215	175	16	276	11	48	18	136	45	.75	37	.274	.323	.379

Carlton Fisk

Bats: Right **Throws:** Right **Pos:** C   **Ht:** 6' 2" **Wt:** 223 **Born:** 12/26/47 **Age:** 46

							BATTING												BASERUNNING				PERCENTAGES		
Year Team	Lg	G	AB	H	2B	3B	HR	(Hm	Rd)	TB	R	RBI	TBB	IBB	SO	HBP	SH	SF	SB	CS	SB%	GDP	Avg	OBP	SLG
1969 Boston	AL	2	5	0	0	0	0	(0	0)	0	0	0	0	0	2	0	0	0	0	0	.00	0	.000	.000	.000

1971 Boston	AL	14	48	15	2	1	2	(0 2)	25	7	6	1	0	10	0	0	0	0	0	.00	1	.313	.327	.521
1972 Boston	AL	131	457	134	28	9	22	(13 9)	246	74	61	52	6	83	4	1	0	5	2	.71	11	.293	.370	.538
1973 Boston	AL	135	508	125	21	0	26	(16 10)	224	65	71	37	2	99	10	1	2	7	2	.78	11	.246	.309	.441
1974 Boston	AL	52	187	56	12	1	11	(5 6)	103	36	26	24	2	23	2	2	1	5	1	.83	5	.299	.383	.551
1975 Boston	AL	79	263	87	14	4	10	(6 4)	139	47	52	27	4	32	2	0	2	4	3	.57	7	.331	.395	.529
1976 Boston	AL	134	487	124	17	5	17	(10 7)	202	76	58	56	3	71	6	3	5	12	5	.71	11	.255	.336	.415
1977 Boston	AL	152	536	169	26	3	26	(15 11)	279	106	102	75	3	85	9	2	10	7	6	.54	9	.315	.402	.521
1978 Boston	AL	157	571	162	39	5	20	(8 12)	271	94	88	71	6	83	7	3	6	7	2	.78	10	.284	.366	.475
1979 Boston	AL	91	320	87	23	2	10	(5 5)	144	49	42	10	0	38	6	1	3	3	0	1.00	9	.272	.304	.450
1980 Boston	AL	131	478	138	25	3	18	(12 6)	223	73	62	36	6	62	13	0	3	11	5	.69	12	.289	.353	.467
1981 Chicago	AL	96	338	89	12	0	7	(4 3)	122	44	45	38	3	37	12	1	5	3	2	.60	9	.263	.354	.361
1982 Chicago	AL	135	476	127	17	3	14	(7 7)	192	66	65	46	7	60	6	4	4	17	2	.89	12	.267	.336	.403
1983 Chicago	AL	138	488	141	26	4	26	(17 9)	253	85	86	46	3	88	6	2	3	9	6	.60	8	.289	.355	.518
1984 Chicago	AL	102	359	83	20	1	21	(11 10)	168	54	43	26	4	60	5	1	4	6	0	1.00	7	.231	.289	.468
1985 Chicago	AL	153	543	129	23	1	37	(20 17)	265	85	107	52	12	81	17	2	6	17	9	.65	9	.238	.320	.488
1986 Chicago	AL	125	457	101	11	0	14	(5 9)	154	42	63	22	2	92	6	0	6	2	4	.33	10	.221	.263	.337
1987 Chicago	AL	135	454	116	22	1	23	(5 18)	209	68	71	39	8	72	8	1	6	1	4	.20	9	.256	.321	.460
1988 Chicago	AL	76	253	70	8	1	19	(9 10)	137	37	50	37	9	40	5	1	2	0	0	.00	6	.277	.377	.542
1989 Chicago	AL	103	375	110	25	2	13	(4 9)	178	47	68	36	8	60	3	0	5	1	0	1.00	15	.293	.356	.475
1990 Chicago	AL	137	452	129	21	0	18	(5 13)	204	65	65	61	8	73	7	0	1	7	2	.78	12	.285	.378	.451
1991 Chicago	AL	134	460	111	25	0	18	(9 9)	190	42	74	32	4	86	7	0	2	1	2	.33	19	.241	.299	.413
1992 Chicago	AL	62	188	43	4	1	3	(2 1)	58	12	21	23	5	38	1	0	2	3	0	1.00	2	.229	.313	.309
1993 Chicago	AL	25	53	10	0	0	1	(0 1)	13	2	4	2	0	11	1	1	1	0	1	.00	0	.189	.228	.245
24 ML YEARS		2499	8756	2356	421	47	376	(188 188)	3999	1276	1330	849	105	1386	143	26	79	128	58	.69	204	.269	.341	.457

John Flaherty

Bats: Right **Throws:** Right **Pos:** C   **Ht:** 6' 1" **Wt:** 195 **Born:** 10/21/67 **Age:** 26

								BATTING											BASERUNNING				PERCENTAGES		
Year Team	Lg	G	AB	H	2B	3B	HR	(Hm Rd)	TB	R	RBI	TBB	IBB	SO	HBP	SH	SF	SB	CS	SB%	GDP	Avg	OBP	SLG
1988 Elmira	A	46	162	38	3	0	3	-- --	50	17	16	12	0	23	2	3	1	2	1	.67	5	.235	.294	.309
1989 Winter Havn	A	95	334	87	14	2	4	-- --	117	31	28	20	1	44	3	2	2	1	0	1.00	19	.260	.306	.350
1990 Lynchburg	A	1	4	0	0	0	0	-- --	0	0	1	0	0	1	0	0	1	0	0	.00	0	.000	.000	.000
Pawtucket	AAA	99	317	72	18	0	4	-- --	102	35	32	24	0	43	2	2	2	1	1	.50	11	.227	.284	.322
1991 Pawtucket	AAA	45	156	29	7	0	3	-- --	45	18	13	15	0	14	0	4	0	0	1	.00	1	.186	.257	.288
New Britain	AA	67	225	65	9	0	3	-- --	83	27	18	31	1	22	1	0	2	0	2	.00	5	.289	.375	.369
1992 Pawtucket	AAA	31	104	26	3	0	0	-- --	29	11	7	5	0	8	1	1	0	0	0	.00	6	.250	.291	.279
1993 Pawtucket	AAA	105	365	99	22	0	6	-- --	139	29	35	26	1	41	5	2	2	0	2	.00	9	.271	.327	.381
1992 Boston	AL	35	66	13	2	0	0	(0 0)	15	3	2	3	0	7	0	1	1	0	0	.00	5	.197	.229	.227
1993 Boston	AL	13	25	3	2	0	0	(0 0)	5	3	2	2	0	6	1	1	0	0	0	.00	0	.120	.214	.200
2 ML YEARS		48	91	16	4	0	0	(0 0)	20	6	4	5	0	13	1	2	1	0	0	.00	5	.176	.224	.220

Dave Fleming

Pitches: Left **Bats:** Left **Pos:** SP   **Ht:** 6' 3" **Wt:** 200 **Born:** 11/07/69 **Age:** 24

					HOW MUCH HE PITCHED			WHAT HE GAVE UP											THE RESULTS				
Year Team	Lg	G	GS	CG	GF	IP	BFP	H	R	ER	HR	SH	SF	HB	TBB	IBB	SO	WP	Bk	W	L	Pct.	ShO	Sv	ERA
1993 Jacksnville *	AA	4	4	0	0	16.1	71	16	9	8	2	2	0	1	7	0	10	0	0	0	2	.000	0	0	4.41
1991 Seattle	AL	9	3	0	3	17.2	73	19	13	13	3	0	0	3	3	0	11	1	0	1	0	1.000	0	0	6.62
1992 Seattle	AL	33	33	7	0	228.1	946	225	95	86	13	3	2	4	60	3	112	8	1	17	10	.630	4	0	3.39
1993 Seattle	AL	26	26	1	0	167.1	737	189	84	81	15	4	8	6	67	6	75	2	0	12	5	.706	1	0	4.36
3 ML YEARS		68	62	8	3	413.1	1756	433	192	180	31	7	10	13	130	9	198	11	1	30	15	.667	5	0	3.92

Huck Flener

Pitches: Left **Bats:** Both **Pos:** RP   **Ht:** 5'11" **Wt:** 175 **Born:** 02/25/69 **Age:** 25

					HOW MUCH HE PITCHED			WHAT HE GAVE UP											THE RESULTS				
Year Team	Lg	G	GS	CG	GF	IP	BFP	H	R	ER	HR	SH	SF	HB	TBB	IBB	SO	WP	Bk	W	L	Pct.	ShO	Sv	ERA
1990 St. Cath	A	14	7	0	3	61.2	258	45	29	23	4	3	0	1	33	0	46	4	3	4	3	.571	0	1	3.36
1991 Myrtle Bch	A	55	0	0	44	79.1	334	58	28	16	1	5	3	0	41	0	107	7	2	6	4	.600	0	13	1.82
1992 Dunedin	A	41	8	0	19	112.1	451	70	35	28	4	5	2	7	50	2	93	2	1	7	3	.700	0	8	2.24
1993 Knoxville	AA	38	16	2	10	136.1	556	130	56	50	9	6	4	3	39	1	114	9	8	13	6	.684	2	4	3.30
1993 Toronto	AL	6	0	0	1	6.2	30	7	3	3	0	0	0	0	4	1	2	1	0	0	0	.000	0	0	4.05

Darrin Fletcher

Bats: Left **Throws:** Right **Pos:** C   **Ht:** 6' 1" **Wt:** 195 **Born:** 10/03/66 **Age:** 27

								BATTING											BASERUNNING				PERCENTAGES		
Year Team	Lg	G	AB	H	2B	3B	HR	(Hm Rd)	TB	R	RBI	TBB	IBB	SO	HBP	SH	SF	SB	CS	SB%	GDP	Avg	OBP	SLG
1989 Los Angeles	NL	5	8	4	0	0	1	(1 0)	7	1	2	1	0	0	0	0	0	0	0	.00	0	.500	.556	.875
1990 2 ML Teams		11	23	3	1	0	0	(0 0)	4	3	1	0	0	6	0	0	0	0	0	.00	0	.130	.167	.174

Year	Team	Lg	G	AB	H	2B	3B	HR	(Hm	Rd)	TB	R	RBI	TBB	IBB	SO	HBP	SH	SF	SB	CS	SB%	GDP	Avg	OBP	SLG
1991	Philadelphia	NL	46	136	31	8	0	1	(1	0)	42	5	12	5	0	15	0	1	0	0	1	.00	2	.228	.255	.309
1992	Montreal	NL	83	222	54	10	2	2	(0	2)	74	13	26	14	3	28	2	2	4	0	2	.00	8	.243	.289	.333
1993	Montreal	NL	133	396	101	20	1	9	(5	4)	150	33	60	34	2	40	6	5	4	0	0	.00	7	.255	.320	.379
1990	Los Angeles	NL	2	1	0	0	0	0	(0	0)	0	0	0	0	0	1	0	0	0	0	0	.00	0	.000	.000	.000
	Philadelphia	NL	9	22	3	1	0	0	(0	0)	4	3	1	1	0	5	0	0	0	0	0	.00	0	.136	.174	.182
5 ML YEARS			278	785	193	39	3	13	(7	6)	277	55	101	55	5	89	8	8	8	0	3	.00	17	.246	.299	.353

Paul Fletcher

Pitches: Right **Bats:** Right **Pos:** RP **Ht:** 6'1" **Wt:** 185 **Born:** 01/14/67 **Age:** 27

Year	Team	Lg	G	GS	CG	GF	IP	BFP	H	R	ER	HR	SH	SF	HB	TBB	IBB	SO	WP	Bk	W	L	Pct.	ShO	Sv	ERA
1988	Martinsville	R	15	14	1	1	69.1	320	81	44	36	4	1	3	4	33	0	61	3	1	1	3	.250	0	1	4.67
1989	Batavia	A	14	14	3	0	82.1	339	77	41	30	13	2	2	3	28	0	58	3	1	7	5	.583	0	0	3.28
1990	Spartanburg	A	9	9	1	0	49.1	207	46	24	18	3	1	1	2	18	0	53	7	1	2	4	.333	0	0	3.28
	Clearwater	A	20	18	2	1	117.1	498	104	56	44	3	6	6	13	49	0	106	7	2	5	8	.385	0	1	3.38
1991	Clearwater	A	14	4	0	5	29.1	119	22	6	4	1	1	2	0	8	1	27	2	0	0	1	.000	0	1	1.23
	Reading	AA	21	19	3	1	120.2	517	111	56	47	12	3	2	1	56	3	90	6	1	7	9	.438	1	0	3.51
1992	Reading	AA	22	20	2	0	127	521	103	45	40	10	1	1	5	47	2	103	7	0	9	4	.692	1	0	2.83
	Scranton/wb	AAA	4	4	0	0	22.2	85	17	8	7	1	0	0	1	2	0	26	2	0	3	0	1.000	0	0	2.78
1993	Scranton/wb	AAA	34	19	2	5	140	625	146	99	88	21	4	4	9	60	3	116	21	0	4	12	.250	0	0	5.66
1993	Philadelphia	NL	1	0	0	0	0.1	1	0	0	0	0	0	0	0	0	0	0	1	0	0	0	.000	0	0	0.00

Scott Fletcher

Bats: Right **Throws:** Right **Pos:** 2B **Ht:** 5'11" **Wt:** 173 **Born:** 07/30/58 **Age:** 35

Year	Team	Lg	G	AB	H	2B	3B	HR	(Hm	Rd)	TB	R	RBI	TBB	IBB	SO	HBP	SH	SF	SB	CS	SB%	GDP	Avg	OBP	SLG
1981	Chicago	NL	19	46	10	4	0	0	(0	0)	14	6	1	2	0	4	0	0	0	0	0	.00	0	.217	.250	.304
1982	Chicago	NL	11	24	4	0	0	0	(0	0)	4	4	1	4	0	5	0	0	0	1	0	1.00	0	.167	.286	.167
1983	Chicago	AL	114	262	62	16	5	3	(1	2)	97	42	31	29	0	22	2	7	2	5	1	.83	8	.237	.315	.370
1984	Chicago	AL	149	456	114	13	3	3	(2	1)	142	46	35	46	2	46	8	9	2	10	4	.71	5	.250	.328	.311
1985	Chicago	AL	119	301	77	8	1	2	(0	2)	93	38	31	35	0	47	0	11	1	5	5	.50	9	.256	.332	.309
1986	Texas	AL	147	530	159	34	5	3	(2	1)	212	82	50	47	0	59	4	10	3	12	11	.52	10	.300	.360	.400
1987	Texas	AL	156	588	169	28	4	5	(4	1)	220	82	63	61	3	66	5	12	2	13	12	.52	14	.287	.358	.374
1988	Texas	AL	140	515	142	19	4	0	(0	0)	169	59	47	62	1	34	12	15	5	8	5	.62	13	.276	.364	.328
1989	2 ML Teams		142	546	138	25	2	1	(0	1)	170	77	43	64	1	60	3	11	5	2	1	.67	12	.253	.332	.311
1990	Chicago	AL	151	509	123	18	3	4	(1	3)	159	54	56	45	3	63	3	11	5	1	3	.25	10	.242	.304	.312
1991	Chicago	AL	90	248	51	10	1	1	(0	1)	66	14	28	17	0	26	3	6	3	0	2	.00	3	.206	.262	.266
1992	Milwaukee	AL	123	386	106	18	3	3	(2	1)	139	53	51	30	1	33	7	6	4	17	10	.63	4	.275	.335	.360
1993	Boston	AL	121	480	137	31	5	5	(2	3)	193	81	45	37	1	35	5	6	3	16	3	.84	12	.285	.341	.402
1989	Texas	AL	83	314	75	14	1	0	(0	0)	91	47	22	38	1	41	2	2	2	1	0	1.00	4	.239	.323	.290
	Chicago	AL	59	232	63	11	1	1	(0	0)	79	30	21	26	0	19	1	9	3	1	1	.50	4	.272	.344	.341
13 ML YEARS			1482	4891	1292	224	36	30	(14	16)	1678	638	482	479	12	500	52	104	35	90	57	.61	100	.264	.334	.343

Cliff Floyd

Bats: Left **Throws:** Left **Pos:** 1B **Ht:** 6'4" **Wt:** 220 **Born:** 12/05/72 **Age:** 21

Year	Team	Lg	G	AB	H	2B	3B	HR	(Hm	Rd)	TB	R	RBI	TBB	IBB	SO	HBP	SH	SF	SB	CS	SB%	GDP	Avg	OBP	SLG
1991	Expos	R	56	214	56	9	3	6	--	--	89	35	30	19	1	36	5	1	1	13	3	.81	3	.262	.335	.416
1992	Albany	A	134	516	157	24	16	16	--	--	261	83	97	45	9	75	9	0	3	32	11	.74	4	.304	.368	.506
	Wst Plm Bch	A	4	4	0	0	0	0	--	--	0	0	1	0	0	1	0	0	1	0	0	.00	0	.000	.000	.000
1993	Harrisburg	AA	101	380	125	17	4	26	--	--	228	82	101	54	12	71	5	0	2	31	10	.76	8	.329	.417	.600
	Ottawa	AAA	32	125	30	2	2	2	--	--	42	12	18	16	3	34	1	0	1	2	2	.50	1	.240	.329	.336
1993	Montreal	NL	10	31	7	0	0	1	(0	1)	10	3	2	0	0	0	0	0	0	0	0	.00	0	.226	.226	.323

Tom Foley

Bats: Left **Throws:** Right **Pos:** 2B/1B **Ht:** 6'1" **Wt:** 175 **Born:** 09/09/59 **Age:** 34

Year	Team	Lg	G	AB	H	2B	3B	HR	(Hm	Rd)	TB	R	RBI	TBB	IBB	SO	HBP	SH	SF	SB	CS	SB%	GDP	Avg	OBP	SLG
1983	Cincinnati	NL	68	98	20	4	1	0	(0	0)	26	7	9	13	2	17	0	2	0	1	0	1.00	1	.204	.297	.265
1984	Cincinnati	NL	106	277	70	8	3	5	(0	0)	99	26	27	24	7	36	0	1	2	3	2	.60	2	.253	.310	.357
1985	2 ML Teams		89	250	60	13	4	1	(2	1)	84	24	23	19	8	34	0	0	0	2	3	.40	2	.240	.294	.336
1986	2 ML Teams		103	263	70	15	3	1	(1	0)	94	26	23	30	6	37	0	2	4	10	3	.77	4	.266	.337	.357
1987	Montreal	NL	106	280	82	18	3	5	(3	2)	121	35	28	11	0	40	1	1	0	6	10	.38	6	.293	.322	.432
1988	Montreal	NL	127	377	100	21	3	5	(0	0)	142	33	43	30	10	49	1	0	3	2	7	.22	11	.265	.319	.377
1989	Montreal	NL	122	375	86	19	2	7	(4	3)	130	34	39	45	4	53	3	4	4	2	3	.40	2	.229	.314	.347
1990	Montreal	NL	73	164	35	2	1	0	(0	0)	39	11	12	12	2	22	0	1	1	0	1	.00	4	.213	.266	.238
1991	Montreal	NL	86	168	35	11	1	0	(0	0)	48	12	15	14	4	30	1	1	3	2	0	1.00	4	.208	.269	.286
1992	Montreal	NL	72	115	20	3	1	0	(0	0)	25	7	5	8	2	21	1	3	0	3	0	1.00	6	.174	.230	.217

	Lg	G	AB	H	2B	3B	HR	(Hm	Rd)	TB	R	RBI	TBB	IBB	SO	HBP	SH	SF	SB	CS	SB%	GDP	Avg	OBP	SLG
1993 Pittsburgh	NL	86	194	49	11	1	3	(1	2)	71	18	22	11	1	26	0	2	4	0	0	.00	4	.253	.287	.366
1985 Cincinnati	NL	43	92	18	5	1	0	(0	0)	25	7	6	6	1	16	0	0	0	1	0	1.00	0	.196	.245	.272
Philadelphia	NL	46	158	42	8	0	3	(2	1)	59	17	17	13	7	18	0	0	0	1	3	.25	2	.266	.322	.373
1986 Philadelphia	NL	39	61	18	2	1	0	(0	0)	22	8	5	10	1	11	0	0	1	2	0	1.00	1	.295	.389	.361
Montreal	NL	64	202	52	13	2	1	(1	0)	72	18	18	20	5	26	0	2	3	8	3	.73	3	.257	.320	.356
11 ML YEARS		1038	2561	627	125	20	29	(16	13)	879	233	246	217	46	365	7	17	23	31	29	.52	46	.245	.303	.343

Tony Fossas

Pitches: Left **Bats:** Left **Pos:** RP   **Ht:** 6' 0" **Wt:** 187 **Born:** 09/23/57 **Age:** 36

		HOW MUCH HE PITCHED						WHAT HE GAVE UP												THE RESULTS					
Year Team	Lg	G	GS	CG	GF	IP	BFP	H	R	ER	HR	SH	SF	HB	TBB	IBB	SO	WP	Bk	W	L	Pct.	ShO	Sv	ERA
1988 Texas	AL	5	0	0	1	5.2	28	11	3	3	0	0	0	0	2	0	0	1	0	0	0	.000	0	0	4.76
1989 Milwaukee	AL	51	0	0	16	61	256	57	27	24	3	7	3	1	22	7	42	1	3	2	2	.500	0	0	3.54
1990 Milwaukee	AL	32	0	0	9	29.1	146	44	23	21	5	2	1	0	10	2	24	0	0	2	3	.400	0	0	6.44
1991 Boston	AL	64	0	0	18	57	244	49	27	22	3	5	0	3	28	9	29	2	0	3	2	.600	0	1	3.47
1992 Boston	AL	60	0	0	17	29.2	129	31	9	8	1	3	0	1	14	3	19	0	0	1	2	.333	0	2	2.43
1993 Boston	AL	71	0	0	19	40	175	38	28	23	4	0	1	2	15	4	39	1	1	1	1	.500	0	0	5.18
6 ML YEARS		283	0	0	80	222.2	978	230	117	101	16	17	5	7	91	25	153	5	4	9	10	.474	0	4	4.08

Kevin Foster

Pitches: Right **Bats:** Right **Pos:** SP   **Ht:** 6' 1" **Wt:** 160 **Born:** 01/13/69 **Age:** 25

		HOW MUCH HE PITCHED						WHAT HE GAVE UP												THE RESULTS					
Year Team	Lg	G	GS	CG	GF	IP	BFP	H	R	ER	HR	SH	SF	HB	TBB	IBB	SO	WP	Bk	W	L	Pct.	ShO	Sv	ERA
1990 Expos	R	4	0	0	1	10.2	47	9	6	6	0	1	0	1	6	0	11	0	0	2	0	1.000	0	0	5.06
Gate City	R	10	10	0	0	55	248	43	42	28	3	0	1	6	34	0	52	10	0	1	7	.125	0	0	4.58
1991 Sumter	A	34	11	1	9	102	445	62	36	31	3	1	5	9	68	1	114	5	4	10	4	.714	1	1	2.74
1992 Wst Plm Bch	A	16	11	0	2	69.1	279	45	19	15	4	0	2	3	31	1	66	1	1	7	2	.778	0	0	1.95
1993 Jacksnville	AA	12	12	1	0	65.2	278	53	32	29	2	0	2	4	29	0	72	4	1	4	4	.500	1	0	3.97
Scranton/wb	AAA	17	9	1	0	71	304	63	32	31	7	0	0	3	29	0	59	5	0	1	1	.500	0	0	3.93
1993 Philadelphia	NL	2	1	0	0	6.2	40	13	11	11	3	0	0	0	7	0	6	2	0	0	1	.000	0	0	14.85

Steve Foster

Pitches: Right **Bats:** Right **Pos:** RP   **Ht:** 6' 0" **Wt:** 180 **Born:** 08/16/66 **Age:** 27

		HOW MUCH HE PITCHED						WHAT HE GAVE UP												THE RESULTS					
Year Team	Lg	G	GS	CG	GF	IP	BFP	H	R	ER	HR	SH	SF	HB	TBB	IBB	SO	WP	Bk	W	L	Pct.	ShO	Sv	ERA
1991 Cincinnati	NL	11	0	0	5	14	53	7	5	3	1	0	0	0	4	0	11	0	0	0	0	.000	0	0	1.93
1992 Cincinnati	NL	31	1	0	7	50	209	52	16	16	4	5	2	0	13	1	34	1	0	1	1	.500	0	2	2.88
1993 Cincinnati	NL	17	0	0	7	25.2	105	23	8	5	1	1	0	1	5	2	16	0	0	2	2	.500	0	0	1.75
3 ML YEARS		59	1	0	19	89.2	367	82	29	24	6	6	2	1	22	3	61	1	0	3	3	.500	0	2	2.41

Eric Fox

Bats: Both **Throws:** Left **Pos:** CF   **Ht:** 5'10" **Wt:** 180 **Born:** 08/15/63 **Age:** 30

		BATTING																BASERUNNING				PERCENTAGES		
Year Team	Lg	G	AB	H	2B	3B	HR	(Hm	Rd)	TB	R	RBI	TBB	IBB	SO	HBP	SH	SF	SB	CS	SB%	GDP	Avg	OBP	SLG
1986 Salinas	A	133	526	137	17	3	5	--	--	175	80	42	69	7	78	1	9	4	41	27	.60	1	.260	.345	.333
1987 Chattanooga	AA	134	523	139	28	10	8	--	--	211	76	54	40	5	93	2	4	5	22	10	.69	2	.266	.318	.403
1988 Vermont	AA	129	478	120	20	6	3	--	--	161	55	39	39	3	69	2	7	4	33	12	.73	1	.251	.308	.337
1989 Huntsville	AA	139	498	125	10	5	15	--	--	190	84	51	72	1	85	0	11	2	49	15	.77	3	.251	.344	.382
1990 Tacoma	AAA	62	221	61	9	2	4	--	--	86	37	34	20	0	34	0	5	2	8	8	.50	2	.276	.333	.389
1991 Tacoma	AAA	127	522	141	24	8	4	--	--	193	85	52	57	4	82	2	9	4	17	11	.61	6	.270	.342	.370
1992 Huntsville	AA	59	240	65	16	2	5	--	--	100	42	14	27	4	43	0	0	3	16	5	.76	2	.271	.341	.417
Tacoma	AAA	37	121	24	3	1	1	--	--	32	16	7	16	1	25	0	2	2	5	0	1.00	2	.198	.288	.264
1993 Tacoma	AAA	92	317	99	14	5	11	--	--	156	49	52	41	3	48	1	7	3	18	8	.69	4	.312	.390	.492
1992 Oakland	AL	51	143	34	5	2	3	(0	3)	52	24	13	13	0	29	0	6	1	3	4	.43	1	.238	.299	.364
1993 Oakland	AL	29	56	8	1	0	1	(1	0)	12	5	5	2	0	7	0	3	0	0	2	.00	0	.143	.172	.214
2 ML YEARS		80	199	42	6	2	4	(1	3)	64	29	18	15	0	36	0	9	1	3	6	.33	1	.211	.265	.322

John Franco

Pitches: Left **Bats:** Left **Pos:** RP   **Ht:** 5'10" **Wt:** 185 **Born:** 09/17/60 **Age:** 33

		HOW MUCH HE PITCHED						WHAT HE GAVE UP												THE RESULTS					
Year Team	Lg	G	GS	CG	GF	IP	BFP	H	R	ER	HR	SH	SF	HB	TBB	IBB	SO	WP	Bk	W	L	Pct.	ShO	Sv	ERA
1984 Cincinnati	NL	54	0	0	30	79.1	335	74	28	23	3	4	4	2	36	4	55	2	0	6	2	.750	0	4	2.61
1985 Cincinnati	NL	67	0	0	33	99	407	83	27	24	5	11	1	1	40	8	61	4	0	12	3	.800	0	12	2.18
1986 Cincinnati	NL	74	0	0	52	101	429	90	40	33	7	8	3	2	44	12	84	4	0	6	6	.500	0	29	2.94
1987 Cincinnati	NL	68	0	0	44	82	344	76	26	23	6	5	2	0	27	6	61	1	0	8	5	.615	0	32	2.52
1988 Cincinnati	NL	70	0	0	61	86	336	60	18	15	3	5	1	0	27	3	46	1	2	6	6	.500	0	39	1.57
1989 Cincinnati	NL	60	0	0	50	80.2	345	77	35	28	3	7	3	0	36	8	60	3	2	4	8	.333	0	32	3.12

Year	Team	Lg	G	GS	CG	GF	IP	BFP	H	R	ER	HR	SH	SF	HB	TBB	IBB	SO	WP	Bk	W	L	Pct.	ShO	Sv	ERA
1990	New York	NL	55	0	0	48	67.2	287	66	22	19	4	3	1	0	21	2	56	7	2	5	3	.625	0	33	2.53
1991	New York	NL	52	0	0	48	55.1	247	61	27	18	2	3	0	1	18	4	45	6	0	5	9	.357	0	30	2.93
1992	New York	NL	31	0	0	30	33	128	24	6	6	1	0	2	0	11	2	20	0	0	6	2	.750	0	15	1.64
1993	New York	NL	35	0	0	30	36.1	172	46	24	21	6	4	1	1	19	3	29	5	0	4	3	.571	0	10	5.20
	10 ML YEARS		566	0	0	442	720.1	3030	657	253	210	40	50	18	7	279	52	517	33	8	62	47	.569	0	236	2.62

Julio Franco

Bats: Right **Throws:** Right **Pos:** DH   **Ht:** 6' 1" **Wt:** 188 **Born:** 08/23/61 **Age:** 32

						BATTING														BASERUNNING				PERCENTAGES		
Year	Team	Lg	G	AB	H	2B	3B	HR	(Hm Rd)	TB	R	RBI	TBB	IBB	SO	HBP	SH	SF	SB	CS	SB%	GDP	Avg	OBP	SLG
1982	Philadelphia	NL	16	29	8	1	0	0	(0 0)	9	3	3	2	1	4	0	1	0	0	2	.00	1	.276	.323	.310
1983	Cleveland	AL	149	560	153	24	8	8	(6 2)	217	68	80	27	1	50	2	3	6	32	12	.73	21	.273	.306	.388
1984	Cleveland	AL	160	658	188	22	5	3	(1 2)	229	82	79	43	1	68	6	1	10	19	10	.66	23	.286	.331	.348
1985	Cleveland	AL	160	636	183	33	4	6	(3 3)	242	97	90	54	2	74	4	0	9	13	9	.59	26	.288	.343	.381
1986	Cleveland	AL	149	599	183	30	5	10	(4 6)	253	80	74	32	1	66	0	0	5	10	7	.59	28	.306	.338	.422
1987	Cleveland	AL	128	495	158	24	3	8	(5 3)	212	86	52	57	2	56	3	0	5	32	9	.78	23	.319	.389	.428
1988	Cleveland	AL	152	613	186	23	6	10	(3 7)	251	88	54	56	4	72	2	1	4	25	11	.69	17	.303	.361	.409
1989	Texas	AL	150	548	173	31	5	13	(9 4)	253	80	92	66	11	69	1	0	6	21	3	.88	27	.316	.386	.462
1990	Texas	AL	157	582	172	27	1	11	(4 7)	234	96	69	82	3	83	2	2	2	31	10	.76	12	.296	.383	.402
1991	Texas	AL	146	589	201	27	3	15	(7 8)	279	108	78	65	8	78	3	0	2	36	9	.80	13	.341	.408	.474
1992	Texas	AL	35	107	25	7	0	2	(2 0)	38	19	8	15	2	17	0	1	0	1	1	.50	3	.234	.328	.355
1993	Texas	AL	144	532	154	31	3	14	(6 8)	233	85	84	62	4	95	1	5	7	9	3	.75	16	.289	.360	.438
	12 ML YEARS		1546	5948	1784	280	43	100	(50 50)	2450	892	763	561	40	732	24	14	56	229	86	.73	210	.300	.360	.412

Lou Frazier

Bats: Both **Throws:** Right **Pos:** LF   **Ht:** 6' 2" **Wt:** 175 **Born:** 01/26/65 **Age:** 29

						BATTING														BASERUNNING				PERCENTAGES		
Year	Team	Lg	G	AB	H	2B	3B	HR	(Hm Rd)	TB	R	RBI	TBB	IBB	SO	HBP	SH	SF	SB	CS	SB%	GDP	Avg	OBP	SLG
1986	Astros	R	51	178	51	7	2	1	(-- --)	65	39	23	32	0	25	1	3	1	17	8	.68	3	.287	.396	.365
1987	Asheville	A	108	399	103	9	2	1	(-- --)	119	83	33	68	1	89	2	4	3	75	24	.76	3	.258	.367	.298
1988	Osceola	A	130	468	110	11	3	0	(-- --)	127	79	34	90	5	104	4	5	1	87	16	.84	9	.235	.362	.271
1989	Columbus	AA	135	460	106	10	1	4	(-- --)	130	65	31	76	2	101	1	2	2	43	14	.75	7	.230	.340	.283
1990	London	AA	81	242	53	4	1	0	(-- --)	59	29	15	27	0	52	0	1	1	20	3	.87	5	.219	.296	.244
1991	London	AA	122	439	105	9	4	3	(-- --)	131	69	40	77	5	86	1	3	1	42	17	.71	8	.239	.353	.298
1992	London	AA	129	477	120	16	3	0	(-- --)	142	85	34	95	1	107	0	2	2	58	23	.72	3	.252	.375	.298
1993	Montreal	NL	112	189	54	7	1	1	(1 0)	66	27	16	16	0	24	0	5	1	17	2	.89	3	.286	.340	.349

Scott Fredrickson

Pitches: Right **Bats:** Right **Pos:** RP   **Ht:** 6' 3" **Wt:** 215 **Born:** 08/19/67 **Age:** 26

			HOW MUCH HE PITCHED						WHAT HE GAVE UP											THE RESULTS					
Year	Team	Lg	G	GS	CG	GF	IP	BFP	H	R	ER	HR	SH	SF	HB	TBB	IBB	SO	WP	Bk	W	L	Pct.	ShO	Sv	ERA
1990	Spokane	A	26	1	0	15	46.2	197	35	22	17	3	4	1	2	17	1	61	6	4	3	3	.500	0	8	3.28
1991	Waterloo	A	26	0	0	22	38.1	153	24	9	5	1	1	2	1	15	3	40	3	2	3	5	.375	0	6	1.17
	High Desert	A	23	0	0	19	35	154	31	15	9	2	1	1	1	18	2	26	6	0	4	1	.800	0	7	2.31
1992	Wichita	AA	56	0	0	22	73.1	303	50	29	26	9	2	5	2	38	3	66	11	0	4	7	.364	0	5	3.19
1993	Colo Sprngs	AAA	23	0	0	18	26.1	119	25	16	16	3	2	1	0	19	3	20	2	0	1	3	.250	0	7	5.47
1993	Colorado	NL	25	0	0	4	29	137	33	25	20	3	2	2	1	17	2	20	4	1	0	1	.000	0	0	6.21

Marvin Freeman

Pitches: Right **Bats:** Right **Pos:** RP   **Ht:** 6' 7" **Wt:** 222 **Born:** 04/10/63 **Age:** 31

			HOW MUCH HE PITCHED						WHAT HE GAVE UP											THE RESULTS					
Year	Team	Lg	G	GS	CG	GF	IP	BFP	H	R	ER	HR	SH	SF	HB	TBB	IBB	SO	WP	Bk	W	L	Pct.	ShO	Sv	ERA
1993	Richmond *	AAA	2	2	0	0	4	18	4	1	1	0	0	0	1	1	0	5	0	0	0	0	.000	0	0	2.25
1986	Philadelphia	NL	3	3	0	0	16	61	6	4	4	0	0	1	0	10	0	8	1	0	2	0	1.000	0	0	2.25
1988	Philadelphia	NL	11	11	0	0	51.2	249	55	36	35	2	5	1	1	43	2	37	3	1	2	3	.400	0	0	6.10
1989	Philadelphia	NL	1	1	0	0	3	16	2	2	2	0	0	0	0	5	0	0	0	1	0	0	.000	0	0	6.00
1990	2 ML Teams	NL	25	3	0	5	48	207	41	24	20	5	2	0	5	17	2	38	4	0	1	2	.333	0	1	4.31
1991	Atlanta	NL	34	0	0	0	48	190	37	19	16	2	1	1	2	13	1	34	4	0	1	0	1.000	0	1	3.00
1992	Atlanta	NL	58	0	0	15	64.1	276	61	26	23	7	2	1	1	29	7	41	4	0	7	5	.583	0	3	3.22
1993	Atlanta	NL	21	0	0	5	23.2	103	24	16	16	1	0	0	1	10	2	25	3	0	2	0	1.000	0	3	6.08
1990	Philadelphia	NL	16	3	0	4	32.1	147	34	21	20	5	1	0	3	14	2	26	4	0	0	2	.000	0	1	5.57
	Atlanta	NL	9	0	0	1	15.2	60	7	3	3	0	1	0	0	3	0	12	0	0	1	0	1.000	0	0	1.72
	7 ML YEARS		153	18	0	31	254.2	1102	226	127	119	17	10	4	10	127	14	183	19	2	15	10	.600	0	5	4.21

Steve Frey

Pitches: Left   **Bats:** Right   **Pos:** RP   **Ht:** 5'9"   **Wt:** 170   **Born:** 07/29/63   **Age:** 30

		HOW MUCH HE PITCHED				WHAT HE GAVE UP								THE RESULTS						
Year Team	Lg	G	GS	CG	GF	IP	BFP	H	R	ER	HR	SH	SF	HB	TBB	IBB	SO	WP	Bk	W	L	Pct.	ShO	Sv	ERA
1989 Montreal	NL	20	0	0	11	21.1	103	29	15	13	4	0	2	1	11	1	15	1	1	3	2	.600	0	0	5.48
1990 Montreal	NL	51	0	0	21	55.2	236	44	15	13	4	3	2	1	29	6	29	0	0	8	2	.800	0	9	2.10
1991 Montreal	NL	31	0	0	5	39.2	182	43	31	22	3	3	2	1	23	4	21	3	1	0	1	.000	0	1	4.99
1992 California	AL	51	0	0	20	45.1	193	39	18	18	6	2	3	2	22	3	24	1	0	4	2	.667	0	4	3.57
1993 California	AL	55	0	0	28	48.1	212	41	20	16	1	4	1	3	26	1	22	3	0	2	3	.400	0	13	2.98
5 ML YEARS		208	0	0	85	210.1	926	196	99	82	18	12	10	8	111	15	111	8	2	17	10	.630	0	27	3.51

Todd Frohwirth

Pitches: Right   **Bats:** Right   **Pos:** RP   **Ht:** 6'4"   **Wt:** 211   **Born:** 09/28/62   **Age:** 31

		HOW MUCH HE PITCHED				WHAT HE GAVE UP								THE RESULTS						
Year Team	Lg	G	GS	CG	GF	IP	BFP	H	R	ER	HR	SH	SF	HB	TBB	IBB	SO	WP	Bk	W	L	Pct.	ShO	Sv	ERA
1987 Philadelphia	NL	10	0	0	2	11	43	12	0	0	0	0	0	0	2	0	9	0	0	1	0	1.000	0	0	0.00
1988 Philadelphia	NL	12	0	0	6	12	62	16	11	11	2	1	1	0	11	6	11	1	0	1	2	.333	0	0	8.25
1989 Philadelphia	NL	45	0	0	11	62.2	258	56	26	25	4	3	1	3	18	0	39	1	1	1	0	1.000	0	0	3.59
1990 Philadelphia	NL	5	0	0	0	1	12	3	2	2	0	0	0	0	6	2	1	1	0	0	1	.000	0	0	18.00
1991 Baltimore	AL	51	0	0	10	96.1	372	64	24	20	2	4	1	1	29	3	77	0	0	7	3	.700	0	3	1.87
1992 Baltimore	AL	65	0	0	23	106	444	97	33	29	4	7	1	3	41	4	58	1	0	4	3	.571	0	4	2.46
1993 Baltimore	AL	70	0	0	30	96.1	411	91	47	41	7	7	2	3	44	8	50	1	0	6	7	.462	0	3	3.83
7 ML YEARS		258	0	0	82	385.1	1602	339	143	128	19	22	6	10	151	23	245	5	1	20	16	.556	0	10	2.99

Jeff Frye

Bats: Right   **Throws:** Right   **Pos:** 2B   **Ht:** 5'9"   **Wt:** 165   **Born:** 08/31/66   **Age:** 27

		BATTING											BASERUNNING			PERCENTAGES		
Year Team	Lg	G	AB	H	2B	3B	HR	(Hm	Rd)	TB	R	RBI	TBB	IBB	SO	HBP	SH	SF	SB	CS	SB%	GDP	Avg	OBP	SLG
1988 Butte	R	55	185	53	7	1	0	--	--	62	47	14	55	1	24	1	1	1	16	1	.94	2	.286	.401	.335
1989 Gastonia	A	125	464	145	26	3	1	--	--	180	85	40	72	5	53	1	5	1	33	13	.72	4	.313	.405	.388
1990 Charlotte	A	131	503	137	16	7	0	--	--	167	77	50	80	5	66	2	7	4	28	6	.82	5	.272	.372	.332
1991 Tulsa	AA	131	503	152	32	11	4	--	--	218	92	41	71	0	60	1	5	3	15	8	.65	8	.302	.388	.433
1992 Okla City	AAA	87	337	101	26	2	2	--	--	137	64	28	51	0	39	11	8	0	11	9	.55	9	.300	.409	.407
1992 Texas	AL	67	199	51	9	1	1	(0	1)	65	24	12	16	0	27	3	11	1	1	3	.25	2	.256	.320	.327

Travis Fryman

Bats: Right   **Throws:** Right   **Pos:** SS/3B   **Ht:** 6'1"   **Wt:** 194   **Born:** 03/25/69   **Age:** 25

		BATTING											BASERUNNING			PERCENTAGES		
Year Team	Lg	G	AB	H	2B	3B	HR	(Hm | Rd)	TB	R	RBI	TBB	IBB	SO	HBP	SH	SF	SB	CS	SB%	GDP	Avg	OBP	SLG
1990 Detroit	AL	66	232	69	11	1	9	(5 | 4)	109	32	27	17	0	51	1	1	0	3	3	.50	3	.297	.348	.470
1991 Detroit	AL	149	557	144	36	3	21	(8 | 13)	249	65	91	40	0	149	3	6	6	12	5	.71	13	.259	.309	.447
1992 Detroit	AL	161	659	175	31	4	20	(9 | 11)	274	87	96	45	1	144	6	5	6	8	4	.67	13	.266	.316	.416
1993 Detroit	AL	151	607	182	37	5	22	(13 | 9)	295	98	97	77	1	128	4	1	6	9	4	.69	8	.300	.379	.486
4 ML YEARS		527	2055	570	115	13	72	(35 | 37)	927	282	311	179	2	472	14	13	18	32	16	.67	37	.277	.337	.451

Gary Gaetti

Bats: Right   **Throws:** Right   **Pos:** 3B/1B   **Ht:** 6'0"   **Wt:** 200   **Born:** 08/19/58   **Age:** 35

		BATTING											BASERUNNING			PERCENTAGES		
Year Team	Lg	G	AB	H	2B	3B	HR	(Hm | Rd)	TB	R	RBI	TBB	IBB	SO	HBP	SH	SF	SB	CS	SB%	GDP	Avg	OBP	SLG
1981 Minnesota	AL	9	26	5	0	0	2	(1 | 1)	11	4	3	0	0	6	0	0	0	0	0	.00	1	.192	.192	.423
1982 Minnesota	AL	145	508	117	25	4	25	(15 | 10)	225	59	84	37	2	107	3	4	13	0	4	.00	16	.230	.280	.443
1983 Minnesota	AL	157	584	143	30	3	21	(7 | 14)	242	81	78	54	2	121	4	0	8	7	1	.88	18	.245	.309	.414
1984 Minnesota	AL	162	588	154	29	4	5	(2 | 3)	206	55	65	44	1	81	4	3	5	11	5	.69	9	.262	.315	.350
1985 Minnesota	AL	160	560	138	31	0	20	(10 | 10)	229	71	63	37	3	89	7	3	1	13	5	.72	15	.246	.301	.409
1986 Minnesota	AL	157	596	171	34	1	34	(16 | 18)	309	91	108	52	4	108	6	1	6	14	15	.48	18	.287	.347	.518
1987 Minnesota	AL	154	584	150	36	2	31	(18 | 13)	283	95	109	37	7	92	3	1	3	10	7	.59	25	.257	.303	.485
1988 Minnesota	AL	133	468	141	29	2	28	(9 | 19)	258	66	88	36	5	85	5	1	6	7	6	.54	10	.301	.353	.551
1989 Minnesota	AL	130	498	125	11	4	19	(10 | 9)	201	63	75	25	5	87	3	1	9	6	2	.75	12	.251	.286	.404
1990 Minnesota	AL	154	577	132	27	5	16	(7 | 9)	217	61	85	36	1	101	3	1	8	6	1	.86	22	.229	.274	.376
1991 California	AL	152	586	144	22	1	18	(12 | 6)	222	58	66	33	3	104	8	2	5	5	5	.50	13	.246	.293	.379
1992 California	AL	130	456	103	13	2	12	(8 | 4)	156	41	48	21	4	79	6	0	3	3	1	.75	9	.226	.267	.342
1993 2 ML Teams		102	331	81	20	1	14	(6 | 8)	145	40	50	21	0	87	8	2	7	1	3	.25	5	.245	.300	.438
1993 California	AL	20	50	9	2	0	0	(0 | 0)	11	3	4	5	0	12	0	0	1	1	0	1.00	3	.180	.250	.220
Kansas City	AL	82	281	72	18	1	14	(6 | 8)	134	37	46	16	0	75	8	2	6	0	3	.00	2	.256	.309	.477
13 ML YEARS		1745	6362	1604	307	29	245	(121 | 124)	2704	785	922	433	37	1147	60	19	74	83	53	.61	173	.252	.303	.425

Greg Gagne

Bats: Right **Throws:** Right **Pos:** SS   **Ht:** 5'11" **Wt:** 180 **Born:** 11/12/61 **Age:** 32

							BATTING											BASERUNNING				PERCENTAGES		
Year	Team	Lg	G	AB	H	2B	3B	HR	(Hm | Rd)	TB	R	RBI	TBB	IBB	SO	HBP	SH	SF	SB	CS	SB%	GDP	Avg	OBP	SLG
1983	Minnesota	AL	10	27	3	1	0	0	(0 | 0)	4	2	3	0	0	6	0	0	2	0	0	.00	0	.111	.103	.148
1984	Minnesota	AL	2	1	0	0	0	0	(0 | 0)	0	0	0	0	0	0	0	0	0	0	0	.00	0	.000	.000	.000
1985	Minnesota	AL	114	293	66	15	3	2	(0 | 2)	93	37	23	20	0	57	3	3	3	10	4	.71	5	.225	.279	.317
1986	Minnesota	AL	156	472	118	22	6	12	(10 | 2)	188	63	54	30	0	108	6	13	3	12	10	.55	4	.250	.301	.398
1987	Minnesota	AL	137	437	116	28	7	10	(7 | 3)	188	68	40	25	0	84	4	10	2	6	6	.50	3	.265	.310	.430
1988	Minnesota	AL	149	461	109	20	6	14	(5 | 9)	183	70	48	27	2	110	7	11	1	15	7	.68	13	.236	.288	.397
1989	Minnesota	AL	149	460	125	29	7	9	(5 | 4)	195	69	48	17	0	80	2	7	5	11	4	.73	10	.272	.298	.424
1990	Minnesota	AL	138	388	91	22	3	7	(3 | 4)	140	38	38	24	0	76	1	8	2	8	8	.50	5	.235	.280	.361
1991	Minnesota	AL	139	408	108	23	3	8	(3 | 5)	161	52	42	26	0	72	3	5	5	11	9	.55	15	.265	.310	.395
1992	Minnesota	AL	146	439	108	23	0	7	(1 | 6)	152	53	39	19	0	83	2	12	1	6	7	.46	11	.246	.280	.346
1993	Kansas City	AL	159	540	151	32	3	10	(3 | 7)	219	66	57	33	1	93	0	4	4	10	12	.45	7	.280	.319	.406
11 ML YEARS			1299	3926	995	215	38	79	(37 | 42)	1523	518	392	221	3	769	28	73	28	89	67	.57	73	.253	.296	.388

Jay Gainer

Bats: Left **Throws:** Left **Pos:** 1B   **Ht:** 6' 0" **Wt:** 188 **Born:** 10/08/66 **Age:** 27

							BATTING											BASERUNNING				PERCENTAGES		
Year	Team	Lg	G	AB	H	2B	3B	HR	(Hm	Rd)	TB	R	RBI	TBB	IBB	SO	HBP	SH	SF	SB	CS	SB%	GDP	Avg	OBP	SLG
1990	Spokane	A	74	281	100	21	0	10	--	--	151	41	54	31	3	49	5	1	4	4	3	.57	4	.356	.424	.537
1991	High Desert	A	127	499	131	17	0	32	--	--	244	83	120	52	3	105	3	0	16	4	3	.57	8	.263	.326	.489
1992	Wichita	AA	105	376	98	12	1	23	--	--	181	57	67	46	6	101	0	1	6	4	2	.67	5	.261	.336	.481
1993	Colo Sprngs	AAA	86	293	86	11	3	10	--	--	133	51	74	22	2	70	1	1	4	4	2	.67	6	.294	.341	.454
1993	Colorado	NL	23	41	7	0	0	3	(1	2)	16	4	6	4	0	12	0	0	0	1	1	.50	0	.171	.244	.390

Andres Galarraga

Bats: Right **Throws:** Right **Pos:** 1B   **Ht:** 6' 3" **Wt:** 235 **Born:** 06/18/61 **Age:** 33

							BATTING											BASERUNNING				PERCENTAGES		
Year	Team	Lg	G	AB	H	2B	3B	HR	(Hm | Rd)	TB	R	RBI	TBB	IBB	SO	HBP	SH	SF	SB	CS	SB%	GDP	Avg	OBP	SLG
1985	Montreal	NL	24	75	14	1	0	2	(0 | 2)	21	9	4	3	0	18	1	0	0	1	2	.33	0	.187	.228	.280
1986	Montreal	NL	105	321	87	13	0	10	(4 | 6)	130	39	42	30	5	79	3	1	1	6	5	.55	8	.271	.338	.405
1987	Montreal	NL	147	551	168	40	3	13	(7 | 6)	253	72	90	41	13	127	10	0	4	7	10	.41	11	.305	.361	.459
1988	Montreal	NL	157	609	184	42	8	29	(14 | 15)	329	99	92	39	9	153	10	0	3	13	4	.76	12	.302	.352	.540
1989	Montreal	NL	152	572	147	30	1	23	(13 | 10)	248	76	85	48	10	158	13	0	3	12	5	.71	12	.257	.327	.434
1990	Montreal	NL	155	579	148	29	0	20	(6 | 14)	237	65	87	40	8	169	4	0	5	10	1	.91	14	.256	.306	.409
1991	Montreal	NL	107	375	82	13	2	9	(3 | 6)	126	34	33	23	5	86	2	0	0	5	6	.45	6	.219	.268	.336
1992	St. Louis	NL	95	325	79	14	2	10	(4 | 6)	127	38	39	11	0	69	8	0	3	5	4	.56	8	.243	.282	.391
1993	Colorado	NL	120	470	174	35	4	22	(13 | 9)	283	71	98	24	12	73	6	0	6	2	4	.33	9	.370	.403	.602
9 ML YEARS			1062	3877	1083	217	20	138	(64 | 74)	1754	503	570	259	62	932	57	1	25	61	41	.60	80	.279	.332	.452

Dave Gallagher

Bats: Right **Throws:** Right **Pos:** CF/LF/RF   **Ht:** 6' 0" **Wt:** 185 **Born:** 09/20/60 **Age:** 33

							BATTING											BASERUNNING				PERCENTAGES		
Year	Team	Lg	G	AB	H	2B	3B	HR	(Hm | Rd)	TB	R	RBI	TBB	IBB	SO	HBP	SH	SF	SB	CS	SB%	GDP	Avg	OBP	SLG
1987	Cleveland	AL	15	36	4	1	1	0	(0 | 0)	7	2	1	2	0	5	0	1	0	2	0	1.00	1	.111	.158	.194
1988	Chicago	AL	101	347	105	15	3	5	(1 | 4)	141	59	31	29	3	40	0	6	2	5	4	.56	8	.303	.354	.406
1989	Chicago	AL	161	601	160	22	2	1	(1 | 0)	189	74	46	46	1	79	2	16	2	5	6	.45	9	.266	.320	.314
1990	2 ML Teams		68	126	32	4	1	0	(0 | 0)	38	12	7	7	0	12	1	1	1	1	2	.33	3	.254	.296	.302
1991	California	AL	90	270	79	17	0	1	(0 | 1)	99	32	30	24	0	43	2	10	0	2	4	.33	6	.293	.355	.367
1992	New York	NL	98	175	42	11	1	1	(1 | 0)	58	20	21	19	0	16	1	3	7	4	5	.44	7	.240	.307	.331
1993	New York	NL	99	201	55	12	2	6	(1 | 5)	89	34	28	20	1	18	0	7	1	1	1	.50	7	.274	.338	.443
1990	Chicago	AL	45	75	21	3	1	0	(0 | 0)	26	5	5	3	0	9	1	5	0	1	0	1.00	3	.280	.316	.347
	Baltimore	AL	23	51	11	1	0	0	(0 | 0)	12	7	2	4	0	3	0	2	1	1	1	.50	0	.216	.268	.235
7 ML YEARS			632	1756	477	82	10	14	(4 | 10)	621	233	164	147	5	213	6	50	13	20	22	.48	41	.272	.328	.354

Mike Gallego

Bats: Right **Throws:** Right **Pos:** SS/2B/3B   **Ht:** 5' 8" **Wt:** 175 **Born:** 10/31/60 **Age:** 33

							BATTING											BASERUNNING				PERCENTAGES		
Year	Team	Lg	G	AB	H	2B	3B	HR	(Hm | Rd)	TB	R	RBI	TBB	IBB	SO	HBP	SH	SF	SB	CS	SB%	GDP	Avg	OBP	SLG
1985	Oakland	AL	76	77	16	5	1	1	(0 | 1)	26	13	9	12	0	14	1	2	1	1	1	.50	2	.208	.319	.338
1986	Oakland	AL	20	37	10	2	0	0	(0 | 0)	12	2	4	1	0	6	0	2	0	0	2	.00	0	.270	.289	.324
1987	Oakland	AL	72	124	31	6	2	2	(0 | 2)	43	18	14	12	0	21	1	5	1	0	1	.00	5	.250	.319	.347
1988	Oakland	AL	129	277	58	8	0	2	(2 | 0)	72	38	20	34	0	53	1	8	0	2	3	.40	6	.209	.298	.260
1989	Oakland	AL	133	357	90	14	2	3	(2 | 1)	117	45	30	35	0	43	6	8	3	7	5	.58	10	.252	.327	.328
1990	Oakland	AL	140	389	80	13	2	3	(1 | 2)	106	36	34	35	0	50	4	17	2	5	5	.50	13	.206	.277	.272

Year Team	Lg	G	AB	H	2B	3B	HR	(Hm	Rd)	TB	R	RBI	TBB	IBB	SO	HBP	SH	SF	SB	CS	SB%	GDP	Avg	OBP	SLG
1991 Oakland	AL	159	482	119	15	4	12	(6	6)	178	67	49	67	3	84	5	10	3	6	9	.40	8	.247	.343	.369
1992 New York	AL	53	173	44	7	1	3	(1	2)	62	24	14	20	0	22	4	3	1	0	1	.00	5	.254	.343	.358
1993 New York	AL	119	403	114	20	1	10	(5	5)	166	63	54	50	0	65	4	3	5	3	2	.60	16	.283	.364	.412
9 ML YEARS		901	2319	562	90	11	36	(17	19)	782	306	228	266	3	358	26	58	16	24	29	.45	65	.242	.325	.337

Ron Gant

Bats: Right   **Throws:** Right   **Pos:** LF   **Ht:** 6' 0"   **Wt:** 172   **Born:** 03/02/65   **Age:** 29

							BATTING												BASERUNNING				PERCENTAGES		
Year Team	Lg	G	AB	H	2B	3B	HR	(Hm	Rd)	TB	R	RBI	TBB	IBB	SO	HBP	SH	SF	SB	CS	SB%	GDP	Avg	OBP	SLG
1987 Atlanta	NL	21	83	22	4	0	2	(1	1)	32	9	9	1	0	11	0	1	1	4	2	.67	3	.265	.271	.386
1988 Atlanta	NL	146	563	146	28	8	19	(7	12)	247	85	60	46	4	118	3	2	4	19	10	.66	7	.259	.317	.439
1989 Atlanta	NL	75	260	46	8	3	9	(5	4)	87	26	25	20	0	63	1	2	2	9	6	.60	0	.177	.237	.335
1990 Atlanta	NL	152	575	174	34	3	32	(18	14)	310	107	84	50	0	86	1	1	4	33	16	.67	8	.303	.357	.539
1991 Atlanta	NL	154	561	141	35	3	32	(18	14)	278	101	105	71	8	104	5	0	5	34	15	.69	6	.251	.338	.496
1992 Atlanta	NL	153	544	141	22	6	17	(10	7)	226	74	80	45	5	101	7	0	6	32	10	.76	10	.259	.321	.415
1993 Atlanta	NL	157	606	166	27	4	36	(17	19)	309	113	117	67	2	117	2	0	7	26	9	.74	14	.274	.345	.510
7 ML YEARS		858	3192	836	158	27	147	(76	71)	1489	515	480	300	19	600	19	6	29	157	68	.70	48	.262	.326	.466

Rich Garces

Pitches: Right   **Bats:** Right   **Pos:** RP   **Ht:** 6' 0"   **Wt:** 215   **Born:** 05/18/71   **Age:** 23

		HOW MUCH HE PITCHED						WHAT HE GAVE UP								THE RESULTS					
Year Team	Lg	G	GS	CG	GF	IP	BFP	H	R	ER	HR	SH	SF	HB	TBB	IBB	SO	WP	Bk	W	L	Pct.	ShO	Sv	ERA
1988 Elizabethtn	R	17	3	1	10	59	254	51	22	15	1	2	1	1	27	2	69	7	0	5	4	.556	0	5	2.29
1989 Kenosha	A	24	24	4	0	142.2	596	117	70	54	5	5	5	5	62	1	84	5	6	9	10	.474	1	0	3.41
1990 Visalia	A	47	0	0	42	54.2	212	33	14	11	2	1	1	1	16	0	75	6	0	2	2	.500	0	28	1.81
Orlando	AA	15	0	0	14	17.1	81	17	4	4	0	1	0	0	14	2	22	2	0	2	1	.667	0	8	2.08
1991 Portland	AAA	10	0	0	8	13	58	10	7	7	1	0	0	1	8	1	13	0	1	0	1	.000	0	3	4.85
Orlando	AA	10	0	0	5	16.1	75	12	6	6	0	2	1	2	14	2	17	0	0	2	1	.667	0	0	3.31
1992 Orlando	AA	58	0	0	42	73.1	334	76	46	37	6	8	7	2	39	1	72	6	0	3	3	.500	0	13	4.54
1993 Portland	AAA	35	7	0	5	54	293	70	55	50	4	3	2	0	64	0	48	3	3	1	3	.250	0	0	8.33
1990 Minnesota	AL	5	0	0	3	5.2	24	4	2	1	0	0	0	0	4	0	1	0	0	0	0	.000	0	2	1.59
1993 Minnesota	AL	3	0	0	1	4	18	4	2	0	0	0	0	0	2	0	3	0	0	0	0	.000	0	0	0.00
2 ML YEARS		8	0	0	4	9.2	42	8	4	1	0	0	0	0	6	0	4	0	0	0	0	.000	0	2	0.93

Carlos Garcia

Bats: Right   **Throws:** Right   **Pos:** 2B   **Ht:** 6' 1"   **Wt:** 185   **Born:** 10/15/67   **Age:** 26

							BATTING												BASERUNNING				PERCENTAGES		
Year Team	Lg	G	AB	H	2B	3B	HR	(Hm	Rd)	TB	R	RBI	TBB	IBB	SO	HBP	SH	SF	SB	CS	SB%	GDP	Avg	OBP	SLG
1987 Macon	A	110	373	95	14	3	3	--	--	124	44	38	23	2	80	6	2	2	20	10	.67	6	.255	.307	.332
1988 Augusta	A	73	269	78	13	2	1	--	--	98	32	45	22	0	46	1	2	1	11	6	.65	5	.290	.345	.364
Salem	A	62	236	65	9	3	1	--	--	83	21	28	10	0	32	1	0	3	8	2	.80	9	.275	.304	.352
1989 Salem	A	81	304	86	12	4	7	--	--	127	45	49	18	0	51	4	1	5	19	6	.76	3	.283	.326	.418
Harrisburg	AA	54	188	53	5	5	3	--	--	77	28	25	8	0	36	0	0	1	6	4	.60	4	.282	.310	.410
1990 Harrisburg	AA	65	242	67	11	2	5	--	--	97	36	25	16	0	36	3	1	1	12	1	.92	6	.277	.328	.401
Buffalo	AAA	63	197	52	10	0	5	--	--	77	23	18	16	2	40	2	1	2	7	4	.64	5	.264	.323	.391
1991 Buffalo	AAA	127	463	123	21	6	7	--	--	177	62	60	33	5	78	7	6	3	30	7	.81	6	.266	.322	.382
1992 Buffalo	AAA	113	426	129	28	9	13	--	--	214	73	70	24	2	64	4	4	5	21	7	.75	7	.303	.342	.502
1990 Pittsburgh	NL	4	4	2	0	0	0	(0	0)	2	1	0	0	0	2	0	0	0	0	0	.00	0	.500	.500	.500
1991 Pittsburgh	NL	12	24	6	0	0	0	(0	0)	10	2	1	1	0	8	0	0	0	0	0	.00	1	.250	.280	.417
1992 Pittsburgh	NL	22	39	8	1	0	0	(0	0)	9	4	4	0	0	9	0	1	2	0	0	.00	1	.205	.195	.231
1993 Pittsburgh	NL	141	546	147	25	5	12	(7	5)	218	77	47	31	2	67	9	6	5	18	11	.62	9	.269	.316	.399
4 ML YEARS		179	613	163	26	7	12	(7	5)	239	84	52	32	2	86	9	7	7	18	11	.62	11	.266	.309	.390

Mike Gardiner

Pitches: Right   **Bats:** Both   **Pos:** RP   **Ht:** 6' 0"   **Wt:** 200   **Born:** 10/19/65   **Age:** 28

		HOW MUCH HE PITCHED						WHAT HE GAVE UP								THE RESULTS					
Year Team	Lg	G	GS	CG	GF	IP	BFP	H	R	ER	HR	SH	SF	HB	TBB	IBB	SO	WP	Bk	W	L	Pct.	ShO	Sv	ERA
1993 Ottawa *	AAA	5	5	0	0	25	101	17	8	6	2	1	2	0	9	0	25	1	0	1	1	.500	0	0	2.16
Toledo *	AAA	4	0	0	2	5	22	6	3	3	0	0	0	0	2	0	10	2	0	0	1	.000	0	1	5.40
1990 Seattle	AL	5	3	0	1	12.2	66	22	17	15	1	0	1	2	5	0	6	0	0	0	2	.000	0	0	10.66
1991 Boston	AL	22	22	0	0	130	562	140	79	70	18	1	3	0	47	2	91	1	0	9	10	.474	0	0	4.85
1992 Boston	AL	28	18	0	3	130.2	566	126	78	69	12	3	5	2	58	2	79	8	0	4	10	.286	0	0	4.75
1993 2 ML Teams		34	2	0	4	49.1	224	52	33	27	3	2	3	1	26	3	25	2	0	2	3	.400	0	0	4.93
1993 Montreal	NL	24	2	0	3	38	173	40	28	22	3	1	3	1	19	2	21	0	0	2	3	.400	0	0	5.21
Detroit	AL	10	0	0	1	11.1	51	12	5	5	0	1	0	0	7	1	4	2	0	0	0	.000	0	0	3.97
4 ML YEARS		89	45	0	8	322.2	1418	340	207	181	34	6	12	5	136	7	201	11	0	15	25	.375	0	0	5.05

Jeff Gardner

Bats: Left **Throws:** Right **Pos:** 2B **Ht:** 5'11" **Wt:** 175 **Born:** 02/04/64 **Age:** 30

Year	Team	Lg	G	AB	H	2B	3B	HR	(Hm	Rd)	TB	R	RBI	TBB	IBB	SO	HBP	SH	SF	SB	CS	SB%	GDP	Avg	OBP	SLG
1985	Columbia	A	123	401	118	9	1	0	--	--	129	80	50	142	1	40	5	10	1	31	5	.86	9	.294	.483	.322
1986	Lynchburg	A	111	334	91	11	2	1	--	--	109	59	39	81	3	33	4	8	3	6	4	.60	10	.272	.417	.326
1987	Jackson	AA	119	399	109	10	3	0	--	--	125	55	30	58	1	55	3	5	2	1	5	.17	7	.273	.368	.313
1988	Jackson	AA	134	432	109	15	2	0	--	--	128	46	33	69	7	52	1	14	1	13	8	.62	6	.252	.356	.296
	Tidewater	AAA	2	8	3	1	1	0	--	--	6	3	2	1	0	1	0	0	0	0	0	.00	0	.375	.444	.750
1989	Tidewater	AAA	101	269	75	11	0	0	--	--	86	28	24	25	1	27	0	4	3	0	0	.00	7	.279	.337	.320
1990	Tidewater	AAA	138	463	125	11	1	0	--	--	138	55	33	84	3	33	1	4	1	3	3	.50	12	.270	.383	.298
1991	Tidewater	AAA	136	504	147	23	4	1	--	--	181	73	56	84	4	48	3	7	5	6	5	.55	8	.292	.393	.359
1992	Las Vegas	AAA	120	439	147	30	5	1	--	--	190	82	51	67	6	48	2	7	2	7	2	.78	9	.335	.424	.433
1991	New York	NL	13	37	6	0	0	0	(0	0)	6	3	1	4	0	6	0	0	1	0	0	.00	0	.162	.238	.162
1992	San Diego	NL	15	19	2	0	0	0	(0	0)	2	0	0	1	0	8	0	0	0	0	0	.00	0	.105	.150	.105
1993	San Diego	NL	140	404	106	21	7	1	(1	0)	144	53	24	45	1	69	1	1	1	2	6	.25	3	.262	.337	.356
	3 ML YEARS		168	460	114	21	7	1	(1	0)	152	56	25	50	1	83	1	1	2	2	6	.25	3	.248	.322	.330

Mark Gardner

Pitches: Right **Bats:** Right **Pos:** SP **Ht:** 6' 1" **Wt:** 205 **Born:** 03/01/62 **Age:** 32

Year	Team	Lg	G	GS	CG	GF	IP	BFP	H	R	ER	HR	SH	SF	HB	TBB	IBB	SO	WP	Bk	W	L	Pct.	ShO	Sv	ERA
1993	Omaha *	AAA	8	8	1	0	48.1	193	34	17	15	7	1	1	1	19	2	41	1	0	4	2	.667	0	0	2.79
1989	Montreal	NL	7	4	0	1	26.1	117	26	16	15	2	0	0	2	11	1	21	0	0	0	3	.000	0	0	5.13
1990	Montreal	NL	27	26	3	1	152.2	642	129	62	58	13	4	7	9	61	5	135	2	4	7	9	.438	0	0	3.42
1991	Montreal	NL	27	27	0	0	168.1	692	139	78	72	17	7	2	4	75	1	107	2	1	9	11	.450	2	0	3.85
1992	Montreal	NL	33	30	0	1	179.2	778	179	91	87	15	12	7	9	60	2	132	2	0	12	10	.545	0	0	4.36
1993	Kansas City	AL	17	16	0	0	91.2	387	92	65	63	17	1	7	4	36	0	54	2	0	4	6	.400	0	0	6.19
	5 ML YEARS		111	103	3	3	618.2	2616	565	312	295	64	24	23	28	243	9	449	8	5	32	39	.451	3	0	4.29

Brent Gates

Bats: Both **Throws:** Right **Pos:** 2B **Ht:** 6' 1" **Wt:** 180 **Born:** 03/14/70 **Age:** 24

Year	Team	Lg	G	AB	H	2B	3B	HR	(Hm	Rd)	TB	R	RBI	TBB	IBB	SO	HBP	SH	SF	SB	CS	SB%	GDP	Avg	OBP	SLG
1991	Sou Oregon	A	58	219	63	11	0	3	--	--	83	41	26	30	2	33	2	5	2	8	2	.80	5	.288	.375	.379
	Madison	A	4	12	4	2	0	0	--	--	6	4	1	3	0	2	0	0	0	1	0	1.00	0	.333	.467	.500
1992	Modesto	A	133	505	162	39	2	10	--	--	235	94	88	85	9	60	2	2	9	9	7	.56	9	.321	.414	.465
1993	Huntsville	AA	12	45	15	4	0	1	--	--	22	7	11	7	0	9	0	1	0	0	0	.00	3	.333	.423	.489
	Tacoma	AAA	12	44	15	7	0	1	--	--	25	7	4	4	1	6	1	0	0	2	0	1.00	1	.341	.408	.568
1993	Oakland	AL	139	535	155	29	2	7	(4	3)	209	64	69	56	4	75	4	6	8	7	3	.70	17	.290	.357	.391

Bob Geren

Bats: Right **Throws:** Right **Pos:** C **Ht:** 6' 3" **Wt:** 228 **Born:** 09/22/61 **Age:** 32

Year	Team	Lg	G	AB	H	2B	3B	HR	(Hm	Rd)	TB	R	RBI	TBB	IBB	SO	HBP	SH	SF	SB	CS	SB%	GDP	Avg	OBP	SLG
1988	New York	AL	10	10	1	0	0	0	(0	0)	1	0	0	2	0	3	0	0	0	0	0	.00	0	.100	.250	.100
1989	New York	AL	65	205	59	5	1	9	(4	5)	93	26	27	12	0	44	1	6	1	0	0	.00	10	.288	.329	.454
1990	New York	AL	110	277	59	7	0	8	(4	4)	90	21	31	13	1	73	5	6	2	0	0	.00	0	.213	.259	.325
1991	New York	AL	64	128	28	3	0	2	(1	1)	37	7	12	9	0	31	0	3	0	0	1	.00	5	.219	.270	.289
1993	San Diego	NL	58	145	31	6	0	3	(1	2)	46	8	6	13	4	28	0	4	0	0	0	.00	4	.214	.278	.317
	5 ML YEARS		307	765	178	21	1	22	(10	12)	267	62	76	49	5	179	6	19	3	0	1	.00	26	.233	.283	.349

Kirk Gibson

Bats: Left **Throws:** Left **Pos:** DH/CF **Ht:** 6' 3" **Wt:** 225 **Born:** 05/28/57 **Age:** 37

Year	Team	Lg	G	AB	H	2B	3B	HR	(Hm	Rd)	TB	R	RBI	TBB	IBB	SO	HBP	SH	SF	SB	CS	SB%	GDP	Avg	OBP	SLG
1979	Detroit	AL	12	38	9	3	0	1	(0	1)	15	3	4	1	0	3	0	0	0	3	3	.50	0	.237	.256	.395
1980	Detroit	AL	51	175	46	2	1	9	(3	6)	77	23	16	10	0	45	1	1	2	4	7	.36	0	.263	.303	.440
1981	Detroit	AL	83	290	95	11	3	9	(4	5)	139	41	40	18	1	64	2	1	2	17	5	.77	9	.328	.369	.479
1982	Detroit	AL	69	266	74	16	2	8	(4	4)	118	34	35	25	2	41	1	1	1	9	7	.56	2	.278	.341	.444
1983	Detroit	AL	128	401	91	12	9	15	(5	10)	166	60	51	53	3	96	4	5	4	14	3	.82	2	.227	.320	.414
1984	Detroit	AL	149	531	150	23	10	27	(11	16)	274	92	91	63	6	103	8	3	6	29	9	.76	4	.282	.363	.516
1985	Detroit	AL	154	581	167	37	5	29	(16	13)	301	96	97	71	16	137	5	3	10	30	4	.88	5	.287	.364	.518
1986	Detroit	AL	119	441	118	11	2	28	(15	13)	217	84	86	68	4	107	7	1	4	34	6	.85	8	.268	.371	.492
1987	Detroit	AL	128	487	135	25	3	24	(14	10)	238	95	79	71	8	117	5	1	4	26	7	.79	5	.277	.372	.489
1988	Los Angeles	NL	150	542	157	28	1	25	(14	11)	262	106	76	73	14	120	7	3	7	31	4	.89	8	.290	.377	.483
1989	Los Angeles	NL	71	253	54	8	2	9	(4	5)	93	35	28	35	5	55	2	0	2	12	3	.80	5	.213	.312	.368
1990	Los Angeles	NL	89	315	82	20	0	8	(2	6)	126	59	38	39	0	65	3	0	2	26	2	.93	4	.260	.345	.400

74

Year	Team	Lg	G	AB	H	2B	3B	HR	(Hm	Rd)	TB	R	RBI	TBB	IBB	SO	HBP	SH	SF	SB	CS	SB%	GDP	Avg	OBP	SLG
1991	Kansas City	AL	132	462	109	17	6	16	(4	12)	186	81	55	69	3	103	6	1	2	18	4	.82	9	.236	.341	.403
1992	Pittsburgh	NL	16	56	11	0	0	2	(0	2)	17	6	5	3	0	12	0	1	0	3	1	.75	1	.196	.237	.304
1993	Detroit	AL	116	403	105	18	6	13	(5	8)	174	62	62	44	4	87	4	0	3	15	6	.71	2	.261	.337	.432
	15 ML YEARS		1467	5241	1403	231	50	223	(103	120)	2403	877	763	643	66	1155	55	21	49	271	71	.79	64	.268	.351	.459

Paul Gibson

Pitches: Left Bats: Right Pos: RP **Ht: 6' 1" Wt: 185 Born: 01/04/60 Age: 34**

			HOW MUCH HE PITCHED						WHAT HE GAVE UP									THE RESULTS						
Year	Team	Lg	G	GS	CG	GF	IP	BFP	H	R	ER	HR	SH	SF	HB	TBB	IBB	SO	WP	Bk	W	L	Pct.	ShO	Sv	ERA
1993	Norfolk *	AAA	14	0	0	11	21	79	10	2	2	0	1	0	0	5	0	29	0	0	1	1	.500	0	7	0.86
	Columbus *	AAA	3	1	0	1	7	25	4	0	0	0	0	0	0	1	0	7	0	0	1	0	1.000	0	1	0.00
1988	Detroit	AL	40	1	0	18	92	390	83	33	30	6	3	5	2	34	8	50	3	1	4	2	.667	0	0	2.93
1989	Detroit	AL	45	13	0	16	132	573	129	71	68	11	7	5	6	57	12	77	4	1	4	8	.333	0	0	4.64
1990	Detroit	AL	61	0	0	17	97.1	422	99	36	33	10	4	5	1	44	12	56	1	1	5	4	.556	0	3	3.05
1991	Detroit	AL	68	0	0	28	96	432	112	51	49	10	2	2	3	48	8	52	4	0	5	7	.417	0	8	4.59
1992	New York	NL	43	1	0	12	62	273	70	37	36	7	3	1	0	25	0	49	1	0	0	1	.000	0	0	5.23
1993	2 ML Teams		28	0	0	10	44	184	45	21	17	5	0	3	0	11	0	37	1	0	3	1	.750	0	0	3.48
1993	New York	NL	8	0	0	1	8.2	42	14	6	5	1	0	0	0	2	0	12	1	0	1	1	.500	0	0	5.19
	New York	AL	20	0	0	9	35.1	142	31	15	12	4	0	3	0	9	0	25	0	0	2	0	1.000	0	0	3.06
	6 ML YEARS		285	15	0	101	523.1	2274	538	249	233	49	19	21	12	219	40	321	14	3	21	23	.477	0	11	4.01

Benji Gil

Bats: Right Throws: Right Pos: SS **Ht: 6' 2" Wt: 180 Born: 10/06/72 Age: 21**

			BATTING																BASERUNNING				PERCENTAGES		
Year	Team	Lg	G	AB	H	2B	3B	HR	(Hm	Rd)	TB	R	RBI	TBB	IBB	SO	HBP	SH	SF	SB	CS	SB%	GDP	Avg	OBP	SLG
1991	Butte	R	32	129	37	4	3	2	--	--	53	25	15	14	1	36	0	0	1	9	3	.75	0	.287	.354	.411
1992	Gastonia	A	132	482	132	21	1	9	--	--	182	75	55	50	0	106	3	3	4	26	13	.67	16	.274	.343	.378
1993	Tulsa	AA	101	342	94	9	1	17	--	--	156	45	59	35	2	89	7	0	3	20	12	.63	9	.275	.351	.456
1993	Texas	AL	22	57	7	0	0	0	(0	0)	7	3	2	5	0	22	0	4	0	1	2	.33	0	.123	.194	.123

Bernard Gilkey

Bats: Right Throws: Right Pos: LF **Ht: 6' 0" Wt: 190 Born: 09/24/66 Age: 27**

			BATTING																BASERUNNING				PERCENTAGES		
Year	Team	Lg	G	AB	H	2B	3B	HR	(Hm	Rd)	TB	R	RBI	TBB	IBB	SO	HBP	SH	SF	SB	CS	SB%	GDP	Avg	OBP	SLG
1990	St. Louis	NL	18	64	19	5	2	1	(0	1)	31	11	3	8	0	5	0	0	0	6	1	.86	1	.297	.375	.484
1991	St. Louis	NL	81	268	58	7	2	5	(2	3)	84	28	20	39	0	33	1	1	2	14	8	.64	14	.216	.316	.313
1992	St. Louis	NL	131	384	116	19	4	7	(3	4)	164	56	43	39	1	52	1	3	4	18	12	.60	5	.302	.364	.427
1993	St. Louis	NL	137	557	170	40	5	16	(7	9)	268	99	70	56	2	66	4	0	5	15	10	.60	16	.305	.370	.481
	4 ML YEARS		367	1273	363	71	13	29	(12	17)	547	194	136	142	3	156	6	4	11	53	31	.63	36	.285	.357	.430

Joe Girardi

Bats: Right Throws: Right Pos: C **Ht: 5'11" Wt: 195 Born: 10/14/64 Age: 29**

			BATTING																BASERUNNING				PERCENTAGES		
Year	Team	Lg	G	AB	H	2B	3B	HR	(Hm	Rd)	TB	R	RBI	TBB	IBB	SO	HBP	SH	SF	SB	CS	SB%	GDP	Avg	OBP	SLG
1993	Colo Sprngs *	AAA	8	31	11	1	1	1	--	--	21	6	6	0	0	3	0	0	0	1	0	1.00	0	.484	.484	.677
1989	Chicago	NL	59	157	39	10	0	1	(0	1)	52	15	14	11	5	26	2	1	1	2	1	.67	4	.248	.304	.331
1990	Chicago	NL	133	419	113	24	2	1	(1	0)	144	36	38	17	11	50	3	4	4	8	3	.73	13	.270	.300	.344
1991	Chicago	NL	21	47	9	2	0	0	(0	0)	11	3	6	6	1	6	0	1	0	0	0	.00	0	.191	.283	.234
1992	Chicago	NL	91	270	73	3	1	1	(1	0)	81	19	12	19	3	38	1	0	1	0	2	.00	4	.270	.320	.300
1993	Colorado	NL	86	310	90	14	5	3	(2	1)	123	35	31	24	0	41	3	12	1	6	6	.50	6	.290	.346	.397
	5 ML YEARS		390	1203	324	53	8	6	(4	2)	411	108	101	77	20	161	9	18	7	16	12	.57	31	.269	.316	.342

Dan Gladden

Bats: Right Throws: Right Pos: LF/CF **Ht: 5'11" Wt: 184 Born: 07/07/57 Age: 36**

			BATTING																BASERUNNING				PERCENTAGES		
Year	Team	Lg	G	AB	H	2B	3B	HR	(Hm	Rd)	TB	R	RBI	TBB	IBB	SO	HBP	SH	SF	SB	CS	SB%	GDP	Avg	OBP	SLG
1993	Toledo *	AAA	7	28	11	1	0	1	--	--	15	6	7	0	0	6	0	1	0	1	0	1.00	1	.393	.393	.536
1983	San Francisco	NL	18	63	14	2	0	1	(1	0)	19	6	9	5	0	11	0	3	1	4	3	.57	3	.222	.275	.302
1984	San Francisco	NL	86	342	120	17	2	4	(4	0)	153	71	31	33	2	37	2	6	1	31	16	.66	3	.351	.410	.447
1985	San Francisco	NL	142	502	122	15	8	7	(6	1)	174	64	41	40	1	78	7	10	2	32	15	.68	10	.243	.307	.347
1986	San Francisco	NL	102	351	97	16	1	4	(1	3)	127	55	29	39	3	59	5	7	0	27	10	.73	5	.276	.357	.362
1987	Minnesota	AL	121	438	109	21	2	8	(4	4)	158	69	38	38	2	72	3	1	2	25	9	.74	8	.249	.312	.361
1988	Minnesota	AL	141	576	155	32	6	11	(8	3)	232	91	62	46	4	74	4	2	5	28	8	.78	9	.269	.325	.403
1989	Minnesota	AL	121	461	136	23	3	8	(1	7)	189	69	46	23	3	53	5	5	7	23	7	.77	6	.295	.331	.410
1990	Minnesota	AL	136	534	147	27	6	5	(2	3)	201	64	40	26	2	67	6	1	4	25	9	.74	17	.275	.314	.376
1991	Minnesota	AL	126	461	114	14	9	6	(3	3)	164	65	52	36	1	60	5	5	4	15	9	.63	13	.247	.306	.356
1992	Detroit	AL	113	417	106	20	1	7	(3	4)	149	57	42	30	0	64	2	5	5	4	2	.67	10	.254	.304	.357

Year Team	Lg	G	AB	H	2B	3B	HR	(Hm	Rd)	TB	R	RBI	TBB	IBB	SO	HBP	SH	SF	SB	CS	SB%	GDP	Avg	OBP	SLG
1993 Detroit	AL	91	356	95	16	2	13	(11	2)	154	52	56	21	0	50	3	4	2	8	5	.62	14	.267	.312	.433
11 ML YEARS		1197	4501	1215	203	40	74	(44	30)	1720	663	446	337	18	625	42	49	33	222	93	.70	98	.270	.324	.382

Tom Glavine

Pitches: Left   **Bats:** Left   **Pos:** SP   **Ht:** 6' 1"   **Wt:** 190   **Born:** 03/25/66   **Age:** 28

		HOW MUCH HE PITCHED						WHAT HE GAVE UP									THE RESULTS					
Year Team	Lg	G	GS	CG	GF	IP	BFP	H	R	ER	HR	SH	SF	HB	TBB	IBB	SO	WP	Bk	W	L	Pct.	ShO	Sv	ERA
1987 Atlanta	NL	9	9	0	0	50.1	238	55	34	31	5	2	3	3	33	4	20	1	1	2	4	.333	0	0	5.54
1988 Atlanta	NL	34	34	1	0	195.1	844	201	111	99	12	17	11	8	63	7	84	2	2	7	17	.292	0	0	4.56
1989 Atlanta	NL	29	29	6	0	186	766	172	88	76	20	11	4	2	40	3	90	2	0	14	8	.636	4	0	3.68
1990 Atlanta	NL	33	33	1	0	214.1	929	232	111	102	18	21	2	1	78	10	129	8	1	10	12	.455	0	0	4.28
1991 Atlanta	NL	34	34	9	0	246.1	989	201	83	70	17	7	6	2	69	6	192	10	2	20	11	.645	1	0	2.56
1992 Atlanta	NL	33	33	7	0	225	919	197	81	69	6	2	6	2	70	7	129	5	0	20	8	.714	5	0	2.76
1993 Atlanta	NL	36	36	4	0	239.1	1014	236	91	85	16	10	2	2	90	7	120	4	0	22	6	.786	2	0	3.20
7 ML YEARS		208	208	28	0	1356.2	5699	1294	599	532	94	70	34	20	443	44	764	32	6	95	66	.590	12	0	3.53

Jerry Goff

Bats: Left   **Throws:** Right   **Pos:** C   **Ht:** 6' 3"   **Wt:** 210   **Born:** 04/12/64   **Age:** 30

		BATTING																	BASERUNNING				PERCENTAGES		
Year Team	Lg	G	AB	H	2B	3B	HR	(Hm	Rd)	TB	R	RBI	TBB	IBB	SO	HBP	SH	SF	SB	CS	SB%	GDP	Avg	OBP	SLG
1993 Buffalo *	AAA	104	362	91	27	3	14	--	--	166	52	69	55	4	82	1	0	7	1	1	.50	3	.251	.346	.459
1990 Montreal	NL	52	119	27	1	0	3	(0	3)	37	14	7	21	4	36	0	1	0	0	2	.00	0	.227	.343	.311
1992 Montreal	NL	3	3	0	0	0	0	(0	0)	0	0	0	0	0	3	0	0	0	0	0	.00	0	.000	.000	.000
1993 Pittsburgh	NL	14	37	11	2	0	2	(2	0)	19	5	6	8	1	9	0	1	0	0	0	.00	0	.297	.422	.514
3 ML YEARS		69	159	38	3	0	5	(2	3)	56	19	13	29	5	48	0	2	0	0	2	.00	0	.239	.356	.352

Greg Gohr

Pitches: Right   **Bats:** Right   **Pos:** RP   **Ht:** 6' 3"   **Wt:** 205   **Born:** 10/29/67   **Age:** 26

		HOW MUCH HE PITCHED						WHAT HE GAVE UP									THE RESULTS					
Year Team	Lg	G	GS	CG	GF	IP	BFP	H	R	ER	HR	SH	SF	HB	TBB	IBB	SO	WP	Bk	W	L	Pct.	ShO	Sv	ERA
1989 Fayetteville	A	4	4	0	0	11.1	50	11	9	9	3	0	1	0	6	0	10	0	0	0	2	.000	0	0	7.15
1990 Lakeland	A	25	25	0	0	137.2	577	125	52	40	0	2	1	5	50	0	90	11	6	13	5	.722	0	0	2.62
1991 London	AA	2	2	0	0	11	42	9	0	0	0	0	0	0	2	0	10	0	0	0	0	.000	0	0	0.00
Toledo	AAA	26	26	2	0	148.1	627	125	86	76	11	9	5	3	66	0	96	14	3	10	8	.556	1	0	4.61
1992 Toledo	AAA	22	20	2	0	130.2	551	124	65	58	9	3	3	3	46	1	94	5	1	8	10	.444	0	0	3.99
1993 Toledo	AAA	18	17	2	1	107	484	127	74	69	16	1	8	5	38	2	77	5	0	3	10	.231	0	0	5.80
1993 Detroit	AL	16	0	0	9	22.2	108	26	15	15	1	1	1	2	14	2	23	1	0	0	0	.000	0	0	5.96

Chris Gomez

Bats: Right   **Throws:** Right   **Pos:** SS/2B   **Ht:** 6' 1"   **Wt:** 183   **Born:** 06/16/71   **Age:** 23

		BATTING																	BASERUNNING				PERCENTAGES		
Year Team	Lg	G	AB	H	2B	3B	HR	(Hm	Rd)	TB	R	RBI	TBB	IBB	SO	HBP	SH	SF	SB	CS	SB%	GDP	Avg	OBP	SLG
1992 London	AA	64	220	59	13	2	1	--	--	79	20	19	34	3	0	0	1	3	.25	11	.268	.337	.359
1993 Toledo	AAA	87	277	68	12	2	0	--	--	84	29	20	23	0	37	3	6	2	6	2	.75	4	.245	.308	.303
1993 Detroit	AL	46	128	32	7	1	0	(0	0)	41	11	11	9	0	17	1	3	0	2	2	.50	2	.250	.304	.320

Leo Gomez

Bats: Right   **Throws:** Right   **Pos:** 3B   **Ht:** 6' 0"   **Wt:** 208   **Born:** 03/02/67   **Age:** 27

		BATTING																	BASERUNNING				PERCENTAGES		
Year Team	Lg	G	AB	H	2B	3B	HR	(Hm	Rd)	TB	R	RBI	TBB	IBB	SO	HBP	SH	SF	SB	CS	SB%	GDP	Avg	OBP	SLG
1993 Rochester *	AAA	4	15	3	1	0	0	--	--	4	3	1	3	0	4	0	0	0	0	0	.00	1	.200	.333	.267
1990 Baltimore	AL	12	39	9	0	0	0	(0	0)	9	3	1	8	0	7	0	1	0	0	0	.00	2	.231	.362	.231
1991 Baltimore	AL	118	391	91	17	2	16	(7	9)	160	40	45	40	0	82	2	5	7	1	1	.50	11	.233	.302	.409
1992 Baltimore	AL	137	468	124	24	0	17	(6	11)	199	62	64	63	4	78	8	5	8	2	3	.40	14	.265	.356	.425
1993 Baltimore	AL	71	244	48	7	0	10	(7	3)	85	30	25	32	1	60	3	3	2	0	1	.00	2	.197	.295	.348
4 ML YEARS		338	1142	272	48	2	43	(20	23)	453	135	135	143	5	227	13	14	17	3	5	.38	29	.238	.325	.397

Pat Gomez

Pitches: Left   **Bats:** Left   **Pos:** RP   **Ht:** 5'11"   **Wt:** 185   **Born:** 03/17/68   **Age:** 26

		HOW MUCH HE PITCHED						WHAT HE GAVE UP									THE RESULTS					
Year Team	Lg	G	GS	CG	GF	IP	BFP	H	R	ER	HR	SH	SF	HB	TBB	IBB	SO	WP	Bk	W	L	Pct.	ShO	Sv	ERA
1986 Wytheville	R	11	11	0	0	54	265	57	51	31	4	2	6	1	46	0	55	13	3	3	6	.333	0	0	5.17
1987 Peoria	A	20	17	1	3	94	435	88	55	45	4	5	3	1	71	2	95	13	3	3	6	.333	0	0	4.31
1988 Chston-Wv	A	36	9	0	14	78.2	357	75	53	47	1	5	1	3	52	0	97	3	14	2	7	.222	0	5	5.38
1989 Winston-Sal	A	23	21	3	0	137.2	579	115	59	42	6	7	3	5	60	2	127	8	6	11	6	.647	0	0	2.75
Charlotte	AA	2	2	0	0	14.1	57	14	5	4	0	1	0	0	3	0	11	4	2	1	0	1.000	0	0	2.51

Year	Team	Lg	G	GS	CG	GF	IP	BFP	H	R	ER	HR	SH	SF	HB	TBB	IBB	SO	WP	Bk	W	L	Pct.	ShO	Sv	ERA
1990	Richmond	AAA	4	4	0	0	15.1	74	19	16	15	1	0	0	0	10	1	8	3	1	1	1	.500	0	0	8.80
	Greenville	AA	23	21	0	1	124.1	557	126	75	62	9	4	3	2	71	1	94	16	12	6	8	.429	0	0	4.49
1991	Greenville	AA	13	13	0	0	79.2	318	58	20	16	1	3	2	3	31	1	71	7	1	5	2	.714	0	0	1.81
	Richmond	AAA	16	14	0	0	82	376	99	55	40	3	3	2	2	41	0	41	3	1	2	9	.182	0	0	4.39
1992	Richmond	AAA	23	11	0	3	71	330	79	47	43	10	1	1	2	42	2	48	3	2	3	5	.375	0	0	5.45
	Greenville	AA	8	8	1	0	47.2	177	25	8	6	1	1	0	0	19	0	38	3	0	7	0	1.000	1	0	1.13
1993	San Diego	NL	27	1	0	6	31.2	144	35	19	18	2	1	4	0	19	4	26	2	0	1	3	.333	0	0	5.12

Larry Gonzales

Bats: Right   Throws: Right   Pos: C   **Ht: 6' 3"   Wt: 200   Born: 03/28/67   Age: 27**

									BATTING												BASERUNNING				PERCENTAGES		
Year	Team	Lg	G	AB	H	2B	3B	HR	(Hm	Rd)	TB	R	RBI	TBB	IBB	SO	HBP	SH	SF	SB	CS	SB%	GDP	Avg	OBP	SLG
1988	Palm Sprngs	A	35	100	20	0	0	0	--	--	20	11	11	22	0	25	1	1	0	0	0	.00	0	.200	.350	.200
1989	Quad City	A	69	195	38	3	1	6	--	--	61	24	20	39	1	34	4	2	1	2	5	.29	3	.195	.339	.313
1990	Quad City	A	99	309	95	16	1	8	--	--	137	44	75	36	1	56	8	2	2	2	1	.67	9	.307	.392	.443
1991	Edmonton	AAA	2	3	0	0	0	0	--	--	0	0	0	1	0	1	0	0	0	0	0	.00	0	.000	.250	.000
	Midland	AA	78	257	82	13	0	4	--	--	107	27	56	22	0	33	6	3	6	2	2	.50	9	.319	.378	.416
1992	Edmonton	AAA	80	241	79	10	0	3	--	--	98	37	47	38	0	24	4	3	4	2	1	.67	10	.328	.422	.407
1993	Vancouver	AAA	81	264	69	9	0	2	--	--	84	30	27	26	2	28	4	2	5	5	1	.83	9	.261	.329	.318
1993	California	AL	2	2	1	0	0	0	(0	0)	1	0	1	1	0	0	0	0	0	0	0	.00	0	.500	.667	.500

Rene Gonzales

Bats: Right   Throws: Right   Pos: 3B/1B   **Ht: 6' 3"   Wt: 215   Born: 09/03/61   Age: 32**

									BATTING												BASERUNNING				PERCENTAGES		
Year	Team	Lg	G	AB	H	2B	3B	HR	(Hm	Rd)	TB	R	RBI	TBB	IBB	SO	HBP	SH	SF	SB	CS	SB%	GDP	Avg	OBP	SLG
1984	Montreal	NL	29	30	7	1	0	0	(0	0)	8	5	2	2	0	5	1	0	0	0	0	.00	0	.233	.303	.267
1986	Montreal	NL	11	26	3	0	0	0	(0	0)	3	1	0	2	0	7	0	1	0	0	2	.00	0	.115	.179	.115
1987	Baltimore	AL	37	60	16	2	1	1	(1	0)	23	14	7	3	0	11	0	2	0	1	0	1.00	2	.267	.302	.383
1988	Baltimore	AL	92	237	51	6	0	2	(1	1)	63	13	15	13	0	32	3	5	2	2	0	1.00	5	.215	.263	.266
1989	Baltimore	AL	71	166	36	4	0	1	(0	1)	43	16	11	12	0	30	0	6	1	5	3	.63	6	.217	.268	.259
1990	Baltimore	AL	67	103	22	3	1	1	(1	0)	30	13	12	12	0	14	0	6	0	1	2	.33	3	.214	.296	.291
1991	Toronto	AL	71	118	23	3	0	1	(1	0)	29	16	6	12	0	22	4	6	1	0	0	.00	5	.195	.289	.246
1992	California	AL	104	329	91	17	1	7	(6	1)	131	47	38	41	1	46	4	5	1	7	4	.64	17	.277	.363	.398
1993	California	AL	117	335	84	17	0	2	(1	1)	107	34	31	49	2	45	1	2	2	5	5	.50	12	.251	.346	.319
9 ML YEARS			599	1404	333	53	3	15	(11	4)	437	159	122	146	3	212	13	32	7	21	16	.57	50	.237	.313	.311

Juan Gonzalez

Bats: Right   Throws: Right   Pos: LF   **Ht: 6' 3"   Wt: 210   Born: 10/16/69   Age: 24**

									BATTING												BASERUNNING				PERCENTAGES		
Year	Team	Lg	G	AB	H	2B	3B	HR	(Hm	Rd)	TB	R	RBI	TBB	IBB	SO	HBP	SH	SF	SB	CS	SB%	GDP	Avg	OBP	SLG
1989	Texas	AL	24	60	9	3	0	1	(1	0)	15	6	7	6	0	17	0	2	0	0	0	.00	4	.150	.227	.250
1990	Texas	AL	25	90	26	7	1	4	(3	1)	47	11	12	2	0	18	2	0	1	0	1	.00	2	.289	.316	.522
1991	Texas	AL	142	545	144	34	1	27	(7	20)	261	78	102	42	7	118	5	0	3	4	4	.50	10	.264	.321	.479
1992	Texas	AL	155	584	152	24	2	43	(19	24)	309	77	109	35	1	143	5	0	8	0	1	.00	16	.260	.304	.529
1993	Texas	AL	140	536	166	33	4	46	(24	22)	339	105	118	37	7	99	13	0	1	4	1	.80	11	.310	.368	.632
5 ML YEARS			486	1815	497	101	5	121	(54	67)	971	277	348	122	15	395	25	2	13	8	7	.53	43	.274	.326	.535

Luis Gonzalez

Bats: Left   Throws: Right   Pos: LF   **Ht: 6' 2"   Wt: 180   Born: 09/03/67   Age: 26**

									BATTING												BASERUNNING				PERCENTAGES		
Year	Team	Lg	G	AB	H	2B	3B	HR	(Hm	Rd)	TB	R	RBI	TBB	IBB	SO	HBP	SH	SF	SB	CS	SB%	GDP	Avg	OBP	SLG
1990	Houston	NL	12	21	4	2	0	0	(0	0)	6	1	0	2	1	5	0	0	0	0	0	.00	0	.190	.261	.286
1991	Houston	NL	137	473	120	28	9	13	(4	9)	205	51	69	40	4	101	8	1	4	10	7	.59	9	.254	.320	.433
1992	Houston	NL	122	387	94	19	3	10	(4	6)	149	40	55	24	3	52	2	1	2	7	7	.50	9	.243	.289	.385
1993	Houston	NL	154	540	162	34	3	15	(8	7)	247	82	72	47	7	83	10	3	10	20	9	.69	9	.300	.361	.457
4 ML YEARS			425	1421	380	83	15	38	(16	22)	607	174	196	113	15	241	20	5	16	37	23	.62	24	.267	.327	.427

Dwight Gooden

Pitches: Right   Bats: Right   Pos: SP   **Ht: 6' 3"   Wt: 210   Born: 11/16/64   Age: 29**

			HOW MUCH HE PITCHED						WHAT HE GAVE UP												THE RESULTS					
Year	Team	Lg	G	GS	CG	GF	IP	BFP	H	R	ER	HR	SH	SF	HB	TBB	IBB	SO	WP	Bk	W	L	Pct.	ShO	Sv	ERA
1984	New York	NL	31	31	7	0	218	879	161	72	63	7	3	2	2	73	2	276	3	7	17	9	.654	3	0	2.60
1985	New York	NL	35	35	16	0	276.2	1065	198	51	47	13	6	2	2	69	4	268	6	2	24	4	.857	8	0	1.53
1986	New York	NL	33	33	12	0	250	1020	197	92	79	17	10	8	4	80	3	200	4	4	17	6	.739	2	0	2.84
1987	New York	NL	25	25	7	0	179.2	730	162	68	64	11	5	5	2	53	2	148	1	1	15	7	.682	3	0	3.21
1988	New York	NL	34	34	10	0	248.1	1024	242	98	88	8	10	6	4	57	4	175	5	5	18	9	.667	3	0	3.19
1989	New York	NL	19	17	0	1	118.1	497	93	42	38	9	4	3	2	47	2	101	7	5	9	4	.692	0	1	2.89

Year	Team	Lg	G	GS	CG	GF	IP	BFP	H	R	ER	HR	SH	SF	HB	TBB	IBB	SO	WP	Bk	W	L	Pct.	ShO	Sv	ERA
1990	New York	NL	34	34	2	0	232.2	983	229	106	99	10	10	7	7	70	3	223	6	3	19	7	.731	1	0	3.83
1991	New York	NL	27	27	3	0	190	789	185	80	76	12	5	4	3	56	2	150	5	2	13	7	.650	1	0	3.60
1992	New York	NL	31	31	3	0	206	863	197	93	84	11	10	7	3	70	7	145	3	1	10	13	.435	0	0	3.67
1993	New York	NL	29	29	7	0	208.2	866	188	89	80	16	11	7	9	61	1	149	5	2	12	15	.444	2	0	3.45
10 ML YEARS			298	296	67	1	2128.1	8716	1852	791	718	114	74	51	40	636	30	1835	45	32	154	81	.655	23	1	3.04

Tom Goodwin

Bats: Left   **Throws: Right**   **Pos: LF**   **Ht: 6' 1"**   **Wt: 170**   **Born: 07/27/68**   **Age: 25**

							BATTING												BASERUNNING				PERCENTAGES		
Year	Team	Lg	G	AB	H	2B	3B	HR	(Hm | Rd)	TB	R	RBI	TBB	IBB	SO	HBP	SH	SF	SB	CS	SB%	GDP	Avg	OBP	SLG
1993	Albuquerque *	AAA	85	289	75	5	5	1	--	--	93	48	28	30	2	51	2	5	4	21	5	.81	1	.260	.329	.322
1991	Los Angeles	NL	16	7	1	0	0	0	(0 | 0)	1	3	0	0	0	0	0	0	0	1	1	.50	0	.143	.143	.143
1992	Los Angeles	NL	57	73	17	1	1	0	(0 | 0)	20	15	3	6	0	10	0	0	0	7	3	.70	0	.233	.291	.274
1993	Los Angeles	NL	30	17	5	1	0	0	(0 | 0)	6	6	1	1	0	4	0	0	0	1	2	.33	1	.294	.333	.353
3 ML YEARS			103	97	23	2	1	0	(0 | 0)	27	24	4	7	0	14	0	0	0	9	6	.60	1	.237	.288	.278

Keith Gordon

Bats: Right   **Throws: Right**   **Pos: LF**   **Ht: 6' 2"**   **Wt: 200**   **Born: 01/22/69**   **Age: 25**

							BATTING												BASERUNNING				PERCENTAGES		
Year	Team	Lg	G	AB	H	2B	3B	HR	(Hm	Rd)	TB	R	RBI	TBB	IBB	SO	HBP	SH	SF	SB	CS	SB%	GDP	Avg	OBP	SLG
1990	Billings	R	49	154	36	5	1	1	--	--	46	21	14	24	1	49	3	2	1	6	4	.60	2	.234	.346	.299
1991	Chston-Wv	A	123	388	104	14	10	8	--	--	162	63	46	50	2	134	5	7	1	25	9	.74	5	.268	.358	.418
1992	Cedar Rapds	A	114	375	94	19	3	12	--	--	155	59	63	43	2	135	3	1	4	21	10	.68	5	.251	.329	.413
1993	Chattanooga	AA	116	419	122	26	3	14	--	--	196	69	59	19	0	132	4	0	2	13	17	.43	15	.291	.327	.468
1993	Cincinnati	NL	3	6	1	0	0	0	(0	0)	1	0	0	0	0	2	0	0	0	0	0	.00	0	.167	.167	.167

Tom Gordon

Pitches: Right   **Bats: Right**   **Pos: RP/SP**   **Ht: 5' 9"**   **Wt: 180**   **Born: 11/18/67**   **Age: 26**

				HOW MUCH HE PITCHED					WHAT HE GAVE UP										THE RESULTS					
Year	Team	Lg	G	GS	CG	GF	IP	BFP	H	R	ER	HR	SH	SF	HB	TBB	IBB	SO	WP	Bk	W	L	Pct.	ShO	Sv	ERA
1988	Kansas City	AL	5	2	0	0	15.2	67	16	9	9	1	0	0	0	7	0	18	0	0	0	2	.000	0	0	5.17
1989	Kansas City	AL	49	16	1	16	163	677	122	67	66	10	4	4	1	86	4	153	12	0	17	9	.654	1	1	3.64
1990	Kansas City	AL	32	32	6	0	195.1	858	192	99	81	17	8	2	3	99	1	175	11	0	12	11	.522	1	0	3.73
1991	Kansas City	AL	45	14	1	11	158	684	129	76	68	16	5	3	4	87	6	167	5	0	9	14	.391	0	1	3.87
1992	Kansas City	AL	40	11	0	13	117.2	516	116	67	60	9	2	6	4	55	4	98	5	2	6	10	.375	0	0	4.59
1993	Kansas City	AL	48	14	2	18	155.2	651	125	65	62	11	6	6	1	77	5	143	17	0	12	6	.667	0	1	3.58
6 ML YEARS			219	89	10	58	805.1	3453	700	383	346	64	25	21	13	411	20	754	50	2	56	52	.519	2	3	3.87

Goose Gossage

Pitches: Right   **Bats: Right**   **Pos: RP**   **Ht: 6' 3"**   **Wt: 225**   **Born: 07/05/51**   **Age: 42**

				HOW MUCH HE PITCHED					WHAT HE GAVE UP										THE RESULTS					
Year	Team	Lg	G	GS	CG	GF	IP	BFP	H	R	ER	HR	SH	SF	HB	TBB	IBB	SO	WP	Bk	W	L	Pct.	ShO	Sv	ERA
1972	Chicago	AL	36	1	0	7	80	352	72	44	38	2	10	2	4	44	3	57	7	0	7	1	.875	0	2	4.28
1973	Chicago	AL	20	4	1	4	50	232	57	44	41	9	5	4	3	37	2	33	6	0	0	4	.000	0	0	7.38
1974	Chicago	AL	39	3	0	19	89	397	92	45	41	4	6	4	2	47	7	64	2	1	4	6	.400	0	1	4.15
1975	Chicago	AL	62	0	0	49	142	582	99	32	29	3	15	0	5	70	15	130	3	0	9	8	.529	0	26	1.84
1976	Chicago	AL	31	29	15	1	224	956	214	104	98	16	8	7	9	90	3	135	6	0	9	17	.346	0	1	3.94
1977	Pittsburgh	NL	72	0	0	55	133	523	78	27	24	9	7	6	2	49	6	151	2	0	11	9	.550	0	26	1.62
1978	New York	AL	63	0	0	55	134	543	87	41	30	9	9	8	2	59	8	122	5	0	10	11	.476	0	27	2.01
1979	New York	AL	36	0	0	33	58	234	48	18	17	5	4	0	0	19	4	41	3	0	5	3	.625	0	18	2.64
1980	New York	AL	64	0	0	58	99	401	74	29	25	5	8	4	1	37	3	103	4	0	6	2	.750	0	33	2.27
1981	New York	AL	32	0	0	30	47	173	22	6	4	2	1	1	1	14	1	48	1	0	3	2	.600	0	20	0.77
1982	New York	AL	56	0	0	43	93	356	63	23	23	5	5	2	0	28	5	102	1	0	4	5	.444	0	30	2.23
1983	New York	AL	57	0	0	47	87.1	367	82	27	22	5	5	6	1	25	5	90	0	0	13	5	.722	0	22	2.27
1984	San Diego	NL	62	0	0	51	102.1	412	75	34	33	6	4	3	1	36	4	84	2	2	10	6	.625	0	25	2.90
1985	San Diego	NL	50	0	0	38	79	308	64	21	16	1	3	4	1	17	1	52	0	0	5	3	.625	0	26	1.82
1986	San Diego	NL	45	0	0	38	64.2	281	69	36	32	8	2	4	2	20	0	63	4	0	5	7	.417	0	21	4.45
1987	San Diego	NL	40	0	0	30	52	217	47	18	18	4	2	3	0	19	6	44	2	0	5	4	.556	0	11	3.12
1988	Chicago	NL	46	0	0	33	43.2	194	50	23	21	3	3	1	3	15	5	30	3	2	4	4	.500	0	13	4.33
1989	2 ML Teams		42	0	0	28	58	238	46	22	19	2	3	2	1	30	4	30	3	0	3	1	.750	0	5	2.95
1991	Texas	AL	44	0	0	16	40.1	167	33	16	16	4	3	0	3	16	1	28	0	0	4	2	.667	0	1	3.57
1992	Oakland	AL	30	0	0	13	38	163	32	13	12	5	1	2	2	19	4	26	0	0	0	2	.000	0	0	2.84
1993	Oakland	AL	39	0	0	12	47.2	213	49	24	24	6	0	2	1	26	2	40	4	0	4	5	.444	0	1	4.53
1989	San Francisco	NL	31	0	0	22	43.2	182	32	16	13	2	2	2	0	27	3	24	2	0	2	1	.667	0	4	2.68
	New York	AL	11	0	0	6	14.1	56	14	6	6	0	1	0	1	3	1	6	1	0	1	0	1.000	0	1	3.77
21 ML YEARS			966	37	16	660	1762	7309	1453	647	583	113	104	65	44	717	89	1473	61	5	121	107	.531	0	309	2.98

78

Jim Gott

Pitches: Right **Bats:** Right **Pos:** RP   **Ht:** 6' 4" **Wt:** 229 **Born:** 08/03/59 **Age:** 34

			HOW MUCH HE PITCHED					WHAT HE GAVE UP									THE RESULTS				
Year	Team	Lg	G	GS	CG	GF	IP	BFP	H	R	ER	HR	SH	SF	HB	TBB	IBB	SO	WP	Bk	W	L	Pct.	ShO	Sv	ERA
1982	Toronto	AL	30	23	1	4	136	600	134	76	67	15	3	2	3	66	0	82	8	0	5	10	.333	1	0	4.43
1983	Toronto	AL	34	30	6	2	176.2	776	195	103	93	15	4	3	5	68	5	121	2	0	9	14	.391	1	0	4.74
1984	Toronto	AL	35	12	1	11	109.2	464	93	54	49	7	7	6	3	49	3	73	1	0	7	6	.538	1	2	4.02
1985	San Francisco	NL	26	26	2	0	148.1	629	144	73	64	10	6	4	1	51	3	78	3	2	7	10	.412	0	0	3.88
1986	San Francisco	NL	9	2	0	3	13	66	16	12	11	0	1	1	0	13	2	9	1	1	0	0	.000	0	1	7.62
1987	2 ML Teams		55	3	0	30	87	382	81	43	33	4	2	1	2	40	7	90	5	0	1	2	.333	0	13	3.41
1988	Pittsburgh	NL	67	0	0	59	77.1	314	68	30	30	9	7	3	2	22	5	76	1	6	6	6	.500	0	34	3.49
1989	Pittsburgh	NL	1	0	0	0	0.2	4	1	0	0	0	0	0	0	1	0	1	0	0	0	0	.000	0	0	0.00
1990	Los Angeles	NL	50	0	0	24	62	270	59	27	20	5	2	4	0	34	7	44	4	0	3	5	.375	0	3	2.90
1991	Los Angeles	NL	55	0	0	26	76	322	63	28	25	5	6	1	1	32	7	73	6	3	4	3	.571	0	2	2.96
1992	Los Angeles	NL	68	0	0	28	88	369	72	27	24	4	6	1	1	41	13	75	9	3	3	3	.500	0	6	2.45
1993	Los Angeles	NL	62	0	0	45	77.2	313	71	23	20	6	7	2	1	17	5	67	5	0	4	8	.333	0	25	2.32
1987	Los Angeles	NL	30	3	0	8	56	253	53	32	28	4	1	1	2	32	5	63	3	0	1	0	1.000	0	0	4.50
	Pittsburgh	NL	25	0	0	22	31	129	28	11	5	0	1	0	0	8	2	27	2	0	0	2	.000	0	13	1.45
	12 ML YEARS		492	96	10	232	1052.1	4509	997	496	436	80	51	28	19	434	57	789	45	15	49	67	.422	3	86	3.73

Mauro Gozzo

Pitches: Right **Bats:** Right **Pos:** RP   **Ht:** 6' 3" **Wt:** 212 **Born:** 03/07/66 **Age:** 28

			HOW MUCH HE PITCHED					WHAT HE GAVE UP									THE RESULTS				
Year	Team	Lg	G	GS	CG	GF	IP	BFP	H	R	ER	HR	SH	SF	HB	TBB	IBB	SO	WP	Bk	W	L	Pct.	ShO	Sv	ERA
1993	Norfolk *	AAA	28	28	2	0	190.1	798	208	88	73	10	4	5	9	49	7	97	6	0	8	11	.421	0	0	3.45
1989	Toronto	AL	9	3	0	2	31.2	133	35	19	17	1	0	2	1	9	1	10	0	0	4	1	.800	0	0	4.83
1990	Cleveland	AL	2	0	0	1	3	13	2	0	0	0	0	0	0	2	0	2	0	0	0	0	.000	0	0	0.00
1991	Cleveland	AL	2	2	0	0	4.2	28	9	10	10	0	0	1	0	7	0	3	2	0	0	0	.000	0	0	19.29
1992	Minnesota	AL	2	0	0	0	1.2	12	7	5	5	2	0	0	0	0	0	1	0	0	0	0	.000	0	0	27.00
1993	New York	NL	10	0	0	5	14	57	11	5	4	1	0	0	0	5	1	6	0	0	0	1	.000	0	1	2.57
	5 ML YEARS		25	5	0	8	55	243	64	39	36	4	0	3	1	23	2	22	3	0	4	2	.667	0	1	5.89

Mark Grace

Bats: Left **Throws:** Left **Pos:** 1B   **Ht:** 6' 2" **Wt:** 190 **Born:** 06/28/64 **Age:** 30

			BATTING																BASERUNNING				PERCENTAGES		
Year	Team	Lg	G	AB	H	2B	3B	HR	(Hm	Rd)	TB	R	RBI	TBB	IBB	SO	HBP	SH	SF	SB	CS	SB%	GDP	Avg	OBP	SLG
1988	Chicago	NL	134	486	144	23	4	7	(0	7)	196	65	57	60	5	43	0	0	4	3	3	.50	12	.296	.371	.403
1989	Chicago	NL	142	510	160	28	3	13	(8	5)	233	74	79	80	13	42	0	3	3	14	7	.67	13	.314	.405	.457
1990	Chicago	NL	157	589	182	32	1	9	(4	5)	243	72	82	59	5	54	5	1	8	15	6	.71	10	.309	.372	.413
1991	Chicago	NL	160	619	169	28	5	8	(5	3)	231	87	58	70	7	53	3	4	7	3	4	.43	6	.273	.346	.373
1992	Chicago	NL	158	603	185	37	5	9	(5	4)	259	72	79	72	8	36	4	2	8	6	1	.86	14	.307	.380	.430
1993	Chicago	NL	155	594	193	39	4	14	(5	9)	282	86	98	71	14	32	1	1	9	8	4	.67	25	.325	.393	.475
	6 ML YEARS		906	3401	1033	187	22	60	(27	33)	1444	456	453	412	52	260	13	11	39	49	25	.66	80	.304	.377	.425

Joe Grahe

Pitches: Right **Bats:** Right **Pos:** RP   **Ht:** 6' 0" **Wt:** 200 **Born:** 08/14/67 **Age:** 26

			HOW MUCH HE PITCHED					WHAT HE GAVE UP									THE RESULTS				
Year	Team	Lg	G	GS	CG	GF	IP	BFP	H	R	ER	HR	SH	SF	HB	TBB	IBB	SO	WP	Bk	W	L	Pct.	ShO	Sv	ERA
1993	Vancouver *	AAA	4	4	0	0	6	26	4	3	3	1	0	0	0	2	0	5	1	0	1	1	.500	0	0	4.50
1990	California	AL	8	8	0	0	43.1	200	51	30	24	3	0	0	3	23	1	25	1	0	3	4	.429	0	0	4.98
1991	California	AL	18	10	1	2	73	330	84	43	39	2	1	1	3	33	0	40	2	0	3	7	.300	0	0	4.81
1992	California	AL	46	7	0	31	94.2	399	85	37	37	5	4	4	6	39	2	39	3	0	5	6	.455	0	21	3.52
1993	California	AL	45	0	0	32	56.2	247	54	22	18	5	2	3	2	25	4	31	3	0	4	1	.800	0	11	2.86
	4 ML YEARS		117	25	1	65	267.2	1176	274	132	118	15	7	8	14	120	7	135	9	0	15	18	.455	0	32	3.97

Jeff Granger

Pitches: Left **Bats:** Left **Pos:** RP   **Ht:** 6' 4" **Wt:** 190 **Born:** 12/16/71 **Age:** 22

			HOW MUCH HE PITCHED					WHAT HE GAVE UP									THE RESULTS				
Year	Team	Lg	G	GS	CG	GF	IP	BFP	H	R	ER	HR	SH	SF	HB	TBB	IBB	SO	WP	Bk	W	L	Pct.	ShO	Sv	ERA
1993	Eugene	A	8	7	0	0	36	146	28	17	12	2	1	0	1	10	1	56	1	0	3	3	.500	0	0	3.00
1993	Kansas City	AL	1	0	0	0	1	8	3	3	3	0	0	0	0	2	0	1	0	0	0	0	.000	0	0	27.00

Mark Grant

Pitches: Right **Bats:** Right **Pos:** RP

Ht: 6' 2" **Wt:** 215 **Born:** 10/24/63 **Age:** 30

Year	Team	Lg	HOW MUCH HE PITCHED						WHAT HE GAVE UP										THE RESULTS				
			G	GS	CG	GF	IP	BFP	H	R	ER	HR	SH	SF	HB	TBB	IBB	SO	WP	Bk	W	L	Pct.	ShO	Sv	ERA
1993	Tucson *	AAA	4	0	0	1	8.1	34	5	1	1	0	1	0	0	4	0	10	0	0	1	0	1.000	0	0	1.08
	Vancouver *	AAA	1	0	0	1	2	8	0	0	0	0	1	0	0	2	0	1	0	0	0	0	.000	0	0	0.00
1984	San Francisco	NL	11	10	0	1	53.2	231	56	40	38	6	2	3	1	19	0	32	3	0	1	4	.200	0	1	6.37
1986	San Francisco	NL	4	1	0	3	10	39	6	4	4	0	0	0	0	5	0	5	0	1	0	1	.000	0	0	3.60
1987	2 ML Teams		33	25	2	2	163.1	720	170	88	77	22	15	1	1	73	8	90	8	3	7	9	.438	1	1	4.24
1988	San Diego	NL	33	11	0	9	97.2	410	97	41	40	14	6	4	2	36	6	61	5	0	2	8	.200	0	0	3.69
1989	San Diego	NL	50	0	0	19	116.1	466	105	45	43	11	5	2	3	32	6	69	2	0	8	2	.800	0	2	3.33
1990	2 ML Teams		59	1	0	21	91.1	411	108	53	48	9	6	5	1	37	11	69	2	1	2	3	.400	0	3	4.73
1992	Seattle	AL	23	10	0	4	81	352	100	39	35	6	5	1	2	22	2	42	2	0	2	4	.333	0	0	3.89
1993	2 ML Teams		20	0	0	9	25.1	114	34	24	21	4	0	2	0	11	3	14	2	0	0	1	.000	0	1	7.46
1987	San Francisco	NL	16	8	0	2	61	264	66	29	24	6	7	1	1	21	5	32	2	2	1	2	.333	1	1	3.54
	San Diego	NL	17	17	2	0	102.1	456	104	59	53	16	8	0	0	52	3	58	6	1	6	7	.462	1	0	4.66
1990	San Diego	NL	26	0	0	5	39	180	47	23	21	5	4	3	0	19	8	29	1	1	1	1	.500	0	0	4.85
	Atlanta	NL	33	1	0	16	52.1	231	61	30	27	4	2	2	1	18	3	40	1	0	1	2	.333	0	3	4.64
1993	Houston	NL	6	0	0	3	11	46	11	4	1	0	0	1	0	5	2	6	0	0	0	0	.000	0	0	0.82
	Colorado	NL	14	0	0	6	14.1	68	23	20	20	4	0	1	0	6	1	8	2	0	0	1	.000	0	1	12.56
	8 ML YEARS		233	58	2	68	638.2	2743	676	334	306	72	39	18	10	235	36	382	24	5	22	32	.407	1	8	4.31

Mark Grater

Pitches: Right **Bats:** Right **Pos:** RP

Ht: 5'10" **Wt:** 205 **Born:** 01/19/64 **Age:** 30

Year	Team	Lg	HOW MUCH HE PITCHED						WHAT HE GAVE UP										THE RESULTS				
			G	GS	CG	GF	IP	BFP	H	R	ER	HR	SH	SF	HB	TBB	IBB	SO	WP	Bk	W	L	Pct.	ShO	Sv	ERA
1986	Johnson Cty	R	24	0	0	19	41.1	163	25	14	11	2	0	2	2	14	3	46	7	0	5	2	.714	0	8	2.40
1987	Savannah	A	50	0	0	28	74	319	54	35	25	4	5	1	6	48	9	59	11	1	6	10	.375	0	6	3.04
1988	Springfield	A	53	0	0	28	81	318	60	23	16	1	4	1	4	27	7	66	5	3	7	2	.778	0	11	1.78
1989	St.Pete	A	56	0	0	49	67.1	279	44	23	14	1	4	3	7	24	4	59	2	0	3	8	.273	0	32	1.87
1990	Louisville	AAA	24	0	0	15	28.1	124	24	13	10	0	3	2	0	15	4	18	0	0	0	2	.000	0	3	3.18
	Arkansas	AA	29	0	0	22	44	182	31	18	14	1	2	1	4	18	0	43	6	0	2	0	1.000	0	17	2.86
1991	Louisville	AAA	58	0	0	41	80.1	329	68	20	18	1	6	0	3	33	7	53	4	0	3	5	.375	0	12	2.02
1992	Louisville	AAA	54	0	0	45	76	314	74	26	18	2	6	1	3	15	2	46	2	0	7	8	.467	0	24	2.13
1993	Toledo	AAA	28	0	0	20	31	145	42	31	28	8	0	1	0	12	0	31	2	0	1	2	.333	0	4	8.13
	Calgary	AAA	9	0	0	7	11.2	62	19	10	10	1	0	0	2	6	0	4	2	0	0	0	.000	0	0	7.71
1991	St. Louis	NL	3	0	0	2	3	15	5	0	0	0	0	0	0	2	0	0	0	0	0	0	.000	0	0	0.00
1993	Detroit	AL	6	0	0	1	5	25	6	3	3	0	0	0	0	4	1	4	1	0	0	0	.000	0	0	5.40
	2 ML YEARS		9	0	0	3	8	40	11	3	3	0	0	0	0	6	1	4	1	0	0	0	.000	0	0	3.38

Craig Grebeck

Bats: Right **Throws:** Right **Pos:** SS/2B/3B

Ht: 5' 7" **Wt:** 148 **Born:** 12/29/64 **Age:** 29

Year	Team	Lg	BATTING																		BASERUNNING				PERCENTAGES		
			G	AB	H	2B	3B	HR	(Hm	Rd)	TB	R	RBI	TBB	IBB	SO	HBP	SH	SF	SB	CS	SB%	GDP	Avg	OBP	SLG
1990	Chicago	AL	59	119	20	3	1	1	(1	0)	28	7	9	8	0	24	2	3	3	0	0	.00	2	.168	.227	.235
1991	Chicago	AL	107	224	63	16	3	6	(3	3)	103	37	31	38	0	40	1	4	1	1	3	.25	3	.281	.386	.460
1992	Chicago	AL	88	287	77	21	2	3	(2	1)	111	24	35	30	0	34	3	10	3	0	3	.00	5	.268	.341	.387
1993	Chicago	AL	72	190	43	5	0	1	(0	1)	51	25	12	26	0	26	0	7	0	1	2	.33	9	.226	.319	.268
	4 ML YEARS		326	820	203	45	6	11	(6	5)	293	93	87	102	0	124	6	24	7	2	8	.20	19	.248	.333	.357

Shawn Green

Bats: Left **Throws:** Left **Pos:** RF

Ht: 6' 4" **Wt:** 190 **Born:** 11/10/72 **Age:** 21

Year	Team	Lg	BATTING																		BASERUNNING				PERCENTAGES		
			G	AB	H	2B	3B	HR	(Hm	Rd)	TB	R	RBI	TBB	IBB	SO	HBP	SH	SF	SB	CS	SB%	GDP	Avg	OBP	SLG
1992	Dunedin	A	114	417	114	21	3	1	--	--	144	44	49	28	0	66	4	5	8	22	9	.71	9	.273	.319	.345
1993	Knoxville	AA	99	360	102	14	2	4	--	--	132	40	34	26	2	72	5	6	1	4	9	.31	6	.283	.339	.367
1993	Toronto	AL	3	6	0	0	0	0	(0	0)	0	0	0	0	0	0	0	0	0	0	0	.00	0	.000	.000	.000

Tyler Green

Pitches: Right **Bats:** Right **Pos:** SP

Ht: 6' 5" **Wt:** 185 **Born:** 02/18/70 **Age:** 24

Year	Team	Lg	HOW MUCH HE PITCHED						WHAT HE GAVE UP										THE RESULTS				
			G	GS	CG	GF	IP	BFP	H	R	ER	HR	SH	SF	HB	TBB	IBB	SO	WP	Bk	W	L	Pct.	ShO	Sv	ERA
1991	Batavia	A	3	3	0	0	15	58	7	2	2	0	0	0	2	6	0	19	2	0	1	0	1.000	0	0	1.20
	Clearwater	A	2	2	0	0	13	50	3	2	2	0	0	0	0	8	0	20	2	0	2	0	1.000	0	0	1.38
1992	Reading	AA	12	12	0	0	62.1	249	46	16	13	2	4	1	1	20	0	67	5	0	6	3	.667	0	0	1.88
	Scranton/wb	AAA	2	2	0	0	10.1	50	7	7	7	1	0	0	1	12	0	15	0	1	0	1	.000	0	0	6.10
1993	Scranton/wb	AAA	28	14	4	6	118.1	496	102	62	52	8	3	4	5	43	2	87	8	2	6	10	.375	0	0	3.95
1993	Philadelphia	NL	3	2	0	1	7.1	41	16	9	6	0	0	0	0	5	0	7	2	0	0	0	.000	0	0	7.36

Tommy Greene

Pitches: Right **Bats:** Right **Pos:** SP   **Ht:** 6' 5" **Wt:** 219 **Born:** 04/06/67 **Age:** 27

			HOW MUCH HE PITCHED					WHAT HE GAVE UP									THE RESULTS				
Year Team	Lg	G	GS	CG	GF	IP	BFP	H	R	ER	HR	SH	SF	HB	TBB	IBB	SO	WP	Bk	W	L	Pct.	ShO	Sv	ERA
1989 Atlanta	NL	4	4	1	0	26.1	103	22	12	12	5	1	2	0	6	1	17	1	0	1	2	.333	0	0	4.10
1990 2 ML Teams		15	9	0	1	51.1	227	50	31	29	8	5	0	1	26	1	21	1	0	3	3	.500	0	0	5.08
1991 Philadelphia	NL	36	27	3	3	207.2	857	177	85	78	19	9	11	3	66	4	154	9	1	13	7	.650	2	0	3.38
1992 Philadelphia	NL	13	12	0	0	64.1	298	75	39	38	5	4	2	0	34	2	39	1	0	3	3	.500	0	0	5.32
1993 Philadelphia	NL	31	30	7	0	200	834	175	84	76	12	9	9	3	62	3	167	15	0	16	4	.800	2	0	3.42
1990 Atlanta	NL	5	2	0	0	12.1	61	14	11	11	3	2	0	1	9	0	4	0	0	1	0	1.000	0	0	8.03
Philadelphia		10	7	0	1	39	166	36	20	18	5	3	0	0	17	1	17	1	0	2	3	.400	0	0	4.15
5 ML YEARS		99	82	11	4	549.2	2319	499	251	233	49	28	24	7	194	11	398	27	1	36	19	.655	5	0	3.82

Willie Greene

Bats: Left **Throws:** Right **Pos:** SS   **Ht:** 5'11" **Wt:** 180 **Born:** 09/23/71 **Age:** 22

				BATTING														BASERUNNING				PERCENTAGES		
Year Team	Lg	G	AB	H	2B	3B	HR	(Hm	Rd)	TB	R	RBI	TBB	IBB	SO	HBP	SH	SF	SB	CS	SB%	GDP	Avg	OBP	SLG
1989 Pirates	R	23	86	24	3	3	5	--	--	48	17	11	9	1	6	1	0	0	4	3	.57	0	.279	.354	.558
Princeton	R	39	136	44	6	4	2	--	--	64	22	24	9	1	29	2	0	0	4	4	.50	0	.324	.374	.471
1990 Augusta	A	86	291	75	12	4	11	--	--	128	59	47	61	3	58	3	1	5	6	5	.55	5	.258	.386	.440
Salem	A	17	60	11	1	1	3	--	--	23	9	9	7	1	18	1	0	1	0	1	.00	1	.183	.275	.383
Rockford	A	11	35	14	3	0	0	--	--	17	4	2	6	0	7	0	0	0	2	1	.67	0	.400	.488	.486
1991 Wst Plm Bch	A	99	322	70	9	3	12	--	--	121	46	43	50	2	92	3	1	3	9	7	.56	3	.217	.325	.376
1992 Cedar Rapds	A	34	120	34	8	2	12	--	--	82	26	40	18	0	27	2	0	2	3	4	.43	3	.283	.380	.683
Chattanooga	AA	96	349	97	19	2	15	--	--	165	47	66	46	3	90	3	1	5	9	9	.50	8	.278	.362	.473
1993 Indianapols	AAA	98	341	91	19	2	22	--	--	176	62	58	51	2	83	1	2	2	2	4	.33	5	.267	.362	.516
1992 Cincinnati	NL	29	93	25	5	2	2	(2	0)	40	10	13	10	0	23	0	0	1	0	2	.00	1	.269	.337	.430
1993 Cincinnati	NL	15	50	8	1	1	2	(2	0)	17	7	5	2	0	19	0	0	1	0	0	.00	1	.160	.189	.340
2 ML YEARS		44	143	33	6	3	4	(4	0)	57	17	18	12	0	42	0	0	2	0	2	.00	2	.231	.287	.399

Mike Greenwell

Bats: Left **Throws:** Right **Pos:** LF   **Ht:** 6' 0" **Wt:** 205 **Born:** 07/18/63 **Age:** 30

				BATTING														BASERUNNING				PERCENTAGES		
Year Team	Lg	G	AB	H	2B	3B	HR	(Hm	Rd)	TB	R	RBI	TBB	IBB	SO	HBP	SH	SF	SB	CS	SB%	GDP	Avg	OBP	SLG
1985 Boston	AL	17	31	10	1	0	4	(1	3)	23	7	8	3	1	4	0	0	0	1	0	1.00	0	.323	.382	.742
1986 Boston	AL	31	35	11	2	0	0	(0	0)	13	4	4	5	0	7	0	0	0	0	0	.00	1	.314	.400	.371
1987 Boston	AL	125	412	135	31	6	19	(8	11)	235	71	89	35	1	40	6	0	3	5	4	.56	7	.328	.386	.570
1988 Boston	AL	158	590	192	39	8	22	(12	10)	313	86	119	87	18	38	9	0	7	16	8	.67	11	.325	.416	.531
1989 Boston	AL	145	578	178	36	0	14	(6	8)	256	87	95	56	15	44	3	0	4	13	5	.72	21	.308	.370	.443
1990 Boston	AL	159	610	181	30	6	14	(6	8)	265	71	73	65	12	43	4	0	3	8	7	.53	19	.297	.367	.434
1991 Boston	AL	147	544	163	26	6	9	(5	4)	228	76	83	43	6	35	3	1	7	15	5	.75	11	.300	.350	.419
1992 Boston	AL	49	180	42	2	0	2	(0	2)	50	16	18	18	1	19	2	0	2	2	3	.40	8	.233	.307	.278
1993 Boston	AL	146	540	170	38	6	13	(6	7)	259	77	72	54	12	46	4	2	3	5	4	.56	17	.315	.379	.480
9 ML YEARS		977	3520	1082	205	32	97	(44	53)	1642	495	561	366	66	276	31	3	29	65	36	.64	95	.307	.375	.466

Ken Greer

Pitches: Right **Bats:** Right **Pos:** RP   **Ht:** 6' 3" **Wt:** 210 **Born:** 05/12/67 **Age:** 27

			HOW MUCH HE PITCHED					WHAT HE GAVE UP									THE RESULTS				
Year Team	Lg	G	GS	CG	GF	IP	BFP	H	R	ER	HR	SH	SF	HB	TBB	IBB	SO	WP	Bk	W	L	Pct.	ShO	Sv	ERA
1988 Oneonta	A	15	15	4	0	112.1	470	109	46	30	0	5	4	7	18	2	60	6	6	5	5	.500	0	0	2.40
1989 Pr William	A	29	13	3	7	111.2	461	101	56	52	3	2	2	7	22	0	44	4	1	7	3	.700	1	2	4.19
1990 Ft.Lauderdle	A	38	5	0	11	89.1	417	115	64	54	5	9	5	7	33	2	55	3	3	4	9	.308	0	1	5.44
Pr William	A	1	1	0	0	7.2	32	7	2	2	0	0	1	0	2	0	7	0	0	1	0	1.000	0	0	2.35
1991 Ft.Lauderdle	A	31	1	0	12	57.1	245	49	31	27	3	1	1	7	22	2	46	5	0	4	3	.571	0	0	4.24
1992 Pr William	A	13	0	0	6	27	112	25	11	11	1	0	0	1	9	0	30	1	0	1	2	.333	0	1	3.67
Albany	AA	40	1	0	18	68.2	280	48	19	14	1	2	1	0	30	4	53	6	0	4	1	.800	0	4	1.83
Columbus	AAA	1	0	0	1	3	13	3	2	1	0	0	1	0	1	0	1	0	0	0	0	.000	0	0	9.00
1993 Columbus	AAA	46	0	0	21	79.1	347	78	41	39	5	4	4	2	36	6	50	2	0	9	4	.692	0	6	4.42
1993 New York	NL	1	0	0	1	1	3	0	0	0	0	0	0	0	0	0	2	0	0	1	0	1.000	0	0	0.00

Tommy Gregg

Bats: Left **Throws:** Left **Pos:** LF   **Ht:** 6' 1" **Wt:** 190 **Born:** 07/29/63 **Age:** 30

				BATTING														BASERUNNING				PERCENTAGES		
Year Team	Lg	G	AB	H	2B	3B	HR	(Hm	Rd)	TB	R	RBI	TBB	IBB	SO	HBP	SH	SF	SB	CS	SB%	GDP	Avg	OBP	SLG
1993 Indianapols *	AAA	71	198	63	12	5	7	--	--	106	34	30	26	0	28	1	1	3	3	5	.38	3	.318	.398	.535
1987 Pittsburgh	NL	10	8	2	1	0	0	(0	0)	3	3	0	0	0	2	0	0	0	0	0	.00	2	.250	.250	.375
1988 2 ML Teams		25	44	13	4	0	1	(0	1)	20	5	7	3	1	6	0	0	1	0	0	.00	1	.295	.333	.455
1989 Atlanta	NL	102	276	67	8	0	6	(2	4)	93	24	23	18	2	45	0	3	1	3	4	.43	4	.243	.288	.337

Year	Team	Lg	G	AB	H	2B	3B	HR	(Hm	Rd)	TB	R	RBI	TBB	IBB	SO	HBP	SH	SF	SB	CS	SB%	GDP	Avg	OBP	SLG
1990	Atlanta	NL	124	239	63	13	1	5	(2	3)	93	18	32	20	4	39	1	0	1	4	3	.57	1	.264	.322	.389
1991	Atlanta	NL	72	107	20	8	1	1	(1	0)	33	13	4	12	2	24	1	0	0	2	2	.50	1	.187	.275	.308
1992	Atlanta	NL	18	19	5	0	0	1	(1	0)	8	1	1	1	0	7	0	0	0	1	0	1.00	1	.263	.300	.421
1993	Cincinnati	NL	10	12	2	0	0	0	(0	0)	2	1	1	0	0	0	0	0	1	0	0	.00	0	.167	.154	.167
1988	Pittsburgh	NL	14	15	3	1	0	1	(0	1)	7	4	3	1	0	4	0	0	1	0	1	.00	0	.200	.235	.467
	Atlanta	NL	11	29	10	3	0	0	(0	0)	13	1	4	2	1	2	0	0	0	0	0	.00	0	.345	.387	.448
7 ML YEARS			361	705	172	34	2	14	(6	8)	252	65	68	54	9	123	2	3	4	10	10	.50	10	.244	.298	.357

Ken Griffey Jr

Bats: Left **Throws:** Left **Pos:** CF/DH **Ht:** 6' 3" **Wt:** 205 **Born:** 11/21/69 **Age:** 24

					BATTING															BASERUNNING				PERCENTAGES		
Year	Team	Lg	G	AB	H	2B	3B	HR	(Hm	Rd)	TB	R	RBI	TBB	IBB	SO	HBP	SH	SF	SB	CS	SB%	GDP	Avg	OBP	SLG
1989	Seattle	AL	127	455	120	23	0	16	(10	6)	191	61	61	44	8	83	2	1	4	16	7	.70	4	.264	.329	.420
1990	Seattle	AL	155	597	179	28	7	22	(8	14)	287	91	80	63	12	81	2	0	4	16	11	.59	12	.300	.366	.481
1991	Seattle	AL	154	548	179	42	1	22	(16	6)	289	76	100	71	21	82	1	4	9	18	6	.75	10	.327	.399	.527
1992	Seattle	AL	142	565	174	39	4	27	(16	11)	302	83	103	44	15	67	5	0	3	10	5	.67	15	.308	.361	.535
1993	Seattle	AL	156	582	180	38	3	45	(21	24)	359	113	109	96	25	91	6	0	7	17	9	.65	14	.309	.408	.617
5 ML YEARS			734	2747	832	170	15	132	(71	61)	1428	424	453	318	81	404	16	5	27	77	38	.67	55	.303	.375	.520

Alfredo Griffin

Bats: Both **Throws:** Right **Pos:** SS/2B **Ht:** 5'11" **Wt:** 167 **Born:** 03/06/57 **Age:** 37

					BATTING															BASERUNNING				PERCENTAGES		
Year	Team	Lg	G	AB	H	2B	3B	HR	(Hm	Rd)	TB	R	RBI	TBB	IBB	SO	HBP	SH	SF	SB	CS	SB%	GDP	Avg	OBP	SLG
1976	Cleveland	AL	12	4	1	0	0	0	(0	0)	1	0	0	0	0	2	0	0	0	0	1	.00	0	.250	.250	.250
1977	Cleveland	AL	14	41	6	1	0	0	(0	0)	7	5	3	3	0	5	0	0	0	2	2	.50	1	.146	.205	.171
1978	Cleveland	AL	5	4	2	1	0	0	(0	0)	3	1	0	2	0	1	0	0	0	0	0	.00	0	.500	.667	.750
1979	Toronto	AL	153	624	179	22	10	2	(2	0)	227	81	31	40	0	59	5	16	4	21	16	.57	10	.287	.333	.364
1980	Toronto	AL	155	653	166	26	15	2	(1	1)	228	63	41	24	2	58	4	10	5	18	23	.44	8	.254	.283	.349
1981	Toronto	AL	101	388	81	19	6	0	(0	0)	112	30	21	17	1	38	1	6	2	8	12	.40	6	.209	.243	.289
1982	Toronto	AL	162	539	130	20	8	1	(0	1)	169	57	48	22	0	48	0	11	4	10	8	.56	7	.241	.269	.314
1983	Toronto	AL	162	528	132	22	9	4	(2	2)	184	62	47	27	0	44	3	11	3	8	11	.42	5	.250	.289	.348
1984	Toronto	AL	140	419	101	8	2	4	(1	3)	125	53	30	4	0	33	1	13	4	11	3	.79	5	.241	.248	.298
1985	Oakland	AL	162	614	166	18	7	2	(0	2)	204	75	64	20	1	50	0	5	7	24	9	.73	6	.270	.290	.332
1986	Oakland	AL	162	594	169	23	6	4	(1	3)	216	74	51	35	6	52	2	12	6	33	16	.67	5	.285	.323	.364
1987	Oakland	AL	144	494	130	23	5	3	(2	1)	172	69	60	28	2	41	4	10	3	26	13	.67	9	.263	.306	.348
1988	Los Angeles	NL	95	316	63	8	3	1	(0	1)	80	39	27	24	7	30	2	11	1	7	5	.58	3	.199	.259	.253
1989	Los Angeles	NL	136	506	125	27	2	0	(0	0)	156	49	29	29	2	57	0	11	1	10	7	.59	5	.247	.287	.308
1990	Los Angeles	NL	141	461	97	11	3	1	(0	1)	117	38	35	29	11	65	2	6	4	6	3	.67	5	.210	.258	.254
1991	Los Angeles	NL	109	350	85	6	2	0	(0	0)	95	27	27	22	5	49	1	7	5	5	4	.56	5	.243	.286	.271
1992	Toronto	AL	63	150	35	7	0	0	(0	0)	42	21	10	9	0	19	0	3	2	3	1	.75	3	.233	.273	.280
1993	Toronto	AL	46	95	20	3	0	0	(0	0)	23	15	3	3	0	13	0	4	0	0	0	.00	3	.211	.235	.242
18 ML YEARS			1962	6780	1688	245	78	24	(9	15)	2161	759	527	338	37	664	25	136	51	192	134	.59	86	.249	.285	.319

Jason Grimsley

Pitches: Right **Bats:** Right **Pos:** SP **Ht:** 6' 3" **Wt:** 182 **Born:** 08/07/67 **Age:** 26

			HOW MUCH HE PITCHED						WHAT HE GAVE UP										THE RESULTS					
Year	Team	Lg	G	GS	CG	GF	IP	BFP	H	R	ER	HR	SH	SF	HB	TBB	IBB	SO	WP	Bk	W	L	Pct.	ShO	Sv	ERA
1993	Charlotte *	AAA	28	19	3	5	135.1	579	138	64	51	10	3	1	1	49	1	102	18	0	6	6	.500	1	0	3.39
1989	Philadelphia	NL	4	4	0	0	18.1	91	19	13	12	2	1	0	0	19	1	7	2	0	1	3	.250	0	0	5.89
1990	Philadelphia	NL	11	11	0	0	57.1	255	47	21	21	1	2	1	2	43	0	41	6	1	3	2	.600	0	0	3.30
1991	Philadelphia	NL	12	12	0	0	61	272	54	34	33	4	3	2	3	41	3	42	14	0	1	7	.125	0	0	4.87
1993	Cleveland	AL	10	6	0	1	42.1	194	52	26	25	3	1	0	1	20	1	27	2	0	3	4	.429	0	0	5.31
4 ML YEARS			37	33	0	1	179	812	172	94	91	10	7	3	6	123	5	117	24	1	8	16	.333	0	0	4.58

Marquis Grissom

Bats: Right **Throws:** Right **Pos:** CF **Ht:** 5'11" **Wt:** 190 **Born:** 04/17/67 **Age:** 27

					BATTING															BASERUNNING				PERCENTAGES		
Year	Team	Lg	G	AB	H	2B	3B	HR	(Hm	Rd)	TB	R	RBI	TBB	IBB	SO	HBP	SH	SF	SB	CS	SB%	GDP	Avg	OBP	SLG
1989	Montreal	NL	26	74	19	2	0	1	(0	1)	24	16	2	12	0	21	0	1	0	1	0	1.00	1	.257	.360	.324
1990	Montreal	NL	98	288	74	14	2	3	(2	1)	101	42	29	27	2	40	0	4	1	22	2	.92	3	.257	.320	.351
1991	Montreal	NL	148	558	149	23	9	6	(3	3)	208	73	39	34	0	89	1	4	0	76	17	.82	8	.267	.310	.373
1992	Montreal	NL	159	653	180	39	6	14	(8	6)	273	99	66	42	6	81	5	3	4	78	13	.86	12	.276	.322	.418
1993	Montreal	NL	157	630	188	27	2	19	(9	10)	276	104	95	52	6	76	3	0	8	53	10	.84	10	.298	.351	.438
5 ML YEARS			588	2203	610	105	19	43	(22	21)	882	334	231	167	14	307	9	12	13	230	42	.85	34	.277	.329	.400

Buddy Groom

Pitches: Left **Bats:** Left **Pos:** RP/SP   **Ht:** 6' 2" **Wt:** 200 **Born:** 07/10/65 **Age:** 28

		HOW MUCH HE PITCHED						WHAT HE GAVE UP												THE RESULTS					
Year Team	Lg	G	GS	CG	GF	IP	BFP	H	R	ER	HR	SH	SF	HB	TBB	IBB	SO	WP	Bk	W	L	Pct.	ShO	Sv	ERA
1987 White Sox	R	4	1	0	1	12	48	12	1	1	0	1	0	1	2	0	8	0	0	1	0	1.000	0	1	0.75
Daytona Bch	A	11	10	2	0	67.2	290	60	30	27	4	1	0	2	33	1	29	2	0	7	2	.778	0	0	3.59
1988 Tampa	A	27	27	8	0	195	801	181	69	55	7	2	10	6	51	1	118	11	6	13	10	.565	0	0	2.54
1989 Birmingham	AA	26	26	3	0	167.1	735	172	101	84	13	10	8	2	78	1	94	11	3	13	8	.619	1	0	4.52
1990 Birmingham	AA	20	20	0	0	115.1	519	135	81	65	10	3	1	2	48	1	66	6	2	6	8	.429	0	0	5.07
1991 London	AA	11	7	0	2	51.2	220	51	20	20	7	0	0	2	12	1	39	2	0	7	1	.875	0	0	3.48
Toledo	AAA	24	6	0	4	75	320	73	39	36	7	5	2	4	25	2	49	1	1	2	5	.286	0	1	4.32
1992 Toledo	AAA	16	16	1	0	109.1	443	102	41	34	8	3	4	1	23	1	71	5	0	7	7	.500	0	0	2.80
1993 Toledo	AAA	16	15	0	0	102	421	98	34	31	5	1	2	2	30	1	78	2	0	9	3	.750	0	0	2.74
1992 Detroit	AL	12	7	0	3	38.2	177	48	28	25	4	3	2	0	22	4	15	0	1	0	5	.000	0	0	5.82
1993 Detroit	AL	19	3	0	8	36.2	170	48	25	25	4	2	4	2	13	5	15	2	1	0	2	.000	0	0	6.14
2 ML YEARS		31	10	0	11	75.1	347	96	53	50	8	5	6	2	35	9	30	2	2	0	7	.000	0	1	5.97

Kevin Gross

Pitches: Right **Bats:** Right **Pos:** SP   **Ht:** 6' 5" **Wt:** 227 **Born:** 06/08/61 **Age:** 33

		HOW MUCH HE PITCHED						WHAT HE GAVE UP												THE RESULTS					
Year Team	Lg	G	GS	CG	GF	IP	BFP	H	R	ER	HR	SH	SF	HB	TBB	IBB	SO	WP	Bk	W	L	Pct.	ShO	Sv	ERA
1983 Philadelphia	NL	17	17	1	0	96	418	100	46	38	13	2	1	3	35	3	66	4	1	4	6	.400	1	0	3.56
1984 Philadelphia	NL	44	14	1	9	129	566	140	66	59	8	9	3	5	44	4	84	4	4	8	5	.615	0	1	4.12
1985 Philadelphia	NL	38	31	6	0	205.2	873	194	86	78	11	7	5	7	81	6	151	2	0	15	13	.536	2	0	3.41
1986 Philadelphia	NL	37	36	7	0	241.2	1040	240	115	108	28	8	5	8	94	2	154	2	1	12	12	.500	2	0	4.02
1987 Philadelphia	NL	34	33	3	1	200.2	878	205	107	97	26	8	6	10	87	7	110	3	7	9	16	.360	1	0	4.35
1988 Philadelphia	NL	33	33	5	0	231.2	989	209	101	95	18	9	4	11	89	5	162	5	7	12	14	.462	1	0	3.69
1989 Montreal	NL	31	31	4	0	201.1	867	188	105	98	20	10	3	6	88	6	158	5	5	11	12	.478	3	0	4.38
1990 Montreal	NL	31	26	2	3	163.1	712	171	86	83	9	6	9	4	65	7	111	4	1	9	12	.429	1	0	4.57
1991 Los Angeles	NL	46	10	0	16	115.2	509	123	55	46	10	6	4	2	50	6	95	3	0	10	11	.476	0	3	3.58
1992 Los Angeles	NL	34	30	4	0	204.2	856	182	82	72	11	14	6	3	77	10	158	4	2	8	13	.381	3	0	3.17
1993 Los Angeles	NL	33	32	3	1	202.1	892	224	110	93	15	11	6	5	74	7	150	2	5	13	13	.500	0	0	4.14
11 ML YEARS		378	293	36	30	1992	8600	1976	959	867	169	90	52	64	784	63	1399	38	33	111	127	.466	14	4	3.92

Kip Gross

Pitches: Right **Bats:** Right **Pos:** RP   **Ht:** 6' 2" **Wt:** 190 **Born:** 08/24/64 **Age:** 29

		HOW MUCH HE PITCHED						WHAT HE GAVE UP												THE RESULTS					
Year Team	Lg	G	GS	CG	GF	IP	BFP	H	R	ER	HR	SH	SF	HB	TBB	IBB	SO	WP	Bk	W	L	Pct.	ShO	Sv	ERA
1993 Albuquerque*	AAA	59	0	0	25	124.1	521	115	58	56	7	7	1	2	41	6	96	9	3	13	7	.650	0	13	4.05
1990 Cincinnati	NL	5	0	0	2	6.1	25	6	3	3	0	0	0	0	2	0	3	0	0	0	0	.000	0	0	4.26
1991 Cincinnati	NL	29	9	1	6	85.2	381	93	43	33	8	6	2	0	40	2	40	5	1	6	4	.600	0	0	3.47
1992 Los Angeles	NL	16	1	0	7	23.2	109	32	14	11	1	0	0	0	10	1	14	1	1	1	1	.500	0	0	4.18
1993 Los Angeles	NL	10	0	0	0	15	59	13	1	1	0	0	0	0	4	0	12	0	0	0	0	.000	0	0	0.60
4 ML YEARS		60	10	1	15	130.2	574	144	61	48	9	6	3	0	56	3	69	6	2	7	5	.583	0	0	3.31

Kelly Gruber

Bats: Right **Throws:** Right **Pos:** 3B   **Ht:** 6' 0" **Wt:** 185 **Born:** 02/26/62 **Age:** 32

		BATTING																	BASERUNNING				PERCENTAGES		
Year Team	Lg	G	AB	H	2B	3B	HR	(Hm	Rd)	TB	R	RBI	TBB	IBB	SO	HBP	SH	SF	SB	CS	SB%	GDP	Avg	OBP	SLG
1993 Palm Sprngs*	A	5	9	2	0	0	0	--	--	2	0	1	1	0	2	0	0	0	0	0	.00	0	.222	.300	.222
Vancouver*	AAA	8	24	11	1	0	1	--	--	15	4	5	0	2	0	0	0	1	0	0	.00	0	.458	.462	.625
1984 Toronto	AL	15	16	1	0	0	1	(0	1)	4	1	2	0	0	5	0	0	0	0	0	.00	1	.063	.063	.250
1985 Toronto	AL	5	13	3	0	0	0	(0	0)	3	0	1	0	0	3	0	0	0	0	0	.00	0	.231	.231	.231
1986 Toronto	AL	87	143	28	4	1	5	(4	1)	49	20	15	5	0	27	0	2	2	2	5	.29	4	.196	.220	.343
1987 Toronto	AL	138	341	80	14	3	12	(5	7)	136	50	36	17	2	70	7	1	2	12	2	.86	11	.235	.283	.399
1988 Toronto	AL	158	569	158	33	5	16	(5	11)	249	75	81	38	1	92	7	5	4	23	5	.82	20	.278	.328	.438
1989 Toronto	AL	135	545	158	24	4	18	(8	10)	244	83	73	30	0	60	3	0	5	10	5	.67	13	.290	.328	.448
1990 Toronto	AL	150	592	162	36	6	31	(23	8)	303	92	118	48	2	94	8	1	13	14	2	.88	14	.274	.330	.512
1991 Toronto	AL	113	429	108	18	2	20	(8	12)	190	58	65	31	5	70	6	3	5	12	7	.63	7	.252	.308	.443
1992 Toronto	AL	120	446	102	16	3	11	(7	4)	157	42	43	26	3	72	4	1	4	7	7	.50	14	.229	.275	.352
1993 California	AL	18	65	18	3	0	3	(1	2)	30	10	9	2	0	11	1	2	0	0	0	.00	0	.277	.309	.462
10 ML YEARS		939	3159	818	148	24	117	(61	56)	1365	431	443	197	13	504	36	15	35	80	33	.71	86	.259	.307	.432

Eddie Guardado

Pitches: Left **Bats:** Right **Pos:** SP **Ht:** 5'10" **Wt:** 200 **Born:** 10/02/70 **Age:** 23

Year	Team	Lg	G	GS	CG	GF	IP	BFP	H	R	ER	HR	SH	SF	HB	TBB	IBB	SO	WP	Bk	W	L	Pct.	ShO	Sv	ERA
1991	Elizabethtn	R	14	13	3	1	92	376	67	30	19	5	5	1	2	31	0	106	6	2	8	4	.667	1	0	1.86
1992	Kenosha	A	18	18	2	0	101	429	106	57	49	5	6	2	4	30	0	103	2	7	5	10	.333	1	0	4.37
	Visalia	A	7	7	1	0	49.1	195	47	13	9	1	2	1	0	10	0	39	0	1	7	0	1.000	1	0	1.64
1993	Nashville	AA	10	10	2	0	65.1	255	53	10	9	1	2	1	2	10	0	57	2	0	4	0	1.000	2	0	1.24
1993	Minnesota	AL	19	16	0	2	94.2	426	123	68	65	13	1	3	1	36	2	46	0	0	3	8	.273	0	0	6.18

Mark Gubicza

Pitches: Right **Bats:** Right **Pos:** RP/SP **Ht:** 6'5" **Wt:** 230 **Born:** 08/14/62 **Age:** 31

Year	Team	Lg	G	GS	CG	GF	IP	BFP	H	R	ER	HR	SH	SF	HB	TBB	IBB	SO	WP	Bk	W	L	Pct.	ShO	Sv	ERA
1984	Kansas City	AL	29	29	4	0	189	800	172	90	85	13	4	9	5	75	0	111	3	1	10	14	.417	2	0	4.05
1985	Kansas City	AL	29	28	0	0	177.1	760	160	88	80	14	1	6	5	77	0	99	12	0	14	10	.583	0	0	4.06
1986	Kansas City	AL	35	24	3	2	180.2	765	155	77	73	8	4	8	5	84	2	118	15	0	12	6	.667	2	0	3.64
1987	Kansas City	AL	35	35	10	0	241.2	1036	231	114	107	18	6	11	6	120	3	166	14	1	13	18	.419	2	0	3.98
1988	Kansas City	AL	35	35	8	0	269.2	1111	237	94	81	11	3	6	6	83	3	183	12	4	20	8	.714	4	0	2.70
1989	Kansas City	AL	36	36	8	0	255	1060	252	100	86	10	11	8	5	63	8	173	9	0	15	11	.577	2	0	3.04
1990	Kansas City	AL	16	16	2	0	94	409	101	48	47	5	6	4	4	38	4	71	2	1	4	7	.364	0	0	4.50
1991	Kansas City	AL	26	26	0	0	133	601	168	90	84	10	3	5	6	42	1	89	5	0	9	12	.429	0	0	5.68
1992	Kansas City	AL	18	18	2	0	111.1	470	110	47	46	8	5	3	1	36	3	81	5	1	7	6	.538	1	0	3.72
1993	Kansas City	AL	49	6	0	12	104.1	474	128	61	54	2	6	6	2	43	8	80	12	0	5	8	.385	0	0	4.66
	10 ML YEARS		308	253	37	14	1756	7486	1714	809	743	99	49	66	45	661	32	1171	89	8	109	100	.522	13	2	3.81

Lee Guetterman

Pitches: Left **Bats:** Left **Pos:** RP **Ht:** 6'8" **Wt:** 230 **Born:** 11/22/58 **Age:** 35

Year	Team	Lg	G	GS	CG	GF	IP	BFP	H	R	ER	HR	SH	SF	HB	TBB	IBB	SO	WP	Bk	W	L	Pct.	ShO	Sv	ERA
1993	Louisville *	AAA	25	0	0	7	33.2	145	35	11	11	0	1	1	2	12	3	20	3	1	2	1	.667	0	2	2.94
1984	Seattle	AL	3	0	0	1	4.1	22	9	2	2	0	0	0	0	2	0	2	1	0	0	0	.000	0	0	4.15
1986	Seattle	AL	41	4	1	8	76	353	108	67	62	7	3	5	4	30	3	38	2	0	0	4	.000	0	0	7.34
1987	Seattle	AL	25	17	2	3	113.1	483	117	60	48	13	2	5	2	35	2	42	3	0	11	4	.733	1	0	3.81
1988	New York	AL	20	2	0	7	40.2	177	49	21	21	2	1	1	1	14	0	15	2	0	1	2	.333	0	0	4.65
1989	New York	AL	70	0	0	38	103	412	98	31	28	6	4	2	0	26	9	51	4	0	5	5	.500	0	13	2.45
1990	New York	AL	64	0	0	21	93	376	80	37	35	6	8	3	0	26	7	48	1	1	11	7	.611	0	2	3.39
1991	New York	AL	64	0	0	37	88	376	91	42	36	6	4	4	3	25	5	35	4	0	3	4	.429	0	6	3.68
1992	2 ML Teams		58	0	0	22	66	310	92	52	52	10	2	5	1	27	8	20	4	0	4	5	.444	0	2	7.09
1993	St. Louis	NL	40	0	0	14	46	192	41	18	15	1	1	2	2	16	5	19	1	0	3	3	.500	0	1	2.93
1992	New York	AL	15	0	0	7	22.2	114	35	24	24	5	0	2	0	13	3	5	1	0	1	1	.500	0	0	9.53
	New York	NL	43	0	0	15	43.1	196	57	28	28	5	2	3	1	14	5	15	3	0	3	4	.429	0	2	5.82
	9 ML YEARS		385	23	3	151	630.1	2701	685	330	299	51	25	27	13	201	39	270	22	1	38	34	.528	1	24	4.27

Ozzie Guillen

Bats: Left **Throws:** Right **Pos:** SS **Ht:** 5'11" **Wt:** 164 **Born:** 01/20/64 **Age:** 30

Year	Team	Lg	G	AB	H	2B	3B	HR	(Hm	Rd)	TB	R	RBI	TBB	IBB	SO	HBP	SH	SF	SB	CS	SB%	GDP	Avg	OBP	SLG
1985	Chicago	AL	150	491	134	21	9	1	(1	0)	176	71	33	12	1	36	1	8	1	7	4	.64	5	.273	.291	.358
1986	Chicago	AL	159	547	137	19	4	2	(1	1)	170	58	47	12	1	52	1	12	5	8	4	.67	14	.250	.265	.311
1987	Chicago	AL	149	560	156	22	7	2	(2	0)	198	64	51	22	2	52	1	13	8	25	8	.76	10	.279	.303	.354
1988	Chicago	AL	156	566	148	16	7	0	(0	0)	178	58	39	25	3	40	2	10	3	25	13	.66	14	.261	.294	.314
1989	Chicago	AL	155	597	151	20	8	1	(0	1)	190	63	54	15	3	48	0	11	3	36	17	.68	8	.253	.270	.318
1990	Chicago	AL	160	516	144	21	4	1	(1	0)	176	61	58	26	8	37	1	15	5	13	17	.43	6	.279	.312	.341
1991	Chicago	AL	154	524	143	20	3	3	(1	2)	178	52	49	11	1	38	0	13	7	21	15	.58	7	.273	.284	.340
1992	Chicago	AL	12	40	8	4	0	0	(0	0)	12	5	7	1	0	5	0	1	1	1	0	1.00	1	.200	.214	.300
1993	Chicago	AL	134	457	128	23	4	4	(3	1)	171	44	50	10	0	41	0	13	6	5	4	.56	6	.280	.292	.374
	9 ML YEARS		1229	4298	1149	166	46	14	(9	5)	1449	476	388	134	19	349	6	96	39	141	82	.63	71	.267	.288	.337

Bill Gullickson

Pitches: Right **Bats:** Right **Pos:** SP **Ht:** 6'3" **Wt:** 225 **Born:** 02/20/59 **Age:** 35

Year	Team	Lg	G	GS	CG	GF	IP	BFP	H	R	ER	HR	SH	SF	HB	TBB	IBB	SO	WP	Bk	W	L	Pct.	ShO	Sv	ERA
1993	Lakeland *	A	5	5	0	0	18.1	84	24	14	14	2	1	1	1	4	0	9	1	0	1	0	1.000	0	0	6.87
	Toledo *	AAA	1	1	0	0	6	26	8	6	6	4	0	0	0	0	0	4	0	0	1	0	1.000	0	0	9.00
1979	Montreal	NL	1	0	0	1	1	4	2	0	0	0	0	0	0	0	0	0	0	0	0	0	.000	0	0	0.00
1980	Montreal	NL	24	19	5	1	141	593	127	53	47	6	3	4	2	50	2	120	5	0	10	5	.667	2	0	3.00
1981	Montreal	NL	22	22	3	0	157	640	142	54	49	3	5	2	4	34	4	115	4	0	7	9	.438	2	0	2.81

Year	Team	Lg	G	GS	CG	GF	IP	BFP	H	R	ER	HR	SH	SF	HB	TBB	IBB	SO	WP	Bk	W	L	Pct.	ShO	Sv	ERA
1982	Montreal	NL	34	34	6	0	236.2	990	231	101	94	25	9	6	4	61	2	155	11	3	12	14	.462	0	0	3.57
1983	Montreal	NL	34	34	10	0	242.1	990	230	108	101	19	4	7	4	59	4	120	4	1	17	12	.586	1	0	3.75
1984	Montreal	NL	32	32	3	0	226.2	919	230	100	91	27	8	4	1	37	7	100	5	0	12	9	.571	0	0	3.61
1985	Montreal	NL	29	29	4	0	181.1	759	187	78	71	8	12	8	1	47	9	68	1	1	14	12	.538	1	0	3.52
1986	Cincinnati	NL	37	37	6	0	244.2	1014	245	103	92	24	12	13	2	60	10	121	3	0	15	12	.556	2	0	3.38
1987	2 ML Teams		35	35	4	0	213	896	218	128	115	40	8	8	3	50	7	117	4	1	14	13	.519	1	0	4.86
1990	Houston	NL	32	32	2	0	193.1	846	221	100	82	21	6	8	2	61	14	73	3	2	10	14	.417	1	0	3.82
1991	Detroit	AL	35	35	4	0	226.1	954	256	109	98	22	8	8	4	44	13	91	4	0	20	9	.690	0	0	3.90
1992	Detroit	AL	34	34	4	0	221.2	919	228	109	107	35	7	9	0	50	5	64	6	0	14	13	.519	1	0	4.34
1993	Detroit	AL	28	28	2	0	159.1	699	186	106	95	28	6	7	3	44	3	70	2	0	13	9	.591	0	0	5.37
1987	Cincinnati	NL	27	27	3	0	165	698	172	99	89	33	6	6	2	39	6	89	4	1	10	11	.476	1	0	4.85
	New York	AL	8	8	1	0	48	198	46	29	26	7	2	2	1	11	1	28	0	0	4	2	.667	0	0	4.88
	13 ML YEARS		377	371	53	0	2444.1	10223	2503	1149	1042	258	88	84	30	597	80	1214	52	8	158	131	.547	11	0	3.84

Mark Guthrie

Pitches: Left **Bats:** Both **Pos:** RP **Ht:** 6' 4" **Wt:** 206 **Born:** 09/22/65 **Age:** 28

Year	Team	Lg	HOW MUCH HE PITCHED						WHAT HE GAVE UP												THE RESULTS					
			G	GS	CG	GF	IP	BFP	H	R	ER	HR	SH	SF	HB	TBB	IBB	SO	WP	Bk	W	L	Pct.	ShO	Sv	ERA
1989	Minnesota	AL	13	8	0	2	57.1	254	66	32	29	7	1	5	1	21	1	38	1	0	2	4	.333	0	0	4.55
1990	Minnesota	AL	24	21	3	0	144.2	603	154	65	61	8	6	0	1	39	3	101	9	0	7	9	.438	1	0	3.79
1991	Minnesota	AL	41	12	0	13	98	432	116	52	47	11	4	3	1	41	2	72	7	0	7	5	.583	0	2	4.32
1992	Minnesota	AL	54	0	0	15	75	303	59	27	24	7	4	2	0	23	7	76	2	0	2	3	.400	0	5	2.88
1993	Minnesota	AL	22	0	0	2	21	94	20	11	11	2	1	2	0	16	2	15	1	3	2	1	.667	0	0	4.71
	5 ML YEARS		154	41	3	32	396	1686	415	187	172	35	16	12	3	140	15	302	20	3	20	22	.476	1	7	3.91

Ricky Gutierrez

Bats: Right **Throws:** Right **Pos:** SS **Ht:** 6' 1" **Wt:** 175 **Born:** 05/23/70 **Age:** 24

Year	Team	Lg	BATTING																	BASERUNNING				PERCENTAGES		
			G	AB	H	2B	3B	HR	(Hm	Rd)	TB	R	RBI	TBB	IBB	SO	HBP	SH	SF	SB	CS	SB%	GDP	Avg	OBP	SLG
1988	Bluefield	R	62	208	51	8	2	2	--	--	69	35	19	44	0	40	5	2	4	5	3	.63	4	.245	.383	.332
1989	Frederick	A	127	456	106	16	2	3	--	--	135	48	41	39	2	86	3	1	5	15	10	.60	12	.232	.294	.296
1990	Hagerstown	AA	20	64	15	0	1	0	--	--	17	4	6	3	0	8	0	1	1	2	0	1.00	2	.234	.265	.266
	Frederick	A	112	425	117	16	4	1	--	--	144	54	46	38	0	59	6	9	3	12	6	.67	11	.275	.341	.339
1991	Hagerstown	AA	84	292	69	6	4	0	--	--	83	47	30	57	0	52	2	3	2	11	0	1.00	8	.236	.363	.284
	Rochester	AAA	49	157	48	5	3	0	--	--	59	23	15	24	1	27	0	3	1	4	1	.80	3	.306	.396	.376
1992	Rochester	AAA	125	431	109	9	3	0	--	--	124	54	41	53	2	77	0	3	5	14	12	.54	12	.253	.331	.288
	Las Vegas	AAA	3	6	1	0	0	0	--	--	1	0	1	1	0	3	0	0	1	0	0	.00	0	.167	.250	.167
1993	Las Vegas	AAA	5	24	10	4	0	0	--	--	14	4	4	0	0	4	0	0	0	4	1	.80	0	.417	.417	.583
1993	San Diego	NL	133	438	110	10	5	5	(5	0)	145	76	26	50	2	97	5	1	1	4	3	.57	7	.251	.334	.331

Jose Guzman

Pitches: Right **Bats:** Right **Pos:** SP **Ht:** 6' 3" **Wt:** 195 **Born:** 04/09/63 **Age:** 31

Year	Team	Lg	HOW MUCH HE PITCHED						WHAT HE GAVE UP												THE RESULTS					
			G	GS	CG	GF	IP	BFP	H	R	ER	HR	SH	SF	HB	TBB	IBB	SO	WP	Bk	W	L	Pct.	ShO	Sv	ERA
1985	Texas	AL	5	5	0	0	32.2	140	27	13	10	3	0	0	0	14	1	24	1	0	3	2	.600	0	0	2.76
1986	Texas	AL	29	29	2	0	172.1	757	199	101	87	23	7	4	6	60	2	87	3	0	9	15	.375	0	0	4.54
1987	Texas	AL	37	30	6	1	208.1	880	196	115	108	30	6	8	3	82	0	143	6	5	14	14	.500	2	0	4.67
1988	Texas	AL	30	30	6	0	206.2	876	180	99	85	20	4	6	5	82	3	157	10	12	11	13	.458	2	0	3.70
1991	Texas	AL	25	25	5	0	169.2	730	152	67	58	10	2	3	4	84	1	125	8	1	13	7	.650	1	0	3.08
1992	Texas	AL	33	33	5	0	224	947	229	103	91	17	9	7	4	73	0	179	6	0	16	11	.593	0	0	3.66
1993	Chicago	NL	30	30	2	0	191	819	188	98	92	25	8	5	3	74	6	163	6	5	12	10	.545	1	0	4.34
	7 ML YEARS		189	182	26	1	1204.2	5149	1171	596	531	128	36	33	25	469	13	878	40	23	78	72	.520	4	0	3.97

Juan Guzman

Pitches: Right **Bats:** Right **Pos:** SP **Ht:** 5'11" **Wt:** 195 **Born:** 10/28/66 **Age:** 27

Year	Team	Lg	HOW MUCH HE PITCHED						WHAT HE GAVE UP												THE RESULTS					
			G	GS	CG	GF	IP	BFP	H	R	ER	HR	SH	SF	HB	TBB	IBB	SO	WP	Bk	W	L	Pct.	ShO	Sv	ERA
1991	Toronto	AL	23	23	1	0	138.2	574	98	53	46	6	2	5	4	66	0	123	10	0	10	3	.769	0	0	2.99
1992	Toronto	AL	28	28	1	0	180.2	733	135	56	53	6	5	3	1	72	2	165	14	1	16	5	.762	0	0	2.64
1993	Toronto	AL	33	33	2	0	221	963	211	107	98	17	5	9	3	110	2	194	26	1	14	3	.824	1	0	3.99
	3 ML YEARS		84	84	4	0	540.1	2270	444	216	197	29	12	17	8	248	4	482	50	3	40	11	.784	1	0	3.28

Chris Gwynn

Bats: Left **Throws:** Left **Pos:** LF/RF **Ht:** 6' 0" **Wt:** 220 **Born:** 10/13/64 **Age:** 29

Year	Team	Lg	G	AB	H	2B	3B	HR	(Hm	Rd)	TB	R	RBI	TBB	IBB	SO	HBP	SH	SF	SB	CS	SB%	GDP	Avg	OBP	SLG
1987	Los Angeles	NL	17	32	7	1	0	0	(0	0)	8	2	2	1	0	7	0	1	0	0	0	.00	0	.219	.242	.250
1988	Los Angeles	NL	12	11	2	0	0	0	(0	0)	2	1	0	1	0	2	0	0	0	0	0	.00	0	.182	.250	.182
1989	Los Angeles	NL	32	68	16	4	1	0	(0	0)	22	8	7	2	0	9	0	2	1	1	0	1.00	1	.235	.254	.324
1990	Los Angeles	NL	101	141	40	2	1	5	(0	5)	59	19	22	7	2	28	0	0	3	1	0	1.00	1	.284	.311	.418
1991	Los Angeles	NL	94	139	35	5	1	5	(3	2)	57	18	22	10	1	23	1	1	3	1	0	1.00	5	.252	.301	.410
1992	Kansas City	AL	34	84	24	3	2	1	(0	1)	34	10	7	3	0	10	0	1	2	0	0	.00	1	.286	.303	.405
1993	Kansas City	AL	103	287	86	14	4	1	(0	1)	111	36	25	24	5	34	1	2	2	0	1	.00	7	.300	.354	.387
	7 ML YEARS		393	762	210	29	9	12	(3	9)	293	94	85	48	8	113	2	7	11	2	2	.50	16	.276	.316	.385

Tony Gwynn

Bats: Left **Throws:** Left **Pos:** RF **Ht:** 5'11" **Wt:** 215 **Born:** 05/09/60 **Age:** 34

Year	Team	Lg	G	AB	H	2B	3B	HR	(Hm	Rd)	TB	R	RBI	TBB	IBB	SO	HBP	SH	SF	SB	CS	SB%	GDP	Avg	OBP	SLG
1982	San Diego	NL	54	190	55	12	2	1	(0	1)	74	33	17	14	0	16	0	4	1	8	3	.73	5	.289	.337	.389
1983	San Diego	NL	86	304	94	12	2	1	(0	1)	113	34	37	23	5	21	0	4	3	7	4	.64	9	.309	.355	.372
1984	San Diego	NL	158	606	213	21	10	5	(3	2)	269	88	71	59	13	23	2	6	2	33	18	.65	15	.351	.410	.444
1985	San Diego	NL	154	622	197	29	5	6	(3	3)	254	90	46	45	4	33	2	1	1	14	11	.56	17	.317	.364	.408
1986	San Diego	NL	160	642	211	33	7	14	(8	6)	300	107	59	52	11	35	3	2	2	37	9	.80	20	.329	.381	.467
1987	San Diego	NL	157	589	218	36	13	7	(5	2)	301	119	54	82	26	35	3	2	4	56	12	.82	13	.370	.447	.511
1988	San Diego	NL	133	521	163	22	5	7	(3	4)	216	64	70	51	13	40	0	4	2	26	11	.70	11	.313	.373	.415
1989	San Diego	NL	158	604	203	27	7	4	(3	1)	256	82	62	56	16	30	1	11	7	40	16	.71	12	.336	.389	.424
1990	San Diego	NL	141	573	177	29	10	4	(2	2)	238	79	72	44	20	23	1	7	4	17	8	.68	13	.309	.357	.415
1991	San Diego	NL	134	530	168	27	11	4	(1	3)	229	69	62	34	8	19	0	1	5	8	8	.50	11	.317	.355	.432
1992	San Diego	NL	128	520	165	27	3	6	(4	2)	216	77	41	46	12	16	0	0	3	3	6	.33	13	.317	.371	.415
1993	San Diego	NL	122	489	175	41	3	7	(4	3)	243	70	59	36	11	19	1	1	7	14	1	.93	18	.358	.398	.497
	12 ML YEARS		1585	6190	2039	316	78	66	(36	30)	2709	912	650	542	139	310	13	42	41	263	107	.71	157	.329	.382	.438

Dave Haas

Pitches: Right **Bats:** Right **Pos:** RP **Ht:** 6' 1" **Wt:** 200 **Born:** 10/19/65 **Age:** 28

			HOW MUCH HE PITCHED						WHAT HE GAVE UP										THE RESULTS					
Year	Team	Lg	G	GS	CG	GF	IP	BFP	H	R	ER	HR	SH	SF	HB	TBB	IBB	SO	WP	Bk	W	L	Pct.	ShO	Sv	ERA
1993	Toledo *	AAA	2	2	0	0	4.1	27	8	9	9	0	0	0	1	6	0	2	1	0	0	0	.000	0	0	18.69
1991	Detroit	AL	11	0	0	0	10.2	50	8	8	8	1	2	2	1	12	3	6	1	0	1	0	1.000	0	0	6.75
1992	Detroit	AL	12	11	1	1	61.2	264	68	30	27	8	1	0	1	16	1	29	2	0	5	3	.625	1	0	3.94
1993	Detroit	AL	20	0	0	5	28	131	45	20	19	9	2	1	0	8	5	17	0	0	2	2	.333	0	0	6.11
	3 ML YEARS		43	11	1	6	100.1	445	121	58	54	18	5	3	2	36	9	52	3	0	7	5	.583	1	0	4.84

John Habyan

Pitches: Right **Bats:** Right **Pos:** RP **Ht:** 6' 2" **Wt:** 195 **Born:** 01/29/64 **Age:** 30

			HOW MUCH HE PITCHED						WHAT HE GAVE UP										THE RESULTS					
Year	Team	Lg	G	GS	CG	GF	IP	BFP	H	R	ER	HR	SH	SF	HB	TBB	IBB	SO	WP	Bk	W	L	Pct.	ShO	Sv	ERA
1985	Baltimore	AL	2	0	0	1	2.2	12	3	1	0	0	0	0	0	0	0	2	0	0	1	0	1.000	0	0	0.00
1986	Baltimore	AL	6	5	0	1	26.1	117	24	17	13	3	2	1	0	18	2	14	1	0	1	3	.250	0	0	4.44
1987	Baltimore	AL	27	13	0	4	116.1	493	110	67	62	20	4	4	2	40	1	64	3	0	6	7	.462	0	0	4.80
1988	Baltimore	AL	7	0	0	1	14.2	68	22	10	7	2	0	2	0	4	0	4	1	1	1	0	1.000	0	0	4.30
1990	New York	AL	6	0	0	1	8.2	37	10	2	2	0	0	0	1	2	0	4	1	0	0	0	.000	0	0	2.08
1991	New York	AL	66	0	0	16	90	349	73	28	23	2	2	1	2	20	2	70	1	2	4	2	.667	0	2	2.30
1992	New York	AL	56	0	0	20	72.2	316	84	32	31	6	5	3	2	21	5	44	2	1	5	6	.455	0	7	3.84
1993	2 ML Teams		48	0	0	23	56.1	239	59	27	26	6	2	2	0	20	4	39	0	2	2	1	.667	0	1	4.15
1993	New York	AL	36	0	0	21	42.1	181	45	20	19	5	0	2	0	16	2	29	0	2	2	1	.667	0	1	4.04
	Kansas City	AL	12	0	0	2	14	58	14	7	7	1	0	0	0	4	2	10	0	0	0	0	.000	0	0	4.50
	8 ML YEARS		218	18	0	67	387.2	1631	385	184	164	39	13	13	7	125	14	241	9	6	20	19	.513	0	11	3.81

Chip Hale

Bats: Left **Throws:** Right **Pos:** 2B/3B/DH **Ht:** 5'11" **Wt:** 180 **Born:** 12/02/64 **Age:** 29

Year	Team	Lg	G	AB	H	2B	3B	HR	(Hm	Rd)	TB	R	RBI	TBB	IBB	SO	HBP	SH	SF	SB	CS	SB%	GDP	Avg	OBP	SLG
1987	Kenosha	A	87	339	117	12	7	7	--	--	164	65	65	33	4	26	4	0	7	3	3	.50	4	.345	.402	.484
1988	Orlando	AA	133	482	126	20	1	11	--	--	181	62	65	64	3	31	3	5	3	8	3	.73	12	.261	.350	.376
1989	Portland	AAA	108	411	112	16	9	2	--	--	152	49	34	35	2	55	1	5	2	3	2	.60	11	.273	.330	.370
1990	Portland	AAA	130	479	134	24	2	3	--	--	171	71	40	68	3	57	1	7	7	6	6	.50	16	.280	.366	.357
1991	Portland	AAA	110	352	85	16	3	1	--	--	110	45	37	47	4	22	0	5	5	3	3	.50	5	.241	.327	.313
1992	Portland	AAA	132	474	135	25	8	1	--	--	179	77	53	73	11	45	0	4	4	3	3	.50	7	.285	.376	.378

86

Year Team	Lg	G	AB	H	2B	3B	HR	(Hm	Rd)	TB	R	RBI	TBB	IBB	SO	HBP	SH	SF	SB	CS	SB%	GDP	Avg	OBP	SLG
1993 Portland	AAA	55	211	59	15	3	1	--	--	83	37	24	21	1	13	0	3	1	2	1	.67	6	.280	.343	.393
1989 Minnesota	AL	28	67	14	3	0	0	(0	0)	17	6	4	1	0	6	0	1	2	0	0	.00	0	.209	.214	.254
1990 Minnesota	AL	1	2	0	0	0	0	(0	0)	0	0	2	0	0	1	0	0	2	0	0	.00	0	.000	.000	.000
1993 Minnesota	AL	69	186	62	6	1	3	(1	2)	79	25	27	18	0	17	6	2	1	2	1	.67	3	.333	.408	.425
3 ML YEARS		98	255	76	9	1	3	(1	2)	96	31	33	19	0	24	6	3	5	2	1	.67	3	.298	.354	.376

Bob Hamelin

Bats: Left **Throws:** Left **Pos:** 1B   **Ht:** 6' 0" **Wt:** 230 **Born:** 11/29/67 **Age:** 26

| | | | | | | | | BATTING | | | | | | | | | | | BASERUNNING | | | | PERCENTAGES | | |
Year Team	Lg	G	AB	H	2B	3B	HR	(Hm	Rd)	TB	R	RBI	TBB	IBB	SO	HBP	SH	SF	SB	CS	SB%	GDP	Avg	OBP	SLG
1988 Eugene	A	70	235	70	19	1	17	--	--	142	42	61	56	4	67	5	0	8	9	1	.90	7	.298	.431	.604
1989 Memphis	AA	68	211	65	12	5	16	--	--	135	45	47	52	7	52	5	0	1	3	6	.33	2	.308	.454	.640
1990 Omaha	AAA	90	271	63	11	2	8	--	--	102	31	30	62	5	78	4	1	2	2	2	.50	1	.232	.381	.376
1991 Omaha	AAA	37	127	24	3	1	1	--	--	41	13	19	16	0	32	0	1	4	0	0	.00	4	.189	.272	.323
1992 Baseball Cy	A	11	44	12	0	1	1	--	--	17	7	6	2	0	11	0	0	0	0	0	.00	0	.273	.304	.386
Memphis	AA	35	120	40	8	0	6	--	--	66	23	22	26	2	17	0	0	0	0	1	.00	2	.333	.452	.550
Omaha	AAA	27	95	19	3	1	5	--	--	39	9	15	14	0	15	0	0	3	0	0	.00	1	.200	.295	.411
1993 Omaha	AAA	137	479	124	19	3	29	--	--	236	77	84	82	9	94	5	0	9	8	3	.73	8	.259	.367	.493
1993 Kansas City	AL	16	49	11	3	0	2	(1	1)	20	2	5	6	0	15	0	0	0	0	0	.00	2	.224	.309	.408

Darryl Hamilton

Bats: Left **Throws:** Right **Pos:** RF/LF/CF   **Ht:** 6' 1" **Wt:** 180 **Born:** 12/03/64 **Age:** 29

| | | | | | | | | BATTING | | | | | | | | | | | BASERUNNING | | | | PERCENTAGES | | |
Year Team	Lg	G	AB	H	2B	3B	HR	(Hm	Rd)	TB	R	RBI	TBB	IBB	SO	HBP	SH	SF	SB	CS	SB%	GDP	Avg	OBP	SLG
1988 Milwaukee	AL	44	103	19	4	0	1	(1	0)	26	14	11	12	0	9	1	0	1	7	3	.70	2	.184	.274	.252
1990 Milwaukee	AL	89	156	46	5	0	1	(1	0)	54	27	18	9	0	12	0	3	0	10	3	.77	2	.295	.333	.346
1991 Milwaukee	AL	122	405	126	15	6	1	(0	1)	156	64	57	33	2	38	0	7	3	16	6	.73	10	.311	.361	.385
1992 Milwaukee	AL	128	470	140	19	7	5	(1	4)	188	67	62	45	0	42	1	4	7	41	14	.75	10	.298	.356	.400
1993 Milwaukee	AL	135	520	161	21	1	9	(5	4)	211	74	48	45	5	62	3	4	1	21	13	.62	9	.310	.367	.406
5 ML YEARS		518	1654	492	64	14	17	(8	9)	635	246	196	144	7	163	5	18	12	95	39	.71	33	.297	.353	.384

Chris Hammond

Pitches: Left **Bats:** Left **Pos:** SP   **Ht:** 6' 1" **Wt:** 190 **Born:** 01/21/66 **Age:** 28

| | | | | | HOW MUCH HE PITCHED | | | WHAT HE GAVE UP | | | | | | | | | | THE RESULTS | | | | | |
Year Team	Lg	G	GS	CG	GF	IP	BFP	H	R	ER	HR	SH	SF	HB	TBB	IBB	SO	WP	Bk	W	L	Pct.	ShO	Sv	ERA
1990 Cincinnati	NL	3	3	0	0	11.1	56	13	9	8	2	1	0	0	12	1	4	1	3	0	2	.000	0	0	6.35
1991 Cincinnati	NL	20	18	0	0	99.2	425	92	51	45	4	6	1	2	48	3	50	3	0	7	7	.500	0	0	4.06
1992 Cincinnati	NL	28	26	0	1	147.1	627	149	75	69	13	5	3	3	55	6	79	6	0	7	10	.412	0	0	4.21
1993 Florida	NL	32	32	1	0	191	826	207	106	99	18	10	2	1	66	2	108	10	5	11	12	.478	0	0	4.66
4 ML YEARS		83	79	1	1	449.1	1934	461	241	221	37	22	6	6	181	12	241	20	8	25	31	.446	0	0	4.43

Jeffrey Hammonds

Bats: Right **Throws:** Right **Pos:** LF   **Ht:** 6' 0" **Wt:** 195 **Born:** 03/05/71 **Age:** 23

| | | | | | | | | BATTING | | | | | | | | | | | BASERUNNING | | | | PERCENTAGES | | |
Year Team	Lg	G	AB	H	2B	3B	HR	(Hm	Rd)	TB	R	RBI	TBB	IBB	SO	HBP	SH	SF	SB	CS	SB%	GDP	Avg	OBP	SLG
1993 Rochester	AAA	36	151	47	9	1	5	--	--	73	25	23	5	0	27	2	1	2	6	3	.67	2	.311	.338	.483
Bowie	AA	24	92	26	3	0	3	--	--	38	13	10	9	0	18	2	1	1	4	3	.57	1	.283	.356	.413
1993 Baltimore	AL	33	105	32	8	0	3	(2	1)	49	10	19	2	1	16	0	0	2	4	0	1.00	3	.305	.312	.467

Mike Hampton

Pitches: Left **Bats:** Right **Pos:** RP/SP   **Ht:** 5'10" **Wt:** 180 **Born:** 09/09/72 **Age:** 21

| | | | | | HOW MUCH HE PITCHED | | | WHAT HE GAVE UP | | | | | | | | | | THE RESULTS | | | | | |
Year Team	Lg	G	GS	CG	GF	IP	BFP	H	R	ER	HR	SH	SF	HB	TBB	IBB	SO	WP	Bk	W	L	Pct.	ShO	Sv	ERA
1990 Mariners	R	14	13	0	0	64.1	292	49	32	19	0	1	2	5	40	0	60	10	6	7	2	.778	0	0	2.66
1991 San Berndno	A	18	15	1	1	73.2	341	71	58	43	3	2	1	6	47	1	57	12	3	1	7	.125	1	0	5.25
Bellingham	A	9	9	0	0	57	225	32	15	10	0	2	0	0	26	0	65	6	3	5	2	.714	0	0	1.58
1992 San Berndno	A	25	25	6	0	170	720	163	75	59	8	4	8	3	66	0	132	10	4	13	8	.619	2	0	3.12
Jacksnville	AA	2	2	1	0	10.1	42	13	5	5	0	0	0	0	1	0	6	0	0	0	1	.000	0	0	4.35
1993 Jacksnville	AA	15	14	1	1	87.1	356	71	43	36	3	2	1	4	33	1	84	2	4	6	4	.600	0	0	3.71
1993 Seattle	AL	13	3	0	2	17	95	28	20	18	3	1	1	0	17	3	8	1	1	1	3	.250	0	1	9.53

Chris Haney

Pitches: Left **Bats:** Left **Pos:** SP   **Ht:** 6' 3" **Wt:** 195 **Born:** 11/16/68 **Age:** 25

| | | | | | HOW MUCH HE PITCHED | | | WHAT HE GAVE UP | | | | | | | | | | THE RESULTS | | | | | |
Year Team	Lg	G	GS	CG	GF	IP	BFP	H	R	ER	HR	SH	SF	HB	TBB	IBB	SO	WP	Bk	W	L	Pct.	ShO	Sv	ERA
1993 Omaha *	AAA	8	7	2	0	47.2	185	43	13	12	2	0	1	1	14	0	32	2	0	6	1	.857	0	0	2.27

1991 Montreal	NL	16	16	0	0	84.2	387	94	49	38	6	6	1	1	43	1	51	9	0	3	7	.300	0	0	4.04
1992 2 ML Teams		16	13	2	2	80	339	75	43	41	11	0	6	4	26	2	54	5	1	4	6	.400	2	0	4.61
1993 Kansas City	AL	23	23	1	0	124	556	141	87	83	13	3	4	3	53	2	65	6	1	9	9	.500	1	0	6.02
1992 Montreal	NL	9	6	1	2	38	165	40	25	23	6	0	3	4	10	0	27	5	1	2	3	.400	1	0	5.45
Kansas City	AL	7	7	1	0	42	174	35	18	18	5	0	3	0	16	2	27	0	0	2	3	.400	1	0	3.86
3 ML YEARS		55	52	3	2	288.2	1282	310	179	162	30	9	11	8	122	5	170	20	2	16	22	.421	3	0	5.05

Dave Hansen

Bats: Left **Throws:** Right **Pos:** 3B   **Ht:** 6' 0" **Wt:** 195 **Born:** 11/24/68 **Age:** 25

						BATTING												BASERUNNING				PERCENTAGES		
Year Team	Lg	G	AB	H	2B	3B	HR	(Hm | Rd)	TB	R	RBI	TBB	IBB	SO	HBP	SH	SF	SB	CS	SB%	GDP	Avg	OBP	SLG
1990 Los Angeles	NL	5	7	1	0	0	0	(0 | 0)	1	0	1	0	0	3	0	0	0	0	0	.00	0	.143	.143	.143
1991 Los Angeles	NL	53	56	15	4	0	1	(0 | 1)	22	3	5	2	0	12	0	1	0	1	0	1.00	0	.268	.293	.393
1992 Los Angeles	NL	132	341	73	11	0	6	(1 | 5)	102	30	22	34	3	49	1	0	2	0	2	.00	9	.214	.286	.299
1993 Los Angeles	NL	84	105	38	3	0	4	(2 | 2)	53	13	30	21	3	13	0	0	1	0	1	.00	0	.362	.465	.505
4 ML YEARS		274	509	127	18	0	11	(3	8)	178	46	58	57	6	77	1	0	3	3	25	11	.250	.325	.350

Erik Hanson

Pitches: Right **Bats:** Right **Pos:** SP   **Ht:** 6' 6" **Wt:** 215 **Born:** 05/18/65 **Age:** 29

		HOW MUCH HE PITCHED						WHAT HE GAVE UP									THE RESULTS					
Year Team	Lg	G	GS	CG	GF	IP	BFP	H	R	ER	HR	SH	SF	HB	TBB	IBB	SO	WP	Bk	W	L	Pct.	ShO	Sv	ERA
1988 Seattle	AL	6	6	0	0	41.2	168	35	17	15	4	3	0	1	12	1	36	2	2	2	3	.400	0	0	3.24
1989 Seattle	AL	17	17	1	0	113.1	465	103	44	40	7	4	1	5	32	1	75	3	0	9	5	.643	0	0	3.18
1990 Seattle	AL	33	33	5	0	236	964	205	88	85	15	5	6	2	68	6	211	10	1	18	9	.667	1	0	3.24
1991 Seattle	AL	27	27	2	0	174.2	744	182	82	74	16	2	8	2	56	2	143	14	1	8	8	.500	1	0	3.81
1992 Seattle	AL	31	30	6	0	186.2	809	209	110	100	14	8	9	7	57	1	112	6	0	8	17	.320	1	0	4.82
1993 Seattle	AL	31	30	7	0	215	898	215	91	83	17	10	4	5	60	6	163	8	0	11	12	.478	0	0	3.47
6 ML YEARS		145	143	21	0	967.1	4048	949	432	397	73	32	28	22	285	17	740	43	4	56	54	.509	3	0	3.69

Mike Harkey

Pitches: Right **Bats:** Right **Pos:** SP   **Ht:** 6' 5" **Wt:** 235 **Born:** 10/25/66 **Age:** 27

		HOW MUCH HE PITCHED						WHAT HE GAVE UP									THE RESULTS					
Year Team	Lg	G	GS	CG	GF	IP	BFP	H	R	ER	HR	SH	SF	HB	TBB	IBB	SO	WP	Bk	W	L	Pct.	ShO	Sv	ERA
1993 Orlando *	AA	1	1	0	0	5.1	21	4	1	1	0	0	0	0	2	0	5	0	0	0	0	.000	0	0	1.69
1988 Chicago	NL	5	5	0	0	34.2	155	33	14	10	0	5	0	2	15	3	18	2	1	0	3	.000	0	0	2.60
1990 Chicago	NL	27	27	2	0	173.2	728	153	71	63	14	5	4	7	59	8	94	8	1	12	6	.667	1	0	3.26
1991 Chicago	NL	4	4	0	0	18.2	84	21	11	11	3	0	1	0	6	1	15	1	0	0	2	.000	0	0	5.30
1992 Chicago	NL	7	7	0	0	38	159	34	13	8	4	1	2	1	15	0	21	3	1	4	0	1.000	0	0	1.89
1993 Chicago	NL	28	28	1	0	157.1	676	187	100	92	17	8	8	3	43	4	67	1	3	10	10	.500	0	0	5.26
5 ML YEARS		71	71	3	0	422.1	1802	428	209	184	38	19	15	13	138	16	215	15	6	26	21	.553	1	0	3.92

Pete Harnisch

Pitches: Right **Bats:** Right **Pos:** SP   **Ht:** 6' 0" **Wt:** 207 **Born:** 09/23/66 **Age:** 27

		HOW MUCH HE PITCHED						WHAT HE GAVE UP									THE RESULTS					
Year Team	Lg	G	GS	CG	GF	IP	BFP	H	R	ER	HR	SH	SF	HB	TBB	IBB	SO	WP	Bk	W	L	Pct.	ShO	Sv	ERA
1988 Baltimore	AL	2	2	0	0	13	61	13	8	8	1	2	0	0	9	1	10	1	0	0	2	.000	0	0	5.54
1989 Baltimore	AL	18	17	2	1	103.1	468	97	55	53	10	4	5	5	64	3	70	5	1	5	9	.357	0	0	4.62
1990 Baltimore	AL	31	31	3	0	188.2	821	189	96	91	17	6	5	1	86	5	122	2	2	11	11	.500	0	0	4.34
1991 Houston	NL	33	33	4	0	216.2	900	169	71	65	14	9	7	5	83	3	172	5	2	12	9	.571	2	0	2.70
1992 Houston	NL	34	34	0	0	206.2	859	182	92	85	18	5	5	5	64	3	164	4	1	9	10	.474	0	0	3.70
1993 Houston	NL	33	33	5	0	217.2	896	171	84	72	20	9	4	6	79	5	185	3	1	16	9	.640	4	0	2.98
6 ML YEARS		151	150	14	1	946	4005	821	406	374	80	35	26	22	385	20	723	20	7	53	50	.515	6	0	3.56

Brian Harper

Bats: Right **Throws:** Right **Pos:** C   **Ht:** 6' 2" **Wt:** 206 **Born:** 10/16/59 **Age:** 34

						BATTING												BASERUNNING				PERCENTAGES		
Year Team	Lg	G	AB	H	2B	3B	HR	(Hm | Rd)	TB	R	RBI	TBB	IBB	SO	HBP	SH	SF	SB	CS	SB%	GDP	Avg	OBP	SLG
1979 California	AL	1	2	0	0	0	0	(0 | 0)	0	0	0	0	0	1	0	0	0	0	0	.00	0	.000	.000	.000
1981 California	AL	4	11	3	0	0	0	(0 | 0)	3	1	1	0	0	0	0	0	1	1	0	1.00	0	.273	.250	.273
1982 Pittsburgh	NL	20	29	8	1	0	2	(0 | 2)	15	4	4	1	1	4	0	1	0	0	0	.00	0	.276	.300	.517
1983 Pittsburgh	NL	61	131	29	4	1	7	(5 | 2)	56	16	20	2	0	15	1	2	4	0	0	.00	3	.221	.232	.427
1984 Pittsburgh	NL	46	112	29	4	0	2	(1 | 1)	39	4	11	5	0	11	2	1	1	0	0	.00	4	.259	.300	.348
1985 St. Louis	NL	43	52	13	4	0	0	(0 | 0)	17	5	8	2	0	3	0	0	1	0	0	.00	2	.250	.273	.327
1986 Detroit	AL	19	36	5	1	0	0	(0 | 0)	6	2	3	3	0	3	0	0	1	0	0	.00	0	.139	.200	.167
1987 Oakland	AL	11	17	4	1	0	0	(0 | 0)	5	1	3	0	0	4	0	1	1	0	0	.00	1	.235	.222	.294
1988 Minnesota	AL	60	166	49	11	1	3	(0 | 3)	71	15	20	10	1	12	3	2	1	0	3	.00	12	.295	.344	.428
1989 Minnesota	AL	126	385	125	24	0	8	(4 | 4)	173	43	57	13	3	16	6	4	4	2	4	.33	11	.325	.353	.449

Year	Team	Lg	G	AB	H	2B	3B	HR	(Hm	Rd)	TB	R	RBI	TBB	IBB	SO	HBP	SH	SF	SB	CS	SB%	GDP	Avg	OBP	SLG
1990	Minnesota	AL	134	479	141	42	3	6	(1	5)	207	61	54	19	2	27	7	0	4	3	2	.60	20	.294	.328	.432
1991	Minnesota	AL	123	441	137	28	1	10	(4	6)	197	54	69	14	3	22	6	2	6	1	2	.33	14	.311	.336	.447
1992	Minnesota	AL	140	502	154	25	0	9	(3	6)	206	58	73	26	7	22	7	1	10	0	1	.00	15	.307	.343	.410
1993	Minnesota	AL	147	530	161	26	1	12	(6	6)	225	52	73	29	9	29	9	0	5	1	3	.25	15	.304	.347	.425
14 ML YEARS			935	2893	858	171	7	59	(24	35)	1220	316	396	124	26	169	41	15	39	8	15	.35	99	.297	.330	.422

Donald Harris

Bats: Right **Throws:** Right **Pos:** CF/RF   **Ht:** 6' 1" **Wt:** 185 **Born:** 11/12/67 **Age:** 26

									BATTING											BASERUNNING				PERCENTAGES		
Year	Team	Lg	G	AB	H	2B	3B	HR	(Hm	Rd)	TB	R	RBI	TBB	IBB	SO	HBP	SH	SF	SB	CS	SB%	GDP	Avg	OBP	SLG
1989	Butte	R	65	264	75	7	8	6	--	--	116	50	37	12	0	54	6	0	3	14	4	.78	6	.284	.326	.439
1990	Tulsa	AA	64	213	34	5	1	1	--	--	44	16	15	7	0	69	3	3	0	7	3	.70	0	.160	.197	.207
	Gastonia	A	58	221	46	10	0	3	--	--	65	27	13	14	0	63	2	4	0	15	8	.65	2	.208	.262	.294
1991	Tulsa	AA	130	450	102	17	8	11	--	--	168	47	53	26	1	118	7	7	2	9	6	.60	11	.227	.278	.373
1992	Tulsa	AA	83	303	77	15	2	11	--	--	129	39	39	9	1	85	7	3	1	4	3	.57	11	.254	.291	.426
1993	Okla City	AAA	96	367	93	13	9	6	--	--	142	48	40	23	0	89	4	4	5	4	4	.50	5	.253	.301	.387
1991	Texas	AL	18	8	3	0	0	1	(0	1)	6	4	2	1	0	3	0	0	0	1	0	1.00	0	.375	.444	.750
1992	Texas	AL	24	33	6	1	0	0	(0	0)	7	3	1	0	0	15	0	0	0	1	0	1.00	0	.182	.182	.212
1993	Texas	AL	40	76	15	2	0	1	(1	0)	20	10	8	5	0	18	1	3	1	0	1	.00	0	.197	.253	.263
3 ML YEARS			82	117	24	3	0	2	(1	1)	33	17	11	6	0	36	1	3	1	2	1	.67	0	.205	.248	.282

Gene Harris

Pitches: Right **Bats:** Right **Pos:** RP   **Ht:** 5'11" **Wt:** 190 **Born:** 12/05/64 **Age:** 29

			HOW MUCH HE PITCHED						WHAT HE GAVE UP										THE RESULTS					
Year	Team	Lg	G	GS	CG	GF	IP	BFP	H	R	ER	HR	SH	SF	HB	TBB	IBB	SO	WP	Bk	W	L	Pct.	ShO	Sv	ERA
1989	2 ML Teams		21	6	0	9	53.1	236	63	38	35	4	7	4	1	25	1	25	3	0	2	5	.286	0	1	5.91
1990	Seattle	AL	25	0	0	12	38	176	31	25	20	5	0	2	1	30	5	43	2	0	1	2	.333	0	0	4.74
1991	Seattle	AL	8	0	0	3	13.1	66	15	8	6	1	1	0	0	10	3	6	1	0	0	0	.000	0	1	4.05
1992	2 ML Teams		22	1	0	4	30.1	130	23	15	14	3	3	0	1	15	0	25	1	2	0	2	.000	0	0	4.15
1993	San Diego	NL	59	0	0	48	59.1	269	57	27	20	3	5	2	1	37	8	39	7	0	6	6	.500	0	23	3.03
1989	Montreal	NL	11	0	0	7	20	84	16	11	11	1	7	1	0	10	0	11	3	0	1	1	.500	0	0	4.95
	Seattle	AL	10	6	0	2	33.1	152	47	27	24	3	0	3	1	15	1	14	0	0	1	4	.200	0	1	6.48
1992	Seattle	AL	8	0	0	2	9	40	8	7	7	3	0	0	0	6	0	6	0	1	0	0	.000	0	0	7.00
	San Diego	NL	14	1	0	2	21.1	90	15	8	7	0	3	0	1	9	0	19	1	1	0	2	.000	0	0	2.95
5 ML YEARS			135	7	0	76	194.1	877	189	113	95	16	16	8	4	117	17	138	14	2	9	15	.375	0	25	4.40

Greg Harris

Pitches: Right **Bats:** Both **Pos:** RP   **Ht:** 6' 0" **Wt:** 175 **Born:** 11/02/55 **Age:** 38

			HOW MUCH HE PITCHED						WHAT HE GAVE UP										THE RESULTS					
Year	Team	Lg	G	GS	CG	GF	IP	BFP	H	R	ER	HR	SH	SF	HB	TBB	IBB	SO	WP	Bk	W	L	Pct.	ShO	Sv	ERA
1981	New York	NL	16	14	0	2	69	300	65	36	34	8	4	1	2	28	2	54	3	2	3	5	.375	0	1	4.43
1982	Cincinnati	NL	34	10	1	9	91.1	398	96	56	49	12	5	3	2	37	1	67	2	2	2	6	.250	0	1	4.83
1983	Cincinnati	NL	1	0	0	0	1	9	2	3	3	0	1	0	1	3	2	1	0	0	0	0	.000	0	0	27.00
1984	2 ML Teams		34	0	0	14	54.1	226	38	18	15	3	2	3	4	25	1	45	3	0	2	2	.500	0	3	2.48
1985	Texas	AL	58	0	0	35	113	450	74	35	31	7	3	2	5	43	3	111	2	1	5	4	.556	0	11	2.47
1986	Texas	AL	73	0	0	63	111.1	462	103	40	35	12	3	6	1	42	6	95	2	1	10	8	.556	0	20	2.83
1987	Texas	AL	42	19	0	14	140.2	629	157	92	76	18	7	3	4	56	3	106	4	2	5	10	.333	0	0	4.86
1988	Philadelphia	NL	66	1	0	19	107	446	80	34	28	7	6	2	4	52	14	71	8	2	4	6	.400	0	1	2.36
1989	2 ML Teams		59	0	0	24	103.1	442	85	46	38	8	4	3	2	58	9	76	12	0	4	4	.500	0	1	3.31
1990	Boston	AL	34	30	1	3	184.1	803	186	90	82	13	8	9	6	77	7	117	8	1	13	9	.591	0	0	4.00
1991	Boston	AL	53	21	1	15	173	731	157	79	74	13	4	8	5	69	5	127	6	1	11	12	.478	0	2	3.85
1992	Boston	AL	70	2	1	22	107.2	459	82	38	30	6	8	5	4	60	11	73	5	0	4	9	.308	0	4	2.51
1993	Boston	AL	80	0	0	24	112.1	494	95	55	47	7	10	4	10	60	14	103	8	1	6	7	.462	0	8	3.77
1984	Montreal	NL	15	0	0	4	17.2	68	10	4	4	0	1	0	2	7	1	15	0	0	0	1	.000	0	2	2.04
	San Diego	NL	19	0	0	10	36.2	158	28	14	11	3	1	3	2	18	0	30	3	0	2	1	.667	0	1	2.70
1989	Philadelphia	NL	44	0	0	17	75.1	324	64	34	30	7	3	2	2	43	7	51	10	0	2	2	.500	0	1	3.58
	Boston	AL	15	0	0	7	28	118	21	12	8	1	1	1	0	15	2	25	2	0	2	2	.500	0	0	2.57
13 ML YEARS			620	98	4	244	1368.1	5849	1220	622	542	114	65	49	50	610	78	1046	63	13	69	82	.457	0	52	3.56

Greg W. Harris

Pitches: Right **Bats:** Right **Pos:** SP   **Ht:** 6' 2" **Wt:** 195 **Born:** 12/01/63 **Age:** 30

			HOW MUCH HE PITCHED						WHAT HE GAVE UP										THE RESULTS					
Year	Team	Lg	G	GS	CG	GF	IP	BFP	H	R	ER	HR	SH	SF	HB	TBB	IBB	SO	WP	Bk	W	L	Pct.	ShO	Sv	ERA
1988	San Diego	NL	3	1	1	2	18	68	13	3	3	0	0	0	0	3	0	15	0	0	2	0	1.000	0	0	1.50
1989	San Diego	NL	56	8	0	25	135	554	106	43	39	8	5	2	2	52	9	106	3	3	8	9	.471	0	6	2.60
1990	San Diego	NL	73	0	0	33	117.1	488	92	35	30	6	9	7	4	49	13	97	2	3	8	8	.500	0	9	2.30
1991	San Diego	NL	20	20	3	0	133	537	116	42	33	16	9	2	1	27	6	95	2	0	9	5	.643	2	0	2.23
1992	San Diego	NL	20	20	1	0	118	496	113	62	54	13	8	3	2	35	2	66	2	1	4	8	.333	0	0	4.12
1993	2 ML Teams		35	35	4	0	225.1	975	239	127	115	33	14	4	7	69	9	123	6	6	11	17	.393	0	0	4.59

1993 San Diego	NL	22	22	4	0	152	639	151	65	62	18	8	2	3	39	6	83	2	3	10	9	.526	0	0	3.67
Colorado	NL	13	13	0	0	73.1	336	88	62	53	15	6	2	4	30	3	40	4	3	1	8	.111	0	0	6.50
6 ML YEARS		207	84	9	60	746.2	3118	679	312	274	76	45	18	16	235	39	502	15	13	42	47	.472	2	15	3.30

Lenny Harris

Bats: Left **Throws:** Right **Pos:** 2B/3B   **Ht:** 5'10" **Wt:** 204 **Born:** 10/28/64 **Age:** 29

								BATTING												BASERUNNING				PERCENTAGES		
Year Team	Lg	G	AB	H	2B	3B	HR	(Hm	Rd)	TB	R	RBI	TBB	IBB	SO	HBP	SH	SF	SB	CS	SB%	GDP	Avg	OBP	SLG
1988	NL	16	43	16	1	0	0	(0	0)	17	7	8	5	0	4	0	1	2	4	1	.80	0	.372	.420	.395
1989 2 ML Teams		115	335	79	10	1	3	(1	2)	100	36	26	20	0	33	2	1	0	14	9	.61	14	.236	.283	.299
1990 Los Angeles	NL	137	431	131	16	4	2	(0	2)	161	61	29	29	2	31	1	3	1	15	10	.60	8	.304	.348	.374
1991 Los Angeles	NL	145	429	123	16	1	3	(1	2)	150	59	38	37	5	32	5	12	2	12	3	.80	16	.287	.349	.350
1992 Los Angeles	NL	135	347	94	11	0	0	(0	0)	105	28	30	24	3	24	1	6	2	19	7	.73	10	.271	.318	.303
1993 Los Angeles	NL	107	160	38	6	1	2	(0	2)	52	20	11	15	4	15	0	1	0	3	1	.75	4	.238	.303	.325
1989 Cincinnati	NL	61	188	42	4	0	2	(0	2)	52	17	11	9	0	20	1	1	0	10	6	.63	5	.223	.263	.277
Los Angeles	NL	54	147	37	6	1	1	(1	0)	48	19	15	11	0	13	1	0	0	4	3	.57	9	.252	.308	.327
6 ML YEARS		655	1745	481	60	7	10	(2	8)	585	211	142	130	14	139	9	24	7	67	31	.68	52	.276	.328	.335

Mike Hartley

Pitches: Right **Bats:** Right **Pos:** RP   **Ht:** 6' 1" **Wt:** 195 **Born:** 08/31/61 **Age:** 32

			HOW MUCH HE PITCHED							WHAT HE GAVE UP											THE RESULTS				
Year Team	Lg	G	GS	CG	GF	IP	BFP	H	R	ER	HR	SH	SF	HB	TBB	IBB	SO	WP	Bk	W	L	Pct.	ShO	Sv	ERA
1989 Los Angeles	NL	5	0	0	3	6	20	2	1	1	0	0	0	0	4	0	0	0	0	0	1	.000	0	1	1.50
1990 Los Angeles	NL	32	6	1	8	79.1	325	58	32	26	7	2	1	2	30	2	76	3	0	6	3	.667	1	1	2.95
1991 2 ML Teams		58	0	0	16	83.1	368	74	40	39	11	2	1	6	47	8	63	10	2	4	1	.800	0	2	4.21
1992 Philadelphia	NL	46	0	0	15	55	243	54	23	21	5	5	1	2	23	6	53	4	0	7	6	.538	0	3	3.44
1993 Minnesota	AL	53	0	0	21	81	359	86	38	36	4	4	6	7	36	3	57	8	0	1	2	.333	0	1	4.00
1991 Los Angeles	NL	40	0	0	11	57	258	53	29	28	7	1	1	3	37	7	44	8	1	2	0	1.000	0	1	4.42
Philadelphia	NL	18	0	0	5	26.1	110	21	11	11	4	1	0	3	10	1	19	2	1	2	1	.667	0	1	3.76
5 ML YEARS		194	6	1	63	304.2	1315	274	134	123	27	13	9	17	136	19	253	25	2	18	13	.581	1	4	3.63

Bryan Harvey

Pitches: Right **Bats:** Right **Pos:** RP   **Ht:** 6' 2" **Wt:** 212 **Born:** 06/02/63 **Age:** 31

			HOW MUCH HE PITCHED							WHAT HE GAVE UP											THE RESULTS				
Year Team	Lg	G	GS	CG	GF	IP	BFP	H	R	ER	HR	SH	SF	HB	TBB	IBB	SO	WP	Bk	W	L	Pct.	ShO	Sv	ERA
1987 California	AL	3	0	0	2	5	22	6	0	0	0	0	0	0	2	0	3	3	0	0	0	.000	0	0	0.00
1988 California	AL	50	0	0	38	76	303	59	22	18	4	3	3	1	20	6	67	4	1	7	5	.583	0	17	2.13
1989 California	AL	51	0	0	42	55	245	36	21	21	6	5	2	0	41	1	78	5	0	3	3	.500	0	25	3.44
1990 California	AL	54	0	0	47	64.1	267	45	24	23	4	4	4	0	35	6	82	7	1	4	4	.500	0	25	3.22
1991 California	AL	67	0	0	63	78.2	309	51	20	14	6	3	2	1	17	3	101	2	2	2	4	.333	0	46	1.60
1992 California	AL	25	0	0	22	28.2	122	22	12	9	4	2	3	0	11	1	34	4	0	0	4	.000	0	13	2.83
1993 Florida	NL	59	0	0	54	69	264	45	14	13	4	3	6	0	13	2	73	0	1	1	5	.167	0	45	1.70
7 ML YEARS		309	0	0	268	376.2	1532	264	113	98	28	20	20	2	139	19	438	25	5	17	25	.405	0	171	2.34

Bill Haselman

Bats: Right **Throws:** Right **Pos:** C   **Ht:** 6' 3" **Wt:** 215 **Born:** 05/25/66 **Age:** 28

								BATTING												BASERUNNING				PERCENTAGES		
Year Team	Lg	G	AB	H	2B	3B	HR	(Hm	Rd)	TB	R	RBI	TBB	IBB	SO	HBP	SH	SF	SB	CS	SB%	GDP	Avg	OBP	SLG
1987 Gastonia	A	61	235	72	13	1	8	--	--	111	35	33	19	0	46	1	0	1	1	2	.33	3	.306	.359	.472
1988 Charlotte	A	122	453	111	17	2	10	--	--	162	56	54	45	3	99	3	1	2	8	5	.62	10	.245	.316	.358
1989 Tulsa	AA	107	352	95	17	2	7	--	--	137	38	36	40	0	88	3	1	2	5	10	.33	7	.270	.348	.389
1990 Tulsa	AA	120	430	137	38	2	18	--	--	233	68	80	43	1	96	6	3	3	3	7	.30	11	.319	.386	.542
1991 Okla City	AAA	126	442	113	22	2	9	--	--	166	57	59	61	1	89	1	1	4	10	6	.63	14	.256	.344	.376
1992 Okla City	AAA	17	58	14	5	0	1	--	--	22	8	9	13	0	12	0	0	0	1	0	1.00	2	.241	.380	.379
Calgary	AAA	88	302	77	14	2	19	--	--	152	49	53	41	4	89	2	1	3	3	3	.50	9	.255	.345	.503
1990 Texas	AL	7	13	2	0	0	0	(0	0)	2	0	3	1	0	5	0	0	0	0	0	.00	0	.154	.214	.154
1992 Seattle	AL	8	19	5	0	0	0	(0	0)	5	1	0	0	0	7	0	0	0	0	0	.00	1	.263	.263	.263
1993 Seattle	AL	58	137	35	8	0	5	(3	2)	58	21	16	12	0	19	1	2	2	2	1	.67	5	.255	.316	.423
3 ML YEARS		73	169	42	8	0	5	(3	2)	65	22	19	13	0	31	1	2	2	2	1	.67	6	.249	.303	.385

Billy Hatcher

Bats: Right **Throws:** Right **Pos:** CF   **Ht:** 5'10" **Wt:** 190 **Born:** 10/04/60 **Age:** 33

								BATTING												BASERUNNING				PERCENTAGES		
Year Team	Lg	G	AB	H	2B	3B	HR	(Hm	Rd)	TB	R	RBI	TBB	IBB	SO	HBP	SH	SF	SB	CS	SB%	GDP	Avg	OBP	SLG
1984 Chicago	NL	8	9	1	0	0	0	(0	0)	1	1	0	1	1	0	0	0	0	2	0	1.00	0	.111	.200	.111
1985 Chicago	NL	53	163	40	12	1	2	(2	0)	60	24	10	8	0	12	3	2	2	2	4	.33	9	.245	.290	.368
1986 Houston	NL	127	419	108	15	4	6	(2	4)	149	55	36	22	1	52	5	6	1	38	14	.73	3	.258	.302	.356

Year	Team	Lg	G	AB	H	2B	3B	HR	(Hm	Rd)	TB	R	RBI	TBB	IBB	SO	HBP	SH	SF	SB	CS	SB%	GDP	Avg	OBP	SLG
1987	Houston	NL	141	564	167	28	3	11	(3	8)	234	96	63	42	1	70	9	7	5	53	9	.85	11	.296	.352	.415
1988	Houston	NL	145	530	142	25	4	7	(3	4)	196	79	52	37	4	56	8	8	8	32	13	.71	6	.268	.321	.370
1989	2 ML Teams		135	481	111	19	3	4	(0	4)	148	59	51	30	2	62	2	3	4	24	7	.77	4	.231	.277	.308
1990	Cincinnati	NL	139	504	139	28	5	5	(2	3)	192	68	25	33	5	42	6	1	1	30	10	.75	4	.276	.327	.381
1991	Cincinnati	NL	138	442	116	25	3	4	(2	2)	159	45	41	26	4	55	7	4	3	11	9	.55	9	.262	.312	.360
1992	2 ML Teams		118	409	102	19	2	3	(1	2)	134	47	33	22	1	52	3	6	4	4	8	.33	11	.249	.290	.328
1993	Boston	AL	136	508	146	24	3	9	(5	4)	203	71	57	28	4	46	11	11	4	14	7	.67	14	.287	.336	.400
1989	Houston	NL	108	395	90	15	3	3	(0	3)	120	49	44	30	2	53	1	3	4	22	6	.79	3	.228	.281	.304
	Pittsburgh	NL	27	86	21	4	0	1	(0	1)	28	10	7	0	0	9	1	0	0	2	1	.67	1	.244	.253	.326
1992	Cincinnati	NL	43	94	27	3	0	2	(0	2)	36	10	10	5	0	11	0	0	3	0	2	.00	2	.287	.314	.383
	Boston	AL	75	315	75	16	2	1	(1	0)	98	37	23	17	1	41	3	6	1	4	6	.40	9	.238	.283	.311
	10 ML YEARS		1140	4029	1072	195	28	51	(20	31)	1476	545	368	249	23	447	54	48	32	210	81	.72	71	.266	.315	.366

Hilly Hathaway

Pitches: Left **Bats:** Left **Pos:** SP **Ht:** 6' 4" **Wt:** 195 **Born:** 09/12/69 **Age:** 24

			HOW MUCH HE PITCHED					WHAT HE GAVE UP											THE RESULTS					
Year	Team	Lg	G	GS	CG	GF	IP	BFP	H	R	ER	HR	SH	SF	HB	TBB	IBB	SO	WP	Bk	W	L	Pct.	ShO	Sv	ERA
1990	Boise	A	15	15	0	0	86.1	337	57	18	14	1	1	3	2	25	0	113	7	5	8	2	.800	0	0	1.46
1991	Quad City	A	20	20	1	0	129	545	126	58	48	5	4	1	7	41	1	110	11	3	9	6	.600	0	0	3.35
1992	Palm Sprngs	A	3	3	2	0	24	98	25	5	4	1	0	0	0	3	0	17	0	0	2	1	.667	1	0	1.50
	Midland	AA	14	14	1	0	95.1	378	90	39	34	2	1	1	8	10	0	69	2	2	7	2	.778	0	0	3.21
1993	Vancouver	AAA	12	12	0	0	70.1	291	60	38	32	5	1	2	2	27	0	44	4	1	7	0	1.000	0	0	4.09
1992	California	AL	2	1	0	0	5.2	29	8	5	5	1	1	1	0	3	0	1	0	0	0	0	.000	0	0	7.94
1993	California	AL	11	11	0	0	57.1	253	71	35	32	6	1	3	5	26	1	11	5	1	4	3	.571	0	0	5.02
	2 ML YEARS		13	12	0	0	63	282	79	40	37	7	2	4	5	29	1	12	5	1	4	3	.571	0	0	5.29

Charlie Hayes

Bats: Right **Throws:** Right **Pos:** 3B **Ht:** 6' 0" **Wt:** 205 **Born:** 05/29/65 **Age:** 29

						BATTING													BASERUNNING			PERCENTAGES		
Year	Team	Lg	G	AB	H	2B	3B	HR	(Hm | Rd)	TB	R	RBI	TBB	IBB	SO	HBP	SH	SF	SB	CS	SB%	GDP	Avg	OBP	SLG
1988	San Francisco	NL	7	11	1	0	0	0	(0 | 0)	1	0	0	0	0	3	0	0	0	0	0	.00	0	.091	.091	.091
1989	2 ML Teams		87	304	78	15	1	8	(3 | 5)	119	26	43	11	1	50	0	2	3	3	1	.75	6	.257	.280	.391
1990	Philadelphia	NL	152	561	145	20	0	10	(3 | 7)	195	56	57	28	3	91	2	0	6	4	4	.50	12	.258	.293	.348
1991	Philadelphia	NL	142	460	106	23	1	12	(6 | 6)	167	34	53	16	3	75	1	2	1	3	3	.50	13	.230	.257	.363
1992	New York	AL	142	509	131	19	2	18	(7 | 11)	208	52	66	28	0	100	3	3	6	3	5	.38	12	.257	.297	.409
1993	Colorado	NL	157	573	175	45	2	25	(17 | 8)	299	89	98	43	6	82	5	1	8	11	6	.65	25	.305	.355	.522
1989	San Francisco	NL	3	5	1	0	0	0	(0 | 0)	1	0	0	0	0	1	0	0	0	0	0	.00	0	.200	.200	.200
	Philadelphia	NL	84	299	77	15	1	8	(3 | 5)	118	26	43	11	1	49	0	2	3	3	1	.75	6	.258	.281	.395
	6 ML YEARS		687	2418	636	122	6	73	(36 | 37)	989	257	317	126	13	401	11	8	24	24	19	.56	68	.263	.300	.409

Neal Heaton

Pitches: Left **Bats:** Left **Pos:** RP **Ht:** 6' 0" **Wt:** 200 **Born:** 03/03/60 **Age:** 34

			HOW MUCH HE PITCHED					WHAT HE GAVE UP											THE RESULTS					
Year	Team	Lg	G	GS	CG	GF	IP	BFP	H	R	ER	HR	SH	SF	HB	TBB	IBB	SO	WP	Bk	W	L	Pct.	ShO	Sv	ERA
1982	Cleveland	AL	8	4	0	0	31	142	32	21	18	1	1	2	0	16	0	14	4	0	0	2	.000	0	0	5.23
1983	Cleveland	AL	39	16	4	19	149.1	637	157	79	69	11	3	5	1	44	10	75	1	0	11	7	.611	3	7	4.16
1984	Cleveland	AL	38	34	4	2	198.2	880	231	128	115	21	6	10	0	75	5	75	3	1	12	15	.444	1	0	5.21
1985	Cleveland	AL	36	33	5	2	207.2	921	244	119	103	19	7	8	7	80	2	82	2	2	9	17	.346	1	0	4.90
1986	2 ML Teams		33	29	5	2	198.2	850	201	102	90	26	6	5	2	81	8	90	4	0	7	15	.318	0	1	4.08
1987	Montreal	NL	32	32	3	0	193.1	807	207	103	97	25	5	5	3	37	3	105	2	5	13	10	.565	1	0	4.52
1988	Montreal	NL	32	11	0	7	97.1	415	98	54	54	14	5	3	3	43	5	43	1	5	3	10	.231	0	2	4.99
1989	Pittsburgh	NL	42	18	1	5	147.1	620	127	55	50	12	12	3	6	55	12	67	4	5	6	7	.462	0	0	3.05
1990	Pittsburgh	NL	30	24	0	2	146	599	143	66	56	17	10	6	2	38	1	68	4	1	12	9	.571	0	0	3.45
1991	Pittsburgh	NL	42	1	0	5	68.2	293	72	37	33	6	3	3	4	21	2	34	0	1	3	3	.500	0	0	4.33
1992	2 ML Teams		32	0	0	9	42	189	43	21	19	5	2	3	1	23	2	31	3	1	3	1	.750	0	0	4.07
1993	New York	AL	18	0	0	9	27	128	34	19	18	6	0	1	3	11	1	15	2	1	1	0	1.000	0	0	6.00
1986	Cleveland	AL	12	12	2	0	74.1	324	73	42	35	8	2	0	1	34	4	24	2	0	3	6	.333	0	0	4.24
	Minnesota		21	17	3	2	124.1	526	128	60	55	18	4	5	1	47	4	66	2	0	4	9	.308	0	1	3.98
1992	Kansas City	AL	31	0	0	8	41	185	43	21	19	5	2	3	1	22	2	29	3	1	3	1	.750	0	0	4.17
	Milwaukee	AL	1	0	0	1	1	4	0	0	0	0	0	0	0	2	0	2	0	0	0	0	.000	0	0	0.00
	12 ML YEARS		382	202	22	62	1507	6481	1589	804	732	163	60	54	32	524	51	699	30	21	80	96	.455	6	10	4.37

Eric Helfand

Bats: Left **Throws:** Right **Pos:** C **Ht:** 6' 0" **Wt:** 195 **Born:** 03/25/69 **Age:** 25

						BATTING													BASERUNNING			PERCENTAGES		
Year	Team	Lg	G	AB	H	2B	3B	HR	(Hm | Rd)	TB	R	RBI	TBB	IBB	SO	HBP	SH	SF	SB	CS	SB%	GDP	Avg	OBP	SLG
1990	Sou Oregon	A	57	207	59	12	0	2	(-- | --)	77	29	39	20	1	49	7	0	1	0	0	1.00	3	.285	.366	.372
1991	Modesto	A	67	242	62	15	1	7	(-- | --)	100	35	38	37	2	56	2	2	2	0	1	.00	6	.256	.357	.413

Year	Team	Lg	G	AB	H	2B	3B	HR	(Hm	Rd)	TB	R	RBI	TBB	IBB	SO	HBP	SH	SF	SB	CS	SB%	GDP	Avg	OBP	SLG
1992	Modesto	A	72	249	72	15	0	10	--	--	117	40	44	47	4	46	6	1	3	0	1	.00	5	.289	.410	.470
	Huntsville	AA	37	114	26	7	0	2	--	--	39	13	9	5	0	32	1	0	0	0	0	.00	4	.228	.267	.342
1993	Huntsville	AA	100	302	69	15	2	10	--	--	118	38	48	43	2	78	8	3	7	1	1	.50	5	.228	.333	.391
1993	Oakland	AL	8	13	3	0	0	0	(0	0)	3	1	1	0	0	1	0	0	0	0	0	.00	0	.231	.231	.231

Scott Hemond

Bats: Right **Throws:** Right **Pos:** C **Ht:** 6' 0" **Wt:** 205 **Born:** 11/18/65 **Age:** 28

Year	Team	Lg	G	AB	H	2B	3B	HR	(Hm	Rd)	TB	R	RBI	TBB	IBB	SO	HBP	SH	SF	SB	CS	SB%	GDP	Avg	OBP	SLG
1989	Oakland	AL	4	0	0	0	0	0	(0	0)	0	2	0	0	0	0	0	0	0	0	0	.00	0	.000	.000	.000
1990	Oakland	AL	7	13	2	0	0	0	(0	0)	2	1	0	0	0	5	0	0	0	0	0	.00	0	.154	.154	.154
1991	Oakland	AL	23	23	5	0	0	0	(0	0)	5	4	0	1	0	7	0	0	0	1	2	.33	0	.217	.250	.217
1992	2 ML Teams		25	40	9	2	0	0	(0	0)	11	8	2	4	0	13	0	0	1	1	0	1.00	2	.225	.289	.275
1993	Oakland	AL	91	215	55	16	0	6	(3	3)	89	31	26	32	0	55	1	6	1	14	5	.74	2	.256	.353	.414
1992	Oakland	AL	17	27	6	1	0	0	(0	0)	7	7	1	3	0	7	0	0	0	1	0	1.00	2	.222	.300	.259
	Chicago	AL	8	13	3	1	0	0	(0	0)	4	1	1	1	0	6	0	0	1	0	0	.00	0	.231	.267	.308
	5 ML YEARS		150	291	71	18	0	6	(3	3)	107	45	29	37	0	80	1	6	2	16	7	.70	4	.244	.329	.368

Dave Henderson

Bats: Right **Throws:** Right **Pos:** CF/RF/DH **Ht:** 6' 2" **Wt:** 220 **Born:** 07/21/58 **Age:** 35

Year	Team	Lg	G	AB	H	2B	3B	HR	(Hm	Rd)	TB	R	RBI	TBB	IBB	SO	HBP	SH	SF	SB	CS	SB%	GDP	Avg	OBP	SLG
1993	Tacoma *	AAA	3	11	2	1	0	0	--	--	3	1	2	0	0	2	0	0	0	0	0	.00	0	.182	.167	.273
1981	Seattle	AL	59	126	21	3	0	6	(5	1)	42	17	13	16	1	24	1	1	1	2	1	.67	4	.167	.264	.333
1982	Seattle	AL	104	324	82	17	1	14	(8	6)	143	47	48	36	2	67	0	1	1	2	5	.29	5	.253	.327	.441
1983	Seattle	AL	137	484	130	24	5	17	(9	8)	215	50	55	28	3	93	1	2	6	9	3	.75	5	.269	.306	.444
1984	Seattle	AL	112	350	98	23	0	14	(8	6)	163	42	43	19	0	56	2	2	1	5	5	.50	4	.280	.320	.466
1985	Seattle	AL	139	502	121	28	2	14	(8	6)	195	70	68	48	2	104	3	1	2	6	1	.86	11	.241	.310	.388
1986	2 ML Teams		139	388	103	22	4	15	(10	5)	178	59	47	39	4	110	2	2	1	2	3	.40	6	.265	.335	.459
1987	2 ML Teams		90	205	48	12	0	8	(4	4)	84	32	26	30	0	53	0	1	2	3	1	.75	3	.234	.329	.410
1988	Oakland	AL	146	507	154	38	1	24	(12	12)	266	100	94	47	1	92	4	5	7	2	4	.33	14	.304	.363	.525
1989	Oakland	AL	152	579	145	24	3	15	(10	5)	220	77	80	54	1	131	3	1	6	8	5	.62	13	.250	.315	.380
1990	Oakland	AL	127	450	122	28	0	20	(11	9)	210	65	63	40	1	105	1	1	2	3	1	.75	5	.271	.331	.467
1991	Oakland	AL	150	572	158	33	0	25	(15	10)	266	86	85	58	3	113	4	1	2	6	6	.50	9	.276	.346	.465
1992	Oakland	AL	20	63	9	1	0	0	(0	0)	10	1	2	2	0	16	0	0	0	0	0	.00	0	.143	.169	.159
1993	Oakland	AL	107	382	84	19	0	20	(7	13)	163	37	53	32	0	113	0	0	8	0	3	.00	1	.220	.275	.427
1986	Seattle	AL	103	337	93	19	4	14	(10	4)	162	51	44	37	4	95	2	1	1	1	3	.25	5	.276	.350	.481
	Boston	AL	36	51	10	3	0	1	(0	1)	16	8	3	2	0	15	0	1	0	1	0	1.00	1	.196	.226	.314
1987	Boston	AL	75	184	43	10	0	8	(4	4)	77	30	25	22	0	48	0	1	2	1	1	.50	3	.234	.313	.418
	San Francisco	NL	15	21	5	2	0	0	(0	0)	7	2	1	8	0	5	0	0	0	2	0	1.00	0	.238	.448	.333
	13 ML YEARS		1482	4932	1275	272	16	192	(107	85)	2155	683	677	449	18	1077	21	18	39	48	38	.56	80	.259	.321	.437

Rickey Henderson

Bats: Right **Throws:** Left **Pos:** LF/DH **Ht:** 5'10" **Wt:** 190 **Born:** 12/25/58 **Age:** 35

Year	Team	Lg	G	AB	H	2B	3B	HR	(Hm	Rd)	TB	R	RBI	TBB	IBB	SO	HBP	SH	SF	SB	CS	SB%	GDP	Avg	OBP	SLG
1979	Oakland	AL	89	351	96	13	3	1	(1	0)	118	49	26	34	0	39	2	8	3	33	11	.75	4	.274	.338	.336
1980	Oakland	AL	158	591	179	22	4	9	(3	6)	236	111	53	117	7	54	5	6	3	100	26	.79	6	.303	.420	.399
1981	Oakland	AL	108	423	135	18	7	6	(5	1)	185	89	35	64	4	68	2	0	4	56	22	.72	7	.319	.408	.437
1982	Oakland	AL	149	536	143	24	4	10	(5	5)	205	119	51	116	1	94	2	0	2	130	42	.76	5	.267	.398	.382
1983	Oakland	AL	145	513	150	25	7	9	(5	4)	216	105	48	103	8	80	4	1	1	108	19	.85	11	.292	.414	.421
1984	Oakland	AL	142	502	147	27	4	16	(7	9)	230	113	58	86	1	81	5	1	3	66	18	.79	7	.293	.399	.458
1985	New York	AL	143	547	172	28	5	24	(8	16)	282	146	72	99	1	65	3	0	5	80	10	.89	8	.314	.419	.516
1986	New York	AL	153	608	160	31	5	28	(13	15)	285	130	74	89	2	81	2	0	2	87	18	.83	12	.263	.358	.469
1987	New York	AL	95	358	104	17	3	17	(10	7)	178	78	37	80	1	52	2	0	0	41	8	.84	10	.291	.423	.497
1988	New York	AL	140	554	169	30	2	6	(2	4)	221	118	50	82	1	54	3	2	6	93	13	.88	6	.305	.394	.399
1989	2 ML Teams		150	541	148	26	3	12	(7	5)	216	113	57	126	5	68	3	0	4	77	14	.85	8	.274	.411	.399
1990	Oakland	AL	136	489	159	33	3	28	(8	20)	282	119	61	97	2	60	4	2	2	65	10	.87	13	.325	.439	.577
1991	Oakland	AL	134	470	126	17	1	18	(8	10)	199	105	57	98	7	73	7	0	3	58	18	.76	7	.268	.400	.423
1992	Oakland	AL	117	396	112	18	3	15	(10	5)	181	77	46	95	5	56	6	0	3	48	11	.81	5	.283	.426	.457
1993	2 ML Teams		134	481	139	22	2	21	(10	11)	228	114	59	120	7	65	4	1	4	53	8	.87	9	.289	.432	.474
1989	New York	AL	65	235	58	13	1	3	(1	2)	82	41	22	56	0	29	1	0	1	25	8	.76	0	.247	.392	.349
	Oakland	AL	85	306	90	13	2	9	(6	3)	134	72	35	70	5	39	2	0	3	52	6	.90	8	.294	.425	.438
1993	Oakland	AL	90	318	104	19	1	17	(8	9)	176	77	47	85	6	46	2	0	2	31	6	.84	8	.327	.469	.553
	Toronto	AL	44	163	35	3	1	4	(2	2)	52	37	12	35	1	19	2	1	2	22	2	.92	1	.215	.356	.319
	15 ML YEARS		1993	7360	2139	351	56	220	(102	118)	3262	1586	784	1406	52	990	54	21	45	1095	248	.82	118	.291	.406	.443

Tom Henke

Pitches: Right **Bats:** Right **Pos:** RP **Ht:** 6' 5" **Wt:** 225 **Born:** 12/21/57 **Age:** 36

Year	Team	Lg	G	GS	CG	GF	IP	BFP	H	R	ER	HR	SH	SF	HB	TBB	IBB	SO	WP	Bk	W	L	Pct.	ShO	Sv	ERA
1982	Texas	AL	8	0	0	6	15.2	67	14	2	2	0	1	0	1	8	2	9	0	0	1	0	1.000	0	0	1.15
1983	Texas	AL	8	0	0	5	16	65	16	6	6	1	0	0	0	4	0	17	0	0	1	0	1.000	0	1	3.38
1984	Texas	AL	25	0	0	13	28.1	141	36	21	20	0	1	4	1	20	2	25	2	2	1	1	.500	0	2	6.35
1985	Toronto	AL	28	0	0	22	40	153	29	12	9	4	2	2	0	8	2	42	0	0	3	3	.500	0	13	2.03
1986	Toronto	AL	63	0	0	51	91.1	370	63	39	34	6	2	6	1	32	4	118	3	1	9	5	.643	0	27	3.35
1987	Toronto	AL	72	0	0	62	94	363	62	27	26	10	3	5	0	25	3	128	5	0	0	6	.000	0	34	2.49
1988	Toronto	AL	52	0	0	44	68	285	60	23	22	6	4	2	2	24	3	66	0	0	4	4	.500	0	25	2.91
1989	Toronto	AL	64	0	0	56	89	356	66	20	19	5	4	3	2	25	4	116	2	0	8	3	.727	0	20	1.92
1990	Toronto	AL	61	0	0	58	74.2	297	58	18	18	8	4	1	1	19	2	75	6	0	2	4	.333	0	32	2.17
1991	Toronto	AL	49	0	0	43	50.1	190	33	13	13	4	0	0	0	11	2	53	1	0	0	2	.000	0	32	2.32
1992	Toronto	AL	57	0	0	50	55.2	228	40	19	14	5	0	3	0	22	2	46	4	0	3	2	.600	0	34	2.26
1993	Texas	AL	66	0	0	60	74.1	302	55	25	24	7	3	3	1	27	3	79	3	0	5	5	.500	0	40	2.91
	12 ML YEARS		553	0	0	470	697.1	2817	532	225	207	56	24	29	9	225	29	774	26	3	37	35	.514	0	260	2.67

Mike Henneman

Pitches: Right **Bats:** Right **Pos:** RP **Ht:** 6' 4" **Wt:** 205 **Born:** 12/11/61 **Age:** 32

Year	Team	Lg	G	GS	CG	GF	IP	BFP	H	R	ER	HR	SH	SF	HB	TBB	IBB	SO	WP	Bk	W	L	Pct.	ShO	Sv	ERA
1987	Detroit	AL	55	0	0	28	96.2	399	86	36	32	8	2	3	3	30	5	75	7	0	11	3	.786	0	7	2.98
1988	Detroit	AL	65	0	0	51	91.1	364	72	23	19	7	5	2	2	24	10	58	8	1	9	6	.600	0	22	1.87
1989	Detroit	AL	60	0	0	35	90	401	84	46	37	4	7	3	5	51	15	69	0	1	11	4	.733	0	8	3.70
1990	Detroit	AL	69	0	0	53	94.1	399	90	36	32	4	5	2	3	33	12	50	3	0	8	6	.571	0	22	3.05
1991	Detroit	AL	60	0	0	50	84.1	358	81	29	27	2	5	5	0	34	8	61	5	0	10	2	.833	0	21	2.88
1992	Detroit	AL	60	0	0	53	77.1	321	75	36	34	6	3	5	0	20	10	58	7	0	2	6	.250	0	24	3.96
1993	Detroit	AL	63	0	0	50	71.2	316	69	28	21	4	5	2	2	32	8	58	4	0	5	3	.625	0	24	2.64
	7 ML YEARS		432	0	0	320	605.2	2558	557	234	202	35	32	21	15	224	68	429	34	2	56	30	.651	0	128	3.00

Butch Henry

Pitches: Left **Bats:** Left **Pos:** SP/RP **Ht:** 6' 1" **Wt:** 195 **Born:** 10/07/68 **Age:** 25

Year	Team	Lg	G	GS	CG	GF	IP	BFP	H	R	ER	HR	SH	SF	HB	TBB	IBB	SO	WP	Bk	W	L	Pct.	ShO	Sv	ERA
1987	Billings	R	9	5	0	2	35	151	37	21	18	3	0	1	1	12	1	38	4	1	4	0	1.000	0	1	4.63
1988	Cedar Rapds	A	27	27	1	0	187	745	144	59	47	14	7	4	6	56	2	163	6	8	16	2	.889	1	0	2.26
1989	Chattanooga	AA	7	7	0	0	26.1	110	22	12	10	2	1	1	0	12	1	19	2	0	1	3	.250	0	0	3.42
1990	Chattanooga	AA	24	22	2	0	143	622	151	74	67	15	9	5	3	58	0	95	12	2	8	8	.500	0	0	4.22
1991	Tucson	AAA	27	27	2	0	153.2	671	192	92	82	10	8	5	1	42	2	97	5	4	10	11	.476	0	0	4.80
1993	Ottawa	AAA	5	5	1	0	31.1	125	34	15	13	2	0	1	0	1	0	25	0	0	3	1	.750	0	0	3.73
1992	Houston	NL	28	28	2	0	165.2	710	185	81	74	16	12	7	1	41	7	96	2	2	6	9	.400	1	0	4.02
1993	2 ML Teams		30	16	1	4	103	467	135	76	70	15	6	6	1	28	2	47	1	0	3	9	.250	0	0	6.12
1993	Colorado	NL	20	15	1	1	84.2	390	117	66	62	14	6	5	1	24	2	39	1	0	2	8	.200	0	0	6.59
	Montreal	NL	10	1	0	3	18.1	77	18	10	8	1	0	1	0	4	0	8	0	0	1	1	.500	0	0	3.93
	2 ML YEARS		58	44	3	4	268.2	1177	320	157	144	31	18	13	2	69	9	143	3	2	9	18	.333	1	0	4.82

Doug Henry

Pitches: Right **Bats:** Right **Pos:** RP **Ht:** 6' 4" **Wt:** 185 **Born:** 12/10/63 **Age:** 30

Year	Team	Lg	G	GS	CG	GF	IP	BFP	H	R	ER	HR	SH	SF	HB	TBB	IBB	SO	WP	Bk	W	L	Pct.	ShO	Sv	ERA
1991	Milwaukee	AL	32	0	0	25	36	137	16	4	4	1	1	2	0	14	1	28	0	0	2	1	.667	0	15	1.00
1992	Milwaukee	AL	68	0	0	56	65	277	64	34	29	6	1	2	0	24	4	52	0	0	1	4	.200	0	29	4.02
1993	Milwaukee	AL	54	0	0	41	55	260	67	37	34	7	5	4	3	25	8	38	4	0	4	4	.500	0	17	5.56
	3 ML YEARS		154	0	0	122	156	674	147	75	67	14	7	8	3	63	13	118	8	0	7	9	.438	0	61	3.87

Dwayne Henry

Pitches: Right **Bats:** Right **Pos:** RP **Ht:** 6' 3" **Wt:** 230 **Born:** 02/16/62 **Age:** 32

Year	Team	Lg	G	GS	CG	GF	IP	BFP	H	R	ER	HR	SH	SF	HB	TBB	IBB	SO	WP	Bk	W	L	Pct.	ShO	Sv	ERA
1984	Texas	AL	3	0	0	1	4.1	25	5	4	4	0	1	0	0	7	0	2	0	0	0	1	.000	0	0	8.31
1985	Texas	AL	16	0	0	10	21	86	16	7	6	0	2	1	0	7	0	20	1	0	2	2	.500	0	3	2.57
1986	Texas	AL	19	0	0	4	19.1	93	14	11	10	1	1	2	1	22	0	17	7	1	1	0	1.000	0	4	4.66
1987	Texas	AL	5	0	0	1	10	60	12	10	10	2	0	0	0	9	0	7	1	0	0	0	.000	0	0	9.00
1988	Texas	AL	11	0	0	5	10.1	59	15	10	10	1	0	1	3	9	1	10	3	1	0	1	.000	0	1	8.71
1989	Atlanta	NL	12	0	0	6	12.2	55	12	6	6	2	2	0	0	5	1	16	1	0	0	2	.000	0	1	4.26

Year Team	Lg	G	GS	CG	GF	IP	BFP	H	R	ER	HR	SH	SF	HB	TBB	IBB	SO	WP	Bk	W	L	Pct.	ShO	Sv	ERA
1990 Atlanta	NL	34	0	0	14	38.1	176	41	26	24	3	0	1	0	25	0	34	2	1	2	2	.500	0	0	5.63
1991 Houston	NL	52	0	0	25	67.2	282	51	25	24	7	6	2	2	39	7	51	5	0	3	2	.600	0	2	3.19
1992 Cincinnati	NL	60	0	0	11	83.2	352	59	31	31	4	7	3	1	44	6	72	12	0	3	3	.500	0	0	3.33
1993 2 ML Teams		34	1	0	16	58.2	275	62	48	42	6	3	4	2	39	5	37	8	0	2	2	.500	0	2	6.44
1993 Cincinnati	NL	3	0	0	1	4.2	26	6	8	2	0	0	0	0	4	1	2	1	0	0	1	.000	0	0	3.86
Seattle	AL	31	1	0	15	54	249	56	40	40	6	3	4	2	35	4	35	7	0	2	1	.667	0	2	6.67
10 ML YEARS		246	1	0	93	326	1453	287	178	167	26	22	14	9	206	20	266	40	3	13	15	.464	0	9	4.61

Pat Hentgen

Pitches: Right **Bats:** Right **Pos:** SP   **Ht:** 6' 2" **Wt:** 200 **Born:** 11/13/68 **Age:** 25

		HOW MUCH HE PITCHED						WHAT HE GAVE UP												THE RESULTS					
Year Team	Lg	G	GS	CG	GF	IP	BFP	H	R	ER	HR	SH	SF	HB	TBB	IBB	SO	WP	Bk	W	L	Pct.	ShO	Sv	ERA
1991 Toronto	AL	3	1	0	1	7.1	30	5	2	2	1	1	0	2	3	0	3	1	0	0	0	.000	0	0	2.45
1992 Toronto	AL	28	2	0	10	50.1	229	49	30	30	7	2	2	0	32	5	39	2	1	5	2	.714	0	0	5.36
1993 Toronto	AL	34	32	3	0	216.1	926	215	103	93	27	6	5	7	74	5	122	11	1	19	9	.679	0	0	3.87
3 ML YEARS		65	35	3	11	274	1185	269	135	125	35	9	7	9	109	5	164	14	2	24	11	.686	0	0	4.11

Gil Heredia

Pitches: Right **Bats:** Right **Pos:** RP/SP   **Ht:** 6' 1" **Wt:** 190 **Born:** 10/26/65 **Age:** 28

		HOW MUCH HE PITCHED						WHAT HE GAVE UP												THE RESULTS					
Year Team	Lg	G	GS	CG	GF	IP	BFP	H	R	ER	HR	SH	SF	HB	TBB	IBB	SO	WP	Bk	W	L	Pct.	ShO	Sv	ERA
1993 Ottawa *	AAA	16	16	1	0	102.2	429	97	46	34	7	4	0	3	26	2	66	6	0	8	4	.667	0	0	2.98
1991 San Francisco	NL	7	4	0	1	33	126	27	14	14	4	2	1	0	7	2	13	1	0	0	2	.000	0	0	3.82
1992 2 ML Teams		20	5	0	4	44.2	187	44	23	21	4	2	1	1	20	1	22	1	0	2	3	.400	0	0	4.23
1993 Montreal	NL	20	9	1	2	57.1	246	66	28	25	4	4	1	2	14	2	40	0	0	4	2	.667	0	2	3.92
1992 San Francisco	NL	13	4	0	3	30	132	32	20	18	3	0	0	1	16	1	15	1	0	2	3	.400	0	0	5.40
Montreal	NL	7	1	0	1	14.2	55	12	3	3	1	2	1	0	4	0	7	0	0	0	0	.000	0	0	1.84
3 ML YEARS		47	18	1	7	135	559	137	65	60	12	8	3	3	41	5	75	2	0	6	7	.462	0	2	4.00

Carlos Hernandez

Bats: Right **Throws:** Right **Pos:** C   **Ht:** 5'11" **Wt:** 208 **Born:** 05/24/67 **Age:** 27

		BATTING																BASERUNNING				PERCENTAGES		
Year Team	Lg	G	AB	H	2B	3B	HR	(Hm	Rd)	TB	R	RBI	TBB	IBB	SO	HBP	SH	SF	SB	CS	SB%	GDP	Avg	OBP	SLG
1990 Los Angeles	NL	10	20	4	1	0	0	(0	0)	5	2	1	0	0	2	0	0	0	0	0	.00	0	.200	.200	.250
1991 Los Angeles	NL	15	14	3	1	0	0	(0	0)	4	1	1	0	0	5	1	0	1	1	0	1.00	2	.214	.250	.286
1992 Los Angeles	NL	69	173	45	4	0	3	(1	2)	58	11	17	11	1	21	4	0	2	0	1	.00	8	.260	.316	.335
1993 Los Angeles	NL	50	99	25	5	0	2	(1	1)	36	6	7	2	0	11	0	1	0	0	0	.00	0	.253	.267	.364
4 ML YEARS		144	306	77	11	0	5	(2	3)	103	20	26	13	1	39	5	1	3	1	1	.50	10	.252	.291	.337

Cesar Hernandez

Bats: Right **Throws:** Right **Pos:** LF   **Ht:** 6' 0" **Wt:** 170 **Born:** 09/28/66 **Age:** 27

		BATTING																BASERUNNING				PERCENTAGES		
Year Team	Lg	G	AB	H	2B	3B	HR	(Hm	Rd)	TB	R	RBI	TBB	IBB	SO	HBP	SH	SF	SB	CS	SB%	GDP	Avg	OBP	SLG
1986 Burlington	A	38	104	26	11	0	1	--	--	40	12	12	7	0	24	4	1	2	7	0	1.00	2	.250	.316	.385
1987 Wst Plm Bch	A	32	106	25	3	1	2	--	--	36	14	6	4	0	29	1	0	1	6	1	.86	1	.236	.268	.340
1988 Rockford	A	117	411	101	20	4	19	--	--	186	71	60	25	1	109	4	1	1	28	8	.78	11	.246	.295	.453
1989 Wst Plm Bch	A	42	158	45	8	3	1	--	--	62	16	15	8	1	32	5	1	2	16	4	.80	2	.285	.335	.392
Jacksnville	AA	81	222	47	9	1	3	--	--	67	25	13	22	2	60	0	1	0	11	4	.73	3	.212	.283	.302
1990 Jacksnville	AA	118	393	94	21	7	10	--	--	159	58	50	18	3	75	7	1	6	16	11	.59	4	.239	.281	.405
1991 Harrisburg	AA	128	418	106	16	2	13	--	--	165	58	52	25	2	106	8	1	6	34	8	.81	7	.254	.304	.395
1992 Nashville	AAA	1	2	2	0	0	0	--	--	2	0	0	0	0	0	0	0	0	1	0	1.000	0	1.000	1.000	1.000
Chattanooga	AA	93	328	91	24	4	3	--	--	132	50	27	19	1	65	4	2	0	12	9	.57	5	.277	.325	.402
1993 Indianapols	AAA	84	272	70	12	4	5	--	--	105	30	22	9	0	63	3	1	2	5	7	.42	2	.257	.287	.386
1992 Cincinnati	NL	34	51	14	4	0	0	(0	0)	18	6	4	0	0	10	0	0	0	3	1	.75	1	.275	.275	.353
1993 Cincinnati	NL	27	24	2	0	0	0	(0	0)	2	3	1	1	0	8	0	1	0	1	2	.33	0	.083	.120	.083
2 ML YEARS		61	75	16	4	0	0	(0	0)	20	9	5	1	0	18	0	1	0	4	3	.57	1	.213	.224	.267

Jeremy Hernandez

Pitches: Right **Bats:** Right **Pos:** RP   **Ht:** 6' 6" **Wt:** 195 **Born:** 07/07/66 **Age:** 27

		HOW MUCH HE PITCHED						WHAT HE GAVE UP												THE RESULTS					
Year Team	Lg	G	GS	CG	GF	IP	BFP	H	R	ER	HR	SH	SF	HB	TBB	IBB	SO	WP	Bk	W	L	Pct.	ShO	Sv	ERA
1991 San Diego	NL	9	0	0	7	14.1	56	8	1	0	0	0	0	0	5	0	9	2	0	0	0	.000	0	2	0.00
1992 San Diego	NL	26	0	0	11	36.2	157	39	17	17	4	6	5	1	11	5	25	0	0	1	4	.200	0	1	4.17
1993 2 ML Teams		70	0	0	31	111.2	467	116	52	45	14	4	6	0	34	7	70	2	2	6	7	.462	0	8	3.63
1993 San Diego	NL	21	0	0	9	34.1	146	41	19	18	2	2	1	0	7	1	26	0	2	0	2	.000	0	0	4.72
Cleveland	AL	49	0	0	22	77.1	321	75	33	27	12	2	5	0	27	6	44	2	0	6	5	.545	0	8	3.14
3 ML YEARS		105	0	0	49	162.2	680	163	70	62	18	10	11	1	50	12	104	4	2	7	11	.389	0	11	3.43

94

Roberto Hernandez

Pitches: Right **Bats:** Right **Pos:** RP **Ht:** 6' 4" **Wt:** 235 **Born:** 11/11/64 **Age:** 29

		HOW MUCH HE PITCHED					WHAT HE GAVE UP								THE RESULTS				
Year	Team	Lg	G	GS	CG	GF	IP	BFP	H	R	ER	HR	SH	SF	HB	TBB	IBB	SO	WP	Bk	W	L	Pct.	ShO	Sv	ERA
1991	Chicago	AL	9	3	0	1	15	69	18	15	13	1	0	0	0	7	0	6	1	0	1	0	1.000	0	0	7.80
1992	Chicago	AL	43	0	0	27	71	277	45	15	13	4	0	3	4	20	1	68	2	0	7	3	.700	0	12	1.65
1993	Chicago	AL	70	0	0	67	78.2	314	66	21	20	6	2	2	0	20	1	71	2	0	3	4	.429	0	38	2.29
	3 ML YEARS		122	3	0	95	164.2	660	129	51	46	11	2	5	4	47	2	145	5	0	11	7	.611	0	50	2.51

Xavier Hernandez

Pitches: Right **Bats:** Left **Pos:** RP **Ht:** 6' 2" **Wt:** 185 **Born:** 08/16/65 **Age:** 28

		HOW MUCH HE PITCHED					WHAT HE GAVE UP								THE RESULTS				
Year	Team	Lg	G	GS	CG	GF	IP	BFP	H	R	ER	HR	SH	SF	HB	TBB	IBB	SO	WP	Bk	W	L	Pct.	ShO	Sv	ERA
1989	Toronto	AL	7	0	0	2	22.2	101	25	15	12	2	2	1	2	8	0	7	1	0	1	0	1.000	0	0	4.76
1990	Houston	NL	34	1	0	10	62.1	268	60	34	32	8	2	4	4	24	5	24	6	0	2	1	.667	0	0	4.62
1991	Houston	NL	32	6	0	8	63	285	66	34	33	6	1	1	0	32	7	55	0	0	2	7	.222	0	3	4.71
1992	Houston	NL	77	0	0	25	111	454	81	31	26	5	3	2	3	42	7	96	5	0	9	1	.900	0	7	2.11
1993	Houston	NL	72	0	0	29	96.2	389	75	37	28	6	3	3	1	28	3	101	6	0	4	5	.444	0	9	2.61
	5 ML YEARS		222	7	0	74	355.2	1497	307	151	131	27	9	12	9	134	22	283	18	0	18	14	.563	0	19	3.31

Orel Hershiser

Pitches: Right **Bats:** Right **Pos:** SP **Ht:** 6' 3" **Wt:** 198 **Born:** 09/16/58 **Age:** 35

		HOW MUCH HE PITCHED					WHAT HE GAVE UP								THE RESULTS				
Year	Team	Lg	G	GS	CG	GF	IP	BFP	H	R	ER	HR	SH	SF	HB	TBB	IBB	SO	WP	Bk	W	L	Pct.	ShO	Sv	ERA
1983	Los Angeles	NL	8	0	0	4	8	37	7	6	3	1	1	0	0	6	0	5	1	0	0	0	.000	0	1	3.38
1984	Los Angeles	NL	45	20	8	10	189.2	771	160	65	56	9	2	3	4	50	8	150	8	1	11	8	.579	4	2	2.66
1985	Los Angeles	NL	36	34	9	1	239.2	953	179	72	54	8	5	4	6	68	5	157	5	0	19	3	.864	5	0	2.03
1986	Los Angeles	NL	35	35	8	0	231.1	988	213	112	99	13	14	6	5	86	11	153	12	3	14	14	.500	1	0	3.85
1987	Los Angeles	NL	37	35	10	2	264.2	1093	247	105	90	17	8	2	9	74	5	190	11	2	16	16	.500	1	1	3.06
1988	Los Angeles	NL	35	34	15	1	267	1068	208	73	67	18	9	6	4	73	10	178	6	5	23	8	.742	8	1	2.26
1989	Los Angeles	NL	35	33	8	0	256.2	1047	226	75	66	9	19	6	3	77	14	178	8	4	15	15	.500	4	0	2.31
1990	Los Angeles	NL	4	4	0	0	25.1	106	26	12	12	1	1	0	1	4	0	16	0	1	1	1	.500	0	0	4.26
1991	Los Angeles	NL	21	21	0	0	112	473	112	43	43	3	2	1	5	32	6	73	2	4	7	2	.778	0	0	3.46
1992	Los Angeles	NL	33	33	1	0	210.2	910	209	101	86	15	15	6	8	69	13	130	10	0	10	15	.400	0	0	3.67
1993	Los Angeles	NL	33	33	5	0	215.2	913	201	106	86	17	12	4	7	72	13	141	7	0	12	14	.462	1	0	3.59
	11 ML YEARS		322	282	64	18	2020.2	8359	1788	770	662	111	88	38	52	611	85	1371	70	20	128	96	.571	24	5	2.95

Joe Hesketh

Pitches: Left **Bats:** Left **Pos:** RP/SP **Ht:** 6' 2" **Wt:** 173 **Born:** 02/15/59 **Age:** 35

		HOW MUCH HE PITCHED					WHAT HE GAVE UP								THE RESULTS				
Year	Team	Lg	G	GS	CG	GF	IP	BFP	H	R	ER	HR	SH	SF	HB	TBB	IBB	SO	WP	Bk	W	L	Pct.	ShO	Sv	ERA
1984	Montreal	NL	11	5	1	2	45	182	38	12	9	2	2	2	0	15	3	32	1	3	2	2	.500	1	1	1.80
1985	Montreal	NL	25	25	2	0	155.1	618	125	52	43	10	8	2	2	45	2	113	3	3	10	5	.667	1	0	2.49
1986	Montreal	NL	15	15	0	0	82.2	362	92	46	46	11	2	2	2	31	4	67	4	3	6	5	.545	0	0	5.01
1987	Montreal	NL	18	0	0	3	28.2	128	23	12	10	2	2	0	2	15	3	31	1	0	0	0	.000	0	1	3.14
1988	Montreal	NL	60	0	0	23	72.2	304	63	30	23	1	5	4	0	35	9	64	5	1	4	3	.571	0	9	2.85
1989	Montreal	NL	43	0	0	17	48.1	219	54	34	31	5	6	2	0	26	6	44	1	3	6	4	.600	0	3	5.77
1990	3 ML Teams		45	2	0	19	59.2	269	69	35	30	7	0	1	1	25	2	50	8	0	1	6	.143	0	5	4.53
1991	Boston	AL	39	17	0	5	153.1	631	142	59	56	19	7	3	0	53	3	104	8	0	12	4	.750	0	0	3.29
1992	Boston	AL	30	25	1	1	148.2	659	162	84	72	15	5	6	2	58	9	104	6	0	8	9	.471	0	1	4.36
1993	Boston	AL	28	5	0	8	53.1	246	62	35	30	4	4	2	0	29	4	34	4	2	3	4	.429	0	1	5.06
1990	Montreal	NL	2	0	0	0	3	12	2	0	0	0	0	0	0	2	1	3	0	0	1	0	1.000	0	0	0.00
	Atlanta	NL	31	0	0	15	31	135	30	23	20	5	0	1	1	12	0	21	5	0	0	2	.000	0	5	5.81
	Boston	AL	12	2	0	4	25.2	122	37	12	10	2	0	0	0	11	1	26	3	0	0	4	.000	0	0	3.51
	10 ML YEARS		314	94	4	78	847.2	3618	830	399	350	76	41	24	7	332	45	643	41	15	52	42	.553	2	21	3.72

Phil Hiatt

Bats: Right **Throws:** Right **Pos:** 3B **Ht:** 6' 3" **Wt:** 200 **Born:** 05/01/69 **Age:** 25

								BATTING												BASERUNNING				PERCENTAGES		
Year	Team	Lg	G	AB	H	2B	3B	HR	(Hm	Rd)	TB	R	RBI	TBB	IBB	SO	HBP	SH	SF	SB	CS	SB%	GDP	Avg	OBP	SLG
1990	Eugene	A	73	289	85	18	5	2	--	--	119	33	44	17	1	69	1	1	4	15	4	.79	1	.294	.331	.412
1991	Baseball Cy	A	81	315	94	21	6	5	--	--	142	41	33	22	4	70	3	1	2	28	14	.67	4	.298	.348	.451
	Memphis	AA	56	206	47	7	1	6	--	--	74	29	33	9	1	63	3	0	6	6	1	.86	3	.228	.263	.359
1992	Memphis	AA	129	487	119	20	5	27	--	--	230	71	83	25	1	157	5	1	3	5	10	.33	11	.244	.287	.472
	Omaha	AAA	5	14	3	0	0	2	--	--	9	3	4	2	0	3	0	0	0	1	0	1.00	0	.214	.313	.643
1993	Omaha	AAA	12	51	12	2	0	3	--	--	23	8	10	4	0	20	1	0	0	0	0	.00	0	.235	.304	.451
1993	Kansas City	AL	81	238	52	12	1	7	(4	3)	87	30	36	16	0	82	7	0	2	6	3	.67	8	.218	.285	.366

Greg Hibbard

Pitches: Left   **Bats:** Left   **Pos:** SP   **Ht:** 6' 0" **Wt:** 185 **Born:** 09/13/64 **Age:** 29

		HOW MUCH HE PITCHED						WHAT HE GAVE UP												THE RESULTS					
Year Team	Lg	G	GS	CG	GF	IP	BFP	H	R	ER	HR	SH	SF	HB	TBB	IBB	SO	WP	Bk	W	L	Pct.	ShO	Sv	ERA
1989 Chicago	AL	23	23	2	0	137.1	581	142	58	49	5	5	4	2	41	0	55	4	0	6	7	.462	0	0	3.21
1990 Chicago	AL	33	33	3	0	211	871	202	80	74	11	8	10	6	55	2	92	2	1	14	9	.609	1	0	3.16
1991 Chicago	AL	32	29	5	1	194	806	196	107	93	23	8	2	2	57	1	71	1	0	11	11	.500	0	0	4.31
1992 Chicago	AL	31	28	0	2	176	755	187	92	86	17	10	6	7	57	2	69	1	1	10	7	.588	0	1	4.40
1993 Chicago	NL	31	31	1	0	191	800	209	96	84	19	9	10	3	47	9	82	1	2	15	11	.577	0	0	3.96
5 ML YEARS		150	144	11	3	909.1	3813	936	433	386	75	40	32	20	257	14	369	9	4	56	45	.554	1	1	3.82

Bryan Hickerson

Pitches: Left   **Bats:** Left   **Pos:** RP/SP   **Ht:** 6' 2" **Wt:** 203 **Born:** 10/13/63 **Age:** 30

		HOW MUCH HE PITCHED						WHAT HE GAVE UP												THE RESULTS					
Year Team	Lg	G	GS	CG	GF	IP	BFP	H	R	ER	HR	SH	SF	HB	TBB	IBB	SO	WP	Bk	W	L	Pct.	ShO	Sv	ERA
1991 San Francisco	NL	17	6	0	4	50	212	53	20	20	3	2	0	0	17	3	43	2	0	2	2	.500	0	0	3.60
1992 San Francisco	NL	61	1	0	8	87.1	345	74	31	30	7	4	5	1	21	2	68	4	1	5	3	.625	0	0	3.09
1993 San Francisco	NL	47	15	0	5	120.1	525	137	58	57	14	11	4	1	39	3	69	4	0	7	5	.583	0	0	4.26
3 ML YEARS		125	22	0	17	257.2	1082	264	109	107	24	17	9	2	77	8	180	10	1	14	10	.583	0	0	3.74

Kevin Higgins

Bats: Left   **Throws:** Right   **Pos:** C   **Ht:** 5'11" **Wt:** 170 **Born:** 01/22/67 **Age:** 27

		BATTING																	BASERUNNING				PERCENTAGES		
Year Team	Lg	G	AB	H	2B	3B	HR	(Hm	Rd)	TB	R	RBI	TBB	IBB	SO	HBP	SH	SF	SB	CS	SB%	GDP	Avg	OBP	SLG
1989 Spokane	A	71	295	98	9	3	2	--	--	119	54	52	30	1	13	5	1	9	2	4	.33	8	.332	.392	.403
1990 Las Vegas	AAA	9	26	7	1	1	0	--	--	10	4	3	4	0	3	1	0	1	0	0	.00	1	.269	.375	.385
Riverside	A	49	176	53	5	1	2	--	--	66	27	18	27	3	15	2	2	1	0	1	.00	6	.301	.398	.375
Wichita	AA	52	187	67	7	1	1	--	--	79	24	23	16	3	8	1	1	4	5	0	1.00	6	.358	.404	.422
1991 Las Vegas	AAA	130	403	116	12	4	3	--	--	145	53	45	47	5	38	2	10	3	3	2	.60	13	.288	.363	.360
1992 Las Vegas	AAA	124	355	90	12	3	0	--	--	108	49	40	41	2	31	3	5	7	6	4	.60	10	.254	.330	.304
1993 Las Vegas	AAA	40	142	51	8	0	1	--	--	62	22	22	18	1	8	0	1	1	1	1	.50	3	.359	.429	.437
1993 San Diego	NL	71	181	40	4	1	0	(0	0)	46	17	13	16	0	17	3	1	1	0	1	.00	6	.221	.294	.254

Teddy Higuera

Pitches: Left   **Bats:** Both   **Pos:** SP   **Ht:** 5'10" **Wt:** 178 **Born:** 11/09/58 **Age:** 35

		HOW MUCH HE PITCHED						WHAT HE GAVE UP												THE RESULTS					
Year Team	Lg	G	GS	CG	GF	IP	BFP	H	R	ER	HR	SH	SF	HB	TBB	IBB	SO	WP	Bk	W	L	Pct.	ShO	Sv	ERA
1993 New Orleans *	AAA	1	1	0	0	8	42	11	11	8	1	0	2	0	7	0	7	1	1	0	1	.000	0	0	9.00
1985 Milwaukee	AL	32	30	7	2	212.1	874	186	105	92	22	5	10	3	63	0	127	4	3	15	8	.652	2	0	3.90
1986 Milwaukee	AL	34	34	15	0	248.1	1031	226	84	77	26	7	11	3	74	5	207	3	0	20	11	.645	4	0	2.79
1987 Milwaukee	AL	35	35	14	0	261.2	1084	236	120	112	24	6	9	2	87	2	240	4	2	18	10	.643	3	0	3.85
1988 Milwaukee	AL	31	31	8	0	227.1	895	168	66	62	15	10	7	6	59	4	192	0	6	16	9	.640	1	0	2.45
1989 Milwaukee	AL	22	22	2	0	135.1	567	125	56	52	9	6	5	4	48	2	91	0	1	9	6	.600	1	0	3.46
1990 Milwaukee	AL	27	27	4	0	170	720	167	80	71	16	10	4	3	50	2	129	2	1	11	10	.524	1	0	3.76
1991 Milwaukee	AL	7	6	0	1	36.1	153	37	18	18	2	0	1	1	10	0	33	0	0	3	2	.600	0	0	4.46
1993 Milwaukee	AL	8	8	0	0	30	148	43	24	24	4	1	1	1	16	2	27	0	3	1	3	.250	0	0	7.20
8 ML YEARS		196	193	50	3	1321.1	5472	1188	553	508	118	45	48	23	407	17	1046	13	16	93	59	.612	12	0	3.46

Glenallen Hill

Bats: Right   **Throws:** Right   **Pos:** RF/LF/DH   **Ht:** 6' 2" **Wt:** 210 **Born:** 03/22/65 **Age:** 29

		BATTING																	BASERUNNING				PERCENTAGES		
Year Team	Lg	G	AB	H	2B	3B	HR	(Hm	Rd)	TB	R	RBI	TBB	IBB	SO	HBP	SH	SF	SB	CS	SB%	GDP	Avg	OBP	SLG
1989 Toronto	AL	19	52	15	0	0	1	(1	0)	18	4	7	3	0	12	0	0	0	2	1	.67	0	.288	.327	.346
1990 Toronto	AL	84	260	60	11	3	12	(7	5)	113	47	32	18	0	62	0	0	0	8	3	.73	5	.231	.281	.435
1991 2 ML Teams		72	221	57	8	2	8	(3	5)	93	29	25	23	0	54	0	1	3	6	4	.60	7	.258	.324	.421
1992 Cleveland	AL	102	369	89	16	1	18	(7	11)	161	38	49	20	0	73	4	0	1	9	6	.60	11	.241	.287	.436
1993 2 ML Teams		97	261	69	14	2	15	(5	10)	132	33	47	17	1	71	1	1	4	8	3	.73	4	.264	.307	.506
1991 Toronto	AL	35	99	25	5	2	3	(2	1)	43	14	11	7	0	24	0	0	2	2	2	.50	2	.253	.296	.434
Cleveland	AL	37	122	32	3	0	5	(1	4)	50	15	14	16	0	30	0	1	1	4	2	.67	5	.262	.345	.410
1993 Cleveland	AL	66	174	39	7	2	5	(0	5)	65	19	25	11	1	50	1	0	3	7	3	.70	3	.224	.268	.374
Chicago	NL	31	87	30	7	0	10	(5	5)	67	14	22	6	0	21	0	0	0	1	0	1.00	1	.345	.387	.770
5 ML YEARS		374	1163	290	49	8	54	(23	31)	517	151	160	81	2	272	5	2	8	33	17	.66	27	.249	.299	.445

Ken Hill

Pitches: Right **Bats:** Right **Pos:** SP 　　　　**Ht:** 6' 2" **Wt:** 195 **Born:** 12/14/65 **Age:** 28

Year Team	Lg	G	GS	CG	GF	IP	BFP	H	R	ER	HR	SH	SF	HB	TBB	IBB	SO	WP	Bk	W	L	Pct.	ShO	Sv	ERA
1993 Ottawa *	AAA	1	1	0	0	4	13	1	0	0	0	0	0	0	1	0	0	0	0	0	0	.000	0	0	0.00
1988 St. Louis	NL	4	1	0	0	14	62	16	9	8	0	0	0	0	6	0	6	1	0	0	1	.000	0	0	5.14
1989 St. Louis	NL	33	33	2	0	196.2	862	186	92	83	9	14	5	5	99	6	112	11	2	7	15	.318	1	0	3.80
1990 St. Louis	NL	17	14	1	1	78.2	343	79	49	48	7	5	5	1	33	1	58	5	0	5	6	.455	0	0	5.49
1991 St. Louis	NL	30	30	0	0	181.1	743	147	76	72	15	7	7	6	67	4	121	7	1	11	10	.524	0	0	3.57
1992 Montreal	NL	33	33	3	0	218	908	187	76	65	13	15	3	3	75	4	150	11	4	16	9	.640	3	0	2.68
1993 Montreal	NL	28	28	2	0	183.2	780	163	84	66	7	9	7	6	74	7	90	6	2	9	7	.563	0	0	3.23
6 ML YEARS		145	139	8	1	872.1	3698	778	386	342	51	50	27	21	354	22	537	41	9	48	48	.500	4	0	3.53

Milt Hill

Pitches: Right **Bats:** Right **Pos:** RP 　　　　**Ht:** 6' 0" **Wt:** 180 **Born:** 08/22/65 **Age:** 28

Year Team	Lg	G	GS	CG	GF	IP	BFP	H	R	ER	HR	SH	SF	HB	TBB	IBB	SO	WP	Bk	W	L	Pct.	ShO	Sv	ERA
1993 Indianapolis *	AAA	20	5	0	9	53	227	53	27	24	1	5	0	3	17	4	45	3	0	3	5	.375	0	2	4.08
1991 Cincinnati	NL	22	0	0	8	33.1	137	36	14	14	1	4	3	0	8	2	20	1	0	1	1	.500	0	0	3.78
1992 Cincinnati	NL	14	0	0	5	20	80	15	9	7	1	2	1	1	5	2	10	0	0	0	0	.000	0	1	3.15
1993 Cincinnati	NL	19	0	0	2	28.2	125	34	18	18	5	0	3	0	9	1	23	1	0	3	0	1.000	0	0	5.65
3 ML YEARS		55	0	0	15	82	342	85	41	39	7	6	7	1	22	5	53	2	0	4	1	.800	0	1	4.28

Shawn Hillegas

Pitches: Right **Bats:** Right **Pos:** SP/RP 　　　　**Ht:** 6' 2" **Wt:** 223 **Born:** 08/21/64 **Age:** 29

Year Team	Lg	G	GS	CG	GF	IP	BFP	H	R	ER	HR	SH	SF	HB	TBB	IBB	SO	WP	Bk	W	L	Pct.	ShO	Sv	ERA
1993 Tacoma *	AAA	9	9	0	0	47.2	217	62	31	29	4	1	3	1	13	0	29	0	0	2	3	.400	0	0	5.48
1987 Los Angeles	NL	12	10	0	1	58	252	52	27	23	5	4	1	0	31	0	51	4	0	4	3	.571	0	0	3.57
1988 2 ML Teams		17	16	0	0	96.2	405	84	42	40	9	1	4	4	35	1	56	3	0	6	6	.500	0	0	3.72
1989 Chicago	AL	50	13	0	12	119.2	533	132	67	63	12	4	2	3	51	4	76	4	1	7	11	.389	0	3	4.74
1990 Chicago	AL	7	0	0	3	11.1	42	4	1	1	0	1	1	0	5	1	5	2	0	0	0	.000	0	0	0.79
1991 Cleveland	AL	51	3	0	31	83	359	67	42	40	7	4	7	2	46	7	66	5	0	3	4	.429	0	7	4.34
1992 2 ML Teams		26	9	1	6	86	385	104	57	50	13	2	3	0	37	2	49	2	0	1	8	.111	1	0	5.23
1993 Oakland	AL	18	11	0	4	60.2	288	78	48	47	8	3	2	4	33	1	29	1	0	3	6	.333	0	0	6.97
1988 Los Angeles	NL	11	10	0	0	56.2	239	54	26	26	5	1	2	3	17	1	30	3	0	3	4	.429	0	0	4.13
Chicago	AL	6	6	0	0	40	166	30	16	14	4	0	2	1	18	0	26	0	0	3	2	.600	0	0	3.15
1992 New York	AL	21	9	1	4	78.1	351	96	52	48	12	1	3	0	33	1	46	2	0	1	8	.111	1	0	5.51
Oakland	AL	5	0	0	2	7.2	34	8	5	2	1	1	0	0	4	1	3	0	0	0	0	.000	0	0	2.35
7 ML YEARS		181	62	1	57	515.1	2265	521	284	264	54	19	20	13	238	16	332	21	1	24	38	.387	1	10	4.61

Eric Hillman

Pitches: Left **Bats:** Left **Pos:** SP/RP 　　　　**Ht:** 6'10" **Wt:** 225 **Born:** 04/27/66 **Age:** 28

Year Team	Lg	G	GS	CG	GF	IP	BFP	H	R	ER	HR	SH	SF	HB	TBB	IBB	SO	WP	Bk	W	L	Pct.	ShO	Sv	ERA
1987 Little Fls	A	13	13	2	0	79	346	84	44	37	4	2	5	3	30	2	80	8	1	6	4	.600	1	0	4.22
1988 Columbia	A	17	13	0	4	73	320	54	45	32	2	2	2	6	43	0	60	5	3	1	6	.143	0	1	3.95
1989 Columbia	A	9	7	0	2	33.2	151	28	17	7	1	1	2	4	21	0	33	1	0	2	1	.667	0	1	1.87
St.Lucie	A	19	14	1	1	88.1	404	96	59	54	3	3	2	3	53	0	67	15	1	6	6	.500	0	0	5.50
1990 St. Lucie	A	4	3	0	0	27	99	15	2	2	0	1	0	1	8	0	23	3	0	2	0	1.000	0	0	0.67
Jackson	AA	15	15	0	0	89.1	386	93	42	39	2	1	1	4	30	1	61	7	2	6	5	.545	0	0	3.93
1991 Tidewater	AAA	27	27	2	0	161.2	710	184	89	72	9	15	6	10	58	0	91	12	3	5	12	.294	0	0	4.01
1992 Tidewater	AAA	34	9	0	7	91.1	380	93	39	37	6	2	4	2	27	1	49	6	2	9	2	.818	0	0	3.65
1993 Norfolk	AAA	10	9	3	1	61	238	52	18	15	2	2	2	2	12	1	27	2	0	6	2	.750	1	0	2.21
1992 New York	NL	11	8	0	2	52.1	227	67	31	31	9	3	1	2	10	2	16	1	0	2	2	.500	0	0	5.33
1993 New York	NL	27	22	3	1	145	627	173	83	64	12	10	10	4	24	2	60	0	1	2	9	.182	1	0	3.97
2 ML YEARS		38	30	3	3	197.1	854	240	114	95	21	13	11	6	34	4	76	1	1	4	11	.267	1	0	4.33

Sterling Hitchcock

Pitches: Left **Bats:** Left **Pos:** SP 　　　　**Ht:** 6' 1" **Wt:** 195 **Born:** 04/29/71 **Age:** 23

Year Team	Lg	G	GS	CG	GF	IP	BFP	H	R	ER	HR	SH	SF	HB	TBB	IBB	SO	WP	Bk	W	L	Pct.	ShO	Sv	ERA
1989 Yankees	R	13	13	0	0	76.2	299	48	16	14	1	3	1	4	27	0	98	5	0	9	1	.900	0	0	1.64
1990 Greensboro	A	27	27	6	0	173.1	694	122	68	56	7	5	2	8	60	1	171	6	2	12	12	.500	5	0	2.91
1991 Pr William	A	19	19	2	0	119.1	500	111	49	35	2	3	4	3	26	0	101	5	2	7	7	.500	0	0	2.64
1992 Albany	AA	24	24	2	0	146.2	600	116	51	42	6	3	1	9	42	0	155	9	2	6	9	.400	0	0	2.58
1993 Oneonta	A	1	0	0	0	1	3	0	0	0	0	0	0	0	0	0	0	1	0	0	0	.000	0	0	0.00
Columbus	AAA	16	16	0	0	76.2	334	80	43	41	8	0	0	6	28	0	85	1	0	3	5	.375	0	0	4.81

Year	Team	Lg	G	GS	CG	GF	IP	BFP	H	R	ER	HR	SH	SF	HB	TBB	IBB	SO	WP	Bk	W	L	Pct.	ShO	Sv	ERA
1992	New York	AL	3	3	0	0	13	68	23	12	12	2	0	0	1	6	0	6	0	0	0	2	.000	0	0	8.31
1993	New York	AL	6	6	0	0	31	135	32	18	16	4	0	2	1	14	1	26	3	2	1	2	.333	0	0	4.65
	2 ML YEARS		9	9	0	0	44	203	55	30	28	6	0	2	2	20	1	32	3	2	1	4	.200	0	0	5.73

Denny Hocking

Bats: Both   Throws: Right   Pos: SS **Ht: 5'10"   Wt: 155   Born: 04/02/70   Age: 24**

								BATTING													BASERUNNING				PERCENTAGES		
Year	Team	Lg	G	AB	H	2B	3B	HR	(Hm	Rd)	TB	R	RBI	TBB	IBB	SO	HBP	SH	SF	SB	CS	SB%	GDP	Avg	OBP	SLG
1990	Elizabethtn	R	54	201	59	6	2	6	--	--	87	45	30	40	1	25	6	1	2	13	4	.76	6	.294	.422	.433
1991	Kenosha	A	125	432	110	17	8	2	--	--	149	72	36	69	4	69	6	3	4	22	10	.69	6	.255	.372	.345
1992	Visalia	A	135	550	182	34	9	7	--	--	255	117	81	72	1	77	8	2	2	38	18	.68	7	.331	.415	.464
1993	Nashville	AA	107	409	109	9	4	8	--	--	150	54	50	34	0	66	4	3	2	15	5	.75	12	.267	.327	.367
1993	Minnesota	AL	15	36	5	1	0	0	(0	0)	6	7	0	6	0	8	0	0	0	1	0	1.00	1	.139	.262	.167

Trevor Hoffman

Pitches: Right   Bats: Right   Pos: RP **Ht: 6'1"   Wt: 200   Born: 10/13/67   Age: 26**

						HOW MUCH HE PITCHED				WHAT HE GAVE UP										THE RESULTS					
Year	Team	Lg	G	GS	CG	GF	IP	BFP	H	R	ER	HR	SH	SF	HB	TBB	IBB	SO	WP	Bk	W	L	Pct.	ShO	Sv	ERA
1991	Cedar Rapids	A	27	0	0	25	33.2	133	22	8	7	0	2	0	1	13	0	52	2	1	1	1	.500	0	12	1.87
	Chattanooga	AA	14	0	0	13	14	59	10	4	3	0	0	0	0	7	0	23	1	0	1	0	1.000	0	8	1.93
1992	Chattanooga	AA	6	6	0	0	29.2	118	22	6	5	1	1	1	1	11	1	31	3	0	3	0	1.000	0	0	1.52
	Nashville	AAA	42	5	0	23	65.1	278	57	32	31	6	1	0	1	32	3	63	4	0	4	6	.400	0	6	4.27
1993	2 ML Teams		67	0	0	26	90	391	80	43	39	10	4	5	1	39	13	79	5	0	4	6	.400	0	5	3.90
1993	Florida	NL	28	0	0	13	35.2	152	24	13	13	5	2	1	0	19	7	26	3	0	2	2	.500	0	2	3.28
	San Diego	NL	39	0	0	13	54.1	239	56	30	26	5	2	4	1	20	6	53	2	0	2	4	.333	0	3	4.31

Chris Hoiles

Bats: Right   Throws: Right   Pos: C **Ht: 6'0"   Wt: 213   Born: 03/20/65   Age: 29**

								BATTING													BASERUNNING				PERCENTAGES		
Year	Team	Lg	G	AB	H	2B	3B	HR	(Hm	Rd)	TB	R	RBI	TBB	IBB	SO	HBP	SH	SF	SB	CS	SB%	GDP	Avg	OBP	SLG
1989	Baltimore	AL	6	9	1	1	0	0	(0	0)	2	0	1	1	0	3	0	0	0	0	0	.00	0	.111	.200	.222
1990	Baltimore	AL	23	63	12	3	0	1	(1	0)	18	7	6	5	1	12	0	0	0	0	0	.00	0	.190	.250	.286
1991	Baltimore	AL	107	341	83	15	0	11	(5	6)	131	36	31	29	1	61	1	0	1	0	2	.00	11	.243	.304	.384
1992	Baltimore	AL	96	310	85	10	1	20	(8	12)	157	49	40	55	2	60	2	1	3	0	2	.00	8	.274	.384	.506
1993	Baltimore	AL	126	419	130	28	0	29	(16	13)	245	80	82	69	4	94	9	3	3	1	1	.50	10	.310	.416	.585
	5 ML YEARS		358	1142	311	57	1	61	(30	31)	553	172	160	159	8	230	12	4	7	1	5	.17	29	.272	.365	.484

Dave Hollins

Bats: Both   Throws: Right   Pos: 3B **Ht: 6'1"   Wt: 207   Born: 05/25/66   Age: 28**

								BATTING													BASERUNNING				PERCENTAGES		
Year	Team	Lg	G	AB	H	2B	3B	HR	(Hm	Rd)	TB	R	RBI	TBB	IBB	SO	HBP	SH	SF	SB	CS	SB%	GDP	Avg	OBP	SLG
1990	Philadelphia	NL	72	114	21	0	0	5	(2	3)	36	14	15	10	3	28	1	0	2	0	0	.00	1	.184	.252	.316
1991	Philadelphia	NL	56	151	45	10	2	6	(3	3)	77	18	21	17	1	26	3	0	1	1	1	.50	2	.298	.378	.510
1992	Philadelphia	NL	156	586	158	28	4	27	(14	13)	275	104	93	76	4	110	19	0	4	9	6	.60	8	.270	.369	.469
1993	Philadelphia	NL	143	543	148	30	4	18	(9	9)	240	104	93	85	5	109	5	0	7	2	3	.40	15	.273	.372	.442
	4 ML YEARS		427	1394	372	68	10	56	(28	28)	628	240	222	188	13	273	28	0	14	12	10	.55	26	.267	.362	.451

Brad Holman

Pitches: Right   Bats: Right   Pos: RP **Ht: 6'5"   Wt: 200   Born: 02/09/68   Age: 26**

						HOW MUCH HE PITCHED				WHAT HE GAVE UP										THE RESULTS					
Year	Team	Lg	G	GS	CG	GF	IP	BFP	H	R	ER	HR	SH	SF	HB	TBB	IBB	SO	WP	Bk	W	L	Pct.	ShO	Sv	ERA
1990	Eugene	A	17	4	0	3	43.1	184	43	28	23	3	2	0	4	17	0	31	4	2	0	3	.000	0	0	4.78
1991	Peninsula	A	47	0	0	35	78.1	334	70	34	28	4	5	3	2	33	7	71	5	3	6	6	.500	0	10	3.22
1992	Peninsula	A	13	0	0	12	17.2	74	15	8	6	0	0	0	0	4	1	19	2	0	1	1	.500	0	5	3.06
	Jacksnville	AA	35	0	0	15	73.2	305	67	24	21	6	0	2	4	21	3	76	3	0	3	3	.500	0	4	2.57
1993	Calgary	AAA	21	13	1	2	98.2	427	109	59	52	5	3	6	3	42	0	54	7	1	8	4	.667	0	0	4.74
1993	Seattle	AL	19	0	0	9	36.1	152	27	17	15	1	1	0	5	16	2	17	2	0	1	3	.250	0	3	3.72

Darren Holmes

Pitches: Right   Bats: Right   Pos: RP **Ht: 6'0"   Wt: 199   Born: 04/25/66   Age: 28**

						HOW MUCH HE PITCHED				WHAT HE GAVE UP										THE RESULTS					
Year	Team	Lg	G	GS	CG	GF	IP	BFP	H	R	ER	HR	SH	SF	HB	TBB	IBB	SO	WP	Bk	W	L	Pct.	ShO	Sv	ERA
1993	Colo Springs *	AAA	3	2	0	0	8.2	29	1	1	0	0	0	0	0	1	0	9	0	0	1	0	1.000	0	0	0.00
1990	Los Angeles	NL	14	0	0	1	17.1	77	15	10	10	1	1	2	0	11	3	19	1	0	0	1	.000	0	0	5.19
1991	Milwaukee	AL	40	0	0	9	76.1	344	90	43	40	6	8	3	1	27	1	59	6	0	1	4	.200	0	3	4.72
1992	Milwaukee	AL	41	0	0	25	42.1	173	35	12	12	1	4	0	2	11	4	31	0	0	4	4	.500	0	6	2.55
1993	Colorado	NL	62	0	0	51	66.2	274	56	31	30	6	0	0	2	20	1	60	2	1	3	3	.500	0	25	4.05
	4 ML YEARS		157	0	0	86	202.2	868	196	96	92	14	13	5	5	69	9	169	9	1	8	12	.400	0	34	4.09

Mark Holzemer

Pitches: Left   **Bats:** Left   **Pos:** SP   **Ht:** 6' 0"   **Wt:** 165   **Born:** 08/20/69   **Age:** 24

			HOW MUCH HE PITCHED					WHAT HE GAVE UP										THE RESULTS					
Year Team	Lg	G	GS	CG	GF	IP	BFP	H	R	ER	HR	SH	SF	HB	TBB	IBB	SO	WP	Bk	W	L	Pct.	ShO	Sv	ERA
1988 Bend	A	13	13	1	0	68.2	311	59	51	40	3	0	1	6	47	1	72	8	6	4	6	.400	1	0	5.24
1989 Quad City	A	25	25	3	0	139.1	603	122	68	52	4	3	5	5	64	1	131	12	4	12	7	.632	1	0	3.36
1990 Midland	AA	15	15	1	0	77	363	92	55	45	10	2	1	6	41	0	54	6	0	1	7	.125	0	0	5.26
1991 Midland	AA	2	2	0	0	6.1	28	3	2	1	0	1	0	1	5	0	7	2	0	0	0	.000	0	0	1.42
1992 Palm Sprngs	A	5	5	2	0	30	124	23	10	10	2	1	0	3	13	0	32	0	0	3	2	.600	0	0	3.00
Midland	AA	7	7	2	0	44.2	188	45	22	19	4	0	1	1	13	0	36	3	1	2	5	.286	0	0	3.83
Edmonton	AAA	17	16	4	1	89	416	114	69	66	12	2	6	7	55	1	49	6	1	5	7	.417	0	0	6.67
1993 Vancouver	AAA	24	23	2	0	145.2	642	158	94	78	9	6	4	4	70	2	80	5	5	9	6	.600	0	0	4.82
1993 California	AL	5	4	0	1	23.1	117	34	24	23	2	1	0	3	13	0	10	1	0	0	3	.000	0	0	8.87

Rick Honeycutt

Pitches: Left   **Bats:** Left   **Pos:** RP   **Ht:** 6' 1"   **Wt:** 191   **Born:** 06/29/54   **Age:** 40

			HOW MUCH HE PITCHED					WHAT HE GAVE UP										THE RESULTS					
Year Team	Lg	G	GS	CG	GF	IP	BFP	H	R	ER	HR	SH	SF	HB	TBB	IBB	SO	WP	Bk	W	L	Pct.	ShO	Sv	ERA
1977 Seattle	AL	10	3	0	3	29	125	26	16	14	7	0	2	3	11	2	17	2	1	0	1	.000	0	0	4.34
1978 Seattle	AL	26	24	4	0	134	594	150	81	73	12	9	7	3	49	5	50	3	0	5	11	.313	1	0	4.90
1979 Seattle	AL	33	28	8	2	194	839	201	103	87	22	11	6	6	67	7	83	5	1	11	12	.478	1	0	4.04
1980 Seattle	AL	30	30	9	0	203	871	221	99	89	22	11	7	3	60	7	79	4	0	10	17	.370	1	0	3.95
1981 Texas	AL	20	20	8	0	128	509	120	49	47	12	5	0	0	17	1	40	1	0	11	6	.647	2	0	3.30
1982 Texas	AL	30	26	4	3	164	728	201	103	96	20	4	8	3	54	4	64	3	1	5	17	.227	1	0	5.27
1983 2 ML Teams		34	32	6	0	213.2	865	214	85	72	15	5	6	8	50	6	74	1	3	16	11	.593	2	0	3.03
1984 Los Angeles	NL	29	28	6	0	183.2	762	180	72	58	11	6	5	2	51	11	75	1	2	10	9	.526	2	0	2.84
1985 Los Angeles	NL	31	25	1	2	142	600	141	71	54	9	5	4	1	49	7	67	2	0	8	12	.400	0	1	3.42
1986 Los Angeles	NL	32	28	0	2	171	713	164	71	61	9	6	1	3	45	4	100	4	1	11	9	.550	0	0	3.32
1987 2 ML Teams		34	24	1	1	139.1	631	158	91	73	13	1	3	4	54	4	102	5	1	3	16	.158	1	0	4.72
1988 Oakland	AL	55	0	0	17	79.2	330	74	36	31	6	3	6	3	25	2	47	3	8	3	2	.600	0	7	3.50
1989 Oakland	AL	64	0	0	24	76.2	305	56	26	20	5	5	2	1	26	3	52	6	1	2	2	.500	0	12	2.35
1990 Oakland	AL	63	0	0	13	63.1	256	46	23	19	2	2	6	1	22	2	38	1	1	2	2	.500	0	7	2.70
1991 Oakland	AL	43	0	0	7	37.2	167	37	16	15	3	4	1	2	20	3	26	0	1	2	4	.333	0	0	3.58
1992 Oakland	AL	54	0	0	7	39	169	41	19	16	2	4	1	3	10	3	32	2	0	1	4	.200	0	3	3.69
1993 Oakland	AL	52	0	0	7	41.2	174	30	18	13	2	7	4	1	20	6	21	0	0	1	2	.200	0	1	2.81
1983 Texas	AL	25	25	5	0	174.2	693	168	59	47	9	3	6	6	37	2	56	1	2	14	8	.636	2	0	2.42
Los Angeles	NL	9	7	1	0	39	172	46	26	25	6	2	0	2	13	4	18	0	1	2	3	.400	0	0	5.77
1987 Los Angeles	NL	27	20	1	0	115.2	525	133	74	59	10	0	0	2	45	4	92	4	0	2	12	.143	1	0	4.59
Oakland	AL	7	4	0	1	23.2	106	25	17	14	3	1	3	2	9	0	10	1	1	1	4	.200	0	0	5.32
17 ML YEARS		640	268	47	88	2039.2	8638	2060	979	840	172	86	69	47	630	77	967	43	20	101	139	.421	11	31	3.71

John Hope

Pitches: Right   **Bats:** Right   **Pos:** SP   **Ht:** 6' 3"   **Wt:** 190   **Born:** 12/21/70   **Age:** 23

			HOW MUCH HE PITCHED					WHAT HE GAVE UP										THE RESULTS					
Year Team	Lg	G	GS	CG	GF	IP	BFP	H	R	ER	HR	SH	SF	HB	TBB	IBB	SO	WP	Bk	W	L	Pct.	ShO	Sv	ERA
1989 Pirates	R	4	3	0	0	15	68	15	12	8	0	1	3	1	6	0	14	0	1	0	1	.000	0	0	4.80
1991 Welland	A	3	3	0	0	17	67	12	1	1	0	0	0	2	3	0	15	0	0	2	0	1.000	0	0	0.53
Augusta	A	7	7	0	0	46.1	188	29	20	18	1	0	1	4	19	0	37	2	1	4	2	.667	0	0	3.50
Salem	A	6	5	0	1	27.2	122	38	20	19	5	0	1	0	4	0	18	0	0	2	2	.500	0	0	6.18
1992 Salem	A	27	27	4	0	176.1	726	169	75	68	13	2	4	10	46	0	106	10	3	11	8	.579	0	0	3.47
1993 Carolina	AA	21	20	0	0	111.1	478	123	69	54	7	2	6	8	29	4	66	10	2	9	4	.692	0	0	4.37
Buffalo	AAA	4	4	0	0	21.1	92	30	16	15	4	0	0	1	2	0	6	2	0	2	1	.667	0	0	6.33
1993 Pittsburgh	NL	7	7	0	0	38	166	47	19	17	2	5	1	2	8	3	8	1	0	0	2	.000	0	0	4.03

Sam Horn

Bats: Left   **Throws:** Left   **Pos:** DH   **Ht:** 6' 5"   **Wt:** 247   **Born:** 11/02/63   **Age:** 30

				BATTING															BASERUNNING				PERCENTAGES		
Year Team	Lg	G	AB	H	2B	3B	HR	(Hm	Rd)	TB	R	RBI	TBB	IBB	SO	HBP	SH	SF	SB	CS	SB%	GDP	Avg	OBP	SLG
1993 Charlotte*	AAA	122	402	108	17	1	38	--	--	241	62	96	60	8	131	2	0	7	0	0	1.00	10	.269	.361	.600
1987 Boston	AL	46	158	44	7	0	14	(6	8)	93	31	34	17	0	55	2	0	0	0	0	.00	5	.278	.356	.589
1988 Boston	AL	24	61	9	0	0	2	(2	0)	15	4	8	11	3	20	0	0	1	0	0	.00	1	.148	.274	.246
1989 Boston	AL	33	54	8	2	0	0	(0	0)	10	1	4	8	1	16	0	0	0	0	0	.00	0	.148	.258	.185
1990 Baltimore	AL	79	246	61	13	0	14	(8	6)	116	30	45	32	1	62	0	0	2	0	0	.00	8	.248	.332	.472
1991 Baltimore	AL	121	317	74	16	0	23	(12	11)	159	45	61	41	4	99	3	0	1	0	0	.00	10	.233	.326	.502
1992 Baltimore	AL	63	162	38	10	1	5	(2	3)	65	13	19	21	2	60	1	0	0	0	0	.00	8	.235	.324	.401

| 1993 Cleveland | AL | 12 | 33 | 15 | 1 | 0 | 4 | (2 | 2) | 28 | 8 | 8 | 1 | 0 | 5 | 1 | 0 | 1 | 0 | 0 | .00 | 1 | .455 | .472 | .848 |
| 7 ML YEARS | | 378 | 1031 | 249 | 49 | 1 | 62 | (32 | 30) | 486 | 132 | 179 | 131 | 11 | 317 | 7 | 0 | 6 | 0 | 1 | .00 | 37 | .242 | .329 | .471 |

Vince Horsman

Pitches: Left **Bats:** Right **Pos:** RP **Ht:** 6' 2" **Wt:** 180 **Born:** 03/09/67 **Age:** 27

		HOW MUCH HE PITCHED						WHAT HE GAVE UP										THE RESULTS					
Year Team	Lg	G	GS	CG	GF	IP	BFP	H	R	ER	HR	SH	SF	HB	TBB	IBB	SO	WP	Bk	W	L	Pct.	ShO	Sv	ERA
1993 Tacoma *	AAA	26	0	0	10	33.2	149	37	25	16	11	1	2	0	9	2	23	1	1	1	2	.333	0	3	4.28
1991 Toronto	AL	4	0	0	2	4	16	2	0	0	0	1	0	0	3	1	2	0	0	0	0	.000	0	0	0.00
1992 Oakland	AL	58	0	0	9	43.1	180	39	13	12	3	3	1	0	21	4	18	1	0	2	1	.667	0	1	2.49
1993 Oakland	AL	40	0	0	5	25	116	25	15	15	2	0	0	3	15	1	17	1	0	2	0	1.000	0	0	5.40
3 ML YEARS		102	0	0	16	72.1	312	66	28	27	5	4	1	3	39	6	37	2	0	4	1	.800	0	1	3.36

Steve Hosey

Bats: Right **Throws:** Right **Pos:** RF **Ht:** 6' 3" **Wt:** 218 **Born:** 04/02/69 **Age:** 25

		BATTING															BASERUNNING				PERCENTAGES		
Year Team	Lg	G	AB	H	2B	3B	HR	(Hm | Rd)	TB	R	RBI	TBB	IBB	SO	HBP	SH	SF	SB	CS	SB%	GDP	Avg	OBP	SLG
1989 Everett	A	73	288	83	14	3	13	--	--	142	44	59	27	2	84	10	0	2	15	3	.83	3	.288	.367	.493
1990 San Jose	A	139	479	111	13	6	16	--	--	184	85	78	71	2	139	5	1	4	16	17	.48	7	.232	.335	.384
1991 Shreveport	AA	126	409	120	21	5	17	--	--	202	79	74	56	5	87	6	5	4	24	11	.69	7	.293	.383	.494
1992 Phoenix	AAA	125	462	132	28	7	10	--	--	204	64	65	39	4	98	6	0	5	15	15	.50	11	.286	.346	.442
1993 Phoenix	AAA	129	455	133	40	4	16	--	--	229	70	85	66	5	129	3	0	5	16	10	.62	5	.292	.382	.503
1992 San Francisco	NL	21	56	14	1	0	1	(1 | 0)	18	6	6	0	0	15	0	0	0	1	1	.50	1	.250	.241	.321
1993 San Francisco	NL	3	2	1	1	0	0	(0 | 0)	2	0	1	1	0	1	0	0	0	0	0	.00	0	.500	.667	1.000
2 ML YEARS		24	58	15	2	0	1	(1 | 0)	20	6	7	1	0	16	0	0	2	1	1	.50	1	.259	.262	.345

Charlie Hough

Pitches: Right **Bats:** Right **Pos:** SP **Ht:** 6' 2" **Wt:** 190 **Born:** 01/05/48 **Age:** 46

		HOW MUCH HE PITCHED						WHAT HE GAVE UP										THE RESULTS					
Year Team	Lg	G	GS	CG	GF	IP	BFP	H	R	ER	HR	SH	SF	HB	TBB	IBB	SO	WP	Bk	W	L	Pct.	ShO	Sv	ERA
1970 Los Angeles	NL	8	0	0	5	17	79	18	11	10	7	0	0	0	11	0	8	0	0	0	0	.000	0	2	5.29
1971 Los Angeles	NL	4	0	0	3	4	19	3	3	2	1	1	0	0	3	0	4	0	0	0	0	.000	0	0	4.50
1972 Los Angeles	NL	2	0	0	2	3	13	2	1	1	0	0	0	1	2	0	4	0	0	0	0	.000	0	0	3.00
1973 Los Angeles	NL	37	0	0	18	72	309	52	24	22	3	4	3	6	45	2	70	2	0	4	2	.667	0	5	2.75
1974 Los Angeles	NL	49	0	0	16	96	389	65	45	40	12	6	8	4	40	2	63	4	0	9	4	.692	0	1	3.75
1975 Los Angeles	NL	38	0	0	24	61	266	43	25	20	3	3	0	8	34	0	34	4	1	3	7	.300	0	4	2.95
1976 Los Angeles	NL	77	0	0	55	143	600	102	43	35	6	4	1	8	77	3	81	9	0	12	8	.600	0	18	2.20
1977 Los Angeles	NL	70	1	0	53	127	551	98	53	47	10	10	4	7	70	6	105	8	0	6	12	.333	0	22	3.33
1978 Los Angeles	NL	55	0	0	31	93	390	69	38	34	6	0	0	5	48	4	66	6	0	5	5	.500	0	7	3.29
1979 Los Angeles	NL	42	14	0	10	151	662	152	88	80	16	9	4	8	66	2	76	9	1	7	5	.583	0	0	4.77
1980 2 ML Teams		35	3	2	12	93	426	91	51	47	6	7	4	5	58	2	72	11	0	3	5	.375	1	1	4.55
1981 Texas	AL	21	5	2	9	82	330	61	30	27	4	1	1	3	31	1	69	4	0	4	1	.800	0	1	2.96
1982 Texas	AL	34	34	12	0	228	954	217	111	100	21	7	4	7	72	5	128	9	0	16	13	.552	2	0	3.95
1983 Texas	AL	34	33	11	1	252	1030	219	96	89	22	5	5	3	95	0	152	6	1	15	13	.536	3	0	3.18
1984 Texas	AL	36	36	17	0	266	1133	260	127	111	26	5	7	9	94	3	164	12	2	16	14	.533	1	0	3.76
1985 Texas	AL	34	34	14	0	250.1	1018	198	102	92	23	1	7	7	83	1	141	11	3	14	16	.467	1	0	3.31
1986 Texas	AL	33	33	7	0	230.1	958	188	115	97	32	9	1	9	89	2	146	16	0	17	10	.630	2	0	3.79
1987 Texas	AL	40	40	13	0	285.1	1231	238	159	120	36	5	14	19	124	1	223	12	9	18	13	.581	0	0	3.79
1988 Texas	AL	34	34	10	0	252	1067	202	111	93	20	8	8	12	126	1	174	10	0	15	16	.484	0	0	3.32
1989 Texas	AL	30	30	5	0	182	795	168	97	88	28	3	6	6	95	2	94	7	5	10	13	.435	1	0	4.35
1990 Texas	AL	32	32	5	0	218.2	950	190	108	99	24	2	11	11	119	2	114	4	0	12	12	.500	0	0	4.07
1991 Chicago	AL	31	29	4	1	199.1	858	167	98	89	21	8	16	11	94	0	107	5	1	9	10	.474	1	0	4.02
1992 Chicago	AL	27	27	4	0	176.1	751	160	88	77	19	2	6	7	66	2	76	10	1	7	12	.368	0	0	3.93
1993 Florida	NL	34	34	0	0	204.1	876	202	109	97	20	11	7	8	71	2	126	11	4	9	16	.360	0	0	4.27
1980 Los Angeles	NL	19	1	0	5	32	156	37	21	20	4	3	3	2	21	0	25	3	0	1	3	.250	0	1	5.63
Texas	AL	16	2	2	7	61	270	54	30	27	2	4	1	3	37	2	47	8	0	2	2	.500	1	0	3.98
24 ML YEARS		837	419	106	240	3686.2	15655	3165	1733	1517	366	111	117	164	1613	43	2297	170	38	211	207	.505	12	61	3.70

Wayne Housie

Bats: Both **Throws:** Right **Pos:** RF **Ht:** 5' 9" **Wt:** 165 **Born:** 05/20/65 **Age:** 29

		BATTING															BASERUNNING				PERCENTAGES		
Year Team	Lg	G	AB	H	2B	3B	HR	(Hm | Rd)	TB	R	RBI	TBB	IBB	SO	HBP	SH	SF	SB	CS	SB%	GDP	Avg	OBP	SLG
1986 Gastonia	A	90	336	87	10	6	2	--	--	115	55	29	43	0	85	4	4	1	38	13	.75	4	.259	.349	.342
1987 Lakeland	A	125	458	118	12	7	1	--	--	147	58	45	39	2	74	3	6	6	26	11	.70	7	.258	.316	.321
1988 Glens Falls	AA	63	202	38	4	2	1	--	--	49	26	16	28	1	34	3	5	2	9	5	.64	2	.188	.294	.243
Lakeland	A	55	212	57	11	3	0	--	--	74	31	23	13	0	40	3	2	1	24	6	.80	5	.269	.319	.349
1989 London	AA	127	434	103	17	2	5	--	--	139	56	28	52	3	90	4	3	3	23	14	.62	5	.237	.323	.320
1990 Salinas	A	92	367	99	20	6	5	--	--	146	51	49	26	1	72	4	5	3	27	11	.71	5	.270	.316	.398

100

Year	Team	Lg	G	AB	H	2B	3B	HR	(Hm	Rd)	TB	R	RBI	TBB	IBB	SO	HBP	SH	SF	SB	CS	SB%	GDP	Avg	OBP	SLG
	New Britain	AA	30	113	31	8	3	1	--	--	48	13	12	6	0	33	1	5	0	7	2	.78	0	.274	.317	.425
1991	New Britain	AA	113	444	123	24	2	6	--	--	169	58	26	55	2	86	3	6	0	43	14	.75	5	.277	.361	.381
	Pawtucket	AAA	21	79	26	9	0	2	--	--	41	14	8	6	0	20	1	0	0	2	2	.50	0	.329	.384	.519
1992	Pawtucket	AAA	134	456	100	22	5	2	--	--	138	53	28	32	1	102	3	10	1	20	8	.71	7	.219	.274	.303
1993	Norfolk	AAA	16	67	14	0	0	1	--	--	17	5	5	3	0	13	0	1	1	7	0	1.00	2	.209	.239	.254
	New Orleans	AAA	64	113	31	6	1	0	--	--	39	22	7	18	0	21	1	4	0	6	2	.75	2	.274	.379	.345
1991	Boston	AL	11	8	2	1	0	0	(0	0)	3	2	0	1	0	3	0	1	0	1	0	1.00	1	.250	.333	.375
1993	New York	NL	18	16	3	1	0	0	(0	0)	4	2	1	1	0	1	0	0	0	0	0	.00	0	.188	.235	.250
	2 ML YEARS		29	24	5	2	0	0	(0	0)	7	4	1	2	0	4	0	1	0	1	0	1.00	1	.208	.269	.292

Chris Howard

Bats: Right **Throws:** Right **Pos:** C   **Ht:** 6' 2" **Wt:** 200 **Born:** 02/27/66 **Age:** 28

									BATTING											BASERUNNING				PERCENTAGES		
Year	Team	Lg	G	AB	H	2B	3B	HR	(Hm	Rd)	TB	R	RBI	TBB	IBB	SO	HBP	SH	SF	SB	CS	SB%	GDP	Avg	OBP	SLG
1988	Bellingham	A	2	9	3	0	0	1	--	--	6	3	3	1	0	2	0	0	0	0	0	.00	0	.333	.400	.667
	Wausau	A	61	187	45	10	1	7	--	--	78	20	20	18	0	60	3	0	1	1	3	.25	4	.241	.316	.417
1989	Wausau	A	36	125	30	8	0	4	--	--	50	13	32	13	1	35	1	0	1	0	0	.00	2	.240	.314	.400
	Williamsprt	AA	86	296	75	13	0	9	--	--	115	30	36	28	0	79	5	2	0	1	1	.00	10	.253	.328	.389
1990	Williamsprt	AA	118	401	95	19	1	5	--	--	131	48	49	37	1	91	3	4	4	3	1	.75	16	.237	.303	.327
1991	Calgary	AAA	82	293	72	12	1	8	--	--	110	32	36	16	1	56	2	3	1	1	1	.50	10	.246	.288	.375
1992	Calgary	AAA	97	319	76	16	0	8	--	--	116	29	45	14	0	73	5	3	2	3	7	.30	9	.238	.279	.364
1993	Calgary	AAA	94	331	106	23	0	6	--	--	147	40	55	23	1	62	5	5	2	1	5	.17	4	.320	.371	.444
1991	Seattle	AL	9	6	1	1	0	0	(0	0)	2	1	0	1	0	2	0	0	0	0	0	.00	0	.167	.286	.333
1993	Seattle	AL	4	1	0	0	0	0	(0	0)	0	0	0	0	0	0	0	0	0	0	0	.00	0	.000	.000	.000
	2 ML YEARS		13	7	1	1	0	0	(0	0)	2	1	0	1	0	2	0	0	0	0	0	.00	0	.143	.250	.286

Chris Howard

Pitches: Left **Bats:** Right **Pos:** RP   **Ht:** 6' 0" **Wt:** 185 **Born:** 11/18/65 **Age:** 28

				HOW MUCH HE PITCHED					WHAT HE GAVE UP									THE RESULTS					
Year	Team	Lg	G	GS	CG	GF	IP	BFP	H	R	ER	HR	SH	SF	HB	TBB	IBB	SO	WP	Bk	W	L	Pct.	ShO	Sv	ERA
1990	Albany	AA	2	0	0	1	5	30	9	8	8	0	0	1	0	7	0	2	0	0	0	0	.000	0	0	14.40
	Kinston	A	8	0	0	3	14.2	73	21	5	4	0	0	0	2	6	0	16	0	2	1	1	.500	0	0	2.45
1991	Birmingham	AA	38	0	0	24	53	219	43	14	12	2	6	2	3	16	1	52	2	1	6	1	.857	0	9	2.04
1992	White Sox	R	1	0	0	0	2	9	3	1	1	0	0	0	0	0	0	3	0	1	0	0	.000	0	0	4.50
	Vancouver	AAA	20	0	0	5	24.2	111	18	9	8	3	6	2	0	22	3	23	0	1	3	1	.750	0	0	2.92
1993	Nashville	AAA	43	0	0	17	66.2	271	55	32	25	9	3	5	0	16	4	53	7	2	4	3	.571	0	3	3.38
1993	Chicago	AL	3	0	0	0	2.1	10	2	0	0	0	0	0	0	3	1	1	0	0	1	0	1.000	0	0	0.00

Dave Howard

Bats: Both **Throws:** Right **Pos:** 2B   **Ht:** 6' 0" **Wt:** 165 **Born:** 02/26/67 **Age:** 27

									BATTING											BASERUNNING				PERCENTAGES		
Year	Team	Lg	G	AB	H	2B	3B	HR	(Hm	Rd)	TB	R	RBI	TBB	IBB	SO	HBP	SH	SF	SB	CS	SB%	GDP	Avg	OBP	SLG
1993	Omaha *	AAA	47	157	40	8	2	0	--	--	52	15	18	7	0	20	1	4	3	3	1	.75	3	.255	.286	.331
1991	Kansas City	AL	94	236	51	7	0	1	(0	1)	61	20	17	16	0	45	1	9	2	3	2	.60	1	.216	.267	.258
1992	Kansas City	AL	74	219	49	6	2	1	(1	0)	62	19	18	15	0	43	0	8	2	3	4	.43	3	.224	.271	.283
1993	Kansas City	AL	15	24	8	0	1	0	(0	0)	10	5	2	2	0	5	0	2	1	1	0	1.00	0	.333	.370	.417
	3 ML YEARS		183	479	108	13	3	2	(1	1)	133	44	37	33	0	93	1	19	5	7	6	.54	4	.225	.274	.278

Thomas Howard

Bats: Both **Throws:** Right **Pos:** LF/CF/RF   **Ht:** 6' 2" **Wt:** 205 **Born:** 12/11/64 **Age:** 29

									BATTING											BASERUNNING				PERCENTAGES		
Year	Team	Lg	G	AB	H	2B	3B	HR	(Hm	Rd)	TB	R	RBI	TBB	IBB	SO	HBP	SH	SF	SB	CS	SB%	GDP	Avg	OBP	SLG
1990	San Diego	NL	20	44	12	2	0	0	(0	0)	14	4	0	0	0	11	0	1	0	0	1	.00	1	.273	.273	.318
1991	San Diego	NL	106	281	70	12	3	4	(4	0)	100	30	22	24	4	57	1	2	1	10	7	.59	4	.249	.309	.356
1992	2 ML Teams		122	361	100	15	2	2	(1	1)	125	37	32	17	1	60	0	11	2	15	8	.65	4	.277	.308	.346
1993	2 ML Teams		112	319	81	15	3	7	(5	2)	123	48	36	24	0	63	0	0	5	10	7	.59	4	.254	.302	.386
1992	San Diego	NL	5	3	1	0	0	0	(0	0)	1	1	0	0	0	0	0	1	0	0	0	.00	0	.333	.333	.333
	Cleveland	AL	117	358	99	15	2	2	(1	1)	124	36	32	17	1	60	0	10	2	15	8	.65	4	.277	.308	.346
1993	Cleveland	AL	74	178	42	7	0	3	(3	0)	58	26	23	12	0	42	0	0	4	5	1	.83	5	.236	.278	.326
	Cincinnati	NL	38	141	39	8	3	4	(2	2)	65	22	13	12	0	21	0	0	1	5	6	.45	4	.277	.331	.461
	4 ML YEARS		360	1005	263	44	8	13	(10	3)	362	119	90	65	5	191	1	14	8	35	23	.60	18	.262	.305	.360

Steve Howe

Pitches: Left **Bats:** Left **Pos:** RP   **Ht:** 5'11" **Wt:** 198 **Born:** 03/10/58 **Age:** 36

				HOW MUCH HE PITCHED					WHAT HE GAVE UP									THE RESULTS					
Year	Team	Lg	G	GS	CG	GF	IP	BFP	H	R	ER	HR	SH	SF	HB	TBB	IBB	SO	WP	Bk	W	L	Pct.	ShO	Sv	ERA
1993	Columbus *	AAA	2	2	0	0	2.2	15	6	3	3	0	0	0	0	1	0	1	0	0	0	1	.000	0	0	10.13

Year	Team	Lg	G	GS	CG	GF	IP	BFP	H	R	ER	HR	SH	SF	HB	TBB	IBB	SO	WP	Bk	W	L	Pct.	ShO	Sv	ERA
1980	Los Angeles	NL	59	0	0	36	85	359	83	33	25	1	8	3	2	22	10	39	1	0	7	9	.438	0	17	2.65
1981	Los Angeles	NL	41	0	0	25	54	227	51	17	15	2	4	4	0	18	7	32	0	0	5	3	.625	0	8	2.50
1982	Los Angeles	NL	66	0	0	41	99.1	393	87	27	23	3	10	3	0	17	11	49	1	- 0	7	5	.583	0	13	2.08
1983	Los Angeles	NL	46	0	0	33	68.2	274	55	15	11	2	5	3	1	12	7	52	3	0	4	7	.364	0	18	1.44
1985	2 ML Teams		32	0	0	19	41	198	58	33	25	3	2	5	1	12	4	21	3	0	3	4	.429	0	3	5.49
1987	Texas	AL	24	0	0	15	31.1	131	33	15	15	2	2	0	3	8	1	19	2	1	3	3	.500	0	1	4.31
1991	New York	AL	37	0	0	10	48.1	189	39	12	9	1	2	1	3	7	2	34	2	0	3	1	.750	0	3	1.68
1992	New York	AL	20	0	0	10	22	79	9	7	6	1	1	1	0	3	1	12	1	0	3	0	1.000	0	6	2.45
1993	New York	AL	51	0	0	19	50.2	215	58	31	28	7	5	2	3	10	4	19	0	0	3	5	.375	0	4	4.97
1985	Los Angeles	NL	19	0	0	14	22	104	30	17	12	2	2	2	1	5	2	11	2	0	1	1	.500	0	3	4.91
	Minnesota	AL	13	0	0	5	19	94	28	16	13	1	0	3	0	7	2	10	1	0	2	3	.400	0	0	6.16
	9 ML YEARS		376	0	0	208	500.1	2065	473	190	157	22	39	22	13	109	47	277	13	1	38	37	.507	0	73	2.82

Jay Howell

Pitches: Right **Bats:** Right **Pos:** RP   **Ht:** 6' 3" **Wt:** 215 **Born:** 11/26/55 **Age:** 38

			HOW MUCH HE PITCHED						WHAT HE GAVE UP												THE RESULTS					
Year	Team	Lg	G	GS	CG	GF	IP	BFP	H	R	ER	HR	SH	SF	HB	TBB	IBB	SO	WP	Bk	W	L	Pct.	ShO	Sv	ERA
1980	Cincinnati	NL	5	0	0	1	3	19	8	5	5	0	0	1	1	0	0	1	0	0	0	0	.000	0	0	15.00
1981	Chicago	NL	10	2	0	1	22	97	23	13	12	3	1	1	2	10	2	10	0	0	2	0	1.000	0	0	4.91
1982	New York	AL	6	6	0	0	28	138	42	25	24	1	0	2	0	13	0	21	1	0	2	3	.400	0	0	7.71
1983	New York	AL	19	12	2	3	82	368	89	53	49	7	1	5	3	35	0	61	2	1	1	5	.167	0	0	5.38
1984	New York	AL	61	1	0	23	103.2	426	86	33	31	5	3	3	0	34	3	109	4	0	9	4	.692	0	7	2.69
1985	Oakland	AL	63	0	0	58	98	414	98	32	31	5	3	4	1	31	3	68	4	1	9	8	.529	0	29	2.85
1986	Oakland	AL	38	0	0	33	53.1	230	53	23	20	3	3	1	1	23	4	42	4	0	3	6	.333	0	16	3.38
1987	Oakland	AL	36	0	0	27	44.1	200	48	30	29	6	3	2	1	21	1	35	4	0	3	4	.429	0	16	5.89
1988	Los Angeles	NL	50	0	0	38	65	262	44	16	15	1	3	3	1	21	2	70	2	2	5	3	.625	0	21	2.08
1989	Los Angeles	NL	56	0	0	41	79.2	312	60	15	14	3	4	2	0	22	6	55	1	0	5	3	.625	0	28	1.58
1990	Los Angeles	NL	45	0	0	35	66	271	59	17	16	5	1	0	6	20	3	59	4	1	5	5	.500	0	16	2.18
1991	Los Angeles	NL	44	0	0	35	51	202	39	19	18	3	5	2	1	11	3	40	0	0	6	5	.545	0	16	3.18
1992	Los Angeles	NL	41	0	0	26	46.2	203	41	9	8	2	5	1	1	18	5	36	3	1	1	3	.250	0	4	1.54
1993	Atlanta	NL	54	0	0	22	58.1	233	48	16	15	3	3	4	0	16	4	37	0	2	3	3	.500	0	0	2.31
	14 ML YEARS		528	21	2	343	801	3375	738	306	287	47	35	31	18	275	36	644	29	8	54	52	.509	0	153	3.22

Dann Howitt

Bats: Left **Throws:** Right **Pos:** LF/RF   **Ht:** 6' 5" **Wt:** 205 **Born:** 02/13/64 **Age:** 30

			BATTING																BASERUNNING				PERCENTAGES		
Year	Team	Lg	G	AB	H	2B	3B	HR	(Hm	Rd)	TB	R	RBI	TBB	IBB	SO	HBP	SH	SF	SB	CS	SB%	GDP	Avg	OBP	SLG
1993	Calgary *	AAA	95	333	93	20	1	21	--	--	178	.57	77	39	2	67	1	1	7	7	5	.58	4	.279	.350	.535
1989	Oakland	AL	3	3	0	0	0	0	(0	0)	0	0	0	0	0	2	0	0	0	0	0	.00	0	.000	.000	.000
1990	Oakland	AL	14	22	3	0	1	0	(0	0)	5	3	1	3	0	12	0	0	0	0	0	.00	0	.136	.240	.227
1991	Oakland	AL	21	42	7	1	0	1	(0	1)	11	5	3	1	0	12	0	0	1	0	0	.00	1	.167	.182	.262
1992	2 ML Teams		35	85	16	4	1	2	(1	1)	28	7	10	8	1	9	0	1	3	1	1	.50	6	.188	.250	.329
1993	Seattle	AL	32	76	16	3	1	2	(1	1)	27	6	8	4	0	18	0	0	0	0	0	.00	0	.211	.250	.355
1992	Oakland	AL	22	48	6	0	0	1	(0	1)	9	1	2	5	1	4	0	1	0	0	0	.00	4	.125	.208	.188
	Seattle	AL	13	37	10	4	1	1	(1	0)	19	6	8	3	0	5	0	0	3	1	1	.50	2	.270	.302	.514
	5 ML YEARS		105	228	42	8	3	5	(2	3)	71	21	22	16	1	53	0	1	4	1	1	.50	7	.184	.234	.311

Kent Hrbek

Bats: Left **Throws:** Right **Pos:** 1B   **Ht:** 6' 4" **Wt:** 252 **Born:** 05/21/60 **Age:** 34

			BATTING																BASERUNNING				PERCENTAGES		
Year	Team	Lg	G	AB	H	2B	3B	HR	(Hm	Rd)	TB	R	RBI	TBB	IBB	SO	HBP	SH	SF	SB	CS	SB%	GDP	Avg	OBP	SLG
1981	Minnesota	AL	24	67	16	5	0	1	(0	1)	24	5	7	5	1	9	1	0	0	0	0	.00	0	.239	.301	.358
1982	Minnesota	AL	140	532	160	21	4	23	(11	12)	258	82	92	54	12	80	0	1	4	3	1	.75	11	.301	.363	.485
1983	Minnesota	AL	141	515	153	41	5	16	(7	9)	252	75	84	57	5	71	3	0	7	4	6	.40	12	.297	.366	.489
1984	Minnesota	AL	149	559	174	31	3	27	(15	12)	292	80	107	65	15	87	4	1	6	1	1	.50	17	.311	.383	.522
1985	Minnesota	AL	158	593	165	31	2	21	(10	11)	263	78	93	67	12	87	2	0	4	1	1	.50	12	.278	.351	.444
1986	Minnesota	AL	149	550	147	27	1	29	(18	11)	263	85	91	71	9	81	6	0	7	2	2	.50	15	.267	.353	.478
1987	Minnesota	AL	143	477	136	20	1	34	(20	14)	260	85	90	84	12	60	0	0	5	5	2	.71	13	.285	.389	.545
1988	Minnesota	AL	143	510	159	31	0	25	(13	12)	265	75	76	67	7	54	0	2	7	0	3	.00	9	.312	.387	.520
1989	Minnesota	AL	109	375	102	17	0	25	(17	8)	194	59	84	53	4	35	1	1	4	3	0	1.00	6	.272	.360	.517
1990	Minnesota	AL	143	492	141	26	0	22	(8	14)	233	61	79	69	8	45	7	2	8	5	2	.71	17	.287	.377	.474
1991	Minnesota	AL	132	462	131	20	1	20	(10	10)	213	72	89	67	4	48	0	3	2	4	5	.44	15	.284	.373	.461
1992	Minnesota	AL	112	394	96	20	0	15	(10	5)	161	52	58	71	9	56	0	2	3	5	2	.71	12	.244	.357	.409
1993	Minnesota	AL	123	392	95	11	1	25	(12	13)	183	60	83	71	6	57	1	3	4	4	2	.67	12	.242	.357	.467
	13 ML YEARS		1666	5918	1675	301	18	283	(152	131)	2861	869	1033	801	104	770	25	15	61	37	26	.59	157	.283	.368	.483

Michael Huff

Bats: Right **Throws:** Right **Pos:** LF   **Ht:** 6' 1" **Wt:** 180 **Born:** 08/11/63 **Age:** 30

Year	Team	Lg	G	AB	H	2B	3B	HR	(Hm	Rd)	TB	R	RBI	TBB	IBB	SO	HBP	SH	SF	SB	CS	SB%	GDP	Avg	OBP	SLG
1993	Nashville*	AAA	92	344	101	12	6	8	--	--	149	65	32	64	0	43	6	1	2	18	7	.72	4	.294	.411	.433
1989	Los Angeles	NL	12	25	5	1	0	1	(0	1)	9	4	2	3	0	6	1	1	0	0	1	.00	0	.200	.310	.360
1991	2 ML Teams	AL	102	243	61	10	2	3	(1	2)	84	42	25	37	2	48	6	6	2	14	4	.78	7	.251	.361	.346
1992	Chicago	AL	60	115	24	5	0	0	(0	0)	29	13	8	10	1	24	1	2	2	1	2	.33	2	.209	.273	.252
1993	Chicago	AL	43	44	8	2	0	1	(0	1)	13	4	6	9	0	15	1	1	2	1	0	1.00	0	.182	.321	.295
1991	Cleveland	AL	51	146	35	6	1	2	(1	1)	49	28	10	25	0	30	4	3	1	11	2	.85	2	.240	.364	.336
	Chicago	AL	51	97	26	4	1	1	(0	1)	35	14	15	12	2	18	2	3	1	3	2	.60	5	.268	.357	.361
	4 ML YEARS		217	427	98	18	2	5	(1	4)	135	63	41	59	3	93	9	10	6	16	7	.70	9	.230	.331	.316

Keith Hughes

Bats: Left **Throws:** Left **Pos:** LF   **Ht:** 6' 3" **Wt:** 210 **Born:** 09/12/63 **Age:** 30

Year	Team	Lg	G	AB	H	2B	3B	HR	(Hm	Rd)	TB	R	RBI	TBB	IBB	SO	HBP	SH	SF	SB	CS	SB%	GDP	Avg	OBP	SLG
1993	Indianapolis*	AAA	82	283	81	28	4	13	--	--	156	55	42	41	2	61	2	1	1	5	0	1.00	3	.286	.379	.551
1987	2 ML Teams		41	80	20	2	0	0	(0	0)	22	8	10	7	0	13	1	0	0	0	0	.00	1	.250	.318	.275
1988	Baltimore	AL	41	108	21	4	2	2	(1	1)	35	10	14	16	1	27	0	0	2	1	0	1.00	0	.194	.294	.324
1990	New York	NL	8	9	0	0	0	0	(0	0)	0	0	0	0	0	4	0	0	0	0	0	.00	0	.000	.000	.000
1993	Cincinnati	NL	3	4	0	0	0	0	(0	0)	0	0	0	0	0	0	0	0	0	0	0	.00	0	.000	.000	.000
1987	New York	AL	4	4	0	0	0	0	(0	0)	0	0	0	0	0	2	0	0	0	0	0	.00	0	.000	.000	.000
	Philadelphia	NL	37	76	20	2	0	0	(0	0)	22	8	10	7	0	11	1	0	0	0	0	.00	1	.263	.333	.289
	4 ML YEARS		93	201	41	6	2	2	(1	1)	57	18	24	23	1	44	1	0	2	1	0	1.00	4	.204	.286	.284

Tim Hulett

Bats: Right **Throws:** Right **Pos:** 3B   **Ht:** 6' 0" **Wt:** 200 **Born:** 01/12/60 **Age:** 34

Year	Team	Lg	G	AB	H	2B	3B	HR	(Hm	Rd)	TB	R	RBI	TBB	IBB	SO	HBP	SH	SF	SB	CS	SB%	GDP	Avg	OBP	SLG
1983	Chicago	AL	6	5	1	0	0	0	(0	0)	1	0	0	0	0	0	0	0	0	1	0	1.00	0	.200	.200	.200
1984	Chicago	AL	8	7	0	0	0	0	(0	0)	0	1	0	1	0	4	0	0	0	1	0	1.00	0	.000	.125	.000
1985	Chicago	AL	141	395	106	19	4	5	(3	2)	148	52	37	30	1	81	4	4	3	6	4	.60	8	.268	.324	.375
1986	Chicago	AL	150	520	120	16	5	17	(7	10)	197	53	44	21	0	91	1	6	4	4	1	.80	11	.231	.260	.379
1987	Chicago	AL	68	240	52	10	0	7	(3	4)	83	20	28	10	1	41	0	5	2	0	2	.00	6	.217	.246	.346
1989	Baltimore	AL	33	97	27	5	0	3	(2	1)	41	12	18	10	0	17	0	1	1	0	0	.00	3	.278	.343	.423
1990	Baltimore	AL	53	153	39	7	1	3	(2	1)	57	16	16	15	0	41	0	1	0	1	0	1.00	2	.255	.321	.373
1991	Baltimore	AL	79	206	42	9	0	7	(1	6)	72	29	18	13	0	49	1	1	0	0	1	.00	3	.204	.255	.350
1992	Baltimore	AL	57	142	41	7	2	2	(1	1)	58	11	21	10	1	31	1	0	0	0	1	.00	7	.289	.340	.408
1993	Baltimore	AL	85	260	78	15	0	2	(2	0)	99	40	23	23	1	56	3	1	2	1	2	.33	5	.300	.361	.381
	10 ML YEARS		680	2025	506	88	12	46	(20	26)	756	234	205	133	4	411	10	19	12	14	11	.56	45	.250	.298	.373

David Hulse

Bats: Left **Throws:** Left **Pos:** CF   **Ht:** 5'11" **Wt:** 170 **Born:** 02/25/68 **Age:** 26

Year	Team	Lg	G	AB	H	2B	3B	HR	(Hm	Rd)	TB	R	RBI	TBB	IBB	SO	HBP	SH	SF	SB	CS	SB%	GDP	Avg	OBP	SLG
1990	Butte	R	64	257	92	12	2	2	--	--	114	54	36	25	1	31	2	2	0	24	5	.83	4	.358	.419	.444
1991	Charlotte	A	88	310	86	4	5	0	--	--	100	41	17	36	2	75	1	6	0	44	7	.86	4	.277	.354	.323
1992	Tulsa	AA	88	354	101	14	3	3	--	--	130	40	20	20	2	86	3	1	0	17	10	.63	2	.285	.329	.367
	Okla City	AAA	8	30	7	1	1	0	--	--	10	7	3	1	0	4	1	1	0	2	2	.50	0	.233	.281	.333
1992	Texas	AL	32	92	28	4	0	0	(0	0)	32	14	2	3	0	18	0	2	0	3	1	.75	0	.304	.326	.348
1993	Texas	AL	114	407	118	9	10	1	(0	1)	150	71	29	26	1	57	1	5	2	29	9	.76	9	.290	.333	.369
	2 ML YEARS		146	499	146	13	10	1	(0	1)	182	85	31	29	1	75	1	7	2	32	10	.76	9	.293	.331	.365

Mike Humphreys

Bats: Right **Throws:** Right **Pos:** LF   **Ht:** 6' 0" **Wt:** 185 **Born:** 04/10/67 **Age:** 27

Year	Team	Lg	G	AB	H	2B	3B	HR	(Hm	Rd)	TB	R	RBI	TBB	IBB	SO	HBP	SH	SF	SB	CS	SB%	GDP	Avg	OBP	SLG
1988	Spokane	A	76	303	93	16	5	6	--	--	137	67	59	46	1	57	0	0	4	21	4	.84	9	.307	.394	.452
1989	Riverside	A	117	420	121	26	1	13	--	--	188	77	66	72	4	79	7	3	5	23	10	.70	9	.288	.397	.448
1990	Wichita	AA	116	421	116	21	4	17	--	--	196	92	79	67	4	79	5	2	4	37	9	.80	6	.276	.378	.466
	Las Vegas	AAA	12	42	10	1	0	2	--	--	17	7	6	4	0	11	1	2	0	1	0	1.00	0	.238	.319	.405
1991	Columbus	AAA	117	413	117	23	5	9	--	--	177	71	53	63	3	61	3	1	6	34	9	.79	10	.283	.377	.429
1992	Columbus	AAA	114	408	115	18	6	6	--	--	163	83	46	59	0	70	1	3	5	37	13	.74	9	.282	.370	.400
1993	Columbus	AAA	92	330	95	16	2	6	--	--	133	59	42	52	2	57	3	2	2	18	15	.55	6	.288	.388	.403
1991	New York	AL	25	40	8	0	0	0	(0	0)	8	9	3	9	0	7	0	1	0	2	0	1.00	2	.200	.347	.200
1992	New York	AL	4	10	1	0	0	0	(0	0)	1	0	0	0	0	1	0	0	0	0	0	.00	2	.100	.100	.100
1993	New York	AL	25	35	6	2	1	1	(1	0)	13	6	6	4	0	11	0	0	1	2	1	.67	0	.171	.250	.371
	3 ML YEARS		54	85	15	2	1	1	(1	0)	22	15	9	13	0	19	0	1	1	4	1	.80	2	.176	.283	.259

Todd Hundley

Bats: Both **Throws:** Right **Pos:** C **Ht:** 5'11" **Wt:** 185 **Born:** 05/27/69 **Age:** 25

								BATTING											BASERUNNING				PERCENTAGES		
Year Team	Lg	G	AB	H	2B	3B	HR	(Hm	Rd)	TB	R	RBI	TBB	IBB	SO	HBP	SH	SF	SB	CS	SB%	GDP	Avg	OBP	SLG
1990 New York	NL	36	67	14	6	0	0	(0	0)	20	8	2	6	0	18	0	1	0	0	0	.00	1	.209	.274	.299
1991 New York	NL	21	60	8	0	1	1	(1	0)	13	5	7	6	0	14	1	1	1	0	0	.00	3	.133	.221	.217
1992 New York	NL	123	358	75	17	0	7	(2	5)	113	32	32	19	4	76	4	7	2	3	0	1.00	8	.209	.256	.316
1993 New York	NL	130	417	95	17	2	11	(5	6)	149	40	53	23	7	62	2	2	4	1	1	.50	10	.228	.269	.357
4 ML YEARS		310	902	192	40	3	19	(8	11)	295	85	94	54	11	170	7	11	7	4	1	.80	22	.213	.261	.327

Brian Hunter

Bats: Right **Throws:** Left **Pos:** 1B **Ht:** 6'0" **Wt:** 195 **Born:** 03/04/68 **Age:** 26

								BATTING											BASERUNNING				PERCENTAGES		
Year Team	Lg	G	AB	H	2B	3B	HR	(Hm	Rd)	TB	R	RBI	TBB	IBB	SO	HBP	SH	SF	SB	CS	SB%	GDP	Avg	OBP	SLG
1993 Richmond *	AAA	30	99	24	7	0	6	--	--	49	16	26	10	0	21	3	0	0	4	2	.67	2	.242	.330	.495
1991 Atlanta	NL	97	271	68	16	1	12	(7	5)	122	32	50	17	0	48	1	0	2	0	2	.00	6	.251	.296	.450
1992 Atlanta	NL	102	238	57	13	2	14	(9	5)	116	34	41	21	3	50	0	1	8	1	2	.33	2	.239	.292	.487
1993 Atlanta	NL	37	80	11	3	1	0	(0	0)	16	4	8	2	1	15	0	0	3	0	0	.00	1	.138	.153	.200
3 ML YEARS		236	589	136	32	4	26	(16	10)	254	70	99	40	4	113	1	1	13	1	4	.20	9	.231	.275	.431

Bruce Hurst

Pitches: Left **Bats:** Left **Pos:** SP **Ht:** 6'3" **Wt:** 220 **Born:** 03/24/58 **Age:** 36

		HOW MUCH HE PITCHED						WHAT HE GAVE UP												THE RESULTS					
Year Team	Lg	G	GS	CG	GF	IP	BFP	H	R	ER	HR	SH	SF	HB	TBB	IBB	SO	WP	Bk	W	L	Pct.	ShO	Sv	ERA
1993 Las Vegas *	AAA	1	1	0	0	5	24	8	6	5	1	1	2	0	0	0	7	0	0	0	1	.000	0	0	9.00
Rancho Cuca*	A	1	1	0	0	4.1	20	4	5	4	0	0	0	0	1	0	6	0	0	0	0	.000	0	0	8.31
Colo Sprngs *	AAA	3	3	0	0	14.2	67	22	13	12	0	2	0	0	4	1	8	0	0	1	1	.500	0	0	7.36
1980 Boston	AL	12	7	0	2	31	147	39	33	31	4	0	2	2	16	0	16	4	2	2	2	.500	0	0	9.00
1981 Boston	AL	5	5	0	0	23	104	23	11	11	1	0	2	1	12	2	11	2	0	2	0	1.000	0	0	4.30
1982 Boston	AL	28	19	0	3	117	535	161	87	75	16	2	7	3	40	2	53	5	0	3	7	.300	0	0	5.77
1983 Boston	AL	33	32	6	0	211.1	903	241	102	96	22	3	4	3	62	5	115	1	2	12	12	.500	2	0	4.09
1984 Boston	AL	33	33	9	0	218	958	232	106	95	25	3	4	6	88	3	136	1	1	12	12	.500	2	0	3.92
1985 Boston	AL	35	31	6	0	229.1	973	243	123	115	31	6	3	3	70	4	189	3	4	11	13	.458	1	0	4.51
1986 Boston	AL	25	25	11	0	174.1	721	169	63	58	18	5	3	3	50	2	167	6	0	13	8	.619	4	0	2.99
1987 Boston	AL	33	33	15	0	238.2	1001	239	124	117	35	5	5	1	76	5	190	3	1	15	13	.536	3	0	4.41
1988 Boston	AL	33	32	7	0	216.2	922	222	98	88	21	8	5	2	65	1	166	5	3	18	6	.750	1	0	3.66
1989 San Diego	NL	33	33	10	0	244.2	990	214	84	73	16	18	3	0	66	7	179	8	0	15	11	.577	2	0	2.69
1990 San Diego	NL	33	33	9	0	223.2	903	188	85	78	21	15	1	1	63	5	162	7	1	11	9	.550	4	0	3.14
1991 San Diego	NL	31	31	4	0	221.2	909	201	89	81	17	8	4	3	59	3	141	5	1	15	8	.652	0	0	3.29
1992 San Diego	NL	32	32	6	0	217.1	902	223	96	93	22	12	4	0	51	3	131	4	3	14	9	.609	4	0	3.85
1993 2 ML Teams		5	5	0	0	13	60	15	12	11	1	1	0	0	6	0	9	1	1	0	2	.000	0	0	7.62
1993 San Diego	NL	2	2	0	0	4.1	26	9	7	6	0	1	0	0	3	0	3	0	0	0	1	.000	0	0	12.46
Colorado	NL	3	3	0	0	8.2	34	6	5	5	1	0	0	0	3	0	6	1	1	0	1	.000	0	0	5.19
14 ML YEARS		371	351	83	5	2379.2	10028	2410	1113	1022	250	86	51	28	724	42	1665	55	19	143	112	.561	23	0	3.87

Butch Huskey

Bats: Right **Throws:** Right **Pos:** 3B **Ht:** 6'3" **Wt:** 240 **Born:** 11/10/71 **Age:** 22

								BATTING											BASERUNNING				PERCENTAGES		
Year Team	Lg	G	AB	H	2B	3B	HR	(Hm	Rd)	TB	R	RBI	TBB	IBB	SO	HBP	SH	SF	SB	CS	SB%	GDP	Avg	OBP	SLG
1989 Mets	R	54	190	50	14	2	6	--	--	86	27	34	14	0	36	1	0	1	4	1	.80	2	.263	.317	.453
1990 Kingsport	R	72	279	75	12	0	14	--	--	129	39	53	24	0	74	2	0	5	4	3	.57	2	.269	.326	.462
1991 Columbia	A	134	492	141	27	5	26	--	--	256	88	99	54	6	90	4	1	7	22	10	.69	11	.287	.357	.520
1992 St. Lucie	A	134	493	125	17	1	18	--	--	198	65	75	33	6	74	1	0	5	7	3	.70	5	.254	.299	.402
1993 Binghamton	AA	139	526	132	23	1	25	--	--	232	72	98	48	3	102	2	0	8	11	2	.85	14	.251	.312	.441
1993 New York	NL	13	41	6	1	0	0	(0	0)	7	2	3	1	1	13	0	0	2	0	0	.00	0	.146	.159	.171

Jeff Huson

Bats: Left **Throws:** Right **Pos:** SS **Ht:** 6'3" **Wt:** 180 **Born:** 08/15/64 **Age:** 29

								BATTING											BASERUNNING				PERCENTAGES		
Year Team	Lg	G	AB	H	2B	3B	HR	(Hm	Rd)	TB	R	RBI	TBB	IBB	SO	HBP	SH	SF	SB	CS	SB%	GDP	Avg	OBP	SLG
1993 Okla City *	AAA	24	76	22	5	0	1	--	--	30	11	10	13	0	10	0	0	0	1	3	.25	1	.289	.393	.395
1988 Montreal	NL	20	42	13	2	0	0	(0	0)	15	7	3	4	2	3	0	0	0	2	1	.67	2	.310	.370	.357
1989 Montreal	NL	32	74	12	5	0	0	(0	0)	17	1	2	6	3	6	0	3	0	3	0	1.00	6	.162	.225	.230
1990 Texas	AL	145	396	95	12	2	0	(0	0)	111	57	28	46	0	54	2	7	3	12	4	.75	8	.240	.320	.280
1991 Texas	AL	119	268	57	8	3	2	(1	1)	77	36	26	39	0	32	0	9	4	8	3	.73	6	.213	.312	.287
1992 Texas	AL	123	318	83	14	3	4	(0	4)	115	49	24	41	2	43	1	8	6	18	6	.75	7	.261	.342	.362
1993 Texas	AL	23	45	6	1	0	0	(0	0)	9	3	2	0	0	10	0	1	0	0	0	.00	0	.133	.133	.200
6 ML YEARS		462	1143	266	42	9	6	(1	5)	344	153	85	136	7	148	3	28	10	43	14	.75	29	.233	.313	.301

Mark Hutton

Pitches: Right **Bats:** Right **Pos:** SP   **Ht:** 6' 6" **Wt:** 225 **Born:** 02/06/70 **Age:** 24

Year	Team	Lg	G	GS	CG	GF	IP	BFP	H	R	ER	HR	SH	SF	HB	TBB	IBB	SO	WP	Bk	W	L	Pct.	ShO	Sv	ERA
1989	Oneonta	A	12	12	0	0	66.1	283	70	39	30	1	2	4	1	24	0	62	5	2	6	2	.750	0	0	4.07
1990	Greensboro	A	21	19	0	1	81.1	394	77	78	57	2	2	3	7	62	0	72	14	1	1	10	.091	0	0	6.31
1991	Ft.Lauderdale	A	24	24	3	0	147	606	98	54	40	5	6	1	11	65	5	117	4	4	5	8	.385	0	0	2.45
	Columbus	AAA	1	1	0	0	6	24	3	2	1	0	0	0	0	5	0	5	0	0	1	0	1.000	0	0	1.50
1992	Albany	AA	25	25	1	0	165.1	703	146	75	66	6	2	3	11	66	1	128	2	1	13	7	.650	0	0	3.59
	Columbus	AAA	1	0	0	0	5	22	7	4	3	0	0	0	0	2	0	4	0	0	0	1	.000	0	0	5.40
1993	Columbus	AAA	21	21	0	0	133	544	98	52	47	14	2	0	10	53	0	112	2	1	10	4	.714	0	0	3.18
1993	New York	AL	7	4	0	2	22	104	24	17	14	2	2	2	1	17	0	12	0	0	1	1	.500	0	0	5.73

Mike Ignasiak

Pitches: Right **Bats:** Both **Pos:** RP   **Ht:** 5'11" **Wt:** 175 **Born:** 03/12/66 **Age:** 28

Year	Team	Lg	G	GS	CG	GF	IP	BFP	H	R	ER	HR	SH	SF	HB	TBB	IBB	SO	WP	Bk	W	L	Pct.	ShO	Sv	ERA
1988	Helena	R	7	0	0	7	11.2	53	10	5	4	1	0	0	1	7	0	18	2	0	2	0	1.000	0	1	3.09
	Beloit	A	9	9	1	0	56.1	232	52	21	17	4	3	2	2	12	1	66	1	1	2	4	.333	0	0	2.72
1989	Stockton	A	28	28	4	0	179	763	140	67	54	4	4	5	5	97	0	142	12	1	11	6	.647	4	0	2.72
1990	Stockton	A	6	6	1	0	32	130	18	14	14	3	0	0	2	17	0	23	2	1	3	1	.750	1	0	3.94
	El Paso	AA	15	15	1	0	82.2	368	96	45	40	5	2	3	1	34	1	39	4	3	6	3	.667	0	0	4.35
1991	Denver	AAA	24	22	1	1	137.2	587	119	68	65	14	1	1	6	57	2	103	4	1	9	5	.643	0	1	4.25
1992	Denver	AAA	62	0	0	34	92	388	83	37	30	6	8	2	1	33	4	64	3	3	7	4	.636	0	10	2.93
1993	New Orleans	AAA	35	0	0	18	57.2	220	26	10	7	4	4	3	1	20	2	61	3	1	6	0	1.000	0	9	1.09
1991	Milwaukee	AL	4	1	0	0	12.2	51	7	8	8	2	0	0	0	8	0	10	0	0	2	1	.667	0	0	5.68
1993	Milwaukee	AL	27	0	0	4	37	158	32	17	15	2	1	1	2	21	4	28	0	0	1	1	.500	0	0	3.65
	2 ML YEARS		31	1	0	4	49.2	209	39	25	23	4	1	1	2	29	4	38	0	0	3	2	.600	0	0	4.17

Pete Incaviglia

Bats: Right **Throws:** Right **Pos:** LF   **Ht:** 6' 1" **Wt:** 225 **Born:** 04/02/64 **Age:** 30

Year	Team	Lg	G	AB	H	2B	3B	HR	(Hm	Rd)	TB	R	RBI	TBB	IBB	SO	HBP	SH	SF	SB	CS	SB%	GDP	Avg	OBP	SLG
1986	Texas	AL	153	540	135	21	2	30	(17	13)	250	82	88	55	2	185	4	0	7	3	2	.60	9	.250	.320	.463
1987	Texas	AL	139	509	138	26	4	27	(11	16)	253	85	80	48	1	168	1	0	5	9	3	.75	8	.271	.332	.497
1988	Texas	AL	116	418	104	19	3	22	(12	10)	195	59	54	39	3	153	7	0	3	6	4	.60	6	.249	.321	.467
1989	Texas	AL	133	453	107	27	4	21	(13	8)	205	48	81	32	0	136	6	0	4	5	7	.42	12	.236	.293	.453
1990	Texas	AL	153	529	123	27	0	24	(15	9)	222	59	85	45	5	146	9	0	4	3	4	.43	18	.233	.302	.420
1991	Detroit	AL	97	337	72	12	1	11	(6	5)	119	38	38	36	0	92	1	1	2	1	3	.25	6	.214	.290	.353
1992	Houston	NL	113	349	93	22	1	11	(6	5)	150	31	44	25	2	99	3	0	2	2	2	.50	6	.266	.319	.430
1993	Philadelphia	NL	116	368	104	16	3	24	(15	9)	195	60	89	21	1	82	6	0	7	1	1	.50	9	.274	.318	.530
	8 ML YEARS		1020	3503	873	170	18	170	(95	75)	1589	462	559	301	14	1061	37	1	34	30	26	.54	74	.249	.313	.454

Jeff Innis

Pitches: Right **Bats:** Right **Pos:** RP   **Ht:** 6' 1" **Wt:** 170 **Born:** 07/05/62 **Age:** 31

Year	Team	Lg	G	GS	CG	GF	IP	BFP	H	R	ER	HR	SH	SF	HB	TBB	IBB	SO	WP	Bk	W	L	Pct.	ShO	Sv	ERA
1987	New York	NL	17	1	0	8	25.2	109	29	9	9	5	0	0	1	4	1	28	1	1	0	1	.000	0	0	3.16
1988	New York	NL	12	0	0	7	19	80	19	6	4	0	1	1	0	2	1	14	0	0	1	1	.500	0	0	1.89
1989	New York	NL	29	0	0	12	39.2	160	38	16	14	2	1	1	1	8	0	16	0	0	0	1	.000	0	0	3.18
1990	New York	NL	18	0	0	12	26.1	104	19	9	7	4	0	2	1	10	3	12	1	1	1	3	.250	0	1	2.39
1991	New York	NL	69	0	0	28	84.2	336	66	30	25	2	6	5	0	23	6	47	4	0	0	2	.000	0	0	2.66
1992	New York	NL	76	0	0	28	88	373	85	32	28	4	7	4	6	36	4	39	1	0	6	9	.400	0	1	2.86
1993	New York	NL	67	0	0	30	76.2	345	81	39	35	5	4	1	6	38	12	36	3	1	2	3	.400	0	3	4.11
	7 ML YEARS		288	1	0	126	360	1507	337	141	122	22	24	14	15	121	27	192	10	3	10	20	.333	0	5	3.05

Bo Jackson

Bats: Right **Throws:** Right **Pos:** DH/LF/RF   **Ht:** 6' 1" **Wt:** 225 **Born:** 11/30/62 **Age:** 31

Year	Team	Lg	G	AB	H	2B	3B	HR	(Hm	Rd)	TB	R	RBI	TBB	IBB	SO	HBP	SH	SF	SB	CS	SB%	GDP	Avg	OBP	SLG
1986	Kansas City	AL	25	82	17	2	1	2	(1	1)	27	9	9	7	0	34	2	0	0	3	1	.75	1	.207	.286	.329
1987	Kansas City	AL	116	396	93	17	2	22	(14	8)	180	46	53	30	0	158	5	1	2	10	4	.71	3	.235	.296	.455
1988	Kansas City	AL	124	439	108	16	4	25	(10	15)	207	63	68	25	6	146	1	1	2	27	6	.82	6	.246	.287	.472

Year	Team	Lg	G	AB	H	2B	3B	HR	(Hm	Rd)	TB	R	RBI	TBB	IBB	SO	HBP	SH	SF	SB	CS	SB%	GDP	Avg	OBP	SLG
1989	Kansas City	AL	135	515	132	15	6	32	(11	21)	255	86	105	39	8	172	3	0	4	26	9	.74	10	.256	.310	.495
1990	Kansas City	AL	111	405	110	16	1	28	(12	16)	212	74	78	44	2	128	2	0	5	15	9	.63	10	.272	.342	.523
1991	Chicago	AL	23	71	16	4	0	3	(3	0)	29	8	14	12	1	25	0	0	1	0	1	.00	3	.225	.333	.408
1993	Chicago	AL	85	284	66	9	0	16	(9	7)	123	32	45	23	1	106	0	0	1	0	2	.00	5	.232	.289	.433
7	ML YEARS		619	2192	542	79	14	128	(60	68)	1033	318	372	180	18	769	13	2	15	81	32	.72	38	.247	.306	.471

Danny Jackson

Pitches: Left   Bats: Right   Pos: SP   **Ht: 6' 0"   Wt: 205   Born: 01/05/62   Age: 32**

			HOW MUCH HE PITCHED						WHAT HE GAVE UP												THE RESULTS					
Year	Team	Lg	G	GS	CG	GF	IP	BFP	H	R	ER	HR	SH	SF	HB	TBB	IBB	SO	WP	Bk	W	L	Pct.	ShO	Sv	ERA
1983	Kansas City	AL	4	3	0	0	19	87	26	12	11	1	1	0	0	6	0	9	0	0	0	0	.500	0	0	5.21
1984	Kansas City	AL	15	11	1	3	76	338	84	41	36	4	3	0	5	35	0	40	3	2	2	6	.250	0	0	4.26
1985	Kansas City	AL	32	32	4	0	208	893	209	94	79	7	5	4	6	76	2	114	4	2	14	12	.538	3	0	3.42
1986	Kansas City	AL	32	27	4	3	185.2	789	177	83	66	13	10	4	4	79	1	115	7	0	11	12	.478	1	1	3.20
1987	Kansas City	AL	36	34	11	1	224	981	219	115	100	11	8	7	7	109	1	152	5	0	9	18	.333	2	0	4.02
1988	Cincinnati	NL	35	35	15	0	260.2	1034	206	86	79	13	13	5	2	71	6	161	5	2	23	8	.742	6	0	2.73
1989	Cincinnati	NL	20	20	1	0	115.2	519	122	78	72	10	6	4	1	57	7	70	3	2	6	11	.353	0	0	5.60
1990	Cincinnati	NL	22	21	0	1	117.1	499	119	54	47	11	4	5	2	40	4	76	3	1	6	6	.500	0	0	3.61
1991	Chicago	NL	17	14	0	0	70.2	347	89	59	53	8	8	2	1	48	4	31	1	1	1	5	.167	0	0	6.75
1992	2 ML Teams		34	34	0	0	201.1	883	211	99	86	6	17	10	4	77	6	97	2	2	8	13	.381	0	0	3.84
1993	Philadelphia	NL	32	32	2	0	210.1	919	214	105	88	12	14	8	4	80	2	120	4	0	12	11	.522	1	0	3.77
1992		NL	19	19	0	0	113	501	117	59	53	5	11	5	3	48	3	51	1	2	4	9	.308	0	0	4.22
	Pittsburgh	NL	15	15	0	0	88.1	382	94	40	33	1	6	5	1	29	3	46	1	0	4	4	.500	0	0	3.36
11	ML YEARS		279	263	38	8	1688.2	7289	1676	826	717	96	89	49	36	678	33	985	37	12	93	103	.474	13	1	3.82

Darrin Jackson

Bats: Right   Throws: Right   Pos: RF/CF   **Ht: 6' 0"   Wt: 185   Born: 08/22/63   Age: 30**

			BATTING																BASERUNNING				PERCENTAGES		
Year	Team	Lg	G	AB	H	2B	3B	HR	(Hm	Rd)	TB	R	RBI	TBB	IBB	SO	HBP	SH	SF	SB	CS	SB%	GDP	Avg	OBP	SLG
1985	Chicago	NL	5	11	1	0	0	0	(0	0)	1	0	0	0	0	3	0	0	0	0	0	.00	0	.091	.091	.091
1987	Chicago	NL	7	5	4	1	0	0	(0	0)	5	2	0	0	0	0	0	0	0	0	0	.00	0	.800	.800	1.000
1988	Chicago	NL	100	188	50	11	3	6	(3	3)	85	29	20	5	1	28	1	2	1	4	1	.80	3	.266	.287	.452
1989	2 ML Teams		70	170	37	7	0	4	(1	3)	56	17	20	13	5	34	0	0	2	1	4	.20	2	.218	.270	.329
1990	San Diego	NL	58	113	29	3	0	3	(1	2)	41	10	9	5	1	24	0	1	1	3	0	1.00	1	.257	.286	.363
1991	San Diego	NL	122	359	94	12	1	21	(12	9)	171	51	49	27	2	66	2	3	3	5	3	.63	5	.262	.315	.476
1992	San Diego	NL	155	587	146	23	5	17	(11	6)	230	72	70	26	4	106	4	6	5	14	3	.82	21	.249	.283	.392
1993	2 ML Teams		77	263	55	9	0	6	(4	2)	82	19	26	10	0	75	0	6	1	0	2	.00	9	.209	.237	.312
1989	Chicago	NL	45	83	19	4	0	1	(0	1)	26	7	8	6	1	17	0	0	0	1	2	.33	1	.229	.281	.313
	San Diego		25	87	18	3	0	3	(1	2)	30	10	12	7	4	17	0	0	2	0	2	.00	1	.207	.260	.345
1993	Toronto	AL	46	176	38	8	0	5	(4	1)	61	15	19	8	0	53	0	5	0	0	2	.00	9	.216	.250	.347
	New York	NL	31	87	17	1	0	1	(0	1)	21	4	7	2	0	22	0	1	1	0	0	.00	0	.195	.211	.241
8	ML YEARS		594	1696	416	66	9	71	(32	25)	671	200	194	86	13	336	7	18	13	27	13	.68	41	.245	.282	.396

Mike Jackson

Pitches: Right   Bats: Right   Pos: RP   **Ht: 6' 2"   Wt: 223   Born: 12/22/64   Age: 29**

			HOW MUCH HE PITCHED						WHAT HE GAVE UP												THE RESULTS					
Year	Team	Lg	G	GS	CG	GF	IP	BFP	H	R	ER	HR	SH	SF	HB	TBB	IBB	SO	WP	Bk	W	L	Pct.	ShO	Sv	ERA
1986	Philadelphia	NL	9	0	0	4	13.1	54	12	5	5	2	0	0	2	4	1	3	0	0	0	0	.000	0	0	3.38
1987	Philadelphia	NL	55	7	0	8	109.1	468	88	55	51	16	3	4	3	56	6	93	6	8	3	10	.231	0	1	4.20
1988	Seattle	AL	62	0	0	29	99.1	412	74	37	29	10	3	10	2	43	10	76	6	6	6	5	.545	0	4	2.63
1989	Seattle	AL	65	0	0	27	99.1	431	81	43	35	8	6	2	6	54	6	94	1	2	4	6	.400	0	7	3.17
1990	Seattle	AL	63	0	0	28	77.1	338	64	42	39	8	8	5	2	44	12	69	9	2	5	7	.417	0	3	4.54
1991	Seattle	AL	72	0	0	35	88.2	363	64	35	32	5	4	0	6	34	11	74	3	0	7	7	.500	0	14	3.25
1992	San Francisco	NL	67	0	0	24	82	346	76	35	34	7	5	2	4	33	10	80	1	0	6	6	.500	0	2	3.73
1993	San Francisco	NL	81	0	0	17	77.1	317	58	28	26	7	4	2	3	24	6	70	2	2	6	6	.500	0	1	3.03
8	ML YEARS		474	7	0	172	646.2	2729	517	280	251	63	33	25	28	292	62	559	28	20	37	47	.440	0	32	3.49

John Jaha

Bats: Right   Throws: Right   Pos: 1B   **Ht: 6' 1"   Wt: 195   Born: 05/27/66   Age: 28**

			BATTING																BASERUNNING				PERCENTAGES		
Year	Team	Lg	G	AB	H	2B	3B	HR	(Hm	Rd)	TB	R	RBI	TBB	IBB	SO	HBP	SH	SF	SB	CS	SB%	GDP	Avg	OBP	SLG
1985	Helena	R	24	68	18	3	0	2	--	--	27	13	14	14	0	23	0	0	1	4	1	1.00	0	.265	.386	.397
1986	Tri-Cities	A	73	258	82	13	2	15	--	--	144	65	67	70	4	75	5	0	2	9	4	.69	2	.318	.469	.558
1987	Beloit	A	122	376	101	22	0	7	--	--	144	68	47	102	2	86	4	2	3	10	5	.67	11	.269	.427	.383
1988	Stockton	A	99	302	77	14	6	8	--	--	127	58	54	69	0	85	2	2	1	10	6	.63	10	.255	.396	.421
1989	Stockton	A	140	479	140	26	5	25	--	--	251	83	91	112	6	115	5	2	13	8	11	.42	15	.292	.422	.524
1990	Stockton	A	26	84	22	5	0	4	--	--	39	12	19	18	0	25	2	0	0	0	0	.00	1	.262	.404	.464

Year	Team	Lg	G	AB	H	2B	3B	HR	(Hm	Rd)	TB	R	RBI	TBB	IBB	SO	HBP	SH	SF	SB	CS	SB%	GDP	Avg	OBP	SLG
1991	El Paso	AA	130	486	167	38	3	30	--	--	301	121	134	78	6	101	8	1	5	12	6	.67	9	.344	.438	.619
1992	Denver	AAA	79	274	88	18	2	18	--	--	164	61	69	50	1	60	6	1	2	6	4	.60	3	.321	.434	.599
1992	Milwaukee	AL	47	133	30	3	1	2	(1	1)	41	17	10	12	1	30	2	1	4	10	1	1.00	1	.226	.291	.308
1993	Milwaukee	AL	153	515	136	21	0	19	(5	14)	214	78	70	51	4	109	8	4	4	13	9	.59	6	.264	.337	.416
	2 ML YEARS		200	648	166	24	1	21	(6	15)	255	95	80	63	5	139	10	5	8	23	9	.72	7	.256	.328	.394

Chris James

Bats: Right **Throws:** Right **Pos:** RF/LF **Ht:** 6' 1" **Wt:** 202 **Born:** 10/04/62 **Age:** 31

						BATTING														BASERUNNING				PERCENTAGES		
Year	Team	Lg	G	AB	H	2B	3B	HR	(Hm	Rd)	TB	R	RBI	TBB	IBB	SO	HBP	SH	SF	SB	CS	SB%	GDP	Avg	OBP	SLG
1986	Philadelphia	NL	16	46	13	3	0	1	(0	1)	19	5	5	1	0	13	0	1	0	0	0	.00	1	.283	.298	.413
1987	Philadelphia	NL	115	358	105	20	6	17	(9	8)	188	48	54	27	0	67	2	1	3	3	1	.75	4	.293	.344	.525
1988	Philadelphia	NL	150	566	137	24	1	19	(10	9)	220	57	66	31	2	73	3	0	5	7	4	.64	15	.242	.283	.389
1989	2 ML Teams		132	482	117	17	2	13	(7	6)	177	55	65	26	2	68	1	4	3	5	2	.71	20	.243	.281	.367
1990	Cleveland	AL	140	528	158	32	4	12	(6	6)	234	62	70	31	4	71	4	3	3	4	3	.57	11	.299	.341	.443
1991	Cleveland	AL	115	437	104	16	2	5	(1	4)	139	31	41	18	2	61	4	2	1	3	4	.43	9	.238	.273	.318
1992	San Francisco	NL	111	248	60	10	4	5	(3	2)	93	25	32	14	2	45	2	0	3	2	3	.40	2	.242	.285	.375
1993	2 ML Teams		73	160	44	11	1	9	(6	3)	84	24	26	18	2	40	1	1	2	2	0	1.00	2	.275	.348	.525
1989	Philadelphia	NL	45	179	37	4	0	2	(1	1)	47	14	19	4	0	23	0	1	1	3	1	.75	9	.207	.223	.263
	San Diego	NL	87	303	80	13	2	11	(6	5)	130	41	46	22	2	45	1	3	2	2	1	.67	11	.264	.314	.429
1993	Houston	NL	65	129	33	10	1	6	(6	0)	63	19	19	15	2	34	1	1	2	2	0	1.00	2	.256	.333	.488
	Texas	AL	8	31	11	1	0	3	(0	3)	21	5	7	3	0	6	0	0	0	0	0	.00	0	.355	.412	.677
	8 ML YEARS		852	2825	738	133	20	81	(42	39)	1154	307	359	166	14	438	17	12	21	26	17	.60	64	.261	.304	.408

Dion James

Bats: Left **Throws:** Left **Pos:** LF/CF **Ht:** 6' 1" **Wt:** 185 **Born:** 11/09/62 **Age:** 31

						BATTING														BASERUNNING				PERCENTAGES		
Year	Team	Lg	G	AB	H	2B	3B	HR	(Hm	Rd)	TB	R	RBI	TBB	IBB	SO	HBP	SH	SF	SB	CS	SB%	GDP	Avg	OBP	SLG
1983	Milwaukee	AL	11	20	2	0	0	0	(0	0)	2	1	1	2	0	2	0	0	0	1	0	1.00	0	.100	.182	.100
1984	Milwaukee	AL	128	387	114	19	5	1	(1	0)	146	52	30	32	1	41	3	6	3	10	10	.50	7	.295	.351	.377
1985	Milwaukee	AL	18	49	11	1	0	0	(0	0)	12	5	3	6	0	6	0	0	0	0	0	.00	0	.224	.309	.245
1987	Atlanta	NL	134	494	154	37	6	10	(5	5)	233	80	61	70	2	63	2	5	3	10	8	.56	8	.312	.397	.472
1988	Atlanta	NL	132	386	99	17	5	3	(1	2)	135	46	30	58	5	59	1	2	2	9	9	.50	12	.256	.353	.350
1989	2 ML Teams		134	415	119	18	0	5	(1	4)	152	41	40	49	6	49	1	5	1	2	7	.22	9	.287	.363	.366
1990	Cleveland	AL	87	248	68	15	2	1	(0	1)	90	28	22	27	3	23	1	3	1	5	3	.63	6	.274	.347	.363
1992	New York	AL	67	145	38	8	0	3	(2	1)	55	24	17	22	0	15	1	0	2	1	0	1.00	3	.262	.359	.379
1993	New York	AL	115	343	114	21	2	7	(5	2)	160	62	36	31	1	31	2	1	1	0	0	.00	5	.332	.390	.466
1989	Cleveland	NL	63	170	44	7	0	1	(0	1)	54	15	11	25	2	23	1	3	1	1	3	.25	4	.259	.355	.318
	Cleveland	AL	71	245	75	11	0	4	(1	3)	98	26	29	24	4	26	0	2	0	1	4	.20	5	.306	.368	.400
	9 ML YEARS		826	2487	719	136	20	30	(15	15)	985	339	240	297	18	289	11	22	13	38	37	.51	50	.289	.366	.396

Stan Javier

Bats: Both **Throws:** Right **Pos:** LF/1B/CF/RF **Ht:** 6' 0" **Wt:** 185 **Born:** 01/09/64 **Age:** 30

						BATTING														BASERUNNING				PERCENTAGES		
Year	Team	Lg	G	AB	H	2B	3B	HR	(Hm	Rd)	TB	R	RBI	TBB	IBB	SO	HBP	SH	SF	SB	CS	SB%	GDP	Avg	OBP	SLG
1984	New York	AL	7	7	1	0	0	0	(0	0)	1	1	0	0	0	1	0	0	0	0	0	.00	0	.143	.143	.143
1986	Oakland	AL	59	114	23	8	0	0	(0	0)	31	13	8	16	0	27	1	0	0	8	0	1.00	0	.202	.305	.272
1987	Oakland	AL	81	151	28	3	1	2	(1	1)	39	22	9	19	3	33	0	6	0	3	2	.60	2	.185	.276	.258
1988	Oakland	AL	125	397	102	13	3	2	(0	2)	127	49	35	32	1	63	2	6	3	20	1	.95	13	.257	.313	.320
1989	Oakland	AL	112	310	77	12	3	1	(1	0)	98	42	28	31	1	45	1	4	2	12	2	.86	6	.248	.317	.316
1990	2 ML Teams		123	309	92	9	6	3	(1	2)	122	60	27	40	2	50	0	6	3	15	7	.68	6	.298	.376	.395
1991	Los Angeles	NL	121	176	36	5	3	1	(0	1)	50	21	11	16	0	36	0	3	2	7	1	.88	4	.205	.268	.284
1992	2 ML Teams		130	334	83	17	1	1	(1	0)	105	42	29	37	2	54	3	3	2	18	3	.86	4	.249	.322	.314
1993	California	AL	92	237	69	10	4	3	(0	3)	96	33	28	27	1	33	1	1	3	12	2	.86	7	.291	.362	.405
1990	Oakland	AL	19	33	8	0	2	0	(0	0)	12	4	3	3	0	6	0	0	0	0	0	.00	0	.242	.306	.364
	Los Angeles	NL	104	276	84	9	4	3	(1	2)	110	56	24	37	2	44	0	6	2	15	7	.68	6	.304	.384	.399
1992	San Jose	NL	56	58	11	3	0	1	(1	0)	17	6	5	6	2	11	1	1	0	1	2	.33	0	.190	.277	.293
	Philadelphia	NL	74	276	72	14	1	0	(0	0)	88	36	24	31	0	43	2	2	2	17	1	.94	4	.261	.338	.319
	9 ML YEARS		850	2035	511	77	21	13	(4	9)	669	283	175	218	10	342	8	29	14	95	18	.84	44	.251	.324	.329

Domingo Jean

Pitches: Right **Bats:** Right **Pos:** SP **Ht:** 6' 2" **Wt:** 175 **Born:** 01/09/69 **Age:** 25

						HOW MUCH HE PITCHED				WHAT HE GAVE UP									THE RESULTS					
Year	Team	Lg	G	GS	CG	GF	IP	BFP	H	R	ER	HR	SH	SF	HB	TBB	IBB	SO	WP	Bk	W	L	Pct.	ShO	Sv	ERA
1990	White Sox	R	13	13	1	0	78.2	312	55	32	20	1	0	1	6	16	0	65	10	2	2	5	.286	0	0	2.29
1991	South Bend	A	25	25	2	0	158	680	121	75	58	7	3	7	10	65	0	141	17	5	12	8	.600	0	0	3.30
1992	Ft. Laud.	A	23	23	5	0	158.2	637	118	57	46	3	7	6	6	49	1	172	4	1	6	11	.353	1	0	2.61
	Albany	AA	1	1	0	0	4	17	3	2	1	0	0	0	0	3	0	6	1	0	0	0	.000	0	0	2.25
1993	Albany	AA	11	11	1	0	61	257	42	24	17	1	1	1	5	33	0	41	4	0	5	3	.625	0	0	2.51

Year Team	Lg	G	GS	CG	GF	IP	BFP	H	R	ER	HR	SH	SF	HB	TBB	IBB	SO	WP	Bk	W	L	Pct.	ShO	Sv	ERA
Columbus	AAA	7	7	1	0	44.2	180	40	15	14	2	0	2	2	13	1	39	3	0	2	2	.500	0	0	2.82
Pr William	A	1	0	0	0	1.2	6	1	0	0	0	0	0	0	0	0	1	0	0	0	0	.000	0	0	0.00
1993 New York	AL	10	6	0	1	40.1	176	37	20	20	7	0	1	0	19	1	20	1	0	1	1	.500	0	0	4.46

Gregg Jefferies

Bats: Both   Throws: Right   Pos: 1B   Ht: 5'10"   Wt: 185   Born: 08/01/67   Age: 26

Year Team	Lg	G	AB	H	2B	3B	HR	Hm	Rd	TB	R	RBI	TBB	IBB	SO	HBP	SH	SF	SB	CS	SB%	GDP	Avg	OBP	SLG
1987 New York	NL	6	6	3	1	0	0	(0	0)	4	0	2	0	0	0	0	0	0	0	0	.00	0	.500	.500	.667
1988 New York	NL	29	109	35	8	2	6	(3	3)	65	19	17	8	0	10	0	0	1	5	1	.83	1	.321	.364	.596
1989 New York	NL	141	508	131	28	2	12	(7	5)	199	72	56	39	8	46	5	2	5	21	6	.78	16	.258	.314	.392
1990 New York	NL	153	604	171	40	3	15	(9	6)	262	96	68	46	2	40	5	0	4	11	2	.85	12	.283	.337	.434
1991 New York	NL	136	486	132	19	2	9	(5	4)	182	59	62	47	2	38	2	1	3	26	5	.84	12	.272	.336	.374
1992 Kansas City	AL	152	604	172	36	3	10	(3	7)	244	66	75	43	4	29	1	0	9	19	9	.68	24	.285	.329	.404
1993 St. Louis	NL	142	544	186	24	3	16	(10	6)	264	89	83	62	7	32	2	0	4	46	9	.84	15	.342	.408	.485
7 ML YEARS		759	2861	830	156	15	68	(37	31)	1220	401	363	245	23	195	15	3	26	128	32	.80	80	.290	.346	.426

Reggie Jefferson

Bats: Both   Throws: Left   Pos: DH/1B   Ht: 6' 4"   Wt: 215   Born: 09/25/68   Age: 25

Year Team	Lg	G	AB	H	2B	3B	HR	Hm	Rd	TB	R	RBI	TBB	IBB	SO	HBP	SH	SF	SB	CS	SB%	GDP	Avg	OBP	SLG
1991 2 ML Teams		31	108	21	3	0	3	(2	1)	33	11	13	4	0	24	0	1	0	0	0	.00	1	.194	.221	.306
1992 Cleveland	AL	24	89	30	6	2	1	(1	0)	43	8	6	1	0	17	1	0	0	0	0	.00	2	.337	.352	.483
1993 Cleveland	AL	113	366	91	11	2	10	(4	6)	136	35	34	28	7	78	5	3	1	1	3	.25	7	.249	.310	.372
1991 Cincinnati	NL	5	7	1	0	0	1	(0	1)	4	1	1	1	0	2	0	0	0	0	0	.00	0	.143	.250	.571
Cleveland	AL	26	101	20	3	0	2	(1	1)	29	10	12	3	0	22	0	0	1	0	0	.00	1	.198	.219	.287
3 ML YEARS		168	563	142	20	4	14	(7	7)	212	54	53	33	7	119	6	3	2	1	3	.25	10	.252	.300	.377

Doug Jennings

Bats: Left   Throws: Left   Pos: 1B   Ht: 5'10"   Wt: 175   Born: 09/30/64   Age: 29

Year Team	Lg	G	AB	H	2B	3B	HR	Hm	Rd	TB	R	RBI	TBB	IBB	SO	HBP	SH	SF	SB	CS	SB%	GDP	Avg	OBP	SLG
1993 Iowa *	AAA	65	228	67	20	1	7	--	--	110	38	37	29	2	64	4	0	2	3	4	.43	5	.294	.380	.482
1988 Oakland	AL	71	101	21	6	0	1	(0	1)	30	9	15	21	1	28	2	1	3	1	0	1.00	1	.208	.346	.297
1989 Oakland	AL	4	4	0	0	0	0	(0	0)	0	0	0	0	0	2	0	0	0	0	0	.00	0	.000	.000	.000
1990 Oakland	AL	64	156	30	7	2	2	(1	1)	47	19	14	17	0	48	2	2	3	0	3	.00	1	.192	.275	.301
1991 Oakland	AL	8	9	1	0	0	0	(0	0)	1	0	0	2	0	2	0	0	0	0	1	.00	0	.111	.273	.111
1993 Chicago	NL	42	52	13	3	1	2	(2	0)	24	8	8	3	0	10	2	0	0	0	0	.00	1	.250	.316	.462
5 ML YEARS		189	322	65	16	3	5	(3	2)	102	36	37	43	1	90	6	3	6	0	5	.00	3	.202	.302	.317

Miguel Jimenez

Pitches: Right   Bats: Right   Pos: SP   Ht: 6' 2"   Wt: 205   Born: 08/19/69   Age: 24

Year Team	Lg	G	GS	CG	GF	IP	BFP	H	R	ER	HR	SH	SF	HB	TBB	IBB	SO	WP	Bk	W	L	Pct.	ShO	Sv	ERA
1993 Oakland	AL	5	4	0	0	27	120	27	12	12	5	0	0	1	16	0	13	0	0	1	0	1.000	0	0	4.00

Dave Johnson

Pitches: Right   Bats: Right   Pos: RP   Ht: 5'11"   Wt: 181   Born: 10/24/59   Age: 34

Year Team	Lg	G	GS	CG	GF	IP	BFP	H	R	ER	HR	SH	SF	HB	TBB	IBB	SO	WP	Bk	W	L	Pct.	ShO	Sv	ERA
1993 Toledo *	AAA	9	0	0	0	17.1	60	6	0	0	0	2	0	0	5	1	8	0	0	1	0	1.000	0	0	0.00
1987 Pittsburgh	NL	5	0	0	3	6.1	31	13	7	7	1	0	0	0	2	0	4	0	0	0	0	.000	0	0	9.95
1989 Baltimore	AL	14	14	4	0	89.1	378	90	44	42	11	3	3	4	28	1	26	0	2	4	7	.364	0	0	4.23
1990 Baltimore	AL	30	29	3	0	180	758	196	83	82	30	5	7	3	43	2	68	1	2	13	9	.591	0	0	4.10
1991 Baltimore	AL	22	14	0	4	84	393	127	68	66	18	0	1	4	24	3	38	0	0	4	8	.333	0	0	7.07
1993 Detroit	AL	6	0	0	2	8.1	46	13	13	12	3	0	1	2	5	1	7	1	0	1	1	.500	0	0	12.96
5 ML YEARS		77	57	7	9	368	1606	439	215	209	63	8	12	13	102	7	143	2	4	22	25	.468	0	0	5.11

Erik Johnson

Bats: Right   Throws: Right   Pos: 2B   Ht: 5'11"   Wt: 165   Born: 10/11/65   Age: 28

Year Team	Lg	G	AB	H	2B	3B	HR	Hm	Rd	TB	R	RBI	TBB	IBB	SO	HBP	SH	SF	SB	CS	SB%	GDP	Avg	OBP	SLG
1987 Pocatello	R	43	129	34	7	0	4	--	--	53	19	12	13	0	21	0	3	0	6	2	.75	1	.264	.331	.411
Shreveport	AA	9	21	2	1	0	0	--	--	3	1	3	0	0	5	0	0	0	0	1	.00	0	.095	.095	.143
1988 Clinton	A	90	322	72	12	3	5	--	--	105	29	38	26	3	39	3	4	2	4	7	.36	6	.224	.290	.326
San Jose	A	44	160	40	3	1	1	--	--	48	25	16	18	0	29	2	1	0	4	2	.67	5	.250	.333	.300
1989 Shreveport	AA	87	246	56	5	4	3	--	--	78	28	29	23	3	37	1	4	4	3	2	.60	10	.228	.292	.317

Year Team	Lg	G	AB	H	2B	3B	HR	(Hm	Rd)	TB	R	RBI	TBB	IBB	SO	HBP	SH	SF	SB	CS	SB%	GDP	Avg	OBP	SLG
1990 Phoenix	AAA	2	3	0	0	0	0	--	--	0	0	0	1	0	1	0	0	0	0	0	.00	1	.000	.250	.000
Shreveport	AA	91	270	60	6	0	1	--	--	69	35	15	22	3	38	3	3	0	6	6	.50	8	.222	.288	.256
1991 Phoenix	AAA	16	34	11	1	1	0	--	--	14	6	4	3	1	5	0	0	1	0	0	.00	0	.324	.368	.412
Shreveport	AA	58	146	32	7	0	2	--	--	45	27	20	16	4	20	1	4	0	6	2	.75	3	.219	.301	.308
1992 Phoenix	AAA	90	229	55	5	1	0	--	--	62	24	19	20	2	38	2	5	1	8	10	.44	9	.240	.306	.271
1993 Phoenix	AAA	101	363	90	8	5	0	--	--	108	33	33	29	2	51	1	2	3	3	9	.25	13	.248	.303	.298
1993 San Francisco	NL	4	5	2	2	0	0	(0	0)	4	1	0	0	0	1	0	0	0	0	0	.00	0	.400	.400	.800

Howard Johnson

Bats: Both **Throws:** Right **Pos:** 3B   **Ht:** 5'10" **Wt:** 195 **Born:** 11/29/60 **Age:** 33

BATTING / BASERUNNING / PERCENTAGES

Year Team	Lg	G	AB	H	2B	3B	HR	(Hm	Rd)	TB	R	RBI	TBB	IBB	SO	HBP	SH	SF	SB	CS	SB%	GDP	Avg	OBP	SLG
1982 Detroit	AL	54	155	49	5	0	4	(1	3)	66	23	14	16	1	30	1	1	0	7	4	.64	3	.316	.384	.426
1983 Detroit	AL	27	66	14	0	0	3	(2	1)	23	11	5	7	0	10	1	0	0	0	0	.00	1	.212	.297	.348
1984 Detroit	AL	116	355	88	14	1	12	(4	8)	140	43	50	40	1	67	1	4	2	10	6	.63	6	.248	.324	.394
1985 New York	NL	126	389	94	18	4	11	(5	6)	153	38	46	34	10	78	0	1	4	6	4	.60	6	.242	.300	.393
1986 New York	NL	88	220	54	14	0	10	(5	5)	98	30	39	31	8	64	1	1	0	8	1	.89	2	.245	.341	.445
1987 New York	NL	157	554	147	22	1	36	(13	23)	279	93	99	83	18	113	5	0	3	32	10	.76	8	.265	.364	.504
1988 New York	NL	148	495	114	21	1	24	(9	15)	209	85	68	86	25	104	3	2	8	23	7	.77	6	.230	.343	.422
1989 New York	NL	153	571	164	41	3	36	(19	17)	319	104	101	77	8	126	1	0	6	41	8	.84	4	.287	.369	.559
1990 New York	NL	154	590	144	37	3	23	(13	10)	256	89	90	69	12	100	0	0	9	34	8	.81	4	.244	.319	.434
1991 New York	NL	156	564	146	34	4	38	(21	17)	302	108	117	78	12	120	1	0	15	30	16	.65	4	.259	.342	.535
1992 New York	NL	100	350	78	19	0	7	(2	5)	118	48	43	55	5	79	2	0	3	22	5	.81	7	.223	.329	.337
1993 New York	NL	72	235	56	8	2	7	(3	4)	89	32	26	43	3	43	0	0	2	6	4	.60	3	.238	.354	.379
12 ML YEARS		1351	4544	1148	233	19	211	(97	114)	2052	704	698	619	103	934	16	9	52	219	73	.75	57	.253	.341	.452

Jeff Johnson

Pitches: Left **Bats:** Right **Pos:** SP   **Ht:** 6' 3" **Wt:** 200 **Born:** 08/04/66 **Age:** 27

HOW MUCH HE PITCHED / WHAT HE GAVE UP / THE RESULTS

Year Team	Lg	G	GS	CG	GF	IP	BFP	H	R	ER	HR	SH	SF	HB	TBB	IBB	SO	WP	Bk	W	L	Pct.	ShO	Sv	ERA
1993 Columbus *	AAA	19	17	3	0	114.2	500	125	55	44	7	6	2	5	47	2	59	4	0	7	6	.538	1	0	3.45
1991 New York	AL	23	23	0	0	127	562	156	89	83	15	7	4	6	33	1	62	5	1	6	11	.353	0	0	5.88
1992 New York	AL	13	8	0	3	52.2	245	71	44	39	4	2	2	2	23	0	14	1	0	2	3	.400	0	0	6.66
1993 New York	AL	2	2	0	0	2.2	22	12	10	9	1	0	0	0	2	0	0	0	0	0	0	.000	0	0	30.38
3 ML YEARS		38	33	0	3	182.1	829	239	143	131	20	9	6	8	58	1	76	6	1	8	16	.333	0	0	6.47

Lance Johnson

Bats: Left **Throws:** Left **Pos:** CF   **Ht:** 5'11" **Wt:** 160 **Born:** 07/06/63 **Age:** 30

BATTING / BASERUNNING / PERCENTAGES

Year Team	Lg	G	AB	H	2B	3B	HR	(Hm	Rd)	TB	R	RBI	TBB	IBB	SO	HBP	SH	SF	SB	CS	SB%	GDP	Avg	OBP	SLG
1987 St. Louis	NL	33	59	13	2	1	0	(0	0)	17	4	7	4	1	6	0	0	0	6	1	.86	2	.220	.270	.288
1988 Chicago	AL	33	124	23	4	1	0	(0	0)	29	11	6	6	0	11	0	2	0	6	2	.75	1	.185	.223	.234
1989 Chicago	AL	50	180	54	8	2	0	(0	0)	66	28	16	17	0	24	0	2	0	16	3	.84	1	.300	.360	.367
1990 Chicago	AL	151	541	154	18	9	1	(0	1)	193	76	51	33	2	45	1	8	4	36	22	.62	12	.285	.325	.357
1991 Chicago	AL	160	588	161	14	13	0	(0	0)	201	72	49	26	2	58	1	6	3	26	11	.70	14	.274	.304	.342
1992 Chicago	AL	157	567	158	15	12	3	(2	1)	206	67	47	34	4	33	1	4	5	41	14	.75	20	.279	.318	.363
1993 Chicago	AL	147	540	168	18	14	0	(0	0)	214	75	47	36	1	33	0	3	0	35	7	.83	10	.311	.354	.396
7 ML YEARS		731	2599	731	79	52	4	(2	2)	926	333	223	156	10	210	3	25	12	166	60	.73	60	.281	.321	.356

Randy Johnson

Pitches: Left **Bats:** Right **Pos:** SP   **Ht:** 6'10" **Wt:** 225 **Born:** 09/10/63 **Age:** 30

HOW MUCH HE PITCHED / WHAT HE GAVE UP / THE RESULTS

Year Team	Lg	G	GS	CG	GF	IP	BFP	H	R	ER	HR	SH	SF	HB	TBB	IBB	SO	WP	Bk	W	L	Pct.	ShO	Sv	ERA
1988 Montreal	NL	4	4	1	0	26	109	23	8	7	3	0	0	0	7	0	25	3	0	3	0	1.000	0	0	2.42
1989 2 ML Teams		29	28	2	1	160.2	715	147	100	86	13	10	13	3	96	2	130	7	7	7	13	.350	0	0	4.82
1990 Seattle	AL	33	33	5	0	219.2	944	174	103	89	26	7	6	5	120	2	194	4	2	14	11	.560	2	0	3.65
1991 Seattle	AL	33	33	2	0	201.1	889	151	96	89	15	9	8	12	152	0	228	12	3	13	10	.565	1	0	3.98
1992 Seattle	AL	31	31	6	0	210.1	922	154	104	88	13	3	8	18	144	1	241	13	1	12	14	.462	2	0	3.77
1993 Seattle	AL	35	34	10	1	255.1	1043	185	97	92	22	8	7	16	99	1	308	8	2	19	8	.704	3	1	3.24
1989 Montreal	NL	7	6	0	1	29.2	143	29	25	22	2	3	4	0	26	1	26	2	2	0	4	.000	0	0	6.67
Seattle	AL	22	22	2	0	131	572	118	75	64	11	7	9	3	70	1	104	5	5	7	9	.438	0	0	4.40
6 ML YEARS		165	163	26	2	1073.1	4622	834	508	451	92	37	42	54	618	6	1126	47	14	68	56	.548	8	1	3.78

Joel Johnston

Pitches: Right **Bats:** Right **Pos:** RP **Ht:** 6' 4" **Wt:** 220 **Born:** 03/08/67 **Age:** 27

Year	Team	Lg	G	GS	CG	GF	IP	BFP	H	R	ER	HR	SH	SF	HB	TBB	IBB	SO	WP	Bk	W	L	Pct.	ShO	Sv	ERA
1988	Eugene	A	14	14	0	0	64	295	64	49	37	1	4	3	7	34	0	64	7	6	4	7	.364	0	0	5.20
1989	Baseball Cy	A	26	26	0	0	131.2	586	135	84	72	6	2	6	11	63	2	76	8	5	9	4	.692	0	0	4.92
1990	Memphis	AA	4	3	0	1	6.2	40	5	9	5	1	0	0	0	16	0	6	3	0	0	0	.000	0	0	6.75
	Baseball Cy	A	31	7	1	18	55.1	251	36	37	30	2	6	3	3	49	0	60	6	1	2	4	.333	0	7	4.88
	Omaha	AAA	2	0	0	0	3	9	1	0	0	0	0	0	0	1	0	3	0	0	0	0	.000	0	0	0.00
1991	Omaha	AAA	47	0	0	27	74.1	318	60	43	43	12	4	0	1	42	2	63	6	0	4	7	.364	0	8	5.21
1992	Omaha	AAA	42	0	0	22	74.2	342	80	54	53	9	5	5	4	45	2	48	6	1	5	2	.714	0	2	6.39
1993	Buffalo	AAA	26	0	0	14	31.1	150	30	28	27	5	4	3	3	25	2	26	5	0	1	3	.250	0	1	7.76
1991	Kansas City	AL	13	0	0	1	22.1	85	9	1	1	0	1	0	0	9	3	21	0	0	1	0	1.000	0	0	0.40
1992	Kansas City	AL	5	0	0	1	2.2	13	3	4	4	2	0	0	0	2	0	6	1	0	0	0	.000	0	0	13.50
1993	Pittsburgh	NL	33	0	0	16	53.1	210	38	20	20	7	4	0	0	19	5	31	1	0	2	4	.333	0	2	3.38
3 ML YEARS			51	0	0	18	78.1	308	50	25	25	9	5	0	0	30	8	52	2	0	3	4	.429	0	2	2.87

John Johnstone

Pitches: Right **Bats:** Right **Pos:** RP **Ht:** 6' 3" **Wt:** 195 **Born:** 11/25/68 **Age:** 25

Year	Team	Lg	G	GS	CG	GF	IP	BFP	H	R	ER	HR	SH	SF	HB	TBB	IBB	SO	WP	Bk	W	L	Pct.	ShO	Sv	ERA
1987	Kingsport	R	17	1	0	4	29	144	42	28	24	3	0	3	0	20	0	21	4	1	1	1	.500	0	0	7.45
1988	Mets	R	12	12	3	0	74	314	65	29	22	0	1	3	4	25	0	57	5	1	3	4	.429	0	2	2.68
1989	Pittsfield	A	15	15	2	0	104	444	101	47	32	4	1	3	3	28	1	60	4	1	11	2	.846	1	0	2.77
1990	St. Lucie	A	25	25	9	0	172.2	708	145	53	43	3	4	5	5	60	1	120	16	2	15	6	.714	3	0	2.24
1991	Williamsprt	AA	27	27	2	0	165.1	720	159	94	73	5	7	6	5	79	1	99	8	0	7	9	.438	0	0	3.97
1992	Binghamton	AA	24	24	2	0	149.1	615	132	66	62	8	7	4	9	36	0	121	3	0	7	7	.500	0	0	3.74
1993	Edmonton	AAA	30	21	1	6	144.1	645	167	95	83	16	5	8	6	59	2	126	9	2	4	15	.211	0	4	5.18
1993	Florida	NL	7	0	0	3	10.2	54	16	8	7	1	0	0	0	7	0	5	1	0	0	2	.000	0	0	5.91

Barry Jones

Pitches: Right **Bats:** Right **Pos:** RP **Ht:** 6' 4" **Wt:** 225 **Born:** 02/15/63 **Age:** 31

Year	Team	Lg	G	GS	CG	GF	IP	BFP	H	R	ER	HR	SH	SF	HB	TBB	IBB	SO	WP	Bk	W	L	Pct.	ShO	Sv	ERA
1993	Nashville *	AAA	7	0	0	2	17.1	70	16	5	5	3	0	0	0	2	0	19	2	0	0	0	.000	0	2	2.60
1986	Pittsburgh	NL	26	0	0	10	37.1	159	29	16	12	3	2	1	0	21	2	29	2	0	3	4	.429	0	3	2.89
1987	Pittsburgh	NL	32	0	0	10	43.1	203	55	34	27	6	3	2	0	23	6	28	3	0	2	4	.333	0	1	5.61
1988	2 ML Teams		59	0	0	25	82.1	347	72	28	26	6	5	5	1	38	7	48	13	2	3	3	.500	0	3	2.84
1989	Chicago	AL	22	0	0	8	30.1	125	22	12	8	2	4	2	1	8	0	17	1	0	3	2	.600	0	1	2.37
1990	Chicago	AL	65	0	0	9	74	310	62	20	19	2	7	5	1	33	7	45	0	1	11	4	.733	0	1	2.31
1991	Montreal	NL	77	0	0	46	88.2	353	76	35	33	8	7	3	1	33	8	46	1	1	4	9	.308	0	13	3.35
1992	2 ML Teams		61	0	0	17	69.2	319	85	46	44	3	3	3	2	35	7	30	2	2	7	6	.538	0	1	5.68
1993	Chicago	AL	6	0	0	1	7.1	38	14	8	7	2	1	0	0	3	0	7	0	0	0	1	.000	0	0	8.59
1988	Pittsburgh	NL	42	0	0	15	56.1	241	57	21	19	3	5	4	1	21	6	31	7	1	1	1	.500	0	2	3.04
	Chicago	AL	17	0	0	10	26	106	15	7	7	3	0	1	0	17	1	17	6	1	2	2	.500	0	1	2.42
1992	Philadelphia	NL	44	0	0	10	54.1	243	65	30	28	3	2	2	2	24	4	19	1	2	5	6	.455	0	0	4.64
	New York	NL	17	0	0	7	15.1	76	20	16	16	0	1	1	0	11	3	11	1	0	2	0	1.000	0	1	9.39
8 ML YEARS			348	0	0	126	433	1850	415	199	176	32	32	21	6	194	37	250	22	6	33	33	.500	0	23	3.66

Bobby Jones

Pitches: Right **Bats:** Right **Pos:** SP **Ht:** 6' 4" **Wt:** 210 **Born:** 02/10/70 **Age:** 24

Year	Team	Lg	G	GS	CG	GF	IP	BFP	H	R	ER	HR	SH	SF	HB	TBB	IBB	SO	WP	Bk	W	L	Pct.	ShO	Sv	ERA
1991	Columbia	A	5	5	0	0	24.1	98	20	5	5	2	1	0	2	3	0	35	0	4	3	1	.750	0	0	1.85
1992	Binghamton	AA	24	24	4	0	158	625	118	40	33	5	4	6	8	43	0	143	3	1	12	4	.750	4	0	1.88
1993	Norfolk	AAA	24	24	6	0	166	671	149	72	67	9	3	5	11	32	2	126	11	0	12	10	.545	3	0	3.63
1993	New York	NL	9	9	0	0	61.2	265	61	35	25	6	5	3	2	22	3	35	1	0	2	4	.333	0	0	3.65

Chipper Jones

Bats: Both **Throws:** Right **Pos:** SS **Ht:** 6' 3" **Wt:** 185 **Born:** 04/24/72 **Age:** 22

Year	Team	Lg	G	AB	H	2B	3B	HR	(Hm	Rd)	TB	R	RBI	TBB	IBB	SO	HBP	SH	SF	SB	CS	SB%	GDP	Avg	OBP	SLG
1990	Braves	R	44	140	32	1	1	1	--	--	38	20	18	14	1	25	6	2	2	5	3	.63	3	.229	.321	.271
1991	Macon	A	136	473	153	24	11	15	--	--	244	104	98	69	4	70	3	1	10	39	11	.78	6	.323	.405	.516
1992	Durham	A	70	264	73	22	1	4	--	--	109	43	31	31	2	34	2	1	3	10	8	.56	5	.277	.353	.413
	Greenville	AA	67	266	92	17	11	9	--	--	158	43	42	11	1	32	0	4	4	14	1	.93	5	.346	.367	.594
1993	Richmond	AAA	139	536	174	31	12	13	--	--	268	97	89	57	5	70	1	3	6	23	7	.77	8	.325	.387	.500
1993	Atlanta	NL	8	3	2	1	0	0	(0	0)	3	2	0	1	0	1	0	0	0	0	0	.00	0	.667	.750	1.000

Chris Jones

Bats: Right **Throws:** Right **Pos:** CF/LF ⬤ **Ht:** 6' 2" **Wt:** 205 **Born:** 12/16/65 **Age:** 28

		BATTING																BASERUNNING				PERCENTAGES		
Year Team	Lg	G	AB	H	2B	3B	HR	(Hm | Rd)	TB	R	RBI	TBB	IBB	SO	HBP	SH	SF	SB	CS	SB%	GDP	Avg	OBP	SLG
1993 Colo Sprngs *	AAA	46	168	47	5	5	12	--	--	98	41	40	19	2	47	2	0	4	8	2	.80	2	.280	.352	.583
1991 Cincinnati	NL	52	89	26	1	2	2	(0 | 2)	37	14	6	2	0	31	0	0	1	2	1	.67	2	.292	.304	.416
1992 Houston	NL	54	63	12	2	1	1	(1 | 0)	19	7	4	7	0	21	0	3	0	3	0	1.00	1	.190	.271	.302
1993 Colorado	NL	86	209	57	11	4	6	(2 | 4)	94	29	31	10	1	48	0	5	1	9	4	.69	6	.273	.305	.450
3 ML YEARS		192	361	95	14	7	9	(3 | 6)	150	50	41	19	1	100	0	8	2	14	5	.74	9	.263	.298	.416

Doug Jones

Pitches: Right **Bats:** Right **Pos:** RP ⬤ **Ht:** 6' 2" **Wt:** 195 **Born:** 06/24/57 **Age:** 37

		HOW MUCH HE PITCHED						WHAT HE GAVE UP										THE RESULTS				
Year Team	Lg	G	GS	CG	GF	IP	BFP	H	R	ER	HR	SH	SF	HB	TBB	IBB	SO	WP	Bk	W	L	Pct.	ShO	Sv	ERA
1982 Milwaukee	AL	4	0	0	2	2.2	14	5	3	3	1	0	0	0	1	0	1	0	0	0	0	.000	0	0	10.13
1986 Cleveland	AL	11	0	0	5	18	79	18	5	5	0	1	1	1	6	1	12	0	0	1	0	1.000	0	1	2.50
1987 Cleveland	AL	49	0	0	29	91.1	400	101	45	32	4	5	5	6	24	5	87	0	0	6	5	.545	0	8	3.15
1988 Cleveland	AL	51	0	0	46	83.1	338	69	26	21	1	3	0	2	16	3	72	2	3	3	4	.429	0	37	2.27
1989 Cleveland	AL	59	0	0	53	80.2	331	76	25	21	4	8	6	1	13	4	65	1	1	7	10	.412	0	32	2.34
1990 Cleveland	AL	66	0	0	64	84.1	331	66	26	24	5	2	2	2	22	4	55	2	0	5	5	.500	0	43	2.56
1991 Cleveland	AL	36	4	0	29	63.1	293	87	42	39	7	2	2	0	17	5	48	1	0	4	8	.333	0	7	5.54
1992 Houston	NL	80	0	0	70	111.2	440	96	29	23	5	9	0	5	17	5	93	2	1	11	8	.579	0	36	1.85
1993 Houston	NL	71	0	0	60	85.1	381	102	46	43	7	9	4	5	21	6	66	3	0	4	10	.286	0	26	4.54
9 ML YEARS		427	4	0	358	620.2	2607	620	247	211	34	39	20	22	137	33	499	11	5	41	50	.451	0	190	3.06

Jimmy Jones

Pitches: Right **Bats:** Right **Pos:** SP/RP ⬤ **Ht:** 6' 2" **Wt:** 190 **Born:** 04/20/64 **Age:** 30

		HOW MUCH HE PITCHED						WHAT HE GAVE UP										THE RESULTS				
Year Team	Lg	G	GS	CG	GF	IP	BFP	H	R	ER	HR	SH	SF	HB	TBB	IBB	SO	WP	Bk	W	L	Pct.	ShO	Sv	ERA
1993 Ottawa *	AAA	3	3	0	0	15	59	10	2	2	0	1	0	0	5	0	12	0	0	1	0	1.000	0	0	1.20
1986 San Diego	NL	3	3	1	0	18	65	10	6	5	1	1	0	0	3	0	15	0	0	2	0	1.000	1	0	2.50
1987 San Diego	NL	30	22	2	4	145.2	639	154	65	67	14	5	5	5	54	2	51	3	2	9	7	.563	1	0	4.14
1988 San Diego	NL	29	29	3	0	179	760	192	98	82	14	11	9	3	44	3	82	4	1	9	14	.391	0	0	4.12
1989 New York	AL	11	6	0	3	48	211	56	29	28	7	1	1	2	16	1	25	1	0	2	1	.667	0	0	5.25
1990 New York	AL	17	7	0	9	50	238	72	42	35	8	1	4	1	23	0	25	3	0	1	2	.333	0	0	6.30
1991 Houston	NL	26	22	1	0	135.1	593	143	73	66	9	7	2	3	51	3	88	4	0	6	8	.429	1	0	4.39
1992 Houston	NL	25	23	0	1	139.1	579	135	64	63	13	7	4	5	39	3	69	4	1	10	6	.625	0	0	4.07
1993 Montreal	NL	12	6	0	3	39.2	175	47	34	28	6	1	0	0	9	0	21	1	1	4	1	.800	0	0	6.35
8 ML YEARS		153	118	7	20	755	3260	809	431	374	72	34	25	19	239	12	376	20	5	43	39	.524	3	0	4.46

Tim Jones

Bats: Left **Throws:** Right **Pos:** SS ⬤ **Ht:** 5'10" **Wt:** 175 **Born:** 12/01/62 **Age:** 31

		BATTING																BASERUNNING				PERCENTAGES		
Year Team	Lg	G	AB	H	2B	3B	HR	(Hm	Rd)	TB	R	RBI	TBB	IBB	SO	HBP	SH	SF	SB	CS	SB%	GDP	Avg	OBP	SLG
1993 Louisville *	AAA	101	408	118	22	10	5	--	--	175	72	46	44	1	67	2	2	4	13	8	.62	4	.289	.358	.429
1988 St. Louis	NL	31	52	14	0	0	0	(0	0)	14	2	3	4	0	10	0	0	0	4	1	.80	1	.269	.321	.269
1989 St. Louis	NL	42	75	22	6	0	0	(0	0)	28	11	7	7	1	8	1	1	2	1	0	1.00	2	.293	.353	.373
1990 St. Louis	NL	67	128	28	7	1	1	(1	0)	40	9	12	12	1	20	1	4	0	3	4	.43	1	.219	.291	.313
1991 St. Louis	NL	16	24	4	2	0	0	(0	0)	6	1	2	2	1	6	0	0	1	0	1	.00	0	.167	.222	.250
1992 St. Louis	NL	67	145	29	4	0	0	(0	0)	33	9	3	11	1	29	0	2	0	5	2	.71	1	.200	.256	.228
1993 St. Louis	NL	29	61	16	6	0	0	(0	0)	22	13	1	9	0	8	1	2	0	2	2	.50	0	.262	.366	.361
6 ML YEARS		252	485	113	25	1	1	(1	0)	143	45	28	45	4	81	3	9	3	15	10	.60	5	.233	.300	.295

Todd Jones

Pitches: Right **Bats:** Left **Pos:** RP ⬤ **Ht:** 6' 3" **Wt:** 200 **Born:** 04/24/68 **Age:** 26

		HOW MUCH HE PITCHED						WHAT HE GAVE UP										THE RESULTS				
Year Team	Lg	G	GS	CG	GF	IP	BFP	H	R	ER	HR	SH	SF	HB	TBB	IBB	SO	WP	Bk	W	L	Pct.	ShO	Sv	ERA
1989 Auburn	A	11	9	1	1	49.2	241	47	39	30	2	1	0	2	42	1	71	9	1	2	3	.400	0	0	5.44
1990 Osceola	A	27	27	1	0	151.1	678	124	81	59	2	7	2	3	109	1	106	16	3	12	10	.545	0	0	3.51
1991 Osceola	A	14	14	0	0	72.1	311	68	38	35	2	1	2	3	35	0	52	4	0	4	4	.500	0	0	4.35
Jackson	AA	10	10	0	0	55.1	258	51	37	30	2	2	1	4	39	1	37	6	2	4	3	.571	0	0	4.88
1992 Jackson	AA	61	0	0	48	66	295	52	28	23	3	5	0	2	44	3	60	5	1	3	7	.300	0	25	3.14
Tucson	AAA	3	0	0	2	4	23	1	2	2	0	0	0	0	10	1	4	1	0	0	1	.000	0	0	4.50
1993 Tucson	AAA	41	0	0	28	48.2	220	49	26	24	5	3	1	0	31	2	45	5	0	4	2	.667	0	12	4.44
1993 Houston	NL	27	0	0	8	37.1	150	28	14	13	4	2	1	1	15	2	25	1	1	1	2	.333	0	2	3.13

111

Brian Jordan

Bats: Right **Throws:** Right **Pos:** CF/LF/RF **Ht:** 6' 1" **Wt:** 205 **Born:** 03/29/67 **Age:** 27

Year Team	Lg	G	AB	H	2B	3B	HR	Hm	Rd	TB	R	RBI	TBB	IBB	SO	HBP	SH	SF	SB	CS	SB%	GDP	Avg	OBP	SLG
1988 Hamilton	A	19	71	22	3	1	4	--	--	39	12	12	6	1	15	3	1	0	3	3	.50	0	.310	.388	.549
1989 St.Pete	A	11	43	15	4	1	2	--	--	27	7	11	0	0	8	2	0	0	0	2	.00	1	.349	.378	.628
1990 Arkansas	AA	16	50	8	1	0	0	--	--	9	4	0	0	0	11	1	0	0	0	0	.00	1	.160	.176	.180
St. Pete	A	9	30	5	0	1	0	--	--	7	3	1	2	0	11	0	0	0	0	2	.00	0	.167	.219	.233
1991 Louisville	AAA	61	212	56	11	4	4	--	--	87	35	24	17	1	41	8	1	0	10	4	.71	5	.264	.342	.410
1992 Louisville	AAA	43	155	45	3	1	4	--	--	62	23	16	8	1	21	4	0	2	13	2	.87	1	.290	.337	.400
1993 Louisville	AAA	38	144	54	13	2	5	--	--	86	24	35	16	0	17	3	0	2	9	4	.69	3	.375	.442	.597
1992 St. Louis	NL	55	193	40	9	4	5	(3	2)	72	17	22	10	1	48	1	0	0	7	2	.78	6	.207	.250	.373
1993 St. Louis	NL	67	223	69	10	6	10	(4	6)	121	33	44	12	0	35	4	0	3	6	6	.50	5	.309	.351	.543
2 ML YEARS		122	416	109	19	10	15	(7	8)	193	50	66	22	1	83	5	0	3	13	8	.62	12	.262	.305	.464

Ricky Jordan

Bats: Right **Throws:** Right **Pos:** 1B **Ht:** 6' 3" **Wt:** 205 **Born:** 05/26/65 **Age:** 29

Year Team	Lg	G	AB	H	2B	3B	HR	Hm	Rd	TB	R	RBI	TBB	IBB	SO	HBP	SH	SF	SB	CS	SB%	GDP	Avg	OBP	SLG
1988 Philadelphia	NL	69	273	84	15	1	11	(6	5)	134	41	43	7	2	39	0	0	1	1	1	.50	5	.308	.324	.491
1989 Philadelphia	NL	144	523	149	22	3	12	(7	5)	213	63	75	23	5	62	5	0	8	4	3	.57	19	.285	.317	.407
1990 Philadelphia	NL	92	324	78	21	0	5	(2	3)	114	32	44	13	6	39	5	0	4	2	0	1.00	9	.241	.277	.352
1991 Philadelphia	NL	101	301	82	21	3	9	(5	4)	136	38	49	14	2	49	2	0	5	0	2	.00	11	.272	.304	.452
1992 Philadelphia	NL	94	276	84	19	0	4	(2	2)	115	33	34	5	0	44	0	0	3	3	0	1.00	8	.304	.313	.417
1993 Philadelphia	NL	90	159	46	4	1	5	(3	2)	67	21	18	8	1	32	1	0	0	0	0	.00	2	.289	.324	.421
6 ML YEARS		590	1856	523	102	8	46	(25	21)	779	228	263	70	16	265	13	0	23	10	6	.63	54	.282	.309	.420

Terry Jorgensen

Bats: Right **Throws:** Right **Pos:** 3B **Ht:** 6' 4" **Wt:** 213 **Born:** 09/02/66 **Age:** 27

Year Team	Lg	G	AB	H	2B	3B	HR	Hm	Rd	TB	R	RBI	TBB	IBB	SO	HBP	SH	SF	SB	CS	SB%	GDP	Avg	OBP	SLG
1987 Kenosha	A	67	254	80	17	0	7	--	--	118	37	33	18	0	43	2	0	1		0	1.00		.315	.364	.465
1988 Orlando	AA	135	472	116	27	4	3	--	--	160	53	43	40	3	62	6	2	6	4	1	.80	11	.246	.309	.339
1989 Orlando	AA	135	514	135	27	5	13	--	--	211	84	101	76	4	78	5	0	9	1	1	.50	6	.263	.358	.411
1990 Portland	AAA	123	440	114	28	3	10	--	--	178	43	50	44	2	83	0	1	4		4	.00	11	.259	.324	.405
1991 Portland	AAA	126	456	136	29	0	11	--	--	198	74	59	54	1	41	4	2	2	1	0	1.00	22	.298	.376	.434
1992 Portland	AAA	135	505	149	32	2	14	--	--	227	78	71	54	3	58	4	3	5	2	0	1.00	22	.295	.364	.450
1993 Portland	AAA	61	238	73	18	2	4	--	--	107	37	44	19	2	28	1	1	0	1	0	1.00	11	.307	.360	.450
1989 Minnesota	AL	10	23	4	1	0	0	(0	0)	5	1	2	4	0	5	0	0	0	0	0	.00	1	.174	.296	.217
1992 Minnesota	AL	22	58	18	1	0	0	(0	0)	19	5	5	3	0	11	1	0	1	1	2	.33	4	.310	.349	.328
1993 Minnesota	AL	59	152	34	7	0	1	(0	1)	44	15	12	10	0	21	0	0	1	1	0	1.00	7	.224	.270	.289
3 ML YEARS		91	233	56	9	0	1	(0	1)	68	21	19	17	0	37	1	0	2	2	2	.50	12	.240	.292	.292

Felix Jose

Bats: Both **Throws:** Right **Pos:** RF **Ht:** 6' 1" **Wt:** 220 **Born:** 05/08/65 **Age:** 29

Year Team	Lg	G	AB	H	2B	3B	HR	Hm	Rd	TB	R	RBI	TBB	IBB	SO	HBP	SH	SF	SB	CS	SB%	GDP	Avg	OBP	SLG
1988 Oakland	AL	8	6	2	1	0	0	(0	0)	3	2	1	0	0	1	0	0	0	0	1	1.00	0	.333	.333	.500
1989 Oakland	AL	20	57	11	2	0	0	(0	0)	13	3	5	4	0	13	0	0	0	0	1	.00	2	.193	.246	.228
1990 2 ML Teams		126	426	113	16	1	6	(5	6)	164	54	52	24	0	81	5	2	1	12	6	.67	9	.265	.311	.385
1991 St. Louis	NL	154	568	173	40	6	8	(3	5)	249	69	77	50	4	113	2	0	1	20	12	.63	12	.305	.360	.438
1992 St. Louis	NL	131	509	150	22	3	14	(12	2)	220	62	75	40	8	100	1	0	1	28	12	.70	9	.295	.347	.432
1993 Kansas City	AL	149	499	126	24	3	6	(2	4)	174	64	43	36	5	95	1	1	2	31	13	.70	5	.253	.303	.349
1990 Oakland	AL	101	341	90	12	0	8	(3	5)	126	42	39	16	0	65	5	2	1	8	2	.80	8	.264	.306	.370
St. Louis	NL	25	85	23	4	1	3			38	12	13	8	0	16	0	0	0	4	4	.50	1	.271	.333	.447
6 ML YEARS		588	2065	575	105	13	39	(22	17)	823	254	253	154	21	403	9	3	9	92	44	.68	37	.278	.330	.399

Wally Joyner

Bats: Left **Throws:** Left **Pos:** 1B **Ht:** 6' 2" **Wt:** 200 **Born:** 06/16/62 **Age:** 32

Year Team	Lg	G	AB	H	2B	3B	HR	Hm	Rd	TB	R	RBI	TBB	IBB	SO	HBP	SH	SF	SB	CS	SB%	GDP	Avg	OBP	SLG
1986 California	AL	154	593	172	27	3	22	(11	11)	271	82	100	57	8	58	2	10	12	5	2	.71	11	.290	.348	.457
1987 California	AL	149	564	161	33	1	34	(19	15)	298	100	117	72	12	64	5	2	10	8	2	.80	14	.285	.366	.528
1988 California	AL	158	597	176	31	2	13	(5	8)	250	81	85	55	14	51	5	0	6	8	2	.80	16	.295	.356	.419
1989 California	AL	159	593	167	30	2	16	(8	8)	249	78	79	46	7	58	6	1	8	3	2	.60	15	.282	.335	.420
1990 California	AL	83	310	83	15	0	8	(5	3)	122	35	41	41	4	34	1	1	5	2	1	.67	10	.268	.350	.394
1991 California	AL	143	551	166	34	3	21	(10	11)	269	79	96	52	4	66	1	2	5	2	0	1.00	11	.301	.360	.488

Year	Team	Lg	G	AB	H	2B	3B	HR	(Hm	Rd)	TB	R	RBI	TBB	IBB	SO	HBP	SH	SF	SB	CS	SB%	GDP	Avg	OBP	SLG
1992	Kansas City	AL	149	572	154	36	2	9	(1	8)	221	66	66	55	4	50	4	0	2	11	5	.69	19	.269	.336	.386
1993	Kansas City	AL	141	497	145	36	3	15	(4	11)	232	83	65	66	13	67	3	2	5	5	9	.36	6	.292	.375	.467
	8 ML YEARS		1136	4277	1224	242	16	138	(64	74)	1912	604	649	444	66	448	27	18	53	44	23	.66	102	.286	.353	.447

Jeff Juden

Pitches: Right **Bats:** Right **Pos:** RP **Ht:** 6' 7" **Wt:** 245 **Born:** 01/19/71 **Age:** 23

			HOW MUCH HE PITCHED					WHAT HE GAVE UP													THE RESULTS					
Year	Team	Lg	G	GS	CG	GF	IP	BFP	H	R	ER	HR	SH	SF	HB	TBB	IBB	SO	WP	Bk	W	L	Pct.	ShO	Sv	ERA
1989	Astros	R	9	8	0	0	39.2	177	33	21	15	0	1	3	3	17	0	49	7	2	1	4	.200	0	0	3.40
1990	Osceola	A	15	15	2	0	91	390	72	37	33	2	3	1	5	42	0	85	7	4	10	1	.909	0	0	2.27
	Columbus	AA	11	11	0	0	52	250	55	36	31	2	2	1	4	42	2	40	9	2	1	3	.250	0	0	5.37
1991	Jackson	AA	16	16	0	0	95.2	408	84	43	33	4	8	4	3	44	0	75	5	2	6	3	.667	0	0	3.10
	Tucson	AAA	10	10	0	0	56.2	245	56	28	20	2	4	3	0	25	0	51	7	0	3	2	.600	0	0	3.18
1992	Tucson	AAA	26	26	0	0	147	655	149	84	66	11	12	7	7	71	1	120	12	7	9	10	.474	0	0	4.04
1993	Tucson	AAA	27	27	0	0	169	755	174	102	87	8	5	5	9	76	0	156	15	0	11	6	.647	0	0	4.63
1991	Houston	NL	4	3	0	0	18	81	19	14	12	3	2	3	0	7	1	11	0	1	0	2	.000	0	0	6.00
1993	Houston	NL	2	0	0	1	5	23	4	3	3	1	0	1	0	4	1	7	0	0	0	1	.000	0	0	5.40
	2 ML YEARS		6	3	0	1	23	104	23	17	15	4	2	4	0	11	2	18	0	1	0	3	.000	0	0	5.87

Dave Justice

Bats: Left **Throws:** Left **Pos:** RF **Ht:** 6' 3" **Wt:** 200 **Born:** 04/14/66 **Age:** 28

			BATTING																	BASERUNNING				PERCENTAGES		
Year	Team	Lg	G	AB	H	2B	3B	HR	(Hm	Rd)	TB	R	RBI	TBB	IBB	SO	HBP	SH	SF	SB	CS	SB%	GDP	Avg	OBP	SLG
1989	Atlanta	NL	16	51	12	3	0	1	(1	0)	18	7	3	3	1	9	1	1	0	2	1	.67	1	.235	.291	.353
1990	Atlanta	NL	127	439	124	23	2	28	(19	9)	235	76	78	64	4	92	0	0	1	11	6	.65	2	.282	.373	.535
1991	Atlanta	NL	109	396	109	25	1	21	(11	10)	199	67	87	65	9	81	3	0	5	8	8	.50	4	.275	.377	.503
1992	Atlanta	NL	144	484	124	19	5	21	(10	11)	216	78	72	79	8	85	2	0	6	2	4	.33	1	.256	.359	.446
1993	Atlanta	NL	157	585	158	15	4	40	(18	22)	301	90	120	78	12	90	3	0	4	3	5	.38	10	.270	.357	.515
	5 ML YEARS		553	1955	527	85	12	111	(59	52)	969	318	360	289	34	357	9	1	16	26	24	.52	18	.270	.364	.496

Jeff Kaiser

Pitches: Left **Bats:** Right **Pos:** RP **Ht:** 6' 3" **Wt:** 195 **Born:** 07/24/60 **Age:** 33

			HOW MUCH HE PITCHED					WHAT HE GAVE UP													THE RESULTS					
Year	Team	Lg	G	GS	CG	GF	IP	BFP	H	R	ER	HR	SH	SF	HB	TBB	IBB	SO	WP	Bk	W	L	Pct.	ShO	Sv	ERA
1993	Indianapolis*	AAA	1	0	0	0	1	3	0	0	0	0	0	0	0	0	0	2	0	0	0	0	.000	0	0	0.00
	Norfolk*	AAA	21	0	0	15	22.1	95	23	15	14	2	0	1	0	6	0	23	3	0	1	1	.500	0	9	5.64
1985	Oakland	AL	15	0	0	4	16.2	97	25	32	27	6	1	2	1	20	2	10	2	0	0	0	.000	0	0	14.58
1987	Cleveland	AL	2	0	0	0	3.1	18	4	6	6	1	0	0	1	3	0	2	0	0	0	0	.000	0	0	16.20
1988	Cleveland	AL	3	0	0	1	2.2	11	2	0	0	0	2	1	0	1	0	0	0	0	0	0	.000	0	0	0.00
1989	Cleveland	AL	6	0	0	1	3.2	22	5	5	3	1	0	1	0	5	0	4	1	0	0	1	.000	0	0	7.36
1990	Cleveland	AL	5	0	0	0	12.2	60	16	5	5	2	0	1	0	7	1	9	0	0	0	0	.000	0	0	3.55
1991	Detroit	AL	10	0	0	4	5	26	6	5	5	1	0	0	0	5	2	4	0	0	0	1	.000	0	2	9.00
1993	2 ML Teams		9	0	0	3	8	37	10	7	7	1	0	1	0	5	1	9	0	0	0	0	.000	0	0	7.88
1993	Cincinnati	NL	3	0	0	1	3.1	16	4	1	1	0	0	0	0	2	1	4	0	0	0	0	.000	0	0	2.70
	New York	NL	6	0	0	2	4.2	21	6	6	6	1	0	1	0	3	0	5	0	0	0	0	.000	0	0	11.57
	7 ML YEARS		50	0	0	13	52	271	68	60	53	12	3	6	2	46	6	38	3	0	0	2	.000	0	2	9.17

Scott Kamieniecki

Pitches: Right **Bats:** Right **Pos:** SP/RP **Ht:** 6' 0" **Wt:** 195 **Born:** 04/19/64 **Age:** 30

			HOW MUCH HE PITCHED					WHAT HE GAVE UP													THE RESULTS					
Year	Team	Lg	G	GS	CG	GF	IP	BFP	H	R	ER	HR	SH	SF	HB	TBB	IBB	SO	WP	Bk	W	L	Pct.	ShO	Sv	ERA
1993	Columbus*	AAA	1	1	0	0	6	22	5	1	1	0	0	0	0	0	0	4	0	0	1	0	1.000	0	0	1.50
1991	New York	AL	9	9	0	0	55.1	239	54	24	24	8	2	1	3	22	1	34	1	0	4	4	.500	0	0	3.90
1992	New York	AL	28	28	4	0	188	804	193	100	91	13	5	5	5	74	9	88	9	1	6	14	.300	0	0	4.36
1993	New York	AL	30	20	2	4	154.1	659	163	73	70	17	3	5	3	59	7	72	2	0	10	7	.588	0	1	4.08
	3 ML YEARS		67	57	6	4	397.2	1702	410	197	185	38	8	11	11	155	17	194	12	1	20	25	.444	0	1	4.19

Ron Karkovice

Bats: Right **Throws:** Right **Pos:** C **Ht:** 6' 1" **Wt:** 219 **Born:** 08/08/63 **Age:** 30

			BATTING																	BASERUNNING				PERCENTAGES		
Year	Team	Lg	G	AB	H	2B	3B	HR	(Hm	Rd)	TB	R	RBI	TBB	IBB	SO	HBP	SH	SF	SB	CS	SB%	GDP	Avg	OBP	SLG
1986	Chicago	AL	37	97	24	7	0	4	(1	3)	43	13	13	9	0	37	1	1	1	1	0	1.00	3	.247	.315	.443
1987	Chicago	AL	39	85	6	0	0	2	(1	1)	12	7	7	7	0	40	2	1	0	3	0	1.00	2	.071	.160	.141
1988	Chicago	AL	46	115	20	4	0	3	(1	2)	33	10	9	7	0	30	1	3	0	4	2	.67	1	.174	.228	.287
1989	Chicago	AL	71	182	48	9	2	3	(0	3)	70	21	24	10	0	56	2	7	2	0	0	.00	0	.264	.306	.385
1990	Chicago	AL	68	183	45	10	0	6	(0	6)	73	30	20	16	1	52	1	7	1	2	0	1.00	2	.246	.308	.399
1991	Chicago	AL	75	167	41	13	0	5	(0	5)	69	25	22	15	1	42	1	9	1	0	0	.00	2	.246	.310	.413

Year	Team	Lg	G	AB	H	2B	3B	HR	(Hm	Rd)	TB	R	RBI	TBB	IBB	SO	HBP	SH	SF	SB	CS	SB%	GDP	Avg	OBP	SLG
1992	Chicago	AL	123	342	81	12	1	13	(5	8)	134	39	50	30	1	89	3	4	2	10	4	.71	3	.237	.302	.392
1993	Chicago	AL	128	403	92	17	1	20	(6	14)	171	60	54	29	1	126	6	11	4	2	2	.50	12	.228	.287	.424
	8 ML YEARS		587	1574	357	72	4	56	(14	42)	605	205	199	123	4	472	17	43	11	22	8	.73	24	.227	.288	.384

Eric Karros

Bats: Right **Throws:** Right **Pos:** 1B **Ht:** 6' 4" **Wt:** 216 **Born:** 11/04/67 **Age:** 26

							BATTING													BASERUNNING				PERCENTAGES		
Year	Team	Lg	G	AB	H	2B	3B	HR	(Hm	Rd)	TB	R	RBI	TBB	IBB	SO	HBP	SH	SF	SB	CS	SB%	GDP	Avg	OBP	SLG
1991	Los Angeles	NL	14	14	1	0	0	0	(0	0)	1	0	1	1	0	6	0	0	0	0	0	.00	0	.071	.133	.143
1992	Los Angeles	NL	149	545	140	30	1	20	(6	14)	232	63	88	37	3	103	2	0	5	2	4	.33	15	.257	.304	.426
1993	Los Angeles	NL	158	619	153	27	2	23	(13	10)	253	74	80	34	1	82	2	0	3	0	1	.00	17	.247	.287	.409
	3 ML YEARS		321	1178	294	58	3	43	(19	24)	487	137	169	72	4	191	4	0	8	2	5	.29	32	.250	.293	.413

Steve Karsay

Pitches: Right **Bats:** Right **Pos:** SP **Ht:** 6' 3" **Wt:** 180 **Born:** 03/24/72 **Age:** 22

				HOW MUCH HE PITCHED						WHAT HE GAVE UP									THE RESULTS					
Year	Team	Lg	G	GS	CG	GF	IP	BFP	H	R	ER	HR	SH	SF	HB	TBB	IBB	SO	WP	Bk	W	L	Pct.	ShO	Sv	ERA
1990	St. Cath	A	5	5	0	0	22.2	90	11	4	2	0	0	0	0	12	0	25	0	3	1	1	.500	0	0	0.79
1991	Myrtle Bch	A	20	20	1	0	110.2	460	96	58	44	7	4	3	5	48	0	100	8	5	4	9	.308	0	0	3.58
1992	Dunedin	A	16	16	3	0	85.2	334	56	32	26	6	1	1	4	29	0	87	2	3	6	3	.667	2	0	2.73
1993	Knoxville	AA	19	18	1	0	104	434	98	42	39	9	3	3	6	32	1	100	5	0	8	4	.667	1	0	3.38
	Huntsville	AA	2	2	0	0	14	56	13	8	8	2	1	0	1	3	0	22	0	0	0	0	.000	0	0	5.14
1993	Oakland	AL	8	8	0	0	49	210	49	23	22	4	0	2	2	16	1	33	1	0	3	3	.500	0	0	4.04

Bobby Kelly

Bats: Right **Throws:** Right **Pos:** CF **Ht:** 6' 2" **Wt:** 190 **Born:** 10/01/64 **Age:** 29

							BATTING													BASERUNNING				PERCENTAGES		
Year	Team	Lg	G	AB	H	2B	3B	HR	(Hm	Rd)	TB	R	RBI	TBB	IBB	SO	HBP	SH	SF	SB	CS	SB%	GDP	Avg	OBP	SLG
1987	New York	AL	23	52	14	3	0	1	(0	1)	20	12	7	5	0	15	0	1	0	9	3	.75	0	.269	.328	.385
1988	New York	AL	38	77	19	4	1	1	(1	0)	28	9	7	3	0	15	0	3	1	5	2	.71	0	.247	.272	.364
1989	New York	AL	137	441	133	18	3	9	(2	7)	184	65	48	41	3	89	6	8	0	35	12	.74	9	.302	.369	.417
1990	New York	AL	162	641	183	32	4	15	(5	10)	268	85	61	33	0	148	4	4	4	42	17	.71	7	.285	.323	.418
1991	New York	AL	126	486	130	22	2	20	(11	9)	216	68	69	45	2	77	5	2	5	32	9	.78	14	.267	.333	.444
1992	New York	AL	152	580	158	31	2	10	(6	4)	223	81	66	41	4	96	4	1	6	28	5	.85	19	.272	.322	.384
1993	Cincinnati	NL	78	320	102	17	3	9	(4	5)	152	44	35	17	0	43	2	0	3	21	5	.81	10	.319	.354	.475
	7 ML YEARS		716	2597	739	127	15	65	(29	36)	1091	364	293	185	9	483	21	19	20	172	53	.76	59	.285	.335	.420

Pat Kelly

Bats: Right **Throws:** Right **Pos:** 2B **Ht:** 6' 0" **Wt:** 182 **Born:** 10/14/67 **Age:** 26

							BATTING													BASERUNNING				PERCENTAGES		
Year	Team	Lg	G	AB	H	2B	3B	HR	(Hm	Rd)	TB	R	RBI	TBB	IBB	SO	HBP	SH	SF	SB	CS	SB%	GDP	Avg	OBP	SLG
1991	New York	AL	96	298	72	12	4	3	(3	0)	101	35	23	15	0	52	5	5	2	12	1	.92	5	.242	.288	.339
1992	New York	AL	106	318	72	22	2	7	(3	4)	119	38	27	25	1	72	10	6	3	8	5	.62	6	.226	.301	.374
1993	New York	AL	127	406	111	24	1	7	(4	3)	158	49	51	24	0	68	5	10	6	14	11	.56	9	.273	.317	.389
	3 ML YEARS		329	1022	255	58	7	17	(10	7)	378	122	101	64	1	192	20	18	11	34	17	.67	20	.250	.303	.370

Jeff Kent

Bats: Right **Throws:** Right **Pos:** 2B/3B **Ht:** 6' 1" **Wt:** 185 **Born:** 03/07/68 **Age:** 26

							BATTING													BASERUNNING				PERCENTAGES		
Year	Team	Lg	G	AB	H	2B	3B	HR	(Hm	Rd)	TB	R	RBI	TBB	IBB	SO	HBP	SH	SF	SB	CS	SB%	GDP	Avg	OBP	SLG
1989	St.Cathmes	A	73	268	72	14	1	13	--	--	115	34	37	33	2	81	6	0	4	5	1	.83	2	.224	.318	.429
1990	Dunedin	A	132	447	124	32	2	16	--	--	208	72	60	53	5	98	6	3	3	17	7	.71	4	.277	.360	.465
1991	Knoxville	AA	139	445	114	34	1	12	--	--	186	68	61	80	2	104	10	2	3	25	6	.81	3	.256	.379	.418
1992	2 ML Teams		102	305	73	21	2	11	(4	7)	131	52	50	27	0	76	7	0	4	2	3	.40	5	.239	.312	.430
1993	New York	NL	140	496	134	24	0	21	(9	12)	221	65	80	30	2	88	8	6	4	4	4	.50	11	.270	.320	.446
1992	Toronto	AL	65	192	46	13	1	8	(2	6)	85	36	35	20	0	47	6	0	4	2	1	.67	3	.240	.324	.443
	New York	NL	37	113	27	8	1	3	(2	1)	46	16	15	7	0	29	1	0	0	0	2	.00	2	.239	.289	.407
	2 ML YEARS		242	801	207	45	2	32	(13	19)	352	117	130	57	2	164	15	6	8	6	7	.46	16	.258	.317	.439

Keith Kessinger

Bats: Both **Throws:** Right **Pos:** SS **Ht:** 6' 2" **Wt:** 185 **Born:** 02/19/67 **Age:** 27

							BATTING													BASERUNNING				PERCENTAGES		
Year	Team	Lg	G	AB	H	2B	3B	HR	(Hm	Rd)	TB	R	RBI	TBB	IBB	SO	HBP	SH	SF	SB	CS	SB%	GDP	Avg	OBP	SLG
1989	Bluefield	R	28	99	27	4	0	2	--	--	37	17	9	8	0	12	1	2	0	1	0	1.00	1	.273	.333	.374
1990	Wausau	A	37	134	29	8	0	0	--	--	37	17	9	6	0	23	3	0	0	1	1	.50	2	.216	.266	.276
	Frederick	A	64	145	22	4	0	0	--	--	26	18	8	20	0	36	3	5	0	0	0	.00	2	.152	.268	.179
1991	Frederick	A	26	56	10	3	0	0	--	--	13	5	4	8	0	12	1	0	0	2	1	.67	3	.179	.281	.232

Year	Team	Lg	G	AB	R	2B	3B	HR			H	TBB	IBB	SO	SB	CS					Avg	OBP	SLG
	Cedar Rapds	A	59	206	42	5	0	1	--	--	50	15	15	23	1	46	3	5	1	0	1 .00	4	.204 .292 .243
1992	Cedar Rapds	A	95	308	73	15	1	4	--	--	102	41	38	36	2	57	1	5	1	2	0 1.00	7	.237 .318 .331
1993	Chattanooga	AA	56	161	50	9	0	3	--	--	68	24	28	24	2	18	0	5	0	0	3 .00	0	.311 .400 .422
	Indianapols	AAA	35	120	34	9	0	2	--	--	49	17	15	14	4	14	1	1	0	0	1 .00	0	.283 .363 .408
1993	Cincinnati	NL	11	27	7	1	0	1	(1	0)	11	4	3	4	0	4	0	0	0	0	0 .00	1	.259 .344 .407

Jimmy Key

Pitches: Left **Bats:** Right **Pos:** SP   **Ht:** 6' 1" **Wt:** 185 **Born:** 04/22/61 **Age:** 33

			HOW MUCH HE PITCHED						WHAT HE GAVE UP										THE RESULTS						
Year	Team	Lg	G	GS	CG	GF	IP	BFP	H	R	ER	HR	SH	SF	HB	TBB	IBB	SO	WP	Bk	W	L	Pct.	ShO	Sv	ERA
1984	Toronto	AL	63	0	0	24	62	285	70	37	32	8	6	1	1	32	8	44	3	1	4	5	.444	0	10	4.65
1985	Toronto	AL	35	32	3	0	212.2	856	188	77	71	22	5	5	2	50	1	85	6	1	14	6	.700	0	0	3.00
1986	Toronto	AL	36	35	4	0	232	959	222	98	92	24	10	6	3	74	1	141	3	0	14	11	.560	2	0	3.57
1987	Toronto	AL	36	36	8	0	261	1033	210	80	80	24	11	3	2	66	6	161	8	5	17	8	.680	1	0	**2.76**
1988	Toronto	AL	21	21	2	0	131.1	551	127	55	48	13	4	3	5	30	2	65	1	0	12	5	.706	2	0	3.29
1989	Toronto	AL	33	33	5	0	216	886	226	99	93	18	9	9	3	27	2	118	4	1	13	14	.481	1	0	3.88
1990	Toronto	AL	27	27	0	0	154.2	636	169	79	73	20	5	6	1	22	2	88	0	1	13	7	.650	0	0	4.25
1991	Toronto	AL	33	33	2	0	209.1	877	207	84	71	12	10	5	3	44	3	125	1	0	16	12	.571	2	0	3.05
1992	Toronto	AL	33	33	4	0	216.2	900	205	88	85	24	2	7	1	59	0	117	5	0	13	13	.500	2	0	3.53
1993	New York	AL	34	34	4	0	236.2	948	219	84	79	26	6	9	1	43	1	173	3	0	18	6	.750	0	0	3.00
	10 ML YEARS		351	284	32	24	1932.1	7931	1843	794	724	191	68	54	25	447	26	1117	34	9	134	87	.606	12	10	3.37

Mark Kiefer

Pitches: Right **Bats:** Right **Pos:** RP   **Ht:** 6' 4" **Wt:** 175 **Born:** 11/13/68 **Age:** 25

			HOW MUCH HE PITCHED						WHAT HE GAVE UP										THE RESULTS						
Year	Team	Lg	G	GS	CG	GF	IP	BFP	H	R	ER	HR	SH	SF	HB	TBB	IBB	SO	WP	Bk	W	L	Pct.	ShO	Sv	ERA
1988	Helena	R	15	9	2	4	68	296	76	30	20	3	3	0	6	17	0	51	4	3	4	4	.500	0	0	2.65
1989	Beloit	A	30	15	7	5	131.2	533	106	44	34	4	1	4	8	32	2	100	6	0	9	6	.600	2	1	2.32
1990	Brewers	R	1	1	0	0	2.1	10	3	1	1	0	0	0	0	1	0	2	0	0	0	0	.000	0	0	3.86
	Stockton	A	11	10	0	1	60	261	65	23	22	5	0	1	8	17	0	37	3	1	5	2	.714	0	0	3.30
1991	El Paso	AA	12	12	0	0	75.2	325	62	33	28	4	2	2	1	43	2	72	6	0	7	1	.875	0	0	3.33
	Denver	AAA	17	17	3	0	101.1	449	104	55	52	7	4	1	9	41	0	68	6	0	9	5	.643	2	0	4.62
1992	Denver	AAA	27	26	1	0	162.2	706	168	95	83	25	3	4	9	65	1	145	8	3	7	13	.350	0	0	4.59
1993	El Paso	AA	11	11	0	0	51.2	221	48	29	23	5	1	0	2	19	0	44	6	3	3	4	.429	0	0	4.01
	New Orleans	AAA	5	5	0	0	28.1	126	28	20	16	4	1	1	0	17	0	23	4	0	3	2	.600	0	0	5.08
1993	Milwaukee	AL	6	0	0	4	9.1	37	3	0	0	0	0	0	1	5	0	7	0	0	0	0	.000	0	1	0.00

John Kiely

Pitches: Right **Bats:** Right **Pos:** RP   **Ht:** 6' 3" **Wt:** 215 **Born:** 10/04/64 **Age:** 29

			HOW MUCH HE PITCHED						WHAT HE GAVE UP										THE RESULTS						
Year	Team	Lg	G	GS	CG	GF	IP	BFP	H	R	ER	HR	SH	SF	HB	TBB	IBB	SO	WP	Bk	W	L	Pct.	ShO	Sv	ERA
1993	Toledo *	AAA	37	0	0	16	58	261	65	34	25	8	1	2	1	25	1	48	2	0	3	4	.429	0	4	3.88
1991	Detroit	AL	7	0	0	3	6.2	42	13	11	11	0	2	1	1	9	2	1	1	0	0	1	.000	0	0	14.85
1992	Detroit	AL	39	0	0	20	55	231	44	14	13	2	4	3	0	28	3	18	0	0	4	2	.667	0	0	2.13
1993	Detroit	AL	8	0	0	5	11.2	59	13	11	10	2	1	0	1	13	5	5	2	0	0	2	.000	0	0	7.71
	3 ML YEARS		54	0	0	28	73.1	332	70	36	34	4	7	4	2	50	10	24	3	0	4	5	.444	0	0	4.17

Darryl Kile

Pitches: Right **Bats:** Right **Pos:** SP/RP   **Ht:** 6' 5" **Wt:** 185 **Born:** 12/02/68 **Age:** 25

			HOW MUCH HE PITCHED						WHAT HE GAVE UP										THE RESULTS						
Year	Team	Lg	G	GS	CG	GF	IP	BFP	H	R	ER	HR	SH	SF	HB	TBB	IBB	SO	WP	Bk	W	L	Pct.	ShO	Sv	ERA
1991	Houston	NL	37	22	0	5	153.2	689	144	81	63	16	9	5	6	84	4	100	5	4	7	11	.389	0	0	3.69
1992	Houston	NL	22	22	2	0	125.1	554	124	61	55	8	5	6	4	63	4	90	3	4	5	10	.333	0	0	3.95
1993	Houston	NL	32	26	4	0	171.2	733	152	73	67	12	5	7	15	69	1	141	9	3	15	8	.652	2	0	3.51
	3 ML YEARS		91	70	6	5	450.2	1976	420	215	185	36	19	18	25	216	9	331	17	11	27	29	.482	2	0	3.69

Paul Kilgus

Pitches: Left **Bats:** Left **Pos:** RP   **Ht:** 6' 1" **Wt:** 185 **Born:** 02/02/62 **Age:** 32

			HOW MUCH HE PITCHED						WHAT HE GAVE UP										THE RESULTS						
Year	Team	Lg	G	GS	CG	GF	IP	BFP	H	R	ER	HR	SH	SF	HB	TBB	IBB	SO	WP	Bk	W	L	Pct.	ShO	Sv	ERA
1993	Louisville *	AAA	9	9	4	0	68	275	59	21	20	10	2	0	1	19	0	54	3	0	7	1	.875	1	0	2.65
1987	Texas	AL	25	12	0	2	89.1	385	95	45	41	14	2	0	2	31	2	42	0	0	2	7	.222	0	0	4.13
1988	Texas	AL	32	32	5	0	203.1	871	190	105	94	18	4	4	10	71	2	88	6	4	12	15	.444	3	0	4.16
1989	Chicago	NL	35	23	0	5	145.2	642	164	90	71	9	5	4	5	49	6	61	3	2	6	10	.375	0	0	4.39
1990	Toronto	AL	11	0	0	4	16.1	74	19	11	11	2	1	3	1	7	1	7	0	0	0	0	.000	0	0	6.06
1991	Baltimore	AL	38	0	0	14	62	267	60	38	35	8	2	4	3	24	2	32	2	0	0	2	.000	0	1	5.08
1993	St. Louis	NL	22	1	0	7	28.2	109	18	2	2	1	0	0	1	8	1	21	0	0	1	0	1.000	0	0	0.63
	6 ML YEARS		163	68	5	32	545.1	2348	546	291	254	52	14	15	22	190	14	251	11	6	21	34	.382	3	4	4.19

Jeff King

Bats: Right   **Throws:** Right   **Pos:** 3B   **Ht:** 6' 1"   **Wt:** 180   **Born:** 12/26/64   **Age:** 29

								BATTING												BASERUNNING				PERCENTAGES		
Year Team	Lg	G	AB	H	2B	3B	HR	(Hm	Rd)	TB	R	RBI	TBB	IBB	SO	HBP	SH	SF		SB	CS	SB%	GDP	Avg	OBP	SLG
1989 Pittsburgh	NL	75	215	42	13	3	5	(3	2)	76	31	19	20	1	34	2	2	4		4	2	.67	3	.195	.266	.353
1990 Pittsburgh	NL	127	371	91	17	1	14	(9	5)	152	46	53	21	1	50	1	2	7		3	3	.50	12	.245	.283	.410
1991 Pittsburgh	NL	33	109	26	1	1	4	(3	1)	41	16	18	14	3	15	1	0	1		3	1	.75	3	.239	.328	.376
1992 Pittsburgh	NL	130	480	111	21	2	14	(6	8)	178	56	65	27	3	56	2	8	5		4	6	.40	8	.231	.272	.371
1993 Pittsburgh	NL	158	611	180	35	3	9	(4	5)	248	82	98	59	4	54	4	1	8		8	6	.57	17	.295	.356	.406
5 ML YEARS		523	1786	450	87	10	46	(25	21)	695	231	253	141	12	209	10	13	25		22	18	.55	43	.252	.306	.389

Kevin King

Pitches: Left   **Bats:** Left   **Pos:** RP   **Ht:** 6' 4"   **Wt:** 170   **Born:** 02/11/69   **Age:** 25

		HOW MUCH HE PITCHED						WHAT HE GAVE UP										THE RESULTS					
Year Team	Lg	G	GS	CG	GF	IP	BFP	H	R	ER	HR	SH	SF	HB	TBB	IBB	SO	WP	Bk	W	L	Pct.	ShO	Sv	ERA
1990 Bellingham	A	6	6	0	0	32	140	37	18	17	3	1	0	0	10	0	27	1	1	3	2	.600	0	0	4.78
Peninsula	A	7	7	0	0	36.1	159	42	23	18	2	2	1	0	13	0	20	2	3	4	2	.667	0	0	4.46
1991 Peninsula	A	17	17	2	0	92.2	405	99	55	45	8	5	2	0	38	0	59	5	2	6	7	.462	1	0	4.37
1992 San Berndno	A	27	27	0	0	165.2	744	226	118	98	14	2	11	2	55	0	101	10	2	7	16	.304	0	0	5.32
1993 Riverside	A	25	0	0	14	46	184	37	10	8	0	1	3	1	20	1	28	1	0	3	2	.600	0	5	1.57
Jacksnville	AA	16	0	0	8	28.2	116	25	10	10	3	3	1	1	7	2	13	3	0	2	0	1.000	0	1	3.14
1993 Seattle	AL	13	0	0	3	11.2	49	9	8	8	3	3	2	1	4	1	8	0	0	0	1	.000	0	0	6.17

Wayne Kirby

Bats: Left   **Throws:** Right   **Pos:** RF/CF   **Ht:** 5'10"   **Wt:** 185   **Born:** 01/22/64   **Age:** 30

								BATTING												BASERUNNING				PERCENTAGES		
Year Team	Lg	G	AB	H	2B	3B	HR	(Hm	Rd)	TB	R	RBI	TBB	IBB	SO	HBP	SH	SF		SB	CS	SB%	GDP	Avg	OBP	SLG
1984 Vero Beach	A	76	224	61	6	3	0	--	--	73	39	21	21	2	30	6	5	2		11	9	.55	3	.272	.348	.326
Great Falls	R	20	84	26	2	2	1	--	--	35	19	11	12	2	9	0	1	1		19	3	.86	2	.310	.392	.417
Bakersfield	A	23	84	23	3	0	0	--	--	26	14	10	4	0	5	0	2	1		8	3	.73	0	.274	.303	.310
1985 Vero Beach	A	122	437	123	9	3	0	--	--	138	70	28	41	1	41	3	4	3		31	14	.69	3	.281	.345	.316
1986 Vero Beach	A	114	387	101	9	4	2	--	--	124	60	31	37	3	30	1	2	2		28	17	.62	5	.261	.326	.320
1987 San Antonio	AA	24	80	19	1	2	1	--	--	27	7	9	4	0	7	0	3	0		6	4	.60	0	.238	.274	.338
Bakersfield	A	105	416	112	14	3	0	--	--	132	77	34	49	1	41	3	5	2		56	21	.73	3	.269	.349	.317
1988 Bakersfield	A	12	47	13	0	1	0	--	--	15	12	4	11	0	4	0	0	0		9	2	.82	0	.277	.414	.319
San Antonio	AA	100	334	80	9	2	0	--	--	93	50	21	21	2	42	3	10	1		26	10	.72	5	.240	.290	.278
1989 San Antonio	AA	44	140	30	3	1	0	--	--	35	14	7	18	0	17	1	2	1		11	6	.65	4	.214	.306	.250
Albuquerque	AAA	78	310	106	18	8	0	--	--	140	62	30	26	1	27	1	5	1		29	14	.67	2	.342	.393	.452
1990 Albuquerque	AAA	119	342	95	14	5	0	--	--	119	56	30	28	1	36	3	4	3		29	7	.81	2	.278	.335	.348
1991 Colo Sprngs	AAA	118	385	113	14	4	1	--	--	138	66	39	34	2	36	2	5	3		29	14	.67	3	.294	.351	.358
1992 Colo Sprngs	AAA	123	470	162	18	16	11	--	--	245	101	74	36	4	28	2	4	2		51	20	.72	7	.345	.392	.521
1993 Charlotte	AAA	17	76	22	6	2	3	--	--	41	10	7	3	0	10	0	0	0		4	2	.67	1	.289	.316	.539
1991 Cleveland	AL	21	43	9	2	0	0	(0	0)	11	4	5	2	0	6	0	1	1		1	2	.33	2	.209	.239	.256
1992 Cleveland	AL	21	18	3	1	0	1	(0	1)	7	9	1	3	0	2	0	0	0		0	3	.00	1	.167	.286	.389
1993 Cleveland	AL	131	458	123	19	5	6	(4	2)	170	71	60	37	2	58	3	7	6		17	5	.77	8	.269	.323	.371
3 ML YEARS		173	519	135	22	5	7	(4	3)	188	84	66	42	2	66	3	8	7		18	10	.64	11	.260	.315	.362

Ryan Klesko

Bats: Left   **Throws:** Left   **Pos:** 1B   **Ht:** 6' 3"   **Wt:** 220   **Born:** 06/12/71   **Age:** 23

								BATTING												BASERUNNING				PERCENTAGES		
Year Team	Lg	G	AB	H	2B	3B	HR	(Hm	Rd)	TB	R	RBI	TBB	IBB	SO	HBP	SH	SF		SB	CS	SB%	GDP	Avg	OBP	SLG
1989 Braves	R	17	57	23	5	4	1	--	--	39	14	16	6	2	6	0	0	1		4	3	.57	2	.404	.453	.684
Sumter	A	25	90	26	6	0	1	--	--	35	17	12	11	1	14	0	1	1		1	0	1.00	5	.289	.363	.389
1990 Sumter	A	63	231	85	15	1	10	--	--	132	41	38	31	5	30	1	0	5		13	1	.93	6	.368	.437	.571
Durham	A	77	292	80	16	1	7	--	--	119	40	47	32	4	53	2	0	6		10	5	.67	8	.274	.343	.408
1991 Greenville	AA	126	419	122	22	3	14	--	--	192	64	67	75	14	60	6	3	3		14	17	.45	5	.291	.404	.458
1992 Richmond	AAA	123	418	105	22	2	17	--	--	182	63	59	41	6	72	4	1	2		3	5	.38	14	.251	.323	.435
1993 Richmond	AAA	98	343	94	14	2	22	--	--	178	59	74	47	4	69	2	0	4		4	3	.57	8	.274	.361	.519
1992 Atlanta	NL	13	14	0	0	0	0	(0	0)	0	0	1	0	0	5	1	0	0		0	0	.00	0	.000	.067	.000
1993 Atlanta	NL	22	17	6	1	0	2	(2	0)	13	3	5	3	1	4	0	0	0		0	0	.00	0	.353	.450	.765
2 ML YEARS		35	31	6	1	0	2	(2	0)	13	3	6	3	1	9	1	0	0		0	0	.00	0	.194	.286	.419

Joe Klink

Pitches: Left   **Bats:** Left   **Pos:** RP   **Ht:** 5'11"   **Wt:** 175   **Born:** 02/03/62   **Age:** 32

		HOW MUCH HE PITCHED						WHAT HE GAVE UP										THE RESULTS					
Year Team	Lg	G	GS	CG	GF	IP	BFP	H	R	ER	HR	SH	SF	HB	TBB	IBB	SO	WP	Bk	W	L	Pct.	ShO	Sv	ERA
1987 Minnesota	AL	12	0	0	5	23	116	37	18	17	4	1	1	0	11	0	17	1	0	0	1	.000	0	0	6.65

1990 Oakland	AL	40	0	0	19	39.2	165	34	9	9	1	1	0	0	18	0	19	3	1	0	0	.000	0	1	2.04
1991 Oakland	AL	62	0	0	10	62	266	60	30	30	4	8	0	5	21	5	34	4	0	10	3	.769	0	2	4.35
1993 Florida	NL	59	0	0	10	37.2	168	37	22	21	0	2	3	0	24	4	22	1	2	0	0	.000	0	0	5.02
4 ML YEARS		173	0	0	44	162.1	715	168	79	77	9	12	4	5	74	9	92	9	3	10	6	.625	0	3	4.27

Joe Kmak

Bats: Right   **Throws:** Right   **Pos:** C   **Ht:** 6' 0"   **Wt:** 185   **Born:** 05/03/63   **Age:** 31

								BATTING											BASERUNNING				PERCENTAGES		
Year	Team	Lg	G	AB	H	2B	3B	HR	(Hm	Rd)	TB	R	RBI	TBB	IBB	SO	HBP	SH	SF	SB	CS	SB%	GDP	Avg	OBP	SLG
1985	Everett	A	40	129	40	10	1	1	--	--	55	21	14	20	0	23	3	0	2	0	1	.00	3	.310	.409	.426
1986	Fresno	A	60	163	44	5	0	1	--	--	52	23	9	15	0	38	3	0	1	3	2	.60	6	.270	.341	.319
1987	Fresno	A	48	154	34	8	0	0	--	--	42	18	12	15	0	32	3	3	0	1	2	.33	3	.221	.302	.273
	Shreveport	AA	15	41	8	0	1	0	--	--	10	5	3	3	0	4	1	0	0	0	0	.00	1	.195	.267	.244
1988	Shreveport	AA	71	178	40	5	2	1	--	--	52	16	14	11	2	19	4	1	1	0	0	.00	3	.225	.284	.292
1989	Reno	A	78	248	68	10	5	4	--	--	100	39	34	40	1	41	5	0	1	8	4	.67	9	.274	.384	.403
1990	El Paso	AA	35	109	31	3	2	2	--	--	44	8	11	7	0	22	2	3	2	0	0	.00	2	.284	.333	.404
	Denver	AAA	28	95	22	3	0	1	--	--	28	12	10	4	0	16	3	5	0	1	1	.50	3	.232	.284	.295
1991	Denver	AAA	100	294	70	17	2	1	--	--	94	34	33	28	0	44	5	8	1	7	3	.70	5	.238	.314	.320
1992	Denver	AAA	67	225	70	11	4	3	--	--	98	27	31	19	0	39	3	5	2	6	3	.67	5	.311	.369	.436
1993	New Orleans	AAA	24	76	23	3	2	1	--	--	33	9	13	8	0	14	0	0	0	1	0	1.00	1	.303	.369	.434
1993	Milwaukee	AL	51	110	24	5	0	0	(0	0)	29	9	7	14	0	13	2	1	0	6	2	.75	2	.218	.317	.264

Chuck Knoblauch

Bats: Right   **Throws:** Right   **Pos:** 2B   **Ht:** 5' 9"   **Wt:** 180   **Born:** 07/07/68   **Age:** 25

								BATTING											BASERUNNING				PERCENTAGES		
Year	Team	Lg	G	AB	H	2B	3B	HR	(Hm	Rd)	TB	R	RBI	TBB	IBB	SO	HBP	SH	SF	SB	CS	SB%	GDP	Avg	OBP	SLG
1991	Minnesota	AL	151	565	159	24	6	1	(1	0)	198	78	50	59	0	40	4	1	5	25	5	.83	8	.281	.351	.350
1992	Minnesota	AL	155	600	178	19	6	2	(0	2)	215	104	56	88	1	60	5	2	12	34	13	.72	8	.297	.384	.358
1993	Minnesota	AL	153	602	167	27	4	2	(2	0)	208	82	41	65	1	44	9	4	5	29	11	.73	11	.277	.354	.346
3 ML YEARS			459	1767	504	70	16	5	(3	2)	621	264	147	212	2	144	18	7	22	88	29	.75	27	.285	.364	.351

Randy Knorr

Bats: Right   **Throws:** Right   **Pos:** C   **Ht:** 6' 2"   **Wt:** 205   **Born:** 11/12/68   **Age:** 25

								BATTING											BASERUNNING				PERCENTAGES		
Year	Team	Lg	G	AB	H	2B	3B	HR	(Hm	Rd)	TB	R	RBI	TBB	IBB	SO	HBP	SH	SF	SB	CS	SB%	GDP	Avg	OBP	SLG
1986	Medicne Hat	R	55	215	58	13	0	4	--	--	83	21	32	17	0	53	0	3	3	0	0	.00	6	.270	.319	.386
1987	Medicne Hat	R	26	106	31	7	0	10	--	--	68	21	24	5	3	26	1	0	3	0	0	.00	1	.292	.322	.642
	Myrtle Bch	A	46	129	34	4	0	6	--	--	56	17	21	6	0	46	0	0	2	0	0	.00	1	.264	.292	.434
1988	Myrtle Bch	A	117	364	85	13	0	9	--	--	125	43	42	41	0	91	0	9	2	0	1	.00	7	.234	.310	.343
1989	Dunedin	A	33	122	32	6	0	6	--	--	56	13	23	6	0	21	0	0	2	0	2	.00	0	.262	.292	.459
1990	Knoxville	AA	116	392	108	12	1	13	--	--	161	51	64	31	2	83	2	4	6	0	3	.00	7	.276	.327	.411
1991	Knoxville	AA	24	74	13	4	0	0	--	--	17	7	4	10	1	18	1	0	1	2	0	1.00	0	.176	.279	.230
	Syracuse	AAA	91	342	89	20	0	5	--	--	124	29	44	23	3	58	3	0	4	1	0	1.00	17	.260	.309	.363
1992	Syracuse	AAA	61	228	62	13	1	11	--	--	110	27	27	17	1	38	0	0	3	1	0	1.00	5	.272	.319	.482
1991	Toronto	AL	3	1	0	0	0	0	(0	0)	0	0	0	1	0	1	0	0	0	0	0	.00	0	.000	.500	.000
1992	Toronto	AL	8	19	5	0	0	1	(0	1)	8	1	2	1	1	5	0	0	0	0	0	.00	0	.263	.300	.421
1993	Toronto	AL	39	101	25	3	2	4	(2	2)	44	11	20	9	0	29	0	2	0	0	0	.00	2	.248	.309	.436
3 ML YEARS			50	121	30	3	2	5	(2	3)	52	12	22	11	1	35	0	2	0	0	0	.00	2	.248	.311	.430

Kurt Knudsen

Pitches: Right   **Bats:** Right   **Pos:** RP   **Ht:** 6' 3"   **Wt:** 200   **Born:** 02/20/67   **Age:** 27

			HOW MUCH HE PITCHED					WHAT HE GAVE UP										THE RESULTS					
Year	Team	Lg	G	GS	CG	GF	IP	BFP	H	R	ER	HR	SH	SF	HB	TBB	IBB	SO	WP	Bk	W	L	Pct.	ShO	Sv	ERA
1988	Bristol	R	2	0	0	2	2.1	14	4	3	0	0	0	0	0	1	0	0	0	0	0	0	.000	0	0	0.00
	Fayettevlle	A	12	0	0	5	20	77	8	4	3	1	2	1	1	9	1	22	1	1	3	1	.750	0	1	1.35
	Lakeland	A	7	0	0	4	9.1	39	7	2	1	0	0	0	0	7	0	6	2	0	0	0	.000	0	0	0.96
1989	Lakeland	A	45	0	0	26	54.1	225	43	16	13	1	5	2	1	22	7	68	2	3	3	2	.600	0	10	2.15
1990	Lakeland	A	14	8	0	5	67	253	42	18	17	2	2	1	0	22	0	70	5	2	5	0	1.000	0	3	2.28
	London	AA	15	0	0	8	26	102	15	6	6	1	0	1	2	11	0	26	2	1	2	1	.667	0	1	2.08
1991	London	AA	34	0	0	18	51.2	226	42	29	20	1	4	5	1	30	2	56	4	1	2	3	.400	0	6	3.48
	Toledo	AAA	12	0	0	3	18.1	79	13	11	3	1	0	0	0	10	1	28	2	0	1	2	.333	0	1	1.47
1992	Toledo	AAA	12	0	0	8	21.2	82	11	5	5	1	1	1	1	6	0	19	1	0	3	1	.750	0	1	2.08
1993	Toledo	AAA	23	0	0	15	33.1	136	24	15	14	3	1	0	0	11	1	39	2	2	2	2	.500	0	6	3.78
1992	Detroit	AL	48	1	0	14	70.2	313	70	39	36	9	4	2	1	41	9	51	5	0	2	3	.400	0	5	4.58
1993	Detroit	AL	30	0	0	7	37.2	171	41	22	20	9	2	3	4	16	2	29	2	0	3	2	.600	0	2	4.78
2 ML YEARS			78	1	0	21	108.1	484	111	61	56	18	6	5	5	57	11	80	7	0	5	5	.500	0	7	4.65

Mark Knudson

Pitches: Right **Bats:** Right **Pos:** RP   **Ht:** 6' 5" **Wt:** 200 **Born:** 10/28/60 **Age:** 33

Year Team	Lg	G	GS	CG	GF	IP	BFP	H	R	ER	HR	SH	SF	HB	TBB	IBB	SO	WP	Bk	W	L	Pct.	ShO	Sv	ERA
1993 Colo Sprngs *	AAA	5	5	1	0	28	120	30	12	7	0	0	1	0	8	0	15	1	0	3	1	.750	1	0	2.25
1985 Houston	NL	2	2	0	0	11	53	21	11	11	0	1	0	0	3	0	4	0	0	0	2	.000	0	0	9.00
1986 2 ML Teams		13	8	0	2	60.1	273	70	38	35	12	3	0	1	20	6	29	2	0	1	6	.143	0	0	5.22
1987 Milwaukee	AL	15	8	1	3	62	288	88	46	37	7	3	5	0	14	1	26	1	0	4	4	.500	0	0	5.37
1988 Milwaukee	AL	5	0	0	3	16	63	17	3	2	1	0	0	0	2	0	7	1	0	0	0	.000	0	0	1.13
1989 Milwaukee	AL	40	7	1	16	123.2	499	110	50	46	15	2	1	3	29	2	47	2	0	8	5	.615	0	0	3.35
1990 Milwaukee	AL	30	27	4	0	168.1	719	187	84	77	14	3	9	3	40	1	56	6	0	10	9	.526	2	0	4.12
1991 Milwaukee	AL	12	7	0	3	35	174	54	33	31	8	3	3	1	15	0	23	1	0	1	3	.250	0	0	7.97
1993 Colorado	NL	4	0	0	2	5.2	39	16	14	14	4	0	0	0	5	0	3	2	0	0	0	.000	0	0	22.24
1986 Houston	NL	9	7	0	1	42.2	191	48	23	20	5	3	0	1	15	5	20	1	0	1	5	.167	0	0	4.22
Milwaukee	AL	4	1	0	1	17.2	82	22	15	15	7	0	0	0	5	1	9	1	0	0	1	.000	0	0	7.64
8 ML YEARS		121	59	6	29	482	2108	563	279	253	61	15	18	8	128	10	195	15	0	24	29	.453	2	0	4.72

Brian Koelling

Bats: Right **Throws:** Right **Pos:** 2B   **Ht:** 6' 1" **Wt:** 185 **Born:** 06/11/69 **Age:** 25

Year Team	Lg	G	AB	H	2B	3B	HR	(Hm	Rd)	TB	R	RBI	TBB	IBB	SO	HBP	SH	SF	SB	CS	SB%	GDP	Avg	OBP	SLG
1991 Billings	R	22	85	30	7	1	2	--	--	45	17	12	14	0	23	1	0	0	6	2	.75	0	.353	.450	.529
Cedar Rapds	A	35	147	38	6	0	1	--	--	47	27	12	14	0	39	3	0	1	22	6	.79	0	.259	.333	.320
1992 Cedar Rapds	A	129	460	121	18	7	5	--	--	168	81	43	49	0	137	1	9	2	47	16	.75	3	.263	.334	.365
1993 Chattanooga	AA	110	430	119	17	6	4	--	--	160	64	47	32	1	105	2	4	3	34	13	.72	2	.277	.328	.372
Indianapols	AAA	2	9	2	0	0	0	--	--	2	1	0	0	0	1	1	0	0	0	1	.00	0	.222	.300	.222
1993 Cincinnati	NL	7	15	1	0	0	0	(0	0)	1	2	0	0	0	2	1	0	0	0	0	.00	0	.067	.125	.067

Kevin Koslofski

Bats: Left **Throws:** Right **Pos:** RF   **Ht:** 5' 8" **Wt:** 175 **Born:** 09/24/66 **Age:** 27

Year Team	Lg	G	AB	H	2B	3B	HR	(Hm	Rd)	TB	R	RBI	TBB	IBB	SO	HBP	SH	SF	SB	CS	SB%	GDP	Avg	OBP	SLG
1984 Eugene	A	53	155	29	2	2	1	--	--	38	23	10	25	0	37	0	1	1	10	2	.83	3	.187	.298	.245
1985 Royals	R	33	108	27	4	2	0	--	--	35	17	11	12	0	19	3	2		7	2	.78	1	.250	.341	.324
1986 Ft. Myers	A	103	331	84	13	5	0	--	--	107	44	29	47	2	59	2	7	4	12	6	.67	6	.254	.346	.323
1987 Ft. Myers	A	109	330	80	12	3	0	--	--	98	46	25	46	3	64	7	3	2	25	9	.74	4	.242	.345	.297
1988 Baseball Cy	A	108	368	97	7	8	3	--	--	129	52	30	44	5	71	4	3	2	32	11	.74	4	.264	.347	.351
1989 Baseball Cy	A	116	343	89	10	3	4	--	--	117	65	33	51	2	57	5	5	3	41	14	.75	9	.259	.361	.341
1990 Memphis	AA	118	367	78	11	5	3	--	--	108	52	32	54	1	89	2	7	3	12	7	.63	4	.213	.315	.294
1991 Memphis	AA	81	287	93	15	3	7	--	--	135	41	39	33	3	56	4	4	4	10	13	.43	2	.324	.396	.470
Omaha	AAA	25	94	28	3	2	2	--	--	41	13	19	15	0	19	1	2	1	4	3	.57	1	.298	.396	.436
1992 Omaha	AAA	78	280	87	12	5	4	--	--	121	29	32	21	3	47	2	7	1	8	3	.73	2	.311	.362	.432
1993 Omaha	AAA	111	395	109	22	5	7	--	--	162	58	45	43	3	73	2	3	2	15	7	.68	9	.276	.348	.410
1992 Kansas City	AL	55	133	33	0	2	3	(1	2)	46	20	13	12	0	23	1	3	1	2	1	.67	2	.248	.313	.346
1993 Kansas City	AL	15	26	7	0	0	1	(0	1)	10	4	2	4	0	5	1	1	0	0	1	.00	1	.269	.387	.385
2 ML YEARS		70	159	40	0	2	4	(1	3)	56	24	15	16	0	28	2	4	1	2	2	.50	3	.252	.326	.352

Tom Kramer

Pitches: Right **Bats:** Both **Pos:** RP/SP   **Ht:** 6' 0" **Wt:** 205 **Born:** 01/09/68 **Age:** 26

Year Team	Lg	G	GS	CG	GF	IP	BFP	H	R	ER	HR	SH	SF	HB	TBB	IBB	SO	WP	Bk	W	L	Pct.	ShO	Sv	ERA
1987 Burlington	R	12	11	2	1	71.2	292	57	31	24	2	0	1	1	26	0	71	0	0	7	3	.700	1	1	3.01
1988 Waterloo	A	27	27	10	0	198.2	814	173	70	56	9	10	3	3	60	3	152	5	3	14	7	.667	2	0	2.54
1989 Kinston	A	18	17	5	1	131.2	527	97	44	38	7	5	3	4	42	3	89	4	1	9	5	.643	1	0	2.60
Canton-Akrn	AA	10	8	1	0	43.1	202	58	34	30	6	3	4	0	20	0	26	3	0	1	6	.143	0	0	6.23
1990 Kinston	A	16	16	2	0	98	402	82	34	31	5	1	2	2	29	0	96	2	1	7	4	.636	1	0	2.85
Canton-Akrn	AA	12	10	2	0	72	287	67	25	24	3	2	1	0	14	1	46	1	0	6	3	.667	0	0	3.00
1991 Canton-Akrn	AA	35	5	0	13	79.1	320	61	23	21	5	6	1	1	34	3	61	3	0	7	3	.700	0	6	2.38
Colo Sprngs	AAA	10	1	0	6	11.1	43	5	1	1	1	0	0	0	5	0	18	1	0	1	0	1.000	0	4	0.79
1992 Colo Sprngs	AAA	38	3	0	11	75.2	344	88	43	41	2	4	3	1	43	2	72	0	0	8	3	.727	0	3	4.88
1991 Cleveland	AL	4	0	0	1	4.2	30	10	9	9	1	0	3	0	6	0	4	0	0	0	0	.000	0	0	17.36
1993 Cleveland	AL	39	16	1	6	121	535	126	60	54	19	3	2	2	59	7	71	1	0	7	3	.700	0	0	4.02
2 ML YEARS		43	16	1	7	125.2	565	136	69	63	20	3	5	2	65	7	75	1	0	7	3	.700	0	0	4.51

Chad Kreuter

Bats: Both **Throws:** Right **Pos:** C   **Ht:** 6' 2" **Wt:** 190 **Born:** 08/26/64 **Age:** 29

				BATTING															BASERUNNING				PERCENTAGES		
Year Team	Lg	G	AB	H	2B	3B	HR	(Hm	Rd)	TB	R	RBI	TBB	IBB	SO	HBP	SH	SF	SB	CS	SB%	GDP	Avg	OBP	SLG
1988 Texas	AL	16	51	14	2	1	1	(0	1)	21	3	5	7	0	13	0	0	0	0	0	.00	1	.275	.362	.412
1989 Texas	AL	87	158	24	3	0	5	(2	3)	42	16	9	27	0	40	0	6	1	0	1	.00	4	.152	.274	.266
1990 Texas	AL	22	22	1	1	0	0	(0	0)	2	2	2	8	0	9	0	1	1	0	0	.00	0	.045	.290	.091
1991 Texas	AL	3	4	0	0	0	0	(0	0)	0	0	0	0	0	1	0	0	0	0	0	.00	0	.000	.000	.000
1992 Detroit	AL	67	190	48	9	0	2	(2	0)	63	22	16	20	1	38	0	3	2	0	1	.00	8	.253	.321	.332
1993 Detroit	AL	119	374	107	23	3	15	(9	6)	181	59	51	49	4	92	3	2	3	2	1	.67	5	.286	.371	.484
6 ML YEARS		314	799	194	38	4	23	(13	10)	309	102	83	111	5	193	3	12	7	2	3	.40	18	.243	.335	.387

Bill Krueger

Pitches: Left **Bats:** Left **Pos:** RP/SP   **Ht:** 6' 5" **Wt:** 205 **Born:** 04/24/58 **Age:** 36

		HOW MUCH HE PITCHED						WHAT HE GAVE UP												THE RESULTS					
Year Team	Lg	G	GS	CG	GF	IP	BFP	H	R	ER	HR	SH	SF	HB	TBB	IBB	SO	WP	Bk	W	L	Pct.	ShO	Sv	ERA
1993 Toledo *	AAA	3	3	0	0	11.1	47	11	2	2	0	0	0	0	3	0	8	0	0	1	0	1.000	0	0	1.59
1983 Oakland	AL	17	16	2	0	109.2	473	104	54	44	7	0	5	2	53	1	58	1	1	7	6	.538	0	0	3.61
1984 Oakland	AL	26	24	1	0	142	647	156	95	75	9	4	8	2	85	2	61	5	1	10	10	.500	0	0	4.75
1985 Oakland	AL	32	23	2	4	151.1	674	165	95	76	13	1	5	2	69	1	56	6	3	9	10	.474	0	0	4.52
1986 Oakland	AL	11	3	0	4	34.1	149	40	25	23	4	1	2	0	13	0	10	3	1	1	2	.333	0	1	6.03
1987 2 ML Teams		11	0	0	1	8	46	12	9	6	0	0	0	0	9	3	4	0	1	0	3	.000	0	0	6.75
1988 Los Angeles	NL	1	1	0	0	2.1	14	4	3	3	0	0	0	1	2	1	1	0	0	0	0	.000	0	0	11.57
1989 Milwaukee	AL	34	5	0	8	93.2	403	96	43	40	9	5	1	0	33	3	72	10	1	3	2	.600	0	3	3.84
1990 Milwaukee	AL	30	17	0	4	129	566	137	70	57	10	3	10	3	54	6	64	8	0	6	8	.429	0	0	3.98
1991 Seattle	AL	35	25	1	2	175	751	194	82	70	15	6	9	4	60	4	91	10	1	11	8	.579	0	0	3.60
1992 2 ML Teams		36	29	2	3	178.2	765	189	95	90	18	4	1	4	53	2	99	12	0	10	8	.556	2	0	4.53
1993 Detroit	AL	32	7	0	7	82	356	90	43	31	6	3	3	4	30	5	60	8	0	6	4	.600	0	0	3.40
1987 Oakland	AL	9	0	0	1	5.2	33	9	7	6	0	0	0	0	8	3	2	0	1	0	3	.000	0	0	9.53
Los Angeles	NL	2	0	0	0	2.1	13	3	2	0	0	0	0	0	1	0	2	0	0	0	0	.000	0	0	0.00
1992 Minnesota	AL	27	27	2	0	161.1	684	166	82	77	18	4	1	3	46	2	86	11	0	10	6	.625	2	0	4.30
Montreal	NL	9	2	0	3	17.1	81	23	13	13	0	0	0	1	7	0	13	1	0	0	2	.000	0	0	6.75
11 ML YEARS		265	150	8	33	1106	4844	1187	614	515	91	27	44	22	461	28	576	63	9	63	61	.508	2	4	4.19

John Kruk

Bats: Left **Throws:** Left **Pos:** 1B   **Ht:** 5'10" **Wt:** 214 **Born:** 02/09/61 **Age:** 33

				BATTING															BASERUNNING				PERCENTAGES		
Year Team	Lg	G	AB	H	2B	3B	HR	(Hm	Rd)	TB	R	RBI	TBB	IBB	SO	HBP	SH	SF	SB	CS	SB%	GDP	Avg	OBP	SLG
1986 San Diego	NL	122	278	86	16	2	4	(1	3)	118	33	38	45	0	58	0	2	2	4	.33	11	.309	.403	.424
1987 San Diego	NL	138	447	140	14	2	20	(8	12)	218	72	91	73	15	93	0	3	4	18	10	.64	6	.313	.406	.488
1988 San Diego	NL	120	378	91	17	1	9	(8	1)	137	54	44	80	12	68	0	3	5	5	3	.63	7	.241	.369	.362
1989 2 ML Teams		112	357	107	13	6	8	(6	2)	156	53	44	44	2	53	0	2	3	3	0	1.00	10	.300	.374	.437
1990 Philadelphia	NL	142	443	129	25	8	7	(2	5)	191	52	67	69	16	70	0	2	1	10	5	.67	11	.291	.386	.431
1991 Philadelphia	NL	152	538	158	27	6	21	(8	13)	260	84	92	67	16	100	1	0	9	7	0	1.00	11	.294	.367	.483
1992 Philadelphia	NL	144	507	164	30	4	10	(7	3)	232	86	70	92	8	88	1	0	7	3	5	.38	11	.323	.423	.458
1993 Philadelphia	NL	150	535	169	33	5	14	(8	6)	254	100	85	111	10	87	0	0	5	6	2	.75	10	.316	.430	.475
1989 San Diego	NL	31	76	14	0	0	3	(2	1)	23	7	6	17	0	14	0	1	0	0	0	.00	5	.184	.333	.303
Philadelphia	NL	81	281	93	13	6	5	(4	1)	133	46	38	27	2	39	0	1	3	3	0	1.00	5	.331	.386	.473
8 ML YEARS		1080	3483	1044	175	34	93	(48	45)	1566	534	531	581	79	617	2	12	36	54	29	.65	77	.300	.397	.450

Steve Lake

Bats: Right **Throws:** Right **Pos:** C   **Ht:** 6' 1" **Wt:** 195 **Born:** 03/14/57 **Age:** 37

				BATTING															BASERUNNING				PERCENTAGES		
Year Team	Lg	G	AB	H	2B	3B	HR	(Hm	Rd)	TB	R	RBI	TBB	IBB	SO	HBP	SH	SF	SB	CS	SB%	GDP	Avg	OBP	SLG
1983 Chicago	NL	38	85	22	4	1	1	(1	0)	31	9	7	2	2	6	1	0	0	0	0	.00	4	.259	.284	.365
1984 Chicago	NL	25	54	12	4	0	2	(1	1)	22	4	7	0	0	7	1	1	1	0	0	.00	0	.222	.232	.407
1985 Chicago	NL	58	119	18	2	0	1	(1	0)	23	5	11	3	1	21	1	4	1	1	0	1.00	3	.151	.177	.193
1986 2 ML Teams		36	68	20	2	0	2	(0	2)	28	8	14	3	1	7	0	1	0	0	0	.00	3	.294	.324	.412
1987 St. Louis	NL	74	179	45	7	2	2	(1	1)	62	19	19	10	4	18	0	5	1	0	0	.00	2	.251	.289	.346
1988 St. Louis	NL	36	54	15	3	0	1	(1	0)	21	5	4	3	0	15	2	0	0	0	0	.00	0	.278	.339	.389
1989 Philadelphia	NL	58	155	39	5	1	2	(1	1)	52	9	14	12	4	20	0	1	1	0	0	.00	6	.252	.304	.335
1990 Philadelphia	NL	29	80	20	2	0	0	(0	0)	22	4	6	3	1	12	1	0	0	0	0	.00	0	.250	.286	.275
1991 Philadelphia	NL	58	158	36	4	1	1	(0	1)	45	12	11	2	1	26	0	4	0	0	0	.00	5	.228	.238	.285
1992 Philadelphia	NL	20	53	13	2	0	1	(1	0)	18	3	2	1	0	8	0	0	1	0	0	.00	1	.245	.255	.340
1993 Chicago	NL	44	120	27	6	0	5	(1	4)	48	11	13	4	3	19	0	2	0	0	0	.00	8	.225	.250	.400
1986 Chicago	NL	10	19	8	1	0	0	(0	0)	9	4	4	1	1	2	0	1	0	0	0	.00	1	.421	.450	.474

Year Team	Lg	G	AB	H	2B	3B	HR	(Hm	Rd)	TB	R	RBI	TBB	IBB	SO	HBP	SH	SF	SB	CS	SB%	GDP	Avg	OBP	SLG
St. Louis	NL	26	49	12	1	0	2	(0	2)	19	4	10	2	0	5	0	0	0	0	0	.00	2	.245	.275	.388
11 ML YEARS		476	1125	267	41	5	18	(8	10)	372	89	108	43	17	159	6	18	5	1	0	1.00	33	.237	.268	.331

Tim Laker

Bats: Right **Throws:** Right **Pos:** C **Ht:** 6' 3" **Wt:** 195 **Born:** 11/27/69 **Age:** 24

							BATTING												BASERUNNING				PERCENTAGES		
Year Team	Lg	G	AB	H	2B	3B	HR	(Hm	Rd)	TB	R	RBI	TBB	IBB	SO	HBP	SH	SF	SB	CS	SB%	GDP	Avg	OBP	SLG
1988 Jamestown	A	47	152	34	9	0	0	--	--	43	14	17	8	0	30	0	2	1	2	1	.67	4	.224	.261	.283
1989 Rockford	A	14	48	11	1	1	0	--	--	14	4	4	3	0	6	0	0	0	1	0	1.00	1	.229	.275	.292
Jamestown	A	58	216	48	9	1	2	--	--	65	25	24	16	1	40	2	0	3	8	4	.67	4	.222	.278	.301
1990 Rockford	A	120	425	94	18	3	7	--	--	139	46	57	32	1	83	1	1	8	7	2	.78	9	.221	.273	.327
Wst Plm Bch	A	2	3	0	0	0	0	--	--	0	0	0	0	0	1	0	0	0	0	0	.00	0	.000	.000	.000
1991 Harrisburg	AA	11	35	10	1	0	1	--	--	14	4	5	2	0	5	1	0	0	0	1	.00	1	.286	.342	.400
Wst Plm Bch	A	100	333	77	15	2	5	--	--	111	36	33	22	0	52	2	0	4	10	1	.91	9	.231	.280	.333
1992 Harrisburg	AA	117	409	99	19	3	15	--	--	169	55	68	39	2	89	5	0	5	3	1	.75	10	.242	.312	.413
1993 Ottawa	AAA	56	204	47	10	0	4	--	--	69	26	23	21	0	41	1	0	1	3	2	.60	10	.230	.304	.338
1992 Montreal	NL	28	46	10	3	0	0	(0	0)	13	8	4	2	0	14	0	0	0	1	1	.50	1	.217	.250	.283
1993 Montreal	NL	43	86	17	2	1	0	(0	0)	21	3	7	2	0	16	1	3	1	2	0	1.00	2	.198	.222	.244
2 ML YEARS		71	132	27	5	1	0	(0	0)	34	11	11	4	0	30	1	3	1	3	1	.75	3	.205	.232	.258

Tom Lampkin

Bats: Left **Throws:** Right **Pos:** C **Ht:** 5'11" **Wt:** 183 **Born:** 03/04/64 **Age:** 30

							BATTING												BASERUNNING				PERCENTAGES		
Year Team	Lg	G	AB	H	2B	3B	HR	(Hm	Rd)	TB	R	RBI	TBB	IBB	SO	HBP	SH	SF	SB	CS	SB%	GDP	Avg	OBP	SLG
1993 New Orleans *	AAA	25	80	26	5	0	2	--	--	37	18	10	18	2	4	3	1	0	5	4	.56	2	.325	.465	.463
1988 Cleveland	AL	4	4	0	0	0	0	(0	0)	0	0	0	1	0	0	0	0	0	0	0	.00	1	.000	.200	.000
1990 San Diego	NL	26	63	14	0	1	1	(1	0)	19	4	4	4	1	9	0	0	0	0	1	.00	2	.222	.269	.302
1991 San Diego	NL	38	58	11	3	1	0	(0	0)	16	4	3	3	0	9	0	0	0	0	0	.00	0	.190	.230	.276
1992 San Diego	NL	9	17	4	0	0	0	(0	0)	4	3	0	6	0	1	1	0	0	2	0	1.00	0	.235	.458	.235
1993 Milwaukee	AL	73	162	32	8	0	4	(1	3)	52	22	25	20	3	26	0	2	4	7	3	.70	2	.198	.280	.321
5 ML YEARS		150	304	61	11	2	5	(2	3)	91	33	32	34	4	45	1	2	4	9	4	.69	5	.201	.280	.299

Les Lancaster

Pitches: Right **Bats:** Right **Pos:** RP **Ht:** 6' 2" **Wt:** 200 **Born:** 04/21/62 **Age:** 32

		HOW MUCH HE PITCHED						WHAT HE GAVE UP										THE RESULTS					
Year Team	Lg	G	GS	CG	GF	IP	BFP	H	R	ER	HR	SH	SF	HB	TBB	IBB	SO	WP	Bk	W	L	Pct.	ShO	Sv	ERA
1987 Chicago	NL	27	18	0	4	132.1	578	138	76	72	14	5	6	1	51	5	78	7	8	8	3	.727	0	0	4.90
1988 Chicago	NL	44	3	1	15	85.2	371	89	42	36	4	3	7	1	34	7	36	3	3	4	6	.400	0	5	3.78
1989 Chicago	NL	42	0	0	15	72.2	288	60	12	11	2	3	4	0	15	1	56	2	1	4	2	.667	0	8	1.36
1990 Chicago	NL	55	6	1	26	109	479	121	57	56	11	6	5	1	40	8	65	7	0	9	5	.643	1	6	4.62
1991 Chicago	NL	64	11	1	21	156	653	150	68	61	13	9	4	4	49	7	102	2	2	9	7	.563	0	3	3.52
1992 Detroit	AL	41	1	0	17	86.2	404	101	66	61	11	2	4	3	51	12	35	2	0	3	4	.429	0	0	6.33
1993 St. Louis	NL	50	0	0	12	61.1	259	56	24	20	5	5	1	1	21	5	36	5	0	4	1	.800	0	0	2.93
7 ML YEARS		323	39	3	110	703.2	3032	715	345	317	60	33	31	11	261	45	408	28	14	41	28	.594	1	22	4.05

Bill Landrum

Pitches: Right **Bats:** Right **Pos:** RP **Ht:** 6' 2" **Wt:** 205 **Born:** 08/17/58 **Age:** 35

		HOW MUCH HE PITCHED						WHAT HE GAVE UP										THE RESULTS					
Year Team	Lg	G	GS	CG	GF	IP	BFP	H	R	ER	HR	SH	SF	HB	TBB	IBB	SO	WP	Bk	W	L	Pct.	ShO	Sv	ERA
1986 Cincinnati	NL	10	0	0	4	13.1	65	23	11	10	0	1	1	0	4	0	14	0	0	0	0	.000	0	0	6.75
1987 Cincinnati	NL	44	2	0	14	65	276	68	35	34	3	7	2	0	34	6	42	4	1	3	2	.600	0	2	4.71
1988 Chicago	NL	7	0	0	5	12.1	55	19	8	8	1	0	0	0	3	0	6	1	1	1	0	1.000	0	0	5.84
1989 Pittsburgh	NL	56	0	0	40	81	325	60	18	15	2	3	2	0	28	8	51	2	0	2	3	.400	0	26	1.67
1990 Pittsburgh	NL	54	0	0	41	71.2	292	69	22	17	4	5	3	0	21	5	39	1	1	7	3	.700	0	13	2.13
1991 Pittsburgh	NL	61	0	0	43	76.1	322	76	32	27	4	1	1	0	19	5	45	3	2	4	4	.500	0	17	3.18
1992 Montreal	NL	18	0	0	6	20	95	27	16	16	3	1	0	2	9	2	7	0	0	1	1	.500	0	0	7.20
1993 Cincinnati	NL	18	0	0	6	21.2	86	18	9	9	1	2	0	0	6	1	14	0	0	0	0	.000	0	0	3.74
8 ML YEARS		268	2	0	159	361.1	1516	360	151	136	18	20	9	2	124	27	218	11	5	18	15	.545	0	58	3.39

Ced Landrum

Bats: Left **Throws:** Right **Pos:** LF **Ht:** 5' 7" **Wt:** 167 **Born:** 09/03/63 **Age:** 30

							BATTING												BASERUNNING				PERCENTAGES		
Year Team	Lg	G	AB	H	2B	3B	HR	(Hm	Rd)	TB	R	RBI	TBB	IBB	SO	HBP	SH	SF	SB	CS	SB%	GDP	Avg	OBP	SLG
1986 Geneva	A	64	213	67	6	2	3	--	--	86	51	16	40	1	33	3	4	3	49	10	.83	1	.315	.425	.404
1987 Winston-Sal	A	126	458	129	13	7	4	--	--	168	82	49	78	3	50	6	1	4	79	18	.81	6	.282	.390	.367
1988 Pittsfield	AA	128	445	109	15	8	1	--	--	143	82	39	55	2	63	8	10	4	69	17	.80	4	.245	.336	.321
1989 Charlotte	AA	123	361	92	11	2	6	--	--	125	72	37	48	0	54	5	5	2	45	9	.83	4	.255	.349	.346

1990	Iowa	AAA	123	372	110	10	4	0	--	--	128	71	24	43	1	63	1	5	3	46	16	.74	4	.296	.368	.344
1991	Iowa	AAA	38	131	44	8	2	1	--	--	59	14	11	5	0	21	0	2	0	13	4	.76	2	.336	.360	.450
1992	Iowa	AAA	8	20	6	0	0	0	--	--	6	4	0	4	0	1	1	0	0	1	1	.50	0	.300	.440	.300
	Denver	AAA	43	144	45	7	0	1	--	--	55	20	19	13	0	16	0	4	2	15	9	.63	1	.313	.365	.382
1993	Portland	AAA	4	4	0	0	0	0	--	--	0	0	0	0	0	0	0	0	0	1	0	1.00	0	.000	.000	.000
	Norfolk	AAA	69	275	80	13	5	5	--	--	118	39	29	19	2	30	1	3	0	16	6	.73	5	.291	.339	.429
1991	Chicago	NL	56	86	20	2	1	0	(0	0)	24	28	6	10	0	18	0	3	0	27	5	.84	2	.233	.313	.279
1993	New York	NL	22	19	5	1	0	0	(0	0)	6	2	1	0	0	5	0	1	0	0	0	.00	0	.263	.263	.316
	2 ML YEARS		78	105	25	3	1	0	(0	0)	30	30	7	10	0	23	0	4	0	27	5	.84	2	.238	.304	.286

Mark Langston

Pitches: Left **Bats:** Right **Pos:** SP   **Ht:** 6' 2" **Wt:** 184 **Born:** 08/20/60 **Age:** 33

			HOW MUCH HE PITCHED					WHAT HE GAVE UP										THE RESULTS					
Year	Team	Lg	G	GS	CG	GF	IP	BFP	H	R	ER	HR	SH	SF	HB	TBB	IBB	SO	WP	Bk	W	L	Pct.	ShO	Sv	ERA
1984	Seattle	AL	35	33	5	0	225	965	188	99	85	16	13	7	8	118	5	204	4	2	17	10	.630	2	0	3.40
1985	Seattle	AL	24	24	2	0	126.2	577	122	85	77	22	3	2	2	91	2	72	3	3	7	14	.333	0	0	5.47
1986	Seattle	AL	37	36	9	1	239.1	1057	234	142	129	30	5	8	4	123	1	245	10	3	12	14	.462	0	0	4.85
1987	Seattle	AL	35	35	14	0	272	1152	242	132	116	30	12	6	5	114	0	262	9	2	19	13	.594	3	0	3.84
1988	Seattle	AL	35	35	9	0	261.1	1078	222	108	97	32	6	5	3	110	2	235	7	4	15	11	.577	3	0	3.34
1989	2 ML Teams		34	34	8	0	250	1037	198	87	76	16	9	7	4	112	6	235	6	4	16	14	.533	5	0	2.74
1990	California	AL	33	33	5	0	223	950	215	120	109	13	6	6	5	104	1	195	8	0	10	17	.370	1	0	4.40
1991	California	AL	34	34	7	0	246.1	992	190	89	82	30	4	6	2	96	3	183	6	0	19	8	.704	0	0	3.00
1992	California	AL	32	32	9	0	229	941	206	103	93	14	4	5	6	74	2	174	5	0	13	14	.481	2	0	3.66
1993	California	AL	35	35	7	0	256.1	1039	220	100	91	22	3	8	1	85	2	196	10	2	16	11	.593	0	0	3.20
1989	Seattle	AL	10	10	2	0	73.1	297	60	30	29	3	0	3	4	19	0	60	1	2	4	5	.444	1	0	3.56
	Montreal	NL	24	24	6	0	176.2	740	138	57	47	13	9	4	0	93	6	175	5	2	12	9	.571	4	0	2.39
	10 ML YEARS		334	331	75	1	2329	9788	2037	1065	955	225	65	60	40	1027	24	2001	68	20	144	126	.533	16	0	3.69

Ray Lankford

Bats: Left **Throws:** Left **Pos:** CF   **Ht:** 5'11" **Wt:** 198 **Born:** 06/05/67 **Age:** 27

			BATTING															BASERUNNING				PERCENTAGES		
Year	Team	Lg	G	AB	H	2B	3B	HR	(Hm | Rd)	TB	R	RBI	TBB	IBB	SO	HBP	SH	SF	SB	CS	SB%	GDP	Avg	OBP	SLG
1990	St. Louis	NL	39	126	36	10	1	3	(2 | 1)	57	12	12	13	0	27	0	0	0	8	2	.80	1	.286	.353	.452
1991	St. Louis	NL	151	566	142	23	15	9	(4 | 5)	222	83	69	41	1	114	1	4	3	44	20	.69	4	.251	.301	.392
1992	St. Louis	NL	153	598	175	40	6	20	(13 | 7)	287	87	86	72	6	147	5	2	5	42	24	.64	5	.293	.371	.480
1993	St. Louis	NL	127	407	97	17	3	7	(6 | 1)	141	64	45	81	7	111	3	1	3	14	14	.50	5	.238	.366	.346
	4 ML YEARS		470	1697	450	90	25	39	(25 | 14)	707	246	212	207	14	399	9	7	11	108	60	.64	15	.265	.346	.417

Mike Lansing

Bats: Right **Throws:** Right **Pos:** 3B/2B/SS   **Ht:** 6' 0" **Wt:** 180 **Born:** 04/03/68 **Age:** 26

			BATTING															BASERUNNING				PERCENTAGES		
Year	Team	Lg	G	AB	H	2B	3B	HR	(Hm	Rd)	TB	R	RBI	TBB	IBB	SO	HBP	SH	SF	SB	CS	SB%	GDP	Avg	OBP	SLG
1990	Miami	A	61	207	50	5	2	2	--	--	65	20	11	29	0	35	1	3	0	15	5	.75	3	.242	.338	.314
1991	Miami	A	103	384	110	20	7	6	--	--	162	54	55	40	1	75	4	1	6	29	6	.83	3	.286	.355	.422
1992	Harrisburg	AA	128	483	135	20	6	6	--	--	185	66	54	52	3	64	4	1	3	46	9	.84	15	.280	.352	.383
1993	Montreal	NL	141	491	141	29	1	3	(1	2)	181	64	45	46	2	56	5	10	3	23	5	.82	16	.287	.352	.369

Barry Larkin

Bats: Right **Throws:** Right **Pos:** SS   **Ht:** 6' 0" **Wt:** 190 **Born:** 04/28/64 **Age:** 30

			BATTING															BASERUNNING				PERCENTAGES		
Year	Team	Lg	G	AB	H	2B	3B	HR	(Hm | Rd)	TB	R	RBI	TBB	IBB	SO	HBP	SH	SF	SB	CS	SB%	GDP	Avg	OBP	SLG
1986	Cincinnati	NL	41	159	45	4	3	3	(3 | 0)	64	27	19	9	1	21	0	0	1	8	0	1.00	2	.283	.320	.403
1987	Cincinnati	NL	125	439	107	16	2	12	(6 | 6)	163	64	43	36	3	52	5	5	3	21	6	.78	8	.244	.306	.371
1988	Cincinnati	NL	151	588	174	32	5	12	(9 | 3)	252	91	56	41	3	24	8	10	5	40	7	.85	7	.296	.347	.429
1989	Cincinnati	NL	97	325	111	14	4	4	(1 | 3)	145	47	36	20	5	23	2	2	8	10	5	.67	7	.342	.375	.446
1990	Cincinnati	NL	158	614	185	25	6	7	(4 | 3)	243	85	67	49	3	49	7	7	4	30	5	.86	14	.301	.358	.396
1991	Cincinnati	NL	123	464	140	27	4	20	(16 | 4)	235	88	69	55	1	64	3	3	2	24	6	.80	7	.302	.378	.506
1992	Cincinnati	NL	140	533	162	32	6	12	(8 | 4)	242	76	78	63	8	58	4	2	7	15	4	.79	13	.304	.377	.454
1993	Cincinnati	NL	100	384	121	20	3	8	(4 | 4)	171	57	51	51	6	33	1	1	3	14	1	.93	13	.315	.394	.445
	8 ML YEARS		935	3506	1045	170	33	78	(51 | 27)	1515	535	419	324	30	324	30	30	33	162	34	.83	71	.298	.359	.432

Gene Larkin

Bats: Both **Throws:** Right **Pos:** RF/1B   **Ht:** 6' 3" **Wt:** 205 **Born:** 10/24/62 **Age:** 31

			BATTING															BASERUNNING				PERCENTAGES		
Year	Team	Lg	G	AB	H	2B	3B	HR	(Hm | Rd)	TB	R	RBI	TBB	IBB	SO	HBP	SH	SF	SB	CS	SB%	GDP	Avg	OBP	SLG
1987	Minnesota	AL	85	233	62	11	2	4	(0 | 4)	89	23	28	25	3	31	2	0	2	1	4	.20	4	.266	.340	.382
1988	Minnesota	AL	149	505	135	30	2	8	(5 | 3)	193	56	70	68	8	55	15	1	5	3	2	.60	12	.267	.368	.382

1989 Minnesota	AL	136	446	119	25	1	6	(3	3)	164	61	46	54	6	57	9	5	6	5	2	.71	13	.267	.353	.368
1990 Minnesota	AL	119	401	108	26	4	5	(5	0)	157	46	42	42	2	55	5	5	4	5	3	.63	6	.269	.343	.392
1991 Minnesota	AL	98	255	73	14	1	2	(0	2)	95	34	19	30	3	21	1	3	2	2	3	.40	9	.286	.361	.373
1992 Minnesota	AL	115	337	83	18	1	6	(5	1)	121	38	42	28	6	43	4	0	4	7	2	.78	7	.246	.308	.359
1993 Minnesota	AL	56	144	38	7	1	1	(1	0)	50	17	19	21	3	16	2	2	4	0	1	.00	5	.264	.357	.347
7 ML YEARS		758	2321	618	131	12	32	(19	13)	869	275	266	268	31	278	38	16	27	23	17	.58	56	.266	.348	.374

Mike LaValliere

Bats: Left **Throws:** Right **Pos:** C **Ht:** 5' 9" **Wt:** 210 **Born:** 08/18/60 **Age:** 33

						BATTING														BASERUNNING				PERCENTAGES		
Year Team	Lg	G	AB	H	2B	3B	HR	(Hm	Rd)	TB	R	RBI	TBB	IBB	SO	HBP	SH	SF	SB	CS	SB%	GDP	Avg	OBP	SLG
1993 Sarasota *	A	32	108	33	2	0	0	--	--	35	6	14	19	1	5	1	0	3	2	0	1.00	4	.306	.405	.324
1984 Philadelphia	NL	6	7	0	0	0	0	(0	0)	0	0	0	2	0	2	0	0	0	0	0	.00	0	.000	.222	.000
1985 St. Louis	NL	12	34	5	1	0	0	(0	0)	6	2	6	7	0	3	0	0	3	0	0	.00	2	.147	.273	.176
1986 St. Louis	NL	110	303	71	10	2	3	(1	2)	94	18	30	36	5	37	1	10	0	0	1	.00	7	.234	.318	.310
1987 Pittsburgh	NL	121	340	102	19	0	1	(1	0)	124	33	36	43	9	32	1	3	3	0	0	.00	4	.300	.377	.365
1988 Pittsburgh	NL	120	352	92	18	0	2	(0	2)	116	24	47	50	10	34	2	1	4	3	2	.60	8	.261	.353	.330
1989 Pittsburgh	NL	68	190	60	10	0	2	(2	0)	76	15	23	29	7	24	0	4	0	0	2	.00	4	.316	.406	.400
1990 Pittsburgh	NL	96	279	72	15	0	3	(2	1)	96	27	31	44	8	20	2	4	1	0	3	.00	6	.258	.362	.344
1991 Pittsburgh	NL	108	336	97	11	2	3	(1	2)	121	25	41	33	4	27	2	1	5	2	1	.67	10	.289	.351	.360
1992 Pittsburgh	NL	95	293	75	13	1	2	(1	1)	96	22	29	44	14	21	1	0	5	0	3	.00	8	.256	.350	.328
1993 2 ML Teams		38	102	26	2	0	0	(0	0)	28	6	8	4	0	14	0	7	2	0	1	.00	1	.255	.278	.275
1993 Pittsburgh	NL	1	5	1	0	0	0	(0	0)	1	0	0	0	0	0	0	0	0	0	0	.00	0	.200	.200	.200
Chicago	AL	37	97	25	2	0	0	(0	0)	27	6	8	4	0	14	0	7	2	0	1	.00	1	.258	.282	.278
10 ML YEARS		774	2236	600	99	5	16	(8	8)	757	172	251	292	57	214	9	30	23	5	13	.28	50	.268	.352	.339

Tim Layana

Pitches: Right **Bats:** Right **Pos:** RP **Ht:** 6' 2" **Wt:** 190 **Born:** 03/02/64 **Age:** 30

		HOW MUCH HE PITCHED					WHAT HE GAVE UP										THE RESULTS				
Year Team	Lg	G	GS	CG	GF	IP	BFP	H	R	ER	HR	SH	SF	HB	TBB	IBB	SO	WP	Bk	W	L	Pct.	ShO	Sv	ERA
1993 Phoenix *	AAA	55	0	0	38	67.1	306	80	42	36	5	4	6	5	24	4	55	8	2	3	2	.600	0	9	4.81
1990 Cincinnati	NL	55	0	0	17	80	344	71	33	31	7	4	3	2	44	5	53	5	4	5	3	.625	0	2	3.49
1991 Cincinnati	NL	22	0	0	9	20.2	95	23	18	16	1	1	0	0	11	0	14	3	0	0	2	.000	0	0	6.97
1993 San Francisco	NL	1	0	0	0	2	15	7	5	5	1	1	0	0	1	1	1	0	0	0	0		0	0	22.50
3 ML YEARS		78	0	0	26	102.2	454	101	56	52	9	6	3	2	56	6	68	8	4	5	5	.500	0	2	4.56

Terry Leach

Pitches: Right **Bats:** Right **Pos:** RP **Ht:** 6' 0" **Wt:** 194 **Born:** 03/13/54 **Age:** 40

		HOW MUCH HE PITCHED					WHAT HE GAVE UP										THE RESULTS				
Year Team	Lg	G	GS	CG	GF	IP	BFP	H	R	ER	HR	SH	SF	HB	TBB	IBB	SO	WP	Bk	W	L	Pct.	ShO	Sv	ERA
1993 Nashville *	AAA	5	0	0	1	5.2	20	4	2	2	0	1	0	0	0	0	4	0	0	0	0	.000	0	1	3.18
Birmingham *	AA	4	0	0	1	4.1	19	4	2	2	0	0	0	0	2	1	5	0	0	0	0	.000	0	1	4.15
1981 New York	NL	21	1	0	3	35	139	26	11	10	2	0	0	0	12	1	16	0	0	1	1	.500	0	0	2.57
1982 New York	NL	21	1	1	12	45.1	194	46	22	21	2	5	1	0	18	5	30	0	0	2	1	.667	1	3	4.17
1985 New York	NL	22	4	1	4	55.2	226	48	19	18	3	5	2	1	14	3	30	0	0	3	4	.429	1	1	2.91
1986 New York	NL	6	0	0	1	6.2	30	6	3	2	0	0	0	0	3	0	4	0	0	0	0	.000	0	0	2.70
1987 New York	NL	44	12	1	7	131.1	542	132	54	47	14	8	1	1	29	5	61	0	1	11	1	.917	1	0	3.22
1988 New York	NL	52	0	0	21	92	392	95	32	26	5	8	3	3	24	4	51	0	0	7	2	.778	0	3	2.54
1989 2 ML Teams		40	3	0	10	95	413	97	57	44	5	6	6	2	40	9	36	1	1	5	6	.455	0	0	4.17
1990 Minnesota	AL	55	0	0	29	81.2	344	84	31	29	2	7	2	1	21	10	46	1	0	2	5	.286	0	2	3.20
1991 Minnesota	AL	50	0	0	22	67.1	292	82	28	27	3	3	1	0	14	5	32	1	0	1	2	.333	0	1	3.61
1992 Chicago	AL	51	0	0	21	73.2	292	57	17	16	2	2	1	4	20	5	22	0	0	6	5	.545	0	0	1.95
1993 Chicago	AL	14	0	0	8	16	64	15	5	5	0	0	1	1	2	1	3	0	0	0	0	.000	0	1	2.81
1989 New York	NL	10	0	0	4	21.1	85	19	11	10	1	0	2	1	4	0	2	0	0	0	0	.000	0	0	4.22
Kansas City	AL	30	3	0	6	73.2	328	78	46	34	4	6	4	1	36	9	34	1	1	5	6	.455	0	0	4.15
11 ML YEARS		376	21	3	138	699.2	2928	688	279	245	38	44	18	13	197	48	331	3	3	38	27	.585	3	10	3.15

Tim Leary

Pitches: Right **Bats:** Right **Pos:** SP/RP **Ht:** 6' 3" **Wt:** 220 **Born:** 12/23/58 **Age:** 35

		HOW MUCH HE PITCHED					WHAT HE GAVE UP										THE RESULTS				
Year Team	Lg	G	GS	CG	GF	IP	BFP	H	R	ER	HR	SH	SF	HB	TBB	IBB	SO	WP	Bk	W	L	Pct.	ShO	Sv	ERA
1981 New York	NL	1	1	0	0	2	7	0	0	0	0	0	0	0	1	0	3	1	0	0	0	.000	0	0	0.00
1983 New York	NL	2	2	1	0	10.2	53	15	10	4	0	1	1	0	4	0	9	0	1	1	1	.500	0	0	3.38
1984 New York	NL	20	7	0	3	53.2	237	61	28	24	2	1	2	2	18	3	29	2	3	3	3	.500	0	0	4.02
1985 Milwaukee	AL	5	5	0	0	33.1	146	40	18	15	5	2	0	1	8	0	29	1	0	1	4	.200	0	0	4.05
1986 Milwaukee	AL	33	30	3	2	188.1	817	216	97	88	20	4	6	7	53	4	110	7	0	12	12	.500	2	0	4.21
1987 Los Angeles	NL	39	12	0	11	107.2	469	121	62	57	15	6	1	2	36	5	61	3	1	3	11	.214	0	1	4.76

Year	Team	Lg	G	GS	CG	GF	IP	BFP	H	R	ER	HR	SH	SF	HB	TBB	IBB	SO	WP	Bk	W	L	Pct.	ShO	Sv	ERA
1988	Los Angeles	NL	35	34	9	0	228.2	932	201	87	74	13	7	3	6	56	4	180	9	6	17	11	.607	6	0	2.91
1989	2 ML Teams		33	31	2	0	207	874	205	84	81	17	7	8	5	68	15	123	10	0	8	14	.364	0	0	3.52
1990	New York	AL	31	31	6	0	208	881	202	105	95	18	7	4	7	78	1	138	23	0	9	19	.321	1	0	4.11
1991	New York	AL	28	18	1	4	120.2	551	150	89	87	20	7	2	4	57	1	83	10	0	4	10	.286	0	0	6.49
1992	2 ML Teams		26	23	3	2	141	624	131	89	84	12	6	11	9	87	5	46	9	0	8	10	.444	0	0	5.36
1993	Seattle	AL	33	27	0	6	169.1	746	202	104	95	21	5	1	8	58	5	68	6	2	11	9	.550	0	0	5.05
1989	Los Angeles	NL	19	17	2	0	117.1	481	107	45	44	9	4	4	2	37	7	59	4	0	6	7	.462	0	0	3.38
	Cincinnati	NL	14	14	0	0	89.2	393	98	39	37	8	3	4	3	31	8	64	6	0	2	7	.222	0	0	3.71
1992	New York	AL	18	15	2	2	97	414	84	62	60	9	4	6	4	57	2	34	7	0	5	6	.455	0	0	5.57
	Seattle	AL	8	8	1	0	44	210	47	27	24	3	2	5	5	30	3	12	2	0	3	4	.429	0	0	4.91
12 ML YEARS			286	221	25	28	1470.1	6337	1544	773	704	143	53	39	51	524	43	879	81	13	77	104	.425	9	1	4.31

Derek Lee

Bats: Left **Throws:** Right **Pos:** LF   **Ht:** 6' 0" **Wt:** 195 **Born:** 07/28/66 **Age:** 27

							BATTING													BASERUNNING				PERCENTAGES		
Year	Team	Lg	G	AB	H	2B	3B	HR	(Hm	Rd)	TB	R	RBI	TBB	IBB	SO	HBP	SH	SF	SB	CS	SB%	GDP	Avg	OBP	SLG
1988	Utica	A	76	252	86	7	5	2	--	--	109	51	47	50	5	48	3	3	4	54	15	.78	2	.341	.450	.433
1989	South Bend	A	125	448	128	24	4	11	--	--	199	89	48	87	4	83	9	4	2	45	26	.63	5	.286	.410	.444
1990	Birmingham	AA	126	411	105	21	3	7	--	--	153	68	75	71	5	93	6	3	5	14	10	.58	4	.255	.369	.372
1991	Birmingham	AA	45	154	50	10	2	5	--	--	79	36	16	46	5	23	6	0	1	9	7	.56	1	.325	.493	.513
	Vancouver	AAA	87	319	94	28	5	6	--	--	150	54	44	35	2	62	2	3	1	4	2	.67	1	.295	.367	.470
1992	Vancouver	AAA	115	381	104	20	6	7	--	--	157	58	50	56	7	65	6	4	2	17	7	.71	11	.273	.373	.412
1993	Portland	AAA	106	381	120	30	7	10	--	--	194	79	80	60	2	51	4	4	4	16	5	.76	10	.315	.410	.509
1993	Minnesota	AL	15	33	5	1	0	0	(0	0)	6	3	4	1	0	4	0	0	0	0	0	.00	0	.152	.176	.182

Manuel Lee

Bats: Both **Throws:** Right **Pos:** SS   **Ht:** 5' 9" **Wt:** 166 **Born:** 06/17/65 **Age:** 29

							BATTING													BASERUNNING				PERCENTAGES		
Year	Team	Lg	G	AB	H	2B	3B	HR	(Hm	Rd)	TB	R	RBI	TBB	IBB	SO	HBP	SH	SF	SB	CS	SB%	GDP	Avg	OBP	SLG
1985	Toronto	AL	64	40	8	0	0	0	(0	0)	8	9	0	2	0	9	0	1	0	1	4	.20	2	.200	.238	.200
1986	Toronto	AL	35	78	16	0	1	1	(1	0)	21	8	7	4	0	10	0	2	1	0	1	.00	5	.205	.241	.269
1987	Toronto	AL	56	121	31	2	3	1	(0	1)	42	14	11	6	0	13	0	1	1	2	0	1.00	1	.256	.289	.347
1988	Toronto	AL	116	381	111	16	3	2	(2	0)	139	38	38	26	1	64	0	4	4	3	3	.50	13	.291	.333	.365
1989	Toronto	AL	99	300	78	9	2	3	(1	2)	100	27	34	20	1	60	0	1	1	4	2	.67	8	.260	.305	.333
1990	Toronto	AL	117	391	95	12	4	6	(2	4)	133	45	41	26	0	90	0	1	3	3	1	.75	9	.243	.288	.340
1991	Toronto	AL	138	445	104	18	3	0	(0	0)	128	41	29	24	0	107	2	10	4	7	2	.78	11	.234	.274	.288
1992	Toronto	AL	128	396	104	10	1	3	(1	2)	125	49	39	50	0	73	0	8	3	6	2	.75	8	.263	.343	.316
1993	Texas	AL	73	205	45	3	1	1	(0	1)	53	31	12	22	3	39	2	9	1	2	4	.33	2	.220	.300	.259
9 ML YEARS			826	2357	592	70	18	17	(7	10)	749	262	211	180	5	465	4	37	18	28	19	.60	59	.251	.303	.318

Craig Lefferts

Pitches: Left **Bats:** Left **Pos:** RP/SP   **Ht:** 6' 1" **Wt:** 210 **Born:** 09/29/57 **Age:** 36

			HOW MUCH HE PITCHED						WHAT HE GAVE UP											THE RESULTS					
Year	Team	Lg	G	GS	CG	GF	IP	BFP	H	R	ER	HR	SH	SF	HB	TBB	IBB	SO	WP	Bk	W	L	Pct.	ShO	Sv	ERA
1993	Okla City *	AAA	1	1	0	0	6	27	9	5	5	1	0	1	0	2	0	1	0	0	0	1	.000	0	0	7.50
1983	Chicago	NL	56	5	0	10	89	367	80	35	31	13	7	0	2	29	3	60	2	0	3	4	.429	0	1	3.13
1984	San Diego	NL	62	0	0	29	105.2	420	88	29	25	4	4	6	1	24	1	56	2	2	3	4	.429	0	10	2.13
1985	San Diego	NL	60	0	0	24	83.1	345	75	34	31	7	7	1	0	30	4	48	2	0	7	6	.538	0	2	3.35
1986	San Diego	NL	83	0	0	36	107.2	446	98	41	37	7	9	5	1	44	11	72	1	1	9	8	.529	0	4	3.09
1987	2 ML Teams		77	0	0	22	98.2	416	92	47	42	13	6	2	2	33	11	57	6	3	5	5	.500	0	6	3.83
1988	San Francisco	NL	64	0	0	30	92.1	362	74	33	30	7	6	3	1	23	5	58	4	0	3	8	.273	0	11	2.92
1989	San Francisco	NL	70	0	0	32	107	430	93	38	32	11	4	4	1	22	5	71	4	1	2	4	.333	0	20	2.69
1990	San Diego	NL	56	0	0	44	78.2	327	68	26	22	10	5	1	1	22	4	60	1	0	7	5	.583	0	23	2.52
1991	San Diego	NL	54	0	0	40	69	290	74	35	30	5	10	5	1	14	3	48	3	1	1	6	.143	0	23	3.91
1992	2 ML Teams		32	32	1	0	196.1	820	214	95	82	19	14	6	0	41	2	104	5	1	14	12	.538	0	0	3.76
1993	Texas	AL	52	0	0	9	83.1	373	102	57	56	17	6	3	1	28	3	58	0	1	3	9	.250	0	0	6.05
1987	San Diego	NL	33	0	0	8	51.1	225	56	29	25	9	2	0	2	15	5	39	5	2	2	2	.500	0	2	4.38
	San Francisco		44	0	0	14	47.1	191	36	18	17	4	4	2	0	18	6	18	1	1	3	3	.500	0	0	3.23
1992	San Diego	NL	27	27	1	0	163.1	684	180	76	67	16	12	5	0	35	2	81	4	1	13	9	.591	0	0	3.69
	Baltimore	AL	5	5	1	0	33	136	34	19	15	3	2	1	0	6	0	23	1	0	1	3	.250	0	0	4.09
11 ML YEARS			666	45	1	276	1111	4596	1058	470	418	113	78	36	11	310	52	692	30	10	57	71	.445	0	100	3.39

Phil Leftwich

Pitches: Right **Bats:** Right **Pos:** SP   **Ht:** 6' 5" **Wt:** 205 **Born:** 05/19/69 **Age:** 25

			HOW MUCH HE PITCHED						WHAT HE GAVE UP											THE RESULTS					
Year	Team	Lg	G	GS	CG	GF	IP	BFP	H	R	ER	HR	SH	SF	HB	TBB	IBB	SO	WP	Bk	W	L	Pct.	ShO	Sv	ERA
1990	Boise	A	15	15	0	0	92	373	88	36	19	0	0	4	1	23	1	81	3	2	8	2	.800	0	0	1.86

Year Team	Lg	G	GS	CG	GF	IP	BFP	H	R	ER	HR	SH	SF	HB	TBB	IBB	SO	WP	Bk	W	L	Pct.	ShO	Sv	ERA
1991 Quad City	A	26	26	5	0	173	716	158	70	63	6	7	2	3	59	0	163	8	2	11	9	.550	1	0	3.28
Midland	AA	1	1	0	0	6	27	5	2	2	0	0	0	0	5	0	3	0	0	1	0	1.000	0	0	3.00
1992 Midland	AA	21	21	0	0	121	546	156	90	79	10	6	3	4	37	1	85	2	1	6	9	.400	0	0	5.88
1993 Vancouver	AAA	20	20	3	0	126	552	138	74	65	8	3	4	2	45	1	102	4	0	7	7	.500	1	0	4.64
1993 California	AL	12	12	1	0	80.2	343	81	35	34	5	3	1	3	27	1	31	1	0	4	6	.400	0	0	3.79

Charlie Leibrandt

Pitches: Left **Bats:** Right **Pos:** SP　　**Ht:** 6' 3" **Wt:** 200 **Born:** 10/04/56 **Age:** 37

		HOW MUCH HE PITCHED						WHAT HE GAVE UP												THE RESULTS					
Year Team	Lg	G	GS	CG	GF	IP	BFP	H	R	ER	HR	SH	SF	HB	TBB	IBB	SO	WP	Bk	W	L	Pct.	ShO	Sv	ERA
1979 Cincinnati	NL	3	0	0	1	4	16	2	2	0	0	0	1	0	2	0	1	0	0	0	0	.000	0	0	0.00
1980 Cincinnati	NL	36	27	5	3	174	754	200	84	82	15	12	2	2	54	4	62	1	6	10	9	.526	2	0	4.24
1981 Cincinnati	NL	7	4	1	0	30	128	28	12	12	0	4	2	0	15	2	9	0	0	1	1	.500	1	0	3.60
1982 Cincinnati	NL	36	11	0	10	107.2	484	130	68	61	4	10	2	2	48	9	34	6	1	5	7	.417	0	2	5.10
1984 Kansas City	AL	23	23	0	0	143.2	621	158	65	58	11	3	7	3	38	2	53	5	1	11	7	.611	0	0	3.63
1985 Kansas City	AL	33	33	8	0	237.2	983	223	86	71	17	8	5	2	68	3	108	4	3	17	9	.654	3	0	2.69
1986 Kansas City	AL	35	34	8	0	231.1	975	238	112	105	18	14	5	4	63	0	108	2	1	14	11	.560	1	0	4.09
1987 Kansas City	AL	35	35	8	0	240.1	1015	235	104	91	23	5	5	1	74	2	151	9	3	16	11	.593	3	0	3.41
1988 Kansas City	AL	35	35	7	0	243	1002	244	98	86	20	5	7	4	62	3	125	10	4	13	12	.520	2	0	3.19
1989 Kansas City	AL	33	27	3	3	161	712	196	98	92	13	8	4	2	54	4	73	9	2	5	11	.313	1	0	5.14
1990 Atlanta	NL	24	24	5	0	162.1	680	164	72	57	9	7	6	4	35	3	76	4	3	9	11	.450	2	0	3.16
1991 Atlanta	NL	36	36	1	0	229.2	949	212	105	89	18	19	6	4	56	3	128	5	3	15	13	.536	1	0	3.49
1992 Atlanta	NL	32	31	5	0	193	799	191	78	72	9	7	4	5	42	4	104	3	2	15	7	.682	2	0	3.36
1993 Texas	AL	26	26	1	0	150.1	656	169	84	76	15	8	4	4	45	5	89	5	2	9	10	.474	0	0	4.55
14 ML YEARS		394	346	52	17	2308	9774	2390	1068	952	172	110	60	37	656	44	1121	63	31	140	119	.541	18	2	3.71

Al Leiter

Pitches: Left **Bats:** Left **Pos:** RP/SP　　**Ht:** 6' 3" **Wt:** 215 **Born:** 10/23/65 **Age:** 28

		HOW MUCH HE PITCHED						WHAT HE GAVE UP												THE RESULTS					
Year Team	Lg	G	GS	CG	GF	IP	BFP	H	R	ER	HR	SH	SF	HB	TBB	IBB	SO	WP	Bk	W	L	Pct.	ShO	Sv	ERA
1987 New York	AL	4	4	0	0	22.2	104	24	16	16	2	1	0	0	15	0	28	4	0	2	2	.500	0	0	6.35
1988 New York	AL	14	14	0	0	57.1	251	49	27	25	7	1	0	5	33	0	60	1	4	4	4	.500	0	0	3.92
1989 2 ML Teams		5	5	0	0	33.1	154	32	23	21	2	1	1	2	23	0	26	2	1	1	2	.333	0	0	5.67
1990 Toronto	AL	4	0	0	2	6.1	22	1	0	0	0	0	0	0	2	0	5	0	0	0	0	.000	0	0	0.00
1991 Toronto	AL	3	0	0	1	1.2	13	3	5	5	0	1	0	0	5	0	1	0	0	0	0	.000	0	0	27.00
1992 Toronto	AL	1	0	0	0	1	7	1	1	1	0	0	0	0	2	0	0	0	0	0	0	.000	0	0	9.00
1993 Toronto	AL	34	12	1	4	105	454	93	52	48	8	3	3	4	56	2	66	2	2	9	6	.600	1	2	4.11
1989 New York	AL	4	4	0	0	26.2	123	23	20	18	1	1	1	2	21	0	22	1	1	1	2	.333	0	0	6.08
Toronto	AL	1	1	0	0	6.2	31	9	3	3	1	0	0	0	2	0	4	1	0	0	0	.000	0	0	4.05
7 ML YEARS		65	35	1	7	227.1	1005	203	124	116	19	7	4	11	136	2	186	9	7	16	14	.533	1	2	4.59

Mark Leiter

Pitches: Right **Bats:** Right **Pos:** RP/SP　　**Ht:** 6' 3" **Wt:** 210 **Born:** 04/13/63 **Age:** 31

		HOW MUCH HE PITCHED						WHAT HE GAVE UP												THE RESULTS					
Year Team	Lg	G	GS	CG	GF	IP	BFP	H	R	ER	HR	SH	SF	HB	TBB	IBB	SO	WP	Bk	W	L	Pct.	ShO	Sv	ERA
1990 New York	AL	8	3	0	2	26.1	119	33	20	20	5	2	1	2	9	0	21	0	0	1	1	.500	0	0	6.84
1991 Detroit	AL	38	15	1	7	134.2	578	125	66	63	16	5	6	6	50	4	103	2	0	9	7	.563	0	1	4.21
1992 Detroit	AL	35	14	1	7	112	475	116	57	52	9	2	8	3	43	5	75	3	0	8	5	.615	0	0	4.18
1993 Detroit	AL	27	13	1	4	106.2	471	111	61	56	17	3	5	3	44	5	70	5	0	6	6	.500	0	0	4.72
4 ML YEARS		108	45	3	20	379.2	1643	385	204	191	47	12	20	14	146	14	269	10	0	24	19	.558	0	1	4.53

Scott Leius

Bats: Right **Throws:** Right **Pos:** SS　　**Ht:** 6' 3" **Wt:** 195 **Born:** 09/24/65 **Age:** 28

		BATTING															BASERUNNING			PERCENTAGES		
Year Team	Lg	G	AB	H	2B	3B	HR	(Hm | Rd)	TB	R	RBI	TBB	IBB	SO	HBP	SH	SF	SB	CS	SB%	GDP	Avg	OBP	SLG
1990 Minnesota	AL	14	25	6	1	0	1	(0 | 1)	10	4	4	2	0	2	0	1	0	0	0	.00	2	.240	.296	.400
1991 Minnesota	AL	109	199	57	7	2	5	(2 | 3)	83	35	20	30	1	35	0	5	1	5	5	.50	4	.286	.378	.417
1992 Minnesota	AL	129	409	102	18	2	2	(2 | 0)	130	50	35	34	0	61	1	5	0	6	5	.55	10	.249	.309	.318
1993 Minnesota	AL	10	18	3	0	0	0	(0 | 0)	3	4	2	2	0	4	0	0	2	0	0	.00	1	.167	.227	.167
4 ML YEARS		262	651	168	26	4	8	(4 | 4)	226	93	61	68	1	102	1	11	3	11	10	.52	17	.258	.328	.347

Mark Lemke

Bats: Both **Throws:** Right **Pos:** 2B　　**Ht:** 5' 9" **Wt:** 167 **Born:** 08/13/65 **Age:** 28

		BATTING															BASERUNNING			PERCENTAGES		
Year Team	Lg	G	AB	H	2B	3B	HR	(Hm | Rd)	TB	R	RBI	TBB	IBB	SO	HBP	SH	SF	SB	CS	SB%	GDP	Avg	OBP	SLG
1988 Atlanta	NL	16	58	13	4	0	0	(0 | 0)	17	8	2	4	0	5	0	2	0	0	2	.00	1	.224	.274	.293
1989 Atlanta	NL	14	55	10	2	1	2	(1 | 1)	20	4	10	5	0	7	0	0	0	0	1	.00	1	.182	.250	.364

Year	Team	Lg	G	AB	H	2B	3B	HR	(Hm	Rd)	TB	R	RBI	TBB	IBB	SO	HBP	SH	SF	SB	CS	SB%	GDP	Avg	OBP	SLG
1990	Atlanta	NL	102	239	54	13	0	0	(0	0)	67	22	21	21	3	22	0	4	2	0	1	.00	6	.226	.286	.280
1991	Atlanta	NL	136	269	63	11	2	2	(2	0)	84	36	23	29	2	27	0	6	4	1	2	.33	9	.234	.305	.312
1992	Atlanta	NL	155	427	97	7	4	6	(4	2)	130	38	26	50	11	39	0	12	2	0	3	.00	9	.227	.307	.304
1993	Atlanta	NL	151	493	124	19	2	7	(3	4)	168	52	49	65	13	50	0	5	6	1	2	.33	20	.252	.335	.341
	6 ML YEARS		574	1541	361	56	9	17	(10	7)	486	160	131	174	29	150	0	29	14	2	11	.15	46	.234	.309	.315

Mark Leonard

Bats: Left Throws: Right Pos: LF　　　　**Ht: 6' 0" Wt: 195 Born: 08/14/64 Age: 29**

						BATTING													BASERUNNING				PERCENTAGES		
Year	Team	Lg	G	AB	H	2B	3B	HR	(Hm	Rd)	TB	R	RBI	TBB	IBB	SO	HBP	SH	SF	SB	CS	SB%	GDP	Avg	OBP	SLG
1993	Rochester *	AAA	97	330	91	23	1	17	(Hm	--	167	57	58	60	4	81	10	0	6	0	1	.00	4	.276	.397	.506
1990	San Francisco	NL	11	17	3	1	0	1	(0	1)	7	3	2	3	0	8	0	0	0	0	0	.00	0	.176	.300	.412
1991	San Francisco	NL	64	129	31	7	1	2	(0	2)	46	14	14	12	1	25	1	1	2	0	1	.00	3	.240	.306	.357
1992	San Francisco	NL	55	128	30	7	0	4	(3	1)	49	13	16	16	0	31	3	0	1	0	1	.00	3	.234	.331	.383
1993	Baltimore	AL	10	15	1	1	0	0	(0	0)	2	1	3	3	0	7	0	0	3	0	0	.00	0	.067	.190	.133
	4 ML YEARS		140	289	65	16	1	7	(3	4)	104	31	35	34	1	71	4	1	6	0	2	.00	6	.225	.309	.360

Curt Leskanic

Pitches: Right Bats: Right Pos: RP/SP　　　　**Ht: 6' 0" Wt: 180 Born: 04/02/68 Age: 26**

			HOW MUCH HE PITCHED					WHAT HE GAVE UP									THE RESULTS					
Year	Team	Lg	G	GS	CG	GF	IP	BFP	H	R	ER	HR	SH	SF	HB	TBB	IBB	SO	WP	Bk	W	L	Pct.	ShO	Sv	ERA
1990	Kinston	A	14	14	2	0	73.1	303	61	34	30	6	2	2	2	30	1	71	10	8	6	5	.545	0	0	3.68
1991	Kinston	A	28	28	0	0	174.1	730	143	63	54	10	1	1	3	91	0	163	16	1	15	8	.652	0	0	2.79
1992	Orlando	AA	26	23	3	1	152.2	664	158	84	73	15	2	3	9	64	0	126	10	1	9	11	.450	0	0	4.30
	Portland	AAA	5	3	0	2	15.1	68	16	17	17	1	1	0	0	8	0	14	0	1	1	2	.333	0	0	9.98
1993	Wichita	AA	7	7	0	0	44.1	185	37	20	17	3	2	2	3	17	0	42	4	0	3	2	.600	0	0	3.45
	Colo Sprngs	AAA	9	7	1	1	44.1	195	39	24	22	3	2	2	2	26	0	38	1	2	4	3	.571	1	0	4.47
1993	Colorado	NL	18	8	0	1	57	260	59	40	34	7	5	4	2	27	1	30	8	2	1	5	.167	0	0	5.37

Jesse Levis

Bats: Left Throws: Right Pos: C　　　　**Ht: 5' 9" Wt: 180 Born: 04/14/68 Age: 26**

						BATTING													BASERUNNING				PERCENTAGES		
Year	Team	Lg	G	AB	H	2B	3B	HR	(Hm	Rd)	TB	R	RBI	TBB	IBB	SO	HBP	SH	SF	SB	CS	SB%	GDP	Avg	OBP	SLG
1989	Colo Sprngs	AAA	1	1	0	0	0	0	--	--	0	0	0	0	0	0	0	0	0	0	0	.00	1	.000	.000	.000
	Burlington	R	27	93	32	4	0	4	--	--	48	11	16	10	3	7	2	0	1	1	0	1.00	3	.344	.415	.516
	Kinston	A	27	87	26	6	0	2	--	--	38	11	11	12	0	15	2	0	0	1	0	1.00	3	.299	.396	.437
1990	Kinston	A	107	382	113	18	3	7	--	--	158	63	64	64	1	42	5	1	6	4	1	.80	5	.296	.398	.414
1991	Canton-Akrn	AA	115	382	101	17	3	6	--	--	142	31	45	40	5	36	0	4	2	2	5	.29	11	.264	.333	.372
1992	Colo Sprngs	AAA	87	253	92	20	1	6	--	--	132	39	44	37	0	25	1	3	2	1	3	.25	3	.364	.444	.522
1993	Charlotte	AAA	47	129	32	6	1	2	--	--	46	10	20	15	1	12	1	1	2	0	2	.00	7	.248	.327	.357
1992	Cleveland	AL	28	43	12	4	0	1	(0	1)	19	2	3	0	0	5	0	0	0	0	0	.00	1	.279	.279	.442
1993	Cleveland	AL	31	63	11	2	0	0	(0	0)	13	7	4	2	0	10	0	1	1	0	0	.00	0	.175	.197	.206
	2 ML YEARS		59	106	23	6	0	1	(0	1)	32	9	7	2	0	15	0	1	1	0	0	.00	1	.217	.229	.302

Darren Lewis

Bats: Right Throws: Right Pos: CF　　　　**Ht: 6' 0" Wt: 189 Born: 08/28/67 Age: 26**

						BATTING													BASERUNNING				PERCENTAGES		
Year	Team	Lg	G	AB	H	2B	3B	HR	(Hm	Rd)	TB	R	RBI	TBB	IBB	SO	HBP	SH	SF	SB	CS	SB%	GDP	Avg	OBP	SLG
1990	Oakland	AL	25	35	8	0	0	0	(0	0)	8	4	1	7	0	4	1	3	0	2	0	1.00	2	.229	.372	.229
1991	San Francisco	NL	72	222	55	5	3	1	(0	1)	69	41	15	36	0	30	2	7	0	13	7	.65	1	.248	.358	.311
1992	San Francisco	NL	100	320	74	8	1	1	(1	0)	87	38	18	29	0	46	1	10	2	28	8	.78	3	.231	.295	.272
1993	San Francisco	NL	136	522	132	17	7	2	(2	0)	169	84	48	30	1	40	7	12	1	46	15	.75	4	.253	.302	.324
	4 ML YEARS		333	1099	269	30	11	4	(3	1)	333	167	82	102	0	120	11	32	3	89	30	.75	10	.245	.314	.303

Mark Lewis

Bats: Right Throws: Right Pos: SS　　　　**Ht: 6' 1" Wt: 190 Born: 11/30/69 Age: 24**

						BATTING													BASERUNNING				PERCENTAGES		
Year	Team	Lg	G	AB	H	2B	3B	HR	(Hm	Rd)	TB	R	RBI	TBB	IBB	SO	HBP	SH	SF	SB	CS	SB%	GDP	Avg	OBP	SLG
1993	Charlotte *	AAA	126	507	144	30	4	17	--	--	233	93	67	34	4	76	2	8	3	9	5	.64	19	.284	.330	.460
1991	Cleveland	AL	84	314	83	15	1	0	(0	0)	100	29	30	15	0	45	0	2	5	2	2	.50	12	.264	.293	.318
1992	Cleveland	AL	122	413	109	21	0	5	(2	3)	145	44	30	25	1	69	3	1	4	4	5	.44	12	.264	.308	.351
1993	Cleveland	AL	14	52	13	2	0	1	(1	0)	18	6	5	0	0	7	0	1	0	3	0	1.00	1	.250	.250	.346
	3 ML YEARS		220	779	205	38	1	6	(3	3)	263	79	65	40	1	121	3	4	9	9	7	.56	25	.263	.298	.338

Richie Lewis

Pitches: Right Bats: Right Pos: RP   **Ht:** 5'10" **Wt:** 175 **Born:** 01/25/66 **Age:** 28

		HOW MUCH HE PITCHED					WHAT HE GAVE UP										THE RESULTS					
Year Team	Lg	G	GS	CG	GF	IP	BFP	H	R	ER	HR	SH	SF	HB	TBB	IBB	SO	WP	Bk	W	L	Pct.	ShO	Sv	ERA
1987 Indianapols	AAA	2	0	0	2	3.2	19	6	4	4	2	0	0	0	2	0	3	0	0	0	0	.000	0	0	9.82
1988 Jacksnville	AA	12	12	1	0	61.1	275	37	32	23	2	0	3	3	56	0	60	7	4	5	3	.625	0	0	3.38
1989 Jacksnville	AA	17	17	0	0	94.1	414	80	37	27	2	7	1	2	55	0	105	8	2	5	4	.556	0	0	2.58
1990 Wst Plm Bch	A	10	0	0	6	15	68	12	8	5	0	1	0	0	11	0	14	1	0	0	1	.000	0	2	3.00
Jacksnville	AA	11	0	0	8	14.1	54	7	2	2	0	0	1	0	5	0	14	3	0	0	0	.000	0	5	1.26
1991 Harrisburg	AA	34	6	0	16	74.2	318	67	33	31	2	3	2	2	40	1	82	5	2	6	5	.545	0	5	3.74
Indianapols	AAA	5	4	0	0	27.2	131	35	12	11	1	0	1	0	20	1	22	2	0	1	0	1.000	0	0	3.58
Rochester	AAA	2	2	0	0	16	62	13	5	5	1	0	0	0	7	0	18	1	0	1	0	1.000	0	0	2.81
1992 Rochester	AAA	24	23	6	1	159.1	668	136	63	58	15	1	4	3	61	2	154	13	2	10	9	.526	1	0	3.28
1992 Baltimore	AL	2	2	0	0	6.2	40	13	8	8	1	0	1	0	7	0	4	0	0	1	1	.500	0	0	10.80
1993 Florida	NL	57	0	0	14	77.1	341	68	37	28	7	8	4	1	43	6	65	9	1	6	3	.667	0	3	3.26
2 ML YEARS		59	2	0	14	84	381	81	45	36	8	8	5	1	50	6	69	9	1	7	4	.636	0	3	3.86

Scott Lewis

Pitches: Right Bats: Right Pos: RP/SP   **Ht:** 6'3" **Wt:** 178 **Born:** 12/05/65 **Age:** 28

		HOW MUCH HE PITCHED					WHAT HE GAVE UP										THE RESULTS					
Year Team	Lg	G	GS	CG	GF	IP	BFP	H	R	ER	HR	SH	SF	HB	TBB	IBB	SO	WP	Bk	W	L	Pct.	ShO	Sv	ERA
1993 Midland *	AA	1	1	0	0	6	25	6	1	1	0	0	1	0	0	0	2	0	0	1	0	1.000	0	0	1.50
Vancouver *	AAA	24	0	0	18	39.1	156	31	7	6	1	2	1	2	9	2	38	1	0	3	1	.750	0	9	1.37
1990 California	AL	2	2	1	0	16.1	60	10	4	4	2	0	0	0	2	0	9	0	0	1	1	.500	0	0	2.20
1991 California	AL	16	11	0	0	60.1	281	81	43	42	9	2	0	2	21	0	37	3	0	3	5	.375	0	0	6.27
1992 California	AL	21	2	0	7	38.1	160	36	18	17	3	0	3	2	14	1	18	1	1	4	0	1.000	0	0	3.99
1993 California	AL	15	4	0	2	32	142	37	16	15	3	2	7	2	12	1	10	1	0	1	2	.333	0	0	4.22
4 ML YEARS		54	19	1	9	147	643	164	81	78	17	4	10	6	49	2	74	5	1	9	8	.529	0	0	4.78

Jim Leyritz

Bats: Right Throws: Right Pos: 1B/C/RF/DH   **Ht:** 6'0" **Wt:** 195 **Born:** 12/27/63 **Age:** 30

		BATTING																	BASERUNNING				PERCENTAGES		
Year Team	Lg	G	AB	H	2B	3B	HR	(Hm	Rd)	TB	R	RBI	TBB	IBB	SO	HBP	SH	SF	SB	CS	SB%	GDP	Avg	OBP	SLG
1990 New York	AL	92	303	78	13	1	5	(1	4)	108	28	25	27	1	51	7	1	1	2	3	.40	11	.257	.331	.356
1991 New York	AL	32	77	14	3	0	0	(0	0)	17	8	4	13	0	15	0	1	0	0	1	.00	0	.182	.300	.221
1992 New York	AL	63	144	37	6	0	7	(3	4)	64	17	26	14	1	22	6	0	3	0	1	.00	2	.257	.341	.444
1993 New York	AL	95	259	80	14	0	14	(6	8)	136	43	53	37	3	59	8	0	1	0	0	.00	12	.309	.410	.525
4 ML YEARS		282	783	209	36	1	26	(10	16)	325	96	108	91	5	147	21	2	5	2	5	.29	25	.267	.357	.415

Derek Lilliquist

Pitches: Left Bats: Left Pos: RP   **Ht:** 5'10" **Wt:** 195 **Born:** 02/20/66 **Age:** 28

		HOW MUCH HE PITCHED					WHAT HE GAVE UP										THE RESULTS					
Year Team	Lg	G	GS	CG	GF	IP	BFP	H	R	ER	HR	SH	SF	HB	TBB	IBB	SO	WP	Bk	W	L	Pct.	ShO	Sv	ERA
1989 Atlanta	NL	32	30	0	0	165.2	718	202	87	73	16	8	3	2	34	5	79	4	3	8	10	.444	0	0	3.97
1990 2 ML Teams		28	18	1	3	122	537	136	74	72	16	9	5	3	42	5	63	2	3	5	11	.313	1	0	5.31
1991 San Diego	NL	6	2	0	1	14.1	70	25	14	14	3	0	0	0	4	1	7	0	0	0	2	.000	0	0	8.79
1992 Cleveland	AL	71	0	0	22	61.2	239	39	13	12	5	5	4	2	18	6	47	2	0	5	3	.625	0	6	1.75
1993 Cleveland	AL	56	2	0	28	64	271	64	20	16	5	6	2	1	19	5	40	1	0	4	4	.500	0	10	2.25
1990 Atlanta	NL	12	11	0	1	61.2	279	75	45	43	10	6	4	1	19	4	34	0	2	2	8	.200	0	0	6.28
San Diego	NL	16	7	1	2	60.1	258	61	29	29	6	3	1	2	23	1	29	2	1	3	3	.500	1	0	4.33
5 ML YEARS		193	52	1	54	427.2	1835	466	208	187	45	28	14	8	117	22	236	9	6	22	30	.423	1	16	3.94

Jose Lind

Bats: Right Throws: Right Pos: 2B   **Ht:** 5'11" **Wt:** 170 **Born:** 05/01/64 **Age:** 30

		BATTING																	BASERUNNING				PERCENTAGES		
Year Team	Lg	G	AB	H	2B	3B	HR	(Hm	Rd)	TB	R	RBI	TBB	IBB	SO	HBP	SH	SF	SB	CS	SB%	GDP	Avg	OBP	SLG
1987 Pittsburgh	NL	35	143	46	8	4	0	(0	0)	62	21	11	8	1	12	0	6	0	2	1	.67	5	.322	.358	.434
1988 Pittsburgh	NL	154	611	160	24	4	2	(1	1)	198	82	49	42	0	75	0	12	3	15	4	.79	11	.262	.308	.324
1989 Pittsburgh	NL	153	578	134	21	3	2	(2	0)	167	52	48	39	7	64	2	13	5	15	1	.94	13	.232	.280	.289
1990 Pittsburgh	NL	152	514	134	28	5	1	(1	0)	175	46	48	35	19	52	1	4	7	8	0	1.00	20	.261	.305	.340
1991 Pittsburgh	NL	150	502	133	16	6	3	(2	1)	170	53	54	30	10	56	2	5	6	7	4	.64	20	.265	.306	.339
1992 Pittsburgh	NL	135	468	110	14	1	0	(0	0)	126	38	39	26	12	29	1	7	4	3	1	.75	14	.235	.275	.269
1993 Kansas City	AL	136	431	107	13	2	0	(0	0)	124	33	37	13	0	36	2	13	5	3	2	.60	7	.248	.271	.288
7 ML YEARS		915	3247	824	124	25	8	(6	2)	1022	325	286	193	49	324	8	60	30	53	13	.80	90	.254	.295	.315

Jim Lindeman

Bats: Right **Throws:** Right **Pos:** 1B **Ht:** 6' 1" **Wt:** 200 **Born:** 01/10/62 **Age:** 32

								BATTING											BASERUNNING				PERCENTAGES		
Year Team	Lg	G	AB	H	2B	3B	HR	(Hm	Rd)	TB	R	RBI	TBB	IBB	SO	HBP	SH	SF	SB	CS	SB%	GDP	Avg	OBP	SLG
1993 Tucson *	AAA	101	390	141	28	7	12	(--	--)	219	72	88	41	4	68	5	0	7	5	0	1.00	9	.362	.422	.562
1986 St. Louis	NL	19	55	14	1	0	1	(0	1)	18	7	6	2	0	10	0	0	1	1	1	.50	2	.255	.276	.327
1987 St. Louis	NL	75	207	43	13	0	8	(2	6)	80	20	28	11	0	56	3	2	4	3	1	.75	4	.208	.253	.386
1988 St. Louis	NL	17	43	9	1	0	2	(0	2)	16	3	7	2	0	9	0	1	0	0	0	.00	1	.209	.244	.372
1989 St. Louis	NL	73	45	5	1	0	0	(0	0)	6	8	2	3	0	18	0	1	1	0	0	.00	2	.111	.163	.133
1990 Detroit	AL	12	32	7	1	0	2	(2	0)	14	5	8	2	0	13	0	0	0	0	0	.00	0	.219	.265	.438
1991 Philadelphia	NL	65	95	32	5	0	0	(0	0)	37	13	12	13	1	14	0	2	1	0	0	.00	1	.337	.413	.389
1992 Philadelphia	NL	29	39	10	1	0	1	(1	0)	14	6	6	3	0	11	0	0	0	0	0	.00	0	.256	.310	.359
1993 Houston	NL	9	23	8	3	0	0	(0	0)	11	2	0	0	0	7	0	0	0	0	0	.00	0	.348	.348	.478
8 ML YEARS		299	539	128	26	0	14	(5	9)	196	64	69	36	1	138	3	6	7	4	3	.57	11	.237	.285	.364

Doug Lindsey

Bats: Right **Throws:** Right **Pos:** C **Ht:** 6' 2" **Wt:** 200 **Born:** 09/22/67 **Age:** 26

								BATTING											BASERUNNING				PERCENTAGES		
Year Team	Lg	G	AB	H	2B	3B	HR	(Hm	Rd)	TB	R	RBI	TBB	IBB	SO	HBP	SH	SF	SB	CS	SB%	GDP	Avg	OBP	SLG
1987 Utica	A	52	169	41	7	0	1	(--	--)	51	23	25	22	2	34	1	0	3	1	3	.25	2	.243	.328	.302
1988 Spartanburg	A	90	324	76	19	0	4	(--	--)	107	29	46	29	1	68	4	2	3	4	2	.67	5	.235	.303	.330
1989 Spartanburg	A	39	136	31	7	0	3	(--	--)	47	14	17	23	2	31	0	1	1	2	2	.50	7	.228	.338	.346
Clearwater	A	36	118	23	3	0	0	(--	--)	26	8	9	5	0	18	0	0	2	0	0	.00	4	.195	.224	.220
1990 Reading	AA	107	323	56	11	0	1	(--	--)	70	16	32	26	1	78	1	6	3	2	1	.67	10	.173	.235	.217
1991 Reading	AA	94	313	81	13	0	1	(--	--)	97	26	34	21	0	49	2	4	4	1	0	1.00	12	.259	.306	.310
1992 Scranton/wb	AAA	87	274	57	9	0	4	(--	--)	78	28	27	37	4	66	1	1	2	0	2	.00	11	.208	.303	.285
1993 Scranton/wb	AAA	38	121	21	4	1	2	(--	--)	33	9	7	5	0	24	0	0	0	0	0	.00	6	.174	.206	.273
1991 Philadelphia	NL	1	3	0	0	0	0	(0	0)	0	0	0	0	0	3	0	0	0	0	0	.00	0	.000	.000	.000
1993 2 ML Teams		4	3	1	0	0	0	(0	0)	0	0	0	0	0	1	0	0	0	0	0	.00	0	.333	.333	.333
1993 Philadelphia	NL	2	2	1	0	0	0	(0	0)	1	0	0	0	0	1	0	0	0	0	0	.00	0	.500	.500	.500
Chicago	AL	2	1	0	0	0	0	(0	0)	0	0	0	0	0	0	0	0	0	0	0	.00	0	.000	.000	.000
2 ML YEARS		5	6	1	0	0	0	(0	0)	0	0	0	0	0	4	0	0	0	0	0	.00	0	.167	.167	.167

Doug Linton

Pitches: Right **Bats:** Right **Pos:** RP **Ht:** 6' 1" **Wt:** 180 **Born:** 02/09/65 **Age:** 29

		HOW MUCH HE PITCHED						WHAT HE GAVE UP												THE RESULTS					
Year Team	Lg	G	GS	CG	GF	IP	BFP	H	R	ER	HR	SH	SF	HB	TBB	IBB	SO	WP	Bk	W	L	Pct.	ShO	Sv	ERA
1987 Myrtle Bch	A	20	19	2	1	122	480	94	34	21	9	0	2	2	25	0	155	8	1	14	2	.875	0	1	1.55
Knoxville	AA	1	1	0	0	3	16	5	3	3	0	0	0	1	1	0	1	0	1	0	0	.000	0	0	9.00
1988 Dunedin	A	12	0	0	6	27.2	111	19	5	5	0	1	1	0	9	1	28	2	2	2	1	.667	0	2	1.63
1989 Dunedin	A	9	1	0	5	27.1	117	27	12	9	1	0	1	0	9	0	35	1	0	1	2	.333	0	2	2.96
Knoxville	AA	14	13	3	0	90	355	68	28	26	2	3	1	2	23	2	93	6	1	5	4	.556	2	0	2.60
1990 Syracuse	AAA	26	26	8	0	177.1	753	174	77	67	14	2	10	8	67	3	113	4	1	10	10	.500	3	0	3.40
1991 Syracuse	AAA	30	26	3	1	161.2	710	181	108	90	21	6	10	10	56	2	93	5	0	10	12	.455	1	0	5.01
1992 Syracuse	AAA	25	25	7	0	170.2	741	176	83	71	17	5	4	7	70	3	126	12	1	12	10	.545	1	0	3.74
1993 Syracuse	AAA	13	7	0	4	47.1	206	48	29	28	11	2	1	3	14	3	42	2	0	2	6	.250	0	0	5.32
1992 Toronto	AL	8	3	0	2	24	116	31	23	23	5	1	2	0	17	0	16	2	0	1	3	.250	0	0	8.63
1993 2 ML Teams		23	1	0	6	36.2	178	46	30	30	8	0	3	1	23	1	23	2	0	2	1	.667	0	0	7.36
1993 Toronto	AL	4	1	0	0	11	55	11	8	8	0	0	2	1	9	0	4	0	0	0	1	.000	0	0	6.55
California	AL	19	0	0	6	25.2	123	35	22	22	8	0	1	0	14	1	19	2	0	2	0	1.000	0	0	7.71
2 ML YEARS		31	4	0	8	60.2	294	77	53	53	13	1	5	1	40	1	39	4	0	3	4	.429	0	0	7.86

Nelson Liriano

Bats: Both **Throws:** Right **Pos:** SS/2B **Ht:** 5'10" **Wt:** 172 **Born:** 06/03/64 **Age:** 30

								BATTING											BASERUNNING				PERCENTAGES		
Year Team	Lg	G	AB	H	2B	3B	HR	(Hm	Rd)	TB	R	RBI	TBB	IBB	SO	HBP	SH	SF	SB	CS	SB%	GDP	Avg	OBP	SLG
1993 Central Val *	A	6	22	8	0	2	0	(--	--)	12	3	4	6	0	0	0	0	0	0	2	.00	0	.364	.500	.545
Colo Sprngs *	AAA	79	293	105	23	6	6	(--	--)	158	48	46	32	1	34	1	2	3	9	13	.41	11	.358	.419	.539
1987 Toronto	AL	37	158	38	6	2	2	(1	1)	54	29	10	16	2	22	0	2	0	13	2	.87	5	.241	.310	.342
1988 Toronto	AL	99	276	73	6	2	3	(0	3)	92	36	23	11	0	40	2	5	1	12	5	.71	4	.264	.297	.333
1989 Toronto	AL	132	418	110	26	3	5	(3	2)	157	51	53	43	0	51	2	10	5	16	7	.70	10	.263	.331	.376
1990 2 ML Teams		103	355	83	12	9	1	(1	0)	116	46	28	38	0	44	1	4	2	8	7	.53	8	.234	.308	.327
1991 Kansas City	AL	10	22	9	0	0	0	(0	0)	9	5	1	0	0	2	0	1	0	0	1	.00	0	.409	.409	.409
1993 Colorado	NL	48	151	46	6	3	2	(0	2)	64	28	15	18	2	22	0	5	1	6	4	.60	6	.305	.376	.424
1990 Toronto	AL	50	170	36	7	2	1	(1	0)	50	16	15	16	0	20	1	1	1	3	5	.38	5	.212	.282	.294
Minnesota	AL	53	185	47	5	7	0	(0	0)	66	30	13	22	0	24	0	3	1	5	2	.71	3	.254	.332	.357
6 ML YEARS		429	1380	359	56	19	13	(5	8)	492	195	130	126	4	181	5	27	9	55	26	.68	31	.260	.322	.357

Pat Listach

Bats: Both **Throws:** Right **Pos:** SS **Ht:** 5' 9" **Wt:** 170 **Born:** 09/12/67 **Age:** 26

						BATTING												BASERUNNING				PERCENTAGES		
Year	Team	Lg	G	AB	H	2B	3B	HR	(Hm	Rd)	TB	R	RBI	TBB	IBB	SO	HBP	SH	SF	SB	CS	SB%	GDP	Avg	OBP	SLG
1988	Beloit	A	53	200	48	5	1	1	--	--	58	40	18	18	0	20	6	4	2	20	9	.69	6	.240	.319	.290
1989	Stockton	A	132	480	110	11	4	2	--	--	135	73	34	58	1	106	4	7	1	37	19	.66	10	.229	.317	.281
1990	Stockton	A	139	503	137	21	6	2	--	--	176	116	39	105	2	122	6	3	1	78	25	.74	8	.272	.403	.350
1991	El Paso	AA	49	186	47	5	2	0	--	--	56	40	13	25	0	56	5	2	0	14	2	.88	3	.253	.356	.301
	Denver	AAA	89	286	72	10	4	1	--	--	93	51	31	45	1	67	0	3	4	23	7	.77	2	.252	.349	.325
1993	Beloit	A	4	12	3	0	0	0	--	--	3	2	1	1	0	2	1	0	0	2	0	1.00	0	.250	.357	.250
1992	Milwaukee	AL	149	579	168	19	6	1	(0	1)	202	93	47	55	0	124	1	12	2	54	18	.75	3	.290	.352	.349
1993	Milwaukee	AL	98	356	87	15	1	3	(0	3)	113	50	30	37	0	70	3	5	2	18	9	.67	7	.244	.319	.317
	2 ML YEARS		247	935	255	34	7	4	(0	4)	315	143	77	92	0	194	4	17	4	72	27	.73	10	.273	.339	.337

Greg Litton

Bats: Right **Throws:** Right **Pos:** LF/1B/2B/DH **Ht:** 6' 0" **Wt:** 175 **Born:** 07/13/64 **Age:** 29

						BATTING												BASERUNNING				PERCENTAGES		
Year	Team	Lg	G	AB	H	2B	3B	HR	(Hm	Rd)	TB	R	RBI	TBB	IBB	SO	HBP	SH	SF	SB	CS	SB%	GDP	Avg	OBP	SLG
1993	Calgary *	AAA	49	170	54	16	3	6	--	--	94	35	27	25	0	36	1	0	2	3	1	.75	3	.318	.404	.553
1989	San Francisco	NL	71	143	36	5	3	4	(3	1)	59	12	17	7	0	29	1	4	0	0	2	.00	3	.252	.291	.413
1990	San Francisco	NL	93	204	50	9	1	1	(0	1)	64	17	24	11	0	45	1	2	2	1	0	1.00	6	.245	.284	.314
1991	San Francisco	NL	59	127	23	7	1	1	(0	1)	35	13	15	11	0	25	1	3	1	0	2	.00	2	.181	.250	.276
1992	San Francisco	NL	68	140	32	5	0	4	(2	2)	49	9	15	11	0	33	0	3	0	0	1	.00	2	.229	.285	.350
1993	Seattle	AL	72	174	52	17	0	3	(3	0)	78	25	25	18	2	30	1	5	1	0	0	.00	5	.299	.366	.448
	5 ML YEARS		363	788	193	43	5	13	(8	5)	285	76	96	58	2	162	4	17	4	1	6	.14	18	.245	.299	.362

Scott Livingstone

Bats: Left **Throws:** Right **Pos:** 3B/DH **Ht:** 6' 0" **Wt:** 198 **Born:** 07/15/65 **Age:** 28

						BATTING												BASERUNNING				PERCENTAGES		
Year	Team	Lg	G	AB	H	2B	3B	HR	(Hm	Rd)	TB	R	RBI	TBB	IBB	SO	HBP	SH	SF	SB	CS	SB%	GDP	Avg	OBP	SLG
1991	Detroit	AL	44	127	37	5	0	2	(1	1)	48	19	11	10	0	25	0	1	1	2	1	.67	0	.291	.341	.378
1992	Detroit	AL	117	354	100	21	0	4	(2	2)	133	43	46	21	1	36	0	3	4	1	3	.25	8	.282	.319	.376
1993	Detroit	AL	98	304	89	10	2	2	(1	1)	109	39	39	19	1	32	0	1	6	1	3	.25	4	.293	.328	.359
	3 ML YEARS		259	785	226	36	2	8	(4	4)	290	101	96	50	2	93	0	5	11	4	7	.36	12	.288	.326	.369

Graeme Lloyd

Pitches: Left **Bats:** Left **Pos:** RP **Ht:** 6' 7" **Wt:** 215 **Born:** 04/09/67 **Age:** 27

			HOW MUCH HE PITCHED					WHAT HE GAVE UP											THE RESULTS					
Year	Team	Lg	G	GS	CG	GF	IP	BFP	H	R	ER	HR	SH	SF	HB	TBB	IBB	SO	WP	Bk	W	L	Pct.	ShO	Sv	ERA
1988	Myrtle Bch	A	41	0	0	18	59.2	281	71	33	24	2	1	0	6	30	5	43	5	2	3	2	.600	0	2	3.62
1989	Dunedin	A	2	0	0	0	2.2	14	6	3	3	0	0	0	0	1	0	0	1	0	0	0	.000	0	0	10.13
	Myrtle Bch	A	1	1	0	0	5	21	5	4	3	1	0	0	0	1	0	3	1	0	0	0	.000	0	0	5.40
1990	Myrtle Bch	A	19	6	0	8	49.2	216	51	20	15	3	0	0	0	16	1	42	1	1	5	2	.714	0	6	2.72
1991	Dunedin	A	50	0	0	39	60.1	260	54	17	15	1	2	0	1	25	2	39	4	0	2	5	.286	0	24	2.24
	Knoxville	AA	2	0	0	1	1.2	7	1	0	0	0	0	0	0	1	0	2	0	0	0	0	.000	0	0	0.00
1992	Knoxville	AA	49	7	1	33	92	376	79	30	20	2	1	2	3	25	2	65	8	0	4	8	.333	0	14	1.96
1993	Milwaukee	AL	55	0	0	12	63.2	269	64	24	20	5	1	2	3	13	3	31	4	0	3	4	.429	0	0	2.83

Kenny Lofton

Bats: Left **Throws:** Left **Pos:** CF **Ht:** 6' 0" **Wt:** 180 **Born:** 05/31/67 **Age:** 27

						BATTING												BASERUNNING				PERCENTAGES		
Year	Team	Lg	G	AB	H	2B	3B	HR	(Hm	Rd)	TB	R	RBI	TBB	IBB	SO	HBP	SH	SF	SB	CS	SB%	GDP	Avg	OBP	SLG
1991	Houston	NL	20	74	15	1	0	0	(0	0)	16	9	0	5	0	19	0	0	0	2	1	.67	0	.203	.253	.216
1992	Cleveland	AL	148	576	164	15	8	5	(3	2)	210	96	42	68	3	54	2	4	1	66	12	.85	7	.285	.362	.365
1993	Cleveland	AL	148	569	185	28	8	1	(0	1)	232	116	42	81	6	83	1	2	4	70	14	.83	8	.325	.408	.408
	3 ML YEARS		316	1219	364	44	16	6	(4	2)	458	221	84	154	9	156	3	6	5	138	27	.84	15	.299	.377	.376

Tony Longmire

Bats: Left **Throws:** Right **Pos:** LF **Ht:** 6' 1" **Wt:** 197 **Born:** 08/12/68 **Age:** 25

						BATTING												BASERUNNING				PERCENTAGES		
Year	Team	Lg	G	AB	H	2B	3B	HR	(Hm	Rd)	TB	R	RBI	TBB	IBB	SO	HBP	SH	SF	SB	CS	SB%	GDP	Avg	OBP	SLG
1986	Pirates	R	15	40	11	2	1	0	--	--	15	6	6	2	0	2	1	0	1	1	2	.33	2	.275	.318	.375
1987	Macon	A	127	445	117	15	4	5	--	--	155	63	62	41	6	73	5	3	6	18	7	.72	8	.263	.328	.348
1988	Harrisburg	AA	32	94	14	2	2	0	--	--	20	7	4	9	0	12	1	0	0	2	2	.00	3	.149	.231	.213
	Salem	A	64	218	60	12	2	11	--	--	109	46	40	36	1	44	1	1	0	4	3	.57	5	.275	.380	.500
1989	Pirates	R	2	5	0	0	0	0	--	--	0	0	0	1	0	1	0	0	0	0	0	.00	0	.000	.167	.000
	Salem	A	14	62	20	3	1	1	--	--	28	8	6	1	0	13	0	0	0	1	0	.00	1	.323	.333	.452

128

Year	Team	Lg	G	AB	H	2B	3B	HR	(Hm	Rd)	TB	R	RBI	TBB	IBB	SO	HBP	SH	SF	SB	CS	SB%	GDP	Avg	OBP	SLG
	Harrisburg	AA	37	127	37	7	0	3	--	--	53	15	22	12	0	21	1	1	0	1	0	1.00	2	.291	.357	.417
1990	Harrisburg	AA	24	91	27	6	0	1	--	--	36	9	13	7	0	11	0	0	1	5	1	.83	1	.297	.343	.396
1991	Scranton-Wb	AAA	36	111	29	3	2	0	--	--	36	11	9	8	1	20	0	1	0	4	4	.50	1	.261	.311	.324
	Reading	AA	85	323	93	23	1	9	--	--	145	43	56	32	6	45	2	1	4	10	7	.59	9	.288	.352	.449
1993	Scranton/wb	AAA	120	447	136	36	4	6	--	--	198	63	67	41	6	71	3	4	4	12	4	.75	6	.304	.364	.443
1993	Philadelphia	NL	11	13	3	0	0	0	(0	0)	3	1	1	0	0	1	0	0	0	0	0	.00	0	.231	.231	.231

Brian Looney

Pitches: Left **Bats:** Left **Pos:** RP **Ht:** 5'10" **Wt:** 180 **Born:** 09/26/69 **Age:** 24

			HOW MUCH HE PITCHED						WHAT HE GAVE UP												THE RESULTS					
Year	Team	Lg	G	GS	CG	GF	IP	BFP	H	R	ER	HR	SH	SF	HB	TBB	IBB	SO	WP	Bk	W	L	Pct.	ShO	Sv	ERA
1991	Jamestown	A	11	11	2	0	62.1	246	42	12	8	0	2	2	0	28	0	64	6	0	7	1	.875	1	0	1.16
1992	Rockford	A	17	0	0	5	31.1	141	28	13	11	0	2	0	1	23	0	34	1	0	3	1	.750	0	0	3.16
	Albany	A	11	11	1	0	67.1	265	51	22	16	1	1	3	0	30	0	56	4	0	3	2	.600	1	0	2.14
1993	Wst Plm Bch	A	18	16	0	1	106	451	108	48	37	2	7	3	5	29	0	109	2	1	4	6	.400	0	0	3.14
	Harrisburg	AA	8	8	1	0	56.2	221	36	15	15	2	1	1	1	17	1	76	0	0	3	2	.600	0	0	2.38
1993	Montreal	NL	3	1	0	1	6	28	8	2	2	0	0	0	0	2	0	7	0	1	0	0	.000	0	0	3.00

Albie Lopez

Pitches: Right **Bats:** Right **Pos:** SP **Ht:** 6'1" **Wt:** 205 **Born:** 08/18/71 **Age:** 22

			HOW MUCH HE PITCHED						WHAT HE GAVE UP												THE RESULTS					
Year	Team	Lg	G	GS	CG	GF	IP	BFP	H	R	ER	HR	SH	SF	HB	TBB	IBB	SO	WP	Bk	W	L	Pct.	ShO	Sv	ERA
1991	Burlington	R	13	13	0	0	73.1	302	61	33	28	4	2	2	3	23	0	81	4	0	4	5	.444	0	0	3.44
1992	Columbus	A	16	16	1	0	97	402	80	41	31	4	0	4	2	33	0	117	9	7	7	2	.778	0	0	2.88
	Kinston	A	10	10	1	0	64	268	56	28	25	5	1	2	1	26	1	44	4	0	5	2	.714	1	0	3.52
1993	Canton-Akrn	AA	16	16	2	0	110	449	79	44	38	10	1	6	5	47	0	80	6	1	9	4	.692	0	0	3.11
	Charlotte	AAA	3	2	0	0	12	47	8	3	3	1	0	0	2	2	0	7	0	0	1	0	1.000	0	0	2.25
1993	Cleveland	AL	9	9	0	0	49.2	222	49	34	33	7	1	1	1	32	1	25	0	0	3	1	.750	0	0	5.98

Javy Lopez

Bats: Right **Throws:** Right **Pos:** C **Ht:** 6'3" **Wt:** 210 **Born:** 11/05/70 **Age:** 23

			BATTING																	BASERUNNING			PERCENTAGES		
Year	Team	Lg	G	AB	H	2B	3B	HR	(Hm	Rd)	TB	R	RBI	TBB	IBB	SO	HBP	SH	SF	SB	CS	SB%	GDP	Avg	OBP	SLG
1988	Braves	R	31	94	18	4	0	1	--	--	25	8	9	3	0	19	0	1	1	1	0	1.00	0	.191	.214	.266
1989	Pulaski	R	51	153	40	8	1	3	--	--	59	27	27	5	0	35	1	0	3	3	2	.60	8	.261	.284	.386
1990	Burlington	A	116	422	112	17	3	11	--	--	168	48	55	14	2	84	5	4	0	10	2	.77	10	.265	.297	.398
1991	Durham	A	113	384	94	14	2	11	--	--	145	43	51	25	4	87	3	0	3	10	3	.77	10	.245	.294	.378
1992	Greenville	AA	115	442	142	28	3	16	--	--	224	63	60	24	1	47	5	1	2	7	3	.70	8	.321	.362	.507
1993	Richmond	AAA	100	380	116	23	2	17	--	--	194	56	74	12	1	53	6	0	3	1	6	.14	8	.305	.334	.511
1992	Atlanta	NL	9	16	6	2	0	0	(0	0)	8	3	2	0	0	1	0	0	0	0	0	.00	0	.375	.375	.500
1993	Atlanta	NL	8	16	6	1	1	1	(0	1)	12	1	2	0	0	2	1	0	0	0	0	.00	0	.375	.412	.750
	2 ML YEARS		17	32	12	3	1	1	(0	1)	20	4	4	0	0	3	1	0	0	0	0	.00	0	.375	.394	.625

Luis Lopez

Bats: Both **Throws:** Right **Pos:** 2B **Ht:** 5'11" **Wt:** 175 **Born:** 09/04/70 **Age:** 23

			BATTING																	BASERUNNING			PERCENTAGES		
Year	Team	Lg	G	AB	H	2B	3B	HR	(Hm	Rd)	TB	R	RBI	TBB	IBB	SO	HBP	SH	SF	SB	CS	SB%	GDP	Avg	OBP	SLG
1988	Spokane	A	70	312	95	13	1	0	--	--	110	50	35	18	0	59	4	2	2	14	5	.74	7	.304	.348	.353
1989	Chston-Sc	A	127	460	102	15	1	1	--	--	122	50	29	17	0	85	2	7	3	12	9	.57	9	.222	.251	.265
1990	Riverside	A	14	46	17	3	1	1	--	--	25	5	4	3	2	3	0	1	0	4	2	.67	1	.370	.408	.543
1991	Wichita	AA	125	452	121	17	1	1	--	--	143	43	41	18	3	70	8	4	4	6	7	.46	8	.268	.305	.316
1992	Las Vegas	AAA	120	395	92	8	8	1	--	--	119	44	31	19	1	65	3	7	3	6	4	.60	12	.233	.271	.301
1993	Las Vegas	AAA	131	491	150	36	6	6	--	--	216	52	58	27	3	62	5	13	3	8	0	1.00	7	.305	.346	.440
1993	San Diego	NL	17	43	5	1	0	0	(0	0)	6	1	1	0	0	8	0	0	1	0	0	.00	0	.116	.114	.140

Torey Lovullo

Bats: Both **Throws:** Right **Pos:** 2B/3B **Ht:** 6'0" **Wt:** 185 **Born:** 07/25/65 **Age:** 28

			BATTING																	BASERUNNING			PERCENTAGES		
Year	Team	Lg	G	AB	H	2B	3B	HR	(Hm	Rd)	TB	R	RBI	TBB	IBB	SO	HBP	SH	SF	SB	CS	SB%	GDP	Avg	OBP	SLG
1988	Detroit	AL	12	21	8	1	1	1	(0	1)	14	2	2	1	0	2	0	1	0	0	0	.00	1	.381	.409	.667
1989	Detroit	AL	29	87	10	2	0	1	(0	1)	15	8	4	14	0	20	0	1	2	0	0	.00	3	.115	.233	.172
1991	New York	AL	22	51	9	2	0	0	(0	0)	11	0	2	5	1	7	0	3	0	0	0	.00	0	.176	.250	.216
1993	California	AL	116	367	92	20	0	6	(4	4)	130	42	30	36	1	49	1	3	2	7	6	.54	8	.251	.318	.354
	4 ML YEARS		179	526	119	25	1	8	(4	4)	170	52	38	56	2	78	1	8	4	7	6	.54	12	.226	.300	.323

Larry Luebbers

Pitches: Right **Bats:** Right **Pos:** SP **Ht:** 6' 6" **Wt:** 190 **Born:** 10/11/69 **Age:** 24

Year	Team	Lg	G	GS	CG	GF	IP	BFP	H	R	ER	HR	SH	SF	HB	TBB	IBB	SO	WP	Bk	W	L	Pct.	ShO	Sv	ERA
1990	Billings	R	13	13	1	0	72.1	319	74	46	36	3	2	3	6	31	0	48	7	1	5	4	.556	1	0	4.48
1991	Cedar Rapids	A	28	28	3	0	184.2	781	177	85	64	8	12	6	10	64	5	98	11	4	8	10	.444	0	0	3.12
1992	Cedar Rapids	A	14	14	1	0	82.1	355	71	33	24	2	4	3	8	33	0	56	1	1	7	0	1.000	0	0	2.62
	Chattanooga	AA	14	14	1	0	87.1	368	86	34	22	5	2	1	4	34	1	56	5	2	6	5	.545	0	0	2.27
1993	Indianapols	AAA	15	15	0	0	84.1	380	81	45	39	7	6	2	6	47	5	51	1	0	4	7	.364	0	0	4.16
1993	Cincinnati	NL	14	14	0	0	77.1	332	74	49	39	7	4	5	1	38	3	38	4	0	2	5	.286	0	0	4.54

Mitch Lyden

Bats: Right **Throws:** Right **Pos:** C **Ht:** 6' 3" **Wt:** 225 **Born:** 12/14/64 **Age:** 29

Year	Team	Lg	G	AB	H	2B	3B	HR	(Hm	Rd)	TB	R	RBI	TBB	IBB	SO	HBP	SH	SF	SB	CS	SB%	GDP	Avg	OBP	SLG
1984	Greensboro	A	14	32	7	1	0	1	--	--	11	3	2	1	1	9	0	0	0	0	0	.00	0	.219	.242	.344
	Yankees	R	54	200	47	4	0	1	--	--	54	21	21	13	1	36	4	1	2	3	1	.75	3	.235	.292	.270
1985	Ft.Laudrdle	A	116	400	102	21	1	10	--	--	155	43	58	27	0	93	5	1	5	1	2	.33	15	.255	.307	.388
1986	Yankees	R	17	50	17	7	0	3	--	--	33	8	16	7	0	7	0	0	1	0	0	.00	1	.340	.414	.660
	Albany	AA	46	159	48	14	1	8	--	--	88	19	29	4	1	39	2	0	2	0	1	.00	5	.302	.323	.553
	Columbus	AAA	2	7	0	0	0	0	--	--	0	0	0	1	0	1	0	0	0	0	0	.00	0	.000	.125	.000
1987	Columbus	AAA	29	100	22	3	0	0	--	--	25	7	8	4	0	22	1	1	3	1	0	1.00	7	.220	.250	.250
	Albany	AA	71	233	59	12	2	8	--	--	99	25	36	11	0	47	2	1	1	0	0	.00	4	.253	.291	.425
1988	Pr William	A	67	234	66	12	2	17	--	--	133	42	47	19	3	59	4	0	2	1	0	1.00	5	.282	.344	.568
	Albany	AA	20	78	32	7	1	8	--	--	65	16	21	5	1	15	0	0	1	0	2	.00	3	.410	.440	.833
1989	Albany	AA	53	181	43	2	0	6	--	--	63	24	21	12	3	51	2	1	1	0	1	.00	5	.238	.292	.348
	Pr William	A	30	105	29	2	1	7	--	--	54	17	28	8	0	26	8	0	1	1	0	1.00	2	.276	.369	.514
1990	Albany	AA	85	311	92	22	1	17	--	--	167	55	63	24	1	67	9	0	4	1	0	1.00	13	.296	.359	.537
	Columbus	AAA	41	147	33	8	0	7	--	--	62	18	20	7	0	34	4	0	1	0	0	.00	9	.224	.277	.422
1991	Toledo	AAA	101	340	76	11	2	18	--	--	145	34	55	15	3	108	0	0	7	0	0	.00	11	.224	.251	.426
1992	Tidewater	AAA	91	299	77	13	0	14	--	--	132	34	52	12	0	95	3	0	4	1	2	.33	11	.258	.289	.441
1993	Edmonton	AAA	50	160	49	15	1	8	--	--	90	34	31	5	0	34	0	0	2	1	1	.50	2	.306	.323	.563
1993	Florida	NL	6	10	3	0	0	1	(0	1)	6	2	1	0	0	3	0	0	0	0	0	.00	0	.300	.300	.600

Scott Lydy

Bats: Right **Throws:** Right **Pos:** LF/RF **Ht:** 6' 5" **Wt:** 195 **Born:** 10/26/68 **Age:** 25

Year	Team	Lg	G	AB	H	2B	3B	HR	(Hm	Rd)	TB	R	RBI	TBB	IBB	SO	HBP	SH	SF	SB	CS	SB%	GDP	Avg	OBP	SLG
1990	Madison	A	54	174	33	6	3	4	--	--	55	33	19	25	1	62	1	0	2	7	5	.58	1	.190	.292	.316
	Athletics	R	18	50	17	6	0	2	--	--	29	8	11	10	0	14	0	0	0	0	0	.00	1	.340	.450	.580
1991	Madison	A	127	464	120	26	2	12	--	--	186	64	69	66	5	109	5	0	4	24	9	.73	10	.259	.354	.401
1992	Reno	A	33	124	49	13	2	2	--	--	72	29	27	26	2	30	0	0	4	9	4	.69	1	.395	.500	.581
	Huntsville	AA	109	387	118	20	3	9	--	--	171	64	65	67	5	95	4	0	4	16	5	.76	4	.305	.409	.442
1993	Tacoma	AAA	95	341	100	22	6	9	--	--	161	70	41	50	3	87	1	2	3	12	4	.75	8	.293	.382	.472
1993	Oakland	AL	41	102	23	5	0	2	(1	1)	34	11	7	8	0	39	1	0	0	2	0	1.00	1	.225	.288	.333

Steve Lyons

Bats: Left **Throws:** Right **Pos:** 2B **Ht:** 6' 3" **Wt:** 205 **Born:** 06/03/60 **Age:** 34

Year	Team	Lg	G	AB	H	2B	3B	HR	(Hm	Rd)	TB	R	RBI	TBB	IBB	SO	HBP	SH	SF	SB	CS	SB%	GDP	Avg	OBP	SLG
1993	Pawtucket *	AAA	67	177	42	6	0	4	--	--	60	24	18	26	3	50	0	2	1	3	4	.43	2	.213	.304	.305
1985	Boston	AL	133	371	98	14	3	5	(4	1)	133	52	30	32	0	64	1	2	3	12	9	.57	2	.264	.322	.358
1986	2 ML Teams		101	247	56	9	2	1	(1	0)	74	30	20	19	2	47	1	4	4	4	6	.40	4	.227	.280	.300
1987	Chicago	AL	76	193	54	11	1	1	(0	1)	70	26	19	12	0	37	0	4	1	3	1	.75	4	.280	.320	.363
1988	Chicago	AL	146	472	127	28	3	5	(1	4)	176	59	45	32	1	59	1	15	6	12	2	.33	6	.269	.313	.373
1989	Chicago	AL	140	443	117	21	3	2	(0	2)	150	51	50	35	3	68	1	12	3	9	6	.60	3	.264	.317	.339
1990	Chicago	AL	94	146	28	6	1	1	(0	1)	39	22	11	10	1	41	1	4	2	1	0	1.00	1	.192	.245	.267
1991	Boston	AL	87	212	51	10	1	4	(2	2)	75	15	17	11	2	35	0	3	1	10	3	.77	1	.241	.277	.354
1992	3 ML Teams		48	55	11	0	2	0	(0	0)	15	5	4	3	0	8	0	1	0	1	3	.25	2	.200	.241	.273
1993	Boston	AL	28	23	3	1	0	0	(0	0)	4	4	0	2	0	5	0	0	0	1	2	.33	0	.130	.200	.174
1986	Boston	AL	59	124	31	7	2	1	(1	0)	45	20	14	12	2	23	0	1	2	2	3	.40	3	.250	.312	.363
	Chicago	AL	42	123	25	2	1	0	(0	0)	29	10	6	7	0	24	1	3	2	2	3	.40	1	.203	.248	.300
1992	Atlanta	NL	11	14	1	0	1	0	(0	0)	3	3	0	1	0	4	0	0	0	0	0	.00	0	.071	.071	.214
	Montreal	NL	16	13	3	0	0	0	(0	0)	3	2	1	1	0	3	0	0	1	1	2	.33	1	.231	.286	.231
	Boston	AL	21	28	7	0	1	0	(0	0)	9	3	2	2	0	1	0	0	0	1	0	.00	1	.250	.300	.321
	9 ML YEARS		853	2162	545	100	17	19	(8	11)	736	264	196	156	9	364	5	45	20	42	32	.57	23	.252	.301	.340

Kevin Maas

Bats: Left   **Throws:** Left   **Pos:** DH/1B   **Ht:** 6' 3"   **Wt:** 204   **Born:** 01/20/65   **Age:** 29

Year Team	Lg	G	AB	H	2B	3B	HR	(Hm	Rd)	TB	R	RBI	TBB	IBB	SO	HBP	SH	SF	SB	CS	SB%	GDP	Avg	OBP	SLG
1993 Columbus *	AAA	28	104	29	6	0	4	--	--	47	14	18	19	2	22	1	0	1	0	1	.00	1	.279	.392	.452
1990 New York	AL	79	254	64	9	0	21	(12	9)	136	42	41	43	10	76	3	0	0	1	2	.33	2	.252	.367	.535
1991 New York	AL	148	500	110	14	1	23	(8	15)	195	69	63	83	3	128	4	0	5	5	1	.83	4	.220	.333	.390
1992 New York	AL	98	286	71	12	0	11	(7	4)	116	35	35	25	4	63	0	0	4	3	1	.75	1	.248	.305	.406
1993 New York	AL	59	151	31	4	0	9	(7	2)	62	20	25	24	2	32	1	0	1	1	1	.50	2	.205	.316	.411
4 ML YEARS		384	1191	276	39	1	64	(34	30)	509	166	164	175	19	299	8	0	10	10	5	.67	9	.232	.332	.427

Bob MacDonald

Pitches: Left   **Bats:** Left   **Pos:** RP   **Ht:** 6' 3"   **Wt:** 208   **Born:** 04/27/65   **Age:** 29

Year Team	Lg	G	GS	CG	GF	IP	BFP	H	R	ER	HR	SH	SF	HB	TBB	IBB	SO	WP	Bk	W	L	Pct.	ShO	Sv	ERA
1990 Toronto	AL	4	0	0	1	2.1	8	0	0	0	0	0	0	0	2	0	0	0	0	0	0	.000	0	0	0.00
1991 Toronto	AL	45	0	0	10	53.2	231	51	19	17	5	2	2	0	25	4	24	1	1	3	3	.500	0	0	2.85
1992 Toronto	AL	27	0	0	9	47.1	204	50	24	23	4	1	1	1	16	3	26	0	0	1	0	1.000	0	0	4.37
1993 Detroit	AL	68	0	0	24	65.2	293	67	42	39	8	4	5	1	33	5	39	3	1	3	3	.500	0	3	5.35
4 ML YEARS		144	0	0	44	169	736	168	85	79	17	7	8	2	76	12	89	4	2	7	6	.538	0	3	4.21

Mike Macfarlane

Bats: Right   **Throws:** Right   **Pos:** C   **Ht:** 6' 1"   **Wt:** 205   **Born:** 04/12/64   **Age:** 30

Year Team	Lg	G	AB	H	2B	3B	HR	(Hm	Rd)	TB	R	RBI	TBB	IBB	SO	HBP	SH	SF	SB	CS	SB%	GDP	Avg	OBP	SLG
1987 Kansas City	AL	8	19	4	1	0	0	(0	0)	5	0	3	2	0	2	0	0	0	0	0	.00	1	.211	.286	.263
1988 Kansas City	AL	70	211	56	15	0	4	(2	2)	83	25	26	21	2	37	1	1	0	0	0	.00	8	.265	.332	.393
1989 Kansas City	AL	69	157	35	6	0	2	(0	2)	47	13	19	7	0	27	2	0	1	0	0	.00	8	.223	.263	.299
1990 Kansas City	AL	124	400	102	24	4	6	(1	5)	152	37	58	25	2	69	7	1	6	1	0	1.00	9	.255	.306	.380
1991 Kansas City	AL	84	267	74	18	2	13	(6	7)	135	34	41	17	0	52	6	1	4	1	0	1.00	4	.277	.330	.506
1992 Kansas City	AL	129	402	94	28	3	17	(7	10)	179	51	48	30	2	89	15	1	2	1	5	.17	8	.234	.310	.445
1993 Kansas City	AL	117	388	106	27	0	20	(7	13)	193	55	67	40	2	83	16	1	6	2	5	.29	8	.273	.360	.497
7 ML YEARS		601	1844	471	119	9	62	(23	39)	794	215	262	142	8	359	47	5	21	5	10	.33	43	.255	.321	.431

Shane Mack

Bats: Right   **Throws:** Right   **Pos:** CF/LF   **Ht:** 6' 0"   **Wt:** 188   **Born:** 12/07/63   **Age:** 30

Year Team	Lg	G	AB	H	2B	3B	HR	(Hm	Rd)	TB	R	RBI	TBB	IBB	SO	HBP	SH	SF	SB	CS	SB%	GDP	Avg	OBP	SLG
1987 San Diego	NL	105	238	57	11	3	4	(2	2)	86	28	25	18	0	47	3	6	2	4	6	.40	11	.239	.299	.361
1988 San Diego	NL	56	119	29	3	0	0	(0	0)	32	13	12	14	0	21	3	3	1	5	1	.83	2	.244	.336	.269
1990 Minnesota	AL	125	313	102	10	4	8	(5	3)	144	50	44	29	1	69	5	6	0	13	4	.76	7	.326	.392	.460
1991 Minnesota	AL	143	442	137	27	8	18	(4	14)	234	79	74	34	1	79	6	2	5	13	9	.59	11	.310	.363	.529
1992 Minnesota	AL	156	600	189	31	6	16	(10	6)	280	101	75	64	1	106	15	11	2	26	14	.65	8	.315	.394	.467
1993 Minnesota	AL	128	503	139	30	4	10	(3	7)	207	66	61	41	1	76	4	3	2	15	5	.75	13	.276	.335	.412
6 ML YEARS		713	2215	653	112	25	56	(24	32)	983	337	291	200	4	398	36	31	12	76	39	.66	52	.295	.361	.444

Lonnie Maclin

Bats: Left   **Throws:** Left   **Pos:** LF   **Ht:** 5'11"   **Wt:** 185   **Born:** 02/17/67   **Age:** 27

Year Team	Lg	G	AB	H	2B	3B	HR	(Hm	Rd)	TB	R	RBI	TBB	IBB	SO	HBP	SH	SF	SB	CS	SB%	GDP	Avg	OBP	SLG
1987 Johnson Cty	R	62	229	69	6	1	3	--	--	86	45	22	24	0	32	1	0	1	22	5	.81	2	.301	.369	.376
1988 St. Pete	A	51	175	33	3	1	3	--	--	47	22	12	18	1	41	2	2	0	9	7	.56	2	.189	.272	.269
Savannah	A	46	119	28	3	0	0	--	--	31	10	9	12	1	19	0	0	2	8	4	.67	3	.235	.301	.261
1989 Springfield	A	103	315	78	10	3	3	--	--	103	33	34	21	0	56	2	4	1	18	14	.56	3	.248	.298	.327
1990 St. Pete	A	31	119	46	6	3	2	--	--	64	18	17	11	0	12	0	0	1	6	2	.75	4	.387	.435	.538
Arkansas	AA	74	263	81	14	5	2	--	--	111	32	25	20	1	35	0	5	2	11	7	.61	4	.308	.354	.422
Louisville	AAA	17	58	18	3	2	0	--	--	25	9	6	7	0	11	1	1	1	1	4	.20	1	.310	.388	.431
1991 Louisville	AAA	84	327	94	12	2	4	--	--	122	35	37	16	0	50	0	2	1	19	14	.58	5	.287	.320	.373
1992 Louisville	AAA	111	290	94	17	3	1	--	--	120	29	18	22	1	31	5	4	7	4	7	.36	1	.324	.373	.414
1993 Louisville	AAA	62	220	61	10	3	4	--	--	89	29	18	16	2	48	2	0	0	4	4	.50	4	.277	.332	.405
1993 St. Louis	NL	12	13	1	0	0	0	(0	0)	1	2	1	0	0	5	0	0	1	1	0	1.00	0	.077	.071	.077

Greg Maddux

Pitches: Right **Bats:** Right **Pos:** SP   **Ht:** 6' 0" **Wt:** 175 **Born:** 04/14/66 **Age:** 28

Year Team	Lg	G	GS	CG	GF	IP	BFP	H	R	ER	HR	SH	SF	HB	TBB	IBB	SO	WP	Bk	W	L	Pct.	ShO	Sv	ERA
1986 Chicago	NL	6	5	1	1	31	144	44	20	19	3	1	0	1	11	2	20	2	0	2	4	.333	0	0	5.52
1987 Chicago	NL	30	27	1	2	155.2	701	181	111	97	17	7	1	4	74	13	101	4	7	6	14	.300	1	0	5.61
1988 Chicago	NL	34	34	9	0	249	1047	230	97	88	13	11	2	9	81	16	140	3	6	18	8	.692	3	0	3.18
1989 Chicago	NL	35	35	7	0	238.1	1002	222	90	78	13	18	6	6	82	13	135	5	3	19	12	.613	1	0	2.95
1990 Chicago	NL	35	35	8	0	237	1011	242	116	91	11	18	5	4	71	10	144	5	3	15	15	.500	2	0	3.46
1991 Chicago	NL	37	37	7	0	263	1070	232	113	98	18	16	3	6	66	9	198	6	3	15	11	.577	2	0	3.35
1992 Chicago	NL	35	35	9	0	268	1061	201	68	65	7	15	3	14	70	7	199	5	0	20	11	.645	4	0	2.18
1993 Atlanta	NL	36	36	8	0	267	1064	228	85	70	14	15	7	6	52	7	197	5	1	20	10	.667	1	0	2.36
8 ML YEARS		248	244	50	3	1709	7100	1580	700	606	96	101	27	50	507	77	1134	33	23	115	85	.575	14	0	3.19

Mike Maddux

Pitches: Right **Bats:** Left **Pos:** RP   **Ht:** 6' 2" **Wt:** 188 **Born:** 08/27/61 **Age:** 32

Year Team	Lg	G	GS	CG	GF	IP	BFP	H	R	ER	HR	SH	SF	HB	TBB	IBB	SO	WP	Bk	W	L	Pct.	ShO	Sv	ERA
1986 Philadelphia	NL	16	16	0	0	78	351	88	56	47	6	3	3	3	34	4	44	4	2	3	7	.300	0	0	5.42
1987 Philadelphia	NL	7	2	0	0	17	72	17	5	5	0	0	0	0	5	0	15	1	0	2	0	1.000	0	0	2.65
1988 Philadelphia	NL	25	11	0	4	88.2	380	91	41	37	6	7	3	5	34	4	59	4	2	4	3	.571	0	0	3.76
1989 Philadelphia	NL	16	4	2	1	43.2	191	52	29	25	3	3	1	2	14	3	26	3	1	1	3	.250	1	1	5.15
1990 Los Angeles	NL	11	2	0	3	20.2	88	24	15	15	3	0	1	1	4	0	11	2	0	0	1	.000	0	0	6.53
1991 San Diego	NL	64	1	0	27	98.2	388	78	30	27	4	5	2	1	27	3	57	5	0	7	2	.778	0	5	2.46
1992 San Diego	NL	50	1	0	14	79.2	330	71	25	21	2	2	3	0	24	4	60	4	1	2	2	.500	0	5	2.37
1993 New York	NL	58	0	0	31	75	320	67	34	30	3	7	6	4	27	7	57	4	1	3	8	.273	0	0	3.60
8 ML YEARS		247	37	2	80	501.1	2120	488	235	207	27	27	19	16	169	25	329	27	7	22	26	.458	1	16	3.72

Dave Magadan

Bats: Left **Throws:** Right **Pos:** 3B/1B   **Ht:** 6' 3" **Wt:** 205 **Born:** 09/30/62 **Age:** 31

Year Team	Lg	G	AB	H	2B	3B	HR	(Hm	Rd)	TB	R	RBI	TBB	IBB	SO	HBP	SH	SF	SB	CS	SB%	GDP	Avg	OBP	SLG
1986 New York	NL	10	18	8	0	0	0	(0	0)	8	3	3	3	0	1	0	0	0	0	0	.00	1	.444	.524	.444
1987 New York	NL	85	192	61	13	1	3	(2	1)	85	21	24	22	2	22	0	1	1	0	0	.00	5	.318	.386	.443
1988 New York	NL	112	314	87	15	0	1	(1	0)	105	39	35	60	4	39	2	1	3	0	1	.00	9	.277	.393	.334
1989 New York	NL	127	374	107	22	3	4	(3	1)	147	47	41	49	6	37	1	1	4	1	0	1.00	2	.286	.367	.393
1990 New York	NL	144	451	148	28	6	6	(2	4)	206	74	72	74	4	55	2	4	10	2	1	.67	11	.328	.417	.457
1991 New York	NL	124	418	108	23	0	4	(2	2)	143	58	51	83	8	50	2	7	7	1	1	.50	5	.258	.378	.342
1992 New York	NL	99	321	91	9	1	3	(2	1)	111	33	28	56	3	44	0	2	0	1	0	1.00	6	.283	.390	.346
1993 2 ML Teams		137	455	124	23	0	5	(3	2)	162	49	50	80	7	63	1	2	6	2	1	.67	12	.273	.378	.356
1993 Florida	NL	66	227	65	12	0	4	(3	1)	89	22	29	44	4	30	1	0	3	0	1	.00	3	.286	.400	.392
Seattle	AL	71	228	59	11	0	1	(0	1)	73	27	21	36	3	33	0	2	3	2	0	1.00	9	.259	.356	.320
8 ML YEARS		838	2543	734	133	11	26	(15	11)	967	324	304	427	29	311	8	18	31	7	4	.64	51	.289	.389	.380

Mike Magnante

Pitches: Left **Bats:** Left **Pos:** SP   **Ht:** 6' 1" **Wt:** 180 **Born:** 06/17/65 **Age:** 29

Year Team	Lg	G	GS	CG	GF	IP	BFP	H	R	ER	HR	SH	SF	HB	TBB	IBB	SO	WP	Bk	W	L	Pct.	ShO	Sv	ERA
1993 Omaha *	AAA	33	13	0	5	105.1	428	97	46	43	7	2	6	4	29	2	74	6	0	2	6	.250	0	2	3.67
1991 Kansas City	AL	38	0	0	10	55	236	55	19	15	3	2	1	0	23	3	42	1	0	0	1	.000	0	0	2.45
1992 Kansas City	AL	44	12	0	11	89.1	403	115	53	49	5	5	7	2	35	5	31	2	0	4	9	.308	0	0	4.94
1993 Kansas City	AL	7	6	0	0	35.1	145	37	16	16	3	1	1	1	11	1	16	1	0	1	2	.333	0	0	4.08
3 ML YEARS		89	18	0	21	179.2	784	207	88	80	11	8	9	3	69	9	89	4	0	5	12	.294	0	0	4.01

Joe Magrane

Pitches: Left **Bats:** Right **Pos:** SP   **Ht:** 6' 6" **Wt:** 230 **Born:** 07/02/64 **Age:** 29

Year Team	Lg	G	GS	CG	GF	IP	BFP	H	R	ER	HR	SH	SF	HB	TBB	IBB	SO	WP	Bk	W	L	Pct.	ShO	Sv	ERA
1987 St. Louis	NL	27	26	4	0	170.1	722	157	75	67	9	9	3	10	60	6	101	9	7	9	7	.563	2	0	3.54
1988 St. Louis	NL	24	24	4	0	165.1	677	133	57	40	6	8	4	2	51	4	100	8	8	5	9	.357	3	0	2.18
1989 St. Louis	NL	34	33	9	1	234.2	971	219	81	76	5	14	8	6	72	7	127	14	5	18	9	.667	3	0	2.91
1990 St. Louis	NL	31	31	3	0	203.1	855	204	86	81	10	8	6	8	59	7	100	11	1	10	17	.370	2	0	3.59
1992 St. Louis	NL	5	5	0	0	31.1	143	34	15	14	2	3	1	2	15	0	20	4	0	1	2	.333	0	0	4.02
1993 2 ML Teams		30	28	0	2	164	708	175	95	85	19	10	10	5	58	3	62	8	0	11	12	.478	0	0	4.66
1993 St. Louis	NL	22	20	0	2	116	499	127	68	64	15	6	7	5	37	3	38	4	0	8	10	.444	0	0	4.97
California	AL	8	8	0	0	48	209	48	27	21	4	4	3	0	21	0	24	4	0	3	2	.600	0	0	3.94
6 ML YEARS		151	147	20	3	969	4076	922	409	363	51	52	32	33	315	27	510	54	21	54	56	.491	10	0	3.37

132

Pat Mahomes

Pitches: Right **Bats:** Right **Pos:** RP/SP | **Ht:** 6' 1" **Wt:** 210 **Born:** 08/09/70 **Age:** 23

			HOW MUCH HE PITCHED						WHAT HE GAVE UP										THE RESULTS				
Year Team	Lg	G	GS	CG	GF	IP	BFP	H	R	ER	HR	SH	SF	HB	TBB	IBB	SO	WP	Bk	W	L	Pct.	ShO	Sv	ERA
1988 Elizabethtn	R	13	13	3	0	78	344	66	45	32	4	3	1	0	51	0	93	9	2	6	3	.667	0	0	3.69
1989 Kenosha	A	25	25	3	0	156.1	668	120	66	57	4	0	9	2	100	3	167	9	3	13	7	.650	1	0	3.28
1990 Visalia	A	28	28	5	0	185.1	784	136	77	68	14	3	4	4	118	1	178	19	1	11	11	.500	1	0	3.30
1991 Orlando	AA	18	17	2	0	116	463	77	30	23	5	0	3	3	57	0	136	3	0	8	5	.615	0	0	1.78
Portland	AAA	9	9	2	0	55	244	50	26	21	2	2	3	0	36	1	41	2	1	3	5	.375	0	0	3.44
1992 Portland	AAA	17	16	3	1	111	455	97	43	42	7	0	0	1	43	1	87	4	0	9	5	.643	3	1	3.41
1993 Portland	AAA	17	16	3	1	115.2	467	89	47	39	11	4	2	1	54	1	94	4	0	11	4	.733	1	0	3.03
1992 Minnesota	AL	14	13	0	1	69.2	302	73	41	39	5	0	3	0	37	0	44	2	1	3	4	.429	0	0	5.04
1993 Minnesota	AL	12	5	0	4	37.1	173	47	34	32	8	1	3	1	16	0	23	3	0	1	5	.167	0	0	7.71
2 ML YEARS		26	18	0	5	107	475	120	75	71	13	1	6	1	53	0	67	5	1	4	9	.308	0	0	5.97

Mike Maksudian

Bats: Left **Throws:** Right **Pos:** 1B | **Ht:** 5'11" **Wt:** 220 **Born:** 05/28/66 **Age:** 28

					BATTING														BASERUNNING				PERCENTAGES		
Year Team	Lg	G	AB	H	2B	3B	HR	(Hm	Rd)	TB	R	RBI	TBB	IBB	SO	HBP	SH	SF	SB	CS	SB%	GDP	Avg	OBP	SLG
1987 White Sox	R	34	109	38	11	3	1	--	--	58	23	28	19	4	13	1	0	2	7	2	.78	2	.349	.443	.532
1988 South Bend	A	102	366	111	26	3	4	--	--	155	51	50	60	9	59	3	0	2	5	3	.63	5	.303	.404	.423
Tampa	A	1	3	2	1	0	0	--	--	3	1	2	0	0	1	0	0	0	0	0	.00	0	.667	.667	1.000
St. Lucie	A	13	42	9	2	1	0	--	--	13	7	1	8	0	6	0	0	1	0	0	.00	1	.214	.333	.310
1989 Miami	A	83	288	90	18	4	9	--	--	143	36	42	28	2	42	0	0	2	6	4	.60	11	.313	.371	.497
1990 Knoxville	AA	121	422	121	22	5	8	--	--	177	51	55	50	6	66	2	0	1	6	4	.60	9	.287	.364	.419
1991 Syracuse	AAA	31	97	32	6	3	1	--	--	47	13	13	10	0	17	0	1	0	0	0	.00	2	.330	.393	.485
Knoxville	AA	71	231	59	12	3	5	--	--	92	32	35	37	5	43	0	0	5	2	2	.50	3	.255	.352	.398
1992 Syracuse	AAA	101	339	95	17	1	13	--	--	153	38	58	32	6	63	1	0	1	4	1	.80	7	.280	.343	.451
1993 Portland	AAA	76	264	83	16	7	10	--	--	143	57	49	45	3	51	0	0	4	5	1	.83	1	.314	.409	.542
1992 Toronto	AL	3	3	0	0	0	0	(0	0)	0	0	0	0	0	0	0	0	0	0	0	.00	0	.000	.000	.000
1993 Minnesota	AL	5	12	2	1	0	0	(0	0)	3	2	2	4	0	2	0	0	1	0	0	.00	0	.167	.353	.250
2 ML YEARS		8	15	2	1	0	0	(0	0)	3	2	2	4	0	2	0	0	1	0	0	.00	0	.133	.300	.200

Candy Maldonado

Bats: Right **Throws:** Right **Pos:** RF/LF | **Ht:** 6' 0" **Wt:** 205 **Born:** 09/05/60 **Age:** 33

					BATTING														BASERUNNING				PERCENTAGES		
Year Team	Lg	G	AB	H	2B	3B	HR	(Hm	Rd)	TB	R	RBI	TBB	IBB	SO	HBP	SH	SF	SB	CS	SB%	GDP	Avg	OBP	SLG
1981 Los Angeles	NL	11	12	1	0	0	0	(0	0)	1	0	0	0	0	5	0	0	0	0	0	.00	0	.083	.083	.083
1982 Los Angeles	NL	6	4	0	0	0	0	(0	0)	0	0	0	1	1	2	0	0	0	0	0	.00	0	.000	.200	.000
1983 Los Angeles	NL	42	62	12	1	1	1	(1	0)	18	5	6	5	0	14	0	1	0	0	0	.00	1	.194	.254	.290
1984 Los Angeles	NL	116	254	68	14	0	5	(1	4)	97	25	28	19	0	29	1	1	3	0	3	.00	6	.268	.318	.382
1985 Los Angeles	NL	121	213	48	7	1	5	(2	3)	72	20	19	19	4	40	0	2	1	1	1	.50	3	.225	.288	.338
1986 San Francisco	NL	133	405	102	31	3	18	(6	12)	193	49	85	20	4	77	3	0	4	4	4	.50	12	.252	.289	.477
1987 San Francisco	NL	118	442	129	28	4	20	(14	6)	225	69	85	34	4	78	6	0	7	8	8	.50	9	.292	.346	.509
1988 San Francisco	NL	142	499	127	23	1	12	(5	7)	188	53	68	37	1	89	7	3	6	6	5	.55	13	.255	.311	.377
1989 San Francisco	NL	129	345	75	23	0	9	(1	8)	125	39	41	37	4	69	3	1	3	4	1	.80	8	.217	.296	.362
1990 Cleveland	AL	155	590	161	32	2	22	(12	10)	263	76	95	49	4	134	5	0	7	3	5	.38	13	.273	.330	.446
1991 2 ML Teams		86	288	72	15	0	12	(7	5)	123	37	48	36	4	76	6	0	3	4	0	1.00	8	.250	.342	.427
1992 Toronto	AL	137	489	133	25	4	20	(8	12)	226	64	66	59	3	112	7	2	3	2	2	.50	13	.272	.357	.462
1993 2 ML Teams		98	221	46	7	0	8	(5	3)	77	19	35	24	2	58	*1	1	1	0	1	.00	5	.208	.287	.348
1991 Milwaukee	AL	34	111	23	6	0	5	(3	2)	44	11	20	13	0	23	0	0	1	1	0	1.00	4	.207	.288	.396
Toronto	AL	52	177	49	9	0	7	(4	3)	79	26	28	23	4	53	6	0	2	3	0	1.00	4	.277	.375	.446
1993 Chicago	NL	70	140	26	5	0	3	(1	2)	40	8	15	13	0	40	1	0	0	0	1	.00	5	.186	.296	.286
Cleveland	AL	28	81	20	2	0	5	(4	1)	37	11	20	11	2	18	0	1	1	0	0	.00	0	.247	.333	.457
13 ML YEARS		1294	3824	974	206	16	132	(62	70)	1608	456	576	340	31	783	39	11	38	32	30	.52	91	.255	.319	.421

Carlos Maldonado

Pitches: Right **Bats:** Right **Pos:** RP | **Ht:** 6' 2" **Wt:** 215 **Born:** 10/18/66 **Age:** 27

			HOW MUCH HE PITCHED						WHAT HE GAVE UP										THE RESULTS				
Year Team	Lg	G	GS	CG	GF	IP	BFP	H	R	ER	HR	SH	SF	HB	TBB	IBB	SO	WP	Bk	W	L	Pct.	ShO	Sv	ERA
1993 New Orleans *	AAA	12	0	0	9	19.1	77	13	1	1	0	1	1	0	7	1	14	0	0	1	0	1.000	0	7	0.47
1990 Kansas City	AL	4	0	0	1	6	31	9	6	6	0	0	1	0	4	0	9	1	0	0	0	.000	0	0	9.00
1991 Kansas City	AL	5	0	0	2	7.2	43	11	9	7	0	1	0	0	9	1	1	4	0	0	0	.000	0	0	8.22
1993 Milwaukee	AL	29	0	0	9	37.1	167	40	20	19	2	4	4	0	17	5	18	1	0	2	2	.500	0	1	4.58
3 ML YEARS		38	0	0	12	51	241	60	35	32	2	5	5	0	30	6	28	6	0	2	2	.500	0	1	5.65

133

Jeff Manto

Bats: Right **Throws:** Right **Pos:** 3B   **Ht:** 6' 3" **Wt:** 210 **Born:** 08/23/64 **Age:** 29

Year	Team	Lg	G	AB	H	2B	3B	HR	(Hm	Rd)	TB	R	RBI	TBB	IBB	SO	HBP	SH	SF	SB	CS	SB%	GDP	Avg	OBP	SLG
1993	Scranton/wb *	AAA	106	388	112	30	1	17	--	--	195	62	88	55	3	58	5	0	6	4	1	.80	9	.289	.379	.503
1990	Cleveland	AL	30	76	17	5	1	2	(1	1)	30	12	14	21	1	18	0	0	0	0	1	.00	0	.224	.392	.395
1991	Cleveland	AL	47	128	27	7	0	2	(0	2)	40	15	13	14	0	22	4	1	1	2	0	1.00	3	.211	.306	.313
1993	Philadelphia	NL	8	18	1	0	0	0	(0	0)	1	0	0	0	0	3	1	0	0	0	0	.00	0	.056	.105	.056
	3 ML YEARS		85	222	45	12	1	4	(1	3)	71	27	27	35	1	43	5	1	1	2	1	.67	3	.203	.323	.320

Kirt Manwaring

Bats: Right **Throws:** Right **Pos:** C   **Ht:** 5'11" **Wt:** 203 **Born:** 07/15/65 **Age:** 28

Year	Team	Lg	G	AB	H	2B	3B	HR	(Hm	Rd)	TB	R	RBI	TBB	IBB	SO	HBP	SH	SF	SB	CS	SB%	GDP	Avg	OBP	SLG
1987	San Francisco	NL	6	7	1	0	0	0	(0	0)	1	0	0	0	0	1	1	0	0	0	0	.00	1	.143	.250	.143
1988	San Francisco	NL	40	116	29	7	0	1	(0	1)	39	12	15	2	0	21	3	1	1	0	1	.00	1	.250	.279	.336
1989	San Francisco	NL	85	200	42	4	2	0	(0	0)	50	14	18	11	1	28	4	7	1	0	1	.67	5	.210	.264	.250
1990	San Francisco	NL	8	13	2	0	1	0	(0	0)	4	0	1	0	0	3	0	0	0	0	0	.00	0	.154	.154	.308
1991	San Francisco	NL	67	178	40	9	0	0	(0	0)	49	16	19	9	0	22	3	7	2	1	1	.50	2	.225	.271	.275
1992	San Francisco	NL	109	349	85	10	5	4	(1	3)	117	24	26	29	0	42	5	6	0	2	1	.67	12	.244	.311	.335
1993	San Francisco	NL	130	432	119	15	1	5	(3	2)	151	48	49	41	13	76	6	5	2	1	3	.25	14	.275	.345	.350
	7 ML YEARS		445	1295	318	45	9	10	(4	6)	411	114	128	92	14	193	22	26	6	7		.46	35	.246	.305	.317

Josias Manzanillo

Pitches: Right **Bats:** Right **Pos:** RP   **Ht:** 6' 0" **Wt:** 190 **Born:** 10/16/67 **Age:** 26

Year	Team	Lg	G	GS	CG	GF	IP	BFP	H	R	ER	HR	SH	SF	HB	TBB	IBB	SO	WP	Bk	W	L	Pct.	ShO	Sv	ERA
1984	Elmira	A	14	0	0	7	25.2	128	27	24	15	1	1	1	1	26	1	15	9	0	2	3	.400	0	1	5.26
1985	Greensboro	A	7	0	0	2	12	62	12	13	13	1	0	0	0	18	0	10	2	0	1	1	.500	0	0	9.75
	Elmira	A	19	4	0	10	39.2	181	36	19	17	1	0	1	2	36	4	43	12	0	2	4	.333	0	1	3.86
1986	Winter Havn	A	23	21	3	2	142.2	601	110	51	36	3	6	4	3	81	0	102	9	0	13	5	.722	2	0	2.27
1987	New Britain	AA	2	2	0	0	10	45	8	5	5	1	0	0	0	8	0	12	0	0	2	0	1.000	0	0	4.50
1989	New Britain	AA	26	26	3	0	147.2	657	129	78	60	11	4	5	5	85	7	93	16	2	9	10	.474	1	0	3.66
1990	New Britain	AA	12	12	2	0	74	317	66	34	28	3	1	0	2	37	1	51	7	3	4	4	.500	1	0	3.41
	Pawtucket	AAA	15	15	5	0	82.2	368	75	57	51	9	1	2	2	45	0	77	8	0	4	7	.364	0	0	5.55
1991	Pawtucket	AAA	7	7	0	0	49.2	212	37	25	16	0	5	0	1	28	1	35	2	1	2	2	.500	0	0	2.90
	Pawtucket	AAA	20	16	0	0	102.2	459	109	69	64	12	2	4	4	53	0	65	9	1	5	5	.500	0	0	5.61
1992	Memphis	AA	2	0	0	0	7.1	33	6	6	6	0	0	0	1	6	0	8	2	0	0	2	.000	0	0	7.36
	Omaha	AAA	26	21	0	2	136.1	603	138	76	66	12	8	7	7	71	0	114	9	0	7	10	.412	0	0	4.36
1993	New Orleans	AAA	1	0	0	1	1	4	1	1	1	1	0	0	0	0	0	3	0	0	0	1	.000	0	0	9.00
	Norfolk	AAA	14	12	2	1	84	350	82	40	29	3	1	4	2	25	1	79	0	0	1	5	.167	1	0	3.11
1991	Boston	AL	1	0	0	1	1	8	2	2	2	0	0	0	0	3	0	1	0	0	0	0	.000	0	0	18.00
1993	2 ML Teams		16	1	0	6	29	140	30	27	22	2	3	3	2	19	3	21	1	0	1	1	.500	0	0	6.83
1993	Milwaukee	AL	10	1	0	4	17	86	22	20	18	1	2	2	2	10	3	10	1	0	1	1	.500	0	1	9.53
	New York	NL	6	0	0	2	12	54	8	7	4	1	1	1	0	9	0	11	0	0	0	0	.000	0	0	3.00
	2 ML YEARS		17	1	0	7	30	148	32	29	24	2	3	3	2	22	3	22	1	0	1	1	.500	0	1	7.20

Oreste Marrero

Bats: Left **Throws:** Left **Pos:** 1B   **Ht:** 6' 0" **Wt:** 195 **Born:** 10/31/69 **Age:** 24

Year	Team	Lg	G	AB	H	2B	3B	HR	(Hm	Rd)	TB	R	RBI	TBB	IBB	SO	HBP	SH	SF	SB	CS	SB%	GDP	Avg	OBP	SLG
1987	Helena	R	51	154	50	8	2	7	--	--	83	30	34	18	3	31	1	1	0	2	1	.67	1	.325	.399	.539
1988	Beloit	A	19	52	9	2	0	1	--	--	14	5	7	3	0	16	0	0	0	0	1	.00	0	.173	.218	.269
	Helena	R	67	240	85	15	0	16	--	--	148	52	44	42	2	48	0	1	1	3	4	.43	4	.354	.449	.617
1989	Beloit	A	14	40	5	1	0	0	--	--	6	1	3	3	0	20	0	0	1	1	0	1.00	0	.125	.182	.150
	Brewers	R	10	44	18	0	1	3	--	--	29	13	9	2	0	5	0	0	1	2	2	.50	0	.409	.426	.659
	Boise	A	54	203	56	8	1	11	--	--	99	38	43	30	3	60	0	0	4	1	2	.33	3	.276	.363	.488
1990	Beloit	A	119	400	110	25	1	16	--	--	185	59	55	45	3	107	0	0	1	8	4	.67	12	.275	.348	.463
1991	Stockton	A	123	438	110	15	2	13	--	--	168	63	61	57	8	98	0	0	1	4	5	.44	5	.251	.333	.384
1992	El Paso	AA	18	54	10	2	1	1	--	--	17	8	8	4	0	13	0	0	1	1	0	1.00	0	.185	.237	.315
	Stockton	A	76	243	67	17	0	7	--	--	105	35	51	44	6	49	1	1	1	3	2	.60	0	.276	.388	.432
1993	Harrisburg	AA	85	255	85	18	1	10	--	--	135	39	49	22	2	46	0	3	4	3	3	.50	2	.333	.381	.529
1993	Montreal	NL	32	81	17	5	1	1	(1	0)	27	10	4	14	0	16	0	0	0	1	3	.25	0	.210	.326	.333

Al Martin

Bats: Left **Throws:** Left **Pos:** LF/CF **Ht:** 6' 2" **Wt:** 220 **Born:** 11/24/67 **Age:** 26

Year Team	Lg	G	AB	H	2B	3B	HR	(Hm	Rd)	TB	R	RBI	TBB	IBB	SO	HBP	SH	SF	SB	CS	SB%	GDP	Avg	OBP	SLG
1985 Braves	R	40	138	32	3	0	0	--	--	35	16	9	19	2	36	2	0	1	1	4	.20	4	.232	.331	.254
1986 Sumter	A	44	156	38	5	0	1	--	--	46	23	24	23	1	36	0	0	0	6	2	.75	6	.244	.341	.295
Idaho Falls	R	63	242	80	17	6	4	--	--	121	39	44	20	0	53	2	0	0	11	2	.85	1	.331	.386	.500
1987 Sumter	A	117	375	95	18	5	12	--	--	159	59	64	44	5	69	2	1	4	27	8	.77	5	.253	.332	.424
1988 Burlington	A	123	480	134	21	3	7	--	--	182	69	42	30	5	88	4	5	5	40	12	.77	6	.279	.324	.379
1989 Durham	A	128	457	124	26	3	9	--	--	183	84	48	34	0	107	3	0	3	27	14	.66	6	.271	.324	.400
1990 Greenville	AA	133	455	110	17	5	10	--	--	167	64	50	43	4	102	3	1	3	20	7	.74	9	.242	.310	.367
1991 Greenville	AA	86	301	73	13	3	7	--	--	113	38	38	32	4	84	8	1	1	19	7	.73	2	.243	.330	.375
Richmond	AAA	44	151	42	11	1	5	--	--	70	20	18	7	0	33	1	0	0	11	2	.85	0	.278	.314	.464
1992 Buffalo	AAA	125	420	128	16	15	20	--	--	234	85	59	35	4	93	6	3	5	20	5	.80	1	.305	.363	.557
1992 Pittsburgh	NL	12	12	2	0	1	0	(0	0)	4	1	2	0	0	5	0	0	1	0	0	.00	0	.167	.154	.333
1993 Pittsburgh	NL	143	480	135	26	8	18	(15	3)	231	85	64	42	5	122	1	2	3	16	9	.64	5	.281	.338	.481
2 ML YEARS		155	492	137	26	9	18	(15	3)	235	86	66	42	5	127	1	2	4	16	9	.64	5	.278	.334	.478

Norberto Martin

Bats: Right **Throws:** Right **Pos:** 2B **Ht:** 5'10" **Wt:** 164 **Born:** 12/10/66 **Age:** 27

Year Team	Lg	G	AB	H	2B	3B	HR	(Hm	Rd)	TB	R	RBI	TBB	IBB	SO	HBP	SH	SF	SB	CS	SB%	GDP	Avg	OBP	SLG
1984 White Sox	R	56	205	56	8	2	1	--	--	71	36	30	21	0	31	4	1	4	18	5	.78	3	.273	.346	.346
1985 Appleton	A	30	96	19	2	0	0	--	--	21	15	5	9	0	23	0	3	0	2	2	.50	1	.198	.267	.219
Niagara Fls	A	60	217	55	9	0	1	--	--	67	22	13	7	0	41	1	5	0	6	4	.60	2	.253	.280	.309
1986 Appleton	A	9	33	10	2	0	0	--	--	12	4	2	2	0	5	0	0	0	1	0	1.00	1	.303	.343	.364
1987 Chston-Wv	A	68	250	78	14	1	5	--	--	109	44	35	17	1	40	4	4	3	14	4	.78	1	.312	.361	.436
Peninsula	A	41	162	42	6	1	1	--	--	53	21	18	18	0	19	1	0	4	11	6	.65	3	.259	.330	.327
1988 Tampa	A	101	360	93	10	4	2	--	--	117	44	33	17	0	49	3	7	3	24	5	.83	13	.258	.295	.325
1990 Vancouver	AAA	130	508	135	20	4	3	--	--	172	77	45	27	0	63	5	8	6	10	7	.59	14	.266	.306	.339
1991 Vancouver	AAA	93	338	94	9	0	0	--	--	103	39	20	21	0	38	3	10	2	11	7	.61	14	.278	.324	.305
1992 Vancouver	AAA	135	497	143	12	7	0	--	--	169	72	29	29	1	44	2	14	2	29	12	.71	11	.288	.328	.340
1993 Nashville	AAA	137	580	179	21	6	9	--	--	239	87	74	26	0	59	2	12	6	31	5	.86	17	.309	.337	.412
1993 Chicago	AL	8	14	5	0	0	0	(0	0)	5	3	2	1	0	1	0	0	0	0	0	.00	0	.357	.400	.357

Carlos Martinez

Bats: Right **Throws:** Right **Pos:** 3B/1B/DH **Ht:** 6' 5" **Wt:** 215 **Born:** 08/11/65 **Age:** 28

Year Team	Lg	G	AB	H	2B	3B	HR	(Hm	Rd)	TB	R	RBI	TBB	IBB	SO	HBP	SH	SF	SB	CS	SB%	GDP	Avg	OBP	SLG
1993 Charlotte *	AAA	20	79	29	7	1	3	--	--	47	17	12	4	0	15	1	0	0	2	0	1.00	2	.367	.405	.595
1988 Chicago	AL	17	55	9	1	0	0	(0	0)	10	5	0	0	0	12	0	0	0	1	0	1.00	1	.164	.164	.182
1989 Chicago	AL	109	350	105	22	0	5	(2	3)	142	44	32	21	2	57	1	6	1	4	1	.80	14	.300	.340	.406
1990 Chicago	AL	92	272	61	6	5	4	(2	2)	89	18	24	10	2	40	0	1	0	0	4	.00	8	.224	.252	.327
1991 Cleveland	AL	72	257	73	14	0	5	(3	2)	102	22	30	10	2	43	2	1	5	3	2	.60	10	.284	.310	.397
1992 Cleveland	AL	69	228	60	9	1	5	(2	3)	86	23	35	7	0	21	1	1	4	1	2	.33	5	.263	.283	.377
1993 Cleveland	AL	80	262	64	10	0	5	(2	3)	89	26	31	20	3	29	0	0	3	1	1	.50	5	.244	.295	.340
6 ML YEARS		439	1424	372	62	6	24	(11	13)	518	138	152	68	9	202	4	9	13	10	10	.50	43	.261	.294	.364

Chito Martinez

Bats: Left **Throws:** Left **Pos:** RF **Ht:** 5'10" **Wt:** 185 **Born:** 12/19/65 **Age:** 28

Year Team	Lg	G	AB	H	2B	3B	HR	(Hm	Rd)	TB	R	RBI	TBB	IBB	SO	HBP	SH	SF	SB	CS	SB%	GDP	Avg	OBP	SLG
1993 Bowie *	AA	5	13	1	0	0	0	--	--	1	5	0	2	0	2	0	0	0	0	0	.00	1	.077	.200	.077
Rochester *	AAA	43	145	38	11	0	5	--	--	64	14	23	11	0	34	0	2	0	0	0	.00	2	.262	.314	.441
1991 Baltimore	AL	67	216	58	12	1	13	(8	5)	111	32	33	11	0	51	0	0	1	1	1	.50	2	.269	.303	.514
1992 Baltimore	AL	83	198	53	10	1	5	(2	3)	80	26	25	31	4	47	2	0	4	0	1	.00	9	.268	.366	.404
1993 Baltimore	AL	8	15	0	0	0	0	(0	0)	0	0	0	4	2	4	0	0	0	0	0	.00	0	.000	.211	.000
3 ML YEARS		158	429	111	22	2	18	(10	8)	191	58	58	46	6	102	2	0	5	1	2	.33	11	.259	.330	.445

Dave Martinez

Bats: Left **Throws:** Left **Pos:** CF/RF **Ht:** 5'10" **Wt:** 175 **Born:** 09/26/64 **Age:** 29

Year Team	Lg	G	AB	H	2B	3B	HR	(Hm	Rd)	TB	R	RBI	TBB	IBB	SO	HBP	SH	SF	SB	CS	SB%	GDP	Avg	OBP	SLG
1993 Phoenix *	AAA	3	15	7	0	0	0	--	--	7	4	2	1	0	0	0	0	0	1	0	1.00	0	.467	.500	.467
1986 Chicago	NL	53	108	15	1	1	1	(1	0)	21	13	7	6	0	22	1	0	1	4	2	.67	0	.139	.190	.194
1987 Chicago	NL	142	459	134	18	8	8	(5	3)	192	70	36	57	4	96	2	1	1	16	8	.67	4	.292	.372	.418
1988 2 ML Teams		138	447	114	13	6	6	(2	4)	157	51	46	38	8	94	2	2	5	23	9	.72	3	.255	.313	.351

Year	Team	Lg	G	AB	H	2B	3B	HR	(Hm	Rd)	TB	R	RBI	TBB	IBB	SO	HBP	SH	SF	SB	CS	SB%	GDP	Avg	OBP	SLG
1989	Montreal	NL	126	361	99	16	7	3	(1	2)	138	41	27	27	2	57	0	7	1	23	4	.85	1	.274	.324	.382
1990	Montreal	NL	118	391	109	13	5	11	(5	6)	165	60	39	24	2	48	1	3	2	13	11	.54	8	.279	.321	.422
1991	Montreal	NL	124	396	117	18	5	7	(3	4)	166	47	42	20	3	54	3	5	3	16	7	.70	3	.295	.332	.419
1992	Cincinnati	NL	135	393	100	20	5	3	(3	0)	139	47	31	42	4	54	0	6	4	12	8	.60	6	.254	.323	.354
1993	San Francisco	NL	91	241	58	12	1	5	(1	4)	87	28	27	27	3	39	0	0	0	6	3	.67	5	.241	.317	.361
1988	Chicago	NL	75	256	65	10	1	4	(2	2)	89	27	34	21	5	46	2	0	4	7	3	.70	2	.254	.311	.348
	Montreal	NL	63	191	49	3	5	2	(0	2)	68	24	12	17	3	48	0	2	1	16	6	.73	1	.257	.316	.356
8 ML YEARS			927	2796	746	111	38	44	(21	23)	1065	357	255	241	26	464	9	24	17	113	52	.68	31	.267	.325	.381

Dennis Martinez

Pitches: Right **Bats:** Right **Pos:** SP **Ht:** 6' 1" **Wt:** 180 **Born:** 05/14/55 **Age:** 39

			HOW MUCH HE PITCHED						WHAT HE GAVE UP											THE RESULTS					
Year	Team	Lg	G	GS	CG	GF	IP	BFP	H	R	ER	HR	SH	SF	HB	TBB	IBB	SO	WP	Bk	W	L	Pct.	ShO	Sv	ERA
1976	Baltimore	AL	4	2	1	1	28	106	23	8	8	1	1	0	0	8	0	18	1	0	1	2	.333	0	0	2.57
1977	Baltimore	AL	42	13	5	19	167	709	157	86	76	10	8	8	8	64	5	107	5	0	14	7	.667	0	4	4.10
1978	Baltimore	AL	40	38	15	0	276	1140	257	121	108	20	8	7	3	93	4	142	8	0	16	11	.593	2	0	3.52
1979	Baltimore	AL	40	39	18	0	292	1206	279	129	119	28	12	12	1	78	1	132	9	2	15	16	.484	3	0	3.67
1980	Baltimore	AL	25	12	2	8	100	428	103	44	44	12	1	3	2	44	6	42	0	1	6	4	.600	0	1	3.96
1981	Baltimore	AL	25	24	9	0	179	753	173	84	66	10	2	5	2	62	1	88	6	1	14	5	.737	2	0	3.32
1982	Baltimore	AL	40	39	10	0	252	1093	262	123	118	30	11	7	7	87	2	111	7	1	16	12	.571	2	0	4.21
1983	Baltimore	AL	32	25	4	3	153	688	209	108	94	21	3	5	2	45	0	71	2	0	7	16	.304	0	0	5.53
1984	Baltimore	AL	34	20	2	4	141.2	599	145	81	79	26	0	5	5	37	2	77	13	0	6	9	.400	0	0	5.02
1985	Baltimore	AL	33	31	3	1	180	789	203	110	103	29	0	11	9	63	3	68	4	1	13	11	.542	1	0	5.15
1986	2 ML Teams		23	15	1	2	104.2	449	114	57	55	11	8	2	3	30	4	65	3	2	3	6	.333	1	0	4.73
1987	Montreal	NL	22	22	2	0	144.2	599	133	59	53	9	4	3	6	40	2	84	4	2	11	4	.733	1	0	3.30
1988	Montreal	NL	34	34	9	0	235.1	968	215	94	71	21	2	6	6	55	3	120	5	10	15	13	.536	2	0	2.72
1989	Montreal	NL	34	33	5	1	232	950	227	88	82	21	8	2	7	49	4	142	5	2	16	7	.696	2	0	3.18
1990	Montreal	NL	32	32	7	0	226	908	191	80	74	16	11	3	6	49	9	156	1	1	10	11	.476	2	0	2.95
1991	Montreal	NL	31	31	9	0	222	905	187	70	59	9	7	3	4	62	3	123	3	0	14	11	.560	5	0	2.39
1992	Montreal	NL	32	32	6	0	226.1	900	172	75	62	12	12	5	9	60	3	147	2	0	16	11	.593	0	0	2.47
1993	Montreal	NL	35	34	2	1	224.2	945	211	110	96	27	10	4	11	64	7	138	2	4	15	9	.625	0	1	3.85
1986	Baltimore	AL	4	0	0	1	6.2	33	11	5	5	0	0	1	0	2	0	2	1	0	0	0	.000	0	0	6.75
	Montreal	NL	19	15	1	1	98	416	103	52	50	11	8	1	3	28	4	63	2	2	3	6	.333	1	0	4.59
18 ML YEARS			558	476	110	40	3384.1	14135	3261	1527	1367	313	108	91	91	990	59	1831	80	27	208	165	.558	23	6	3.64

Domingo Martinez

Bats: Right **Throws:** Right **Pos:** 1B **Ht:** 6' 2" **Wt:** 215 **Born:** 08/04/67 **Age:** 26

			BATTING																BASERUNNING				PERCENTAGES		
Year	Team	Lg	G	AB	H	2B	3B	HR	(Hm | Rd)	TB	R	RBI	TBB	IBB	SO	HBP	SH	SF	SB	CS	SB%	GDP	Avg	OBP	SLG
1985	Blue Jays	R	58	219	65	10	2	4	--	--	91	36	19	12	0	42	2	0	0	3	4	.43	3	.297	.339	.416
1986	Ventura	A	129	455	113	19	6	9	--	--	171	51	57	36	2	127	4	3	3	9	9	.50	15	.248	.307	.376
1987	Dunedin	A	118	435	112	32	2	8	--	--	172	53	65	41	2	88	3	0	2	8	3	.73	9	.257	.324	.395
1988	Knoxville	AA	143	516	136	25	2	13	--	--	204	54	70	40	3	88	5	0	7	2	7	.22	13	.264	.319	.395
1989	Knoxville	AA	120	415	102	19	2	10	--	--	155	56	53	42	3	82	9	1	5	2	2	.50	7	.246	.325	.373
1990	Knoxville	AA	128	463	119	20	3	17	--	--	196	52	67	51	1	81	5	1	2	3	4	.40	24	.257	.336	.423
1991	Syracuse	AAA	126	467	146	16	2	17	--	--	217	61	83	41	0	107	6	5	6	6	4	.60	10	.313	.371	.465
1992	Syracuse	AAA	116	438	120	22	0	21	--	--	205	55	62	33	5	95	8	0	4	6	0	1.00	11	.274	.333	.468
1993	Syracuse	AAA	127	465	127	24	2	24	--	--	227	50	79	31	6	115	10	0	4	4	5	.44	11	.273	.329	.488
1992	Toronto	AL	7	8	5	0	0	1	(1 | 0)	8	2	3	0	0	1	0	0	0	0	0	.00	0	.625	.625	1.000
1993	Toronto	AL	8	14	4	0	0	1	(0 | 1)	7	2	3	1	0	7	0	0	0	0	0	.00	0	.286	.333	.500
2 ML YEARS			15	22	9	0	0	2	(1 | 1)	15	4	6	1	0	8	0	0	0	0	0	.00	0	.409	.435	.682

Edgar Martinez

Bats: Right **Throws:** Right **Pos:** DH/3B **Ht:** 5'11" **Wt:** 190 **Born:** 01/02/63 **Age:** 31

			BATTING																BASERUNNING				PERCENTAGES		
Year	Team	Lg	G	AB	H	2B	3B	HR	(Hm | Rd)	TB	R	RBI	TBB	IBB	SO	HBP	SH	SF	SB	CS	SB%	GDP	Avg	OBP	SLG
1993	Jacksonville *	AA	4	14	5	0	0	1	--	--	8	2	3	2	0	0	0	0	0	0	0	.00	1	.357	.438	.571
1987	Seattle	AL	13	43	16	5	2	0	(0 | 0)	25	6	5	2	0	5	1	0	0	0	0	.00	0	.372	.413	.581
1988	Seattle	AL	14	32	9	4	0	0	(0 | 0)	13	0	5	4	0	7	0	1	1	0	0	.00	0	.281	.351	.406
1989	Seattle	AL	65	171	41	5	0	2	(1 | 1)	52	20	20	17	1	26	3	2	3	2	1	.67	3	.240	.314	.304
1990	Seattle	AL	144	487	147	27	2	11	(3 | 8)	211	71	49	74	3	62	5	1	3	1	4	.20	13	.302	.397	.433
1991	Seattle	AL	150	544	167	35	1	14	(8 | 6)	246	98	52	84	9	72	8	2	4	0	3	.00	19	.307	.405	.452
1992	Seattle	AL	135	528	181	46	3	18	(11 | 7)	287	100	73	54	2	61	4	1	5	14	4	.78	15	.343	.404	.544
1993	Seattle	AL	42	135	32	7	0	4	(1 | 3)	51	20	13	28	1	19	0	1	1	0	0	.00	4	.237	.366	.378
7 ML YEARS			563	1940	593	129	8	49	(23 | 26)	885	315	217	263	16	252	21	8	17	17	12	.59	54	.306	.391	.456

Pedro Martinez

Pitches: Right **Bats:** Right **Pos:** RP **Ht:** 5'11" **Wt:** 150 **Born:** 07/25/71 **Age:** 22

Year Team	Lg	G	GS	CG	GF	IP	BFP	H	R	ER	HR	SH	SF	HB	TBB	IBB	SO	WP	Bk	W	L	Pct.	ShO	Sv	ERA
1990 Great Falls	R	14	14	0	0	77	346	74	39	31	5	2	2	8	40	1	82	6	1	8	3	.727	0	0	3.62
1991 Bakersfield	A	10	10	0	0	61.1	243	41	17	14	3	0	2	5	19	0	83	1	1	8	0	1.000	0	0	2.05
San Antonio	AA	12	12	4	0	76.2	310	57	21	15	1	5	0	3	31	1	74	5	1	7	5	.583	3	0	1.76
Albuquerque	AAA	6	6	0	0	39.1	157	28	17	16	3	1	1	0	16	0	35	3	0	3	3	.500	0	0	3.66
1992 Albuquerque	AAA	20	20	3	0	125.1	527	104	57	53	10	4	2	9	57	0	124	2	0	7	6	.538	1	0	3.81
1993 Albuquerque	AAA	1	1	0	0	3	11	1	1	1	0	0	0	0	1	0	4	0	0	0	0	.000	0	0	3.00
1992 Los Angeles	NL	2	1	0	1	8	31	6	2	2	0	0	0	0	1	0	8	0	0	0	1	.000	0	0	2.25
1993 Los Angeles	NL	65	2	0	20	107	444	76	34	31	5	0	5	4	57	4	119	3	1	10	5	.667	0	2	2.61
2 ML YEARS		67	3	0	21	115	475	82	36	33	5	0	5	4	58	4	127	3	1	10	6	.625	0	2	2.58

Pedro A. Martinez

Pitches: Left **Bats:** Left **Pos:** RP **Ht:** 6'2" **Wt:** 155 **Born:** 11/29/68 **Age:** 25

Year Team	Lg	G	GS	CG	GF	IP	BFP	H	R	ER	HR	SH	SF	HB	TBB	IBB	SO	WP	Bk	W	L	Pct.	ShO	Sv	ERA
1987 Spokane	A	18	5	1	4	51.2	240	57	31	22	1	3	2	0	36	1	42	5	2	4	1	.800	0	0	3.83
1988 Spokane	A	15	15	1	0	99.2	433	108	55	47	1	2	6	2	32	0	89	4	5	8	3	.727	0	0	4.24
1989 Chston-Sc	A	27	27	5	0	187	750	147	53	41	5	4	5	2	64	1	158	4	2	14	8	.636	2	0	1.97
1990 Wichita	AA	24	23	2	0	129.1	576	139	83	69	14	5	2	3	70	2	88	4	0	6	10	.375	0	0	4.80
1991 Wichita	AA	26	26	3	0	156.2	677	169	99	91	21	8	6	3	57	2	95	7	0	11	10	.524	2	0	5.23
1992 Wichita	AA	26	26	1	0	168.1	694	153	66	56	12	4	4	3	52	0	142	3	0	11	7	.611	0	0	2.99
1993 Las Vegas	AAA	15	14	1	0	87.2	381	94	49	46	8	2	4	1	40	4	65	3	1	3	5	.375	0	0	4.72
1993 San Diego	NL	32	0	0	9	37	148	23	11	10	4	0	0	1	13	1	32	0	0	3	1	.750	0	0	2.43

Ramon Martinez

Pitches: Right **Bats:** Left **Pos:** SP **Ht:** 6'4" **Wt:** 176 **Born:** 03/22/68 **Age:** 26

Year Team	Lg	G	GS	CG	GF	IP	BFP	H	R	ER	HR	SH	SF	HB	TBB	IBB	SO	WP	Bk	W	L	Pct.	ShO	Sv	ERA
1988 Los Angeles	NL	9	6	0	0	35.2	151	27	17	15	0	4	0	0	22	1	23	1	0	1	3	.250	0	0	3.79
1989 Los Angeles	NL	15	15	2	0	98.2	410	79	39	35	11	4	0	5	41	1	89	1	0	6	4	.600	2	0	3.19
1990 Los Angeles	NL	33	33	12	0	234.1	950	191	89	76	22	7	5	4	67	5	223	3	3	20	6	.769	3	0	2.92
1991 Los Angeles	NL	33	33	6	0	220.1	916	190	89	80	18	8	4	7	69	4	150	6	0	17	13	.567	4	0	3.27
1992 Los Angeles	NL	25	25	1	0	150.2	662	141	82	67	11	12	1	5	69	4	101	9	0	8	11	.421	1	0	4.00
1993 Los Angeles	NL	32	32	4	0	211.2	918	202	88	81	15	12	5	4	**104**	9	127	2	2	10	12	.455	3	0	3.44
6 ML YEARS		147	144	25	0	951.1	4007	830	404	354	77	47	15	25	372	24	713	22	5	62	49	.559	13	0	3.35

Tino Martinez

Bats: Left **Throws:** Right **Pos:** 1B **Ht:** 6'2" **Wt:** 210 **Born:** 12/07/67 **Age:** 26

Year Team	Lg	G	AB	H	2B	3B	HR	(Hm	Rd)	TB	R	RBI	TBB	IBB	SO	HBP	SH	SF	SB	CS	SB%	GDP	Avg	OBP	SLG
1990 Seattle	AL	24	68	15	4	0	0	(0	0)	19	4	5	9	0	9	0	0	1	0	0	.00	0	.221	.308	.279
1991 Seattle	AL	36	112	23	2	0	4	(3	1)	37	11	9	11	0	24	0	0	2	0	0	.00	2	.205	.272	.330
1992 Seattle	AL	136	460	118	19	2	16	(10	6)	189	53	66	42	9	77	2	1	8	2	1	.67	24	.257	.316	.411
1993 Seattle	AL	109	408	108	25	1	17	(9	8)	186	48	60	45	9	56	5	3	3	0	3	.00	7	.265	.343	.456
4 ML YEARS		305	1048	264	50	3	37	(22	15)	431	116	140	107	18	166	7	4	14	2	4	.33	33	.252	.321	.411

Roger Mason

Pitches: Right **Bats:** Right **Pos:** RP **Ht:** 6'6" **Wt:** 220 **Born:** 09/18/58 **Age:** 35

Year Team	Lg	G	GS	CG	GF	IP	BFP	H	R	ER	HR	SH	SF	HB	TBB	IBB	SO	WP	Bk	W	L	Pct.	ShO	Sv	ERA
1984 Detroit	AL	5	2	0	2	22	97	23	11	11	1	0	2	0	10	0	15	2	0	1	1	.500	0	1	4.50
1985 San Francisco	NL	5	5	1	0	29.2	128	28	13	7	1	2	0	0	11	1	26	0	0	1	3	.250	1	0	2.12
1986 San Francisco	NL	11	11	1	0	60	262	56	35	32	5	2	3	3	30	3	43	1	0	3	4	.429	0	0	4.80
1987 San Francisco	NL	5	5	0	0	26	110	30	15	13	4	1	0	0	10	0	18	1	1	1	1	.500	0	0	4.50
1989 Houston	NL	2	0	0	1	1.1	8	2	3	3	0	0	0	0	2	0	3	0	0	0	0	.000	0	0	20.25
1991 Pittsburgh	NL	24	0	0	6	29.2	114	21	11	10	2	1	1	1	6	1	21	2	0	3	2	.600	0	3	3.03
1992 Pittsburgh	NL	65	0	0	26	88	374	80	41	40	11	8	4	4	33	8	56	3	0	5	7	.417	0	8	4.09
1993 2 ML Teams		68	0	0	29	99.2	417	90	48	45	10	7	5	2	34	5	71	2	3	5	12	.294	0	4	4.06
1993 San Diego	NL	34	0	0	14	50	207	43	20	18	1	6	3	2	18	4	39	1	2	0	7	.000	0	0	3.24
Philadelphia	NL	34	0	0	15	49.2	210	47	28	27	9	1	2	0	16	1	32	1	1	5	5	.500	0	4	4.89
8 ML YEARS		185	23	2	64	356.1	1510	330	177	161	34	21	15	10	136	18	253	11	4	19	30	.388	1	12	4.07

Don Mattingly

Bats: Left **Throws:** Left **Pos:** 1B   **Ht:** 6' 0" **Wt:** 200 **Born:** 04/20/61 **Age:** 33

Year Team	Lg	G	AB	H	2B	3B	HR	(Hm	Rd)	TB	R	RBI	TBB	IBB	SO	HBP	SH	SF	SB	CS	SB%	GDP	Avg	OBP	SLG
1982 New York	AL	7	12	2	0	0	0	(0	0)	2	0	1	0	0	1	0	0	1	0	0	.00	2	.167	.154	.167
1983 New York	AL	91	279	79	15	4	4	(0	4)	114	34	32	21	5	31	1	2	2	0	0	.00	8	.283	.333	.409
1984 New York	AL	153	603	207	44	2	23	(12	11)	324	91	110	41	8	33	1	8	9	1	1	.50	15	.343	.381	.537
1985 New York	AL	159	652	211	48	3	35	(22	13)	370	107	145	56	13	41	2	2	15	2	2	.50	15	.324	.371	.567
1986 New York	AL	162	677	238	53	2	31	(17	14)	388	117	113	53	11	35	1	1	10	0	0	.00	17	.352	.394	.573
1987 New York	AL	141	569	186	38	2	30	(17	13)	318	93	115	51	13	38	1	0	8	1	4	.20	16	.327	.378	.559
1988 New York	AL	144	599	186	37	0	18	(11	7)	277	94	88	41	14	29	3	0	8	1	0	1.00	13	.311	.353	.462
1989 New York	AL	158	631	191	37	2	23	(19	4)	301	79	113	51	18	30	1	0	10	3	0	1.00	15	.303	.351	.477
1990 New York	AL	102	394	101	16	0	5	(4	1)	132	40	42	28	13	20	3	0	3	1	0	1.00	13	.256	.308	.335
1991 New York	AL	152	587	169	35	0	9	(7	2)	231	64	68	46	11	42	4	0	9	2	0	1.00	21	.288	.339	.394
1992 New York	AL	157	640	184	40	0	14	(6	8)	266	89	86	39	7	43	1	0	6	3	0	1.00	11	.288	.327	.416
1993 New York	AL	134	530	154	27	2	17	(8	9)	236	78	86	61	9	42	2	0	3	0	0	.00	19	.291	.364	.445
12 ML YEARS		1560	6173	1908	390	17	209	(123	86)	2959	886	999	488	122	385	20	13	84	14	7	.67	165	.309	.357	.479

Tim Mauser

Pitches: Right **Bats:** Right **Pos:** RP   **Ht:** 6' 0" **Wt:** 185 **Born:** 10/04/66 **Age:** 27

Year Team	Lg	G	GS	CG	GF	IP	BFP	H	R	ER	HR	SH	SF	HB	TBB	IBB	SO	WP	Bk	W	L	Pct.	ShO	Sv	ERA
1993 Scranton/wb *	AAA	19	0	0	19	20.2	79	10	2	2	0	0	0	0	5	0	25	4	0	2	0	1.000	0	10	0.87
1991 Philadelphia	NL	3	0	0	1	10.2	53	18	10	9	3	1	0	0	3	0	6	0	0	0	0	.000	0	0	7.59
1993 2 ML Teams		36	0	0	16	54	235	51	28	24	6	1	1	1	24	5	46	2	0	0	1	.000	0	0	4.00
1993 Philadelphia	NL	8	0	0	1	16.1	71	15	9	9	1	0	0	1	7	0	14	1	0	0	0	.000	0	0	4.96
San Diego	NL	28	0	0	15	37.2	164	36	19	15	5	1	1	0	17	5	32	1	0	0	1	.000	0	0	3.58
2 ML YEARS		39	0	0	17	64.2	288	69	38	33	9	2	1	1	27	5	52	2	0	0	1	.000	0	0	4.59

Derrick May

Bats: Left **Throws:** Right **Pos:** LF   **Ht:** 6' 4" **Wt:** 225 **Born:** 07/14/68 **Age:** 25

Year Team	Lg	G	AB	H	2B	3B	HR	(Hm	Rd)	TB	R	RBI	TBB	IBB	SO	HBP	SH	SF	SB	CS	SB%	GDP	Avg	OBP	SLG
1990 Chicago	NL	17	61	15	3	0	1	(1	0)	21	8	11	2	0	7	0	0	0	1	0	1.00	1	.246	.270	.344
1991 Chicago	NL	15	22	5	2	0	1	(1	0)	10	4	3	2	0	1	0	0	0	0	0	.00	1	.227	.280	.455
1992 Chicago	NL	124	351	96	11	0	8	(3	5)	131	33	45	14	4	40	3	2	1	5	3	.63	10	.274	.306	.373
1993 Chicago	NL	128	465	137	25	2	10	(3	7)	196	62	77	31	6	41	1	0	6	10	3	.77	15	.295	.336	.422
4 ML YEARS		284	899	253	41	2	20	(8	12)	358	107	136	49	10	89	4	2	8	16	6	.73	27	.281	.319	.398

Brent Mayne

Bats: Left **Throws:** Right **Pos:** C   **Ht:** 6' 1" **Wt:** 190 **Born:** 04/19/68 **Age:** 26

Year Team	Lg	G	AB	H	2B	3B	HR	(Hm	Rd)	TB	R	RBI	TBB	IBB	SO	HBP	SH	SF	SB	CS	SB%	GDP	Avg	OBP	SLG
1990 Kansas City	AL	5	13	3	0	0	0	(0	0)	3	2	1	3	0	3	0	0	0	0	1	.00	0	.231	.375	.231
1991 Kansas City	AL	85	231	58	8	0	3	(2	1)	75	22	31	23	4	42	0	2	3	2	4	.33	6	.251	.315	.325
1992 Kansas City	AL	82	213	48	10	0	0	(0	0)	58	16	18	11	0	26	0	2	3	0	4	.00	5	.225	.260	.272
1993 Kansas City	AL	71	205	52	9	1	2	(0	2)	69	22	22	18	7	31	1	1	3	3	2	.60	6	.254	.317	.337
4 ML YEARS		243	662	161	27	1	5	(2	3)	205	62	72	55	11	102	1	1	7	6	5	.31	17	.243	.300	.310

Matt Maysey

Pitches: Right **Bats:** Right **Pos:** RP   **Ht:** 6' 4" **Wt:** 225 **Born:** 01/08/67 **Age:** 27

Year Team	Lg	G	GS	CG	GF	IP	BFP	H	R	ER	HR	SH	SF	HB	TBB	IBB	SO	WP	Bk	W	L	Pct.	ShO	Sv	ERA
1985 Spokane	A	7	4	0	2	29	0	27	18	15	3	0	0	1	16	0	18	5	0	0	3	.000	0	0	4.66
1986 Charleston	A	18	5	0	11	43	196	43	28	24	5	3	0	3	24	2	39	5	2	3	2	.600	0	1	5.02
1987 Chston-Sc	A	41	18	5	21	150.1	623	112	71	53	13	8	7	5	59	4	143	13	3	14	11	.560	0	7	3.17
1988 Wichita	AA	28	28	4	0	187	789	180	88	77	15	7	6	5	68	1	120	18	5	9	9	.500	0	0	3.71
1989 Las Vegas	AAA	28	28	4	0	176.1	773	173	94	80	19	3	1	2	84	3	96	12	3	8	12	.400	1	0	4.08
1990 Las Vegas	AAA	26	25	1	1	137.2	634	155	97	86	10	6	5	5	88	5	72	12	1	6	10	.375	0	0	5.62
1991 Harrisburg	AA	15	15	2	0	104.2	419	90	26	22	3	2	3	2	28	0	86	8	0	6	5	.545	2	0	1.89
Indianapolis	AAA	12	12	0	0	63	272	60	45	36	7	0	1	2	33	2	45	6	0	3	6	.333	0	0	5.14
1992 Indianapolis	AAA	35	1	0	14	67	286	63	32	32	9	4	2	0	28	5	38	2	1	5	3	.625	0	5	4.30
1993 New Orleans	AAA	29	5	0	6	52.1	215	48	25	24	8	1	2	0	14	1	40	2	1	0	3	.000	0	2	4.13
1992 Montreal	NL	2	0	0	1	2.1	12	4	1	1	1	0	0	0	0	0	1	0	0	0	0	.000	0	0	3.86
1993 Milwaukee	AL	23	0	0	12	22	105	28	14	14	4	2	2	1	13	1	10	4	0	1	2	.333	0	1	5.73
2 ML YEARS		25	0	0	13	24.1	117	32	15	15	5	2	2	2	13	1	11	4	0	1	2	.333	0	1	5.55

Dave McCarty

Bats: Right **Throws:** Left **Pos:** LF/1B/RF **Ht:** 6' 5" **Wt:** 210 **Born:** 11/23/69 **Age:** 24

								BATTING											BASERUNNING				PERCENTAGES		
Year Team	Lg	G	AB	H	2B	3B	HR	(Hm	Rd)	TB	R	RBI	TBB	IBB	SO	HBP	SH	SF	SB	CS	SB%	GDP	Avg	OBP	SLG
1991 Visalia	A	15	50	19	3	0	3	--	--	31	16	8	13	0	7	3	0	0	3	1	.75	0	.380	.530	.620
Orlando	AA	28	88	23	4	0	3	--	--	36	18	11	10	0	20	2	0	0	0	1	.00	1	.261	.350	.409
1992 Orlando	AA	129	456	124	16	2	18	--	--	198	75	79	55	5	89	8	1	6	6	6	.50	8	.272	.356	.434
Portland	AAA	7	26	13	2	0	1	--	--	18	7	8	5	0	3	1	0	1	1	0	1.00	1	.500	.594	.692
1993 Portland	AAA	40	143	55	11	0	8	--	--	90	42	31	27	2	25	1	0	3	5	2	.71	3	.385	.477	.629
1993 Minnesota	AL	98	350	75	15	2	2	(2	0)	100	36	21	19	0	80	1	1	0	2	6	.25	13	.214	.257	.286

Kirk McCaskill

Pitches: Right **Bats:** Right **Pos:** RP/SP **Ht:** 6' 1" **Wt:** 205 **Born:** 04/09/61 **Age:** 33

				HOW MUCH HE PITCHED						WHAT HE GAVE UP									THE RESULTS					
Year Team	Lg	G	GS	CG	GF	IP	BFP	H	R	ER	HR	SH	SF	HB	TBB	IBB	SO	WP	Bk	W	L	Pct.	ShO	Sv	ERA
1993 South Bend *		1	1	0	0	6	25	3	2	1	0	0	0	0	3	0	5	0	0	1	0	1.000	0	0	1.50
1985 California	AL	30	29	6	0	189.2	807	189	105	99	23	2	5	4	64	1	102	5	0	12	12	.500	1	0	4.70
1986 California	AL	34	33	10	1	246.1	1013	207	98	92	19	6	5	5	92	1	202	10	2	17	10	.630	2	0	3.36
1987 California	AL	14	13	1	0	74.2	334	84	52	47	14	3	1	2	34	0	56	1	0	4	6	.400	1	0	5.67
1988 California	AL	23	23	4	0	146.1	635	155	78	70	9	1	6	1	61	3	98	13	2	8	6	.571	2	0	4.31
1989 California	AL	32	32	6	0	212	864	202	73	69	16	3	4	3	59	1	107	7	2	15	10	.600	4	0	2.93
1990 California	AL	29	29	2	0	174.1	738	161	77	63	9	3	1	2	72	1	78	6	1	12	11	.522	1	0	3.25
1991 California	AL	30	30	1	0	177.2	762	193	93	84	19	6	6	3	66	1	71	6	0	10	19	.345	0	0	4.26
1992 Chicago	AL	34	34	0	0	209	911	193	116	97	11	7	7	6	95	5	109	6	2	12	13	.480	0	0	4.18
1993 Chicago	AL	30	14	0	6	113.2	502	144	71	66	12	2	3	1	36	6	65	6	0	4	8	.333	0	2	5.23
9 ML YEARS		256	237	30	7	1543.2	6566	1528	763	687	132	33	38	27	579	19	888	60	9	94	95	.497	11	2	4.01

Lloyd McClendon

Bats: Right **Throws:** Right **Pos:** RF/LF **Ht:** 6' 0" **Wt:** 212 **Born:** 01/11/59 **Age:** 35

								BATTING											BASERUNNING				PERCENTAGES		
Year Team	Lg	G	AB	H	2B	3B	HR	(Hm	Rd)	TB	R	RBI	TBB	IBB	SO	HBP	SH	SF	SB	CS	SB%	GDP	Avg	OBP	SLG
1987 Cincinnati	NL	45	72	15	5	0	2	(0	2)	26	8	13	4	0	15	0	0	1	1	0	1.00	1	.208	.247	.361
1988 Cincinnati	NL	72	137	30	4	0	3	(0	3)	43	9	14	15	1	22	2	1	2	4	0	1.00	6	.219	.301	.314
1989 Chicago	NL	92	259	74	12	1	12	(9	3)	124	47	40	37	3	31	1	1	7	6	4	.60	3	.286	.368	.479
1990 2 ML Teams	NL	53	110	18	3	0	2	(0	2)	27	6	12	14	2	22	0	0	1	1	0	1.00	2	.164	.256	.245
1991 Pittsburgh	NL	85	163	47	7	0	7	(2	5)	75	24	24	18	0	23	2	0	0	2	1	.67	2	.288	.366	.460
1992 Pittsburgh	NL	84	190	48	8	1	3	(3	0)	67	26	20	28	0	24	2	1	3	1	3	.25	5	.253	.350	.353
1993 Pittsburgh	NL	88	181	40	11	1	2	(1	1)	59	21	19	23	1	17	0	1	2	0	3	.00	4	.221	.306	.326
1990 Chicago	NL	49	107	17	3	0	1	(0	1)	23	5	10	14	2	21	0	0	1	1	0	1.00	2	.159	.254	.215
Pittsburgh	NL	4	3	1	0	0	1	(0	1)	4	1	2	0	0	1	0	0	0	0	0	.00	0	.333	.333	1.333
7 ML YEARS		519	1112	272	50	3	31	(15	16)	421	141	142	139	7	154	7	4	16	15	11	.58	23	.245	.328	.379

Bob McClure

Pitches: Left **Bats:** Right **Pos:** RP **Ht:** 5'11" **Wt:** 188 **Born:** 04/29/53 **Age:** 41

				HOW MUCH HE PITCHED						WHAT HE GAVE UP									THE RESULTS					
Year Team	Lg	G	GS	CG	GF	IP	BFP	H	R	ER	HR	SH	SF	HB	TBB	IBB	SO	WP	Bk	W	L	Pct.	ShO	Sv	ERA
1975 Kansas City	AL	12	0	0	4	15	66	4	0	0	0	0	0	0	14	2	15	0	2	1	0	1.000	0	1	0.00
1976 Kansas City	AL	8	0	0	0	4	22	3	4	4	0	0	0	0	8	0	3	0	0	0	0	.000	0	0	9.00
1977 Milwaukee	AL	68	0	0	31	71	302	64	25	20	2	5	5	1	34	5	57	1	2	2	1	.667	0	6	2.54
1978 Milwaukee	AL	44	0	0	29	65	283	53	30	27	8	7	2	6	30	4	47	1	1	2	6	.250	0	9	3.74
1979 Milwaukee	AL	36	0	0	16	51	229	53	29	22	6	2	3	3	24	0	37	5	0	5	2	.714	0	5	3.88
1980 Milwaukee	AL	52	5	2	23	91	390	83	34	31	6	1	5	2	37	2	47	0	2	5	8	.385	1	10	3.07
1981 Milwaukee	AL	4	0	0	1	8	34	7	3	3	1	0	0	0	4	1	6	0	0	0	0	.000	0	0	3.38
1982 Milwaukee	AL	34	26	5	5	172.2	734	160	90	81	21	6	4	4	74	4	99	5	5	12	7	.632	0	0	4.22
1983 Milwaukee	AL	24	23	4	0	142	625	152	75	71	11	0	4	5	68	1	68	4	6	9	9	.500	0	0	4.50
1984 Milwaukee	AL	39	18	1	5	139.2	616	154	76	68	9	8	8	2	52	4	68	1	3	4	8	.333	0	1	4.38
1985 Milwaukee	AL	38	1	0	12	85.2	370	91	43	41	10	3	2	3	30	2	57	5	0	4	1	.800	0	3	4.31
1986 2 ML Teams	AL	65	0	0	22	79	332	71	29	28	4	4	3	1	33	3	53	1	1	4	6	.400	0	6	3.19
1987 Montreal	NL	52	0	0	16	52.1	222	47	30	20	8	5	2	0	20	3	33	0	1	6	1	.857	0	5	3.44
1988 2 ML Teams		33	0	0	13	30	133	35	18	18	4	3	2	2	8	0	19	1	3	2	3	.400	0	3	5.40
1989 California	AL	48	0	0	27	52.1	205	39	14	9	2	1	4	1	15	1	36	1	2	6	1	.857	0	3	1.55
1990 California	AL	11	0	0	1	7	30	7	6	5	0	1	0	0	6	0	6	0	1	2	0	1.000	0	0	6.43
1991 2 ML Teams	AL	45	0	0	11	32.2	146	37	19	18	4	1	4	2	13	2	20	2	1	1	1	.500	0	0	4.96
1992 St. Louis	NL	71	0	0	16	54	230	52	21	19	6	1	3	2	25	5	24	1	0	2	2	.500	0	0	3.17
1993 Florida	NL	14	0	0	1	6.1	36	12	5	5	2	0	0	0	5	0	6	0	0	1	1	.500	0	0	7.11
1986 Milwaukee	AL	13	0	0	7	16.1	75	18	7	7	2	1	0	1	10	1	11	0	0	2	1	.667	0	0	3.86
Montreal	NL	52	0	0	15	62.2	257	53	22	21	2	3	2	1	23	2	42	1	1	2	5	.286	0	6	3.02

Year Team	Lg	G	GS	CG	GF	IP	BFP	H	R	ER	HR	SH	SF	HB	TBB	IBB	SO	WP	Bk	W	L	Pct.	ShO	Sv	ERA
1988 Montreal	NL	19	0	0	8	19	87	23	13	13	3	3	2	1	6	0	12	0	3	1	3	.250	0	2	6.16
New York	NL	14	0	0	5	11	46	12	5	5	1	0	0	1	2	0	7	1	0	1	0	1.000	0	1	4.09
1991 California	AL	13	0	0	2	9.2	48	13	11	10	3	0	1	1	5	0	5	2	1	0	0	.000	0	0	9.31
St. Louis	NL	32	0	0	9	23	98	24	8	8	1	1	3	1	8	2	15	0	0	1	1	.500	0	0	3.13
19 ML YEARS		698	73	12	233	1158.2	5005	1125	551	490	104	48	51	34	497	39	701	29	30	68	57	.544	1	52	3.81

Ben McDonald

Pitches: Right **Bats:** Right **Pos:** SP   **Ht:** 6' 7" **Wt:** 213 **Born:** 11/24/67 **Age:** 26

Year Team	Lg	G	GS	CG	GF	IP	BFP	H	R	ER	HR	SH	SF	HB	TBB	IBB	SO	WP	Bk	W	L	Pct.	ShO	Sv	ERA
1989 Baltimore	AL	6	0	0	2	7.1	33	8	7	7	2	0	1	0	4	0	3	1	1	1	0	1.000	0	0	8.59
1990 Baltimore	AL	21	15	3	2	118.2	472	88	36	32	9	3	5	0	35	0	65	5	0	8	5	.615	2	0	2.43
1991 Baltimore	AL	21	21	1	0	126.1	532	126	71	68	16	2	3	1	43	2	85	3	0	6	8	.429	0	0	4.84
1992 Baltimore	AL	35	35	4	0	227	958	213	113	107	32	6	6	9	74	5	158	3	2	13	13	.500	2	0	4.24
1993 Baltimore	AL	34	34	7	0	220.1	914	185	92	83	17	7	4	5	86	4	171	7	1	13	14	.481	1	0	3.39
5 ML YEARS		117	105	15	4	699.2	2909	620	319	297	76	18	19	15	242	11	482	19	4	41	40	.506	5	0	3.82

Jack McDowell

Pitches: Right **Bats:** Right **Pos:** SP   **Ht:** 6' 5" **Wt:** 188 **Born:** 01/16/66 **Age:** 28

Year Team	Lg	G	GS	CG	GF	IP	BFP	H	R	ER	HR	SH	SF	HB	TBB	IBB	SO	WP	Bk	W	L	Pct.	ShO	Sv	ERA
1987 Chicago	AL	4	4	0	0	28	103	16	6	6	1	0	0	2	6	0	15	0	0	3	0	1.000	0	0	1.93
1988 Chicago	AL	26	26	1	0	158.2	687	147	85	70	12	6	7	7	68	5	84	11	1	5	10	.333	0	0	3.97
1990 Chicago	AL	33	33	4	0	205	866	189	93	87	20	1	5	7	77	0	165	7	1	14	9	.609	0	0	3.82
1991 Chicago	AL	35	35	15	0	253.2	1028	212	97	96	19	8	4	4	82	2	191	10	1	17	10	.630	3	0	3.41
1992 Chicago	AL	34	34	13	0	260.2	1079	247	95	92	21	8	6	7	75	9	178	6	0	20	10	.667	1	0	3.18
1993 Chicago	AL	34	34	10	0	256.2	1067	261	104	96	20	8	6	3	69	6	158	8	1	22	10	.688	4	0	3.37
6 ML YEARS		166	166	43	0	1162.2	4830	1072	480	447	93	31	28	30	377	22	791	42	4	81	49	.623	8	0	3.46

Roger McDowell

Pitches: Right **Bats:** Right **Pos:** RP   **Ht:** 6' 1" **Wt:** 197 **Born:** 12/21/60 **Age:** 33

Year Team	Lg	G	GS	CG	GF	IP	BFP	H	R	ER	HR	SH	SF	HB	TBB	IBB	SO	WP	Bk	W	L	Pct.	ShO	Sv	ERA
1985 New York	NL	62	2	0	36	127.1	516	108	43	40	9	6	2	1	37	8	70	6	2	6	5	.545	0	17	2.83
1986 New York	NL	75	0	0	52	128	524	107	48	43	4	7	3	3	42	5	65	3	3	14	9	.609	0	22	3.02
1987 New York	NL	56	0	0	45	88.2	384	95	41	41	7	5	5	2	28	4	32	3	1	7	5	.583	0	25	4.16
1988 New York	NL	62	0	0	41	89	378	80	31	26	1	3	5	3	31	7	46	6	1	5	5	.500	0	16	2.63
1989 2 ML Teams		69	0	0	56	92	387	79	36	20	3	6	1	3	38	8	47	3	1	4	8	.333	0	23	1.96
1990 Philadelphia	NL	72	0	0	60	86.1	373	92	41	37	2	10	4	2	35	9	39	1	1	6	8	.429	0	22	3.86
1991 2 ML Teams		71	0	0	34	101.1	445	100	40	33	4	11	3	2	48	20	50	2	0	9	9	.500	0	10	2.93
1992 Los Angeles	NL	65	0	0	39	83.2	393	103	46	38	3	10	3	1	42	13	50	4	1	6	10	.375	0	14	4.09
1993 Los Angeles	NL	54	0	0	19	68	300	76	32	17	2	3	1	2	30	10	27	5	0	5	3	.625	0	2	2.25
1989 New York	NL	25	0	0	15	35.1	156	34	21	13	1	3	1	2	16	3	15	3	1	1	5	.167	0	4	3.31
Philadelphia	NL	44	0	0	41	56.2	231	45	15	7	2	3	0	1	22	5	32	0	0	3	3	.500	0	19	1.11
1991 Los Angeles	NL	38	0	0	16	59	271	61	28	21	1	7	1	2	32	12	28	1	0	3	6	.333	0	3	3.20
Los Angeles	NL	33	0	0	18	42.1	174	39	12	12	3	4	2	0	16	8	22	1	0	6	3	.667	0	7	2.55
9 ML YEARS		586	2	0	382	864.1	3700	840	358	295	35	61	27	19	331	84	426	33	10	62	62	.500	0	151	3.07

Chuck McElroy

Pitches: Left **Bats:** Left **Pos:** RP   **Ht:** 6' 0" **Wt:** 195 **Born:** 10/01/67 **Age:** 26

Year Team	Lg	G	GS	CG	GF	IP	BFP	H	R	ER	HR	SH	SF	HB	TBB	IBB	SO	WP	Bk	W	L	Pct.	ShO	Sv	ERA
1993 Iowa *	AAA	9	0	0	4	15.2	73	19	10	8	1	0	0	0	9	0	13	1	0	0	1	.000	0	2	4.60
1989 Philadelphia	NL	11	0	0	4	10.1	46	12	2	2	1	0	0	0	4	1	9	0	0	0	0	.000	0	0	1.74
1990 Philadelphia	NL	16	0	0	8	14	76	24	13	12	0	0	1	0	10	2	16	0	0	0	1	.000	0	0	7.71
1991 Chicago	NL	71	0	0	12	101.1	419	73	33	22	7	9	6	0	57	7	92	1	0	6	2	.750	0	3	1.95
1992 Chicago	NL	72	0	0	30	83.2	369	73	40	33	5	5	5	0	51	10	83	3	0	4	7	.364	0	6	3.55
1993 Chicago	NL	49	0	0	11	47.1	214	51	30	24	4	5	1	1	25	5	31	3	0	2	2	.500	0	0	4.56
5 ML YEARS		219	0	0	65	256.2	1124	233	118	93	17	19	13	1	147	25	230	7	0	12	12	.500	0	9	3.26

Willie McGee

Bats: Both **Throws:** Right **Pos:** RF   **Ht:** 6' 1" **Wt:** 185 **Born:** 11/02/58 **Age:** 35

Year Team	Lg	G	AB	H	2B	3B	HR	(Hm	Rd)	TB	R	RBI	TBB	IBB	SO	HBP	SH	SF	SB	CS	SB%	GDP	Avg	OBP	SLG
1982 St. Louis	NL	123	422	125	12	8	4	(2	2)	165	43	56	12	2	58	2	2	1	24	12	.67	9	.296	.318	.391
1983 St. Louis	NL	147	601	172	22	8	5	(4	1)	225	75	75	26	2	98	0	1	3	39	8	.83	8	.286	.314	.374
1984 St. Louis	NL	145	571	166	19	11	6	(2	4)	225	82	50	29	2	80	1	0	3	43	10	.81	12	.291	.325	.394
1985 St. Louis	NL	152	612	216	26	18	10	(3	7)	308	114	82	34	2	86	0	1	5	56	16	.78	3	.353	.384	.503

Year	Team	Lg	G	AB	H	2B	3B	HR	(Hm	Rd)	TB	R	RBI	TBB	IBB	SO	HBP	SH	SF	SB	CS	SB%	GDP	Avg	OBP	SLG
1986	St. Louis	NL	124	497	127	22	7	7	(7	0)	184	65	48	37	7	82	1	0	4	19	16	.54	8	.256	.306	.370
1987	St. Louis	NL	153	620	177	37	11	11	(6	5)	269	76	105	24	5	90	2	1	5	16	4	.80	24	.285	.312	.434
1988	St. Louis	NL	137	562	164	24	6	3	(1	2)	209	73	50	32	5	84	1	2	3	41	6	.87	10	.292	.329	.372
1989	St. Louis	NL	58	199	47	10	2	3	(1	2)	70	23	17	10	0	34	1	0	1	8	6	.57	2	.236	.275	.352
1990	2 ML Teams		154	614	199	35	7	3	(1	2)	257	99	77	48	6	104	1	0	2	31	9	.78	13	.324	.373	.419
1991	San Francisco	NL	131	497	155	30	3	4	(2	2)	203	67	43	34	3	74	2	8	2	17	9	.65	11	.312	.357	.408
1992	San Francisco	NL	138	474	141	20	2	1	(0	1)	168	56	36	29	3	88	1	5	1	13	4	.76	7	.297	.339	.354
1993	San Francisco	NL	130	475	143	28	1	4	(0	4)	185	53	46	38	7	67	1	3	2	10	9	.53	12	.301	.353	.389
1990	St. Louis	NL	125	501	168	32	5	3	(1	2)	219	76	62	38	6	86	1	0	2	28	9	.76	9	.335	.382	.437
	Oakland	AL	29	113	31	3	2	0	(0	0)	38	23	15	10	0	18	0	0	0	3	0	1.00	4	.274	.333	.336
12 ML YEARS			1592	6144	1832	285	84	61	(29	32)	2468	826	685	353	44	945	13	23	32	317	109	.74	119	.298	.336	.402

Kevin McGehee

Pitches: Right **Bats:** Right **Pos:** RP **Ht:** 6' 0" **Wt:** 190 **Born:** 01/18/69 **Age:** 25

			HOW MUCH HE PITCHED					WHAT HE GAVE UP											THE RESULTS					
Year	Team	Lg	G	GS	CG	GF	IP	BFP	H	R	ER	HR	SH	SF	HB	TBB	IBB	SO	WP	Bk	W	L	Pct.	ShO	Sv	ERA
1990	Everett	A	15	14	1	0	73.2	333	74	48	39	6	3	2	4	38	0	86	16	5	4	8	.333	0	0	4.76
1991	San Jose	A	26	26	2	0	174	735	129	58	45	1	5	6	8	87	2	171	11	2	13	6	.684	0	0	2.33
1992	Shreveport	AA	25	24	1	0	158.1	654	146	61	52	10	3	7	5	42	0	140	8	1	9	7	.563	0	0	2.96
1993	Phoenix	AAA	4	4	0	0	22	104	28	16	12	1	1	3	5	8	1	16	1	0	0	3	.000	0	0	4.91
	Rochester	AAA	20	20	2	0	133.2	551	124	53	44	14	1	3	7	37	1	92	3	0	7	6	.538	0	0	2.96
1993	Baltimore	AL	5	0	0	1	16.2	75	18	11	11	5	1	1	2	7	2	7	1	0	0	0	.000	0	0	5.94

Fred McGriff

Bats: Left **Throws:** Left **Pos:** 1B **Ht:** 6' 3" **Wt:** 210 **Born:** 10/31/63 **Age:** 30

			BATTING																BASERUNNING				PERCENTAGES		
Year	Team	Lg	G	AB	H	2B	3B	HR	(Hm	Rd)	TB	R	RBI	TBB	IBB	SO	HBP	SH	SF	SB	CS	SB%	GDP	Avg	OBP	SLG
1986	Toronto	AL	3	5	1	0	0	0	(0	0)	1	1	0	0	0	2	0	0	0	0	0	.00	0	.200	.200	.200
1987	Toronto	AL	107	295	73	16	0	20	(7	13)	149	58	43	60	4	104	1	0	0	3	2	.60	3	.247	.376	.505
1988	Toronto	AL	154	536	151	35	4	34	(18	16)	296	100	82	79	3	149	4	0	4	6	1	.86	15	.282	.376	.552
1989	Toronto	AL	161	551	148	27	3	36	(18	18)	289	98	92	119	12	132	4	1	5	7	4	.64	14	.269	.399	.525
1990	Toronto	AL	153	557	167	21	1	35	(14	21)	295	91	88	94	12	108	2	1	4	5	3	.63	7	.300	.400	.530
1991	San Diego	NL	153	528	147	19	1	31	(18	13)	261	84	106	105	26	135	2	0	7	4	1	.80	14	.278	.396	.494
1992	San Diego	NL	152	531	152	30	4	35	(21	14)	295	79	104	96	23	108	1	0	4	8	6	.57	14	.286	.394	.556
1993	2 ML Teams		151	557	162	29	2	37	(15	22)	306	111	101	76	6	106	2	0	5	5	3	.63	14	.291	.375	.549
1993	San Diego	NL	83	302	83	11	1	18	(7	11)	150	52	46	42	4	55	1	0	4	4	3	.57	9	.275	.361	.497
	Atlanta	NL	68	255	79	18	1	19	(8	11)	156	59	55	34	2	51	1	0	1	1	0	1.00	5	.310	.392	.612
8 ML YEARS			1034	3560	1001	177	15	228	(111	117)	1892	622	616	629	86	844	16	2	29	38	20	.66	81	.281	.389	.531

Terry McGriff

Bats: Right **Throws:** Right **Pos:** C **Ht:** 6' 2" **Wt:** 195 **Born:** 09/23/63 **Age:** 30

			BATTING																BASERUNNING				PERCENTAGES		
Year	Team	Lg	G	AB	H	2B	3B	HR	(Hm	Rd)	TB	R	RBI	TBB	IBB	SO	HBP	SH	SF	SB	CS	SB%	GDP	Avg	OBP	SLG
1993	Edmonton *	AAA	105	339	117	29	2	7	(--	--)	171	62	55	49	2	29	1	0	3	2	1	.67	10	.345	.426	.504
1987	Cincinnati	NL	34	89	20	3	0	2	(1	1)	29	6	11	8	0	17	0	0	0	0	0	.00	3	.225	.289	.326
1988	Cincinnati	NL	35	96	19	3	0	1	(1	0)	25	9	4	12	0	31	0	0	0	1	0	1.00	4	.198	.284	.260
1989	Cincinnati	NL	6	11	3	0	0	0	(0	0)	3	1	2	2	1	3	0	0	0	0	0	.00	0	.273	.385	.273
1990	2 ML Teams		6	9	0	0	0	0	(0	0)	0	0	0	0	0	1	0	0	0	0	0	.00	0	.000	.000	.000
1993	Florida	NL	3	7	0	0	0	0	(0	0)	0	0	0	1	0	2	0	0	0	0	0			.000	.125	.000
1990	Cincinnati	NL	2	4	0	0	0	0	(0	0)	0	0	0	0	0	1	0	0	0	0	0	.00	0	.000	.000	.000
	Houston	NL	4	5	0	0	0	0	(0	0)	0	0	0	0	0	0	0	0	0	0	0	.00	0	.000	.000	.000
5 ML YEARS			84	212	42	6	0	3	(2	1)	57	16	17	23	1	54	0	0	1	1	0	1.00	6	.198	.275	.269

Mark McGwire

Bats: Right **Throws:** Right **Pos:** 1B **Ht:** 6' 5" **Wt:** 225 **Born:** 10/01/63 **Age:** 30

			BATTING																BASERUNNING				PERCENTAGES		
Year	Team	Lg	G	AB	H	2B	3B	HR	(Hm	Rd)	TB	R	RBI	TBB	IBB	SO	HBP	SH	SF	SB	CS	SB%	GDP	Avg	OBP	SLG
1986	Oakland	AL	18	53	10	1	0	3	(1	2)	20	10	9	4	0	18	1	0	0	0	1	.00	0	.189	.259	.377
1987	Oakland	AL	151	557	161	28	4	49	(21	28)	344	97	118	71	8	131	5	0	8	1	1	.50	6	.289	.370	.618
1988	Oakland	AL	155	550	143	22	1	32	(12	20)	263	87	99	76	4	117	4	1	4	0	0	.00	15	.260	.352	.478
1989	Oakland	AL	143	490	113	17	0	33	(12	21)	229	74	95	83	5	94	3	0	11	1	1	.50	23	.231	.339	.467
1990	Oakland	AL	156	523	123	16	0	39	(14	25)	256	87	108	110	9	116	7	1	9	2	1	.67	13	.235	.370	.489
1991	Oakland	AL	154	483	97	22	0	22	(15	7)	185	62	75	93	3	116	3	1	5	2	1	.67	13	.201	.330	.383
1992	Oakland	AL	139	467	125	22	0	42	(24	18)	273	87	104	90	12	105	5	0	9	0	0	.00	11	.268	.385	.585
1993	Oakland	AL	27	84	28	6	0	9	(5	4)	61	16	24	21	1	19	1	0	1	0	0	.00	0	.333	.467	.726
8 ML YEARS			943	3207	800	134	5	229	(104	125)	1631	520	632	548	46	716	29	3	47	6	7	.46	80	.249	.359	.509

Tim McIntosh

Bats: Right **Throws:** Right **Pos:** C   **Ht:** 5'11" **Wt:** 195 **Born:** 03/21/65 **Age:** 29

Year Team	Lg	G	AB	H	2B	3B	HR	Hm	Rd	TB	R	RBI	TBB	IBB	SO	HBP	SH	SF	SB	CS	SB%	GDP	Avg	OBP	SLG
1993 Ottawa *	AAA	27	106	31	7	1	6	--	--	58	15	21	10	2	22	0	0	2	1	0	1.00	3	.292	.347	.547
1990 Milwaukee	AL	5	5	1	0	0	1	1	0	4	1	1	0	0	2	0	0	0	0	0	.00	0	.200	.200	.800
1991 Milwaukee	AL	7	11	4	1	0	1	1	0	8	2	1	0	0	4	0	0	0	0	0	.00	0	.364	.364	.727
1992 Milwaukee	AL	35	77	14	3	0	0	0	0	17	7	6	3	0	9	2	1	1	1	3	.25	0	.182	.229	.221
1993 2 ML Teams		21	21	2	1	0	0	0	0	3	2	2	0	0	7	0	0	0	0	0	.00	0	.095	.095	.143
1993 Milwaukee	AL	1	0	0	0	0	0	0	0	0	0	0	0	0	0	0	0	0	0	0	.00	0	.000	.000	.000
Montreal	NL	20	21	2	1	0	0	0	0	3	2	2	0	0	7	0	0	0	0	0	.00	0	.095	.095	.143
4 ML YEARS		68	114	21	5	0	2	2	0	32	12	10	3	0	22	2	1	1	1	3	.25	1	.184	.217	.281

Jeff McKnight

Bats: Both **Throws:** Right **Pos:** SS/2B   **Ht:** 6'0" **Wt:** 180 **Born:** 02/18/63 **Age:** 31

Year Team	Lg	G	AB	H	2B	3B	HR	Hm	Rd	TB	R	RBI	TBB	IBB	SO	HBP	SH	SF	SB	CS	SB%	GDP	Avg	OBP	SLG
1989 New York	NL	6	12	3	0	0	0	0	0	3	2	0	2	0	1	0	0	0	0	0	.00	1	.250	.357	.250
1990 Baltimore	AL	29	75	15	2	0	1	1	0	20	11	4	5	0	17	1	3	0	0	0	.00	0	.200	.259	.267
1991 Baltimore	AL	16	41	7	1	0	0	0	0	8	2	2	2	0	7	0	0	0	1	0	1.00	2	.171	.209	.195
1992 New York	NL	31	85	23	3	1	2	1	1	34	10	13	2	0	8	0	0	0	0	1	.00	2	.271	.287	.400
1993 New York	NL	105	164	42	3	1	2	2	0	53	19	13	13	0	31	1	3	2	0	0	.00	3	.256	.311	.323
5 ML YEARS		187	377	90	9	2	5	4	1	118	44	32	24	0	64	2	6	2	1	1	.50	8	.239	.286	.313

Mark McLemore

Bats: Both **Throws:** Right **Pos:** RF/2B   **Ht:** 5'11" **Wt:** 195 **Born:** 10/04/64 **Age:** 29

Year Team	Lg	G	AB	H	2B	3B	HR	Hm	Rd	TB	R	RBI	TBB	IBB	SO	HBP	SH	SF	SB	CS	SB%	GDP	Avg	OBP	SLG
1986 California	AL	5	4	0	0	0	0	0	0	0	0	0	1	0	2	0	1	0	0	1	.00	0	.000	.200	.000
1987 California	AL	138	433	102	13	3	3	3	0	130	61	41	48	0	72	0	15	3	25	8	.76	3	.236	.310	.300
1988 California	AL	77	233	56	11	2	2	1	1	77	38	16	25	0	28	0	5	2	13	7	.65	6	.240	.312	.330
1989 California	AL	32	103	25	3	1	0	0	0	30	12	14	7	0	19	1	3	1	6	1	.86	2	.243	.295	.291
1990 2 ML Teams		28	60	9	2	0	0	0	0	11	6	2	4	0	15	0	1	0	1	0	1.00	1	.150	.203	.183
1991 Houston	NL	21	61	9	1	0	0	0	0	10	6	2	6	0	13	0	0	1	0	1	.00	1	.148	.221	.164
1992 Baltimore	AL	101	228	56	7	2	0	0	0	67	40	27	21	1	26	0	6	1	11	5	.69	6	.246	.308	.294
1993 Baltimore	AL	148	581	165	27	5	4	2	2	214	81	72	64	4	92	1	11	6	21	15	.58	21	.284	.353	.368
1990 California	AL	20	48	7	2	0	0	0	0	9	4	2	4	0	9	0	1	0	1	0	1.00	1	.146	.212	.188
Cleveland	AL	8	12	2	0	0	0	0	0	2	2	0	0	0	6	0	0	0	0	0	.00	0	.167	.167	.167
8 ML YEARS		550	1703	422	64	13	9	6	3	539	244	174	176	5	267	2	42	14	77	38	.67	44	.248	.317	.317

Greg McMichael

Pitches: Right **Bats:** Right **Pos:** RP   **Ht:** 6'3" **Wt:** 195 **Born:** 12/01/66 **Age:** 27

		HOW MUCH HE PITCHED						WHAT HE GAVE UP												THE RESULTS					
Year Team	Lg	G	GS	CG	GF	IP	BFP	H	R	ER	HR	SH	SF	HB	TBB	IBB	SO	WP	Bk	W	L	Pct.	ShO	Sv	ERA
1988 Burlington	R	3	3	1	0	21	86	17	9	6	0	0	0	0	4	0	20	1	1	2	0	1.000	1	0	2.57
Kinston	A	11	11	2	0	77.1	307	57	31	23	3	3	6	3	18	1	35	4	1	4	2	.667	0	0	2.68
1989 Canton-Akrn	AA	26	26	8	0	170	704	164	81	66	10	3	5	6	64	1	101	9	1	11	11	.500	5	0	3.49
1990 Canton-Akrn	AA	13	4	0	4	40.1	172	39	17	15	3	2	2	1	17	1	19	3	0	2	3	.400	0	0	3.35
Colo Sprngs	AAA	12	12	1	0	59	279	72	45	38	5	2	4	0	30	0	34	6	0	2	3	.400	1	0	5.80
1991 Durham	A	36	6	0	13	79.2	350	83	34	32	3	6	2	3	29	6	82	6	2	5	6	.455	0	2	3.62
1992 Greenville	AA	15	4	0	4	46.1	186	37	14	7	2	1	2	0	13	2	53	2	0	4	2	.667	0	1	1.36
Richmond	AAA	19	13	0	2	90.1	382	89	52	44	5	6	2	1	34	3	86	1	1	6	5	.545	2	1	4.38
1993 Atlanta	NL	74	0	0	40	91.2	365	68	22	21	3	4	2	0	29	4	89	6	1	2	3	.400	0	19	2.06

Jim McNamara

Bats: Left **Throws:** Right **Pos:** C   **Ht:** 6'4" **Wt:** 210 **Born:** 06/10/65 **Age:** 29

Year Team	Lg	G	AB	H	2B	3B	HR	Hm	Rd	TB	R	RBI	TBB	IBB	SO	HBP	SH	SF	SB	CS	SB%	GDP	Avg	OBP	SLG
1986 Everett	A	46	158	39	1	2	8	--	--	68	23	30	18	2	39	3	0	2	0	0	.00	3	.247	.331	.430
1987 Clinton	A	110	385	95	22	1	5	--	--	134	43	53	19	1	52	0	2	7	4	2	.67	15	.247	.277	.348
1988 San Jose	A	93	315	59	9	0	1	--	--	71	27	41	43	1	76	2	0	2	3	4	.43	18	.187	.287	.225
1989 Salinas	A	49	155	37	8	0	0	--	--	45	9	10	22	2	24	1	0	3	3	1	.75	3	.239	.333	.290
Phoenix	AAA	27	69	12	3	0	0	--	--	15	3	4	4	0	13	0	2	0	1	2	.33	2	.174	.219	.217
San Jose	A	19	65	18	2	0	1	--	--	23	2	8	1	0	13	0	1	0	0	1	.00	3	.277	.284	.354
1990 San Jose	A	53	158	32	2	2	1	--	--	41	20	22	18	0	30	1	1	1	0	4	.00	3	.203	.287	.259
Phoenix	AAA	6	20	9	0	0	0	--	--	9	2	1	3	0	4	0	0	0	0	0	.00	0	.450	.522	.450
Shreveport	AA	28	79	19	1	0	0	--	--	26	2	13	7	0	9	0	0	0	0	1	.00	7	.241	.302	.329
1991 Phoenix	AAA	17	53	9	1	0	0	--	--	10	3	2	6	0	12	0	0	0	0	0	.00	3	.170	.254	.189

Year Team	Lg	G	AB	H	2B	3B	HR	(Hm	Rd)	TB	R	RBI	TBB	IBB	SO	HBP	SH	SF	SB	CS	SB%	GDP	Avg	OBP	SLG
Shreveport	AA	39	109	30	8	2	2	--	--	48	13	20	21	3	11	0	1	1	2	1	.67	2	.275	.389	.440
1992 Phoenix	AAA	23	67	14	3	0	0	--	--	17	5	3	14	3	13	0	0	0	0	0	.00	5	.209	.346	.254
1993 Phoenix	AAA	50	158	31	5	0	1	--	--	39	10	23	12	1	29	0	1	2	1	0	1.00	8	.196	.250	.247
1992 San Francisco	NL	30	74	16	1	0	1	(1	0)	20	6	9	6	2	25	0	0	2	0	0	.00	1	.216	.275	.270
1993 San Francisco	NL	4	7	1	0	0	0	(0	0)	1	0	1	0	0	1	0	0	0	0	0	.00		.143	.143	.143
2 ML YEARS		34	81	17	1	0	1	(1	0)	21	6	10	6	2	26	0	0	2	0	0	.00	1	.210	.264	.259

Jeff McNeely

Bats: Right **Throws:** Right **Pos:** CF   **Ht:** 6' 2" **Wt:** 190 **Born:** 10/18/69 **Age:** 24

							BATTING												BASERUNNING				PERCENTAGES		
Year Team	Lg	G	AB	H	2B	3B	HR	(Hm	Rd)	TB	R	RBI	TBB	IBB	SO	HBP	SH	SF	SB	CS	SB%	GDP	Avg	OBP	SLG
1989 Red Sox	R	9	32	13	1	1	0	--	--	16	10	4	7	0	3	0	0	1	5	1	.83	1	.406	.500	.500
Elmira	A	61	208	52	7	0	2	--	--	65	20	21	26	0	54	4	1	0	16	8	.67	4	.250	.345	.313
1990 Winter Havn	A	16	62	10	0	0	0	--	--	10	4	3	3	0	19	0	0	0	7	1	.88	1	.161	.200	.161
Elmira	A	73	246	77	4	5	6	--	--	109	41	37	40	5	60	3	8	2	39	10	.80	7	.313	.412	.443
1991 Lynchburg	A	106	382	123	16	5	4	--	--	161	58	38	74	3	74	4	4	1	38	21	.64	5	.322	.436	.421
1992 New Britain	AA	85	261	57	8	4	2	--	--	79	30	11	26	0	78	2	4	0	10	5	.67	10	.218	.294	.303
1993 Pawtucket	AAA	129	498	130	14	3	2	--	--	156	65	35	43	1	102	3	10	2	40	7	.85	4	.261	.322	.313
1993 Boston	AL	21	37	11	1	1	0	(0	0)	14	10	1	7	0	9	0	0	0	6	0	1.00	0	.297	.409	.378

Brian McRae

Bats: Both **Throws:** Right **Pos:** CF   **Ht:** 6' 0" **Wt:** 185 **Born:** 08/27/67 **Age:** 26

							BATTING												BASERUNNING				PERCENTAGES		
Year Team	Lg	G	AB	H	2B	3B	HR	(Hm	Rd)	TB	R	RBI	TBB	IBB	SO	HBP	SH	SF	SB	CS	SB%	GDP	Avg	OBP	SLG
1990 Kansas City	AL	46	168	48	8	3	2	(1	1)	68	21	23	9	0	29	0	3	2	4	3	.57	5	.286	.318	.405
1991 Kansas City	AL	152	629	164	28	9	8	(3	5)	234	86	64	24	1	99	2	3	5	20	11	.65	12	.261	.288	.372
1992 Kansas City	AL	149	533	119	23	5	4	(2	2)	164	63	52	42	1	88	6	7	4	18	5	.78	10	.223	.285	.308
1993 Kansas City	AL	153	627	177	28	9	12	(5	7)	259	78	69	37	1	105	4	14	3	23	14	.62	8	.282	.325	.413
4 ML YEARS		500	1957	508	87	26	26	(11	15)	725	248	208	112	3	321	12	27	14	65	33	.66	35	.260	.302	.370

Kevin McReynolds

Bats: Right **Throws:** Right **Pos:** LF   **Ht:** 6' 1" **Wt:** 225 **Born:** 10/16/59 **Age:** 34

							BATTING												BASERUNNING				PERCENTAGES		
Year Team	Lg	G	AB	H	2B	3B	HR	(Hm	Rd)	TB	R	RBI	TBB	IBB	SO	HBP	SH	SF	SB	CS	SB%	GDP	Avg	OBP	SLG
1983 San Diego	NL	39	140	31	3	1	4	(3	1)	48	15	14	12	1	29	0	0	3	2	1	.67	1	.221	.277	.343
1984 San Diego	NL	147	525	146	26	6	20	(10	10)	244	68	75	34	8	69	0	3	9	3	6	.33	14	.278	.317	.465
1985 San Diego	NL	152	564	132	24	4	15	(6	9)	209	61	75	43	6	81	3	2	4	4	0	1.00	17	.234	.290	.371
1986 San Diego	NL	158	560	161	31	6	26	(14	12)	282	89	96	66	6	83	1	5	9	8	6	.57	9	.288	.358	.504
1987 New York	NL	151	590	163	32	5	29	(18	11)	292	86	95	39	5	70	1	1	8	14	1	.93	13	.276	.318	.495
1988 New York	NL	147	552	159	30	2	27	(13	14)	274	82	99	38	3	56	4	1	5	21	0	1.00	6	.288	.336	.496
1989 New York	NL	148	545	148	25	3	22	(12	10)	245	74	85	46	10	74	1	0	7	15	7	.68	8	.272	.326	.450
1990 New York	NL	147	521	140	23	1	24	(11	13)	237	75	82	71	11	61	1	0	8	9	2	.82	8	.269	.353	.455
1991 New York	NL	143	522	135	32	1	16	(7	9)	217	65	74	49	7	46	2	1	4	6	6	.50	8	.259	.322	.416
1992 Kansas City	AL	109	373	92	25	0	13	(4	9)	156	45	49	67	3	48	0	0	5	7	1	.88	6	.247	.357	.418
1993 Kansas City	AL	110	351	86	22	4	11	(8	3)	149	44	42	37	6	56	1	1	3	2	2	.50	8	.245	.316	.425
11 ML YEARS		1451	5243	1393	273	33	207	(106	101)	2353	704	786	502	66	673	14	14	65	91	32	.74	98	.266	.328	.449

Rusty Meacham

Pitches: Right **Bats:** Right **Pos:** RP   **Ht:** 6' 2" **Wt:** 175 **Born:** 01/27/68 **Age:** 26

		HOW MUCH HE PITCHED						WHAT HE GAVE UP										THE RESULTS					
Year Team	Lg	G	GS	CG	GF	IP	BFP	H	R	ER	HR	SH	SF	HB	TBB	IBB	SO	WP	Bk	W	L	Pct.	ShO	Sv	ERA
1993 Omaha *	AAA	7	0	0	2	9.1	37	10	5	5	1	0	0	0	1	0	10	0	0	0	0	.000	0	0	4.82
1991 Detroit	AL	10	4	0	1	27.2	126	35	17	16	4	1	3	0	11	0	14	0	1	2	1	.667	0	0	5.20
1992 Kansas City	AL	64	0	0	20	101.2	412	88	39	31	5	3	9	1	21	5	64	4	0	10	4	.714	0	2	2.74
1993 Kansas City	AL	15	0	0	11	21	104	31	15	13	2	0	1	3	5	1	13	0	0	2	2	.500	0	0	5.57
3 ML YEARS		89	4	0	32	150.1	642	154	71	60	11	4	13	4	37	6	91	4	1	14	7	.667	0	2	3.59

Pat Meares

Bats: Right **Throws:** Right **Pos:** SS   **Ht:** 5'11" **Wt:** 180 **Born:** 09/06/68 **Age:** 25

							BATTING												BASERUNNING				PERCENTAGES		
Year Team	Lg	G	AB	H	2B	3B	HR	(Hm	Rd)	TB	R	RBI	TBB	IBB	SO	HBP	SH	SF	SB	CS	SB%	GDP	Avg	OBP	SLG
1990 Kenosha	A	52	197	47	10	2	4	--	--	73	26	22	25	2	45	4	2	1	2	1	.67	1	.239	.335	.371
1991 Visalia	A	89	360	109	21	4	6	--	--	156	53	44	24	0	63	5	0	4	15	5	.75	11	.303	.351	.433
1992 Orlando	AA	81	300	76	19	0	3	--	--	104	42	23	11	1	57	7	0	2	5	5	.50	6	.253	.294	.347

143

Year Team	Lg	G	AB	H	2B	3B	HR	(Hm	Rd)	TB	R	RBI	TBB	IBB	SO	HBP	SH	SF	SB	CS	SB%	GDP	Avg	OBP	SLG
1993 Portland	AAA	18	54	16	5	0	0	--	--	21	6	3	3	0	11	1	2	0	0	0	.00	0	.296	.345	.389
1993 Minnesota	AL	111	346	87	14	3	0	(0	0)	107	33	33	7	0	52	1	4	3	4	5	.44	11	.251	.266	.309

Roberto Mejia

Bats: Right Throws: Right Pos: 2B   **Ht: 5'11" Wt: 160 Born: 04/14/72 Age: 22**

Year Team	Lg	G	AB	H	2B	3B	HR	(Hm	Rd)	TB	R	RBI	TBB	IBB	SO	HBP	SH	SF	SB	CS	SB%	GDP	Avg	OBP	SLG
1991 Great Falls	R	23	84	22	6	2	2	--	--	38	17	14	7	0	22	1	0	1	3	1	.75	0	.262	.323	.452
1992 Vero Beach	A	96	330	82	17	1	12	--	--	137	42	40	37	0	60	2	0	5	14	10	.58	6	.248	.324	.415
1993 Colo Sprngs	AAA	77	291	87	15	2	14	--	--	148	51	48	18	0	56	1	0	3	12	5	.71	6	.299	.339	.509
1993 Colorado	NL	65	229	53	14	5	5	(3	2)	92	31	20	13	1	63	1	4	1	4	1	.80	2	.231	.275	.402

Jose Melendez

Pitches: Right Bats: Right Pos: RP   **Ht: 6' 2" Wt: 175 Born: 09/02/65 Age: 28**

Year Team	Lg	G	GS	CG	GF	IP	BFP	H	R	ER	HR	SH	SF	HB	TBB	IBB	SO	WP	Bk	W	L	Pct.	ShO	Sv	ERA
1993 Pawtucket *	AAA	19	0	0	10	35	156	37	24	21	7	2	2	2	7	0	31	2	0	2	3	.400	0	2	5.40
1990 Seattle	AL	3	0	0	1	5.1	28	8	8	7	2	0	0	1	3	0	7	1	0	0	0	.000	0	0	11.81
1991 San Diego	NL	31	9	0	10	93.2	381	77	35	34	11	2	6	1	24	3	60	3	2	6	5	.615	0	3	3.27
1992 San Diego	NL	56	3	0	18	89.1	363	82	32	29	9	7	4	3	20	7	82	1	1	6	7	.462	0	0	2.92
1993 Boston	AL	9	0	0	5	16	63	10	4	4	2	0	2	0	5	3	14	0	0	2	1	.667	0	0	2.25
4 ML YEARS		99	12	0	34	204.1	835	177	79	74	24	9	12	5	52	13	163	5	3	16	13	.552	0	3	3.26

Bob Melvin

Bats: Right Throws: Right Pos: C   **Ht: 6' 4" Wt: 205 Born: 10/28/61 Age: 32**

Year Team	Lg	G	AB	H	2B	3B	HR	(Hm	Rd)	TB	R	RBI	TBB	IBB	SO	HBP	SH	SF	SB	CS	SB%	GDP	Avg	OBP	SLG
1985 Detroit	AL	41	82	18	4	1	0	(0	0)	24	10	4	3	0	21	0	2	0	0	0	.00	1	.220	.247	.293
1986 San Francisco	NL	89	268	60	14	2	5	(2	3)	93	24	25	15	1	69	0	3	3	3	2	.60	7	.224	.262	.347
1987 San Francisco	NL	84	246	49	8	0	11	(6	5)	90	31	31	17	3	44	0	0	2	0	4	.00	7	.199	.249	.366
1988 San Francisco	NL	92	273	64	13	1	8	(4	4)	103	23	27	13	0	46	0	1	1	0	2	.00	5	.234	.268	.377
1989 Baltimore	AL	85	278	67	10	1	1	(0	1)	82	22	32	15	3	53	0	7	1	1	4	.20	10	.241	.279	.295
1990 Baltimore	AL	93	301	73	14	1	5	(3	2)	104	30	37	11	1	53	0	3	3	0	1	.00	8	.243	.267	.346
1991 Baltimore	AL	79	228	57	10	0	1	(0	1)	70	11	23	11	2	46	0	1	5	0	0	.00	5	.250	.279	.307
1992 Kansas City	AL	32	70	22	5	0	0	(0	0)	27	5	6	5	0	13	0	0	2	0	0	.00	3	.314	.351	.386
1993 Boston	AL	77	176	39	7	0	3	(1	2)	55	13	23	7	0	44	1	3	0	0	0	.00	2	.222	.251	.313
9 ML YEARS		672	1922	449	85	6	34	(16	18)	648	169	208	97	10	389	1	20	20	4	13	.24	48	.234	.268	.337

Tony Menendez

Pitches: Right Bats: Right Pos: RP   **Ht: 6' 2" Wt: 189 Born: 02/20/65 Age: 29**

Year Team	Lg	G	GS	CG	GF	IP	BFP	H	R	ER	HR	SH	SF	HB	TBB	IBB	SO	WP	Bk	W	L	Pct.	ShO	Sv	ERA
1984 White Sox	R	6	6	0	0	37	148	26	19	13	2	0	1	0	13	0	30	2	0	3	2	.600	0	0	3.16
1985 Buffalo	AAA	1	1	0	0	2.1	15	9	5	5	0	0	0	0	1	1	2	0	0	0	1	.000	0	0	19.29
Appleton	A	24	24	2	0	148	620	134	67	45	8	6	3	4	55	0	100	11	1	13	4	.765	0	0	2.74
1986 Peninsula	A	11	10	1	1	63	279	58	35	32	9	1	6	4	29	0	43	6	0	4	4	.500	1	0	4.57
Birmingham	AA	17	17	0	0	96.1	470	132	71	61	17	0	3	7	50	0	52	14	0	7	8	.467	0	0	5.70
1987 Birmingham	AA	27	27	4	0	173.1	776	193	111	93	19	3	7	7	76	1	102	12	2	10	10	.500	1	0	4.83
1988 Birmingham	AA	24	24	3	0	153	642	131	79	67	14	4	8	2	64	0	112	6	4	6	11	.353	0	0	3.94
1989 Birmingham	AA	27	18	2	6	144	596	123	61	51	14	5	1	4	53	2	115	7	2	10	4	.714	1	1	3.19
1990 Vancouver	AAA	24	9	2	2	72.2	307	63	34	30	6	3	5	6	28	1	48	1	0	2	5	.286	1	0	3.72
1991 Tulsa	AA	3	2	0	1	14	54	9	2	2	0	0	0	0	4	0	14	0	1	3	0	1.000	0	0	1.29
Okla City	AAA	21	19	0	1	116	504	107	70	67	6	5	8	6	62	3	82	8	1	5	5	.500	0	0	5.20
1992 Nashville	AAA	50	2	0	11	106.2	458	98	53	48	10	8	5	3	47	6	92	3	0	3	5	.375	0	1	4.05
1993 Buffalo	AAA	54	0	0	39	63.1	255	50	20	17	5	1	3	3	21	2	48	5	0	4	5	.444	0	24	2.42
1992 Cincinnati	NL	3	0	0	1	4.2	15	1	1	1	1	0	0	0	0	0	5	0	0	1	0	1.000	0	0	1.93
1993 Pittsburgh	NL	14	0	0	3	21	85	20	8	7	4	1	1	1	4	0	13	0	0	2	0	1.000	0	0	3.00
2 ML YEARS		17	0	0	4	25.2	100	21	9	8	5	1	1	1	4	0	18	0	0	3	0	1.000	0	0	2.81

Orlando Merced

Bats: Left Throws: Right Pos: RF/1B   **Ht: 5'11" Wt: 170 Born: 11/02/66 Age: 27**

Year Team	Lg	G	AB	H	2B	3B	HR	(Hm	Rd)	TB	R	RBI	TBB	IBB	SO	HBP	SH	SF	SB	CS	SB%	GDP	Avg	OBP	SLG
1990 Pittsburgh	NL	25	24	5	1	0	0	(0	0)	6	3	0	1	0	9	0	0	0	0	0	.00	1	.208	.240	.250
1991 Pittsburgh	NL	120	411	113	17	2	10	(5	5)	164	83	50	64	4	81	1	1	1	8	4	.67	6	.275	.373	.399

144

Year	Team	Lg	G	AB	H	2B	3B	HR	(Hm	Rd)	TB	R	RBI	TBB	IBB	SO	HBP	SH	SF	SB	CS	SB%	GDP	Avg	OBP	SLG
1992	Pittsburgh	NL	134	405	100	28	5	6	(4	2)	156	50	60	52	8	63	2	1	5	5	4	.56	6	.247	.332	.385
1993	Pittsburgh	NL	137	447	140	26	4	8	(3	5)	198	68	70	77	10	64	1	0	2	3	3	.50	9	.313	.414	.443
4 ML YEARS			416	1287	358	72	11	24	(12	12)	524	204	180	194	22	217	4	2	8	16	11	.59	22	.278	.372	.407

Henry Mercedes

Bats: Right **Throws:** Right **Pos:** C   **Ht:** 5'11" **Wt:** 185 **Born:** 07/23/69 **Age:** 24

									BATTING											BASERUNNING				PERCENTAGES		
Year	Team	Lg	G	AB	H	2B	3B	HR	(Hm	Rd)	TB	R	RBI	TBB	IBB	SO	HBP	SH	SF	SB	CS	SB%	GDP	Avg	OBP	SLG
1988	Athletics	R	2	5	2	0	0	0	--	--	2	1	0	0	0	0	0	0	0	0	0	.00	0	.400	.400	.400
1989	Madison	A	51	152	32	3	0	2	--	--	41	11	13	22	1	46	1	3	0	0	0	.00	1	.211	.314	.270
	Modesto	A	16	37	3	0	0	1	--	--	6	6	3	7	0	22	0	0	0	0	0	.00	2	.081	.227	.162
	Sou Oregon	A	22	61	10	0	1	0	--	--	12	6	1	10	0	24	1	0	0	2	0	.00	0	.164	.292	.197
1990	Tacoma	AAA	12	31	6	1	0	0	--	--	7	3	2	3	0	7	0	2	0	0	1	.00	2	.194	.265	.226
	Madison	A	90	282	64	13	2	3	--	--	90	29	38	30	0	100	1	6	2	6	0	1.00	5	.227	.302	.319
1991	Modesto	A	116	388	100	17	3	4	--	--	135	55	61	68	1	110	2	3	3	5	8	.38	6	.258	.369	.348
1992	Tacoma	AAA	85	246	57	9	2	0	--	--	70	36	20	26	0	60	0	4	0	1	3	.25	8	.232	.305	.285
1993	Tacoma	AAA	85	256	61	13	1	4	--	--	88	37	32	31	2	53	1	3	7	1	2	.33	7	.238	.315	.344
1992	Oakland	AL	9	5	4	0	1	0	(0	0)	6	1	1	0	0	1	0	0	0	0	0	.00	0	.800	.800	1.200
1993	Oakland	AL	20	47	10	2	0	0	(0	0)	12	5	3	2	0	15	1	0	0	1	1	.50	0	.213	.260	.255
2 ML YEARS			29	52	14	2	1	0	(0	0)	18	6	4	2	0	16	1	0	0	1	1	.50	0	.269	.309	.346

Luis Mercedes

Bats: Right **Throws:** Right **Pos:** RF   **Ht:** 6' 3" **Wt:** 193 **Born:** 02/20/68 **Age:** 26

									BATTING											BASERUNNING				PERCENTAGES		
Year	Team	Lg	G	AB	H	2B	3B	HR	(Hm	Rd)	TB	R	RBI	TBB	IBB	SO	HBP	SH	SF	SB	CS	SB%	GDP	Avg	OBP	SLG
1988	Bluefield	R	59	215	59	8	4	0	--	--	75	36	20	32	0	39	2	3	1	16	11	.59	6	.274	.372	.349
1989	Frederick	A	108	502	155	12	5	3	--	--	155	62	36	30	2	62	3	2	2	29	11	.73	7	.309	.360	.387
1990	Hagerstown	AA	108	416	139	12	4	3	--	--	168	71	37	34	2	70	6	6	2	38	14	.73	13	.334	.391	.404
1991	Rochester	AAA	102	374	125	14	5	2	--	--	155	68	36	65	0	63	5	6	4	23	14	.62	10	.334	.435	.414
1992	Rochester	AAA	103	409	128	15	1	3	--	--	154	62	29	44	2	56	1	3	3	35	14	.71	11	.313	.379	.377
1993	Phoenix	AAA	70	244	71	5	3	0	--	--	82	28	15	36	0	30	4	1	1	14	6	.70	5	.291	.389	.336
1991	Baltimore	AL	19	54	11	2	0	0	(0	0)	13	10	2	4	0	9	0	1	0	0	0	.00	1	.204	.259	.241
1992	Baltimore	AL	23	50	7	2	0	0	(0	0)	9	7	4	8	0	9	1	2	1	0	1	.00	2	.140	.267	.180
1993	2 ML Teams		28	49	11	2	1	0	(0	0)	15	2	3	6	0	7	2	2	0	1	2	.33	1	.224	.333	.306
1993	Baltimore	AL	10	24	7	2	0	0	(0	0)	9	1	0	5	0	4	0	1	0	1	1	.50	1	.292	.414	.375
	San Francisco	NL	18	25	4	0	1	0	(0	0)	6	1	3	1	0	3	2	1	0	0	1	.00	0	.160	.250	.240
3 ML YEARS			70	153	29	6	1	0	(0	0)	37	19	9	18	0	25	3	5	1	3	3	.25	4	.190	.286	.242

Kent Mercker

Pitches: Left **Bats:** Left **Pos:** RP/SP   **Ht:** 6' 2" **Wt:** 195 **Born:** 02/01/68 **Age:** 26

				HOW MUCH HE PITCHED						WHAT HE GAVE UP									THE RESULTS					
Year	Team	Lg	G	GS	CG	GF	IP	BFP	H	R	ER	HR	SH	SF	HB	TBB	IBB	SO	WP	Bk	W	L	Pct.	ShO	Sv	ERA
1989	Atlanta	NL	2	1	0	1	4.1	26	8	6	6	0	0	0	0	6	0	4	0	0	0	0	.000	0	0	12.46
1990	Atlanta	NL	36	0	0	28	48.1	211	43	22	17	6	1	2	2	24	3	39	2	0	4	7	.364	0	7	3.17
1991	Atlanta	NL	50	4	0	28	73.1	306	56	23	21	5	2	2	1	35	3	62	4	1	5	3	.625	0	6	2.58
1992	Atlanta	NL	53	0	0	18	68.1	289	51	27	26	4	4	1	3	35	1	49	6	0	3	2	.600	0	6	3.42
1993	Atlanta	NL	43	6	0	9	66	283	52	24	21	2	0	0	2	36	3	59	5	1	3	1	.750	0	0	2.86
5 ML YEARS			184	11	0	84	260.1	1115	210	102	91	17	7	5	8	136	10	213	17	2	15	13	.536	0	19	3.15

Brett Merriman

Pitches: Right **Bats:** Right **Pos:** RP   **Ht:** 6' 2" **Wt:** 180 **Born:** 07/15/66 **Age:** 27

				HOW MUCH HE PITCHED						WHAT HE GAVE UP									THE RESULTS					
Year	Team	Lg	G	GS	CG	GF	IP	BFP	H	R	ER	HR	SH	SF	HB	TBB	IBB	SO	WP	Bk	W	L	Pct.	ShO	Sv	ERA
1988	Burlington	R	8	8	0	0	45.1	190	39	20	13	1	2	2	1	13	1	45	6	4	0	4	.000	0	0	2.58
1989	Miami	A	5	5	0	0	19	105	30	21	17	1	1	3	4	17	0	8	3	0	0	4	.000	0	0	8.05
	Watertown	A	14	14	2	0	92	402	75	50	27	1	5	2	8	44	0	64	3	0	7	5	.583	2	0	2.64
1990	Palm Sprngs	A	24	16	0	0	100.2	460	106	60	42	2	3	1	9	55	2	53	8	0	3	10	.231	0	0	3.75
	Midland	AA	2	0	0	1	4	18	7	1	1	0	0	0	0	0	0	1	0	0	1	0	1.000	0	0	2.25
1991	Palm Sprngs	A	34	0	0	17	41.1	188	36	20	9	0	3	1	2	30	5	23	4	0	4	1	.800	0	2	1.96
1992	Midland	AA	38	0	0	27	53.1	214	49	26	16	3	1	2	3	10	1	32	7	0	3	4	.429	0	4	2.70
	Edmonton	AAA	22	0	0	14	31.2	136	31	16	5	0	0	1	2	10	3	15	2	0	1	3	.250	0	4	1.42
1993	Portland	AAA	39	0	0	33	48	206	46	19	16	0	1	2	3	18	0	29	2	0	5	0	1.000	0	15	3.00
1993	Minnesota	AL	19	0	0	10	27	135	36	29	29	3	2	1	3	23	2	14	1	0	1	1	.500	0	0	9.67

Matt Merullo

Bats: Left **Throws:** Right **Pos:** DH **Ht:** 6' 2" **Wt:** 200 **Born:** 08/04/65 **Age:** 28

Year Team	Lg	G	AB	H	2B	3B	HR	(Hm	Rd)	TB	R	RBI	TBB	IBB	SO	HBP	SH	SF	SB	CS	SB%	GDP	Avg	OBP	SLG
1993 Nashville *	AAA	103	352	117	30	1	12	--	--	185	50	65	28	6	47	3	1	2	0	2	.00	12	.332	.384	.526
1989 Chicago	AL	31	81	18	1	0	1	(1	0)	22	5	8	6	0	14	0	2	1	0	1	.00	2	.222	.273	.272
1991 Chicago	AL	80	140	32	1	0	5	(1	4)	48	8	21	9	1	18	0	1	4	0	0	.00	1	.229	.268	.343
1992 Chicago	AL	24	50	9	1	1	0	(0	0)	12	3	3	1	0	8	1	0	1	0	0	.00	1	.180	.208	.240
1993 Chicago	AL	8	20	1	0	0	0	(0	0)	1	1	0	0	0	1	0	1	0	0	0	.00	1	.050	.050	.050
4 ML YEARS		143	291	60	3	1	6	(2	4)	83	17	32	16	1	41	1	4	6	0	1	.00	4	.206	.245	.285

Jose Mesa

Pitches: Right **Bats:** Right **Pos:** SP **Ht:** 6' 3" **Wt:** 225 **Born:** 05/22/66 **Age:** 28

Year Team	Lg	G	GS	CG	GF	IP	BFP	H	R	ER	HR	SH	SF	HB	TBB	IBB	SO	WP	Bk	W	L	Pct.	ShO	Sv	ERA
1987 Baltimore	AL	6	5	0	0	31.1	143	38	23	21	7	0	0	0	15	0	17	4	0	1	3	.250	0	0	6.03
1990 Baltimore	AL	7	7	0	0	46.2	202	37	20	20	2	2	2	1	27	2	24	1	1	3	2	.600	0	0	3.86
1991 Baltimore	AL	23	23	2	0	123.2	566	151	86	82	11	5	4	3	62	2	64	3	0	6	11	.353	1	0	5.97
1992 2 ML Teams		28	27	1	1	160.2	700	169	86	82	14	2	5	4	70	1	62	2	0	7	12	.368	1	0	4.59
1993 Cleveland	AL	34	33	3	0	208.2	897	232	122	114	21	9	9	7	62	2	118	8	2	10	12	.455	0	0	4.92
1992 Baltimore	AL	13	12	0	1	67.2	300	77	41	39	9	0	3	2	27	1	22	2	0	3	8	.273	0	0	5.19
Cleveland	AL	15	15	1	0	93	400	92	45	43	5	2	2	2	43	0	40	0	0	4	4	.500	1	0	4.16
5 ML YEARS		98	95	6	1	571	2508	627	337	319	55	18	20	15	236	7	285	18	3	27	40	.403	2	0	5.03

Hensley Meulens

Bats: Right **Throws:** Right **Pos:** LF **Ht:** 6' 3" **Wt:** 212 **Born:** 06/23/67 **Age:** 27

Year Team	Lg	G	AB	H	2B	3B	HR	(Hm	Rd)	TB	R	RBI	TBB	IBB	SO	HBP	SH	SF	SB	CS	SB%	GDP	Avg	OBP	SLG
1993 Columbus *	AAA	75	279	57	14	0	14	--	--	113	39	45	32	0	92	3	0	3	6	2	.75	7	.204	.290	.405
1989 New York	AL	8	28	5	0	0	0	(0	0)	5	2	1	2	0	8	0	0	0	1	0	.00	2	.179	.233	.179
1990 New York	AL	23	83	20	7	0	3	(2	1)	36	12	10	9	0	25	3	0	0	1	0	1.00	3	.241	.337	.434
1991 New York	AL	96	288	64	8	1	6	(4	2)	92	37	29	18	1	97	4	1	2	3	0	1.00	3	.222	.276	.319
1992 New York	AL	2	5	3	0	0	1	(1	0)	6	1	1	0	0	0	0	0	0	0	0	.00	0	.600	.667	1.200
1993 New York	AL	30	53	9	1	1	2	(1	1)	18	8	5	8	0	19	0	0	0	0	0	.00	2	.170	.279	.340
5 ML YEARS		159	457	101	16	2	12	(8	4)	157	60	46	38	1	149	7	1	2	4	2	.67	15	.221	.290	.344

Danny Miceli

Pitches: Right **Bats:** Right **Pos:** RP **Ht:** 6' 1" **Wt:** 185 **Born:** 09/09/70 **Age:** 23

Year Team	Lg	G	GS	CG	GF	IP	BFP	H	R	ER	HR	SH	SF	HB	TBB	IBB	SO	WP	Bk	W	L	Pct.	ShO	Sv	ERA
1990 Royals	R	27	0	0	13	53	228	45	27	23	0	4	1	2	29	5	48	4	0	3	4	.429	0	4	3.91
1991 Eugene	A	25	0	0	21	33.2	135	18	8	8	1	1	1	1	18	0	43	2	0	0	1	.000	0	10	2.14
1992 Appleton	A	23	0	0	22	23.1	89	12	6	5	0	1	0	1	4	1	44	1	0	1	1	.500	0	9	1.93
Memphis	AA	32	0	0	16	37.2	145	20	10	8	5	2	4	1	13	0	46	1	0	3	0	1.000	0	4	1.91
1993 Memphis	AA	40	0	0	29	58.2	271	54	30	30	7	2	3	4	39	3	68	4	1	6	4	.600	0	7	4.60
Carolina	AA	13	0	0	12	12.1	51	11	8	7	2	0	0	0	4	1	19	0	0	0	2	.000	0	10	5.11
1993 Pittsburgh	NL	9	0	0	1	5.1	25	6	3	3	0	0	0	0	3	0	4	0	0	0	0	.000	0	0	5.06

Matt Mieske

Bats: Right **Throws:** Right **Pos:** RF **Ht:** 6' 0" **Wt:** 185 **Born:** 02/13/68 **Age:** 26

Year Team	Lg	G	AB	H	2B	3B	HR	(Hm	Rd)	TB	R	RBI	TBB	IBB	SO	HBP	SH	SF	SB	CS	SB%	GDP	Avg	OBP	SLG
1990 Spokane	A	76	291	99	20	0	12	--	--	155	59	63	45	3	43	6	1	6	25	12	.68	6	.340	.431	.533
1991 High Desert	A	133	492	168	36	6	15	--	--	261	108	119	94	6	82	13	0	4	39	12	.76	13	.341	.456	.530
1992 Denver	AAA	134	524	140	29	11	19	--	--	248	80	77	39	2	90	3	4	5	13	9	.59	15	.267	.319	.473
1993 New Orleans	AAA	60	219	57	14	2	8	--	--	99	36	22	27	3	46	3	2	0	6	4	.60	5	.260	.349	.452
1993 Milwaukee	AL	23	58	14	0	0	3	(1	2)	23	9	7	4	0	14	0	1	0	0	0	.00	2	.241	.290	.397

Bob Milacki

Pitches: Right **Bats:** Right **Pos:** RP **Ht:** 6' 4" **Wt:** 232 **Born:** 07/28/64 **Age:** 29

Year Team	Lg	G	GS	CG	GF	IP	BFP	H	R	ER	HR	SH	SF	HB	TBB	IBB	SO	WP	Bk	W	L	Pct.	ShO	Sv	ERA
1993 Charlotte *	AAA	21	7	0	8	71.2	288	59	31	27	6	2	2	0	19	1	46	4	0	4	3	.571	0	4	3.39
1988 Baltimore	AL	3	3	1	0	25	91	9	2	2	1	0	0	0	9	0	18	0	0	2	0	1.000	1	0	0.72
1989 Baltimore	AL	37	36	3	1	243	1022	233	105	101	21	7	6	2	88	4	113	1	1	14	12	.538	2	0	3.74
1990 Baltimore	AL	27	24	1	0	135.1	594	143	73	67	18	5	5	0	61	2	60	2	1	5	8	.385	1	0	4.46
1991 Baltimore	AL	31	26	3	1	184	758	175	86	82	17	7	5	1	53	3	108	1	2	10	9	.526	1	0	4.01

1992 Baltimore	AL	23	20	0	1	115.2	525	140	78	75	16	3	3	2	44	2	51	7	1	6	8	.429	0	1	5.84
1993 Cleveland	AL	5	2	0	0	16	74	19	8	6	3	0	0	0	11	0	7	0	0	1	1	.500	0	0	3.38
6 ML YEARS		126	111	8	3	719	3064	719	352	333	76	22	19	5	266	11	357	11	5	38	38	.500	5	1	4.17

Sam Militello

Pitches: Right **Bats:** Right **Pos:** SP   **Ht:** 6' 3" **Wt:** 195 **Born:** 11/26/69 **Age:** 24

		HOW MUCH HE PITCHED						WHAT HE GAVE UP												THE RESULTS					
Year Team	Lg	G	GS	CG	GF	IP	BFP	H	R	ER	HR	SH	SF	HB	TBB	IBB	SO	WP	Bk	W	L	Pct.	ShO	Sv	ERA
1990 Oneonta	A	13	13	3	0	88.2	332	53	14	12	2	0	2	1	24	0	119	0	2	8	2	.800	2	0	1.22
1991 Pr William	A	16	16	1	0	103.1	397	65	19	14	1	1	4	4	27	1	113	1	1	12	2	.857	0	0	1.22
Albany	AA	7	7	0	0	46	191	40	14	12	3	1	1	3	19	1	55	0	0	2	2	.500	0	0	2.35
1992 Columbus	AAA	22	21	3	0	141.1	576	104	45	36	5	2	5	11	46	1	152	4	1	12	2	.857	2	0	2.29
1993 Columbus	AAA	7	7	0	0	33	151	36	22	21	7	1	0	1	20	0	39	4	0	1	3	.250	0	0	5.73
1992 New York	AL	9	9	0	0	60	255	43	24	23	6	0	0	2	32	1	42	1	0	3	3	.500	0	0	3.45
1993 New York	AL	3	2	0	0	9.1	46	10	8	7	1	0	0	2	7	1	5	0	0	1	1	.500	0	0	6.75
2 ML YEARS		12	11	0	0	69.1	301	53	32	30	7	0	0	4	39	2	47	1	0	4	4	.500	0	0	3.89

Keith Miller

Bats: Right **Throws:** Right **Pos:** 3B   **Ht:** 5'11" **Wt:** 185 **Born:** 06/12/63 **Age:** 31

		BATTING																	BASERUNNING				PERCENTAGES		
Year Team	Lg	G	AB	H	2B	3B	HR	(Hm	Rd)	TB	R	RBI	TBB	IBB	SO	HBP	SH	SF	SB	CS	SB%	GDP	Avg	OBP	SLG
1993 Omaha *	AAA	6	24	7	1	1	0	--	--	10	2	2	0	0	2	0	0	0	1	0	1.00	2	.292	.292	.417
1987 New York	NL	25	51	19	2	2	0	(0	0)	25	14	1	2	0	6	1	3	0	8	1	.89	1	.373	.407	.490
1988 New York	NL	40	70	15	1	1	1	(1	0)	21	9	5	6	0	10	0	3	0	0	5	.00	1	.214	.276	.300
1989 New York	NL	57	143	33	7	0	1	(0	1)	43	15	7	5	0	27	1	3	0	6	0	1.00	3	.231	.262	.301
1990 New York	NL	88	233	60	8	0	1	(1	0)	71	42	12	23	1	46	2	2	2	16	3	.84	2	.258	.327	.305
1991 New York	NL	98	275	77	22	1	4	(2	2)	113	41	23	23	0	44	5	0	1	14	4	.78	2	.280	.345	.411
1992 Kansas City	AL	106	416	118	24	4	4	(1	3)	162	57	38	31	0	46	14	1	2	16	6	.73	1	.284	.352	.389
1993 Kansas City	AL	37	108	18	3	0	0	(0	0)	21	9	3	8	0	19	1	0	1	3	1	.75	3	.167	.229	.194
7 ML YEARS		451	1296	340	67	8	11	(5	6)	456	187	89	98	1	198	24	12	6	63	20	.76	13	.262	.324	.352

Paul Miller

Pitches: Right **Bats:** Right **Pos:** SP   **Ht:** 6' 5" **Wt:** 220 **Born:** 04/27/65 **Age:** 29

		HOW MUCH HE PITCHED						WHAT HE GAVE UP												THE RESULTS					
Year Team	Lg	G	GS	CG	GF	IP	BFP	H	R	ER	HR	SH	SF	HB	TBB	IBB	SO	WP	Bk	W	L	Pct.	ShO	Sv	ERA
1987 Pirates	R	12	12	1	0	70.1	292	55	34	25	3	4	1	2	26	0	62	3	0	3	6	.333	1	0	3.20
1988 Augusta	A	15	15	2	0	90.1	374	80	34	29	3	3	5	4	28	1	51	8	5	6	5	.545	2	0	2.89
1989 Salem	A	26	20	2	0	133.2	599	138	86	62	17	2	4	8	64	0	82	8	1	6	12	.333	1	0	4.17
1990 Salem	A	22	22	5	0	150.2	628	145	58	41	6	3	6	7	33	1	83	5	1	8	6	.571	1	0	2.45
Harrisburg	AA	5	5	2	0	37	148	27	9	9	1	1	2	2	10	0	11	0	0	2	1	.667	1	0	2.19
1991 Carolina	AA	15	15	1	0	89.1	369	69	29	24	4	7	1	3	35	4	69	5	1	7	2	.778	0	0	2.42
Buffalo	AAA	10	10	2	0	67	272	41	17	11	2	4	0	5	29	0	30	1	1	5	2	.714	0	0	1.48
1992 Buffalo	AAA	8	7	0	0	32.1	150	38	23	14	3	3	1	1	16	0	18	0	0	2	3	.400	0	0	3.90
1993 Carolina	AA	6	6	0	0	38.1	152	31	15	12	3	1	1	0	12	1	33	4	1	2	2	.500	0	0	2.82
Buffalo	AAA	10	10	0	0	52.1	220	57	28	26	2	2	0	1	14	1	25	0	0	3	1	.750	0	0	4.47
1991 Pittsburgh	NL	1	1	0	0	5	21	4	3	3	0	0	0	0	3	0	3	2	0	0	0	.000	0	0	5.40
1992 Pittsburgh	NL	6	0	0	1	11.1	46	11	3	3	0	1	1	0	1	0	5	1	0	1	0	1.000	0	0	2.38
1993 Pittsburgh	NL	3	2	0	1	10	47	15	6	6	2	2	0	0	2	0	2	1	0	0	0	.000	0	0	5.40
3 ML YEARS		10	3	0	2	26.1	114	30	12	12	2	3	1	0	6	0	9	2	0	1	0	1.000	0	0	4.10

Joe Millette

Bats: Right **Throws:** Right **Pos:** SS   **Ht:** 6' 1" **Wt:** 175 **Born:** 08/12/66 **Age:** 27

		BATTING																	BASERUNNING				PERCENTAGES		
Year Team	Lg	G	AB	H	2B	3B	HR	(Hm	Rd)	TB	R	RBI	TBB	IBB	SO	HBP	SH	SF	SB	CS	SB%	GDP	Avg	OBP	SLG
1989 Batavia	A	11	42	10	3	0	0	--	--	13	4	4	4	0	6	0	0	0	3	0	1.00	1	.238	.304	.310
Spartanburg	A	60	209	50	4	3	0	--	--	60	27	18	28	0	36	7	3	3	4	2	.67	5	.239	.344	.287
1990 Clearwater	A	108	295	54	5	0	0	--	--	59	31	18	29	0	53	7	7	6	4	4	.50	5	.183	.267	.200
1991 Clearwater	A	18	55	14	2	0	0	--	--	16	6	6	7	0	6	1	3	2	1	2	.33	1	.255	.338	.291
Reading	AA	115	353	87	9	4	3	--	--	113	52	28	36	2	54	7	10	3	6	6	.50	5	.246	.326	.320
1992 Scranton/wb	AAA	78	256	68	11	1	1	--	--	84	24	23	15	0	30	6	7	0	3	2	.60	8	.266	.321	.328
1993 Scranton/wb	AAA	107	343	77	15	2	1	--	--	99	27	24	19	2	56	5	7	1	5	4	.56	9	.224	.274	.289
1992 Philadelphia	NL	33	78	16	0	0	0	(0	0)	16	5	2	5	2	10	2	2	0	1	0	1.00	8	.205	.271	.205
1993 Philadelphia	NL	10	10	2	0	0	0	(0	0)	2	3	2	1	0	2	0	3	0	0	0	.00	1	.200	.273	.200
2 ML YEARS		43	88	18	0	0	0	(0	0)	18	8	4	6	2	12	2	5	0	1	0	1.00	9	.205	.271	.205

Randy Milligan

Bats: Right **Throws:** Right **Pos:** 1B   **Ht:** 6' 1" **Wt:** 225 **Born:** 11/27/61 **Age:** 32

							BATTING												BASERUNNING				PERCENTAGES		
Year Team	Lg	G	AB	H	2B	3B	HR	(Hm	Rd)	TB	R	RBI	TBB	IBB	SO	HBP	SH	SF	SB	CS	SB%	GDP	Avg	OBP	SLG
1987 New York	NL	3	1	0	0	0	0	(0	0)	0	0	0	1	0	1	0	0	0	0	0	.00	0	.000	.500	.000
1988 Pittsburgh	NL	40	82	18	5	0	3	(1	2)	32	10	8	20	0	24	1	0	0	1	2	.33	2	.220	.379	.390
1989 Baltimore	AL	124	365	98	23	5	12	(6	6)	167	56	45	74	2	75	3	0	2	9	5	.64	12	.268	.394	.458
1990 Baltimore	AL	109	362	96	20	1	20	(11	9)	178	64	60	88	3	68	2	0	4	6	3	.67	11	.265	.394	.492
1991 Baltimore	AL	141	483	127	17	2	16	(8	8)	196	57	70	84	4	108	2	0	2	0	5	.00	23	.263	.373	.406
1992 Baltimore	AL	137	462	111	21	1	11	(7	4)	167	71	53	106	0	81	4	0	5	0	1	.00	15	.240	.383	.361
1993 2 ML Teams		102	281	84	18	1	6	(5	1)	122	37	36	60	0	53	1	0	1	0	2	.00	3	.299	.423	.434
1993 Cincinnati	NL	83	234	64	11	1	6	(5	1)	95	30	29	46	0	49	1	0	1	0	2	.00	3	.274	.394	.406
Cleveland	AL	19	47	20	7	0	0	(0	0)	27	7	7	14	0	4	0	0	0	0	0	.00	0	.426	.557	.574
7 ML YEARS		656	2036	534	104	10	68	(38	30)	862	295	272	433	9	410	13	0	14	16	18	.47	66	.262	.393	.423

Alan Mills

Pitches: Right **Bats:** Both **Pos:** RP   **Ht:** 6' 1" **Wt:** 192 **Born:** 10/18/66 **Age:** 27

					HOW MUCH HE PITCHED				WHAT HE GAVE UP									THE RESULTS				
Year Team	Lg	G	GS	CG	GF	IP	BFP	H	R	ER	HR	SH	SF	HB	TBB	IBB	SO	WP	Bk	W	L	Pct.	ShO	Sv	ERA
1990 New York	AL	36	0	0	18	41.2	200	48	21	19	4	4	1	1	33	6	24	3	0	1	5	.167	0	0	4.10
1991 New York	AL	6	2	0	3	16.1	72	16	9	8	1	0	1	0	8	0	11	2	0	1	1	.500	0	0	4.41
1992 Baltimore	AL	35	3	0	12	103.1	428	78	33	30	5	6	5	1	54	10	60	2	0	10	4	.714	0	2	2.61
1993 Baltimore	AL	45	0	0	18	100.1	421	80	39	36	14	4	6	4	51	5	68	3	0	5	4	.556	0	4	3.23
4 ML YEARS		122	5	0	51	261.2	1121	222	102	93	24	14	13	6	146	21	163	10	0	17	14	.548	0	6	3.20

Nate Minchey

Pitches: Right **Bats:** Right **Pos:** SP   **Ht:** 6' 7" **Wt:** 210 **Born:** 08/31/69 **Age:** 24

					HOW MUCH HE PITCHED				WHAT HE GAVE UP									THE RESULTS				
Year Team	Lg	G	GS	CG	GF	IP	BFP	H	R	ER	HR	SH	SF	HB	TBB	IBB	SO	WP	Bk	W	L	Pct.	ShO	Sv	ERA
1987 Expos	R	12	11	2	0	54.2	252	62	45	30	1	0	0	2	28	0	61	6	0	3	4	.429	0	0	4.94
1988 Rockford	A	28	27	0	0	150.1	673	148	93	80	4	4	8	4	87	1	63	14	5	11	12	.478	0	0	4.79
1989 Rockford	A	15	15	0	0	87	395	85	51	46	2	4	2	3	54	0	53	14	1	3	6	.333	0	0	4.76
Burlington	A	11	11	1	0	69	294	69	37	35	6	2	5	2	28	0	34	8	0	2	6	.250	0	0	4.57
1990 Durham	A	25	24	2	0	133	579	143	75	56	11	4	3	5	46	0	100	13	2	4	11	.267	2	0	3.79
1991 Miami	A	13	13	4	0	95.1	378	81	31	20	1	2	1	4	32	0	61	1	2	5	3	.625	1	0	1.89
Durham	A	15	12	3	0	89	354	72	31	28	3	0	1	3	29	0	77	6	0	6	6	.500	0	0	2.83
1992 Greenville	AA	28	25	5	1	172	684	137	51	44	7	3	3	7	40	2	115	9	0	13	6	.684	4	0	2.30
Pawtucket	AAA	2	0	0	2	7	23	3	0	0	0	0	0	0	0	0	4	0	0	2	0	1.000	0	0	0.00
1993 Pawtucket	AAA	29	29	7	0	194.2	814	182	103	87	22	7	5	10	50	1	113	8	0	7	14	.333	2	0	4.02
1993 Boston	AL	5	5	1	0	33	141	35	16	13	5	1	0	0	8	2	18	2	0	1	2	.333	0	0	3.55

Blas Minor

Pitches: Right **Bats:** Right **Pos:** RP   **Ht:** 6' 3" **Wt:** 195 **Born:** 03/20/66 **Age:** 28

					HOW MUCH HE PITCHED				WHAT HE GAVE UP									THE RESULTS				
Year Team	Lg	G	GS	CG	GF	IP	BFP	H	R	ER	HR	SH	SF	HB	TBB	IBB	SO	WP	Bk	W	L	Pct.	ShO	Sv	ERA
1988 Princeton	R	15	0	0	14	16.1	77	18	10	8	2	0	0	0	5	0	23	0	0	0	1	.000	0	7	4.41
1989 Salem	A	39	4	0	25	86.2	377	91	43	35	6	4	1	2	31	6	62	3	1	3	5	.375	0	4	3.63
1990 Harrisburg	AA	38	6	0	23	94	391	81	41	32	5	8	4	0	29	7	98	3	1	6	4	.600	0	5	3.06
Buffalo	AAA	1	0	0	0	2.2	12	2	1	1	0	0	0	0	2	0	2	0	0	0	1	.000	0	0	3.38
1991 Buffalo	AAA	17	3	0	3	36	168	46	27	23	7	2	1	0	15	0	25	1	0	2	2	.500	0	0	5.75
Carolina	AA	3	2	0	1	12.2	52	9	4	4	0	1	0	0	7	0	18	1	0	0	0	.000	0	0	2.84
1992 Buffalo	AAA	45	7	0	29	96.1	379	72	30	26	7	4	2	1	26	2	60	2	1	5	4	.556	0	18	2.43
1992 Pittsburgh	NL	1	0	0	0	2	9	3	2	1	0	0	0	0	0	0	0	1	0	0	0	.000	0	0	4.50
1993 Pittsburgh	NL	65	0	0	18	94.1	398	94	43	43	8	6	4	4	26	3	84	5	0	8	6	.571	0	2	4.10
2 ML YEARS		66	0	0	18	96.1	407	97	45	44	8	6	4	4	26	3	84	6	0	8	6	.571	0	2	4.11

Gino Minutelli

Pitches: Left **Bats:** Left **Pos:** RP   **Ht:** 6' 0" **Wt:** 185 **Born:** 05/23/64 **Age:** 30

					HOW MUCH HE PITCHED				WHAT HE GAVE UP									THE RESULTS				
Year Team	Lg	G	GS	CG	GF	IP	BFP	H	R	ER	HR	SH	SF	HB	TBB	IBB	SO	WP	Bk	W	L	Pct.	ShO	Sv	ERA
1985 Tri-Cities	A	20	10	0	7	57		61	57	51	3	0	0	6	57	0	79	6	0	4	8	.333	0	0	8.05
1986 Cedar Rapds	A	27	27	3	0	152.2	671	133	73	62	14	4	6	5	76	1	149	16	2	15	5	.750	2	0	3.66
1987 Tampa	A	17	15	5	0	104.1	461	98	51	44	4	10	3	5	48	4	70	13	1	7	6	.538	1	0	3.80
Vermont	AA	6	6	0	0	39.2	168	34	15	14	3	0	0	2	16	0	39	2	1	4	1	.800	0	0	3.18
1988 Chattanooga	AA	2	2	0	0	5.2	27	6	2	1	0	0	0	1	4	0	3	0	2	0	1	.000	0	0	1.59
1989 Reds	R	1	1	0	0	1	4	0	0	0	0	0	0	0	1	0	0	0	1	0	0	.000	0	0	0.00
Chattanooga	AA	6	6	1	0	29	140	28	19	17	1	0	0	6	23	0	20	8	1	4	1	.500	0	0	5.28

1990 Chattanooga	AA	17	17	5	0	108.1	467	106	52	48	9	5	2	2	46	1	75	5	13	9	5	.643	0	0	3.99
Nashville	AAA	11	11	3	0	78.1	315	65	34	28	5	1	1	1	31	0	61	1	0	5	2	.714	0	0	3.22
1991 Chston-Wv	A	2	2	0	0	8	28	2	0	0	0	0	0	0	4	0	8	0	0	1	0	1.000	0	0	0.00
Nashville	AAA	13	13	1	0	80.1	325	57	25	17	3	6	2	1	35	2	64	6	1	4	7	.364	1	0	1.90
1992 Nashville	AAA	29	29	1	0	158	722	177	96	75	18	13	5	5	76	1	110	11	1	4	12	.250	0	0	4.27
1993 Phoenix	AAA	49	0	0	34	53.2	235	55	28	24	1	1	3	0	26	0	57	6	1	2	2	.500	0	11	4.02
1990 Cincinnati	NL	2	0	0	0	1	6	0	1	1	0	0	0	1	2	0	1	0	0	0	0	.000	0	0	9.00
1991 Cincinnati	NL	16	3	0	2	25.1	124	30	17	17	5	0	2	0	18	1	21	3	0	0	2	.000	0	0	6.04
1993 San Francisco	NL	9	0	0	4	14.1	64	7	9	6	2	1	2	0	15	0	10	1	0	0	0	.000	0	0	3.77
3 ML YEARS		27	3	0-	6	40.2	194	37	27	24	7	1	4	1	35	1	31	5	0	0	3	.000	0		5.31

Angel Miranda

Pitches: Left **Bats:** Left **Pos:** SP/RP **Ht:** 6' 1" **Wt:** 190 **Born:** 11/09/69 **Age:** 24

		HOW MUCH HE PITCHED						WHAT HE GAVE UP												THE RESULTS					
Year Team	Lg	G	GS	CG	GF	IP	BFP	H	R	ER	HR	SH	SF	HB	TBB	IBB	SO	WP	Bk	W	L	Pct.	ShO	Sv	ERA
1987 Butte	R	12	0	0	5	21.2	91	15	13	9	3	1	0	1	10	0	28	1	1	1	1	.500	0	0	3.74
Helena	R	13	0	0	8	21.2	95	12	9	6	1	2	0	0	16	2	32	0	0	0	1	.000	0	3	2.49
1988 Stockton	A	16	0	0	5	26.1	139	20	30	21	1	2	0	2	37	0	36	7	0	0	1	.000	0	2	7.18
Helena	R	14	11	0	1	60.2	284	54	32	26	2	0	1	2	58	0	75	6	3	5	2	.714	0	0	3.86
1989 Beloit	A	43	0	0	40	63	264	39	13	6	1	7	5	1	32	6	88	3	1	6	5	.545	0	16	0.86
1990 Stockton	A	52	9	2	40	108.1	443	75	37	32	7	6	4	2	49	1	138	2	1	9	4	.692	1	24	2.66
1991 El Paso	AA	38	0	0	24	74.1	317	55	27	21	2	1	4	1	41	1	86	7	0	4	2	.667	0	11	2.54
Denver	AAA	11	0	0	8	11.2	60	10	9	8	0	2	0	0	17	1	14	1	0	0	1	.000	0	2	6.17
1992 Denver	AAA	28	27	1	0	160.1	714	183	100	85	16	6	3	1	77	0	122	9	6	6	12	.333	1	0	4.77
1993 New Orleans	AAA	9	2	0	1	18.1	72	11	8	7	3	1	0	0	10	0	24	2	0	0	1	.000	0	0	3.44
1993 Milwaukee	AL	22	17	2	0	120	502	100	53	44	12	3	3	2	52	4	88	4	2	4	5	.444	0	0	3.30

Kevin Mitchell

Bats: Right **Throws:** Right **Pos:** LF **Ht:** 5'11" **Wt:** 210 **Born:** 01/13/62 **Age:** 32

		BATTING																BASERUNNING				PERCENTAGES		
Year Team	Lg	G	AB	H	2B	3B	HR	(Hm | Rd)	TB	R	RBI	TBB	IBB	SO	HBP	SH	SF	SB	CS	SB%	GDP	Avg	OBP	SLG
1984 New York	NL	7	14	3	0	0	0	(0 | 0)	3	0	1	0	0	3	0	0	0	0	1	.00	0	.214	.214	.214
1986 New York	NL	108	328	91	22	2	12	(4 | 8)	153	51	43	33	0	61	1	1	1	3	3	.50	5	.277	.344	.466
1987 2 ML Teams		131	464	130	20	2	22	(9 | 13)	220	68	70	48	4	88	2	0	1	9	6	.60	10	.280	.350	.474
1988 San Francisco	NL	148	505	127	25	7	19	(10 | 9)	223	60	80	48	7	85	5	1	7	5	5	.50	9	.251	.319	.442
1989 San Francisco	NL	154	543	158	34	6	47	(22 | 25)	345	100	125	87	32	115	3	0	7	3	4	.43	6	.291	.388	.635
1990 San Francisco	NL	140	524	152	24	2	35	(15 | 20)	285	90	93	58	9	87	2	0	5	4	7	.36	8	.290	.360	.544
1991 San Francisco	NL	113	371	95	13	1	27	(9 | 18)	191	52	69	43	8	57	5	0	4	2	3	.40	6	.256	.338	.515
1992 Seattle	AL	99	360	103	24	0	9	(5 | 4)	154	48	67	35	6	46	3	0	4	0	2	.00	4	.286	.351	.428
1993 Cincinnati	NL	93	323	110	21	3	19	(10 | 9)	194	56	64	25	4	48	1	0	4	1	0	1.00	14	.341	.385	.601
1987 San Diego	NL	62	196	48	7	1	7	(2 | 5)	78	19	26	20	3	38	0	0	1	0	0	.00	5	.245	.313	.398
San Francisco	NL	69	268	82	13	1	15	(7 | 8)	142	49	44	28	1	50	2	0	0	9	6	.60	5	.306	.376	.530
9 ML YEARS		993	3432	969	183	23	190	(84 | 106)	1768	525	612	377	68	590	22	2	33	27	31	.47	63	.282	.354	.515

Dave Mlicki

Pitches: Right **Bats:** Right **Pos:** SP **Ht:** 6' 4" **Wt:** 190 **Born:** 06/08/68 **Age:** 26

		HOW MUCH HE PITCHED						WHAT HE GAVE UP												THE RESULTS					
Year Team	Lg	G	GS	CG	GF	IP	BFP	H	R	ER	HR	SH	SF	HB	TBB	IBB	SO	WP	Bk	W	L	Pct.	ShO	Sv	ERA
1990 Burlington	R	8	1	0	2	18	81	16	11	7	1	0	1	1	6	0	17	0	0	3	1	.750	0	0	3.50
Watertown	A	7	4	0	3	32	139	33	15	12	3	0	1	0	11	0	28	2	0	3	0	1.000	0	0	3.38
1991 Columbus	A	22	19	2	1	115.2	516	101	70	54	3	0	1	6	70	1	136	10	2	8	6	.571	0	0	4.20
1992 Canton-Akrn	AA	27	27	2	0	172.2	720	143	77	69	8	5	7	3	80	3	146	9	1	11	9	.550	2	0	3.60
1993 Canton-Akrn	AA	6	6	0	0	23	92	15	2	1	0	0	1	2	8	0	21	2	0	2	1	.667	0	0	0.39
1992 Cleveland	AL	4	4	0	0	21.2	101	23	14	12	3	2	0	1	16	0	16	1	0	0	2	.000	0	0	4.98
1993 Cleveland	AL	3	3	0	0	13.1	58	11	6	5	2	0	0	2	6	0	7	2	0	0	0	.000	0	0	3.38
2 ML YEARS		7	7	0	0	35	159	34	20	17	5	2	0	3	22	0	23	3	0	0	2	.000	0	0	4.37

Dennis Moeller

Pitches: Left **Bats:** Right **Pos:** RP **Ht:** 6' 2" **Wt:** 195 **Born:** 09/15/67 **Age:** 26

		HOW MUCH HE PITCHED						WHAT HE GAVE UP												THE RESULTS					
Year Team	Lg	G	GS	CG	GF	IP	BFP	H	R	ER	HR	SH	SF	HB	TBB	IBB	SO	WP	Bk	W	L	Pct.	ShO	Sv	ERA
1986 Eugene	A	14	14	0	0	61.2		54	22	21	1	0	0	2	34	0	65	7	2	4	0	1.000	0	0	3.06
1987 Appleton	A	18	13	0	0	55	292	72	63	44	5	2	3	1	45	3	49	6	0	2	5	.286	0	0	7.20
1988 Appleton	A	20	18	0	1	99	421	94	46	35	4	4	3	4	34	1	88	5	2	3	5	.375	0	0	3.18
1989 Baseball Cy	A	12	11	2	1	71	280	59	17	14	2	0	3	1	20	1	64	1	1	9	0	1.000	1	0	1.77
Memphis	AA	5	5	0	0	25.1	100	16	9	8	2	2	0	1	10	0	21	0	0	1	1	.500	0	0	2.84
1990 Memphis	AA	14	14	0	0	67.2	307	79	55	47	11	3	3	2	30	1	42	3	2	7	6	.538	0	0	6.25
Omaha	AAA	11	11	1	0	65	274	63	29	29	8	1	0	1	30	0	53	0	5	5	2	.714	1	0	4.02

Year	Team	Lg	G	GS	CG	GF	IP	BFP	H	R	ER	HR	SH	SF	HB	TBB	IBB	SO	WP	Bk	W	L	Pct.	ShO	Sv	ERA
1991	Memphis	AA	10	10	0	0	53	224	52	24	15	6	1	1	1	21	0	54	1	1	4	5	.444	0	0	2.55
	Omaha	AAA	14	14	0	0	78.1	342	70	36	28	4	3	1	3	40	0	51	3	3	7	3	.700	0	0	3.22
1992	Omaha	AAA	23	16	3	2	120.2	496	121	36	33	9	3	1	4	34	1	56	5	3	8	5	.615	1	2	2.46
1993	Buffalo	AAA	24	11	0	4	76.2	326	85	43	37	13	5	5	1	21	3	38	4	5	3	4	.429	0	0	4.34
1992	Kansas City	AL	5	4	0	1	18	89	24	17	14	5	3	3	0	11	2	6	1	1	0	3	.000	0	0	7.00
1993	Pittsburgh	NL	10	0	0	3	16.1	82	26	20	18	2	1	0	1	7	1	13	1	2	1	0	1.000	0	0	9.92
	2 ML YEARS		15	4	0	4	34.1	171	50	37	32	7	4	3	1	18	3	19	2	3	1	3	.250	0	0	8.39

Mike Mohler

Pitches: Left **Bats:** Right **Pos:** RP/SP   **Ht:** 6' 2" **Wt:** 195 **Born:** 07/26/68 **Age:** 25

			HOW MUCH HE PITCHED						WHAT HE GAVE UP										THE RESULTS					
Year	Team	Lg	G	GS	CG	GF	IP	BFP	H	R	ER	HR	SH	SF	HB	TBB	IBB	SO	WP	Bk	W	L	Pct.	ShO	Sv	ERA
1990	Madison	A	42	2	0	10	63.1	280	56	34	24	8	2	8	2	32	0	72	4	1	1	1	.500	0	1	3.41
1991	Modesto	A	21	20	1	0	122.2	505	106	48	39	5	2	3	2	45	1	98	7	1	9	4	.692	0	0	2.86
	Huntsville	AA	8	8	0	0	53	225	55	22	21	5	2	0	2	20	0	27	3	0	4	2	.667	0	0	3.57
1992	Huntsville	AA	44	6	0	19	80.1	346	72	41	32	5	5	4	3	39	1	56	2	1	3	8	.273	0	3	3.59
1993	Oakland	AL	42	9	0	4	64.1	290	57	45	40	10	5	2	2	44	4	42	0	1	1	6	.143	0	0	5.60

Paul Molitor

Bats: Right **Throws:** Right **Pos:** DH/1B   **Ht:** 6' 0" **Wt:** 185 **Born:** 08/22/56 **Age:** 37

			BATTING																	BASERUNNING				PERCENTAGES		
Year	Team	Lg	G	AB	H	2B	3B	HR	(Hm	Rd)	TB	R	RBI	TBB	IBB	SO	HBP	SH	SF	SB	CS	SB%	GDP	Avg	OBP	SLG
1978	Milwaukee	AL	125	521	142	26	4	6	(4	2)	194	73	45	19	2	54	4	7	5	30	12	.71	6	.273	.301	.372
1979	Milwaukee	AL	140	584	188	27	16	9	(3	6)	274	88	62	48	5	48	2	6	5	33	13	.72	9	.322	.372	.469
1980	Milwaukee	AL	111	450	137	29	2	9	(2	7)	197	81	37	48	4	48	3	6	5	34	7	.83	9	.304	.372	.438
1981	Milwaukee	AL	64	251	67	11	0	2	(1	1)	84	45	19	25	1	29	3	5	0	10	6	.63	3	.267	.341	.335
1982	Milwaukee	AL	160	666	201	26	8	19	(9	10)	300	136	71	69	1	93	1	10	5	41	9	.82	9	.302	.366	.450
1983	Milwaukee	AL	152	608	164	28	6	15	(9	6)	249	95	47	59	4	74	2	7	6	41	8	.84	12	.270	.333	.410
1984	Milwaukee	AL	13	46	10	1	0	0	(0	0)	11	3	6	2	0	8	0	0	1	1	0	1.00	0	.217	.245	.239
1985	Milwaukee	AL	140	576	171	28	3	10	(6	4)	235	93	48	54	6	80	1	7	4	21	7	.75	12	.297	.356	.408
1986	Milwaukee	AL	105	437	123	24	6	9	(5	4)	186	62	55	40	0	81	0	2	3	20	5	.80	9	.281	.340	.426
1987	Milwaukee	AL	118	465	164	41	5	16	(7	9)	263	114	75	69	2	67	2	5	1	45	10	.82	5	.353	.438	.566
1988	Milwaukee	AL	154	609	190	34	6	13	(9	4)	275	115	60	71	8	54	2	5	3	41	10	.80	10	.312	.384	.452
1989	Milwaukee	AL	155	615	194	35	4	11	(6	5)	270	84	56	64	4	67	4	4	9	27	11	.71	11	.315	.379	.439
1990	Milwaukee	AL	103	418	119	27	6	12	(6	6)	194	64	45	37	4	51	1	0	2	18	3	.86	7	.285	.343	.464
1991	Milwaukee	AL	158	665	216	32	13	17	(7	10)	325	133	75	77	16	62	6	0	1	19	8	.70	11	.325	.399	.489
1992	Milwaukee	AL	158	609	195	36	7	12	(4	8)	281	89	89	73	12	66	3	4	11	31	6	.84	13	.320	.389	.461
1993	Toronto	AL	160	636	211	37	5	22	(13	9)	324	121	111	77	3	71	3	1	8	22	4	.85	13	.332	.402	.509
	16 ML YEARS		2016	8156	2492	442	91	182	(91	91)	3662	1396	901	832	72	953	37	69	69	434	119	.78	138	.306	.370	.449

Raul Mondesi

Bats: Right **Throws:** Right **Pos:** LF/RF   **Ht:** 5'11" **Wt:** 150 **Born:** 03/12/71 **Age:** 23

			BATTING																	BASERUNNING				PERCENTAGES		
Year	Team	Lg	G	AB	H	2B	3B	HR	(Hm	Rd)	TB	R	RBI	TBB	IBB	SO	HBP	SH	SF	SB	CS	SB%	GDP	Avg	OBP	SLG
1990	Great Falls	R	44	175	53	10	4	8	--	--	95	35	31	11	1	30	2	0	1	30	6	.83	0	.303	.349	.543
1991	Bakersfield	A	28	106	30	7	2	3	--	--	50	23	13	5	1	21	3	0	1	9	4	.69	1	.283	.330	.472
	San Antonio	AA	53	213	58	10	5	5	--	--	93	32	26	8	0	47	4	0	3	7	3	.70	1	.272	.307	.437
	Albuquerque	AAA	2	9	3	0	1	0	--	--	5	3	0	0	0	1	0	0	0	1	0	1.00	0	.333	.333	.556
1992	Albuquerque	AAA	35	138	43	4	7	4	--	--	73	23	15	9	4	35	1	0	0	2	3	.40	0	.312	.358	.529
	San Antonio	AA	18	68	18	2	2	2	--	--	30	8	14	1	0	24	0	0	3	3	2	.60	1	.265	.264	.441
1993	Albuquerque	AAA	110	425	119	22	7	12	--	--	191	65	65	18	4	85	2	0	5	13	10	.57	4	.280	.309	.449
1993	Los Angeles	NL	42	86	25	3	1	4	(2	2)	42	13	10	4	0	16	0	1	0	4	1	.80	1	.291	.322	.488

Rich Monteleone

Pitches: Right **Bats:** Right **Pos:** RP   **Ht:** 6' 3" **Wt:** 214 **Born:** 03/22/63 **Age:** 31

			HOW MUCH HE PITCHED						WHAT HE GAVE UP										THE RESULTS					
Year	Team	Lg	G	GS	CG	GF	IP	BFP	H	R	ER	HR	SH	SF	HB	TBB	IBB	SO	WP	Bk	W	L	Pct.	ShO	Sv	ERA
1987	Seattle	AL	3	0	0	1	7	34	10	5	5	2	0	0	1	4	0	2	0	0	0	0	.000	0	0	6.43
1988	California	AL	3	0	0	2	4.1	20	4	0	0	0	0	0	1	1	1	3	0	1	0	0	.000	0	0	0.00
1989	California	AL	24	0	0	8	39.2	170	39	15	14	3	1	2	1	13	1	27	2	0	2	2	.500	0	0	3.18
1990	New York	AL	5	0	0	2	7.1	31	8	5	5	0	0	0	0	2	0	8	0	0	0	1	.000	0	0	6.14
1991	New York	AL	26	0	0	10	47	201	42	27	19	5	2	2	0	19	3	34	1	1	3	1	.750	0	0	3.64
1992	New York	AL	47	0	0	15	92.2	380	82	35	34	7	3	1	0	27	3	62	0	3	7	3	.700	0	0	3.30
1993	New York	AL	42	0	0	11	85.2	369	85	52	47	14	4	5	0	35	10	50	1	0	7	4	.636	0	0	4.94
	7 ML YEARS		150	0	0	49	283.2	1205	270	139	124	31	10	10	3	101	18	186	4	5	19	11	.633	0	0	3.93

Jeff Montgomery

Pitches: Right **Bats:** Right **Pos:** RP   **Ht:** 5'11" **Wt:** 180 **Born:** 01/07/62 **Age:** 32

		HOW MUCH HE PITCHED						WHAT HE GAVE UP												THE RESULTS					
Year Team	Lg	G	GS	CG	GF	IP	BFP	H	R	ER	HR	SH	SF	HB	TBB	IBB	SO	WP	Bk	W	L	Pct.	ShO	Sv	ERA
1987 Cincinnati	NL	14	1	0	6	19.1	89	25	15	14	2	0	0	0	9	1	13	1	1	2	2	.500	0	1	6.52
1988 Kansas City	AL	45	0	0	13	62.2	271	54	25	24	6	3	2	2	30	1	47	3	6	7	2	.778	0	1	3.45
1989 Kansas City	AL	63	0	0	39	92	363	66	16	14	3	1	1	2	25	4	94	6	1	7	3	.700	0	18	1.37
1990 Kansas City	AL	73	0	0	59	94.1	400	81	36	25	6	2	2	5	34	8	94	3	0	6	5	.545	0	24	2.39
1991 Kansas City	AL	67	0	0	55	90	376	83	32	29	6	6	2	2	28	2	77	6	0	4	4	.500	0	33	2.90
1992 Kansas City	AL	65	0	0	62	82.2	333	61	23	20	5	4	2	3	27	2	69	2	0	1	6	.143	0	39	2.18
1993 Kansas City	AL	69	0	0	63	87.1	347	65	22	22	3	5	1	2	23	4	66	3	0	7	5	.583	0	45	2.27
7 ML YEARS		396	1	0	297	528.1	2179	435	169	148	31	21	10	16	176	22	460	24	8	34	27	.557	0	160	2.52

Charlie Montoyo

Bats: Right **Throws:** Right **Pos:** 2B   **Ht:** 5'10" **Wt:** 170 **Born:** 10/17/65 **Age:** 28

		BATTING																		BASERUNNING				PERCENTAGES		
Year Team	Lg	G	AB	H	2B	3B	HR	(Hm	Rd)	TB	R	RBI	TBB	IBB	SO	HBP	SH	SF		SB	CS	SB%	GDP	Avg	OBP	SLG
1987 Helena	R	13	45	13	1	2	0	--	--	18	12	2	12	0	3	0	0	1		2	1	.67	0	.289	.431	.400
Beloit	A	55	188	50	9	2	5	--	--	78	46	19	52	0	22	4	1	1		8	0	1.00	1	.266	.433	.415
1988 Stockton	A	132	450	115	14	1	3	--	--	140	103	61	156	0	93	5	6	2		16	6	.73	7	.256	.450	.311
1989 Stockton	A	129	448	111	22	2	0	--	--	137	69	48	102	3	40	11	6	4		13	9	.59	7	.248	.396	.306
1990 El Paso	AA	94	322	93	13	3	3	--	--	121	71	44	72	1	43	8	1	2		9	0	1.00	4	.289	.428	.376
1991 Denver	AAA	120	394	94	13	1	12	--	--	145	68	45	69	0	51	5	6	4		15	4	.79	6	.239	.356	.368
1992 Denver	AAA	84	259	84	7	4	2	--	--	105	40	34	47	0	36	1	2	1		3	5	.38	10	.324	.429	.405
1993 Ottawa	AAA	99	319	89	18	2	1	--	--	114	43	43	71	0	37	4	6	5		0	9	.00	11	.279	.411	.357
1993 Montreal	NL	4	5	2	1	0	0	(0	0)	3	1	3	0	0	0	0	0	0		0	0	.00	0	.400	.400	.600

Marcus Moore

Pitches: Right **Bats:** Both **Pos:** RP   **Ht:** 6'5" **Wt:** 195 **Born:** 11/02/70 **Age:** 23

		HOW MUCH HE PITCHED						WHAT HE GAVE UP												THE RESULTS					
Year Team	Lg	G	GS	CG	GF	IP	BFP	H	R	ER	HR	SH	SF	HB	TBB	IBB	SO	WP	Bk	W	L	Pct.	ShO	Sv	ERA
1989 Bend	A	14	14	1	0	81.2	373	84	55	41	2	3	4	5	51	1	74	14	6	2	5	.286	0	0	4.52
1990 Quad City	A	27	27	2	0	160.1	717	150	83	59	6	2	7	3	106	0	160	13	9	16	5	.762	1	0	3.31
1991 Dunedin	A	27	25	2	1	160.2	694	139	78	66	3	9	5	4	99	3	115	12	9	6	13	.316	0	0	3.70
1992 Knoxville	AA	36	14	1	18	106.1	493	110	82	66	10	3	7	5	79	0	85	17	5	5	10	.333	0	0	5.59
1993 Central Val	A	8	0	0	8	12	53	7	3	1	0	1	0	0	9	0	15	1	0	1	0	1.000	0	2	0.75
Colo Sprngs	AAA	30	0	0	14	44.1	209	54	26	22	3	3	1	1	29	0	38	4	0	1	5	.167	0	4	4.47
1993 Colorado	NL	27	0	0	8	26.1	128	30	25	20	4	0	4	1	20	0	13	4	0	3	1	.750	0	0	6.84

Mike Moore

Pitches: Right **Bats:** Right **Pos:** SP   **Ht:** 6'4" **Wt:** 205 **Born:** 11/26/59 **Age:** 34

		HOW MUCH HE PITCHED						WHAT HE GAVE UP												THE RESULTS					
Year Team	Lg	G	GS	CG	GF	IP	BFP	H	R	ER	HR	SH	SF	HB	TBB	IBB	SO	WP	Bk	W	L	Pct.	ShO	Sv	ERA
1982 Seattle	AL	28	27	1	0	144.1	651	159	91	86	21	8	4	2	79	0	73	6	0	7	14	.333	1	0	5.36
1983 Seattle	AL	22	21	3	1	128	556	130	75	67	10	1	6	3	60	4	108	7	0	6	8	.429	2	0	4.71
1984 Seattle	AL	34	33	6	0	212	937	236	127	117	16	5	6	5	85	10	158	7	2	7	17	.292	0	0	4.97
1985 Seattle	AL	35	34	14	1	247	1016	230	100	95	18	2	7	4	70	2	155	10	3	17	10	.630	2	0	3.46
1986 Seattle	AL	38	37	11	1	266	1145	279	141	127	28	10	6	12	94	6	146	4	1	11	13	.458	1	1	4.30
1987 Seattle	AL	33	33	12	0	231	1020	268	145	121	29	9	8	0	84	3	115	4	2	9	19	.321	0	0	4.71
1988 Seattle	AL	37	32	9	3	228.2	918	196	104	96	24	3	3	3	63	6	182	4	3	9	15	.375	3	1	3.78
1989 Oakland	AL	35	35	6	0	241.2	976	193	82	70	14	5	6	2	83	1	172	17	0	19	11	.633	3	0	2.61
1990 Oakland	AL	33	33	3	0	199.1	862	204	113	103	14	4	7	3	84	2	73	13	0	13	15	.464	0	0	4.65
1991 Oakland	AL	33	33	3	0	210	887	176	75	69	11	5	4	5	105	3	153	14	0	17	8	.680	0	0	2.96
1992 Oakland	AL	36	36	2	0	223	982	229	113	102	20	7	11	8	103	5	117	22	0	17	12	.586	0	0	4.12
1993 Detroit	AL	36	36	4	0	213.2	942	227	135	124	35	4	8	3	89	10	89	9	0	13	9	.591	3	0	5.22
12 ML YEARS		400	390	74	6	2544.2	10892	2527	1301	1177	240	63	76	50	999	50	1541	117	11	145	151	.490	16	2	4.16

Mickey Morandini

Bats: Left **Throws:** Right **Pos:** 2B   **Ht:** 5'11" **Wt:** 171 **Born:** 04/22/66 **Age:** 28

		BATTING																		BASERUNNING				PERCENTAGES		
Year Team	Lg	G	AB	H	2B	3B	HR	(Hm	Rd)	TB	R	RBI	TBB	IBB	SO	HBP	SH	SF		SB	CS	SB%	GDP	Avg	OBP	SLG
1990 Philadelphia	NL	25	79	19	4	0	1	(1	0)	26	9	3	6	0	19	0	2	0		3	0	1.00	1	.241	.294	.329
1991 Philadelphia	NL	98	325	81	11	4	1	(1	0)	103	38	20	29	0	45	2	6	2		13	2	.87	7	.249	.313	.317
1992 Philadelphia	NL	127	422	112	8	8	3	(2	1)	145	47	30	25	2	64	0	6	2		8	3	.73	4	.265	.305	.344
1993 Philadelphia	NL	120	425	105	19	9	3	(2	1)	151	57	33	34	2	73	5	4	2		13	2	.87	6	.247	.309	.355
4 ML YEARS		370	1251	317	42	21	8	(6	2)	425	151	86	94	4	201	7	18	6		37	7	.84	18	.253	.308	.340

Mike Morgan

Pitches: Right **Bats:** Right **Pos:** SP   **Ht:** 6' 2" **Wt:** 220 **Born:** 10/08/59 **Age:** 34

Year Team	Lg	G	GS	CG	GF	IP	BFP	H	R	ER	HR	SH	SF	HB	TBB	IBB	SO	WP	Bk	W	L	Pct.	ShO	Sv	ERA
1978 Oakland	AL	3	3	1	0	12	60	19	12	10	1	1	0	0	8	0	0	0	0	0	3	.000	0	0	7.50
1979 Oakland	AL	13	13	2	0	77	368	102	57	51	7	4	4	3	50	0	17	7	0	2	10	.167	0	0	5.96
1982 New York	AL	30	23	2	2	150.1	661	167	77	73	15	2	4	2	67	5	71	6	0	7	11	.389	0	0	4.37
1983 Toronto	AL	16	4	0	2	45.1	198	48	26	26	6	0	1	0	21	0	22	3	0	0	3	.000	0	0	5.16
1985 Seattle	AL	2	2	0	0	6	33	11	8	8	2	0	0	0	5	0	2	1	0	1	1	.500	0	0	12.00
1986 Seattle	AL	37	33	9	2	216.1	951	243	122	109	24	7	3	4	86	3	116	8	1	11	17	.393	1	1	4.53
1987 Seattle	AL	34	31	8	2	207	898	245	117	107	25	8	5	5	53	3	85	11	0	12	17	.414	2	0	4.65
1988 Baltimore	AL	22	10	2	6	71.1	299	70	45	43	6	1	0	1	23	1	29	5	0	1	6	.143	0	1	5.43
1989 Los Angeles	NL	40	19	0	7	152.2	604	130	51	43	6	8	6	2	33	8	72	6	0	8	11	.421	0	0	2.53
1990 Los Angeles	NL	33	33	6	0	211	891	216	100	88	19	11	4	5	60	5	106	4	1	11	15	.423	4	0	3.75
1991 Los Angeles	NL	34	33	5	1	236.1	949	197	85	73	12	10	4	3	61	10	140	6	0	14	10	.583	1	1	2.78
1992 Chicago	NL	34	34	6	0	240	966	203	80	68	14	10	5	3	79	10	123	11	0	16	8	.667	1	0	2.55
1993 Chicago	NL	32	32	1	0	207.2	883	206	100	93	15	11	5	7	74	8	111	8	2	10	15	.400	1	0	4.03
13 ML YEARS		330	270	42	22	1833	7761	1857	880	792	152	73	41	35	620	53	894	76	4	93	127	.423	10	3	3.89

Hal Morris

Bats: Left **Throws:** Left **Pos:** 1B   **Ht:** 6' 4" **Wt:** 215 **Born:** 04/09/65 **Age:** 29

Year Team	Lg	G	AB	H	2B	3B	HR	(Hm	Rd)	TB	R	RBI	TBB	IBB	SO	HBP	SH	SF	SB	CS	SB%	GDP	Avg	OBP	SLG
1993 Indianapols *	AAA	3	13	6	0	1	1	--	--	11	4	5	1	0	2	0	0	0	0	1	.00	0	.462	.500	.846
1988 New York	AL	15	20	2	0	0	0	(0	0)	2	1	0	0	0	9	0	0	0	0	0	.00	0	.100	.100	.100
1989 New York	AL	15	18	5	0	0	0	(0	0)	5	2	4	1	0	4	0	0	0	0	0	.00	2	.278	.316	.278
1990 Cincinnati	NL	107	309	105	22	3	7	(3	4)	154	50	36	21	4	32	1	3	2	9	3	.75	12	.340	.381	.498
1991 Cincinnati	NL	136	478	152	33	1	14	(9	5)	229	72	59	46	7	61	1	5	7	10	4	.71	4	.318	.374	.479
1992 Cincinnati	NL	115	395	107	21	3	6	(3	3)	152	41	53	45	8	53	2	2	2	6	6	.50	12	.271	.347	.385
1993 Cincinnati	NL	101	379	120	18	0	7	(2	5)	159	48	49	34	4	51	2	0	6	2	2	.50	5	.317	.371	.420
6 ML YEARS		489	1599	491	94	7	34	(17	17)	701	214	201	147	23	210	6	10	17	27	15	.64	35	.307	.364	.438

Jack Morris

Pitches: Right **Bats:** Right **Pos:** SP   **Ht:** 6' 3" **Wt:** 200 **Born:** 05/16/55 **Age:** 39

Year Team	Lg	G	GS	CG	GF	IP	BFP	H	R	ER	HR	SH	SF	HB	TBB	IBB	SO	WP	Bk	W	L	Pct.	ShO	Sv	ERA
1977 Detroit	AL	7	6	1	0	46	189	38	20	19	4	3	1	0	23	0	28	2	0	1	1	.500	0	0	3.72
1978 Detroit	AL	28	7	0	10	106	469	107	57	51	8	8	9	3	49	5	48	4	0	3	5	.375	0	0	4.33
1979 Detroit	AL	27	27	9	0	198	806	179	76	72	19	3	6	4	59	4	113	9	1	17	7	.708	1	0	3.27
1980 Detroit	AL	36	36	11	0	250	1074	252	125	116	20	10	13	4	87	5	112	6	2	16	15	.516	2	0	4.18
1981 Detroit	AL	25	25	15	0	198	798	153	69	67	14	8	9	2	78	11	97	2	2	14	7	.667	1	0	3.05
1982 Detroit	AL	37	37	17	0	266.1	1107	247	131	120	37	4	5	0	96	7	135	10	0	17	16	.515	3	0	4.06
1983 Detroit	AL	37	37	20	0	293.2	1204	257	117	109	30	8	9	3	83	5	232	18	0	20	13	.606	1	0	3.34
1984 Detroit	AL	35	35	9	0	240.1	1015	221	108	96	20	5	3	2	87	7	148	14	0	19	11	.633	1	0	3.60
1985 Detroit	AL	35	35	13	0	257	1077	212	102	95	21	11	7	5	110	7	191	15	3	16	11	.593	4	0	3.33
1986 Detroit	AL	35	35	15	0	267	1092	229	105	97	40	7	3	0	82	7	223	12	0	21	8	.724	6	0	3.27
1987 Detroit	AL	34	34	13	0	266	1101	227	111	100	39	6	5	1	93	7	208	24	1	18	11	.621	0	0	3.38
1988 Detroit	AL	34	34	10	0	235	997	225	115	103	20	12	3	4	83	7	168	11	11	15	13	.536	2	0	3.94
1989 Detroit	AL	24	24	10	0	170.1	743	189	102	92	23	6	7	2	59	3	115	12	1	6	14	.300	0	0	4.86
1990 Detroit	AL	36	36	11	0	249.2	1073	231	144	125	26	7	10	6	97	13	162	16	2	15	18	.455	3	0	4.51
1991 Minnesota	AL	35	35	10	0	246.2	1032	226	107	94	18	5	8	5	92	5	163	15	0	18	12	.600	2	0	3.43
1992 Toronto	AL	34	34	6	0	240.2	1005	222	114	108	18	4	7	10	80	2	132	9	2	21	6	.778	1	0	4.04
1993 Toronto	AL	27	27	4	0	152.2	702	189	116	105	18	4	3	3	65	2	103	14	1	7	12	.368	1	0	6.19
17 ML YEARS		526	504	174	10	3683.1	15484	3404	1719	1569	375	111	110	54	1323	97	2378	193	27	244	180	.575	28	0	3.83

Jamie Moyer

Pitches: Left **Bats:** Left **Pos:** SP   **Ht:** 6' 0" **Wt:** 170 **Born:** 11/18/62 **Age:** 31

Year Team	Lg	G	GS	CG	GF	IP	BFP	H	R	ER	HR	SH	SF	HB	TBB	IBB	SO	WP	Bk	W	L	Pct.	ShO	Sv	ERA
1993 Rochester *	AAA	8	8	1	0	54	217	42	13	10	2	1	1	3	13	0	41	0	0	6	0	1.000	1	0	1.67
1986 Chicago	NL	16	16	1	0	87.1	395	107	52	49	10	3	3	3	42	1	45	3	3	7	4	.636	1	0	5.05
1987 Chicago	NL	35	33	1	1	201	899	210	127	114	28	14	7	5	97	9	147	11	2	12	15	.444	0	0	5.10
1988 Chicago	NL	34	30	3	1	202	855	212	84	78	20	14	4	4	55	7	121	4	0	9	15	.375	1	0	3.48
1989 Texas	AL	15	15	1	0	76	337	84	51	41	10	1	4	2	33	0	44	1	0	4	9	.308	0	0	4.86
1990 Texas	AL	33	10	1	6	102.1	447	115	59	53	6	1	7	4	39	4	58	1	0	2	6	.250	0	0	4.66
1991 St. Louis	NL	8	7	0	1	31.1	142	38	21	20	5	4	2	1	16	0	20	2	1	0	5	.000	0	0	5.74

Year Team	Lg	G	GS	CG	GF	IP	BFP	H	R	ER	HR	SH	SF	HB	TBB	IBB	SO	WP	Bk	W	L	Pct.	ShO	Sv	ERA
1993 Baltimore	AL	25	25	3	0	152	630	154	63	58	11	3	1	6	38	2	90	1	1	12	9	.571	1	0	3.43
7 ML YEARS		166	136	10	9	852	3705	920	457	413	90	40	28	25	320	23	525	23	7	46	63	.422	3	0	4.36

Terry Mulholland

Pitches: Left **Bats:** Right **Pos:** SP **Ht:** 6' 2" **Wt:** 215 **Born:** 03/09/63 **Age:** 31

Year Team	Lg	G	GS	CG	GF	IP	BFP	H	R	ER	HR	SH	SF	HB	TBB	IBB	SO	WP	Bk	W	L	Pct.	ShO	Sv	ERA
1986 San Francisco	NL	15	10	0	1	54.2	245	51	33	30	3	5	1	1	35	2	27	6	0	1	7	.125	0	0	4.94
1988 San Francisco	NL	9	6	2	1	46	191	50	20	19	3	5	0	1	7	0	18	1	0	2	1	.667	1	0	3.72
1989 2 ML Teams		25	18	2	4	115.1	513	137	66	63	8	7	1	4	36	3	66	3	0	4	7	.364	1	0	4.92
1990 Philadelphia	NL	33	26	6	2	180.2	746	172	78	67	15	7	12	2	42	7	75	7	2	9	10	.474	1	0	3.34
1991 Philadelphia	NL	34	34	8	0	232	956	231	100	93	15	11	6	3	49	2	142	3	0	16	13	.552	3	0	3.61
1992 Philadelphia	NL	32	32	12	0	229	937	227	101	97	14	10	7	3	46	3	125	3	0	13	11	.542	2	0	3.81
1993 Philadelphia	NL	29	28	7	0	191	786	177	80	69	20	5	4	3	40	2	116	5	0	12	9	.571	2	0	3.25
1989 San Francisco	NL	5	1	0	2	11	51	15	5	5	0	0	0	0	4	0	6	0	0	0	0	.000	0	0	4.09
Philadelphia	NL	20	17	2	2	104.1	462	122	61	58	8	7	1	4	32	3	60	3	0	4	7	.364	1	0	5.00
7 ML YEARS		177	154	37	8	1048.2	4374	1045	478	438	78	50	31	17	255	19	569	28	2	57	58	.496	10	0	3.76

Bobby Munoz

Pitches: Right **Bats:** Right **Pos:** RP **Ht:** 6' 7" **Wt:** 237 **Born:** 03/03/68 **Age:** 26

Year Team	Lg	G	GS	CG	GF	IP	BFP	H	R	ER	HR	SH	SF	HB	TBB	IBB	SO	WP	Bk	W	L	Pct.	ShO	Sv	ERA
1989 Yankees	R	2	2	0	0	10.1	41	5	4	4	0	0	0	0	4	0	13	1	1	1	1	.500	0	0	3.48
Ft.Laudrdle	A	3	3	0	0	13.1	58	16	8	7	2	0	0	0	7	0	2	0	1	1	2	.333	0	0	4.72
1990 Greensboro	A	25	24	0	0	132.2	581	134	70	55	4	2	2	5	58	1	100	4	6	5	12	.294	0	0	3.73
1991 Ft.Laudrdle	A	19	19	4	0	108	443	91	45	28	4	2	4	4	40	0	53	6	2	5	8	.385	2	0	2.33
Columbus	AAA	1	1	0	0	3	21	8	8	8	0	0	0	0	3	0	2	0	0	0	1	.000	0	0	24.00
1992 Albany	AA	22	22	0	0	112.1	491	96	55	41	2	2	4	4	70	0	66	8	0	7	5	.583	0	0	3.28
1993 Columbus	AAA	22	1	0	18	31.1	124	24	6	5	0	1	0	0	8	0	16	1	0	3	1	.750	0	10	1.44
1993 New York	AL	38	0	0	12	45.2	208	48	27	27	1	1	3	0	26	5	33	2	0	3	3	.500	0	0	5.32

Mike Munoz

Pitches: Left **Bats:** Left **Pos:** RP **Ht:** 6' 2" **Wt:** 200 **Born:** 07/12/65 **Age:** 28

Year Team	Lg	G	GS	CG	GF	IP	BFP	H	R	ER	HR	SH	SF	HB	TBB	IBB	SO	WP	Bk	W	L	Pct.	ShO	Sv	ERA
1993 Colo Sprngs *	AAA	40	0	0	13	37.2	167	46	10	7	0	3	2	0	9	0	30	2	0	1	2	.333	0	3	1.67
1989 Los Angeles	NL	3	0	0	1	2.2	14	5	5	5	1	0	0	0	2	0	3	0	0	0	0	.000	0	0	16.88
1990 Los Angeles	NL	8	0	0	3	5.2	24	6	2	2	0	1	0	0	3	0	2	0	0	0	0	.000	0	0	3.18
1991 Detroit	AL	6	0	0	4	9.1	46	14	10	10	0	0	1	0	5	0	3	1	0	0	0	.000	0	0	9.64
1992 Detroit	AL	65	0	0	15	48	210	44	16	16	3	4	2	0	25	6	23	2	0	1	2	.333	0	2	3.00
1993 2 ML Teams		29	0	0	10	21	101	25	14	11	2	3	2	0	15	4	17	2	0	2	2	.500	0	4	4.71
1993 Detroit	AL	8	0	0	3	3	19	4	2	2	1	0	0	0	6	1	1	0	0	0	1	.000	0	0	6.00
Colorado	NL	21	0	0	7	18	82	21	12	9	1	3	2	0	9	3	16	2	0	2	1	.667	0	4	4.50
5 ML YEARS		111	0	0	33	86.2	395	94	47	44	6	8	5	0	50	10	48	5	0	3	5	.375	0	2	4.57

Pedro Munoz

Bats: Right **Throws:** Right **Pos:** LF/RF **Ht:** 5'10" **Wt:** 207 **Born:** 09/19/68 **Age:** 25

Year Team	Lg	G	AB	H	2B	3B	HR	(Hm	Rd)	TB	R	RBI	TBB	IBB	SO	HBP	SH	SF	SB	CS	SB%	GDP	Avg	OBP	SLG
1990 Minnesota	AL	22	85	23	4	1	1	(0	0)	29	13	5	2	0	16	0	1	2	3	0	1.00	3	.271	.281	.341
1991 Minnesota	AL	51	138	39	7	1	7	(4	3)	69	15	26	9	0	31	1	1	2	3	0	1.00	2	.283	.327	.500
1992 Minnesota	AL	127	418	113	16	3	12	(8	4)	171	44	71	17	1	90	1	0	3	4	5	.44	18	.270	.298	.409
1993 Minnesota	AL	104	326	76	11	1	13	(2	11)	128	34	38	25	2	97	3	0	0	1	2	.33	7	.233	.294	.393
4 ML YEARS		304	967	251	38	6	32	(14	18)	397	106	140	53	3	234	5	2	7	11	7	.61	30	.260	.299	.411

Dale Murphy

Bats: Right **Throws:** Right **Pos:** RF **Ht:** 6' 4" **Wt:** 221 **Born:** 03/12/56 **Age:** 38

Year Team	Lg	G	AB	H	2B	3B	HR	(Hm	Rd)	TB	R	RBI	TBB	IBB	SO	HBP	SH	SF	SB	CS	SB%	GDP	Avg	OBP	SLG
1976 Atlanta	NL	19	65	17	6	0	0	(0	0)	23	3	9	7	0	9	0	0	0	0	0	.00	0	.262	.333	.354
1977 Atlanta	NL	18	76	24	8	1	2	(0	2)	40	5	14	0	0	8	0	0	0	0	1	.00	3	.316	.316	.526
1978 Atlanta	NL	151	530	120	14	3	23	(17	6)	209	66	79	42	3	145	3	3	5	11	7	.61	15	.226	.284	.394
1979 Atlanta	NL	104	384	106	7	2	21	(12	9)	180	53	57	38	5	67	2	0	5	6	1	.86	12	.276	.340	.469
1980 Atlanta	NL	156	569	160	27	2	33	(17	16)	290	98	89	59	9	133	1	2	2	9	6	.60	8	.281	.349	.510
1981 Atlanta	NL	104	369	91	12	1	13	(9	4)	144	43	50	44	8	72	0	1	2	14	5	.74	10	.247	.325	.390
1982 Atlanta	NL	162	598	168	23	2	36	(24	12)	303	113	109	93	9	134	3	0	4	23	11	.68	10	.281	.378	.507
1983 Atlanta	NL	162	589	178	24	4	36	(17	19)	318	131	121	90	12	110	2	0	6	30	4	.88	15	.302	.393	.540

Year	Team	Lg	G	AB	H	2B	3B	HR	(Hm	Rd)	TB	R	RBI	TBB	IBB	SO	HBP	SH	SF	SB	CS	SB%	GDP	Avg	OBP	SLG
1984	Atlanta	NL	**162**	607	176	32	8	**36**	(18	18)	**332**	94	100	79	20	134	2	0	3	19	7	.73	13	.290	.372	**.547**
1985	Atlanta	NL	**162**	616	185	32	2	37	(19	18)	332	**118**	111	**90**	15	**141**	1	0	5	10	3	.77	14	.300	.388	.539
1986	Atlanta	NL	160	614	163	29	7	29	(17	12)	293	89	83	75	5	141	2	0	1	7	7	.50	10	.265	.347	.477
1987	Atlanta	NL	159	566	167	27	1	44	(25	19)	328	115	105	115	29	136	7	0	5	16	6	.73	11	.295	.417	.580
1988	Atlanta	NL	156	592	134	35	4	24	(14	10)	249	77	77	74	16	125	2	0	3	3	5	.38	**24**	.226	.313	.421
1989	Atlanta	NL	154	574	131	16	0	20	(9	11)	207	60	84	65	10	142	2	0	6	3	2	.60	14	.228	.306	.361
1990	2 ML Teams		154	563	138	23	1	24	(9	15)	235	60	83	61	14	130	1	0	4	9	3	.75	**22**	.245	.318	.417
1991	Philadelphia	NL	153	544	137	33	1	18	(9	9)	226	66	81	48	3	93	0	0	7	1	0	1.00	20	.252	.309	.415
1992	Philadelphia	NL	18	62	10	1	0	2	(2	0)	17	5	7	1	0	13	0	0	0	0	0	.00	3	.161	.175	.274
1993	Colorado	NL	26	42	6	1	0	0	(0	0)	7	1	7	5	1	15	0	0	2	0	0	.00	5	.143	.224	.167
1990	Atlanta	NL	97	349	81	14	0	17	(8	9)	146	38	55	41	11	84	1	0	3	9	2	.82	11	.232	.312	.418
	Philadelphia	NL	57	214	57	9	1	7	(1	6)	89	22	28	20	3	46	0	0	1	0	1	.00	11	.266	.328	.416
	18 ML YEARS		2180	7960	2111	350	39	398	(217	181)	3733	1197	1266	986	159	1748	28	6	60	161	68	.70	209	.265	.346	.469

Rob Murphy

Pitches: Left **Bats:** Left **Pos:** RP **Ht:** 6' 2" **Wt:** 215 **Born:** 05/26/60 **Age:** 34

			HOW MUCH HE PITCHED						WHAT HE GAVE UP										THE RESULTS					
Year	Team	Lg	G	GS	CG	GF	IP	BFP	H	R	ER	HR	SH	SF	HB	TBB	IBB	SO	WP	Bk	W	L	Pct.	ShO	Sv	ERA
1985	Cincinnati	NL	2	0	0	2	3	12	2	2	2	1	0	0	0	2	0	1	0	0	0	0	.000	0	0	6.00
1986	Cincinnati	NL	34	0	0	12	50.1	195	26	4	4	0	3	3	0	21	2	36	5	0	6	0	1.000	0	1	0.72
1987	Cincinnati	NL	87	0	0	21	100.2	415	91	37	34	7	1	2	0	32	5	99	1	0	8	5	.615	0	3	3.04
1988	Cincinnati	NL	**76**	0	0	28	84.2	350	69	31	29	3	9	1	1	38	6	74	5	1	0	6	.000	0	3	3.08
1989	Boston	AL	74	0	0	27	105	438	97	38	32	7	7	3	1	41	8	107	6	0	5	7	.417	0	9	2.74
1990	Boston	AL	68	0	0	20	57	285	85	46	40	10	4	4	1	32	3	54	4	0	0	6	.000	0	7	6.32
1991	Seattle	AL	57	0	0	26	48	211	47	17	16	4	3	0	1	19	4	34	4	0	0	1	.000	0	4	3.00
1992	Houston	NL	59	0	0	6	55.2	242	56	28	25	2	3	3	0	21	4	42	4	0	3	1	.750	0	4	4.04
1993	St. Louis	NL	73	0	0	23	64.2	279	73	37	35	8	4	2	1	20	6	41	5	0	5	7	.417	0	1	4.87
	9 ML YEARS		530	0	0	165	569	2427	546	240	217	42	34	18	5	226	38	488	34	1	27	33	.450	0	28	3.43

Eddie Murray

Bats: Both **Throws:** Right **Pos:** 1B **Ht:** 6' 2" **Wt:** 220 **Born:** 02/24/56 **Age:** 38

			BATTING																BASERUNNING				PERCENTAGES		
Year	Team	Lg	G	AB	H	2B	3B	HR	(Hm | Rd)	TB	R	RBI	TBB	IBB	SO	HBP	SH	SF	SB	CS	SB%	GDP	Avg	OBP	SLG
1977	Baltimore	AL	160	611	173	29	2	27	(14 | 13)	287	81	88	48	6	104	1	0	6	0	1	.00	22	.283	.333	.470
1978	Baltimore	AL	161	610	174	32	3	27	(10 | 17)	293	85	95	70	7	97	1	1	6	6	5	.55	15	.285	.356	.480
1979	Baltimore	AL	159	606	179	30	2	25	(10 | 15)	288	90	99	72	9	78	2	1	6	10	2	.83	16	.295	.369	.475
1980	Baltimore	AL	158	621	186	36	2	32	(10 | 22)	322	100	116	54	10	71	2	0	6	7	2	.78	18	.300	.354	.519
1981	Baltimore	AL	99	378	111	21	2	**22**	(12 | 10)	202	57	**78**	40	10	43	1	0	3	2	3	.40	10	.294	.360	.534
1982	Baltimore	AL	151	550	174	30	1	32	(18 | 14)	302	87	110	70	**18**	82	1	0	6	7	2	.78	17	.316	.391	.549
1983	Baltimore	AL	156	582	178	30	3	33	(16 | 17)	313	115	111	86	13	90	3	0	9	5	1	.83	13	.306	.393	.538
1984	Baltimore	AL	**162**	588	180	26	3	29	(18 | 11)	299	97	110	**107**	**25**	87	2	0	8	10	2	.83	9	.306	**.410**	.509
1985	Baltimore	AL	156	583	173	37	1	31	(15 | 16)	305	111	124	84	12	68	2	0	8	5	2	.71	8	.297	.383	.523
1986	Baltimore	AL	137	495	151	25	1	17	(9 | 8)	229	61	84	78	7	49	0	0	5	3	0	1.00	17	.305	.396	.463
1987	Baltimore	AL	160	618	171	28	3	30	(14 | 16)	295	89	91	73	6	80	0	0	3	1	2	.33	15	.277	.352	.477
1988	Baltimore	AL	161	603	171	27	2	28	(14 | 14)	286	75	84	75	8	78	0	0	3	5	2	.71	20	.284	.361	.474
1989	Los Angeles	NL	160	594	147	29	1	20	(4 | 16)	238	66	88	87	24	85	2	0	7	7	2	.78	12	.247	.342	.401
1990	Los Angeles	NL	155	558	184	22	3	26	(12 | 14)	290	96	95	82	**21**	64	1	0	4	8	5	.62	19	.330	.414	.520
1991	Los Angeles	NL	153	576	150	23	1	19	(11 | 8)	232	69	96	55	17	74	0	0	8	10	3	.77	17	.260	.321	.403
1992	New York	NL	156	551	144	37	2	16	(7 | 9)	233	64	93	66	8	74	0	0	8	4	2	.67	15	.261	.336	.423
1993	New York	NL	154	610	174	28	1	27	(15 | 12)	285	77	100	40	4	61	0	0	9	2	2	.50	24	.285	.325	.467
	17 ML YEARS		2598	9734	2820	490	33	441	(209 | 232)	4699	1420	1662	1187	205	1285	18	2	107	92	38	.71	267	.290	.364	.483

Mike Mussina

Pitches: Right **Bats:** Right **Pos:** SP **Ht:** 6' 2" **Wt:** 185 **Born:** 12/08/68 **Age:** 25

			HOW MUCH HE PITCHED						WHAT HE GAVE UP										THE RESULTS					
Year	Team	Lg	G	GS	CG	GF	IP	BFP	H	R	ER	HR	SH	SF	HB	TBB	IBB	SO	WP	Bk	W	L	Pct.	ShO	Sv	ERA
1993	Bowie *	AA	2	2	0	0	8	30	5	2	2	0	0	0	0	1	0	10	0	0	1	0	1.000	0	0	2.25
1991	Baltimore	AL	12	12	2	0	87.2	349	77	31	28	7	3	2	1	21	0	52	3	1	4	5	.444	0	0	2.87
1992	Baltimore	AL	32	32	8	0	241	957	212	70	68	16	**13**	6	2	48	2	130	6	0	18	5	**.783**	4	0	2.54
1993	Baltimore	AL	25	25	3	0	167.2	693	163	84	83	20	6	4	3	44	2	117	5	0	14	6	.700	2	0	4.46
	3 ML YEARS		69	69	13	0	496.1	1999	452	185	179	43	22	12	6	113	4	299	14	1	36	16	.692	6	0	3.25

Jeff Mutis

Pitches: Left **Bats:** Left **Pos:** SP   **Ht:** 6' 2" **Wt:** 185 **Born:** 12/20/66 **Age:** 27

Year	Team	Lg	G	GS	CG	GF	IP	BFP	H	R	ER	HR	SH	SF	HB	TBB	IBB	SO	WP	Bk	W	L	Pct.	ShO	Sv	ERA
1988	Burlington	R	3	3	0	0	22	79	8	1	1	0	0	0	0	6	0	20	1	2	3	0	1.000	0	0	0.41
	Kinston	A	1	1	0	0	5.2	24	6	1	1	0	1	0	0	3	0	2	1	0	1	0	1.000	0	0	1.59
1989	Kinston	A	16	15	5	1	99.2	406	87	42	29	6	1	4	2	20	0	68	3	2	7	3	.700	2	0	2.62
1990	Canton-Akrn	AA	26	26	7	0	165	702	178	73	58	6	3	2	3	44	2	94	5	1	11	10	.524	3	0	3.16
1991	Canton-Akrn	AA	25	24	7	0	169.2	682	138	42	34	0	8	4	6	51	2	89	3	1	11	5	.688	4	0	1.80
1992	Colo Sprngs	AAA	25	24	4	0	145.1	652	177	99	82	8	6	8	5	57	1	77	8	4	9	9	.500	0	0	5.08
1993	Charlotte	AAA	12	11	3	0	75.2	315	64	27	22	1	1	2	3	25	3	59	1	1	6	0	1.000	0	0	2.62
1991	Cleveland	AL	3	3	0	0	12.1	68	23	16	16	1	2	1	0	7	1	6	1	0	0	3	.000	0	0	11.68
1992	Cleveland	AL	3	2	0	0	11.1	64	24	14	12	4	0	2	0	6	0	8	2	0	0	2	.000	0	0	9.53
1993	Cleveland	AL	17	13	1	1	81	364	93	56	52	14	0	2	7	33	2	29	1	0	3	6	.333	1	0	5.78
	3 ML YEARS		23	18	1	1	104.2	496	140	86	80	19	2	5	7	46	3	43	4	0	3	11	.214	1	0	6.88

Greg Myers

Bats: Left **Throws:** Right **Pos:** C   **Ht:** 6' 2" **Wt:** 205 **Born:** 04/14/66 **Age:** 28

Year	Team	Lg	G	AB	H	2B	3B	HR	(Hm	Rd)	TB	R	RBI	TBB	IBB	SO	HBP	SH	SF	SB	CS	SB%	GDP	Avg	OBP	SLG
1987	Toronto	AL	7	9	1	0	0	0	(0	0)	1	1	0	0	0	3	0	0	0	0	0	.00	0	.111	.111	.111
1989	Toronto	AL	17	44	5	2	0	0	(0	0)	7	0	1	2	0	9	0	0	0	0	1	.00	2	.114	.152	.159
1990	Toronto	AL	87	250	59	7	1	5	(3	2)	83	33	22	22	0	33	0	1	4	0	1	.00	12	.236	.293	.332
1991	Toronto	AL	107	309	81	22	0	8	(5	3)	127	25	36	21	4	45	0	4	3	0	0	.00	13	.262	.306	.411
1992	2 ML Teams		30	78	18	7	0	1	(0	1)	28	4	13	5	0	11	0	1	2	0	0	.00	2	.231	.271	.359
1993	California	AL	108	290	74	10	0	7	(4	3)	105	27	40	17	2	47	2	3	3	3	3	.50	8	.255	.298	.362
1992	Toronto	AL	22	61	14	6	0	1	(0	1)	23	4	13	5	0	5	0	0	2	0	0	.00	2	.230	.279	.377
	California	AL	8	17	4	1	0	0	(0	0)	5	0	0	0	0	6	0	1	0	0	0	.00	0	.235	.235	.294
	6 ML YEARS		356	980	238	48	1	21	(12	9)	351	90	112	67	6	148	2	5	12	3	5	.38	39	.243	.289	.358

Randy Myers

Pitches: Left **Bats:** Left **Pos:** RP   **Ht:** 6' 1" **Wt:** 225 **Born:** 09/19/62 **Age:** 31

Year	Team	Lg	G	GS	CG	GF	IP	BFP	H	R	ER	HR	SH	SF	HB	TBB	IBB	SO	WP	Bk	W	L	Pct.	ShO	Sv	ERA
1985	New York	NL	1	0	0	1	2	7	0	0	0	0	0	0	0	1	0	2	0	0	0	0	.000	0	0	0.00
1986	New York	NL	10	0	0	5	10.2	53	11	5	5	1	0	0	1	9	1	13	0	0	0	0	.000	0	0	4.22
1987	New York	NL	54	0	0	18	75	314	61	36	33	6	7	6	0	30	5	92	3	0	3	6	.333	0	6	3.96
1988	New York	NL	55	0	0	44	68	261	45	15	13	5	3	2	2	17	2	69	2	0	7	3	.700	0	26	1.72
1989	New York	NL	65	0	0	47	84.1	349	62	23	22	4	6	2	0	40	4	88	3	0	7	4	.636	0	24	2.35
1990	Cincinnati	NL	66	0	0	59	86.2	353	59	24	20	6	4	2	3	38	8	98	2	1	4	6	.400	0	31	2.08
1991	Cincinnati	NL	58	12	1	18	132	575	116	61	52	8	8	6	1	80	5	108	2	1	6	13	.316	0	6	3.55
1992	San Diego	NL	66	0	0	57	79.2	348	84	38	38	7	7	5	1	34	3	66	5	0	3	6	.333	0	38	4.29
1993	Chicago	NL	73	0	0	69	75.1	313	65	26	26	7	1	2	1	26	2	86	3	0	2	4	.333	0	53	3.11
	9 ML YEARS		448	12	1	318	613.2	2573	503	228	209	44	36	25	9	275	30	622	20	2	32	42	.432	0	184	3.07

Chris Nabholz

Pitches: Left **Bats:** Left **Pos:** SP/RP   **Ht:** 6' 5" **Wt:** 212 **Born:** 01/05/67 **Age:** 27

Year	Team	Lg	G	GS	CG	GF	IP	BFP	H	R	ER	HR	SH	SF	HB	TBB	IBB	SO	WP	Bk	W	L	Pct.	ShO	Sv	ERA
1993	Ottawa *	AAA	5	5	0	0	26.2	109	24	15	13	1	1	0	0	7	0	20	0	0	1	1	.500	0	0	4.39
1990	Montreal	NL	11	11	1	0	70	282	43	23	22	6	1	2	2	32	1	53	1	0	6	2	.750	1	0	2.83
1991	Montreal	NL	24	24	1	0	153.2	631	134	66	62	5	2	4	2	57	4	99	3	1	8	7	.533	0	0	3.63
1992	Montreal	NL	32	32	1	0	195	812	176	80	72	11	7	4	5	74	2	130	5	1	11	12	.478	1	0	3.32
1993	Montreal	NL	26	21	1	2	116.2	505	100	57	53	9	7	4	8	63	4	74	7	0	9	8	.529	0	0	4.09
	4 ML YEARS		93	88	4	2	535.1	2230	453	226	209	31	17	14	17	226	11	356	16	3	34	29	.540	2	0	3.51

Tim Naehring

Bats: Right **Throws:** Right **Pos:** 2B   **Ht:** 6' 2" **Wt:** 205 **Born:** 02/01/67 **Age:** 27

Year	Team	Lg	G	AB	H	2B	3B	HR	(Hm	Rd)	TB	R	RBI	TBB	IBB	SO	HBP	SH	SF	SB	CS	SB%	GDP	Avg	OBP	SLG
1993	Pawtucket *	AAA	55	202	62	9	1	7	--	--	94	38	36	35	3	27	0	3	1	0	2	.00	5	.307	.408	.465
1990	Boston	AL	24	85	23	6	0	2	(2	0)	35	10	12	8	1	15	0	0	0	0	0	.00	2	.271	.333	.412
1991	Boston	AL	20	55	6	1	0	0	(0	0)	7	1	3	6	0	15	0	4	0	0	0	.00	0	.109	.197	.127
1992	Boston	AL	72	186	43	8	0	3	(0	3)	60	12	14	18	0	31	3	6	1	0	0	.00	1	.231	.308	.323
1993	Boston	AL	39	127	42	10	0	1	(0	1)	55	14	17	10	0	26	0	3	1	0	1	1.00	6	.331	.377	.433
	4 ML YEARS		155	453	114	25	0	6	(2	4)	157	37	46	42	1	87	3	13	2	0	1	1.00	6	.252	.318	.347

Charles Nagy

Pitches: Right **Bats:** Left **Pos:** SP **Ht:** 6' 3" **Wt:** 200 **Born:** 05/05/67 **Age:** 27

		HOW MUCH HE PITCHED					WHAT HE GAVE UP										THE RESULTS					
Year Team	Lg	G	GS	CG	GF	IP	BFP	H	R	ER	HR	SH	SF	HB	TBB	IBB	SO	WP	Bk	W	L	Pct.	ShO	Sv	ERA
1993 Canton-Akrn *	AA	2	2	0	0	8	32	8	1	1	0	0	0	0	2	0	4	0	0	0	0	.000	0	0	1.13
1990 Cleveland	AL	9	8	0	1	45.2	208	58	31	30	7	1	1	1	21	1	26	1	1	2	4	.333	0	0	5.91
1991 Cleveland	AL	33	33	6	0	211.1	914	228	103	97	15	5	9	6	66	7	109	6	2	10	15	.400	1	0	4.13
1992 Cleveland	AL	33	33	10	0	252	1018	245	91	83	11	6	9	2	57	1	169	7	0	17	10	.630	3	0	2.96
1993 Cleveland	AL	9	9	1	0	48.2	223	66	38	34	6	2	1	2	13	1	30	2	0	2	6	.250	0	0	6.29
4 ML YEARS		84	83	17	1	557.2	2363	597	263	244	39	14	20	11	157	10	334	16	3	31	35	.470	4	0	3.94

Bob Natal

Bats: Right **Throws:** Right **Pos:** C **Ht:** 5'11" **Wt:** 190 **Born:** 11/13/65 **Age:** 28

		BATTING																	BASERUNNING				PERCENTAGES		
Year Team	Lg	G	AB	H	2B	3B	HR	(Hm	Rd)	TB	R	RBI	TBB	IBB	SO	HBP	SH	SF	SB	CS	SB%	GDP	Avg	OBP	SLG
1987 Jamestown	A	57	180	58	8	4	7	--	--	95	26	32	12	1	25	3	0	3	6	4	.60	3	.322	.369	.528
1988 Wst Plm Bch	A	113	387	93	17	0	6	--	--	128	47	51	29	0	50	9	3	3	3	2	.60	8	.240	.306	.331
1989 Jacksnville	A	46	141	29	8	1	0	--	--	39	12	11	9	0	24	0	2	3	2	1	.67	1	.206	.248	.277
Wst Plm Bch	A	15	48	6	0	0	1	--	--	9	5	2	9	1	9	2	0	1	1	0	1.00	1	.125	.288	.188
1990 Jacksnville	AA	62	171	42	7	1	7	--	--	72	23	25	14	2	42	5	1	2	0	1	.00	2	.246	.318	.421
1991 Indianapols	AAA	16	41	13	4	0	0	--	--	17	2	9	6	1	9	0	0	1	1	0	1.00	0	.317	.396	.415
Harrisburg	AA	100	336	86	16	3	13	--	--	147	47	53	49	3	90	8	2	5	1	1	.50	5	.256	.359	.438
1992 Indianapols	AAA	96	344	104	19	3	12	--	--	165	50	50	28	1	42	4	1	3	3	0	1.00	7	.302	.359	.480
1993 Edmonton	AAA	17	66	21	6	1	3	--	--	38	16	16	8	0	10	1	0	0	0	0	.00	0	.318	.400	.576
1992 Montreal	NL	5	6	0	0	0	0	(0	0)	0	0	0	1	0	1	0	0	0	0	0	.00	1	.000	.143	.000
1993 Florida	NL	41	117	25	4	1	1	(0	1)	34	3	6	6	0	22	4	3	1	1	0	1.00	6	.214	.273	.291
2 ML YEARS		46	123	25	4	1	1	(0	1)	34	3	6	7	0	23	4	3	1	1	0	1.00	6	.203	.267	.276

Jaime Navarro

Pitches: Right **Bats:** Right **Pos:** SP **Ht:** 6' 4" **Wt:** 210 **Born:** 03/27/68 **Age:** 26

		HOW MUCH HE PITCHED						WHAT HE GAVE UP											THE RESULTS					
Year Team	Lg	G	GS	CG	GF	IP	BFP	H	R	ER	HR	SH	SF	HB	TBB	IBB	SO	WP	Bk	W	L	Pct.	ShO	Sv	ERA
1989 Milwaukee	AL	19	17	1	1	109.2	470	119	47	38	6	5	2	1	32	3	56	3	0	7	8	.467	0	0	3.12
1990 Milwaukee	AL	32	22	3	2	149.1	654	176	83	74	11	4	5	4	41	3	75	6	5	8	7	.533	0	1	4.46
1991 Milwaukee	AL	34	34	10	0	234	1002	237	117	102	18	7	8	6	73	3	114	10	0	15	12	.556	2	0	3.92
1992 Milwaukee	AL	34	34	5	0	246	1004	224	98	91	14	9	13	6	64	4	100	6	0	17	11	.607	3	0	3.33
1993 Milwaukee	AL	35	34	5	0	214.1	955	254	135	127	21	6	17	11	73	4	114	11	0	11	12	.478	1	0	5.33
5 ML YEARS		154	141	24	3	953.1	4085	1010	480	432	70	31	45	28	283	17	459	36	5	58	50	.537	6	1	4.08

Tito Navarro

Bats: Both **Throws:** Right **Pos:** SS **Ht:** 5'10" **Wt:** 155 **Born:** 09/12/70 **Age:** 23

		BATTING																	BASERUNNING				PERCENTAGES		
Year Team	Lg	G	AB	H	2B	3B	HR	(Hm	Rd)	TB	R	RBI	TBB	IBB	SO	HBP	SH	SF	SB	CS	SB%	GDP	Avg	OBP	SLG
1988 Kingsport	R	54	172	42	3	2	0	--	--	49	26	23	30	0	27	3	2	3	3	4	.43	4	.244	.361	.285
1989 Pittsfield	A	46	157	44	6	2	0	--	--	54	26	14	18	0	30	0	3	1	13	3	.81	8	.280	.352	.344
1990 Columbia	A	136	497	156	25	4	0	--	--	189	87	54	69	1	56	2	7	7	50	14	.78	4	.314	.395	.380
Jackson	AA	3	11	2	1	0	0	--	--	3	0	1	2	0	2	0	0	0	0	1	.00	0	.182	.308	.273
1991 Williamsprt	AA	128	482	139	9	4	2	--	--	162	69	42	73	2	63	1	12	4	42	19	.69	10	.288	.380	.336
1993 Mets	R	4	14	4	1	1	0	--	--	7	2	5	3	0	1	0	0	2	1	0	1.00	0	.286	.368	.500
Norfolk	AAA	96	273	77	11	1	0	--	--	90	35	16	33	1	39	0	7	2	19	3	.86	10	.282	.357	.330
1993 New York	NL	12	17	1	0	0	0	(0	0)	1	1	1	4	0	1	0	0	2	0	0	.00	1	.059	.059	.059

Denny Neagle

Pitches: Left **Bats:** Left **Pos:** RP/SP **Ht:** 6' 2" **Wt:** 215 **Born:** 09/13/68 **Age:** 25

		HOW MUCH HE PITCHED						WHAT HE GAVE UP											THE RESULTS					
Year Team	Lg	G	GS	CG	GF	IP	BFP	H	R	ER	HR	SH	SF	HB	TBB	IBB	SO	WP	Bk	W	L	Pct.	ShO	Sv	ERA
1993 Buffalo *	AAA	3	0	0	0	3.1	14	3	0	0	0	0	0	0	2	0	6	0	0	0	0	.000	0	0	0.00
1991 Minnesota	AL	7	3	0	2	20	92	28	9	9	3	0	0	0	7	2	14	1	0	0	1	.000	0	0	4.05
1992 Pittsburgh	NL	55	6	0	8	86.1	380	81	46	43	9	4	3	2	43	8	77	3	2	4	6	.400	0	2	4.48
1993 Pittsburgh	NL	50	7	0	13	81.1	360	82	49	48	10	1	1	3	37	3	73	5	0	3	5	.375	0	1	5.31
3 ML YEARS		112	16	0	23	187.2	832	191	104	100	22	5	4	5	87	13	164	9	2	7	12	.368	0	3	4.80

156

Troy Neel

Bats: Left **Throws:** Right **Pos:** DH/1B **Ht:** 6'4" **Wt:** 215 **Born:** 09/14/65 **Age:** 28

					BATTING															BASERUNNING				PERCENTAGES		
Year	Team	Lg	G	AB	H	2B	3B	HR	(Hm	Rd)	TB	R	RBI	TBB	IBB	SO	HBP	SH	SF	SB	CS	SB%	GDP	Avg	OBP	SLG
1986	Batavia	A	4	13	0	0	0	0	--	--	0	0	1	0	0	8	0	0	0	0	0	.00	0	.000	.000	.000
1987	Burlington	R	59	192	54	17	0	10	--	--	101	36	59	25	4	59	3	0	5	0	0	.00	3	.281	.364	.526
1988	Waterloo	A	91	331	96	20	1	8	--	--	142	49	57	38	3	76	6	0	3	0	1	.00	11	.290	.370	.429
1989	Canton-Akrn	AA	124	404	118	21	2	21	--	--	206	58	73	51	6	87	9	0	5	5	9	.36	10	.292	.380	.510
1990	Colo Spngs	AAA	98	288	81	15	0	6	--	--	114	39	50	43	1	52	2	0	4	5	4	.56	5	.281	.374	.396
1991	Tacoma	AAA	18	59	14	3	1	0	--	--	19	7	7	7	0	14	1	0	0	0	0	.00	0	.237	.328	.322
	Huntsville	AA	110	364	101	21	0	23	--	--	191	64	68	82	18	75	5	0	7	1	3	.25	7	.277	.410	.525
1992	Tacoma	AAA	112	396	139	36	3	17	--	--	232	61	74	60	11	84	6	0	5	2	5	.29	8	.351	.439	.586
1993	Tacoma	AAA	13	50	18	4	0	1	--	--	25	11	9	6	2	9	0	0	0	2	1	.67	0	.360	.429	.500
1992	Oakland	AL	24	53	14	3	0	3	(2	1)	26	8	9	5	0	15	1	0	0	0	1	.00	1	.264	.339	.491
1993	Oakland	AL	123	427	124	21	0	19	(11	8)	202	59	63	49	5	101	4	0	2	3	5	.38	7	.290	.367	.473
	2 ML YEARS		147	480	138	24	0	22	(13	9)	228	67	72	54	5	116	5	0	2	3	6	.33	8	.288	.364	.475

Gene Nelson

Pitches: Right **Bats:** Right **Pos:** RP **Ht:** 6'0" **Wt:** 174 **Born:** 12/03/60 **Age:** 33

			HOW MUCH HE PITCHED						WHAT HE GAVE UP											THE RESULTS					
Year	Team	Lg	G	GS	CG	GF	IP	BFP	H	R	ER	HR	SH	SF	HB	TBB	IBB	SO	WP	Bk	W	L	Pct.	ShO	Sv	ERA
1981	New York	AL	8	7	0	0	39	179	40	24	21	5	0	2	1	23	1	16	2	0	3	1	.750	0	0	4.85
1982	Seattle	AL	22	19	2	2	122.2	545	133	70	63	16	4	2	2	60	1	71	4	2	6	9	.400	1	0	4.62
1983	Seattle	AL	10	5	1	2	32	153	38	29	28	6	2	0	1	21	2	11	1	0	0	3	.000	0	0	7.88
1984	Chicago	AL	20	9	2	4	74.2	304	72	38	37	9	1	2	1	17	0	36	4	1	3	5	.375	0	1	4.46
1985	Chicago	AL	46	18	1	11	145.2	643	144	74	69	23	9	2	7	67	4	101	11	1	10	10	.500	0	2	4.26
1986	Chicago	AL	54	1	0	26	114.2	488	118	52	49	7	7	1	3	41	5	70	3	0	6	6	.500	0	6	3.85
1987	Oakland	AL	54	6	0	15	123.2	530	120	58	54	12	3	5	5	35	0	94	7	0	6	5	.545	0	3	3.93
1988	Oakland	AL	54	1	0	20	111.2	456	93	42	38	9	3	4	3	38	4	67	4	6	9	6	.600	0	3	3.06
1989	Oakland	AL	50	0	0	15	80	335	60	33	29	5	3	4	2	30	3	70	5	0	3	5	.375	0	3	3.26
1990	Oakland	AL	51	0	0	17	74.2	291	55	14	13	5	1	5	3	17	1	38	1	0	3	3	.500	0	5	1.57
1991	Oakland	AL	44	0	0	11	48.2	229	60	38	37	12	3	4	3	23	1	23	0	0	1	5	.167	0	0	6.84
1992	Oakland	AL	28	2	0	8	51.2	234	68	37	37	5	4	5	0	22	5	23	2	0	3	1	.750	0	0	6.45
1993	2 ML Teams		52	0	0	22	60.2	265	60	28	21	3	3	4	2	24	5	35	2	0	0	5	.000	0	5	3.12
1993	California	AL	46	0	0	20	52.2	231	50	25	18	3	3	4	2	23	4	31	1	0	0	5	.000	0	4	3.08
	Texas	AL	6	0	0	2	8	34	10	3	3	0	0	0	0	1	1	4	1	0	0	0	.000	0	1	3.38
	13 ML YEARS		493	68	6	153	1079.2	4652	1061	537	496	117	43	40	33	418	32	655	46	10	53	64	.453	1	28	4.13

Jeff Nelson

Pitches: Right **Bats:** Right **Pos:** RP **Ht:** 6'8" **Wt:** 225 **Born:** 11/17/66 **Age:** 27

			HOW MUCH HE PITCHED						WHAT HE GAVE UP											THE RESULTS					
Year	Team	Lg	G	GS	CG	GF	IP	BFP	H	R	ER	HR	SH	SF	HB	TBB	IBB	SO	WP	Bk	W	L	Pct.	ShO	Sv	ERA
1984	Great Falls	R	1	0	0	0	0.2	13	3	4	4	1	0	0	1	3	0	1	0	0	0	0	.000	0	0	54.00
	Dodgers	R	9	0	0	3	13.1	56	6	3	2	0	0	0	1	6	0	7	1	1	0	0	.000	0	0	1.35
1985	Dodgers	R	14	7	0	3	47.1	242	72	50	29	1	0	1	0	32	0	31	8	1	0	5	.000	0	0	5.51
1986	Great Falls	R	3	0	0	2	2	12	5	3	3	0	0	0	0	3	2	1	2	0	0	0	.000	0	0	13.50
	Bakersfield	A	24	11	0	6	71.1	412	79	83	53	9	1	9	4	84	1	37	10	0	0	7	.000	0	0	6.69
1987	Salinas	A	17	16	1	0	80	389	80	61	51	2	4	3	4	71	0	43	17	0	3	7	.300	0	0	5.74
1988	San Berndno	A	27	27	1	0	149.1	677	163	115	92	9	2	8	8	91	2	94	20	0	8	9	.471	1	0	5.54
1989	Williamsprt	AA	15	15	2	0	92.1	392	72	41	34	2	0	3	4	53	1	61	9	1	7	5	.583	0	0	3.31
1990	Williamsprt	AA	10	10	0	0	43.1	203	65	35	31	2	0	2	2	18	1	14	2	0	1	4	.200	0	0	6.44
	Peninsula	A	18	7	1	8	60	247	47	21	21	5	1	0	1	25	1	49	2	0	2	2	.500	1	6	3.15
1991	Jacksnville	AA	21	0	0	20	28.1	113	23	5	4	0	2	0	0	9	0	34	2	0	4	0	1.000	0	12	1.27
	Calgary	AAA	28	0	0	21	32.1	146	39	19	14	1	2	3	0	15	3	26	2	1	3	4	.429	0	7	3.90
1992	Calgary	AAA	2	0	0	2	3.2	10	0	0	0	0	0	0	0	1	0	0	0	0	1	0	1.000	0	0	0.00
1993	Calgary	AAA	5	0	0	4	7.2	31	6	1	1	0	1	0	1	2	0	6	2	0	1	0	1.000	0	1	1.17
1992	Seattle	AL	66	0	0	27	81	352	71	34	31	7	9	3	6	44	12	46	2	0	1	7	.125	0	6	3.44
1993	Seattle	AL	71	0	0	13	60	269	57	30	29	5	2	4	8	34	10	61	2	0	5	3	.625	0	1	4.35
	2 ML YEARS		137	0	0	40	141	621	128	64	60	12	11	7	14	78	22	107	4	0	6	10	.375	0	7	3.83

Robb Nen

Pitches: Right **Bats:** Right **Pos:** RP/SP **Ht:** 6'4" **Wt:** 190 **Born:** 11/28/69 **Age:** 24

			HOW MUCH HE PITCHED						WHAT HE GAVE UP											THE RESULTS					
Year	Team	Lg	G	GS	CG	GF	IP	BFP	H	R	ER	HR	SH	SF	HB	TBB	IBB	SO	WP	Bk	W	L	Pct.	ShO	Sv	ERA
1987	Rangers	R	2	0	0	0	2.1	13	4	2	2	0	0	0	0	3	1	4	0	0	0	0	.000	0	0	7.71
1988	Gastonia	A	14	10	0	1	48.1	269	69	57	40	5	1	4	2	45	0	36	5	2	0	5	.000	0	0	7.45
	Butte	R	14	13	0	0	48.1	257	65	55	47	4	0	2	1	45	0	30	12	1	4	5	.444	0	0	8.75

Year Team	Lg	G	GS	CG	GF	IP	BFP	H	R	ER	HR	SH	SF	HB	TBB	IBB	SO	WP	Bk	W	L	Pct	ShO	Sv	ERA
1989 Gastonia	A	24	24	1	0	138.1	580	96	47	37	7	2	3	6	76	0	146	15	4	7	4	.636	1	0	2.41
1990 Charlotte	A	11	11	1	0	53.2	231	44	28	22	1	2	2	0	36	0	38	6	0	1	4	.200	0	0	3.69
Tulsa	AA	7	7	0	0	26.2	120	23	20	15	1	1	2	0	21	0	21	3	0	0	5	.000	0	0	5.06
1991 Tulsa	AA	6	6	0	0	28	124	24	21	18	6	1	2	2	20	0	23	3	1	0	2	.000	0	0	5.79
1992 Tulsa	AA	4	4	1	0	25	98	21	7	6	1	0	1	1	2	0	20	4	0	1	1	.500	0	0	2.16
1993 Okla City	AAA	6	5	0	0	28.1	141	45	22	21	3	2	1	2	18	0	12	2	0	0	2	.000	0	0	6.67
1993 2 ML Teams		24	4	0	5	56	272	63	45	42	6	1	2	0	46	0	39	6	1	2	1	.667	0	0	6.75
1993 Texas	AL	9	3	0	3	22.2	113	28	17	16	1	0	1	0	26	0	12	2	1	1	1	.500	0	0	6.35
Florida	NL	15	1	0	2	33.1	159	35	28	26	5	1	1	0	20	0	27	4	0	1	0	1.000	0	0	7.02

Marc Newfield

Bats: Right Throws: Right Pos: DH/LF   **Ht: 6' 4" Wt: 205 Born: 10/19/72 Age: 21**

Year Team	Lg	G	AB	H	2B	3B	HR	Hm	Rd	TB	R	RBI	TBB	IBB	SO	HBP	SH	SF	SB	CS	SB%	GDP	Avg	OBP	SLG
1990 Mariners	A	49	185	60	13	2	6	--	--	95	34	38	23	0	20	2	0	2	4	4	.50	3	.324	.401	.514
1991 San Berndno	A	125	440	132	22	3	11	--	--	193	64	68	59	9	90	10	0	5	12	6	.67	14	.300	.391	.439
Jacksnville	AA	6	26	6	3	0	0	--	--	9	4	2	0	0	8	1	0	0	0	0	.00	0	.231	.259	.346
1992 Jacksnville	AA	45	162	40	12	0	4	--	--	64	15	19	12	0	34	3	1	1	1	5	.17	3	.247	.309	.395
1993 Jacksnville	AA	91	336	103	18	0	19	--	--	178	48	51	33	1	35	5	0	3	1	1	.50	12	.307	.374	.530
1993 Seattle	AL	22	66	15	3	0	1	(1	0)	21	5	7	2	0	8	1	0	1	0	1	.00	2	.227	.257	.318

Warren Newson

Bats: Left Throws: Left Pos: DH   **Ht: 5' 7" Wt: 190 Born: 07/03/64 Age: 29**

Year Team	Lg	G	AB	H	2B	3B	HR	Hm	Rd	TB	R	RBI	TBB	IBB	SO	HBP	SH	SF	SB	CS	SB%	GDP	Avg	OBP	SLG
1993 Nashville	AAA	61	176	60	8	2	4	--	--	84	40	21	38	4	38	1	0	3	5	2	.71	4	.341	.454	.477
1991 Chicago	AL	71	132	39	5	0	4	(1	3)	56	20	25	28	1	34	0	0	0	2	2	.50	4	.295	.419	.424
1992 Chicago	AL	63	136	30	3	0	1	(1	0)	36	19	11	37	2	38	0	0	0	3	0	1.00	4	.221	.387	.265
1993 Chicago	AL	26	40	12	0	0	2	(2	0)	18	9	6	9	1	12	0	0	0	0	0	.00	2	.300	.429	.450
3 ML YEARS		160	308	81	8	0	7	(4	3)	110	48	42	74	4	84	0	0	0	5	2	.71	10	.263	.406	.357

Rod Nichols

Pitches: Right Bats: Right Pos: RP   **Ht: 6' 2" Wt: 190 Born: 12/29/64 Age: 29**

Year Team	Lg	G	GS	CG	GF	IP	BFP	H	R	ER	HR	SH	SF	HB	TBB	IBB	SO	WP	Bk	W	L	Pct	ShO	Sv	ERA
1993 Albuquerque *	AAA	21	21	3	0	127.2	552	132	68	61	16	6	3		50	3	79	9	3	8	5	.615	1	0	4.30
1988 Cleveland	AL	11	10	3	1	69.1	297	73	41	39	5	2	2	2	23	1	31	2	3	1	7	.125	0	0	5.06
1989 Cleveland	AL	15	11	0	2	71.2	315	81	42	35	9	3	2	2	24	0	42	0	0	4	6	.400	0	0	4.40
1990 Cleveland	AL	4	2	0	0	16	79	24	14	14	5	1	0	2	6	0	3	0	0	0	3	.000	0	0	7.88
1991 Cleveland	AL	31	16	3	4	137.1	578	145	63	54	6	6	4	6	30	3	76	3	0	2	11	.154	1	1	3.54
1992 Cleveland	AL	30	9	0	5	105.1	456	114	58	53	13	1	5	2	31	1	56	3	0	4	3	.571	0	0	4.53
1993 Los Angeles	NL	4	0	0	2	6.1	28	7	1	1	0	1	0	0	2	2	3	0	0	0	1	.000	0	0	5.68
6 ML YEARS		95	48	6	14	406	1753	446	223	199	39	14	13	14	116	7	211	8	3	11	31	.262	1	1	4.41

Dave Nied

Pitches: Right Bats: Right Pos: SP   **Ht: 6' 2" Wt: 185 Born: 12/22/68 Age: 25**

Year Team	Lg	G	GS	CG	GF	IP	BFP	H	R	ER	HR	SH	SF	HB	TBB	IBB	SO	WP	Bk	W	L	Pct	ShO	Sv	ERA
1988 Sumter	A	27	27	3	0	165.1	701	156	78	69	15	7	3	12	53	1	133	6	2	12	9	.571	0	0	3.76
1989 Durham	A	12	12	0	0	58.1	275	74	47	43	10	2	1	5	23	1	38	1	0	5	2	.714	0	0	6.63
Burlington	A	13	12	2	0	80	341	78	38	34	3	3	2	5	23	0	73	3	1	5	6	.455	1	0	3.83
1990 Durham	A	10	10	0	0	42.1	176	38	19	18	3	2	1	1	14	0	27	4	0	5	5	.500	0	0	3.83
Burlington	A	10	9	1	1	64	252	55	21	16	2	2	2	1	10	0	66	3	0	5	3	.625	1	0	2.25
1991 Durham	A	13	12	2	1	80.2	312	46	19	14	2	1	1	3	23	0	77	0	0	8	3	.727	2	0	1.56
Greenville	AA	15	15	1	0	89.2	367	79	26	24	0	3	2	6	20	3	101	1	0	7	3	.700	0	0	2.41
1992 Richmond	AAA	26	26	7	0	168	680	144	73	53	15	8	7	3	44	2	159	1	0	14	9	.609	2	0	2.84
1993 Central Val	A	1	1	0	0	3	16	3	2	1	0	0	0	0	3	0	3	0	0	0	0	.000	0	0	3.00
Colo Sprngs	AAA	3	3	0	0	15	73	24	17	15	3	0	1	2	6	0	11	0	0	0	2	.000	0	0	9.00
1992 Atlanta	NL	6	2	0	0	23	83	10	3	3	1	0	1	0	5	0	19	0	0	3	0	1.000	0	0	1.17
1993 Colorado	NL	16	16	1	0	87	394	99	53	50	8	9	7	1	42	4	46	1	1	5	9	.357	0	0	5.17
2 ML YEARS		22	18	1	0	110	477	109	56	53	8	10	7	1	47	4	65	1	1	8	9	.471	0	0	4.34

Jerry Nielsen

Pitches: Left Bats: Left Pos: RP   **Ht: 6' 1" Wt: 180 Born: 08/05/66 Age: 27**

Year Team	Lg	G	GS	CG	GF	IP	BFP	H	R	ER	HR	SH	SF	HB	TBB	IBB	SO	WP	Bk	W	L	Pct	ShO	Sv	ERA
1988 Oneonta	A	19	1	0	8	38	158	27	6	3	0	3	0	3	18	0	35	0	4	6	2	.750	0	0	0.71

Year Team		G	GS	CG	SV	IP	BFP	H	R	ER	HR	SH	SF	HB	TBB	IBB	SO	WP	Bk	W	L	Pct.	ShO	Sv	ERA
1989 Pr William	A	39	0	0	16	49.1	198	26	14	12	0	2	4	6	25	0	45	6	0	3	2	.600	0	4	2.19
1990 Pr William	A	26	26	1	0	151.2	665	149	76	66	9	4	2	11	79	1	119	9	2	7	12	.368	1	0	3.92
1991 Ft.Laudrdle	A	42	0	0	14	64.2	275	50	29	20	2	5	5	3	31	4	66	7	0	3	3	.500	0	4	2.78
Albany	AA	6	0	0	2	8	38	9	6	5	1	1	0	0	8	0	5	0	0	0	1	.000	0	0	5.63
1992 Albany	AA	36	0	0	21	53	207	38	8	7	1	1	0	1	15	2	59	5	0	3	5	.375	0	11	1.19
Columbus	AAA	4	0	0	2	5	18	2	1	1	0	0	2	1	2	0	5	1	0	0	0	.000	0	1	1.80
1993 Vancouver	AAA	33	5	0	10	55.2	252	70	32	26	4	7	2	0	20	3	45	2	1	2	5	.286	0	0	4.20
1992 New York	AL	20	0	0	12	19.2	90	17	10	10	1	1	1	0	18	2	12	1	0	1	0	1.000	0	0	4.58
1993 California	AL	10	0	0	3	12.1	62	18	13	11	1	1	3	1	4	0	8	0	1	0	0	.000	0	0	8.03
2 ML YEARS		30	0	0	15	32	152	35	23	21	2	2	4	1	22	2	20	1	1	1	0	1.000	0	0	5.91

Melvin Nieves

Bats: Both   Throws: Right   Pos: RF   Ht: 6' 2"   Wt: 200   Born: 12/28/71   Age: 22

Year Team	Lg	G	AB	H	2B	3B	HR	(Hm	Rd)	TB	R	RBI	TBB	IBB	SO	HBP	SH	SF	SB	CS	SB%	GDP	Avg	OBP	SLG
1988 Braves	R	56	176	30	6	0	1	--	--	39	16	12	20	0	53	2	1	1	5	4	.56	2	.170	.261	.222
1989 Pulaski	R	64	231	64	16	3	9	--	--	113	43	46	30	4	59	1	3	4	6	4	.60	2	.277	.357	.489
1990 Sumter	A	126	459	130	24	7	9	--	--	195	60	59	53	4	125	9	1	9	10	6	.63	7	.283	.362	.425
1991 Durham	A	64	201	53	11	0	9	--	--	91	31	25	40	2	53	5	0	1	3	8	.27	1	.264	.397	.453
1992 Durham	A	31	106	32	9	1	8	--	--	67	18	32	17	3	33	2	0	4	4	2	.67	1	.302	.395	.632
Greenville	AA	100	350	99	23	5	18	--	--	186	61	76	52	2	98	6	2	4	6	4	.60	4	.283	.381	.531
1993 Richmond	AAA	78	273	76	10	3	10	--	--	122	38	36	25	4	84	2	1	1	4	3	.57	4	.278	.342	.447
Las Vegas	AAA	43	159	49	10	1	7	--	--	82	31	24	18	0	42	2	0	0	2	2	.50	1	.308	.385	.516
1992 Atlanta	NL	12	19	4	1	0	0	(0	0)	5	0	1	2	0	7	0	0	0	0	0	.00	0	.211	.286	.263
1993 San Diego	NL	19	47	9	0	0	2	(2	0)	15	4	3	3	0	21	1	0	0	0	0	.00	0	.191	.255	.319
2 ML YEARS		31	66	13	1	0	2	(2	0)	20	4	4	5	0	28	1	0	0	0	0	.00	0	.197	.264	.303

Dave Nilsson

Bats: Left   Throws: Right   Pos: C   Ht: 6' 3"   Wt: 185   Born: 12/14/69   Age: 24

Year Team	Lg	G	AB	H	2B	3B	HR	(Hm	Rd)	TB	R	RBI	TBB	IBB	SO	HBP	SH	SF	SB	CS	SB%	GDP	Avg	OBP	SLG
1987 Helena	R	55	188	74	13	0	1	--	--	90	36	21	22	2	14	0	1	2	0	1	.00	4	.394	.453	.479
1988 Beloit	A	95	332	74	15	2	4	--	--	105	28	41	25	2	49	2	0	5	2	5	.29	10	.223	.277	.316
1989 Stockton	A	125	472	115	16	6	5	--	--	158	59	56	51	1	75	1	4	4	2	1	.67	20	.244	.316	.335
1990 Stockton	A	107	359	104	22	3	7	--	--	153	70	47	43	3	36	0	0	4	6	5	.55	6	.290	.362	.426
1991 El Paso	AA	65	249	104	24	3	5	--	--	149	52	57	27	4	14	1	0	2	4	0	1.00	4	.418	.473	.598
Denver	AAA	28	95	22	8	0	1	--	--	33	10	14	17	0	16	0	0	0	1	1	.50	2	.232	.348	.347
1992 Denver	AAA	66	240	76	16	7	3	--	--	115	38	39	23	2	19	0	2	5	10	4	.71	3	.317	.369	.479
1993 El Paso	AA	5	17	8	1	0	1	--	--	12	5	7	2	0	4	0	0	1	1	1	.50	0	.471	.500	.706
New Orleans	AAA	17	61	21	6	0	1	--	--	30	9	9	5	0	6	0	1	1	0	1	.00	1	.344	.388	.492
1992 Milwaukee	AL	51	164	38	8	0	4	(1	3)	58	15	25	17	1	18	0	2	0	2	2	.50	1	.232	.304	.354
1993 Milwaukee	AL	100	296	76	10	2	7	(5	2)	111	35	40	37	5	36	0	4	3	3	6	.33	9	.257	.336	.375
2 ML YEARS		151	460	114	18	2	11	(6	5)	169	50	65	54	6	54	0	6	3	5	8	.38	10	.248	.325	.367

Otis Nixon

Bats: Both   Throws: Right   Pos: CF   Ht: 6' 2"   Wt: 180   Born: 01/09/59   Age: 35

Year Team	Lg	G	AB	H	2B	3B	HR	(Hm	Rd)	TB	R	RBI	TBB	IBB	SO	HBP	SH	SF	SB	CS	SB%	GDP	Avg	OBP	SLG
1983 New York	AL	13	14	2	0	0	0	(0	0)	2	2	0	1	0	5	0	0	0	2	0	1.00	0	.143	.200	.143
1984 Cleveland	AL	49	91	14	0	0	0	(0	0)	14	16	1	8	0	11	0	3	1	12	6	.67	2	.154	.220	.154
1985 Cleveland	AL	104	162	38	4	0	3	(1	2)	51	34	9	8	0	27	0	4	0	20	11	.65	2	.235	.271	.315
1986 Cleveland	AL	105	95	25	4	1	0	(0	0)	31	33	8	13	0	12	0	2	0	23	6	.79	1	.263	.352	.326
1987 Cleveland	AL	19	17	1	0	0	0	(0	0)	1	2	1	3	0	4	0	0	0	2	3	.40	0	.059	.200	.059
1988 Montreal	NL	90	271	66	8	2	0	(0	0)	78	47	15	28	0	42	0	4	2	46	13	.78	0	.244	.312	.288
1989 Montreal	NL	126	258	56	7	2	0	(0	0)	67	41	21	33	1	36	0	2	0	37	12	.76	4	.217	.306	.260
1990 Montreal	NL	119	231	58	6	2	1	(0	1)	71	46	20	28	0	33	0	3	1	50	13	.79	2	.251	.331	.307
1991 Atlanta	NL	124	401	119	10	1	0	(0	0)	131	81	26	47	3	40	2	7	3	72	21	.77	5	.297	.371	.327
1992 Atlanta	NL	120	456	134	14	2	2	(1	1)	158	79	22	39	0	54	0	5	2	41	18	.69	4	.294	.348	.346
1993 Atlanta	NL	134	461	124	12	3	1	(1	0)	145	77	24	61	2	63	0	5	5	47	13	.78	9	.269	.351	.315
11 ML YEARS		1003	2457	637	65	13	7	(3	4)	749	458	147	269	6	327	2	35	14	352	116	.75	29	.259	.331	.305

Matt Nokes

Bats: Left   Throws: Right   Pos: C/DH   Ht: 6' 1"   Wt: 210   Born: 10/31/63   Age: 30

Year Team	Lg	G	AB	H	2B	3B	HR	(Hm	Rd)	TB	R	RBI	TBB	IBB	SO	HBP	SH	SF	SB	CS	SB%	GDP	Avg	OBP	SLG
1985 San Francisco	NL	19	53	11	2	0	2	(1	1)	19	3	5	1	0	9	1	0	0	0	0	.00	0	.208	.236	.358
1986 Detroit	AL	7	24	8	1	0	1	(0	1)	12	2	2	1	1	1	0	0	0	0	0	.00	1	.333	.360	.500

Year	Team	Lg	G	AB	H	2B	3B	HR	(Hm	Rd)	TB	R	RBI	TBB	IBB	SO	HBP	SH	SF	SB	CS	SB%	GDP	Avg	OBP	SLG
1987	Detroit	AL	135	461	133	14	2	32	(14	18)	247	69	87	35	2	70	6	3	3	2	1	.67	13	.289	.345	.536
1988	Detroit	AL	122	382	96	18	0	16	(9	7)	162	53	53	34	3	58	1	6	2	0	1	.00	11	.251	.313	.424
1989	Detroit	AL	87	268	67	10	0	9	(7	2)	104	15	39	17	1	37	2	1	2	1	0	1.00	7	.250	.298	.388
1990	2 ML Teams		136	351	87	9	1	11	(4	7)	131	33	40	24	6	47	6	0	1	2	2	.50	11	.248	.306	.373
1991	New York	AL	135	456	122	20	0	24	(13	11)	214	52	77	25	5	49	5	0	7	3	2	.60	6	.268	.308	.469
1992	New York	AL	121	384	86	9	1	22	(18	4)	163	42	59	37	11	62	3	0	6	0	1	.00	13	.224	.293	.424
1993	New York	AL	76	217	54	8	0	10	(4	6)	92	25	35	16	2	31	2	0	3	0	0	.00	4	.249	.303	.424
1990	Detroit	AL	44	111	30	5	1	3	(1	2)	46	12	8	4	3	14	2	0	1	0	0	.00	5	.270	.305	.414
	New York		92	240	57	4	0	8	(3	5)	85	21	32	20	3	33	4	0	0	2	2	.50	6	.238	.307	.354
	9 ML YEARS		838	2596	664	91	4	127	(70	57)	1144	294	397	190	31	364	26	10	24	8	7	.53	68	.256	.310	.441

Rafael Novoa

Pitches: Left **Bats:** Left **Pos:** RP/SP **Ht:** 6' 1" **Wt:** 180 **Born:** 10/26/67 **Age:** 26

			HOW MUCH HE PITCHED						WHAT HE GAVE UP										THE RESULTS					
Year	Team	Lg	G	GS	CG	GF	IP	BFP	H	R	ER	HR	SH	SF	HB	TBB	IBB	SO	WP	Bk	W	L	Pct.	ShO	Sv	ERA
1989	Everett	A	3	3	0	0	15	73	20	11	8	2	0	0	1	8	0	20	3	1	0	1	.000	0	0	4.80
	Clinton	A	13	10	0	0	63.2	267	58	20	18	1	9	1	4	18	1	61	1	6	4	5	.556	0	0	2.54
1990	Clinton	A	15	14	3	0	97.2	397	73	32	26	6	2	3	4	30	0	113	2	2	9	2	.818	1	0	2.40
	Shreveport	AA	11	10	2	1	71.2	297	60	21	21	3	1	2	3	25	0	66	1	0	5	4	.556	1	0	2.64
1991	Phoenix	AAA	17	17	0	0	93.2	450	135	83	62	16	5	6	5	37	3	46	3	1	6	6	.500	0	0	5.96
1992	El Paso	AA	22	21	6	1	146.1	617	143	63	53	6	4	3	9	48	3	124	8	1	10	7	.588	0	0	3.26
1993	New Orleans	AAA	20	18	2	0	113	471	105	55	43	20	1	3	5	38	3	74	4	1	10	5	.667	1	0	3.42
1990	San Francisco	NL	7	2	0	2	18.2	88	21	14	14	3	0	1	0	13	1	14	0	0	0	1	.000	0	1	6.75
1993	Milwaukee	AL	15	7	2	0	56	249	58	32	28	7	4	2	4	22	2	17	1	0	0	3	.000	0	0	4.50
	2 ML YEARS		22	9	2	2	74.2	337	79	46	42	10	4	3	4	35	3	31	1	0	0	4	.000	0	1	5.06

Edwin Nunez

Pitches: Right **Bats:** Right **Pos:** RP **Ht:** 6' 5" **Wt:** 240 **Born:** 05/27/63 **Age:** 31

			HOW MUCH HE PITCHED						WHAT HE GAVE UP										THE RESULTS					
Year	Team	Lg	G	GS	CG	GF	IP	BFP	H	R	ER	HR	SH	SF	HB	TBB	IBB	SO	WP	Bk	W	L	Pct.	ShO	Sv	ERA
1982	Seattle	AL	8	5	0	0	35.1	153	36	18	18	7	3	0	0	16	0	27	0	2	1	2	.333	0	0	4.58
1983	Seattle	AL	14	5	0	4	37	170	40	21	18	3	1	0	3	22	1	35	0	2	0	4	.000	0	0	4.54
1984	Seattle	AL	37	0	0	23	67.2	280	55	26	24	8	1	3	3	21	2	57	1	0	2	2	.500	0	7	3.19
1985	Seattle	AL	70	0	0	53	90.1	378	79	36	31	13	4	3	0	34	5	58	2	1	7	3	.700	0	16	3.09
1986	Seattle	AL	14	1	0	6	21.2	93	25	15	14	5	0	0	0	5	1	17	0	0	1	2	.333	0	0	5.82
1987	Seattle	AL	48	0	0	40	47.1	198	45	20	20	7	3	4	1	18	3	34	2	0	3	4	.429	0	12	3.80
1988	2 ML Teams		24	3	0	6	43.1	210	66	40	33	5	2	4	2	17	3	27	1	1	2	4	.333	0	0	6.85
1989	Detroit	AL	27	0	0	12	54	238	49	33	25	6	6	3	0	36	13	41	2	1	3	4	.429	0	1	4.17
1990	Detroit	AL	42	0	0	15	80.1	343	65	26	20	4	5	1	2	37	6	66	4	0	3	1	.750	0	6	2.24
1991	Milwaukee	AL	23	0	0	18	25.1	119	28	20	17	6	3	2	0	13	2	24	0	1	2	1	.667	0	8	6.04
1992	2 ML Teams		49	0	0	16	59.1	263	63	34	32	6	0	4	2	22	0	49	5	0	1	3	.250	0	3	4.85
1993	Oakland	AL	56	0	0	16	75.2	341	89	36	32	2	5	2	6	29	2	58	4	2	3	6	.333	0	1	3.81
1988	Seattle	AL	14	3	0	2	29.1	145	45	33	26	4	2	4	0	14	3	19	0	1	1	4	.200	0	0	7.98
	New York	NL	10	0	0	4	14	65	21	7	7	1	0	0	0	3	0	8	1	0	1	0	1.000	0	0	4.50
1992	Milwaukee	AL	10	0	0	5	13.2	58	12	5	4	1	0	0	0	6	0	10	0	0	1	1	.500	0	0	2.63
	Texas	AL	39	0	0	11	45.2	205	51	29	28	5	0	4	2	16	0	39	5	0	0	2	.000	0	3	5.52
	12 ML YEARS		412	14	0	209	637.1	2786	640	325	284	72	33	26	19	270	38	493	21	10	28	36	.438	0	54	4.01

Charlie O'Brien

Bats: Right **Throws:** Right **Pos:** C **Ht:** 6' 2" **Wt:** 205 **Born:** 05/01/61 **Age:** 33

			BATTING																BASERUNNING				PERCENTAGES		
Year	Team	Lg	G	AB	H	2B	3B	HR	(Hm	Rd)	TB	R	RBI	TBB	IBB	SO	HBP	SH	SF	SB	CS	SB%	GDP	Avg	OBP	SLG
1985	Oakland	AL	16	11	3	1	0	0	(0	0)	4	3	1	3	0	3	0	0	0	0	0	.00	0	.273	.429	.364
1987	Milwaukee	AL	10	35	7	3	1	0	(0	0)	12	2	0	4	0	4	0	1	0	0	1	.00	0	.200	.282	.343
1988	Milwaukee	AL	40	118	26	6	0	2	(2	0)	38	12	9	5	0	16	0	4	0	0	0	.00	3	.220	.252	.322
1989	Milwaukee	AL	62	188	44	10	0	6	(4	2)	72	22	35	21	1	11	9	8	0	0	0	.00	11	.234	.339	.383
1990	2 ML Teams		74	213	38	10	2	0	(0	0)	52	17	20	21	3	34	3	10	2	0	0	.00	4	.178	.259	.244
1991	New York	NL	69	168	31	6	0	2	(1	1)	43	16	14	17	1	25	4	0	2	0	2	.00	5	.185	.272	.256
1992	New York	NL	68	156	33	12	0	2	(1	1)	51	15	13	18	1	18	1	4	0	0	1	.00	4	.212	.289	.327
1993	New York	NL	67	188	48	11	0	4	(1	3)	71	15	23	14	1	14	2	3	1	0	0	.50	4	.255	.312	.378
1990	Milwaukee	AL	46	145	27	7	2	0	(0	0)	38	11	11	11	1	26	2	8	0	0	0	.00	3	.186	.253	.262
	New York	NL	28	68	11	3	0	0	(0	0)	14	6	9	10	2	8	1	2	2	0	0	.00	1	.162	.272	.206
	8 ML YEARS		406	1077	230	59	3	16	(9	7)	343	102	115	101	7	125	19	30	5	1	6	.14	31	.214	.291	.318

160

Pete O'Brien

Bats: Left **Throws:** Left **Pos:** DH **Ht:** 6' 2" **Wt:** 205 **Born:** 02/09/58 **Age:** 36

									BATTING										BASERUNNING				PERCENTAGES		
Year	Team	Lg	G	AB	H	2B	3B	HR	(Hm	Rd)	TB	R	RBI	TBB	IBB	SO	HBP	SH	SF	SB	CS	SB%	GDP	Avg	OBP	SLG
1982	Texas	AL	20	67	16	4	1	4	(2	2)	34	13	13	6	0	8	0	0	1	1	0	1.00	0	.239	.297	.507
1983	Texas	AL	154	524	124	24	5	8	(4	4)	182	53	53	58	2	62	1	3	2	5	4	.56	12	.237	.313	.347
1984	Texas	AL	142	520	149	26	2	18	(7	11)	233	57	80	53	8	50	0	1	7	3	5	.38	11	.287	.348	.448
1985	Texas	AL	159	573	153	34	3	22	(12	10)	259	69	92	69	4	53	1	3	9	5	10	.33	18	.267	.342	.452
1986	Texas	AL	156	551	160	23	3	23	(11	12)	258	86	90	87	11	66	0	0	3	4	4	.50	19	.290	.385	.468
1987	Texas	AL	159	569	163	26	1	23	(9	14)	260	84	88	59	6	61	0	0	10	0	4	.00	9	.286	.348	.457
1988	Texas	AL	156	547	149	24	1	16	(6	10)	223	57	71	72	9	73	0	1	8	1	4	.20	12	.272	.352	.408
1989	Cleveland	AL	155	554	144	24	1	12	(5	7)	206	75	55	83	17	48	2	2	5	3	1	.75	10	.260	.356	.372
1990	Seattle	AL	108	366	82	18	0	5	(3	2)	115	32	27	44	1	33	2	1	4	0	0	.00	12	.224	.308	.314
1991	Seattle	AL	152	560	139	29	3	17	(12	5)	225	58	88	44	7	61	1	3	9	0	1	.00	14	.248	.300	.402
1992	Seattle	AL	134	396	88	15	1	14	(6	8)	147	40	52	40	8	27	0	1	7	2	1	.67	8	.222	.289	.371
1993	Seattle	AL	72	210	54	7	0	7	(1	6)	82	30	27	26	4	21	0	0	8	0	0	.00	8	.257	.335	.390
	12 ML YEARS		1567	5437	1421	254	21	169	(78	91)	2224	654	736	641	77	563	7	15	68	24	34	.41	133	.261	.336	.409

John O'Donoghue

Pitches: Left **Bats:** Left **Pos:** RP **Ht:** 6' 6" **Wt:** 198 **Born:** 05/26/69 **Age:** 25

			HOW MUCH HE PITCHED						WHAT HE GAVE UP											THE RESULTS					
Year	Team	Lg	G	GS	CG	GF	IP	BFP	H	R	ER	HR	SH	SF	HB	TBB	IBB	SO	WP	Bk	W	L	Pct.	ShO	Sv	ERA
1990	Bluefield	R	10	6	2	3	49.1	200	49	13	11	2	2	0	1	10	0	67	2	1	4	2	.667	2	0	2.01
	Frederick	A	1	1	0	0	4	18	5	2	2	0	0	0	0	0	0	3	0	0	0	1	.000	0	0	4.50
1991	Frederick	A	22	21	2	1	133.2	567	131	55	43	6	0	2	2	50	2	128	8	1	7	8	.467	1	0	2.90
1992	Hagerstown	AA	17	16	2	1	112.1	459	78	37	28	6	4	2	4	40	0	87	7	4	7	4	.636	0	0	2.24
	Rochester	AAA	13	10	3	1	69.2	282	60	31	25	5	4	0	0	19	1	47	5	0	5	4	.556	1	0	3.23
1993	Rochester	AAA	22	20	2	1	127.2	543	122	60	55	11	8	3	3	41	0	111	3	0	7	4	.636	1	0	3.88
1993	Baltimore	AL	11	1	0	3	19.2	90	22	12	10	4	0	0	1	10	1	16	0	0	0	1	.000	0	0	4.58

Troy O'Leary

Bats: Left **Throws:** Left **Pos:** LF **Ht:** 6' 0" **Wt:** 175 **Born:** 08/04/69 **Age:** 24

									BATTING										BASERUNNING				PERCENTAGES		
Year	Team	Lg	G	AB	H	2B	3B	HR	(Hm	Rd)	TB	R	RBI	TBB	IBB	SO	HBP	SH	SF	SB	CS	SB%	GDP	Avg	OBP	SLG
1987	Helena	R	3	5	2	0	0	0	--	--	2	0	1	0	0	0	0	0	0	0	0	.00	0	.400	.400	.400
1988	Helena	R	67	203	70	11	1	0	--	--	83	40	27	30	1	32	2	3	5	10	8	.56	4	.345	.425	.409
1989	Beloit	A	42	115	21	4	0	0	--	--	25	7	8	15	1	20	0	0	0	1	7	.13	3	.183	.277	.217
	Helena	R	68	263	89	16	3	11	--	--	144	54	56	28	1	43	2	9	3	9	8	.53	6	.338	.402	.548
1990	Beloit	A	118	436	130	29	1	6	--	--	179	73	62	41	2	90	0	6	3	12	12	.50	4	.298	.356	.411
	Stockton	A	2	6	3	1	0	0	--	--	4	1	0	2	1	1	0	0	0	0	0	.00	0	.500	.625	.667
1991	Stockton	A	126	418	110	20	4	5	--	--	153	63	46	73	5	96	5	1	3	4	9	.31	6	.263	.377	.366
1992	El Paso	AA	135	506	169	27	8	5	--	--	227	92	79	59	6	87	1	3	8	28	16	.64	7	.334	.399	.449
1993	New Orleans	AAA	111	388	106	32	1	7	--	--	161	65	59	43	7	61	2	6	5	6	3	.67	7	.273	.345	.415
1993	Milwaukee	AL	19	41	12	3	0	0	(0	0)	15	3	3	5	0	9	0	3	0	0	0	.00	1	.293	.370	.366

Paul O'Neill

Bats: Left **Throws:** Left **Pos:** RF/LF **Ht:** 6' 4" **Wt:** 215 **Born:** 02/25/63 **Age:** 31

									BATTING										BASERUNNING				PERCENTAGES		
Year	Team	Lg	G	AB	H	2B	3B	HR	(Hm	Rd)	TB	R	RBI	TBB	IBB	SO	HBP	SH	SF	SB	CS	SB%	GDP	Avg	OBP	SLG
1985	Cincinnati	NL	5	12	4	1	0	0	(0	0)	5	1	1	0	0	2	0	0	0	0	0	.00	0	.333	.333	.417
1986	Cincinnati	NL	3	2	0	0	0	0	(0	0)	0	0	1	0	1	0	0	0	0	0	0	.00	0	.000	.333	.000
1987	Cincinnati	NL	84	160	41	14	1	7	(4	3)	78	24	28	18	1	29	0	0	0	2	1	.67	3	.256	.331	.488
1988	Cincinnati	NL	145	485	122	25	3	16	(12	4)	201	58	73	38	5	65	2	3	5	8	6	.57	4	.252	.306	.414
1989	Cincinnati	NL	117	428	118	24	2	15	(11	4)	191	49	74	46	8	64	2	0	4	20	5	.80	7	.276	.346	.446
1990	Cincinnati	NL	145	503	136	28	0	16	(10	6)	212	59	78	53	13	103	2	1	5	13	11	.54	12	.270	.339	.421
1991	Cincinnati	NL	152	532	136	36	0	28	(20	8)	256	71	91	73	14	107	1	0	1	12	7	.63	8	.256	.346	.481
1992	Cincinnati	NL	148	496	122	19	1	14	(6	8)	185	59	66	77	15	85	2	3	6	6	3	.67	10	.246	.346	.373
1993	New York	AL	141	498	155	34	1	20	(8	12)	251	71	75	44	5	69	2	0	3	2	4	.33	13	.311	.367	.504
	9 ML YEARS		940	3116	834	181	8	116	(71	45)	1379	392	486	350	61	525	11	7	24	63	37	.63	60	.268	.341	.443

Sherman Obando

Bats: Right **Throws:** Right **Pos:** DH/RF **Ht:** 6' 4" **Wt:** 215 **Born:** 01/23/70 **Age:** 24

									BATTING										BASERUNNING				PERCENTAGES		
Year	Team	Lg	G	AB	H	2B	3B	HR	(Hm	Rd)	TB	R	RBI	TBB	IBB	SO	HBP	SH	SF	SB	CS	SB%	GDP	Avg	OBP	SLG
1988	Yankees	R	49	172	44	10	2	4	--	--	70	26	27	16	2	32	3	0	1	8	5	.62	3	.256	.328	.407
1989	Oneonta	A	70	276	86	23	3	6	--	--	133	50	45	16	1	45	6	1	2	8	5	.62	3	.312	.360	.482

Year	Team	Lg	G	AB	H	2B	3B	HR	(Hm	Rd)	TB	R	RBI	TBB	IBB	SO	HBP	SH	SF	SB	CS	SB%	GDP	Avg	OBP	SLG
1990	Pr William	A	121	439	117	24	6	10	--	--	183	67	67	42	1	85	11	0	6	5	3	.63	7	.267	.341	.417
1991	Yankees	R	4	17	5	2	0	0	--	--	7	3	1	1	0	2	1	0	0	0	0	.00	0	.294	.368	.412
	Pr William	A	42	140	37	11	1	7	--	--	71	25	31	19	2	28	2	0	2	0	1	.00	0	.264	.356	.507
1992	Albany	AA	109	381	107	19	3	17	--	--	183	71	56	32	1	67	8	2	4	3	1	.75	12	.281	.346	.480
1993	Bowie	AA	19	58	14	2	0	3	--	--	25	8	12	9	0	11	1	0	3	1	0	1.00	1	.241	.338	.431
1993	Baltimore	AL	31	92	25	2	0	3	(2	1)	36	8	15	4	0	26	1	0	0	0	0	.00	1	.272	.309	.391

Jose Offerman

Bats: Both **Throws:** Right **Pos:** SS **Ht:** 6' 0" **Wt:** 165 **Born:** 11/08/68 **Age:** 25

										BATTING										BASERUNNING				PERCENTAGES		
Year	Team	Lg	G	AB	H	2B	3B	HR	(Hm	Rd)	TB	R	RBI	TBB	IBB	SO	HBP	SH	SF	SB	CS	SB%	GDP	Avg	OBP	SLG
1990	Los Angeles	NL	29	58	9	0	0	1	(1	0)	12	7	7	4	1	14	0	1	0	1	0	1.00	0	.155	.210	.207
1991	Los Angeles	NL	52	113	22	2	0	0	(0	0)	24	10	3	25	2	32	1	1	0	3	2	.60	5	.195	.345	.212
1992	Los Angeles	NL	149	534	139	20	8	1	(1	0)	178	67	30	57	4	98	1	0	5	23	16	.59	5	.260	.331	.333
1993	Los Angeles	NL	158	590	159	21	6	1	(1	0)	195	77	62	71	7	75	2	25	8	30	13	.70	12	.269	.346	.331
	4 ML YEARS		388	1295	329	43	14	3	(3	0)	409	161	102	157	14	219	3	32	10	57	31	.65	22	.254	.334	.316

Bobby Ojeda

Pitches: Left **Bats:** Left **Pos:** SP **Ht:** 6' 1" **Wt:** 195 **Born:** 12/17/57 **Age:** 36

						HOW MUCH HE PITCHED			WHAT HE GAVE UP									THE RESULTS					
Year	Team	Lg	G	GS	CG	GF	IP	BFP	H	R	ER	HR	SH	SF	HB	TBB	IBB	SO	WP	Bk	W	L	Pct.	ShO	Sv	ERA
1980	Boston	AL	7	7	0	0	26	122	39	20	20	2	0	0	0	14	1	12	1	0	1	1	.500	0	0	6.92
1981	Boston	AL	10	10	2	0	66	267	50	25	23	6	3	1	2	25	2	28	0	0	6	2	.750	0	0	3.14
1982	Boston	AL	22	14	0	6	78.1	352	95	53	49	13	0	1	1	29	0	52	5	0	4	6	.400	0	0	5.63
1983	Boston	AL	29	28	5	0	173.2	746	173	85	78	15	6	11	3	73	2	94	2	0	12	7	.632	0	0	4.04
1984	Boston	AL	33	32	8	0	216.2	928	211	106	96	17	8	6	2	96	2	137	0	1	12	12	.500	5	0	3.99
1985	Boston	AL	39	22	5	10	157.2	671	166	74	70	11	10	3	2	48	9	102	3	3	9	11	.450	0	1	4.00
1986	New York	NL	32	30	7	1	217.1	871	185	72	62	15	10	3	2	52	3	148	2	1	18	5	.783	2	0	2.57
1987	New York	NL	10	7	0	0	46.1	192	45	23	20	5	3	1	0	10	1	21	1	0	3	5	.375	0	0	3.88
1988	New York	NL	29	29	5	0	190.1	752	158	74	61	6	6	6	4	33	2	133	4	7	10	13	.435	5	0	2.88
1989	New York	NL	31	31	5	0	192	824	179	83	74	16	6	7	2	78	5	95	0	2	13	11	.542	2	0	3.47
1990	New York	NL	38	12	0	9	118	500	123	53	48	10	3	3	2	40	4	62	2	3	7	6	.538	0	0	3.66
1991	Los Angeles	NL	31	31	2	0	189.1	802	181	78	67	15	15	9	3	70	9	120	4	2	12	9	.571	1	0	3.18
1992	Los Angeles	NL	29	29	2	0	166.1	731	169	80	67	8	11	7	1	81	8	94	3	0	6	9	.400	1	0	3.63
1993	Cleveland	AL	9	7	0	0	43	194	48	22	21	5	4	3	0	21	0	27	3	0	2	1	.667	0	0	4.40
	14 ML YEARS		349	289	41	26	1881	7952	1822	848	756	144	85	61	24	670	48	1125	30	19	115	98	.540	16	1	3.62

John Olerud

Bats: Left **Throws:** Left **Pos:** 1B/DH **Ht:** 6' 5" **Wt:** 218 **Born:** 08/05/68 **Age:** 25

										BATTING										BASERUNNING				PERCENTAGES		
Year	Team	Lg	G	AB	H	2B	3B	HR	(Hm	Rd)	TB	R	RBI	TBB	IBB	SO	HBP	SH	SF	SB	CS	SB%	GDP	Avg	OBP	SLG
1989	Toronto	AL	6	8	3	0	0	0	(0	0)	3	2	0	0	0	1	0	0	0	0	0	.00	0	.375	.375	.375
1990	Toronto	AL	111	358	95	15	1	14	(11	3)	154	43	48	57	6	75	1	1	4	0	2	.00	6	.265	.364	.430
1991	Toronto	AL	139	454	116	30	1	17	(7	10)	199	64	68	68	9	84	6	3	10	0	2	.00	12	.256	.353	.438
1992	Toronto	AL	138	458	130	28	0	16	(4	12)	206	68	66	70	11	61	1	1	7	1	0	1.00	15	.284	.375	.450
1993	Toronto	AL	158	551	200	54	2	24	(9	15)	330	109	107	114	33	65	7	0	7	0	2	.00	12	.363	.473	.599
	5 ML YEARS		552	1829	544	127	4	71	(31	40)	892	286	289	309	59	286	15	5	28	1	6	.14	44	.297	.398	.488

Omar Olivares

Pitches: Right **Bats:** Right **Pos:** RP/SP **Ht:** 6' 1" **Wt:** 193 **Born:** 07/06/67 **Age:** 26

						HOW MUCH HE PITCHED			WHAT HE GAVE UP									THE RESULTS					
Year	Team	Lg	G	GS	CG	GF	IP	BFP	H	R	ER	HR	SH	SF	HB	TBB	IBB	SO	WP	Bk	W	L	Pct.	ShO	Sv	ERA
1990	St. Louis	NL	9	6	0	0	49.1	201	45	17	16	2	1	0	2	17	0	20	1	1	1	1	.500	0	0	2.92
1991	St. Louis	NL	28	24	0	2	167.1	688	148	72	69	13	11	2	5	61	1	91	3	1	11	7	.611	0	1	3.71
1992	St. Louis	NL	32	30	1	1	197	818	189	84	84	20	8	7	4	63	5	124	2	0	9	9	.500	0	0	3.84
1993	St. Louis	NL	58	9	0	11	118.2	537	134	60	55	10	4	4	9	54	7	63	4	3	5	3	.625	0	1	4.17
	4 ML YEARS		127	69	1	14	532.1	2244	516	233	224	45	24	13	20	195	13	298	10	5	26	20	.565	0	2	3.79

Darren Oliver

Pitches: Left **Bats:** Right **Pos:** RP **Ht:** 6' 0" **Wt:** 170 **Born:** 10/06/70 **Age:** 23

						HOW MUCH HE PITCHED			WHAT HE GAVE UP									THE RESULTS					
Year	Team	Lg	G	GS	CG	GF	IP	BFP	H	R	ER	HR	SH	SF	HB	TBB	IBB	SO	WP	Bk	W	L	Pct.	ShO	Sv	ERA
1988	Rangers	R	12	9	0	0	54.1	216	39	16	13	0	2	1	2	18	0	59	3	2	5	1	.833	0	0	2.15
1989	Gastonia	A	24	23	2	0	122.1	525	86	54	43	4	3	3	5	82	1	108	15	2	8	7	.533	1	0	3.16
1990	Rangers	R	3	3	0	0	6	21	1	1	0	0	0	0	1	1	0	7	1	0	0	0	.000	0	0	0.00
	Gastonia	A	1	1	0	0	2	11	1	3	3	0	0	0	0	4	0	2	0	1	0	0	.000	0	0	13.50
1991	Charlotte	A	2	2	0	0	8	33	6	4	4	1	0	0	0	3	0	12	1	0	0	1	.000	0	0	4.50

162

Year	Team	Lg	G	GS	CG	GF	IP	BFP	H	R	ER	HR	SH	SF	HB	TBB	IBB	SO	WP	Bk	W	L	Pct.	ShO	Sv	ERA
1992	Charlotte	A	8	2	1	2	25	95	11	2	2	0	0	0	2	10	2	33	3	0	1	0	1.000	1	2	0.72
	Tulsa	AA	3	3	0	0	14.1	66	15	9	5	1	1	0	0	4	0	14	0	0	0	1	.000	0	0	3.14
1993	Tulsa	AA	46	0	0	25	73.1	315	51	18	16	1	5	1	9	41	5	77	9	0	7	5	.583	0	6	1.96
1993	Texas	AL	2	0	0	0	3.1	14	2	1	1	1	0	0	0	1	1	4	0	0	0	0	.000	0	0	2.70

Joe Oliver

Bats: Right **Throws:** Right **Pos:** C/1B   **Ht:** 6' 3" **Wt:** 210 **Born:** 07/24/65 **Age:** 28

								BATTING										BASERUNNING				PERCENTAGES		
Year	Team	Lg	G	AB	H	2B	3B	HR	(Hm | Rd)	TB	R	RBI	TBB	IBB	SO	HBP	SH	SF	SB	CS	SB%	GDP	Avg	OBP	SLG
1989	Cincinnati	NL	49	151	41	8	0	3	(1 | 2)	58	13	23	6	1	28	1	1	2	0	0	.00	3	.272	.300	.384
1990	Cincinnati	NL	121	364	84	23	0	8	(3 | 5)	131	34	52	37	15	75	2	5	1	1	1	.50	6	.231	.304	.360
1991	Cincinnati	NL	94	269	58	11	0	11	(7 | 4)	102	21	41	18	5	53	0	4	0	0	0	.00	14	.216	.265	.379
1992	Cincinnati	NL	143	485	131	25	1	10	(7 | 3)	188	42	57	35	19	75	1	6	7	2	3	.40	12	.270	.316	.388
1993	Cincinnati	NL	139	482	115	28	0	14	(7 | 7)	185	40	75	27	2	91	1	2	9	0	0	.00	13	.239	.276	.384
	5 ML YEARS		546	1751	429	95	1	46	(25 | 21)	664	150	248	123	42	322	5	18	19	3	4	.43	48	.245	.293	.379

Greg Olson

Bats: Right **Throws:** Right **Pos:** C   **Ht:** 6' 0" **Wt:** 200 **Born:** 09/06/60 **Age:** 33

								BATTING										BASERUNNING				PERCENTAGES		
Year	Team	Lg	G	AB	H	2B	3B	HR	(Hm | Rd)	TB	R	RBI	TBB	IBB	SO	HBP	SH	SF	SB	CS	SB%	GDP	Avg	OBP	SLG
1989	Minnesota	AL	3	2	1	0	0	0	(0 | 0)	1	0	0	0	0	0	0	0	0	0	0	.00	0	.500	.500	.500
1990	Atlanta	NL	100	298	78	12	1	7	(4 | 3)	113	36	36	30	4	51	2	1	1	1	1	.50	9	.262	.332	.379
1991	Atlanta	NL	133	411	99	25	0	6	(6 | 0)	142	46	44	44	3	48	3	2	4	1	1	.50	13	.241	.316	.345
1992	Atlanta	NL	95	302	72	14	2	3	(0 | 3)	99	27	27	34	4	31	1	1	2	2	1	.67	8	.238	.316	.328
1993	Atlanta	NL	83	262	59	10	0	4	(3 | 1)	81	23	24	29	0	27	1	2	1	1	0	1.00	11	.225	.304	.309
	5 ML YEARS		414	1275	309	61	3	20	(13 | 7)	436	132	131	137	11	157	7	6	8	5	3	.63	40	.242	.317	.342

Gregg Olson

Pitches: Right **Bats:** Right **Pos:** RP   **Ht:** 6' 4" **Wt:** 206 **Born:** 10/11/66 **Age:** 27

							HOW MUCH HE PITCHED			WHAT HE GAVE UP										THE RESULTS					
Year	Team	Lg	G	GS	CG	GF	IP	BFP	H	R	ER	HR	SH	SF	HB	TBB	IBB	SO	WP	Bk	W	L	Pct.	ShO	Sv	ERA
1988	Baltimore	AL	10	0	0	4	11	51	10	4	4	1	0	0	0	10	1	9	0	1	1	1	.500	0	0	3.27
1989	Baltimore	AL	64	0	0	52	85	356	57	17	16	1	4	1	1	46	10	90	9	3	5	2	.714	0	27	1.69
1990	Baltimore	AL	64	0	0	58	74.1	305	57	20	20	3	1	2	3	31	3	74	5	0	6	5	.545	0	37	2.42
1991	Baltimore	AL	72	0	0	62	73.2	319	74	28	26	1	5	1	1	29	5	72	8	1	4	6	.400	0	31	3.18
1992	Baltimore	AL	60	0	0	56	61.1	244	46	14	14	3	0	2	0	24	0	58	4	0	1	5	.167	0	36	2.05
1993	Baltimore	AL	50	0	0	45	45	188	37	9	8	1	2	2	0	18	3	44	5	0	0	2	.000	0	29	1.60
	6 ML YEARS		320	0	0	277	350.1	1463	281	92	88	10	12	8	5	158	22	347	31	5	17	21	.447	0	160	2.26

Steve Ontiveros

Pitches: Right **Bats:** Right **Pos:** RP   **Ht:** 6' 0" **Wt:** 197 **Born:** 03/05/61 **Age:** 33

							HOW MUCH HE PITCHED			WHAT HE GAVE UP										THE RESULTS					
Year	Team	Lg	G	GS	CG	GF	IP	BFP	H	R	ER	HR	SH	SF	HB	TBB	IBB	SO	WP	Bk	W	L	Pct.	ShO	Sv	ERA
1993	Portland *	AAA	20	16	2	2	103.1	418	90	40	33	5	2	6	4	20	0	73	5	2	7	6	.538	0	0	2.87
1985	Oakland	AL	39	0	0	18	74.2	284	45	17	16	4	2	2	2	19	2	36	1	0	1	3	.250	0	8	1.93
1986	Oakland	AL	46	0	0	27	72.2	305	72	40	38	10	1	6	1	25	3	54	4	0	2	2	.500	0	10	4.71
1987	Oakland	AL	35	22	2	6	150.2	645	141	78	67	19	6	2	4	50	3	97	4	1	10	8	.556	1	1	4.00
1988	Oakland	AL	10	10	0	0	54.2	241	57	32	28	4	5	0	0	21	1	30	5	5	3	4	.429	0	0	4.61
1989	Philadelphia	NL	6	5	0	0	30.2	134	34	15	13	2	1	0	0	15	1	12	2	0	2	1	.667	0	0	3.82
1990	Philadelphia	NL	5	0	0	1	10	43	9	3	3	1	0	0	0	3	0	6	0	0	0	0	.000	0	0	2.70
1993	Seattle	AL	14	0	0	8	18	72	18	3	2	0	1	0	0	6	2	13	1	0	0	2	.000	0	0	1.00
	7 ML YEARS		155	37	2	60	411.1	1724	376	188	167	40	16	10	7	139	12	248	17	6	18	20	.474	1	19	3.65

Jose Oquendo

Bats: Both **Throws:** Right **Pos:** SS/2B   **Ht:** 5'10" **Wt:** 171 **Born:** 07/04/63 **Age:** 30

								BATTING										BASERUNNING				PERCENTAGES		
Year	Team	Lg	G	AB	H	2B	3B	HR	(Hm | Rd)	TB	R	RBI	TBB	IBB	SO	HBP	SH	SF	SB	CS	SB%	GDP	Avg	OBP	SLG
1983	New York	NL	120	328	70	7	0	1	(0 | 1)	80	29	17	19	2	60	2	3	1	8	9	.47	10	.213	.260	.244
1984	New York	NL	81	189	42	5	0	0	(0 | 0)	47	23	10	15	2	26	2	3	2	10	1	.91	2	.222	.284	.249
1986	St. Louis	NL	76	138	41	4	1	0	(0 | 0)	47	20	13	15	4	20	0	2	3	2	3	.40	3	.297	.359	.341
1987	St. Louis	NL	116	248	71	9	0	1	(0 | 1)	83	43	24	54	6	29	0	6	4	4	4	.50	6	.286	.408	.335
1988	St. Louis	NL	148	451	125	10	1	7	(4 | 3)	158	36	46	52	7	40	0	12	3	4	6	.40	8	.277	.350	.350
1989	St. Louis	NL	163	556	162	28	7	1	(0 | 1)	207	59	48	79	7	59	0	7	8	3	5	.38	12	.291	.375	.372
1990	St. Louis	NL	156	469	118	17	5	1	(1 | 0)	148	38	37	74	8	46	0	5	5	1	1	.50	7	.252	.350	.316
1991	St. Louis	NL	127	366	88	11	4	1	(0 | 1)	110	37	26	67	13	48	1	4	3	1	2	.33	5	.240	.357	.301
1992	St. Louis	NL	14	35	9	3	1	0	(0 | 0)	14	3	3	5	1	3	0	0	0	0	0	.00	0	.257	.350	.400
1993	St. Louis	NL	46	73	15	0	0	0	(0 | 0)	15	7	4	12	1	8	0	0	3	0	0	.00	5	.205	.314	.205
	10 ML YEARS		1047	2853	741	94	19	12	(5 | 7)	909	295	228	392	51	339	5	45	30	33	31	.52	58	.260	.347	.319

Mike Oquist

Pitches: Right **Bats:** Right **Pos:** RP **Ht:** 6' 2" **Wt:** 170 **Born:** 05/30/68 **Age:** 26

Year Team	Lg	G	GS	CG	GF	IP	BFP	H	R	ER	HR	SH	SF	HB	TBB	IBB	SO	WP	Bk	W	L	Pct.	ShO	Sv	ERA
1989 Erie	A	15	15	1	0	97.2	402	86	43	39	7	2	1	3	25	0	109	1	1	7	4	.636	1	0	3.59
1990 Frederick	A	25	25	3	0	166.1	678	134	64	52	11	6	6	4	48	3	170	9	1	9	8	.529	1	0	2.81
1991 Hagerstown	AA	27	26	1	1	166.1	717	168	82	75	15	4	7	0	62	4	136	7	1	10	9	.526	0	0	4.06
1992 Rochester	AAA	26	24	5	0	153.1	665	164	80	70	17	5	4	5	45	1	111	6	1	10	12	.455	0	0	4.11
1993 Rochester	AAA	28	21	2	1	149.1	617	144	62	58	20	5	1	2	41	1	128	5	1	9	8	.529	1	0	3.50
1993 Baltimore	AL	5	0	0	2	11.2	50	12	5	5	0	0	0	0	4	1	8	0	0	0	0	.000	0	0	3.86

Jesse Orosco

Pitches: Left **Bats:** Right **Pos:** RP **Ht:** 6' 2" **Wt:** 185 **Born:** 04/21/57 **Age:** 37

Year Team	Lg	G	GS	CG	GF	IP	BFP	H	R	ER	HR	SH	SF	HB	TBB	IBB	SO	WP	Bk	W	L	Pct.	ShO	Sv	ERA
1979 New York	NL	18	2	0	6	35	154	33	20	19	4	3	0	2	22	0	22	0	0	1	2	.333	0	0	4.89
1981 New York	NL	8	0	0	4	17	69	13	4	3	2	2	0	0	6	2	18	0	1	0	1	.000	0	1	1.59
1982 New York	NL	54	2	0	22	109.1	451	92	37	33	7	5	4	2	40	2	89	3	2	4	10	.286	0	4	2.72
1983 New York	NL	62	0	0	42	110	432	76	27	18	3	4	3	1	38	7	84	1	2	13	7	.650	0	17	1.47
1984 New York	NL	60	0	0	52	87	355	58	29	25	7	3	3	2	34	6	85	1	1	10	6	.625	0	31	2.59
1985 New York	NL	54	0	0	39	79	331	66	26	24	6	1	1	0	34	7	68	4	0	8	6	.571	0	17	2.73
1986 New York	NL	58	0	0	40	81	338	64	23	21	6	2	3	3	35	3	62	2	0	8	6	.571	0	21	2.33
1987 New York	NL	58	0	0	41	77	335	78	41	38	5	5	4	2	31	9	78	2	0	3	9	.250	0	16	4.44
1988 Los Angeles	NL	55	0	0	21	53	229	41	18	16	4	3	3	2	30	3	43	1	0	3	2	.600	0	9	2.72
1989 Cleveland	AL	69	0	0	29	78	312	54	20	18	7	8	3	2	26	4	79	0	0	3	4	.429	0	3	2.08
1990 Cleveland	AL	55	0	0	28	64.2	289	58	35	28	9	5	3	0	38	7	55	1	0	5	4	.556	0	2	3.90
1991 Cleveland	AL	47	0	0	20	45.2	202	52	20	19	4	1	3	1	15	8	36	1	1	2	0	1.000	0	0	3.74
1992 Milwaukee	AL	59	0	0	14	39	158	33	15	14	5	0	2	1	13	1	40	2	0	3	1	.750	0	1	3.23
1993 Milwaukee	AL	57	0	0	27	56.2	233	47	25	20	2	1	2	3	17	3	67	3	1	3	5	.375	0	8	3.18
14 ML YEARS		714	4	0	385	932.1	3888	765	340	296	71	43	34	21	379	62	826	21	8	66	63	.512	0	130	2.86

Joe Orsulak

Bats: Left **Throws:** Left **Pos:** LF/CF/RF **Ht:** 6' 1" **Wt:** 205 **Born:** 05/31/62 **Age:** 32

Year Team	Lg	G	AB	H	2B	3B	HR	(Hm	Rd)	TB	R	RBI	TBB	IBB	SO	HBP	SH	SF	SB	CS	SB%	GDP	Avg	OBP	SLG
1983 Pittsburgh	NL	7	11	2	0	0	0	(0	0)	2	0	1	0	0	2	0	0	1	0	1	.00	0	.182	.167	.182
1984 Pittsburgh	NL	32	67	17	1	2	0	(0	0)	22	12	3	1	0	7	1	3	1	3	1	.75	0	.254	.271	.328
1985 Pittsburgh	NL	121	397	119	14	6	0	(0	0)	145	54	21	26	3	27	1	9	3	24	11	.69	5	.300	.342	.365
1986 Pittsburgh	NL	138	401	100	19	6	2	(0	2)	137	60	19	28	2	38	1	6	1	24	11	.69	4	.249	.299	.342
1988 Baltimore	AL	125	379	109	21	3	8	(3	5)	160	48	27	23	2	30	3	8	3	9	8	.53	7	.288	.331	.422
1989 Baltimore	AL	123	390	111	22	5	7	(0	7)	164	59	55	41	6	35	2	7	6	5	3	.63	8	.285	.351	.421
1990 Baltimore	AL	124	413	111	14	3	11	(9	2)	164	49	57	46	9	48	1	4	1	6	8	.43	7	.269	.343	.397
1991 Baltimore	AL	143	486	135	22	1	5	(3	2)	174	57	43	28	1	45	4	0	3	6	2	.75	9	.278	.321	.358
1992 Baltimore	AL	117	391	116	18	3	4	(2	2)	149	45	39	28	5	34	4	4	1	5	4	.56	3	.289	.342	.381
1993 New York	NL	134	409	116	15	4	8	(5	3)	163	59	35	28	1	25	2	0	2	5	4	.56	6	.284	.331	.399
10 ML YEARS		1064	3344	933	146	33	45	(22	23)	1280	443	300	249	29	291	19	41	22	87	53	.62	49	.279	.330	.383

Junior Ortiz

Bats: Right **Throws:** Right **Pos:** C **Ht:** 5'11" **Wt:** 185 **Born:** 10/24/59 **Age:** 34

Year Team	Lg	G	AB	H	2B	3B	HR	(Hm	Rd)	TB	R	RBI	TBB	IBB	SO	HBP	SH	SF	SB	CS	SB%	GDP	Avg	OBP	SLG
1982 Pittsburgh	NL	7	15	3	1	0	0	(0	0)	4	1	0	1	0	3	0	0	0	0	0	.00	1	.200	.250	.267
1983 2 ML Teams		73	193	48	5	0	0	(0	0)	53	11	12	4	0	34	1	2	0	1	0	1.00	1	.249	.268	.275
1984 New York	NL	40	91	18	3	0	0	(0	0)	21	6	11	5	0	15	0	0	2	1	0	1.00	1	.198	.235	.231
1985 Pittsburgh	NL	23	72	21	2	0	1	(0	1)	26	4	5	3	1	17	0	1	0	1	0	1.00	1	.292	.320	.361
1986 Pittsburgh	NL	49	110	37	6	0	0	(0	0)	43	11	14	9	0	13	0	1	2	0	1	.00	4	.336	.380	.391
1987 Pittsburgh	NL	75	192	52	8	1	0	(0	1)	65	16	22	15	1	23	0	5	1	0	2	.00	6	.271	.322	.339
1988 Pittsburgh	NL	49	118	33	6	0	2	(1	1)	45	8	18	9	0	9	2	1	2	1	4	.20	6	.280	.336	.381
1989 Pittsburgh	NL	91	230	50	6	1	1	(0	1)	61	16	22	20	4	20	2	3	3	2	2	.50	9	.217	.282	.265
1990 Minnesota	AL	71	170	57	7	1	0	(0	0)	66	18	18	12	0	16	2	2	1	0	4	.00	4	.335	.384	.388
1991 Minnesota	AL	61	134	28	5	1	0	(0	0)	35	9	11	15	0	12	1	1	0	0	1	.00	6	.209	.293	.261
1992 Cleveland	AL	86	244	61	7	0	0	(0	0)	68	20	24	12	0	23	4	2	0	1	3	.25	7	.250	.296	.279
1993 Cleveland	AL	95	249	55	13	0	0	(0	0)	68	19	20	11	1	26	5	4	1	1	0	1.00	10	.221	.267	.273
1983 Pittsburgh	NL	5	8	1	0	0	0	(0	0)	1	1	0	1	0	0	0	1	0	0	0	.00	0	.125	.222	.125
New York	NL	68	185	47	5	0	0	(0	0)	52	10	12	3	0	34	1	1	0	0	1	1.00	1	.254	.270	.281
12 ML YEARS		720	1818	463	69	4	5	(1	4)	555	139	177	116	7	211	17	22	12	8	17	.32	57	.255	.304	.305

Luis Ortiz

Bats: Right **Throws:** Right **Pos:** 3B   **Ht:** 6' 0" **Wt:** 188 **Born:** 05/25/70 **Age:** 24

										BATTING									BASERUNNING				PERCENTAGES		
Year Team	Lg	G	AB	H	2B	3B	HR	(Hm	Rd)	TB	R	RBI	TBB	IBB	SO	HBP	SH	SF	SB	CS	SB%	GDP	Avg	OBP	SLG
1991 Red Sox	R	42	153	51	11	2	4	--	--	78	21	29	7	0	9	2	1	1	2	1	.67	1	.333	.368	.510
1992 Lynchburg	A	94	355	103	27	1	10	--	--	162	43	61	22	3	55	2	0	5	4	2	.67	8	.290	.331	.456
1993 Pawtucket	AAA	102	402	118	28	1	18	--	--	202	45	81	13	3	74	2	0	4	1	1	.50	10	.294	.316	.502
1993 Boston	AL	9	12	3	0	0	0	(0	0)	3	1	0	0	0	2	0	0	0	0	0	.00	0	.250	.250	.250

John Orton

Bats: Right **Throws:** Right **Pos:** C   **Ht:** 6' 1" **Wt:** 192 **Born:** 12/08/65 **Age:** 28

										BATTING									BASERUNNING				PERCENTAGES		
Year Team	Lg	G	AB	H	2B	3B	HR	(Hm	Rd)	TB	R	RBI	TBB	IBB	SO	HBP	SH	SF	SB	CS	SB%	GDP	Avg	OBP	SLG
1993 Palm Sprngs *	A	2	7	0	0	0	0	--	--	0	0	0	1	0	1	0	0	0	0	0	.00	0	.000	.125	.000
1989 California	AL	16	39	7	1	0	0	(0	0)	8	4	4	2	0	17	0	1	0	0	0	.00	0	.179	.220	.205
1990 California	AL	31	84	16	5	0	1	(0	1)	24	8	6	5	0	31	1	2	0	0	1	.00	0	.190	.244	.286
1991 California	AL	29	69	14	4	0	0	(0	0)	18	7	3	10	0	17	1	4	0	0	1	.00	2	.203	.313	.261
1992 California	AL	43	114	25	3	0	2	(1	1)	34	11	12	7	0	32	2	2	0	1	1	.50	1	.219	.276	.298
1993 California	AL	37	95	18	5	0	1	(0	1)	26	5	4	7	0	24	1	2	0	1	2	.33	1	.189	.252	.274
5 ML YEARS		156	401	80	18	0	4	(1	3)	110	35	29	31	0	121	5	11	0	2	5	.29	6	.200	.265	.274

Donovan Osborne

Pitches: Left **Bats:** Left **Pos:** SP   **Ht:** 6' 2" **Wt:** 195 **Born:** 06/21/69 **Age:** 25

						HOW MUCH HE PITCHED							WHAT HE GAVE UP							THE RESULTS			
Year Team	Lg	G	GS	CG	GF	IP	BFP	H	R	ER	HR	SH	SF	HB	TBB	IBB	SO	WP	Bk	W	L	Pct.	ShO	Sv	ERA
1990 Hamilton	A	4	4	0	0	20	86	21	8	8	0	1	1	0	5	1	14	1	2	0	2	.000	0	0	3.60
Savannah	A	6	6	1	0	41.1	169	40	20	12	2	1	1	3	7	0	28	2	3	2	2	.500	0	0	2.61
1991 Arkansas	AA	26	26	3	0	166	696	177	82	67	6	9	4	4	43	3	130	4	4	8	12	.400	0	0	3.63
1992 St. Louis	NL	34	29	0	2	179	754	193	91	75	14	7	4	2	38	2	104	6	0	11	9	.550	0	0	3.77
1993 St. Louis	NL	26	26	1	0	155.2	657	153	73	65	18	6	2	7	47	4	83	4	0	10	7	.588	0	0	3.76
2 ML YEARS		60	55	1	2	334.2	1411	346	164	140	32	13	6	9	85	6	187	10	0	21	16	.568	0	0	3.76

Al Osuna

Pitches: Left **Bats:** Right **Pos:** RP   **Ht:** 6' 3" **Wt:** 200 **Born:** 08/10/65 **Age:** 28

						HOW MUCH HE PITCHED							WHAT HE GAVE UP							THE RESULTS			
Year Team	Lg	G	GS	CG	GF	IP	BFP	H	R	ER	HR	SH	SF	HB	TBB	IBB	SO	WP	Bk	W	L	Pct.	ShO	Sv	ERA
1993 Tucson *	AAA	13	4	0	3	30	133	26	16	15	1	0	1	5	17	0	38	4	0	3	1	.750	0	1	4.50
1990 Houston	NL	12	0	0	2	11.1	48	10	6	6	1	0	2	3	6	1	6	3	0	2	0	1.000	0	0	4.76
1991 Houston	NL	71	0	0	32	81.2	353	59	39	31	6	5	5	3	46	5	68	3	1	7	6	.538	0	12	3.42
1992 Houston	NL	66	0	0	17	61.2	270	52	29	29	8	5	6	1	38	5	37	3	1	6	3	.667	0	0	4.23
1993 Houston	NL	44	0	0	6	25.1	107	17	10	9	3	4	4	1	13	2	21	3	0	1	1	.500	0	2	3.20
4 ML YEARS		193	0	0	57	180	778	138	84	75	17	15	17	8	103	13	132	12	1	16	10	.615	0	14	3.75

Dave Otto

Pitches: Left **Bats:** Left **Pos:** RP/SP   **Ht:** 6' 7" **Wt:** 210 **Born:** 11/12/64 **Age:** 29

						HOW MUCH HE PITCHED							WHAT HE GAVE UP							THE RESULTS			
Year Team	Lg	G	GS	CG	GF	IP	BFP	H	R	ER	HR	SH	SF	HB	TBB	IBB	SO	WP	Bk	W	L	Pct.	ShO	Sv	ERA
1987 Oakland	AL	3	0	0	3	6	24	7	6	6	1	0	0	0	1	0	3	0	0	0	0	.000	0	0	9.00
1988 Oakland	AL	3	2	0	1	10	43	9	2	2	0	0	0	0	6	0	7	0	1	0	0	.000	0	0	1.80
1989 Oakland	AL	1	1	0	0	6.2	26	6	2	2	0	1	0	0	2	0	4	0	0	0	0	.000	0	0	2.70
1990 Oakland	AL	2	0	0	2	2.1	13	3	3	2	0	0	0	0	3	0	2	0	0	0	0	.000	0	0	7.71
1991 Cleveland	AL	18	14	1	0	100	425	108	52	47	7	8	4	4	27	6	47	3	0	2	8	.200	0	0	4.23
1992 Cleveland	AL	18	16	0	0	80.1	368	110	64	63	12	3	1	1	33	0	32	5	0	5	9	.357	0	0	7.06
1993 Pittsburgh	NL	28	8	0	7	68	306	85	40	38	9	6	1	3	28	1	30	4	0	3	4	.429	0	0	5.03
7 ML YEARS		73	41	1	13	273.1	1205	328	169	160	29	18	6	8	100	7	125	12	1	10	21	.323	0	0	5.27

Spike Owen

Bats: Both **Throws:** Right **Pos:** SS   **Ht:** 5'10" **Wt:** 170 **Born:** 04/19/61 **Age:** 33

										BATTING									BASERUNNING				PERCENTAGES		
Year Team	Lg	G	AB	H	2B	3B	HR	(Hm	Rd)	TB	R	RBI	TBB	IBB	SO	HBP	SH	SF	SB	CS	SB%	GDP	Avg	OBP	SLG
1983 Seattle	AL	80	306	60	11	3	2	(1	1)	83	36	21	24	0	44	2	5	3	10	6	.63	2	.196	.257	.271
1984 Seattle	AL	152	530	130	18	8	3	(2	1)	173	67	43	46	0	63	3	9	2	16	8	.67	5	.245	.308	.326
1985 Seattle	AL	118	352	91	10	6	6	(3	3)	131	41	37	34	0	27	0	5	2	11	5	.69	5	.259	.322	.372
1986 2 ML Teams		154	528	122	24	7	1	(0	1)	163	67	45	51	1	51	2	9	3	4	4	.50	13	.231	.300	.309
1987 Boston	AL	132	437	113	17	7	2	(2	0)	150	50	48	53	2	43	1	9	4	11	8	.58	9	.259	.337	.343
1988 Boston	AL	89	257	64	14	1	5	(2	3)	95	40	18	27	0	27	2	7	1	0	1	.00	7	.249	.324	.370
1989 Montreal	NL	142	437	102	17	4	6	(5	1)	145	52	41	76	25	44	3	3	3	3	2	.60	11	.233	.349	.332

Year Team	Lg	G	AB	H	2B	3B	HR	(Hm	Rd)	TB	R	RBI	TBB	IBB	SO	HBP	SH	SF	SB	CS	SB%	GDP	Avg	OBP	SLG
1990 Montreal	NL	149	453	106	24	5	5	(2	3)	155	55	35	70	12	60	0	5	5	8	6	.57	6	.234	.333	.342
1991 Montreal	NL	139	424	108	22	8	3	(1	2)	155	39	26	42	11	61	1	4	4	2	6	.25	11	.255	.321	.366
1992 Montreal	NL	122	386	104	16	3	7	(3	4)	147	52	40	50	3	30	0	4	6	9	4	.69	10	.269	.348	.381
1993 New York	AL	103	334	78	16	2	2	(1	1)	104	41	20	29	2	30	0	3	1	3	2	.60	5	.234	.294	.311
1986 Seattle	AL	112	402	99	22	6	0	(0	0)	133	46	35	34	1	42	1	7	2	1	3	.25	11	.246	.305	.331
Boston	AL	42	126	23	2	1	1	(0	1)	30	21	10	17	0	9	1	2	1	3	1	.75	2	.183	.283	.238
11 ML YEARS		1380	4444	1078	189	54	42	(22	20)	1501	540	374	502	56	480	14	63	34	77	52	.60	84	.243	.319	.338

Jayhawk Owens

Bats: Right **Throws:** Right **Pos:** C   **Ht:** 6' 1" **Wt:** 200 **Born:** 02/10/69 **Age:** 25

				BATTING															BASERUNNING				PERCENTAGES		
Year Team	Lg	G	AB	H	2B	3B	HR	(Hm	Rd)	TB	R	RBI	TBB	IBB	SO	HBP	SH	SF	SB	CS	SB%	GDP	Avg	OBP	SLG
1990 Kenosha	A	66	216	51	9	2	5	--	--	79	31	30	39	0	59	13	1	1	15	7	.68	8	.236	.383	.366
1991 Visalia	A	65	233	57	16	1	6	--	--	93	33	33	35	1	70	8	0	2	14	6	.70	4	.245	.360	.399
1992 Orlando	AA	102	330	88	24	0	4	--	--	124	50	30	36	0	67	11	0	5	10	2	.83	5	.267	.353	.376
1993 Colo Sprngs	AAA	55	174	54	11	3	6	--	--	89	24	43	21	0	56	5	0	3	5	3	.63	6	.310	.394	.511
1993 Colorado	NL	33	86	18	5	0	3	(2	1)	32	12	6	6	1	30	2	0	0	1	0	1.00	1	.209	.277	.372

Mike Pagliarulo

Bats: Left **Throws:** Right **Pos:** 3B   **Ht:** 6' 2" **Wt:** 201 **Born:** 03/15/60 **Age:** 34

				BATTING															BASERUNNING				PERCENTAGES		
Year Team	Lg	G	AB	H	2B	3B	HR	(Hm	Rd)	TB	R	RBI	TBB	IBB	SO	HBP	SH	SF	SB	CS	SB%	GDP	Avg	OBP	SLG
1984 New York	AL	67	201	48	15	3	7	(4	3)	90	24	34	15	0	46	0	0	3	0	0	.00	5	.239	.288	.448
1985 New York	AL	138	380	91	16	2	19	(8	11)	168	55	62	45	4	86	4	3	3	0	0	.00	6	.239	.324	.442
1986 New York	AL	149	504	120	24	3	28	(14	14)	234	71	71	54	10	120	4	1	2	4	1	.80	10	.238	.316	.464
1987 New York	AL	150	522	122	26	3	32	(17	15)	250	76	87	53	9	111	2	2	3	1	3	.25	9	.234	.305	.479
1988 New York	AL	125	444	96	20	1	15	(8	7)	163	46	67	37	9	104	2	1	6	1	0	1.00	5	.216	.276	.367
1989 2 ML Teams		124	371	73	17	0	7	(5	2)	111	31	30	37	4	82	3	1	0	3	1	.75	5	.197	.275	.299
1990 San Diego	NL	128	398	101	23	2	7	(1	6)	149	29	38	39	3	66	3	2	4	1	3	.25	12	.254	.322	.374
1991 Minnesota	AL	121	365	102	20	0	6	(4	2)	140	38	36	21	3	55	3	2	2	1	2	.33	9	.279	.322	.384
1992 Minnesota	AL	42	105	21	4	0	0	(0	0)	25	10	9	1	0	17	1	0	1	0	1	.00	1	.200	.213	.238
1993 2 ML Teams		116	370	112	25	4	9	(5	4)	172	55	44	26	2	49	6	2	1	6	6	.50	7	.303	.357	.465
1989 New York	AL	74	223	44	10	0	4	(3	1)	66	19	16	19	0	43	2	0	0	1	1	.50	2	.197	.266	.296
San Diego	NL	50	148	29	7	0	3	(2	1)	45	12	14	18	4	39	1	1	0	2	0	1.00	3	.196	.287	.304
1993 Minnesota	AL	83	253	74	16	4	3	(2	1)	107	31	23	18	2	34	5	2	1	6	6	.50	5	.292	.350	.423
Baltimore	AL	33	117	38	9	0	6	(3	3)	65	24	21	8	0	15	1	0	0	0	0	.00	2	.325	.373	.556
10 ML YEARS		1160	3660	886	190	18	130	(66	64)	1502	435	478	328	44	736	28	14	25	18	16	.53	69	.242	.307	.410

Tom Pagnozzi

Bats: Right **Throws:** Right **Pos:** C   **Ht:** 6' 1" **Wt:** 190 **Born:** 07/30/62 **Age:** 31

				BATTING															BASERUNNING				PERCENTAGES		
Year Team	Lg	G	AB	H	2B	3B	HR	(Hm	Rd)	TB	R	RBI	TBB	IBB	SO	HBP	SH	SF	SB	CS	SB%	GDP	Avg	OBP	SLG
1993 Louisville *	AAA	12	43	12	3	0	1	--	--	18	5	1	2	0	3	0	0	0	0	0	.00	1	.279	.311	.419
1987 St. Louis	NL	27	48	9	1	0	2	(2	0)	16	8	9	4	2	13	0	1	0	1	0	1.00	0	.188	.250	.333
1988 St. Louis	NL	81	195	55	9	0	0	(0	0)	64	17	15	11	1	32	0	2	1	0	0	.00	5	.282	.319	.328
1989 St. Louis	NL	52	80	12	2	0	0	(0	0)	14	3	3	6	2	19	1	0	1	0	0	.00	7	.150	.216	.175
1990 St. Louis	NL	69	220	61	15	0	2	(2	0)	82	20	23	14	1	37	1	0	2	1	1	.50	0	.277	.321	.373
1991 St. Louis	NL	140	459	121	24	5	2	(2	0)	161	38	57	36	6	63	4	6	5	9	13	.41	10	.264	.319	.351
1992 St. Louis	NL	139	485	121	26	3	7	(3	4)	174	33	44	28	9	64	1	6	3	2	5	.29	15	.249	.290	.359
1993 St. Louis	NL	92	330	85	15	1	7	(1	6)	123	31	41	19	6	30	1	0	5	1	0	1.00	7	.258	.296	.373
7 ML YEARS		600	1817	464	92	9	20	(10	10)	634	150	192	118	27	258	8	15	17	14	19	.42	44	.255	.301	.349

Lance Painter

Pitches: Left **Bats:** Left **Pos:** SP   **Ht:** 6' 1" **Wt:** 195 **Born:** 07/21/67 **Age:** 26

			HOW MUCH HE PITCHED					WHAT HE GAVE UP										THE RESULTS				
Year Team	Lg	G	GS	CG	GF	IP	BFP	H	R	ER	HR	SH	SF	HB	TBB	IBB	SO	WP	Bk	W	L	Pct.	ShO	Sv	ERA
1990 Spokane	A	23	1	0	10	71.2	281	45	18	12	4	5	1	2	16	0	104	3	3	7	3	.700	0	3	1.51
1991 Waterloo	A	28	28	7	0	200	788	162	64	51	14	5	4	2	57	7	201	3	1	14	8	.636	4	0	2.30
1992 Wichita	AA	27	27	1	0	163.1	680	138	74	64	11	8	3	10	55	1	137	6	3	10	5	.667	1	0	3.53
1993 Colo Sprngs	AAA	23	22	4	0	138	610	165	90	66	10	10	5	5	44	2	91	6	0	9	7	.563	1	0	4.30
1993 Colorado	NL	10	6	1	2	39	166	52	26	26	5	1	0	0	9	0	16	2	0	2	2	.500	0	0	6.00

Donn Pall

Pitches: Right **Bats:** Right **Pos:** RP   **Ht:** 6' 1" **Wt:** 180 **Born:** 01/11/62 **Age:** 32

			HOW MUCH HE PITCHED					WHAT HE GAVE UP										THE RESULTS				
Year Team	Lg	G	GS	CG	GF	IP	BFP	H	R	ER	HR	SH	SF	HB	TBB	IBB	SO	WP	Bk	W	L	Pct.	ShO	Sv	ERA
1988 Chicago	AL	17	0	0	6	28.2	130	39	11	11	1	2	1	0	8	1	16	1	0	0	2	.000	0	0	3.45

166

Year Team	Lg	G																							
1989 Chicago	AL	53	0	0	27	87	370	90	35	32	9	8	2	8	19	3	58	4	1	4	5	.444	0	6	3.31
1990 Chicago	AL	56	0	0	11	76	306	63	33	28	7	4	2	4	24	8	39	2	0	3	5	.375	0	2	3.32
1991 Chicago	AL	51	0	0	7	71	282	59	22	19	7	4	0	3	20	3	40	2	0	7	2	.778	0	0	2.41
1992 Chicago	AL	39	0	0	12	73	323	79	43	40	9	1	3	2	27	8	27	1	2	5	2	.714	0	1	4.93
1993 2 ML Teams		47	0	0	11	76.1	320	77	32	26	6	7	1	2	14	3	40	3	1	3	3	.500	0	1	3.07
1993 Chicago	AL	39	0	0	9	58.2	251	62	25	21	5	6	1	2	11	3	29	3	0	2	3	.400	0	1	3.22
Philadelphia	NL	8	0	0	2	17.2	69	15	7	5	1	1	0	0	3	0	11	0	1	1	0	1.000	0	0	2.55
6 ML YEARS		263	0	0	74	412	1731	407	176	156	39	26	9	19	112	26	220	13	4	22	19	.537	0	10	3.41

Rafael Palmeiro

Bats: Left Throws: Left Pos: 1B **Ht: 6' 0" Wt: 188 Born: 09/24/64 Age: 29**

Year Team	Lg	G	AB	H	2B	3B	HR	(Hm	Rd)	TB	R	RBI	TBB	IBB	SO	HBP	SH	SF	SB	CS	SB%	GDP	Avg	OBP	SLG
1986 Chicago	NL	22	73	18	4	0	3	(1	2)	31	9	12	4	0	6	1	0	0	1	1	.50	4	.247	.295	.425
1987 Chicago	NL	84	221	61	15	1	14	(5	9)	120	32	30	20	1	26	1	0	2	2	2	.50	2	.276	.336	.543
1988 Chicago	NL	152	580	178	41	5	8	(8	0)	253	75	53	38	6	34	3	2	6	12	2	.86	11	.307	.349	.436
1989 Texas	AL	156	559	154	23	4	8	(4	4)	209	76	64	63	3	48	6	2	2	4	3	.57	18	.275	.354	.374
1990 Texas	AL	154	598	191	35	6	14	(9	5)	280	72	89	40	6	59	3	2	8	3	3	.50	24	.319	.361	.468
1991 Texas	AL	159	631	203	49	3	26	(12	14)	336	115	88	68	10	72	6	2	7	4	3	.57	17	.322	.389	.532
1992 Texas	AL	159	608	163	27	4	22	(8	14)	264	84	85	72	8	83	10	5	6	2	3	.40	10	.268	.352	.434
1993 Texas	AL	160	597	176	40	2	37	(22	15)	331	124	105	73	22	85	5	2	9	22	3	.88	8	.295	.371	.554
8 ML YEARS		1046	3867	1144	234	25	132	(69	63)	1824	587	526	378	56	413	35	15	40	50	20	.71	96	.296	.360	.472

Dean Palmer

Bats: Right Throws: Right Pos: 3B **Ht: 6' 2" Wt: 195 Born: 12/27/68 Age: 25**

Year Team	Lg	G	AB	H	2B	3B	HR	(Hm	Rd)	TB	R	RBI	TBB	IBB	SO	HBP	SH	SF	SB	CS	SB%	GDP	Avg	OBP	SLG
1989 Texas	AL	16	19	2	2	0	0	(0	0)	4	0	1	0	0	12	0	0	1	0	0	.00	0	.105	.100	.211
1991 Texas	AL	81	268	50	9	2	15	(6	9)	108	38	37	32	0	98	3	1	0	0	2	.00	4	.187	.281	.403
1992 Texas	AL	152	541	124	25	0	26	(11	15)	227	74	72	62	2	154	4	2	4	10	4	.71	9	.229	.311	.420
1993 Texas	AL	148	519	127	31	2	33	(12	21)	261	88	96	53	4	154	8	0	5	11	10	.52	5	.245	.321	.503
4 ML YEARS		397	1347	303	67	4	74	(29	45)	600	200	206	147	6	418	15	3	10	21	16	.57	18	.225	.306	.445

Erik Pappas

Bats: Right Throws: Right Pos: C/RF **Ht: 6' 0" Wt: 190 Born: 04/25/66 Age: 28**

Year Team	Lg	G	AB	H	2B	3B	HR	(Hm	Rd)	TB	R	RBI	TBB	IBB	SO	HBP	SH	SF	SB	CS	SB%	GDP	Avg	OBP	SLG
1993 Louisville *	AAA	21	71	24	6	1	4	--	--	44	19	13	11	0	12	0	0	0	0	2	.00	1	.338	.427	.620
1991 Chicago	NL	7	17	3	0	0	0	(0	0)	3	1	2	1	0	5	0	0	0	0	0	.00	0	.176	.222	.176
1993 St. Louis	NL	82	228	63	12	0	1	(1	0)	78	25	28	35	2	35	0	0	3	1	3	.25	7	.276	.368	.342
2 ML YEARS		89	245	66	12	0	1	(1	0)	81	26	30	36	2	40	0	0	3	1	3	.25	7	.269	.359	.331

Craig Paquette

Bats: Right Throws: Right Pos: 3B **Ht: 6' 0" Wt: 190 Born: 03/28/69 Age: 25**

Year Team	Lg	G	AB	H	2B	3B	HR	(Hm	Rd)	TB	R	RBI	TBB	IBB	SO	HBP	SH	SF	SB	CS	SB%	GDP	Avg	OBP	SLG
1989 Sou Oregon	A	71	277	93	22	3	14	--	--	163	53	56	30	4	46	2	0	1	9	4	.69	6	.336	.403	.588
1990 Modesto	A	130	495	118	23	4	15	--	--	194	65	59	47	1	123	3	0	4	8	5	.62	10	.238	.306	.392
1991 Huntsville	AA	102	378	99	18	1	8	--	--	143	50	60	28	0	87	3	2	5	0	5	.00	16	.262	.314	.378
1992 Huntsville	AA	115	450	116	25	4	17	--	--	200	59	71	29	0	118	2	1	3	13	10	.57	12	.258	.304	.444
Tacoma	AAA	17	66	18	7	0	2	--	--	31	10	11	2	0	16	0	0	0	3	1	.75	3	.273	.294	.470
1993 Tacoma	AAA	50	183	49	8	0	8	--	--	81	29	29	14	0	54	1	0	2	3	3	.50	6	.268	.320	.443
1993 Oakland	AL	105	393	86	20	4	12	(8	4)	150	35	46	14	2	108	0	1	1	4	2	.67	7	.219	.245	.382

Mark Parent

Bats: Right Throws: Right Pos: C **Ht: 6' 5" Wt: 225 Born: 09/16/61 Age: 32**

Year Team	Lg	G	AB	H	2B	3B	HR	(Hm	Rd)	TB	R	RBI	TBB	IBB	SO	HBP	SH	SF	SB	CS	SB%	GDP	Avg	OBP	SLG
1993 Rochester *	AAA	92	332	82	15	0	14	--	--	139	47	56	40	0	71	0	0	1	0	1	.00	12	.247	.327	.419
1986 San Diego	NL	8	14	2	0	0	0	(0	0)	2	1	0	1	0	3	0	0	0	0	0	.00	1	.143	.200	.143
1987 San Diego	NL	12	25	2	0	0	0	(0	0)	2	0	2	0	0	9	0	0	0	0	0	.00	0	.080	.080	.080
1988 San Diego	NL	41	118	23	3	0	6	(4	2)	44	9	15	6	0	23	0	0	1	0	0	.00	0	.195	.232	.373
1989 San Diego	NL	52	141	27	4	0	7	(6	1)	52	12	21	8	2	34	0	1	4	1	0	1.00	5	.191	.229	.369
1990 San Diego	NL	65	189	42	11	0	3	(1	2)	62	13	16	16	3	29	0	3	0	1	0	1.00	2	.222	.283	.328
1991 Texas	AL	3	1	0	0	0	0	(0	0)	0	0	0	0	0	1	0	0	0	0	0	.00	0	.000	.000	.000
1992 Baltimore	AL	17	34	8	1	0	2	(0	2)	15	4	4	3	0	7	1	2	0	0	0	.00	0	.235	.316	.441

	Lg	G	AB	H	2B	3B	HR	(Hm	Rd)	TB	R	RBI	TBB	IBB	SO	HBP	SH	SF	SB	CS	SB%	GDP	Avg	OBP	SLG
1993 Baltimore	AL	22	54	14	2	0	4	(1	3)	28	7	12	3	0	14	0	3	1	0	0	.00	1	.259	.293	.519
8 ML YEARS		220	576	118	21	0	22	(12	10)	205	46	70	37	5	120	1	9	6	2	0	1.00	10	.205	.252	.356

Rick Parker

Bats: Right **Throws:** Right **Pos:** CF **Ht:** 6' 0" **Wt:** 185 **Born:** 03/20/63 **Age:** 31

					BATTING														BASERUNNING				PERCENTAGES		
Year Team	Lg	G	AB	H	2B	3B	HR	(Hm	Rd)	TB	R	RBI	TBB	IBB	SO	HBP	SH	SF	SB	CS	SB%	GDP	Avg	OBP	SLG
1993 Tucson *	AAA	29	120	37	9	3	2	--	--	58	28	12	14	1	20	0	0	0	6	2	.75	2	.308	.381	.483
1990 San Francisco	NL	54	107	26	5	0	2	(0	2)	37	19	14	10	0	15	1	3	0	6	1	.86	1	.243	.314	.346
1991 San Francisco	NL	13	14	1	0	0	0	(0	0)	1	0	1	1	0	5	0	0	0	0	0	.00	0	.071	.133	.071
1993 Houston	NL	45	45	15	3	0	0	(0	0)	18	11	4	3	0	8	0	1	0	1	2	.33	2	.333	.375	.400
3 ML YEARS		112	166	42	8	0	2	(0	2)	56	30	19	14	0	28	1	4	0	7	3	.70	3	.253	.315	.337

Derek Parks

Bats: Right **Throws:** Right **Pos:** C **Ht:** 6' 0" **Wt:** 205 **Born:** 09/29/68 **Age:** 25

					BATTING														BASERUNNING				PERCENTAGES		
Year Team	Lg	G	AB	H	2B	3B	HR	(Hm	Rd)	TB	R	RBI	TBB	IBB	SO	HBP	SH	SF	SB	CS	SB%	GDP	Avg	OBP	SLG
1986 Elizabethtn	R	62	224	53	10	1	10	--	--	95	39	40	23	0	58	5	0	3	1	0	1.00	3	.237	.318	.424
1987 Kenosha	A	129	466	115	19	2	24	--	--	210	70	94	77	5	111	10	0	6	1	1	.50	12	.247	.361	.451
1988 Orlando	AA	118	400	94	15	0	7	--	--	130	52	42	49	1	81	15	0	5	1	1	.50	12	.235	.337	.325
1989 Orlando	AA	31	95	18	3	0	2	--	--	27	16	10	19	0	27	6	0	0	1	0	1.00	1	.189	.358	.284
1990 Portland	AAA	76	231	41	8	1	11	--	--	84	27	27	18	0	56	8	0	1	0	0	.00	6	.177	.260	.364
1991 Orlando	AA	92	256	55	14	0	6	--	--	87	31	31	31	1	64	12	2	3	0	0	.00	4	.215	.325	.340
1992 Portland	AAA	79	249	61	12	0	12	--	--	109	33	49	25	0	47	4	4	6	0	2	.00	6	.245	.317	.438
1993 Portland	AAA	107	363	113	23	1	17	--	--	189	63	71	48	1	57	4	0	6	0	0	.00	12	.311	.392	.521
1992 Minnesota	AL	7	6	2	0	0	0	(0	0)	2	1	0	1	0	1	1	0	0	0	0	.00	0	.333	.500	.333
1993 Minnesota	AL	7	20	4	0	0	0	(0	0)	4	3	1	1	0	2	0	0	0	0	0	.00	0	.200	.238	.200
2 ML YEARS		14	26	6	0	0	0	(0	0)	6	4	1	2	0	3	1	0	0	0	0	.00	0	.231	.310	.231

Jeff Parrett

Pitches: Right **Bats:** Right **Pos:** RP/SP **Ht:** 6' 3" **Wt:** 195 **Born:** 08/26/61 **Age:** 32

			HOW MUCH HE PITCHED						WHAT HE GAVE UP									THE RESULTS					
Year Team	Lg	G	GS	CG	GF	IP	BFP	H	R	ER	HR	SH	SF	HB	TBB	IBB	SO	WP	Bk	W	L	Pct.	ShO	Sv	ERA
1986 Montreal	NL	12	0	0	6	20.1	91	19	11	11	3	0	1	0	13	0	21	2	0	0	1	.000	0	0	4.87
1987 Montreal	NL	45	0	0	26	62	267	53	33	29	8	5	1	0	30	4	56	6	1	7	6	.538	0	6	4.21
1988 Montreal	NL	61	0	0	34	91.2	369	66	29	27	8	9	6	1	45	9	62	4	1	12	4	.750	0	6	2.65
1989 Philadelphia	NL	72	0	0	34	105.2	444	90	43	35	6	7	5	0	44	13	98	7	3	12	6	.667	0	6	2.98
1990 2 ML Teams		67	5	0	19	108.2	479	119	62	56	11	7	5	2	55	10	86	5	1	5	10	.333	0	2	4.64
1991 Atlanta	NL	18	0	0	9	21.1	109	31	18	15	2	2	0	0	12	2	14	4	0	1	2	.333	0	1	6.33
1992 Oakland	AL	66	0	0	14	98.1	410	81	35	33	7	4	4	2	42	3	78	13	0	9	1	.900	0	0	3.02
1993 Colorado	NL	40	6	0	13	73.2	341	78	47	44	6	4	5	2	45	9	66	11	1	3	3	.500	0	1	5.38
1990 Philadelphia	NL	47	5	0	14	81.2	355	92	51	47	10	3	1	1	36	8	69	3	1	4	9	.308	0	1	5.18
Atlanta	NL	20	0	0	5	27	124	27	11	9	1	4	4	1	19	2	17	2	0	1	1	.500	0	1	3.00
8 ML YEARS		381	11	0	155	581.2	2510	537	278	250	51	38	27	7	286	50	481	52	7	49	33	.598	0	22	3.87

Lance Parrish

Bats: Right **Throws:** Right **Pos:** C **Ht:** 6' 3" **Wt:** 224 **Born:** 06/15/56 **Age:** 38

					BATTING														BASERUNNING				PERCENTAGES		
Year Team	Lg	G	AB	H	2B	3B	HR	(Hm	Rd)	TB	R	RBI	TBB	IBB	SO	HBP	SH	SF	SB	CS	SB%	GDP	Avg	OBP	SLG
1993 Albuquerque *	AAA	11	33	9	2	0	0	--	--	11	4	1	5	0	4	3	0	0	0	0	.00	1	.273	.415	.333
1977 Detroit	AL	12	46	9	2	0	3	(2	1)	20	10	7	5	0	12	0	0	0	0	0	.00	2	.196	.275	.435
1978 Detroit	AL	85	288	63	11	3	14	(7	7)	122	37	41	11	0	71	3	1	1	0	0	.00	6	.219	.254	.424
1979 Detroit	AL	143	493	136	26	3	19	(8	11)	225	65	65	49	2	105	2	3	1	6	7	.46	15	.276	.343	.456
1980 Detroit	AL	144	553	158	34	6	24	(7	17)	276	79	82	31	3	109	3	2	3	6	4	.60	24	.286	.325	.499
1981 Detroit	AL	96	348	85	18	2	10	(8	2)	137	39	46	34	0	52	0	1	1	2	3	.40	16	.244	.311	.394
1982 Detroit	AL	133	486	138	19	2	32	(22	10)	257	75	87	40	5	99	1	0	2	3	4	.43	5	.284	.338	.529
1983 Detroit	AL	155	605	163	42	3	27	(12	15)	292	80	114	44	7	106	1	0	13	1	3	.25	21	.269	.314	.483
1984 Detroit	AL	147	578	137	16	2	33	(13	20)	256	75	98	41	6	120	2	2	6	2	4	.33	12	.237	.287	.443
1985 Detroit	AL	140	549	150	27	1	28	(11	17)	263	64	98	41	5	90	2	3	5	2	6	.25	10	.273	.323	.479
1986 Detroit	AL	91	327	84	6	1	22	(8	14)	158	53	62	38	3	83	5	1	3	0	0	.00	3	.257	.340	.483
1987 Philadelphia	NL	130	466	114	21	0	17	(5	12)	186	42	67	47	2	104	1	1	3	0	1	.00	23	.245	.313	.399
1988 Philadelphia	NL	123	424	91	17	2	15	(11	4)	157	44	60	47	7	93	2	0	5	0	0	.00	11	.215	.293	.370
1989 California	AL	124	433	103	12	1	17	(8	9)	168	48	50	42	6	104	2	1	5	1	1	.50	10	.238	.306	.388
1990 California	AL	133	470	126	14	0	24	(14	10)	212	54	70	46	4	107	5	0	2	2	2	.50	11	.268	.338	.451
1991 California	AL	119	402	87	12	0	19	(9	10)	156	38	51	35	2	117	5	0	3	0	1	.00	7	.216	.285	.388
1992 2 ML Teams		93	275	64	13	1	12	(7	5)	115	26	32	24	3	70	1	1	3	1	1	.50	7	.233	.294	.418
1993 Cleveland	AL	10	20	4	1	0	1	(1	0)	8	2	2	4	0	5	0	0	0	0	0	1.00	2	.200	.333	.400

168

Year	Team	Lg	G	AB	H	2B	3B	HR	(Hm	Rd)	TB	R	RBI	TBB	IBB	SO	HBP	SH	SF	SB	CS	SB%	GDP	Avg	OBP	SLG
1992	California	AL	24	83	19	2	0	4	(1	3)	33	7	11	5	1	22	0	1	1	0	0	.00	1	.229	.270	.398
	Seattle	AL	69	192	45	11	1	8	(6	2)	82	19	21	19	2	48	1	0	2	1	1	.50	6	.234	.304	.427
17 ML YEARS			1878	6763	1712	291	27	317	(153	164)	3008	831	1032	579	61	1447	35	16	55	27	36	.43	188	.253	.313	.445

Dan Pasqua

Bats: Left   **Throws:** Left   **Pos:** 1B/LF/RF   **Ht:** 6' 0"   **Wt:** 218   **Born:** 10/17/61   **Age:** 32

									BATTING											BASERUNNING				PERCENTAGES		
Year	Team	Lg	G	AB	H	2B	3B	HR	(Hm	Rd)	TB	R	RBI	TBB	IBB	SO	HBP	SH	SF	SB	CS	SB%	GDP	Avg	OBP	SLG
1985	New York	AL	60	148	31	3	1	9	(7	2)	63	17	25	16	4	38	1	0	1	0	0	.00	1	.209	.289	.426
1986	New York	AL	102	280	82	17	0	16	(9	7)	147	44	45	47	3	78	3	1	1	2	0	1.00	4	.293	.399	.525
1987	New York	AL	113	318	74	7	1	17	(6	11)	134	42	42	40	3	99	1	2	1	0	2	.00	7	.233	.319	.421
1988	Chicago	AL	129	422	96	16	2	20	(11	9)	176	48	50	46	5	100	3	2	2	1	0	1.00	10	.227	.307	.417
1989	Chicago	AL	73	246	61	9	1	11	(5	6)	105	26	47	25	1	58	1	1	4	1	2	.33	0	.248	.315	.427
1990	Chicago	AL	112	325	89	27	3	13	(4	9)	161	43	58	37	7	66	2	0	5	1	1	.50	4	.274	.347	.495
1991	Chicago	AL	134	417	108	22	5	18	(10	8)	194	71	66	62	4	86	3	1	1	0	2	.00	9	.259	.358	.465
1992	Chicago	AL	93	265	56	16	1	6	(2	4)	92	26	33	36	1	57	1	1	3	2	1	.00	4	.211	.305	.347
1993	Chicago	AL	78	176	36	10	1	5	(2	3)	63	22	20	26	1	51	0	1	3	2	2	.50	3	.205	.302	.358
9 ML YEARS			894	2597	633	127	15	115	(56	59)	1135	339	386	335	29	633	15	9	21	7	10	.41	42	.244	.331	.437

Bob Patterson

Pitches: Left   **Bats:** Right   **Pos:** RP   **Ht:** 6' 2"   **Wt:** 185   **Born:** 05/16/59   **Age:** 35

				HOW MUCH HE PITCHED						WHAT HE GAVE UP								THE RESULTS					
Year	Team	Lg	G	GS	CG	GF	IP	BFP	H	R	ER	HR	SH	SF	HB	TBB	IBB	SO	WP	Bk	W	L	Pct.	ShO	Sv	ERA
1985	San Diego	NL	3	0	0	2	4	26	13	11	11	2	0	0	0	3	0	1	0	1	0	0	.000	0	0	24.75
1986	Pittsburgh	NL	11	5	0	2	36.1	159	49	20	20	0	1	1	0	5	2	20	0	1	2	3	.400	0	0	4.95
1987	Pittsburgh	NL	15	7	0	2	43	201	49	34	32	5	6	3	1	22	4	27	1	0	1	4	.200	0	0	6.70
1989	Pittsburgh	NL	12	3	0	2	26.2	109	23	13	12	3	1	1	0	8	2	20	0	0	4	3	.571	0	1	4.05
1990	Pittsburgh	NL	55	5	0	19	94.2	386	88	33	31	9	5	3	3	21	7	70	1	2	8	5	.615	0	5	2.95
1991	Pittsburgh	NL	54	1	0	19	65.2	270	67	32	30	7	2	2	0	15	1	57	0	0	4	3	.571	0	2	4.11
1992	Pittsburgh	NL	60	0	0	26	64.2	268	59	22	21	7	3	2	0	23	6	43	3	0	6	3	.667	0	9	2.92
1993	Texas	AL	52	0	0	29	52.2	224	59	28	28	8	1	2	1	11	0	46	0	0	2	4	.333	0	1	4.78
8 ML YEARS			262	21	0	101	387.2	1643	407	193	185	41	19	14	5	108	22	284	5	4	27	25	.519	0	18	4.29

John Patterson

Bats: Both   **Throws:** Right   **Pos:** PH   **Ht:** 5' 9"   **Wt:** 168   **Born:** 02/11/67   **Age:** 27

									BATTING											BASERUNNING				PERCENTAGES		
Year	Team	Lg	G	AB	H	2B	3B	HR	(Hm	Rd)	TB	R	RBI	TBB	IBB	SO	HBP	SH	SF	SB	CS	SB%	GDP	Avg	OBP	SLG
1988	Everett	A	58	232	58	10	4	0	--	--	76	37	26	18	0	27	0	0	1	21	3	.88	1	.250	.303	.328
1990	San Jose	A	131	530	160	23	6	4	--	--	207	91	66	46	2	74	9	5	6	29	17	.63	7	.302	.364	.391
1991	Shreveport	AA	117	464	137	31	13	4	--	--	206	81	56	30	3	63	11	3	3	40	19	.68	9	.295	.350	.444
1992	Phoenix	AAA	93	362	109	20	6	2	--	--	147	52	37	33	4	45	5	0	2	22	18	.55	3	.301	.366	.406
1993	San Jose	A	16	68	16	7	0	1	--	--	26	8	14	7	1	12	2	0	0	6	0	1.00	0	.235	.325	.382
1992	San Francisco	NL	32	103	19	1	1	0	(0	0)	22	10	4	5	0	24	1	0	0	5	1	.83	2	.184	.229	.214
1993	San Francisco	NL	16	16	3	0	0	1	(0	1)	6	1	2	0	0	5	0	0	0	0	1	.00	0	.188	.188	.375
2 ML YEARS			48	119	22	1	1	1	(0	1)	28	11	6	5	0	29	1	0	0	5	2	.71	2	.185	.224	.235

Ken Patterson

Pitches: Left   **Bats:** Left   **Pos:** RP   **Ht:** 6' 4"   **Wt:** 210   **Born:** 07/08/64   **Age:** 29

				HOW MUCH HE PITCHED						WHAT HE GAVE UP								THE RESULTS					
Year	Team	Lg	G	GS	CG	GF	IP	BFP	H	R	ER	HR	SH	SF	HB	TBB	IBB	SO	WP	Bk	W	L	Pct.	ShO	Sv	ERA
1988	Chicago	AL	9	2	0	3	20.2	92	25	11	11	2	0	0	0	7	0	8	1	1	0	2	.000	0	1	4.79
1989	Chicago	AL	50	1	0	18	65.2	284	64	37	33	11	1	4	2	28	3	43	3	1	6	1	.857	0	0	4.52
1990	Chicago	AL	43	0	0	15	66.1	283	58	27	25	6	2	5	2	34	1	40	2	0	2	1	.667	0	2	3.39
1991	Chicago	AL	43	0	0	13	63.2	265	48	22	20	5	3	2	1	35	1	32	2	0	3	0	1.000	0	1	2.83
1992	Chicago	NL	32	1	0	4	41.2	191	41	25	18	7	6	4	1	27	6	23	3	1	2	3	.400	0	0	3.89
1993	California	AL	46	0	0	9	59	255	54	30	30	7	2	1	0	35	5	36	2	0	1	1	.500	0	1	4.58
6 ML YEARS			223	4	0	62	317	1370	290	152	137	38	14	16	6	166	16	182	13	3	14	8	.636	0	5	3.89

Roger Pavlik

Pitches: Right   **Bats:** Right   **Pos:** SP   **Ht:** 6' 2"   **Wt:** 220   **Born:** 10/04/67   **Age:** 26

				HOW MUCH HE PITCHED						WHAT HE GAVE UP								THE RESULTS					
Year	Team	Lg	G	GS	CG	GF	IP	BFP	H	R	ER	HR	SH	SF	HB	TBB	IBB	SO	WP	Bk	W	L	Pct.	ShO	Sv	ERA
1987	Gastonia	A	15	14	0	0	67.1	303	66	46	37	3	1	4	5	42	0	55	6	0	2	7	.222	0	0	4.95
1988	Gastonia	A	18	16	0	1	84.1	408	94	65	43	3	4	0	6	58	2	89	10	3	2	12	.143	0	0	4.59
	Butte	R	8	8	1	0	49	223	45	29	25	2	2	1	7	34	0	56	3	0	4	0	1.000	1	0	4.59
1989	Charlotte	A	26	22	1	2	118.2	511	92	60	45	5	4	4	8	72	1	98	12	4	3	8	.273	1	1	3.41
1990	Charlotte	A	11	11	1	0	66.1	279	50	21	18	1	2	0	5	40	3	76	6	1	5	3	.625	0	0	2.44

169

Year Team	Lg	G	GS	CG	GF	IP	BFP	H	R	ER	HR	SH	SF	HB	TBB	IBB	SO	WP	Bk	W	L	Pct.	ShO	Sv	ERA
Tulsa	AA	16	16	2	0	100.1	418	66	29	26	4	3	1	5	71	2	91	7	2	6	5	.545	1	0	2.33
1991 Okla City	AAA	8	7	0	0	26	126	19	21	15	1	0	1	1	26	1	43	5	1	0	5	.000	0	0	5.19
1992 Okla City	AAA	18	18	0	0	117.2	485	90	44	39	7	3	8	4	51	0	104	14	1	7	5	.583	0	0	2.98
1993 Okla City	AAA	6	6	0	0	37	150	26	12	7	1	2	0	2	14	0	32	1	0	3	2	.600	0	0	1.70
1992 Texas	AL	13	12	1	0	62	275	66	32	29	3	0	2	3	34	0	45	9	0	4	4	.500	0	0	4.21
1993 Texas	AL	26	26	2	0	166.1	712	151	67	63	18	6	4	5	80	3	131	7	0	12	6	.667	0	0	3.41
2 ML YEARS		39	38	3	0	228.1	987	217	99	92	21	6	6	8	114	3	176	16	0	16	10	.615	0	0	3.63

Bill Pecota

Bats: Right **Throws:** Right **Pos:** 3B   **Ht:** 6' 2" **Wt:** 195 **Born:** 02/16/60 **Age:** 34

				BATTING														BASERUNNING				PERCENTAGES		
Year Team	Lg	G	AB	H	2B	3B	HR	(Hm Rd)	TB	R	RBI	TBB	IBB	SO	HBP	SH	SF	SB	CS	SB%	GDP	Avg	OBP	SLG
1986 Kansas City	AL	12	29	6	2	0	0	(0 0)	8	3	2	3	0	3	1	0	1	0	2	.00	1	.207	.294	.276
1987 Kansas City	AL	66	156	43	5	1	3	(0 3)	59	22	14	15	0	25	1	0	0	5	0	1.00	3	.276	.343	.378
1988 Kansas City	AL	90	178	37	3	3	1	(0 1)	49	25	15	18	0	34	2	7	1	7	2	.78	1	.208	.286	.275
1989 Kansas City	AL	65	83	17	4	2	3	(0 1)	34	21	5	7	1	9	1	1	0	5	0	1.00	4	.205	.275	.410
1990 Kansas City	AL	87	240	58	15	2	5	(3 2)	92	43	20	33	0	39	1	6	0	8	5	.62	5	.242	.336	.383
1991 Kansas City	AL	125	398	114	23	2	6	(4 2)	159	53	45	41	6	45	2	7	0	16	7	.70	12	.286	.356	.399
1992 New York	NL	117	269	61	13	0	2	(1 1)	80	28	26	25	3	40	1	5	2	9	3	.75	7	.227	.293	.297
1993 Atlanta	NL	72	62	20	2	1	0	(0 0)	24	17	5	2	0	5	0	1	0	1	1	.50	0	.323	.344	.387
8 ML YEARS		634	1415	356	67	11	20	(8 12)	505	212	132	144	10	200	9	27	4	51	20	.72	33	.252	.324	.357

Dan Peltier

Bats: Left **Throws:** Left **Pos:** RF   **Ht:** 6' 1" **Wt:** 200 **Born:** 06/30/68 **Age:** 26

				BATTING														BASERUNNING				PERCENTAGES		
Year Team	Lg	G	AB	H	2B	3B	HR	(Hm Rd)	TB	R	RBI	TBB	IBB	SO	HBP	SH	SF	SB	CS	SB%	GDP	Avg	OBP	SLG
1989 Butte	R	33	122	49	7	1	7	-- --	79	35	28	25	2	16	1	0	0	10	1	.91	4	.402	.507	.648
1990 Tulsa	AA	117	446	125	19	4	11	-- --	185	66	57	40	2	67	6	1	2	8	6	.57	8	.279	.345	.413
1991 Okla City	AAA	94	345	79	16	4	3	-- --	112	38	31	43	2	71	0	2	0	6	5	.55	8	.229	.313	.325
1992 Okla City	AAA	125	450	133	30	7	7	-- --	198	65	53	60	3	72	3	3	1	1	7	.13	14	.296	.381	.440
1993 Okla City	AAA	48	187	60	15	4	5	-- --	98	28	33	19	4	27	0	0	2	2	2	.50	4	.321	.380	.524
1992 Texas	AL	12	24	4	0	0	0	(0 0)	4	1	2	0	0	3	0	0	0	0	0	.00	0	.167	.167	.167
1993 Texas	AL	65	160	43	7	1	1	(1 0)	55	23	17	20	0	27	1	1	1	0	4	.00	3	.269	.352	.344
2 ML YEARS		77	184	47	7	1	1	(1 0)	59	24	19	20	0	30	1	1	1	0	4	.00	3	.255	.330	.321

Alejandro Pena

Pitches: Right **Bats:** Right **Pos:** RP   **Ht:** 6' 1" **Wt:** 203 **Born:** 06/25/59 **Age:** 35

		HOW MUCH HE PITCHED						WHAT HE GAVE UP												THE RESULTS					
Year Team	Lg	G	GS	CG	GF	IP	BFP	H	R	ER	HR	SH	SF	HB	TBB	IBB	SO	WP	Bk	W	L	Pct.	ShO	Sv	ERA
1981 Los Angeles	NL	14	0	0	7	25	104	18	8	8	2	0	0	1	11	1	14	0	0	1	1	.500	0	2	2.88
1982 Los Angeles	NL	29	0	0	11	35.2	160	37	24	19	2	2	0	1	21	7	20	1	1	0	2	.000	0	0	4.79
1983 Los Angeles	NL	34	26	4	4	177	730	152	61	54	7	8	5	1	51	7	120	2	1	12	9	.571	3	1	2.75
1984 Los Angeles	NL	28	28	8	0	199.1	813	186	67	55	7	6	2	3	46	7	135	5	1	12	6	.667	4	0	2.48
1985 Los Angeles	NL	2	1	0	0	4.1	23	7	5	4	1	0	0	0	3	1	2	0	0	0	1	.000	0	0	8.31
1986 Los Angeles	NL	24	10	0	6	70	309	74	40	38	6	3	1	1	30	5	46	1	1	1	2	.333	0	1	4.89
1987 Los Angeles	NL	37	7	0	17	87.1	377	82	41	34	9	5	6	2	37	5	76	0	1	2	7	.222	0	11	3.50
1988 Los Angeles	NL	60	0	0	31	94.1	378	75	29	20	4	3	3	1	27	6	83	3	2	6	7	.462	0	12	1.91
1989 Los Angeles	NL	53	0	0	28	76	306	62	20	18	6	3	1	2	18	4	75	1	1	4	3	.571	0	5	2.13
1990 New York	NL	52	0	0	32	76	320	71	31	27	4	1	6	1	22	5	76	0	0	3	3	.500	0	5	3.20
1991 2 ML Teams		59	0	0	36	82.1	331	74	23	22	6	3	4	0	22	4	62	1	2	8	1	.889	0	15	2.40
1992 Atlanta	NL	41	0	0	31	42	173	40	19	19	7	2	1	0	13	5	34	0	0	1	6	.143	0	15	4.07
1991 New York	NL	44	0	0	24	63	261	63	20	19	5	2	4	0	19	4	49	1	2	6	1	.857	0	4	2.71
Atlanta	NL	15	0	0	12	19.1	70	11	3	3	1	1	0	0	3	0	13	0	0	2	0	1.000	0	11	1.40
12 ML YEARS		433	72	12	203	969.1	4024	878	374	318	61	36	29	12	301	57	743	14	10	50	48	.510	7	67	2.95

Geronimo Pena

Bats: Both **Throws:** Right **Pos:** 2B   **Ht:** 6' 1" **Wt:** 195 **Born:** 03/29/67 **Age:** 27

				BATTING														BASERUNNING				PERCENTAGES		
Year Team	Lg	G	AB	H	2B	3B	HR	(Hm Rd)	TB	R	RBI	TBB	IBB	SO	HBP	SH	SF	SB	CS	SB%	GDP	Avg	OBP	SLG
1993 Louisville *	AAA	7	23	4	1	0	0	(0 0)	5	4	0	1	0	4	1	0	1	0	1	1.00	0	.174	.240	.217
1990 St. Louis	NL	18	45	11	2	0	0	(0 0)	13	5	2	4	0	14	1	0	1	1	1	.50	0	.244	.314	.289
1991 St. Louis	NL	104	185	45	8	3	5	(2 3)	74	38	17	18	1	45	5	1	3	15	5	.75	0	.243	.322	.400
1992 St. Louis	NL	62	203	62	12	1	7	(4 3)	97	31	31	24	0	37	5	0	4	13	8	.62	1	.305	.386	.478
1993 St. Louis	NL	74	254	65	19	2	5	(2 3)	103	34	30	25	0	71	4	4	2	13	5	.72	3	.256	.330	.406
4 ML YEARS		258	687	183	41	6	17	(7 10)	287	108	80	71	1	167	15	5	10	42	19	.69	4	.266	.344	.418

Tony Pena

Bats: Right **Throws:** Right **Pos:** C **Ht:** 6' 0" **Wt:** 185 **Born:** 06/04/57 **Age:** 37

								BATTING											BASERUNNING				PERCENTAGES		
Year Team	Lg	G	AB	H	2B	3B	HR	(Hm	Rd)	TB	R	RBI	TBB	IBB	SO	HBP	SH	SF	SB	CS	SB%	GDP	Avg	OBP	SLG
1980 Pittsburgh	NL	8	21	9	1	1	0	(0	0)	12	1	1	0	0	4	0	0	0	0	1	.00	1	.429	.429	.571
1981 Pittsburgh	NL	66	210	63	9	1	2	(1	1)	80	16	17	8	2	23	1	2	2	1	2	.33	4	.300	.326	.381
1982 Pittsburgh	NL	138	497	147	28	4	11	(5	6)	216	53	63	17	3	57	4	3	2	2	5	.29	17	.296	.323	.435
1983 Pittsburgh	NL	151	542	163	22	3	15	(8	7)	236	51	70	31	8	73	0	6	1	6	7	.46	13	.301	.338	.435
1984 Pittsburgh	NL	147	546	156	27	2	15	(7	8)	232	77	78	36	5	79	4	4	2	12	8	.60	14	.286	.333	.425
1985 Pittsburgh	NL	147	546	136	27	2	10	(2	8)	197	53	59	29	4	67	0	7	5	12	8	.60	19	.249	.284	.361
1986 Pittsburgh	NL	144	510	147	26	2	10	(5	5)	207	56	52	53	6	69	1	0	1	9	10	.47	21	.288	.356	.406
1987 St. Louis	NL	116	384	82	13	4	5	(1	4)	118	40	44	36	9	54	1	2	2	6	1	.86	19	.214	.281	.307
1988 St. Louis	NL	149	505	133	23	1	10	(4	6)	188	55	51	33	11	60	1	3	4	6	2	.75	12	.263	.308	.372
1989 St. Louis	NL	141	424	110	17	2	4	(3	1)	143	36	37	35	19	33	2	2	1	5	3	.63	19	.259	.318	.337
1990 Boston	AL	143	491	129	19	1	7	(3	4)	171	62	56	43	3	71	1	2	3	8	6	.57	23	.263	.322	.348
1991 Boston	AL	141	464	107	23	2	5	(2	3)	149	45	48	37	1	53	4	4	3	8	3	.73	23	.231	.291	.321
1992 Boston	AL	133	410	99	21	1	1	(1	0)	125	39	38	24	0	61	1	13	2	3	2	.60	11	.241	.284	.305
1993 Boston	AL	126	304	55	11	0	4	(2	2)	78	20	19	25	0	46	2	13	3	1	3	.25	12	.181	.246	.257
14 ML YEARS		1750	5854	1536	267	26	99	(44	55)	2152	604	633	407	71	750	22	61	31	79	61	.56	208	.262	.311	.368

Terry Pendleton

Bats: Both **Throws:** Right **Pos:** 3B **Ht:** 5' 9" **Wt:** 195 **Born:** 07/16/60 **Age:** 33

								BATTING											BASERUNNING				PERCENTAGES		
Year Team	Lg	G	AB	H	2B	3B	HR	(Hm	Rd)	TB	R	RBI	TBB	IBB	SO	HBP	SH	SF	SB	CS	SB%	GDP	Avg	OBP	SLG
1984 St. Louis	NL	67	262	85	16	3	1	(0	1)	110	37	33	16	3	32	0	0	5	20	5	.80	7	.324	.357	.420
1985 St. Louis	NL	149	559	134	16	3	5	(3	2)	171	56	69	37	4	75	0	3	3	17	12	.59	18	.240	.285	.306
1986 St. Louis	NL	159	578	138	26	5	1	(0	1)	177	56	59	34	10	59	1	6	7	24	6	.80	12	.239	.279	.306
1987 St. Louis	NL	159	583	167	29	4	12	(5	7)	240	82	96	70	6	74	2	3	9	19	12	.61	18	.286	.360	.412
1988 St. Louis	NL	110	391	99	20	2	6	(3	3)	141	44	53	21	4	51	2	4	3	3	3	.50	9	.253	.293	.361
1989 St. Louis	NL	162	613	162	28	5	13	(8	5)	239	83	74	44	3	81	0	2	2	9	5	.64	16	.264	.313	.390
1990 St. Louis	NL	121	447	103	20	2	6	(6	0)	145	46	58	30	8	58	1	0	6	7	5	.58	12	.230	.277	.324
1991 Atlanta	NL	153	586	187	34	8	22	(13	9)	303	94	86	43	8	70	1	7	7	10	2	.83	16	.319	.363	.517
1992 Atlanta	NL	160	640	199	39	1	21	(13	8)	303	98	105	37	8	67	0	5	7	5	2	.71	16	.311	.345	.473
1993 Atlanta	NL	161	633	172	33	1	17	(9	8)	258	81	84	36	5	97	3	3	7	5	1	.83	18	.272	.311	.408
10 ML YEARS		1401	5292	1446	261	34	104	(60	44)	2087	677	717	368	59	664	10	33	56	119	53	.69	142	.273	.319	.394

Brad Pennington

Pitches: Left **Bats:** Left **Pos:** RP **Ht:** 6' 5" **Wt:** 205 **Born:** 04/14/69 **Age:** 25

					HOW MUCH HE PITCHED				WHAT HE GAVE UP												THE RESULTS				
Year Team	Lg	G	GS	CG	GF	IP	BFP	H	R	ER	HR	SH	SF	HB	TBB	IBB	SO	WP	Bk	W	L	Pct.	ShO	Sv	ERA
1989 Bluefield	R	15	14	0	0	64.1	319	50	58	47	2	1	3	6	74	0	81	14	8	2	7	.222	0	0	6.58
1990 Wausau	A	32	18	1	7	106	523	81	89	61	12	6	4	4	121	1	142	10	1	4	9	.308	0	0	5.18
1991 Kane County	A	23	0	0	19	23	112	16	17	15	1	0	0	0	25	0	43	6	0	0	2	.000	0	4	5.87
Frederick	A	36	0	0	27	43.2	203	32	23	19	4	3	2	2	44	0	58	4	0	1	4	.200	0	13	3.92
1992 Frederick	A	8	0	0	6	9	38	5	3	2	0	1	1	1	4	0	16	1	0	1	0	1.000	0	2	2.00
Hagerstown	AA	19	0	0	16	28.1	121	20	9	8	0	4	3	3	17	0	33	4	0	1	2	.333	0	7	2.54
Rochester	AAA	29	0	0	17	39	158	12	10	9	2	4	1	1	33	2	56	2	0	1	3	.250	0	5	2.08
1993 Rochester	AAA	17	0	0	14	15.2	73	12	11	6	0	0	0	0	13	0	19	1	1	1	2	.333	0	8	3.45
1993 Baltimore	AL	34	0	0	16	33	158	34	25	24	7	2	1	2	25	0	39	3	0	3	2	.600	0	4	6.55

William Pennyfeather

Bats: Right **Throws:** Right **Pos:** CF **Ht:** 6' 2" **Wt:** 195 **Born:** 05/25/68 **Age:** 26

								BATTING											BASERUNNING				PERCENTAGES		
Year Team	Lg	G	AB	H	2B	3B	HR	(Hm	Rd)	TB	R	RBI	TBB	IBB	SO	HBP	SH	SF	SB	CS	SB%	GDP	Avg	OBP	SLG
1988 Pirates	R	17	74	18	2	1	1	(--	--)	25	6	7	2	0	18	0	0	1	3	3	.50	0	.243	.260	.338
Princeton	R	16	57	19	2	0	1	(--	--)	24	11	5	6	0	15	0	0	0	7	2	.78	0	.333	.397	.421
1989 Welland	A	75	289	55	10	1	3	(--	--)	76	34	26	12	1	75	2	1	6	18	5	.78	6	.190	.223	.263
1990 Augusta	A	122	465	122	14	4	4	(--	--)	156	69	48	23	0	85	3	3	3	21	10	.68	7	.262	.300	.335
1991 Salem	A	81	319	85	17	3	8	(--	--)	132	35	46	8	0	52	1	1	2	11	8	.58	9	.266	.285	.414
Carolina	AA	42	149	41	5	0	0	(--	--)	46	13	9	7	0	17	1	1	1	3	2	.60	8	.275	.310	.309
1992 Carolina	AA	51	199	67	13	1	6	(--	--)	100	28	25	9	1	34	0	0	3	7	6	.54	5	.337	.360	.503
Buffalo	AAA	55	160	38	6	2	1	(--	--)	51	19	12	2	0	24	3	2	0	3	2	.60	4	.238	.261	.319
1993 Buffalo	AAA	112	457	114	18	3	14	(--	--)	180	54	41	18	2	92	0	8	1	10	12	.45	3	.249	.277	.394
1992 Pittsburgh	NL	15	9	2	0	0	0	(0	0)	2	2	0	0	0	0	0	0	1	0	0	.00	1	.222	.222	.222
1993 Pittsburgh	NL	21	34	7	1	0	0	(0	0)	8	4	2	0	0	6	0	0	0	0	0	.00	1	.206	.206	.235
2 ML YEARS		36	43	9	1	0	0	(0	0)	10	6	2	0	0	6	0	0	1	0	0	.00	2	.209	.209	.233

Eduardo Perez

Bats: Right **Throws:** Right **Pos:** 3B   **Ht:** 6' 4" **Wt:** 215 **Born:** 09/11/69 **Age:** 24

								BATTING												BASERUNNING				PERCENTAGES		
Year Team	Lg	G	AB	H	2B	3B	HR	(Hm	Rd)	TB	R	RBI	TBB	IBB	SO	HBP	SH	SF	SB	CS	SB%	GDP	Avg	OBP	SLG
1991 Boise	A	46	160	46	13	0	1	--	--	62	35	22	19	0	39	4	1	1	12	3	.80	4	.288	.375	.388
1992 Palm Sprngs	A	54	204	64	8	4	3	--	--	89	37	35	23	0	33	3	0	3	14	3	.82	5	.314	.386	.436
Midland	AA	62	235	54	8	1	3	--	--	73	27	23	22	1	49	1	1	3	19	7	.73	7	.230	.295	.311
1993 Vancouver	AAA	96	363	111	23	6	12	--	--	182	66	70	28	5	83	3	1	0	21	7	.75	5	.306	.360	.501
1993 California	AL	52	180	45	6	2	4	(2	2)	67	16	30	9	0	39	2	0	1	5	4	.56	4	.250	.292	.372

Melido Perez

Pitches: Right **Bats:** Right **Pos:** SP   **Ht:** 6' 4" **Wt:** 180 **Born:** 02/15/66 **Age:** 28

			HOW MUCH HE PITCHED						WHAT HE GAVE UP											THE RESULTS					
Year Team	Lg	G	GS	CG	GF	IP	BFP	H	R	ER	HR	SH	SF	HB	TBB	IBB	SO	WP	Bk	W	L	Pct.	ShO	Sv	ERA
1987 Kansas City	AL	3	3	0	0	10.1	53	18	12	9	2	0	0	0	5	0	5	0	0	1	1	.500	0	0	7.84
1988 Chicago	AL	32	32	3	0	197	836	186	105	83	26	5	8	2	72	0	138	13	3	12	10	.545	1	0	3.79
1989 Chicago	AL	31	31	2	0	183.1	810	187	106	102	23	5	4	3	90	3	141	12	5	11	14	.440	0	0	5.01
1990 Chicago	AL	35	35	3	0	197	833	177	111	101	14	4	6	2	86	1	161	8	4	13	14	.481	3	0	4.61
1991 Chicago	AL	49	8	0	16	135.2	553	111	49	47	15	4	1	1	52	0	128	11	1	8	7	.533	0	1	3.12
1992 New York	AL	33	33	10	0	247.2	1013	212	94	79	16	6	8	5	93	5	218	13	0	13	16	.448	1	0	2.87
1993 New York	AL	25	25	0	0	163	718	173	103	94	22	4	2	1	64	5	148	3	1	6	14	.300	0	0	5.19
7 ML YEARS		208	167	18	16	1134	4816	1064	580	515	118	28	29	14	462	14	939	60	14	64	76	.457	5	1	4.09

Mike Perez

Pitches: Right **Bats:** Right **Pos:** RP   **Ht:** 6' 0" **Wt:** 187 **Born:** 10/19/64 **Age:** 29

			HOW MUCH HE PITCHED						WHAT HE GAVE UP											THE RESULTS					
Year Team	Lg	G	GS	CG	GF	IP	BFP	H	R	ER	HR	SH	SF	HB	TBB	IBB	SO	WP	Bk	W	L	Pct.	ShO	Sv	ERA
1993 Arkansas *	AA	4	0	0	0	3.2	19	7	3	3	0	0	1	0	1	0	0	4	0	0	0	0	.000	0	0	7.36
1990 St. Louis	NL	13	0	0	7	13.2	55	12	6	6	0	0	2	0	3	0	5	0	0	1	0	1.000	0	1	3.95
1991 St. Louis	NL	14	0	0	2	17	75	19	11	11	1	1	0	1	7	2	7	0	1	0	2	.000	0	0	5.82
1992 St. Louis	NL	77	0	0	22	93	377	70	23	19	4	7	4	1	32	9	46	4	0	9	3	.750	0	0	1.84
1993 St. Louis	NL	65	0	0	25	72.2	298	65	24	20	4	5	5	1	20	1	58	2	0	7	2	.778	0	7	2.48
4 ML YEARS		169	0	0	56	196.1	805	166	64	56	9	13	11	3	62	12	116	6	1	17	7	.708	0	8	2.57

Gerald Perry

Bats: Left **Throws:** Right **Pos:** 1B   **Ht:** 6' 0" **Wt:** 201 **Born:** 10/30/60 **Age:** 33

								BATTING												BASERUNNING				PERCENTAGES		
Year Team	Lg	G	AB	H	2B	3B	HR	(Hm	Rd)	TB	R	RBI	TBB	IBB	SO	HBP	SH	SF	SB	CS	SB%	GDP	Avg	OBP	SLG
1983 Atlanta	NL	27	39	14	2	0	1	(0	1)	19	5	6	5	0	4	0	0	1	0	1	.00	1	.359	.422	.487
1984 Atlanta	NL	122	347	92	12	2	7	(3	4)	129	52	47	61	5	38	2	2	7	15	12	.56	9	.265	.372	.372
1985 Atlanta	NL	110	238	51	5	0	3	(3	0)	65	22	13	28	1	28	0	0	1	9	5	.64	7	.214	.282	.273
1986 Atlanta	NL	29	70	19	2	0	2	(2	0)	27	6	11	8	1	4	0	1	1	0	1	.00	4	.271	.342	.386
1987 Atlanta	NL	142	533	144	35	2	12	(2	10)	219	77	74	48	1	63	1	3	5	42	16	.72	18	.270	.329	.411
1988 Atlanta	NL	141	547	164	29	1	8	(4	4)	219	61	74	36	9	49	1	1	10	29	14	.67	18	.300	.338	.400
1989 Atlanta	NL	72	266	67	11	0	4	(2	2)	90	24	21	32	5	28	3	0	2	10	6	.63	5	.252	.337	.338
1990 Kansas City	AL	133	465	118	22	2	8	(3	5)	168	57	57	39	4	56	3	0	5	17	4	.81	14	.254	.313	.361
1991 St. Louis	NL	109	242	58	8	4	6	(1	5)	92	29	36	22	1	34	0	0	3	15	8	.65	2	.240	.300	.380
1992 St. Louis	NL	87	143	34	8	0	1	(1	0)	45	13	18	15	4	23	1	0	2	3	6	.33	3	.238	.311	.315
1993 St. Louis	NL	96	98	33	5	0	4	(3	1)	50	21	16	18	2	23	0	0	0	1	1	.50	4	.337	.440	.510
11 ML YEARS		1068	2988	794	139	11	56	(24	32)	1123	367	373	307	33	350	11	7	37	141	74	.66	85	.266	.333	.376

Mark Petkovsek

Pitches: Right **Bats:** Right **Pos:** RP   **Ht:** 6' 0" **Wt:** 185 **Born:** 11/18/65 **Age:** 28

			HOW MUCH HE PITCHED						WHAT HE GAVE UP											THE RESULTS					
Year Team	Lg	G	GS	CG	GF	IP	BFP	H	R	ER	HR	SH	SF	HB	TBB	IBB	SO	WP	Bk	W	L	Pct.	ShO	Sv	ERA
1987 Rangers	R	3	1	0	0	5.2	26	4	2	2	0	0	0	2	2	0	7	0	0	0	0	.000	0	0	3.18
Charlotte	A	11	10	0	1	56	249	67	36	25	2	3	3	0	17	0	23	5	1	3	4	.429	0	0	4.02
1988 Charlotte	A	28	28	7	0	175.2	708	156	71	58	5	6	7	3	42	2	95	11	4	10	11	.476	5	0	2.97
1989 Okla City	AAA	6	6	0	0	30.2	147	39	27	25	3	1	1	3	18	1	8	2	0	0	4	.000	0	0	7.34
Tulsa	AA	21	21	1	0	140	585	144	63	54	7	6	7	3	35	0	66	5	0	8	5	.615	0	0	3.47
1990 Okla City	AAA	28	28	2	0	151	669	187	103	88	9	3	2	4	42	1	81	8	0	7	14	.333	1	0	5.25
1991 Okla City	AAA	25	24	3	0	149.2	646	162	89	82	9	5	9	7	38	2	67	10	1	9	8	.529	1	0	4.93
1992 Buffalo	AAA	32	22	1	1	150.1	632	150	76	59	9	12	3	7	44	1	49	5	0	8	8	.500	0	1	3.53
1993 Buffalo	AAA	14	11	1	0	70.2	291	74	38	34	8	2	1	2	16	0	27	4	0	3	4	.429	0	0	4.33
1991 Texas	AL	4	1	0	0	9.1	53	21	16	15	4	0	1	0	4	0	6	2	0	0	1	.000	0	0	14.46
1993 Pittsburgh	NL	26	0	0	9	32.1	145	43	25	25	7	4	1	0	9	2	14	4	0	3	0	1.000	0	0	6.96
2 ML YEARS		30	1	0	9	41.2	198	64	41	40	11	4	2	0	13	2	20	6	0	3	1	.750	0	0	8.64

Geno Petralli

Bats: Both **Throws:** Right **Pos:** C **Ht:** 6' 1" **Wt:** 190 **Born:** 09/25/59 **Age:** 34

Year	Team	Lg	G	AB	H	2B	3B	HR	(Hm	Rd)	TB	R	RBI	TBB	IBB	SO	HBP	SH	SF	SB	CS	SB%	GDP	Avg	OBP	SLG
1993	Okla City *	AAA	6	20	4	1	0	1	--	--	8	2	1	3	0	3	0	0	0	0	0	.00	1	.200	.304	.400
1982	Toronto	AL	16	44	16	2	0	0	(0	0)	18	3	1	4	0	6	0	1	0	0	0	.00	1	.364	.417	.409
1983	Toronto	AL	6	4	0	0	0	0	(0	0)	0	0	0	1	0	1	0	0	0	0	0	.00	0	.000	.200	.000
1984	Toronto	AL	3	3	0	0	0	0	(0	0)	0	0	0	0	0	0	0	0	0	0	0	.00	0	.000	.000	.000
1985	Texas	AL	42	100	27	2	0	0	(0	0)	29	7	11	8	0	12	1	3	4	1	0	1.00	4	.270	.319	.290
1986	Texas	AL	69	137	35	9	3	2	(1	1)	56	17	18	5	0	14	0	0	0	3	0	1.00	7	.255	.282	.409
1987	Texas	AL	101	202	61	11	2	7	(4	3)	97	28	31	27	2	29	2	0	1	0	2	.00	4	.302	.388	.480
1988	Texas	AL	129	351	99	14	2	7	(1	6)	138	35	36	41	5	52	2	1	5	0	1	.00	12	.282	.356	.393
1989	Texas	AL	70	184	56	7	0	4	(1	3)	75	18	23	17	1	24	2	1	1	0	0	.00	5	.304	.368	.408
1990	Texas	AL	133	325	83	13	1	0	(0	0)	98	28	21	50	3	49	3	1	3	0	2	.00	12	.255	.357	.302
1991	Texas	AL	87	199	54	8	1	2	(0	2)	70	21	20	21	1	25	0	7	1	2	1	.67	4	.271	.339	.352
1992	Texas	AL	94	192	38	12	0	1	(0	1)	53	11	18	20	2	34	0	1	0	0	0	.00	8	.198	.274	.276
1993	Texas	AL	59	133	32	5	0	1	(1	0)	40	16	13	22	3	17	0	1	0	2	0	1.00	5	.241	.348	.301
12 ML YEARS			809	1874	501	83	9	24	(8	16)	674	184	192	216	17	263	10	16	15	8	6	.57	62	.267	.344	.360

J.R. Phillips

Bats: Left **Throws:** Left **Pos:** 1B **Ht:** 6' 1" **Wt:** 185 **Born:** 04/29/70 **Age:** 24

Year	Team	Lg	G	AB	H	2B	3B	HR	(Hm	Rd)	TB	R	RBI	TBB	IBB	SO	HBP	SH	SF	SB	CS	SB%	GDP	Avg	OBP	SLG
1988	Bend	A	56	210	40	8	0	4	--	--	60	24	23	21	1	70	1	1	3	3	1	.75	5	.190	.264	.286
1989	Quad City	A	125	442	85	29	1	8	--	--	140	41	50	49	2	146	4	4	4	3	3	.50	5	.192	.277	.317
1990	Palm Sprngs	A	46	162	32	4	1	1	--	--	41	14	15	10	1	58	1	1	1	3	1	.75	7	.198	.247	.253
	Boise	A	68	238	46	6	0	10	--	--	82	30	34	19	0	78	0	1	2	1	1	.50	4	.193	.251	.345
1991	Palm Sprngs	A	130	471	117	22	2	20	--	--	203	64	70	57	4	144	3	1	2	15	13	.54	8	.248	.332	.431
1992	Midland	AA	127	497	118	32	4	14	--	--	200	58	77	32	4	165	2	1	4	5	3	.63	9	.237	.284	.402
1993	Phoenix	AAA	134	506	133	35	2	27	--	--	253	80	94	53	9	127	6	0	6	7	5	.58	2	.263	.336	.500
1993	San Francisco	NL	11	16	5	1	1	1	(0	1)	11	1	4	0	0	5	0	0	0	0	0	.00	0	.313	.313	.688

Tony Phillips

Bats: Both **Throws:** Right **Pos:** LF/2B/RF **Ht:** 5'10" **Wt:** 175 **Born:** 04/25/59 **Age:** 35

Year	Team	Lg	G	AB	H	2B	3B	HR	(Hm	Rd)	TB	R	RBI	TBB	IBB	SO	HBP	SH	SF	SB	CS	SB%	GDP	Avg	OBP	SLG
1982	Oakland	AL	40	81	17	2	2	0	(0	0)	23	11	8	12	0	26	2	5	0	2	3	.40	0	.210	.326	.284
1983	Oakland	AL	148	412	102	12	3	4	(1	3)	132	54	35	48	1	70	2	11	3	16	5	.76	5	.248	.327	.320
1984	Oakland	AL	154	451	120	24	3	4	(2	2)	162	62	37	42	1	86	0	7	5	10	6	.63	5	.266	.325	.359
1985	Oakland	AL	42	161	45	12	2	4	(2	2)	73	23	17	13	0	34	0	3	1	3	2	.60	1	.280	.331	.453
1986	Oakland	AL	118	441	113	14	5	5	(3	2)	157	76	52	76	0	82	3	9	5	15	10	.60	2	.256	.367	.345
1987	Oakland	AL	111	379	91	20	0	10	(5	5)	141	48	46	57	1	76	0	2	3	7	6	.54	9	.240	.337	.372
1988	Oakland	AL	79	212	43	8	4	2	(2	0)	65	32	17	36	0	50	1	1	1	0	2	.00	6	.203	.320	.307
1989	Oakland	AL	143	451	118	15	6	4	(2	2)	157	48	47	58	2	66	3	5	7	3	8	.27	17	.262	.345	.348
1990	Detroit	AL	152	573	144	23	5	8	(4	4)	201	97	55	99	0	85	4	9	2	19	9	.68	10	.251	.364	.351
1991	Detroit	AL	146	564	160	28	4	17	(9	8)	247	87	72	79	5	95	3	3	6	10	5	.67	8	.284	.371	.438
1992	Detroit	AL	159	606	167	32	3	10	(3	7)	235	114	64	114	2	93	1	5	7	12	10	.55	13	.276	.387	.388
1993	Detroit	AL	151	566	177	27	0	7	(3	4)	225	113	57	132	5	102	4	1	4	16	11	.59	11	.313	.443	.398
12 ML YEARS			1443	4897	1297	217	37	75	(36	39)	1813	765	507	766	17	865	23	61	42	113	77	.59	87	.265	.364	.370

Mike Piazza

Bats: Right **Throws:** Right **Pos:** C **Ht:** 6' 3" **Wt:** 197 **Born:** 09/04/68 **Age:** 25

Year	Team	Lg	G	AB	H	2B	3B	HR	(Hm	Rd)	TB	R	RBI	TBB	IBB	SO	HBP	SH	SF	SB	CS	SB%	GDP	Avg	OBP	SLG
1989	Salem	A	57	198	53	11	0	8	--	--	88	22	25	13	0	51	2	0	1	0	0	.00	11	.268	.318	.444
1990	Vero Beach	A	88	272	68	20	0	6	--	--	106	27	45	11	0	68	1	0	1	0	1	.00	6	.250	.281	.390
1991	Bakersfield	A	117	448	124	27	2	29	--	--	242	71	80	47	2	83	3	0	8	0	3	.00	19	.277	.344	.540
1992	San Antonio	AA	31	114	43	11	0	7	--	--	75	18	21	13	2	18	0	0	0	0	0	.00	2	.377	.441	.658
	Albuquerque	AAA	94	358	122	22	5	16	--	--	202	54	69	37	4	57	2	0	1	1	3	.25	9	.341	.405	.564
1992	Los Angeles	NL	21	69	16	3	0	1	(1	0)	22	5	7	4	0	12	1	0	0	0	0	.00	0	.232	.284	.319
1993	Los Angeles	NL	149	547	174	24	2	35	(21	14)	307	81	112	46	6	86	3	0	6	3	4	.43	10	.318	.370	.561
2 ML YEARS			170	616	190	27	2	36	(22	14)	329	86	119	50	6	98	4	0	6	3	4	.43	11	.308	.361	.534

Hipolito Pichardo

Pitches: Right **Bats:** Right **Pos:** SP/RP **Ht:** 6' 1" **Wt:** 185 **Born:** 08/22/69 **Age:** 24

			HOW MUCH HE PITCHED					WHAT HE GAVE UP									THE RESULTS					
Year	Team	Lg	G	GS	CG	GF	IP	BFP	H	R	ER	HR	SH	SF	HB	TBB	IBB	SO	WP	Bk	W	L	Pct.	ShO	Sv	ERA
1988	Royals	R	1	0	0	0	1.1	9	3	2	2	0	0	0	1	1	0	3	0	0	0	0	.000	0	0	13.50
1989	Appleton	A	12	12	2	0	75.2	300	58	29	25	4	2	1	5	18	0	50	5	4	5	4	.556	0	0	2.97
1990	Baseball Cy	A	11	10	0	0	45	201	47	28	19	1	2	2	1	25	0	40	4	2	1	6	.143	0	0	3.80
1991	Memphis	AA	34	11	0	5	99	447	116	56	47	4	7	4	4	38	5	75	6	1	3	11	.214	0	0	4.27
1992	Memphis	AA	2	2	0	0	14	55	13	2	1	0	1	0	0	1	0	10	0	0	2	0	.000	0	0	0.64
1992	Kansas City	AL	31	24	1	0	143.2	615	148	71	63	9	4	5	3	49	1	59	3	1	9	6	.600	1	0	3.95
1993	Kansas City	AL	30	25	2	2	165	720	183	85	74	10	3	8	6	53	2	70	5	3	7	8	.467	0	0	4.04
	2 ML YEARS		61	49	3	2	308.2	1335	331	156	137	19	7	13	9	102	3	129	8	4	16	14	.533	1	0	3.99

Greg Pirkl

Bats: Right **Throws:** Right **Pos:** 1B **Ht:** 6' 5" **Wt:** 225 **Born:** 08/07/70 **Age:** 23

			BATTING																BASERUNNING				PERCENTAGES		
Year	Team	Lg	G	AB	H	2B	3B	HR	(Hm	Rd)	TB	R	RBI	TBB	IBB	SO	HBP	SH	SF	SB	CS	SB%	GDP	Avg	OBP	SLG
1988	Bellingham	A	65	246	59	6	0	6	--	--	83	22	35	12	0	59	6	0	2	1	1	.50	8	.240	.289	.337
1989	Bellingham	A	70	265	68	6	0	8	--	--	98	31	36	23	2	51	3	1	3	4	1	.80	8	.257	.320	.370
1990	San Berndno	A	58	207	61	10	0	5	--	--	86	37	28	13	0	34	3	0	1	3	0	1.00	4	.295	.344	.415
1991	Peninsula	A	64	239	63	16	0	6	--	--	97	20	41	9	0	41	7	0	3	0	0	.00	9	.264	.306	.406
	San Berndno	A	63	239	75	13	1	14	--	--	132	32	53	12	1	43	2	0	6	4	0	1.00	5	.314	.344	.552
1992	Jacksnville	AA	59	227	66	11	1	10	--	--	109	25	29	9	1	45	7	0	4	0	0	.00	10	.291	.332	.480
	Calgary	AAA	79	286	76	21	3	6	--	--	121	30	32	14	0	64	3	0	2	4	3	.57	8	.266	.305	.423
1993	Calgary	AAA	115	445	137	24	1	21	--	--	226	67	94	13	1	50	6	1	10	3	3	.50	15	.308	.329	.508
1993	Seattle	AL	7	23	4	0	0	1	(1	0)	7	1	4	0	0	4	0	0	0	0	0	.00	2	.174	.174	.304

Erik Plantenberg

Pitches: Left **Bats:** Both **Pos:** RP **Ht:** 6' 1" **Wt:** 180 **Born:** 10/30/68 **Age:** 25

			HOW MUCH HE PITCHED					WHAT HE GAVE UP									THE RESULTS					
Year	Team	Lg	G	GS	CG	GF	IP	BFP	H	R	ER	HR	SH	SF	HB	TBB	IBB	SO	WP	Bk	W	L	Pct.	ShO	Sv	ERA
1990	Elmira	A	16	5	0	4	40.1	186	44	26	18	2	6	1	0	19	0	36	4	1	2	3	.400	0	1	4.02
1991	Lynchburg	A	20	20	0	0	103	461	116	59	43	3	4	2	4	51	1	73	8	0	11	5	.688	0	0	3.76
1992	Lynchburg	A	21	12	0	4	81.2	384	112	69	47	7	2	4	5	36	0	62	6	0	2	3	.400	0	0	5.18
1993	Jacksnville	AA	34	0	0	13	44.2	182	38	11	10	0	1	0	0	14	1	49	1	0	2	1	.667	0	1	2.01
1993	Seattle	AL	20	0	0	4	9.2	53	11	7	7	0	1	0	1	12	1	3	1	0	0	0	.000	0	0	6.52

Phil Plantier

Bats: Left **Throws:** Right **Pos:** LF **Ht:** 5'11" **Wt:** 195 **Born:** 01/27/69 **Age:** 25

			BATTING																BASERUNNING				PERCENTAGES		
Year	Team	Lg	G	AB	H	2B	3B	HR	(Hm	Rd)	TB	R	RBI	TBB	IBB	SO	HBP	SH	SF	SB	CS	SB%	GDP	Avg	OBP	SLG
1990	Boston	AL	14	15	2	1	0	0	(0	0)	3	1	3	4	0	6	1	0	1	0	0	.00	1	.133	.333	.200
1991	Boston	AL	53	148	49	7	1	11	(6	5)	91	27	35	23	2	38	1	0	1	1	0	1.00	2	.331	.420	.615
1992	Boston	AL	108	349	86	19	0	7	(5	2)	126	46	30	44	8	83	2	2	2	2	3	.40	9	.246	.332	.361
1993	San Diego	NL	138	462	111	20	1	34	(16	18)	235	67	100	61	7	124	7	1	5	4	5	.44	4	.240	.335	.509
	4 ML YEARS		313	974	248	47	2	52	(27	25)	455	141	168	132	17	251	11	3	10	7	8	.47	16	.255	.347	.467

Dan Plesac

Pitches: Left **Bats:** Left **Pos:** RP **Ht:** 6' 5" **Wt:** 215 **Born:** 02/04/62 **Age:** 32

			HOW MUCH HE PITCHED					WHAT HE GAVE UP									THE RESULTS					
Year	Team	Lg	G	GS	CG	GF	IP	BFP	H	R	ER	HR	SH	SF	HB	TBB	IBB	SO	WP	Bk	W	L	Pct.	ShO	Sv	ERA
1986	Milwaukee	AL	51	0	0	33	91	377	81	34	30	5	6	5	0	29	1	75	4	0	10	7	.588	0	14	2.97
1987	Milwaukee	AL	57	0	0	47	79.1	325	63	30	23	8	1	2	3	23	1	89	6	0	5	6	.455	0	23	2.61
1988	Milwaukee	AL	50	0	0	48	52.1	211	46	14	10	2	0	2	0	12	2	52	4	6	1	2	.333	0	30	2.41
1989	Milwaukee	AL	52	0	0	51	61.1	242	47	16	16	6	0	4	0	17	1	52	0	0	3	4	.429	0	33	2.35
1990	Milwaukee	AL	66	0	0	52	69	299	67	36	34	5	2	2	3	31	6	65	2	0	3	7	.300	0	24	4.43
1991	Milwaukee	AL	45	10	0	25	92.1	402	92	49	44	12	3	7	3	39	1	61	2	1	2	7	.222	0	8	4.29
1992	Milwaukee	AL	44	4	0	13	79	330	64	28	26	5	8	4	3	35	5	54	3	1	5	4	.556	0	1	2.96
1993	Chicago	NL	57	0	0	12	62.2	276	74	37	33	10	4	3	0	21	6	47	5	2	2	1	.667	0	0	4.74
	8 ML YEARS		422	14	0	281	587	2462	534	244	220	53	26	27	12	207	23	495	26	10	31	38	.449	0	133	3.37

Eric Plunk

Pitches: Right **Bats:** Right **Pos:** RP **Ht:** 6' 5" **Wt:** 220 **Born:** 09/03/63 **Age:** 30

			HOW MUCH HE PITCHED					WHAT HE GAVE UP									THE RESULTS					
Year	Team	Lg	G	GS	CG	GF	IP	BFP	H	R	ER	HR	SH	SF	HB	TBB	IBB	SO	WP	Bk	W	L	Pct.	ShO	Sv	ERA
1986	Oakland	AL	26	15	0	2	120.1	537	91	75	71	14	2	3	5	102	2	98	9	6	4	7	.364	0	0	5.31
1987	Oakland	AL	32	11	0	11	95	432	91	53	50	8	3	5	2	62	3	90	5	2	4	6	.400	0	2	4.74

174

1988 Oakland	AL	49	0	0	22	78	331	62	27	26	6	3	2	1	39	4	79	4	7	7	2	.778	0	5	3.00
1989 2 ML Teams		50	7	0	17	104.1	445	82	43	38	10	3	4	1	64	2	85	10	3	8	6	.571	0	1	3.28
1990 New York	AL	47	0	0	16	72.2	310	58	27	22	6	7	0	2	43	4	67	4	2	6	3	.667	0	0	2.72
1991 New York	AL	43	8	0	6	111.2	521	128	69	59	18	6	4	1	62	1	103	6	2	2	5	.286	0	0	4.76
1992 Cleveland	AL	58	0	0	20	71.2	309	61	31	29	5	3	2	0	38	2	50	5	0	9	6	.600	0	4	3.64
1993 Cleveland	AL	70	0	0	40	71	306	61	29	22	5	4	2	0	30	4	77	6	0	4	5	.444	0	15	2.79
1989 Oakland	AL	23	0	0	12	28.2	113	17	7	7	1	1	0	1	12	0	24	4	0	1	1	.500	0	1	2.20
New York	AL	27	7	0	5	75.2	332	65	36	31	9	2	4	0	52	2	61	6	3	7	5	.583	0	0	3.69
8 ML YEARS		375	41	0	134	724.2	3191	634	354	317	72	31	22	12	440	22	649	49	22	44	40	.524	0	27	3.94

Gus Polidor

Bats: Right **Throws:** Right **Pos:** 2B **Ht:** 6' 0" **Wt:** 184 **Born:** 10/26/61 **Age:** 32

								BATTING											BASERUNNING				PERCENTAGES		
Year Team	Lg	G	AB	H	2B	3B	HR	(Hm	Rd)	TB	R	RBI	TBB	IBB	SO	HBP	SH	SF	SB	CS	SB%	GDP	Avg	OBP	SLG
1993 Edmonton *	AAA	72	249	71	16	2	3	--	--	100	26	40	17	3	17	2	5	1	1	1	.50	11	.285	.335	.402
1985 California	AL	2	1	1	0	0	0	(0	0)	1	1	0	0	0	0	0	0	0	0	0	.00	0	1.000	1.000	1.000
1986 California	AL	6	19	5	1	0	0	(0	0)	6	1	1	1	0	0	0	0	0	0	0	.00	2	.263	.300	.316
1987 California	AL	63	137	36	3	0	2	(0	2)	45	12	15	2	0	15	1	0	1	0	0	.00	3	.263	.277	.328
1988 California	AL	54	81	12	3	0	0	(0	0)	15	4	4	3	0	11	0	3	0	0	0	.00	0	.148	.179	.185
1989 Milwaukee	AL	79	175	34	7	0	0	(0	0)	41	15	14	6	0	18	2	3	0	3	0	1.00	6	.194	.230	.234
1990 Milwaukee	AL	18	15	1	0	0	0	(0	0)	1	0	0	0	0	1	0	0	0	0	0	.00	0	.067	.067	.067
1993 Florida	NL	7	6	1	1	0	0	(0	0)	2	0	0	0	0	2	0	0	0	0	0	.00	0	.167	.167	.333
7 ML YEARS		229	434	90	15	0	2	(0	2)	111	33	35	12	0	47	3	6	1	3	0	1.00	13	.207	.233	.256

Luis Polonia

Bats: Left **Throws:** Left **Pos:** LF **Ht:** 5' 8" **Wt:** 150 **Born:** 10/12/64 **Age:** 29

								BATTING											BASERUNNING				PERCENTAGES		
Year Team	Lg	G	AB	H	2B	3B	HR	(Hm	Rd)	TB	R	RBI	TBB	IBB	SO	HBP	SH	SF	SB	CS	SB%	GDP	Avg	OBP	SLG
1987 Oakland	AL	125	435	125	16	10	4	(1	3)	173	78	49	32	1	64	0	1	1	29	7	.81	4	.287	.335	.398
1988 Oakland	AL	84	288	84	11	4	2	(1	1)	109	51	27	21	0	40	0	2	1	24	9	.73	3	.292	.338	.378
1989 2 ML Teams		125	433	130	17	6	3	(1	2)	168	70	46	25	1	44	2	2	4	22	8	.73	13	.300	.338	.388
1990 2 ML Teams		120	403	135	7	9	2	(2	0)	166	52	35	25	1	43	1	3	4	21	14	.60	9	.335	.372	.412
1991 California	AL	150	604	179	28	8	2	(1	1)	229	92	50	52	4	74	1	2	3	48	23	.68	11	.296	.352	.379
1992 California	AL	149	577	165	17	4	0	(0	0)	190	83	35	45	6	64	1	8	4	51	21	.71	18	.286	.337	.329
1993 California	AL	152	576	156	17	6	1	(0	1)	188	75	32	48	7	53	2	8	3	55	24	.70	7	.271	.328	.326
1989 Oakland	AL	59	206	59	6	4	1	(0	1)	76	31	17	9	0	15	0	2	1	13	4	.76	5	.286	.315	.369
New York	AL	66	227	71	11	2	2	(1	1)	92	39	29	16	1	29	2	0	3	9	4	.69	8	.313	.359	.405
1990 New York	AL	11	22	7	0	0	0	(0	0)	7	2	3	0	0	1	0	0	1	1	0	1.00	1	.318	.304	.318
California	AL	109	381	128	7	9	2	(2	0)	159	50	32	25	1	42	1	3	3	20	14	.59	8	.336	.376	.417
7 ML YEARS		905	3316	974	113	47	14	(6	8)	1223	501	274	248	20	382	7	26	21	250	106	.70	65	.294	.342	.369

Jim Poole

Pitches: Left **Bats:** Left **Pos:** RP **Ht:** 6' 2" **Wt:** 203 **Born:** 04/28/66 **Age:** 28

		HOW MUCH HE PITCHED						WHAT HE GAVE UP											THE RESULTS					
Year Team	Lg	G	GS	CG	GF	IP	BFP	H	R	ER	HR	SH	SF	HB	TBB	IBB	SO	WP	Bk	W	L	Pct.	ShO	Sv	ERA
1990 Los Angeles	NL	16	0	0	4	10.2	46	7	5	5	1	0	0	0	8	4	6	1	0	0	0	.000	0	0	4.22
1991 2 ML Teams		29	0	0	5	42	166	29	14	11	3	3	3	0	12	2	38	2	0	3	2	.600	0	1	2.36
1992 Baltimore	AL	6	0	0	1	3.1	14	3	0	0	0	0	0	0	1	0	3	0	0	0	0	.000	0	0	2.36
1993 Baltimore	AL	55	0	0	11	50.1	197	30	18	12	2	3	2	0	21	5	29	0	0	2	1	.667	0	2	2.15
1991 Texas	AL	5	0	0	2	6	31	10	4	3	0	0	1	0	3	0	4	0	0	0	0	.000	0	1	4.50
Baltimore	AL	24	0	0	3	36	135	19	10	8	3	3	2	0	9	2	34	2	0	3	2	.600	0	0	2.00
4 ML YEARS		106	0	0	21	106.1	423	69	40	28	6	6	5	0	42	11	76	3	0	5	3	.625	0	3	2.37

Mark Portugal

Pitches: Right **Bats:** Right **Pos:** SP **Ht:** 6' 0" **Wt:** 190 **Born:** 10/30/62 **Age:** 31

		HOW MUCH HE PITCHED						WHAT HE GAVE UP											THE RESULTS					
Year Team	Lg	G	GS	CG	GF	IP	BFP	H	R	ER	HR	SH	SF	HB	TBB	IBB	SO	WP	Bk	W	L	Pct.	ShO	Sv	ERA
1985 Minnesota	AL	6	4	0	0	24.1	105	24	16	15	3	0	2	0	14	0	12	1	1	1	3	.250	0	0	5.55
1986 Minnesota	AL	27	15	3	7	112.2	481	112	56	54	10	5	3	1	50	1	67	5	0	6	10	.375	0	1	4.31
1987 Minnesota	AL	13	7	0	3	44	204	58	40	38	13	0	1	1	24	1	28	2	0	1	3	.250	0	0	7.77
1988 Minnesota	AL	26	0	0	9	57.2	242	60	30	29	11	2	3	1	17	1	31	2	2	3	3	.500	0	3	4.53
1989 Houston	NL	20	15	2	1	108	440	91	34	33	7	8	1	2	37	0	86	3	0	7	1	.875	1	0	2.75
1990 Houston	NL	32	32	1	0	196.2	831	187	90	79	21	7	6	4	67	4	136	6	0	11	10	.524	0	0	3.62
1991 Houston	NL	32	27	1	3	168.1	710	163	91	84	19	6	6	2	59	5	120	4	1	10	12	.455	0	1	4.49
1992 Houston	NL	18	16	1	0	101.1	405	76	32	30	7	5	1	1	41	3	62	1	1	6	3	.667	1	0	2.66
1993 Houston	NL	33	33	1	0	208	876	194	75	64	10	11	3	4	77	3	131	9	2	18	4	**.818**	1	0	2.77
9 ML YEARS		207	149	9	23	1021	4294	965	464	426	101	44	26	16	386	18	673	33	7	63	49	.563	3	5	3.76

Scott Pose

Bats: Left **Throws:** Right **Pos:** CF   **Ht:** 5'11" **Wt:** 165 **Born:** 02/11/67 **Age:** 27

								BATTING												BASERUNNING				PERCENTAGES		
Year Team	Lg	G	AB	H	2B	3B	HR	(Hm	Rd)	TB	R	RBI	TBB	IBB	SO	HBP	SH	SF	SB	CS	SB%	GDP	Avg	OBP	SLG
1989 Billings	R	60	210	74	7	2	0	--	--	85	52	25	54	3	31	1	1	1	26	3	.90	2	.352	.485	.405
1990 Chston-Wv	A	135	480	143	13	5	0	--	--	166	106	46	114	8	56	7	5	6	49	21	.70	5	.298	.435	.346
1991 Nashville	AAA	15	52	10	0	0	0	--	--	10	7	3	2	0	9	2	2	0	3	1	.75	0	.192	.250	.192
Chattanooga	AA	117	402	110	8	5	1	--	--	131	61	31	69	3	50	2	7	3	17	13	.57	7	.274	.380	.326
1992 Chattanooga	AA	136	526	180	22	8	2	--	--	224	87	45	63	5	66	4	4	3	21	27	.44	8	.342	.414	.426
1993 Edmonton	AAA	109	398	113	8	6	0	--	--	133	61	27	42	3	36	1	5	1	19	9	.68	8	.284	.353	.334
1993 Florida	NL	15	41	8	2	0	0	(0	0)	10	0	3	2	0	4	0	0	0	0	2	.00	0	.195	.233	.244

Dennis Powell

Pitches: Left **Bats:** Right **Pos:** RP   **Ht:** 6'3" **Wt:** 200 **Born:** 08/13/63 **Age:** 30

		HOW MUCH HE PITCHED						WHAT HE GAVE UP											THE RESULTS					
Year Team	Lg	G	GS	CG	GF	IP	BFP	H	R	ER	HR	SH	SF	HB	TBB	IBB	SO	WP	Bk	W	L	Pct.	ShO	Sv	ERA
1993 Calgary*	AAA	12	4	0	2	40	164	37	16	16	3	1	0	1	19	1	30	0	0	3	2	.600	0	1	3.60
1985 Los Angeles	NL	16	2	0	6	29.1	133	30	19	17	7	4	1	1	13	3	19	3	0	1	1	.500	0	1	5.22
1986 Los Angeles	NL	27	6	0	5	65.1	272	65	32	31	5	5	2	1	25	7	31	7	2	2	7	.222	0	0	4.27
1987 Seattle	AL	16	3	0	1	32.1	147	32	13	12	3	2	2	0	15	0	17	0	0	1	3	.250	0	0	3.15
1988 Seattle	AL	12	2	0	1	18.2	95	29	20	18	2	0	2	0	11	2	15	0	0	1	3	.250	0	0	8.68
1989 Seattle	AL	43	1	0	9	45	201	49	25	25	6	3	3	2	21	0	27	1	0	2	2	.500	0	2	5.00
1990 2 ML Teams		11	7	0	2	42.1	214	64	40	33	0	2	2	2	21	0	23	2	0	0	4	.000	0	0	7.02
1992 Seattle	AL	49	0	0	11	57	243	49	30	29	5	5	0	3	29	2	35	2	0	4	2	.667	0	0	4.58
1993 Seattle	AL	33	2	0	7	47.2	197	42	22	22	7	5	2	1	24	2	32	2	0	0	0	.000	0	0	4.15
1990 Seattle	AL	2	0	0	1	3	17	5	3	3	0	0	0	1	2	0	0	0	0	0	0	.000	0	0	9.00
Milwaukee	AL	9	7	0	1	39.1	197	59	37	30	0	2	2	1	19	0	23	2	0	0	4	.000	0	0	6.86
8 ML YEARS		207	23	0	42	339.2	1502	360	201	187	35	26	14	12	159	16	199	17	2	11	22	.333	0	3	4.95

Ross Powell

Pitches: Left **Bats:** Left **Pos:** RP   **Ht:** 6'0" **Wt:** 175 **Born:** 01/24/68 **Age:** 26

		HOW MUCH HE PITCHED						WHAT HE GAVE UP											THE RESULTS					
Year Team	Lg	G	GS	CG	GF	IP	BFP	H	R	ER	HR	SH	SF	HB	TBB	IBB	SO	WP	Bk	W	L	Pct.	ShO	Sv	ERA
1989 Cedar Rapids	A	13	13	1	0	76.1	319	68	37	30	4	1	1	1	23	0	58	4	3	7	4	.636	1	0	3.54
1990 Chattanooga	AA	29	27	6	1	185	783	172	89	73	10	11	8	6	57	5	132	11	2	8	14	.364	1	0	3.55
Nashville	AAA	3	0	0	1	2.2	9	1	1	1	0	2	0	0	0	0	4	0	0	0	0	.000	0	0	3.38
1991 Nashville	AAA	24	24	1	0	129.2	568	125	74	63	10	5	2	2	63	1	82	3	0	8	8	.500	0	0	4.37
1992 Chattanooga	AA	14	5	0	2	57.1	224	43	9	8	2	3	2	0	17	1	56	3	1	4	1	.800	0	1	1.26
Nashville	AAA	25	12	0	4	93.1	403	89	37	35	5	4	2	3	42	1	84	2	1	4	8	.333	0	0	3.38
1993 Indianapols	AAA	28	27	4	1	179.2	764	159	89	82	27	1	2	5	71	1	133	13	2	10	10	.500	0	0	4.11
1993 Cincinnati	NL	9	1	0	1	16.1	66	13	8	8	1	2	0	0	6	0	17	0	0	0	3	.000	0	0	4.41

Ted Power

Pitches: Right **Bats:** Right **Pos:** RP   **Ht:** 6'4" **Wt:** 215 **Born:** 01/31/55 **Age:** 39

		HOW MUCH HE PITCHED						WHAT HE GAVE UP											THE RESULTS					
Year Team	Lg	G	GS	CG	GF	IP	BFP	H	R	ER	HR	SH	SF	HB	TBB	IBB	SO	WP	Bk	W	L	Pct.	ShO	Sv	ERA
1993 Canton-Akrn*	AA	7	3	0	0	17.1	79	22	10	9	2	1	0	1	8	0	16	0	0	0	0	.000	0	0	4.67
1981 Los Angeles	NL	5	5	0	1	14	66	16	6	5	0	0	2	1	7	2	7	0	0	1	3	.250	0	0	3.21
1982 Los Angeles	NL	12	4	0	4	32.3	160	38	27	25	4	4	1	0	23	1	15	3	3	1	1	.500	0	0	6.68
1983 Cincinnati	NL	49	6	1	14	111	480	120	62	56	10	4	6	1	49	3	57	1	0	5	6	.455	0	2	4.54
1984 Cincinnati	NL	78	0	0	42	108.2	456	93	37	34	4	9	8	0	46	8	81	3	0	9	7	.563	0	11	2.82
1985 Cincinnati	NL	64	0	0	50	80	342	65	27	24	2	6	4	1	45	8	42	1	0	8	6	.571	0	27	2.70
1986 Cincinnati	NL	56	10	0	30	129	537	115	59	53	13	9	6	1	52	10	95	5	1	10	6	.625	0	1	3.70
1987 Cincinnati	NL	34	34	2	0	204	887	213	115	102	28	8	7	3	71	7	133	3	2	10	13	.435	1	0	4.50
1988 2 ML Teams		26	14	2	3	99	443	121	67	65	8	2	4	3	38	7	57	4	2	6	7	.462	2	0	5.91
1989 St. Louis	NL	23	15	0	2	97	407	96	47	40	7	5	3	1	21	3	43	1	2	7	7	.500	0	0	3.71
1990 Pittsburgh	NL	40	0	0	25	51.2	218	50	23	21	5	3	2	0	17	6	42	1	0	1	3	.250	0	7	3.66
1991 Cincinnati	NL	68	0	0	22	87	371	87	37	35	6	6	4	2	31	5	51	6	1	5	3	.625	0	3	3.62
1992 Cleveland	AL	64	0	0	16	99.1	409	88	33	28	7	7	8	4	35	9	51	2	1	3	3	.500	0	6	2.54
1993 2 ML Teams		45	0	0	24	45.1	206	57	28	27	3	3	2	0	17	4	27	2	0	2	4	.333	0	13	5.36
1988 Kansas City	AL	22	12	2	3	80.1	360	98	54	53	7	2	4	3	30	3	44	3	2	5	6	.455	2	0	5.94
Detroit	AL	4	2	0	0	18.2	83	23	13	12	1	0	0	0	8	4	13	1	0	1	1	.500	0	0	5.79
1993 Cleveland	AL	20	0	0	6	20	101	30	17	16	2	2	1	0	8	3	11	1	0	0	2	.000	0	0	7.20
Seattle	AL	25	0	0	18	25.1	105	27	11	11	1	1	1	0	9	1	16	1	0	2	2	.500	0	13	3.91
13 ML YEARS		564	85	5	233	1159.2	4982	1159	568	515	97	66	57	17	452	73	701	32	10	68	69	.496	3	70	4.00

Todd Pratt

Bats: Right **Throws:** Right **Pos:** C **Ht:** 6' 3" **Wt:** 227 **Born:** 02/09/67 **Age:** 27

Year	Team	Lg	G	AB	H	2B	3B	HR	(Hm	Rd)	TB	R	RBI	TBB	IBB	SO	HBP	SH	SF	SB	CS	SB%	GDP	Avg	OBP	SLG
1985	Elmira	A	39	119	16	1	1	0	--	--	19	7	5	10	0	27	1	3	1	0	1	.00	6	.134	.206	.160
1986	Greensboro	A	107	348	84	16	0	12	--	--	136	63	56	74	0	114	5	4	4	0	1	.00	10	.241	.378	.391
1987	Winter Havn	A	118	407	105	22	0	12	--	--	163	57	65	70	4	94	1	0	6	0	1	.00	10	.258	.364	.400
1988	New Britain	AA	124	395	89	15	2	8	--	--	132	41	49	41	2	110	3	1	6	1	4	.20	7	.225	.299	.334
1989	New Britain	AA	109	338	77	17	1	2	--	--	102	30	35	44	1	66	7	1	5	1	2	.33	10	.228	.325	.302
1990	New Britain	AA	70	195	45	14	1	2	--	--	67	15	22	18	0	56	0	3	2	0	1	.00	7	.231	.293	.344
1991	Pawtucket	AAA	68	219	64	16	0	11	--	--	113	27	41	23	2	42	3	5	0	0	3	.00	9	.292	.367	.516
1992	Reading	AA	41	132	44	6	1	6	--	--	70	20	26	24	0	28	0	1	0	2	0	1.00	1	.333	.436	.530
	Scranton/wb	AAA	41	125	40	9	1	7	--	--	72	20	28	30	0	14	0	1	2	1	0	1.00	5	.320	.446	.576
1993	Scranton/wb	AAA	3	9	2	1	0	0	--	--	3	1	1	3	0	1	0	0	0	0	0	.00	0	.222	.417	.333
1992	Philadelphia	NL	16	46	13	1	0	2	(2	0)	20	6	10	4	0	12	0	0	0	0	0	.00	2	.283	.340	.435
1993	Philadelphia	NL	33	87	25	6	0	5	(4	1)	46	8	13	5	0	19	1	1	1	0	0	.00	2	.287	.330	.529
	2 ML YEARS		49	133	38	7	0	7	(6	1)	66	14	23	9	0	31	1	1	1	0	0	.00	4	.286	.333	.496

Curtis Pride

Bats: Left **Throws:** Right **Pos:** LF **Ht:** 5'11" **Wt:** 195 **Born:** 12/17/68 **Age:** 25

Year	Team	Lg	G	AB	H	2B	3B	HR	(Hm	Rd)	TB	R	RBI	TBB	IBB	SO	HBP	SH	SF	SB	CS	SB%	GDP	Avg	OBP	SLG
1986	Kingsport.	R	27	46	5	0	0	1	--	--	8	5	4	6	0	24	1	0	0	5	0	1.00	0	.109	.226	.174
1987	Kingsport	R	31	104	25	4	0	1	--	--	32	22	9	16	0	34	1	2	0	14	5	.74	0	.240	.347	.308
1988	Kingsport	R	70	268	76	13	1	8	--	--	115	59	27	50	1	48	1	2	1	23	7	.77	2	.284	.397	.429
1989	Pittsfield	A	55	212	55	7	3	6	--	--	86	35	23	25	1	47	2	2	1	9	2	.82	1	.259	.342	.406
1990	Columbia	A	53	191	52	4	4	6	--	--	82	38	25	21	3	45	0	0	1	11	8	.58	3	.272	.343	.429
1991	St. Lucie	A	116	392	102	21	7	9	--	--	164	57	37	43	4	94	2	3	0	24	5	.83	8	.260	.336	.418
1992	Binghamton	AA	118	388	88	15	3	10	--	--	139	54	42	47	1	110	4	0	1	14	11	.56	5	.227	.316	.358
1993	Harrisburg	AA	50	180	64	6	3	15	--	--	121	51	39	12	0	36	4	2	2	21	6	.78	2	.356	.404	.672
	Ottawa	AAA	69	262	79	11	4	6	--	--	116	55	22	34	7	61	3	2	0	29	12	.71	3	.302	.388	.443
1993	Montreal	NL	10	9	4	1	1	1	(0	1)	10	3	5	0	0	3	0	0	0	1	0	1.00	0	.444	.444	1.111

Tom Prince

Bats: Right **Throws:** Right **Pos:** C **Ht:** 5'11" **Wt:** 185 **Born:** 08/13/64 **Age:** 29

Year	Team	Lg	G	AB	H	2B	3B	HR	(Hm	Rd)	TB	R	RBI	TBB	IBB	SO	HBP	SH	SF	SB	CS	SB%	GDP	Avg	OBP	SLG
1987	Pittsburgh	NL	4	9	2	1	0	1	(0	1)	6	1	2	0	0	2	0	0	0	0	0	.00	0	.222	.222	.667
1988	Pittsburgh	NL	29	74	13	2	0	0	(0	0)	15	3	6	4	0	15	0	2	0	0	0	.00	5	.176	.218	.203
1989	Pittsburgh	NL	21	52	7	4	0	0	(0	0)	11	1	5	6	1	12	0	0	1	1	1	.50	1	.135	.220	.212
1990	Pittsburgh	NL	4	10	1	0	0	0	(0	0)	1	1	0	1	0	2	0	0	0	0	1	.00	0	.100	.182	.100
1991	Pittsburgh	NL	26	34	9	3	0	1	(0	1)	15	4	2	7	0	3	1	0	0	0	0	.00	3	.265	.405	.441
1992	Pittsburgh	NL	27	44	4	2	0	0	(0	0)	6	1	5	6	0	9	0	0	2	1	1	.50	2	.091	.192	.136
1993	Pittsburgh	NL	66	179	35	14	0	2	(2	0)	55	14	24	13	2	38	7	2	3	1	1	.50	5	.196	.272	.307
	7 ML YEARS		177	402	71	26	0	4	(2	2)	109	25	44	37	3	81	8	4	6	3	4	.43	16	.177	.256	.271

Kirby Puckett

Bats: Right **Throws:** Right **Pos:** CF/RF/DH **Ht:** 5' 9" **Wt:** 220 **Born:** 03/14/61 **Age:** 33

Year	Team	Lg	G	AB	H	2B	3B	HR	(Hm	Rd)	TB	R	RBI	TBB	IBB	SO	HBP	SH	SF	SB	CS	SB%	GDP	Avg	OBP	SLG
1984	Minnesota	AL	128	557	165	12	5	0	(0	0)	187	63	31	16	1	69	4	4	2	14	7	.67	11	.296	.320	.336
1985	Minnesota	AL	161	691	199	29	13	4	(2	2)	266	80	74	41	0	87	4	5	3	21	12	.64	9	.288	.330	.385
1986	Minnesota	AL	161	680	223	37	6	31	(14	17)	365	119	96	34	4	99	7	2	0	20	12	.63	14	.328	.366	.537
1987	Minnesota	AL	157	624	207	32	5	28	(18	10)	333	96	99	32	7	91	6	0	6	12	7	.63	16	.332	.367	.534
1988	Minnesota	AL	158	657	234	42	5	24	(13	11)	358	109	121	23	4	83	2	0	9	6	7	.46	17	.356	.375	.545
1989	Minnesota	AL	159	635	215	45	4	9	(7	2)	295	75	85	41	9	59	3	0	5	11	4	.73	21	.339	.379	.465
1990	Minnesota	AL	146	551	164	40	3	12	(6	6)	246	82	80	57	11	73	3	1	3	5	4	.56	15	.298	.365	.446
1991	Minnesota	AL	152	611	195	29	6	15	(7	8)	281	92	89	31	4	78	4	8	7	11	5	.69	27	.319	.352	.460
1992	Minnesota	AL	160	639	210	38	4	19	(9	10)	313	104	110	44	13	97	6	1	6	17	7	.71	17	.329	.374	.490
1993	Minnesota	AL	156	622	184	39	3	22	(12	10)	295	89	89	47	7	93	7	1	5	8	6	.57	15	.296	.349	.474
	10 ML YEARS		1538	6267	1996	343	54	164	(88	76)	2939	909	874	366	60	829	46	22	46	125	71	.64	162	.318	.358	.469

Tim Pugh

Pitches: Right **Bats:** Right **Pos:** SP **Ht:** 6' 6" **Wt:** 225 **Born:** 01/26/67 **Age:** 27

Year	Team	Lg	G	GS	CG	GF	IP	BFP	H	R	ER	HR	SH	SF	HB	TBB	IBB	SO	WP	Bk	W	L	Pct.	ShO	Sv	ERA
1989	Billings	R	13	13	2	0	77.2	333	81	44	34	4	6	2	5	25	0	72	4	6	2	6	.250	0	0	3.94

Year	Team	Lg	G	GS	CG	GF	IP	BFP	H	R	ER	HR	SH	SF	HB	TBB	IBB	SO	WP	Bk	W	L	Pct.	ShO	Sv	ERA
1990	Chston-Wv	A	27	27	8	0	177.1	733	142	58	37	5	5	3	7	56	0	154	10	0	15	6	.714	2	0	1.88
1991	Chattanooga	AA	5	5	0	0	38.1	143	20	7	7	2	1	1	4	11	0	24	0	0	3	1	.750	0	0	1.64
	Nashville	AAA	23	23	3	0	148.2	612	130	68	63	9	3	6	10	56	2	89	9	1	7	11	.389	1	0	3.81
1992	Nashville	AAA	27	27	3	0	169.2	725	165	75	67	10	6	5	8	65	3	117	4	0	12	9	.571	2	0	3.55
1992	Cincinnati	NL	7	7	0	0	45.1	187	47	15	13	2	2	1	1	13	3	18	0	0	4	2	.667	0	0	2.58
1993	Cincinnati	NL	31	27	3	3	164.1	738	200	102	96	19	6	5	7	59	1	94	3	2	10	15	.400	1	0	5.26
	2 ML YEARS		38	34	3	3	209.2	925	247	117	109	21	8	6	8	72	4	112	3	2	14	17	.452	1	0	4.68

Harvey Pulliam

Bats: Right **Throws:** Right **Pos:** RF/LF **Ht:** 6' 0" **Wt:** 205 **Born:** 10/20/67 **Age:** 26

Year	Team	Lg	G	AB	H	2B	3B	HR	(Hm	Rd)	TB	R	RBI	TBB	IBB	SO	HBP	SH	SF	SB	CS	SB%	GDP	Avg	OBP	SLG
1993	Omaha *	AAA	54	208	55	10	0	5	(--	--)	80	28	26	17	1	36	1	0	0	0	1	1.00	6	.264	.323	.385
1991	Kansas City	AL	18	33	9	1	0	3	(2	1)	19	4	4	3	1	9	0	1	0	0	0	.00	1	.273	.333	.576
1992	Kansas City	AL	4	5	1	1	0	0	(0	0)	2	2	0	1	0	3	0	0	0	0	0	.00	0	.200	.333	.400
1993	Kansas City	AL	27	62	16	5	0	1	(0	1)	24	7	6	2	0	14	1	0	0	0	0	.00	3	.258	.292	.387
	3 ML YEARS		49	100	26	7	0	4	(2	2)	45	13	10	6	1	26	1	1	0	0	0	.00	4	.260	.308	.450

Paul Quantrill

Pitches: Right **Bats:** Left **Pos:** RP/SP **Ht:** 6' 1" **Wt:** 185 **Born:** 11/03/68 **Age:** 25

Year	Team	Lg	G	GS	CG	GF	IP	BFP	H	R	ER	HR	SH	SF	HB	TBB	IBB	SO	WP	Bk	W	L	Pct.	ShO	Sv	ERA
1989	Red Sox	R	2	0	0	2	5	18	2	0	0	0	0	0	0	0	0	5	0	0	0	0	.000	0	2	0.00
	Elmira	A	20	7	5	7	76	326	90	37	29	5	4	3	6	12	2	57	1	2	5	4	.556	0	2	3.43
1990	Winter Havn	A	7	7	1	0	45.2	182	46	24	21	3	0	2	6	6	0	14	3	0	2	5	.286	0	0	4.14
	New Britain	AA	22	22	1	0	132.2	549	149	65	52	3	4	7	4	23	2	53	3	2	7	11	.389	1	0	3.53
1991	New Britain	AA	5	5	1	0	35	142	32	14	8	2	3	1	1	8	0	18	0	0	2	1	.667	0	0	2.06
	Pawtucket	AAA	25	23	6	0	155.2	645	169	81	77	14	9	2	4	30	1	75	2	2	10	7	.588	2	0	4.45
1992	Pawtucket	AAA	19	18	4	1	119	504	143	63	59	16	3	1	4	20	1	56	1	1	6	8	.429	1	0	4.46
1992	Boston	AL	27	0	0	10	49.1	213	55	18	12	1	4	2	1	15	5	24	1	0	2	3	.400	0	1	2.19
1993	Boston	AL	49	14	1	8	138	594	151	73	60	13	4	2	2	44	14	66	0	1	6	12	.333	1	1	3.91
	2 ML YEARS		76	14	1	18	187.1	807	206	91	72	14	8	4	3	59	19	90	1	1	8	15	.348	1	2	3.46

Carlos Quintana

Bats: Right **Throws:** Right **Pos:** 1B/RF **Ht:** 6' 2" **Wt:** 220 **Born:** 08/26/65 **Age:** 28

Year	Team	Lg	G	AB	H	2B	3B	HR	(Hm	Rd)	TB	R	RBI	TBB	IBB	SO	HBP	SH	SF	SB	CS	SB%	GDP	Avg	OBP	SLG
1988	Boston	AL	5	6	2	0	0	0	(0	0)	2	1	2	2	0	3	0	0	0	0	0	.00	0	.333	.500	.333
1989	Boston	AL	34	77	16	5	0	0	(0	0)	21	6	6	7	0	12	0	0	0	0	0	.00	5	.208	.274	.273
1990	Boston	AL	149	512	147	28	0	7	(3	4)	196	56	67	52	0	74	2	4	2	1	2	.33	19	.287	.354	.383
1991	Boston	AL	149	478	141	21	1	11	(2	9)	197	69	71	61	2	66	2	6	3	1	0	1.00	15	.295	.375	.412
1993	Boston	AL	101	303	74	5	0	1	(0	1)	82	31	19	31	2	52	2	5	2	1	0	1.00	13	.244	.317	.271
	5 ML YEARS		438	1376	380	59	1	19	(5	14)	498	163	165	153	4	207	6	15	7	3	2	.60	54	.276	.350	.362

Scott Radinsky

Pitches: Left **Bats:** Left **Pos:** RP **Ht:** 6' 3" **Wt:** 204 **Born:** 03/03/68 **Age:** 26

Year	Team	Lg	G	GS	CG	GF	IP	BFP	H	R	ER	HR	SH	SF	HB	TBB	IBB	SO	WP	Bk	W	L	Pct.	ShO	Sv	ERA
1990	Chicago	AL	62	0	0	18	52.1	237	47	29	28	1	2	2	2	36	1	46	2	1	6	1	.857	0	4	4.82
1991	Chicago	AL	67	0	0	19	71.1	289	53	18	16	4	4	4	1	23	2	49	0	0	5	5	.500	0	8	2.02
1992	Chicago	AL	68	0	0	33	59.1	261	54	21	18	3	2	1	2	34	5	48	3	0	3	7	.300	0	15	2.73
1993	Chicago	AL	73	0	0	24	54.2	250	61	33	26	3	2	0	1	19	3	44	0	4	8	2	.800	0	4	4.28
	4 ML YEARS		270	0	0	94	237.2	1037	215	101	88	11	10	7	6	112	11	187	5	5	22	15	.595	0	31	3.33

Tim Raines

Bats: Both **Throws:** Right **Pos:** LF **Ht:** 5' 8" **Wt:** 186 **Born:** 09/16/59 **Age:** 34

Year	Team	Lg	G	AB	H	2B	3B	HR	(Hm	Rd)	TB	R	RBI	TBB	IBB	SO	HBP	SH	SF	SB	CS	SB%	GDP	Avg	OBP	SLG
1993	Nashville *	AAA	3	11	5	1	0	0	(--	--)	6	3	2	2	0	0	0	0	0	2	1	.67	0	.455	.538	.545
1979	Montreal	NL	6	0	0	0	0	0	(0	0)	0	3	0	0	0	0	0	0	0	2	0	1.00	0	.000	.000	.000
1980	Montreal	NL	15	20	1	0	0	0	(0	0)	1	5	0	6	0	3	0	1	0	5	0	1.00	0	.050	.269	.050
1981	Montreal	NL	88	313	95	13	7	5	(3	2)	137	61	37	45	5	31	2	0	3	71	11	.87	7	.304	.391	.438
1982	Montreal	NL	156	647	179	32	8	4	(1	3)	239	90	43	75	9	83	2	6	1	78	16	.83	6	.277	.353	.369
1983	Montreal	NL	156	615	183	32	8	11	(5	6)	264	133	71	97	9	70	2	2	4	90	14	.87	12	.298	.393	.429
1984	Montreal	NL	160	622	192	38	9	8	(2	6)	272	106	60	87	7	69	2	3	4	75	10	.88	7	.309	.393	.437
1985	Montreal	NL	150	575	184	30	13	11	(4	7)	273	115	41	81	13	60	3	3	3	70	9	.89	9	.320	.405	.475
1986	Montreal	NL	151	580	194	35	10	9	(4	5)	276	91	62	78	9	60	2	1	3	70	9	.89	6	.334	.413	.476
1987	Montreal	NL	139	530	175	34	8	18	(9	9)	279	123	68	90	26	52	4	0	3	50	5	.91	9	.330	.429	.526

Year	Team	Lg	G	AB	H	2B	3B	HR	Hm	Rd	TB	R	RBI	TBB	IBB	SO	HBP	SH	SF	SB	CS	SB%	GDP	Avg	OBP	SLG
1988	Montreal	NL	109	429	116	19	7	12	(5	7)	185	66	48	53	14	44	2	0	4	33	7	.83	8	.270	.350	.431
1989	Montreal	NL	145	517	148	29	6	9	(6	3)	216	76	60	93	18	48	3	0	5	41	9	.82	8	.286	.395	.418
1990	Montreal	NL	130	457	131	11	5	9	(6	3)	179	65	62	70	8	43	3	0	8	49	16	.75	9	.287	.379	.392
1991	Chicago	AL	155	609	163	20	6	5	(1	4)	210	102	50	83	9	68	5	9	3	51	15	.77	7	.268	.359	.345
1992	Chicago	AL	144	551	162	22	9	7	(4	3)	223	102	54	81	4	48	0	4	8	45	6	.88	5	.294	.380	.405
1993	Chicago	AL	115	415	127	16	4	16	(7	9)	199	75	54	64	4	35	3	2	2	21	7	.75	7	.306	.401	.480
15 ML YEARS			1819	6880	2050	331	100	124	(57	67)	2953	1213	710	1003	135	714	33	31	51	751	134	.85	100	.298	.387	.429

Manny Ramirez

Bats: Right Throws: Right Pos: DH/RF Ht: 6' 0" Wt: 190 Born: 05/30/72 Age: 22

Year	Team	Lg	G	AB	H	2B	3B	HR	Hm	Rd	TB	R	RBI	TBB	IBB	SO	HBP	SH	SF	SB	CS	SB%	GDP	Avg	OBP	SLG
1991	Burlington	R	59	215	70	11	4	19	--	--	146	44	63	34	5	41	6	0	3	7	8	.47	4	.326	.426	.679
1992	Kinston	A	81	291	81	18	4	13	--	--	146	52	63	45	3	74	4	1	3	1	3	.25	9	.278	.379	.502
1993	Canton-Akrn	AA	89	344	117	32	0	17	--	--	200	67	79	45	10	68	2	0	5	2	2	.50	11	.340	.414	.581
	Charlotte	AAA	40	145	46	12	0	14	--	--	100	38	36	27	1	35	2	0	3	1	1	.50	1	.317	.424	.690
1993	Cleveland	AL	22	53	9	1	0	2	(0	2)	16	5	5	2	0	8	0	0	0	0	0	.00	3	.170	.200	.302

Pat Rapp

Pitches: Right Bats: Right Pos: SP Ht: 6' 3" Wt: 195 Born: 07/13/67 Age: 26

Year	Team	Lg	G	GS	CG	GF	IP	BFP	H	R	ER	HR	SH	SF	HB	TBB	IBB	SO	WP	Bk	W	L	Pct.	ShO	Sv	ERA
1989	Pocatello	R	16	12	1	1	73	333	90	54	43	5	3	2	8	29	1	40	6	0	4	6	.400	0	0	5.30
1990	Clinton	A	27	26	4	1	167.1	692	132	60	49	2	6	2	7	79	2	132	8	3	14	10	.583	0	0	2.64
1991	San Jose	A	16	15	1	0	90	396	88	41	25	1	1	2	10	37	0	73	1	0	7	5	.583	0	0	2.50
	Shreveport	AA	10	10	1	0	60.1	257	52	23	18	1	3	2	3	22	0	46	1	0	6	2	.750	1	0	2.69
1992	Phoenix	AAA	39	12	2	17	121	516	115	54	41	2	8	10	2	40	3	79	1	1	7	8	.467	1	3	3.05
1993	Edmonton	AAA	17	17	4	0	107.2	440	89	45	41	8	7	5	1	34	0	93	2	1	8	3	.727	1	0	3.43
1992	San Francisco	NL	3	2	0	1	10	43	8	8	8	0	2	0	1	6	1	3	0	0	0	2	.000	0	0	7.20
1993	Florida	NL	16	16	1	0	94	412	101	49	42	7	8	4	2	39	1	57	6	0	4	6	.400	0	0	4.02
2 ML YEARS			19	18	1	1	104	455	109	57	50	7	10	4	3	45	2	60	6	0	4	8	.333	0	0	4.33

Dennis Rasmussen

Pitches: Left Bats: Left Pos: RP/SP Ht: 6' 7" Wt: 240 Born: 04/18/59 Age: 35

Year	Team	Lg	G	GS	CG	GF	IP	BFP	H	R	ER	HR	SH	SF	HB	TBB	IBB	SO	WP	Bk	W	L	Pct.	ShO	Sv	ERA
1993	Omaha *	AAA	17	17	3	0	105.2	451	124	68	59	16	4	5	1	27	0	59	4	2	7	8	.467	0	0	5.03
1983	San Diego	NL	4	1	0	1	13.2	58	10	5	3	1	0	0	0	8	0	13	1	0	0	0	.000	0	0	1.98
1984	New York	AL	24	24	1	0	147.2	616	127	79	75	16	3	7	4	60	0	110	8	2	9	6	.600	0	0	4.57
1985	New York	AL	22	16	2	0	101.2	429	97	56	45	10	1	5	1	42	1	63	3	1	3	5	.375	0	0	3.98
1986	New York	AL	31	31	3	0	202	819	160	91	87	28	1	5	2	74	0	131	5	0	18	6	.750	1	0	3.88
1987	2 ML Teams		33	32	2	0	191.1	814	184	100	97	36	8	6	5	67	1	128	7	2	13	8	.619	0	0	4.56
1988	2 ML Teams		31	31	7	0	204.2	854	199	84	78	17	10	4	4	58	4	112	7	5	16	10	.615	1	0	3.43
1989	San Diego	NL	33	33	1	0	183.2	799	190	100	87	18	9	11	3	72	6	87	4	2	10	10	.500	1	0	4.26
1990	San Diego	NL	32	32	3	0	187.2	825	217	110	94	28	14	4	3	62	4	86	9	1	11	15	.423	1	0	4.51
1991	San Diego	NL	24	24	1	0	146.2	633	155	74	61	12	4	6	2	49	3	75	1	1	6	13	.316	1	0	3.74
1992	2 ML Teams		8	6	1	1	42.2	158	52	29	12	3	2	1	1	8	1	12	3	0	4	1	.800	1	0	2.53
1993	Kansas City	AL	9	4	0	3	29	138	40	25	24	4	0	1	1	14	1	12	2	0	1	2	.333	0	0	7.45
1987	New York	AL	26	25	2	0	146	627	145	78	77	31	5	5	4	55	1	89	6	0	9	7	.563	0	0	4.75
	Cincinnati	NL	7	7	0	0	45.1	187	39	22	20	5	3	1	1	12	0	39	1	2	4	1	.800	0	0	3.97
1988	Cincinnati	NL	11	11	1	0	56.1	255	68	36	36	8	2	2	2	22	4	27	1	5	2	6	.250	1	0	5.75
	San Diego	NL	20	20	6	0	148.1	599	131	48	42	9	8	2	2	36	0	85	6	0	14	4	.778	1	0	2.55
1992	Chicago	NL	3	1	0	1	5	24	7	6	6	2	0	1	1	2	1	0	0	0	0	0	.000	0	0	10.80
	Kansas City	AL	5	5	1	0	37.2	134	25	7	6	0	1	0	0	6	0	12	3	0	4	1	.800	1	0	1.43
11 ML YEARS			251	234	21	6	1450.2	6143	1411	737	663	172	51	50	26	514	21	829	50	14	91	76	.545	5	0	4.11

Randy Ready

Bats: Right Throws: Right Pos: 2B/1B Ht: 5'11" Wt: 180 Born: 01/08/60 Age: 34

Year	Team	Lg	G	AB	H	2B	3B	HR	Hm	Rd	TB	R	RBI	TBB	IBB	SO	HBP	SH	SF	SB	CS	SB%	GDP	Avg	OBP	SLG
1993	Rochester *	AAA	84	305	88	17	3	9	--	--	138	48	46	50	2	37	1	1	3	4	0	1.00	7	.289	.387	.452
1983	Milwaukee	AL	12	37	15	3	2	1	(0	1)	25	8	6	6	1	3	0	0	0	0	1	.00	0	.405	.488	.676
1984	Milwaukee	AL	37	123	23	6	1	3	(3	0)	40	13	13	14	0	18	0	3	0	0	0	.00	2	.187	.270	.325
1985	Milwaukee	AL	48	181	48	9	5	1	(0	1)	70	29	21	14	0	23	1	2	2	0	0	.00	6	.265	.318	.387
1986	2 ML Teams		24	82	15	4	0	1	(0	1)	22	8	4	9	0	10	0	1	0	2	0	1.00	3	.183	.264	.268
1987	San Diego	NL	124	350	108	26	6	12	(7	5)	182	69	54	67	2	44	3	2	1	7	3	.70	7	.309	.423	.520
1988	San Diego	NL	114	331	88	16	2	7	(3	4)	129	43	39	39	1	38	3	4	3	6	2	.75	3	.266	.346	.390
1989	2 ML Teams		100	254	67	13	2	8	(3	5)	108	37	26	42	0	37	2	1	4	4	3	.57	4	.264	.368	.425

Year	Team	Lg	G	AB	H	2B	3B	HR	(Hm	Rd)	TB	R	RBI	TBB	IBB	SO	HBP	SH	SF	SB	CS	SB%	GDP	Avg	OBP	SLG
1990	Philadelphia	NL	101	217	53	9	1	1	(0	1)	67	26	26	29	0	35	1	3	3	3	2	.60	3	.244	.332	.309
1991	Philadelphia	NL	76	205	51	10	1	1	(1	0)	66	32	20	47	3	25	1	1	4	2	1	.67	5	.249	.385	.322
1992	Oakland	AL	61	125	25	2	0	3	(1	2)	36	17	17	25	1	23	0	2	2	1	0	1.00	1	.200	.329	.288
1993	Montreal	NL	40	134	34	8	1	1	(0	1)	47	22	10	23	0	8	1	1	0	2	1	.67	4	.254	.367	.351
1986	Milwaukee	AL	23	79	15	4	0	1	(0	1)	22	8	4	9	0	9	0	1	0	2	0	1.00	0	.190	.273	.278
	San Diego	NL	1	3	0	0	0	0	(0	0)	0	0	0	0	0	1	0	0	0	0	0	.00	0	.000	.000	.000
1989	San Diego	NL	28	67	17	2	1	0	(0	0)	21	4	5	11	0	6	0	1	1	0	0	.00	2	.254	.354	.313
	Philadelphia	NL	72	187	50	11	1	8	(3	5)	87	33	21	31	0	31	2	0	3	4	3	.57	7	.267	.372	.465
11 ML YEARS			737	2039	527	106	21	39	(18	21)	792	304	236	315	8	264	12	20	19	27	13	.68	38	.258	.358	.388

Jeff Reardon

Pitches: Right **Bats:** Right **Pos:** RP **Ht:** 6' 0" **Wt:** 205 **Born:** 10/01/55 **Age:** 38

			HOW MUCH HE PITCHED						WHAT HE GAVE UP										THE RESULTS					
Year	Team	Lg	G	GS	CG	GF	IP	BFP	H	R	ER	HR	SH	SF	HB	TBB	IBB	SO	WP	Bk	W	L	Pct.	ShO	Sv	ERA
1979	New York	NL	18	0	0	10	21	81	12	7	4	2	2	1	0	9	3	10	2	0	1	2	.333	0	2	1.71
1980	New York	NL	61	0	0	35	110	475	96	36	32	10	8	5	0	47	15	101	2	0	8	7	.533	0	6	2.62
1981	2 ML Teams		43	0	0	33	70.1	279	48	17	17	5	3	1	2	21	4	49	1	0	3	0	1.000	0	8	2.18
1982	Montreal	NL	75	0	0	53	109	444	87	28	25	8	4	4	2	36	4	86	2	0	7	4	.636	0	26	2.06
1983	Montreal	NL	66	0	0	53	92	403	87	34	31	7	8	2	1	44	9	78	2	0	7	9	.438	0	21	3.03
1984	Montreal	NL	68	0	0	58	87	363	70	31	28	5	3	2	3	37	7	79	4	0	7	7	.500	0	23	2.90
1985	Montreal	NL	63	0	0	50	87.2	356	68	31	31	7	3	1	1	26	4	67	2	0	2	8	.200	0	41	3.18
1986	Montreal	NL	62	0	0	48	89	368	83	42	39	12	9	1	1	26	2	67	0	0	7	9	.438	0	35	3.94
1987	Minnesota	AL	63	0	0	58	80.1	337	70	41	40	14	1	3	3	28	4	83	2	0	8	8	.500	0	31	4.48
1988	Minnesota	AL	63	0	0	58	73	299	68	21	20	6	4	1	2	15	2	56	0	3	2	4	.333	0	42	2.47
1989	Minnesota	AL	65	0	0	61	73	297	68	33	33	8	1	5	3	12	3	46	1	1	5	4	.556	0	31	4.07
1990	Boston	AL	47	0	0	37	51.1	210	39	19	18	5	1	0	1	19	4	33	0	0	5	3	.625	0	21	3.16
1991	Boston	AL	57	0	0	51	59.1	248	54	21	20	9	0	2	1	16	3	44	0	0	1	4	.200	0	40	3.03
1992	2 ML Teams		60	0	0	50	58	245	67	22	22	6	2	2	2	9	1	39	0	0	5	2	.714	0	30	3.41
1993	Cincinnati	NL	58	0	0	32	61.2	267	66	34	28	4	4	4	5	10	0	35	2	0	4	6	.400	0	8	4.09
1981	New York	NL	18	0	0	14	28.2	124	27	11	11	2	0	1	1	12	4	28	0	0	1	0	1.000	0	2	3.45
	Montreal	NL	25	0	0	19	41.2	155	21	6	6	3	3	0	1	9	0	21	1	0	2	0	1.000	0	6	1.30
1992	Boston	AL	46	0	0	39	42.1	183	53	20	20	6	1	2	1	7	0	32	0	0	2	2	.500	0	27	4.25
	Atlanta	NL	14	0	0	11	15.2	62	14	2	2	0	1	0	1	2	1	7	0	0	3	0	1.000	0	3	1.15
15 ML YEARS			869	0	0	687	1122.2	4672	983	417	388	106	57	34	27	355	65	873	20	4	72	77	.483	0	365	3.11

Jeff Reboulet

Bats: Right **Throws:** Right **Pos:** SS/2B/3B **Ht:** 6' 0" **Wt:** 165 **Born:** 04/30/64 **Age:** 30

			BATTING																BASERUNNING				PERCENTAGES		
Year	Team	Lg	G	AB	H	2B	3B	HR	(Hm	Rd)	TB	R	RBI	TBB	IBB	SO	HBP	SH	SF	SB	CS	SB%	GDP	Avg	OBP	SLG
1986	Visalia	A	72	254	73	13	1	0	--	--	88	54	29	54	1	33	1	5	2	14	11	.56	4	.287	.412	.346
1987	Orlando	AA	129	422	108	15	1	1	--	--	128	52	35	58	0	56	1	5	0	9	5	.64	9	.256	.347	.303
1988	Orlando	AA	125	439	112	24	2	4	--	--	152	57	41	53	0	55	3	7	2	18	8	.69	5	.255	.338	.346
	Portland	AAA	4	12	1	0	0	0	--	--	1	0	1	3	0	2	0	0	0	0	0	.00	1	.083	.267	.083
1989	Portland	AAA	26	65	16	1	0	0	--	--	17	9	3	12	0	11	0	0	2	2	1	.67	2	.246	.354	.262
	Orlando	AA	81	291	63	5	1	0	--	--	70	43	26	49	0	33	1	2	3	11	6	.65	7	.216	.328	.241
1990	Orlando	AA	97	287	66	12	2	2	--	--	88	43	34	57	1	37	2	5	4	10	5	.67	5	.230	.357	.307
1991	Portland	AAA	134	391	97	27	3	3	--	--	139	50	46	57	2	52	2	17	2	5	2	.71	9	.248	.345	.355
1992	Portland	AAA	48	161	46	11	1	2	--	--	65	21	21	35	0	18	1	4	1	3	3	.50	7	.286	.414	.404
1992	Minnesota	AL	73	137	26	7	1	1	(1	0)	38	15	16	23	0	26	1	7	0	3	2	.60	0	.190	.311	.277
1993	Minnesota	AL	109	240	62	8	0	1	(0	1)	73	33	15	35	0	37	2	5	1	5	5	.50	6	.258	.356	.304
2 ML YEARS			182	377	88	15	1	2	(1	1)	111	48	31	58	0	63	3	12	1	8	7	.53	6	.233	.339	.294

Gary Redus

Bats: Right **Throws:** Right **Pos:** RF/CF **Ht:** 6' 1" **Wt:** 195 **Born:** 11/01/56 **Age:** 37

			BATTING																BASERUNNING				PERCENTAGES		
Year	Team	Lg	G	AB	H	2B	3B	HR	(Hm	Rd)	TB	R	RBI	TBB	IBB	SO	HBP	SH	SF	SB	CS	SB%	GDP	Avg	OBP	SLG
1982	Cincinnati	NL	20	83	18	3	2	1	(1	0)	28	12	7	5	0	21	0	0	1	11	2	.85	0	.217	.258	.337
1983	Cincinnati	NL	125	453	112	20	9	17	(6	11)	201	90	51	71	4	111	3	2	2	39	14	.74	6	.247	.352	.444
1984	Cincinnati	NL	123	394	100	21	3	7	(4	3)	148	69	22	52	3	71	1	3	5	48	11	.81	4	.254	.338	.376
1985	Cincinnati	NL	101	246	62	14	4	6	(4	2)	102	51	28	44	2	52	1	2	1	48	12	.80	0	.252	.366	.415
1986	Philadelphia	NL	90	340	84	22	4	11	(8	3)	147	62	33	47	4	78	3	1	1	25	7	.78	2	.247	.343	.432
1987	Chicago	AL	130	475	112	26	6	12	(4	8)	186	78	48	69	0	90	0	3	7	52	11	.83	7	.236	.328	.392
1988	2 ML Teams		107	333	83	12	4	8	(3	5)	127	54	38	48	1	71	3	0	8	31	4	.89	6	.249	.342	.381
1989	Pittsburgh	NL	98	279	79	18	7	6	(3	3)	129	42	33	40	3	51	1	1	3	25	6	.81	5	.283	.372	.462
1990	Pittsburgh	NL	96	227	56	15	3	6	(2	4)	95	32	23	33	0	38	2	1	5	11	5	.69	1	.247	.341	.419
1991	Pittsburgh	NL	98	252	62	12	2	7	(3	4)	99	45	24	28	2	39	3	1	4	17	3	.85	0	.246	.324	.393
1992	Pittsburgh	NL	76	176	45	7	3	3	(1	2)	67	26	12	17	0	25	0	0	0	11	4	.73	1	.256	.321	.381
1993	Texas	AL	77	222	64	12	4	6	(2	4)	102	28	31	23	1	35	0	0	3	4	4	.50	3	.288	.351	.459

Year	Team	Lg	G	AB	H	2B	3B	HR	(Hm	Rd)	TB	R	RBI	TBB	IBB	SO	HBP	SH	SF	SB	CS	SB%	GDP	Avg	OBP	SLG
1988	Chicago	AL	77	262	69	10	4	6	(1	5)	105	42	34	33	1	52	2	0	7	26	2	.93	5	.263	.342	.401
	Pittsburgh	NL	30	71	14	2	0	2	(2	0)	22	12	4	15	0	19	1	0	1	5	2	.71	1	.197	.341	.310
	12 ML YEARS		1141	3480	877	182	51	90	(41	49)	1431	589	350	477	20	682	17	14	40	322	83	.80	35	.252	.342	.411

Jeff Reed

Bats: Left **Throws:** Right **Pos:** C **Ht:** 6' 2" **Wt:** 190 **Born:** 11/12/62 **Age:** 31

			BATTING																	BASERUNNING				PERCENTAGES		
Year	Team	Lg	G	AB	H	2B	3B	HR	(Hm	Rd)	TB	R	RBI	TBB	IBB	SO	HBP	SH	SF	SB	CS	SB%	GDP	Avg	OBP	SLG
1993	San Jose *	A	4	10	5	1	0	0	--	--	6	2	2	1	0	0	0	0	0	0	0	.00	0	.500	.545	.600
1984	Minnesota	AL	18	21	3	3	0	0	(0	0)	6	3	1	2	0	6	0	1	0	0	0	.00	0	.143	.217	.286
1985	Minnesota	AL	7	10	2	0	0	0	(0	0)	2	2	0	0	0	3	0	0	0	0	0	.00	0	.200	.200	.200
1986	Minnesota	AL	68	165	39	6	1	2	(1	1)	53	13	9	16	0	19	1	3	0	1	0	1.00	0	.236	.308	.321
1987	Montreal	NL	75	207	44	11	0	1	(1	0)	58	15	21	12	1	20	1	4	4	0	1	.00	8	.213	.254	.280
1988	2 ML Teams		92	265	60	9	2	1	(1	0)	76	20	16	28	1	41	0	1	1	1	0	1.00	5	.226	.299	.287
1989	Cincinnati	NL	102	287	64	11	0	3	(1	2)	84	16	23	34	5	46	2	3	4	0	0	.00	6	.223	.306	.293
1990	Cincinnati	NL	72	175	44	8	1	3	(2	1)	63	12	16	24	5	26	0	5	1	0	0	.00	4	.251	.340	.360
1991	Cincinnati	NL	91	270	72	15	2	3	(1	2)	100	20	31	23	3	38	1	1	5	0	1	.00	4	.267	.321	.370
1992	Cincinnati	NL	15	25	4	0	0	0	(0	0)	4	2	2	1	1	4	0	0	1	0	1	.00	1	.160	.192	.160
1993	San Francisco	NL	66	119	31	3	0	6	(5	1)	52	10	12	16	4	22	0	0	1	0	1	.00	2	.261	.346	.437
1988	Montreal	NL	43	123	27	3	2	0	(0	0)	34	10	9	13	1	22	0	1	1	1	0	1.00	3	.220	.292	.276
	Cincinnati	NL	49	142	33	6	0	1	(1	0)	42	10	7	15	0	19	0	0	0	0	0	.00	2	.232	.306	.296
	10 ML YEARS		606	1544	363	66	6	19	(12	7)	498	113	131	156	20	225	5	18	16	2	3	.40	34	.235	.304	.323

Jody Reed

Bats: Right **Throws:** Right **Pos:** 2B **Ht:** 5' 9" **Wt:** 165 **Born:** 07/26/62 **Age:** 31

			BATTING																	BASERUNNING				PERCENTAGES		
Year	Team	Lg	G	AB	H	2B	3B	HR	(Hm	Rd)	TB	R	RBI	TBB	IBB	SO	HBP	SH	SF	SB	CS	SB%	GDP	Avg	OBP	SLG
1987	Boston	AL	9	30	9	1	1	0	(0	0)	12	4	8	4	0	0	1	0	1	1	1	.50	0	.300	.382	.400
1988	Boston	AL	109	338	99	23	1	1	(1	0)	127	60	28	45	1	21	4	11	2	1	3	.25	5	.293	.380	.376
1989	Boston	AL	146	524	151	42	2	3	(2	1)	206	76	40	73	0	44	4	13	5	4	5	.44	12	.288	.376	.393
1990	Boston	AL	155	598	173	45	0	5	(3	2)	233	70	51	75	4	65	4	11	3	4	4	.50	19	.289	.371	.390
1991	Boston	AL	153	618	175	42	2	5	(3	2)	236	87	60	60	2	53	4	11	3	6	5	.55	15	.283	.349	.382
1992	Boston	AL	143	550	136	27	1	3	(2	1)	174	64	40	62	2	44	0	10	4	7	8	.47	17	.247	.321	.316
1993	Los Angeles	NL	132	445	123	21	2	2	(0	2)	154	48	31	38	10	40	1	17	3	1	3	.25	16	.276	.333	.346
	7 ML YEARS		847	3103	866	201	9	19	(11	8)	1142	409	258	357	19	267	17	74	20	24	29	.45	84	.279	.355	.368

Rick Reed

Pitches: Right **Bats:** Right **Pos:** RP **Ht:** 6' 0" **Wt:** 200 **Born:** 08/16/64 **Age:** 29

			HOW MUCH HE PITCHED					WHAT HE GAVE UP										THE RESULTS					
Year	Team	Lg	G	GS	CG	GF	IP	BFP	H	R	ER	HR	SH	SF	HB	TBB	IBB	SO	WP	Bk	W	L	Pct.	ShO	Sv	ERA
1993	Omaha *	AAA	19	19	3	0	128.1	502	116	48	44	19	1	5	2	14	1	58	1	0	11	4	.733	2	0	3.09
	Okla City *	AAA	5	5	1	0	34.1	144	43	20	16	2	1	1	1	2	0	21	2	0	1	3	.250	0	0	4.19
1988	Pittsburgh	NL	2	2	0	0	12	47	10	4	4	1	2	0	0	2	0	6	0	0	1	0	1.000	0	0	3.00
1989	Pittsburgh	NL	15	7	0	2	54.2	232	62	35	34	5	2	3	2	11	3	34	0	3	1	4	.200	0	0	5.60
1990	Pittsburgh	NL	13	8	1	2	53.2	238	62	32	26	6	2	1	1	12	6	27	0	0	2	3	.400	1	1	4.36
1991	Pittsburgh	NL	1	1	0	0	4.1	21	8	6	5	1	0	0	0	1	0	2	0	0	0	0	.000	0	0	10.38
1992	Kansas City	AL	19	18	1	0	100.1	419	105	47	41	10	2	5	5	20	3	49	0	0	3	7	.300	1	0	3.68
1993	2 ML Teams		3	0	0	0	7.2	36	12	5	5	1	0	0	2	2	0	5	0	0	1	0	1.000	0	0	5.87
1993	Kansas City	AL	1	0	0	0	3.2	18	6	4	4	0	0	0	1	1	0	3	0	0	0	0	.000	0	0	9.82
	Texas	AL	2	0	0	0	4	18	6	1	1	1	0	0	1	1	0	2	0	0	1	0	1.000	0	0	2.25
	6 ML YEARS		53	36	2	4	232.2	993	259	129	115	24	8	9	10	48	12	123	0	3	8	14	.364	2	1	4.45

Steve Reed

Pitches: Right **Bats:** Right **Pos:** RP **Ht:** 6' 2" **Wt:** 202 **Born:** 03/11/66 **Age:** 28

			HOW MUCH HE PITCHED					WHAT HE GAVE UP										THE RESULTS					
Year	Team	Lg	G	GS	CG	GF	IP	BFP	H	R	ER	HR	SH	SF	HB	TBB	IBB	SO	WP	Bk	W	L	Pct.	ShO	Sv	ERA
1988	Pocatello	R	31	0	0	29	46	192	42	20	13	3	3	2	2	8	1	49	0	1	4	1	.800	0	13	2.54
1989	Clinton	A	60	0	0	50	94.2	370	54	16	11	1	4	5	7	38	10	104	0	1	5	3	.625	0	26	1.05
	San Jose	A	2	0	0	1	2	7	0	0	0	0	0	0	1	0	0	0	0	0	0	0	.000	0	0	0.00
1990	Shreveport	AA	45	0	0	28	60.1	255	53	20	11	2	2	1	2	20	6	59	0	1	3	1	.750	0	8	1.64
1991	Shreveport	AA	15	0	0	14	21.2	81	17	2	2	1	0	0	0	3	0	26	0	0	2	0	1.000	0	7	0.83
	Phoenix	AAA	41	0	0	24	56.1	241	62	33	27	5	3	2	2	12	0	46	1	0	2	3	.400	0	6	4.31
1992	Shreveport	AA	27	0	0	25	29	105	18	3	2	1	0	1	1	0	0	33	0	0	1	0	1.000	0	23	0.62
	Phoenix	AAA	29	0	0	28	31	128	27	13	12	2	2	2	0	10	3	30	1	0	0	1	.000	0	20	3.48
1993	Colo Sprngs	AAA	11	0	0	10	12.1	49	8	1	0	0	1	0	0	1	0	10	1	0	0	0	.000	0	7	0.00
1992	San Francisco	NL	18	0	0	2	15.2	63	13	5	4	2	0	0	1	3	0	11	0	0	1	0	1.000	0	0	2.30
1993	Colorado	NL	64	0	0	14	84.1	347	80	47	42	13	2	3	3	30	5	51	1	0	9	5	.643	0	3	4.48
	2 ML YEARS		82	0	0	16	100	410	93	52	46	15	2	3	4	33	5	62	1	0	10	5	.667	0	3	4.14

Kevin Reimer

Bats: Left   **Throws:** Right   **Pos:** DH/LF   **Ht:** 6' 2"   **Wt:** 230   **Born:** 06/28/64   **Age:** 30

Year Team	Lg	G	AB	H	2B	3B	HR	(Hm	Rd)	TB	R	RBI	TBB	IBB	SO	HBP	SH	SF	SB	CS	SB%	GDP	Avg	OBP	SLG
1988 Texas	AL	12	25	3	0	0	1	(0	1)	6	2	2	0	0	6	0	0	1	0	0	.00	0	.120	.115	.240
1989 Texas	AL	3	5	0	0	0	0	(0	0)	0	0	0	0	0	1	0	0	0	0	0	.00	1	.000	.000	.000
1990 Texas	AL	64	100	26	9	1	2	(0	2)	43	5	15	10	0	22	1	0	0	0	1	.00	3	.260	.333	.430
1991 Texas	AL	136	394	106	22	0	20	(13	7)	188	46	69	33	6	93	7	0	6	0	3	.00	10	.269	.332	.477
1992 Texas	AL	148	494	132	32	2	16	(10	6)	216	56	58	42	5	103	10	0	1	2	4	.33	10	.267	.336	.437
1993 Milwaukee	AL	125	437	109	22	1	13	(8	5)	172	53	60	30	4	72	5	1	4	5	4	.56	12	.249	.303	.394
6 ML YEARS		488	1455	376	85	4	52	(31	21)	625	162	204	115	15	297	23	1	12	7	12	.37	36	.258	.320	.430

Rich Renteria

Bats: Right   **Throws:** Right   **Pos:** 2B/3B   **Ht:** 5' 9"   **Wt:** 175   **Born:** 12/25/61   **Age:** 32

Year Team	Lg	G	AB	H	2B	3B	HR	(Hm	Rd)	TB	R	RBI	TBB	IBB	SO	HBP	SH	SF	SB	CS	SB%	GDP	Avg	OBP	SLG
1986 Pittsburgh	NL	10	12	3	1	0	0	(0	0)	4	2	1	0	0	4	0	0	0	1	0	.00	0	.250	.250	.333
1987 Seattle	AL	12	10	1	1	0	0	(0	0)	2	2	0	1	0	2	0	0	0	1	0	1.00	1	.100	.182	.200
1988 Seattle	AL	31	88	18	9	0	0	(0	0)	27	6	6	2	0	8	0	1	0	1	3	.25	3	.205	.222	.307
1993 Florida	NL	103	263	67	9	2	2	(2	0)	86	27	30	21	1	31	2	3	1	2	2	.00	8	.255	.314	.327
4 ML YEARS		156	373	89	20	2	2	(2	0)	119	37	37	24	1	45	2	4	1	2	5	.29	12	.239	.288	.319

Harold Reynolds

Bats: Both   **Throws:** Right   **Pos:** 2B   **Ht:** 5'11"   **Wt:** 165   **Born:** 11/26/60   **Age:** 33

Year Team	Lg	G	AB	H	2B	3B	HR	(Hm	Rd)	TB	R	RBI	TBB	IBB	SO	HBP	SH	SF	SB	CS	SB%	GDP	Avg	OBP	SLG
1983 Seattle	AL	20	59	12	4	1	0	(0	0)	18	8	1	2	0	9	0	1	1	0	2	.00	1	.203	.226	.305
1984 Seattle	AL	10	10	3	0	0	0	(0	0)	3	3	0	0	0	1	1	1	0	1	1	.50	0	.300	.364	.300
1985 Seattle	AL	67	104	15	3	1	0	(0	0)	20	15	6	17	0	14	0	1	0	3	2	.60	0	.144	.264	.192
1986 Seattle	AL	126	445	99	19	4	1	(1	0)	129	46	24	29	0	42	3	9	0	30	12	.71	6	.222	.275	.290
1987 Seattle	AL	160	530	146	31	8	1	(1	0)	196	73	35	39	0	34	2	8	5	60	20	.75	7	.275	.325	.370
1988 Seattle	AL	158	598	169	26	11	4	(4	0)	229	61	41	51	1	51	2	10	2	35	29	.55	9	.283	.340	.383
1989 Seattle	AL	153	613	184	24	9	0	(0	0)	226	87	43	55	1	45	3	3	3	25	18	.58	4	.300	.359	.369
1990 Seattle	AL	160	642	162	36	5	5	(0	5)	223	100	55	81	3	52	3	5	6	31	16	.66	9	.252	.336	.347
1991 Seattle	AL	161	631	160	34	6	3	(1	2)	215	95	57	72	2	63	5	14	6	28	8	.78	11	.254	.332	.341
1992 Seattle	AL	140	458	113	23	3	3	(2	1)	151	55	33	45	1	41	3	11	4	15	12	.56	12	.247	.316	.330
1993 Baltimore	AL	145	485	122	20	4	4	(2	2)	162	64	47	66	3	47	4	10	5	12	11	.52	4	.252	.343	.334
11 ML YEARS		1300	4575	1185	220	52	21	(11	10)	1572	607	342	457	11	399	26	73	32	240	131	.65	63	.259	.328	.344

Shane Reynolds

Pitches: Right   **Bats:** Right   **Pos:** RP   **Ht:** 6' 3"   **Wt:** 210   **Born:** 03/26/68   **Age:** 26

Year Team	Lg	G	GS	CG	GF	IP	BFP	H	R	ER	HR	SH	SF	HB	TBB	IBB	SO	WP	Bk	W	L	Pct.	ShO	Sv	ERA
1989 Auburn	A	6	6	1	0	35	150	36	16	9	1	1	0	4	14	0	23	1	1	3	2	.600	0	0	2.31
Asheville	A	8	8	2	0	51.1	224	53	25	21	2	2	2	1	21	0	33	1	4	5	3	.625	1	0	3.68
1990 Columbus	AA	29	27	2	1	155.1	710	182	104	83	14	11	5	5	70	1	92	6	6	9	10	.474	1	0	4.81
1991 Jackson	AA	27	27	2	0	151	673	165	93	75	8	8	7	2	62	1	116	3	3	8	9	.471	0	0	4.47
1992 Tucson	AAA	25	22	2	1	142	605	156	73	58	4	3	4	4	34	2	106	4	1	9	8	.529	0	1	3.68
1993 Tucson	AAA	25	20	2	1	139.1	584	147	74	56	4	6	5	3	21	0	106	4	0	10	6	.625	0	1	3.62
1992 Houston	NL	8	5	0	0	25.1	122	42	22	20	2	6	1	0	6	1	10	1	1	1	3	.250	0	0	7.11
1993 Houston	NL	5	1	0	0	11	49	11	4	1	0	0	0	0	6	1	10	0	0	0	0	.000	0	0	0.82
2 ML YEARS		13	6	0	0	36.1	171	53	26	21	2	6	1	0	12	2	20	1	1	1	3	.250	0	0	5.20

Armando Reynoso

Pitches: Right   **Bats:** Right   **Pos:** SP   **Ht:** 6' 0"   **Wt:** 186   **Born:** 05/01/66   **Age:** 28

Year Team	Lg	G	GS	CG	GF	IP	BFP	H	R	ER	HR	SH	SF	HB	TBB	IBB	SO	WP	Bk	W	L	Pct.	ShO	Sv	ERA
1990 Richmond	AAA	4	3	0	0	24	102	26	7	6	3	1	1	0	7	0	15	0	3	3	1	.750	0	0	2.25
1991 Richmond	AAA	22	19	3	1	131	544	117	44	38	9	7	3	10	39	1	97	8	6	10	6	.625	3	0	2.61
1992 Richmond	AAA	28	27	4	1	169.1	693	156	65	50	12	3	5	7	52	6	108	8	5	12	9	.571	1	0	2.66
1993 Colo Sprngs	AAA	4	4	0	0	22.1	93	19	10	8	1	2	2	1	8	0	22	2	0	2	1	.667	0	0	3.22
1991 Atlanta	NL	6	5	0	1	23.1	103	26	18	16	4	3	0	3	10	1	10	2	0	2	1	.667	0	0	6.17
1992 Atlanta	NL	3	1	0	0	7.2	32	11	4	4	2	1	0	1	2	1	2	0	0	1	0	1.000	0	0	4.70
1993 Colorado	NL	30	30	4	0	189	830	206	101	84	22	5	8	9	63	7	117	7	6	12	11	.522	0	0	4.00
3 ML YEARS		39	36	4	2	220	965	243	123	104	28	9	8	13	75	9	129	9	6	15	12	.556	0	1	4.25

Arthur Rhodes

Pitches: Left **Bats:** Left **Pos:** SP   **Ht:** 6' 2" **Wt:** 206 **Born:** 10/24/69 **Age:** 24

				HOW MUCH HE PITCHED					WHAT HE GAVE UP												THE RESULTS					
Year Team	Lg	G	GS	CG	GF	IP	BFP	H	R	ER	HR	SH	SF	HB	TBB	IBB	SO	WP	Bk	W	L	Pct.	ShO	Sv	ERA
1993 Rochester*	AAA	6	6	0	0	26.2	115	26	12	12	5	0	0	0	15	0	33	5	1	1	1	.500	0	0	4.05
1991 Baltimore	AL	8	8	0	0	36	174	47	35	32	4	1	3	0	23	0	23	2	0	0	3	.000	0	0	8.00
1992 Baltimore	AL	15	15	2	0	94.1	394	87	39	38	6	5	1	1	38	2	77	2	1	7	5	.583	1	0	3.63
1993 Baltimore	AL	17	17	0	0	85.2	387	91	62	62	16	2	3	1	49	1	49	2	0	5	6	.455	0	0	6.51
3 ML YEARS		40	40	2	0	216	955	225	136	132	26	8	7	2	110	3	149	6	1	12	14	.462	1	0	5.50

Karl Rhodes

Bats: Left **Throws:** Left **Pos:** CF   **Ht:** 5'11" **Wt:** 170 **Born:** 08/21/68 **Age:** 25

								BATTING												BASERUNNING				PERCENTAGES		
Year Team	Lg	G	AB	H	2B	3B	HR	(Hm	Rd)	TB	R	RBI	TBB	IBB	SO	HBP	SH	SF	SB	CS	SB%	GDP	Avg	OBP	SLG
1993 Omaha*	AAA	88	365	116	31	2	23	--	--	220	81	64	38	4	60	1	2	4	10	5	.67	8	.318	.380	.603
Iowa*	AAA	35	125	40	12	1	7	--	--	75	31	25	20	4	22	1	2	1	6	3	.67		.320	.415	.600
1990 Houston	NL	38	86	21	6	1	1	(0	1)	32	12	3	13	3	12	0	1	1	4	1	.80	1	.244	.340	.372
1991 Houston	NL	44	136	29	3	1	1	(0	1)	37	7	12	14	3	26	1	0	1	2	2	.50	3	.213	.289	.272
1992 Houston	NL	5	4	0	0	0	0	(0	0)	0	0	0	0	0	2	0	0	0	0	0	.00	0	.000	.000	.000
1993 2 ML Teams		20	54	15	2	1	3	(0	3)	28	12	7	11	0	9	0	0	0	2	0	1.00	0	.278	.400	.519
1993 Houston	NL	5	2	0	0	0	0	(0	0)	0	0	0	0	0	0	0	0	0	0	0	.00	0	.000	.000	.000
Chicago	NL	15	52	15	2	1	3	(0	3)	28	12	7	11	0	9	0	0	0	2	0	1.00	0	.288	.413	.538
4 ML YEARS		107	280	65	11	3	5	(0	5)	97	31	22	38	6	49	1	1	2	8	3	.73	4	.232	.324	.346

Jeff Richardson

Bats: Right **Throws:** Right **Pos:** 2B   **Ht:** 6' 2" **Wt:** 180 **Born:** 08/26/65 **Age:** 28

								BATTING												BASERUNNING				PERCENTAGES		
Year Team	Lg	G	AB	H	2B	3B	HR	(Hm	Rd)	TB	R	RBI	TBB	IBB	SO	HBP	SH	SF	SB	CS	SB%	GDP	Avg	OBP	SLG
1993 Pawtucket*	AAA	9	28	9	1	0	0	--	--	10	2	1	6	0	1	0		0	0	0	.00	1	.321	.333	.357
1989 Cincinnati	NL	53	125	21	4	0	2	(1	1)	31	10	11	10	0	23	1	3	1	1	0	1.00	3	.168	.234	.248
1991 Pittsburgh	NL	6	4	1	0	0	0	(0	0)	1	0	0	0	0	3	0	0	0	0	0	.00	0	.250	.250	.250
1993 Boston	AL	15	24	5	2	0	0	(0	0)	7	3	2	1	0	3	0	2	0	0	0	.00	0	.208	.240	.292
3 ML YEARS		74	153	27	6	0	2	(1	1)	39	13	13	11	0	29	1	5	1	1	0	1.00	3	.176	.235	.255

Dave Righetti

Pitches: Left **Bats:** Left **Pos:** RP   **Ht:** 6' 4" **Wt:** 219 **Born:** 11/28/58 **Age:** 35

				HOW MUCH HE PITCHED					WHAT HE GAVE UP												THE RESULTS					
Year Team	Lg	G	GS	CG	GF	IP	BFP	H	R	ER	HR	SH	SF	HB	TBB	IBB	SO	WP	Bk	W	L	Pct.	ShO	Sv	ERA
1979 New York	AL	3	3	0	0	17	67	10	7	7	2	1	1	0	10	0	13	0	0	0	1	.000	0	0	3.71
1981 New York	AL	15	15	2	0	105	422	75	25	24	1	0	2	0	38	0	89	1	1	8	4	.667	0	0	2.06
1982 New York	AL	33	27	4	3	183	804	155	88	77	11	8	5	6	108	4	163	9	5	11	10	.524	0	1	3.79
1983 New York	AL	31	31	7	0	217	900	194	96	83	12	10	4	2	67	2	169	10	1	14	8	.636	2	0	3.44
1984 New York	AL	64	0	0	53	96.1	400	79	29	25	5	4	4	0	37	7	90	0	2	5	6	.455	0	31	2.34
1985 New York	AL	74	0	0	60	107	452	96	36	33	5	6	3	0	45	3	92	7	0	12	7	.632	0	29	2.78
1986 New York	AL	74	0	0	68	106.2	435	88	31	29	4	5	4	2	35	7	83	1	0	8	8	.500	0	46	2.45
1987 New York	AL	60	0	0	54	95	419	95	45	37	9	6	5	2	44	4	77	1	3	8	6	.571	0	31	3.51
1988 New York	AL	60	0	0	41	87	377	86	35	34	5	4	0	1	37	2	70	2	4	5	4	.556	0	25	3.52
1989 New York	AL	55	0	0	53	69	300	73	32	23	3	7	2	1	26	6	51	0	0	2	6	.250	0	25	3.00
1990 New York	AL	53	0	0	47	53	235	48	24	21	8	1	1	2	26	2	43	2	0	1	1	.500	0	36	3.57
1991 San Francisco	NL	61	0	0	49	71.2	304	64	29	27	4	4	2	3	28	6	51	1	1	2	7	.222	0	24	3.39
1992 San Francisco	NL	54	4	0	23	78.1	340	79	47	44	4	6	4	0	36	5	47	5	2	2	7	.222	0	3	5.06
1993 San Francisco	NL	51	0	0	15	47.1	210	58	31	30	11	2	0	1	17	0	31	1	0	3	1	.500	0	1	5.70
14 ML YEARS		688	80	13	466	1333.1	5665	1200	555	494	84	64	37	20	554	48	1069	40	19	79	76	.510	2	252	3.33

Jose Rijo

Pitches: Right **Bats:** Right **Pos:** SP   **Ht:** 6' 2" **Wt:** 210 **Born:** 05/13/65 **Age:** 29

				HOW MUCH HE PITCHED					WHAT HE GAVE UP												THE RESULTS					
Year Team	Lg	G	GS	CG	GF	IP	BFP	H	R	ER	HR	SH	SF	HB	TBB	IBB	SO	WP	Bk	W	L	Pct.	ShO	Sv	ERA
1984 New York	AL	24	5	0	8	62.1	289	74	40	33	5	6	1	1	33	1	47	2	1	2	8	.200	0	2	4.76
1985 Oakland	AL	12	9	0	1	63.2	272	57	26	25	6	5	0	1	28	2	65	0	0	6	4	.600	0	0	3.53
1986 Oakland	AL	39	26	4	9	193.2	856	172	116	100	24	10	9	4	108	7	176	6	4	9	11	.450	0	1	4.65
1987 Oakland	AL	21	14	1	3	82.1	394	106	67	54	10	0	3	2	41	1	67	5	2	2	7	.222	0	0	5.90
1988 Cincinnati	NL	49	19	0	12	162	653	120	47	43	7	8	5	3	63	7	160	1	4	13	8	.619	0	0	2.39
1989 Cincinnati	NL	19	19	1	0	111	464	101	39	35	3	6	2	2	48	3	86	4	3	7	6	.538	1	0	2.84
1990 Cincinnati	NL	29	29	7	0	197	801	151	65	59	10	8	1	2	78	1	152	2	5	14	8	.636	1	0	2.70

Year	Team	Lg	G	GS	CG	GF	IP	BFP	H	R	ER	HR	SH	SF	HB	TBB	IBB	SO	WP	Bk	W	L	Pct.	ShO	Sv	ERA
1991	Cincinnati	NL	30	30	3	0	204.1	825	165	69	57	8	4	8	3	55	4	172	2	4	15	6	.714	1	0	2.51
1992	Cincinnati	NL	33	33	2	0	211	836	185	67	60	15	9	4	3	44	1	171	2	1	15	10	.600	0	0	2.56
1993	Cincinnati	NL	36	36	2	0	257.1	1029	218	76	71	19	13	3	2	62	2	227	0	1	14	9	.609	1	0	2.48
	10 ML YEARS		292	220	20	33	1544.2	6419	1349	612	537	110	66	40	23	560	29	1323	24	25	97	77	.557	4	3	3.13

Ernest Riles

Bats: Left **Throws:** Right **Pos:** 2B/3B/DH 　　**Ht:** 6' 1" **Wt:** 180 **Born:** 10/02/60 **Age:** 33

									BATTING											BASERUNNING				PERCENTAGES		
Year	Team	Lg	G	AB	H	2B	3B	HR	(Hm	Rd)	TB	R	RBI	TBB	IBB	SO	HBP	SH	SF	SB	CS	SB%	GDP	Avg	OBP	SLG
1993	Pawtucket *	AAA	6	18	5	0	0	2	--	--	11	4	6	3	0	0	0	0	2	0	0	.00	1	.278	.348	.611
1985	Milwaukee	AL	116	448	128	12	7	5	(2	3)	169	54	45	36	0	54	0	2	6	2	2	.50	16	.286	.339	.377
1986	Milwaukee	AL	145	524	132	24	2	9	(2	7)	187	69	47	54	0	80	1	6	3	7	7	.50	14	.252	.321	.357
1987	Milwaukee	AL	83	276	72	11	1	4	(1	3)	97	38	38	30	1	47	1	3	6	3	4	.43	6	.261	.329	.351
1988	2 ML Teams		120	314	87	13	3	4	(4	0)	118	33	37	17	2	59	0	1	4	3	4	.43	8	.277	.310	.376
1989	San Francisco	NL	122	302	84	13	2	7	(5	2)	122	43	40	28	3	50	2	1	4	0	6	.00	7	.278	.339	.404
1990	San Francisco	NL	92	155	31	2	1	8	(7	1)	59	22	21	26	3	26	0	2	1	0	0	.00	2	.200	.313	.381
1991	Oakland	AL	108	281	60	8	4	5	(3	2)	91	30	32	31	3	42	1	4	4	3	2	.60	8	.214	.290	.324
1992	Houston	NL	39	61	16	1	0	1	(0	1)	20	5	4	2	0	11	0	0	1	1	0	1.00	3	.262	.281	.328
1993	Boston	AL	94	143	27	8	0	5	(2	3)	50	15	20	20	3	40	2	2	3	1	3	.25	3	.189	.292	.350
1988	Milwaukee	AL	41	127	32	6	1	1	(1	0)	43	7	9	7	0	26	0	1	0	2	2	.50	3	.252	.291	.339
	San Francisco	NL	79	187	55	7	2	3	(3	0)	75	26	28	10	2	33	0	0	4	1	2	.33	5	.294	.323	.401
	9 ML YEARS		919	2504	637	92	20	48	(26	22)	913	309	284	244	15	409	9	25	29	20	28	.42	64	.254	.319	.365

Billy Ripken

Bats: Right **Throws:** Right **Pos:** 2B/SS 　　**Ht:** 6' 1" **Wt:** 187 **Born:** 12/16/64 **Age:** 29

									BATTING											BASERUNNING				PERCENTAGES		
Year	Team	Lg	G	AB	H	2B	3B	HR	(Hm	Rd)	TB	R	RBI	TBB	IBB	SO	HBP	SH	SF	SB	CS	SB%	GDP	Avg	OBP	SLG
1987	Baltimore	AL	58	234	72	9	0	2	(0	2)	87	27	20	21	0	23	0	1	1	4	1	.80	3	.308	.363	.372
1988	Baltimore	AL	150	512	106	18	1	2	(0	2)	132	52	34	33	0	63	5	6	3	8	2	.80	14	.207	.260	.258
1989	Baltimore	AL	115	318	76	11	2	2	(0	2)	97	31	26	22	0	53	0	19	5	1	2	.33	12	.239	.284	.305
1990	Baltimore	AL	129	406	118	28	1	3	(2	1)	157	48	38	28	2	43	4	17	1	5	2	.71	7	.291	.342	.387
1991	Baltimore	AL	104	287	62	11	1	0	(0	0)	75	24	14	15	0	31	0	11	2	0	1	.00	14	.216	.253	.261
1992	Baltimore	AL	111	330	76	15	0	4	(3	1)	103	35	36	18	1	26	3	10	2	2	3	.40	10	.230	.275	.312
1993	Texas	AL	50	132	25	4	0	0	(0	0)	29	12	11	11	0	19	4	5	1	0	2	.00	6	.189	.270	.220
	7 ML YEARS		717	2219	535	96	5	13	(5	8)	680	229	179	148	3	258	16	69	15	20	13	.61	66	.241	.291	.306

Cal Ripken

Bats: Right **Throws:** Right **Pos:** SS 　　**Ht:** 6' 4" **Wt:** 220 **Born:** 08/24/60 **Age:** 33

									BATTING											BASERUNNING				PERCENTAGES		
Year	Team	Lg	G	AB	H	2B	3B	HR	(Hm	Rd)	TB	R	RBI	TBB	IBB	SO	HBP	SH	SF	SB	CS	SB%	GDP	Avg	OBP	SLG
1981	Baltimore	AL	23	39	5	0	0	0	(0	0)	5	1	0	1	0	8	0	0	0	0	0	.00	4	.128	.150	.128
1982	Baltimore	AL	160	598	158	32	5	28	(11	17)	284	90	93	46	3	95	3	2	6	3	3	.50	16	.264	.317	.475
1983	Baltimore	AL	162	663	211	47	2	27	(12	15)	343	121	102	58	0	97	0	0	5	0	4	.00	24	.318	.371	.517
1984	Baltimore	AL	162	641	195	37	7	27	(16	11)	327	103	86	71	1	89	2	0	2	2	1	.67	16	.304	.374	.510
1985	Baltimore	AL	161	642	181	32	5	26	(15	11)	301	116	110	67	1	68	1	0	8	2	3	.40	32	.282	.347	.469
1986	Baltimore	AL	162	627	177	35	1	25	(10	15)	289	98	81	70	5	60	4	0	6	4	2	.67	19	.282	.355	.461
1987	Baltimore	AL	162	624	157	28	3	27	(17	10)	272	97	98	81	0	77	1	0	11	3	5	.38	19	.252	.333	.436
1988	Baltimore	AL	161	575	152	25	1	23	(11	12)	248	87	81	102	7	69	2	0	10	2	2	.50	10	.264	.372	.431
1989	Baltimore	AL	162	646	166	30	0	21	(13	8)	259	80	93	57	5	72	3	0	6	3	2	.60	22	.257	.317	.401
1990	Baltimore	AL	161	600	150	28	4	21	(8	13)	249	78	84	82	18	66	5	1	7	3	1	.75	12	.250	.341	.415
1991	Baltimore	AL	162	650	210	46	5	34	(16	18)	368	99	114	53	15	46	5	0	6	6	1	.86	19	.323	.374	.566
1992	Baltimore	AL	162	637	160	29	1	14	(5	9)	233	73	72	64	14	50	7	0	7	4	3	.57	13	.251	.323	.366
1993	Baltimore	AL	162	641	165	26	3	24	(14	10)	269	87	90	65	19	58	6	0	6	1	4	.20	17	.257	.329	.420
	13 ML YEARS		1962	7583	2087	395	37	297	(148	149)	3447	1130	1104	817	88	855	39	3	83	33	31	.52	223	.275	.345	.455

Bill Risley

Pitches: Right **Bats:** Right **Pos:** RP 　　**Ht:** 6' 2" **Wt:** 210 **Born:** 05/29/67 **Age:** 27

							HOW MUCH HE PITCHED			WHAT HE GAVE UP											THE RESULTS				
Year	Team	Lg	G	GS	CG	GF	IP	BFP	H	R	ER	HR	SH	SF	HB	TBB	IBB	SO	WP	Bk	W	L	Pct.	ShO	Sv	ERA
1987	Reds	R	11	11	0	0	52.1	226	38	24	11	0	1	3	3	26	3	50	6	2	1	4	.200	0	0	1.89
1988	Greensboro	A	23	23	3	0	120.1	515	82	60	55	2	3	9	11	84	0	135	9	19	8	4	.667	3	0	4.11
1989	Cedar Rapids	A	27	27	2	0	140.2	581	87	72	61	9	1	9	6	81	2	128	19	8	9	10	.474	0	0	3.90
1990	Cedar Rapids	A	22	22	7	0	137.2	579	99	51	43	8	6	4	7	68	1	123	13	3	8	9	.471	1	0	2.81
1991	Chattanooga	AA	19	19	3	0	108.1	465	81	48	38	3	3	6	9	60	2	77	5	5	5	7	.417	0	0	3.16
	Nashville	AAA	8	8	1	0	44	199	45	27	24	7	3	1	1	26	1	32	3	0	3	5	.375	0	0	4.91
1992	Indianapolis	AAA	25	15	0	1	95.2	434	105	69	68	11	3	5	4	47	0	64	2	4	5	8	.385	0	0	6.40
1993	Ottawa	AAA	41	0	0	12	63.2	277	51	26	18	7	6	3	3	34	3	74	5	0	2	4	.333	0	1	2.54

Year	Team	Lg	G	GS	CG	GF	IP	BFP	H	R	ER	HR	SH	SF	HB	TBB	IBB	SO	WP	Bk	W	L	Pct.	ShO	Sv	ERA
1992	Montreal	NL	1	1	0	0	5	19	4	1	1	0	1	0	0	1	0	2	0	0	1	0	1.000	0	0	1.80
1993	Montreal	NL	2	0	0	1	3	14	2	3	2	1	1	0	1	2	0	2	0	0	0	0	.000	0	0	6.00
	2 ML YEARS		3	1	0	1	8	33	6	4	3	1	2	0	1	3	0	4	0	0	1	0	1.000	0	0	3.38

Ben Rivera

Pitches: Right **Bats:** Right **Pos:** SP **Ht:** 6' 6" **Wt:** 230 **Born:** 01/11/69 **Age:** 25

			HOW MUCH HE PITCHED						WHAT HE GAVE UP												THE RESULTS					
Year	Team	Lg	G	GS	CG	GF	IP	BFP	H	R	ER	HR	SH	SF	HB	TBB	IBB	SO	WP	Bk	W	L	Pct.	ShO	Sv	ERA
1987	Braves	R	16	5	0	2	49.2	220	55	26	18	0	1	2	2	19	1	29	2	2	1	5	.167	0	0	3.26
1988	Sumter	A	27	27	3	0	173.1	724	167	77	61	12	2	5	7	52	0	99	6	7	9	11	.450	2	0	3.17
1989	Durham	A	23	22	1	0	102.1	462	113	55	51	6	4	3	5	51	1	58	10	3	5	7	.417	0	0	4.49
1990	Greenville	AA	13	13	0	0	52	243	68	40	38	6	2	1	3	26	0	32	10	0	1	4	.200	0	0	6.58
	Durham	A	16	13	1	3	75	327	69	41	30	7	2	3	5	33	1	64	4	2	5	3	.625	1	1	3.60
1991	Greenville	AA	26	26	3	0	158.2	683	155	76	63	13	2	1	3	75	4	116	8	4	11	8	.579	2	0	3.57
1992	Scranton/wb	AAA	2	2	1	0	12	41	4	0	0	0	0	1	0	2	0	10	0	1	2	0	1.000	1	0	0.00
1992	2 ML Teams		28	14	4	7	117.1	487	99	40	40	9	5	2	4	45	4	77	5	0	7	4	.636	1	0	3.07
1993	Philadelphia	NL	30	28	1	1	163	742	175	99	91	16	5	5	6	85	4	123	13	0	13	9	.591	0	0	5.02
1992	Atlanta	NL	8	0	0	3	15.1	78	21	8	8	1	0	1	2	13	2	11	0	0	0	1	.000	0	0	4.70
	Philadelphia	NL	20	14	4	4	102	409	78	32	32	8	5	1	2	32	2	66	5	0	7	3	.700	1	0	2.82
	2 ML YEARS		58	42	5	8	280.1	1229	274	139	131	25	10	7	10	130	8	200	18	0	20	13	.606	1	0	4.21

Luis Rivera

Bats: Right **Throws:** Right **Pos:** 2B/SS **Ht:** 5'10" **Wt:** 175 **Born:** 01/03/64 **Age:** 30

			BATTING																BASERUNNING				PERCENTAGES		
Year	Team	Lg	G	AB	H	2B	3B	HR	(Hm | Rd)	TB	R	RBI	TBB	IBB	SO	HBP	SH	SF	SB	CS	SB%	GDP	Avg	OBP	SLG
1986	Montreal	NL	55	166	34	11	1	0	(0 | 0)	47	20	13	17	0	33	2	1	1	1	1	.50	1	.205	.285	.283
1987	Montreal	NL	18	32	5	2	0	0	(0 | 0)	7	0	1	1	0	8	0	0	0	0	0	.00	0	.156	.182	.219
1988	Montreal	NL	123	371	83	17	3	4	(2 | 2)	118	35	30	24	4	69	1	3	3	3	4	.43	9	.224	.271	.318
1989	Boston	AL	93	323	83	17	1	5	(4 | 1)	117	35	29	20	1	60	1	4	1	2	3	.40	7	.257	.301	.362
1990	Boston	AL	118	346	78	20	0	7	(4 | 3)	119	38	45	25	0	58	1	12	1	4	3	.57	10	.225	.279	.344
1991	Boston	AL	129	414	107	22	3	8	(4 | 4)	159	64	40	35	0	86	3	12	4	4	4	.50	10	.258	.318	.384
1992	Boston	AL	102	288	62	11	1	0	(0 | 0)	75	17	29	26	0	56	3	5	0	4	3	.57	5	.215	.287	.260
1993	Boston	AL	62	130	27	8	1	1	(1 | 0)	40	13	7	11	0	36	1	2	1	1	2	.33	2	.208	.273	.308
	8 ML YEARS		700	2070	479	108	10	25	(15 | 10)	682	222	194	159	5	406	12	39	11	19	20	.49	44	.231	.289	.329

Kevin Roberson

Bats: Both **Throws:** Right **Pos:** RF/LF **Ht:** 6' 4" **Wt:** 210 **Born:** 01/29/68 **Age:** 26

			BATTING																BASERUNNING				PERCENTAGES		
Year	Team	Lg	G	AB	H	2B	3B	HR	(Hm | Rd)	TB	R	RBI	TBB	IBB	SO	HBP	SH	SF	SB	CS	SB%	GDP	Avg	OBP	SLG
1988	Wytheville	R	63	225	47	12	2	3	--	--	72	39	29	40	0	86	3	0	2	3	2	.60	0	.209	.333	.320
1989	Chston-Wv	A	126	429	109	19	1	13	--	--	169	49	57	70	4	149	5	2	3	3	6	.33	7	.254	.363	.394
1990	Winston-Sal	A	85	313	84	23	3	5	--	--	128	49	45	25	0	70	3	1	2	7	3	.70	6	.268	.327	.409
	Charlotte	AA	31	119	29	6	2	5	--	--	54	14	16	8	0	23	0	1	2	2	0	1.00	3	.244	.287	.454
1991	Charlotte	AA	136	507	130	23	2	19	--	--	214	77	67	39	1	125	9	0	5	17	3	.85	10	.256	.318	.422
1992	Iowa	AAA	51	197	60	15	4	6	--	--	101	25	34	5	1	46	2	1	1	0	0	.00	4	.305	.327	.513
1993	Iowa	AAA	67	263	80	20	1	16	--	--	150	48	50	19	3	66	4	0	3	3	2	.60	4	.304	.356	.570
1993	Chicago	NL	62	180	34	4	1	9	(4 | 5)	67	23	27	12	0	48	3	0	0	0	1	.00	2	.189	.251	.372

Bip Roberts

Bats: Both **Throws:** Right **Pos:** 2B/LF **Ht:** 5' 7" **Wt:** 165 **Born:** 10/27/63 **Age:** 30

			BATTING																BASERUNNING				PERCENTAGES		
Year	Team	Lg	G	AB	H	2B	3B	HR	(Hm | Rd)	TB	R	RBI	TBB	IBB	SO	HBP	SH	SF	SB	CS	SB%	GDP	Avg	OBP	SLG
1986	San Diego	NL	101	241	61	5	2	1	(0 | 1)	73	34	12	14	1	29	0	2	1	14	12	.54	2	.253	.293	.303
1988	San Diego	NL	5	9	3	0	0	0	(0 | 0)	3	1	0	1	0	2	0	0	0	0	2	.00	0	.333	.400	.333
1989	San Diego	NL	117	329	99	15	8	3	(2 | 1)	139	81	25	49	0	45	1	6	2	21	11	.66	3	.301	.391	.422
1990	San Diego	NL	149	556	172	36	3	9	(4 | 5)	241	104	44	55	1	65	6	8	4	46	12	.79	8	.309	.375	.433
1991	San Diego	NL	117	424	119	13	3	3	(3 | 0)	147	66	32	37	0	71	4	4	3	26	11	.70	6	.281	.342	.347
1992	Cincinnati	NL	147	532	172	34	6	4	(3 | 1)	230	92	45	62	4	54	2	1	4	44	16	.73	7	.323	.393	.432
1993	Cincinnati	NL	83	292	70	13	0	1	(0 | 1)	86	46	18	38	1	46	3	0	3	26	6	.81	2	.240	.330	.295
	7 ML YEARS		719	2383	696	116	22	21	(12 | 9)	919	424	176	256	7	312	16	21	17	177	70	.72	28	.292	.362	.386

Rich Robertson

Pitches: Left **Bats:** Left **Pos:** RP **Ht:** 6' 4" **Wt:** 170 **Born:** 09/15/68 **Age:** 25

			HOW MUCH HE PITCHED						WHAT HE GAVE UP												THE RESULTS					
Year	Team	Lg	G	GS	CG	GF	IP	BFP	H	R	ER	HR	SH	SF	HB	TBB	IBB	SO	WP	Bk	W	L	Pct.	ShO	Sv	ERA
1990	Welland	A	16	13	0	0	64.1	293	51	34	22	4	1	2	1	55	2	80	6	2	3	4	.429	0	0	3.08

Year Team	Lg	G	GS	CG	GF	IP	BFP	H	R	ER	HR	SH	SF	HB	TBB	IBB	SO	WP	Bk	W	L	Pct.	ShO	Sv	ERA
1991 Salem	A	12	11	0	0	45.2	210	34	32	25	2	1	0	3	42	0	32	4	0	2	4	.333	0	0	4.93
Augusta	A	13	12	1	1	74	348	73	52	41	4	2	1	1	51	0	62	3	1	4	7	.364	0	0	4.99
1992 Salem	A	6	6	0	0	37	152	29	18	14	6	0	1	1	10	0	27	1	1	3	0	1.000	0	0	3.41
Carolina	AA	20	20	1	0	124.2	534	127	51	42	7	1	2	4	41	2	107	4	1	6	7	.462	1	0	3.03
1993 Buffalo	AAA	23	23	2	0	132.1	569	141	67	63	9	3	5	2	52	2	71	10	1	9	8	.529	0	0	4.28
1993 Pittsburgh	NL	9	0	0	2	9	44	15	6	6	1	0	0	1	4	0	5	0	0	0	1	.000	0	0	6.00

Henry Rodriguez

Bats: Left   **Throws:** Left   **Pos:** LF/1B/RF   **Ht:** 6' 1"   **Wt:** 180   **Born:** 11/08/67   **Age:** 26

								BATTING											BASERUNNING				PERCENTAGES		
Year Team	Lg	G	AB	H	2B	3B	HR	(Hm	Rd)	TB	R	RBI	TBB	IBB	SO	HBP	SH	SF	SB	CS	SB%	GDP	Avg	OBP	SLG
1987 Dodgers	R	49	148	49	7	3	0	(Hm	--)	62	23	15	16	7	15	3	1	2	3	1	.75	5	.331	.402	.419
1988 Salem	A	72	291	84	14	4	2	--	--	112	47	39	21	1	42	4	1	6	14	2	.88	7	.289	.339	.385
1989 Vero Beach	A	126	433	123	33	1	10	--	--	188	53	73	48	11	58	2	1	6	7	6	.54	12	.284	.354	.434
Bakersfield	A	3	9	2	0	0	1	--	--	5	2	2	0	0	3	0	0	0	0	0	.00	0	.222	.222	.556
1990 San Antonio	AA	129	495	144	21	9	28	--	--	267	82	109	61	9	66	2	1	14	5	4	.56	10	.291	.362	.539
1991 Albuquerque	AAA	121	446	121	22	5	10	--	--	183	61	67	25	3	62	1	1	5	4	5	.44	11	.271	.308	.410
1992 Albuquerque	AAA	94	365	111	21	5	14	--	--	184	59	72	31	5	57	1	2	10	1	5	.17	11	.304	.351	.504
1993 Albuquerque	AAA	46	179	53	13	5	4	--	--	88	26	30	14	0	37	2	0	3	1	2	.33	5	.296	.348	.492
1992 Los Angeles	NL	53	146	32	7	0	3	(2	1)	48	11	14	8	0	30	0	1	1	0	0	.00	2	.219	.258	.329
1993 Los Angeles	NL	76	176	39	10	0	8	(5	3)	73	20	23	11	2	39	0	0	1	1	0	1.00	1	.222	.266	.415
2 ML YEARS		129	322	71	17	0	11	(7	4)	121	31	37	19	2	69	0	1	2	1	0	1.00	3	.220	.262	.376

Ivan Rodriguez

Bats: Right   **Throws:** Right   **Pos:** C   **Ht:** 5' 9"   **Wt:** 205   **Born:** 11/30/71   **Age:** 22

								BATTING											BASERUNNING				PERCENTAGES		
Year Team	Lg	G	AB	H	2B	3B	HR	(Hm	Rd)	TB	R	RBI	TBB	IBB	SO	HBP	SH	SF	SB	CS	SB%	GDP	Avg	OBP	SLG
1991 Texas	AL	88	280	74	16	0	3	(3	0)	99	24	27	5	0	42	0	2	1	0	1	.00	10	.264	.276	.354
1992 Texas	AL	123	420	109	16	1	8	(4	4)	151	39	37	24	2	73	1	7	2	0	0	.00	15	.260	.300	.360
1993 Texas	AL	137	473	129	28	4	10	(7	3)	195	56	66	29	3	70	4	5	8	8	7	.53	16	.273	.315	.412
3 ML YEARS		348	1173	312	60	5	21	(14	7)	445	119	130	58	5	185	5	14	11	8	8	.50	41	.266	.301	.379

Rich Rodriguez

Pitches: Left   **Bats:** Right   **Pos:** RP   **Ht:** 6' 0"   **Wt:** 200   **Born:** 03/01/63   **Age:** 31

		HOW MUCH HE PITCHED						WHAT HE GAVE UP												THE RESULTS					
Year Team	Lg	G	GS	CG	GF	IP	BFP	H	R	ER	HR	SH	SF	HB	TBB	IBB	SO	WP	Bk	W	L	Pct.	ShO	Sv	ERA
1990 San Diego	NL	32	0	0	15	47.2	201	52	17	15	2	2	1	1	16	4	22	1	1	1	1	.500	0	1	2.83
1991 San Diego	NL	64	1	0	19	80	335	66	31	29	8	7	2	0	44	8	40	4	1	3	1	.750	0	0	3.26
1992 San Diego	NL	61	1	0	15	91	369	77	28	24	4	2	2	0	29	4	64	1	1	6	3	.667	0	0	2.37
1993 2 ML Teams		70	0	0	21	76	331	73	38	32	10	5	0	2	33	8	43	3	0	2	4	.333	0	3	3.79
1993 San Diego	NL	34	0	0	10	30	133	34	15	11	2	2	0	1	9	3	22	1	0	2	3	.400	0	2	3.30
Florida	NL	36	0	0	11	46	198	39	23	21	8	3	0	1	24	5	21	2	0	0	0	.000	0	1	4.11
4 ML YEARS		227	2	0	70	294.2	1236	268	114	100	24	16	5	3	122	24	169	9	3	12	9	.571	0	4	3.05

Kenny Rogers

Pitches: Left   **Bats:** Left   **Pos:** SP   **Ht:** 6' 1"   **Wt:** 205   **Born:** 11/10/64   **Age:** 29

		HOW MUCH HE PITCHED						WHAT HE GAVE UP												THE RESULTS					
Year Team	Lg	G	GS	CG	GF	IP	BFP	H	R	ER	HR	SH	SF	HB	TBB	IBB	SO	WP	Bk	W	L	Pct.	ShO	Sv	ERA
1989 Texas	AL	73	0	0	24	73.2	314	60	28	24	2	6	3	4	42	9	63	6	0	3	4	.429	0	2	2.93
1990 Texas	AL	69	3	0	46	97.2	428	93	40	34	6	7	4	1	42	5	74	5	0	10	6	.625	0	15	3.13
1991 Texas	AL	63	9	0	20	109.2	511	121	80	66	14	9	5	6	61	7	73	3	1	10	10	.500	0	5	5.42
1992 Texas	AL	81	0	0	38	78.2	337	80	32	27	7	4	1	0	26	8	70	4	1	3	6	.333	0	6	3.09
1993 Texas	AL	35	33	5	0	208.1	885	210	108	95	18	7	5	4	71	2	140	6	5	16	10	.615	0	0	4.10
5 ML YEARS		321	45	5	128	568	2475	564	288	246	47	33	18	15	242	31	420	24	7	42	36	.538	0	28	3.90

Kevin Rogers

Pitches: Left   **Bats:** Both   **Pos:** RP   **Ht:** 6' 1"   **Wt:** 198   **Born:** 08/20/68   **Age:** 25

		HOW MUCH HE PITCHED						WHAT HE GAVE UP												THE RESULTS					
Year Team	Lg	G	GS	CG	GF	IP	BFP	H	R	ER	HR	SH	SF	HB	TBB	IBB	SO	WP	Bk	W	L	Pct.	ShO	Sv	ERA
1988 Pocatello	R	13	13	1	0	69.2	314	73	51	48	4	0	3	2	35	0	71	5	4	2	8	.200	0	0	6.20
1989 Clinton	A	29	28	4	0	169.1	722	128	74	48	4	2	6	6	78	1	168	5	7	13	8	.619	0	0	2.55
1990 San Jose	A	28	26	1	1	172	731	143	86	69	9	6	8	11	68	1	186	19	3	14	5	.737	1	0	3.61
1991 Shreveport	AA	22	22	2	0	118	528	124	63	44	8	5	5	2	54	4	108	11	2	4	6	.400	0	0	3.36
1992 Shreveport	AA	16	16	2	0	101	413	87	34	29	3	2	1	4	29	0	110	7	0	8	5	.615	2	0	2.58
Phoenix	AAA	11	11	1	0	69.2	287	63	34	31	0	5	3	1	22	1	62	2	1	3	3	.500	1	0	4.00
1992 San Francisco	NL	6	6	0	0	34	148	37	17	16	4	2	0	1	13	1	26	2	0	0	2	.000	0	0	4.24
1993 San Francisco	NL	64	0	0	24	80.2	334	71	28	24	3	0	1	4	28	5	62	3	0	2	2	.500	0	0	2.68
2 ML YEARS		70	6	0	24	114.2	482	108	45	40	7	2	1	5	41	6	88	5	0	2	4	.333	0	0	3.14

Mel Rojas

Pitches: Right **Bats:** Right **Pos:** RP   **Ht:** 5'11" **Wt:** 195 **Born:** 12/10/66 **Age:** 27

Year Team	Lg	G	GS	CG	GF	IP	BFP	H	R	ER	HR	SH	SF	HB	TBB	IBB	SO	WP	Bk	W	L	Pct.	ShO	Sv	ERA
1990 Montreal	NL	23	0	0	5	40	173	34	17	16	5	2	0	2	24	4	26	2	0	3	1	.750	0	1	3.60
1991 Montreal	NL	37	0	0	13	48	200	42	21	20	4	0	2	1	13	1	37	3	0	3	3	.500	0	6	3.75
1992 Montreal	NL	68	0	0	26	100.2	399	71	17	16	2	4	2	2	34	8	70	2	0	7	1	.875	0	10	1.43
1993 Montreal	NL	66	0	0	25	88.1	378	80	39	29	6	8	6	4	30	3	48	5	0	5	8	.385	0	10	2.95
4 ML YEARS		194	0	0	69	277	1150	227	94	81	17	14	10	9	101	16	181	12	0	18	13	.581	0	27	2.63

Marc Ronan

Bats: Left **Throws:** Right **Pos:** C   **Ht:** 6'2" **Wt:** 190 **Born:** 09/19/69 **Age:** 24

Year Team	Lg	G	AB	H	2B	3B	HR	(Hm	Rd)	TB	R	RBI	TBB	IBB	SO	HBP	SH	SF	SB	CS	SB%	GDP	Avg	OBP	SLG
1990 Hamilton	A	56	167	38	6	0	1	--	--	47	14	15	15	0	37	1	0	3	1	2	.33	3	.228	.290	.281
1991 Savannah	A	108	343	81	10	1	0	--	--	93	41	45	37	1	54	4	3	1	11	2	.85	13	.236	.317	.271
1992 Springfield	A	110	376	81	19	2	6	--	--	122	45	48	23	2	58	1	0	4	4	5	.44	11	.215	.260	.324
1993 St.Pete	A	25	87	21	5	0	0	--	--	32	13	6	6	0	10	0	3	2	0	0	.00	1	.310	.347	.368
Arkansas	AA	96	281	60	16	1	7	--	--	99	33	34	26	2	47	2	3	3	1	3	.25	7	.214	.282	.352
1993 St. Louis	NL	6	12	1	0	0	0	(0	0)	1	0	0	0	0	5	0	0	0	0	0	.00	0	.083	.083	.083

John Roper

Pitches: Right **Bats:** Right **Pos:** SP   **Ht:** 6'0" **Wt:** 175 **Born:** 11/21/71 **Age:** 22

Year Team	Lg	G	GS	CG	GF	IP	BFP	H	R	ER	HR	SH	SF	HB	TBB	IBB	SO	WP	Bk	W	L	Pct.	ShO	Sv	ERA
1990 Reds	R	13	13	0	0	74	281	41	10	8	1	0	0	3	31	0	76	2	0	7	2	.778	0	0	0.97
1991 Chston-Wv	A	27	27	5	0	186.2	741	133	59	48	5	1	5	4	67	0	189	8	1	14	9	.609	3	0	2.31
1992 Chattanooga	AA	20	20	1	0	120.2	513	115	57	55	11	5	6	4	37	2	99	15	5	10	9	.526	1	0	4.10
1993 Indianapls	AAA	12	12	0	0	54.2	248	56	33	27	12	0	0	3	30	1	42	2	2	3	5	.375	0	0	4.45
1993 Cincinnati	NL	16	15	0	0	80	360	92	51	50	10	5	3	4	36	3	54	5	1	2	5	.286	0	0	5.63

Rico Rossy

Bats: Right **Throws:** Right **Pos:** 2B/3B/SS   **Ht:** 5'10" **Wt:** 175 **Born:** 02/16/64 **Age:** 30

Year Team	Lg	G	AB	H	2B	3B	HR	(Hm	Rd)	TB	R	RBI	TBB	IBB	SO	HBP	SH	SF	SB	CS	SB%	GDP	Avg	OBP	SLG
1993 Omaha *	AAA	37	131	39	10	1	5	--	--	66	25	21	20	1	19	3	0	1	3	2	.60	1	.298	.400	.504
1991 Atlanta	NL	5	1	0	0	0	0	(0	0)	0	0	0	0	0	1	0	0	0	0	0	.00	0	.000	.000	.000
1992 Kansas City	AL	59	149	32	8	1	1	(0	1)	45	21	12	20	1	20	1	7	1	0	3	.00	6	.215	.310	.302
1993 Kansas City	AL	46	86	19	4	0	2	(2	0)	29	10	12	9	0	11	1	1	0	0	0	.00	0	.221	.302	.337
3 ML YEARS		110	236	51	12	1	3	(2	1)	74	31	24	29	1	32	2	8	1	0	3	.00	6	.216	.306	.314

Rich Rowland

Bats: Right **Throws:** Right **Pos:** C   **Ht:** 6'1" **Wt:** 215 **Born:** 02/25/67 **Age:** 27

Year Team	Lg	G	AB	H	2B	3B	HR	(Hm	Rd)	TB	R	RBI	TBB	IBB	SO	HBP	SH	SF	SB	CS	SB%	GDP	Avg	OBP	SLG
1988 Bristol	R	56	186	51	10	1	4	--	--	75	29	41	27	1	39	1	0	3	1	2	.33	2	.274	.364	.403
1989 Fayetteville	A	108	375	102	17	1	9	--	--	148	43	59	54	2	98	3	3	3	4	1	.80	8	.272	.366	.395
1990 London	AA	47	161	46	10	0	8	--	--	80	22	30	20	3	33	3	0	1	1	1	.50	7	.286	.373	.497
Toledo	AAA	62	192	50	12	0	7	--	--	83	28	22	15	0	33	1	3	2	2	3	.40	3	.260	.314	.432
1991 Toledo	AAA	109	383	104	25	0	13	--	--	168	56	68	60	3	77	0	0	1	4	2	.67	8	.272	.374	.439
1992 Toledo	AAA	136	473	111	19	1	25	--	--	207	75	82	56	6	112	3	0	4	9	3	.75	20	.235	.317	.438
1993 Toledo	AAA	96	325	87	24	2	21	--	--	178	58	59	51	3	72	3	0	3	1	6	.14	11	.268	.369	.548
1990 Detroit	AL	7	19	3	1	0	0	(0	0)	4	3	0	2	1	4	0	0	0	0	0	.00	1	.158	.238	.211
1991 Detroit	AL	4	4	1	0	0	0	(0	0)	1	0	1	1	0	2	0	0	1	0	0	.00	0	.250	.333	.250
1992 Detroit	AL	6	14	3	0	0	0	(0	0)	3	2	0	3	0	3	0	0	0	0	0	.00	1	.214	.353	.214
1993 Detroit	AL	21	46	10	3	0	0	(0	0)	13	2	4	5	0	16	0	1	0	0	0	.00	1	.217	.294	.283
4 ML YEARS		38	83	17	4	0	0	(0	0)	21	7	5	11	1	25	0	1	1	0	0	.00	3	.205	.295	.253

Stan Royer

Bats: Right **Throws:** Right **Pos:** 3B   **Ht:** 6'3" **Wt:** 195 **Born:** 08/31/67 **Age:** 26

Year Team	Lg	G	AB	H	2B	3B	HR	(Hm	Rd)	TB	R	RBI	TBB	IBB	SO	HBP	SH	SF	SB	CS	SB%	GDP	Avg	OBP	SLG
1988 Sou Oregon	A	73	286	91	19	3	6	--	--	134	47	48	33	1	71	2	1	4	1	0	1.00	6	.318	.388	.469
1989 Tacoma	AAA	6	19	5	1	0	0	--	--	6	2	2	2	0	6	0	0	0	0	0	.00	1	.263	.333	.316
Modesto	A	127	476	120	28	1	11	--	--	183	54	69	58	3	132	1	2	2	3	2	.60	11	.252	.333	.384
1990 Huntsville	AA	137	527	136	29	3	14	--	--	213	69	89	43	0	113	3	8	4	4	1	.80	13	.258	.315	.404
Louisville	AAA	4	15	4	1	1	0	--	--	7	1	4	2	0	5	0	0	0	0	0	.00	0	.267	.353	.467
1991 Louisville	AAA	138	523	133	29	6	14	--	--	216	48	74	43	1	126	3	0	6	1	2	.33	13	.254	.311	.413

Year	Team	Lg	G	AB	H	2B	3B	HR	(IBB HBP)	TB	R	RBI	BB	IBB	SO	SB	CS	GDP	SH	SF	E	DP	Avg	OBP	Slg
1992	Louisville	AAA	124	444	125	31	2	11	-- --	193	55	77	32	2	74	4	4	4	0	0	.00	17	.282	.333	.435
1993	Louisville	AAA	98	368	103	19	0	16	-- --	170	46	54	33	2	74	0	3	5	2	0	1.00	9	.280	.335	.462
1991	St. Louis	NL	9	21	6	1	0	0	(0 0)	7	1	1	1	0	2	0	0	0	0	0	.00	0	.286	.318	.333
1992	St. Louis	NL	13	31	10	2	0	2	(1 1)	18	6	9	1	0	4	0	0	1	0	0	.00	0	.323	.333	.581
1993	St. Louis	NL	24	46	14	2	0	1	(0 1)	19	4	8	2	0	14	0	0	0	0	0	.00	2	.304	.333	.413
	3 ML YEARS		46	98	30	5	0	3	(1 2)	44	11	18	4	0	20	0	0	1	0	1	.00	2	.306	.330	.449

Kirk Rueter

Pitches: Left **Bats:** Left **Pos:** SP **Ht:** 6' 3" **Wt:** 190 **Born:** 12/01/70 **Age:** 23

			HOW MUCH HE PITCHED					WHAT HE GAVE UP										THE RESULTS					
Year	Team	Lg	G	GS	CG	GF	IP	BFP	H	R	ER	HR	SH	SF	HB	TBB	IBB	SO	WP	Bk	W	L	Pct.	ShO	Sv	ERA
1991	Expos	R	5	4	0	0	19	76	16	5	2	0	2	1	0	4	0	19	1	0	1	1	.500	0	0	0.95
	Sumter	A	8	5	0	1	40.2	160	32	8	6	3	1	0	0	10	0	27	1	0	3	1	.750	0	0	1.33
1992	Rockford	A	26	26	6	0	174.1	697	150	68	50	5	10	3	1	36	2	153	4	1	11	9	.550	2	0	2.58
1993	Harrisburg	AA	9	8	1	1	59.2	225	47	10	9	4	2	0	0	7	0	36	1	0	5	0	1.000	1	0	1.36
	Ottawa	AAA	7	7	1	0	43.1	174	46	20	13	7	1	1	0	3	0	27	0	0	4	2	.667	0	0	2.70
1993	Montreal	NL	14	14	1	0	85.2	341	85	33	26	5	1	0	0	18	1	31	0	0	8	0	1.000	0	0	2.73

Scott Ruffcorn

Pitches: Right **Bats:** Right **Pos:** SP **Ht:** 6' 4" **Wt:** 215 **Born:** 12/29/69 **Age:** 24

			HOW MUCH HE PITCHED					WHAT HE GAVE UP										THE RESULTS					
Year	Team	Lg	G	GS	CG	GF	IP	BFP	H	R	ER	HR	SH	SF	HB	TBB	IBB	SO	WP	Bk	W	L	Pct.	ShO	Sv	ERA
1991	White Sox	R	4	2	0	1	11.1	49	8	7	4	0	0	0	0	5	0	15	1	1	0	0	.000	0	0	3.18
	South Bend	A	9	9	0	0	43.2	193	35	26	19	1	2	1	2	25	0	45	1	2	1	3	.250	0	0	3.92
1992	Sarasota	A	25	24	2	0	160.1	642	122	53	39	7	4	5	3	39	0	140	3	1	14	5	.737	0	0	2.19
1993	Birmingham	AA	20	20	3	0	135	563	108	47	41	6	5	0	4	52	0	141	7	0	9	4	.692	3	0	2.73
	Nashville	AAA	7	6	1	0	45	172	30	16	14	5	2	1	0	8	1	44	3	0	2	2	.500	0	0	2.80
1993	Chicago	AL	3	2	0	1	10	46	9	11	9	2	1	1	0	10	0	2	1	0	0	2	.000	0	0	8.10

Bruce Ruffin

Pitches: Left **Bats:** Both **Pos:** RP/SP **Ht:** 6' 2" **Wt:** 213 **Born:** 10/04/63 **Age:** 30

			HOW MUCH HE PITCHED					WHAT HE GAVE UP										THE RESULTS					
Year	Team	Lg	G	GS	CG	GF	IP	BFP	H	R	ER	HR	SH	SF	HB	TBB	IBB	SO	WP	Bk	W	L	Pct.	ShO	Sv	ERA
1986	Philadelphia	NL	21	21	6	0	146.1	600	138	53	40	6	2	4	1	44	6	70	0	1	9	4	.692	0	0	2.46
1987	Philadelphia	NL	35	35	3	0	204.2	884	236	118	99	17	8	10	2	73	4	93	6	0	11	14	.440	1	0	4.35
1988	Philadelphia	NL	15	15	3	14	144.1	646	151	86	71	7	10	3	3	80	6	82	12	0	6	10	.375	0	3	4.43
1989	Philadelphia	NL	24	23	1	0	125.2	576	152	69	62	10	8	1	0	62	6	70	8	0	6	10	.375	0	0	4.44
1990	Philadelphia	NL	32	25	2	1	149	678	178	99	89	14	10	6	1	62	7	79	3	2	6	13	.316	1	0	5.38
1991	Philadelphia	NL	31	15	1	2	119	508	125	52	50	6	6	4	1	38	3	85	4	0	4	7	.364	1	0	3.78
1992	Milwaukee	AL	25	6	1	6	58	272	66	43	43	7	3	3	0	41	3	45	2	0	1	6	.143	0	0	6.67
1993	Colorado	NL	59	12	0	8	139.2	619	145	71	60	10	4	5	1	69	9	126	8	0	6	5	.545	0	2	3.87
	8 ML YEARS		282	152	17	31	1086.2	4783	1191	591	514	77	51	36	9	469	44	650	43	3	49	69	.415	3	5	4.26

Johnny Ruffin

Pitches: Right **Bats:** Right **Pos:** RP **Ht:** 6' 3" **Wt:** 172 **Born:** 07/29/71 **Age:** 22

			HOW MUCH HE PITCHED					WHAT HE GAVE UP										THE RESULTS					
Year	Team	Lg	G	GS	CG	GF	IP	BFP	H	R	ER	HR	SH	SF	HB	TBB	IBB	SO	WP	Bk	W	L	Pct.	ShO	Sv	ERA
1988	White Sox	R	13	11	1	1	58.2	246	43	27	15	3	1	2	4	22	0	31	9	2	4	2	.667	0	0	2.30
1989	Utica	A	15	15	0	0	88.1	376	67	43	33	3	5	1	1	46	0	92	8	0	4	8	.333	0	0	3.36
1990	South Bend	A	24	24	0	0	123	568	117	86	57	7	1	5	3	82	0	92	17	4	7	6	.538	0	0	4.17
1991	Sarasota	A	26	26	6	0	158.2	655	126	68	57	9	3	5	5	62	0	117	10	2	11	4	.733	2	0	3.23
1992	Birmingham	AA	10	10	0	0	47.2	228	51	48	32	3	1	5	1	34	0	44	9	0	0	7	.000	0	0	6.04
	Sarasota	A	23	8	0	6	62.2	290	56	46	41	5	2	1	4	41	0	61	10	2	3	7	.300	0	0	5.89
1993	Birmingham	AA	11	0	0	10	22.1	92	16	9	7	2	2	1	0	9	1	23	0	0	0	4	.000	0	2	2.82
	Nashville	AAA	29	0	0	11	60	242	48	24	22	5	2	2	1	16	4	69	10	0	3	4	.429	0	1	3.30
	Indianapols	AAA	3	0	0	3	6.2	25	3	1	1	0	1	0	0	2	1	6	0	0	1	1	.500	0	1	1.35
1993	Cincinnati	NL	21	0	0	5	37.2	159	36	16	15	4	1	0	1	11	1	30	2	0	2	1	.667	0	2	3.58

Scott Ruskin

Pitches: Left **Bats:** Right **Pos:** RP **Ht:** 6' 2" **Wt:** 195 **Born:** 06/08/63 **Age:** 31

			HOW MUCH HE PITCHED					WHAT HE GAVE UP										THE RESULTS					
Year	Team	Lg	G	GS	CG	GF	IP	BFP	H	R	ER	HR	SH	SF	HB	TBB	IBB	SO	WP	Bk	W	L	Pct.	ShO	Sv	ERA
1993	Indianapols*	AAA	49	2	0	42	56	245	60	34	32	8	1	1	0	22	3	41	1	0	1	5	.167	0	28	5.14
1990	2 ML Teams		67	0	0	12	75.1	336	75	28	23	4	5	2	2	38	6	57	3	1	3	2	.600	0	2	2.75
1991	Montreal	NL	64	0	0	24	63.2	275	57	31	30	4	5	0	3	30	2	46	5	0	4	4	.500	0	6	4.24
1992	Cincinnati	NL	57	0	0	19	53.2	234	56	31	30	6	7	2	1	20	4	43	1	0	4	3	.571	0	5	5.03
1993	Cincinnati	NL	4	0	0	0	1	8	3	2	2	1	0	0	0	2	0	0	0	0	0	0	.000	0	0	18.00
1990	Pittsburgh	NL	44	0	0	8	47.2	221	50	21	16	2	3	2	2	28	3	34	3	1	2	2	.500	0	2	3.02

Team	Lg	G	GS	CG	GF	IP	BFP	H	R	ER	HR	SH	SF	HB	TBB	IBB	SO	WP	Bk	W	L	Pct.	ShO	Sv	ERA
Montreal	NL	23	0	0	4	27.2	115	25	7	7	2	2	0		10	3	23	0	0	1	0	1.000	0	0	2.28
4 ML YEARS		192	0	0	55	193.2	853	191	92	85	15	17	4	6	90	12	146	9	1	11	9	.550	0	8	3.95

Jeff Russell

Pitches: Right Bats: Right Pos: RP Ht: 6' 3" Wt: 205 Born: 09/02/61 Age: 32

		HOW MUCH HE PITCHED						WHAT HE GAVE UP												THE RESULTS					
Year Team	Lg	G	GS	CG	GF	IP	BFP	H	R	ER	HR	SH	SF	HB	TBB	IBB	SO	WP	Bk	W	L	Pct.	ShO	Sv	ERA
1983 Cincinnati	NL	10	10	2	0	68.1	282	58	30	23	7	6	5	0	22	3	40	1	1	4	5	.444	0	0	3.03
1984 Cincinnati	NL	33	30	4	1	181.2	787	186	97	86	15	8	3	4	65	8	101	3	3	6	18	.250	2	0	4.26
1985 Texas	AL	13	13	0	0	62	295	85	55	52	10	1	3	2	27	1	44	2	0	3	6	.333	0	0	7.55
1986 Texas	AL	37	0	0	9	82	338	74	40	31	11	1	2	1	31	2	54	5	0	5	2	.714	0	2	3.40
1987 Texas	AL	52	2	0	12	97.1	442	109	56	48	9	0	5	2	52	5	56	6	1	5	4	.556	0	3	4.44
1988 Texas	AL	34	24	5	1	188.2	793	183	86	80	15	4	3	7	66	3	88	5	7	10	9	.526	0	0	3.82
1989 Texas	AL	71	0	0	66	72.2	278	45	21	16	4	1	3	3	24	5	77	6	0	6	4	.600	0	38	1.98
1990 Texas	AL	27	0	0	22	25.1	111	23	15	12	1	3	1	0	16	5	16	2	0	1	5	.167	0	10	4.26
1991 Texas	AL	68	0	0	56	79.1	336	71	36	29	11	3	4	1	26	1	52	6	0	6	4	.600	0	30	3.29
1992 2 ML Teams		59	0	0	46	66.1	276	55	14	12	3	1	2	2	25	3	48	3	0	4	3	.571	0	30	1.63
1993 Boston	AL	51	0	0	48	46.2	189	39	16	14	1	1	4	1	14	1	45	2	0	1	4	.200	0	33	2.70
1992 Texas	AL	51	0	0	42	56.2	241	51	14	12	3	1	2	2	22	3	43	3	0	2	3	.400	0	28	1.91
Oakland	AL	8	0	0	4	9.2	35	4	0	0	0	0	0	0	3	0	5	0	0	2	0	1.000	0	2	1.00
11 ML YEARS		455	79	11	261	970.1	4127	928	466	403	87	29	35	23	368	37	621	41	12	51	64	.443	2	146	3.74

John Russell

Bats: Right Throws: Right Pos: C Ht: 6' 0" Wt: 195 Born: 01/05/61 Age: 33

		BATTING																	BASERUNNING				PERCENTAGES		
Year Team	Lg	G	AB	H	2B	3B	HR	(Hm	Rd)	TB	R	RBI	TBB	IBB	SO	HBP	SH	SF	SB	CS	SB%	GDP	Avg	OBP	SLG
1984 Philadelphia	NL	39	99	28	8	1	2	(1	1)	44	11	11	12	2	33	0	0	3	0	1	.00	2	.283	.351	.444
1985 Philadelphia	NL	81	216	47	12	0	9	(6	3)	86	22	23	18	0	72	0	0	0	2	0	1.00	5	.218	.278	.398
1986 Philadelphia	NL	93	315	76	21	2	13	(8	5)	140	35	60	25	2	103	3	1	4	0	1	.00	6	.241	.300	.444
1987 Philadelphia	NL	24	62	9	1	0	3	(1	2)	19	5	8	3	0	17	0	0	0	0	1	.00	4	.145	.185	.306
1988 Philadelphia	NL	22	49	12	1	0	2	(1	1)	19	5	4	3	0	15	1	0	0	0	0	.00	2	.245	.302	.388
1989 Atlanta	NL	74	159	29	2	0	2	(1	1)	37	14	9	8	1	53	1	0	1	0	0	.00	4	.182	.225	.233
1990 Texas	AL	68	128	35	4	0	2	(0	2)	45	16	8	11	2	41	0	1	0	1	0	1.00	3	.273	.331	.352
1991 Texas	AL	22	27	3	0	0	0	(0	0)	3	3	1	1	0	7	0	0	1	0	0	.00	0	.111	.138	.111
1992 Texas	AL	7	10	1	0	0	0	(0	0)	1	1	1	2	1	4	1	0	0	0	0	.00	0	.100	.231	.100
1993 Texas	AL	18	22	5	1	0	1	(1	0)	9	1	3	2	0	10	0	0	0	0	0	.00	0	.227	.292	.409
10 ML YEARS		448	1087	245	50	3	34	(19	15)	403	113	129	84	7	355	6	2	10	3	3	.50	26	.225	.282	.371

Ken Ryan

Pitches: Right Bats: Right Pos: RP Ht: 6' 3" Wt: 215 Born: 10/24/68 Age: 25

		HOW MUCH HE PITCHED						WHAT HE GAVE UP												THE RESULTS					
Year Team	Lg	G	GS	CG	GF	IP	BFP	H	R	ER	HR	SH	SF	HB	TBB	IBB	SO	WP	Bk	W	L	Pct.	ShO	Sv	ERA
1986 Elmira	A	13	1	0	10	21.2	103	20	14	14	0	2	2	1	21	2	22	1	0	2	2	.500	0	0	5.82
1987 Greensboro	A	28	19	2	8	121.1	554	139	88	74	10	1	7	3	63	8	75	10	3	3	12	.200	0	0	5.49
1988 Lynchburg	A	19	14	0	2	71.1	344	79	51	49	4	2	1	3	45	5	49	5	3	2	7	.222	0	0	6.18
1989 Winter Havn	A	24	22	3	1	137	586	114	58	48	5	4	4	7	81	0	78	8	4	8	8	.500	0	0	3.15
1990 Lynchburg	A	28	28	3	0	161.1	735	182	104	92	10	6	5	6	82	0	109	19	1	6	14	.300	1	0	5.13
1991 Winter Havn	A	21	1	0	11	52.2	213	40	15	12	1	0	0	2	19	0	53	3	1	1	3	.250	0	1	2.05
New Britain	AA	14	0	0	6	26	116	23	7	5	2	4	0	1	12	1	26	2	0	1	2	.333	0	1	1.73
Pawtucket	AAA	9	0	0	4	18.1	80	15	11	10	2	2	2	1	11	1	14	2	0	1	0	1.000	0	1	4.91
1992 New Britain	AA	44	0	0	42	50.2	220	44	17	11	0	0	2	1	24	2	51	4	0	1	4	.200	0	22	1.95
Pawtucket	AAA	9	0	0	9	8.2	36	6	2	2	1	0	0	0	4	0	6	0	0	2	0	1.000	0	7	2.08
1993 Pawtucket	AAA	18	0	0	15	25.1	112	18	9	7	1	3	1	2	17	4	22	2	1	0	2	.000	0	8	2.49
1992 Boston	AL	7	0	0	6	7	30	4	5	5	2	1	1	0	5	0	5	0	0	0	0	.000	0	1	6.43
1993 Boston	AL	47	0	0	26	50	223	43	23	20	2	4	4	3	29	5	49	3	0	7	2	.778	0	1	3.60
2 ML YEARS		54	0	0	32	57	253	47	28	25	4	5	5	3	34	5	54	3	0	7	2	.778	0	2	3.95

Nolan Ryan

Pitches: Right Bats: Right Pos: SP Ht: 6' 2" Wt: 212 Born: 01/31/47 Age: 47

		HOW MUCH HE PITCHED						WHAT HE GAVE UP												THE RESULTS					
Year Team	Lg	G	GS	CG	GF	IP	BFP	H	R	ER	HR	SH	SF	HB	TBB	IBB	SO	WP	Bk	W	L	Pct.	ShO	Sv	ERA
1966 New York	NL	2	1	0	0	3	17	5	5	5	1	0	0	0	3	1	6	1	0	0	1	.000	0	0	15.00
1968 New York	NL	21	18	3	1	134	559	93	50	46	12	12	4	4	75	4	133	7	0	6	9	.400	0	0	3.09
1969 New York	NL	25	10	2	4	89	375	60	38	35	3	2	2	1	53	3	92	1	3	6	3	.667	0	1	3.54
1970 New York	NL	27	19	5	4	132	570	86	59	50	10	8	4	4	97	2	125	8	0	7	11	.389	2	1	3.41
1971 New York	NL	30	26	3	1	152	705	125	78	67	8	3	0	15	116	4	137	6	1	10	14	.417	0	0	3.97
1972 California	AL	39	39	20	0	284	1154	166	80	72	14	11	3	10	157	4	329	18	0	19	16	.543	9	0	2.28

Year Team	Lg	G	GS	CG	GF	IP	BFP	H	R	ER	HR	SH	SF	HB	TBB	IBB	SO	WP	Bk	W	L	Pct.	ShO	Sv	ERA
1973 California	AL	41	39	26	2	326	1355	238	113	104	18	7	7	7	**162**	2	**383**	15	0	21	16	.568	4	1	2.87
1974 California	AL	42	41	26	1	332.2	1392	221	127	107	18	12	4	9	**202**	3	**367**	9	0	22	16	.579	3	0	2.89
1975 California	AL	28	28	10	0	198	864	152	90	76	13	6	7	7	132	0	186	12	0	14	12	.538	5	0	3.45
1976 California	AL	39	39	21	0	284	1196	193	117	106	13	13	4	5	**183**	2	**327**	5	2	17	**18**	.486	**7**	0	3.36
1977 California	AL	37	37	**22**	0	299	**1272**	198	110	92	12	**22**	10	9	**204**	7	**341**	21	3	19	16	.543	4	0	2.77
1978 California	AL	31	31	14	0	235	1008	183	106	97	12	11	**14**	3	**148**	7	**260**	**13**	2	10	13	.435	3	0	3.71
1979 California	AL	34	34	17	0	223	937	169	104	89	15	8	10	6	114	3	**223**	9	0	16	14	.533	5	0	3.59
1980 Houston	NL	35	35	4	0	234	982	205	100	87	10	7	7	3	98	1	**200**	10	1	11	10	.524	2	0	3.35
1981 Houston	NL	21	21	5	0	149	605	99	34	28	2	5	3	1	68	1	**140**	**16**	2	11	5	.688	3	0	**1.69**
1982 Houston	NL	35	35	10	0	250.1	1050	196	100	88	20	9	3	**8**	109	3	**245**	18	2	16	12	.571	3	0	3.16
1983 Houston	NL	29	29	5	0	196.1	804	134	74	65	9	7	5	4	101	3	**183**	5	1	14	9	.609	2	0	2.98
1984 Houston	NL	30	30	5	0	183.2	760	143	78	62	12	4	6	4	69	2	**197**	6	3	12	11	.522	2	0	3.04
1985 Houston	NL	35	35	4	0	232	983	205	108	98	12	11	**12**	9	95	8	**209**	14	2	10	12	.455	0	0	3.80
1986 Houston	NL	30	30	1	0	178	729	119	72	66	14	5	4	4	82	5	**194**	**15**	0	12	8	.600	0	0	3.34
1987 Houston	NL	34	34	0	0	211.2	873	154	75	65	14	9	1	4	87	2	**270**	10	2	8	16	.333	0	0	**2.76**
1988 Houston	NL	33	33	4	0	220	930	186	98	86	18	10	8	7	87	6	**228**	10	7	12	11	.522	1	0	3.52
1989 Texas	AL	32	32	6	0	239.1	988	162	96	85	17	9	5	9	98	3	**301**	**19**	1	16	10	.615	2	0	3.20
1990 Texas	AL	30	30	5	0	204	818	137	86	78	18	3	5	7	74	2	**232**	9	1	13	9	.591	2	0	3.44
1991 Texas	AL	27	27	2	0	173	683	102	58	56	12	3	9	5	72	0	203	8	0	12	6	.667	2	0	2.91
1992 Texas	AL	27	27	2	0	157.1	675	138	75	65	9	6	7	12	69	0	157	9	0	5	5	.357	0	0	3.72
1993 Texas	AL	13	13	0	0	66.1	291	54	47	36	5	2	2	1	40	0	46	3	0	5	5	.500	0	0	4.88
27 ML YEARS		807	773	222	13	5386.2	22575	3923	2178	1911	321	205	146	158	2795	78	5714	277	33	324	292	.526	61	3	3.19

Bret Saberhagen

Pitches: Right **Bats:** Right **Pos:** SP   **Ht:** 6' 1" **Wt:** 190 **Born:** 04/11/64 **Age:** 30

		HOW MUCH HE PITCHED						WHAT HE GAVE UP												THE RESULTS				
Year Team	Lg	G	GS	CG	GF	IP	BFP	H	R	ER	HR	SH	SF	HB	TBB	IBB	SO	WP	Bk	W	L	Pct.	ShO	Sv	ERA
1984 Kansas City	AL	38	18	2	9	157.2	634	138	71	61	13	8	5	2	36	4	73	7	1	10	11	.476	1	1	3.48
1985 Kansas City	AL	32	32	10	0	235.1	931	211	79	75	19	9	7	1	38	1	158	1	3	20	6	.769	1	0	2.87
1986 Kansas City	AL	30	25	4	4	156	652	165	77	72	15	3	3	2	29	1	112	1	1	7	12	.368	2	0	4.15
1987 Kansas City	AL	33	33	15	0	257	1048	246	99	96	27	8	5	6	53	2	163	6	1	18	10	.643	4	0	3.36
1988 Kansas City	AL	35	35	9	0	260.2	1089	**271**	122	110	18	8	10	4	59	5	171	9	0	14	16	.467	0	0	3.80
1989 Kansas City	AL	36	35	**12**	0	262.1	1021	209	74	63	13	9	6	2	43	6	193	8	1	**23**	6	**.793**	4	0	**2.16**
1990 Kansas City	AL	20	20	5	0	135	561	146	52	49	9	4	4	1	28	1	87	1	0	5	9	.357	0	0	3.27
1991 Kansas City	AL	28	28	7	0	196.1	789	165	76	67	12	8	3	9	45	5	136	8	1	13	8	.619	2	0	3.07
1992 New York	NL	17	15	1	0	97.2	397	84	39	38	6	3	3	4	27	1	81	1	2	3	5	.375	1	0	3.50
1993 New York	NL	19	19	4	0	139.1	556	131	55	51	11	6	6	3	17	4	93	2	2	7	7	.500	1	0	3.29
10 ML YEARS		288	260	69	13	1897.1	7678	1766	744	682	143	66	52	34	375	30	1267	44	12	120	90	.571	16	1	3.24

Chris Sabo

Bats: Right **Throws:** Right **Pos:** 3B   **Ht:** 6' 0" **Wt:** 185 **Born:** 01/19/62 **Age:** 32

		BATTING														BASERUNNING				PERCENTAGES		
Year Team	Lg	G	AB	H	2B	3B	HR	(Hm | Rd)	TB	R	RBI	TBB	IBB	SO	HBP	SH	SF	SB	CS	SB%	GDP	Avg	OBP	SLG
1988 Cincinnati	NL	137	538	146	40	2	11	(8 | 3)	223	74	44	29	1	52	6	5	4	46	14	.77	12	.271	.314	.414
1989 Cincinnati	NL	82	304	79	21	1	6	(3 | 3)	120	40	29	25	2	33	1	4	2	14	9	.61	2	.260	.316	.395
1990 Cincinnati	NL	148	567	153	38	2	25	(15 | 10)	270	95	71	61	2	58	4	1	3	25	10	.71	8	.270	.343	.476
1991 Cincinnati	NL	153	582	175	35	3	26	(15 | 11)	294	91	88	44	3	79	6	5	3	19	6	.76	13	.301	.354	.505
1992 Cincinnati	NL	96	344	84	19	3	12	(8 | 4)	145	42	43	30	1	54	1	1	6	4	5	.44	12	.244	.302	.422
1993 Cincinnati	NL	148	552	143	33	2	21	(12 | 9)	243	86	82	43	5	105	6	2	8	6	4	.60	10	.259	.315	.440
6 ML YEARS		764	2887	780	186	13	101	(61 | 40)	1295	428	357	232	19	381	24	18	26	114	48	.70	57	.270	.327	.449

Roger Salkeld

Pitches: Right **Bats:** Right **Pos:** SP   **Ht:** 6' 5" **Wt:** 215 **Born:** 03/06/71 **Age:** 23

		HOW MUCH HE PITCHED						WHAT HE GAVE UP												THE RESULTS				
Year Team	Lg	G	GS	CG	GF	IP	BFP	H	R	ER	HR	SH	SF	HB	TBB	IBB	SO	WP	Bk	W	L	Pct.	ShO	Sv	ERA
1989 Bellingham	A	8	6	0	1	42	168	27	17	6	0	0	1	4	10	0	55	3	3	2	2	.500	0	0	1.29
1990 San Berndno	A	25	25	2	0	153.1	677	140	77	58	3	7	1	3	83	0	167	9	2	11	5	.688	0	0	3.40
1991 Jacksnville	AA	23	23	5	0	153.2	634	131	56	52	9	5	5	10	55	1	159	12	2	8	8	.500	0	0	3.05
Calgary	AAA	4	4	0	0	19.1	90	18	16	11	2	1	0	4	13	0	21	1	0	2	1	.667	0	0	5.12
1993 Jacksnville	AA	14	14	0	0	77	334	71	39	28	8	3	5	5	29	1	56	2	1	4	3	.571	0	0	3.27
1993 Seattle	AL	3	2	0	0	14.1	61	13	4	4	0	0	0	1	4	0	13	0	0	0	0	.000	0	0	2.51

190

Tim Salmon

Bats: Right **Throws:** Right **Pos:** RF   **Ht:** 6' 3" **Wt:** 220 **Born:** 08/24/68 **Age:** 25

								BATTING												BASERUNNING				PERCENTAGES		
Year Team	Lg	G	AB	H	2B	3B	HR	(Hm	Rd)	TB	R	RBI	TBB	IBB	SO	HBP	SH	SF	SB	CS	SB%	GDP	Avg	OBP	SLG
1989 Bend	A	55	196	48	6	5	6	--	--	82	37	31	33	0	61	6	1	2	2	4	.33	2	.245	.367	.418
1990 Palm Sprngs	A	36	118	34	6	0	2	--	--	46	19	21	21	0	44	4	0	0	11	1	.92	1	.288	.413	.390
Midland	AA	27	97	26	3	1	3	--	--	40	17	16	18	0	38	1	0	1	1	0	1.00	1	.268	.385	.412
1991 Midland	AA	131	465	114	26	4	23	--	--	217	100	94	89	1	166	6	3	2	12	6	.67	6	.245	.372	.467
1992 Edmonton	AAA	118	409	142	38	4	29	--	--	275	101	105	91	11	103	6	0	4	9	7	.56	9	.347	.469	.672
1992 California	AL	23	79	14	1	0	2	(1	1)	21	8	6	11	1	23	1	0	1	1	1	.50	1	.177	.283	.266
1993 California	AL	142	515	146	35	1	31	(23	8)	276	93	95	82	5	135	5	0	8	5	6	.45	6	.283	.382	.536
2 ML YEARS		165	594	160	36	1	33	(24	9)	297	101	101	93	6	158	6	0	9	6	7	.46	7	.269	.369	.500

Bill Sampen

Pitches: Right **Bats:** Right **Pos:** RP   **Ht:** 6' 2" **Wt:** 200 **Born:** 01/18/63 **Age:** 31

				HOW MUCH HE PITCHED						WHAT HE GAVE UP										THE RESULTS					
Year Team	Lg	G	GS	CG	GF	IP	BFP	H	R	ER	HR	SH	SF	HB	TBB	IBB	SO	WP	Bk	W	L	Pct.	ShO	Sv	ERA
1993 Omaha *	AAA	33	0	0	28	37	160	37	16	14	1	6	0	2	13	1	34	1	0	1	2	.333	0	8	3.41
1990 Montreal	NL	59	4	0	26	90.1	394	94	34	30	7	5	3	2	33	6	69	4	0	12	7	.632	0	2	2.99
1991 Montreal	NL	43	8	0	8	92.1	409	96	49	41	13	4	4	3	46	7	52	3	1	9	5	.643	0	0	4.00
1992 2 ML Teams		52	2	0	13	83	348	83	32	30	4	6	3	4	32	7	37	2	2	1	6	.143	0	0	3.25
1993 Kansas City	AL	18	0	0	3	18.1	89	25	12	12	1	2	0	4	9	0	9	2	0	2	2	.500	0	0	5.89
1992 Montreal	NL	44	1	0	10	63.1	267	62	22	22	4	5	1	1	29	6	23	1	2	1	4	.200	0	0	3.13
Kansas City	AL	8	1	0	3	19.2	81	21	10	8	0	1	2	3	3	1	14	1	0	0	0	.000	0	0	3.66
4 ML YEARS		172	14	0	50	284	1240	298	127	113	25	17	10	13	120	20	167	11	3	24	20	.545	0	2	3.58

Juan Samuel

Bats: Right **Throws:** Right **Pos:** 2B   **Ht:** 5'11" **Wt:** 180 **Born:** 12/09/60 **Age:** 33

								BATTING												BASERUNNING				PERCENTAGES		
Year Team	Lg	G	AB	H	2B	3B	HR	(Hm	Rd)	TB	R	RBI	TBB	IBB	SO	HBP	SH	SF	SB	CS	SB%	GDP	Avg	OBP	SLG
1983 Philadelphia	NL	18	65	18	1	2	2	(1	1)	29	14	5	4	1	16	1	0	1	3	2	.60	1	.277	.324	.446
1984 Philadelphia	NL	160	701	191	36	19	15	(8	7)	310	105	69	28	2	168	7	0	1	72	15	.83	6	.272	.307	.442
1985 Philadelphia	NL	161	663	175	31	13	19	(8	11)	289	101	74	33	2	141	6	2	5	53	19	.74	8	.264	.303	.436
1986 Philadelphia	NL	145	591	157	36	12	16	(10	6)	265	90	78	26	3	142	8	1	7	42	14	.75	8	.266	.302	.448
1987 Philadelphia	NL	160	655	178	37	15	28	(15	13)	329	113	100	60	5	162	5	0	6	35	15	.70	12	.272	.335	.502
1988 Philadelphia	NL	157	629	153	32	9	12	(7	5)	239	68	67	39	6	151	12	0	5	33	10	.77	8	.243	.298	.380
1989 2 ML Teams		137	532	125	16	2	11	(5	6)	178	69	48	42	2	120	11	2	2	42	12	.78	7	.235	.303	.335
1990 Los Angeles	NL	143	492	119	24	3	13	(6	7)	188	62	52	51	5	126	5	5	5	38	20	.66	8	.242	.316	.382
1991 Los Angeles	NL	153	594	161	22	6	12	(4	8)	231	74	58	49	4	133	3	10	3	23	8	.74	8	.271	.328	.389
1992 2 ML Teams		76	224	61	8	4	0	(0	0)	77	22	23	14	4	49	2	4	2	8	3	.73	2	.272	.318	.344
1993 Cincinnati	NL	103	261	60	10	4	4	(1	3)	90	31	26	23	3	53	3	0	2	9	7	.56	2	.230	.298	.345
1989 Philadelphia	NL	51	199	49	3	1	8	(3	5)	78	32	20	18	1	45	1	0	1	11	3	.79	2	.246	.311	.392
New York	NL	86	333	76	13	1	3	(2	1)	100	37	28	24	1	75	10	2	1	31	9	.78	5	.228	.299	.300
1992 Los Angeles	NL	47	122	32	3	1	0	(0	0)	37	7	15	7	3	22	1	4	2	2	2	.50	0	.262	.303	.303
Kansas City	AL	29	102	29	5	3	0	(0	0)	40	15	8	7	1	27	1	0	0	6	1	.86	2	.284	.336	.392
11 ML YEARS		1413	5407	1398	253	89	132	(65	67)	2225	749	600	369	37	1261	63	24	39	358	125	.74	70	.259	.311	.412

Rey Sanchez

Bats: Right **Throws:** Right **Pos:** SS   **Ht:** 5' 9" **Wt:** 170 **Born:** 10/05/67 **Age:** 26

								BATTING												BASERUNNING				PERCENTAGES		
Year Team	Lg	G	AB	H	2B	3B	HR	(Hm	Rd)	TB	R	RBI	TBB	IBB	SO	HBP	SH	SF	SB	CS	SB%	GDP	Avg	OBP	SLG
1991 Chicago	NL	13	23	6	0	0	0	(0	0)	6	1	2	4	0	3	0	0	0	0	0	.00	0	.261	.370	.261
1992 Chicago	NL	74	255	64	14	3	1	(1	0)	87	24	19	10	1	17	3	5	2	2	1	.67	7	.251	.285	.341
1993 Chicago	NL	105	344	97	11	2	0	(0	0)	112	35	28	15	7	22	3	9	2	1	1	.50	8	.282	.316	.326
3 ML YEARS		192	622	167	25	5	1	(1	0)	205	60	49	29	8	42	6	14	4	3	2	.60	15	.268	.306	.330

Ryne Sandberg

Bats: Right **Throws:** Right **Pos:** 2B   **Ht:** 6' 2" **Wt:** 185 **Born:** 09/18/59 **Age:** 34

								BATTING												BASERUNNING				PERCENTAGES		
Year Team	Lg	G	AB	H	2B	3B	HR	(Hm	Rd)	TB	R	RBI	TBB	IBB	SO	HBP	SH	SF	SB	CS	SB%	GDP	Avg	OBP	SLG
1993 Daytona *	A	2	5	1	0	0	1	--	--	4	2	2	1	0	0	0	0	0	0	0	.00	0	.200	.333	.800
Orlando *	AA	4	9	2	0	0	0	--	--	2	0	1	3	1	1	0	0	0	0	0	.00	0	.222	.417	.222
1981 Philadelphia	NL	13	6	1	0	0	0	(0	0)	1	2	0	0	0	1	0	0	0	0	0	.00	0	.167	.167	.167
1982 Chicago	NL	156	635	172	33	5	7	(5	2)	236	103	54	36	3	90	4	7	5	32	12	.73	7	.271	.312	.372
1983 Chicago	NL	158	633	165	25	4	8	(4	4)	219	94	48	51	3	79	3	7	5	37	11	.77	8	.261	.316	.351
1984 Chicago	NL	156	636	200	36	19	19	(11	8)	331	114	84	52	3	101	3	5	4	32	7	.82	7	.314	.367	.520
1985 Chicago	NL	153	609	186	31	6	26	(17	9)	307	113	83	57	5	97	1	2	4	54	11	.83	10	.305	.364	.504
1986 Chicago	NL	154	627	178	28	5	14	(8	6)	258	68	76	46	6	79	0	3	6	34	11	.76	11	.284	.330	.411

Year	Team	Lg	G	AB	H	2B	3B	HR	(Hm	Rd)	TB	R	RBI	TBB	IBB	SO	HBP	SH	SF	SB	CS	SB%	GDP	Avg	OBP	SLG
1987	Chicago	NL	132	523	154	25	2	16	(8	8)	231	81	59	59	4	79	2	1	2	21	2	.91	11	.294	.367	.442
1988	Chicago	NL	155	618	163	23	8	19	(10	9)	259	77	69	54	3	91	1	1	5	25	10	.71	14	.264	.322	.419
1989	Chicago	NL	157	606	176	25	5	30	(16	14)	301	104	76	59	8	85	4	1	2	15	5	.75	9	.290	.356	.497
1990	Chicago	NL	155	615	188	30	3	40	(25	15)	344	116	100	50	8	84	1	0	9	25	7	.78	8	.306	.354	.559
1991	Chicago	NL	158	585	170	32	2	26	(15	11)	284	104	100	87	4	89	2	1	9	22	8	.73	9	.291	.379	.485
1992	Chicago	NL	158	612	186	32	8	26	(16	10)	312	100	87	68	4	73	1	0	6	17	6	.74	13	.304	.371	.510
1993	Chicago	NL	117	456	141	20	0	9	(5	4)	188	67	45	37	1	62	2	2	6	9	2	.82	12	.309	.359	.412
13 ML YEARS			1822	7161	2080	340	67	240	(140	100)	3274	1143	881	656	52	1010	24	30	63	323	92	.78	119	.290	.349	.457

Deion Sanders

Bats: Left **Throws:** Left **Pos:** CF   **Ht:** 6' 1" **Wt:** 195 **Born:** 08/09/67 **Age:** 26

						BATTING														BASERUNNING				PERCENTAGES		
Year	Team	Lg	G	AB	H	2B	3B	HR	(Hm	Rd)	TB	R	RBI	TBB	IBB	SO	HBP	SH	SF	SB	CS	SB%	GDP	Avg	OBP	SLG
1989	New York	AL	14	47	11	2	0	2	(0	2)	19	7	7	3	1	8	0	0	0	1	0	1.00	0	.234	.280	.404
1990	New York	AL	57	133	21	2	2	3	(1	2)	36	24	9	13	0	27	1	1	1	8	2	.80	2	.158	.236	.271
1991	Atlanta	NL	54	110	21	1	2	4	(2	2)	38	16	13	12	0	23	0	1	0	11	3	.79	1	.191	.270	.345
1992	Atlanta	NL	97	303	92	6	14	8	(5	3)	150	54	28	18	0	52	2	1	1	26	9	.74	5	.304	.346	.495
1993	Atlanta	NL	95	272	75	18	6	6	(1	5)	123	42	28	16	3	42	3	1	2	19	7	.73	3	.276	.321	.452
5 ML YEARS			317	865	220	29	24	23	(9	14)	366	143	85	62	4	152	6	3	4	65	21	.76	11	.254	.307	.423

Reggie Sanders

Bats: Right **Throws:** Right **Pos:** RF   **Ht:** 6' 1" **Wt:** 180 **Born:** 12/01/67 **Age:** 26

						BATTING														BASERUNNING				PERCENTAGES		
Year	Team	Lg	G	AB	H	2B	3B	HR	(Hm	Rd)	TB	R	RBI	TBB	IBB	SO	HBP	SH	SF	SB	CS	SB%	GDP	Avg	OBP	SLG
1991	Cincinnati	NL	9	40	8	0	0	1	(0	1)	11	6	3	0	0	9	0	0	0	1	1	.50	1	.200	.200	.275
1992	Cincinnati	NL	116	385	104	26	6	12	(6	6)	178	62	36	48	2	98	4	0	1	16	7	.70	6	.270	.356	.462
1993	Cincinnati	NL	138	496	136	16	4	20	(8	12)	220	90	83	51	7	118	5	3	8	27	10	.73	10	.274	.343	.444
3 ML YEARS			263	921	248	42	10	33	(14	19)	409	158	122	99	9	225	9	3	9	44	18	.71	17	.269	.343	.444

Scott Sanders

Pitches: Right **Bats:** Right **Pos:** SP   **Ht:** 6' 4" **Wt:** 210 **Born:** 03/25/69 **Age:** 25

				HOW MUCH HE PITCHED						WHAT HE GAVE UP										THE RESULTS					
Year	Team	Lg	G	GS	CG	GF	IP	BFP	H	R	ER	HR	SH	SF	HB	TBB	IBB	SO	WP	Bk	W	L	Pct.	ShO	Sv	ERA
1990	Spokane	A	3	3	0	0	19	70	12	3	2	0	1	0	2	5	0	21	0	1	2	1	.667	0	0	0.95
	Waterloo	A	7	7	0	0	37	166	43	24	20	2	2	2	1	21	0	28	0	2	2	2	.500	0	0	4.86
1991	Waterloo	A	4	4	0	0	26.1	102	17	2	2	0	1	0	1	6	0	18	0	0	3	0	1.000	0	0	0.68
	High Desert	A	21	21	4	0	132.2	569	114	72	54	7	4	2	7	72	2	93	8	2	9	6	.600	2	0	3.66
1992	Wichita	AA	14	14	0	0	87.2	377	85	35	34	7	5	4	3	37	2	95	4	0	7	5	.583	0	0	3.49
	Las Vegas	AAA	14	12	1	1	72	340	97	49	44	7	3	1	3	31	1	51	6	0	3	6	.333	1	0	5.50
1993	Las Vegas	AAA	24	24	4	0	152.1	687	170	101	84	19	13	4	6	62	2	161	8	1	5	10	.333	0	0	4.96
1993	San Diego	NL	9	9	0	0	52.1	231	54	32	24	4	1	2	1	23	1	37	0	1	3	3	.500	0	0	4.13

Scott Sanderson

Pitches: Right **Bats:** Right **Pos:** SP   **Ht:** 6' 5" **Wt:** 192 **Born:** 07/22/56 **Age:** 37

				HOW MUCH HE PITCHED						WHAT HE GAVE UP										THE RESULTS					
Year	Team	Lg	G	GS	CG	GF	IP	BFP	H	R	ER	HR	SH	SF	HB	TBB	IBB	SO	WP	Bk	W	L	Pct.	ShO	Sv	ERA
1978	Montreal	NL	10	9	1	1	61	251	52	20	17	3	3	2	1	21	0	50	2	0	4	2	.667	1	0	2.51
1979	Montreal	NL	34	24	5	3	168	696	148	69	64	16	5	7	3	54	4	138	2	3	9	8	.529	3	1	3.43
1980	Montreal	NL	33	33	7	0	211	875	206	76	73	18	11	5	3	56	3	125	6	0	16	11	.593	3	0	3.11
1981	Montreal	NL	22	22	4	0	137	560	122	50	45	10	7	4	1	31	2	77	0	0	9	7	.563	1	0	2.96
1982	Montreal	NL	32	32	7	0	224	922	212	98	86	24	9	6	3	58	5	158	2	1	12	12	.500	0	0	3.46
1983	Montreal	NL	18	16	0	1	81.1	346	98	50	42	12	2	1	0	20	0	55	0	0	6	7	.462	0	1	4.65
1984	Chicago	NL	24	24	3	0	140.2	571	140	54	49	5	6	8	2	24	3	76	3	2	8	5	.615	0	0	3.14
1985	Chicago	NL	19	19	2	0	121	480	100	49	42	13	7	7	0	27	4	80	1	0	5	6	.455	0	0	3.12
1986	Chicago	NL	37	28	1	2	169.2	697	165	85	79	21	6	5	2	37	2	124	3	1	9	11	.450	1	1	4.19
1987	Chicago	NL	32	22	0	5	144.2	631	156	72	69	23	4	5	3	50	5	106	1	0	8	9	.471	0	2	4.29
1988	Chicago	NL	11	0	0	3	15.1	62	13	9	9	1	0	3	0	3	1	6	0	0	1	2	.333	0	0	5.28
1989	Chicago	NL	37	23	2	2	146.1	611	155	69	64	16	8	3	2	31	6	86	1	3	11	9	.550	0	0	3.94
1990	Oakland	AL	34	34	2	0	206.1	885	205	99	89	27	4	8	4	66	2	128	7	1	17	11	.607	1	0	3.88
1991	New York	AL	34	34	2	0	208	837	200	95	88	22	5	5	3	29	0	130	4	1	16	10	.615	2	0	3.81
1992	New York	AL	33	33	2	0	193.1	851	220	116	106	28	3	11	4	64	5	104	4	1	12	11	.522	1	0	4.93
1993	2 ML Teams		32	29	4	1	184	777	201	97	86	27	9	10	6	34	7	102	1	5	11	13	.458	1	0	4.21
1993	California	AL	21	21	4	0	135.1	576	153	77	67	15	6	8	5	27	5	66	1	2	7	11	.389	1	0	4.46
	San Francisco	NL	11	8	0	1	48.2	201	48	20	19	12	3	2	1	7	2	36	0	3	4	2	.667	0	0	3.51
16 ML YEARS			442	382	42	18	2411.2	10052	2393	1108	1008	266	89	90	37	605	49	1545	39	18	154	134	.535	14	5	3.76

Mo Sanford

Pitches: Right **Bats:** Right **Pos:** SP/RP   **Ht:** 6' 6" **Wt:** 220 **Born:** 12/24/66 **Age:** 27

		HOW MUCH HE PITCHED								WHAT HE GAVE UP											THE RESULTS					
Year Team	Lg	G	GS	CG	GF	IP	BFP	H	R	ER	HR	SH	SF	HB	TBB	IBB	SO	WP	Bk	W	L	Pct.	ShO	Sv	ERA
1988 Reds	R	14	11	0	1	53	217	34	24	19	6	0	1	0	25	1	64	3	4	3	4	.429	1	0	3.23
1989 Greensboro	A	25	25	3	0	153.2	629	112	52	48	8	4	2	2	64	0	160	6	3	12	6	.667	1	0	2.81
1990 Cedar Rapds	A	25	25	2	0	157.2	628	112	50	48	15	3	2	4	55	1	180	8	1	13	4	.765	1	0	2.74
1991 Chattanooga	AA	16	16	1	0	95.1	395	69	37	29	7	4	3	1	55	2	124	1	0	7	4	.636	1	0	2.74
Nashville	AAA	5	5	2	0	33.2	140	19	7	6	0	0	0	1	22	0	38	3	0	3	0	1.000	2	0	1.60
1992 Chattanooga	AA	4	4	1	0	26.2	101	13	5	4	2	0	0	2	6	0	28	1	0	4	0	1.000	1	0	1.35
Nashville	AAA	25	25	0	0	122	549	128	81	77	22	6	5	3	65	1	129	2	0	8	8	.500	0	0	5.68
1993 Colo Sprngs	AAA	20	17	0	1	105	456	103	64	61	8	3	6	4	57	2	104	7	1	3	6	.333	0	0	5.23
1991 Cincinnati	NL	5	5	0	0	28	118	19	14	12	3	0	0	1	15	1	31	4	0	1	2	.333	0	0	3.86
1993 Colorado	NL	11	6	0	1	35.2	166	37	25	21	4	4	2	0	27	0	36	2	1	1	2	.333	0	0	5.30
2 ML YEARS		16	11	0	1	63.2	284	56	39	33	7	4	2	1	42	1	67	6	1	2	4	.333	0	0	4.66

Benito Santiago

Bats: Right **Throws:** Right **Pos:** C   **Ht:** 6' 1" **Wt:** 185 **Born:** 03/09/65 **Age:** 29

		BATTING															BASERUNNING				PERCENTAGES		
Year Team	Lg	G	AB	H	2B	3B	HR	(Hm | Rd)	TB	R	RBI	TBB	IBB	SO	HBP	SH	SF	SB	CS	SB%	GDP	Avg	OBP	SLG
1986 San Diego	NL	17	62	18	2	0	3	(2 | 1)	29	10	6	2	0	12	0	0	1	0	1	.00	0	.290	.308	.468
1987 San Diego	NL	146	546	164	33	2	18	(11 | 7)	255	64	79	16	2	112	5	1	4	21	12	.64	12	.300	.324	.467
1988 San Diego	NL	139	492	122	22	2	10	(3 | 7)	178	49	46	24	2	82	1	5	5	15	7	.68	18	.248	.282	.362
1989 San Diego	NL	129	462	109	16	3	16	(8 | 8)	179	50	62	26	6	89	1	3	2	11	6	.65	9	.236	.277	.387
1990 San Diego	NL	100	344	93	8	5	11	(5 | 6)	144	42	53	27	2	55	3	1	7	5	5	.50	4	.270	.323	.419
1991 San Diego	NL	152	580	155	22	3	17	(6 | 11)	234	60	87	23	5	114	4	0	7	8	10	.44	21	.267	.296	.403
1992 San Diego	NL	106	386	97	21	0	10	(8 | 2)	148	37	42	21	1	52	0	0	4	2	5	.29	14	.251	.287	.383
1993 Florida	NL	139	469	108	19	6	13	(6 | 7)	178	49	50	37	2	88	5	0	4	10	7	.59	9	.230	.291	.380
8 ML YEARS		928	3341	866	143	21	98	(49 | 49)	1345	361	425	176	20	604	19	10	34	72	53	.58	87	.259	.297	.403

Nelson Santovenia

Bats: Right **Throws:** Right **Pos:** C   **Ht:** 6' 3" **Wt:** 210 **Born:** 07/27/61 **Age:** 32

		BATTING															BASERUNNING				PERCENTAGES		
Year Team	Lg	G	AB	H	2B	3B	HR	(Hm | Rd)	TB	R	RBI	TBB	IBB	SO	HBP	SH	SF	SB	CS	SB%	GDP	Avg	OBP	SLG
1993 Omaha *	AAA	81	274	65	13	0	11	--	--	111	33	42	12	1	50	3	0	7	0	1	.00	4	.237	.270	.405
1987 Montreal	NL	2	1	0	0	0	0	(0 | 0)	0	0	0	0	0	0	0	0	0	0	0	.00	0	.000	.000	.000
1988 Montreal	NL	92	309	73	20	2	8	(6 | 2)	121	26	41	24	3	77	3	4	4	2	3	.40	4	.236	.294	.392
1989 Montreal	NL	97	304	76	14	1	5	(4 | 1)	107	30	31	24	2	37	3	2	4	2	1	.67	12	.250	.307	.352
1990 Montreal	NL	59	163	31	3	1	6	(4 | 2)	54	13	28	8	0	31	0	0	5	0	3	.00	5	.190	.222	.331
1991 Montreal	NL	41	96	24	5	0	2	(1 | 1)	35	7	14	2	2	18	0	1	0	0	0	.00	4	.250	.255	.365
1992 Chicago	AL	2	3	1	0	0	1	(0 | 1)	4	1	2	0	0	0	0	0	0	0	0	.00	0	.333	.333	1.333
1993 Kansas City	AL	4	8	1	0	0	0	(0 | 0)	1	0	0	1	0	2	0	0	0	0	0	.00	0	.125	.222	.125
7 ML YEARS		297	884	206	42	4	22	(15 | 7)	322	77	116	59	7	165	6	6	17	4	7	.36	25	.233	.281	.364

Mackey Sasser

Bats: Left **Throws:** Right **Pos:** LF/RF/DH   **Ht:** 6' 1" **Wt:** 210 **Born:** 08/03/62 **Age:** 31

		BATTING															BASERUNNING				PERCENTAGES		
Year Team	Lg	G	AB	H	2B	3B	HR	(Hm | Rd)	TB	R	RBI	TBB	IBB	SO	HBP	SH	SF	SB	CS	SB%	GDP	Avg	OBP	SLG
1987 2 ML Teams		14	27	5	0	0	0	(0 | 0)	5	2	2	0	0	2	0	0	0	0	0	.00	1	.185	.185	.185
1988 New York	NL	60	123	35	10	1	1	(0 | 1)	50	9	17	6	4	9	0	0	2	0	0	.00	4	.285	.313	.407
1989 New York	NL	72	182	53	14	2	1	(1 | 0)	74	17	22	7	4	15	0	1	3	0	1	.00	3	.291	.316	.407
1990 New York	NL	100	270	83	14	0	6	(3 | 3)	115	31	41	15	9	19	1	0	2	0	0	.00	7	.307	.344	.426
1991 New York	NL	96	228	62	14	2	5	(3 | 2)	95	18	35	9	2	19	1	1	4	0	2	.00	6	.272	.298	.417
1992 New York	NL	92	141	34	6	0	2	(1 | 1)	46	7	18	3	0	10	0	0	5	0	0	.00	4	.241	.248	.326
1993 Seattle		83	188	41	10	2	1	(0 | 0)	58	18	21	15	6	30	1	0	4	1	0	1.00	7	.218	.274	.309
1987 San Francisco	NL	2	4	0	0	0	0	(0 | 0)	0	0	0	0	0	0	0	0	0	0	0	.00	0	.000	.000	.000
Pittsburgh	NL	12	23	5	0	0	0	(0 | 0)	5	2	2	0	0	2	0	0	0	0	0	.00	1	.217	.217	.217
7 ML YEARS		517	1159	313	68	7	16	(8 | 8)	443	102	156	55	25	104	3	2	18	1	3	.25	32	.270	.300	.382

Doug Saunders

Bats: Right **Throws:** Right **Pos:** 2B   **Ht:** 6' 0" **Wt:** 172 **Born:** 12/13/69 **Age:** 24

		BATTING															BASERUNNING				PERCENTAGES		
Year Team	Lg	G	AB	H	2B	3B	HR	(Hm | Rd)	TB	R	RBI	TBB	IBB	SO	HBP	SH	SF	SB	CS	SB%	GDP	Avg	OBP	SLG
1988 Mets	R	16	64	16	4	1	0	--	--	22	8	10	9	0	14	0	2	0	2	3	.40	0	.250	.342	.344
Little Fls	A	29	100	30	6	1	0	--	--	38	10	11	6	0	15	0	1	0	1	4	.20	2	.300	.340	.380
1989 Columbia	A	115	377	99	18	4	4	--	--	137	53	38	35	2	78	3	4	3	5	5	.50	5	.263	.328	.363
1990 St. Lucie	A	115	408	92	8	4	1	--	--	111	52	43	43	0	96	2	7	2	24	10	.71	7	.225	.301	.272

1991 St. Lucie	A	70	230	54	9	2	2	--	--	73	19	18	25	0	43	4	5	0	5	6	.45	6	.235	.320	.317
1992 Binghamton	AA	130	435	108	16	2	5	--	--	143	45	38	52	0	68	1	5	4	8	12	.40	9	.248	.327	.329
1993 Norfolk	AAA	105	356	88	12	6	2	--	--	118	37	24	44	1	63	3	7	1	6	5	.55	13	.247	.334	.331
1993 New York	NL	28	67	14	2	0	0	(0	0)	16	8	0	3	0	4	0	3	0	0	0	.00	2	.209	.243	.239

Steve Sax

Bats: Right **Throws:** Right **Pos:** LF/DH   **Ht:** 5'11" **Wt:** 189 **Born:** 01/29/60 **Age:** 34

		BATTING																	BASERUNNING				PERCENTAGES		
Year Team	Lg	G	AB	H	2B	3B	HR	(Hm	Rd)	TB	R	RBI	TBB	IBB	SO	HBP	SH	SF	SB	CS	SB%	GDP	Avg	OBP	SLG
1981 Los Angeles	NL	31	119	33	2	0	2	(0	2)	41	15	9	7	1	14	0	1	0	5	7	.42	0	.277	.317	.345
1982 Los Angeles	NL	150	638	180	23	7	4	(2	2)	229	88	47	49	1	53	2	10	0	49	19	.72	10	.282	.335	.359
1983 Los Angeles	NL	155	623	175	18	5	5	(3	2)	218	94	41	58	3	73	1	8	2	56	30	.65	8	.281	.342	.350
1984 Los Angeles	NL	145	569	138	24	4	1	(1	0)	173	70	35	47	3	53	1	2	3	34	19	.64	12	.243	.300	.304
1985 Los Angeles	NL	136	488	136	8	4	1	(1	0)	155	62	42	54	12	43	3	3	3	27	11	.71	15	.279	.352	.318
1986 Los Angeles	NL	157	633	210	43	4	6	(1	5)	279	91	56	59	5	58	3	6	3	40	17	.70	12	.332	.390	.441
1987 Los Angeles	NL	157	610	171	22	7	6	(2	4)	225	84	46	44	5	61	3	5	1	37	11	.77	13	.280	.331	.369
1988 Los Angeles	NL	160	632	175	19	4	5	(2	3)	217	70	57	45	6	51	1	7	2	42	12	.78	11	.277	.325	.343
1989 New York	AL	158	651	205	26	3	5	(2	3)	252	88	63	52	2	44	1	8	5	43	17	.72	19	.315	.364	.387
1990 New York	AL	155	615	160	24	2	4	(3	1)	200	70	42	49	3	46	4	6	6	43	9	.83	13	.260	.316	.325
1991 New York	AL	158	652	198	38	2	10	(6	4)	270	85	56	41	2	38	3	5	6	31	11	.74	15	.304	.345	.414
1992 Chicago	AL	143	567	134	26	4	4	(1	3)	180	74	47	43	4	42	2	12	6	30	12	.71	17	.236	.290	.317
1993 Chicago	AL	57	119	28	5	0	1	(1	0)	36	20	8	8	0	6	1	0	2	7	3	.70	1	.235	.283	.303
13 ML YEARS		1762	6916	1943	278	46	54	(25	29)	2475	911	549	556	47	582	24	75	37	444	178	.71	146	.281	.335	.358

Bob Scanlan

Pitches: Right **Bats:** Right **Pos:** RP   **Ht:** 6'8" **Wt:** 210 **Born:** 08/09/66 **Age:** 27

		HOW MUCH HE PITCHED						WHAT HE GAVE UP										THE RESULTS				
Year Team	Lg	G	GS	CG	GF	IP	BFP	H	R	ER	HR	SH	SF	HB	TBB	IBB	SO	WP	Bk	W	L	Pct.	ShO	Sv	ERA
1991 Chicago	NL	40	13	0	16	111	482	114	60	48	5	8	6	3	40	3	44	5	1	7	8	.467	0	1	3.89
1992 Chicago	NL	69	0	0	41	87.1	360	76	32	28	4	4	2	1	30	6	42	6	1	3	6	.333	0	14	2.89
1993 Chicago	NL	70	0	0	13	75.1	323	79	41	38	6	2	6	3	28	7	44	0	2	4	5	.444	0	0	4.54
3 ML YEARS		179	13	0	70	273.2	1165	269	133	114	15	14	14	7	98	16	130	11	7	14	19	.424	0	15	3.75

Steve Scarsone

Bats: Right **Throws:** Right **Pos:** 2B   **Ht:** 6'2" **Wt:** 170 **Born:** 04/11/66 **Age:** 28

		BATTING																	BASERUNNING				PERCENTAGES		
Year Team	Lg	G	AB	H	2B	3B	HR	(Hm	Rd)	TB	R	RBI	TBB	IBB	SO	HBP	SH	SF	SB	CS	SB%	GDP	Avg	OBP	SLG
1986 Bend	A	65	219	48	10	4	4	--	--	78	42	21	30	0	51	4	1	2	11	2	.85	2	.219	.322	.356
1987 Chston-Wv	A	95	259	56	11	1	1	--	--	72	35	17	31	0	64	3	3	0	8	5	.62	1	.216	.307	.278
1988 Clearwater	A	125	456	120	21	4	8	--	--	173	51	46	18	0	93	8	6	6	14	4	.78	3	.263	.299	.379
1989 Reading	AA	75	240	43	5	0	4	--	--	60	30	22	15	2	67	1	5	4	2	2	.50	5	.179	.227	.250
1990 Clearwater	A	59	211	58	9	5	3	--	--	86	29	20	23	1	57	4	5	1	3	4	.43	2	.275	.345	.408
Reading	AA	74	245	65	12	1	3	--	--	88	26	23	14	0	63	1	4	0	0	0	.00	0	.265	.308	.359
1991 Reading	AA	15	49	15	0	0	3	--	--	24	6	3	4	0	15	0	0	0	2	0	1.00	0	.306	.358	.490
Scranton-Wb	AAA	111	405	111	20	6	6	--	--	161	52	38	19	1	81	7	2	7	10	5	.67	4	.274	.313	.398
1992 Scranton/wb	AAA	89	325	89	23	4	11	--	--	153	43	48	24	3	74	4	5	3	10	7	.59	7	.274	.329	.471
Rochester	AAA	23	82	21	3	0	1	--	--	27	13	12	6	1	12	1	1	3	3	2	.60	3	.256	.304	.329
1993 Phoenix	AAA	19	70	18	1	2	3	--	--	32	13	9	8	1	21	2	0	0	2	0	1.00	0	.257	.350	.457
1992 2 ML Teams		18	30	5	0	0	0	(0	0)	5	3	0	2	0	12	0	1	0	0	0	.00	0	.167	.219	.167
1993 San Francisco	NL	44	103	26	9	0	2	(1	1)	41	16	15	4	0	32	0	4	1	0	1	.00	0	.252	.278	.398
1992 Philadelphia	NL	7	13	2	0	0	0	(0	0)	2	1	0	1	0	6	0	0	0	0	0	.00	0	.154	.214	.154
Baltimore	AL	11	17	3	0	0	0	(0	0)	3	2	0	1	0	6	0	1	0	0	0	.00	0	.176	.222	.176
2 ML YEARS		62	133	31	9	0	2	(1	1)	46	19	15	6	0	44	0	5	1	0	1	.00	0	.233	.264	.346

Curt Schilling

Pitches: Right **Bats:** Right **Pos:** SP   **Ht:** 6'4" **Wt:** 215 **Born:** 11/14/66 **Age:** 27

		HOW MUCH HE PITCHED						WHAT HE GAVE UP										THE RESULTS				
Year Team	Lg	G	GS	CG	GF	IP	BFP	H	R	ER	HR	SH	SF	HB	TBB	IBB	SO	WP	Bk	W	L	Pct.	ShO	Sv	ERA
1988 Baltimore	AL	4	4	0	0	14.2	76	22	19	16	3	0	3	1	10	1	4	2	0	0	3	.000	0	0	9.82
1989 Baltimore	AL	5	1	0	0	8.2	38	10	6	6	2	0	0	0	3	0	6	1	0	0	1	.000	0	0	6.23
1990 Baltimore	AL	35	0	0	16	46	191	38	13	13	1	2	4	0	19	0	32	0	0	1	2	.333	0	3	2.54
1991 Houston	NL	56	0	0	34	75.2	336	79	35	32	2	5	1	0	39	7	71	4	1	3	5	.375	0	8	3.81
1992 Philadelphia	NL	42	26	10	10	226.1	895	165	67	59	11	7	8	1	59	4	147	4	0	14	11	.560	4	2	2.35
1993 Philadelphia	NL	34	34	7	0	235.1	982	234	114	105	23	9	7	4	57	6	186	9	3	16	7	.696	2	0	4.02
6 ML YEARS		176	65	17	60	606.2	2518	548	254	231	42	23	23	6	187	18	446	20	4	34	29	.540	6	13	3.43

194

Dick Schofield

Bats: Right   Throws: Right   Pos: SS Ht: 5'10" Wt: 179 Born: 11/21/62 Age: 31

Year Team	Lg	G	AB	H	2B	3B	HR	(Hm	Rd)	TB	R	RBI	TBB	IBB	SO	HBP	SH	SF	SB	CS	SB%	GDP	Avg	OBP	SLG
1993 Dunedin *	A	11	30	6	2	0	0	--	--	8	4	4	3	0	7	0	2	0	0	1	.00	1	.200	.273	.267
1983 California	AL	21	54	11	2	0	3	(2	1)	22	4	4	6	0	8	1	1	0	0	0	.00	2	.204	.295	.407
1984 California	AL	140	400	77	10	3	4	(0	4)	105	39	21	33	0	79	6	13	0	5	2	.71	7	.193	.264	.263
1985 California	AL	147	438	96	19	3	8	(5	3)	145	50	41	35	0	70	8	12	3	11	4	.73	8	.219	.287	.331
1986 California	AL	139	458	114	17	6	13	(7	6)	182	67	57	48	2	55	5	9	9	23	5	.82	8	.249	.321	.397
1987 California	AL	134	479	120	17	3	9	(4	5)	170	52	46	37	0	63	2	10	3	19	3	.86	4	.251	.305	.355
1988 California	AL	155	527	126	11	6	6	(3	3)	167	61	34	40	0	57	9	11	2	20	5	.80	5	.239	.303	.317
1989 California	AL	91	302	69	11	2	4	(1	3)	96	42	26	28	0	47	3	11	2	9	3	.75	4	.228	.299	.318
1990 California	AL	99	310	79	8	1	1	(1	0)	92	41	18	52	3	61	2	13	2	3	4	.43	3	.255	.363	.297
1991 California	AL	134	427	96	9	3	0	(0	0)	111	44	31	50	2	69	3	7	0	8	4	.67	3	.225	.310	.260
1992 2 ML Teams		143	423	87	18	2	4	(3	1)	121	52	36	61	4	82	5	10	3	11	4	.73	11	.206	.311	.286
1993 Toronto	AL	36	110	21	1	2	0	(0	0)	26	11	5	16	0	25	0	0	2	0	3	1.00	0	.191	.294	.236
1992 California	AL	1	3	1	0	0	0	(0	0)	1	0	0	1	0	0	0	0	0	0	0	.00	0	.333	.500	.333
New York	NL	142	420	86	18	2	4	(3	1)	120	52	36	60	4	82	5	10	3	11	4	.73	11	.205	.309	.286
11 ML YEARS		1239	3928	896	123	31	52	(26	26)	1237	463	319	406	11	616	44	99	24	112	34	.77	56	.228	.306	.315

Mike Schooler

Pitches: Right   Bats: Right   Pos: RP Ht: 6'3" Wt: 220 Born: 08/10/62 Age: 31

Year Team	Lg	G	GS	CG	GF	IP	BFP	H	R	ER	HR	SH	SF	HB	TBB	IBB	SO	WP	Bk	W	L	Pct.	ShO	Sv	ERA
1993 Okla City *	AAA	28	0	0	20	45.2	205	59	33	30	3	1	1	0	11	3	31	5	2	1	3	.250	0	5	5.91
1988 Seattle	AL	40	0	0	33	48.1	214	45	21	19	4	2	3	1	24	4	54	4	1	5	8	.385	0	15	3.54
1989 Seattle	AL	67	0	0	60	77	329	81	27	24	2	3	1	2	19	3	69	6	1	1	7	.125	0	33	2.81
1990 Seattle	AL	49	0	0	45	56	229	47	18	14	5	3	2	1	16	5	45	1	0	1	4	.200	0	30	2.25
1991 Seattle	AL	34	0	0	23	34.1	138	25	14	14	2	1	1	0	10	0	31	2	1	3	3	.500	0	7	3.67
1992 Seattle	AL	53	0	0	36	51.2	232	55	29	27	7	4	3	1	24	6	33	0	0	2	7	.222	0	13	4.70
1993 Texas	AL	17	0	0	0	24.1	111	30	17	15	3	2	0	0	10	1	16	1	0	3	0	1.000	0	0	5.55
6 ML YEARS		260	0	0	197	291.2	1253	283	126	113	23	15	10	5	103	19	248	14	3	15	29	.341	0	98	3.49

Pete Schourek

Pitches: Left   Bats: Left   Pos: RP/SP Ht: 6'5" Wt: 205 Born: 05/10/69 Age: 25

Year Team	Lg	G	GS	CG	GF	IP	BFP	H	R	ER	HR	SH	SF	HB	TBB	IBB	SO	WP	Bk	W	L	Pct.	ShO	Sv	ERA
1991 New York	NL	35	8	0	7	86.1	385	82	49	41	7	5	4	2	43	4	67	1	0	5	4	.556	1	2	4.27
1992 New York	NL	22	21	0	0	136	578	137	60	59	9	4	4	2	44	6	60	4	2	6	8	.429	0	0	3.64
1993 New York	NL	41	18	0	6	128.1	586	168	90	85	13	3	8	3	45	7	72	1	2	5	12	.294	0	0	5.96
3 ML YEARS		98	47	1	13	350.2	1549	387	199	181	29	12	16	7	132	17	199	6	4	16	24	.400	1	2	4.65

Jeff Schwarz

Pitches: Right   Bats: Right   Pos: RP Ht: 6'5" Wt: 190 Born: 05/20/64 Age: 30

Year Team	Lg	G	GS	CG	GF	IP	BFP	H	R	ER	HR	SH	SF	HB	TBB	IBB	SO	WP	Bk	W	L	Pct.	ShO	Sv	ERA
1984 Quad City	A	27	24	2	1	130	606	106	88	73	11	11	3	11	111	2	123	17	0	4	14	.222	0	0	5.05
1985 Peoria	A	27	19	6	3	143.1	605	99	60	51	4	3	7	9	79	2	140	9	0	7	9	.438	2	0	3.20
1986 Winston-Sal	A	4	4	0	1	12	57	10	10	10	3	0	0	1	12	0	11	3	2	0	1	.000	0	0	7.50
1987 Peoria	A	20	13	2	1	92.1	418	79	59	47	7	6	6	8	59	1	91	9	1	5	7	.417	2	0	4.58
1988 Winston-Sal	A	24	24	2	0	151.1	689	133	93	76	10	3	8	6	110	1	153	12	4	7	12	.368	2	0	4.52
Pittsfield	AA	3	3	0	0	14.1	72	19	9	9	1	0	0	0	11	0	5	1	3	0	1	.000	0	0	5.65
1989 Hagerstown	AA	17	9	0	5	69	311	66	45	30	3	4	4	4	41	0	78	7	5	0	6	.000	0	1	3.91
Rochester	AAA	9	0	0	4	12.1	62	5	9	8	0	2	0	1	16	0	12	2	0	0	2	.000	0	2	5.84
1990 Rochester	AAA	5	1	0	0	12.2	60	10	10	10	1	0	3	0	19	0	4	4	0	0	0	.000	0	0	7.11
Stockton	A	19	8	0	0	56.1	265	59	36	30	1	2	0	9	36	0	59	5	1	3	3	.500	0	2	4.79
1991 El Paso	AA	27	24	3	1	141.2	650	139	91	77	11	7	8	8	97	1	134	18	3	11	8	.579	1	0	4.89
1992 Birmingham	AA	21	0	0	16	38.2	147	16	5	5	1	0	0	4	9	2	53	2	0	2	1	.667	0	6	1.16
Vancouver	AAA	23	0	0	17	36	162	26	18	12	0	1	1	0	31	4	42	5	0	1	3	.250	0	3	3.00
1993 Nashville	AAA	7	0	0	2	11	43	3	3	3	0	0	0	2	12	1	8	0	0	0	0	.000	0	0	2.45
1993 Chicago	AL	41	0	0	10	51	218	35	21	21	1	0	3	3	38	2	41	5	1	2	2	.500	0	0	3.71

Mike Scioscia

Bats: Left **Throws: Right** **Pos: C** **Ht: 6' 2"** **Wt: 205** **Born: 11/27/58** **Age: 35**

									BATTING											BASERUNNING				PERCENTAGES		
Year	Team	Lg	G	AB	H	2B	3B	HR	(Hm	Rd)	TB	R	RBI	TBB	IBB	SO	HBP	SH	SF	SB	CS	SB%	GDP	Avg	OBP	SLG
1980	Los Angeles	NL	54	134	34	5	1	1	(1	0)	44	8	8	12	2	9		5	1	1	0	1.00	2	.254	.313	.328
1981	Los Angeles	NL	93	290	80	10	0	2	(0	2)	96	27	29	36	8	18	1	4	4	0	2	.00	8	.276	.353	.331
1982	Los Angeles	NL	129	365	80	11	1	5	(2	3)	108	31	38	44	11	31	1	5	4	2	0	1.00	8	.219	.302	.296
1983	Los Angeles	NL	12	35	11	3	0	1	(0	1)	17	3	7	5	1	2	0	0	0	0	0	.00	1	.314	.400	.486
1984	Los Angeles	NL	114	341	93	18	0	5	(0	5)	126	29	38	52	10	26	1	1	4	2	1	.67	10	.273	.367	.370
1985	Los Angeles	NL	141	429	127	26	3	7	(1	6)	180	47	53	77	9	21	5	11	3	3	3	.50	10	.296	.407	.420
1986	Los Angeles	NL	122	374	94	18	1	5	(2	3)	135	36	26	62	4	23	3	6	4	3	3	.50	11	.251	.359	.345
1987	Los Angeles	NL	142	461	122	26	1	6	(2	4)	168	44	38	55	9	23	1	4	2	7	4	.64	13	.265	.343	.364
1988	Los Angeles	NL	130	408	105	18	0	3	(1	2)	132	29	35	38	12	31	0	3	3	0	3	.00	14	.257	.318	.324
1989	Los Angeles	NL	133	408	102	16	0	10	(4	6)	148	40	44	52	14	29	3	7	1	0	2	.00	4	.250	.338	.363
1990	Los Angeles	NL	135	435	115	25	0	12	(5	7)	176	46	66	55	14	31	3	1	4	4	1	.80	11	.264	.348	.405
1991	Los Angeles	NL	119	345	91	16	2	8	(3	5)	135	39	40	47	3	32	3	5	4	4	3	.57	5	.264	.353	.391
1992	Los Angeles	NL	117	348	77	6	3	3	(1	2)	98	19	24	32	4	31	1	5	3	3	2	.60	9	.221	.286	.282
	13 ML YEARS		1441	4373	1131	198	12	68	(22	46)	1557	398	446	567	101	307	22	57	37	29	24	.55	106	.259	.344	.356

Darryl Scott

Pitches: Right **Bats: Right** **Pos: RP** **Ht: 6' 1"** **Wt: 185** **Born: 08/06/68** **Age: 25**

			HOW MUCH HE PITCHED						WHAT HE GAVE UP												THE RESULTS					
Year	Team	Lg	G	GS	CG	GF	IP	BFP	H	R	ER	HR	SH	SF	HB	TBB	IBB	SO	WP	Bk	W	L	Pct.	ShO	Sv	ERA
1990	Boise	A	27	0	0	11	53.2	221	40	11	8	3	0	1	0	19	1	57	5	0	2	1	.667	0	5	1.34
1991	Quad City	A	47	0	0	36	75.1	285	35	18	13	2	2	0	1	26	4	123	9	1	4	3	.571	0	19	1.55
1992	Midland	AA	27	0	0	22	29.2	126	20	9	6	0	2	2	2	14	1	35	4	0	1	1	.500	0	9	1.82
	Edmonton	AAA	31	0	0	17	36.1	164	41	21	21	1	0	3	0	21	1	48	4	2	0	2	.000	0	6	5.20
1993	Vancouver	AAA	46	0	0	33	51.2	206	35	12	12	4	2	1	1	19	2	57	3	0	7	1	.875	0	15	2.09
1993	California	AL	16	0	0	2	20	90	19	13	13	1	0	2	1	11	1	13	2	0	1	2	.333	0	0	5.85

Tim Scott

Pitches: Right **Bats: Right** **Pos: RP** **Ht: 6' 2"** **Wt: 185** **Born: 11/16/66** **Age: 27**

			HOW MUCH HE PITCHED						WHAT HE GAVE UP												THE RESULTS					
Year	Team	Lg	G	GS	CG	GF	IP	BFP	H	R	ER	HR	SH	SF	HB	TBB	IBB	SO	WP	Bk	W	L	Pct.	ShO	Sv	ERA
1991	San Diego	NL	2	0	0	0	1	5	2	2	1	0	0	0	0	0	0	1	0	0	0	0	.000	0	0	9.00
1992	San Diego	NL	34	0	0	16	37.2	173	39	24	22	4	4	1	1	21	6	30	0	1	4	1	.800	0	0	5.26
1993	2 ML Teams		56	0	0	18	71.2	317	69	28	24	4	3	2	4	34	2	65	2	1	7	2	.778	0	1	3.01
1993	San Diego	NL	24	0	0	2	37.2	169	38	13	10	1	2	2	4	15	0	30	1	1	2	0	1.000	0	0	2.39
	Montreal	NL	32	0	0	16	34	148	31	15	14	3	1	0	0	19	2	35	1	0	5	2	.714	0	1	3.71
	3 ML YEARS		92	0	0	34	110.1	495	110	54	47	8	7	3	5	55	8	96	2	2	11	3	.786	0	1	3.83

Scott Scudder

Pitches: Right **Bats: Right** **Pos: SP** **Ht: 6' 2"** **Wt: 190** **Born: 02/14/68** **Age: 26**

			HOW MUCH HE PITCHED						WHAT HE GAVE UP												THE RESULTS					
Year	Team	Lg	G	GS	CG	GF	IP	BFP	H	R	ER	HR	SH	SF	HB	TBB	IBB	SO	WP	Bk	W	L	Pct.	ShO	Sv	ERA
1993	Charlotte *	AAA	23	22	2	0	136	597	148	92	76	21	0	7	7	52	1	64	5	0	7	7	.500	0	0	5.03
1989	Cincinnati	NL	23	17	0	3	100.1	451	91	54	50	14	7	2	1	61	11	66	0	1	4	9	.308	0	0	4.49
1990	Cincinnati	NL	21	10	0	3	71.2	316	74	41	39	12	3	1	3	30	4	42	2	2	5	5	.500	0	0	4.90
1991	Cincinnati	NL	27	14	0	4	101.1	443	91	52	49	6	8	3	6	56	4	51	7	0	6	9	.400	0	1	4.35
1992	Cleveland	AL	23	22	0	0	109	509	134	80	64	10	6	4	2	55	0	66	7	0	6	10	.375	0	0	5.28
1993	Cleveland	AL	2	1	0	1	4	20	5	4	4	0	0	0	0	4	0	1	0	0	0	1	.000	0	0	9.00
	5 ML YEARS		96	64	0	11	386.1	1739	395	231	206	42	24	10	13	206	19	226	16	3	21	34	.382	0	1	4.80

Rudy Seanez

Pitches: Right **Bats: Right** **Pos: RP** **Ht: 5'10"** **Wt: 185** **Born: 10/20/68** **Age: 25**

			HOW MUCH HE PITCHED						WHAT HE GAVE UP												THE RESULTS					
Year	Team	Lg	G	GS	CG	GF	IP	BFP	H	R	ER	HR	SH	SF	HB	TBB	IBB	SO	WP	Bk	W	L	Pct.	ShO	Sv	ERA
1993	Central Val *	A	5	1	0	1	8.1	46	9	9	9	0	0	1	0	11	0	7	1	0	0	2	.000	0	0	9.72
	Colo Sprngs *	AAA	3	0	0	3	3	13	3	3	3	1	0	0	0	1	0	5	0	0	0	0	.000	0	0	9.00
	Las Vegas *	AAA	14	0	0	8	19.2	90	24	15	14	2	0	1	0	11	0	14	7	1	0	1	.000	0	0	6.41
1989	Cleveland	AL	5	0	0	2	5	20	1	2	2	0	0	2	0	4	1	7	1	1	0	0	.000	0	0	3.60
1990	Cleveland	AL	24	0	0	12	27.1	127	22	17	17	2	0	1	1	25	1	24	5	0	2	1	.667	0	0	5.60
1991	Cleveland	AL	5	0	0	5	5	33	10	12	9	2	0	0	0	7	0	7	2	0	0	0	.000	0	0	16.20
1993	San Diego	NL	3	0	0	3	3.1	20	8	6	5	1	0	1	0	2	0	1	0	0	0	0	.000	0	0	13.50
	4 ML YEARS		37	0	0	17	40.2	200	41	37	33	5	1	3	1	38	2	39	8	1	2	1	.667	0	0	7.30

David Segui

Bats: Both **Throws:** Left **Pos:** 1B · **Ht:** 6'1" **Wt:** 202 **Born:** 07/19/66 **Age:** 27

								BATTING										BASERUNNING				PERCENTAGES		
Year Team	Lg	G	AB	H	2B	3B	HR	(Hm	Rd)	TB	R	RBI	TBB	IBB	SO	HBP	SH	SF	SB	CS	SB%	GDP	Avg	OBP	SLG
1990 Baltimore	AL	40	123	30	7	0	2	(1	1)	43	14	15	11	2	15	1	1	0	0	0	.00	12	.244	.311	.350
1991 Baltimore	AL	86	212	59	7	0	2	(1	1)	72	15	22	12	2	19	0	3	1	1	1	.50	7	.278	.316	.340
1992 Baltimore	AL	115	189	44	9	0	1	(1	0)	56	21	17	20	3	23	0	2	0	1	0	1.00	4	.233	.306	.296
1993 Baltimore	AL	146	450	123	27	0	10	(6	4)	180	54	60	58	4	53	0	3	8	2	1	.67	18	.273	.351	.400
4 ML YEARS		387	974	256	50	0	15	(9	6)	351	104	114	101	11	110	1	9	9	4	2	.67	41	.263	.330	.360

Kevin Seitzer

Bats: Right **Throws:** Right **Pos:** 3B/1B · **Ht:** 5'11" **Wt:** 190 **Born:** 03/26/62 **Age:** 32

								BATTING										BASERUNNING				PERCENTAGES		
Year Team	Lg	G	AB	H	2B	3B	HR	(Hm	Rd)	TB	R	RBI	TBB	IBB	SO	HBP	SH	SF	SB	CS	SB%	GDP	Avg	OBP	SLG
1986 Kansas City	AL	28	96	31	4	1	2	(1	1)	43	16	11	19	0	14	1	0	0	0	0	.00	0	.323	.440	.448
1987 Kansas City	AL	161	641	207	33	8	15	(7	8)	301	105	83	80	0	85	2	1	1	12	7	.63	18	.323	.399	.470
1988 Kansas City	AL	149	559	170	32	5	5	(4	1)	227	90	60	72	4	64	6	3	3	10	8	.56	15	.304	.388	.406
1989 Kansas City	AL	160	597	168	17	2	4	(2	2)	201	78	48	102	7	76	5	4	7	17	8	.68	16	.281	.387	.337
1990 Kansas City	AL	158	622	171	31	5	6	(5	1)	230	91	38	67	2	66	2	4	2	7	5	.58	11	.275	.346	.370
1991 Kansas City	AL	85	234	62	11	3	1	(0	1)	82	28	25	29	3	21	2	1	1	4	1	.80	4	.265	.350	.350
1992 Milwaukee	AL	148	540	146	35	1	5	(2	3)	198	74	71	57	4	44	2	7	9	13	11	.54	16	.270	.337	.367
1993 2 ML Teams		120	417	112	16	2	11	(6	5)	165	45	57	44	1	48	2	3	5	7	7	.50	14	.269	.338	.396
1993 Oakland	AL	73	255	65	10	2	4	(2	2)	91	24	27	27	1	33	1	2	4	4	7	.36	7	.255	.324	.357
Milwaukee	AL	47	162	47	6	0	7	(4	3)	74	21	30	17	0	15	1	1	1	3	0	1.00	7	.290	.359	.457
8 ML YEARS		1009	3706	1067	179	27	49	(27	22)	1447	527	393	470	21	418	22	23	28	70	47	.60	94	.288	.369	.390

Aaron Sele

Pitches: Right **Bats:** Right **Pos:** SP · **Ht:** 6'5" **Wt:** 205 **Born:** 06/25/70 **Age:** 24

			HOW MUCH HE PITCHED					WHAT HE GAVE UP										THE RESULTS				
Year Team	Lg	G	GS	CG	GF	IP	BFP	H	R	ER	HR	SH	SF	HB	TBB	IBB	SO	WP	Bk	W	L	Pct.	ShO	Sv	ERA
1991 Winter Havn	A	13	11	4	1	69	303	65	42	38	2	2	0	6	32	2	51	5	6	3	6	.333	0	1	4.96
1992 Lynchburg	A	20	19	2	0	127	535	104	51	41	5	3	2	14	46	0	112	5	3	13	5	.722	1	0	2.91
New Britain	AA	7	6	1	0	33	162	43	29	23	2	1	0	5	15	0	29	4	1	2	1	.667	0	0	6.27
1993 Pawtucket	AAA	14	14	2	0	94.1	373	74	30	23	8	2	0	5	23	0	87	1	0	8	2	.800	1	0	2.19
1993 Boston	AL	18	18	0	0	111.2	484	100	42	34	5	2	5	7	48	2	93	0	1	7	2	.778	0	0	2.74

Frank Seminara

Pitches: Right **Bats:** Right **Pos:** RP/SP · **Ht:** 6'2" **Wt:** 205 **Born:** 05/16/67 **Age:** 27

			HOW MUCH HE PITCHED					WHAT HE GAVE UP										THE RESULTS				
Year Team	Lg	G	GS	CG	GF	IP	BFP	H	R	ER	HR	SH	SF	HB	TBB	IBB	SO	WP	Bk	W	L	Pct.	ShO	Sv	ERA
1988 Oneonta	A	16	13	0	2	78.1	350	86	49	38	2	3	2	5	32	2	60	11	6	4	7	.364	0	1	4.37
1989 Pr William	A	21	0	0	12	36.2	158	26	23	15	0	1	3	5	22	3	23	5	4	2	4	.333	0	2	3.68
Oneonta	A	11	10	3	0	70	280	51	25	16	0	3	0	3	18	0	70	1	3	7	2	.778	1	0	2.06
1990 Pr William	A	25	25	4	0	170.1	692	136	51	36	5	1	2	10	52	1	132	12	2	16	8	.667	2	0	1.90
1991 Wichita	AA	27	27	6	0	176	761	173	86	66	10	9	5	9	68	0	107	12	3	15	10	.600	1	0	3.38
1992 Las Vegas	AAA	13	13	1	0	80.2	357	92	46	37	2	2	4	3	33	3	48	2	5	6	4	.600	1	0	4.13
1993 Las Vegas	AAA	21	19	0	1	114.1	518	136	79	69	15	6	4	4	52	1	99	2	2	8	5	.615	0	1	5.43
1992 San Diego	NL	19	18	0	0	100.1	435	98	46	41	5	3	2	3	46	3	61	1	1	9	4	.692	0	0	3.68
1993 San Diego	NL	18	7	0	0	46.1	212	53	30	23	5	6	2	3	21	3	22	1	0	3	3	.500	0	0	4.47
2 ML YEARS		37	25	0	0	146.2	647	151	76	64	10	9	4	6	67	6	83	2	1	12	7	.632	0	0	3.93

Scott Servais

Bats: Right **Throws:** Right **Pos:** C · **Ht:** 6'2" **Wt:** 195 **Born:** 06/04/67 **Age:** 27

								BATTING										BASERUNNING				PERCENTAGES		
Year Team	Lg	G	AB	H	2B	3B	HR	(Hm	Rd)	TB	R	RBI	TBB	IBB	SO	HBP	SH	SF	SB	CS	SB%	GDP	Avg	OBP	SLG
1991 Houston	NL	16	37	6	3	0	0	(0	0)	9	0	6	4	0	8	0	1	0	0	0	.00	0	.162	.244	.243
1992 Houston	NL	77	205	49	9	0	0	(0	0)	58	12	15	11	2	25	5	6	0	0	0	.00	7	.239	.294	.283
1993 Houston	NL	85	258	63	11	0	11	(5	6)	107	24	32	22	2	45	5	3	3	0	0	.00	6	.244	.313	.415
3 ML YEARS		178	500	118	23	0	11	(5	6)	174	36	53	37	4	78	10	10	3	0	0	.00	13	.236	.300	.348

Scott Service

Pitches: Right **Bats:** Right **Pos:** RP · **Ht:** 6'6" **Wt:** 240 **Born:** 07/27/67 **Age:** 26

			HOW MUCH HE PITCHED					WHAT HE GAVE UP										THE RESULTS				
Year Team	Lg	G	GS	CG	GF	IP	BFP	H	R	ER	HR	SH	SF	HB	TBB	IBB	SO	WP	Bk	W	L	Pct.	ShO	Sv	ERA
1986 Spartanburg	A	14	9	1	1	58.2	281	68	44	38	3	2	1	7	34	0	49	6	1	1	6	.143	0	0	5.83
Utica	A	10	10	2	0	70.2	299	65	30	21	1	3	2	5	18	0	43	5	1	5	4	.556	0	0	2.67
Clearwater	A	4	4	1	0	25.1	105	20	10	9	2	1	0	2	15	0	19	1	1	1	2	.333	1	0	3.20

Year	Team	Lg	G	GS	CG	GF	IP	BFP	H	R	ER	HR	SH	SF	HB	TBB	IBB	SO	WP	Bk	W	L	Pct.	ShO	Sv	ERA
1987	Reading	AA	5	4	0	0	19.2	95	22	19	17	5	0	0	0	16	1	12	1	0	0	3	.000	0	0	7.78
	Clearwater	A	21	21	5	0	137.2	557	127	46	38	8	2	3	4	32	0	73	1	1	13	4	.765	2	0	2.48
1988	Reading	AA	10	9	1	1	56.2	240	52	25	18	4	1	1	0	22	2	39	1	6	3	4	.429	1	0	2.86
	Maine	AAA	19	18	1	0	110.1	470	109	51	45	10	6	6	2	31	3	87	0	2	8	8	.500	0	0	3.67
1989	Reading	AA	23	10	1	9	85.2	349	71	36	31	8	1	3	8	23	0	82	3	0	6	6	.500	0	1	3.26
	Scr Wil-Bar	AAA	23	0	0	15	33.1	148	27	8	8	2	4	0	2	23	6	23	0	0	3	1	.750	0	6	2.16
1990	Scr Wil-Bar	AAA	45	9	0	11	96.1	427	95	56	51	10	4	2	5	44	1	94	4	0	5	4	.556	0	2	4.76
1991	Indianapols	AAA	18	17	3	1	121.1	477	83	42	40	7	2	3	6	39	0	91	5	1	6	7	.462	1	0	2.97
1992	Indianapols	AAA	13	0	0	7	24.1	95	12	3	2	0	2	0	3	9	0	25	0	0	2	0	1.000	0	2	0.74
	Nashville	AAA	39	2	0	15	70.2	299	54	22	18	2	4	0	2	35	3	87	2	0	6	2	.750	0	4	2.29
1993	Indianapols	AAA	21	1	0	13	30.1	133	25	16	15	5	3	1	0	17	3	28	1	0	4	2	.667	0	2	4.45
1988	Philadelphia	NL	5	0	0	0	5.1	23	7	1	1	0	0	0	1	1	0	6	0	0	0	0	.000	0	0	1.69
1992	Montreal	NL	5	0	0	0	7	41	15	11	11	1	0	0	0	5	0	11	0	0	0	0	.000	0	0	14.14
1993	2 ML Teams		29	0	0	7	46	197	44	24	22	6	2	4	2	16	4	43	0	0	2	2	.500	0	2	4.30
1993	Colorado	NL	3	0	0	0	4.2	24	8	5	5	1	0	2	1	1	0	3	0	0	0	0	.000	0	2	9.64
	Cincinnati	NL	26	0	0	7	41.1	173	36	19	17	5	2	2	1	15	4	40	0	0	2	2	.500	0	2	3.70
	3 ML YEARS		39	0	0	8	58.1	261	66	36	34	7	2	4	3	22	4	60	0	0	2	2	.500	0	2	5.25

Mike Sharperson

Bats: Right   Throws: Right   Pos: 2B   **Ht: 6' 3"   Wt: 205   Born: 10/04/61   Age: 32**

							BATTING													BASERUNNING				PERCENTAGES		
Year	Team	Lg	G	AB	H	2B	3B	HR	(Hm	Rd)	TB	R	RBI	TBB	IBB	SO	HBP	SH	SF	SB	CS	SB%	GDP	Avg	OBP	SLG
1987	2 ML Teams		42	129	29	6	1	0	(0	0)	37	11	10	11	1	20	1	1	0	2	1	.67	3	.225	.291	.287
1988	Los Angeles	NL	46	59	16	1	0	0	(0	0)	17	8	4	1	0	12	1	2	1	0	1	.00	1	.271	.290	.288
1989	Los Angeles	NL	27	28	7	3	0	0	(0	0)	10	2	5	4	1	7	0	1	1	0	1	.00	1	.250	.333	.357
1990	Los Angeles	NL	129	357	106	14	2	3	(1	2)	133	42	36	46	6	39	1	8	3	15	6	.71	5	.297	.376	.373
1991	Los Angeles	NL	105	216	60	11	2	2	(1	1)	81	24	20	25	0	24	1	10	0	1	3	.25	2	.278	.355	.375
1992	Los Angeles	NL	128	317	95	21	0	3	(2	1)	125	48	36	47	1	33	0	5	3	2	2	.50	9	.300	.387	.394
1993	Los Angeles	NL	73	90	23	4	0	2	(1	1)	33	13	10	5	0	17	1	0	1	2	0	1.00	2	.256	.299	.367
1987	Toronto	AL	32	96	20	4	1	0	(0	0)	26	4	9	7	0	15	1	1	0	2	1	.67	2	.208	.269	.271
	Los Angeles	NL	10	33	9	2	0	0	(0	0)	11	7	1	4	1	5	0	0	0	0	0	.00	1	.273	.351	.333
	7 ML YEARS		550	1196	336	60	5	10	(5	5)	436	148	121	139	9	152	5	27	9	22	14	.61	23	.281	.356	.365

Jon Shave

Bats: Right   Throws: Right   Pos: SS   **Ht: 6' 0"   Wt: 180   Born: 11/04/67   Age: 26**

							BATTING													BASERUNNING				PERCENTAGES		
Year	Team	Lg	G	AB	H	2B	3B	HR	(Hm	Rd)	TB	R	RBI	TBB	IBB	SO	HBP	SH	SF	SB	CS	SB%	GDP	Avg	OBP	SLG
1990	Butte	R	64	250	88	9	3	2	--	--	109	41	42	25	0	27	3	2	4	21	7	.75	8	.352	.411	.436
1991	Gastonia	A	55	213	62	11	0	2	--	--	79	29	24	20	0	26	1	3	0	11	9	.55	3	.291	.355	.371
	Charlotte	A	56	189	43	4	1	1	--	--	52	17	20	18	1	30	5	2	4	7	7	.50	3	.228	.306	.275
1992	Tulsa	AA	118	453	130	23	5	2	--	--	169	57	36	37	1	59	4	7	5	6	7	.46	10	.287	.343	.373
1993	Okla City	AAA	100	399	105	17	3	4	--	--	140	58	41	20	0	60	2	9	1	4	3	.57	12	.263	.301	.351
1993	Texas	AL	17	47	15	2	0	0	(0	0)	17	3	3	7	0	8	0	3	2	1	3	.25	0	.319	.306	.362

Jeff Shaw

Pitches: Right   Bats: Right   Pos: RP/SP   **Ht: 6' 2"   Wt: 185   Born: 07/07/66   Age: 27**

			HOW MUCH HE PITCHED						WHAT HE GAVE UP												THE RESULTS					
Year	Team	Lg	G	GS	CG	GF	IP	BFP	H	R	ER	HR	SH	SF	HB	TBB	IBB	SO	WP	Bk	W	L	Pct.	ShO	Sv	ERA
1993	Ottawa *	AAA	2	2	0	0	4	18	5	0	0	0	0	0	0	2	0	1	0	0	0	0	.000	0	0	0.00
1990	Cleveland	AL	12	9	0	0	48.2	229	73	38	36	11	1	3	0	20	0	25	3	0	3	4	.429	0	0	6.66
1991	Cleveland	AL	29	1	0	9	72.1	311	72	34	27	6	1	4	4	27	5	31	6	0	0	5	.000	0	1	3.36
1992	Cleveland	AL	2	1	0	1	7.2	33	7	7	7	2	2	0	0	4	0	3	0	0	0	1	.000	0	0	8.22
1993	Montreal	NL	55	8	0	13	95.2	404	91	47	44	12	5	2	7	32	2	50	2	0	2	7	.222	0	0	4.14
	4 ML YEARS		98	19	0	23	224.1	977	243	126	114	31	9	9	11	83	7	109	11	0	5	17	.227	0	1	4.57

Danny Sheaffer

Bats: Right   Throws: Right   Pos: C   **Ht: 6' 0"   Wt: 185   Born: 08/21/61   Age: 32**

							BATTING													BASERUNNING				PERCENTAGES		
Year	Team	Lg	G	AB	H	2B	3B	HR	(Hm	Rd)	TB	R	RBI	TBB	IBB	SO	HBP	SH	SF	SB	CS	SB%	GDP	Avg	OBP	SLG
1987	Boston	AL	25	66	8	1	0	1	(0	1)	12	5	5	0	0	14	0	1	1	0	0	.00	2	.121	.119	.182
1989	Cleveland	AL	7	16	1	0	0	0	(0	0)	1	1	0	2	0	2	0	1	0	0	0	.00	0	.063	.167	.063
1993	Colorado	NL	82	216	60	9	1	4	(2	2)	83	26	32	8	0	15	1	2	6	2	3	.40	9	.278	.299	.384
	3 ML YEARS		114	298	69	10	1	5	(2	3)	96	32	37	10	0	31	1	4	7	2	3	.40	11	.232	.253	.322

Larry Sheets

Bats: Left **Throws:** Right **Pos:** DH   **Ht:** 6' 3" **Wt:** 236 **Born:** 12/06/59 **Age:** 34

								BATTING											BASERUNNING				PERCENTAGES		
Year Team	Lg	G	AB	H	2B	3B	HR	(Hm	Rd)	TB	R	RBI	TBB	IBB	SO	HBP	SH	SF	SB	CS	SB%	GDP	Avg	OBP	SLG
1993 New Orleans *	AAA	127	457	128	28	1	18	--	--	212	60	98	31	9	52	7	1	10	3	6	.33	10	.280	.329	.464
1984 Baltimore	AL	8	16	7	1	0	1	(0	1)	11	3	2	1	0	3	0	0	0	0	0	.00	0	.438	.471	.688
1985 Baltimore	AL	113	328	86	8	0	17	(5	12)	145	43	50	28	2	52	2	1	1	0	1	.00	15	.262	.323	.442
1986 Baltimore	AL	112	338	92	17	1	18	(10	8)	165	42	60	21	3	56	2	1	2	2	0	1.00	16	.272	.317	.488
1987 Baltimore	AL	135	469	148	23	0	31	(21	10)	264	74	94	31	1	67	3	0	5	1	1	.50	16	.316	.358	.563
1988 Baltimore	AL	136	452	104	19	1	10	(6	4)	155	38	47	42	4	72	6	0	4	1	6	.14	11	.230	.302	.343
1989 Baltimore	AL	102	304	74	12	1	7	(1	6)	109	33	33	26	10	58	3	0	5	1	1	.50	4	.243	.305	.359
1990 Detroit	AL	131	360	94	17	2	10	(7	3)	145	40	52	24	2	42	2	0	4	1	3	.25	13	.261	.308	.403
1993 Seattle	AL	11	17	2	1	0	0	(0	0)	3	0	0	2	0	1	1	0	0	0	0	.00	2	.118	.250	.176
8 ML YEARS		748	2284	607	98	5	94	(50	44)	997	273	339	175	22	351	19	2	21	6	12	.33	77	.266	.321	.437

Gary Sheffield

Bats: Right **Throws:** Right **Pos:** 3B   **Ht:** 5'11" **Wt:** 190 **Born:** 11/18/68 **Age:** 25

								BATTING											BASERUNNING				PERCENTAGES		
Year Team	Lg	G	AB	H	2B	3B	HR	(Hm	Rd)	TB	R	RBI	TBB	IBB	SO	HBP	SH	SF	SB	CS	SB%	GDP	Avg	OBP	SLG
1988 Milwaukee	AL	24	80	19	1	0	4	(1	3)	32	12	12	7	0	7	0	1	1	3	1	.75	5	.238	.295	.400
1989 Milwaukee	AL	95	368	91	18	0	5	(2	3)	124	34	32	27	0	33	4	3	3	10	6	.63	4	.247	.303	.337
1990 Milwaukee	AL	125	487	143	30	1	10	(3	7)	205	67	67	44	1	41	3	4	9	25	10	.71	11	.294	.350	.421
1991 Milwaukee	AL	50	175	34	12	2	2	(2	0)	56	25	22	19	1	15	3	1	5	5	5	.50	3	.194	.277	.320
1992 San Diego	NL	146	557	184	34	3	33	(23	10)	323	87	100	48	5	40	6	0	7	5	6	.45	19	.330	.385	.580
1993 2 ML Teams		140	494	145	20	5	20	(10	10)	235	67	73	47	6	64	9	0	7	17	5	.77	11	.294	.361	.476
1993 San Diego	NL	68	258	76	12	2	10	(6	4)	122	34	36	18	0	30	3	0	3	5	1	.83	9	.295	.344	.473
Florida	NL	72	236	69	8	3	10	(4	6)	113	33	37	29	6	34	6	0	4	12	4	.75	2	.292	.378	.479
6 ML YEARS		580	2161	616	115	11	74	(41	33)	975	292	306	192	13	200	25	9	32	65	33	.66	53	.285	.346	.451

Ben Shelton

Bats: Right **Throws:** Left **Pos:** LF   **Ht:** 6' 3" **Wt:** 210 **Born:** 09/21/69 **Age:** 24

								BATTING											BASERUNNING				PERCENTAGES		
Year Team	Lg	G	AB	H	2B	3B	HR	(Hm	Rd)	TB	R	RBI	TBB	IBB	SO	HBP	SH	SF	SB	CS	SB%	GDP	Avg	OBP	SLG
1987 Pirates	R	38	119	34	8	3	4	--	--	60	22	16	12	1	48	2	0	1	7	2	.78	0	.286	.358	.504
1988 Augusta	A	38	128	25	2	2	5	--	--	46	25	20	30	0	72	2	0	1	3	2	.60	1	.195	.354	.359
Princeton	R	63	204	45	7	3	4	--	--	70	34	20	42	1	82	5	0	3	8	3	.73	1	.221	.362	.343
1989 Augusta	A	122	386	95	16	4	8	--	--	143	67	50	87	1	132	3	0	2	18	4	.82	5	.246	.387	.370
1990 Salem	A	109	320	66	10	2	10	--	--	110	44	36	55	0	116	8	4	4	1	2	.33	5	.206	.333	.344
1991 Salem	A	65	203	53	10	2	14	--	--	109	37	56	45	4	65	5	1	0	3	2	.60	5	.261	.407	.537
Carolina	AA	55	169	39	8	3	1	--	--	56	19	19	29	0	57	4	0	1	2	1	.67	2	.231	.355	.331
1992 Carolina	AA	115	368	86	17	0	10	--	--	133	57	51	68	1	117	8	0	3	4	3	.57	11	.234	.362	.361
1993 Buffalo	AAA	65	173	48	8	1	5	--	--	73	25	22	24	0	44	3	0	0	0	0	.00	2	.277	.375	.422
1993 Pittsburgh	NL	15	24	6	1	0	2	(2	0)	13	3	7	3	0	3	0	0	0	0	0	.00	2	.250	.333	.542

Keith Shepherd

Pitches: Right **Bats:** Right **Pos:** RP   **Ht:** 6' 2" **Wt:** 197 **Born:** 01/21/68 **Age:** 26

				HOW MUCH HE PITCHED					WHAT HE GAVE UP											THE RESULTS					
Year Team	Lg	G	GS	CG	GF	IP	BFP	H	R	ER	HR	SH	SF	HB	TBB	IBB	SO	WP	Bk	W	L	Pct.	ShO	Sv	ERA
1990 Reno	A	5	5	0	0	25	120	22	25	15	1	3	1	2	18	0	16	6	1	1	4	.200	0	0	5.40
Watertown	A	24	0	0	19	54.1	235	41	22	15	1	4	0	4	29	1	55	9	1	3	3	.500	0	3	2.48
1991 South Bend	A	31	0	0	21	35.1	140	17	4	2	0	3	0	1	19	2	38	5	1	1	2	.333	0	10	0.51
Sarasota	A	18	0	0	8	39.2	166	33	16	12	0	3	1	2	20	0	24	1	0	1	1	.500	0	2	2.72
1992 Birmingham	AA	40	0	0	30	71.1	282	50	19	17	1	4	1	1	20	2	64	7	1	3	3	.500	0	7	2.14
Reading	AA	4	3	0	1	22.2	87	7	7	7	1	2	0	0	4	1	9	0	0	0	1	.000	0	0	2.78
1993 Colo Spmgs	AAA	37	1	0	20	67.2	339	90	61	51	2	2	4	4	44	2	57	15	0	3	6	.333	0	8	6.78
1992 Philadelphia	NL	12	0	0	6	22	91	19	10	8	0	4	3	0	6	1	10	1	0	1	1	.500	0	2	3.27
1993 Colorado	NL	14	1	0	3	19.1	85	26	16	15	4	1	1	1	4	0	7	1	0	1	3	.250	0	1	6.98
2 ML YEARS		26	1	0	9	41.1	176	45	26	23	4	5	4	1	10	1	17	2	0	2	4	.333	0	3	5.01

Darrell Sherman

Bats: Left **Throws:** Left **Pos:** LF   **Ht:** 5' 9" **Wt:** 160 **Born:** 12/04/67 **Age:** 26

								BATTING											BASERUNNING				PERCENTAGES		
Year Team	Lg	G	AB	H	2B	3B	HR	(Hm	Rd)	TB	R	RBI	TBB	IBB	SO	HBP	SH	SF	SB	CS	SB%	GDP	Avg	OBP	SLG
1989 Spokane	A	70	258	82	13	1	0	--	--	97	70	29	58	2	29	13	2	4	58	7	.89	1	.318	.459	.376
1990 Riverside	A	131	483	140	10	4	0	--	--	158	97	35	89	2	51	12	6	2	74	26	.74	7	.290	.411	.327
Las Vegas	AAA	4	12	0	0	0	0	--	--	0	1	1	1	0	2	0	0	0	1	0	1.00	0	.000	.077	.000
1991 Wichita	AA	131	502	148	17	3	3	--	--	180	93	48	74	1	28	9	2	6	43	21	.67	7	.295	.391	.359

Year	Team	Lg	G	AB	H	2B	3B	HR	(Hm	Rd)	TB	R	RBI	TBB	IBB	SO	HBP	SH	SF	SB	CS	SB%	GDP	Avg	OBP	SLG
1992	Wichita	AA	64	220	73	11	2	6	--	--	106	60	25	40	2	25	9	2	2	26	7	.79	6	.332	.450	.482
	Las Vegas	AAA	71	269	77	8	1	3	--	--	96	48	22	42	0	41	3	1	1	26	5	.84	3	.286	.387	.357
1993	Las Vegas	AAA	82	272	72	8	2	0	--	--	84	52	11	38	0	27	2	7	1	20	10	.67	1	.265	.358	.309
1993	San Diego	NL	37	63	14	1	0	0	(0	0)	15	8	2	6	0	8	3	1	1	2	1	.67	0	.222	.315	.238

Tommy Shields

Bats: Right   Throws: Right   Pos: 2B   Ht: 6' 0"   Wt: 185   Born: 08/14/64   Age: 29

						BATTING														BASERUNNING				PERCENTAGES		
Year	Team	Lg	G	AB	H	2B	3B	HR	(Hm	Rd)	TB	R	RBI	TBB	IBB	SO	HBP	SH	SF	SB	CS	SB%	GDP	Avg	OBP	SLG
1986	Watertown	A	43	153	44	6	1	4	--	--	64	25	25	17	0	36	7	1	3	15	6	.71	3	.288	.378	.418
	Pr William	A	30	112	31	7	1	1	--	--	43	17	12	9	0	16	5	1	1	4	1	.80	5	.277	.354	.384
1988	Salem	A	45	156	49	5	0	3	--	--	63	20	25	16	0	24	6	1	2	10	3	.77	5	.314	.394	.404
	Harrisburg	AA	57	198	61	4	2	2	--	--	75	30	21	14	1	25	3	2	1	7	3	.70	5	.308	.361	.379
1989	Harrisburg	AA	123	417	120	13	4	5	--	--	156	66	47	25	3	62	9	2	3	17	5	.77	11	.288	.339	.374
1990	Buffalo	AAA	123	380	94	20	3	2	--	--	126	42	30	21	1	72	2	6	3	12	6	.67	11	.247	.288	.332
1991	Rochester	AAA	116	412	119	18	3	6	--	--	161	69	52	32	1	73	11	5	3	16	8	.67	11	.289	.354	.391
1992	Rochester	AAA	121	431	130	23	3	10	--	--	189	58	59	30	1	72	6	4	4	13	7	.65	9	.302	.352	.439
1993	Iowa	AAA	84	314	90	16	1	9	--	--	135	48	48	26	1	46	6	2	2	10	6	.63	9	.287	.351	.430
1992	Baltimore	AL	2	0	0	0	0	0	(0	0)	0	0	0	0	0	0	0	0	0	0	0	.00	0	.000	.000	.000
1993	Chicago	NL	20	34	6	1	0	0	(0	0)	7	4	1	2	0	10	0	0	1	0	0	.00	1	.176	.222	.206
	2 ML YEARS		22	34	6	1	0	0	(0	0)	7	4	1	2	0	10	0	0	1	0	0	.00	1	.176	.222	.206

Zak Shinall

Pitches: Right   Bats: Right   Pos: RP   Ht: 6' 4"   Wt: 220   Born: 10/14/68   Age: 25

					HOW MUCH HE PITCHED					WHAT HE GAVE UP										THE RESULTS				
Year	Team	Lg	G	GS	CG	GF	IP	BFP	H	R	ER	HR	SH	SF	HB	TBB	IBB	SO	WP	Bk	W	L	Pct.	ShO	Sv	ERA
1987	Great Falls	R	1	0	0	0	1.1	15	4	8	7	1	0	0	1	5	0	0	0	1	0	0	.000	0	0	47.25
	Dodgers	R	8	6	0	1	30.1	131	27	17	17	0	2	0	0	15	1	29	4	0	1	2	.333	0	0	5.04
1988	Bakersfield	A	28	19	1	3	113	526	90	65	53	1	3	6	4	104	0	63	20	3	7	8	.467	1	0	4.22
1989	Vero Beach	A	47	4	1	23	86	352	71	32	24	4	5	3	2	29	7	69	4	2	5	7	.417	0	7	2.51
1990	San Antonio	AA	20	15	0	3	91.1	390	93	44	36	2	5	0	1	41	1	43	6	1	6	3	.667	0	0	3.55
1991	San Antonio	AA	25	5	0	19	54.2	234	53	31	17	4	3	1	0	21	2	29	1	2	2	4	.333	0	9	2.80
	Albuquerque	AAA	29	0	0	11	41	176	48	15	14	3	2	0	2	10	0	22	3	0	2	0	1.000	0	1	3.07
1992	Albuquerque	AAA	64	0	0	32	82	363	91	38	30	7	7	2	1	37	11	46	4	0	13	5	.722	0	6	3.29
1993	Charlotte	AAA	1	0	0	0	0.2	6	3	4	0	0	0	0	0	1	0	0	0	0	0	0	.000	0	0	54.00
	Calgary	AAA	33	0	0	19	46.2	211	55	29	26	6	2	1	4	18	3	25	4	0	2	1	.667	0	5	5.01
1993	Seattle	AL	1	0	0	0	2.2	14	4	1	1	1	0	0	0	2	0	0	0	0	0	0	.000	0	0	3.38

Craig Shipley

Bats: Right   Throws: Right   Pos: SS/2B/3B   Ht: 6' 1"   Wt: 185   Born: 01/07/63   Age: 31

						BATTING														BASERUNNING				PERCENTAGES		
Year	Team	Lg	G	AB	H	2B	3B	HR	(Hm	Rd)	TB	R	RBI	TBB	IBB	SO	HBP	SH	SF	SB	CS	SB%	GDP	Avg	OBP	SLG
1986	Los Angeles	NL	12	27	3	1	0	0	(0	0)	4	3	4	2	1	5	1	1	0	0	0	.00	1	.111	.200	.148
1987	Los Angeles	NL	26	35	9	1	0	0	(0	0)	10	3	2	0	0	6	0	0	0	0	0	.00	2	.257	.257	.286
1989	New York	NL	4	7	1	0	0	0	(0	0)	1	3	0	0	0	1	0	0	0	0	0	.00	1	.143	.143	.143
1991	San Diego	NL	37	91	25	3	0	1	(0	1)	31	6	6	2	0	14	1	1	0	0	1	.00	1	.275	.298	.341
1992	San Diego	NL	52	105	26	6	0	0	(0	0)	32	7	7	2	1	21	0	1	0	1	1	.50	2	.248	.262	.305
1993	San Diego	NL	105	230	54	9	0	4	(2	2)	75	25	22	10	0	31	3	1	1	12	3	.80	3	.235	.275	.326
	6 ML YEARS		236	495	118	20	0	5	(2	3)	153	47	41	16	2	78	5	4	1	13	5	.72	9	.238	.269	.309

Brian Shouse

Pitches: Left   Bats: Left   Pos: RP   Ht: 5'11"   Wt: 175   Born: 09/26/68   Age: 25

					HOW MUCH HE PITCHED					WHAT HE GAVE UP										THE RESULTS				
Year	Team	Lg	G	GS	CG	GF	IP	BFP	H	R	ER	HR	SH	SF	HB	TBB	IBB	SO	WP	Bk	W	L	Pct.	ShO	Sv	ERA
1990	Welland	A	17	1	0	7	39.2	177	50	27	23	2	3	2	3	7	0	39	1	2	4	3	.571	0	2	5.22
1991	Augusta	A	26	0	0	25	31	124	22	13	11	1	1	1	3	9	1	32	5	0	2	3	.400	0	8	3.19
	Salem	A	17	0	0	9	33.2	147	35	12	11	2	2	0	0	15	2	25	1	0	2	1	.667	0	3	2.94
1992	Carolina	AA	59	0	0	33	77.1	323	71	31	21	3	8	2	2	28	4	79	4	1	5	6	.455	0	4	2.44
1993	Buffalo	AAA	48	0	0	14	51.2	218	54	24	22	7	0	3	2	17	2	25	1	0	1	0	1.000	0	4	3.83
1993	Pittsburgh	NL	6	0	0	1	4	22	7	4	4	1	0	1	0	2	0	3	1	0	0	0	.000	0	0	9.00

Terry Shumpert

Bats: Right   Throws: Right   Pos: 2B   Ht: 5'11"   Wt: 190   Born: 08/16/66   Age: 27

						BATTING														BASERUNNING				PERCENTAGES		
Year	Team	Lg	G	AB	H	2B	3B	HR	(Hm	Rd)	TB	R	RBI	TBB	IBB	SO	HBP	SH	SF	SB	CS	SB%	GDP	Avg	OBP	SLG
1993	Omaha*	AAA	111	413	124	29	1	14	--	--	197	70	59	41	0	62	6	21	6	36	8	.82	7	.300	.367	.477

Year	Team	Lg	G	AB	H	2B	3B	HR	(Hm	Rd)	TB	R	RBI	TBB	IBB	SO	HBP	SH	SF	SB	CS	SB%	GDP	Avg	OBP	SLG
1990	Kansas City	AL	32	91	25	6	1	0	(0	0)	33	7	8	2	0	17	1	0	2	3	3	.50	4	.275	.292	.363
1991	Kansas City	AL	144	369	80	16	4	5	(1	4)	119	45	34	30	0	75	5	10	3	17	11	.61	10	.217	.283	.322
1992	Kansas City	AL	36	94	14	5	1	1	(0	1)	24	6	11	3	0	17	0	2	0	2	2	.50	2	.149	.175	.255
1993	Kansas City	AL	8	10	1	0	0	0	(0	0)	1	0	0	2	0	2	0	0	0	1	0	1.00	0	.100	.250	.100
4 ML YEARS			220	564	120	27	6	6	(1	5)	177	58	53	37	0	111	6	12	5	23	16	.59	16	.213	.266	.314

Joe Siddall

Bats: Left **Throws:** Right **Pos:** C   **Ht:** 6' 1" **Wt:** 197 **Born:** 10/25/67 **Age:** 26

			BATTING																	BASERUNNING				PERCENTAGES		
Year	Team	Lg	G	AB	H	2B	3B	HR	(Hm	Rd)	TB	R	RBI	TBB	IBB	SO	HBP	SH	SF	SB	CS	SB%	GDP	Avg	OBP	SLG
1988	Jamestown	A	53	178	38	5	3	1	--	--	52	18	16	14	1	29	1	4	2	5	4	.56	3	.213	.272	.292
1989	Rockford	A	98	313	74	15	2	4	--	--	105	36	38	26	2	56	6	5	4	8	5	.62	3	.236	.304	.335
1990	Wst Plm Bch	A	106	348	78	12	1	0	--	--	92	29	32	20	0	55	1	10	2	6	7	.46	7	.224	.267	.264
1991	Harrisburg	AA	76	235	54	6	1	1	--	--	65	28	23	23	2	53	1	2	3	8	3	.73	7	.230	.298	.277
1992	Harrisburg	AA	95	288	68	12	0	2	--	--	86	26	27	29	1	55	3	1	3	4	4	.50	7	.236	.310	.299
1993	Ottawa	AAA	48	136	29	6	0	1	--	--	38	14	16	19	5	33	0	3	2	2	2	.50	6	.213	.306	.279
1993	Montreal	NL	19	20	2	1	0	0	(0	0)	3	0	1	1	1	5	0	0	0	0	0	.00	0	.100	.143	.150

Ruben Sierra

Bats: Both **Throws:** Right **Pos:** RF/DH   **Ht:** 6' 1" **Wt:** 200 **Born:** 10/06/65 **Age:** 28

			BATTING																	BASERUNNING				PERCENTAGES		
Year	Team	Lg	G	AB	H	2B	3B	HR	(Hm	Rd)	TB	R	RBI	TBB	IBB	SO	HBP	SH	SF	SB	CS	SB%	GDP	Avg	OBP	SLG
1986	Texas	AL	113	382	101	13	10	16	(8	8)	182	50	55	22	3	65	1	1	5	7	8	.47	8	.264	.302	.476
1987	Texas	AL	158	643	169	35	4	30	(15	15)	302	97	109	39	4	114	2	0	12	16	11	.59	18	.263	.302	.470
1988	Texas	AL	156	615	156	32	2	23	(15	8)	261	77	91	44	10	91	1	0	8	18	4	.82	15	.254	.301	.424
1989	Texas	AL	162	634	194	35	14	29	(21	8)	344	101	119	43	2	82	2	0	10	8	2	.80	7	.306	.347	.543
1990	Texas	AL	159	608	170	37	2	16	(10	6)	259	70	96	49	13	86	1	0	8	9	0	1.00	15	.280	.330	.426
1991	Texas	AL	161	661	203	44	5	25	(12	13)	332	110	116	56	7	91	0	0	9	16	4	.80	17	.307	.357	.502
1992	2 ML Teams		151	601	167	34	7	17	(10	7)	266	83	87	45	12	68	0	0	10	14	4	.78	11	.278	.323	.443
1993	Oakland	AL	158	630	147	23	5	22	(9	13)	246	77	101	52	16	97	0	0	10	25	5	.83	17	.233	.288	.390
1992	Texas	AL	124	500	139	30	6	14	(8	6)	223	66	70	31	6	59	0	0	8	12	4	.75	9	.278	.315	.446
	Oakland	AL	27	101	28	4	1	3	(2	1)	43	17	17	14	6	9	0	0	2	2	0	1.00	2	.277	.359	.426
8 ML YEARS			1218	4774	1307	253	49	178	(100	78)	2192	665	774	350	67	694	7	1	72	113	38	.75	108	.274	.320	.459

Dave Silvestri

Bats: Right **Throws:** Right **Pos:** SS   **Ht:** 6' 0" **Wt:** 180 **Born:** 09/29/67 **Age:** 26

			BATTING																	BASERUNNING				PERCENTAGES		
Year	Team	Lg	G	AB	H	2B	3B	HR	(Hm	Rd)	TB	R	RBI	TBB	IBB	SO	HBP	SH	SF	SB	CS	SB%	GDP	Avg	OBP	SLG
1989	Osceola	A	129	437	111	20	1	2	--	--	139	67	50	68	1	72	6	8	10	28	13	.68	15	.254	.355	.318
1990	Pr William	A	131	465	120	30	7	5	--	--	179	74	56	77	0	90	6	5	5	37	13	.74	9	.258	.367	.385
	Albany	AA	2	7	2	0	0	0	--	--	2	0	2	0	0	1	0	0	0	0	0	.00	0	.286	.286	.286
1991	Albany	AA	140	512	134	31	8	19	--	--	238	97	83	83	3	126	2	2	2	20	13	.61	18	.262	.366	.465
1992	Columbus	AAA	118	420	117	25	5	13	--	--	191	83	73	58	1	110	8	0	5	19	11	.63	10	.279	.373	.455
1993	Columbus	AAA	120	428	115	26	4	20	--	--	209	76	65	68	4	127	3	0	4	6	9	.40	10	.269	.370	.488
1992	New York	AL	7	13	4	0	2	0	(0	0)	8	3	1	0	0	3	0	0	0	0	0	.00	1	.308	.308	.615
1993	New York	AL	7	21	6	1	0	1	(0	1)	10	4	4	5	0	3	0	0	0	0	0	.00	1	.286	.423	.476
2 ML YEARS			14	34	10	1	2	1	(0	1)	18	7	5	5	0	6	0	0	0	0	0	.00	2	.294	.385	.529

Don Slaught

Bats: Right **Throws:** Right **Pos:** C   **Ht:** 6' 1" **Wt:** 190 **Born:** 09/11/58 **Age:** 35

			BATTING																	BASERUNNING				PERCENTAGES		
Year	Team	Lg	G	AB	H	2B	3B	HR	(Hm	Rd)	TB	R	RBI	TBB	IBB	SO	HBP	SH	SF	SB	CS	SB%	GDP	Avg	OBP	SLG
1982	Kansas City	AL	43	115	32	6	0	3	(0	3)	47	14	8	9	0	12	0	2	0	0	0	.00	3	.278	.331	.409
1983	Kansas City	AL	83	276	86	13	4	0	(0	0)	107	21	28	11	0	27	0	1	2	3	1	.75	8	.312	.336	.388
1984	Kansas City	AL	124	409	108	27	4	4	(1	3)	155	48	42	20	4	55	2	8	7	0	0	.00	8	.264	.297	.379
1985	Texas	AL	102	343	96	17	4	8	(4	4)	145	34	35	20	1	41	6	1	0	5	4	.56	8	.280	.331	.423
1986	Texas	AL	95	314	83	17	1	13	(5	8)	141	39	46	16	0	59	5	3	3	3	2	.60	8	.264	.308	.449
1987	Texas	AL	95	237	53	15	2	8	(5	3)	96	25	16	24	3	51	1	4	0	0	3	.00	7	.224	.298	.405
1988	New York	AL	97	322	91	25	1	9	(7	2)	145	33	43	24	3	54	3	5	4	1	0	1.00	10	.283	.334	.450
1989	New York	AL	117	350	88	21	3	5	(3	2)	130	34	38	30	3	57	5	2	5	1	1	.50	9	.251	.315	.371
1990	Pittsburgh	NL	84	230	69	18	3	4	(1	3)	105	27	29	27	2	27	3	3	4	0	1	.00	2	.300	.375	.457
1991	Pittsburgh	NL	77	220	65	17	1	1	(0	1)	87	19	29	21	1	32	3	5	1	1	0	1.00	6	.295	.363	.395
1992	Pittsburgh	NL	87	255	88	17	3	4	(2	2)	123	26	37	17	5	23	2	6	5	2	2	.50	6	.345	.384	.482
1993	Pittsburgh	NL	116	377	113	19	2	10	(1	9)	166	34	55	29	2	56	6	4	4	2	1	.67	13	.300	.356	.440
12 ML YEARS			1120	3448	972	212	28	69	(29	40)	1447	354	406	248	24	494	36	44	35	18	15	.55	88	.282	.333	.420

Heathcliff Slocumb

Pitches: Right **Bats:** Right **Pos:** RP   **Ht:** 6' 3" **Wt:** 210 **Born:** 06/07/66 **Age:** 28

Year Team	Lg	G	GS	CG	GF	IP	BFP	H	R	ER	HR	SH	SF	HB	TBB	IBB	SO	WP	Bk	W	L	Pct.	ShO	Sv	ERA
1993 Iowa *	AAA	10	0	0	10	12	48	7	2	2	0	1	0	0	8	0	10	0	0	1	0	1.000	0	7	1.50
Charlotte *	AAA	23	0	0	9	30.1	129	25	14	12	2	4	0	0	11	1	25	2	0	3	2	.600	0	1	3.56
1991 Chicago	NL	52	0	0	21	62.2	274	53	29	24	3	6	6	3	30	6	34	9	0	2	1	.667	0	1	3.45
1992 Chicago	NL	30	0	0	11	36	174	52	27	26	3	2	2	1	21	3	27	1	0	0	3	.000	0	1	6.50
1993 2 ML Teams		30	0	0	9	38	164	35	19	17	3	1	3	0	20	2	22	0	0	4	1	.800	0	0	4.03
1993 Chicago	NL	10	0	0	4	10.2	42	7	5	4	0	0	1	0	4	0	4	0	0	1	0	1.000	0	0	3.38
Cleveland	AL	20	0	0	5	27.1	122	28	14	13	3	1	2	0	16	2	18	0	0	3	1	.750	0	0	4.28
3 ML YEARS		112	0	0	41	136.2	612	140	75	67	9	9	11	4	71	11	83	10	0	6	5	.545	0	2	4.41

Joe Slusarski

Pitches: Right **Bats:** Right **Pos:** SP   **Ht:** 6' 4" **Wt:** 195 **Born:** 12/19/66 **Age:** 27

Year Team	Lg	G	GS	CG	GF	IP	BFP	H	R	ER	HR	SH	SF	HB	TBB	IBB	SO	WP	Bk	W	L	Pct.	ShO	Sv	ERA
1993 Tacoma *	AAA	24	21	1	0	113.1	501	133	67	60	6	3	7	1	40	1	61	0	2	7	5	.583	1	0	4.76
1991 Oakland	AL	20	19	1	0	109.1	486	121	69	64	14	0	3	4	52	1	60	4	0	5	7	.417	0	0	5.27
1992 Oakland	AL	15	14	0	1	76	338	85	52	46	15	1	5	6	27	0	38	0	1	5	5	.500	0	0	5.45
1993 Oakland	AL	2	1	0	0	8.2	43	9	5	5	1	2	0	0	11	3	1	0	0	0	0	.000	0	0	5.19
3 ML YEARS		37	34	1	1	194	867	215	126	115	30	3	8	10	90	4	99	4	1	10	12	.455	0	0	5.34

John Smiley

Pitches: Left **Bats:** Left **Pos:** SP   **Ht:** 6' 4" **Wt:** 215 **Born:** 03/17/65 **Age:** 29

Year Team	Lg	G	GS	CG	GF	IP	BFP	H	R	ER	HR	SH	SF	HB	TBB	IBB	SO	WP	Bk	W	L	Pct.	ShO	Sv	ERA
1986 Pittsburgh	NL	12	0	0	2	11.2	42	4	6	5	2	0	0	0	4	0	9	0	0	1	0	1.000	0	0	3.86
1987 Pittsburgh	NL	63	0	0	19	75	336	69	49	48	7	0	3	0	50	8	58	5	1	5	5	.500	0	4	5.76
1988 Pittsburgh	NL	34	32	5	0	205	835	185	81	74	15	11	8	3	46	4	129	6	6	13	11	.542	1	0	3.25
1989 Pittsburgh	NL	28	28	8	0	205.1	835	174	78	64	22	5	7	4	49	5	123	5	2	12	8	.600	1	0	2.81
1990 Pittsburgh	NL	26	25	2	0	149.1	632	161	83	77	15	5	4	2	36	1	86	2	2	9	10	.474	0	0	4.64
1991 Pittsburgh	NL	33	32	2	0	207.2	836	194	78	71	17	11	4	3	44	0	129	3	1	20	8	.714	1	0	3.08
1992 Minnesota	AL	34	34	5	0	241	970	205	93	86	17	4	9	6	65	0	163	4	0	16	9	.640	2	0	3.21
1993 Cincinnati	NL	18	18	2	0	105.2	455	117	69	66	15	10	3	2	31	0	60	2	1	3	9	.250	0	0	5.62
8 ML YEARS		248	169	24	21	1200.2	4941	1109	537	491	110	46	38	20	325	18	757	27	13	79	60	.568	5	4	3.68

Bryn Smith

Pitches: Right **Bats:** Right **Pos:** RP/SP   **Ht:** 6' 2" **Wt:** 205 **Born:** 08/11/55 **Age:** 38

Year Team	Lg	G	GS	CG	GF	IP	BFP	H	R	ER	HR	SH	SF	HB	TBB	IBB	SO	WP	Bk	W	L	Pct.	ShO	Sv	ERA
1981 Montreal	NL	7	0	0	1	13	53	14	4	4	1	0	0	0	3	0	9	2	0	1	0	1.000	0	0	2.77
1982 Montreal	NL	47	1	0	16	79.1	335	81	43	37	5	1	4	0	23	5	50	5	1	2	4	.333	0	3	4.20
1983 Montreal	NL	49	12	5	17	155.1	636	142	51	43	13	14	2	5	43	6	101	5	3	6	11	.353	3	3	2.49
1984 Montreal	NL	28	28	4	0	179	751	178	72	66	15	7	2	3	51	7	101	2	2	12	13	.480	2	0	3.32
1985 Montreal	NL	32	32	4	0	222.1	890	193	85	72	12	13	4	1	41	3	127	1	1	18	5	.783	2	0	2.91
1986 Montreal	NL	30	30	1	0	187.1	807	182	101	82	15	10	3	6	63	6	105	4	2	10	8	.556	0	0	3.94
1987 Montreal	NL	26	26	2	0	150.1	643	164	81	73	16	7	5	2	31	4	94	2	0	10	9	.526	0	0	4.37
1988 Montreal	NL	32	32	1	0	198	791	179	79	66	15	7	6	10	32	2	122	2	5	12	10	.545	0	0	3.00
1989 Montreal	NL	33	32	3	0	215.2	864	177	76	68	16	7	5	4	54	4	129	3	1	10	11	.476	1	0	2.84
1990 St. Louis	NL	26	25	0	0	141.1	605	160	81	67	11	7	5	4	30	1	78	2	0	9	8	.529	0	0	4.27
1991 St. Louis	NL	31	31	3	0	198.2	818	188	95	85	16	10	7	7	45	3	94	3	1	12	9	.571	0	0	3.85
1992 St. Louis	NL	13	1	0	3	21.1	91	20	11	11	3	2	0	3	5	1	9	1	0	4	2	.667	0	0	4.64
1993 Colorado	NL	11	5	0	2	29.2	150	47	29	28	2	2	4	3	11	1	9	1	0	2	4	.333	0	0	8.49
13 ML YEARS		365	255	23	39	1791.1	7434	1725	808	702	140	87	47	48	432	43	1028	33	16	108	94	.535	8	6	3.53

Dwight Smith

Bats: Left **Throws:** Right **Pos:** CF/LF/RF   **Ht:** 5'11" **Wt:** 195 **Born:** 11/08/63 **Age:** 30

Year Team	Lg	G	AB	H	2B	3B	HR	(Hm	Rd)	TB	R	RBI	TBB	IBB	SO	HBP	SH	SF	SB	CS	SB%	GDP	Avg	OBP	SLG
1993 Daytona *	A	5	16	5	4	0	0	--	--	9	3	2	3	0	4	1	0	0	1	0	.00	0	.313	.450	.563
1989 Chicago	NL	109	343	111	19	6	9	(5	4)	169	52	52	31	0	51	2	4	1	9	4	.69	4	.324	.382	.493
1990 Chicago	NL	117	290	76	15	0	6	(3	3)	109	34	27	28	2	46	2	0	2	11	6	.65	7	.262	.329	.376
1991 Chicago	NL	90	167	38	7	2	3	(2	1)	58	16	21	11	2	32	1	1	0	2	3	.40	2	.228	.279	.347
1992 Chicago	NL	109	217	60	10	3	3	(3	0)	85	28	24	13	0	40	1	0	2	9	8	.53	1	.276	.318	.392
1993 Chicago	NL	111	310	93	17	5	11	(6	5)	153	51	35	25	1	51	3	1	3	8	6	.57	3	.300	.355	.494
5 ML YEARS		536	1327	378	68	16	32	(19	13)	574	181	159	108	5	220	9	6	8	39	27	.59	17	.285	.341	.433

Lee Smith

Pitches: Right   **Bats:** Right   **Pos:** RP   **Ht:** 6' 6"   **Wt:** 269   **Born:** 12/04/57   **Age:** 36

		HOW MUCH HE PITCHED						WHAT HE GAVE UP												THE RESULTS					
Year Team	Lg	G	GS	CG	GF	IP	BFP	H	R	ER	HR	SH	SF	HB	TBB	IBB	SO	WP	Bk	W	L	Pct.	ShO	Sv	ERA
1980 Chicago	NL	18	0	0	6	22	97	21	9	7	0	1	1	0	14	5	17	0	0	2	0	1.000	0	0	2.86
1981 Chicago	NL	40	1	0	12	67	280	57	31	26	2	8	2	1	31	8	50	7	1	3	6	.333	0	1	3.49
1982 Chicago	NL	72	5	0	38	117	480	105	38	35	5	6	5	3	37	5	99	6	1	2	5	.286	0	17	2.69
1983 Chicago	NL	66	0	0	56	103.1	413	70	23	19	5	9	2	1	41	14	91	5	2	4	10	.286	0	29	1.65
1984 Chicago	NL	69	0	0	59	101	428	98	42	41	6	4	5	0	35	7	86	6	0	9	7	.563	0	33	3.65
1985 Chicago	NL	65	0	0	57	97.2	397	87	35	33	9	3	1	1	32	6	112	4	0	7	4	.636	0	33	3.04
1986 Chicago	NL	66	0	0	59	90.1	372	69	32	31	7	6	3	0	42	11	93	2	0	9	9	.500	0	31	3.09
1987 Chicago	NL	62	0	0	55	83.2	360	84	30	29	4	4	0	0	32	5	96	4	0	4	10	.286	0	36	3.12
1988 Boston	AL	64	0	0	57	83.2	363	72	34	26	7	3	2	1	37	6	96	2	0	4	5	.444	0	29	2.80
1989 Boston	AL	64	0	0	50	70.2	290	53	30	28	6	2	2	0	33	6	96	1	0	6	1	.857	0	25	3.57
1990 2 ML Teams		64	0	0	53	83	344	71	24	19	3	2	3	0	29	7	87	2	0	5	5	.500	0	31	2.06
1991 St. Louis	NL	67	0	0	61	73	300	70	19	19	5	5	1	0	13	5	67	1	0	6	3	.667	0	47	2.34
1992 St. Louis	NL	70	0	0	55	75	310	62	28	26	4	2	1	0	26	4	60	2	0	4	9	.308	0	43	3.12
1993 2 ML Teams		63	0	0	56	58	239	53	25	25	11	0	3	0	14	2	60	1	0	2	4	.333	0	46	3.88
1990 Boston	AL	11	0	0	8	14.1		13	4	3	0	0	0	0	9	2	17	1	0	2	1	.667	0	4	1.88
St. Louis	NL	53	0	0	45	68.2	280	58	20	16	3	2	3	0	20	5	70	1	0	3	4	.429	0	27	2.10
1993 St. Louis	NL	55	0	0	48	50	206	49	25	25	11	0	2	0	9	1	49	1	0	2	4	.333	0	43	4.50
New York	AL	8	0	0	8	8	33	4	0	0	0	0	0	0	5	1	11	0	0	0	0	.000	0	3	0.00
14 ML YEARS		850	6	0	674	1125.1	4673	972	400	364	74	55	31	7	416	91	1110	43	4	67	78	.462	0	401	2.91

Lonnie Smith

Bats: Right   **Throws:** Right   **Pos:** LF   **Ht:** 5' 9"   **Wt:** 195   **Born:** 12/22/55   **Age:** 38

		BATTING																		BASERUNNING				PERCENTAGES		
Year Team	Lg	G	AB	H	2B	3B	HR	(Hm	Rd)	TB	R	RBI	TBB	IBB	SO	HBP	SH	SF		SB	CS	SB%	GDP	Avg	OBP	SLG
1978 Philadelphia	NL	17	4	0	0	0	0	(0	0)	0	6	0	4	0	3	0	0	0		4	0	1.00	0	.000	.500	.000
1979 Philadelphia	NL	17	30	5	2	0	0	(0	0)	7	4	3	1	0	7	0	0	0		2	1	.67	0	.167	.194	.233
1980 Philadelphia	NL	100	298	101	14	4	3	(2	1)	132	69	20	26	2	48	4	1	2		33	13	.72	5	.339	.397	.443
1981 Philadelphia	NL	62	176	57	14	3	2	(1	1)	83	40	11	18	1	14	5	3	0		21	10	.68	1	.324	.402	.472
1982 St. Louis	NL	156	592	182	35	8	8	(3	5)	257	120	69	64	2	74	9	3	4		68	26	.72	11	.307	.381	.434
1983 St. Louis	NL	130	492	158	31	5	8	(4	4)	223	83	45	41	2	55	9	1	4		43	18	.70	11	.321	.381	.453
1984 St. Louis	NL	145	504	126	20	4	6	(3	3)	172	77	49	70	0	90	9	3	4		50	13	.79	7	.250	.349	.341
1985 2 ML Teams		148	544	140	25	6	6	(2	4)	195	92	48	56	0	89	7	1	5		52	13	.80	4	.257	.332	.358
1986 Kansas City	AL	134	508	146	25	7	8	(2	6)	209	80	44	46	0	78	10	2	2		26	9	.74	10	.287	.357	.411
1987 Kansas City	AL	48	167	42	7	1	3	(1	2)	60	26	8	24	0	31	4	0	2		9	4	.69	1	.251	.355	.359
1988 Atlanta	NL	43	114	27	3	0	3	(2	1)	39	14	9	10	0	25	0	0	1		4	2	.67	0	.237	.296	.342
1989 Atlanta	NL	134	482	152	34	4	21	(10	11)	257	89	79	76	3	95	11	1	7		25	12	.68	7	.315	.415	.533
1990 Atlanta	NL	135	466	142	27	9	9	(2	7)	214	72	42	58	3	69	6	1	6		10	10	.50	2	.305	.384	.459
1991 Atlanta	NL	122	353	97	19	1	7	(6	1)	139	58	44	50	3	64	9	2	2		9	5	.64	4	.275	.377	.394
1992 Atlanta	NL	84	158	39	8	2	6	(3	3)	69	23	33	17	1	37	3	0	4		4	0	1.00	1	.247	.324	.437
1993 2 ML Teams		103	223	62	6	4	8	(6	2)	100	43	27	51	2	52	5	3	2		9	4	.69	3	.278	.420	.448
1985 St. Louis	NL	28	96	25	2	2	0	(0	0)	31	15	7	15	0	20	3	1	0		12	6	.67	2	.260	.377	.323
Kansas City	AL	120	448	115	23	4	6	(2	4)	164	77	41	41	0	69	4	0	5		40	7	.85	2	.257	.321	.366
1993 Pittsburgh	NL	94	199	57	5	4	6	(4	2)	88	35	24	43	2	42	5	3	2		9	4	.69	3	.286	.422	.442
Baltimore	AL	9	24	5	1	0	2	(2	0)	12	8	3	8	0	10	0	0	0		0	0	.00	0	.208	.406	.500
16 ML YEARS		1578	5111	1476	270	58	98	(47	51)	2156	896	531	612	19	831	91	21	45		369	140	.72	67	.289	.372	.422

Ozzie Smith

Bats: Both   **Throws:** Right   **Pos:** SS   **Ht:** 5'10"   **Wt:** 168   **Born:** 12/26/54   **Age:** 39

		BATTING																		BASERUNNING				PERCENTAGES		
Year Team	Lg	G	AB	H	2B	3B	HR	(Hm	Rd)	TB	R	RBI	TBB	IBB	SO	HBP	SH	SF		SB	CS	SB%	GDP	Avg	OBP	SLG
1978 San Diego	NL	159	590	152	17	6	1	(0	1)	184	69	46	47	0	43	0	28	3		40	12	.77	11	.258	.311	.312
1979 San Diego	NL	156	587	124	18	6	0	(0	0)	154	77	27	37	5	37	2	22	1		28	7	.80	11	.211	.260	.262
1980 San Diego	NL	158	609	140	18	5	0	(0	0)	168	67	35	71	1	49	5	23	4		57	15	.79	9	.230	.313	.276
1981 San Diego	NL	110	450	100	11	2	0	(0	0)	115	53	21	41	1	37	5	10	1		22	12	.65	8	.222	.294	.256
1982 St. Louis	NL	140	488	121	24	1	2	(0	2)	153	58	43	68	12	32	2	4	5		25	5	.83	10	.248	.339	.314
1983 St. Louis	NL	159	552	134	30	6	3	(1	2)	185	69	50	64	9	36	1	7	2		34	7	.83	10	.243	.321	.335
1984 St. Louis	NL	124	412	106	20	5	1	(1	0)	139	53	44	56	5	17	2	11	3		35	7	.83	8	.257	.347	.337
1985 St. Louis	NL	158	537	148	22	3	6	(2	4)	194	70	54	65	11	27	2	9	2		31	8	.79	13	.276	.355	.361
1986 St. Louis	NL	153	514	144	19	4	0	(0	0)	171	67	54	79	13	27	2	11	3		31	7	.82	9	.280	.376	.333
1987 St. Louis	NL	158	600	182	40	4	0	(0	0)	230	104	75	89	3	36	1	12	4		43	9	.83	9	.303	.392	.383
1988 St. Louis	NL	153	575	155	27	1	3	(2	1)	193	80	51	74	2	43	1	12	7		57	9	.86	7	.270	.350	.336
1989 St. Louis	NL	155	593	162	30	8	2	(1	1)	214	82	50	55	3	37	2	11	3		29	7	.81	10	.273	.335	.361
1990 St. Louis	NL	143	512	130	21	1	1	(0	1)	156	61	50	61	4	33	2	7	10		32	6	.84	8	.254	.330	.305

	Lg																										
1991 St. Louis	NL	150	550	157	30	3	3	(2	1)	202	96	50	83	2	36	1	6	1	35	9	.80	8	.285	.380	.367
1992 St. Louis	NL	132	518	153	20	2	0	(0	0)	177	73	31	59	4	34	0	12	1	43	9	.83	11	.295	.367	.342
1993 St. Louis	NL	141	545	157	22	6	1	(1	0)	194	75	53	43	1	18	1	7	7	21	8	.72	11	.288	.337	.356
16 ML YEARS		2349	8632	2265	369	63	23	(10	13)	2829	1154	734	992	76	542	29	192	57	563	137	.80	153	.262	.338	.328

Pete Smith

Pitches: Right **Bats:** Right **Pos:** SP/RP **Ht:** 6' 2" **Wt:** 200 **Born:** 02/27/66 **Age:** 28

Year Team	Lg	HOW MUCH HE PITCHED						WHAT HE GAVE UP												THE RESULTS					
		G	GS	CG	GF	IP	BFP	H	R	ER	HR	SH	SF	HB	TBB	IBB	SO	WP	Bk	W	L	Pct.	ShO	Sv	ERA
1987 Atlanta	NL	6	6	0	0	31.2	143	39	21	17	3	0	2	0	14	0	11	3	1	1	2	.333	0	0	4.83
1988 Atlanta	NL	32	32	5	0	195.1	837	183	89	80	15	12	4	1	88	3	124	5	7	7	15	.318	3	0	3.69
1989 Atlanta	NL	28	27	1	0	142	613	144	83	75	13	4	5	0	57	2	115	3	7	5	14	.263	0	0	4.75
1990 Atlanta	NL	13	13	3	0	77	327	77	45	41	11	4	3	0	24	2	56	2	1	5	6	.455	0	0	4.79
1991 Atlanta	NL	14	10	0	2	48	211	48	33	27	5	2	4	0	22	3	29	1	4	1	3	.250	0	0	5.06
1992 Atlanta	NL	12	11	2	0	79	323	63	19	18	3	4	1	0	28	2	43	2	1	7	0	1.000	1	0	2.05
1993 Atlanta	NL	20	14	0	2	90.2	390	92	45	44	15	6	5	2	36	3	53	1	1	4	8	.333	0	0	4.37
7 ML YEARS		125	113	11	4	663.2	2844	646	335	302	65	32	24	3	269	15	431	17	22	30	48	.385	4	0	4.10

Zane Smith

Pitches: Left **Bats:** Left **Pos:** SP **Ht:** 6' 1" **Wt:** 205 **Born:** 12/28/60 **Age:** 33

Year Team	Lg	HOW MUCH HE PITCHED						WHAT HE GAVE UP												THE RESULTS					
		G	GS	CG	GF	IP	BFP	H	R	ER	HR	SH	SF	HB	TBB	IBB	SO	WP	Bk	W	L	Pct.	ShO	Sv	ERA
1993 Carolina *	AA	4	4	0	0	20.2	85	20	10	7	1	0	2	1	5	0	13	1	0	1	2	.333	0	0	3.05
1984 Atlanta	NL	3	3	0	0	20	87	16	7	5	1	1	0	0	13	2	16	0	0	1	0	1.000	0	0	2.25
1985 Atlanta	NL	42	18	2	3	147	631	135	70	62	4	16	1	3	80	2	85	2	0	9	10	.474	2	0	3.80
1986 Atlanta	NL	38	32	3	2	204.2	889	209	109	92	8	13	6	5	105	6	139	8	0	8	16	.333	1	1	4.05
1987 Atlanta	NL	36	36	9	0	242	1035	245	130	110	19	12	5	5	91	6	130	5	1	15	10	.600	3	0	4.09
1988 Atlanta	NL	23	22	3	0	140.1	609	159	72	67	8	15	2	3	44	4	59	2	2	5	10	.333	0	0	4.30
1989 2 ML Teams		48	17	0	10	147	634	141	76	57	7	15	5	3	52	7	93	4	0	1	13	.071	0	2	3.49
1990 2 ML Teams		33	31	4	1	215.1	860	196	77	61	15	3	3	3	50	4	130	2	0	12	9	.571	2	0	2.55
1991 Pittsburgh	NL	35	35	6	0	228	916	234	95	81	15	7	5	2	29	3	120	1	0	16	10	.615	3	0	3.20
1992 Pittsburgh	NL	23	22	4	0	141	566	138	56	48	8	12	4	2	19	3	56	0	0	8	8	.500	2	0	3.06
1993 Pittsburgh	NL	14	14	1	0	83	353	97	43	42	5	6	0	0	22	3	32	2	0	3	7	.300	0	0	4.55
1989 Atlanta	NL	17	17	0	0	99	432	102	65	49	5	10	5	2	33	3	58	3	0	1	12	.077	0	0	4.45
Montreal	NL	31	0	0	10	48	202	39	11	8	2	5	0	1	19	4	35	1	0	0	1	.000	0	2	1.50
1990 Montreal	NL	22	21	1	0	139.1	578	141	57	50	11	2	2	3	41	3	80	1	0	6	7	.462	0	0	3.23
Pittsburgh	NL	11	10	3	1	76	282	55	20	11	4	1	1	0	9	1	50	1	0	6	2	.750	2	0	1.30
10 ML YEARS		295	230	32	16	1568.1	6580	1570	735	625	90	100	31	26	505	43	860	26	3	78	93	.456	14	3	3.59

Roger Smithberg

Pitches: Right **Bats:** Right **Pos:** RP **Ht:** 6' 3" **Wt:** 205 **Born:** 03/21/66 **Age:** 28

Year Team	Lg	HOW MUCH HE PITCHED						WHAT HE GAVE UP												THE RESULTS					
		G	GS	CG	GF	IP	BFP	H	R	ER	HR	SH	SF	HB	TBB	IBB	SO	WP	Bk	W	L	Pct.	ShO	Sv	ERA
1988 Batavia	A	15	15	5	0	103.1	426	90	52	38	2	1	0	2	32	0	72	12	3	9	2	.818	0	0	3.31
1989 Las Vegas	AAA	22	22	4	0	137	604	159	79	68	9	7	4	4	35	2	58	3	4	7	7	.500	0	0	4.47
1990 Riverside	A	3	3	0	0	13	53	12	7	6	1	0	1	0	2	0	5	0	1	1	2	.333	0	0	4.15
Las Vegas	AAA	13	13	0	0	66	325	91	63	51	8	0	4	6	39	0	30	6	1	2	7	.222	0	0	6.95
1991 High Desert	A	3	3	0	0	18	75	12	6	3	0	2	1	1	6	0	11	0	0	1	1	.500	0	0	1.50
Wichita	AA	7	7	0	0	41.1	190	49	28	22	3	2	1	1	16	1	23	3	0	2	3	.400	0	0	4.79
Las Vegas	AAA	17	15	1	0	79	374	112	65	58	8	5	6	3	33	1	34	8	0	3	7	.300	0	0	6.61
1992 Reno	A	10	0	0	5	16.2	80	23	10	6	0	1	1	0	10	3	11	2	0	2	1	.667	0	2	3.24
Huntsville	AA	20	0	0	8	36	159	42	17	16	4	2	2	2	12	1	19	1	0	3	3	.500	0	1	4.00
1993 Huntsville	AA	27	0	0	13	36.2	162	34	15	9	3	2	2	2	16	1	36	2	0	4	2	.667	0	0	2.21
Tacoma	AAA	28	0	0	12	50.2	211	50	14	10	1	5	3	2	11	1	25	2	0	3	3	.500	0	4	1.78
1993 Oakland	AL	13	0	0	9	19.2	76	13	7	6	2	2	0	1	7	2	4	1	0	1	2	.333	0	3	2.75

John Smoltz

Pitches: Right **Bats:** Right **Pos:** SP **Ht:** 6' 3" **Wt:** 185 **Born:** 05/15/67 **Age:** 27

Year Team	Lg	HOW MUCH HE PITCHED						WHAT HE GAVE UP												THE RESULTS					
		G	GS	CG	GF	IP	BFP	H	R	ER	HR	SH	SF	HB	TBB	IBB	SO	WP	Bk	W	L	Pct.	ShO	Sv	ERA
1988 Atlanta	NL	12	12	0	0	64	297	74	40	39	10	2	0	2	33	4	37	2	1	2	7	.222	0	0	5.48
1989 Atlanta	NL	29	29	5	0	208	847	160	79	68	15	10	7	2	72	2	168	8	3	12	11	.522	0	0	2.94
1990 Atlanta	NL	34	34	6	0	231.1	966	206	109	99	20	9	8	1	90	3	170	14	3	14	11	.560	2	0	3.85
1991 Atlanta	NL	36	36	5	0	229.2	947	206	101	97	16	9	9	3	77	1	148	20	1	14	13	.519	2	0	3.80
1992 Atlanta	NL	35	35	9	0	246.2	1021	206	90	78	17	7	8	5	80	5	215	17	1	15	12	.556	3	0	2.85
1993 Atlanta	NL	35	35	3	0	243.2	1028	208	104	98	23	13	4	6	100	12	208	13	1	15	11	.577	1	0	3.62
6 ML YEARS		181	181	28	0	1223.1	5106	1060	523	479	101	50	36	19	452	27	946	74	11	72	65	.526	6	0	3.52

J.T. Snow

Bats: Both **Throws:** Left **Pos:** 1B   **Ht:** 6' 2" **Wt:** 202 **Born:** 02/26/68 **Age:** 26

Year	Team	Lg	G	AB	H	2B	3B	HR	(Hm	Rd)	TB	R	RBI	TBB	IBB	SO	HBP	SH	SF	SB	CS	SB%	GDP	Avg	OBP	SLG
1989	Oneonta	A	73	274	80	18	2	8	--	--	126	41	51	29	6	35	2	2	4	4	1	.80	9	.292	.359	.460
1990	Pr William	A	138	520	133	25	1	8	--	--	184	57	72	46	3	65	5	0	7	2	0	1.00	20	.256	.318	.354
1991	Albany	AA	132	477	133	33	3	13	--	--	211	78	76	67	3	78	3	2	10	5	1	.83	10	.279	.364	.442
1992	Columbus	AAA	135	492	154	26	4	15	--	--	233	81	78	70	11	65	1	1	6	3	3	.50	9	.313	.395	.474
1993	Vancouver	AAA	23	94	32	9	1	5	--	--	58	19	24	10	0	13	1	1	1	0	0	.00	0	.340	.410	.617
1992	New York	AL	7	14	2	1	0	0	(0	0)	3	1	2	5	1	5	0	0	0	0	0	.00	0	.143	.368	.214
1993	California	AL	129	419	101	18	2	16	(10	6)	171	60	57	55	4	88	2	7	6	3	0	1.00	10	.241	.328	.408
	2 ML YEARS		136	433	103	19	2	16	(10	6)	174	61	59	60	5	93	2	7	6	3	0	1.00	10	.238	.329	.402

Cory Snyder

Bats: Right **Throws:** Right **Pos:** RF/1B/3B   **Ht:** 6' 3" **Wt:** 206 **Born:** 11/11/62 **Age:** 31

Year	Team	Lg	G	AB	H	2B	3B	HR	(Hm	Rd)	TB	R	RBI	TBB	IBB	SO	HBP	SH	SF	SB	CS	SB%	GDP	Avg	OBP	SLG
1986	Cleveland	AL	103	416	113	21	1	24	(12	12)	208	58	69	16	0	123	0	1	0	2	3	.40	8	.272	.299	.500
1987	Cleveland	AL	157	577	136	24	2	33	(17	16)	263	74	82	31	4	166	1	0	6	5	1	.83	3	.236	.273	.456
1988	Cleveland	AL	142	511	139	24	3	26	(11	15)	247	71	75	42	7	101	1	0	4	5	1	.83	12	.272	.326	.483
1989	Cleveland	AL	132	489	105	17	0	18	(6	12)	176	49	59	23	1	134	2	0	4	6	5	.55	11	.215	.251	.360
1990	Cleveland	AL	123	438	102	27	3	14	(3	11)	177	46	55	21	3	118	2	1	6	1	4	.20	11	.233	.268	.404
1991	2 ML Teams		71	166	29	4	1	3	(2	1)	44	14	17	9	1	60	0	4	1	0	0	.00	6	.175	.216	.265
1992	San Francisco	NL	124	390	105	22	2	14	(8	6)	173	48	57	23	2	96	2	2	3	4	4	.50	10	.269	.311	.444
1993	Los Angeles	NL	143	516	137	33	1	11	(5	6)	205	61	56	47	3	147	4	2	1	4	1	.80	8	.266	.331	.397
1991	Chicago	AL	50	117	22	4	0	3	(2	1)	35	10	11	6	1	41	0	3	0	0	0	.00	5	.188	.228	.299
	Toronto	AL	21	49	7	0	1	0	(0	0)	9	4	6	3	0	19	0	1	1	0	0	.00	1	.143	.189	.184
	8 ML YEARS		995	3503	866	172	13	143	(64	79)	1493	421	470	212	21	945	12	10	25	27	19	.59	69	.247	.291	.426

Luis Sojo

Bats: Right **Throws:** Right **Pos:** 2B   **Ht:** 5'11" **Wt:** 174 **Born:** 01/03/66 **Age:** 28

Year	Team	Lg	G	AB	H	2B	3B	HR	(Hm	Rd)	TB	R	RBI	TBB	IBB	SO	HBP	SH	SF	SB	CS	SB%	GDP	Avg	OBP	SLG
1993	Syracuse *	AAA	43	142	31	7	2	1	--	--	45	17	12	8	0	12	0	4	0	2	1	.67	6	.218	.260	.317
1990	Toronto	AL	33	80	18	3	0	1	(0	1)	24	14	9	5	0	5	0	0	0	1	1	.50	1	.225	.271	.300
1991	California	AL	113	364	94	14	1	3	(1	2)	119	38	20	14	0	26	5	19	1	4	2	.67	12	.258	.295	.327
1992	California	AL	106	368	100	12	3	7	(2	5)	139	37	43	14	0	24	1	1	1	7	11	.39	14	.272	.299	.378
1993	Toronto	AL	19	47	8	2	0	0	(0	0)	10	5	6	4	0	2	0	2	1	0	0	.00	3	.170	.231	.213
	4 ML YEARS		271	859	220	31	4	11	(3	8)	292	94	78	37	0	57	6	28	2	12	14	.46	30	.256	.291	.340

Paul Sorrento

Bats: Left **Throws:** Right **Pos:** 1B   **Ht:** 6' 2" **Wt:** 220 **Born:** 11/17/65 **Age:** 28

Year	Team	Lg	G	AB	H	2B	3B	HR	(Hm	Rd)	TB	R	RBI	TBB	IBB	SO	HBP	SH	SF	SB	CS	SB%	GDP	Avg	OBP	SLG
1989	Minnesota	AL	14	21	5	0	0	0	(0	0)	5	2	1	5	1	4	0	0	1	0	0	.00	0	.238	.370	.238
1990	Minnesota	AL	41	121	25	4	1	5	(2	3)	46	11	13	12	0	31	1	0	1	1	1	.50	3	.207	.281	.380
1991	Minnesota	AL	26	47	12	2	0	4	(2	2)	26	6	13	4	2	11	0	0	0	0	0	.00	0	.255	.314	.553
1992	Cleveland	AL	140	458	123	24	1	18	(11	7)	203	52	60	51	7	89	1	1	3	0	3	.00	13	.269	.341	.443
1993	Cleveland	AL	148	463	119	26	1	18	(8	10)	201	75	65	58	11	121	2	0	4	3	1	.75	10	.257	.340	.434
	5 ML YEARS		369	1110	284	56	3	45	(23	22)	481	146	152	130	21	256	4	1	9	4	5	.44	29	.256	.334	.433

Sammy Sosa

Bats: Right **Throws:** Right **Pos:** RF/CF   **Ht:** 6' 0" **Wt:** 185 **Born:** 11/12/68 **Age:** 25

Year	Team	Lg	G	AB	H	2B	3B	HR	(Hm	Rd)	TB	R	RBI	TBB	IBB	SO	HBP	SH	SF	SB	CS	SB%	GDP	Avg	OBP	SLG
1989	2 ML Teams		58	183	47	8	0	4	(1	3)	67	27	13	11	2	47	2	5	2	7	5	.58	6	.257	.303	.366
1990	Chicago	AL	153	532	124	26	10	15	(10	5)	215	72	70	33	4	150	6	2	6	32	16	.67	10	.233	.282	.404
1991	Chicago	AL	116	316	64	10	1	10	(3	7)	106	39	33	14	2	98	2	5	1	13	6	.68	5	.203	.240	.335
1992	Chicago	NL	67	262	68	7	2	8	(4	4)	103	41	25	19	1	63	4	4	2	15	7	.68	4	.260	.317	.393
1993	Chicago	NL	159	598	156	25	5	33	(23	10)	290	92	93	38	6	135	4	0	1	36	11	.77	13	.261	.309	.485
1989	Texas	AL	25	84	20	3	0	1	(0	1)	26	8	3	0	0	20	0	4	0	0	2	.00	3	.238	.238	.310
	Chicago	AL	33	99	27	5	0	3	(1	2)	41	19	10	11	2	27	2	1	2	7	3	.70	3	.273	.351	.414
	5 ML YEARS		553	1891	459	76	18	70	(41	29)	781	271	234	115	15	493	18	16	12	103	45	.70	38	.243	.291	.413

Tim Spehr

Bats: Right **Throws:** Right **Pos:** C **Ht:** 6' 2" **Wt:** 195 **Born:** 07/02/66 **Age:** 27

Year Team	Lg	G	AB	H	2B	3B	HR	(Hm	Rd)	TB	R	RBI	TBB	IBB	SO	HBP	SH	SF	SB	CS	SB%	GDP	Avg	OBP	SLG
1993 Ottawa *	AAA	46	141	28	6	1	4	--	--	48	15	13	14	1	35	6	0	1	2	1	.67	4	.199	.296	.340
1991 Kansas City	AL	37	74	14	5	0	3	(1	2)	28	7	14	9	0	18	1	3	1	1	0	1.00	2	.189	.282	.378
1993 Montreal	NL	53	87	20	6	0	2	(0	2)	32	14	10	6	1	20	1	3	2	2	0	1.00	0	.230	.281	.368
2 ML YEARS		90	161	34	11	0	5	(1	4)	60	21	24	15	1	38	2	6	3	3	0	1.00	2	.211	.282	.373

Bill Spiers

Bats: Left **Throws:** Right **Pos:** 2B **Ht:** 6' 2" **Wt:** 190 **Born:** 06/05/66 **Age:** 28

Year Team	Lg	G	AB	H	2B	3B	HR	(Hm	Rd)	TB	R	RBI	TBB	IBB	SO	HBP	SH	SF	SB	CS	SB%	GDP	Avg	OBP	SLG
1989 Milwaukee	AL	114	345	88	9	3	4	(1	3)	115	44	33	21	1	63	1	4	2	10	2	.83	2	.255	.298	.333
1990 Milwaukee	AL	112	363	88	15	3	2	(2	0)	115	44	36	16	1	45	1	6	3	11	6	.65	12	.242	.274	.317
1991 Milwaukee	AL	133	414	117	13	6	8	(1	7)	166	71	54	34	0	55	2	10	4	14	8	.64	9	.283	.337	.401
1992 Milwaukee	AL	12	16	5	2	0	0	(0	0)	7	2	2	1	0	4	0	1	0	1	1	.50	0	.313	.353	.438
1993 Milwaukee	AL	113	340	81	8	4	2	(2	0)	103	43	36	29	2	51	4	9	4	9	8	.53	10	.238	.302	.303
5 ML YEARS		484	1478	379	47	16	16	(6	10)	506	204	161	101	3	218	8	30	13	45	25	.64	33	.256	.305	.342

Jerry Spradlin

Pitches: Right **Bats:** Both **Pos:** RP **Ht:** 6' 7" **Wt:** 230 **Born:** 06/14/67 **Age:** 27

Year Team	Lg	G	GS	CG	GF	IP	BFP	H	R	ER	HR	SH	SF	HB	TBB	IBB	SO	WP	Bk	W	L	Pct.	ShO	Sv	ERA
1988 Billings	R	17	5	0	2	47.2	201	45	25	17	2	1	2	2	14	1	23	3	0	4	1	.800	0	0	3.21
1989 Greensboro	A	42	1	0	22	94.2	389	88	35	29	5	3	7	3	23	0	56	4	0	7	2	.778	0	2	2.76
1990 Cedar Rapids	A	5	0	0	0	12	57	13	8	4	1	1	0	0	5	1	6	0	0	1	0	1.000	0	0	3.00
Chston-Wv	A	43	1	1	34	74.1	308	74	23	21	1	4	1	2	17	5	39	3	1	3	4	.429	0	17	2.54
1991 Chattanooga	AA	48	1	0	22	96	406	95	38	33	2	1	5	4	32	7	73	9	0	7	3	.700	0	4	3.09
1992 Cedar Rapids	A	1	0	0	0	2.1	11	5	2	2	0	0	0	0	0	0	4	0	0	1	0	1.000	0	0	7.71
Chattanooga	AA	59	0	0	53	65.1	248	52	11	10	1	6	1	0	13	3	35	3	0	3	3	.500	0	34	1.38
1993 Indianapols	AAA	34	0	0	8	56.2	239	58	24	22	4	2	0	0	12	2	46	2	0	3	2	.600	0	1	3.49
1993 Cincinnati	NL	37	0	0	16	49	193	44	20	19	4	3	4	0	9	2	24	3	1	2	1	.667	0	2	3.49

Ed Sprague

Bats: Right **Throws:** Right **Pos:** 3B **Ht:** 6' 2" **Wt:** 215 **Born:** 07/25/67 **Age:** 26

Year Team	Lg	G	AB	H	2B	3B	HR	(Hm	Rd)	TB	R	RBI	TBB	IBB	SO	HBP	SH	SF	SB	CS	SB%	GDP	Avg	OBP	SLG
1991 Toronto	AL	61	160	44	7	0	4	(3	1)	63	17	20	19	2	43	3	0	1	0	3	.00	2	.275	.361	.394
1992 Toronto	AL	22	47	11	2	0	1	(1	0)	16	6	7	3	0	7	0	0	0	0	0	.00	0	.234	.280	.340
1993 Toronto	AL	150	546	142	31	1	12	(8	4)	211	50	73	32	1	85	10	2	6	1	0	1.00	23	.260	.310	.386
3 ML YEARS		233	753	197	40	1	17	(12	5)	290	73	100	54	3	135	13	2	7	1	3	.25	25	.262	.319	.385

Russ Springer

Pitches: Right **Bats:** Right **Pos:** SP/RP **Ht:** 6' 4" **Wt:** 195 **Born:** 11/07/68 **Age:** 25

Year Team	Lg	G	GS	CG	GF	IP	BFP	H	R	ER	HR	SH	SF	HB	TBB	IBB	SO	WP	Bk	W	L	Pct.	ShO	Sv	ERA
1989 Yankees	R	6	6	0	0	24	95	14	8	4	0	0	0	1	10	0	34	1	0	3	0	1.000	0	0	1.50
1990 Yankees	R	4	4	0	0	15	62	10	6	2	0	0	0	0	4	0	17	1	1	0	2	.000	0	0	1.20
Greensboro	A	10	10	0	0	56.1	249	51	33	22	3	0	1	1	31	0	51	3	1	2	3	.400	0	0	3.51
1991 Ft.Lauderdle	A	25	25	2	0	152.1	634	118	68	59	9	5	6	6	62	1	138	6	3	5	9	.357	0	0	3.49
Albany	AA	2	2	0	0	15	60	9	4	3	0	0	0	0	6	1	16	0	0	1	0	1.000	0	0	1.80
1992 Columbus	AAA	20	20	1	0	123.2	499	89	46	37	11	1	3	5	54	0	95	4	0	8	5	.615	0	0	2.69
1993 Vancouver	AAA	11	9	1	1	59	263	58	37	28	5	2	1	0	33	0	40	3	0	5	4	.556	0	0	4.27
1992 New York	AL	14	0	0	5	16	75	18	11	11	0	0	0	1	10	0	12	0	0	0	0	.000	0	0	6.19
1993 California	AL	14	9	1	3	60	278	73	48	48	11	1	1	3	32	1	31	6	0	1	6	.143	0	0	7.20
2 ML YEARS		28	9	1	8	76	353	91	59	59	11	1	1	4	42	1	43	6	0	1	6	.143	0	0	6.99

Scott Stahoviak

Bats: Left **Throws:** Right **Pos:** 3B **Ht:** 6' 5" **Wt:** 210 **Born:** 03/06/70 **Age:** 24

Year Team	Lg	G	AB	H	2B	3B	HR	(Hm	Rd)	TB	R	RBI	TBB	IBB	SO	HBP	SH	SF	SB	CS	SB%	GDP	Avg	OBP	SLG
1991 Visalia	A	43	158	44	9	1	1	--	--	58	29	25	22	2	28	3	2	0	9	3	.75	3	.278	.377	.367
1992 Visalia	A	110	409	126	26	3	5	--	--	173	62	68	82	2	66	3	0	2	17	6	.74	6	.308	.425	.423
1993 Nashville	AA	93	331	90	25	1	12	--	--	153	40	56	56	2	95	1	1	4	10	2	.83	5	.272	.375	.462
1993 Minnesota	AL	20	57	11	4	0	0	(0	0)	15	1	3	0		22	0	0	0	0	2	.00	2	.193	.233	.263

Matt Stairs

Bats: Left **Throws:** Right **Pos:** LF   **Ht:** 5' 9" **Wt:** 180 **Born:** 02/27/69 **Age:** 25

						BATTING												BASERUNNING				PERCENTAGES		
Year	Team	Lg	G	AB	H	2B	3B	HR	(Hm | Rd)	TB	R	RBI	TBB	IBB	SO	HBP	SH	SF	SB	CS	SB%	GDP	Avg	OBP	SLG
1989	Jamestown	A	14	43	11	1	0	1	--	--	15	8	5	3	0	5	0	0	0	1	2	.33	0	.256	.304	.349
	Wst Plm Bch	A	36	111	21	3	1	1	--	--	29	12	9	9	0	18	0	1	1	0	0	.00	3	.189	.248	.261
	Rockford	A	44	141	40	9	2	2	--	--	59	20	14	15	3	29	2	2	1	5	4	.56	4	.284	.358	.418
1990	Wst Plm Bch	A	55	184	62	9	3	3	--	--	86	30	30	40	4	19	5	0	2	15	2	.88	5	.337	.463	.467
	Jacksnville	AA	79	280	71	17	0	3	--	--	97	26	34	22	1	42	3	0	5	5	3	.63	5	.254	.310	.346
1991	Harrisburg	AA	129	505	168	30	10	13	--	--	257	87	78	66	8	47	3	2	3	23	11	.68	14	.333	.411	.509
1992	Indianapls	AAA	110	401	107	23	4	11	--	--	171	57	56	49	3	61	4	4	2	11	11	.50	10	.267	.351	.426
1993	Ottawa	AAA	34	125	35	4	2	3	--	--	52	18	20	11	1	15	2	1	0	4	1	.80	3	.280	.348	.416
1992	Montreal	NL	13	30	5	2	0	0	(0 | 0)	7	2	5	7	0	7	0	0	1	0	0	.00	0	.167	.316	.233
1993	Montreal	NL	6	8	3	1	0	0	(0 | 0)	4	1	2	0	0	1	0	0	0	0	0	.00	1	.375	.375	.500
	2 ML YEARS		19	38	8	3	0	0	(0 | 0)	11	3	7	7	0	8	0	0	1	0	0	.00	1	.211	.326	.289

Andy Stankiewicz

Bats: Right **Throws:** Right **Pos:** 2B   **Ht:** 5' 9" **Wt:** 165 **Born:** 08/10/64 **Age:** 29

						BATTING												BASERUNNING				PERCENTAGES		
Year	Team	Lg	G	AB	H	2B	3B	HR	(Hm | Rd)	TB	R	RBI	TBB	IBB	SO	HBP	SH	SF	SB	CS	SB%	GDP	Avg	OBP	SLG
1986	Oneonta	A	59	216	64	8	3	0	--	--	78	51	17	38	0	41	5	4	4	14	3	.82	2	.296	.407	.361
1987	Ft.Laurdrle	A	119	456	140	18	7	2	--	--	178	80	47	62	1	84	4	7	1	26	13	.67	9	.307	.394	.390
1988	Albany	AA	109	414	111	20	2	1	--	--	138	63	33	39	0	53	9	9	2	15	10	.60	6	.268	.343	.333
	Columbus	AAA	29	114	25	0	0	0	--	--	25	4	4	6	0	25	0	1	0	2	0	1.00	4	.219	.258	.219
1989	Albany	AA	133	498	133	26	2	4	--	--	175	74	49	57	2	59	8	3	11	41	9	.82	8	.267	.345	.351
1990	Columbus	AAA	135	446	102	14	4	1	--	--	127	68	48	71	1	63	10	7	4	25	8	.76	11	.229	.345	.285
1991	Columbus	AAA	125	372	101	12	4	1	--	--	124	47	41	29	0	45	8	8	5	29	16	.64	9	.272	.333	.333
1993	Columbus	AAA	90	331	80	12	5	0	--	--	102	45	32	29	0	46	3	4	3	12	8	.60	5	.242	.306	.308
1992	New York	AL	116	400	107	22	2	2	(2 | 0)	139	52	25	38	0	42	5	7	1	9	5	.64	13	.268	.338	.348
1993	New York	AL	16	9	0	0	0	0	(0 | 0)	0	5	0	1	0	1	0	0	0	0	0	.00	0	.000	.100	.000
	2 ML YEARS		132	409	107	22	2	2	(2 | 0)	139	57	25	39	0	43	5	7	1	9	5	.64	13	.262	.333	.340

Mike Stanley

Bats: Right **Throws:** Right **Pos:** C   **Ht:** 6' 0" **Wt:** 192 **Born:** 06/25/63 **Age:** 31

						BATTING												BASERUNNING				PERCENTAGES		
Year	Team	Lg	G	AB	H	2B	3B	HR	(Hm | Rd)	TB	R	RBI	TBB	IBB	SO	HBP	SH	SF	SB	CS	SB%	GDP	Avg	OBP	SLG
1986	Texas	AL	15	30	10	3	0	1	(0 | 1)	16	4	1	3	0	7	0	0	0	1	0	1.00	0	.333	.394	.533
1987	Texas	AL	78	216	59	8	1	6	(3 | 3)	87	34	37	31	0	48	1	1	4	3	0	1.00	6	.273	.361	.403
1988	Texas	AL	94	249	57	8	0	3	(1 | 2)	74	21	27	37	0	62	0	1	5	0	0	.00	6	.229	.323	.297
1989	Texas	AL	67	122	30	3	1	1	(1 | 0)	38	9	11	12	1	29	2	1	0	1	0	1.00	5	.246	.324	.311
1990	Texas	AL	103	189	47	8	1	2	(1 | 1)	63	21	19	30	2	25	0	6	1	1	0	1.00	4	.249	.350	.333
1991	Texas	AL	95	181	45	13	1	3	(1 | 2)	69	25	25	34	0	44	2	5	1	0	0	.00	2	.249	.372	.381
1992	New York	AL	68	173	43	7	0	8	(5 | 3)	74	24	27	33	0	45	1	0	0	0	0	.00	6	.249	.372	.428
1993	New York	AL	130	423	129	17	1	26	(17 | 9)	226	70	84	57	4	85	5	0	6	1	1	.50	10	.305	.389	.534
	8 ML YEARS		650	1583	420	67	5	50	(29 | 21)	647	208	231	237	7	345	11	14	17	7	1	.88	39	.265	.361	.409

Mike Stanton

Pitches: Left **Bats:** Left **Pos:** RP   **Ht:** 5'10" **Wt:** 190 **Born:** 06/02/67 **Age:** 27

						HOW MUCH HE PITCHED			WHAT HE GAVE UP										THE RESULTS				
Year	Team	Lg	G	GS	CG	GF	IP	BFP	H	R	ER	HR	SH	SF	HB	TBB	IBB	SO	WP	Bk	W	L	Pct.	ShO	Sv	ERA
1989	Atlanta	NL	20	0	0	10	24	94	17	4	4	0	4	0	0	8	1	27	1	0	0	0	.000	0	7	1.50
1990	Atlanta	NL	7	0	0	4	7	42	16	16	14	1	1	0	1	4	2	7	1	0	0	3	.000	0	2	18.00
1991	Atlanta	NL	74	0	0	20	78	314	62	27	25	6	6	0	1	21	6	54	0	0	5	5	.500	0	7	2.88
1992	Atlanta	NL	65	0	0	23	63.2	264	59	32	29	6	1	2	2	20	2	44	3	0	5	4	.556	0	8	4.10
1993	Atlanta	NL	63	0	0	41	52	236	51	35	27	4	5	2	0	29	7	43	1	0	4	6	.400	0	27	4.67
	5 ML YEARS		229	0	0	98	224.2	950	205	114	99	17	17	4	4	82	18	175	6	0	14	19	.424	0	51	3.97

Dave Staton

Bats: Right **Throws:** Right **Pos:** 1B   **Ht:** 6' 5" **Wt:** 215 **Born:** 04/12/68 **Age:** 26

						BATTING												BASERUNNING				PERCENTAGES		
Year	Team	Lg	G	AB	H	2B	3B	HR	(Hm | Rd)	TB	R	RBI	TBB	IBB	SO	HBP	SH	SF	SB	CS	SB%	GDP	Avg	OBP	SLG
1989	Spokane	A	70	260	94	18	0	17	--	--	163	52	72	39	4	49	8	0	2	1	1	.50	13	.362	.456	.627
1990	Riverside	A	92	335	97	16	1	20	--	--	175	56	64	52	5	78	2	0	4	4	1	.80	11	.290	.384	.522
	Wichita	AA	45	164	50	11	0	6	--	--	79	26	31	22	0	37	1	0	1	0	0	.00	6	.305	.388	.482
1991	Las Vegas	AAA	107	375	100	19	1	22	--	--	187	61	74	44	4	89	3	0	3	1	0	1.00	12	.267	.346	.499
1992	Las Vegas	AAA	96	335	94	20	0	19	--	--	171	47	76	34	2	95	6	0	5	0	0	.00	14	.281	.353	.510
1993	Wichita	AA	5	12	5	3	0	0	--	--	8	2	2	2	0	3	0	0	0	0	0	.00	0	.417	.500	.667

	Lg	G	AB	H	2B	3B	HR	(Hm	Rd)	TB	R	RBI	TBB	IBB	SO	HBP	SH	SF	SB	CS	SB%	GDP	Avg	OBP	SLG
Rancho Cuca	A	58	221	70	21	0	18	--	--	145	37	58	30	1	52	1	0	1	0	0	.00	6	.317	.399	.656
Las Vegas	AAA	11	37	10	0	0	7	--	--	31	8	11	3	0	9	0	0	1	0	0	.00	3	.270	.317	.838
1993 San Diego	NL	17	42	11	3	0	5	(3	2)	29	7	9	3	0	12	1	0	0	0	0	.00	2	.262	.326	.690

Terry Steinbach

Bats: Right **Throws:** Right **Pos:** C/1B **Ht:** 6' 1" **Wt:** 195 **Born:** 03/02/62 **Age:** 32

		BATTING																	BASERUNNING				PERCENTAGES		
Year Team	Lg	G	AB	H	2B	3B	HR	(Hm	Rd)	TB	R	RBI	TBB	IBB	SO	HBP	SH	SF	SB	CS	SB%	GDP	Avg	OBP	SLG
1986 Oakland	AL	6	15	5	0	0	2	(0	2)	11	3	4	1	0	0	0	0	0	0	0	.00	0	.333	.375	.733
1987 Oakland	AL	122	391	111	16	3	16	(6	10)	181	66	56	32	2	66	9	3	3	1	2	.33	10	.284	.349	.463
1988 Oakland	AL	104	351	93	19	1	9	(6	3)	141	42	51	33	2	47	6	3	5	3	0	1.00	13	.265	.334	.402
1989 Oakland	AL	130	454	124	13	1	7	(5	2)	160	37	42	30	2	66	2	2	3	1	2	.33	14	.273	.319	.352
1990 Oakland	AL	114	379	95	15	2	9	(3	6)	141	32	57	19	1	66	4	5	3	0	1	.00	11	.251	.291	.372
1991 Oakland	AL	129	456	125	31	1	6	(1	5)	176	50	67	22	4	70	7	0	9	2	2	.50	15	.274	.312	.386
1992 Oakland	AL	128	438	122	20	1	12	(3	9)	180	48	53	45	3	58	1	0	3	2	3	.40	20	.279	.345	.411
1993 Oakland	AL	104	389	111	19	1	10	(5	5)	162	47	43	25	1	65	3	0	1	3	3	.50	13	.285	.333	.416
8 ML YEARS		837	2873	786	133	10	71	(29	42)	1152	325	373	207	15	438	32	13	27	12	13	.48	96	.274	.327	.401

Dave Stewart

Pitches: Right **Bats:** Right **Pos:** SP **Ht:** 6' 2" **Wt:** 200 **Born:** 02/19/57 **Age:** 37

		HOW MUCH HE PITCHED						WHAT HE GAVE UP										THE RESULTS					
Year Team	Lg	G	GS	CG	GF	IP	BFP	H	R	ER	HR	SH	SF	HB	TBB	IBB	SO	WP	Bk	W	L	Pct.	ShO	Sv	ERA
1978 Los Angeles	NL	1	0	0	1	2	6	1	0	0	0	0	0	0	0	0	1	0	0	0	0	.000	0	0	0.00
1981 Los Angeles	NL	32	0	0	14	43	184	40	13	12	3	7	3	0	14	5	29	4	0	4	3	.571	0	6	2.51
1982 Los Angeles	NL	45	14	0	9	146.1	616	137	72	62	14	10	5	2	49	11	80	3	0	9	8	.529	0	1	3.81
1983 2 ML Teams		54	9	2	25	135	565	117	43	39	6	9	4	4	50	7	78	3	0	10	4	.714	0	8	2.60
1984 Texas	AL	32	27	3	2	192.1	847	193	106	101	26	4	5	4	87	3	119	12	0	7	14	.333	0	0	4.73
1985 2 ML Teams		46	5	0	32	85.2	383	91	57	52	13	5	2	2	41	5	66	7	1	0	6	.000	0	4	5.46
1986 2 ML Teams		37	17	4	4	161.2	700	152	76	71	16	4	7	3	69	0	111	10	3	9	5	.643	1	0	3.95
1987 Oakland	AL	37	37	8	0	261.1	1103	224	121	107	24	7	5	6	105	2	205	11	0	20	13	.606	1	0	3.68
1988 Oakland	AL	37	37	14	0	275.2	1156	240	111	99	14	7	9	3	110	5	192	14	16	21	12	.636	2	0	3.23
1989 Oakland	AL	36	36	8	0	257.2	1081	260	105	95	23	9	10	6	69	0	155	13	0	21	9	.700	0	0	3.32
1990 Oakland	AL	36	36	11	0	267	1088	226	84	76	16	10	10	5	83	0	166	4	0	22	11	.667	4	0	2.56
1991 Oakland	AL	35	35	2	0	226	1014	245	135	130	24	5	15	9	105	1	144	12	0	11	11	.500	1	0	5.18
1992 Oakland	AL	31	31	2	0	199.1	838	175	96	81	25	5	8	8	79	1	130	3	1	12	10	.545	0	0	3.66
1993 Toronto	AL	26	26	0	0	162	687	146	86	80	23	3	4	4	72	0	96	4	1	12	8	.600	0	0	4.44
1983 Los Angeles	NL	46	1	0	25	76	328	67	28	25	4	7	3	2	33	7	54	2	0	5	2	.714	0	8	2.96
Texas	AL	8	8	2	0	59	237	50	15	14	2	2	1	2	17	0	24	1	0	5	2	.714	0	0	2.14
1985 Texas	AL	42	5	0	29	81.1	361	86	53	49	13	5	2	2	37	5	64	5	1	0	6	.000	0	4	5.42
Philadelphia	NL	4	0	0	3	4.1	22	5	4	3	0	0	0	0	4	0	2	2	0	0	0	.000	0	0	6.23
1986 Philadelphia	NL	8	0	0	2	12.1	56	15	9	9	1	0	3	0	4	0	9	1	3	0	0	.000	0	0	6.57
Oakland	AL	29	17	4	2	149.1	644	137	67	62	15	4	4	3	65	0	102	9	0	9	5	.643	1	0	3.74
14 ML YEARS		485	310	54	87	2415	10268	2247	1105	1005	227	85	87	56	933	41	1572	104	22	158	114	.581	9	19	3.75

Dave Stieb

Pitches: Right **Bats:** Right **Pos:** SP **Ht:** 6' 1" **Wt:** 195 **Born:** 07/22/57 **Age:** 36

		HOW MUCH HE PITCHED						WHAT HE GAVE UP										THE RESULTS					
Year Team	Lg	G	GS	CG	GF	IP	BFP	H	R	ER	HR	SH	SF	HB	TBB	IBB	SO	WP	Bk	W	L	Pct.	ShO	Sv	ERA
1993 Sarasota *	A	2	2	0	0	12.1	61	18	10	8	2	0	0	1	2	0	14	0	0	1	1	.500	0	0	5.84
Nashville *	AAA	1	1	0	0	7	29	9	3	3	0	0	0	0	2	0	3	1	0	0	1	.000	0	0	3.86
Omaha *	AAA	9	8	1	0	47.2	217	63	37	34	10	1	2	2	12	0	18	2	0	3	3	.500	1	0	6.42
1979 Toronto	AL	18	18	7	0	129	563	139	70	62	11	4	4	4	48	3	52	3	1	8	8	.500	1	0	4.33
1980 Toronto	AL	34	32	14	0	243	1004	232	108	100	12	12	9	6	83	6	108	6	2	12	15	.444	4	0	3.70
1981 Toronto	AL	25	25	11	0	184	748	148	70	65	10	5	7	11	61	2	89	1	2	11	10	.524	2	0	3.18
1982 Toronto	AL	38	38	19	0	288.1	1187	271	116	104	27	10	3	5	75	4	141	3	1	17	14	.548	5	0	3.25
1983 Toronto	AL	36	36	14	0	278	1141	223	105	94	21	6	9	14	93	6	187	5	1	17	12	.586	4	0	3.04
1984 Toronto	AL	35	35	11	0	267	1085	215	87	84	19	8	6	11	88	1	198	2	0	16	8	.667	2	0	2.83
1985 Toronto	AL	36	36	8	0	265	1087	206	89	73	22	14	2	9	96	3	167	4	1	14	13	.519	2	0	2.48
1986 Toronto	AL	37	34	1	2	205	919	239	128	108	29	6	6	15	87	1	127	7	0	7	12	.368	1	1	4.74
1987 Toronto	AL	33	31	3	1	185	789	164	92	84	16	5	5	7	87	4	115	4	0	13	9	.591	1	0	4.09
1988 Toronto	AL	32	31	8	1	207.1	844	157	76	70	15	0	4	13	79	0	147	6	4	16	8	.667	4	0	3.04
1989 Toronto	AL	33	33	3	0	206.2	850	164	83	77	12	10	3	13	76	2	101	3	1	17	8	.680	2	0	3.35
1990 Toronto	AL	33	33	2	0	208.2	861	179	73	68	11	6	3	10	64	0	125	5	0	18	6	.750	2	0	2.93
1991 Toronto	AL	9	9	1	0	59.2	244	52	22	21	4	4	1	2	23	0	29	0	0	4	3	.571	0	0	3.17
1992 Toronto	AL	21	14	1	3	96.1	415	98	58	54	9	6	5	4	43	3	45	4	0	4	6	.400	0	0	5.04
1993 Chicago	AL	4	4	0	0	22.1	107	27	17	15	1	2	1	0	14	0	11	0	0	1	3	.250	0	0	6.04
15 ML YEARS		424	409	103	7	2845.1	11844	2514	1194	1079	219	98	68	124	1017	35	1642	51	14	175	135	.565	30	1	3.41

208

Kurt Stillwell

Bats: Both **Throws:** Right **Pos:** SS/2B **Ht:** 5'11" **Wt:** 185 **Born:** 06/04/65 **Age:** 29

Year	Team	Lg	G	AB	H	2B	3B	HR	(Hm	Rd)	TB	R	RBI	TBB	IBB	SO	HBP	SH	SF	SB	CS	SB%	GDP	Avg	OBP	SLG
1986	Cincinnati	NL	104	279	64	6	1	0	(0	0)	72	31	26	30	1	47	2	4	0	6	2	.75	5	.229	.309	.258
1987	Cincinnati	NL	131	395	102	20	7	4	(3	1)	148	54	33	32	2	50	2	2	2	4	6	.40	5	.258	.316	.375
1988	Kansas City	AL	128	459	115	28	5	10	(4	6)	183	63	53	47	0	76	3	6	3	6	5	.55	7	.251	.322	.399
1989	Kansas City	AL	130	463	121	20	7	7	(2	5)	176	52	54	42	2	64	3	5	3	9	6	.60	3	.261	.325	.380
1990	Kansas City	AL	144	506	126	35	4	3	(3	0)	178	60	51	39	1	60	4	4	7	0	2	.00	11	.249	.304	.352
1991	Kansas City	AL	122	385	102	17	1	6	(1	5)	139	44	51	33	5	56	1	5	4	3	4	.43	8	.265	.322	.361
1992	San Diego	NL	114	379	86	15	3	2	(1	1)	113	35	24	26	9	58	1	4	6	4	1	.80	6	.227	.274	.298
1993	2 ML Teams		79	182	42	6	2	1	(1	0)	55	11	14	15	2	33	1	3	2	6	3	.67	4	.231	.290	.302
1993	San Diego	NL	57	121	26	4	0	1	(1	0)	33	9	11	11	2	22	1	2	0	4	3	.57	2	.215	.286	.273
	California	AL	22	61	16	2	2	0	(0	0)	22	2	3	4	0	11	0	1	2	2	0	1.00	2	.262	.299	.361
	8 ML YEARS		952	3048	758	147	30	33	(15	18)	1064	350	306	264	22	444	17	33	27	38	29	.57	49	.249	.310	.349

Kevin Stocker

Bats: Both **Throws:** Right **Pos:** SS **Ht:** 6'1" **Wt:** 175 **Born:** 02/13/70 **Age:** 24

Year	Team	Lg	G	AB	H	2B	3B	HR	(Hm	Rd)	TB	R	RBI	TBB	IBB	SO	HBP	SH	SF	SB	CS	SB%	GDP	Avg	OBP	SLG
1992	Clearwater	A	63	244	69	13	4	1	--	--	93	43	33	27	2	31	4	5	3	15	9	.63	4	.283	.360	.381
	Reading	AA	62	240	60	9	2	1	--	--	76	31	13	22	1	30	2	3	0	17	4	.81	2	.250	.318	.317
1993	Scranton/wb	AAA	83	313	73	14	1	3	--	--	98	54	17	29	2	56	7	8	0	17	6	.74	7	.233	.312	.313
1993	Philadelphia	NL	70	259	84	12	3	2	(1	1)	108	46	31	30	11	43	8	4	1	5	0	1.00	3	.324	.409	.417

Todd Stottlemyre

Pitches: Right **Bats:** Left **Pos:** SP **Ht:** 6'3" **Wt:** 195 **Born:** 05/20/65 **Age:** 29

Year	Team	Lg	G	GS	CG	GF	IP	BFP	H	R	ER	HR	SH	SF	HB	TBB	IBB	SO	WP	Bk	W	L	Pct.	ShO	Sv	ERA
1988	Toronto	AL	28	16	0	2	98	443	109	70	62	15	5	3	4	46	5	67	2	3	4	8	.333	0	0	5.69
1989	Toronto	AL	27	18	0	4	127.2	545	137	56	55	11	3	7	5	44	4	63	4	1	7	7	.500	0	0	3.88
1990	Toronto	AL	33	33	4	0	203	866	214	101	98	18	3	5	8	69	4	115	6	1	13	17	.433	0	0	4.34
1991	Toronto	AL	34	34	1	0	219	921	194	97	92	21	0	8	12	75	3	116	4	0	15	8	.652	0	0	3.78
1992	Toronto	AL	28	27	6	0	174	755	175	99	87	20	2	11	10	63	4	98	7	0	12	11	.522	2	0	4.50
1993	Toronto	AL	30	28	1	0	176.2	786	204	107	95	11	5	11	3	69	5	98	7	1	11	12	.478	1	0	4.84
	6 ML YEARS		180	156	12	6	998.1	4316	1033	530	489	96	18	45	42	366	25	557	30	6	62	63	.496	3	0	4.41

Doug Strange

Bats: Both **Throws:** Right **Pos:** 2B **Ht:** 6'2" **Wt:** 170 **Born:** 04/13/64 **Age:** 30

Year	Team	Lg	G	AB	H	2B	3B	HR	(Hm	Rd)	TB	R	RBI	TBB	IBB	SO	HBP	SH	SF	SB	CS	SB%	GDP	Avg	OBP	SLG
1989	Detroit	AL	64	196	42	4	1	1	(1	0)	51	16	14	17	0	36	1	3	0	3	3	.50	6	.214	.280	.260
1991	Chicago	NL	3	9	4	1	0	0	(0	0)	5	1	0	1	0	1	0	1	0	1	0	1.00	0	.444	.455	.556
1992	Chicago	NL	52	94	15	1	0	1	(0	1)	19	7	5	10	2	15	0	2	0	1	0	1.00	2	.160	.240	.202
1993	Texas	AL	145	484	124	29	0	7	(4	3)	174	58	60	43	3	69	3	8	4	6	4	.60	12	.256	.318	.360
	4 ML YEARS		264	783	185	35	1	9	(5	4)	249	81	80	70	5	121	4	13	5	11	7	.61	20	.236	.301	.318

Darryl Strawberry

Bats: Left **Throws:** Left **Pos:** RF **Ht:** 6'6" **Wt:** 215 **Born:** 03/12/62 **Age:** 32

Year	Team	Lg	G	AB	H	2B	3B	HR	(Hm	Rd)	TB	R	RBI	TBB	IBB	SO	HBP	SH	SF	SB	CS	SB%	GDP	Avg	OBP	SLG
1993	Albuquerque *	AAA	5	19	6	2	0	1	--	--	11	3	2	2	0	5	0	0	0	1	0	1.00	0	.316	.381	.579
1983	New York	NL	122	420	108	15	7	26	(10	16)	215	63	74	47	9	128	4	0	2	19	6	.76	5	.257	.336	.512
1984	New York	NL	147	522	131	27	4	26	(8	18)	244	75	97	75	15	131	0	1	4	27	8	.77	8	.251	.343	.467
1985	New York	NL	111	393	109	15	4	29	(14	15)	219	78	79	73	13	96	1	0	3	26	11	.70	9	.277	.389	.557
1986	New York	NL	136	475	123	27	5	27	(11	16)	241	76	93	72	9	141	6	0	9	28	12	.70	4	.259	.358	.507
1987	New York	NL	154	532	151	32	5	39	(20	19)	310	108	104	97	13	122	7	0	4	36	12	.75	4	.284	.398	.583
1988	New York	NL	153	543	146	27	3	39	(21	18)	296	101	101	85	21	127	3	0	9	29	14	.67	6	.269	.366	.545
1989	New York	NL	134	476	107	26	1	29	(15	14)	222	69	77	61	13	105	1	0	3	11	4	.73	4	.225	.312	.466
1990	New York	NL	152	542	150	18	1	37	(24	13)	281	92	108	70	15	110	4	0	5	15	8	.65	5	.277	.361	.518
1991	Los Angeles	NL	139	505	134	22	4	28	(14	14)	248	86	99	75	4	125	3	0	5	10	8	.56	8	.265	.361	.491
1992	Los Angeles	NL	43	156	37	8	0	5	(3	2)	60	20	25	19	4	34	0	0	1	3	1	.75	2	.237	.322	.385
1993	Los Angeles	NL	32	100	14	2	0	5	(3	2)	31	12	12	16	1	19	2	0	2	1	0	1.00	1	.140	.267	.310
	11 ML YEARS		1323	4664	1210	219	34	290	(143	147)	2367	780	869	690	117	1138	32	1	47	205	84	.71	56	.259	.356	.508

William Suero

Bats: Right **Throws:** Right **Pos:** 2B **Ht:** 5' 9" **Wt:** 175 **Born:** 11/07/66 **Age:** 27

													BATTING								BASERUNNING				PERCENTAGES		
Year	Team	Lg	G	AB	H	2B	3B	HR	(Hm	Rd)	TB	R	RBI	TBB	IBB	SO	HBP	SH	SF	SB	CS	SB%	GDP	Avg	OBP	SLG
1986	Medicne Hat	R	64	273	76	7	5	2	--	--	99	39	28	15	0	36	3	4	2	13	4	.76	7	.278	.321	.363
1987	St.Cathmes	A	77	297	94	12	4	4	--	--	126	43	24	35	1	35	1	2	1	23	11	.68	3	.316	.389	.424
1988	Myrtle Bch	A	125	493	140	21	6	6	--	--	191	88	52	49	2	72	4	3	6	21	7	.75	4	.284	.350	.387
1989	Dunedin	A	51	206	60	10	5	2	--	--	86	35	17	16	0	32	3	1	0	9	3	.75	3	.291	.351	.417
	Knoxville	AA	87	324	84	17	5	4	--	--	123	42	29	34	0	50	3	2	0	7	4	.64	2	.259	.335	.380
1990	Knoxville	AA	133	483	127	29	7	16	--	--	218	80	60	78	3	78	7	6	2	40	21	.66	5	.263	.372	.451
1991	Syracuse	AAA	98	393	78	18	1	1	--	--	101	49	28	38	0	51	7	4	3	17	13	.57	9	.198	.279	.257
	Denver	AAA	20	70	27	3	2	0	--	--	34	20	15	10	0	8	0	2	1	3	0	1.00	3	.386	.457	.486
1992	Denver	AAA	75	276	71	10	9	1	--	--	102	42	25	31	1	33	1	3	2	16	9	.64	5	.257	.332	.370
1993	New Orleans	AAA	46	124	28	4	1	1	--	--	37	14	13	21	0	17	1	2	3	8	7	.53	3	.226	.336	.298
1992	Milwaukee	AL	18	16	3	1	0	0	(0	0)	4	4	0	2	0	1	1	0	0	1	1	.50	2	.188	.316	.250
1993	Milwaukee	AL	15	14	4	0	0	0	(0	0)	4	0	0	1	0	3	0	0	0	0	1	.00	1	.286	.333	.286
	2 ML YEARS		33	30	7	1	0	0	(0	0)	8	4	0	3	0	4	1	0	0	1	2	.33	3	.233	.324	.267

B.J. Surhoff

Bats: Left **Throws:** Right **Pos:** 3B/LF/RF **Ht:** 6' 1" **Wt:** 200 **Born:** 08/04/64 **Age:** 29

													BATTING								BASERUNNING				PERCENTAGES		
Year	Team	Lg	G	AB	H	2B	3B	HR	(Hm	Rd)	TB	R	RBI	TBB	IBB	SO	HBP	SH	SF	SB	CS	SB%	GDP	Avg	OBP	SLG
1987	Milwaukee	AL	115	395	118	22	3	7	(5	2)	167	50	68	36	1	30	0	5	9	11	10	.52	13	.299	.350	.423
1988	Milwaukee	AL	139	493	121	21	0	5	(2	3)	157	47	38	31	9	49	3	11	3	21	6	.78	12	.245	.292	.318
1989	Milwaukee	AL	126	436	108	17	4	5	(3	2)	148	42	55	25	1	29	3	3	10	14	12	.54	8	.248	.287	.339
1990	Milwaukee	AL	135	474	131	21	4	6	(4	2)	178	55	59	41	5	37	1	7	7	18	7	.72	8	.276	.331	.376
1991	Milwaukee	AL	143	505	146	19	4	5	(3	2)	188	57	68	26	2	33	0	13	9	5	8	.38	21	.289	.319	.372
1992	Milwaukee	AL	139	480	121	19	1	4	(3	1)	154	63	62	46	8	41	2	5	10	14	8	.64	9	.252	.314	.321
1993	Milwaukee	AL	148	552	151	38	3	7	(4	3)	216	66	79	36	5	47	2	4	5	12	9	.57	7	.274	.318	.391
	7 ML YEARS		945	3335	896	157	19	39	(24	15)	1208	380	429	241	31	266	11	48	53	95	60	.61	78	.269	.315	.362

Rick Sutcliffe

Pitches: Right **Bats:** Left **Pos:** SP **Ht:** 6' 7" **Wt:** 239 **Born:** 06/21/56 **Age:** 38

				HOW MUCH HE PITCHED					WHAT HE GAVE UP													THE RESULTS					
Year	Team	Lg	G	GS	CG	GF	IP	BFP	H	R	ER	HR	SH	SF	HB	TBB	IBB	SO	WP	Bk	W	L	Pct.	ShO	Sv	ERA
1976	Los Angeles	NL	1	1	0	0	5	17	2	0	0	0	0	0	0	1	0	3	0	0	0	0	.000	0	0	0.00
1978	Los Angeles	NL	2	0	0	0	2	9	2	0	0	0	0	0	1	1	0	0	0	0	0	0	.000	0	0	0.00
1979	Los Angeles	NL	39	30	5	2	242	1016	217	104	93	16	16	9	2	97	6	117	8	6	17	10	.630	1	0	3.46
1980	Los Angeles	NL	42	10	1	19	110	491	122	73	68	10	4	3	1	55	2	59	4	5	3	9	.250	1	5	5.56
1981	Los Angeles	NL	14	6	0	5	47	197	41	24	21	5	1	2	2	20	2	16	0	0	2	2	.500	0	0	4.02
1982	Cleveland	AL	34	27	6	3	216	887	174	81	71	16	7	8	4	98	2	142	6	1	14	8	.636	1	1	2.96
1983	Cleveland	AL	36	35	10	0	243.1	1061	251	131	116	23	8	9	6	102	5	160	7	3	17	11	.607	2	0	4.29
1984	2 ML Teams		35	35	9	0	244.2	1030	234	113	99	16	5	4	3	85	3	213	6	3	20	6	.769	3	0	3.64
1985	Chicago	NL	20	20	6	0	130	549	119	51	46	12	3	4	3	44	3	102	6	0	8	8	.500	3	0	3.18
1986	Chicago	NL	28	27	4	0	176.2	764	166	92	91	18	6	2	1	96	8	122	13	1	5	14	.263	1	0	4.64
1987	Chicago	NL	34	34	6	0	237.1	1012	223	106	97	24	9	8	4	106	14	174	9	4	18	10	.643	1	0	3.68
1988	Chicago	NL	32	32	12	0	226	958	232	97	97	18	17	5	2	70	9	144	11	4	13	14	.481	2	0	3.86
1989	Chicago	NL	35	34	5	0	229	938	202	98	93	18	15	10	2	69	8	153	12	6	16	11	.593	1	0	3.66
1990	Chicago	NL	5	5	0	0	21.1	97	25	14	14	2	1	2	0	12	0	7	4	0	0	2	.000	0	0	5.91
1991	Chicago	NL	19	18	0	0	96.2	422	96	52	44	4	5	8	0	45	2	52	2	2	6	5	.545	0	0	4.10
1992	Baltimore	AL	36	36	5	0	237.1	1018	251	123	118	20	6	11	7	74	4	109	7	2	16	15	.516	2	0	4.47
1993	Baltimore	AL	29	28	3	0	166	763	212	112	106	23	4	3	6	74	5	80	1	0	10	10	.500	0	0	5.75
1984	Cleveland	AL	15	15	2	0	94.1	428	111	60	54	7	4	3	2	46	3	58	3	1	4	5	.444	0	0	5.15
	Chicago	NL	20	20	7	0	150.1	602	123	53	45	9	1	1	1	39	0	155	3	2	16	1	.941	3	0	2.69
	17 ML YEARS		441	378	72	29	2630.1	11229	2569	1271	1174	225	107	88	44	1049	73	1653	96	37	165	135	.550	18	6	4.02

Dale Sveum

Bats: Both **Throws:** Right **Pos:** 1B **Ht:** 6' 3" **Wt:** 185 **Born:** 11/23/63 **Age:** 30

													BATTING								BASERUNNING				PERCENTAGES		
Year	Team	Lg	G	AB	H	2B	3B	HR	(Hm	Rd)	TB	R	RBI	TBB	IBB	SO	HBP	SH	SF	SB	CS	SB%	GDP	Avg	OBP	SLG
1993	Tacoma *	AAA	12	43	15	1	0	2	--	--	22	10	6	6	1	7	1	0	0	2	1	.67	1	.349	.440	.512
	Calgary *	AAA	33	120	36	11	1	6	--	--	67	31	26	24	0	32	0	0	1	0	1	.00	0	.300	.414	.558
1986	Milwaukee	AL	91	317	78	13	2	7	(4	3)	116	35	35	32	0	63	1	5	1	4	3	.57	7	.246	.316	.366
1987	Milwaukee	AL	153	535	135	27	3	25	(9	16)	243	86	95	40	4	133	1	1	5	2	6	.25	11	.252	.303	.454
1988	Milwaukee	AL	129	467	113	14	4	9	(2	7)	162	41	51	21	0	122	1	3	3	1	0	1.00	6	.242	.274	.347
1990	Milwaukee	AL	48	117	23	7	0	1	(1	0)	33	15	12	12	0	30	2	0	2	1	1	.00	2	.197	.278	.282
1991	Milwaukee	AL	90	266	64	19	1	4	(3	1)	97	33	43	32	0	78	1	5	4	2	4	.33	8	.241	.320	.365

Year Team	Lg	G	AB	H	2B	3B	HR	(Hm	Rd)	TB	R	RBI	TBB	IBB	SO	HBP	SH	SF	SB	CS	SB%	GDP	Avg	OBP	SLG
1992 2 ML Teams		94	249	49	13	0	4	(1	3)	74	28	28	28	4	68	0	2	5	1	1	.50	6	.197	.273	.297
1993 Oakland	AL	30	79	14	2	1	2	(0	2)	24	12	6	16	1	21	0	1	0	0	0	.00	2	.177	.316	.304
1992 Philadelphia	NL	54	135	24	4	0	2	(0	2)	34	13	16	16	4	39	0	0	2	0	0	.00	5	.178	.261	.252
Chicago	AL	40	114	25	9	0	2	(1	1)	40	15	12	12	0	29	0	0	3	1	1	.50	1	.219	.287	.351
7 ML YEARS		635	2030	476	95	11	52	(20	32)	749	250	270	181	9	515	6	21	20	10	15	.40	42	.234	.296	.369

Russ Swan

Pitches: Left   Bats: Left   Pos: RP   **Ht: 6' 4"   Wt: 210   Born: 01/03/64   Age: 30**

		HOW MUCH HE PITCHED						WHAT HE GAVE UP												THE RESULTS					
Year Team	Lg	G	GS	CG	GF	IP	BFP	H	R	ER	HR	SH	SF	HB	TBB	IBB	SO	WP	Bk	W	L	Pct.	ShO	Sv	ERA
1993 Calgary*	AAA	9	0	0	3	10.2	51	14	11	10	1	0	0	0	8	0	7	0	0	2	1	.667	0	0	8.44
1989 San Francisco	NL	2	2	0	0	6.2	34	11	10	8	4	2	0	0	4	0	2	0	0	0	2	.000	0	0	10.80
1990 2 ML Teams		13	9	0	0	49.1	213	48	26	20	3	2	3	0	22	2	16	1	1	2	4	.333	0	0	3.65
1991 Seattle	AL	63	0	0	11	78.2	336	81	35	30	8	6	1	0	28	7	33	8	0	6	2	.750	0	2	3.43
1992 Seattle	AL	55	9	1	26	104.1	457	104	60	55	8	7	5	3	45	7	45	6	0	3	10	.231	0	9	4.74
1993 Seattle	AL	23	0	0	6	19.2	100	25	20	20	2	1	0	2	18	1	10	0	0	3	3	.500	0	0	9.15
1990 San Francisco	NL	2	1	0	0	2.1	18	6	4	1	0	0	0	0	4	0	1	1	0	0	1	.000	0	0	3.86
Seattle	AL	11	8	0	0	47	195	42	22	19	3	2	3	0	18	2	15	0	1	2	3	.400	0	0	3.64
5 ML YEARS		156	20	1	43	258.2	1140	269	151	133	25	18	9	5	117	17	106	15	1	14	21	.400	0	11	4.63

Bill Swift

Pitches: Right   Bats: Right   Pos: SP   **Ht: 6' 0"   Wt: 191   Born: 10/27/61   Age: 32**

		HOW MUCH HE PITCHED						WHAT HE GAVE UP												THE RESULTS					
Year Team	Lg	G	GS	CG	GF	IP	BFP	H	R	ER	HR	SH	SF	HB	TBB	IBB	SO	WP	Bk	W	L	Pct.	ShO	Sv	ERA
1985 Seattle	AL	23	21	0	0	120.2	532	131	71	64	8	6	3	5	48	5	55	5	3	6	10	.375	0	0	4.77
1986 Seattle	AL	29	17	1	3	115.1	534	148	85	70	5	5	3	7	55	2	55	2	1	2	9	.182	0	0	5.46
1988 Seattle	AL	38	24	6	4	174.2	757	199	99	89	10	5	3	8	65	3	47	6	2	8	12	.400	1	0	4.59
1989 Seattle	AL	37	16	0	7	130	551	140	72	64	7	4	3	2	38	4	45	4	1	7	3	.700	0	1	4.43
1990 Seattle	AL	55	8	0	18	128	533	135	46	34	4	5	4	7	21	6	42	8	3	6	4	.600	0	6	2.39
1991 Seattle	AL	71	0	0	30	90.1	359	74	22	20	3	2	0	1	26	4	48	2	1	1	2	.333	0	17	1.99
1992 San Francisco	NL	30	22	3	2	164.2	655	144	41	38	6	5	2	3	43	3	77	0	1	10	4	.714	2	1	**2.08**
1993 San Francisco	NL	34	34	1	0	232.2	928	195	82	73	18	4	2	6	55	5	157	4	0	21	8	.724	1	0	2.82
8 ML YEARS		317	142	11	64	1156.1	4849	1166	518	452	61	36	20	39	351	32	526	31	12	61	52	.540	4	25	3.52

Greg Swindell

Pitches: Left   Bats: Right   Pos: SP   **Ht: 6' 3"   Wt: 225   Born: 01/02/65   Age: 29**

		HOW MUCH HE PITCHED						WHAT HE GAVE UP												THE RESULTS					
Year Team	Lg	G	GS	CG	GF	IP	BFP	H	R	ER	HR	SH	SF	HB	TBB	IBB	SO	WP	Bk	W	L	Pct.	ShO	Sv	ERA
1986 Cleveland	AL	9	9	1	0	61.2	255	57	35	29	9	3	1	1	15	0	46	3	2	5	2	.714	0	0	4.23
1987 Cleveland	AL	16	15	4	0	102.1	441	112	62	58	18	4	3	1	37	1	97	0	1	3	8	.273	1	0	5.10
1988 Cleveland	AL	33	33	12	0	242	988	234	97	86	18	9	5	1	45	3	180	5	0	18	14	.563	4	0	3.20
1989 Cleveland	AL	28	28	5	0	184.1	749	170	71	69	16	4	4	0	51	1	129	3	1	13	6	.684	2	0	3.37
1990 Cleveland	AL	34	34	3	0	214.2	912	245	110	105	27	8	6	1	47	2	135	3	2	12	9	.571	0	0	4.40
1991 Cleveland	AL	33	33	7	0	238	971	241	112	92	21	13	8	3	31	1	169	3	1	9	16	.360	0	0	3.48
1992 Cincinnati	NL	31	30	5	0	213.2	867	210	72	64	14	9	7	2	41	4	138	3	2	12	8	.600	3	0	2.70
1993 Houston	NL	31	30	1	0	190.1	818	215	98	88	24	13	3	1	40	3	124	2	2	12	13	.480	1	0	4.16
8 ML YEARS		215	212	38	0	1447	6001	1484	657	591	147	63	37	10	307	15	1018	22	11	84	76	.525	11	0	3.68

Paul Swingle

Pitches: Right   Bats: Right   Pos: RP   **Ht: 6' 0"   Wt: 185   Born: 12/21/66   Age: 27**

		HOW MUCH HE PITCHED						WHAT HE GAVE UP												THE RESULTS					
Year Team	Lg	G	GS	CG	GF	IP	BFP	H	R	ER	HR	SH	SF	HB	TBB	IBB	SO	WP	Bk	W	L	Pct.	ShO	Sv	ERA
1989 Bend	A	9	0	0	2	18.1	81	7	9	6	0	1	0	0	19	0	26	5	1	1	0	1.000	0	0	2.95
1990 Boise	A	14	0	0	12	13.2	51	5	1	1	0	1	0	0	3	1	24	0	0	1	0	1.000	0	5	0.66
1991 Palm Sprngs	A	43	0	0	28	57	268	51	37	28	2	3	3	1	41	8	63	11	0	5	4	.556	0	10	4.42
1992 Midland	AA	25	25	2	0	149.2	648	158	88	78	14	3	6	6	51	1	104	8	2	8	10	.444	0	0	4.69
1993 Vancouver	AAA	37	4	0	11	67.2	318	85	61	52	4	2	4	1	32	1	61	3	1	2	9	.182	0	1	6.92
1993 California	AL	9	0	0	2	9.2	49	15	9	9	2	0	1	0	6	0	6	0	0	0	1	.000	0	0	8.38

Jeff Tackett

Bats: Right   Throws: Right   Pos: C   **Ht: 6' 2"   Wt: 205   Born: 12/01/65   Age: 28**

		BATTING																	BASERUNNING				PERCENTAGES		
Year Team	Lg	G	AB	H	2B	3B	HR	(Hm	Rd)	TB	R	RBI	TBB	IBB	SO	HBP	SH	SF	SB	CS	SB%	GDP	Avg	OBP	SLG
1993 Rochester*	AAA	8	25	8	2	0	0	(--	--)	10	1	2	3	0	8	2	0	1	0	0	.00	0	.320	.419	.400
1991 Baltimore	AL	6	8	1	0	0	0	(0	0)	1	1	0	2	0	2	0	1	0	0	0	.00	0	.125	.300	.125
1992 Baltimore	AL	65	179	43	8	1	5	(4	1)	68	21	24	17	1	28	2	6	4	0	0	.00	11	.240	.307	.380
1993 Baltimore	AL	38	87	15	3	0	0	(0	0)	18	8	9	13	0	28	0	2	1	0	0	.00	0	.172	.277	.207
3 ML YEARS		109	274	59	11	1	5	(4	1)	87	30	33	32	1	58	2	9	5	0	0	.00	16	.215	.297	.318

Frank Tanana

Pitches: Left   **Bats:** Left   **Pos:** SP   **Ht:** 6' 3"   **Wt:** 200   **Born:** 07/03/53   **Age:** 40

		HOW MUCH HE PITCHED						WHAT HE GAVE UP										THE RESULTS					
Year Team	Lg	G	GS	CG	GF	IP	BFP	H	R	ER	HR	SH	SF	HB	TBB	IBB	SO	WP	Bk	W	L	Pct.	ShO	Sv	ERA
1973 California	AL	4	4	2	0	26	108	20	11	9	2	0	0	0	8	0	22	2	0	2	2	.500	1	0	3.12
1974 California	AL	39	35	12	2	269	1127	262	104	93	27	10	4	8	77	4	180	4	2	14	19	.424	4	0	3.11
1975 California	AL	34	33	16	1	257	1029	211	80	75	21	13	4	7	73	6	269	8	1	16	9	.640	5	0	2.63
1976 California	AL	34	34	23	0	288	1142	212	88	78	24	14	3	9	73	5	261	5	0	19	10	.655	2	0	2.44
1977 California	AL	31	31	20	0	241	973	201	72	68	19	8	7	12	61	2	205	8	1	15	9	.625	7	0	2.54
1978 California	AL	33	33	10	0	239	1014	239	108	97	26	8	10	9	60	7	137	5	8	18	12	.600	4	0	3.65
1979 California	AL	18	17	2	0	90	382	93	44	39	9	1	2	2	25	0	46	6	1	7	5	.583	1	0	3.90
1980 California	AL	32	31	7	1	204	870	223	107	94	18	8	4	8	45	0	113	3	1	11	12	.478	0	0	4.15
1981 Boston	AL	24	23	5	0	141	596	142	70	63	17	9	4	4	43	4	78	2	0	4	10	.286	2	0	4.02
1982 Texas	AL	30	30	7	0	194.1	832	199	102	91	16	13	4	7	55	10	87	0	1	7	18	.280	0	0	4.21
1983 Texas	AL	29	22	3	1	159.1	667	144	70	56	14	7	3	7	49	5	108	6	1	7	9	.438	0	0	3.16
1984 Texas	AL	35	35	9	0	246.1	1054	234	117	89	30	6	5	6	81	3	141	12	4	15	15	.500	1	0	3.25
1985 2 ML Teams		33	33	4	0	215	907	220	112	102	28	5	8	3	57	4	159	5	1	12	14	.462	0	0	4.27
1986 Detroit	AL	32	31	3	1	188.1	812	196	95	87	23	8	5	3	65	9	119	7	1	12	9	.571	0	0	4.16
1987 Detroit	AL	34	34	5	0	218.2	924	216	106	95	27	8	11	5	56	5	146	6	0	.15	10	.600	3	0	3.91
1988 Detroit	AL	32	32	2	0	203	876	213	105	95	25	6	3	4	64	7	127	6	0	14	11	.560	0	0	4.21
1989 Detroit	AL	33	33	6	0	223.2	955	227	105	89	21	7	10	8	74	8	147	8	0	10	14	.417	1	0	3.58
1990 Detroit	AL	34	29	1	4	176.1	763	190	104	104	25	3	7	9	66	7	114	5	1	9	8	.529	0	1	5.31
1991 Detroit	AL	33	33	3	0	217.1	920	217	98	89	26	12	9	2	78	9	107	3	1	13	12	.520	2	0	3.69
1992 Detroit	AL	32	31	3	0	186.2	818	188	102	91	22	7	10	7	90	9	91	11	1	13	11	.542	0	0	4.39
1993 2 ML Teams		32	32	0	0	202.2	872	216	110	98	28	12	4	9	55	8	116	7	2	7	17	.292	0	0	4.35
1985 Texas	AL	13	13	0	0	77.2	340	89	53	51	15	2	4	1	23	2	52	3	0	2	7	.222	0	0	5.91
Detroit	AL	20	20	4	0	137.1	567	131	59	51	13	3	4	2	34	6	107	2	1	10	7	.588	0	0	3.34
1993 New York	NL	29	29	0	0	183	784	198	100	91	26	12	4	9	48	7	104	7	2	7	15	.318	0	0	4.48
New York	AL	3	3	0	0	19.2	88	18	10	7	2	0	0	0	7	1	12	0	0	0	2	.000	0	0	3.20
21 ML YEARS		638	616	143	10	4186.2	17641	4063	1910	1702	448	165	117	129	1255	116	2773	119	27	240	236	.504	34	1	3.66

Kevin Tapani

Pitches: Right   **Bats:** Right   **Pos:** SP   **Ht:** 6' 0"   **Wt:** 187   **Born:** 02/18/64   **Age:** 30

		HOW MUCH HE PITCHED						WHAT HE GAVE UP										THE RESULTS					
Year Team	Lg	G	GS	CG	GF	IP	BFP	H	R	ER	HR	SH	SF	HB	TBB	IBB	SO	WP	Bk	W	L	Pct.	ShO	Sv	ERA
1989 2 ML Teams		8	5	0	1	40	169	39	18	17	3	1	2	0	12	1	23	0	1	2	2	.500	0	0	3.83
1990 Minnesota	AL	28	28	1	0	159.1	659	164	75	72	12	3	4	2	29	2	101	1	0	12	8	.600	1	0	4.07
1991 Minnesota	AL	34	34	4	0	244	974	225	84	81	23	9	6	2	40	0	135	3	3	16	9	.640	1	0	2.99
1992 Minnesota	AL	34	34	4	0	220	911	226	103	97	17	8	11	5	48	2	138	4	0	16	11	.593	1	0	3.97
1993 Minnesota	AL	36	35	3	0	225.2	964	243	123	113	21	3	5	6	57	1	150	4	0	12	15	.444	1	0	4.43
1989 New York	NL	3	0	0	0	7.1	31	5	3	3	1	0	1	0	4	0	2	0	1	0	0	.000	0	0	3.68
Minnesota	AL	5	5	0	0	32.2	138	34	15	14	2	1	1	0	8	1	21	0	0	2	2	.500	0	0	3.86
5 ML YEARS		140	136	12	1	889	3677	897	403	378	76	24	28	15	186	6	547	12	4	58	45	.563	4	0	3.83

Tony Tarasco

Bats: Left   **Throws:** Right   **Pos:** RF   **Ht:** 6' 1"   **Wt:** 205   **Born:** 12/09/70   **Age:** 23

		BATTING																	BASERUNNING				PERCENTAGES		
Year Team	Lg	G	AB	H	2B	3B	HR	(Hm	Rd)	TB	R	RBI	TBB	IBB	SO	HBP	SH	SF	SB	CS	SB%	GDP	Avg	OBP	SLG
1988 Idaho Falls	R	7	10	0	0	0	0	--	--	0	1	1	2	0	0	0	0	0	0	1	1.00	1	.000	.333	.000
Braves	R	21	64	15	6	1	0	--	--	23	10	4	7	0	7	1	1	0	3	2	.60	4	.234	.319	.359
1989 Pulaski	R	49	156	53	8	2	2	--	--	71	22	22	21	2	20	0	2	2	7	2	.78	2	.340	.413	.455
1990 Sumter	A	107	355	94	13	3	3	--	--	122	42	37	37	1	57	1	5	3	9	5	.64	6	.265	.333	.344
1991 Durham	A	78	248	62	8	2	12	--	--	110	31	38	21	2	64	1	4	3	11	9	.55	3	.250	.308	.444
1992 Greenville	AA	133	489	140	22	2	15	--	--	211	73	54	27	2	84	1	3	7	33	19	.63	9	.286	.321	.431
1993 Richmond	AAA	93	370	122	15	7	15	--	--	196	73	53	36	3	54	1	4	3	19	11	.63	1	.330	.388	.530
1993 Atlanta	NL	24	35	8	2	0	0	(0	0)	10	6	2	0	0	5	1	0	1	0	1	.00	1	.229	.243	.286

Danny Tartabull

Bats: Right   **Throws:** Right   **Pos:** DH/RF   **Ht:** 6' 1"   **Wt:** 204   **Born:** 10/30/62   **Age:** 31

		BATTING																	BASERUNNING				PERCENTAGES		
Year Team	Lg	G	AB	H	2B	3B	HR	(Hm	Rd)	TB	R	RBI	TBB	IBB	SO	HBP	SH	SF	SB	CS	SB%	GDP	Avg	OBP	SLG
1984 Seattle	AL	10	20	6	1	0	2	(1	1)	13	3	7	2	0	3	1	0	1	0	0	.00	0	.300	.375	.650
1985 Seattle	AL	19	61	20	7	1	1	(0	1)	32	8	7	8	0	14	0	0	0	1	0	1.00	1	.328	.406	.525
1986 Seattle	AL	137	511	138	25	6	25	(13	12)	250	76	96	61	2	157	1	2	3	4	8	.33	10	.270	.347	.489
1987 Kansas City	AL	158	582	180	27	3	34	(15	19)	315	95	101	79	2	136	1	0	5	9	4	.69	14	.309	.390	.541
1988 Kansas City	AL	146	507	139	38	3	26	(15	11)	261	80	102	76	4	119	4	0	6	8	5	.62	10	.274	.369	.515

									(Hm	Rd)																
1989	Kansas City	AL	133	441	118	22	0	18	(9	9)	194	54	62	69	2	123	3	0	2	4	2	.67	12	.268	.369	.440
1990	Kansas City	AL	88	313	84	19	0	15	(5	10)	148	41	60	36	0	93	0	0	3	1	1	.50	9	.268	.341	.473
1991	Kansas City	AL	132	484	153	35	3	31	(13	18)	287	78	100	65	6	121	3	0	5	6	3	.67	9	.316	.397	.593
1992	New York	AL	123	421	112	19	0	25	(11	14)	206	72	85	103	14	115	0	0	2	2	2	.50	7	.266	.409	.489
1993	New York	AL	138	513	128	33	2	31	(11	20)	258	87	102	92	9	156	2	0	4	0	0	.00	8	.250	.363	.503
	10 ML YEARS		1084	3853	1078	226	18	208	(93	115)	1964	594	722	591	39	1037	15	2	31	35	25	.58	80	.280	.375	.510

Jimmy Tatum

Bats: Right **Throws:** Right **Pos:** 1B **Ht:** 6' 2" **Wt:** 200 **Born:** 10/09/67 **Age:** 26

								BATTING												BASERUNNING				PERCENTAGES		
Year	Team	Lg	G	AB	H	2B	3B	HR	(Hm	Rd)	TB	R	RBI	TBB	IBB	SO	HBP	SH	SF	SB	CS	SB%	GDP	Avg	OBP	SLG
1985	Spokane	A	74	281	64	9	1	1	--	--	78	21	32	20	0	60	5	4	1	0	1	.00	7	.228	.290	.278
1986	Charleston	A	120	431	112	19	2	10	--	--	165	55	62	41	2	83	2	4	5	2	4	.33	11	.260	.324	.383
1987	Chston-Sc	A	128	468	131	22	2	9	--	--	184	52	72	46	2	65	8	4	9	8	5	.62	16	.280	.348	.393
1988	Wichita	AA	118	402	105	26	1	8	--	--	157	38	54	30	2	73	5	6	3	2	3	.40	5	.261	.318	.391
1990	Canton-Akrn	AA	30	106	19	6	0	2	--	--	31	6	11	6	1	19	1	0	2	1	0	1.00	2	.179	.226	.292
	Stockton	A	70	260	68	16	0	12	--	--	120	41	59	13	0	49	8	0	4	4	5	.44	7	.262	.312	.462
1991	El Paso	AA	130	493	158	27	8	18	--	--	255	99	128	63	5	79	15	2	20	5	7	.42	21	.320	.399	.517
1992	Denver	AAA	130	492	162	36	3	19	--	--	261	74	101	40	3	87	9	4	11	8	9	.47	11	.329	.382	.530
1993	Colo Sprngs	AAA	13	45	10	2	0	2	--	--	18	5	7	2	0	9	1	0	0	0	1	.00	3	.222	.271	.400
1992	Milwaukee	AL	5	8	1	0	0	0	(0	0)	1	0	0	1	0	2	0	0	0	0	0	.00	0	.125	.222	.125
1993	Colorado	NL	92	98	20	5	0	1	(0	1)	28	7	12	5	0	27	1	0	2	0	0	.00	0	.204	.245	.286
	2 ML YEARS		97	106	21	5	0	1	(0	1)	29	7	12	6	0	29	1	0	2	0	0	.00	0	.198	.243	.274

Eddie Taubensee

Bats: Left **Throws:** Right **Pos:** C **Ht:** 6' 4" **Wt:** 205 **Born:** 10/31/68 **Age:** 25

								BATTING												BASERUNNING				PERCENTAGES		
Year	Team	Lg	G	AB	H	2B	3B	HR	(Hm	Rd)	TB	R	RBI	TBB	IBB	SO	HBP	SH	SF	SB	CS	SB%	GDP	Avg	OBP	SLG
1991	Cleveland	AL	26	66	16	2	1	0	(0	0)	20	5	8	5	1	16	0	0	2	0	0	.00	1	.242	.288	.303
1992	Houston	NL	104	297	66	15	0	5	(2	3)	96	23	28	31	3	78	2	0	1	2	1	.67	4	.222	.299	.323
1993	Houston	NL	94	288	72	11	1	9	(4	5)	112	26	42	21	5	44	0	1	2	1	0	1.00	8	.250	.299	.389
	3 ML YEARS		224	651	154	28	2	14	(6	8)	228	54	78	57	9	138	2	1	5	3	1	.75	13	.237	.298	.350

Julian Tavarez

Pitches: Right **Bats:** Right **Pos:** SP **Ht:** 6' 2" **Wt:** 165 **Born:** 05/22/73 **Age:** 21

			HOW	MUCH	HE	PITCHED			WHAT	HE	GAVE	UP							THE	RESULTS			
Year	Team	Lg	G	GS	CG	GF	IP	BFP	H	R	ER	HR	SH	SF	HB	TBB	IBB	SO	WP	Bk	W	L	Pct.	ShO	Sv	ERA
1992	Burlington	R	14	14	2	0	87.1	370	86	41	26	3	2	1	10	12	0	69	5	1	6	3	.667	2	0	2.68
1993	Kinston	A	18	18	2	0	119	489	102	48	32	6	3	4	7	28	0	107	3	1	11	5	.688	0	0	2.42
	Canton-Akrn	AA	3	2	1	0	19	69	14	2	2	0	0	0	2	1	0	11	0	1	2	1	.667	1	0	0.95
1993	Cleveland	AL	8	7	0	0	37	172	53	29	27	7	0	1	2	13	2	19	3	1	2	2	.500	0	0	6.57

Kerry Taylor

Pitches: Right **Bats:** Right **Pos:** RP/SP **Ht:** 6' 3" **Wt:** 200 **Born:** 01/25/71 **Age:** 23

			HOW	MUCH	HE	PITCHED			WHAT	HE	GAVE	UP							THE	RESULTS			
Year	Team	Lg	G	GS	CG	GF	IP	BFP	H	R	ER	HR	SH	SF	HB	TBB	IBB	SO	WP	Bk	W	L	Pct.	ShO	Sv	ERA
1989	Elizabethtn	R	9	8	0	0	36	157	26	11	6	1	3	1	2	22	0	24	1	0	3	0	1.000	0	0	1.50
1990	Twins	R	14	13	1	1	63	275	57	37	25	2	0	4	4	33	0	59	5	4	3	1	.750	1	0	3.57
1991	Kenosha	A	26	26	2	0	132	586	121	74	56	4	2	5	10	84	1	84	11	1	7	11	.389	1	0	3.82
1992	Kenosha	A	27	27	2	0	170.1	733	150	71	52	3	6	2	10	68	0	158	11	1	10	9	.526	1	0	2.75
1993	San Diego	NL	36	7	0	9	68.1	326	72	53	49	5	10	3	4	49	0	45	4	0	0	5	.000	0	0	6.45

Scott Taylor

Pitches: Left **Bats:** Left **Pos:** RP **Ht:** 6' 1" **Wt:** 190 **Born:** 08/02/67 **Age:** 26

			HOW	MUCH	HE	PITCHED			WHAT	HE	GAVE	UP							THE	RESULTS			
Year	Team	Lg	G	GS	CG	GF	IP	BFP	H	R	ER	HR	SH	SF	HB	TBB	IBB	SO	WP	Bk	W	L	Pct.	ShO	Sv	ERA
1988	Elmira	A	2	1	0	0	3.2	16	2	0	0	0	0	0	0	3	0	8	0	0	1	0	1.000	0	0	0.00
1989	Lynchburg	A	19	9	0	4	81	332	61	33	26	7	2	2	1	25	3	99	3	3	5	3	.625	0	1	2.89
1990	Lynchburg	A	13	13	1	0	89	372	76	36	27	2	3	0	2	30	2	120	7	3	5	6	.455	0	0	2.73
	New Britain	AA	5	5	1	0	27.1	117	23	8	5	0	3	0	1	13	1	27	1	0	0	2	.000	0	0	1.65
1991	New Britain	AA	4	4	0	0	29	109	20	2	2	0	0	0	0	9	0	38	1	0	2	0	1.000	0	0	0.62
	Pawtucket	AAA	7	7	1	0	39	161	32	19	15	3	0	2	1	17	0	35	1	1	3	3	.500	0	0	3.46
1992	Pawtucket	AAA	26	26	5	0	162	694	168	73	66	16	3	5	2	61	1	91	17	0	9	11	.450	0	0	3.67
1993	Pawtucket	AAA	47	8	0	10	122.2	533	132	61	55	12	7	2	3	48	0	88	2	1	7	7	.500	0	1	4.04
1992	Boston	AL	4	1	0	1	14.2	57	13	8	8	4	0	0	0	4	0	7	0	0	1	1	.500	0	0	4.91
1993	Boston	AL	16	0	0	3	11	59	14	10	10	1	1	0	1	12	3	8	0	0	0	1	.000	0	0	8.18
	2 ML YEARS		20	1	0	4	25.2	116	27	18	18	5	1	0	1	16	3	15	0	0	1	2	.333	0	0	6.31

Anthony Telford

Pitches: Right **Bats:** Right **Pos:** RP **Ht:** 6' 0" **Wt:** 184 **Born:** 03/06/66 **Age:** 28

		HOW MUCH HE PITCHED						WHAT HE GAVE UP												THE RESULTS					
Year Team	Lg	G	GS	CG	GF	IP	BFP	H	R	ER	HR	SH	SF	HB	TBB	IBB	SO	WP	Bk	W	L	Pct.	ShO	Sv	ERA
1993 Rochester *	AAA	38	6	0	12	90.2	397	98	51	43	10	2	4	3	33	3	66	6	0	7	7	.500	0	2	4.27
1990 Baltimore	AL	8	8	0	0	36.1	168	43	22	20	4	0	2	1	19	0	20	1	0	3	3	.500	0	0	4.95
1991 Baltimore	AL	9	1	0	4	26.2	109	27	12	12	3	0	1	0	6	1	24	1	0	0	0	.000	0	0	4.05
1993 Baltimore	AL	3	0	0	2	7.1	34	11	8	8	3	0	0	1	1	0	6	1	0	0	0	.000	0	0	9.82
3 ML YEARS		20	9	0	6	70.1	311	81	42	40	10	0	3	2	26	1	50	3	0	3	3	.500	0	0	5.12

Dave Telgheder

Pitches: Right **Bats:** Right **Pos:** RP/SP **Ht:** 6' 3" **Wt:** 212 **Born:** 11/11/66 **Age:** 27

		HOW MUCH HE PITCHED						WHAT HE GAVE UP												THE RESULTS					
Year Team	Lg	G	GS	CG	GF	IP	BFP	H	R	ER	HR	SH	SF	HB	TBB	IBB	SO	WP	Bk	W	L	Pct.	ShO	Sv	ERA
1989 Pittsfield	A	13	7	4	4	58.2	233	43	18	16	2	1	1	2	9	1	65	2	2	5	3	.625	1	2	2.45
1990 Columbia	A	14	13	5	1	99.1	380	79	22	17	2	0	0	0	10	0	81	0	1	9	3	.750	1	0	1.54
St. Lucie	A	14	14	3	0	96	382	84	38	32	3	3	4	3	14	0	77	3	0	9	4	.692	0	0	3.00
1991 Williamsprt	AA	28	26	1	1	167.2	711	185	81	67	7	7	11	5	33	3	90	4	1	13	11	.542	0	0	3.60
1992 Tidewater	AAA	28	27	3	1	169	698	173	87	79	16	4	7	0	36	4	118	1	1	6	14	.300	2	0	4.21
1993 Norfolk	AAA	13	12	0	1	76.1	313	81	29	25	6	3	0	3	19	1	52	1	0	7	3	.700	0	1	2.95
1993 New York	NL	24	7	0	7	75.2	325	82	40	40	10	2	1	4	21	2	35	1	0	6	2	.750	0	0	4.76

Mickey Tettleton

Bats: Both **Throws:** Right **Pos:** 1B/C/LF/RF **Ht:** 6' 2" **Wt:** 212 **Born:** 09/16/60 **Age:** 33

		BATTING																		BASERUNNING				PERCENTAGES		
Year Team	Lg	G	AB	H	2B	3B	HR	(Hm	Rd)	TB	R	RBI	TBB	IBB	SO	HBP	SH	SF	SB	CS	SB%	GDP	Avg	OBP	SLG
1984 Oakland	AL	33	76	20	2	1	1	(1	0)	27	10	5	11	0	21	0	0	1	0	0	.00	3	.263	.352	.355
1985 Oakland	AL	78	211	53	12	0	3	(1	2)	74	23	15	28	0	59	2	5	0	2	2	.50	6	.251	.344	.351
1986 Oakland	AL	90	211	43	9	0	10	(4	6)	82	26	35	39	0	51	1	7	4	7	1	.88	3	.204	.325	.389
1987 Oakland	AL	82	211	41	3	0	8	(5	3)	68	19	26	30	0	65	0	5	2	1	1	.50	3	.194	.292	.322
1988 Baltimore	AL	86	283	74	11	1	11	(7	4)	120	31	37	28	2	70	2	1	2	0	1	.00	9	.261	.330	.424
1989 Baltimore	AL	117	411	106	21	2	26	(15	11)	209	72	65	73	4	117	1	1	3	3	2	.60	8	.258	.369	.509
1990 Baltimore	AL	135	444	99	21	2	15	(8	7)	169	68	51	106	3	160	5	0	4	2	4	.33	7	.223	.376	.381
1991 Detroit	AL	154	501	132	17	2	31	(15	16)	246	85	89	101	9	131	2	0	4	3	3	.50	12	.263	.387	.491
1992 Detroit	AL	157	525	125	25	0	32	(18	14)	246	82	83	122	18	137	1	0	6	0	6	.00	5	.238	.379	.469
1993 Detroit	AL	152	522	128	25	4	32	(16	16)	257	79	110	109	12	139	0	0	6	3	7	.30	5	.245	.372	.492
10 ML YEARS		1084	3395	821	146	12	169	(90	79)	1498	495	516	647	48	950	14	19	32	21	27	.44	61	.242	.363	.441

Tim Teufel

Bats: Right **Throws:** Right **Pos:** 2B **Ht:** 6' 0" **Wt:** 175 **Born:** 07/07/58 **Age:** 35

		BATTING																		BASERUNNING				PERCENTAGES		
Year Team	Lg	G	AB	H	2B	3B	HR	(Hm	Rd)	TB	R	RBI	TBB	IBB	SO	HBP	SH	SF	SB	CS	SB%	GDP	Avg	OBP	SLG
1983 Minnesota	AL	21	78	24	7	1	3	(3	0)	42	11	6	2	0	8	0	2	0	0	0	.00	1	.308	.325	.538
1984 Minnesota	AL	157	568	149	30	3	14	(9	5)	227	76	61	76	8	73	2	2	4	1	3	.25	18	.262	.349	.400
1985 Minnesota	AL	138	434	113	24	3	10	(6	4)	173	58	50	48	2	70	3	7	4	4	2	.67	14	.260	.335	.399
1986 New York	NL	93	279	69	20	1	4	(2	2)	103	35	31	32	1	42	1	3	3	1	2	.33	6	.247	.324	.369
1987 New York	NL	97	299	92	29	0	14	(4	10)	163	55	61	44	2	53	2	3	2	3	2	.60	7	.308	.398	.545
1988 New York	NL	90	273	64	20	0	4	(1	3)	96	35	31	29	1	41	1	2	4	0	1	.00	6	.234	.306	.352
1989 New York	NL	83	219	56	7	2	2	(1	1)	73	27	15	32	1	50	1	0	2	1	3	.25	4	.256	.350	.333
1990 New York	NL	80	175	43	11	0	10	(4	6)	84	28	24	15	1	33	0	1	1	0	0	.00	5	.246	.304	.480
1991 2 ML Teams		117	341	74	16	0	12	(6	6)	126	41	44	51	4	77	1	4	2	9	3	.75	8	.217	.319	.370
1992 San Diego	NL	101	246	55	10	0	6	(2	4)	83	23	25	31	3	45	1	0	1	2	1	.67	7	.224	.312	.337
1993 San Diego	NL	96	200	50	11	2	7	(5	2)	86	26	31	27	0	39	0	3		2	2	.50	9	.250	.338	.430
1991 New York	NL	20	34	4	0	0	1	(1	0)	7	2	2	2	0	8	0	0	0	1	1	.50	0	.118	.167	.206
San Diego	NL	97	307	70	16	0	11	(5	6)	119	39	42	49	4	69	1	4	2	8	2	.80	8	.228	.334	.388
11 ML YEARS		1073	3112	789	185	12	86	(43	43)	1256	415	379	387	23	531	12	27	24	23	19	.55	85	.254	.336	.404

Bob Tewksbury

Pitches: Right **Bats:** Right **Pos:** SP **Ht:** 6' 4" **Wt:** 208 **Born:** 11/30/60 **Age:** 33

		HOW MUCH HE PITCHED						WHAT HE GAVE UP												THE RESULTS					
Year Team	Lg	G	GS	CG	GF	IP	BFP	H	R	ER	HR	SH	SF	HB	TBB	IBB	SO	WP	Bk	W	L	Pct.	ShO	Sv	ERA
1986 New York	AL	23	20	2	0	130.1	558	144	58	48	8	4	7	5	31	0	49	3	2	9	5	.643	0	0	3.31
1987 2 ML Teams		15	9	0	4	51.1	242	79	41	38	6	5	1	1	20	3	22	1	2	1	8	.111	0	0	6.66
1988 Chicago	NL	1	1	0	0	3.1	18	6	5	3	1	0	1	0	2	0	1	0	0	0	0	.000	0	0	8.10
1989 St. Louis	NL	7	4	1	2	30	125	25	12	11	2	1	1	2	10	3	17	0	0	1	0	1.000	1	0	3.30
1990 St. Louis	NL	28	20	3	1	145.1	595	151	67	56	7	5	7	3	15	5	50	2	0	10	9	.526	2	1	3.47
1991 St. Louis	NL	30	30	3	0	191	798	206	86	69	13	12	10	5	38	2	75	0	0	11	12	.478	0	0	3.25

214

Year Team	Lg	G	GS	CG	GF	IP	BFP	H	R	ER	HR	SH	SF	HB	TBB	IBB	SO	WP	Bk	W	L	Pct.	ShO	Sv	ERA
1992 St. Louis	NL	33	32	5	1	233	915	217	63	56	15	9	7	3	20	0	91	2	0	16	5	.762	0	0	2.16
1993 St. Louis	NL	32	32	2	0	213.2	907	258	99	91	15	15	9	6	20	1	97	2	0	17	10	.630	0	0	3.83
1987 New York	AL	8	6	0	1	33.1	149	47	26	25	5	2	0	1	7	0	12	0	0	1	4	.200	0	0	6.75
Chicago	NL	7	3	0	3	18	93	32	15	13	1	3	1	0	13	3	10	1	2	0	4	.000	0	0	6.50
8 ML YEARS		169	148	16	8	998	4158	1086	431	372	67	51	43	25	156	12	402	10	4	65	49	.570	3	1	3.35

Bobby Thigpen

Pitches: Right **Bats:** Right **Pos:** RP **Ht:** 6' 3" **Wt:** 222 **Born:** 07/17/63 **Age:** 30

Year Team	Lg	HOW MUCH HE PITCHED						WHAT HE GAVE UP												THE RESULTS					
		G	GS	CG	GF	IP	BFP	H	R	ER	HR	SH	SF	HB	TBB	IBB	SO	WP	Bk	W	L	Pct.	ShO	Sv	ERA
1986 Chicago	AL	20	0	0	14	35.2	142	26	7	7	1	1	1	1	12	0	20	0	0	2	0	1.000	0	7	1.77
1987 Chicago	AL	51	0	0	37	89	369	86	30	27	10	6	0	3	24	5	52	0	0	7	5	.583	0	16	2.73
1988 Chicago	AL	68	0	0	59	90	398	96	38	33	6	4	5	4	33	3	62	6	2	5	8	.385	0	34	3.30
1989 Chicago	AL	61	0	0	56	79	336	62	34	33	10	5	5	1	40	3	47	2	1	2	6	.250	0	34	3.76
1990 Chicago	AL	77	0	0	73	88.2	347	60	20	18	5	4	3	1	32	3	70	2	0	4	6	.400	0	57	1.83
1991 Chicago	AL	67	0	0	58	69.2	309	63	32	27	10	7	3	4	38	8	47	2	0	7	5	.583	0	30	3.49
1992 Chicago	AL	55	0	0	40	55	253	58	29	29	4	2	4	3	33	5	45	0	0	1	3	.250	0	22	4.75
1993 2 ML Teams		42	0	0	16	54	254	74	38	35	7	2	4	6	21	1	29	0	1	3	1	.750	0	1	5.83
1993 Chicago	AL	25	0	0	11	34.2	166	51	25	22	5	0	3	5	12	0	19	0	0	0	0	.000	0	1	5.71
Philadelphia	NL	17	0	0	5	19.1	88	23	13	13	2	2	1	1	9	1	10	0	1	3	1	.750	0	0	6.05
8 ML YEARS		441	0	0	353	561	2408	525	228	209	53	31	25	23	233	28	372	12	4	31	34	.477	0	201	3.35

Frank Thomas

Bats: Right **Throws:** Right **Pos:** 1B **Ht:** 6' 5" **Wt:** 257 **Born:** 05/27/68 **Age:** 26

Year Team	Lg	BATTING																	BASERUNNING				PERCENTAGES		
		G	AB	H	2B	3B	HR	(Hm	Rd)	TB	R	RBI	TBB	IBB	SO	HBP	SH	SF	SB	CS	SB%	GDP	Avg	OBP	SLG
1990 Chicago	AL	60	191	63	11	3	7	(2	5)	101	39	31	44	0	54	2	0	3	0	1	.00	5	.330	.454	.529
1991 Chicago	AL	158	559	178	31	2	32	(24	8)	309	104	109	138	13	112	1	0	2	1	2	.33	20	.318	.453	.553
1992 Chicago	AL	160	573	185	46	2	24	(10	14)	307	108	115	122	6	88	5	0	11	6	3	.67	19	.323	.439	.536
1993 Chicago	AL	153	549	174	36	0	41	(26	15)	333	106	128	112	23	54	2	0	13	4	2	.67	10	.317	.426	.607
4 ML YEARS		531	1872	600	124	7	104	(62	42)	1050	357	383	416	42	308	10	0	29	11	8	.58	54	.321	.441	.561

Jim Thome

Bats: Left **Throws:** Right **Pos:** 3B **Ht:** 6' 3" **Wt:** 200 **Born:** 08/27/70 **Age:** 23

Year Team	Lg	BATTING																	BASERUNNING				PERCENTAGES		
		G	AB	H	2B	3B	HR	(Hm	Rd)	TB	R	RBI	TBB	IBB	SO	HBP	SH	SF	SB	CS	SB%	GDP	Avg	OBP	SLG
1993 Charlotte *	AAA	115	410	136	21	4	25	--	--	240	85	102	76	8	94	7	0	4	1	3	.25	9	.332	.441	.585
1991 Cleveland	AL	27	98	25	4	2	1	(0	1)	36	7	9	5	1	16	1	0	0	1	1	.50	4	.255	.298	.367
1992 Cleveland	AL	40	117	24	3	1	2	(1	1)	35	8	12	10	2	34	2	0	2	2	1	1.00	4	.205	.275	.299
1993 Cleveland	AL	47	154	41	11	0	7	(5	2)	73	28	22	29	1	36	4	0	5	2	1	.67	3	.266	.385	.474
3 ML YEARS		114	369	90	18	3	10	(6	4)	144	43	43	44	4	86	7	0	7	5	2	.71	10	.244	.330	.390

Milt Thompson

Bats: Left **Throws:** Right **Pos:** LF **Ht:** 5'11" **Wt:** 200 **Born:** 01/05/59 **Age:** 35

Year Team	Lg	BATTING																	BASERUNNING				PERCENTAGES		
		G	AB	H	2B	3B	HR	(Hm	Rd)	TB	R	RBI	TBB	IBB	SO	HBP	SH	SF	SB	CS	SB%	GDP	Avg	OBP	SLG
1984 Atlanta	NL	25	99	30	1	0	2	(0	2)	37	16	4	11	1	11	0	1	0	14	2	.88	1	.303	.373	.374
1985 Atlanta	NL	73	182	55	7	2	0	(0	0)	66	17	6	7	0	36	3	1	0	9	4	.69	1	.302	.339	.363
1986 Philadelphia	NL	96	299	75	7	1	6	(4	2)	102	38	23	26	1	62	1	4	2	19	4	.83	4	.251	.311	.341
1987 Philadelphia	NL	150	527	159	26	9	7	(3	4)	224	86	43	42	2	87	0	3	3	46	10	.82	5	.302	.351	.425
1988 Philadelphia	NL	122	378	109	16	2	2	(1	1)	135	53	33	39	6	59	1	2	3	17	9	.65	8	.288	.354	.357
1989 St. Louis	NL	155	545	158	28	8	4	(2	2)	214	60	68	39	5	91	4	0	3	27	8	.77	12	.290	.340	.393
1990 St. Louis	NL	135	418	91	14	7	6	(3	3)	137	42	30	39	5	60	5	1	0	25	5	.83	4	.218	.292	.328
1991 St. Louis	NL	115	326	100	16	5	6	(4	2)	144	55	34	32	7	53	0	2	1	16	9	.64	4	.307	.368	.442
1992 St. Louis	NL	109	208	61	9	1	4	(1	3)	84	31	17	16	3	39	2	0	0	18	6	.75	3	.293	.350	.404
1993 Philadelphia	NL	129	340	89	14	2	4	(2	2)	119	42	44	40	9	57	2	3	2	9	4	.69	8	.262	.341	.350
10 ML YEARS		1109	3322	927	138	37	41	(20	21)	1262	440	302	291	39	555	18	17	14	200	61	.77	50	.279	.339	.380

Robby Thompson

Bats: Right **Throws:** Right **Pos:** 2B **Ht:** 5'11" **Wt:** 173 **Born:** 05/10/62 **Age:** 32

Year Team	Lg	BATTING																	BASERUNNING				PERCENTAGES		
		G	AB	H	2B	3B	HR	(Hm	Rd)	TB	R	RBI	TBB	IBB	SO	HBP	SH	SF	SB	CS	SB%	GDP	Avg	OBP	SLG
1986 San Francisco	NL	149	549	149	27	3	7	(0	7)	203	73	47	42	0	112	5	18	1	12	15	.44	11	.271	.328	.370
1987 San Francisco	NL	132	420	110	26	5	10	(7	3)	176	62	44	40	3	91	8	6	0	16	11	.59	5	.262	.338	.419
1988 San Francisco	NL	138	477	126	24	6	7	(3	4)	183	66	48	40	0	111	4	14	5	14	5	.74	7	.264	.323	.384
1989 San Francisco	NL	148	547	132	26	11	13	(7	6)	219	91	50	51	0	133	13	9	0	12	2	.86	6	.241	.321	.400
1990 San Francisco	NL	144	498	122	22	3	15	(8	7)	195	67	56	34	0	96	6	8	3	14	4	.78	9	.245	.299	.392
1991 San Francisco	NL	144	492	129	24	5	19	(11	8)	220	74	48	63	2	95	6	11	1	14	7	.67	5	.262	.352	.447

		Lg	G	AB	H	2B	3B	HR	(Hm	Rd)	TB	R	RBI	TBB	IBB	SO	HBP	SH	SF	SB	CS	SB%	GDP	Avg	OBP	SLG
1992	San Francisco	NL	128	443	115	25	1	14	(8	6)	184	54	49	43	1	75	8	7	4	5	9	.36	8	.260	.333	.415
1993	San Francisco	NL	128	494	154	30	2	19	(13	6)	245	85	65	45	0	97	7	9	4	10	4	.71	7	.312	.375	.496
8	ML YEARS		1111	3920	1037	204	36	104	(57	47)	1625	572	407	358	7	810	57	82	18	97	57	.63	61	.265	.334	.415

Ryan Thompson

Bats: Right **Throws:** Right **Pos:** CF　　　　　　　　**Ht:** 6' 3" **Wt:** 200 **Born:** 11/04/67 **Age:** 26

									BATTING											BASERUNNING				PERCENTAGES		
Year	Team	Lg	G	AB	H	2B	3B	HR	(Hm	Rd)	TB	R	RBI	TBB	IBB	SO	HBP	SH	SF	SB	CS	SB%	GDP	Avg	OBP	SLG
1987	Medicne Hat	R	40	110	27	3	1	1	--	--	35	13	9	6	0	34	0	0	0	1	2	.33	1	.245	.284	.318
1988	St.Cathmes	A	23	57	10	4	0	0	--	--	14	13	2	24	0	21	4	1	0	2	2	.50	0	.175	.447	.246
	Dunedin	A	17	29	4	0	0	1	--	--	7	2	2	2	0	12	1	0	0	0	0	.00	0	.138	.219	.241
1989	St.Cathmes	A	74	278	76	14	1	6	--	--	110	39	36	16	0	60	4	0	3	9	6	.60	8	.273	.319	.396
1990	Dunedin	A	117	438	101	15	5	6	--	--	144	56	37	20	1	100	2	3	4	18	5	.78	5	.231	.265	.329
1991	Knoxville	AA	114	403	97	14	3	8	--	--	141	48	40	26	2	88	4	5	3	17	10	.63	11	.241	.291	.350
1992	Syracuse	AAA	112	429	121	20	7	14	--	--	197	74	46	43	1	114	3	2	1	10	4	.71	5	.282	.351	.459
1993	Norfolk	AAA	60	224	58	11	2	12	--	--	109	39	34	24	2	81	5	0	2	6	3	.67	2	.259	.341	.487
1992	New York	NL	30	108	24	7	1	3	(3	0)	42	15	10	8	0	24	0	0	1	2	2	.50	2	.222	.274	.389
1993	New York	NL	80	288	72	19	2	11	(5	6)	128	34	26	19	4	81	3	5	1	2	7	.22	5	.250	.302	.444
2	ML YEARS		110	396	96	26	3	14	(8	6)	170	49	36	27	4	105	3	5	2	4	9	.31	7	.242	.294	.429

Dickie Thon

Bats: Right **Throws:** Right **Pos:** SS/2B/3B/DH　　　　**Ht:** 5'11" **Wt:** 178 **Born:** 06/20/58 **Age:** 36

									BATTING											BASERUNNING				PERCENTAGES		
Year	Team	Lg	G	AB	H	2B	3B	HR	(Hm	Rd)	TB	R	RBI	TBB	IBB	SO	HBP	SH	SF	SB	CS	SB%	GDP	Avg	OBP	SLG
1979	California	AL	35	56	19	3	0	0	(0	0)	22	6	8	5	0	10	0	1	0	0	0	.00	2	.339	.393	.393
1980	California	AL	80	267	68	12	2	0	(0	0)	84	32	15	10	0	28	1	5	2	7	5	.58	5	.255	.282	.315
1981	Houston	NL	49	95	26	6	0	0	(0	0)	32	13	3	9	1	13	0	1	0	6	1	.86	3	.274	.337	.337
1982	Houston	NL	136	496	137	31	10	3	(1	2)	197	73	36	37	2	48	1	5	1	37	8	.82	4	.276	.327	.397
1983	Houston	NL	154	619	177	28	9	20	(4	16)	283	81	79	54	10	73	2	3	8	34	16	.68	12	.286	.341	.457
1984	Houston	NL	5	17	6	0	1	0	(0	0)	8	3	1	0	0	4	1	0	0	0	1	.00	1	.353	.389	.471
1985	Houston	NL	84	251	63	6	1	6	(3	3)	89	26	29	18	4	50	0	1	2	8	3	.73	2	.251	.299	.355
1986	Houston	NL	106	278	69	13	1	3	(0	3)	93	24	21	29	5	49	0	1	1	6	5	.55	8	.248	.318	.335
1987	Houston	NL	32	66	14	1	0	1	(0	1)	18	6	3	16	3	13	0	1	0	3	0	1.00	1	.212	.366	.273
1988	San Diego	NL	95	258	68	12	2	1	(0	1)	87	36	18	33	0	49	1	2	2	19	4	.83	4	.264	.347	.337
1989	Philadelphia	NL	136	435	118	18	4	15	(8	7)	189	45	60	33	6	81	0	1	3	6	3	.67	6	.271	.321	.434
1990	Philadelphia	NL	149	552	141	20	4	8	(3	5)	193	54	48	37	10	77	3	1	2	12	5	.71	14	.255	.305	.350
1991	Philadelphia	NL	146	539	136	18	4	9	(4	5)	189	44	44	25	6	84	0	2	4	11	5	.69	9	.252	.283	.351
1992	Texas	AL	95	275	68	15	3	4	(2	2)	101	30	37	20	1	40	0	3	5	12	2	.86	2	.247	.293	.367
1993	Milwaukee	AL	85	245	66	10	1	1	(0	1)	81	23	33	22	3	39	0	3	5	6	5	.55	4	.269	.324	.331
15	ML YEARS		1387	4449	1176	193	42	71	(25	46)	1666	496	435	348	51	658	9	30	35	167	63	.73	77	.264	.317	.374

Gary Thurman

Bats: Right **Throws:** Right **Pos:** CF/LF/RF　　　　**Ht:** 5'10" **Wt:** 175 **Born:** 11/12/64 **Age:** 29

									BATTING											BASERUNNING				PERCENTAGES		
Year	Team	Lg	G	AB	H	2B	3B	HR	(Hm	Rd)	TB	R	RBI	TBB	IBB	SO	HBP	SH	SF	SB	CS	SB%	GDP	Avg	OBP	SLG
1987	Kansas City	AL	27	81	24	2	0	0	(0	0)	26	12	5	8	0	20	0	1	0	7	2	.78	1	.296	.360	.321
1988	Kansas City	AL	35	66	11	1	0	0	(0	0)	12	6	2	4	0	20	0	0	0	5	1	.83	0	.167	.214	.182
1989	Kansas City	AL	72	87	17	2	1	0	(0	0)	21	24	5	15	0	26	0	2	1	16	0	1.00	0	.195	.311	.241
1990	Kansas City	AL	23	60	14	3	0	0	(0	0)	17	5	3	2	0	12	0	1	0	1	1	.50	2	.233	.258	.283
1991	Kansas City	AL	80	184	51	9	0	2	(1	1)	66	24	13	11	0	42	1	3	1	15	5	.75	4	.277	.320	.359
1992	Kansas City	AL	88	200	49	6	3	0	(0	0)	61	25	20	9	0	34	1	6	0	9	6	.60	3	.245	.281	.305
1993	Detroit	AL	75	89	19	2	2	0	(0	0)	25	22	13	11	0	30	0	1	1	7	0	1.00	2	.213	.297	.281
7	ML YEARS		400	767	185	25	6	2	(1	1)	228	118	61	60	0	184	2	14	3	60	15	.80	12	.241	.297	.297

Mike Timlin

Pitches: Right **Bats:** Right **Pos:** RP　　　　　　　　**Ht:** 6' 4" **Wt:** 205 **Born:** 03/10/66 **Age:** 28

					HOW MUCH HE PITCHED				WHAT HE GAVE UP								THE RESULTS					
Year	Team	Lg	G	GS	CG	GF	IP	BFP	H	R	ER	HR	SH	SF	HB	TBB	IBB	SO	WP	Bk	W	L	Pct.	ShO	Sv	ERA
1993	Dunedin *	A	4	0	0	2	9	30	4	1	1	0	0	0	0	0	0	8	0	0	0	0	.000	0	1	1.00
1991	Toronto	AL	63	3	0	17	108.1	463	94	43	38	6	6	2	1	50	11	85	5	0	11	6	.647	0	3	3.16
1992	Toronto	AL	26	0	0	14	43.2	190	45	23	20	0	2	1	1	20	5	35	0	0	0	2	.000	0	1	4.12
1993	Toronto	AL	54	0	0	27	55.2	254	63	32	29	7	1	3	1	27	3	49	1	0	4	2	.667	0	1	4.69
3	ML YEARS		143	3	0	58	207.2	907	202	98	87	13	9	6	3	97	19	169	6	0	15	10	.600	0	5	3.77

216

Ron Tingley

Bats: Right **Throws:** Right **Pos:** C   **Ht:** 6' 2" **Wt:** 194 **Born:** 05/27/59 **Age:** 35

					BATTING													BASERUNNING				PERCENTAGES		
Year	Team	Lg	G	AB	H	2B	3B	HR	(Hm | Rd)	TB	R	RBI	TBB	IBB	SO	HBP	SH	SF	SB	CS	SB%	GDP	Avg	OBP	SLG
1982	San Diego	NL	8	20	2	0	0	0	(0 | 0)	2	0	0	0	0	7	0	1	0	0	0	.00	0	.100	.100	.100
1988	Cleveland	AL	9	24	4	0	0	1	(0 | 1)	7	1	2	2	0	8	0	0	0	0	0	.00	1	.167	.231	.292
1989	California	AL	4	3	1	0	0	0	(0 | 0)	1	0	0	1	0	0	0	0	0	0	0	.00	0	.333	.500	.333
1990	California	AL	5	3	0	0	0	0	(0 | 0)	0	0	0	1	0	1	0	0	0	0	0	.00	0	.000	.250	.000
1991	California	AL	45	115	23	7	0	1	(1 | 0)	33	11	13	8	0	34	1	4	0	1	1	.50	1	.200	.258	.287
1992	California	AL	71	127	25	2	1	3	(2 | 1)	38	15	8	13	0	35	2	5	0	0	1	.00	4	.197	.282	.299
1993	California	AL	58	90	18	7	0	0	(0 | 0)	25	7	12	9	0	22	1	3	1	1	2	.33	4	.200	.277	.278
	7 ML YEARS		200	382	73	16	1	5	(3 | 2)	106	34	35	34	0	107	4	13	1	2	4	.33	11	.191	.264	.277

Lee Tinsley

Bats: Both **Throws:** Right **Pos:** LF   **Ht:** 5'10" **Wt:** 185 **Born:** 03/04/69 **Age:** 25

					BATTING													BASERUNNING				PERCENTAGES		
Year	Team	Lg	G	AB	H	2B	3B	HR	(Hm	Rd)	TB	R	RBI	TBB	IBB	SO	HBP	SH	SF	SB	CS	SB%	GDP	Avg	OBP	SLG
1987	Medford	A	45	132	23	3	2	0	--	--	30	22	13	35	0	57	2	1	4	9	3	.75	1	.174	.347	.227
1988	Sou Oregon	A	72	256	64	8	2	3	--	--	85	56	28	66	1	106	5	1	1	42	10	.81	1	.250	.412	.332
1989	Madison	A	123	397	72	10	2	6	--	--	104	51	31	67	1	177	9	3	1	19	11	.63	6	.181	.312	.262
1990	Madison	A	132	482	121	14	11	12	--	--	193	88	59	78	7	175	5	3	2	44	11	.80	3	.251	.360	.400
1991	Huntsville	AA	92	303	68	7	6	2	--	--	93	47	24	52	1	97	3	1	4	36	14	.72	6	.224	.340	.307
	Canton-Akrn	AA	38	139	41	7	2	3	--	--	61	26	8	18	2	37	4	2	0	18	5	.78	2	.295	.391	.439
1992	Colo Spmgs	AAA	27	81	19	2	1	0	--	--	23	19	4	16	0	19	1	1	1	3	3	.50	3	.235	.364	.284
	Canton-Akrn	AA	96	349	100	9	8	5	--	--	140	65	38	42	4	82	2	5	2	18	5	.78	13	.287	.365	.401
1993	Calgary	AAA	111	450	136	25	18	10	--	--	227	94	63	50	5	98	2	3	4	34	11	.76	3	.302	.372	.504
1993	Seattle	AL	11	19	3	1	0	1	(0	1)	7	2	2	2	0	9	0	0	0	0	0	.00	1	.158	.238	.368

Fred Toliver

Pitches: Right **Bats:** Right **Pos:** RP   **Ht:** 6' 1" **Wt:** 170 **Born:** 02/03/61 **Age:** 33

					HOW MUCH HE PITCHED				WHAT HE GAVE UP									THE RESULTS					
Year	Team	Lg	G	GS	CG	GF	IP	BFP	H	R	ER	HR	SH	SF	HB	TBB	IBB	SO	WP	Bk	W	L	Pct.	ShO	Sv	ERA
1993	Carolina *	AA	33	0	0	24	40	170	32	16	14	3	5	1	3	24	4	48	3	1	2	2	.500	0	12	3.15
	Buffalo *	AAA	13	0	0	10	12.1	59	13	5	5	0	1	1	0	9	4	11	0	0	1	3	.250	0	1	3.65
1984	Cincinnati	NL	3	1	0	0	10	42	7	2	1	0	1	0	0	7	0	4	0	0	0	0	.000	0	0	0.90
1985	Philadelphia	NL	11	3	0	4	25	117	27	15	13	2	0	1	0	17	1	23	0	0	0	4	.000	0	0	4.68
1986	Philadelphia	NL	5	5	0	0	25.2	112	28	14	10	0	3	0	0	11	0	20	2	0	0	2	.000	0	0	3.51
1987	Philadelphia	NL	10	4	0	2	30.1	139	34	19	19	2	2	2	1	17	3	25	1	1	1	1	.500	0	0	5.64
1988	Minnesota	AL	21	19	0	0	114.2	491	116	57	54	8	7	1	1	52	1	69	10	1	7	6	.538	0	0	4.24
1989	2 ML Teams		16	5	0	3	43	205	56	40	36	7	2	1	2	24	0	25	0	0	1	3	.250	0	0	7.53
1993	Pittsburgh	NL	12	0	0	3	21.2	90	20	10	9	2	2	3	2	8	0	14	0	0	1	0	1.000	0	0	3.74
1989	Minnesota	AL	7	5	0	0	29	140	39	26	25	2	1	0	1	15	0	11	0	0	1	3	.250	0	0	7.76
	San Diego	NL	9	0	0	3	14	65	17	14	11	5	1	1	1	9	0	14	0	0	0	0	.000	0	0	7.07
	7 ML YEARS		78	37	0	12	270.1	1196	288	157	142	21	17	8	6	136	5	180	13	2	10	16	.385	0	0	4.73

Andy Tomberlin

Bats: Left **Throws:** Left **Pos:** LF   **Ht:** 5'11" **Wt:** 160 **Born:** 11/07/66 **Age:** 27

					BATTING													BASERUNNING				PERCENTAGES		
Year	Team	Lg	G	AB	H	2B	3B	HR	(Hm	Rd)	TB	R	RBI	TBB	IBB	SO	HBP	SH	SF	SB	CS	SB%	GDP	Avg	OBP	SLG
1986	Sumter	A	13	1	0	0	0	0	--	--	0	0	0	1	0	1	0	0	0	0	0	.00	0	.000	.500	.000
	Pulaski	R	3	4	1	0	0	0	--	--	1	2	0	2	0	1	0	0	0	0	0	.00	0	.250	.500	.250
1987	Pulaski	R	14	7	2	0	0	0	--	--	2	1	1	0	0	0	0	0	0	0	0	.00	0	.286	.286	.286
1988	Burlington	A	43	134	46	7	3	3	--	--	68	24	18	22	2	33	2	1	1	7	4	.64	0	.343	.440	.507
	Durham	A	83	256	77	16	3	6	--	--	117	43	35	49	3	42	1	2	1	16	8	.67	2	.301	.414	.457
1989	Durham	A	119	363	102	13	2	16	--	--	167	63	61	54	7	82	5	3	1	35	12	.74	4	.281	.381	.460
1990	Greenville	AA	60	196	61	9	1	4	--	--	84	31	25	20	0	35	5	4	1	9	4	.69	1	.311	.387	.429
	Richmond	AAA	80	283	86	19	3	4	--	--	123	36	31	39	7	43	1	4	2	11	4	.73	7	.304	.388	.435
1991	Richmond	AAA	93	329	77	13	2	2	--	--	100	47	24	41	3	85	8	9	1	10	6	.63	6	.234	.332	.304
1992	Richmond	AAA	118	406	110	16	5	9	--	--	163	69	47	41	1	102	8	10	2	12	12	.50	2	.271	.348	.401
1993	Buffalo	AAA	68	221	63	11	6	12	--	--	122	41	45	18	3	48	4	1	2	3	0	1.00	5	.285	.347	.552
1993	Pittsburgh	NL	27	42	12	0	1	1	(0	1)	17	4	5	2	0	14	1	0	0	0	0	.00	0	.286	.333	.405

Randy Tomlin

Pitches: Left **Bats:** Left **Pos:** SP **Ht:** 5'10" **Wt:** 170 **Born:** 06/14/66 **Age:** 28

Year Team	Lg	G	GS	CG	GF	IP	BFP	H	R	ER	HR	SH	SF	HB	TBB	IBB	SO	WP	Bk	W	L	Pct.	ShO	Sv	ERA
1993 Carolina *	AA	2	2	0	0	12	41	7	1	1	1	0	0	0	1	0	9	0	0	1	0	1.000	0	0	0.75
1990 Pittsburgh	NL	12	12	2	0	77.2	297	62	24	22	5	2	2	1	12	1	42	1	3	4	4	.500	0	0	2.55
1991 Pittsburgh	NL	31	27	4	0	175	736	170	75	58	9	5	2	6	54	4	104	2	3	8	7	.533	2	0	2.98
1992 Pittsburgh	NL	35	33	1	0	208.2	866	226	85	79	11	13	5	5	42	4	90	7	2	14	9	.609	1	0	3.41
1993 Pittsburgh	NL	18	18	1	0	98.1	411	109	57	53	11	8	8	5	15	0	44	4	2	4	8	.333	0	0	4.85
4 ML YEARS		96	90	8	0	559.2	2310	567	241	212	36	28	17	17	123	9	280	14	10	30	28	.517	3	0	3.41

Salomon Torres

Pitches: Right **Bats:** Right **Pos:** SP **Ht:** 5' 5" **Wt:** 150 **Born:** 03/11/72 **Age:** 22

Year Team	Lg	G	GS	CG	GF	IP	BFP	H	R	ER	HR	SH	SF	HB	TBB	IBB	SO	WP	Bk	W	L	Pct.	ShO	Sv	ERA
1991 Clinton	A	28	28	8	0	210.2	814	148	48	33	4	4	4	1	47	2	214	6	4	16	5	.762	3	0	1.41
1992 Shreveport	AA	25	25	4	0	162.1	680	167	93	76	10	4	5	2	34	2	151	9	1	6	10	.375	2	0	4.21
1993 Shreveport	AA	12	12	2	0	83.1	324	67	27	25	6	1	1	3	12	0	67	3	0	7	4	.636	1	0	2.70
Phoenix	AAA	14	14	4	0	105.1	437	105	43	41	5	3	2	2	27	0	99	7	2	7	4	.636	0	0	3.50
1993 San Francisco	NL	8	8	0	0	44.2	196	37	21	20	5	7	1	1	27	3	23	3	1	3	5	.375	0	0	4.03

Steve Trachsel

Pitches: Right **Bats:** Right **Pos:** SP **Ht:** 6' 3" **Wt:** 185 **Born:** 10/31/70 **Age:** 23

Year Team	Lg	G	GS	CG	GF	IP	BFP	H	R	ER	HR	SH	SF	HB	TBB	IBB	SO	WP	Bk	W	L	Pct.	ShO	Sv	ERA
1991 Geneva	A	2	2	0	0	14.1	52	10	2	2	0	0	0	0	6	0	7	0	1	1	0	1.000	0	0	1.26
Winston-Sal	A	12	12	1	0	73.2	312	70	38	30	3	5	1	1	19	0	69	1	3	4	4	.500	0	0	3.67
1992 Charlotte	AA	29	29	5	0	191	768	180	76	65	19	6	3	4	35	3	135	7	1	13	8	.619	2	0	3.06
1993 Iowa	AAA	27	26	1	1	170.2	703	170	78	75	20	4	4	6	45	0	135	4	1	13	6	.684	1	0	3.96
1993 Chicago	NL	3	3	0	0	19.2	78	16	10	10	4	1	1	0	3	0	14	1	0	0	2	.000	0	0	4.58

Alan Trammell

Bats: Right **Throws:** Right **Pos:** SS/3B **Ht:** 6' 0" **Wt:** 185 **Born:** 02/21/58 **Age:** 36

Year Team	Lg	G	AB	H	2B	3B	HR	(Hm	Rd)	TB	R	RBI	TBB	IBB	SO	HBP	SH	SF	SB	CS	SB%	GDP	Avg	OBP	SLG
1977 Detroit	AL	19	43	8	0	0	0	(0	0)	8	6	0	4	0	12	0	1	0	0	0	.00	1	.186	.255	.186
1978 Detroit	AL	139	448	120	14	6	2	(0	2)	152	49	34	45	0	56	2	6	3	3	1	.75	12	.268	.335	.339
1979 Detroit	AL	142	460	127	11	4	6	(4	2)	164	68	50	43	0	55	0	12	5	17	14	.55	6	.276	.335	.357
1980 Detroit	AL	146	560	168	21	5	9	(5	4)	226	107	65	69	2	63	3	13	7	12	12	.50	10	.300	.376	.404
1981 Detroit	AL	105	392	101	15	3	2	(2	0)	128	52	31	49	2	31	3	16	3	10	3	.77	10	.258	.342	.327
1982 Detroit	AL	157	489	126	34	3	9	(5	4)	193	66	57	52	0	47	0	9	6	19	8	.70	5	.258	.325	.395
1983 Detroit	AL	142	505	161	31	2	14	(8	6)	238	83	66	57	2	64	0	15	4	30	10	.75	7	.319	.385	.471
1984 Detroit	AL	139	555	174	34	5	14	(7	7)	260	85	69	60	2	63	3	6	2	19	13	.59	8	.314	.382	.468
1985 Detroit	AL	149	605	156	21	7	13	(7	6)	230	79	57	50	4	71	2	11	9	14	5	.74	6	.258	.312	.380
1986 Detroit	AL	151	574	159	33	7	21	(8	13)	269	107	75	59	4	57	5	11	4	25	12	.68	7	.277	.347	.469
1987 Detroit	AL	151	597	205	34	3	28	(13	15)	329	109	105	60	8	47	3	2	6	21	2	.91	11	.343	.402	.551
1988 Detroit	AL	128	466	145	24	1	15	(7	8)	216	73	69	46	8	46	4	0	7	7	4	.64	14	.311	.373	.464
1989 Detroit	AL	121	449	109	20	3	5	(2	3)	150	54	43	45	1	45	4	3	5	10	2	.83	9	.243	.314	.334
1990 Detroit	AL	146	559	170	37	1	14	(9	5)	251	71	89	68	7	55	1	3	6	12	10	.55	11	.304	.377	.449
1991 Detroit	AL	101	375	93	20	0	9	(6	3)	140	57	55	37	1	39	3	5	1	11	2	.85	7	.248	.320	.373
1992 Detroit	AL	29	102	28	7	1	1	(0	1)	40	11	11	15	0	4	1	1	1	2	2	.50	6	.275	.370	.392
1993 Detroit	AL	112	401	132	25	3	12	(6	6)	199	72	60	38	2	38	2	4	2	12	8	.60	7	.329	.388	.496
17 ML YEARS		2077	7580	2182	381	54	174	(89	85)	3193	1149	936	797	43	793	36	118	71	224	108	.67	137	.288	.355	.421

Jeff Treadway

Bats: Left **Throws:** Right **Pos:** 3B/2B **Ht:** 5'11" **Wt:** 170 **Born:** 01/22/63 **Age:** 31

Year Team	Lg	G	AB	H	2B	3B	HR	(Hm	Rd)	TB	R	RBI	TBB	IBB	SO	HBP	SH	SF	SB	CS	SB%	GDP	Avg	OBP	SLG
1987 Cincinnati	NL	23	84	28	4	0	2	(2	0)	38	9	4	2	0	6	1	3	0	1	0	1.00	1	.333	.356	.452
1988 Cincinnati	NL	103	301	76	19	4	2	(2	0)	109	30	23	27	7	30	3	4	6	2	0	1.00	4	.252	.315	.362
1989 Atlanta	NL	134	473	131	18	3	6	(2	6)	179	58	40	30	3	38	0	6	5	3	2	.60	9	.277	.317	.378
1990 Atlanta	NL	128	474	134	20	2	11	(5	6)	191	56	59	25	1	42	3	5	4	3	4	.43	10	.283	.320	.403
1991 Atlanta	NL	106	306	98	17	2	3	(1	2)	128	41	32	23	1	19	2	2	3	2	2	.50	8	.320	.368	.418
1992 Atlanta	NL	61	126	28	6	1	0	(0	0)	36	5	5	9	4	16	0	1	0	1	2	.33	3	.222	.274	.286
1993 Cleveland	AL	97	221	67	14	1	2	(0	2)	89	25	27	14	2	21	2	1	2	1	1	.50	6	.303	.347	.403
7 ML YEARS		652	1985	562	98	13	28	(12	16)	770	224	190	130	18	172	11	22	20	13	11	.54	41	.283	.328	.388

Ricky Trlicek

Pitches: Right Bats: Right Pos: RP   Ht: 6' 2" Wt: 200 Born: 04/26/69 Age: 25

		HOW MUCH HE PITCHED					WHAT HE GAVE UP										THE RESULTS				
Year Team	Lg	G	GS	CG	GF	IP	BFP	H	R	ER	HR	SH	SF	HB	TBB	IBB	SO	WP	Bk	W	L	Pct.	ShO	Sv	ERA
1987 Utica	A	10	8	1	0	37.1	177	43	28	17	2	0	0	1	31	2	22	5	1	2	5	.286	1	0	4.10
1988 Batavia	A	8	8	0	0	31.2	151	27	32	26	2	0	3	4	31	0	26	7	2	2	3	.400	0	0	7.39
1989 Sumter	A	15	15	0	0	93.2	385	73	40	27	7	3	3	4	40	1	72	3	3	6	5	.545	0	0	2.59
Durham	A	1	1	0	0	8	30	3	2	1	0	0	0	1	1	0	4	2	0	0	0	.000	0	0	1.13
1990 Dunedin	A	26	26	0	0	154.1	649	128	74	64	2	6	3	6	72	0	125	22	6	5	8	.385	0	0	3.73
1991 Knoxville	AA	41	0	0	38	51.1	218	36	26	14	3	2	3	0	22	3	55	4	0	2	5	.286	0	16	2.45
1992 Syracuse	AAA	35	0	0	23	43.1	195	37	22	21	2	2	2	0	31	1	35	8	1	1	1	.500	0	10	4.36
1992 Toronto	AL	2	0	0	0	1.2	9	2	2	2	0	0	0	0	2	0	1	0	0	0	0	.000	0	0	10.80
1993 Los Angeles	NL	41	0	0	18	64	267	59	32	29	3	2	0	2	21	4	41	4	1	1	2	.333	0	1	4.08
2 ML YEARS		43	0	0	18	65.2	276	61	34	31	3	2	0	2	23	4	42	4	1	1	2	.333	0	1	4.25

Mike Trombley

Pitches: Right Bats: Right Pos: RP/SP   Ht: 6' 2" Wt: 200 Born: 04/14/67 Age: 27

		HOW MUCH HE PITCHED					WHAT HE GAVE UP										THE RESULTS				
Year Team	Lg	G	GS	CG	GF	IP	BFP	H	R	ER	HR	SH	SF	HB	TBB	IBB	SO	WP	Bk	W	L	Pct.	ShO	Sv	ERA
1989 Kenosha	A	12	3	0	6	49	202	45	23	17	1	1	0	3	13	0	41	4	3	5	1	.833	0	2	3.12
Visalia	A	6	6	2	0	42	165	31	12	10	2	2	0	3	11	0	36	0	2	2	2	.500	1	0	2.14
1990 Visalia	A	27	25	3	1	176	739	163	79	67	12	3	3	11	50	0	164	8	1	14	6	.700	1	0	3.43
1991 Orlando	AA	27	27	7	0	191	773	153	65	54	12	7	6	7	57	3	175	2	1	12	7	.632	2	0	2.54
1992 Portland	AAA	25	25	2	0	165	695	149	70	67	18	5	2	6	58	1	138	1	2	10	8	.556	0	0	3.65
1992 Minnesota	AL	10	7	0	0	46.1	194	43	20	17	5	2	0	1	17	0	38	0	0	3	2	.600	0	0	3.30
1993 Minnesota	AL	44	10	0	8	114.1	506	131	72	62	15	3	7	3	41	4	85	5	0	6	6	.500	0	2	4.88
2 ML YEARS		54	17	0	8	160.2	700	174	92	79	20	5	7	4	58	4	123	5	0	9	8	.529	0	2	4.43

George Tsamis

Pitches: Left Bats: Right Pos: RP   Ht: 6' 2" Wt: 175 Born: 06/14/67 Age: 27

		HOW MUCH HE PITCHED					WHAT HE GAVE UP										THE RESULTS				
Year Team	Lg	G	GS	CG	GF	IP	BFP	H	R	ER	HR	SH	SF	HB	TBB	IBB	SO	WP	Bk	W	L	Pct.	ShO	Sv	ERA
1989 Visalia	A	15	13	3	1	94.1	387	85	36	32	10	3	0	2	34	0	87	9	3	6	3	.667	0	0	3.05
1990 Visalia	A	26	26	4	0	183.2	731	168	62	45	4	3	2	4	61	0	145	7	1	17	4	.810	3	0	2.21
1991 Orlando	AA	1	1	0	0	7	28	3	2	0	0	0	0	0	4	0	5	0	0	0	0	.000	0	0	0.00
Portland	AAA	29	27	2	0	167.2	716	183	75	61	11	8	6	5	66	0	75	7	1	10	8	.556	1	0	3.27
1992 Portland	AAA	39	22	4	6	163.2	700	195	78	71	12	4	5	5	51	1	71	2	0	13	4	.765	1	1	3.90
1993 Portland	AAA	3	3	0	0	14	74	27	15	13	2	0	1	0	5	0	10	0	0	1	2	.333	0	0	8.36
1993 Minnesota	AL	41	0	0	18	68.1	309	86	51	47	9	2	6	3	27	5	30	1	1	1	2	.333	0	1	6.19

Greg Tubbs

Bats: Right Throws: Right Pos: CF/LF   Ht: 5' 9" Wt: 178 Born: 08/31/62 Age: 31

		BATTING																BASERUNNING			PERCENTAGES		
Year Team	Lg	G	AB	H	2B	3B	HR	(Hm | Rd)	TB	R	RBI	TBB	IBB	SO	HBP	SH	SF	SB	CS	SB%	GDP	Avg	OBP	SLG
1984 Braves	R	18	58	21	4	3	0	--	--	31	13	3	15	0	5	0	0	1	5	2	.71	0	.362	.486	.534
Anderson	A	50	174	53	5	2	2	--	--	68	25	11	27	0	29	1	3	0	19	6	.76	0	.305	.401	.391
1985 Sumter	A	61	239	85	11	7	6	--	--	128	53	36	36	0	36	2	1	3	30	18	.63	2	.356	.433	.536
Durham	A	70	266	75	15	6	8	--	--	126	44	32	36	0	52	3	2	1	29	12	.71	6	.282	.373	.474
1986 Greenville	AA	144	536	144	21	7	5	--	--	194	95	56	107	2	74	3	10	3	31	22	.58	14	.269	.391	.362
1987 Greenville	AA	141	540	145	19	7	3	--	--	187	97	40	86	2	86	2	7	1	24	19	.56	9	.269	.370	.346
1988 Greenville	AA	29	101	24	1	1	0	--	--	27	13	12	13	0	20	1	0	0	4	0	1.00	1	.238	.330	.267
Richmond	AAA	78	228	56	14	2	2	--	--	80	43	11	28	0	38	1	3	1	8	8	.50	5	.246	.329	.351
1989 Greenville	AA	11	27	5	0	0	0	--	--	5	4	1	8	0	4	0	0	0	3	0	1.00	1	.185	.371	.185
Richmond	AAA	115	405	122	10	11	4	--	--	166	64	35	47	0	49	1	5	0	19	15	.56	10	.301	.375	.410
1990 Richmond	AAA	11	23	5	0	0	0	--	--	5	3	1	11	0	6	0	1	0	0	2	.00	0	.217	.471	.217
Harrisburg	AA	54	213	60	6	5	3	--	--	85	35	21	23	0	35	0	1	1	8	1	.89	7	.282	.350	.399
1991 Buffalo	AAA	121	373	102	18	11	3	--	--	151	71	34	48	1	62	5	5	2	34	11	.76	11	.273	.362	.405
1992 Buffalo	AAA	110	430	126	20	5	7	--	--	177	69	42	57	2	64	3	3	2	20	19	.51	6	.293	.378	.412
1993 Indianapolis	AAA	97	334	102	21	4	10	--	--	161	59	45	42	3	65	2	1	3	15	11	.58	4	.305	.383	.482
1993 Cincinnati	NL	35	59	11	0	0	1	(1 | 0)	14	10	2	14	0	10	1	0	0	3	1	.75	0	.186	.351	.237

Scooter Tucker

Bats: Right Throws: Right Pos: C   Ht: 6' 2" Wt: 205 Born: 11/18/66 Age: 27

		BATTING																BASERUNNING			PERCENTAGES		
Year Team	Lg	G	AB	H	2B	3B	HR	(Hm | Rd)	TB	R	RBI	TBB	IBB	SO	HBP	SH	SF	SB	CS	SB%	GDP	Avg	OBP	SLG
1988 Everett	A	45	153	40	5	0	3	--	--	54	24	23	30	0	34	3	0	3	0	0	.00	0	.261	.386	.353
1989 Clinton	A	126	426	105	20	2	3	--	--	138	44	43	58	2	80	9	3	4	6	5	.55	11	.246	.346	.324

Year	Team	Lg	G	AB	H	2B	3B	HR	(Hm	Rd)	TB	R	RBI	TBB	IBB	SO	HBP	SH	SF	SB	CS	SB%	GDP	Avg	OBP	SLG
1990	San Jose	A	123	439	123	28	2	5	--	--	170	59	71	71	4	69	13	2	6	9	3	.75	14	.280	.391	.387
1991	Shreveport	AA	110	352	100	29	1	4	--	--	143	49	49	48	1	58	5	6	2	3	4	.43	8	.284	.376	.406
1992	Tucson	AAA	83	288	87	15	1	1	--	--	107	36	29	28	1	35	3	1	2	5	1	.83	12	.302	.368	.372
1993	Tucson	AAA	98	318	87	20	2	1	--	--	114	54	37	47	8	37	2	2	2	1	5	.17	7	.274	.369	.358
1992	Houston	NL	20	50	6	1	0	0	(0	0)	7	5	3	3	0	13	2	1	0	1	1	.50	2	.120	.200	.140
1993	Houston	NL	9	26	5	1	0	0	(0	0)	6	1	3	2	0	3	0	0	0	0	0	.00	0	.192	.250	.231
	2 ML YEARS		29	76	11	2	0	0	(0	0)	13	6	6	5	0	16	2	1	0	1	1	.50	2	.145	.217	.171

Brian Turang

Bats: Right **Throws:** Right **Pos:** LF/CF **Ht:** 5'10" **Wt:** 170 **Born:** 06/14/67 **Age:** 27

									BATTING											BASERUNNING				PERCENTAGES		
Year	Team	Lg	G	AB	H	2B	3B	HR	(Hm	Rd)	TB	R	RBI	TBB	IBB	SO	HBP	SH	SF	SB	CS	SB%	GDP	Avg	OBP	SLG
1989	Bellingham	A	60	207	59	10	3	4	--	--	87	42	11	33	0	50	12	2	0	9	6	.60	1	.285	.413	.420
1990	San Berndno	A	132	487	144	25	5	12	--	--	215	86	67	69	0	98	7	6	4	25	16	.61	8	.296	.388	.441
	Calgary	AAA	3	9	2	0	0	0	--	--	2	1	1	2	0	4	0	0	0	0	0	.00	0	.222	.364	.222
1991	Jacksonville	AA	41	130	28	6	2	0	--	--	38	14	7	13	1	33	2	2	0	5	2	.71	1	.215	.297	.292
	San Berndno	A	34	100	18	2	1	0	--	--	22	9	4	15	0	31	3	1	0	6	6	.50	1	.180	.305	.220
1992	Jacksonville	AA	129	483	121	21	3	14	--	--	190	67	63	44	1	61	12	2	3	19	9	.68	12	.251	.327	.393
1993	Calgary	AAA	110	423	137	20	11	8	--	--	203	84	54	40	2	48	3	5	4	24	8	.75	7	.324	.383	.480
1993	Seattle	AL	40	140	35	11	1	0	(0	0)	48	22	7	17	0	20	2	1	0	6	2	.75	3	.250	.340	.343

Chris Turner

Bats: Right **Throws:** Right **Pos:** C **Ht:** 6'2" **Wt:** 190 **Born:** 03/23/69 **Age:** 25

									BATTING											BASERUNNING				PERCENTAGES		
Year	Team	Lg	G	AB	H	2B	3B	HR	(Hm	Rd)	TB	R	RBI	TBB	IBB	SO	HBP	SH	SF	SB	CS	SB%	GDP	Avg	OBP	SLG
1991	Boise	A	52	163	37	5	0	2	--	--	48	26	29	32	0	32	2	2	5	10	2	.83	3	.227	.351	.294
1992	Quad City	A	109	330	83	18	1	9	--	--	130	66	53	85	5	65	8	6	6	8	7	.53	3	.252	.410	.394
1993	Vancouver	AAA	90	283	78	12	1	4	--	--	104	50	57	49	1	44	3	8	5	6	1	.86	7	.276	.382	.367
1993	California	AL	25	75	21	5	0	1	(0	1)	29	9	13	9	0	16	1	0	1	1	1	.50	1	.280	.360	.387

Matt Turner

Pitches: Right **Bats:** Right **Pos:** RP **Ht:** 6'5" **Wt:** 215 **Born:** 02/18/67 **Age:** 27

				HOW MUCH HE PITCHED					WHAT HE GAVE UP									THE RESULTS				
Year	Team	Lg	G	GS	CG	GF	IP	BFP	H	R	ER	HR	SH	SF	HB	TBB	IBB	SO	WP	Bk	W	L	Pct.	ShO	Sv	ERA
1986	Pulaski	R	18	5	0	7	48.2	229	55	36	25	6	2	2	2	28	1	48	2	0	1	3	.250	0	2	4.62
1987	Sumter	A	39	9	0	17	93.2	423	91	61	49	8	5	4	5	48	2	102	8	6	2	3	.400	0	0	4.71
1988	Burlington	A	7	6	0	1	34.1	161	43	27	25	9	0	1	3	16	0	26	0	3	1	3	.250	0	0	6.55
	Sumter	A	7	0	0	4	15.2	65	17	8	8	0	0	0	2	3	0	7	1	0	1	0	1.000	0	0	4.60
1989	Durham	A	53	3	0	19	118	499	95	38	32	11	3	5	5	47	9	114	5	3	9	9	.500	0	1	2.44
1990	Greenville	AA	40	0	0	26	67.2	289	59	24	20	6	0	1	3	29	2	60	4	2	6	4	.600	0	4	2.66
	Richmond	AAA	22	1	0	11	42	175	44	20	18	6	1	1	2	16	1	36	6	1	2	3	.400	0	2	3.86
1991	Richmond	AAA	23	0	0	17	36	161	33	21	19	5	2	4	2	20	0	33	4	0	1	3	.250	0	5	4.75
	Tucson	AAA	13	0	0	5	26	115	27	12	12	0	0	1	1	14	2	25	1	2	1	1	.500	0	1	4.15
1992	Tucson	AAA	63	0	0	38	100	436	93	52	39	2	7	4	2	40	3	84	5	3	2	8	.200	0	14	3.51
1993	Edmonton	AAA	12	0	0	12	13.2	51	9	1	1	0	1	0	0	2	0	15	0	0	0	0	.000	0	10	0.66
1993	Florida	NL	55	0	0	26	68	279	55	23	22	7	6	4	1	26	9	59	6	1	4	5	.444	0	0	2.91

Tom Urbani

Pitches: Left **Bats:** Left **Pos:** SP/RP **Ht:** 6'1" **Wt:** 190 **Born:** 01/21/68 **Age:** 26

				HOW MUCH HE PITCHED					WHAT HE GAVE UP									THE RESULTS				
Year	Team	Lg	G	GS	CG	GF	IP	BFP	H	R	ER	HR	SH	SF	HB	TBB	IBB	SO	WP	Bk	W	L	Pct.	ShO	Sv	ERA
1990	Johnson Cy	R	9	9	0	0	48.1	217	44	35	18	2	1	0	1	15	0	40	4	0	4	3	.571	0	0	3.35
	Hamilton	A	5	5	0	0	26.1	125	33	26	18	4	0	3	3	15	1	17	1	0	0	4	.000	0	0	6.15
1991	Springfield	A	8	8	0	0	47.2	195	45	20	11	2	2	2	2	6	0	42	1	1	3	2	.600	0	0	2.08
	St. Pete	A	19	19	2	0	118.2	474	109	39	31	3	8	5	2	25	0	64	3	1	8	7	.533	1	0	2.35
1992	Arkansas	AA	10	10	2	0	65.1	263	49	23	14	3	3	0	2	15	1	41	1	0	4	6	.400	1	0	1.93
	Louisville	AAA	16	16	0	0	88.2	384	91	50	46	9	3	4	7	37	1	46	5	1	4	5	.444	0	0	4.67
1993	Louisville	AAA	18	13	0	2	94.2	377	86	29	26	4	3	0	2	23	1	65	0	0	9	5	.643	0	1	2.47
1993	St. Louis	NL	18	9	0	2	62	283	73	44	32	4	4	6	0	26	2	33	1	1	1	3	.250	0	0	4.65

Jose Uribe

Bats: Both **Throws:** Right **Pos:** SS **Ht:** 5'10" **Wt:** 184 **Born:** 01/21/59 **Age:** 35

									BATTING											BASERUNNING				PERCENTAGES		
Year	Team	Lg	G	AB	H	2B	3B	HR	(Hm	Rd)	TB	R	RBI	TBB	IBB	SO	HBP	SH	SF	SB	CS	SB%	GDP	Avg	OBP	SLG
1984	St. Louis	NL	8	19	4	0	0	0	(0	0)	4	4	3	0	0	2	0	1	0	1	0	1.00	1	.211	.211	.211

Year	Team	Lg	G	AB	H	2B	3B	HR	(Hm	Rd)	TB	R	RBI	TBB	IBB	SO	HBP	SH	SF	SB	CS	SB%	GDP	Avg	OBP	SLG
1985	San Francisco	NL	147	476	113	20	4	3	(2	1)	150	46	26	30	8	57	2	5	0	8	2	.80	5	.237	.285	.315
1986	San Francisco	NL	157	453	101	15	1	3	(1	2)	127	46	43	61	19	76	0	3	0	22	11	.67	2	.223	.315	.280
1987	San Francisco	NL	95	309	90	16	5	5	(4	1)	131	44	30	24	9	35	1	5	1	12	2	.86	1	.291	.343	.424
1988	San Francisco	NL	141	493	124	10	7	3	(1	2)	157	47	35	36	10	69	0	4	2	14	10	.58	3	.252	.301	.318
1989	San Francisco	NL	151	453	100	12	6	1	(0	1)	127	34	30	34	12	74	0	6	4	6	6	.50	7	.221	.273	.280
1990	San Francisco	NL	138	415	103	8	6	1	(0	1)	126	35	24	29	13	49	0	4	0	5	9	.36	8	.248	.297	.304
1991	San Francisco	NL	90	231	51	8	4	1	(0	1)	70	23	12	20	6	33	0	1	0	3	4	.43	2	.221	.283	.303
1992	San Francisco	NL	66	162	39	9	1	2	(0	2)	56	24	13	14	3	25	0	4	1	2	2	.50	3	.241	.299	.346
1993	Houston	NL	45	53	13	1	0	0	(0	0)	14	4	3	8	4	5	1	4	0	1	0	1.00	1	.245	.355	.264
10 ML YEARS			1038	3064	738	99	34	19	(8	11)	962	307	219	256	84	425	4	37	8	74	46	.62	33	.241	.300	.314

Sergio Valdez

Pitches: Right **Bats:** Right **Pos:** RP   **Ht:** 6' 1" **Wt:** 190 **Born:** 09/07/65 **Age:** 28

			HOW MUCH HE PITCHED					WHAT HE GAVE UP									THE RESULTS				
Year	Team	Lg	G	GS	CG	GF	IP	BFP	H	R	ER	HR	SH	SF	HB	TBB	IBB	SO	WP	Bk	W	L	Pct.	ShO	Sv	ERA
1993	Ottawa *	AAA	30	4	0	6	83.2	350	77	31	29	3	1	3	6	22	2	53	7	0	5	3	.625	0	1	3.12
1986	Montreal	NL	5	5	0	0	25	120	39	20	19	2	0	0	1	11	0	20	2	0	0	4	.000	0	0	6.84
1989	Atlanta	NL	19	1	0	8	32.2	145	31	24	22	5	2	0	0	17	3	26	2	0	1	2	.333	0	0	6.06
1990	2 ML Teams		30	13	0	7	107.2	466	115	66	58	17	5	5	1	38	2	66	4	0	6	6	.500	0	0	4.85
1991	Cleveland	AL	6	0	0	1	16.1	70	15	11	10	3	1	1	0	5	1	11	1	0	1	0	1.000	0	0	5.51
1992	Montreal	NL	27	0	0	9	37.1	148	25	12	10	2	1	0	0	12	1	32	4	0	0	2	.000	0	0	2.41
1993	Montreal	NL	4	0	0	3	14		4	4	3	1	0	0	0	1	0	2	0	0	0	0	.000	0	0	9.00
1990	Atlanta	NL	6	0	0	3	5.1	26	6	4	4	0	1	0	0	3	0	3	1	0	0	0	.000	0	0	6.75
	Cleveland	AL	24	13	0	4	102.1	440	109	62	54	17	4	5	1	35	2	63	3	0	6	6	.500	0	0	4.75
6 ML YEARS			91	19	0	26	222	963	229	137	122	30	9	6	2	84	7	157	13	0	8	14	.364	0	0	4.95

John Valentin

Bats: Right **Throws:** Right **Pos:** SS   **Ht:** 6' 0" **Wt:** 170 **Born:** 02/18/67 **Age:** 27

			BATTING															BASERUNNING				PERCENTAGES		
Year	Team	Lg	G	AB	H	2B	3B	HR	(Hm | Rd)	TB	R	RBI	TBB	IBB	SO	HBP	SH	SF	SB	CS	SB%	GDP	Avg	OBP	SLG
1988	Elmira	A	60	207	45	5	1	2	--	--	58	18	16	36	1	35	0	5	2	4	4	.56	6	.217	.331	.280
1989	Winter Havn	A	55	215	58	13	1	3	--	--	82	27	18	13	0	29	1	2	1	5	5	.50	7	.270	.310	.381
	Lynchburg	A	75	264	65	7	2	8	--	--	100	47	34	41	1	40	2	2	2	5	2	.71	8	.246	.350	.379
1990	New Britain	AA	94	312	68	18	1	2	--	--	94	20	31	25	1	46	0	11	3	1	2	.33	5	.218	.274	.301
1991	New Britain	AA	23	81	16	3	0	0	--	--	19	8	5	9	0	14	0	1	0	1	1	.50	2	.198	.278	.235
	Pawtucket	AAA	100	329	87	22	4	9	--	--	144	52	49	60	2	42	0	6	4	0	1	.00	8	.264	.374	.438
1992	Pawtucket	AAA	97	331	86	18	1	9	--	--	133	47	29	48	1	50	3	5	1	1	2	.33	9	.260	.358	.402
1993	Pawtucket	AAA	2	9	3	0	0	1	--	--	6	3	1	0	0	1	0	0	0	0	0	.00	1	.333	.333	.667
1992	Boston	AL	58	185	51	13	0	5	(1 | 4)	79	21	25	20	0	17	2	4	1	1	0	1.00	5	.276	.351	.427
1993	Boston	AL	144	468	130	40	3	11	(7 | 4)	209	50	66	49	2	77	2	16	4	3	4	.43	9	.278	.346	.447
2 ML YEARS			202	653	181	53	3	16	(8 | 8)	288	71	91	69	2	94	4	20	5	4	4	.50	14	.277	.347	.441

Jose Valentin

Bats: Both **Throws:** Right **Pos:** SS   **Ht:** 5'10" **Wt:** 175 **Born:** 10/12/69 **Age:** 24

			BATTING															BASERUNNING				PERCENTAGES		
Year	Team	Lg	G	AB	H	2B	3B	HR	(Hm | Rd)	TB	R	RBI	TBB	IBB	SO	HBP	SH	SF	SB	CS	SB%	GDP	Avg	OBP	SLG
1987	Spokane	A	70	244	61	8	2	2	--	--	79	52	24	35	2	38	1	3	0	8	5	.62	4	.250	.346	.324
1988	Chston-Sc	A	133	444	103	20	1	6	--	--	143	56	44	45	3	83	3	9	4	11	4	.73	10	.232	.304	.322
1989	Riverside	A	114	381	74	10	5	10	--	--	124	40	41	37	1	93	5	5	2	8	7	.53	4	.194	.273	.325
	Wichita	AA	18	49	12	1	0	2	--	--	19	8	5	5	1	12	0	3	0	1	0	1.00	1	.245	.315	.388
1990	Wichita	AA	11	36	10	2	0	0	--	--	12	4	2	5	0	7	0	1	0	2	1	.67	1	.278	.366	.333
1991	Wichita	AA	129	447	112	22	5	17	--	--	195	73	68	55	1	115	4	4	5	8	6	.57	5	.251	.335	.436
1992	Denver	AAA	139	492	118	19	11	3	--	--	168	78	45	53	2	99	5	9	6	9	4	.69	8	.240	.317	.341
1993	New Orleans	AAA	122	389	96	22	5	9	--	--	155	56	53	47	2	87	8	14	4	9	10	.47	3	.247	.337	.398
1992	Milwaukee	AL	4	3	0	0	0	0	(0 | 0)	0	1	1	0	0	0	0	0	1	0	0	.00	0	.000	.000	.000
1993	Milwaukee	AL	19	53	13	1	2	1	(1 | 0)	21	10	7	7	1	16	1	2	0	1	0	1.00	1	.245	.344	.396
2 ML YEARS			23	56	13	1	2	1	(1 | 0)	21	11	8	7	1	16	1	2	1	1	0	1.00	1	.232	.323	.375

Fernando Valenzuela

Pitches: Left **Bats:** Left **Pos:** SP   **Ht:** 5'11" **Wt:** 202 **Born:** 11/01/60 **Age:** 33

			HOW MUCH HE PITCHED					WHAT HE GAVE UP									THE RESULTS				
Year	Team	Lg	G	GS	CG	GF	IP	BFP	H	R	ER	HR	SH	SF	HB	TBB	IBB	SO	WP	Bk	W	L	Pct.	ShO	Sv	ERA
1993	Rochester *	AAA	1	1	0	0	3.1	18	6	4	4	0	0	0	0	3	0	1	0	0	0	1	.000	0	0	10.80
	Bowie *	AA	1	1	0	0	6	22	4	1	1	0	1	0	1	0	0	4	0	0	0	0	.000	0	0	1.50
1980	Los Angeles	NL	10	0	0	4	18	66	8	2	0	0	1	1	0	5	0	16	0	1	2	0	1.000	0	1	0.00
1981	Los Angeles	NL	25	25	11	0	192	758	140	55	53	11	9	3	1	61	4	180	4	0	13	7	.650	8	0	2.48
1982	Los Angeles	NL	37	37	18	0	285	1156	247	105	91	13	19	6	2	83	12	199	4	0	19	13	.594	4	0	2.87
1983	Los Angeles	NL	35	35	9	0	257	1094	245	122	107	16	27	5	3	99	10	189	12	1	15	10	.600	4	0	3.75

221

Year	Team	Lg	G	GS	CG	GF	IP	BFP	H	R	ER	HR	SH	SF	HB	TBB	IBB	SO	WP	Bk	W	L	Pct.	ShO	Sv	ERA
1984	Los Angeles	NL	34	34	12	0	261	1078	218	109	88	14	11	7	2	106	4	240	11	1	12	17	.414	2	0	3.03
1985	Los Angeles	NL	35	35	14	0	272.1	1109	211	92	74	14	13	8	1	101	5	208	10	1	17	10	.630	5	0	2.45
1986	Los Angeles	NL	34	34	20	0	269.1	1102	226	104	94	18	15	3	1	85	5	242	13	0	21	11	.656	3	0	3.14
1987	Los Angeles	NL	34	34	12	0	251	1116	254	120	111	25	18	2	4	124	4	190	14	1	14	14	.500	1	0	3.98
1988	Los Angeles	NL	23	22	3	1	142.1	626	142	71	67	11	15	5	0	76	4	64	7	1	5	8	.385	0	1	4.24
1989	Los Angeles	NL	31	31	3	0	196.2	852	185	89	75	11	7	7	2	98	6	116	6	4	10	13	.435	0	0	3.43
1990	Los Angeles	NL	33	33	5	0	204	900	223	112	104	19	11	4	0	77	4	115	13	1	13	13	.500	2	0	4.59
1991	California	AL	2	2	0	0	6.2	36	14	10	9	3	1	1	0	3	0	5	1	0	0	2	.000	0	0	12.15
1993	Baltimore	AL	32	31	5	0	178.2	768	179	104	98	18	4	7	4	79	2	78	8	0	8	10	.444	2	0	4.94
13 ML YEARS			365	353	112	5	2534	10661	2292	1095	971	173	151	59	20	997	60	1842	103	11	149	128	.538	31	2	3.45

Julio Valera

Pitches: Right **Bats:** Right **Pos:** RP/SP   **Ht:** 6' 2" **Wt:** 215 **Born:** 10/13/68 **Age:** 25

			HOW MUCH HE PITCHED						WHAT HE GAVE UP										THE RESULTS					
Year	Team	Lg	G	GS	CG	GF	IP	BFP	H	R	ER	HR	SH	SF	HB	TBB	IBB	SO	WP	Bk	W	L	Pct.	ShO	Sv	ERA
1990	New York	NL	3	3	0	0	13	64	20	11	10	1	0	0	0	7	0	4	0	0	1	1	.500	0	0	6.92
1991	New York	NL	2	0	0	1	2	11	1	0	0	0	0	0	0	4	1	3	0	0	0	0	.000	0	0	0.00
1992	California	AL	30	28	4	0	188	792	188	82	78	15	6	2	2	64	5	113	5	0	8	11	.421	2	0	3.73
1993	California	AL	19	5	0	8	53	246	77	44	39	8	4	1	2	15	2	28	2	0	3	6	.333	0	4	6.62
4 ML YEARS			54	36	4	9	256	1113	286	137	127	24	10	3	4	90	8	148	7	0	12	18	.400	2	4	4.46

Dave Valle

Bats: Right **Throws:** Right **Pos:** C   **Ht:** 6' 2" **Wt:** 220 **Born:** 10/30/60 **Age:** 33

								BATTING											BASERUNNING				PERCENTAGES		
Year	Team	Lg	G	AB	H	2B	3B	HR	(Hm	Rd)	TB	R	RBI	TBB	IBB	SO	HBP	SH	SF	SB	CS	SB%	GDP	Avg	OBP	SLG
1984	Seattle	AL	13	27	8	1	0	1	(1	0)	12	4	4	1	0	5	0	0	0	0	0	.00	0	.296	.321	.444
1985	Seattle	AL	31	70	11	1	0	0	(0	0)	12	2	4	1	0	17	1	1	0	0	0	.00	1	.157	.181	.171
1986	Seattle	AL	22	53	18	3	0	5	(4	1)	36	10	15	7	0	7	0	0	0	0	0	.00	2	.340	.417	.679
1987	Seattle	AL	95	324	83	16	3	12	(8	4)	141	40	53	15	2	46	3	0	4	2	0	1.00	13	.256	.292	.435
1988	Seattle	AL	93	290	67	15	2	10	(5	5)	116	29	50	18	0	38	9	3	2	0	1	.00	13	.231	.295	.400
1989	Seattle	AL	94	316	75	10	3	7	(1	6)	112	32	34	29	2	32	6	1	3	0	0	.00	13	.237	.311	.354
1990	Seattle	AL	107	308	66	15	0	7	(1	6)	102	37	33	45	0	48	7	4	0	1	2	.33	11	.214	.328	.331
1991	Seattle	AL	132	324	63	8	1	8	(0	8)	97	38	32	34	0	49	9	6	3	0	2	.00	19	.194	.286	.299
1992	Seattle	AL	124	367	88	16	1	9	(7	2)	133	39	30	27	1	58	8	7	1	0	0	.00	7	.240	.305	.362
1993	Seattle	AL	135	423	109	19	0	13	(4	9)	167	48	63	48	4	56	17	8	4	1	0	1.00	18	.258	.354	.395
10 ML YEARS			846	2502	588	104	10	72	(31	41)	928	279	318	225	9	356	60	30	17	4	5	.44	97	.235	.311	.371

Ty Van Burkleo

Bats: Left **Throws:** Left **Pos:** 1B   **Ht:** 6' 5" **Wt:** 225 **Born:** 10/07/63 **Age:** 30

								BATTING											BASERUNNING				PERCENTAGES		
Year	Team	Lg	G	AB	H	2B	3B	HR	(Hm	Rd)	TB	R	RBI	TBB	IBB	SO	HBP	SH	SF	SB	CS	SB%	GDP	Avg	OBP	SLG
1992	Edmonton	AAA	135	458	125	28	7	19	--	--	224	83	88	75	6	100	5	0	3	20	5	.80	10	.273	.379	.489
1993	Vancouver	AAA	105	361	99	19	2	6	--	--	140	47	56	51	3	89	2	1	4	7	3	.70	9	.274	.364	.388
1993	California	AL	12	33	5	3	0	1	(1	0)	11	2	1	6	0	9	0	0	0	1	0	1.00	0	.152	.282	.333

Todd Van Poppel

Pitches: Right **Bats:** Right **Pos:** SP   **Ht:** 6' 5" **Wt:** 210 **Born:** 12/09/71 **Age:** 22

			HOW MUCH HE PITCHED						WHAT HE GAVE UP										THE RESULTS					
Year	Team	Lg	G	GS	CG	GF	IP	BFP	H	R	ER	HR	SH	SF	HB	TBB	IBB	SO	WP	Bk	W	L	Pct.	ShO	Sv	ERA
1990	Sou Oregon	A	5	5	0	0	24	92	10	5	3	1	0	1	2	9	0	32	0	0	1	1	.500	0	0	1.13
	Madison	A	3	3	0	0	13.2	61	8	11	6	0	0	1	1	10	0	17	0	0	2	1	.667	0	0	3.95
1991	Huntsville	AA	24	24	1	0	132.1	607	118	69	51	2	4	6	6	90	0	115	12	1	6	13	.316	1	0	3.47
1992	Tacoma	AAA	9	9	0	0	45.1	202	44	22	20	1	3	4	1	35	0	29	1	1	4	2	.667	0	0	3.97
1993	Tacoma	AAA	16	16	0	0	78.2	355	67	53	51	5	3	3	4	54	0	71	2	0	4	8	.333	0	0	5.83
1991	Oakland	AL	1	1	0	0	4.2	21	7	5	5	1	0	0	0	2	0	6	0	0	0	0	.000	0	0	9.64
1993	Oakland	AL	16	16	0	0	84	380	76	50	47	10	1	2	2	62	0	47	3	0	6	6	.500	0	0	5.04
2 ML YEARS			17	17	0	0	88.2	401	83	55	52	11	1	2	2	64	0	53	3	0	6	6	.500	0	0	5.28

Andy Van Slyke

Bats: Left **Throws:** Right **Pos:** CF   **Ht:** 6' 2" **Wt:** 195 **Born:** 12/21/60 **Age:** 33

								BATTING											BASERUNNING				PERCENTAGES		
Year	Team	Lg	G	AB	H	2B	3B	HR	(Hm	Rd)	TB	R	RBI	TBB	IBB	SO	HBP	SH	SF	SB	CS	SB%	GDP	Avg	OBP	SLG
1993	Carolina *	AA	2	4	0	0	0	0	--	--	0	0	1	1	0	3	0	0	0	0	0	.00	0	.000	.200	.000
1983	St. Louis	NL	101	309	81	15	5	8	(3	5)	130	51	38	46	5	64	1	2	3	21	7	.75	4	.262	.357	.421
1984	St. Louis	NL	137	361	88	16	4	7	(3	4)	133	45	50	63	9	71	0	0	2	28	5	.85	5	.244	.354	.368
1985	St. Louis	NL	146	424	110	25	6	13	(5	8)	186	61	55	47	6	54	2	1	1	34	6	.85	5	.259	.335	.439
1986	St. Louis	NL	137	418	113	23	7	13	(6	7)	189	48	61	47	5	85	1	1	3	21	8	.72	2	.270	.343	.452

222

Year Team	Lg	G	AB	H	2B	3B	HR	(Hm	Rd)	TB	R	RBI	TBB	IBB	SO	HBP	SH	SF	SB	CS	SB%	GDP	Avg	OBP	SLG
1987 Pittsburgh	NL	157	564	165	36	11	21	(11	10)	286	93	82	56	4	122	4	3	3	34	8	.81	6	.293	.359	.507
1988 Pittsburgh	NL	154	587	169	23	15	25	(16	9)	297	101	100	57	2	126	1	1	13	30	9	.77	8	.288	.345	.506
1989 Pittsburgh	NL	130	476	113	18	9	9	(4	5)	176	64	53	47	3	100	3	1	4	16	4	.80	13	.237	.308	.370
1990 Pittsburgh	NL	136	493	140	26	6	17	(6	11)	229	67	77	66	2	89	1	3	4	14	4	.78	6	.284	.367	.465
1991 Pittsburgh	NL	138	491	130	24	7	17	(9	8)	219	87	83	71	1	85	4	0	11	10	3	.77	5	.265	.355	.446
1992 Pittsburgh	NL	154	614	199	45	12	14	(6	8)	310	103	89	58	4	99	4	0	9	12	3	.80	9	.324	.381	.505
1993 Pittsburgh	NL	83	323	100	13	4	8	(5	3)	145	42	50	24	5	40	2	0	4	11	2	.85	13	.310	.357	.449
11 ML YEARS		1473	5060	1408	264	86	152	(74	78)	2300	762	738	582	46	935	23	12	57	231	59	.80	78	.278	.352	.455

John VanderWal

Bats: Left **Throws:** Left **Pos:** 1B/LF **Ht:** 6' 2" **Wt:** 190 **Born:** 04/29/66 **Age:** 28

							BATTING												BASERUNNING				PERCENTAGES		
Year Team	Lg	G	AB	H	2B	3B	HR	(Hm	Rd)	TB	R	RBI	TBB	IBB	SO	HBP	SH	SF	SB	CS	SB%	GDP	Avg	OBP	SLG
1991 Montreal	NL	21	61	13	4	1	1	(0	1)	22	4	8	1	0	18	0	0	0	0	0	.00	2	.213	.222	.361
1992 Montreal	NL	105	213	51	8	2	4	(2	2)	75	21	20	24	2	36	0	0	0	3	0	1.00	2	.239	.316	.352
1993 Montreal	NL	106	215	50	7	4	5	(1	4)	80	34	30	27	2	30	1	0	1	6	3	.67	4	.233	.320	.372
3 ML YEARS		232	489	114	19	7	10	(3	7)	177	59	58	52	4	84	1	0	2	9	3	.75	8	.233	.307	.362

Gary Varsho

Bats: Left **Throws:** Right **Pos:** LF **Ht:** 5'11" **Wt:** 185 **Born:** 06/20/61 **Age:** 33

							BATTING												BASERUNNING				PERCENTAGES		
Year Team	Lg	G	AB	H	2B	3B	HR	(Hm	Rd)	TB	R	RBI	TBB	IBB	SO	HBP	SH	SF	SB	CS	SB%	GDP	Avg	OBP	SLG
1993 Indianapols *	AAA	32	121	35	8	1	3	--	--	54	19	18	15	1	13	2	3	1	2	3	.33	1	.289	.377	.446
1988 Chicago	NL	46	73	20	3	0	0	(0	0)	23	6	5	1	0	6	0	0	1	5	0	1.00	0	.274	.280	.315
1989 Chicago	NL	61	87	16	4	2	0	(0	0)	24	10	6	4	1	13	0	0	0	3	0	1.00	0	.184	.220	.276
1990 Chicago	NL	46	48	12	4	0	0	(0	0)	16	10	1	1	1	6	0	0	0	2	0	1.00	1	.250	.265	.333
1991 Pittsburgh	NL	99	187	51	11	2	4	(1	3)	78	23	23	19	2	34	2	1	1	9	2	.82	2	.273	.344	.417
1992 Pittsburgh	NL	103	162	36	6	3	4	(3	1)	60	22	22	10	1	32	0	0	1	5	2	.71	2	.222	.266	.370
1993 Cincinnati	NL	77	95	22	6	0	2	(1	1)	34	8	11	9	0	19	1	3	1	1	0	1.00	1	.232	.302	.358
6 ML YEARS		432	652	157	34	7	10	(5	5)	235	79	68	44	5	110	3	4	4	25	4	.86	6	.241	.290	.360

Greg Vaughn

Bats: Right **Throws:** Right **Pos:** LF/DH **Ht:** 6' 0" **Wt:** 193 **Born:** 07/03/65 **Age:** 28

							BATTING												BASERUNNING				PERCENTAGES		
Year Team	Lg	G	AB	H	2B	3B	HR	(Hm	Rd)	TB	R	RBI	TBB	IBB	SO	HBP	SH	SF	SB	CS	SB%	GDP	Avg	OBP	SLG
1989 Milwaukee	AL	38	113	30	3	0	5	(1	4)	48	18	23	13	0	23	0	0	2	4	1	.80	0	.265	.336	.425
1990 Milwaukee	AL	120	382	84	26	2	17	(9	8)	165	51	61	33	1	91	1	7	6	7	4	.64	11	.220	.280	.432
1991 Milwaukee	AL	145	542	132	24	5	27	(16	11)	247	81	98	62	2	125	1	2	7	2	2	.50	5	.244	.319	.456
1992 Milwaukee	AL	141	501	114	18	2	23	(11	12)	205	77	78	60	1	123	5	2	5	15	15	.50	5	.228	.313	.409
1993 Milwaukee	AL	154	569	152	28	2	30	(12	18)	274	97	97	89	14	118	5	0	4	10	7	.59	6	.267	.369	.482
5 ML YEARS		598	2107	512	99	11	102	(49	53)	939	324	357	257	18	480	12	11	24	38	29	.57	30	.243	.325	.446

Mo Vaughn

Bats: Left **Throws:** Right **Pos:** 1B/DH **Ht:** 6' 1" **Wt:** 225 **Born:** 12/15/67 **Age:** 26

							BATTING												BASERUNNING				PERCENTAGES		
Year Team	Lg	G	AB	H	2B	3B	HR	(Hm	Rd)	TB	R	RBI	TBB	IBB	SO	HBP	SH	SF	SB	CS	SB%	GDP	Avg	OBP	SLG
1991 Boston	AL	74	219	57	12	0	4	(1	3)	81	21	32	26	2	43	2	0	4	2	1	.67	7	.260	.339	.370
1992 Boston	AL	113	355	83	16	2	13	(8	5)	142	42	57	47	7	67	3	0	3	3	3	.50	8	.234	.326	.400
1993 Boston	AL	152	539	160	34	1	29	(13	16)	283	86	101	79	23	130	8	0	7	4	3	.57	14	.297	.390	.525
3 ML YEARS		339	1113	300	62	3	46	(22	24)	506	149	190	152	32	240	13	0	14	9	7	.56	29	.270	.360	.455

Randy Velarde

Bats: Right **Throws:** Right **Pos:** LF/3B/SS **Ht:** 6' 0" **Wt:** 192 **Born:** 11/24/62 **Age:** 31

							BATTING												BASERUNNING				PERCENTAGES		
Year Team	Lg	G	AB	H	2B	3B	HR	(Hm	Rd)	TB	R	RBI	TBB	IBB	SO	HBP	SH	SF	SB	CS	SB%	GDP	Avg	OBP	SLG
1993 Albany *	AA	5	17	4	0	0	1	--	--	7	2	2	2	0	2	0	0	0	0	0	.00	1	.235	.316	.412
1987 New York	AL	8	22	4	0	0	0	(0	0)	4	1	1	0	0	6	0	0	0	0	0	.00	0	.182	.182	.182
1988 New York	AL	48	115	20	6	0	5	(2	3)	41	18	12	8	0	24	2	0	0	1	1	.50	3	.174	.240	.357
1989 New York	AL	33	100	34	4	2	2	(1	1)	48	12	11	7	0	14	1	3	0	0	3	.00	0	.340	.389	.480
1990 New York	AL	95	229	48	6	2	5	(1	4)	73	21	19	20	0	53	1	2	1	0	3	.00	6	.210	.275	.319
1991 New York	AL	80	184	45	11	1	1	(0	1)	61	19	15	18	0	43	3	5	0	3	1	.75	6	.245	.322	.332
1992 New York	AL	121	412	112	24	1	7	(2	5)	159	57	46	38	1	78	2	4	5	7	2	.78	13	.272	.333	.386
1993 New York	AL	85	226	68	13	2	7	(4	3)	106	28	24	18	2	39	4	3	2	2	2	.50	12	.301	.360	.469
7 ML YEARS		470	1288	331	64	8	27	(10	17)	492	156	128	109	3	257	13	17	8	13	12	.52	41	.257	.319	.382

Guillermo Velasquez

Bats: Left   **Throws:** Right   **Pos:** 1B   **Ht:** 6' 3"   **Wt:** 225   **Born:** 04/23/68   **Age:** 26

Year	Team	Lg	G	AB	H	2B	3B	HR	(Hm	Rd)	TB	R	RBI	TBB	IBB	SO	HBP	SH	SF	SB	CS	SB%	GDP	Avg	OBP	SLG
1987	Chston-Sc	A	102	295	65	12	0	3	--	--	86	32	30	16	0	65	0	1	0	2	0	1.00	13	.220	.260	.292
1988	Chston-Sc	A	135	520	149	28	3	11	--	--	216	55	90	34	9	110	1	3	9	1	1	.50	6	.287	.326	.415
1989	Riverside	A	139	544	152	30	2	9	--	--	213	73	69	51	4	91	2	0	10	4	3	.57	14	.279	.338	.392
1990	Wichita	AA	105	377	102	21	2	12	--	--	163	48	72	35	5	66	1	0	4	1	1	.50	9	.271	.331	.432
1991	Wichita	AA	130	501	148	26	3	21	--	--	243	72	100	48	6	75	1	0	7	4	2	.67	6	.295	.354	.485
1992	Las Vegas	AAA	136	512	158	44	4	7	--	--	231	68	99	44	8	94	1	0	9	3	1	.75	7	.309	.359	.451
1993	Las Vegas	AAA	30	129	43	6	1	5	--	--	66	23	24	10	1	19	1	0	2	0	0	.00	2	.333	.380	.512
1992	San Diego	NL	15	23	7	0	0	1	(1	0)	10	1	5	1	0	7	0	0	0	0	0	.00	0	.304	.333	.435
1993	San Diego	NL	79	143	30	2	0	3	(1	2)	41	7	20	13	2	35	0	0	1	0	0	.00	3	.210	.274	.287
	2 ML YEARS		94	166	37	2	0	4	(2	2)	51	8	25	14	2	42	0	0	1	0	0	.00	3	.223	.282	.307

Robin Ventura

Bats: Left   **Throws:** Right   **Pos:** 3B   **Ht:** 6' 1"   **Wt:** 198   **Born:** 07/14/67   **Age:** 26

Year	Team	Lg	G	AB	H	2B	3B	HR	(Hm	Rd)	TB	R	RBI	TBB	IBB	SO	HBP	SH	SF	SB	CS	SB%	GDP	Avg	OBP	SLG
1989	Chicago	AL	16	45	8	3	0	0	(0	0)	11	5	7	8	0	6	1	1	3	0	0	.00	1	.178	.298	.244
1990	Chicago	AL	150	493	123	17	1	5	(2	3)	157	48	54	55	2	53	1	13	3	1	4	.20	5	.249	.324	.318
1991	Chicago	AL	157	606	172	25	1	23	(16	7)	268	92	100	80	3	67	4	8	7	2	4	.33	22	.284	.367	.442
1992	Chicago	AL	157	592	167	38	1	16	(7	9)	255	85	93	93	9	71	0	1	8	2	4	.33	14	.282	.375	.431
1993	Chicago	AL	157	554	145	27	1	22	(12	10)	240	85	94	105	16	82	3	1	6	1	6	.14	15	.262	.379	.433
	5 ML YEARS		637	2290	615	110	4	66	(37	29)	931	315	348	341	30	279	9	24	27	6	18	.25	57	.269	.362	.407

Hector Villanueva

Bats: Right   **Throws:** Right   **Pos:** C   **Ht:** 6' 1"   **Wt:** 220   **Born:** 10/02/64   **Age:** 29

Year	Team	Lg	G	AB	H	2B	3B	HR	(Hm	Rd)	TB	R	RBI	TBB	IBB	SO	HBP	SH	SF	SB	CS	SB%	GDP	Avg	OBP	SLG
1993	Louisville *	AAA	40	124	30	9	0	5	--	--	54	13	20	16	1	18	1	0	1	0	0	.00	5	.242	.331	.435
1990	Chicago	NL	52	114	31	4	1	7	(2	5)	58	14	18	4	2	27	2	0	0	1	0	1.00	3	.272	.308	.509
1991	Chicago	NL	71	192	53	10	1	13	(11	2)	104	23	32	21	1	30	0	0	1	0	0	.00	3	.276	.346	.542
1992	Chicago	NL	51	112	17	6	0	2	(2	0)	29	9	13	11	2	24	0	0	0	0	0	.00	3	.152	.228	.259
1993	St. Louis	NL	17	55	8	1	0	3	(2	1)	18	7	9	4	1	17	0	0	0	0	0	.00	3	.145	.203	.327
	4 ML YEARS		191	473	109	21	2	25	(17	8)	209	53	72	40	6	98	2	0	1	1	0	1.00	14	.230	.293	.442

Fernando Vina

Bats: Left   **Throws:** Right   **Pos:** 2B   **Ht:** 5' 9"   **Wt:** 170   **Born:** 04/16/69   **Age:** 25

Year	Team	Lg	G	AB	H	2B	3B	HR	(Hm	Rd)	TB	R	RBI	TBB	IBB	SO	HBP	SH	SF	SB	CS	SB%	GDP	Avg	OBP	SLG
1991	Columbia	A	129	498	135	23	6	6	--	--	188	77	50	46	1	27	13	5	7	42	22	.66	5	.271	.344	.378
1992	Tidewater	AAA	11	30	6	0	0	0	--	--	6	3	2	0	0	2	0	2	1	0	0	.00	0	.200	.194	.200
	St. Lucie	A	111	421	124	15	5	1	--	--	152	61	42	32	2	26	3	4	2	36	17	.68	7	.295	.347	.361
1993	Norfolk	AAA	73	287	66	6	4	4	--	--	92	24	27	7	2	17	4	4	1	16	11	.59	12	.230	.258	.321
1993	Seattle	AL	24	45	10	2	0	0	(0	0)	12	5	2	4	0	3	3	1	0	6	0	1.00	0	.222	.327	.267

Frank Viola

Pitches: Left   **Bats:** Left   **Pos:** SP   **Ht:** 6' 4"   **Wt:** 210   **Born:** 04/19/60   **Age:** 34

Year	Team	Lg	G	GS	CG	GF	IP	BFP	H	R	ER	HR	SH	SF	HB	TBB	IBB	SO	WP	Bk	W	L	Pct.	ShO	Sv	ERA
1982	Minnesota	AL	22	22	3	0	126	543	152	77	73	22	2	0	0	38	2	84	4	1	4	10	.286	0	0	5.21
1983	Minnesota	AL	35	34	4	0	210	949	242	141	128	34	5	2	8	92	7	127	6	2	7	15	.318	0	0	5.49
1984	Minnesota	AL	35	35	10	0	257.2	1047	225	101	92	28	1	5	4	73	1	149	6	1	18	12	.600	4	0	3.21
1985	Minnesota	AL	36	36	9	0	250.2	1059	262	136	114	26	5	5	2	68	3	135	6	2	18	14	.563	0	0	4.09
1986	Minnesota	AL	37	37	7	0	245.2	1053	257	136	123	37	4	5	3	83	0	191	12	0	16	13	.552	1	0	4.51
1987	Minnesota	AL	36	36	7	0	251.2	1037	230	91	81	29	7	3	6	66	1	197	1	1	17	10	.630	1	0	2.90
1988	Minnesota	AL	35	35	7	0	255.1	1031	236	80	75	20	6	6	3	54	2	193	5	1	24	7	.774	2	0	2.64
1989	2 ML Teams	AL	36	36	9	0	261	1082	246	115	106	22	12	6	4	74	4	211	8	1	13	17	.433	2	0	3.66
1990	New York	NL	35	35	7	0	249.2	1016	227	83	74	15	13	3	2	60	2	182	11	0	20	12	.625	3	0	2.67
1991	New York	NL	35	35	3	0	231.1	980	259	112	102	25	15	5	1	54	4	132	6	1	13	15	.464	0	0	3.97
1992	Boston	AL	35	35	6	0	238	999	214	99	91	13	7	10	7	89	4	121	12	2	13	12	.520	1	0	3.44
1993	Boston	AL	29	29	2	0	183.2	787	180	76	64	12	8	7	6	72	5	91	5	0	11	8	.579	1	0	3.14
1989	Minnesota	AL	24	24	7	0	175.2	731	171	80	74	17	9	4	3	47	1	138	5	1	8	12	.400	1	0	3.79
	New York	NL	12	12	2	0	85.1	351	75	35	32	5	3	2	1	27	3	73	3	0	5	5	.500	1	0	3.38
	12 ML YEARS		406	405	74	0	2760.2	11583	2730	1247	1123	283	85	57	46	823	35	1813	82	12	174	145	.545	16	0	3.66

Jose Vizcaino

Bats: Both **Throws:** Right **Pos:** SS/2B/3B **Ht:** 6' 1" **Wt:** 180 **Born:** 03/26/68 **Age:** 26

			BATTING																		BASERUNNING				PERCENTAGES		
Year Team	Lg	G	AB	H	2B	3B	HR	(Hm	Rd)	TB	R	RBI	TBB	IBB	SO	HBP	SH	SF		SB	CS	SB%	GDP	Avg	OBP	SLG
1989 Los Angeles	NL	7	10	2	0	0	0	(0	0)	2	2	0	0	0	1	0	1	0		0	0	.00	0	.200	.200	.200
1990 Los Angeles	NL	37	51	14	1	1	0	(0	0)	17	3	2	4	1	8	0	0	0		1	1	.50	1	.275	.327	.333
1991 Chicago	NL	93	145	38	5	0	0	(0	0)	43	7	10	5	0	18	0	2	2		2	1	.67	1	.262	.283	.297
1992 Chicago	NL	86	285	64	10	4	1	(0	1)	85	25	17	14	2	35	0	5	1		3	0	1.00	4	.225	.260	.298
1993 Chicago	NL	151	551	158	19	4	4	(1	3)	197	74	54	46	2	71	3	8	9		12	9	.57	9	.287	.340	.358
5 ML YEARS		374	1042	276	35	9	5	(1	4)	344	111	83	69	5	133	3	16	12		18	11	.62	15	.265	.309	.330

Omar Vizquel

Bats: Both **Throws:** Right **Pos:** SS **Ht:** 5' 9" **Wt:** 165 **Born:** 04/24/67 **Age:** 27

			BATTING																		BASERUNNING				PERCENTAGES		
Year Team	Lg	G	AB	H	2B	3B	HR	(Hm	Rd)	TB	R	RBI	TBB	IBB	SO	HBP	SH	SF		SB	CS	SB%	GDP	Avg	OBP	SLG
1989 Seattle	AL	143	387	85	7	3	1	(1	0)	101	45	20	28	0	40	1	13	2		1	4	.20	6	.220	.273	.261
1990 Seattle	AL	81	255	63	3	2	2	(0	2)	76	19	18	18	0	22	0	10	2		4	1	.80	7	.247	.295	.298
1991 Seattle	AL	142	426	98	16	4	1	(1	0)	125	42	41	45	0	37	0	8	3		7	2	.78	8	.230	.302	.293
1992 Seattle	AL	136	483	142	20	4	0	(0	0)	170	49	21	32	0	38	2	9	1		15	13	.54	14	.294	.340	.352
1993 Seattle	AL	158	560	143	14	2	1	(1	1)	167	68	31	50	2	71	4	13	3		12	14	.46	7	.255	.319	.298
5 ML YEARS		660	2111	531	60	15	6	(3	3)	639	223	131	173	2	208	7	53	11		39	34	.53	42	.252	.309	.303

Jack Voigt

Bats: Right **Throws:** Right **Pos:** RF/LF **Ht:** 6' 1" **Wt:** 175 **Born:** 05/17/66 **Age:** 28

			BATTING																		BASERUNNING				PERCENTAGES		
Year Team	Lg	G	AB	H	2B	3B	HR	(Hm	Rd)	TB	R	RBI	TBB	IBB	SO	HBP	SH	SF		SB	CS	SB%	GDP	Avg	OBP	SLG
1987 Newark	A	63	219	70	10	1	11	--	--	115	41	52	33	0	45	0	1	1		1	3	.25	3	.320	.407	.525
Hagerstown	A	2	9	1	0	0	0	--	--	1	0	1	1	0	4	0	0	0		0	0	.00	0	.111	.200	.111
1988 Hagerstown	A	115	367	83	18	2	12	--	--	141	62	42	66	2	92	6	3	2		5	2	.71	7	.226	.351	.384
1989 Frederick	A	127	406	107	26	5	10	--	--	173	61	77	62	4	106	4	2	5		17	2	.89	5	.264	.363	.426
1990 Hagerstown	AA	126	418	106	26	2	12	--	--	172	55	70	59	1	97	5	6	11		5	3	.63	7	.254	.345	.411
1991 Hagerstown	AA	29	90	22	3	0	0	--	--	25	15	6	15	1	19	2	1	0		6	0	1.00	2	.244	.364	.278
Rochester	AAA	83	267	72	11	4	6	--	--	109	46	35	40	2	53	1	5	2		9	1	.90	8	.270	.365	.408
1992 Rochester	AAA	129	443	126	23	4	16	--	--	205	74	64	58	3	102	4	3	0		9	2	.82	10	.284	.372	.463
1993 Rochester	AAA	18	61	22	6	1	3	--	--	39	16	11	9	0	14	0	0	0		1	0	.00	1	.361	.443	.639
1992 Baltimore	AL	1	0	0	0	0	0	(0	0)	0	0	0	0	0	0	0	0	0		0	0	.00	0	.000	.000	.000
1993 Baltimore	AL	64	152	45	11	1	6	(5	1)	76	32	23	25	0	33	0	0	0		1	0	1.00	3	.296	.395	.500
2 ML YEARS		65	152	45	11	1	6	(5	1)	76	32	23	25	0	33	0	0	0		1	0	1.00	3	.296	.395	.500

Paul Wagner

Pitches: Right **Bats:** Right **Pos:** RP/SP **Ht:** 6' 1" **Wt:** 185 **Born:** 11/14/67 **Age:** 26

		HOW MUCH HE PITCHED						WHAT HE GAVE UP											THE RESULTS				
Year Team	Lg	G	GS	CG	GF	IP	BFP	H	R	ER	HR	SH	SF	HB	TBB	IBB	SO	WP	Bk	W	L	Pct.	ShO	Sv	ERA
1989 Welland	A	13	10	0	1	50.1	220	54	34	25	4	1	1	1	15	0	34	4	0	4	5	.444	0	0	4.47
1990 Augusta	A	35	1	0	20	72	313	71	30	22	3	3	3	2	30	3	71	7	0	7	7	.500	0	4	2.75
Salem	A	11	4	0	3	36	159	39	22	20	7	0	0	0	17	1	28	3	0	0	1	.000	0	2	5.00
1991 Salem	A	25	25	5	0	158.2	660	124	70	55	14	4	2	8	60	0	113	11	1	11	6	.647	2	0	3.12
1992 Carolina	AA	19	19	2	0	121.2	513	104	52	41	3	6	5	3	47	1	101	6	0	6	6	.500	1	0	3.03
Buffalo	AAA	8	8	0	0	39.1	181	51	27	24	1	2	1	1	14	0	19	2	0	3	3	.500	0	0	5.49
1992 Pittsburgh	NL	6	1	0	1	13	52	9	1	1	0	0	0	0	5	0	5	1	0	2	0	1.000	0	0	0.69
1993 Pittsburgh	NL	44	17	1	9	141.1	599	143	72	67	15	6	7	1	42	2	114	12	0	8	8	.500	1	2	4.27
2 ML YEARS		50	18	1	10	154.1	651	152	73	68	15	6	7	1	47	2	119	13	0	10	8	.556	1	2	3.97

David Wainhouse

Pitches: Right **Bats:** Left **Pos:** RP **Ht:** 6' 2" **Wt:** 185 **Born:** 11/07/67 **Age:** 26

		HOW MUCH HE PITCHED						WHAT HE GAVE UP											THE RESULTS				
Year Team	Lg	G	GS	CG	GF	IP	BFP	H	R	ER	HR	SH	SF	HB	TBB	IBB	SO	WP	Bk	W	L	Pct.	ShO	Sv	ERA
1989 Wst Plm Bch	A	13	13	0	0	66.1	286	75	35	30	4	3	2	8	19	0	26	6	3	1	5	.167	0	0	4.07
1990 Wst Plm Bch	A	12	12	2	0	76.2	327	68	28	18	1	0	3	5	34	0	58	2	3	6	3	.667	1	0	2.11
Jacksnville	AA	17	16	2	0	95.2	428	97	59	46	8	2	3	7	47	2	59	2	0	7	7	.500	0	0	4.33
1991 Harrisburg	AA	33	0	0	27	52	224	49	17	15	1	2	0	4	17	2	46	3	0	2	2	.500	0	11	2.60
Indianapols	AAA	14	0	0	8	28.2	127	28	14	13	1	2	1	3	15	1	13	3	0	2	0	1.000	0	1	4.08
1992 Indianapols	AAA	44	0	0	41	46	208	48	22	21	4	2	2	2	24	6	37	4	0	5	4	.556	0	21	4.11
1993 Calgary	AAA	13	0	0	10	15.2	62	10	7	7	2	2	2	1	7	1	7	2	0	0	0	.000	0	5	4.02
1991 Montreal	NL	2	0	0	0	2.2	14	2	2	2	0	0	1	0	4	0	1	2	0	0	1	.000	0	0	6.75
1993 Seattle	AL	3	0	0	0	2.1	20	7	7	7	1	0	0	1	5	0	2	0	0	0	0	.000	0	0	27.00
2 ML YEARS		5	0	0	1	5	34	9	9	9	1	0	1	1	9	0	3	2	0	0	1	.000	0	0	16.20

Tim Wakefield

Pitches: Right **Bats:** Right **Pos:** SP 　　　　**Ht:** 6' 2" **Wt:** 195 **Born:** 08/02/66 **Age:** 27

		HOW MUCH HE PITCHED						WHAT HE GAVE UP									THE RESULTS					
Year Team	Lg	G	GS	CG	GF	IP	BFP	H	R	ER	HR	SH	SF	HB	TBB	IBB	SO	WP	Bk	W	L	Pct.	ShO	Sv	ERA
1989 Welland	A	18	1	0	11	39.2	168	30	17	15	1	2	1	2	21	0	42	9	0	1	1	.500	0	2	3.40
1990 Salem	A	28	28	2	0	190.1	824	187	109	100	24	7	6	10	85	2	127	11	0	10	14	.417	0	0	4.73
1991 Buffalo	AAA	1	1	0	0	4.2	23	8	6	6	3	0	0	0	1	0	4	0	0	0	1	.000	0	0	11.57
Carolina	AA	26	25	8	1	183	741	155	68	59	13	6	3	9	51	6	120	2	1	15	8	.652	1	0	2.90
1992 Buffalo	AAA	20	20	6	0	135.1	559	122	52	46	10	3	7	3	51	1	71	9	0	10	3	.769	1	0	3.06
1993 Carolina	AA	9	9	1	0	56.2	265	68	48	44	5	2	4	5	22	0	36	3	0	3	5	.375	0	0	6.99
1992 Pittsburgh	NL	13	13	4	0	92	373	76	26	22	3	6	4	1	35	1	51	3	1	8	1	.889	1	0	2.15
1993 Pittsburgh	NL	24	20	3	1	128.1	595	145	83	80	14	7	5	9	75	2	59	6	0	6	11	.353	0	0	5.61
2 ML YEARS		37	33	7	1	220.1	968	221	109	102	17	13	9	10	110	3	110	9	1	14	12	.538	3	0	4.17

Matt Walbeck

Bats: Both **Throws:** Right **Pos:** C 　　　　**Ht:** 5'11" **Wt:** 195 **Born:** 10/02/69 **Age:** 24

		BATTING																	BASERUNNING				PERCENTAGES		
Year Team	Lg	G	AB	H	2B	3B	HR	(Hm	Rd)	TB	R	RBI	TBB	IBB	SO	HBP	SH	SF	SB	CS	SB%	GDP	Avg	OBP	SLG
1987 Wytheville	R	51	169	53	9	3	1	--	--	71	24	28	22	0	39	0	0	3	0	1	.00	4	.314	.387	.420
1988 Chston-Wv	A	104	312	68	9	0	2	--	--	83	28	24	30	1	44	3	6	1	7	5	.58	8	.218	.292	.266
1989 Peoria	A	94	341	86	19	0	4	--	--	117	38	47	20	1	47	3	1	3	5	2	.71	7	.252	.297	.343
1990 Peoria	A	25	66	15	1	0	0	--	--	16	2	5	5	0	7	2	2	0	1	0	1.00	1	.227	.301	.242
1991 Winston-Sal	A	91	259	70	11	0	3	--	--	90	25	41	20	3	23	2	3	10	3	2	.60	7	.270	.316	.347
1992 Charlotte	AA	105	385	116	22	1	7	--	--	161	48	42	33	3	56	2	3	2	0	7	.00	6	.301	.358	.418
1993 Iowa	AAA	87	331	93	18	2	6	--	--	133	31	43	18	4	47	2	2	2	1	2	.33	6	.281	.320	.402
1993 Chicago	NL	11	30	6	2	0	1	(1	0)	11	2	6	1	0	6	0	0	0	0	0	.00	0	.200	.226	.367

Jim Walewander

Bats: Both **Throws:** Right **Pos:** SS 　　　　**Ht:** 5'10" **Wt:** 155 **Born:** 05/02/61 **Age:** 33

		BATTING																	BASERUNNING				PERCENTAGES		
Year Team	Lg	G	AB	H	2B	3B	HR	(Hm	Rd)	TB	R	RBI	TBB	IBB	SO	HBP	SH	SF	SB	CS	SB%	GDP	Avg	OBP	SLG
1993 Vancouver *	AAA	102	351	107	12	1	1	--	--	124	77	43	60	1	57	9	5	3	36	6	.86	8	.305	.416	.353
1987 Detroit	AL	53	54	13	3	1	1	(1	0)	21	24	4	7	0	6	0	2	0	2	1	.67	2	.241	.328	.389
1988 Detroit	AL	88	175	37	5	0	0	(0	0)	42	23	6	12	0	26	0	10	1	11	4	.73	1	.211	.261	.240
1990 New York	AL	9	5	1	1	0	0	(0	0)	2	1	1	0	0	0	0	0	0	1	1	.50	0	.200	.200	.400
1993 California	AL	12	8	1	0	0	0	(0	0)	1	2	3	5	0	1	0	0	1	1	1	.50	0	.125	.429	.125
4 ML YEARS		162	242	52	9	1	1	(1	0)	66	50	14	24	0	33	0	12	2	15	7	.68	3	.215	.284	.273

Bob Walk

Pitches: Right **Bats:** Right **Pos:** SP 　　　　**Ht:** 6' 3" **Wt:** 217 **Born:** 11/26/56 **Age:** 37

		HOW MUCH HE PITCHED						WHAT HE GAVE UP									THE RESULTS					
Year Team	Lg	G	GS	CG	GF	IP	BFP	H	R	ER	HR	SH	SF	HB	TBB	IBB	SO	WP	Bk	W	L	Pct.	ShO	Sv	ERA
1980 Philadelphia	NL	27	27	2	0	152	673	163	82	77	8	5	5	2	71	2	94	6	3	11	7	.611	0	0	4.56
1981 Atlanta	NL	12	8	0	1	43	189	41	25	22	6	2	0	0	23	0	16	1	0	1	4	.200	0	0	4.60
1982 Atlanta	NL	32	27	3	1	164.1	717	179	101	89	19	8	5	6	59	2	84	7	0	11	9	.550	1	0	4.87
1983 Atlanta	NL	1	1	0	0	3.2	20	7	3	3	0	1	0	0	2	0	4	0	0	0	0	.000	0	0	7.36
1984 Pittsburgh	NL	2	2	0	0	10.1	44	8	5	3	1	0	0	0	4	1	10	0	0	1	1	.500	0	0	2.61
1985 Pittsburgh	NL	9	9	1	0	58.2	248	60	27	24	3	3	1	0	18	2	40	2	3	2	3	.400	1	0	3.68
1986 Pittsburgh	NL	44	15	1	7	141.2	592	129	66	59	14	6	5	3	64	7	78	12	1	7	8	.467	1	2	3.75
1987 Pittsburgh	NL	39	12	1	6	117	498	107	52	43	11	6	2	3	51	2	78	7	3	8	2	.800	1	0	3.31
1988 Pittsburgh	NL	32	32	1	0	212.2	881	183	75	64	6	14	5	2	65	5	81	13	9	12	10	.545	1	0	2.71
1989 Pittsburgh	NL	33	31	2	1	196	843	208	106	96	15	4	2	4	65	1	83	7	4	13	10	.565	0	0	4.41
1990 Pittsburgh	NL	26	24	1	1	129.2	549	136	59	54	17	3	3	4	36	2	73	5	3	7	5	.583	1	1	3.75
1991 Pittsburgh	NL	25	20	0	0	115	484	104	53	46	10	7	4	5	35	2	67	11	2	9	2	.818	0	1	3.60
1992 Pittsburgh	NL	36	19	1	7	135	567	132	54	48	10	5	1	6	43	5	60	7	2	10	6	.625	0	2	3.20
1993 Pittsburgh	NL	32	32	3	0	187	822	214	121	118	23	10	9	5	70	5	80	2	3	13	14	.481	0	0	5.68
14 ML YEARS		350	259	16	24	1666	7127	1671	829	746	143	74	42	40	606	36	848	80	33	105	81	.565	6	5	4.03

Chico Walker

Bats: Both **Throws:** Right **Pos:** 2B/3B/LF 　　　　**Ht:** 5' 9" **Wt:** 185 **Born:** 11/26/58 **Age:** 35

		BATTING																	BASERUNNING				PERCENTAGES		
Year Team	Lg	G	AB	H	2B	3B	HR	(Hm	Rd)	TB	R	RBI	TBB	IBB	SO	HBP	SH	SF	SB	CS	SB%	GDP	Avg	OBP	SLG
1980 Boston	AL	19	57	12	0	0	1	(1	0)	15	3	5	6	1	10	1	1	1	3	2	.60	1	.211	.292	.263
1981 Boston	AL	6	17	6	0	0	0	(0	0)	6	3	2	1	0	2	0	0	0	0	0	.00	0	.353	.389	.353
1983 Boston	AL	4	5	2	0	2	0	(0	0)	6	2	1	0	0	0	0	0	0	0	0	.00	0	.400	.400	1.200
1984 Boston	AL	3	2	0	0	0	0	(0	0)	0	0	1	0	0	1	0	0	0	0	0	.00	0	.000	.000	.000
1985 Chicago	NL	21	12	1	0	0	0	(0	0)	1	3	0	0	0	5	0	0	0	1	0	1.00	0	.083	.083	.083

Year Team	Lg	G	AB	H	2B	3B	HR	(Hm Rd)	TB	R	RBI	TBB	IBB	SO	HBP	SH	SF	SB	CS	SB%	GDP	Avg	OBP	SLG
1986 Chicago	NL	28	101	28	3	2	1	(0 1)	38	21	7	10	0	20	0	0	1	15	4	.79	3	.277	.339	.376
1987 Chicago	NL	47	105	21	4	0	0	(0 0)	25	15	7	12	1	23	0	2	2	11	4	.73	1	.200	.277	.238
1988 California	AL	33	78	12	1	0	0	(0 0)	13	8	2	6	0	15	0	2	0	2	1	.67	2	.154	.214	.167
1991 Chicago	NL	124	374	96	10	1	6	(4 2)	126	51	34	33	2	57	0	1	3	13	5	.72	3	.257	.315	.337
1992 2 ML Teams		126	253	73	12	1	4	(0 4)	99	26	38	27	3	50	0	0	5	15	1	.94	9	.289	.351	.391
1993 New York	NL	115	213	48	7	1	5	(1 4)	72	18	19	14	0	29	0	0	2	7	0	1.00	3	.225	.271	.338
1992 Chicago	NL	19	26	3	0	0	0	(0 0)	3	2	2	3	0	4	0	0	1	1	0	1.00	0	.115	.200	.115
New York	NL	107	227	70	12	1	4	(0 4)	96	24	36	24	3	46	0	0	4	14	1	.93	9	.308	.369	.423
11 ML YEARS		526	1217	299	37	7	17	(6 11)	401	150	116	109	7	212	1	6	15	67	19	.78	22	.246	.305	.329

Larry Walker

Bats: Left **Throws:** Right **Pos:** RF   **Ht:** 6' 3" **Wt:** 215 **Born:** 12/01/66 **Age:** 27

Year Team	Lg	G	AB	H	2B	3B	HR	(Hm Rd)	TB	R	RBI	TBB	IBB	SO	HBP	SH	SF	SB	CS	SB%	GDP	Avg	OBP	SLG
1989 Montreal	NL	20	47	8	0	0	0	(0 0)	8	4	4	5	0	13	1	3	0	1	1	.50	0	.170	.264	.170
1990 Montreal	NL	133	419	101	18	3	19	(9 10)	182	59	51	49	5	112	5	3	2	21	7	.75	8	.241	.326	.434
1991 Montreal	NL	137	487	141	30	2	16	(5 11)	223	59	64	42	2	102	5	1	4	14	9	.61	7	.290	.349	.458
1992 Montreal	NL	143	528	159	31	4	23	(13 10)	267	85	93	41	10	97	6	0	8	18	6	.75	9	.301	.353	.506
1993 Montreal	NL	138	490	130	24	5	22	(13 9)	230	85	86	80	20	76	6	0	6	29	7	.81	8	.265	.371	.469
5 ML YEARS		571	1971	539	103	14	80	(40 40)	910	292	298	217	37	400	23	7	20	83	30	.73	32	.273	.349	.462

Tim Wallach

Bats: Right **Throws:** Right **Pos:** 3B   **Ht:** 6' 3" **Wt:** 202 **Born:** 09/14/57 **Age:** 36

Year Team	Lg	G	AB	H	2B	3B	HR	(Hm Rd)	TB	R	RBI	TBB	IBB	SO	HBP	SH	SF	SB	CS	SB%	GDP	Avg	OBP	SLG
1980 Montreal	NL	5	11	2	0	0	1	(0 1)	5	1	2	1	0	5	0	0	0	0	0	.00	3	.182	.250	.455
1981 Montreal	NL	71	212	50	9	1	4	(1 3)	73	19	13	15	2	37	4	0	0	1	1	.00	3	.236	.299	.344
1982 Montreal	NL	158	596	160	31	3	28	(11 17)	281	89	97	36	4	81	4	5	4	6	4	.60	15	.268	.313	.471
1983 Montreal	NL	156	581	156	33	3	19	(9 10)	252	54	70	55	8	97	6	0	5	0	3	.00	9	.269	.335	.434
1984 Montreal	NL	160	582	143	25	4	18	(4 14)	230	55	72	50	6	101	7	0	4	3	7	.30	12	.246	.311	.395
1985 Montreal	NL	155	569	148	36	3	22	(9 13)	256	70	81	38	8	79	5	0	5	9	9	.50	17	.260	.310	.450
1986 Montreal	NL	134	480	112	22	1	18	(6 12)	190	50	71	44	8	72	10	0	5	8	4	.67	16	.233	.308	.396
1987 Montreal	NL	153	593	177	42	4	26	(13 13)	305	89	123	37	5	98	7	0	7	9	5	.64	6	.298	.343	.514
1988 Montreal	NL	159	592	152	32	5	12	(5 7)	230	52	69	38	7	88	3	0	7	2	6	.25	19	.257	.302	.389
1989 Montreal	NL	154	573	159	42	0	13	(6 7)	240	76	77	58	10	81	1	0	7	3	7	.30	21	.277	.341	.419
1990 Montreal	NL	161	626	185	37	5	21	(9 12)	295	69	98	42	11	80	3	0	7	6	9	.40	12	.296	.339	.471
1991 Montreal	NL	151	577	130	22	1	13	(5 8)	193	60	73	50	8	100	6	0	4	2	4	.33	12	.225	.292	.334
1992 Montreal	NL	150	537	120	29	1	9	(5 4)	178	53	59	50	2	90	8	0	7	2	2	.50	10	.223	.296	.331
1993 Los Angeles	NL	133	477	106	19	1	12	(4 8)	163	42	62	32	2	70	3	1	9	2	0	.00	9	.222	.271	.342
14 ML YEARS		1900	7006	1800	379	32	216	(85 131)	2891	779	967	546	81	1079	67	6	71	50	63	.44	161	.257	.314	.413

Dan Walters

Bats: Right **Throws:** Right **Pos:** C   **Ht:** 6' 4" **Wt:** 235 **Born:** 08/15/66 **Age:** 27

Year Team	Lg	G	AB	H	2B	3B	HR	(Hm Rd)	TB	R	RBI	TBB	IBB	SO	HBP	SH	SF	SB	CS	SB%	GDP	Avg	OBP	SLG
1985 Asheville	A	15	28	1	0	0	0	-- --	1	1	1	1	0	11	0	1	0	0	0	.00	1	.036	.069	.036
Auburn	A	44	144	30	6	0	0	-- --	36	15	10	8	0	23	1	0	3	1	0	1.00	6	.208	.250	.250
1986 Asheville	A	101	366	96	21	1	8	-- --	143	42	46	14	0	59	1	1	2	1	1	.50	12	.262	.290	.391
1987 Osceola	A	99	338	84	8	0	1	-- --	95	23	30	33	2	42	0	5	5	2	4	.33	15	.249	.311	.281
1988 Tucson	AAA	2	7	0	0	0	0	-- --	0	0	0	0	0	2	0	0	0	0	0	.00	0	.000	.000	.000
Columbus	AA	98	305	71	10	1	7	-- --	104	31	28	26	0	42	3	3	4	1	0	1.00	11	.233	.296	.341
1989 Wichita	AA	89	300	82	15	0	6	-- --	115	30	45	25	2	31	3	3	2	0	2	.00	5	.273	.333	.383
1990 Wichita	AA	58	199	59	12	0	7	-- --	92	25	40	21	2	21	1	0	2	0	0	.00	8	.296	.363	.462
Las Vegas	AAA	53	184	47	9	0	3	-- --	65	19	26	13	0	24	0	0	3	0	0	.00	10	.255	.300	.353
1991 Las Vegas	AAA	96	293	93	22	0	4	-- --	127	39	44	22	5	35	0	0	0	0	0	.00	12	.317	.363	.433
1992 Las Vegas	AAA	35	127	50	9	0	2	-- --	65	16	25	10	1	12	2	1	2	0	0	.00	3	.394	.440	.512
1993 Las Vegas	AAA	66	223	64	14	0	5	-- --	93	26	39	14	0	26	1	0	1	1	1	.33	13	.287	.331	.417
1992 San Diego	NL	57	179	45	11	1	4	(3 1)	70	14	22	10	0	28	2	1	2	1	0	1.00	3	.251	.295	.391
1993 San Diego	NL	27	94	19	3	0	1	(1 0)	25	6	10	7	2	13	0	0	1	1	0	.00	2	.202	.255	.266
2 ML YEARS		84	273	64	14	1	5	(4 1)	95	20	32	17	2	41	2	1	3	1	0	1.00	5	.234	.281	.348

Bruce Walton

Pitches: Right **Bats:** Right **Pos:** RP   **Ht:** 6' 2" **Wt:** 195 **Born:** 12/25/62 **Age:** 31

Year Team	Lg	G	GS	CG	GF	IP	BFP	H	R	ER	HR	SH	SF	HB	TBB	IBB	SO	WP	Bk	W	L	Pct.	ShO	Sv	ERA
1985 Pocatello	R	18	9	2	6	76.2		89	46	35	2	0	0	1	27	3	69			3	7	.300	0	0	4.11
1986 Modesto	A	27	27	4	0	176	778	204	96	80	16	10	5	9	41	1	107	7	1	13	7	.650	0	0	4.09

Year Team	Lg	G	GS	CG	GF	IP	BFP	H	R	ER	HR	SH	SF	HB	TBB	IBB	SO	WP	Bk	W	L	Pct.	ShO	Sv	ERA
Madison	A	1	1	0	0	5	21	5	3	3	0	0	0	0	1	0	1	0	0	0	0	.000	0	0	5.40
1987 Modesto	A	16	16	3	0	106.1	437	97	44	34	6	1	3	4	27	0	84	2	0	8	6	.571	1	0	2.88
Huntsville	AA	18	2	0	6	58	248	61	24	20	4	2	3	1	13	1	40	4	2	2	2	.500	0	2	3.10
1988 Huntsville	AA	42	3	0	17	116.1	502	126	64	59	10	5	3	5	23	7	82	2	6	4	5	.444	0	3	4.56
1989 Tacoma	AAA	32	14	1	7	107.2	461	118	59	45	7	4	4	1	27	1	76	3	2	8	6	.571	1	0	3.76
1990 Tacoma	AAA	46	5	0	21	98.1	403	103	42	34	12	4	7	2	23	5	67	1	5	5	5	.500	0	7	3.11
1991 Tacoma	AAA	38	0	0	38	46.2	184	39	11	7	0	2	0	0	5	1	49	2	0	1	1	.500	0	20	1.35
1992 Tacoma	AAA	35	7	2	22	81.1	333	76	29	25	6	1	2	3	21	4	60	1	0	8	2	.800	1	8	2.77
1993 Ottawa	AAA	40	0	0	38	42.2	167	32	12	5	2	2	1	0	8	2	40	1	0	4	4	.500	0	16	1.05
Tucson	AAA	13	0	0	12	15	59	12	4	3	0	0	1	0	3	1	14	1	0	2	0	1.000	0	7	1.80
1991 Oakland	AL	12	0	0	5	13	56	11	9	9	3	0	1	1	6	0	10	3	0	1	0	1.000	0	0	6.23
1992 Oakland	AL	7	0	0	2	10	49	17	11	11	1	0	1	0	3	0	7	0	0	0	0	.000	0	0	9.90
1993 Montreal	NL	4	0	0	3	5.2	32	11	6	6	1	2	0	0	3	0	0	0	0	0	0	.000	0	0	9.53
3 ML YEARS		23	0	0	10	28.2	137	39	26	26	5	2	2	1	12	0	17	3	1	1	0	1.000	0	0	8.16

Jerome Walton

Bats: Right **Throws:** Right **Pos:** DH/LF **Ht:** 6' 1" **Wt:** 175 **Born:** 07/08/65 **Age:** 28

				BATTING															BASERUNNING				PERCENTAGES		
Year Team	Lg	G	AB	H	2B	3B	HR	(Hm	Rd)	TB	R	RBI	TBB	IBB	SO	HBP	SH	SF	SB	CS	SB%	GDP	Avg	OBP	SLG
1993 Vancouver *	AAA	54	176	55	11	1	2	(--	--)	74	34	20	16	0	24	1	8	1	5	4	.56	6	.313	.371	.420
1989 Chicago	NL	116	475	139	23	3	5	(3	2)	183	64	46	27	1	77	6	2	5	24	7	.77	6	.293	.335	.385
1990 Chicago	NL	101	392	103	16	2	2	(2	0)	129	63	21	50	1	70	4	1	2	14	7	.67	4	.263	.350	.329
1991 Chicago	NL	123	270	59	13	1	5	(3	2)	89	42	17	19	0	55	3	3	3	7	3	.70	4	.219	.275	.330
1992 Chicago	NL	30	55	7	0	1	0	(0	0)	9	7	1	9	0	13	2	3	0	1	2	.33	1	.127	.273	.164
1993 California	AL	5	2	0	0	0	0	(0	0)	0	2	0	1	0	2	0	0	0	1	0	1.00	0	.000	.333	.000
5 ML YEARS		375	1194	308	52	7	12	(8	4)	410	178	85	106	2	217	15	9	10	47	19	.71	18	.258	.324	.343

Duane Ward

Pitches: Right **Bats:** Right **Pos:** RP **Ht:** 6' 4" **Wt:** 215 **Born:** 05/28/64 **Age:** 30

		HOW MUCH HE PITCHED						WHAT HE GAVE UP												THE RESULTS					
Year Team	Lg	G	GS	CG	GF	IP	BFP	H	R	ER	HR	SH	SF	HB	TBB	IBB	SO	WP	Bk	W	L	Pct.	ShO	Sv	ERA
1986 2 ML Teams		12	1	0	7	18	88	25	17	16	2	2	1	1	12	0	9	1	1	0	2	.000	0	0	8.00
1987 Toronto	AL	12	1	0	4	11.2	57	14	9	9	0	1	1	0	12	2	10	0	0	1	0	1.000	0	0	6.94
1988 Toronto	AL	64	0	0	32	111.2	487	101	46	41	5	4	5	5	60	8	91	10	3	9	3	.750	0	15	3.30
1989 Toronto	AL	66	0	0	39	114.2	494	94	55	48	4	12	11	5	58	11	122	13	0	4	10	.286	0	15	3.77
1990 Toronto	AL	73	0	0	39	127.2	508	101	51	49	9	6	2	1	42	10	112	5	0	2	8	.200	0	11	3.45
1991 Toronto	AL	81	0	0	46	107.1	428	80	36	33	3	3	4	2	33	3	132	6	0	7	6	.538	0	23	2.77
1992 Toronto	AL	79	0	0	35	101.1	414	76	27	22	5	3	4	1	39	3	103	7	0	7	4	.636	0	12	1.95
1993 Toronto	AL	71	0	0	70	71.2	282	49	17	17	4	0	2	1	25	2	97	7	0	2	3	.400	0	45	2.13
1986 Atlanta	NL	10	0	0	6	16	73	22	13	13	2	2	0	0	8	0	8	0	1	0	1	.000	0	0	7.31
Toronto	AL	2	1	0	1	2	15	3	4	3	0	0	0	1	4	0	1	1	0	0	0	.000	0	0	13.50
8 ML YEARS		458	2	0	272	664	2758	540	258	235	32	31	29	16	281	39	676	49	4	32	36	.471	0	121	3.19

Turner Ward

Bats: Both **Throws:** Right **Pos:** LF/RF **Ht:** 6' 2" **Wt:** 200 **Born:** 04/11/65 **Age:** 29

				BATTING															BASERUNNING				PERCENTAGES		
Year Team	Lg	G	AB	H	2B	3B	HR	(Hm	Rd)	TB	R	RBI	TBB	IBB	SO	HBP	SH	SF	SB	CS	SB%	GDP	Avg	OBP	SLG
1993 Knoxville *	AA	7	23	6	2	0	0	--	--	8	6	2	7	0	3	0	0	0	3	0	1.00	1	.261	.433	.348
1990 Cleveland	AL	14	46	16	2	1	1	(0	1)	23	10	10	3	0	8	0	0	0	3	1	1.00	1	.348	.388	.500
1991 2 ML Teams		48	113	27	7	0	0	(0	0)	34	12	7	11	0	18	0	4	0	0	0	.00	2	.239	.306	.301
1992 Toronto	AL	18	29	10	3	0	1	(0	1)	16	7	3	4	0	4	0	0	0		1	.00	1	.345	.424	.552
1993 Toronto	AL	72	167	32	4	2	4	(2	2)	52	20	28	23	2	26	1	3	4	3	3	.50	7	.192	.287	.311
1991 Cleveland	AL	40	100	23	7	0	0	(0	0)	30	11	5	10	0	16	0	4	0	0	0	.00	1	.230	.300	.300
Toronto	AL	8	13	4	0	0	0	(0	0)	4	1	2	1	0	2	0	0	0	0	0	.00	1	.308	.357	.308
4 ML YEARS		152	355	85	16	3	6	(2	4)	125	49	48	41	2	56	1	7	4	6	4	.60	11	.239	.317	.352

Allen Watson

Pitches: Left **Bats:** Left **Pos:** SP **Ht:** 6' 3" **Wt:** 195 **Born:** 11/18/70 **Age:** 23

		HOW MUCH HE PITCHED						WHAT HE GAVE UP												THE RESULTS					
Year Team	Lg	G	GS	CG	GF	IP	BFP	H	R	ER	HR	SH	SF	HB	TBB	IBB	SO	WP	Bk	W	L	Pct.	ShO	Sv	ERA
1991 Hamilton	A	8	8	0	0	39.1	156	22	14	10	1	0	1	0	17	0	46	1	0	1	1	.500	0	0	2.29
Savannah	A	3	3	0	0	13.2	62	16	7	6	1	0	2	0	8	0	12	1	1	1	1	.500	0	0	3.95
1992 St. Pete	A	14	14	2	0	89.2	374	81	31	19	0	4	1	2	18	2	80	1	0	5	4	.556	0	0	1.91
Arkansas	AA	14	14	3	0	96.1	376	77	24	23	4	4	0	2	23	1	93	0	3	8	5	.615	1	0	2.15
Louisville	AAA	2	2	0	0	12.1	53	8	4	2	1	0	0	0	5	0	9	2	0	1	0	1.000	0	0	1.46
1993 Louisville	AAA	17	17	2	0	120.2	483	101	46	39	13	5	0	4	31	0	86	2	3	5	4	.556	0	0	2.91
1993 St. Louis	NL	16	15	0	1	86	373	90	53	44	11	6	4	3	28	2	49	2	1	6	7	.462	0	0	4.60

Gary Wayne

Pitches: Left **Bats:** Left **Pos:** RP   **Ht:** 6' 3" **Wt:** 195 **Born:** 11/30/62 **Age:** 31

		HOW MUCH HE PITCHED						WHAT HE GAVE UP										THE RESULTS				
Year Team	Lg	G	GS	CG	GF	IP	BFP	H	R	ER	HR	SH	SF	HB	TBB	IBB	SO	WP	Bk	W	L	Pct.	ShO	Sv	ERA
1989 Minnesota	AL	60	0	0	21	71	302	55	28	26	4	4	2	1	36	4	41	7	0	3	4	.429	0	1	3.30
1990 Minnesota	AL	38	0	0	12	38.2	166	38	19	18	5	1	2	1	13	0	28	4	0	1	1	.500	0	1	4.19
1991 Minnesota	AL	8	0	0	2	12.1	52	11	7	7	1	1	1	1	4	0	7	0	0	1	0	1.000	0	0	5.11
1992 Minnesota	AL	41	0	0	13	48	210	46	18	14	2	8	3	3	19	5	29	1	1	3	3	.500	0	0	2.63
1993 Colorado	NL	65	0	0	21	62.1	283	68	40	35	8	3	7	1	26	8	49	9	1	5	3	.625	0	1	5.05
5 ML YEARS		212	0	0	69	232.1	1013	218	112	100	20	17	15	7	98	17	154	21	2	13	11	.542	0	4	3.87

Dave Weathers

Pitches: Right **Bats:** Right **Pos:** RP/SP   **Ht:** 6' 3" **Wt:** 205 **Born:** 09/25/69 **Age:** 24

		HOW MUCH HE PITCHED						WHAT HE GAVE UP										THE RESULTS				
Year Team	Lg	G	GS	CG	GF	IP	BFP	H	R	ER	HR	SH	SF	HB	TBB	IBB	SO	WP	Bk	W	L	Pct.	ShO	Sv	ERA
1988 St.Cathmes	A	15	12	0	2	62.2	267	58	30	21	3	2	0	2	26	0	36	5	4	4	4	.500	0	0	3.02
1989 Myrtle Bch	A	31	31	2	0	172.2	759	163	99	74	3	5	2	7	86	2	111	12	1	11	13	.458	0	0	3.86
1990 Dunedin	A	27	27	2	0	158	675	158	82	65	2	4	7	9	59	0	96	10	9	10	7	.588	0	0	3.70
1991 Knoxville	AA	24	22	5	0	139.1	575	121	51	38	3	1	3	8	49	1	114	7	2	10	7	.588	2	0	2.45
1992 Syracuse	AAA	12	10	0	1	48.1	215	48	29	25	3	2	1	2	21	2	30	2	0	1	4	.200	0	0	4.66
1993 Edmonton	AAA	22	22	3	0	141	611	150	77	60	12	5	3	2	47	2	117	4	1	11	4	.733	1	0	3.83
1991 Toronto	AL	15	0	0	4	14.2	79	15	9	8	1	2	1	2	17	3	13	0	0	1	0	1.000	0	0	4.91
1992 Toronto	AL	2	0	0	0	3.1	15	5	3	3	1	0	0	0	2	0	3	0	0	0	0	.000	0	0	8.10
1993 Florida	NL	14	6	0	2	45.2	202	57	26	26	3	2	0	1	13	1	34	6	0	2	3	.400	0	0	5.12
3 ML YEARS		31	6	0	6	63.2	296	77	38	37	5	4	1	3	32	4	50	6	0	3	3	.500	0	0	5.23

Lenny Webster

Bats: Right **Throws:** Right **Pos:** C   **Ht:** 5' 9" **Wt:** 191 **Born:** 02/10/65 **Age:** 29

		BATTING																BASERUNNING				PERCENTAGES		
Year Team	Lg	G	AB	H	2B	3B	HR	(Hm	Rd)	TB	R	RBI	TBB	IBB	SO	HBP	SH	SF	SB	CS	SB%	GDP	Avg	OBP	SLG
1989 Minnesota	AL	14	20	6	2	0	0	(0	0)	8	3	1	3	0	2	0	0	0	0	0	.00	0	.300	.391	.400
1990 Minnesota	AL	2	6	2	1	0	0	(0	0)	3	1	0	1	0	1	0	0	0	0	0	.00	0	.333	.429	.500
1991 Minnesota	AL	18	34	10	1	0	3	(1	2)	20	7	8	6	0	10	0	0	1	0	0	.00	2	.294	.390	.588
1992 Minnesota	AL	53	118	33	10	1	1	(1	0)	48	10	13	9	0	11	0	2	0	0	2	.00	3	.280	.331	.407
1993 Minnesota	AL	49	106	21	2	0	1	(1	0)	26	14	8	11	1	8	0	0	0	1	0	1.00	1	.198	.274	.245
5 ML YEARS		136	284	72	16	1	5	(3	2)	105	35	30	30	1	32	0	2	1	1	2	.33	6	.254	.324	.370

Mitch Webster

Bats: Both **Throws:** Left **Pos:** LF/RF   **Ht:** 6' 1" **Wt:** 191 **Born:** 05/16/59 **Age:** 35

		BATTING																BASERUNNING				PERCENTAGES		
Year Team	Lg	G	AB	H	2B	3B	HR	(Hm	Rd)	TB	R	RBI	TBB	IBB	SO	HBP	SH	SF	SB	CS	SB%	GDP	Avg	OBP	SLG
1983 Toronto	AL	11	11	2	0	0	0	(0	0)	2	2	0	1	0	1	0	0	0	0	0	.00	0	.182	.250	.182
1984 Toronto	AL	26	22	5	2	1	0	(0	0)	9	9	4	1	0	7	0	0	0	0	0	.00	1	.227	.261	.409
1985 2 ML Teams		78	213	58	8	2	11	(3	8)	103	32	30	20	3	33	0	1	1	15	10	.60	3	.272	.333	.484
1986 Montreal	NL	151	576	167	31	13	8	(2	6)	248	89	49	57	4	78	4	3	5	36	15	.71	9	.290	.355	.431
1987 Montreal	NL	156	588	165	30	8	15	(9	6)	256	101	63	70	5	95	6	8	4	33	10	.77	6	.281	.361	.435
1988 2 ML Teams		151	523	136	16	8	6	(3	3)	186	69	39	55	2	87	8	5	4	22	14	.61	5	.260	.337	.356
1989 Chicago	NL	98	272	70	12	4	3	(1	2)	99	40	19	30	5	55	1	3	2	14	2	.88	3	.257	.331	.364
1990 Cleveland	AL	128	437	110	20	6	12	(6	6)	178	58	55	20	1	61	3	11	6	22	6	.79	5	.252	.285	.407
1991 3 ML Teams		107	203	42	8	5	2	(2	0)	66	23	19	21	1	61	0	2	0	2	3	.40	3	.207	.281	.325
1992 Los Angeles	NL	135	262	70	12	5	6	(1	5)	110	33	35	27	3	49	2	8	5	11	5	.69	1	.267	.334	.420
1993 Los Angeles	NL	88	172	42	6	2	2	(1	1)	58	26	14	11	2	24	2	4	3	4	6	.40	3	.244	.293	.337
1985 Toronto	AL	4	1	0	0	0	0	(0	0)	0	0	0	0	0	0	0	0	0	0	1	.00	0	.000	.000	.000
Montreal	NL	74	212	58	8	2	11	(3	8)	103	32	30	20	3	33	0	1	1	15	9	.63	3	.274	.335	.486
1988 Montreal	NL	81	259	66	5	2	2	(0	2)	81	33	13	36	2	37	5	4	2	12	10	.55	3	.255	.354	.313
Chicago	NL	70	264	70	11	6	4	(3	1)	105	36	26	19	0	50	3	1	2	10	4	.71	2	.265	.319	.398
1991 Cleveland	AL	13	32	4	0	0	0	(0	0)	4	2	0	3	0	9	0	1	0	2	2	.50	1	.125	.200	.125
Pittsburgh	NL	36	97	17	3	4	1	(1	0)	31	9	9	9	1	31	0	0	0	0	0	.00	3	.175	.245	.320
Los Angeles	NL	58	74	21	5	1	1	(1	0)	31	12	10	9	0	21	0	1	0	0	1	.00	0	.284	.361	.419
11 ML YEARS		1129	3279	867	145	54	65	(28	37)	1315	482	327	313	26	551	26	45	30	159	71	.69	39	.264	.331	.401

Eric Wedge

Bats: Right **Throws:** Right **Pos:** C   **Ht:** 6' 3" **Wt:** 215 **Born:** 01/27/68 **Age:** 26

		BATTING																BASERUNNING				PERCENTAGES		
Year Team	Lg	G	AB	H	2B	3B	HR	(Hm	Rd)	TB	R	RBI	TBB	IBB	SO	HBP	SH	SF	SB	CS	SB%	GDP	Avg	OBP	SLG
1989 Elmira	A	41	145	34	6	2	7	--	--	65	20	22	15	0	21	0	0	0	1	1	.50	3	.234	.306	.448
New Britain	AA	14	40	8	2	0	0	--	--	10	3	2	5	0	10	0	2	0	0	0	.00	1	.200	.289	.250
1990 New Britain	AA	103	339	77	13	1	5	--	--	107	36	48	51	2	54	1	0	5	1	3	.25	14	.227	.326	.316

Year	Team	Lg	G	AB	H	2B	3B	HR	(Hm	Rd)	TB	R	RBI	TBB	IBB	SO	HBP	SH	SF	SB	CS	SB%	GDP	Avg	OBP	SLG
1991	New Britain	AA	2	8	2	0	0	0	--	--	2	0	2	0	0	2	0	0	1	0	0	.00	0	.250	.222	.250
	Winter Havn	A	8	21	5	0	0	1	--	--	8	2	1	3	0	7	0	1	0	1	0	1.00	1	.238	.333	.381
	Pawtucket	AAA	53	163	38	14	1	5	--	--	69	24	18	25	0	26	1	2	5	1	2	.33	3	.233	.330	.423
1992	Pawtucket	AAA	65	211	63	9	0	11	--	--	105	28	40	32	3	40	1	0	3	0	0	.00	6	.299	.389	.498
1993	Central Val	A	6	23	7	0	0	3	--	--	16	6	11	2	1	6	0	0	0	0	0	.00	0	.304	.360	.696
	Colo Sprngs	AAA	38	90	24	6	0	3	--	--	39	17	13	16	1	22	2	0	0	0	0	.00	4	.267	.389	.433
1991	Boston	AL	1	1	1	0	0	0	(0	0)	1	0	0	0	0	0	0	0	0	0	0	.00	0	1.000	1.000	1.000
1992	Boston	AL	27	68	17	2	0	5	(3	2)	34	11	11	13	0	18	0	0	0	0	0	.00	0	.250	.370	.500
1993	Colorado	NL	9	11	2	0	0	0	(0	0)	2	2	1	0	0	4	0	0	0	0	0	.00	0	.182	.182	.182
	3 ML YEARS		37	80	20	2	0	5	(3	2)	37	13	12	13	0	22	0	0	0	0	0	.00	0	.250	.355	.463

Bill Wegman

Pitches: Right **Bats:** Right **Pos:** SP   **Ht:** 6' 5" **Wt:** 220 **Born:** 12/19/62 **Age:** 31

Year	Team	Lg	G	GS	CG	GF	IP	BFP	H	R	ER	HR	SH	SF	HB	TBB	IBB	SO	WP	Bk	W	L	Pct.	ShO	Sv	ERA
1985	Milwaukee	AL	3	3	0	0	17.2	73	17	8	7	3	0	1	0	3	0	6	0	1	2	0	1.000	0	0	3.57
1986	Milwaukee	AL	35	32	2	1	198.1	836	217	120	113	32	4	5	7	43	2	82	5	2	5	12	.294	0	0	5.13
1987	Milwaukee	AL	34	33	7	0	225	934	229	113	106	31	4	6	6	53	2	102	0	2	12	11	.522	0	0	4.24
1988	Milwaukee	AL	32	31	4	0	199	847	207	104	91	24	3	10	4	50	5	84	1	1	13	13	.500	1	0	4.12
1989	Milwaukee	AL	11	8	0	1	51	240	69	44	38	6	0	4	0	21	2	27	2	0	2	6	.250	0	0	6.71
1990	Milwaukee	AL	8	5	1	0	29.2	132	37	21	16	6	1	1	0	6	1	20	0	0	2	2	.500	1	0	4.85
1991	Milwaukee	AL	28	28	7	0	193.1	785	176	76	61	16	6	4	7	40	0	89	6	0	15	7	.682	2	0	2.84
1992	Milwaukee	AL	35	35	7	0	261.2	1079	251	104	93	28	7	4	9	55	3	127	1	2	13	14	.481	0	0	3.20
1993	Milwaukee	AL	20	18	5	0	120.2	514	135	70	60	13	3	11	2	34	5	50	0	2	4	14	.222	0	0	4.48
	9 ML YEARS		206	193	33	2	1296.1	5440	1338	660	585	159	28	46	35	305	20	587	15	8	68	79	.463	4	0	4.06

John Wehner

Bats: Right **Throws:** Right **Pos:** CF   **Ht:** 6' 3" **Wt:** 205 **Born:** 06/29/67 **Age:** 27

Year	Team	Lg	G	AB	H	2B	3B	HR	(Hm	Rd)	TB	R	RBI	TBB	IBB	SO	HBP	SH	SF	SB	CS	SB%	GDP	Avg	OBP	SLG
1993	Buffalo *	AAA	89	330	83	22	2	7	--	--	130	61	34	40	2	53	1	2	2	17	3	.85	5	.252	.332	.394
1991	Pittsburgh	NL	37	106	36	7	0	0	(0	0)	43	15	7	7	0	17	0	0	0	3	0	1.00	5	.340	.381	.406
1992	Pittsburgh	NL	55	123	22	6	0	0	(0	0)	28	11	4	12	2	22	0	2	0	3	0	1.00	4	.179	.252	.228
1993	Pittsburgh	NL	29	35	5	0	0	0	(0	0)	5	3	0	6	1	10	0	2	0	0	0	.00	0	.143	.268	.143
	3 ML YEARS		121	264	63	13	0	0	(0	0)	76	29	11	25	3	49	0	4	0	6	0	1.00	4	.239	.304	.288

Walt Weiss

Bats: Both **Throws:** Right **Pos:** SS   **Ht:** 6' 0" **Wt:** 175 **Born:** 11/28/63 **Age:** 30

Year	Team	Lg	G	AB	H	2B	3B	HR	(Hm	Rd)	TB	R	RBI	TBB	IBB	SO	HBP	SH	SF	SB	CS	SB%	GDP	Avg	OBP	SLG
1987	Oakland	AL	16	26	12	4	0	0	(0	0)	16	3	1	2	0	2	0	1	0	1	2	.33	0	.462	.500	.615
1988	Oakland	AL	147	452	113	17	3	3	(0	3)	145	44	39	35	1	56	9	8	7	4	4	.50	9	.250	.312	.321
1989	Oakland	AL	84	236	55	11	0	3	(2	1)	75	30	21	21	0	39	1	5	0	6	1	.86	5	.233	.298	.318
1990	Oakland	AL	138	445	118	17	1	2	(1	1)	143	50	35	46	5	53	4	6	4	9	3	.75	7	.265	.337	.321
1991	Oakland	AL	40	133	30	6	1	0	(0	0)	38	15	13	12	0	14	0	1	2	6	0	1.00	3	.226	.286	.286
1992	Oakland	AL	103	316	67	5	2	0	(0	0)	76	36	21	43	1	39	1	11	4	6	3	.67	10	.212	.305	.241
1993	Florida	NL	158	500	133	14	2	1	(0	1)	154	50	39	79	13	73	3	5	4	7	3	.70	5	.266	.367	.308
	7 ML YEARS		686	2108	528	74	9	9	(3	6)	647	228	169	238	20	276	18	37	21	39	16	.71	39	.250	.329	.307

Bob Welch

Pitches: Right **Bats:** Right **Pos:** SP   **Ht:** 6' 3" **Wt:** 198 **Born:** 11/03/56 **Age:** 37

Year	Team	Lg	G	GS	CG	GF	IP	BFP	H	R	ER	HR	SH	SF	HB	TBB	IBB	SO	WP	Bk	W	L	Pct.	ShO	Sv	ERA
1978	Los Angeles	NL	23	13	4	6	111	439	92	28	25	6	4	6	4	26	2	66	2	2	7	4	.636	3	3	2.03
1979	Los Angeles	NL	25	12	1	10	81	349	82	42	36	7	4	1	3	32	4	64	0	0	5	6	.455	0	5	4.00
1980	Los Angeles	NL	32	32	3	0	214	889	190	85	78	15	12	10	3	79	6	141	7	5	14	9	.609	2	0	3.28
1981	Los Angeles	NL	23	23	2	0	141	601	141	56	54	11	9	4	3	41	0	88	2	0	9	5	.643	1	0	3.45
1982	Los Angeles	NL	36	36	9	0	235.2	965	199	94	88	19	7	4	5	81	5	176	5	1	16	11	.593	3	0	3.36
1983	Los Angeles	NL	31	31	4	0	204	828	164	73	60	13	8	7	3	72	4	156	4	6	15	12	.556	3	0	2.65
1984	Los Angeles	NL	31	29	3	0	178.2	771	191	86	75	11	10	2	2	58	7	126	4	2	13	13	.500	1	0	3.78
1985	Los Angeles	NL	23	23	8	0	167.1	675	141	49	43	16	6	2	6	35	2	96	7	4	14	4	.778	3	0	2.31
1986	Los Angeles	NL	33	33	7	0	235.2	981	227	95	86	14	7	8	7	55	6	183	2	1	7	13	.350	3	0	3.28
1987	Los Angeles	NL	35	35	6	0	251.2	1027	204	94	90	21	10	6	4	86	6	196	4	4	15	9	.625	4	0	3.22
1988	Oakland	AL	36	36	4	0	244.2	1034	237	107	99	22	12	8	10	81	1	158	3	13	17	9	.654	2	0	3.64
1989	Oakland	AL	33	33	1	0	209.2	884	191	82	70	13	3	4	6	78	3	137	5	0	17	8	.680	0	0	3.00
1990	Oakland	AL	35	35	2	0	238	979	214	90	78	26	6	5	5	77	4	127	2	2	27	6	.818	2	0	2.95
1991	Oakland	AL	35	35	7	0	220	950	220	124	112	25	6	6	11	91	3	101	3	2	12	13	.480	1	0	4.58

Year	Team	Lg	G	GS	CG	GF	IP	BFP	H	R	ER	HR	SH	SF	HB	TBB	IBB	SO	WP	Bk	W	L	Pct.	ShO	Sv	ERA
1992	Oakland	AL	20	20	0	0	123.2	513	114	47	45	13	3	3	2	43	0	47	1	0	11	7	.611	0	0	3.27
1993	Oakland	AL	30	28	0	0	166.2	746	208	102	98	25	10	3	7	56	5	63	1	0	9	11	.450	0	0	5.29
	16 ML YEARS		481	454	61	16	3022.2	12631	2815	1254	1137	257	117	79	78	991	58	1925	52	42	208	140	.598	28	8	3.39

David Wells

Pitches: Left **Bats:** Left **Pos:** SP   **Ht:** 6' 4" **Wt:** 225 **Born:** 05/20/63 **Age:** 31

			HOW MUCH HE PITCHED						WHAT HE GAVE UP											THE RESULTS					
Year	Team	Lg	G	GS	CG	GF	IP	BFP	H	R	ER	HR	SH	SF	HB	TBB	IBB	SO	WP	Bk	W	L	Pct.	ShO	Sv	ERA
1987	Toronto	AL	18	2	0	6	29.1	132	37	14	13	0	1	0	0	12	0	32	4	0	4	3	.571	0	1	3.99
1988	Toronto	AL	41	0	0	15	64.1	279	65	36	33	12	2	2	2	31	9	56	6	2	3	5	.375	0	4	4.62
1989	Toronto	AL	54	0	0	19	86.1	352	66	25	23	5	3	2	0	28	7	78	6	3	7	4	.636	0	2	2.40
1990	Toronto	AL	43	25	0	8	189	759	165	72	66	14	9	2	2	45	3	115	7	1	11	6	.647	0	3	3.14
1991	Toronto	AL	40	28	2	3	198.1	811	188	88	82	24	6	6	2	49	1	106	10	3	15	10	.600	0	1	3.72
1992	Toronto	AL	41	14	0	14	120	529	138	84	72	16	3	4	8	36	6	62	3	1	7	9	.438	0	2	5.40
1993	Detroit	AL	32	30	0	0	187	776	183	93	87	26	3	3	7	42	6	139	13	0	11	9	.550	0	0	4.19
	7 ML YEARS		269	99	2	65	874.1	3638	842	412	376	97	27	19	21	243	32	588	49	10	58	46	.558	0	13	3.87

Turk Wendell

Pitches: Right **Bats:** Both **Pos:** SP   **Ht:** 6' 2" **Wt:** 180 **Born:** 05/19/67 **Age:** 27

			HOW MUCH HE PITCHED						WHAT HE GAVE UP											THE RESULTS					
Year	Team	Lg	G	GS	CG	GF	IP	BFP	H	R	ER	HR	SH	SF	HB	TBB	IBB	SO	WP	Bk	W	L	Pct.	ShO	Sv	ERA
1988	Pulaski	R	14	14	6	0	101	418	85	50	43	3	5	2	6	30	0	87	7	6	3	8	.273	1	0	3.83
1989	Burlington	A	22	22	9	0	159	643	127	63	39	7	2	0	3	41	1	153	1	6	9	11	.450	5	0	2.21
	Greenville	AA	1	1	0	0	3.2	19	7	5	4	3	0	0	0	1	0	3	0	0	0	0	.000	0	0	9.82
	Durham	A	3	3	1	0	24	89	13	4	3	0	0	0	0	6	0	27	0	0	2	0	1.000	0	0	1.13
1990	Greenville	AA	36	13	1	13	91	434	105	70	58	5	5	6	11	48	2	85	8	2	4	9	.308	1	2	5.74
	Durham	A	6	5	1	0	38.2	154	24	10	8	3	0	0	2	15	1	26	2	0	1	3	.250	0	0	1.86
1991	Greenville	AA	25	20	1	3	147.2	613	130	47	42	4	2	2	6	51	5	122	11	0	11	3	.786	1	0	2.56
	Richmond	AAA	3	3	1	0	21	97	20	9	8	3	1	0	3	16	0	18	2	0	0	2	.000	0	0	3.43
1992	Iowa	AAA	4	4	0	0	25	107	17	7	4	3	2	1	0	15	0	12	1	0	2	0	1.000	0	0	1.44
1993	Iowa	AAA	25	25	3	0	148.2	639	148	88	76	9	4	6	6	47	0	110	9	3	10	8	.556	0	0	4.60
1993	Chicago	NL	7	4	0	1	22.2	98	24	13	11	0	2	0	0	8	1	15	1	1	1	2	.333	0	0	4.37

Bill Wertz

Pitches: Right **Bats:** Right **Pos:** RP   **Ht:** 6' 6" **Wt:** 220 **Born:** 01/15/67 **Age:** 27

			HOW MUCH HE PITCHED						WHAT HE GAVE UP											THE RESULTS					
Year	Team	Lg	G	GS	CG	GF	IP	BFP	H	R	ER	HR	SH	SF	HB	TBB	IBB	SO	WP	Bk	W	L	Pct.	ShO	Sv	ERA
1989	Indians	R	12	11	1	0	66	282	57	23	23	0	1	4	4	36	0	56	11	0	4	3	.571	1	0	3.14
1990	Reno	A	17	9	0	1	61.1	295	61	58	45	6	3	4	5	52	0	52	12	0	1	3	.250	0	0	6.60
	Watertown	A	14	14	2	0	100.2	431	81	39	32	3	2	3	4	48	0	92	6	0	10	2	.833	0	0	2.86
1991	Columbus	A	49	0	0	31	91	391	81	41	30	6	6	4	6	32	3	95	5	0	6	8	.429	0	9	2.97
1992	Canton-Akrn	AA	57	0	0	24	97.1	382	75	16	13	1	3	2	3	30	6	69	3	0	8	4	.667	0	8	1.20
1993	Charlotte	AAA	28	1	0	9	50.2	207	42	18	11	4	3	0	1	14	4	47	1	0	7	2	.778	0	0	1.95
1993	Cleveland	AL	34	0	0	7	59.2	262	54	28	24	5	1	1	1	32	2	53	0	0	2	3	.400	0	0	3.62

David West

Pitches: Left **Bats:** Left **Pos:** RP   **Ht:** 6' 6" **Wt:** 230 **Born:** 09/01/64 **Age:** 29

			HOW MUCH HE PITCHED						WHAT HE GAVE UP											THE RESULTS					
Year	Team	Lg	G	GS	CG	GF	IP	BFP	H	R	ER	HR	SH	SF	HB	TBB	IBB	SO	WP	Bk	W	L	Pct.	ShO	Sv	ERA
1988	New York	NL	2	1	0	0	6	25	6	2	2	0	0	0	0	3	0	3	0	2	1	0	1.000	0	0	3.00
1989	2 ML Teams		21	7	0	4	63.2	294	73	49	48	9	2	3	3	33	3	50	2	0	3	4	.429	0	0	6.79
1990	Minnesota	AL	29	27	2	0	146.1	646	142	88	83	21	6	4	4	78	1	92	4	1	7	9	.438	0	0	5.10
1991	Minnesota	AL	15	12	0	0	71.1	305	66	37	36	13	2	3	1	28	0	52	3	0	4	4	.500	0	0	4.54
1992	Minnesota	AL	9	3	0	1	28.1	139	32	24	22	3	0	2	1	20	0	19	2	0	1	3	.250	0	0	6.99
1993	Philadelphia	NL	76	0	0	27	86.1	375	60	37	28	6	8	2	5	51	4	87	3	0	6	4	.600	0	3	2.92
1989	New York	NL	11	2	0	0	24.1	112	25	20	20	4	0	1	1	14	2	19	1	0	0	2	.000	0	0	7.40
	Minnesota	AL	10	5	0	4	39.1	182	48	29	28	5	2	2	2	19	1	31	1	0	3	2	.600	0	0	6.41
	6 ML YEARS		152	50	2	32	402	1784	379	237	219	52	18	14	14	213	8	303	14	3	22	24	.478	0	3	4.90

Mickey Weston

Pitches: Right **Bats:** Right **Pos:** RP   **Ht:** 6' 1" **Wt:** 180 **Born:** 03/26/61 **Age:** 33

			HOW MUCH HE PITCHED						WHAT HE GAVE UP											THE RESULTS					
Year	Team	Lg	G	GS	CG	GF	IP	BFP	H	R	ER	HR	SH	SF	HB	TBB	IBB	SO	WP	Bk	W	L	Pct.	ShO	Sv	ERA
1993	Norfolk *	AAA	21	20	3	1	127.1	542	149	77	60	10	3	2	2	18	2	41	4	0	10	9	.526	2	0	4.24
1989	Baltimore	AL	7	0	0	2	13	55	18	8	8	1	0	0	1	2	0	7	0	0	1	0	1.000	0	1	5.54
1990	Baltimore	AL	9	2	0	4	21	94	28	20	18	6	1	0	0	6	1	9	1	0	0	1	.000	0	0	7.71

Year	Team	Lg	G	GS	CG	GF	IP	BFP	H	R	ER	HR	SH	SF	HB	TBB	IBB	SO	WP	Bk	W	L	Pct.	ShO	Sv	ERA
1991	Toronto	AL	2	0	0	2	2	8	1	0	0	0	0	0	0	1	1	1	0	0	0	0	.000	0	0	0.00
1992	Philadelphia	NL	1	1	0	0	3.2	19	7	5	5	1	0	0	1	1	0	0	0	0	0	0	.000	0	0	12.27
1993	New York	NL	4	0	0	0	5.2	30	11	5	5	0	0	0	1	1	0	2	0	0	0	0	.000	0	0	7.94
	5 ML YEARS		23	3	0	8	45.1	206	65	38	36	8	1	0	3	11	2	19	1	0	1	2	.333	0	1	7.15

John Wetteland

Pitches: Right **Bats:** Right **Pos:** RP   **Ht:** 6' 2" **Wt:** 210 **Born:** 08/21/66 **Age:** 27

			HOW MUCH HE PITCHED						WHAT HE GAVE UP										THE RESULTS					
Year	Team	Lg	G	GS	CG	GF	IP	BFP	H	R	ER	HR	SH	SF	HB	TBB	IBB	SO	WP	Bk	W	L	Pct.	ShO	Sv	ERA
1993	Wst Plm Bch *	A	0	0	0	0	0	0	0	0	0	0	0	0	0	0	0	6	0	0	0	0	.000	0	0	0.00
1989	Los Angeles	NL	31	12	0	7	102.2	411	81	46	43	8	4	2	0	34	4	96	16	1	5	8	.385	0	1	3.77
1990	Los Angeles	NL	22	5	0	7	43	190	44	28	23	6	1	1	4	17	3	36	8	0	2	4	.333	0	0	4.81
1991	Los Angeles	NL	6	0	0	3	9	36	5	2	0	0	0	1	1	3	0	9	1	0	1	0	1.000	0	0	0.00
1992	Montreal	NL	67	0	0	58	83.1	347	64	27	27	6	5	1	4	36	3	99	4	0	4	4	.500	0	37	2.92
1993	Montreal	NL	70	0	0	58	85.1	344	58	17	13	3	5	1	2	28	3	113	7	0	9	3	.750	0	43	1.37
	5 ML YEARS		196	17	0	133	323.1	1328	252	120	106	23	15	6	11	118	13	353	36	1	21	19	.525	0	81	2.95

Lou Whitaker

Bats: Left **Throws:** Right **Pos:** 2B   **Ht:** 5'11" **Wt:** 180 **Born:** 05/12/57 **Age:** 37

						BATTING														BASERUNNING				PERCENTAGES		
Year	Team	Lg	G	AB	H	2B	3B	HR	(Hm	Rd)	TB	R	RBI	TBB	IBB	SO	HBP	SH	SF	SB	CS	SB%	GDP	Avg	OBP	SLG
1977	Detroit	AL	11	32	8	1	0	0	(0	0)	9	5	2	4	0	6	0	1	0	2	2	.50	0	.250	.333	.281
1978	Detroit	AL	139	484	138	12	7	3	(2	1)	173	71	58	61	0	65	1	13	8	7	7	.50	9	.285	.361	.357
1979	Detroit	AL	127	423	121	14	8	3	(3	0)	160	75	42	78	2	66	1	14	4	20	10	.67	10	.286	.395	.378
1980	Detroit	AL	145	477	111	19	1	1	(1	0)	135	68	45	73	0	79	0	12	6	8	4	.67	9	.233	.331	.283
1981	Detroit	AL	109	335	88	14	4	5	(4	1)	125	48	36	40	3	42	1	3	3	5	3	.63	5	.263	.340	.373
1982	Detroit	AL	152	560	160	22	8	15	(9	6)	243	76	65	48	4	58	1	6	4	11	3	.79	8	.286	.341	.434
1983	Detroit	AL	161	643	206	40	6	12	(7	5)	294	94	72	67	8	70	0	2	8	17	10	.63	9	.320	.380	.457
1984	Detroit	AL	143	558	161	25	1	13	(8	5)	227	90	56	62	5	63	0	4	5	6	5	.55	9	.289	.357	.407
1985	Detroit	AL	152	609	170	29	8	21	(11	10)	278	102	73	80	9	56	2	5	5	6	4	.60	3	.279	.362	.456
1986	Detroit	AL	144	584	157	26	6	20	(8	12)	255	95	73	63	5	70	0	0	4	13	8	.62	20	.269	.338	.437
1987	Detroit	AL	149	604	160	38	6	16	(10	6)	258	110	59	71	2	108	1	4	4	13	5	.72	5	.265	.341	.427
1988	Detroit	AL	115	403	111	18	2	12	(8	4)	169	54	55	66	5	61	0	6	2	2	0	1.00	8	.275	.376	.419
1989	Detroit	AL	148	509	128	21	1	28	(17	11)	235	77	85	89	6	59	3	1	9	6	3	.67	7	.251	.361	.462
1990	Detroit	AL	132	472	112	22	2	18	(8	10)	192	75	60	74	7	71	0	1	5	8	2	.80	10	.237	.338	.407
1991	Detroit	AL	138	470	131	26	2	23	(15	8)	230	94	78	90	6	45	2	2	8	4	2	.67	3	.279	.391	.489
1992	Detroit	AL	130	453	126	26	0	19	(11	8)	209	77	71	81	5	46	1	5	4	6	4	.60	9	.278	.386	.461
1993	Detroit	AL	119	383	111	32	1	9	(5	4)	172	72	67	78	4	46	4	7	4	3	3	.50	5	.290	.412	.449
	17 ML YEARS		2214	7999	2199	385	63	218	(127	91)	3364	1283	997	1125	71	1011	17	86	83	137	75	.65	129	.275	.362	.421

Derrick White

Bats: Right **Throws:** Right **Pos:** 1B   **Ht:** 6' 1" **Wt:** 215 **Born:** 10/12/69 **Age:** 24

						BATTING														BASERUNNING				PERCENTAGES		
Year	Team	Lg	G	AB	H	2B	3B	HR	(Hm	Rd)	TB	R	RBI	TBB	IBB	SO	HBP	SH	SF	SB	CS	SB%	GDP	Avg	OBP	SLG
1991	Jamestown	A	72	271	89	10	4	6	--	--	125	46	49	40	0	46	7	0	2	8	3	.73	8	.328	.425	.461
1992	Harrisburg	AA	134	495	137	19	2	13	--	--	199	63	81	40	3	73	7	0	2	17	3	.85	16	.277	.338	.402
1993	Wst Plm Bch	A	6	25	5	0	0	0	--	--	5	1	1	1	0	2	0	0	0	2	0	1.00	0	.200	.231	.200
	Ottawa	AAA	67	249	70	15	1	4	--	--	99	32	29	20	2	52	3	0	1	10	7	.59	10	.281	.341	.398
	Harrisburg	AA	21	79	18	1	0	2	--	--	25	14	12	5	0	17	2	0	1	2	0	1.00	2	.228	.287	.316
1993	Montreal	NL	17	49	11	3	0	2	(1	1)	20	6	4	2	1	12	1	0	0	2	0	1.00	1	.224	.269	.408

Devon White

Bats: Both **Throws:** Right **Pos:** CF   **Ht:** 6' 2" **Wt:** 182 **Born:** 12/29/62 **Age:** 31

						BATTING														BASERUNNING				PERCENTAGES		
Year	Team	Lg	G	AB	H	2B	3B	HR	(Hm	Rd)	TB	R	RBI	TBB	IBB	SO	HBP	SH	SF	SB	CS	SB%	GDP	Avg	OBP	SLG
1985	California	AL	21	7	1	0	0	0	(0	0)	1	7	0	1	0	3	1	0	0	3	1	.75	0	.143	.333	.143
1986	California	AL	29	51	12	1	1	1	(0	1)	18	8	3	6	0	8	0	0	0	6	0	1.00	0	.235	.316	.353
1987	California	AL	159	639	168	33	5	24	(11	13)	283	103	87	39	2	135	2	14	2	32	11	.74	8	.263	.306	.443
1988	California	AL	122	455	118	22	2	11	(8	3)	177	76	51	23	1	84	2	5	1	44	8	.68	5	.259	.297	.389
1989	California	AL	156	636	156	18	13	12	(9	3)	236	86	56	31	3	129	2	7	2	44	16	.73	12	.245	.282	.371
1990	California	AL	125	443	96	17	3	11	(5	6)	152	57	44	44	5	116	3	10	3	21	6	.78	6	.217	.290	.343
1991	Toronto	AL	156	642	181	40	10	17	(9	8)	292	110	60	55	1	135	7	5	6	33	10	.77	7	.282	.342	.455
1992	Toronto	AL	153	641	159	26	7	17	(7	10)	250	98	60	47	0	133	5	0	3	37	4	.90	9	.248	.303	.390
1993	Toronto	AL	146	598	163	42	6	15	(10	5)	262	116	52	57	1	127	7	3	3	34	4	.89	3	.273	.341	.438
	9 ML YEARS		1067	4112	1054	199	47	108	(54	54)	1671	661	413	303	13	870	29	44	20	227	60	.79	50	.256	.310	.406

Rondell White

Bats: Right **Throws:** Right **Pos:** LF **Ht:** 6' 1" **Wt:** 193 **Born:** 02/23/72 **Age:** 22

								BATTING											BASERUNNING				PERCENTAGES		
Year	Team	Lg	G	AB	H	2B	3B	HR	(Hm	Rd)	TB	R	RBI	TBB	IBB	SO	HBP	SH	SF	SB	CS	SB%	GDP	Avg	OBP	SLG
1990	Expos	R	57	222	66	8	4	5	--	--	97	33	34	16	0	33	5	0	0	10	7	.59	4	.297	.358	.437
1991	Sumter	A	123	465	121	23	6	12	--	--	192	80	67	57	3	109	8	1	3	51	17	.75	7	.260	.349	.413
1992	Wst Plm Bch	A	111	450	142	10	12	4	--	--	188	80	41	46	4	78	5	3	1	42	16	.72	7	.316	.384	.418
	Harrisburg	AA	21	89	27	7	1	2	--	--	42	22	7	6	0	14	4	0	0	6	1	.86	3	.303	.374	.472
1993	Harrisburg	AA	90	372	122	16	10	12	--	--	194	72	52	22	1	72	5	0	3	21	6	.78	3	.328	.371	.522
	Ottawa	AAA	37	150	57	8	2	7	--	--	90	28	32	12	1	20	3	0	0	10	1	.91	4	.380	.436	.600
1993	Montreal	NL	23	73	19	3	1	2	(1	1)	30	9	15	7	0	16	0	0	2	1	2	.33	2	.260	.321	.411

Wally Whitehurst

Pitches: Right **Bats:** Right **Pos:** SP **Ht:** 6' 3" **Wt:** 185 **Born:** 04/11/64 **Age:** 30

				HOW MUCH HE PITCHED					WHAT HE GAVE UP									THE RESULTS					
Year	Team	Lg	G	GS	CG	GF	IP	BFP	H	R	ER	HR	SH	SF	HB	TBB	IBB	SO	WP	Bk	W	L	Pct.	ShO	Sv	ERA
1993	Wichita *	AA	4	4	0	0	21.1	80	11	4	3	1	0	0	0	5	0	14	4	1	1	0	1.000	0	0	1.27
1989	New York	NL	9	1	0	4	14	64	17	7	7	2	0	1	0	5	0	9	1	0	0	1	.000	0	0	4.50
1990	New York	NL	38	0	0	16	65.2	263	63	27	24	5	3	0	0	9	2	46	2	0	1	0	1.000	0	2	3.29
1991	New York	NL	36	20	0	6	133.1	556	142	67	62	12	6	3	4	25	3	87	3	4	7	12	.368	0	1	4.18
1992	New York	NL	44	11	0	7	97	421	99	45	39	4	6	3	4	33	5	70	2	1	3	9	.250	0	1	3.62
1993	San Diego	NL	21	19	0	1	105.2	441	109	47	45	11	5	8	3	30	5	57	5	1	4	7	.364	0	0	3.83
	5 ML YEARS		148	51	0	34	415.2	1745	430	193	177	34	20	15	11	102	15	269	13	6	15	29	.341	0	3	3.83

Mark Whiten

Bats: Both **Throws:** Right **Pos:** RF/CF **Ht:** 6' 3" **Wt:** 215 **Born:** 11/25/66 **Age:** 27

								BATTING											BASERUNNING				PERCENTAGES		
Year	Team	Lg	G	AB	H	2B	3B	HR	(Hm	Rd)	TB	R	RBI	TBB	IBB	SO	HBP	SH	SF	SB	CS	SB%	GDP	Avg	OBP	SLG
1990	2 ML Teams	AL	33	88	24	1	1	2	(1	1)	33	12	7	7	0	14	0	0	1	2	0	1.00	2	.273	.323	.375
1991	2 ML Teams		116	407	99	18	7	9	(4	5)	158	46	45	30	2	85	3	0	5	4	3	.57	13	.243	.297	.388
1992	Cleveland	AL	148	508	129	19	4	9	(6	3)	183	73	43	72	10	102	2	3	3	16	12	.57	12	.254	.347	.360
1993	St. Louis	NL	152	562	142	13	4	25	(12	13)	238	81	99	58	9	110	2	0	4	15	8	.65	11	.253	.323	.423
1991	Toronto	AL	46	149	33	4	3	2	(2	0)	49	12	19	11	1	35	1	0	3	0	1	.00	5	.221	.274	.329
	Cleveland	AL	70	258	66	14	4	7	(2	5)	109	34	26	19	1	50	2	0	2	4	2	.67	8	.256	.310	.422
	4 ML YEARS		449	1565	394	51	16	45	(23	22)	612	212	194	167	21	311	7	3	13	37	23	.62	38	.252	.324	.391

Matt Whiteside

Pitches: Right **Bats:** Right **Pos:** RP **Ht:** 6' 0" **Wt:** 195 **Born:** 08/08/67 **Age:** 26

				HOW MUCH HE PITCHED					WHAT HE GAVE UP									THE RESULTS					
Year	Team	Lg	G	GS	CG	GF	IP	BFP	H	R	ER	HR	SH	SF	HB	TBB	IBB	SO	WP	Bk	W	L	Pct.	ShO	Sv	ERA
1990	Butte	R	18	5	0	5	57.1	255	57	33	22	4	0	0	9	25	0	45	4	6	4	4	.500	0	2	3.45
1991	Gastonia	A	48	0	0	42	62.2	255	44	19	15	1	1	3	5	21	0	71	3	0	3	1	.750	0	29	2.15
1992	Tulsa	AA	33	0	0	32	33.2	134	31	9	9	2	0	0	1	3	1	30	2	0	0	1	.000	0	21	2.41
	Okla City	AAA	12	0	0	12	11.1	44	7	1	1	1	0	0	0	3	1	13	0	0	1	0	1.000	0	8	0.79
1993	Okla City	AAA	8	0	0	8	11.1	55	17	7	7	1	1	0	0	8	4	10	1	1	2	1	.667	0	1	5.56
1992	Texas	AL	20	0	0	8	28	118	26	8	6	1	0	1	0	11	2	13	2	0	1	1	.500	0	4	1.93
1993	Texas	AL	60	0	0	10	73	305	78	37	35	7	2	1	1	23	6	39	0	2	2	1	.667	0	1	4.32
	2 ML YEARS		80	0	0	18	101	423	104	45	41	8	2	2	1	34	8	52	2	2	3	2	.600	0	5	3.65

Darrell Whitmore

Bats: Left **Throws:** Right **Pos:** RF **Ht:** 6' 1" **Wt:** 210 **Born:** 11/18/68 **Age:** 25

								BATTING											BASERUNNING				PERCENTAGES		
Year	Team	Lg	G	AB	H	2B	3B	HR	(Hm	Rd)	TB	R	RBI	TBB	IBB	SO	HBP	SH	SF	SB	CS	SB%	GDP	Avg	OBP	SLG
1990	Burlington	R	30	112	27	3	2	0	--	--	34	18	13	9	0	30	2	0	1	9	5	.64	0	.241	.306	.304
1991	Watertown	A	6	19	7	2	1	0	--	--	11	2	3	3	0	2	0	0	0	0	0	.00	0	.368	.455	.579
1992	Kinston	A	121	443	124	22	2	10	--	--	180	71	52	56	5	92	5	0	5	17	9	.65	8	.280	.363	.406
1993	Edmonton	AAA	73	273	97	24	2	9	--	--	152	52	62	22	0	53	0	0	3	11	8	.58	12	.355	.399	.557
1993	Florida	NL	76	250	51	8	2	4	(3	1)	75	24	19	10	0	72	5	2	0	4	2	.67	2	.204	.249	.300

Kevin Wickander

Pitches: Left **Bats:** Left **Pos:** RP **Ht:** 6' 3" **Wt:** 200 **Born:** 01/04/65 **Age:** 29

				HOW MUCH HE PITCHED					WHAT HE GAVE UP									THE RESULTS					
Year	Team	Lg	G	GS	CG	GF	IP	BFP	H	R	ER	HR	SH	SF	HB	TBB	IBB	SO	WP	Bk	W	L	Pct.	ShO	Sv	ERA
1993	Indianapolis *	AAA	1	1	0	0	3	11	2	0	0	0	0	0	0	1	0	2	1	0	0	0	.000	0	0	0.00
1989	Cleveland	AL	2	0	0	1	2.2	15	6	1	1	0	0	0	0	2	1	1	0	0	0	0	.000	0	0	3.38
1990	Cleveland	AL	10	0	0	3	12.1	53	14	6	5	0	0	2	1	4	0	10	0	0	0	1	.000	0	0	3.65
1992	Cleveland	AL	44	0	0	10	41	187	39	14	14	1	2	2	4	28	3	38	1	1	2	0	1.000	0	1	3.07
1993	2 ML Teams		44	0	0	9	34	170	47	27	23	4	1	2	0	22	1	23	5	1	1	0	1.000	0	0	6.09

233

1993	Cleveland	AL	11	0	0	1	8.2	44	15	7	4	3	0	0	0	3	0	3	1	0	0	0	.000	0	0	4.15
	Cincinnati	NL	33	0	0	8	25.1	126	32	20	19	5	1	0	2	19	1	20	4	1	1	0	1.000	0	0	6.75
4 ML YEARS			100	0	0	23	90	425	106	48	43	9	3	4	7	56	5	71	6	2	3	1	.750	0	1	4.30

Bob Wickman

Pitches: Right **Bats:** Right **Pos:** RP/SP **Ht:** 6' 1" **Wt:** 212 **Born:** 02/06/69 **Age:** 25

			HOW MUCH HE PITCHED						WHAT HE GAVE UP												THE RESULTS				
Year	Team	Lg	G	GS	CG	GF	IP	BFP	H	R	ER	HR	SH	SF	HB	TBB	IBB	SO	WP	Bk	W	L	Pct.	ShO	Sv	ERA
1990	White Sox	R	2	2	0	0	11	42	7	4	3	0	0	1	0	1	0	15	2	3	2	0	1.000	0	0	2.45
	Sarasota	A	2	2	0	0	13.2	61	17	7	3	0	0	1	0	4	0	8	0	0	0	1	.000	0	0	1.98
	South Bend	A	9	9	3	0	65.1	256	50	16	10	1	3	0	1	16	0	50	0	0	7	2	.778	0	0	1.38
1991	Sarasota	A	7	7	1	0	44	188	43	16	10	2	1	0	1	11	0	32	1	2	5	1	.833	1	0	2.05
	Birmingham	AA	20	20	4	0	131.1	572	127	68	52	5	3	5	5	50	0	81	4	2	6	10	.375	1	0	3.56
1992	Columbus	AAA	23	23	2	0	157	641	131	61	51	12	1	2	5	55	0	108	10	1	12	5	.706	1	0	2.92
1992	New York	AL	8	8	0	0	50.1	213	51	25	23	2	1	3	2	20	0	21	3	0	6	1	.857	0	0	4.11
1993	New York	AL	41	19	1	9	140	629	156	82	72	13	4	1	5	69	7	70	2	0	14	4	.778	1	0	4.63
2 ML YEARS			49	27	1	9	190.1	842	207	107	95	15	5	4	7	89	7	91	5	0	20	5	.800	1	4	4.49

Curt Wilkerson

Bats: Both **Throws:** Right **Pos:** 2B **Ht:** 5' 9" **Wt:** 175 **Born:** 04/26/61 **Age:** 33

			BATTING																BASERUNNING				PERCENTAGES		
Year	Team	Lg	G	AB	H	2B	3B	HR	(Hm | Rd)	TB	R	RBI	TBB	IBB	SO	HBP	SH	SF	SB	CS	SB%	GDP	Avg	OBP	SLG
1983	Texas	AL	16	35	6	0	1	0	(0 | 0)	8	7	1	2	0	5	0	0	0	3	0	1.00	0	.171	.216	.229
1984	Texas	AL	153	484	120	12	0	1	(0 | 1)	135	47	26	22	0	72	2	12	2	12	10	.55	7	.248	.282	.279
1985	Texas	AL	129	360	88	11	6	0	(0 | 0)	111	35	22	22	0	63	4	6	3	14	7	.67	7	.244	.293	.308
1986	Texas	AL	110	236	56	10	3	0	(0 | 0)	72	27	15	11	0	42	1	0	1	9	7	.56	2	.237	.273	.305
1987	Texas	AL	85	138	37	5	3	2	(1 | 1)	54	28	14	6	0	16	2	0	0	6	3	.67	2	.268	.308	.391
1988	Texas	AL	117	338	99	12	5	0	(0 | 0)	121	41	28	26	3	43	2	3	2	9	4	.69	7	.293	.345	.358
1989	Chicago	NL	77	160	39	4	2	1	(1 | 0)	50	18	10	8	0	33	0	1	1	4	2	.67	3	.244	.278	.313
1990	Chicago	NL	77	186	41	5	1	0	(0 | 0)	48	21	16	7	2	36	0	3	0	2	2	.50	4	.220	.249	.258
1991	Pittsburgh	NL	85	191	36	9	1	2	(2 | 0)	53	20	18	15	0	40	0	0	4	2	1	.67	2	.188	.243	.277
1992	Kansas City	AL	111	296	74	10	1	2	(2 | 0)	92	27	29	18	3	47	1	7	4	18	7	.72	4	.250	.292	.311
1993	Kansas City	AL	12	28	4	0	0	0	(0 | 0)	4	1	0	1	0	6	0	0	0	2	0	1.00	1	.143	.172	.143
11 ML YEARS			972	2452	600	78	23	8	(6 | 2)	748	272	179	138	8	403	12	32	17	81	43	.65	39	.245	.286	.305

Rick Wilkins

Bats: Left **Throws:** Right **Pos:** C **Ht:** 6' 2" **Wt:** 215 **Born:** 06/04/67 **Age:** 27

			BATTING																BASERUNNING				PERCENTAGES		
Year	Team	Lg	G	AB	H	2B	3B	HR	(Hm | Rd)	TB	R	RBI	TBB	IBB	SO	HBP	SH	SF	SB	CS	SB%	GDP	Avg	OBP	SLG
1991	Chicago	NL	86	203	45	9	0	6	(2 | 4)	72	21	22	19	2	56	6	7	0	3	3	.50	3	.222	.307	.355
1992	Chicago	NL	83	244	66	9	1	8	(3 | 5)	101	20	22	28	7	53	0	1	1	0	2	.00	6	.270	.344	.414
1993	Chicago	NL	136	446	135	23	1	30	(10 | 20)	250	78	73	50	13	99	3	0	1	2	1	.67	6	.303	.376	.561
3 ML YEARS			305	893	246	41	2	44	(15 | 29)	423	119	117	97	22	208	9	8	2	5	6	.45	15	.275	.352	.474

Bernie Williams

Bats: Both **Throws:** Right **Pos:** CF **Ht:** 6' 2" **Wt:** 200 **Born:** 09/13/68 **Age:** 25

			BATTING																BASERUNNING				PERCENTAGES		
Year	Team	Lg	G	AB	H	2B	3B	HR	(Hm | Rd)	TB	R	RBI	TBB	IBB	SO	HBP	SH	SF	SB	CS	SB%	GDP	Avg	OBP	SLG
1991	New York	AL	85	320	76	19	4	3	(1 | 2)	112	43	34	48	0	57	1	2	3	10	5	.67	4	.238	.336	.350
1992	New York	AL	62	261	73	14	2	5	(3 | 2)	106	39	26	29	1	36	1	2	0	7	6	.54	5	.280	.354	.406
1993	New York	AL	139	567	152	31	4	12	(5 | 7)	227	67	68	53	4	106	4	1	3	9	9	.50	17	.268	.333	.400
3 ML YEARS			286	1148	301	64	10	20	(9 | 11)	445	149	128	130	5	199	6	5	6	26	20	.57	26	.262	.339	.388

Brian Williams

Pitches: Right **Bats:** Right **Pos:** RP/SP **Ht:** 6' 2" **Wt:** 195 **Born:** 02/15/69 **Age:** 25

			HOW MUCH HE PITCHED						WHAT HE GAVE UP												THE RESULTS				
Year	Team	Lg	G	GS	CG	GF	IP	BFP	H	R	ER	HR	SH	SF	HB	TBB	IBB	SO	WP	Bk	W	L	Pct.	ShO	Sv	ERA
1993	Tucson *	AAA	2	0	0	0	3	11	1	0	0	0	0	0	0	0	0	3	0	0	1	0	1.000	0	0	0.00
1991	Houston	NL	2	2	0	0	12	49	11	5	5	2	0	0	1	4	0	4	0	0	0	1	.000	0	0	3.75
1992	Houston	NL	16	16	0	0	96.1	413	92	44	42	10	7	3	0	42	1	54	2	1	7	6	.538	0	0	3.92
1993	Houston	NL	42	5	0	12	82	357	76	48	44	7	5	3	4	38	4	56	9	2	4	4	.500	0	3	4.83
3 ML YEARS			60	23	0	12	190.1	819	179	97	91	19	12	6	5	84	5	114	11	3	11	11	.500	0	3	4.30

Gerald Williams

Bats: Right **Throws:** Right **Pos:** CF/RF **Ht:** 6' 2" **Wt:** 185 **Born:** 08/10/66 **Age:** 27

								BATTING											BASERUNNING				PERCENTAGES		
Year	Team	Lg	G	AB	H	2B	3B	HR	(Hm | Rd)	TB	R	RBI	TBB	IBB	SO	HBP	SH	SF	SB	CS	SB%	GDP	Avg	OBP	SLG
1987	Oneonta	A	29	115	42	6	2	2	--	--	58	26	29	16	0	18	1	0	0	6	2	.75	3	.365	.447	.504
1988	Pr William	A	54	159	29	3	0	2	--	--	38	20	18	15	0	47	0	1	1	6	1	.86	4	.182	.251	.239
	Ft.Laudrdle	A	63	212	40	7	2	2	--	--	57	21	17	16	0	56	3	1	0	4	3	.57	4	.189	.255	.269
1989	Pr William	A	134	454	104	19	6	13	--	--	174	63	69	51	1	120	7	5	1	15	10	.60	7	.229	.316	.383
1990	Ft.Laudrdle	A	50	204	59	4	5	7	--	--	94	25	43	16	1	52	2	0	2	19	5	.79	1	.289	.344	.461
	Albany	AA	96	324	81	17	2	13	--	--	141	54	58	35	1	75	2	1	3	18	8	.69	7	.250	.324	.435
1991	Albany	AA	45	175	50	15	0	5	--	--	80	28	32	18	2	26	0	1	3	18	3	.86	5	.286	.347	.457
	Columbus	AAA	61	198	51	8	3	2	--	--	71	20	27	16	1	39	1	0	5	9	12	.43	3	.258	.309	.359
1992	Columbus	AAA	142	547	156	31	6	16	--	--	247	92	86	38	2	98	5	0	5	36	14	.72	12	.285	.334	.452
1993	Columbus	AAA	87	336	95	19	6	8	--	--	150	53	38	20	1	66	2	1	6	29	12	.71	7	.283	.321	.446
1992	New York	AL	15	27	8	2	0	3	(2 | 1)	19	7	6	0	0	3	0	0	0	2	0	1.00	0	.296	.296	.704
1993	New York	AL	42	67	10	2	3	0	(0 | 0)	18	11	6	1	0	14	2	0	1	2	0	1.00	2	.149	.183	.269
	2 ML YEARS		57	94	18	4	3	3	(2 | 1)	37	18	12	1	0	17	2	0	1	4	0	1.00	2	.191	.214	.394

Matt D. Williams

Bats: Right **Throws:** Right **Pos:** 3B **Ht:** 6' 2" **Wt:** 216 **Born:** 11/28/65 **Age:** 28

								BATTING											BASERUNNING				PERCENTAGES		
Year	Team	Lg	G	AB	H	2B	3B	HR	(Hm | Rd)	TB	R	RBI	TBB	IBB	SO	HBP	SH	SF	SB	CS	SB%	GDP	Avg	OBP	SLG
1987	San Francisco	NL	84	245	46	9	2	8	(5 | 3)	83	28	21	16	4	68	1	3	1	4	3	.57	5	.188	.240	.339
1988	San Francisco	NL	52	156	32	6	1	8	(7 | 1)	64	17	19	8	0	41	2	3	1	0	1	.00	7	.205	.251	.410
1989	San Francisco	NL	84	292	59	18	1	18	(10 | 8)	133	31	50	14	1	72	2	1	2	1	2	.33	5	.202	.242	.455
1990	San Francisco	NL	159	617	171	27	2	33	(20 | 13)	301	87	122	33	9	138	7	2	5	7	4	.64	13	.277	.319	.488
1991	San Francisco	NL	157	589	158	24	5	34	(17 | 17)	294	72	98	33	6	128	6	0	1	5	5	.50	11	.268	.310	.499
1992	San Francisco	NL	146	529	120	13	5	20	(9 | 11)	203	58	66	39	11	109	6	0	2	7	7	.50	15	.227	.286	.384
1993	San Francisco	NL	145	579	170	33	4	38	(19 | 19)	325	105	110	27	4	80	4	0	9	1	3	.25	12	.294	.325	.561
	7 ML YEARS		827	3007	756	130	20	159	(87 | 72)	1403	398	486	170	35	636	28	9	27	25	25	.50	68	.251	.295	.467

Mike Williams

Pitches: Right **Bats:** Right **Pos:** RP/SP **Ht:** 6' 2" **Wt:** 190 **Born:** 07/29/68 **Age:** 25

			HOW MUCH HE PITCHED						WHAT HE GAVE UP											THE RESULTS					
Year	Team	Lg	G	GS	CG	GF	IP	BFP	H	R	ER	HR	SH	SF	HB	TBB	IBB	SO	WP	Bk	W	L	Pct.	ShO	Sv	ERA
1990	Batavia	A	27	0	0	21	47	195	39	17	12	0	3	3	1	14	4	42	1	1	2	3	.400	0	11	2.30
1991	Clearwater	A	14	14	2	0	93.1	348	65	23	18	5	3	1	3	14	0	76	2	6	7	3	.700	1	0	1.74
	Reading	AA	16	15	2	0	102.1	414	93	44	42	1	3	3	2	36	0	51	2	0	7	5	.583	1	0	3.69
1992	Reading	AA	3	3	0	0	15.2	68	17	10	9	1	0	1	0	7	0	12	3	0	1	2	.333	0	0	5.17
	Scranton/wb	AAA	16	16	3	0	92.2	381	84	26	25	4	4	0	0	30	2	59	2	0	9	1	.900	1	0	2.43
1993	Scranton/wb	AAA	14	13	1	0	97.1	385	93	34	31	7	4	2	2	16	0	53	0	0	9	2	.818	1	0	2.87
1992	Philadelphia	NL	5	5	1	0	28.2	121	29	20	17	3	1	1	0	7	0	5	0	0	1	1	.500	0	0	5.34
1993	Philadelphia	NL	17	4	0	2	51	221	50	32	30	5	1	0	0	22	2	33	2	0	1	3	.250	0	0	5.29
	2 ML YEARS		22	9	1	2	79.2	342	79	52	47	8	2	1	0	29	2	38	2	0	2	4	.333	0	0	5.31

Mitch Williams

Pitches: Left **Bats:** Left **Pos:** RP **Ht:** 6' 4" **Wt:** 205 **Born:** 11/17/64 **Age:** 29

			HOW MUCH HE PITCHED						WHAT HE GAVE UP											THE RESULTS					
Year	Team	Lg	G	GS	CG	GF	IP	BFP	H	R	ER	HR	SH	SF	HB	TBB	IBB	SO	WP	Bk	W	L	Pct.	ShO	Sv	ERA
1986	Texas	AL	80	0	0	48	98	435	69	39	39	8	1	3	11	79	8	90	5	5	8	6	.571	0	8	3.58
1987	Texas	AL	85	1	0	32	108.2	469	63	44	39	9	4	3	7	94	7	129	4	2	8	6	.571	0	6	3.23
1988	Texas	AL	67	0	0	51	68	296	48	38	35	4	3	4	6	47	3	61	5	6	2	7	.222	0	18	4.63
1989	Chicago	NL	76	0	0	61	81.2	365	71	27	24	6	2	5	8	52	4	67	6	4	4	4	.500	0	36	2.64
1990	Chicago	NL	59	2	0	39	66.1	310	60	38	29	4	5	3	1	50	6	55	4	2	1	8	.111	0	16	3.93
1991	Philadelphia	NL	69	0	0	60	88.1	386	56	24	23	4	4	4	8	62	5	84	4	1	12	5	.706	0	30	2.34
1992	Philadelphia	NL	66	0	0	56	81	368	69	39	34	4	8	3	6	64	2	74	5	3	5	8	.385	0	29	3.78
1993	Philadelphia	NL	65	0	0	57	62	281	56	30	23	4	2	4	2	44	1	60	6	0	3	7	.300	0	43	3.34
	8 ML YEARS		567	3	0	394	654	2910	492	282	246	42	31	27	49	492	36	620	39	23	43	51	.457	0	186	3.39

Woody Williams

Pitches: Right **Bats:** Right **Pos:** RP **Ht:** 6' 0" **Wt:** 180 **Born:** 08/19/66 **Age:** 27

			HOW MUCH HE PITCHED						WHAT HE GAVE UP											THE RESULTS					
Year	Team	Lg	G	GS	CG	GF	IP	BFP	H	R	ER	HR	SH	SF	HB	TBB	IBB	SO	WP	Bk	W	L	Pct.	ShO	Sv	ERA
1988	St.Cathrnes	A	12	12	1	0	76	294	48	22	13	0	1	3	3	21	0	58	4	1	8	2	.800	0	0	1.54
	Knoxville	AA	6	4	0	0	28.1	120	27	13	12	1	0	0	0	12	0	25	1	0	2	2	.500	0	0	3.81
1989	Dunedin	A	20	9	0	8	81.1	325	63	26	21	3	3	3	2	27	1	60	5	1	3	5	.375	0	3	2.32
	Knoxville	AA	14	12	2	1	71	302	61	32	28	6	3	4	2	33	2	51	1	1	3	5	.375	1	0	3.55

Year Team	Lg	G	GS	CG	GF	IP	BFP	H	R	ER	HR	SH	SF	HB	TBB	IBB	SO	WP	Bk	W	L	Pct.	ShO	Sv	ERA
1990 Syracuse	AAA	3	0	0	0	9	46	15	10	10	1	0	2	0	4	0	8	1	0	0	1	.000	0	0	10.00
Knoxville	AA	42	12	0	19	126	519	111	55	44	7	3	4	2	39	3	74	6	4	7	9	.438	0	5	3.14
1991 Knoxville	AA	18	1	0	8	42.2	177	42	18	17	1	0	1	1	14	0	37	0	0	3	2	.600	0	3	3.59
Syracuse	AAA	31	0	0	16	54.2	243	52	27	25	2	4	1	3	27	3	37	4	1	3	4	.429	0	6	4.12
1992 Syracuse	AAA	25	16	1	3	120.2	503	115	46	42	4	2	2	3	41	0	81	5	1	6	8	.429	0	1	3.13
1993 Syracuse	AAA	12	0	0	11	16.1	67	15	5	4	2	0	1	0	5	3	16	0	0	1	1	.500	0	3	2.20
Dunedin	A	2	0	0	0	4	14	0	0	0	0	0	0	0	2	0	2	0	0	0	0	.000	0	0	0.00
1993 Toronto	AL	30	0	0	9	37	172	40	18	18	2	2	1		22	3	24	2	1	3	1	.750	0	0	4.38

Mark Williamson

Pitches: Right **Bats:** Right **Pos:** RP **Ht:** 6' 0" **Wt:** 185 **Born:** 07/21/59 **Age:** 34

		HOW MUCH HE PITCHED						WHAT HE GAVE UP												THE RESULTS					
Year Team	Lg	G	GS	CG	GF	IP	BFP	H	R	ER	HR	SH	SF	HB	TBB	IBB	SO	WP	Bk	W	L	Pct.	ShO	Sv	ERA
1987 Baltimore	AL	61	2	0	36	125	520	122	59	56	12	5	3	3	41	15	73	3	0	8	9	.471	0	3	4.03
1988 Baltimore	AL	37	10	2	11	117.2	507	125	70	64	14	4	2	2	40	8	69	5	3	5	8	.385	0	2	4.90
1989 Baltimore	AL	65	0	0	38	107.1	445	105	35	35	4	7	3	2	30	9	55	0	0	10	5	.667	0	9	2.93
1990 Baltimore	AL	49	0	0	15	85.1	343	65	25	21	8	6	7	0	28	2	60	1	0	8	2	.800	0	1	2.21
1991 Baltimore	AL	65	0	0	21	80.1	357	87	42	40	9	1	5	0	35	7	53	7	0	5	5	.500	0	4	4.48
1992 Baltimore	AL	12	0	0	6	18.2	78	16	3	2	1	1	0	0	10	1	14	1	0	0	0	.000	0	1	0.96
1993 Baltimore	AL	48	1	0	12	88	386	106	54	48	5	6	6	0	25	8	45	2	0	7	5	.583	0	0	4.91
7 ML YEARS		337	13	2	138	622.1	2636	626	288	266	53	30	26	7	209	50	369	19	3	43	34	.558	0	20	3.85

Carl Willis

Pitches: Right **Bats:** Left **Pos:** RP **Ht:** 6' 4" **Wt:** 211 **Born:** 12/28/60 **Age:** 33

		HOW MUCH HE PITCHED						WHAT HE GAVE UP												THE RESULTS					
Year Team	Lg	G	GS	CG	GF	IP	BFP	H	R	ER	HR	SH	SF	HB	TBB	IBB	SO	WP	Bk	W	L	Pct.	ShO	Sv	ERA
1983 Portland *	AAA	2	0	0	1	4	19	6	2	1	0	0	0	0	1	0	2	0	0	0	0	.000	0	0	2.25
1984 2 ML Teams		17	2	0	5	25.2	113	33	17	17	2	1	0	0	7	2	7	0	0	0	3	.000	0	1	5.96
1985 Cincinnati	NL	11	0	0	6	13.2	69	21	18	14	3	1	2	0	5	0	6	1	0	1	0	1.000	0	1	9.22
1986 Cincinnati	NL	29	0	0	7	52.1	233	54	29	26	4	5	1	1	32	9	24	3	1	1	3	.250	0	4	4.47
1988 Chicago	AL	6	0	0	1	12	55	17	12	11	3	0	1	0	7	1	6	2	0	0	0	.000	0	0	8.25
1991 Minnesota	AL	40	0	0	9	89	355	76	31	26	4	3	4	1	19	2	53	4	1	8	3	.727	0	2	2.63
1992 Minnesota	AL	59	0	0	21	79.1	313	73	25	24	4	2	3	0	11	1	45	2	1	7	3	.700	0	1	2.72
1993 Minnesota	AL	53	0	0	21	58	236	56	23	20	2	2	1	0	17	5	44	3	0	3	0	1.000	0	5	3.10
1984 Detroit	AL	10	2	0	4	16	74	25	13	13	1	0	0	0	5	2	4	0	0	0	2	.000	0	0	7.31
Cincinnati	NL	7	0	0	1	9.2	39	8	4	4	1	1	0	0	2	0	3	0	0	0	1	.000	0	1	3.72
7 ML YEARS		215	2	0	69	330	1374	330	155	138	22	14	12	2	98	20	185	15	3	20	12	.625	0	10	3.76

Craig Wilson

Bats: Right **Throws:** Right **Pos:** 3B **Ht:** 5'11" **Wt:** 210 **Born:** 11/28/64 **Age:** 29

		BATTING															BASERUNNING				PERCENTAGES		
Year Team	Lg	G	AB	H	2B	3B	HR	(Hm | Rd)	TB	R	RBI	TBB	IBB	SO	HBP	SH	SF	SB	CS	SB%	GDP	Avg	OBP	SLG
1993 Omaha *	AAA	65	234	65	13	1	3	--	--	89	26	28	20	0	24	1	1	6	7	4	.64	6	.278	.336	.380
1989 St. Louis	NL	6	4	1	0	0	0	(0 | 0)	1	1	1	1	0	2	0	0	0	0	0	.00	0	.250	.400	.250
1990 St. Louis	NL	55	121	30	2	0	0	(0 | 0)	32	13	7	8	0	14	0	0	2	0	2	.00	7	.248	.290	.264
1991 St. Louis	NL	60	82	14	2	0	0	(0 | 0)	16	5	13	6	2	10	0	0	2	0	0	.00	4	.171	.222	.195
1992 St. Louis	NL	61	106	33	6	0	0	(0 | 0)	39	6	13	10	2	18	0	2	1	1	2	.33	4	.311	.368	.368
1993 Kansas City	AL	21	49	13	1	0	1	(1 | 0)	17	6	3	7	0	6	0	1	0	1	1	.50	0	.265	.357	.347
5 ML YEARS		203	362	91	11	0	1	(1 | 0)	105	31	37	32	4	50	0	3	5	2	5	.29	13	.251	.308	.290

Dan Wilson

Bats: Right **Throws:** Right **Pos:** C **Ht:** 6' 3" **Wt:** 190 **Born:** 03/25/69 **Age:** 25

		BATTING															BASERUNNING				PERCENTAGES		
Year Team	Lg	G	AB	H	2B	3B	HR	(Hm | Rd)	TB	R	RBI	TBB	IBB	SO	HBP	SH	SF	SB	CS	SB%	GDP	Avg	OBP	SLG
1990 Chston-Wv	A	32	113	28	9	1	2	--	--	45	16	17	13	0	18	0	1	1	0	0	.00	1	.248	.323	.398
1991 Chston-Wv	A	52	197	62	11	1	3	--	--	84	25	29	25	0	21	2	0	1	1	1	.50	6	.315	.396	.426
Chattanooga	AA	81	292	75	19	2	2	--	--	104	32	38	21	0	39	0	1	4	2	2	.50	10	.257	.303	.356
1992 Nashville	AAA	106	366	92	16	1	4	--	--	122	27	34	31	3	58	2	2	4	1	4	.20	7	.251	.310	.333
1993 Indianapls	AAA	51	191	50	11	1	0	--	--	66	18	17	19	1	31	1	3	1	1	0	1.00	4	.262	.330	.346
1992 Cincinnati	NL	12	25	9	1	0	0	(0 | 0)	10	2	3	3	0	8	0	0	0	0	0	.00	0	.360	.429	.400
1993 Cincinnati	NL	36	76	17	3	0	0	(0 | 0)	20	6	8	9	4	16	0	2	0	0	0	.00	2	.224	.302	.263
2 ML YEARS		48	101	26	4	0	0	(0 | 0)	30	8	11	12	4	24	0	2	0	0	0	.00	4	.257	.333	.297

Glenn Wilson

Bats: Right **Throws:** Right **Pos:** CF **Ht:** 6' 1" **Wt:** 190 **Born:** 12/22/58 **Age:** 35

Year	Team	Lg	G	AB	H	2B	3B	HR	(Hm	Rd)	TB	R	RBI	TBB	IBB	SO	HBP	SH	SF	SB	CS	SB%	GDP	Avg	OBP	SLG
1993	Buffalo *	AAA	61	201	56	14	1	12	--	--	108	32	43	16	2	38	3	0	4	0	1	.00	8	.279	.335	.537
1982	Detroit	AL	84	322	94	15	1	12	(9	3)	147	39	34	15	0	51	0	3	2	2	3	.40	8	.292	.322	.457
1983	Detroit	AL	144	503	135	25	6	11	(9	2)	205	55	65	25	1	79	3	0	2	1	1	.50	9	.268	.306	.408
1984	Philadelphia	NL	132	341	82	21	3	6	(5	1)	127	28	31	17	1	56	1	1	3	7	1	.88	12	.240	.276	.372
1985	Philadelphia	NL	161	608	167	39	5	14	(7	7)	258	73	102	35	1	117	0	0	7	7	4	.64	24	.275	.311	.424
1986	Philadelphia	NL	155	584	158	30	4	15	(7	8)	241	70	84	42	1	91	4	0	9	5	1	.83	15	.271	.319	.413
1987	Philadelphia	NL	154	569	150	21	2	14	(5	9)	217	55	54	38	2	82	1	0	6	3	6	.33	18	.264	.308	.381
1988	2 ML Teams		115	410	105	18	1	5	(2	3)	140	39	32	18	1	70	1	3	4	1	1	.50	17	.256	.286	.341
1989	2 ML Teams		128	432	115	26	4	11	(4	7)	182	50	64	37	5	53	1	1	6	1	5	.17	11	.266	.321	.421
1990	Houston	NL	118	368	90	14	0	10	(5	5)	134	42	55	26	1	64	1	0	4	0	3	.00	16	.245	.293	.364
1993	Pittsburgh	NL	10	14	2	0	0	0	(0	0)	2	0	0	0	0	2	0	0	0	0	0	.00	0	.143	.143	.143
1988	Seattle	AL	78	284	71	10	1	3	(2	1)	92	28	17	15	0	52	0	1	2	1	1	.50	13	.250	.286	.324
	Pittsburgh	NL	37	126	34	8	0	2	(0	2)	48	11	15	3	1	18	1	2	2	0	0	.00	4	.270	.288	.381
1989	Pittsburgh	NL	100	330	93	20	4	9	(2	7)	148	42	49	32	5	39	1	0	5	1	4	.20	8	.282	.342	.448
	Houston	NL	28	102	22	6	0	2	(2	0)	34	8	15	5	0	14	0	1	1	0	1	.00	3	.216	.250	.333
	10 ML YEARS		1201	4151	1098	209	26	98	(53	45)	1653	451	521	253	13	672	12	8	43	27	25	.52	130	.265	.306	.398

Nigel Wilson

Bats: Left **Throws:** Left **Pos:** LF **Ht:** 6' 1" **Wt:** 185 **Born:** 01/12/70 **Age:** 24

Year	Team	Lg	G	AB	H	2B	3B	HR	(Hm	Rd)	TB	R	RBI	TBB	IBB	SO	HBP	SH	SF	SB	CS	SB%	GDP	Avg	OBP	SLG
1988	St.Cathrnes	A	40	103	21	1	2	2	--	--	32	12	11	12	0	32	4	1	1	8	4	.67	0	.204	.308	.311
1989	St.Cathrnes	A	42	161	35	5	2	4	--	--	56	17	18	11	0	50	4	1	0	8	2	.80	0	.217	.284	.348
1990	Myrtle Bch	A	110	440	120	23	9	16	--	--	209	77	62	30	3	71	6	2	2	22	12	.65	4	.273	.326	.475
1991	Dunedin	A	119	455	137	18	13	12	--	--	217	64	55	29	4	99	9	4	7	26	11	.70	4	.301	.350	.477
1992	Knoxville	AA	137	521	143	34	7	26	--	--	269	85	69	33	5	137	7	2	2	13	8	.62	2	.274	.325	.516
1993	Edmonton	AAA	96	370	108	26	7	17	--	--	199	66	68	25	7	108	10	1	2	8	3	.73	6	.292	.351	.538
1993	Florida	NL	7	16	0	0	0	0	(0	0)	0	0	0	0	0	11	0	0	0	0	0	.00	0	.000	.000	.000

Steve Wilson

Pitches: Left **Bats:** Left **Pos:** RP **Ht:** 6' 4" **Wt:** 224 **Born:** 12/13/64 **Age:** 29

Year	Team	Lg	G	GS	CG	GF	IP	BFP	H	R	ER	HR	SH	SF	HB	TBB	IBB	SO	WP	Bk	W	L	Pct.	ShO	Sv	ERA
1993	Albuquerque *	AAA	13	12	0	0	51.1	220	57	29	25	5	4	1	2	14	0	44	4	2	0	3	.000	0	0	4.38
1988	Texas	AL	3	0	0	1	7.2	31	7	5	5	1	0	0	0	4	1	1	0	0	0	0	.000	0	0	5.87
1989	Chicago	NL	53	8	0	9	85.2	364	83	43	40	6	5	4	1	31	5	65	0	1	6	4	.600	0	2	4.20
1990	Chicago	NL	45	15	1	5	139	597	140	77	74	17	9	3	2	43	6	95	2	1	4	9	.308	0	1	4.79
1991	2 ML Teams		19	0	0	5	20.2	81	14	7	6	1	0	1	0	9	1	14	0	0	0	0	.000	0	2	2.61
1992	Los Angeles	NL	60	0	0	18	66.2	301	74	37	31	6	5	4	1	29	7	54	7	0	2	5	.286	0	0	4.18
1993	Los Angeles	NL	25	0	0	5	25.2	120	30	13	13	2	0	1	0	14	4	23	3	0	1	0	1.000	0	1	4.56
1991	Chicago	NL	8	0	0	2	12.1	53	13	7	6	1	0	1	0	5	1	9	0	0	0	0	.000	0	0	4.38
	Los Angeles	NL	11	0	0	3	8.1	28	1	0	0	0	0	0	0	4	0	5	0	0	0	0	.000	0	2	0.00
	6 ML YEARS		205	23	1	42	345.1	1494	348	182	169	33	20	12	5	130	24	252	12	2	13	18	.419	0	6	4.40

Trevor Wilson

Pitches: Left **Bats:** Left **Pos:** SP **Ht:** 6' 0" **Wt:** 204 **Born:** 06/07/66 **Age:** 28

Year	Team	Lg	G	GS	CG	GF	IP	BFP	H	R	ER	HR	SH	SF	HB	TBB	IBB	SO	WP	Bk	W	L	Pct.	ShO	Sv	ERA
1993	San Jose *	A	2	2	0	0	10	35	4	0	0	0	0	0	0	3	0	8	0	0	1	0	1.000	0	0	0.00
1988	San Francisco	NL	4	4	0	0	22	96	25	14	10	1	3	1	0	8	0	15	0	1	0	2	.000	0	0	4.09
1989	San Francisco	NL	14	4	0	2	39.1	167	28	20	19	2	3	1	4	24	0	22	0	1	2	3	.400	0	0	4.35
1990	San Francisco	NL	27	17	3	3	110.1	457	87	52	49	11	6	2	1	49	3	66	5	2	8	7	.533	2	0	4.00
1991	San Francisco	NL	44	29	2	6	202	841	173	87	80	13	14	5	5	77	4	139	5	3	13	11	.542	1	0	3.56
1992	San Francisco	NL	26	26	1	0	154	661	152	82	72	18	11	6	6	64	5	88	2	7	8	14	.364	1	0	4.21
1993	San Francisco	NL	22	18	1	1	110	455	110	45	44	8	6	3	6	40	3	57	0	0	7	5	.583	0	0	3.60
	6 ML YEARS		137	98	7	12	637.2	2677	575	300	274	53	43	18	22	262	15	387	12	14	38	42	.475	4	0	3.87

Willie Wilson

Bats: Both **Throws:** Right **Pos:** CF **Ht:** 6' 2" **Wt:** 200 **Born:** 07/09/55 **Age:** 38

Year	Team	Lg	G	AB	H	2B	3B	HR	(Hm	Rd)	TB	R	RBI	TBB	IBB	SO	HBP	SH	SF	SB	CS	SB%	GDP	Avg	OBP	SLG
1976	Kansas City	AL	12	6	1	0	0	0	(0	0)	1	0	0	0	0	2	0	0	0	2	1	.67	0	.167	.167	.167
1977	Kansas City	AL	13	34	11	2	0	0	(0	0)	13	10	1	1	0	8	0	1	0	6	3	.67	1	.324	.343	.382

Year	Team	Lg	G	AB	H	2B	3B	HR	(Hm	Rd)	TB	R	RBI	TBB	IBB	SO	HBP	SH	SF	SB	CS	SB%	GDP	Avg	OBP	SLG
1978	Kansas City	AL	127	198	43	8	2	0	(0	0)	55	43	16	16	0	33	2	5	2	46	12	.79	2	.217	.280	.278
1979	Kansas City	AL	154	588	185	18	13	6	(3	3)	247	113	49	28	3	92	7	13	4	**83**	12	**.87**	1	.315	.351	.420
1980	Kansas City	AL	161	**705**	**230**	28	**15**	3	(2	1)	297	**133**	49	28	3	81	6	5	1	79	10	**.89**		.326	.357	.421
1981	Kansas City	AL	102	439	133	10	7	1	(0	1)	160	54	32	18	3	42	4	3	1	34	8	.81	5	.303	.335	.364
1982	Kansas City	AL	136	585	194	19	**15**	3	(2	1)	252	87	46	26	2	81	6	2	2	37	11	.77	4	**.332**	.365	.431
1983	Kansas City	AL	137	576	159	22	8	2	(2	0)	203	90	33	33	2	75	1	1	0	59	8	**.88**	4	.276	.316	.352
1984	Kansas City	AL	128	541	163	24	9	2	(1	1)	211	81	44	39	2	56	3	2	3	47	5	**.90**	7	.301	.350	.390
1985	Kansas City	AL	141	605	168	25	**21**	4	(1	3)	247	87	43	29	3	94	5	2	1	43	11	.80	6	.278	.316	.408
1986	Kansas City	AL	156	631	170	20	7	9	(5	4)	231	77	44	31	1	97	9	3	1	34	8	.81	6	.269	.313	.366
1987	Kansas City	AL	146	610	170	18	**15**	4	(0	4)	230	97	30	32	2	88	6	4	1	59	11	.84	9	.279	.320	.377
1988	Kansas City	AL	147	591	155	17	11	1	(0	1)	197	81	37	22	1	106	2	8	5	35	7	.83	5	.262	.289	.333
1989	Kansas City	AL	112	383	97	17	7	3	(1	2)	137	58	43	27	0	78	1	6	6	24	6	.80	4	.253	.300	.358
1990	Kansas City	AL	115	307	89	13	3	2	(1	1)	114	49	42	30	1	57	2	3	3	24	6	.80	4	.290	.354	.371
1991	Oakland	AL	113	294	70	14	4	0	(0	0)	92	38	28	18	1	43	4	1	1	20	5	.80	11	.238	.290	.313
1992	Oakland	AL	132	396	107	15	5	0	(0	0)	132	38	37	35	2	65	1	2	3	28	8	.78	11	.270	.329	.333
1993	Chicago	NL	105	221	57	11	3	1	(0	1)	77	29	11	11	1	40	3	1	1	7	2	.78	2	.258	.301	.348
18 ML YEARS			2137	7710	2202	281	145	41	(18	23)	2896	1165	585	424	27	1138	62	63	35	667	134	.83	90	.286	.327	.376

Dave Winfield

Bats: Right **Throws:** Right **Pos:** DH/RF   **Ht:** 6' 6" **Wt:** 245 **Born:** 10/03/51 **Age:** 42

			BATTING																	BASERUNNING				PERCENTAGES		
Year	Team	Lg	G	AB	H	2B	3B	HR	(Hm	Rd)	TB	R	RBI	TBB	IBB	SO	HBP	SH	SF	SB	CS	SB%	GDP	Avg	OBP	SLG
1973	San Diego	NL	56	141	39	4	1	3	(2	1)	54	9	12	12	1	19	0	0	1	0	0	.00	5	.277	.331	.383
1974	San Diego	NL	145	498	132	18	4	20	(12	8)	218	57	75	40	2	96	1	0	5	9	7	.56	14	.265	.318	.438
1975	San Diego	NL	143	509	136	20	2	15	(7	8)	205	74	76	69	14	82	3	3	7	23	4	.85	11	.267	.354	.403
1976	San Diego	NL	137	492	139	26	4	13	(4	9)	212	81	69	65	8	78	3	2	5	26	7	.79	14	.283	.366	.431
1977	San Diego	NL	157	615	169	29	7	25	(12	13)	287	104	92	58	10	75	0	0	5	16	7	.70	12	.275	.335	.467
1978	San Diego	NL	158	587	181	30	5	24	(11	13)	293	88	97	55	20	81	2	0	5	21	9	.70	13	.308	.367	.499
1979	San Diego	NL	159	597	184	27	10	34	(16	18)	**333**	97	**118**	85	**24**	71	2	0	2	15	9	.63	9	.308	.395	.558
1980	San Diego	NL	162	558	154	25	6	20	(7	13)	251	89	87	79	14	83	2	0	4	23	7	.77	13	.276	.365	.450
1981	New York	AL	105	388	114	25	1	13	(4	9)	180	52	68	43	3	41	1	1	7	11	1	.92	13	.294	.360	.464
1982	New York	AL	140	539	151	24	8	37	(14	**23**)	302	84	106	45	7	64	0	5	8	3	3	.50	20	.280	.331	.560
1983	New York	AL	152	598	169	26	8	32	(13	19)	307	99	116	58	2	77	2	0	6	15	6	.71	30	.283	.345	.513
1984	New York	AL	141	567	193	34	4	19	(9	10)	292	106	100	53	9	71	0	0	6	6	4	.60	14	.340	.393	.515
1985	New York	AL	155	633	174	34	6	26	(15	11)	298	105	114	52	8	96	0	0	4	19	7	.73	17	.275	.328	.471
1986	New York	AL	154	565	148	31	5	24	(12	12)	261	90	104	77	9	106	2	2	6	6	5	.55	20	.262	.349	.462
1987	New York	AL	156	575	158	22	1	27	(11	16)	263	83	97	76	5	96	0	1	3	5	6	.45	20	.275	.358	.457
1988	New York	AL	149	559	180	37	2	25	(12	13)	296	96	107	69	10	88	2	0	1	9	4	.69	19	.322	.398	.530
1990	2 ML Teams		132	475	127	21	2	21	(13	8)	215	70	78	52	3	81	2	1	7	0	1	.00	17	.267	.338	.453
1991	California	AL	150	568	149	27	4	28	(13	15)	268	75	86	56	4	109	1	2	6	7	2	.78	21	.262	.326	.472
1992	Toronto	AL	156	583	169	33	3	26	(13	13)	286	92	108	82	10	89	1	1	3	2	3	.40	10	.290	.377	.491
1993	Minnesota	AL	143	547	148	27	2	21	(12	9)	242	72	76	45	2	106	0	0	2	3	3	.40	15	.271	.325	.442
1990	New York	AL	20	61	13	3	0	2	(0	2)	22	7	6	4	0	13	1	0	1	0	0	.00	2	.213	.269	.361
	California	AL	112	414	114	18	2	19	(13	6)	193	63	72	48	3	68	1	1	6	0	1	.00	15	.275	.348	.466
20 ML YEARS			2850	10594	3014	520	85	453	(212	241)	5063	1623	1786	1171	165	1609	24	18	93	220	95	.70	307	.285	.354	.478

Bobby Witt

Pitches: Right **Bats:** Right **Pos:** SP   **Ht:** 6' 2" **Wt:** 205 **Born:** 05/11/64 **Age:** 30

			HOW MUCH HE PITCHED						WHAT HE GAVE UP												THE RESULTS					
Year	Team	Lg	G	GS	CG	GF	IP	BFP	H	R	ER	HR	SH	SF	HB	TBB	IBB	SO	WP	Bk	W	L	Pct.	ShO	Sv	ERA
1986	Texas	AL	31	31	0	0	157.2	741	130	104	96	18	3	9	3	**143**	2	174	**22**	3	11	9	.550	0	0	5.48
1987	Texas	AL	26	25	1	0	143	673	114	82	78	10	5	5	3	**140**	1	160	7	2	8	10	.444	0	0	4.91
1988	Texas	AL	22	22	13	0	174.1	736	134	83	76	13	7	6	1	101	2	148	**16**	8	8	10	.444	2	0	3.92
1989	Texas	AL	31	31	5	0	194.1	869	182	123	**111**	14	11	8	2	**114**	3	166	7	4	12	13	.480	1	0	5.14
1990	Texas	AL	33	32	7	1	222	954	197	98	83	12	5	6	4	110	3	221	11	2	17	10	.630	1	0	3.36
1991	Texas	AL	17	16	1	0	88.2	413	84	66	60	4	3	4	1	74	1	82	8	0	3	7	.300	1	0	6.09
1992	2 ML Teams		31	31	0	0	193	848	183	99	92	16	7	10	2	114	2	125	9	1	10	14	.417	0	0	4.29
1993	Oakland	AL	35	33	5	0	220	950	226	112	103	16	9	8	3	91	5	131	6	1	14	13	.519	1	0	4.21
1992	Texas	AL	25	25	0	0	161.1	708	152	87	80	14	5	8	2	95	1	100	6	1	9	13	.409	0	0	4.46
	Oakland	AL	6	6	0	0	31.2	140	31	12	12	2	2	2	0	19	1	25	3	0	1	1	.500	0	0	3.41
8 ML YEARS			226	221	32	1	1393	6184	1250	767	699	103	50	56	19	887	19	1207	88	21	83	86	.491	6	0	4.52

Mike Witt

Pitches: Right **Bats:** Right **Pos:** SP | **Ht:** 6' 7" **Wt:** 203 **Born:** 07/20/60 **Age:** 33

Year Team	Lg	G	GS	CG	GF	IP	BFP	H	R	ER	HR	SH	SF	HB	TBB	IBB	SO	WP	Bk	W	L	Pct.	ShO	Sv	ERA
1993 Albany*	AA	1	0	0	1	2	8	2	0	0	0	0	0	0	0	0	2	0	0	0	0	.000	0	0	0.00
Columbus*	AAA	3	3	0	0	13.2	55	11	3	3	1	0	0	0	5	0	11	0	0	1	0	1.000	0	0	1.98
1981 California	AL	22	21	7	1	129	555	123	60	47	9	3	4	11	47	4	75	2	0	8	9	.471	1	0	3.28
1982 California	AL	33	26	5	2	179.2	748	177	77	70	8	8	5	7	47	2	85	8	1	8	6	.571	1	0	3.51
1983 California	AL	43	19	2	15	154	683	173	90	84	14	5	7	6	75	7	77	8	0	7	14	.333	0	5	4.91
1984 California	AL	34	34	9	0	246.2	1032	227	103	95	17	7	7	5	84	3	196	7	1	15	11	.577	2	0	3.47
1985 California	AL	35	35	6	0	250	1049	228	115	99	22	4	5	4	98	6	180	11	1	15	9	.625	1	0	3.56
1986 California	AL	34	34	14	0	269	1071	218	95	85	22	3	5	3	73	2	208	6	0	18	10	.643	3	0	2.84
1987 California	AL	36	36	10	0	247	1065	252	128	110	34	6	6	4	84	4	192	6	0	16	14	.533	0	0	4.01
1988 California	AL	34	34	12	0	249.2	1080	263	130	115	14	11	10	5	87	7	133	9	2	13	16	.448	2	0	4.15
1989 California	AL	33	33	5	0	220	937	252	119	111	26	10	13	2	48	1	123	7	0	9	15	.375	0	0	4.54
1990 2 ML Teams		26	16	2	4	117	498	106	62	52	9	1	6	5	47	4	74	7	0	5	9	.357	1	1	4.00
1991 New York	AL	2	2	0	0	5.1	26	8	7	6	1	0	0	0	1	0	0	1	0	0	1	.000	0	0	10.13
1993 New York	AL	9	9	0	0	41	183	39	26	24	7	1	0	3	22	0	30	1	0	3	2	.600	0	0	5.27
1990 New York	AL	10	0	0	4	20.1	92	19	9	4	1	1	1	1	13	2	14	1	0	0	3	.000	0	1	1.77
New York	AL	16	16	2	0	96.2	406	87	53	48	8	0	5	4	34	2	60	6	0	5	6	.455	1	0	4.47
12 ML YEARS		341	299	72	22	2108.1	8927	2066	1012	898	183	59	68	55	713	40	1373	73	5	117	116	.502	11	6	3.83

Mark Wohlers

Pitches: Right **Bats:** Right **Pos:** RP | **Ht:** 6' 4" **Wt:** 207 **Born:** 01/23/70 **Age:** 24

Year Team	Lg	G	GS	CG	GF	IP	BFP	H	R	ER	HR	SH	SF	HB	TBB	IBB	SO	WP	Bk	W	L	Pct.	ShO	Sv	ERA
1993 Richmond*	AAA	25	0	0	20	29.1	122	21	7	6	0	2	0	1	11	0	39	2	0	1	3	.250	0	4	1.84
1991 Atlanta	NL	17	0	0	4	19.2	89	17	7	7	1	2	1	2	13	3	13	0	0	3	1	.750	0	2	3.20
1992 Atlanta	NL	32	0	0	16	35.1	140	28	11	10	0	5	1	1	14	4	17	1	0	1	1	.333	0	4	2.55
1993 Atlanta	NL	46	0	0	13	48	199	37	25	24	2	5	1	1	22	3	45	0	0	6	2	.750	0	0	4.50
3 ML YEARS		95	0	0	33	103	428	82	43	41	3	12	3	4	49	10	75	1	0	10	5	.667	0	6	3.58

Tony Womack

Bats: Left **Throws:** Right **Pos:** SS | **Ht:** 5' 9" **Wt:** 160 **Born:** 09/25/69 **Age:** 24

Year Team	Lg	G	AB	H	2B	3B	HR	(Hm	Rd)	TB	R	RBI	TBB	IBB	SO	HBP	SH	SF	SB	CS	SB%	GDP	Avg	OBP	SLG
1991 Welland	A	45	166	46	3	0	1	--	--	52	30	8	17	0	39	0	2	0	26	5	.84	1	.277	.344	.313
1992 Augusta	A	102	380	93	8	3	0	--	--	107	62	18	41	0	59	5	4	2	50	25	.67	2	.245	.325	.282
1993 Salem	A	72	304	91	11	3	2	--	--	114	41	18	13	0	34	2	2	1	28	14	.67	2	.299	.331	.375
Carolina	AA	60	247	75	7	2	0	--	--	86	41	23	17	2	34	1	4	4	21	6	.78	3	.304	.346	.348
1993 Pittsburgh	NL	15	24	2	0	0	0	(0	0)	2	5	0	3	0	3	0	1	0	2	0	1.00	0	.083	.185	.083

Ted Wood

Bats: Left **Throws:** Left **Pos:** LF | **Ht:** 6' 2" **Wt:** 178 **Born:** 01/04/67 **Age:** 27

Year Team	Lg	G	AB	H	2B	3B	HR	(Hm	Rd)	TB	R	RBI	TBB	IBB	SO	HBP	SH	SF	SB	CS	SB%	GDP	Avg	OBP	SLG
1989 Shreveport	AA	114	349	90	13	1	0	--	--	105	44	43	51	2	72	6	10	3	9	7	.56	8	.258	.359	.301
1990 Shreveport	AA	131	456	121	22	11	17	--	--	216	81	72	74	5	76	7	4	7	17	8	.68	8	.265	.375	.474
1991 Phoenix	AAA	137	512	159	38	6	11	--	--	242	90	109	86	4	96	4	0	10	12	7	.63	13	.311	.407	.473
1992 Phoenix	AAA	110	418	127	24	7	7	--	--	186	70	63	48	4	74	4	2	5	9	9	.50	5	.304	.377	.445
1993 Ottawa	AAA	83	231	59	11	4	1	--	--	81	39	21	38	2	54	2	2	1	12	2	.86	4	.255	.364	.351
1991 San Francisco	NL	10	25	3	0	0	0	(0	0)	3	0	1	2	0	11	0	1	0	0	0	.00	0	.120	.185	.120
1992 San Francisco	NL	24	58	12	2	0	1	(0	1)	17	5	3	6	0	15	1	2	0	0	0	.00	4	.207	.292	.293
1993 Montreal	NL	13	26	5	1	0	0	(0	0)	6	4	3	3	1	3	0	0	0	0	0	.00	0	.192	.276	.231
3 ML YEARS		47	109	20	3	0	1	(0	1)	26	9	7	11	1	29	1	6	0	0	0	.00	4	.183	.264	.239

Tracy Woodson

Bats: Right **Throws:** Right **Pos:** 3B/1B | **Ht:** 6' 3" **Wt:** 216 **Born:** 10/05/62 **Age:** 31

Year Team	Lg	G	AB	H	2B	3B	HR	(Hm	Rd)	TB	R	RBI	TBB	IBB	SO	HBP	SH	SF	SB	CS	SB%	GDP	Avg	OBP	SLG
1987 Los Angeles	NL	53	136	31	8	1	1	(1	0)	44	14	11	9	2	21	2	0	1	1	1	.50	2	.228	.284	.324
1988 Los Angeles	NL	65	173	43	4	1	3	(2	1)	58	15	15	7	1	32	1	0	2	1	2	.33	4	.249	.279	.335
1989 Los Angeles	NL	4	6	0	0	0	0	(0	0)	0	0	0	0	0	1	0	0	0	0	0	.00	2	.000	.000	.000
1992 St. Louis	NL	31	114	35	8	0	1	(0	1)	46	9	22	3	0	10	1	1	0	0	0	.00	1	.307	.331	.404
1993 St. Louis	NL	62	77	16	2	0	0	(0	0)	18	4	2	1	0	14	0	1	1	0	0	.00	1	.208	.215	.234
5 ML YEARS		215	506	125	22	2	5	(3	2)	166	42	50	20	3	78	4	1	4	2	3	.40	10	.247	.279	.328

Tim Worrell

Pitches: Right **Bats:** Right **Pos:** SP/RP

Ht: 6' 4" **Wt:** 210 **Born:** 07/05/67 **Age:** 26

Year	Team	Lg	G	GS	CG	GF	IP	BFP	H	R	ER	HR	SH	SF	HB	TBB	IBB	SO	WP	Bk	W	L	Pct.	ShO	Sv	ERA
1990	Chston-Sc	A	20	19	3	0	110.2	478	120	65	57	6	4	4	1	28	2	68	9	1	5	8	.385	2	0	4.64
1991	Waterloo	A	14	14	3	0	86.1	359	70	36	32	5	0	1	3	33	0	83	1	1	8	4	.667	2	0	3.34
	High Desert	A	11	11	2	0	63.2	283	65	32	30	2	3	2	2	33	0	70	3	0	5	2	.714	0	0	4.24
1992	Wichita	AA	19	19	1	0	125.2	508	115	46	40	8	1	3	2	32	0	109	1	3	8	6	.571	1	0	2.86
	Las Vegas	AAA	10	10	1	0	63.1	266	61	32	30	4	0	3	3	19	0	32	3	1	4	2	.667	1	0	4.26
1993	Las Vegas	AAA	15	14	2	0	87	382	102	61	53	13	2	5	2	26	1	89	2	0	5	6	.455	0	0	5.48
1993	San Diego	NL	21	16	0	1	100.2	443	104	63	55	11	8	5	0	43	5	52	3	0	2	7	.222	0	0	4.92

Todd Worrell

Pitches: Right **Bats:** Right **Pos:** RP

Ht: 6' 5" **Wt:** 222 **Born:** 09/28/59 **Age:** 34

Year	Team	Lg	G	GS	CG	GF	IP	BFP	H	R	ER	HR	SH	SF	HB	TBB	IBB	SO	WP	Bk	W	L	Pct.	ShO	Sv	ERA
1993	Bakersfield *	A	2	2	0	0	2	7	1	0	0	0	0	0	0	0	0	5	0	0	0	0	.000	0	0	0.00
	Albuquerque *	AAA	7	2	0	1	8.2	37	7	2	1	1	0	0	0	2	0	13	0	0	1	0	1.000	0	0	1.04
1985	St. Louis	NL	17	0	0	11	21.2	88	17	7	7	2	0	2	0	7	2	17	2	0	3	0	1.000	0	5	2.91
1986	St. Louis	NL	74	0	0	60	103.2	430	86	29	24	9	7	6	1	41	16	73	1	0	9	10	.474	0	36	2.08
1987	St. Louis	NL	75	0	0	54	94.2	395	86	29	28	8	4	2	0	34	11	92	1	0	8	6	.571	0	33	2.66
1988	St. Louis	NL	68	0	0	54	90	366	69	32	30	7	3	5	1	34	14	78	6	2	5	9	.357	0	32	3.00
1989	St. Louis	NL	47	0	0	39	51.2	219	42	21	17	4	3	1	0	26	13	41	3	3	3	5	.375	0	20	2.96
1992	St. Louis	NL	67	0	0	14	64	256	45	15	15	4	3	0	1	25	5	64	1	1	5	3	.625	0	3	2.11
1993	Los Angeles	NL	35	0	0	22	38.2	167	46	28	26	6	3	6	0	11	1	31	1	0	1	1	.500	0	5	6.05
	7 ML YEARS		383	0	0	254	464.1	1921	391	161	147	40	23	22	3	178	62	396	15	6	34	34	.500	0	134	2.85

Rick Wrona

Bats: Right **Throws:** Right **Pos:** C

Ht: 6' 0" **Wt:** 180 **Born:** 12/10/63 **Age:** 30

Year	Team	Lg	G	AB	H	2B	3B	HR	(Hm	Rd)	TB	R	RBI	TBB	IBB	SO	HBP	SH	SF	SB	CS	SB%	GDP	Avg	OBP	SLG
1993	Nashville *	AAA	73	184	39	13	0	3	--	--	61	24	22	11	0	35	2	4	3	1	1	.00	1	.212	.260	.332
1988	Chicago	NL	4	6	0	0	0	0	(0	0)	0	0	0	0	0	1	0	0	0	0	0	.00	0	.000	.000	.000
1989	Chicago	NL	38	92	26	2	1	2	(0	2)	36	11	14	2	1	21	1	0	2	0	0	.00	1	.283	.299	.391
1990	Chicago	NL	16	29	5	0	0	0	(0	0)	5	3	0	2	1	11	0	1	0	1	0	1.00	0	.172	.226	.172
1992	Cincinnati	NL	11	23	4	0	0	0	(0	0)	4	0	0	0	0	3	0	0	0	0	0	.00	2	.174	.174	.174
1993	Chicago	AL	4	8	1	0	0	0	(0	0)	1	0	1	0	0	4	0	0	0	0	0	.00	0	.125	.125	.125
	5 ML YEARS		73	158	36	2	1	2	(0	2)	46	14	15	4	2	40	1	1	2	1	0	1.00	3	.228	.248	.291

Eric Yelding

Bats: Right **Throws:** Right **Pos:** 2B

Ht: 5'11" **Wt:** 165 **Born:** 02/22/65 **Age:** 29

Year	Team	Lg	G	AB	H	2B	3B	HR	(Hm	Rd)	TB	R	RBI	TBB	IBB	SO	HBP	SH	SF	SB	CS	SB%	GDP	Avg	OBP	SLG
1989	Houston	NL	70	90	21	2	0	0	(0	0)	23	19	9	7	0	19	1	2	2	11	5	.69	2	.233	.290	.256
1990	Houston	NL	142	511	130	9	5	1	(0	1)	152	69	28	39	1	87	0	4	5	64	25	.72	11	.254	.305	.297
1991	Houston	NL	78	276	67	11	1	1	(0	1)	83	19	20	13	3	46	0	3	1	11	9	.55	4	.243	.276	.301
1992	Houston	NL	9	8	2	0	0	0	(0	0)	2	1	0	0	0	3	0	0	0	0	0	.00	0	.250	.250	.250
1993	Chicago	NL	69	108	22	5	1	1	(1	0)	32	14	10	11	2	22	0	4	0	3	2	.60	3	.204	.277	.296
	5 ML YEARS		368	993	242	27	7	3	(1	2)	292	122	67	70	6	177	1	13	8	89	41	.68	20	.244	.292	.294

Anthony Young

Pitches: Right **Bats:** Right **Pos:** RP/SP

Ht: 6' 2" **Wt:** 210 **Born:** 01/19/66 **Age:** 28

Year	Team	Lg	G	GS	CG	GF	IP	BFP	H	R	ER	HR	SH	SF	HB	TBB	IBB	SO	WP	Bk	W	L	Pct.	ShO	Sv	ERA
1993	Norfolk *	AAA	3	3	0	0	16	60	14	2	2	1	0	0	0	5	0	8	0	0	1	1	.500	0	0	1.13
1991	New York	NL	10	8	0	2	49.1	202	48	20	17	4	1	1	1	12	1	20	1	0	2	5	.286	0	0	3.10
1992	New York	NL	52	13	1	26	121	517	134	66	56	8	11	4	1	31	5	64	3	1	2	14	.125	0	15	4.17
1993	New York	NL	39	10	1	19	100.1	445	103	62	42	8	11	3	1	42	9	62	0	2	1	16	.059	0	3	3.77
	3 ML YEARS		101	31	2	47	270.2	1164	285	148	115	20	23	8	3	85	15	146	4	3	5	35	.125	0	18	3.82

Cliff Young

Pitches: Left **Bats:** Left **Pos:** RP/SP

Ht: 6' 4" **Wt:** 210 **Born:** 08/02/64 **Age:** 29

Year	Team	Lg	G	GS	CG	GF	IP	BFP	H	R	ER	HR	SH	SF	HB	TBB	IBB	SO	WP	Bk	W	L	Pct.	ShO	Sv	ERA
1993	Charlotte *	AAA	5	5	1	0	37.2	141	30	10	9	4	0	0	0	6	0	21	0	0	3	1	.750	1	0	2.15
1990	California	AL	17	0	0	5	30.2	137	40	14	12	2	2	4	1	7	1	19	1	0	1	1	.500	0	0	3.52
1991	California	AL	11	0	0	6	12.2	49	12	6	6	3	0	0	0	3	1	6	0	0	1	0	1.000	0	0	4.26

Year Team	Lg	G	GS	CG	GF	IP	BFP	H	R	ER	HR	SH	SF	HB	TBB	IBB	SO	WP	Bk	W	L	Pct.	ShO	Sv	ERA
1993 Cleveland	AL	21	7	0	3	60.1	271	74	35	31	9	1	1	3	18	1	31	0	0	3	3	.500	0	1	4.62
3 ML YEARS		49	7	0	14	103.2	457	126	55	49	14	3	5	4	28	3	56	1	0	5	4	.556	0	1	4.25

Curt Young

Pitches: Left **Bats: Right** **Pos: SP**   **Ht: 6' 1"** **Wt: 180** **Born: 04/16/60** **Age: 34**

		HOW MUCH HE PITCHED						WHAT HE GAVE UP												THE RESULTS					
Year Team	Lg	G	GS	CG	GF	IP	BFP	H	R	ER	HR	SH	SF	HB	TBB	IBB	SO	WP	Bk	W	L	Pct.	ShO	Sv	ERA
1993 Tacoma *	AAA	10	10	1	0	65.1	262	53	23	14	2	2	2	1	16	0	31	1	2	0	1	.857	0	0	1.93
1983 Oakland	AL	8	2	0	0	9	50	17	17	16	1	0	0	1	5	0	5	1	0	0	1	.000	0	0	16.00
1984 Oakland	AL	20	17	2	0	108.2	475	118	53	49	9	1	4	8	31	0	41	3	0	9	4	.692	1	0	4.06
1985 Oakland	AL	19	7	0	5	46	214	57	38	37	15	0	1	1	22	0	19	1	0	0	4	.000	0	0	7.24
1986 Oakland	AL	29	27	5	0	198	826	176	88	76	19	8	9	7	57	1	116	7	2	13	9	.591	2	0	3.45
1987 Oakland	AL	31	31	6	0	203	828	194	102	92	38	6	4	3	44	0	124	2	1	13	7	.650	0	0	4.08
1988 Oakland	AL	26	26	1	0	156.1	651	162	77	72	23	3	5	4	50	3	69	3	6	11	8	.579	0	0	4.14
1989 Oakland	AL	25	20	1	2	111	495	117	56	46	10	1	0	3	47	2	55	4	4	5	9	.357	0	0	3.73
1990 Oakland	AL	26	21	0	0	124.1	527	124	70	67	17	4	2	2	53	1	56	3	0	9	6	.600	0	0	4.85
1991 Oakland	AL	41	1	0	6	68.1	306	74	38	38	8	3	1	2	34	2	27	2	1	4	2	.667	0	0	5.00
1992 2 ML Teams		23	7	0	5	67.2	295	80	35	30	2	3	3	2	17	2	20	1	0	4	2	.667	0	0	3.99
1993 Oakland	AL	3	3	0	0	14.2	64	14	7	7	5	0	0	0	6	0	4	0	0	1	1	.500	0	0	4.30
1992 Kansas City	AL	10	2	0	2	24.1	107	29	14	14	1	0	1	0	7	1	7	0	0	1	2	.333	0	0	5.18
New York	AL	13	5	0	3	43.1	188	51	21	16	1	3	2	2	10	1	13	0	0	3	0	1.000	0	0	3.32
11 ML YEARS		251	162	15	18	1107	4731	1133	581	530	147	29	29	33	366	11	536	26	14	69	53	.566	3	0	4.31

Eric Young

Bats: Right **Throws: Right** **Pos: 2B/LF**   **Ht: 5' 9"** **Wt: 180** **Born: 05/18/67** **Age: 27**

		BATTING																	BASERUNNING				PERCENTAGES		
Year Team	Lg	G	AB	H	2B	3B	HR	(Hm	Rd)	TB	R	RBI	TBB	IBB	SO	HBP	SH	SF	SB	CS	SB%	GDP	Avg	OBP	SLG
1989 Dodgers	R	56	197	65	11	5	2	--	--	92	53	22	33	1	16	3	1	0	41	10	.80	1	.330	.432	.467
1990 Vero Beach	A	127	460	132	23	7	2	--	--	175	101	50	69	1	35	6	5	4	76	16	.83	9	.287	.384	.380
1991 San Antonio	AA	127	461	129	17	4	3	--	--	163	82	35	67	0	36	2	8	1	71	26	.73	13	.280	.373	.354
Albuquerque	AAA	1	5	2	0	0	0	--	--	2	2	0	0	0	0	0	0	0	0	0	.00	0	.400	.400	.400
1992 Albuquerque	AAA	94	350	118	16	5	3	--	--	153	61	49	33	0	18	4	13	7	28	11	.72	10	.337	.393	.437
1992 Los Angeles	NL	49	132	34	1	0	1	(0	1)	38	9	11	8	0	9	0	4	0	6	1	.86	3	.258	.300	.288
1993 Colorado	NL	144	490	132	16	8	3	(3	0)	173	82	42	63	3	41	0	2	4	42	19	.69	9	.269	.355	.353
2 ML YEARS		193	622	166	17	8	4	(3	1)	211	91	53	71	3	50	4	8	4	48	20	.71	12	.267	.344	.339

Gerald Young

Bats: Both **Throws: Right** **Pos: RF**   **Ht: 6' 2"** **Wt: 185** **Born: 10/22/64** **Age: 29**

		BATTING																	BASERUNNING				PERCENTAGES		
Year Team	Lg	G	AB	H	2B	3B	HR	(Hm	Rd)	TB	R	RBI	TBB	IBB	SO	HBP	SH	SF	SB	CS	SB%	GDP	Avg	OBP	SLG
1993 Indianapols *	AAA	32	103	31	10	0	1	--	--	44	16	6	18	3	7	1	2	1	7	2	.78	0	.301	.407	.427
Calgary *	AAA	26	104	31	8	2	1	--	--	46	19	10	20	0	16	0	1	0	7	9	.44	1	.298	.411	.442
1987 Houston	NL	71	274	88	9	2	1	(0	1)	104	44	15	26	0	27	1	0	2	26	9	.74	1	.321	.380	.380
1988 Houston	NL	149	576	148	21	9	0	(0	0)	187	79	37	66	1	66	3	5	5	65	27	.71	10	.257	.334	.325
1989 Houston	NL	146	533	124	17	3	0	(0	0)	147	71	38	74	4	60	2	6	5	34	25	.58	7	.233	.326	.276
1990 Houston	NL	57	154	27	4	1	1	(1	0)	36	15	4	20	0	23	0	4	1	6	3	.67	3	.175	.269	.234
1991 Houston	NL	108	142	31	3	1	1	(0	1)	39	26	11	24	0	17	0	1	2	16	5	.76	3	.218	.327	.275
1992 Houston	NL	74	76	14	1	1	0	(0	0)	17	14	4	10	0	11	0	4	0	6	2	.75	2	.184	.279	.224
1993 Colorado	NL	19	19	1	0	0	0	(0	0)	1	5	1	0	0	5	0	0	0	0	1	.00	2	.053	.217	.053
7 ML YEARS		624	1774	433	55	17	3	(1	2)	531	254	110	224	5	205	6	20	15	153	72	.68	28	.244	.328	.299

Kevin Young

Bats: Right **Throws: Right** **Pos: 1B**   **Ht: 6' 2"** **Wt: 213** **Born: 06/16/69** **Age: 25**

		BATTING																	BASERUNNING				PERCENTAGES		
Year Team	Lg	G	AB	H	2B	3B	HR	(Hm	Rd)	TB	R	RBI	TBB	IBB	SO	HBP	SH	SF	SB	CS	SB%	GDP	Avg	OBP	SLG
1990 Welland	A	72	238	58	16	2	5	--	--	93	46	30	31	2	39	7	0	5	10	2	.83	4	.244	.342	.391
1991 Salem	A	56	201	63	11	4	6	--	--	100	38	28	20	0	34	7	0	3	3	2	.60	5	.313	.390	.498
Carolina	AA	75	263	90	19	6	3	--	--	130	36	33	15	1	38	8	0	1	9	3	.75	7	.342	.394	.494
Buffalo	AAA	4	9	2	1	0	0	--	--	3	1	2	0	0	0	1	0	1	1	0	1.00	0	.222	.273	.333
1992 Buffalo	AAA	137	490	154	29	6	8	--	--	219	91	65	67	11	67	11	8	3	18	12	.60	11	.314	.406	.447
1992 Pittsburgh	NL	10	7	4	0	0	0	(0	0)	4	2	4	2	0	0	1	0	0	1	0	1.00	0	.571	.667	.571
1993 Pittsburgh	NL	141	449	106	24	3	6	(6	0)	154	38	47	36	3	82	9	5	9	2	2	.50	9	.236	.300	.343
2 ML YEARS		151	456	110	24	3	6	(6	0)	158	40	51	38	3	82	9	5	9	3	2	.60	9	.241	.307	.346

Matt Young

Pitches: Left **Bats:** Left **Pos:** RP/SP   **Ht:** 6' 3" **Wt:** 210 **Born:** 08/09/58 **Age:** 35

Year Team	Lg	G	GS	CG	GF	IP	BFP	H	R	ER	HR	SH	SF	HB	TBB	IBB	SO	WP	Bk	W	L	Pct.	ShO	Sv	ERA
1993 Charlotte *	AAA	3	3	1	0	17.2	68	11	5	5	1	0	0	3	5	0	17	0	0	3	0	1.000	0	0	2.55
Syracuse *	AAA	7	5	0	1	31.2	125	22	10	8	1	1	0	2	14	0	38	0	0	2	1	.667	0	0	2.27
1983 Seattle	AL	33	32	5	0	203.2	851	178	86	74	17	4	8	7	79	2	130	4	2	11	15	.423	2	0	3.27
1984 Seattle	AL	22	22	1	0	113.1	524	141	81	72	11	1	5	1	57	3	73	3	1	6	8	.429	1	0	5.72
1985 Seattle	AL	37	35	5	2	218.1	951	242	135	119	23	3	7	7	76	3	136	6	2	12	19	.387	2	1	4.91
1986 Seattle	AL	65	5	1	32	103.2	458	108	50	44	9	4	3	8	46	2	82	7	1	8	6	.571	0	13	3.82
1987 Los Angeles	NL	47	0	0	31	54.1	234	62	30	27	3	1	1	0	17	5	42	3	0	5	8	.385	0	11	4.47
1989 Oakland	AL	26	4	0	1	37.1	183	42	31	28	2	4	1	0	31	2	27	5	0	1	4	.200	0	0	6.75
1990 Seattle	AL	34	33	7	0	225.1	963	198	106	88	15	7	7	6	107	7	176	16	0	8	18	.308	1	0	3.51
1991 Boston	AL	19	16	0	1	88.2	404	92	55	51	4	1	2	2	53	2	69	5	0	3	7	.300	0	0	5.18
1992 Boston	AL	28	8	1	4	70.2	321	69	42	36	7	4	3	3	42	2	57	2	0	0	4	.000	0	0	4.58
1993 Cleveland	AL	22	8	0	2	74.1	347	75	45	43	8	4	1	3	57	0	65	5	1	1	6	.143	0	0	5.21
10 ML YEARS		333	163	20	73	1189.2	5236	1207	661	582	99	37	34	37	565	28	857	56	7	55	95	.367	5	25	4.40

Pete Young

Pitches: Right **Bats:** Right **Pos:** RP   **Ht:** 6' 0" **Wt:** 225 **Born:** 03/19/68 **Age:** 26

Year Team	Lg	G	GS	CG	GF	IP	BFP	H	R	ER	HR	SH	SF	HB	TBB	IBB	SO	WP	Bk	W	L	Pct.	ShO	Sv	ERA
1989 Jamestown	A	18	10	0	8	65	269	63	18	14	2	0	1	5	14	0	62	6	0	5	2	.714	0	4	1.94
1990 Wst Plm Bch	A	39	12	0	25	109.1	453	106	36	30	3	3	2	2	27	1	62	6	0	8	3	.727	0	19	2.47
1991 Sumter	A	1	0	0	0	1	5	1	1	1	0	0	0	0	1	0	2	0	0	0	0	.000	0	0	9.00
Harrisburg	AA	54	0	0	29	90	368	82	28	26	9	4	1	2	24	4	74	1	0	7	5	.583	0	13	2.60
1992 Indianapls	AAA	36	0	0	20	48.2	216	53	19	19	5	4	3	1	21	3	34	0	0	6	2	.750	0	7	3.51
1993 Ottawa	AAA	48	0	0	16	72.1	311	63	32	30	5	5	4	6	33	10	46	2	0	4	5	.444	0	1	3.73
1992 Montreal	NL	13	0	0	6	20.1	85	18	9	9	0	0	2	1	9	2	11	1	0	0	0	.000	0	0	3.98
1993 Montreal	NL	4	0	0	2	5.1	20	4	2	2	1	1	0	0	0	0	3	0	0	1	0	1.000	0	0	3.38
2 ML YEARS		17	0	0	8	25.2	105	22	11	11	1	1	2	1	9	2	14	1	0	1	0	1.000	0	0	3.86

Robin Yount

Bats: Right **Throws:** Right **Pos:** CF   **Ht:** 6' 0" **Wt:** 180 **Born:** 09/16/55 **Age:** 38

Year Team	Lg	G	AB	H	2B	3B	HR	(Hm	Rd)	TB	R	RBI	TBB	IBB	SO	HBP	SH	SF	SB	CS	SB%	GDP	Avg	OBP	SLG
1974 Milwaukee	AL	107	344	86	14	5	3	(3	0)	119	48	26	12	0	46	1	5	2	7	7	.50	4	.250	.276	.346
1975 Milwaukee	AL	147	558	149	28	2	8	(4	4)	205	67	52	33	3	69	1	10	5	12	4	.75	8	.267	.307	.367
1976 Milwaukee	AL	161	638	161	19	3	2	(1	1)	192	59	54	38	3	69	0	8	6	16	11	.59	13	.252	.292	.301
1977 Milwaukee	AL	154	605	174	34	4	4	(2	2)	228	66	49	41	1	80	2	11	4	16	7	.70	11	.288	.333	.377
1978 Milwaukee	AL	127	502	147	23	9	9	(5	4)	215	66	71	24	1	43	1	13	5	16	5	.76	5	.293	.323	.428
1979 Milwaukee	AL	149	577	154	26	5	8	(4	4)	214	72	51	35	3	52	1	10	3	11	8	.58	15	.267	.308	.371
1980 Milwaukee	AL	143	611	179	49	10	23	(13	10)	317	121	87	26	1	67	1	6	3	20	5	.80	8	.293	.321	.519
1981 Milwaukee	AL	96	377	103	15	5	10	(1	9)	158	50	49	22	1	37	2	4	6	4	1	.80	4	.273	.312	.419
1982 Milwaukee	AL	156	635	210	46	12	29	(9	20)	367	129	114	54	2	63	1	4	10	14	3	.82	19	.331	.379	.578
1983 Milwaukee	AL	149	578	178	42	10	17	(6	11)	291	102	80	72	6	58	3	1	8	12	5	.71	11	.308	.383	.503
1984 Milwaukee	AL	160	624	186	27	7	16	(8	8)	275	105	80	67	7	67	1	1	9	14	4	.78	22	.298	.362	.441
1985 Milwaukee	AL	122	466	129	26	3	15	(11	4)	206	76	68	49	3	56	2	1	9	10	4	.71	8	.277	.342	.442
1986 Milwaukee	AL	140	522	163	31	7	9	(4	5)	235	82	46	62	7	73	4	5	2	14	5	.74	9	.312	.388	.450
1987 Milwaukee	AL	158	635	198	25	9	21	(12	9)	304	99	103	76	10	94	1	6	5	19	9	.68	9	.312	.384	.479
1988 Milwaukee	AL	162	621	190	38	11	13	(7	6)	289	92	91	63	10	63	3	2	7	22	4	.85	21	.306	.369	.465
1989 Milwaukee	AL	160	614	195	38	9	21	(14	7)	314	101	103	63	9	71	6	3	4	19	3	.86	9	.318	.384	.511
1990 Milwaukee	AL	158	587	145	17	5	17	(8	9)	223	98	77	78	6	89	6	4	8	15	8	.65	7	.247	.337	.380
1991 Milwaukee	AL	130	503	131	20	4	10	(8	2)	189	66	77	54	4	79	4	1	9	6	4	.60	13	.260	.332	.376
1992 Milwaukee	AL	150	557	147	40	3	8	(3	5)	217	71	77	53	9	81	3	4	12	15	6	.71	9	.264	.325	.390
1993 Milwaukee	AL	127	454	117	25	3	8	(1	7)	172	62	51	44	5	93	5	5	6	9	2	.82	12	.258	.326	.379
20 ML YEARS		2856	11008	3142	583	126	251	(124	127)	4730	1632	1406	966	95	1350	48	104	123	271	105	.72	217	.285	.342	.430

Eddie Zambrano

Bats: Right **Throws:** Right **Pos:** RF   **Ht:** 6' 2" **Wt:** 175 **Born:** 02/01/66 **Age:** 28

Year Team	Lg	G	AB	H	2B	3B	HR	(Hm	Rd)	TB	R	RBI	TBB	IBB	SO	HBP	SH	SF	SB	CS	SB%	GDP	Avg	OBP	SLG
1990 Kinston	A	63	204	50	7	2	3	--	--	70	26	30	29	1	36	1	1	2	1	3	.25	6	.245	.339	.343
1991 Carolina	AA	83	269	68	17	3	3	--	--	100	28	39	22	0	57	4	2	7	4	2	.67	4	.253	.311	.372
Buffalo	AAA	48	144	49	8	5	3	--	--	76	19	35	17	1	25	2	2	4	1	1	.50	1	.340	.407	.528

Year Team	Lg	G	AB	H	2B	3B	HR	(Hm	Rd)	TB	R	RBI	TBB	IBB	SO	HBP	SH	SF	SB	CS	SB%	GDP	Avg	OBP	SLG
1992 Buffalo	AAA	126	394	112	22	4	16	--	--	190	47	79	51	2	75	4	3	5	3	2	.60	7	.284	.368	.482
1993 Iowa	AAA	133	469	142	29	2	32	--	--	271	95	115	54	11	93	6	2	7	10	7	.59	10	.303	.377	.578
1993 Chicago	NL	8	17	5	0	0	0	(0	0)	5	1	2	1	0	3	0	0	0	0	0	.00	1	.294	.333	.294

Todd Zeile

Bats: Right   **Throws:** Right   **Pos:** 3B   **Ht:** 6' 1"   **Wt:** 190   **Born:** 09/09/65   **Age:** 28

Year Team	Lg	G	AB	H	2B	3B	HR	(Hm	Rd)	TB	R	RBI	TBB	IBB	SO	HBP	SH	SF	SB	CS	SB%	GDP	Avg	OBP	SLG
1989 St. Louis	NL	28	82	21	3	1	1	(0	1)	29	7	8	9	1	14	0	1	1	0	0	.00	1	.256	.326	.354
1990 St. Louis	NL	144	495	121	25	3	15	(8	7)	197	62	57	67	3	77	2	0	6	2	4	.33	11	.244	.333	.398
1991 St. Louis	NL	155	565	158	36	3	11	(7	4)	233	76	81	62	3	94	5	0	6	17	11	.61	15	.280	.353	.412
1992 St. Louis	NL	126	439	113	18	4	7	(4	3)	160	51	48	68	4	70	0	0	7	7	10	.41	11	.257	.352	.364
1993 St. Louis	NL	157	571	158	36	1	17	(8	9)	247	82	103	70	5	76	0	0	6	5	4	.56	15	.277	.352	.433
5 ML YEARS		610	2152	571	118	12	51	(27	24)	866	278	297	276	16	331	7	1	26	31	29	.52	53	.265	.347	.402

Bob Zupcic

Bats: Right   **Throws:** Right   **Pos:** RF/LF/CF   **Ht:** 6' 4"   **Wt:** 225   **Born:** 08/18/66   **Age:** 27

Year Team	Lg	G	AB	H	2B	3B	HR	(Hm	Rd)	TB	R	RBI	TBB	IBB	SO	HBP	SH	SF	SB	CS	SB%	GDP	Avg	OBP	SLG
1991 Boston	AL	18	25	4	0	0	1	(1	0)	7	3	3	1	0	6	0	1	0	0	0	.00	0	.160	.192	.280
1992 Boston	AL	124	392	108	19	1	3	(3	0)	138	46	43	25	1	60	4	7	4	2	2	.50	6	.276	.322	.352
1993 Boston	AL	141	286	69	24	2	2	(1	1)	103	40	26	27	2	54	2	8	3	5	2	.71	7	.241	.308	.360
3 ML YEARS		283	703	181	43	3	6	(5	1)	248	89	72	53	3	120	6	16	7	7	4	.64	13	.257	.312	.353

1993 Team Statistics

American League Batting

Team	G	AB	H	2B	3B	HR	(Hm	Rd)	TB	R	RBI	TBB	IBB	SO	HBP	SH	SF	SB	CS	SB%	GDP	Avg	OBP	SLG
Detroit	162	5620	1546	282	38	178	(103	75)	2438	899	853	765	50	1122	35	33	52	104	63	.62	101	.275	.362	.434
Toronto	162	5579	1556	317	42	159	(90	69)	2434	847	796	588	57	861	52	46	54	170	49	.78	138	.279	.350	.436
Texas	162	5510	1472	284	39	181	(90	91)	2377	835	780	483	56	984	48	69	56	113	67	.63	111	.267	.329	.431
New York	162	5615	1568	294	24	178	(88	90)	2444	821	793	629	47	910	43	22	50	39	35	.53	149	.279	.353	.435
Cleveland	162	5619	1547	264	31	141	(69	72)	2296	790	747	488	57	843	49	39	72	159	55	.74	131	.275	.335	.409
Baltimore	162	5508	1470	287	24	157	(87	70)	2276	786	744	655	52	930	41	49	56	73	54	.57	131	.267	.346	.413
Chicago	162	5483	1454	228	44	162	(82	80)	2256	776	731	604	52	834	33	72	61	106	57	.65	126	.265	.338	.411
Seattle	162	5494	1429	272	24	161	(74	87)	2232	734	681	624	73	901	56	63	51	91	68	.57	132	.260	.339	.406
Milwaukee	162	5525	1426	240	25	125	(53	72)	2091	733	688	555	52	932	40	57	45	138	93	.60	117	.258	.328	.378
Oakland	162	5543	1408	260	21	158	(78	80)	2184	715	679	622	45	1048	33	46	49	131	59	.69	125	.254	.330	.394
Minnesota	162	5601	1480	261	27	121	(56	65)	2158	693	642	493	35	850	51	27	37	83	59	.58	150	.264	.327	.385
Boston	162	5496	1451	319	29	114	(54	60)	2170	686	644	508	69	871	62	80	49	73	38	.66	146	.264	.330	.395
California	162	5391	1399	259	24	114	(64	50)	2048	684	644	564	39	901	38	50	46	169	100	.63	129	.260	.331	.380
Kansas City	162	5522	1455	294	35	125	(50	75)	2194	675	641	428	50	936	52	48	51	100	75	.57	107	.263	.320	.397
American	1134	77506	20661	3861	427	2074	(1038	1036)	31598	10674	10063	8006	734	12952	633	701	729	1549	872	.64	1793	.267	.337	.408

American League Pitching

Team	G	GS	CG	GF	IP	BFP	H	R	ER	HR	SH	SF	HB	TBB	IBB	SO	WP	Bk	W	L	Pct.	ShO	Sv	ERA
Chicago	162	162	16	146	1454	6173	1398	664	598	125	54	41	40	566	36	974	51	7	94	68	.580	11	48	3.70
Kansas City	162	162	16	146	1445.1	6145	1379	694	649	105	41	52	44	571	36	985	76	7	84	78	.519	6	48	4.04
Boston	162	162	9	153	1452.1	6201	1379	698	609	127	58	60	48	552	87	997	42	11	80	82	.494	11	44	3.77
Seattle	162	162	22	140	1453.2	6254	1421	731	678	135	55	45	66	605	56	1083	57	6	82	80	.506	10	41	4.20
Toronto	162	162	11	151	1441.1	6269	1441	742	674	134	38	52	32	620	38	1023	83	8	95	67	.586	11	50	4.21
Baltimore	162	162	21	141	1442.2	6183	1427	745	691	153	51	42	38	579	50	900	41	2	85	77	.525	10	42	4.31
Texas	162	162	20	142	1438.1	6232	1476	751	684	144	48	42	44	562	42	957	53	14	86	76	.531	6	45	4.28
New York	162	162	11	151	1438.1	6200	1467	761	695	170	50	47	29	552	58	899	33	5	88	74	.543	13	38	4.35
California	162	162	26	136	1430.1	6203	1482	770	690	153	53	61	51	550	35	843	55	7	71	91	.438	6	41	4.34
Milwaukee	162	162	26	136	1447	6285	1511	792	716	153	50	76	60	522	58	810	45	7	69	93	.426	6	29	4.45
Cleveland	162	162	7	155	1445.2	6384	1591	813	735	182	48	41	39	591	53	888	41	5	76	86	.469	8	45	4.58
Minnesota	162	162	5	157	1444.1	6286	1591	830	756	148	42	66	45	514	34	901	43	13	71	91	.438	3	44	4.71
Detroit	162	162	11	151	1436.2	6308	1547	837	742	188	56	57	48	542	92	828	68	5	85	77	.525	7	36	4.65
Oakland	162	162	8	154	1452.1	6456	1551	846	791	157	57	47	49	680	59	864	39	6	68	94	.420	2	42	4.90
American	1134	1134	209	925	20222.1	87579	20661	10674	9708	2074	701	729	633	8006	734	12952	727	103	1134	1134	.500	110	593	4.32

246

National League Batting

Team	G	AB	H	2B	3B	HR	(Hm	Rd)	TB	R	RBI	TBB	IBB	SO	HBP	SH	SF	SB	CS	SB%	GDP	Avg	OBP	SLG
Philadelphia	162	5685	1555	297	51	156	(80	76)	2422	877	811	665	70	1049	42	84	51	91	32	.74	107	.274	.351	.426
San Francisco	162	5557	1534	269	33	168	(82	86)	2373	808	759	516	88	930	46	102	50	120	65	.65	121	.276	.340	.427
Atlanta	162	5515	1444	239	29	169	(78	91)	2248	767	712	560	46	946	36	73	50	125	48	.72	127	.262	.331	.408
St. Louis	162	5551	1508	262	34	118	(59	59)	2192	758	724	588	50	882	27	59	54	153	72	.68	128	.272	.341	.395
Colorado	162	5517	1507	278	59	142	(77	65)	2329	758	704	388	40	944	46	70	52	146	90	.62	125	.273	.323	.422
Chicago	163	5627	1521	259	32	161	(76	85)	2327	738	706	446	61	923	34	67	42	100	43	.70	131	.270	.325	.414
Montreal	163	5493	1410	270	36	122	(62	60)	2118	732	682	542	65	860	48	100	50	228	56	.80	95	.257	.326	.386
Cincinnati	162	5517	1457	261	28	137	(69	68)	2185	722	669	485	42	1025	32	63	66	142	59	.71	104	.264	.324	.396
Houston	162	5464	1459	288	37	138	(62	76)	2235	716	664	497	58	911	40	82	47	103	60	.63	125	.267	.330	.409
Pittsburgh	162	5549	1482	267	50	110	(64	46)	2179	707	664	536	50	972	55	76	52	92	55	.63	129	.267	.335	.393
San Diego	162	5503	1386	239	28	153	(87	66)	2140	679	633	443	43	1046	59	80	50	92	41	.69	111	.252	.312	.389
Los Angeles	162	5588	1458	234	28	130	(66	64)	2138	675	639	492	48	937	27	107	47	126	61	.67	105	.261	.321	.383
New York	162	5448	1350	228	37	158	(75	83)	2126	672	632	498	43	879	24	89	47	79	50	.61	108	.248	.305	.390
Florida	162	5475	1356	197	31	94	(44	50)	1897	581	542	498	39	1054	51	58	43	117	56	.68	122	.248	.314	.346
National	1135	77489	20427	3588	513	1956	(981	975)	30909	10190	9533	7104	743	13358	567	1110	701	1714	788	.69	1638	.264	.327	.399

National League Pitching

Team	G	GS	CG	GF	IP	BFP	H	R	ER	HR	SH	SF	HB	TBB	IBB	SO	WP	Bk	W	L	Pct.	ShO	Sv	ERA
Atlanta	162	162	18	144	1455	6015	1297	559	507	101	77	39	22	480	59	1036	46	9	104	58	.642	16	46	3.14
Houston	162	162	18	144	1441.1	6079	1363	630	559	117	79	43	41	476	52	1056	60	12	85	77	.525	14	42	3.49
San Francisco	162	162	4	158	1456.2	6077	1385	636	585	168	74	38	50	442	46	982	33	18	103	59	.636	9	50	3.61
Los Angeles	162	162	17	145	1472.2	6274	1406	662	573	103	76	48	37	567	68	1043	47	20	81	81	.500	9	36	3.50
Montreal	163	163	8	155	1456.2	6191	1369	682	574	119	82	40	47	521	38	934	46	12	94	68	.580	7	61	3.55
Florida	162	162	4	158	1440.1	6261	1437	724	661	135	80	50	32	598	58	945	85	20	64	98	.395	5	48	4.13
Chicago	163	163	8	155	1449.2	6178	1514	739	673	153	69	51	43	470	61	905	43	21	84	78	.519	5	56	4.18
Philadelphia	162	162	24	138	1472.2	6360	1419	740	647	129	65	42	37	573	33	1117	74	7	97	65	.599	11	46	3.95
New York	162	162	16	146	1438	6151	1483	744	647	139	87	58	50	434	61	867	32	14	59	103	.364	8	22	4.05
St. Louis	162	162	5	157	1453	6196	1553	744	660	152	80	57	43	383	50	775	40	7	87	75	.537	7	54	4.09
San Diego	162	162	8	154	1437.2	6267	1470	772	675	148	89	62	34	558	72	957	57	14	61	101	.377	6	32	4.23
Cincinnati	162	162	11	151	1434	6218	1510	785	718	158	77	40	44	508	36	996	47	8	73	89	.451	8	37	4.51
Pittsburgh	162	162	12	150	1445.2	6247	1557	806	766	153	93	55	46	485	43	832	55	11	75	87	.463	5	34	4.77
Colorado	162	162	9	153	1431.1	6471	1664	967	860	181	82	78	41	609	66	913	82	22	67	95	.414	0	35	5.41
National	1135	1135	162	973	20284.2	86985	20427	10190	9105	1956	1110	701	567	7104	743	13358	747	195	1134	1134	.500	110	599	4.04

1993 Fielding Stats

Fielding statistics and the weather. (We liked that opening sentence three years ago, so we thought we'd try it again.) Thanks to pioneers like Bill James and John Dewan, today one rarely hears a discussion of a player's fielding ability without consideration of his range. We still don't necessarily hear "range factor" or "zone rating", but maybe in a few years those terms will be commonplace. But we also don't hear anymore that Jody Reed is a better second baseman than Mark Lemke because he makes fewer errors each year. (Remember the annual 1970's article on why the Cardinals' Ken Reitz deserved the Gold Glove rather than the Phils' Mike Schmidt?)

But enough patting ourselves on the back. The only important items you'll need to know before digging in are these: All the fielding stats are unofficial. An assist here or a putout there may change when the official stats arrive in December, but these are very close as they are. (Everyone, sing along! Here an A, there an E, everywhere a DP.) The regulars are sorted by range factor, except for the first baseman and the catchers in the first catcher section, who are sorted by fielding percentage. The catchers in the special catcher section are sorted by Catcher ERA (CERA). Remember to consider that pitching staff when looking at those CERA's. (How bad can a CERA be when catching the Braves' staff?) And finally, ties in range or percentage are, in reality, not ties at all, just numbers that don't show enough digits to be unique.

First Basemen - Regulars

Player	Tm	G	Inn	PO	A	E	DP	Pct.	Rng
Mattingly,Don	NYA	130	1118.0	1257	81	3	124	.998	---
Young,Kevin	Pit	135	1056.2	1115	100	3	111	.998	---
Martinez,Tino	Sea	103	909.2	933	60	3	87	.997	---
Grace,Mark	ChN	154	1350.1	1455	109	5	136	.997	---
Palmeiro,Rafael	Tex	160	1395.0	1388	143	5	137	.997	---
Segui,David	Bal	144	1155.0	1152	94	5	122	.996	---
Bream,Sid	Atl	90	638.0	627	60	3	63	.996	---
Milligan,Randy	TOT	79	603.2	569	63	3	64	.995	---
Hrbek,Kent	Min	115	944.2	941	80	5	99	.995	---
Sorrento,Paul	Cle	144	1083.0	1012	86	6	106	.995	---
Snow,J.T.	Cal	129	1059.0	1010	78	6	103	.995	---
Joyner,Wally	KC	140	1194.0	1116	145	7	115	.994	---
Morris,Hal	Cin	98	834.1	745	76	5	61	.994	---
Kruk,John	Phi	144	1243.1	1149	69	8	79	.993	---
Jefferies,Gregg	StL	140	1184.2	1279	75	9	114	.993	---
Bagwell,Jeff	Hou	141	1229.2	1197	111	9	105	.993	---
Jaha,John	Mil	150	1281.1	1187	128	10	116	.992	---
Olerud,John	Tor	137	1205.1	1159	97	10	107	.992	---
Karros,Eric	LA	157	1373.2	1337	146	12	118	.992	---
Fielder,Cecil	Det	119	962.1	971	76	10	84	.991	---
Galarraga,Andres	Col	119	1007.1	1016	100	11	88	.990	---
Thomas,Frank	ChA	150	1300.2	1222	82	15	127	.989	---
Clark,Will	SF	129	1113.1	1079	86	14	114	.988	---
Murray,Eddie	NYN	154	1321.0	1320	109	18	116	.988	---
McGriff,Fred	TOT	150	1290.2	1213	89	17	101	.987	---
Destrade,Orestes	Fla	152	1281.2	1310	89	19	108	.987	---
Vaughn,Mo	Bos	131	1129.1	1110	67	16	103	.987	---
Average	---	133	1120.2	1106	92	8	103	.993	---

First Basemen - The Rest

Player	Tm	G	Inn	PO	A	E	DP	Pct.	Rng
Aldrete,Mike	Oak	59	438.1	368	26	2	39	.995	---
Allanson,Andy	SF	2	7.0	8	0	0	0	1.000	---
Amaral,Rich	Sea	3	7.0	4	0	0	2	1.000	---
Armas,Marcos	Oak	12	71.0	74	4	0	4	1.000	---
Aude,Rich	Pit	7	50.0	48	3	0	6	1.000	---
Barnes,Skeeter	Det	27	107.1	113	9	2	6	.984	---
Bean,Billy	SD	12	53.0	51	3	0	5	1.000	---
Benavides,Freddie	Col	1	2.0	2	0	0	1	1.000	---
Benzinger,Todd	SF	40	280.2	289	15	0	27	1.000	---
Blankenship,Lance	Oak	6	14.0	12	0	0	1	1.000	---
Blowers,Mike	Sea	1	1.0	1	0	0	0	1.000	---
Bolick,Frank	Mon	51	302.2	333	32	3	28	.992	---
Bonilla,Bobby	NYN	6	44.1	50	1	1	4	.981	---
Branson,Jeff	Cin	1	9.0	10	1	0	0	1.000	---
Brewer,Rod	StL	32	102.2	101	5	1	13	.991	---
Brooks,Hubie	KC	3	23.0	19	3	0	1	1.000	---
Brosius,Scott	Oak	11	64.1	68	2	0	7	1.000	---
Browne,Jerry	Oak	2	9.0	8	2	1	3	.909	---
Buechele,Steve	ChN	6	22.1	18	0	0	3	1.000	---
Bush,Randy	Min	4	15.0	13	0	0	2	1.000	---
Cabrera,Francisco	Atl	12	73.0	61	10	0	4	1.000	---
Carey,Paul	Bal	9	60.0	64	0	2	7	.970	---
Carreon,Mark	SF	3	14.0	6	2	0	1	1.000	---
Castellano,Pedro	Col	10	35.0	37	5	2	6	.955	---
Cianfrocco,Archi	Mon	11	40.0	45	2	0	6	1.000	---

First Basemen - The Rest

Player	Tm	G	Inn	PO	A	E	DP	Pct.	Rng
Cianfrocco,Archi	SD	31	170.2	150	19	1	15	.994	---
Clark,Jerald	Col	37	271.2	284	15	5	29	.984	---
Clark,Phil	SD	24	156.0	144	19	4	12	.976	---
Colbrunn,Greg	Mon	61	359.1	372	27	2	31	.995	---
Coles,Darnell	Tor	1	1.0	1	0	0	0	1.000	---
Conine,Jeff	Fla	43	152.2	151	14	0	11	1.000	---
Cooper,Scott	Bos	2	2.0	1	0	0	1	1.000	---
Costo,Tim	Cin	2	7.0	2	1	0	0	1.000	---
Daugherty,Jack	Hou	1	1.0	0	0	0	0	.000	---
Daugherty,Jack	Cin	2	19.0	20	2	0	1	1.000	---
Davis,Glenn	Bal	22	178.1	190	12	2	20	.990	---
Denson,Drew	ChA	3	6.0	4	0	1	1	.800	---
Diaz,Mario	Tex	1	1.0	1	0	0	0	1.000	---
Donnels,Chris	Hou	23	166.2	158	9	2	14	.988	---
Doran,Billy	Mil	4	22.0	16	2	0	2	1.000	---
Dorsett,Brian	Cin	3	10.0	8	0	0	0	1.000	---
Eisenreich,Jim	Phi	1	4.0	5	0	0	0	1.000	---
Floyd,Cliff	Mon	10	68.0	79	4	0	5	1.000	---
Foley,Tom	Pit	12	40.2	31	4	1	3	.972	---
Frazier,Lou	Mon	8	29.0	27	5	1	2	.970	---
Gaetti,Gary	Cal	6	39.0	37	2	0	2	1.000	---
Gaetti,Gary	KC	18	100.1	97	10	1	11	.991	---
Gainer,Jay	Col	7	60.0	52	2	1	3	.982	---
Gallagher,Dave	NYN	9	25.2	22	1	0	0	1.000	---
Geren,Bob	SD	1	1.0	1	0	0	0	1.000	---
Gilkey,Bernard	StL	3	21.0	24	1	0	2	1.000	---
Gonzales,Rene	Cal	31	176.1	163	10	2	24	.989	---
Griffey Jr,Ken	Sea	1	1.0	1	0	0	0	1.000	---
Gwynn,Chris	KC	1	9.0	12	1	0	1	1.000	---
Hale,Chip	Min	1	4.0	5	1	0	1	1.000	---
Hamelin,Bob	KC	15	119.0	129	9	2	11	.986	---
Hemond,Scott	Oak	1	2.0	5	0	0	0	1.000	---
Higgins,Kevin	SD	3	6.0	5	0	0	1	1.000	---
Hunter,Brian	Atl	29	165.2	164	13	1	19	.994	---
James,Dion	NYA	1	1.0	1	0	0	0	1.000	---
Javier,Stan	Cal	12	65.0	64	2	2	2	.971	---
Jefferson,Reggie	Cle	15	111.0	113	10	3	10	.976	---
Jennings,Doug	ChN	11	59.1	80	2	0	8	1.000	---
Jordan,Ricky	Phi	34	234.1	212	4	2	23	.991	---
Jorgensen,Terry	Min	9	39.0	36	6	1	5	.977	---
Klesko,Ryan	Atl	3	5.0	8	0	0	0	1.000	---
Kreuter,Chad	Det	1	4.0	5	1	0	0	1.000	---
Larkin,Gene	Min	18	114.2	122	6	2	10	.985	---
Leyritz,Jim	NYA	29	217.0	260	13	2	23	.993	---
Lindeman,Jim	Hou	9	43.2	39	5	0	5	1.000	---
Litton,Greg	Sea	13	101.0	86	8	0	15	1.000	---
Lovullo,Torey	Cal	1	1.0	0	0	0	0	.000	---
Lyons,Steve	Bos	1	1.0	1	0	1	0	1.000	---
Maas,Kevin	NYA	17	95.0	115	5	2	13	.984	---
Magadan,Dave	Fla	2	6.0	5	1	0	0	1.000	---
Magadan,Dave	Sea	41	319.2	309	18	3	33	.991	---
Maksudian,Mike	Min	4	32.0	28	6	0	3	1.000	---
Marrero,Oreste	Mon	32	201.1	194	15	2	20	.991	---
Martinez,Carlos	Cle	22	145.2	135	7	4	12	.973	---
Martinez,Domingo	Tor	7	27.0	25	4	0	2	1.000	---
McCarty,Dave	Min	36	264.0	278	30	2	24	.994	---
McClendon,Lloyd	Pit	6	14.2	14	2	0	1	1.000	---
McGriff,Fred	SD	84	717.1	650	46	12	50	.983	---

First Basemen - The Rest

Player	Tm	G	Inn	PO	A	E	DP	Pct.	Rng
McGriff,Fred	Atl	66	573.1	563	43	5	51	.992	---
McGwire,Mark	Oak	25	209.2	197	14	0	20	1.000	---
McKnight,Jeff	NYN	10	34.1	35	5	0	5	1.000	---
Melvin,Bob	Bos	1	5.0	5	1	0	1	1.000	---
Merced,Orlando	Pit	42	275.1	275	20	2	23	.993	---
Meulens,Hensley	NYA	3	7.0	5	0	0	0	1.000	---
Milligan,Randy	Cin	61	497.2	468	56	3	49	.994	---
Milligan,Randy	Cle	18	106.0	101	7	0	15	1.000	---
Molitor,Paul	Tor	23	206.0	179	14	3	16	.985	---
Neel,Troy	Oak	34	252.2	236	21	5	25	.981	---
Nilsson,Dave	Mil	4	26.2	27	3	0	3	1.000	---
O'Brien,Pete	Sea	9	69.1	76	8	1	10	.988	---
Oliver,Joe	Cin	12	46.0	34	2	0	5	1.000	---
Orsulak,Joe	NYN	4	12.2	16	1	0	0	1.000	---
Pagliarulo,Mike	Bal	4	27.0	26	2	0	3	1.000	---
Pappas,Erik	StL	2	8.0	6	0	0	1	1.000	---
Pasqua,Dan	ChA	32	143.1	148	9	2	15	.987	---
Peltier,Dan	Tex	5	9.0	8	0	0	1	1.000	---
Perry,Gerald	StL	15	69.2	77	3	2	5	.976	---
Phillips,J.r.	SF	5	28.0	32	2	1	1	.971	---
Piazza,Mike	LA	1	1.0	2	0	0	1	1.000	---
Pirkl,Greg	Sea	5	44.0	42	4	0	8	1.000	---
Quintana,Carlos	Bos	53	314.0	320	21	3	30	.991	---
Ready,Randy	Mon	13	91.1	87	7	4	5	.959	---
Redus,Gary	Tex	5	25.0	21	1	1	5	.957	---
Riles,Ernest	Bos	1	1.0	1	0	0	0	1.000	---
Rodriguez,Henry	LA	13	58.1	71	5	0	2	1.000	---
Royer,Stan	StL	2	17.0	19	1	0	0	1.000	---
Russell,John	Tex	1	8.0	9	0	0	0	1.000	---
Samuel,Juan	Cin	6	11.0	11	3	0	1	1.000	---
Sasser,Mackey	Sea	1	1.0	2	0	0	0	1.000	---
Scarsone,Steve	SF	6	13.2	9	0	0	1	1.000	---
Seitzer,Kevin	Oak	24	169.1	167	18	0	24	1.000	---
Seitzer,Kevin	Mil	7	47.0	43	1	0	4	1.000	---
Sharperson,Mike	LA	1	1.0	0	0	0	0	.000	---
Sheaffer,Danny	Col	7	11.0	6	4	0	1	1.000	---
Shelton,Ben	Pit	2	8.1	10	1	0	1	1.000	---
Shields,Tommy	ChN	1	2.0	0	1	0	0	1.000	---
Siddall,Joe	Mon	1	1.0	0	0	0	0	.000	---
Snyder,Cory	LA	12	29.2	22	3	0	1	1.000	---
Staton,Dave	SD	12	79.0	68	12	0	10	1.000	---
Steinbach,Terry	Oak	15	112.1	102	9	2	9	.982	---
Surhoff,B.J.	Mil	8	30.0	28	2	0	2	1.000	---
Sveum,Dale	Oak	14	109.0	116	5	3	11	.976	---
Tatum,Jimmy	Col	12	44.1	41	4	1	6	.978	---
Tettleton,Mickey	Det	59	363.0	364	24	3	41	.992	---
Teufel,Tim	SD	9	24.2	21	2	1	0	.958	---
Van Burkleo,Ty	Cal	12	90.0	99	2	0	8	1.000	---
VanderWal,John	Mon	42	218.0	237	13	3	17	.988	---
Velasquez,Guillermo	SD	38	239.0	221	20	4	20	.984	---
Ventura,Robin	ChA	4	4.0	7	0	0	1	1.000	---
Voigt,Jack	Bal	5	22.0	26	2	0	3	1.000	---
Walker,Larry	Mon	4	32.0	43	2	0	2	1.000	---
Wallach,Tim	LA	1	9.0	9	1	0	1	1.000	---
Ward,Turner	Tor	1	2.0	3	0	0	0	1.000	---
White,Derrick	Mon	17	114.0	129	7	1	16	.993	---
Winfield,Dave	Min	5	31.0	29	1	0	3	1.000	---
Woodson,Tracy	StL	11	50.0	49	2	1	7	.981	---

First Basemen - The Rest

Player	Tm	G	Inn	PO	A	E	DP	Pct.	Rng
Yount,Robin	Mil	7	40.0	43	1	0	7	1.000	---
Zambrano,Eddie	ChN	2	15.2	13	0	1	1	.929	---

Second Basemen - Regulars

Player	Tm	G	Inn	PO	A	E	DP	Pct.	Rng
Whitaker,Lou	Det	110	864.0	236	320	11	76	.981	5.79
Alicea,Luis	StL	96	779.2	202	280	11	61	.978	5.56
Reed,Jody	LA	132	1134.2	278	412	5	74	.993	5.47
Baerga,Carlos	Cle	150	1303.2	347	444	17	106	.979	5.46
Thompson,Robby	SF	128	1094.2	274	384	8	95	.988	5.41
Fletcher,Scott	Bos	116	982.1	217	370	11	68	.982	5.38
Barberie,Bret	Fla	97	844.1	200	301	9	61	.982	5.34
Lemke,Mark	Atl	150	1299.2	329	442	14	100	.982	5.34
Gates,Brent	Oak	139	1210.1	281	430	14	87	.981	5.29
Young,Eric	Col	79	650.1	154	227	15	43	.962	5.27
Kelly,Pat	NYA	125	1051.2	246	369	14	86	.978	5.26
DeShields,Delino	Mon	123	1073.2	244	381	11	74	.983	5.24
Amaral,Rich	Sea	77	617.2	151	206	9	47	.975	5.20
Strange,Doug	Tex	135	1101.0	272	361	13	81	.980	5.17
Reynolds,Harold	Bal	141	1225.2	306	395	10	111	.986	5.15
Knoblauch,Chuck	Min	148	1273.0	298	426	9	99	.988	5.12
Sandberg,Ryne	ChN	115	989.0	209	347	7	77	.988	5.06
Lovullo,Torey	Cal	91	723.0	185	220	8	66	.981	5.04
Gardner,Jeff	SD	133	907.2	212	295	9	47	.983	5.03
Biggio,Craig	Hou	155	1352.1	307	447	14	89	.982	5.02
Lind,Jose	KC	136	1152.2	269	361	4	75	.994	4.92
Spiers,Bill	Mil	104	804.0	210	226	13	52	.971	4.88
Cora,Joey	ChA	151	1299.0	293	410	19	85	.974	4.87
Garcia,Carlos	Pit	140	1186.0	294	344	11	83	.983	4.84
Morandini,Mickey	Phi	111	928.0	208	287	5	48	.990	4.80
Alomar,Roberto	Tor	151	1305.1	253	439	14	92	.980	4.77
Kent,Jeff	NYN	127	1070.2	250	312	18	67	.969	4.72
Boone,Bret	Sea	74	622.1	139	177	3	54	.991	4.57
Average	---	122	1030.0	245	343	10	75	.982	5.14

Second Basemen - The Rest

Player	Tm	G	Inn	PO	A	E	DP	Pct.	Rng
Abbott,Kurt	Oak	2	3.0	0	0	0	0	.000	.00
Arias,Alex	Fla	30	253.2	59	87	2	15	.986	5.18
Backman,Wally	Sea	1	4.0	0	1	0	0	1.000	2.25
Barnes,Skeeter	Det	10	31.0	7	10	0	1	1.000	4.94
Bell,Juan	Mil	47	389.2	115	115	4	34	.983	5.31
Belliard,Rafael	Atl	24	138.0	26	50	1	7	.987	4.96
Benavides,Freddie	Col	19	110.2	30	39	1	7	.986	5.61
Benjamin,Mike	SF	23	158.2	54	54	1	23	.991	6.13
Blankenship,Lance	Oak	19	157.1	32	56	4	11	.957	5.03
Bogar,Tim	NYN	6	33.2	13	14	1	6	.964	7.22
Bordick,Mike	Oak	1	11.0	5	2	0	2	1.000	5.73
Bournigal,Rafael	LA	4	6.0	0	1	0	0	1.000	1.50
Branson,Jeff	Cin	45	330.2	80	105	5	29	.974	5.04
Browne,Jerry	Oak	3	25.1	5	9	0	1	1.000	4.97
Brumfield,Jacob	Cin	4	25.0	6	10	3	3	.842	5.76
Candaele,Casey	Hou	19	80.0	14	19	0	3	1.000	3.71
Caraballo,Ramon	Atl	5	8.0	4	3	0	1	1.000	7.88

Second Basemen - The Rest

Player	Tm	G	Inn	PO	A	E	DP	Pct.	Rng
Castellano,Pedro	Col	4	33.0	10	7	0	2	1.000	4.64
Cedeno,Domingo	Tor	5	32.0	2	11	0	1	1.000	3.66
Colbert,Craig	SF	2	3.0	0	1	0	0	1.000	3.00
Correia,Rod	Cal	11	78.0	30	19	0	6	1.000	5.65
Curtis,Chad	Cal	3	6.1	2	1	0	0	1.000	4.26
Donnels,Chris	Hou	1	7.0	1	3	0	2	1.000	5.14
Doran,Billy	Mil	17	97.1	28	26	2	5	.964	4.99
Duncan,Mariano	Phi	65	544.2	109	168	9	29	.969	4.58
Easley,Damion	Cal	54	457.0	101	125	5	26	.978	4.45
Espinoza,Alvaro	Cle	2	13.2	6	3	1	2	.900	5.93
Faries,Paul	SF	7	50.2	12	18	0	3	1.000	5.33
Foley,Tom	Pit	35	242.2	71	64	1	19	.993	5.01
Frazier,Lou	Mon	1	6.0	1	1	0	0	1.000	3.00
Gallego,Mike	NYA	52	364.1	83	143	5	37	.978	5.58
Gomez,Chris	Det	17	138.0	36	46	1	7	.988	5.35
Gonzales,Rene	Cal	4	28.0	4	3	0	1	1.000	2.25
Grebeck,Craig	ChA	16	124.0	29	53	0	12	1.000	5.95
Griffin,Alfredo	Tor	11	65.0	22	23	1	6	.978	6.23
Gutierrez,Ricky	SD	6	14.0	1	14	0	0	1.000	9.64
Hale,Chip	Min	21	104.1	22	37	3	8	.952	5.09
Harris,Lenny	LA	35	242.0	56	92	2	11	.987	5.50
Hatcher,Billy	Bos	2	4.0	0	0	0	0	.000	.00
Hemond,Scott	Oak	1	1.0	2	1	0	1	1.000	27.00
Higgins,Kevin	SD	1	2.0	0	0	0	0	.000	.00
Hocking,Denny	Min	1	13.0	4	4	0	2	1.000	5.54
Howard,Dave	KC	7	59.0	15	23	3	2	.927	5.80
Hulett,Tim	Bal	4	33.0	10	8	0	3	1.000	4.91
Huson,Jeff	Tex	5	25.0	8	6	0	2	1.000	5.04
Jaha,John	Mil	1	3.1	1	0	0	0	1.000	2.70
Javier,Stan	Cal	2	3.0	2	0	0	0	1.000	6.00
Jefferies,Gregg	StL	1	3.0	2	1	0	1	1.000	9.00
Johnson,Erik	SF	2	4.1	1	0	0	0	1.000	2.08
Jones,Tim	StL	7	32.0	8	9	0	1	1.000	4.78
King,Jeff	Pit	2	10.0	3	6	1	2	.900	8.10
Koelling,Brian	Cin	3	24.0	4	12	1	1	.941	6.00
Lansing,Mike	Mon	25	148.2	35	52	4	11	.956	5.27
Liriano,Nelson	Col	16	104.0	19	32	3	7	.944	4.41
Litton,Greg	Sea	17	98.0	20	26	0	8	1.000	4.22
Lopez,Luis	SD	15	106.2	23	34	1	5	.983	4.81
Lyons,Steve	Bos	9	34.0	6	15	0	2	1.000	5.56
Martin,Norberto	ChA	5	30.0	13	8	1	4	.955	6.30
McKnight,Jeff	NYN	15	69.1	18	23	3	3	.932	5.32
McLemore,Mark	Bal	25	183.2	53	59	0	19	1.000	5.49
Mejia,Roberto	Col	65	533.1	129	183	12	38	.963	5.27
Miller,Keith	KC	3	17.0	3	6	1	1	.900	4.76
Montoyo,Charlie	Mon	3	6.0	0	0	0	0	.000	.00
Naehring,Tim	Bos	15	113.0	37	34	2	9	.973	5.65
Oquendo,Jose	StL	16	72.1	25	24	0	6	1.000	6.10
Parker,Rick	Hou	1	1.2	1	0	0	0	1.000	5.40
Pecota,Bill	Atl	4	9.1	5	1	0	1	1.000	5.79
Pena,Geronimo	StL	64	566.0	140	200	12	47	.966	5.41
Petralli,Geno	Tex	1	2.0	1	0	0	0	1.000	4.50
Phillips,Tony	Det	51	403.2	106	158	4	33	.985	5.89
Polidor,Gus	Fla	1	1.2	0	0	0	0	.000	.00
Ready,Randy	Mon	28	222.1	46	75	4	16	.968	4.90
Reboulet,Jeff	Min	11	54.0	13	16	0	6	1.000	4.83
Redus,Gary	Tex	1	1.0	0	0	0	0	.000	.00
Renteria,Rich	Fla	45	340.2	70	116	2	17	.989	4.91

Second Basemen - The Rest

Player	Tm	G	Inn	PO	A	E	DP	Pct.	Rng
Richardson,Jeff	Bos	8	42.2	9	24	0	3	1.000	6.96
Riles,Ernest	Bos	20	111.0	22	45	0	8	1.000	5.43
Ripken,Billy	Tex	34	248.0	52	73	1	16	.992	4.54
Rivera,Luis	Bos	27	165.1	36	57	3	13	.969	5.06
Roberts,Bip	Cin	65	525.1	137	173	5	31	.984	5.31
Rossy,Rico	KC	24	136.1	29	48	1	10	.987	5.08
Samuel,Juan	Cin	70	529.0	135	164	9	33	.971	5.09
Saunders,Doug	NYN	22	146.0	36	50	4	18	.956	5.30
Sax,Steve	ChA	1	1.0	0	3	0	1	1.000	27.00
Scarsone,Steve	SF	20	145.1	40	35	0	10	1.000	4.64
Seitzer,Kevin	Oak	2	17.0	2	6	0	1	1.000	4.24
Seitzer,Kevin	Mil	1	0.2	1	1	0	1	1.000	27.00
Sharperson,Mike	LA	17	90.0	24	28	3	8	.945	5.20
Shave,Jon	Tex	8	61.0	9	17	0	3	1.000	3.84
Shields,Tommy	ChN	7	25.0	6	12	0	3	1.000	6.48
Shipley,Craig	SD	12	55.2	11	19	1	1	.968	4.85
Shumpert,Terry	KC	8	34.0	11	11	0	3	1.000	5.82
Sojo,Luis	Tor	8	39.0	9	11	0	2	1.000	4.62
Stankiewicz,Andy	NYA	6	22.0	7	10	0	4	1.000	6.95
Stillwell,Kurt	Cal	18	125.0	39	41	4	6	.952	5.76
Suero,William	Mil	8	26.0	5	12	1	1	.944	5.88
Sveum,Dale	Oak	4	26.2	4	7	0	1	1.000	3.71
Teufel,Tim	SD	52	351.2	85	118	2	22	.990	5.20
Thon,Dickie	Mil	22	126.0	40	32	3	9	.960	5.14
Treadway,Jeff	Cle	19	128.1	29	48	2	6	.949	5.19
Turang,Brian	Sea	1	2.0	1	0	0	0	1.000	4.50
Vina,Fernando	Sea	16	109.2	25	38	0	12	1.000	5.17
Vizcaino,Jose	ChN	34	245.2	67	75	2	23	.986	5.20
Walewander,Jim	Cal	2	10.0	2	3	0	1	1.000	4.50
Walker,Chico	NYN	24	118.1	40	43	2	8	.976	6.31
Wehner,John	Pit	3	7.0	1	4	0	2	1.000	6.43
Wilkerson,Curt	KC	10	39.1	5	16	0	3	1.000	4.81
Wilson,Craig	KC	1	7.0	1	3	1	0	.800	5.14
Yelding,Eric	ChN	32	190.0	48	76	2	14	.984	5.87

Third Basemen - Regulars

Player	Tm	G	Inn	PO	A	E	DP	Pct.	Rng
Lansing,Mike	Mon	81	617.0	50	162	13	19	.942	3.09
Boggs,Wade	NYA	134	1122.2	74	311	12	29	.970	3.09
Gonzales,Rene	Cal	79	646.2	64	154	10	21	.956	3.03
King,Jeff	Pit	156	1366.2	105	354	17	27	.964	3.02
Pendleton,Terry	Atl	161	1392.2	129	318	19	32	.959	2.89
Berry,Sean	Mon	96	686.1	66	153	15	13	.936	2.87
Gaetti,Gary	TOT	79	600.2	51	140	6	15	.970	2.86
Hayes,Charlie	Col	154	1301.1	123	290	20	21	.954	2.86
Magadan,Dave	TOT	90	757.1	66	173	9	18	.964	2.84
Surhoff,B.J.	Mil	121	1013.2	101	217	17	19	.949	2.82
Wallach,Tim	LA	130	1084.2	112	227	15	14	.958	2.81
Caminiti,Ken	Hou	143	1236.2	123	262	24	22	.941	2.80
Blowers,Mike	Sea	117	928.2	65	224	15	13	.951	2.80
Zeile,Todd	StL	153	1299.2	83	309	33	26	.922	2.71
Williams,Matt D.	SF	144	1275.2	117	264	12	35	.969	2.69
Pagliarulo,Mike	TOT	107	861.0	69	184	8	17	.969	2.64
Buechele,Steve	ChN	129	1082.0	79	232	8	22	.975	2.59
Ventura,Robin	ChA	155	1367.0	112	277	14	23	.965	2.56
Sprague,Ed	Tor	150	1291.1	128	231	17	20	.955	2.50

Third Basemen - Regulars

Player	Tm	G	Inn	PO	A	E	DP	Pct.	Rng
Paquette,Craig	Oak	104	888.2	81	165	13	17	.950	2.49
Cooper,Scott	Bos	154	1304.1	111	245	24	20	.937	2.46
Palmer,Dean	Tex	148	1259.0	86	256	29	21	.922	2.44
Seitzer,Kevin	TOT	79	659.1	53	125	12	15	.937	2.43
Sheffield,Gary	TOT	134	1129.2	79	224	34	14	.899	2.41
Sabo,Chris	Cin	148	1265.1	79	241	11	17	.967	2.28
Hollins,Dave	Phi	143	1214.2	73	215	27	8	.914	2.13
Average	---	126	1063.1	87	228	16	19	.950	2.68

Third Basemen - The Rest

Player	Tm	G	Inn	PO	A	E	DP	Pct.	Rng
Alicea,Luis	StL	1	3.0	0	0	0	0	.000	.00
Amaral,Rich	Sea	19	108.0	5	30	1	7	.972	2.92
Arias,Alex	Fla	22	161.1	13	26	1	2	.975	2.18
Backman,Wally	Sea	9	62.0	4	14	3	0	.857	2.61
Barnes,Skeeter	Det	13	65.2	9	17	1	0	.963	3.56
Batiste,Kim	Phi	58	210.2	24	41	3	2	.956	2.78
Bell,Derek	SD	19	152.0	12	28	9	3	.816	2.37
Benavides,Freddie	Col	5	19.0	0	6	0	0	1.000	2.84
Benjamin,Mike	SF	16	123.2	10	34	3	3	.936	3.20
Benzinger,Todd	SF	1	1.0	0	0	0	0	.000	.00
Bogar,Tim	NYN	7	32.2	4	11	0	2	1.000	4.13
Bolick,Frank	Mon	24	112.1	5	30	5	3	.875	2.80
Bonilla,Bobby	NYN	52	426.0	40	101	11	6	.928	2.98
Branson,Jeff	Cin	14	92.0	7	16	1	0	.958	2.25
Brosius,Scott	Oak	10	67.0	2	19	0	1	1.000	2.82
Browne,Jerry	Oak	13	83.2	6	16	3	2	.880	2.37
Brumley,Mike	Hou	1	2.0	0	0	0	0	.000	.00
Candaele,Casey	Hou	4	6.0	0	1	0	0	1.000	1.50
Castellano,Pedro	Col	13	77.0	4	16	2	1	.909	2.34
Cedeno,Andujar	Hou	1	8.2	2	1	0	0	1.000	3.12
Cianfrocco,Archi	SD	64	491.0	48	76	9	8	.932	2.27
Clark,Phil	SD	5	33.0	2	6	0	1	1.000	2.18
Colbert,Craig	SF	1	7.1	1	1	0	1	1.000	2.45
Coles,Darnell	Tor	16	128.0	11	19	4	0	.882	2.11
Cora,Joey	ChA	3	14.0	1	3	0	0	1.000	2.57
Cordero,Wil	Mon	2	14.0	2	3	3	0	.625	3.21
Correia,Rod	Cal	3	6.2	1	0	0	0	1.000	1.35
Costo,Tim	Cin	2	3.0	0	1	0	0	1.000	3.00
Diaz,Mario	Tex	12	95.0	8	19	0	2	1.000	2.56
Donnels,Chris	Hou	31	187.2	11	42	6	5	.898	2.54
Easley,Damion	Cal	14	123.1	10	32	1	3	.977	3.06
Espinoza,Alvaro	Cle	99	519.0	42	107	10	9	.937	2.58
Faries,Paul	SF	1	2.0	0	0	0	0	.000	.00
Felder,Mike	Sea	2	2.0	0	3	0	1	1.000	13.50
Fletcher,Scott	Bos	1	3.0	0	0	0	0	.000	.00
Foley,Tom	Pit	7	38.2	4	19	1	1	.958	5.35
Fryman,Travis	Det	69	599.0	44	118	4	10	.976	2.43
Gaetti,Gary	Cal	7	23.0	1	5	1	0	.857	2.35
Gaetti,Gary	KC	72	577.2	50	135	5	14	.974	2.88
Gallego,Mike	NYA	27	214.2	18	53	2	5	.973	2.98
Gardner,Jeff	SD	1	1.0	0	0	1	0	.000	.00
Geren,Bob	SD	1	3.0	0	3	0	0	1.000	5.40
Gomez,Leo	Bal	70	592.0	48	143	10	16	.950	2.90
Grebeck,Craig	ChA	14	73.0	6	18	2	2	.923	2.96
Greene,Willie	Cin	5	42.0	2	9	0	0	1.000	2.36

Third Basemen - The Rest

Player	Tm	G	Inn	PO	A	E	DP	Pct.	Rng
Griffin,Alfredo	Tor	6	13.0	3	5	0	0	1.000	5.54
Gruber,Kelly	Cal	17	139.0	18	42	4	3	.938	3.88
Gutierrez,Ricky	SD	4	14.0	2	5	0	0	1.000	4.50
Hale,Chip	Min	19	123.2	11	25	1	2	.973	2.62
Hansen,Dave	LA	18	127.2	11	27	3	1	.927	2.68
Harris,Lenny	LA	17	45.0	2	6	1	0	.889	1.60
Hershiser,Orel	LA	1	0.0	0	0	0	0	.000	.00
Hiatt,Phil	KC	70	557.1	45	114	16	6	.909	2.57
Higgins,Kevin	SD	4	7.1	1	1	0	0	1.000	2.45
Howard,Dave	KC	2	3.0	1	0	0	0	1.000	3.00
Hulett,Tim	Bal	75	575.1	47	160	8	23	.963	3.24
Huskey,Butch	NYN	13	105.0	9	27	3	2	.923	3.09
Huson,Jeff	Tex	2	14.0	1	2	1	0	.750	1.93
Jaha,John	Mil	1	0.2	0	0	0	0	.000	.00
Johnson,Erik	SF	1	2.0	0	1	0	0	1.000	4.50
Johnson,Howard	NYN	68	571.1	52	135	11	11	.944	2.95
Jorgensen,Terry	Min	45	341.0	27	85	2	8	.982	2.96
Kent,Jeff	NYN	12	101.1	9	28	3	4	.925	3.29
Larkin,Gene	Min	2	2.0	0	0	0	0	.000	.00
Liriano,Nelson	Col	1	3.0	1	0	0	0	1.000	3.00
Litton,Greg	Sea	7	21.0	1	6	0	1	1.000	3.00
Livingstone,Scott	Det	62	503.1	33	94	6	6	.955	2.27
Lovullo,Torey	Cal	14	101.0	14	25	3	2	.929	3.48
Lyons,Steve	Bos	1	1.0	0	0	0	0	.000	.00
Magadan,Dave	Fla	63	546.1	49	120	7	13	.960	2.78
Magadan,Dave	Sea	27	211.0	17	53	2	5	.972	2.99
Maksudian,Mike	Min	1	1.0	0	0	0	0	.000	.00
Manto,Jeff	Phi	6	37.0	2	7	0	0	1.000	2.19
Martinez,Carlos	Cle	35	263.1	27	44	5	4	.934	2.43
Martinez,Domingo	Tor	1	3.0	0	0	0	0	.000	.00
Martinez,Edgar	Sea	16	119.0	5	11	2	1	.889	1.21
Martinez,Pedro	LA	1	0.0	0	0	0	0	.000	.00
McKnight,Jeff	NYN	9	28.2	3	8	2	0	.846	3.45
McLemore,Mark	Bal	4	26.0	0	8	2	0	.800	2.77
Meulens,Hensley	NYA	1	1.0	0	0	0	0	.000	.00
Miller,Keith	KC	21	159.0	11	29	5	2	.889	2.26
Millette,Joe	Phi	3	10.1	0	4	0	0	1.000	3.48
Naehring,Tim	Bos	9	57.0	6	6	0	2	1.000	1.89
Ortiz,Luis	Bos	5	19.0	2	2	0	1	1.000	1.89
Pagliarulo,Mike	Min	79	620.0	42	137	3	11	.984	2.60
Pagliarulo,Mike	Bal	28	241.0	27	47	5	6	.937	2.76
Pecota,Bill	Atl	23	62.1	3	12	0	0	1.000	2.17
Perez,Eduardo	Cal	45	390.2	24	100	5	7	.961	2.86
Petralli,Geno	Tex	1	1.0	0	0	0	0	.000	.00
Phillips,Tony	Det	1	8.0	0	1	2	0	.333	1.13
Polidor,Gus	Fla	1	2.0	1	0	0	0	1.000	4.50
Ready,Randy	Mon	3	27.0	2	9	0	0	1.000	3.67
Reboulet,Jeff	Min	35	220.2	21	65	2	7	.977	3.51
Renteria,Rich	Fla	25	165.2	14	35	0	4	1.000	2.66
Richardson,Jeff	Bos	1	2.0	1	0	0	0	1.000	4.50
Riles,Ernest	Bos	11	57.0	3	8	0	0	1.000	1.74
Ripken,Billy	Tex	1	2.0	1	1	1	0	.667	9.00
Rivera,Luis	Bos	2	9.0	1	3	0	1	1.000	4.00
Roberts,Bip	Cin	3	19.0	1	4	0	0	1.000	2.37
Rossy,Rico	KC	16	48.0	2	7	0	0	1.000	1.69
Royer,Stan	StL	10	65.0	3	15	3	1	.857	2.49
Russell,John	Tex	1	1.0	0	0	0	0	.000	.00
Samuel,Juan	Cin	4	12.2	2	4	0	0	1.000	4.26

Third Basemen - The Rest

Player	Tm	G	Inn	PO	A	E	DP	Pct.	Rng
Saunders,Doug	NYN	4	9.0	1	2	0	1	1.000	3.00
Scarsone,Steve	SF	8	45.0	4	9	1	1	.929	2.60
Seitzer,Kevin	Oak	46	381.0	31	66	7	7	.933	2.29
Seitzer,Kevin	Mil	33	278.1	22	59	5	8	.942	2.62
Sharperson,Mike	LA	6	13.0	3	2	1	0	.833	3.46
Sheaffer,Danny	Col	1	1.0	0	0	0	0	.000	.00
Sheffield,Gary	SD	68	564.2	41	101	15	10	.904	2.26
Sheffield,Gary	Fla	66	565.0	38	123	19	4	.894	2.56
Shields,Tommy	ChN	7	40.0	2	9	0	1	1.000	2.47
Shipley,Craig	SD	37	117.0	17	20	1	4	.974	2.85
Silvestri,Dave	NYA	3	27.0	0	8	2	0	.800	2.67
Snyder,Cory	LA	23	202.1	12	26	5	3	.884	1.69
Sojo,Luis	Tor	3	6.0	1	1	1	0	.667	3.00
Stahoviak,Scott	Min	19	136.0	9	38	4	1	.922	3.11
Stankiewicz,Andy	NYA	4	15.0	0	5	0	0	1.000	3.00
Stillwell,Kurt	SD	3	9.0	2	3	0	0	1.000	5.00
Strange,Doug	Tex	9	66.0	4	12	0	2	1.000	2.18
Suero,William	Mil	1	2.0	1	1	0	1	1.000	9.00
Sveum,Dale	Oak	7	31.1	5	4	0	1	1.000	2.59
Tatum,Jimmy	Col	6	30.0	3	1	1	1	.800	1.20
Teufel,Tim	SD	9	43.2	3	5	0	0	1.000	1.65
Thome,Jim	Cle	47	380.0	29	86	6	10	.950	2.72
Thon,Dickie	Mil	25	152.1	12	30	1	2	.977	2.48
Trammell,Alan	Det	35	260.2	19	56	5	7	.938	2.59
Treadway,Jeff	Cle	42	283.1	17	66	6	5	.933	2.64
Turang,Brian	Sea	2	2.0	0	0	0	0	.000	.00
Velarde,Randy	NYA	16	57.2	5	16	1	4	.955	3.28
Vizcaino,Jose	ChN	44	286.2	25	68	2	6	.979	2.92
Voigt,Jack	Bal	3	8.0	0	1	0	0	1.000	1.13
Walker,Chico	NYN	23	164.0	12	37	5	0	.907	2.69
Wehner,John	Pit	3	10.2	0	3	0	1	1.000	2.53
Wilson,Craig	KC	15	100.1	7	19	0	4	1.000	2.33
Woodson,Tracy	StL	28	85.1	7	23	3	3	.909	3.16
Yelding,Eric	ChN	7	41.0	3	9	1	1	.923	2.63
Young,Kevin	Pit	6	29.2	6	11	0	0	1.000	5.16

Shortstops - Regulars

Player	Tm	G	Inn	PO	A	E	DP	Pct.	Rng
Offerman,Jose	LA	158	1406.2	251	455	37	96	.950	4.52
Stocker,Kevin	Phi	70	639.2	118	201	14	45	.958	4.49
Listach,Pat	Mil	95	791.0	128	265	10	52	.975	4.47
Guillen,Ozzie	ChA	133	1131.0	189	361	16	82	.972	4.38
Weiss,Walt	Fla	153	1322.1	231	407	15	79	.977	4.34
Cordero,Wil	Mon	134	1114.0	160	368	33	61	.941	4.27
Fermin,Felix	Cle	140	1186.1	211	344	23	86	.960	4.21
Blauser,Jeff	Atl	161	1321.2	189	425	19	85	.970	4.18
Cedeno,Andujar	Hou	149	1224.1	153	373	25	77	.955	3.87
Average	---	128	1088.1	196	369	17	77	.970	4.68

Shortstops - The Rest

Player	Tm	G	Inn	PO	A	E	DP	Pct.	Rng
Abbott,Kurt	Oak	6	32.2	3	12	1	2	.938	4.13
Amaral,Rich	Sea	14	85.0	20	34	0	14	1.000	5.72
Arias,Alex	Fla	18	118.0	22	30	3	7	.945	3.97
Baez,Kevin	NYN	52	344.1	57	117	6	24	.967	4.55
Barnes,Skeeter	Det	2	2.0	0	1	1	0	.500	4.50
Batiste,Kim	Phi	24	180.0	48	66	7	13	.942	5.70
Bell,Juan	Phi	22	173.1	33	57	9	11	.909	4.67
Bell,Juan	Mil	40	311.0	67	109	7	20	.962	5.09
Belliard,Rafael	Atl	58	127.1	27	49	0	11	1.000	5.37
Benavides,Freddie	Col	48	360.0	65	113	12	19	.937	4.45
Benjamin,Mike	SF	23	103.1	10	45	1	7	.982	4.79
Blankenship,Lance	Oak	2	14.0	1	8	0	1	1.000	5.79
Bogar,Tim	NYN	66	507.0	89	193	8	34	.972	5.01
Bournigal,Rafael	LA	4	34.0	5	13	0	3	1.000	4.76
Branson,Jeff	Cin	59	426.1	88	138	5	28	.978	4.77
Brosius,Scott	Oak	6	18.0	0	6	1	2	.857	3.00
Brumley,Mike	Hou	1	1.0	0	1	0	0	1.000	9.00
Candaele,Casey	Hou	14	49.0	9	19	2	1	.933	5.14
Castellano,Pedro	Col	5	20.0	4	5	0	1	1.000	4.05
Cedeno,Domingo	Tor	10	79.0	8	28	1	4	.973	4.10
Cooper,Scott	Bos	1	2.0	0	0	0	0	.000	.00
Correia,Rod	Cal	40	277.1	56	102	3	16	.981	5.13
Cromer,Tripp	StL	9	51.0	13	18	3	3	.912	5.47
Diaz,Mario	Tex	57	419.1	81	135	3	28	.986	4.64
Duncan,Mariano	Phi	59	447.2	71	136	12	21	.945	4.16
Dunston,Shawon	ChN	2	6.0	5	0	0	0	1.000	7.50
Espinoza,Alvaro	Cle	35	147.1	18	47	1	13	.985	3.97
Faries,Paul	SF	4	21.2	3	5	0	0	1.000	3.32
Fernandez,Tony	NYN	48	413.2	83	150	6	28	.975	5.07
Fernandez,Tony	Tor	94	821.2	196	260	7	60	.985	4.99
Fletcher,Scott	Bos	2	2.0	0	0	0	0	.000	.00
Foley,Tom	Pit	6	37.2	11	18	2	6	.935	6.93
Gallego,Mike	NYA	55	400.2	69	172	6	35	.976	5.41
Garcia,Carlos	Pit	3	7.0	3	4	0	3	1.000	9.00
Gardner,Jeff	SD	1	2.0	1	0	0	0	1.000	4.50
Gil,Benji	Tex	22	179.0	27	76	5	10	.954	5.18
Gomez,Chris	Det	29	204.2	32	74	4	16	.964	4.66
Gonzales,Rene	Cal	5	7.0	3	1	0	1	1.000	5.14
Grebeck,Craig	ChA	46	323.0	57	115	3	27	.983	4.79
Greene,Willie	Cin	10	78.2	17	28	1	8	.978	5.15
Griffin,Alfredo	Tor	20	164.0	34	38	3	9	.960	3.95
Hale,Chip	Min	1	0.1	0	0	0	0	.000	.00
Harris,Lenny	LA	3	7.1	2	1	0	0	1.000	3.68

Shortstops - Regulars

Player	Tm	G	Inn	PO	A	E	DP	Pct.	Rng
Sanchez,Rey	ChN	98	762.1	158	317	15	62	.969	5.61
Smith,Ozzie	StL	134	1138.1	251	450	19	98	.974	5.54
Bell,Jay	Pit	154	1349.0	259	525	11	103	.986	5.23
Vizcaino,Jose	ChN	81	680.1	126	264	13	44	.968	5.16
Fernandez,Tony	TOT	142	1235.1	279	410	13	88	.981	5.02
Valentin,John	Bos	144	1221.2	237	431	20	96	.971	4.92
Vizquel,Omar	Sea	155	1330.2	247	476	15	108	.980	4.89
Gagne,Greg	KC	159	1331.0	265	451	10	95	.986	4.84
Fryman,Travis	Det	81	721.1	126	262	19	60	.953	4.84
Owen,Spike	NYA	96	797.0	116	310	14	45	.968	4.81
Meares,Pat	Min	111	890.1	168	304	19	71	.961	4.77
Clayton,Royce	SF	153	1328.2	251	450	27	103	.963	4.75
Castilla,Vinny	Col	104	810.0	140	282	11	67	.975	4.69
DiSarcina,Gary	Cal	126	1072.1	194	364	14	79	.976	4.68
Larkin,Barry	Cin	99	845.2	159	281	16	58	.965	4.68
Gutierrez,Ricky	SD	117	939.0	190	286	14	55	.971	4.56
Bordick,Mike	Oak	159	1374.0	280	416	13	106	.982	4.56
Ripken,Cal	Bal	162	1425.1	227	494	17	101	.977	4.55

Shortstops - The Rest

Player	Tm	G	Inn	PO	A	E	DP	Pct.	Rng
Hayes,Charlie	Col	1	1.0	0	0	0	0	.000	.00
Hocking,Denny	Min	12	71.0	15	19	1	9	.971	4.31
Howard,Dave	KC	3	11.0	1	5	0	0	1.000	4.91
Hulett,Tim	Bal	8	17.0	0	7	0	0	1.000	3.71
Huson,Jeff	Tex	12	76.0	16	34	5	8	.909	5.92
Johnson,Erik	SF	1	3.0	0	0	0	0	.000	.00
Jones,Chipper	Atl	3	6.0	1	1	0	0	1.000	3.00
Jones,Tim	StL	21	128.2	26	54	2	8	.976	5.60
Jorgensen,Terry	Min	6	10.0	2	4	0	0	1.000	5.40
Kent,Jeff	NYN	2	5.0	2	2	1	0	.800	7.20
Kessinger,Keith	Cin	11	72.1	7	22	2	5	.935	3.61
King,Jeff	Pit	2	5.0	0	3	0	0	1.000	5.40
Knoblauch,Chuck	Min	6	15.0	2	6	0	1	1.000	4.80
Koelling,Brian	Cin	2	10.0	2	0	0	0	1.000	1.80
Lansing,Mike	Mon	51	342.2	51	123	7	23	.961	4.57
Lee,Manuel	Tex	72	421.1	96	204	10	35	.968	6.41
Leius,Scott	Min	9	61.0	10	26	2	7	.947	5.31
Lewis,Mark	Cle	13	112.0	22	31	2	10	.964	4.26
Liriano,Nelson	Col	35	240.1	45	71	3	14	.975	4.34
Litton,Greg	Sea	5	21.0	2	8	0	2	1.000	4.29
Lovullo,Torey	Cal	9	20.2	4	4	0	1	1.000	3.48
Manto,Jeff	Phi	1	1.0	0	1	0	0	1.000	9.00
McKnight,Jeff	NYN	29	150.0	31	52	5	11	.943	4.98
Millette,Joe	Phi	7	31.0	3	14	0	1	1.000	4.94
Naehring,Tim	Bos	4	23.0	3	4	0	3	1.000	2.74
Navarro,Tito	NYN	2	17.0	8	7	0	0	1.000	7.94
Oquendo,Jose	StL	22	135.0	27	58	1	9	.988	5.67
Palmer,Dean	Tex	1	1.0	1	0	0	0	1.000	9.00
Parker,Rick	Hou	1	1.0	0	0	0	0	.000	.00
Reboulet,Jeff	Min	62	396.2	85	134	4	27	.982	4.97
Richardson,Jeff	Bos	5	18.0	2	6	0	2	1.000	4.00
Ripken,Billy	Tex	18	127.1	27	50	0	13	1.000	5.44
Rivera,Luis	Bos	27	185.2	28	51	3	13	.963	3.83
Roberts,Bip	Cin	1	1.0	0	0	0	0	.000	.00
Rossy,Rico	KC	11	74.0	11	21	0	7	1.000	3.89
Saunders,Doug	NYN	1	1.0	0	0	0	0	.000	.00
Schofield,Dick	Tor	36	307.0	61	106	4	24	.977	4.90
Seitzer,Kevin	Oak	1	5.0	1	1	0	0	1.000	3.60
Sharperson,Mike	LA	3	15.2	2	8	1	1	.909	5.74
Shave,Jon	Tex	9	62.0	13	20	3	6	.917	4.79
Shipley,Craig	SD	38	276.2	50	82	5	10	.964	4.29
Silvestri,Dave	NYA	4	36.2	9	12	1	4	.955	5.15
Snyder,Cory	LA	2	9.0	4	3	0	3	1.000	7.00
Sojo,Luis	Tor	8	69.2	15	23	1	6	.974	4.91
Spiers,Bill	Mil	4	13.0	1	4	0	2	1.000	3.46
Stankiewicz,Andy	NYA	1	1.0	0	0	0	0	.000	.00
Stillwell,Kurt	SD	30	220.0	45	60	9	12	.921	4.30
Stillwell,Kurt	Cal	7	28.0	7	10	1	3	.944	5.46
Strange,Doug	Tex	1	1.0	0	0	0	0	.000	.00
Sveum,Dale	Oak	1	8.0	3	1	0	0	1.000	4.50
Thon,Dickie	Mil	28	176.1	28	57	3	8	.966	4.34
Trammell,Alan	Det	63	508.2	80	181	3	24	.989	4.62
Uribe,Jose	Hou	41	165.2	35	51	5	20	.945	4.67
Valentin,Jose	Mil	19	155.2	20	51	6	9	.922	4.10
Velarde,Randy	NYA	26	202.2	31	74	3	19	.972	4.66
Vina,Fernando	Sea	4	17.0	3	2	0	1	1.000	2.65
Walewander,Jim	Cal	6	25.0	7	10	0	3	1.000	6.12
Wilkerson,Curt	KC	4	29.1	3	9	0	0	1.000	3.68

Shortstops - The Rest

Player	Tm	G	Inn	PO	A	E	DP	Pct.	Rng
Womack,Tony	Pit	6	47.0	11	22	1	6	.971	6.32
Yelding,Eric	ChN	1	1.0	0	1	1	0	.500	9.00

Left Fielders - Regulars

Player	Tm	G	Inn	PO	A	E	DP	Pct.	Rng
Gonzalez,Luis	Hou	149	1247.2	348	10	8	2	.978	2.58
Belle,Albert	Cle	150	1324.2	338	16	5	7	.986	2.41
Vaughn,Greg	Mil	94	813.0	214	1	3	1	.986	2.38
Davis,Eric	LA	101	849.1	216	7	2	2	.991	2.36
Henderson,Rickey	TOT	118	1006.0	258	6	7	0	.974	2.36
Plantier,Phil	SD	134	1103.0	271	14	3	3	.990	2.33
Clark,Jerald	Col	80	660.0	160	7	7	1	.960	2.28
Polonia,Luis	Cal	141	1181.0	284	12	5	4	.983	2.26
Gonzalez,Juan	Tex	129	1100.0	265	5	4	0	.985	2.21
McReynolds,Kevin	KC	104	812.1	190	5	2	0	.990	2.16
Greenwell,Mike	Bos	134	1125.0	263	6	2	1	.993	2.15
Anderson,Brady	Bal	126	1080.0	247	5	2	0	.992	2.10
Bonds,Barry	SF	157	1370.0	310	7	5	0	.984	2.08
Alou,Moises	Mon	102	796.1	178	6	2	1	.989	2.08
Mitchell,Kevin	Cin	86	640.2	141	6	7	2	.955	2.07
May,Derrick	ChN	121	993.1	217	8	7	1	.970	2.04
Raines,Tim	ChA	112	913.2	201	5	0	1	1.000	2.03
Incaviglia,Pete	Phi	89	690.2	152	3	5	0	.969	2.02
Coleman,Vince	NYN	90	744.1	162	5	3	0	.982	2.02
Thompson,Milt	Phi	102	754.0	162	6	1	1	.994	2.01
Conine,Jeff	Fla	147	1212.1	252	11	2	0	.992	1.95
Felder,Mike	Sea	89	656.1	133	9	2	0	.986	1.95
Gilkey,Bernard	StL	132	1141.1	223	19	8	2	.968	1.91
James,Dion	NYA	91	608.0	124	4	3	1	.977	1.89
Gant,Ron	Atl	155	1384.1	270	5	11	1	.962	1.79
Average	---	117	968.0	223	7	4	1	.982	2.14

Left Fielders - The Rest

Player	Tm	G	Inn	PO	A	E	DP	Pct.	Rng
Abbott,Kurt	Oak	13	102.1	33	1	1	0	.971	2.99
Aldrete,Mike	Oak	17	125.2	34	0	0	0	1.000	2.44
Alicea,Luis	StL	4	29.0	8	1	0	0	1.000	2.79
Amaro,Ruben	Phi	3	16.0	4	0	0	0	1.000	2.25
Ashley,Billy	LA	11	80.0	10	3	0	0	1.000	1.46
Aude,Rich	Pit	1	2.0	0	0	1	0	.000	.00
Barnes,Skeeter	Det	12	80.0	20	0	0	0	1.000	2.25
Bass,Kevin	Hou	12	51.1	10	0	0	0	1.000	1.75
Bean,Billy	SD	11	23.1	3	0	0	0	1.000	1.16
Bell,Derek	SD	1	2.0	0	0	0	0	.000	.00
Benzinger,Todd	SF	7	42.0	10	0	0	0	1.000	2.14
Berroa,Geronimo	Fla	1	9.0	1	1	0	0	1.000	2.00
Blankenship,Lance	Oak	17	136.1	45	0	0	0	1.000	2.97
Blosser,Greg	Bos	9	44.0	11	1	0	0	1.000	2.45
Blowers,Mike	Sea	1	8.0	0	0	0	0	.000	.00
Boston,Daryl	Col	41	318.2	67	1	2	0	.971	1.92
Brewer,Rod	StL	15	80.1	16	0	0	0	1.000	1.79
Briley,Greg	Fla	32	127.1	30	2	1	0	.970	2.26
Brito,Bernardo	Min	10	52.0	12	1	0	0	1.000	2.25
Brooks,Hubie	KC	6	31.0	6	1	1	0	.875	2.03

Left Fielders - The Rest

Left Fielders - The Rest

Player	Tm	G	Inn	PO	A	E	DP	Pct.	Rng
Brosius,Scott	Oak	8	48.0	17	0	0	0	1.000	3.19
Brown,Jarvis	SD	5	28.2	4	1	0	0	1.000	1.57
Browne,Jerry	Oak	30	221.2	65	0	1	0	.985	2.64
Bruett,J.T.	Min	2	16.0	2	0	1	0	.667	1.13
Brumfield,Jacob	Cin	24	77.1	21	0	0	0	1.000	2.44
Brumley,Mike	Hou	1	6.0	1	0	0	0	1.000	1.50
Buford,Damon	Bal	5	25.0	4	0	0	0	1.000	1.44
Butler,Rob	Tor	15	107.0	30	0	1	0	.968	2.52
Calderon,Ivan	Bos	9	58.0	18	0	0	0	1.000	2.79
Canate,Willie	Tor	17	66.0	18	1	0	1	1.000	2.59
Candaele,Casey	Hou	4	11.2	2	0	1	0	.667	1.54
Canseco,Ozzie	StL	5	34.1	1	0	1	0	.500	0.26
Carreon,Mark	SF	9	35.2	4	0	0	0	1.000	1.01
Carrillo,Matias	Fla	4	22.1	2	0	0	0	1.000	0.81
Carter,Joe	Tor	55	465.2	104	1	4	0	.963	2.03
Clark,Dave	Pit	40	266.0	57	1	0	0	1.000	1.96
Clark,Phil	SD	22	145.1	56	4	3	0	.952	3.72
Coles,Darnell	Tor	31	204.1	41	0	1	0	.976	1.81
Costo,Tim	Cin	11	79.0	24	0	1	0	.960	2.73
Cotto,Henry	Sea	23	121.0	32	0	1	0	.970	2.38
Cotto,Henry	Fla	13	29.0	5	0	1	0	.833	1.55
Cummings,Midre	Pit	5	36.2	8	0	0	0	1.000	1.96
Dascenzo,Doug	Tex	16	72.0	17	3	1	1	.952	2.50
Daugherty,Jack	Cin	11	61.0	9	0	1	0	.900	1.33
Davis,Butch	Tex	23	172.0	49	0	1	0	.980	2.56
Diaz,Alex	Mil	4	15.0	5	0	0	0	1.000	3.00
Ducey,Rob	Tex	1	6.0	3	0	0	0	1.000	4.50
Edmonds,Jim	Cal	1	9.0	4	1	0	1	1.000	5.00
Eisenreich,Jim	Phi	1	1.0	0	0	0	0	.000	.00
Espy,Cecil	Cin	18	109.0	25	2	2	0	.931	2.23
Faneyte,Rikkert	SF	1	1.0	0	0	0	0	.000	.00
Fariss,Monty	Fla	1	7.0	3	0	0	0	1.000	3.86
Fox,Eric	Oak	5	25.0	3	0	0	0	1.000	1.08
Frazier,Lou	Mon	52	288.2	64	3	1	0	.985	2.09
Gallagher,Dave	NYN	19	100.1	20	5	0	1	1.000	2.24
Gibson,Kirk	Det	2	4.0	1	0	0	0	1.000	2.25
Gladden,Dan	Det	69	592.1	149	8	3	1	.981	2.39
Goodwin,Tom	LA	6	7.1	2	0	0	0	1.000	2.45
Gordon,Keith	Cin	2	10.0	2	0	0	0	1.000	1.80
Gregg,Tommy	Cin	3	11.0	1	0	0	0	1.000	0.82
Gruber,Kelly	Cal	1	3.0	2	0	0	0	1.000	6.00
Gutierrez,Ricky	SD	3	7.2	1	0	0	0	1.000	1.17
Gwynn,Chris	KC	66	503.0	121	5	1	0	.992	2.25
Hamilton,Darryl	Mil	31	234.2	73	3	0	0	1.000	2.91
Hammonds,Jeffrey	Bal	14	119.2	28	1	1	0	.967	2.18
Harris,Donald	Tex	1	9.0	2	0	0	0	1.000	2.00
Hemond,Scott	Oak	4	9.0	2	0	0	0	1.000	2.00
Henderson,Dave	Oak	2	8.0	2	0	0	0	1.000	2.25
Henderson,Rickey	Oak	74	629.0	182	5	5	0	.974	2.68
Henderson,Rickey	Tor	44	377.0	76	1	2	0	.975	1.84
Hernandez,Cesar	Cin	17	30.0	18	1	1	0	.950	5.70
Higgins,Kevin	SD	1	5.0	0	0	0	0	.000	.00
Hill,Glenallen	Cle	9	65.0	15	0	0	0	1.000	2.08
Hill,Glenallen	ChN	18	139.0	39	2	1	1	.976	2.65
Howard,Thomas	Cle	9	28.0	11	0	0	0	1.000	3.54
Howard,Thomas	Cin	27	200.1	48	2	1	0	.980	2.25
Howitt,Dann	Sea	16	90.2	17	1	0	0	1.000	1.79
Huff,Michael	ChA	31	86.1	24	0	0	0	1.000	2.50

Player	Tm	G	Inn	PO	A	E	DP	Pct.	Rng
Hughes,Keith	Cin	2	3.1	0	0	0	0	.000	.00
Humphreys,Mike	NYA	11	31.0	6	0	0	0	1.000	1.74
Jackson,Bo	ChA	28	201.0	61	2	0	0	1.000	2.82
Jackson,Darrin	NYN	10	65.1	18	1	0	0	1.000	2.62
James,Chris	Hou	16	117.0	36	1	2	0	.949	2.85
James,Chris	Tex	4	27.2	7	0	0	0	1.000	2.28
Javier,Stan	Cal	36	229.1	47	2	2	0	.961	1.92
Johnson,Randy	Sea	1	1.0	0	0	0	0	.000	.00
Jones,Chris	Col	16	68.0	12	0	0	0	1.000	1.59
Jordan,Brian	StL	23	147.0	35	3	0	0	1.000	2.33
Kirby,Wayne	Cle	2	17.0	10	2	0	0	1.000	6.35
Klesko,Ryan	Atl	2	4.0	0	0	0	0	.000	.00
Koslofski,Kevin	KC	3	18.0	6	0	0	0	1.000	3.00
Lampkin,Tom	Mil	2	2.0	0	0	0	0	.000	.00
Landrum,Ced	NYN	3	4.1	0	0	0	0	.000	.00
Larkin,Gene	Min	4	33.0	8	0	0	0	1.000	2.18
Lee,Derek	Min	9	57.0	12	0	0	0	1.000	1.89
Leonard,Mark	Bal	4	16.0	5	0	1	0	.833	2.81
Leyritz,Jim	NYA	6	35.0	14	1	0	0	1.000	3.86
Litton,Greg	Sea	21	131.2	25	3	0	1	1.000	1.91
Longmire,Tony	Phi	2	11.0	4	0	0	0	1.000	3.27
Lydy,Scott	Oak	17	133.2	33	0	0	0	1.000	2.22
Mack,Shane	Min	64	521.0	147	4	5	0	.968	2.61
Maclin,Lonnie	StL	5	20.0	3	0	0	0	1.000	1.35
Maldonado,Candy	ChN	29	166.0	34	2	4	2	.900	1.95
Maldonado,Candy	Cle	2	11.0	2	0	0	0	1.000	1.64
Martin,Al	Pit	81	572.2	133	3	4	0	.971	2.14
Martinez,Dave	SF	3	5.0	0	0	0	0	.000	.00
McCarty,Dave	Min	38	263.0	75	6	3	1	.964	2.77
McClendon,Lloyd	Pit	22	97.1	25	3	1	1	.966	2.59
McIntosh,Tim	Mon	2	6.2	1	0	0	0	1.000	1.35
Mercedes,Luis	SF	1	3.0	0	0	0	0	.000	.00
Meulens,Hensley	NYA	23	123.2	27	0	0	0	1.000	1.96
Mieske,Matt	Mil	1	1.0	0	0	0	0	.000	.00
Miller,Keith	KC	4	26.0	4	0	0	0	1.000	1.38
Milligan,Randy	Cin	9	56.0	9	1	2	0	.833	1.61
Mondesi,Raul	LA	20	85.0	22	1	1	0	.958	2.44
Munoz,Pedro	Min	64	494.1	123	3	2	2	.984	2.29
Murphy,Dale	Col	2	10.0	2	1	0	0	1.000	2.70
Nelson,Jeff	Sea	1	0.1	0	0	0	0	.000	.00
Newfield,Marc	Sea	5	21.0	0	0	0	0	.000	.00
Newson,Warren	ChA	2	7.0	2	0	0	0	1.000	2.57
O'Brien,Pete	Sea	1	6.0	1	0	0	0	1.000	1.50
O'Leary,Troy	Mil	15	86.0	27	1	0	0	1.000	2.93
O'Neill,Paul	NYA	46	351.0	65	3	0	0	1.000	1.74
Obando,Sherman	Bal	1	3.0	0	0	0	0	.000	.00
Orsulak,Joe	NYN	66	458.1	114	4	5	0	.959	2.32
Orton,John	Cal	3	3.0	1	0	0	0	1.000	3.00
Pappas,Erik	StL	1	1.0	0	0	0	0	.000	.00
Paquette,Craig	Oak	1	1.0	1	0	0	0	1.000	9.00
Parker,Rick	Hou	3	6.1	2	0	0	0	1.000	2.84
Pasqua,Dan	ChA	11	74.0	17	1	0	0	1.000	2.19
Peltier,Dan	Tex	2	10.0	2	0	0	0	1.000	1.80
Pennyfeather,William	Pit	1	2.0	0	0	0	0	.000	.00
Phillips,Tony	Det	70	522.2	130	3	2	0	.985	2.29
Pose,Scott	Fla	6	7.1	2	0	0	0	1.000	2.45
Pride,Curtis	Mon	2	2.0	2	0	0	0	1.000	9.00
Puckett,Kirby	Min	1	7.0	1	0	0	0	1.000	1.29

Left Fielders - The Rest

Player	Tm	G	Inn	PO	A	E	DP	Pct.	Rng
Pulliam,Harvey	KC	12	54.0	8	0	1	0	.889	1.33
Quintana,Carlos	Bos	1	2.0	1	0	0	0	1.000	4.50
Reboulet,Jeff	Min	1	1.0	0	0	0	0	.000	.00
Redus,Gary	Tex	5	37.1	7	1	0	0	1.000	1.93
Reimer,Kevin	Mil	28	214.1	57	1	2	0	.967	2.44
Renteria,Rich	Fla	1	1.0	0	0	0	0	.000	.00
Rhodes,Karl	Hou	1	1.0	0	0	0	0	.000	.00
Rhodes,Karl	ChN	6	8.1	1	0	0	0	1.000	1.08
Roberson,Kevin	ChN	14	75.2	11	1	0	0	1.000	1.43
Roberts,Bip	Cin	12	47.2	12	0	1	0	.923	2.27
Rodriguez,Henry	LA	26	183.0	32	1	1	0	.971	1.62
Russell,John	Tex	1	4.0	1	0	0	0	1.000	2.25
Samuel,Juan	Cin	2	8.0	2	0	0	0	1.000	2.25
Sanders,Deion	Atl	5	38.0	6	0	0	0	1.000	1.42
Santiago,Benito	Fla	1	1.2	0	0	0	0	.000	.00
Sasser,Mackey	Sea	26	189.0	33	2	3	0	.921	1.67
Sax,Steve	ChA	26	172.0	32	0	0	0	1.000	1.67
Seitzer,Kevin	Oak	3	11.0	4	0	0	0	1.000	3.27
Sheaffer,Danny	Col	2	3.0	0	0	0	0	.000	.00
Shelton,Ben	Pit	6	33.2	7	1	1	0	.889	2.14
Sherman,Darrell	SD	25	113.2	39	0	0	0	1.000	3.09
Shields,Tommy	ChN	1	1.0	0	0	0	0	.000	.00
Shipley,Craig	SD	2	3.0	0	0	0	0	.000	.00
Siddall,Joe	Mon	1	2.0	0	0	0	0	.000	.00
Smith,Dwight	ChN	14	63.1	12	1	1	0	.929	1.85
Smith,Lonnie	Pit	58	378.1	97	1	1	0	.990	2.33
Smith,Lonnie	Bal	4	31.0	5	1	0	0	1.000	1.74
Snyder,Cory	LA	2	16.0	3	2	0	0	1.000	2.81
Spiers,Bill	Mil	2	6.0	1	0	0	0	1.000	1.50
Stairs,Matt	Mon	1	5.0	1	0	0	0	1.000	1.80
Strawberry,Darryl	LA	4	31.0	3	0	0	0	1.000	0.87
Surhoff,B.J.	Mil	12	75.0	17	1	1	0	.947	2.16
Sveum,Dale	Oak	1	1.0	0	0	0	0	.000	.00
Tarasco,Tony	Atl	4	28.2	5	0	0	0	1.000	1.57
Tatum,Jimmy	Col	2	7.0	1	0	0	0	1.000	1.29
Tettleton,Mickey	Det	18	135.1	23	3	0	1	1.000	1.73
Thurman,Gary	Det	17	66.1	11	2	0	1	1.000	1.76
Tinsley,Lee	Sea	5	25.0	8	0	1	0	.889	2.88
Tomberlin,Andy	Pit	6	52.0	8	1	0	0	1.000	1.56
Trammell,Alan	Det	4	36.0	9	0	1	0	.900	2.25
Tubbs,Greg	Cin	11	36.1	6	0	0	0	1.000	1.49
Turang,Brian	Sea	26	203.2	46	2	1	0	.980	2.12
VanderWal,John	Mon	27	154.2	24	1	1	0	.962	1.45
Varsho,Gary	Cin	13	64.1	12	1	0	1	1.000	1.82
Velarde,Randy	NYA	48	268.2	63	2	4	0	.942	2.18
Velasquez,Guillermo	SD	4	14.0	4	0	0	0	1.000	2.57
Voigt,Jack	Bal	22	167.2	40	0	0	0	1.000	2.15
Walker,Chico	NYN	15	65.1	15	2	1	0	.944	2.34
Walton,Jerome	Cal	1	5.0	2	0	0	0	1.000	3.60
Ward,Turner	Tor	33	221.1	53	1	1	0	.982	2.20
Webster,Mitch	LA	32	221.0	52	1	4	0	.930	2.16
Wehner,John	Pit	4	14.0	6	0	0	0	1.000	3.86
White,Rondell	Mon	19	148.1	30	0	0	0	1.000	1.82
Whitmore,Darrell	Fla	1	0.1	0	0	0	0	.000	.00
Williams,Gerald	NYA	10	20.2	1	0	0	0	1.000	0.44
Wilson,Craig	KC	1	1.0	0	0	0	0	.000	.00
Wilson,Nigel	Fla	3	23.0	4	0	0	0	1.000	1.57
Wood,Ted	Mon	8	53.0	15	0	0	0	1.000	2.55

Left Fielders - The Rest

Player	Tm	G	Inn	PO	A	E	DP	Pct.	Rng
Young,Eric	Col	46	351.0	88	2	2	1	.978	2.31
Young,Gerald	Col	4	13.2	5	0	0	0	1.000	3.29
Zambrano,Eddie	ChN	1	3.0	0	0	0	0	.000	.00
Zupcic,Bob	Bos	48	223.1	48	3	1	0	.981	2.06

Center Fielders - Regulars

Player	Tm	G	Inn	PO	A	E	DP	Pct.	Rng
Thompson,Ryan	NYN	76	656.2	229	4	3	0	.987	3.19
Johnson,Lance	ChA	146	1238.0	425	7	9	1	.980	3.14
Cuyler,Milt	Det	80	616.2	211	2	7	1	.968	3.11
Carr,Chuck	Fla	139	1180.2	393	7	6	2	.985	3.05
Curtis,Chad	Cal	151	1314.1	426	13	9	4	.980	3.01
Lofton,Kenny	Cle	147	1245.0	402	11	9	2	.979	2.99
Dykstra,Lenny	Phi	160	1422.1	469	2	10	0	.979	2.98
Lewis,Darren	SF	131	1080.2	344	4	0	3	1.000	2.90
White,Devon	Tor	145	1265.2	399	6	3	2	.993	2.88
Yount,Robin	Mil	114	949.1	297	6	1	1	.997	2.87
Bell,Derek	SD	120	1019.0	317	8	8	4	.976	2.87
Lankford,Ray	StL	121	1011.2	312	6	7	0	.978	2.83
Grissom,Marquis	Mon	157	1357.0	416	8	7	3	.984	2.81
Nixon,Otis	Atl	145	994.2	306	4	3	1	.990	2.80
Van Slyke,Andy	Pit	78	675.0	204	2	1	1	.995	2.75
Williams,Bernie	NYA	139	1225.0	367	5	4	1	.989	2.73
Kelly,Bobby	Cin	78	663.1	197	3	1	1	.995	2.71
Cole,Alex	Col	93	749.2	218	5	4	1	.982	2.68
McRae,Brian	KC	153	1345.1	394	4	7	3	.983	2.66
Hulse,David	Tex	112	851.2	244	3	3	1	.988	2.61
Finley,Steve	Hou	140	1166.2	327	11	4	4	.988	2.61
Devereaux,Mike	Bal	130	1130.0	310	8	4	3	.988	2.53
Puckett,Kirby	Min	95	807.0	215	9	2	1	.991	2.50
Butler,Brett	LA	155	1381.2	369	6	0	1	1.000	2.44
Griffey Jr,Ken	Sea	139	1208.1	316	8	3	2	.991	2.41
Hatcher,Billy	Bos	129	1098.1	279	6	2	1	.993	2.34
Average	---	124	1063.1	322	6	4	1	.986	2.78

Center Fielders - The Rest

Player	Tm	G	Inn	PO	A	E	DP	Pct.	Rng
Alou,Moises	Mon	12	67.2	23	2	0	0	1.000	3.33
Amaro,Ruben	Phi	8	34.1	8	1	1	0	.900	2.36
Anderson,Brady	Bal	18	134.2	44	2	0	0	1.000	3.07
Anthony,Eric	Hou	23	146.2	32	1	1	0	.971	2.02
Bass,Kevin	Hou	2	10.0	4	0	0	0	1.000	3.60
Bautista,Daniel	Det	9	75.0	24	0	0	0	1.000	2.88
Bean,Billy	SD	17	98.1	28	2	0	0	1.000	2.75
Becker,Rich	Min	3	21.0	7	0	1	0	.875	3.00
Bell,Juan	Mil	1	2.0	0	0	0	0	.000	.00
Bichette,Dante	Col	9	59.1	24	0	0	0	1.000	3.64
Blankenship,Lance	Oak	49	358.2	113	1	1	0	.991	2.86
Boston,Daryl	Col	31	197.1	46	2	0	0	1.000	2.19
Briley,Greg	Fla	1	9.0	1	0	0	0	1.000	1.00
Brosius,Scott	Oak	34	268.0	79	1	0	0	1.000	2.69
Brown,Jarvis	SD	40	282.0	104	1	2	0	.981	3.35
Browne,Jerry	Oak	26	189.2	60	1	1	0	.984	2.89
Bruett,J.T.	Min	4	9.0	6	0	0	0	1.000	6.00

Center Fielders - The Rest

Center Fielders - The Rest

Player	Tm	G	Inn	PO	A	E	DP	Pct.	Rng
Brumfield,Jacob	Cin	68	510.0	146	6	4	1	.974	2.68
Buford,Damon	Bal	24	177.2	55	2	1	2	.983	2.89
Bullett,Scott	Pit	18	116.0	33	1	0	0	1.000	2.64
Burks,Ellis	ChA	21	162.0	49	2	0	0	1.000	2.83
Burnitz,Jeromy	NYN	20	155.1	41	1	0	0	1.000	2.43
Butler,Rob	Tor	1	8.0	2	0	0	0	1.000	2.25
Calderon,Ivan	Bos	2	14.0	6	0	0	0	1.000	3.86
Canate,Willie	Tor	6	34.0	11	0	0	0	1.000	2.91
Candaele,Casey	Hou	12	54.2	19	1	0	0	1.000	3.29
Carreon,Mark	SF	5	33.0	6	0	1	0	.857	1.64
Carrillo,Matias	Fla	5	23.0	7	0	0	0	1.000	2.74
Cotto,Henry	Sea	9	69.1	21	0	0	0	1.000	2.73
Cotto,Henry	Fla	15	102.0	42	0	1	0	.977	3.71
Cummings,Midre	Pit	5	36.0	13	0	0	0	1.000	3.25
Dascenzo,Doug	Tex	35	187.1	50	1	0	1	1.000	2.45
Davis,Butch	Tex	10	62.0	22	2	1	0	.960	3.48
Davis,Eric	LA	3	20.0	5	0	0	0	1.000	2.25
Davis,Eric	Det	18	151.1	52	0	1	0	.981	3.09
Deer,Rob	Det	2	4.0	0	0	0	0	.000	.00
Diaz,Alex	Mil	12	76.0	24	1	1	0	.962	2.96
Ducey,Rob	Tex	14	101.0	22	0	0	0	1.000	1.96
Edmonds,Jim	Cal	1	9.0	5	0	0	0	1.000	5.00
Eisenreich,Jim	Phi	3	6.0	2	0	0	0	1.000	3.00
Everett,Carl	Fla	8	34.2	6	0	1	0	.857	1.56
Faneyte,Rikkert	SF	5	29.0	10	0	0	0	1.000	3.10
Felder,Mike	Sea	7	50.0	10	0	0	0	1.000	1.80
Felix,Junior	Fla	3	25.0	11	0	0	0	1.000	3.96
Fox,Eric	Oak	18	108.2	43	0	0	1	1.000	3.56
Frazier,Lou	Mon	7	16.0	4	0	0	0	1.000	2.25
Gallagher,Dave	NYN	39	212.0	60	1	0	0	1.000	2.59
Gibson,Kirk	Det	30	234.0	74	0	1	0	.987	2.85
Gladden,Dan	Det	28	149.2	47	1	0	0	1.000	2.89
Goodwin,Tom	LA	4	21.0	4	0	0	0	1.000	1.71
Gwynn,Tony	SD	4	4.1	1	0	0	0	1.000	2.08
Hamilton,Darryl	Mil	49	317.2	113	2	2	1	.983	3.26
Harris,Donald	Tex	27	163.2	39	3	2	0	.955	2.31
Hemond,Scott	Oak	1	1.0	0	0	0	0	.000	.00
Henderson,Dave	Oak	60	484.2	168	5	1	1	.994	3.21
Hernandez,Cesar	Cin	7	43.1	12	1	0	0	1.000	2.70
Howard,Dave	KC	1	1.0	0	0	0	0	.000	.00
Howard,Thomas	Cle	11	80.2	25	1	0	1	1.000	2.90
Howard,Thomas	Cin	12	90.1	25	2	0	1	1.000	2.69
Howitt,Dann	Sea	6	16.0	7	0	0	0	1.000	3.94
Huff,Michael	ChA	8	54.0	13	0	0	0	1.000	2.17
Humphreys,Mike	NYA	5	17.1	6	0	0	0	1.000	3.12
Jackson,Darrin	Tor	10	85.2	18	0	1	0	.947	1.89
Jackson,Darrin	NYN	16	122.2	33	3	0	1	1.000	2.64
James,Dion	NYA	14	95.0	15	0	2	0	.882	1.42
Javier,Stan	Cal	16	104.0	26	0	0	0	1.000	2.25
Jones,Chris	Col	52	349.0	95	2	2	0	.980	2.50
Jordan,Brian	StL	37	291.2	82	1	4	0	.954	2.56
Jose,Felix	KC	10	72.0	19	1	0	1	1.000	2.50
Kirby,Wayne	Cle	15	120.0	38	4	0	0	1.000	3.15
Knoblauch,Chuck	Min	1	5.0	2	0	0	0	1.000	3.60
Koslofski,Kevin	KC	4	27.0	10	1	0	1	1.000	3.67
Listach,Pat	Mil	6	31.0	8	0	0	0	1.000	2.32
Lydy,Scott	Oak	5	41.0	12	0	1	0	.923	2.63
Lyons,Steve	Bos	6	14.2	5	0	0	0	1.000	3.07
Mack,Shane	Min	67	578.1	199	4	0	1	1.000	3.16
Martin,Al	Pit	63	487.1	132	3	3	0	.978	2.49
Martinez,Dave	SF	43	285.0	83	4	1	1	.989	2.75
McCarty,Dave	Min	2	19.0	9	0	0	0	1.000	4.26
McNeely,Jeff	Bos	13	101.0	22	0	2	0	.917	1.96
Mercedes,Luis	SF	3	29.0	5	0	0	0	1.000	1.55
Mieske,Matt	Mil	9	68.0	24	0	1	0	.960	3.18
Mondesi,Raul	LA	6	35.0	12	0	0	0	1.000	3.09
Orsulak,Joe	NYN	40	291.1	79	2	0	0	1.000	2.50
Parker,Rick	Hou	13	59.1	15	0	0	0	1.000	2.28
Pennyfeather,William	Pit	15	69.0	21	0	0	0	1.000	2.74
Phillips,Tony	Det	9	56.0	16	0	1	0	.941	2.57
Pose,Scott	Fla	8	66.0	12	0	0	0	1.000	1.64
Reboulet,Jeff	Min	2	5.0	1	0	0	0	1.000	1.80
Redus,Gary	Tex	17	72.1	29	1	0	0	1.000	3.73
Rhodes,Karl	Hou	2	3.2	1	0	0	0	1.000	2.45
Rhodes,Karl	ChN	14	101.2	28	1	1	0	.967	2.57
Roberson,Kevin	ChN	1	0.0	0	0	0	0	.000	.00
Roberts,Bip	Cin	1	7.0	3	0	0	0	1.000	3.86
Salmon,Tim	Cal	1	3.0	2	0	0	0	1.000	6.00
Sanders,Deion	Atl	55	460.1	131	1	2	1	.985	2.58
Sanders,Reggie	Cin	4	31.0	11	0	1	0	.917	3.19
Sherman,Darrell	SD	6	27.0	8	0	0	0	1.000	2.67
Shipley,Craig	SD	3	15.0	6	0	0	0	1.000	3.60
Smith,Dwight	ChN	53	400.1	112	3	6	0	.950	2.59
Smith,Lonnie	Pit	3	17.2	7	0	1	0	.875	3.57
Snyder,Cory	LA	1	9.0	1	0	0	0	1.000	1.00
Sosa,Sammy	ChN	70	527.0	144	5	5	2	.968	2.54
Spiers,Bill	Mil	2	3.0	0	0	0	0	.000	.00
Thompson,Milt	Phi	4	10.0	0	0	0	0	.000	.00
Thurman,Gary	Det	21	119.0	24	0	1	0	.960	1.82
Tinsley,Lee	Sea	1	1.0	1	0	0	0	1.000	9.00
Trammell,Alan	Det	4	31.0	6	1	0	0	1.000	2.03
Tubbs,Greg	Cin	14	89.0	31	1	1	0	.970	3.24
Turang,Brian	Sea	14	109.0	24	0	0	0	1.000	1.98
VanderWal,John	Mon	2	3.0	0	0	0	0	.000	.00
Velarde,Randy	NYA	2	8.2	3	0	1	0	.750	3.12
Ward,Turner	Tor	10	48.0	15	0	0	0	1.000	2.81
Webster,Mitch	LA	2	6.0	1	0	0	0	1.000	1.50
Wehner,John	Pit	8	30.0	9	1	0	0	1.000	3.00
White,Rondell	Mon	5	13.0	3	0	0	0	1.000	2.08
Whiten,Mark	StL	22	149.2	52	1	1	0	.981	3.19
Williams,Gerald	NYA	17	92.0	31	2	2	0	.943	3.23
Wilson,Glenn	Pit	3	14.2	3	2	1	0	.833	3.07
Wilson,Willie	ChN	82	411.2	109	1	1	0	.991	2.40
Yelding,Eric	ChN	1	9.0	1	0	0	0	1.000	1.00
Young,Eric	Col	10	66.1	13	0	1	0	.929	1.76
Young,Gerald	Col	3	9.2	4	0	0	0	1.000	3.72
Zupcic,Bob	Bos	37	224.1	51	1	1	0	.981	2.09

Right Fielders - Regulars

Player	Tm	G	Inn	PO	A	E	DP	Pct.	Rng
Merced,Orlando	Pit	109	766.0	210	11	8	4	.965	2.60
Deer,Rob	TOT	120	1030.1	287	7	8	3	.974	2.57
Salmon,Tim	Cal	141	1219.2	333	12	7	2	.980	2.55
McLemore,Mark	Bal	124	1064.2	282	13	4	4	.987	2.49
Kirby,Wayne	Cle	113	859.1	225	13	5	5	.979	2.49
Eisenreich,Jim	Phi	133	809.0	216	6	1	0	.996	2.47
Bichette,Dante	Col	134	1122.0	284	14	9	3	.971	2.39
Sanders,Reggie	Cin	135	1161.1	302	4	7	0	.978	2.37
Sierra,Ruben	Oak	133	1150.0	291	9	7	3	.977	2.35
Burks,Ellis	ChA	132	1046.0	265	4	6	1	.978	2.31
Sosa,Sammy	ChN	114	836.1	200	12	4	2	.981	2.28
Walker,Larry	Mon	132	1145.0	273	13	6	2	.979	2.25
Whiten,Mark	StL	138	1149.2	277	8	9	1	.969	2.23
Gwynn,Tony	SD	121	1012.1	242	8	5	2	.980	2.22
Justice,Dave	Atl	157	1394.1	324	9	5	1	.985	2.15
Carter,Joe	Tor	96	825.2	184	6	4	0	.979	2.07
McGee,Willie	SF	126	1041.2	224	10	5	1	.979	2.02
O'Neill,Paul	NYA	103	759.1	165	4	2	1	.988	2.00
Bonilla,Bobby	NYN	85	712.2	147	8	5	1	.969	1.96
Anthony,Eric	Hou	121	948.0	201	5	2	0	.990	1.96
Jose,Felix	KC	136	1027.0	218	5	7	2	.970	1.95
Buhner,Jay	Sea	148	1286.1	263	8	6	2	.978	1.90
Snyder,Cory	LA	113	926.1	168	11	4	1	.978	1.74
Average	---	124	1012.2	242	8	5	1	.979	2.23

Right Fielders - The Rest

Player	Tm	G	Inn	PO	A	E	DP	Pct.	Rng
Aldrete,Mike	Oak	3	8.0	3	0	0	0	1.000	3.38
Alou,Moises	Mon	34	236.2	53	3	2	1	.966	2.13
Amaro,Ruben	Phi	6	44.0	13	0	0	0	1.000	2.66
Anderson,Brady	Bal	3	23.0	5	0	0	0	1.000	1.96
Armas,Marcos	Oak	1	5.0	3	0	0	0	1.000	5.40
Barnes,Skeeter	Det	6	36.0	9	0	0	0	1.000	2.25
Bass,Kevin	Hou	51	359.0	69	3	1	0	.986	1.81
Bautista,Daniel	Det	8	55.1	14	2	0	0	1.000	2.60
Bean,Billy	SD	32	184.2	42	4	1	0	.979	2.24
Bell,Derek	SD	6	42.2	8	0	0	0	1.000	1.69
Bell,Juan	Mil	2	11.0	3	0	1	0	.750	2.45
Berroa,Geronimo	Fla	8	54.0	8	0	2	0	.800	1.33
Blankenship,Lance	Oak	2	10.0	4	0	0	0	1.000	3.60
Blowers,Mike	Sea	1	4.0	2	0	0	0	1.000	4.50
Bones,Ricky	Mil	1	1.0	0	0	0	0	.000	.00
Boston,Daryl	Col	9	64.0	12	2	0	1	1.000	1.97
Brewer,Rod	StL	19	109.1	31	1	2	0	.941	2.63
Briley,Greg	Fla	36	152.0	40	0	0	0	1.000	2.37
Brooks,Hubie	KC	34	200.0	47	2	1	1	.980	2.20
Brooks,Jerry	LA	2	5.0	0	0	0	0	.000	.00
Brosius,Scott	Oak	6	45.0	7	1	1	0	.889	1.60
Browne,Jerry	Oak	4	18.0	5	0	0	0	1.000	2.50
Bruett,J.T.	Min	8	21.0	4	0	1	0	.800	1.71
Brumfield,Jacob	Cin	5	23.0	5	0	0	0	1.000	1.96
Brumley,Mike	Hou	1	2.0	0	0	0	0	.000	.00
Brunansky,Tom	Mil	71	522.2	145	4	2	0	.987	2.57
Buford,Damon	Bal	1	7.0	2	0	0	0	1.000	2.57
Bullett,Scott	Pit	1	9.0	2	0	0	0	1.000	2.00
Burnitz,Jeromy	NYN	61	487.0	123	5	4	0	.970	2.37

Right Fielders - The Rest

Player	Tm	G	Inn	PO	A	E	DP	Pct.	Rng
Bush,Randy	Min	1	1.0	0	0	0	0	.000	.00
Calderon,Ivan	Bos	33	241.1	54	2	0	0	1.000	2.09
Canate,Willie	Tor	9	39.0	9	1	0	0	1.000	2.31
Candaele,Casey	Hou	2	3.1	1	0	0	0	1.000	2.70
Canseco,Jose	Tex	49	427.2	94	4	3	2	.970	2.06
Carreon,Mark	SF	30	193.2	38	2	2	0	.952	1.86
Carrillo,Matias	Fla	9	58.0	12	0	0	0	1.000	1.86
Chamberlain,Wes	Phi	76	559.2	131	10	1	4	.993	2.27
Clark,Dave	Pit	53	359.1	76	2	6	1	.929	1.95
Clark,Jerald	Col	17	140.0	31	0	0	0	1.000	1.99
Clark,Phil	SD	15	80.2	18	1	0	0	1.000	2.12
Coles,Darnell	Tor	13	100.0	24	1	2	0	.926	2.25
Costo,Tim	Cin	16	129.2	25	1	0	0	1.000	1.80
Cotto,Henry	Sea	4	13.0	6	0	0	0	1.000	4.15
Cotto,Henry	Fla	21	148.2	38	1	0	0	1.000	2.36
Cummings,Midre	Pit	1	8.0	0	0	0	0	.000	.00
Dascenzo,Doug	Tex	25	78.2	23	1	0	0	1.000	2.75
Daugherty,Jack	Hou	1	1.0	1	0	0	0	1.000	9.00
Daugherty,Jack	Cin	5	11.0	2	0	0	0	1.000	1.64
Davis,Butch	Tex	17	91.0	23	0	2	0	.920	2.27
Dawson,Andre	Bos	20	160.0	42	0	0	0	1.000	2.36
Deer,Rob	Det	84	715.0	193	5	5	3	.975	2.49
Deer,Rob	Bos	36	315.1	94	2	3	0	.970	2.74
Diaz,Alex	Mil	13	78.0	17	0	0	0	1.000	1.96
Ducey,Rob	Tex	13	101.2	26	1	0	0	1.000	2.39
Edmonds,Jim	Cal	15	116.1	37	3	1	1	.976	3.09
Espy,Cecil	Cin	1	1.0	0	0	0	0	.000	.00
Fariss,Monty	Fla	7	45.0	10	0	0	0	1.000	2.00
Felix,Junior	Fla	50	412.2	80	3	6	0	.933	1.81
Fox,Eric	Oak	3	7.0	1	0	0	0	1.000	1.29
Frazier,Lou	Mon	2	10.0	2	0	0	0	1.000	1.80
Gallagher,Dave	NYN	20	128.2	37	0	0	0	1.000	2.59
Gilkey,Bernard	StL	3	19.0	2	0	0	0	1.000	0.95
Goodwin,Tom	LA	2	2.2	2	0	0	0	1.000	6.75
Green,Shawn	Tor	2	7.0	1	0	0	0	1.000	1.29
Gregg,Tommy	Cin	1	8.0	1	0	0	0	1.000	1.13
Gutierrez,Ricky	SD	2	2.0	0	0	0	0	.000	.00
Gwynn,Chris	KC	19	114.0	28	1	0	0	1.000	2.29
Hamilton,Darryl	Mil	70	537.1	156	5	1	0	.994	2.70
Hammonds,Jeffrey	Bal	10	69.0	19	1	1	0	.952	2.61
Harris,Donald	Tex	11	38.0	5	0	1	0	.833	1.18
Harris,Lenny	LA	2	2.0	1	0	0	0	1.000	4.50
Haselman,Bill	Sea	2	5.0	0	0	0	0	.000	.00
Hatcher,Billy	Bos	2	8.0	5	0	0	0	1.000	5.63
Hemond,Scott	Oak	1	3.0	0	0	0	0	.000	.00
Henderson,Dave	Oak	14	119.2	35	2	1	2	.974	2.78
Higgins,Kevin	SD	2	6.0	0	0	0	0	.000	.00
Hill,Glenallen	Cle	30	209.2	46	1	4	0	.922	2.02
Hill,Glenallen	ChN	4	17.0	3	0	1	0	.750	1.59
Hosey,Steve	SF	1	1.0	0	0	0	0	.000	.00
Housie,Wayne	NYN	2	5.0	0	0	0	0	.000	.00
Howard,Thomas	Cle	28	183.2	46	2	2	0	.960	2.35
Howitt,Dann	Sea	12	57.1	18	0	0	0	1.000	2.83
Huff,Michael	ChA	7	19.0	3	0	0	0	1.000	1.42
Humphreys,Mike	NYA	7	33.0	2	0	0	0	1.000	0.55
Hunter,Brian	Atl	17	17.0	4	0	0	0	1.000	2.12
Incaviglia,Pete	Phi	9	67.0	14	1	0	1	1.000	2.01
Jackson,Bo	ChA	19	144.0	28	3	1	1	.969	1.94

Right Fielders - The Rest

Right Fielders - The Rest

Player	Tm	G	Inn	PO	A	E	DP	Pct.	Rng
Jackson,Darrin	Tor	37	318.0	68	2	0	0	1.000	1.98
James,Chris	Hou	18	122.2	29	3	1	0	.970	2.35
James,Chris	Tex	4	29.0	8	0	0	0	1.000	2.48
James,Dion	NYA	1	1.0	0	0	0	0	.000	.00
Javier,Stan	Cal	16	83.1	28	0	0	0	1.000	3.02
Jones,Chris	Col	4	16.0	7	0	0	0	1.000	3.94
Jordan,Brian	StL	11	77.2	25	0	0	0	1.000	2.90
Koslofski,Kevin	KC	7	17.1	4	1	0	1	1.000	2.60
Lampkin,Tom	Mil	1	3.0	0	0	0	0	.000	.00
Larkin,Gene	Min	25	151.0	25	1	0	1	1.000	1.55
Lee,Derek	Min	4	18.1	3	0	0	0	1.000	1.47
Leyritz,Jim	NYA	23	150.2	27	0	0	0	1.000	1.61
Litton,Greg	Sea	2	3.0	0	0	0	0	.000	.00
Lovullo,Torey	Cal	2	11.0	6	0	0	0	1.000	4.91
Lydy,Scott	Oak	16	86.0	22	2	2	0	.923	2.51
Lyons,Steve	Bos	4	6.0	0	0	0	0	.000	.00
Mack,Shane	Min	2	10.0	1	0	0	0	1.000	0.90
Maldonado,Candy	ChN	15	87.0	15	1	1	0	.941	1.66
Maldonado,Candy	Cle	25	167.0	37	1	1	0	.974	2.05
Martin,Al	Pit	6	9.1	2	0	0	0	1.000	1.93
Martinez,Chito	Bal	5	22.0	2	0	0	0	1.000	0.82
Martinez,Dave	SF	34	219.1	47	2	0	1	1.000	2.01
May,Derrick	ChN	2	11.0	3	0	0	0	1.000	2.45
McCarty,Dave	Min	34	265.2	50	2	3	0	.945	1.76
McClendon,Lloyd	Pit	47	276.0	60	2	2	1	.969	2.02
McIntosh,Tim	Mon	6	11.0	2	0	0	0	1.000	1.64
Mercedes,Luis	Bal	8	66.2	11	1	0	1	1.000	1.62
Mercedes,Luis	SF	1	1.0	0	0	0	0	.000	.00
Meulens,Hensley	NYA	1	1.0	0	0	0	0	.000	.00
Mieske,Matt	Mil	12	93.0	19	1	2	0	.909	1.94
Mitchell,Kevin	Cin	2	18.0	7	1	0	0	1.000	4.00
Mondesi,Raul	LA	17	88.0	22	2	2	1	.923	2.45
Munoz,Pedro	Min	41	316.0	49	2	1	0	.981	1.45
Murphy,Dale	Col	11	67.0	14	0	0	0	1.000	1.88
Newson,Warren	ChA	3	15.0	3	0	0	0	1.000	1.80
Nieves,Melvin	SD	15	104.1	27	0	2	0	.931	2.33
Nixon,Otis	Atl	2	4.0	1	0	0	0	1.000	2.25
O'Leary,Troy	Mil	5	30.0	5	0	0	0	1.000	1.50
Obando,Sherman	Bal	7	40.0	13	0	1	0	.929	2.93
Oliver,Joe	Cin	1	8.0	0	0	0	0	.000	.00
Orsulak,Joe	NYN	23	103.2	22	3	0	0	1.000	2.17
Pappas,Erik	StL	15	96.1	37	0	0	0	1.000	3.46
Parker,Rick	Hou	1	3.0	0	0	0	0	.000	.00
Pasqua,Dan	ChA	26	195.0	40	2	1	1	.977	1.94
Pecota,Bill	Atl	1	9.0	1	0	0	0	1.000	1.00
Peltier,Dan	Tex	54	352.2	70	4	4	2	.949	1.89
Pennyfeather,William	Pit	2	2.0	0	0	0	0	.000	.00
Perry,Gerald	StL	1	1.0	2	0	0	0	1.000	18.00
Phillips,Tony	Det	34	246.0	69	2	4	1	.947	2.60
Puckett,Kirby	Min	47	408.1	96	4	0	1	1.000	2.20
Pulliam,Harvey	KC	16	87.0	26	0	0	0	1.000	2.69
Quintana,Carlos	Bos	50	383.1	91	4	0	1	1.000	2.23
Ramirez,Manny	Cle	1	8.0	3	0	0	0	1.000	3.38
Redus,Gary	Tex	46	319.1	67	1	2	0	.971	1.92
Reimer,Kevin	Mil	10	49.0	18	0	1	0	.947	3.31
Rhodes,Karl	Hou	1	2.0	1	0	0	0	1.000	4.50
Rhodes,Karl	ChN	1	3.0	2	0	0	0	1.000	6.00
Roberson,Kevin	ChN	42	326.0	66	1	3	0	.957	1.85

Player	Tm	G	Inn	PO	A	E	DP	Pct.	Rng
Rodriguez,Henry	LA	23	135.1	25	2	0	0	1.000	1.80
Samuel,Juan	Cin	1	6.0	1	1	1	0	.667	3.00
Sasser,Mackey	Sea	11	78.0	17	1	0	0	1.000	2.08
Sax,Steve	ChA	6	35.0	7	0	0	0	1.000	1.80
Seitzer,Kevin	Mil	1	8.0	4	0	0	0	1.000	4.50
Sharperson,Mike	LA	1	1.0	0	0	0	0	.000	.00
Sheets,Larry	Sea	1	5.0	1	0	0	0	1.000	1.80
Sherman,Darrell	SD	1	1.0	2	0	0	0	1.000	18.00
Smith,Dwight	ChN	28	154.1	39	1	1	1	.976	2.33
Sorrento,Paul	Cle	3	18.0	3	0	0	0	1.000	1.50
Spiers,Bill	Mil	4	8.0	2	1	0	0	1.000	3.38
Strawberry,Darryl	LA	25	207.0	34	1	4	0	.897	1.52
Surhoff,B.J.	Mil	14	106.0	20	1	0	0	1.000	1.78
Tarasco,Tony	Atl	8	30.2	6	0	0	0	1.000	1.76
Tartabull,Danny	NYA	50	434.0	88	3	2	2	.978	1.89
Tatum,Jimmy	Col	1	1.0	0	0	0	0	.000	.00
Tettleton,Mickey	Det	39	313.0	68	1	2	0	.972	1.98
Thurman,Gary	Det	15	71.1	19	1	2	0	.909	2.52
Tinsley,Lee	Sea	1	1.0	0	0	0	0	.000	.00
Tomberlin,Andy	Pit	1	5.0	1	0	0	0	1.000	1.80
Tubbs,Greg	Cin	2	10.0	1	0	0	0	1.000	0.90
Turang,Brian	Sea	1	1.0	1	0	0	0	1.000	9.00
VanderWal,John	Mon	10	47.0	10	0	0	0	1.000	1.91
Varsho,Gary	Cin	9	58.0	15	0	0	0	1.000	2.33
Velasquez,Guillermo	SD	2	7.0	0	0	0	0	.000	.00
Voigt,Jack	Bal	23	150.0	35	3	1	0	.974	2.28
Walker,Chico	NYN	1	1.0	1	0	0	0	1.000	9.00
Ward,Turner	Tor	22	151.2	27	1	0	0	1.000	1.66
Webster,Mitch	LA	27	105.1	22	0	0	0	1.000	1.88
Wehner,John	Pit	2	3.0	1	0	0	0	1.000	3.00
Whitmore,Darrell	Fla	69	570.0	140	3	3	1	.979	2.26
Williams,Gerald	NYA	12	59.0	9	0	0	0	1.000	1.37
Wilson,Glenn	Pit	2	8.0	2	0	0	0	1.000	2.25
Winfield,Dave	Min	31	253.0	62	2	0	0	1.000	2.28
Wood,Ted	Mon	1	7.0	1	0	0	0	1.000	1.29
Young,Gerald	Col	5	21.1	6	0	2	0	.750	2.53
Zambrano,Eddie	ChN	3	15.0	1	0	0	0	1.000	0.60
Zupcic,Bob	Bos	54	294.1	78	4	2	0	.976	2.51

Catchers - Regulars

Player	Tm	G	Inn	PO	A	E	DP	PB	Pct.
Manwaring,Kirt	SF	130	1090.2	739	69	2	12	11	.998
Wilkins,Rick	ChN	133	1077.1	717	89	3	8	11	.996
Servais,Scott	Hou	82	653.2	493	40	2	9	4	.996
Stanley,Mike	NYA	122	1001.1	652	46	3	5	6	.996
Valle,Dave	Sea	135	1131.1	880	71	5	13	8	.995
Pena,Tony	Bos	125	915.1	698	53	4	6	5	.995
Karkovice,Ron	ChA	127	1038.2	769	60	5	3	9	.994
Hoiles,Chris	Bal	124	1039.2	696	64	5	11	2	.993
Slaught,Don	Pit	105	874.2	540	50	4	9	10	.993
Oliver,Joe	Cin	133	1102.2	791	66	7	8	11	.992
Taubensee,Eddie	Hou	90	727.2	552	40	5	5	3	.992
Daulton,Darren	Phi	147	1287.0	986	67	9	18	13	.992
Pagnozzi,Tom	StL	92	787.0	421	44	4	4	9	.991
Rodriguez,Ivan	Tex	134	1116.2	800	74	8	7	13	.991
Hemond,Scott	Oak	75	600.0	395	37	4	5	10	.991
Berryhill,Damon	Atl	105	774.0	570	52	6	3	6	.990
Ortiz,Junior	Cle	95	707.2	440	58	5	13	2	.990
Steinbach,Terry	Oak	86	707.2	422	38	5	9	4	.989
Piazza,Mike	LA	146	1243.1	898	99	11	11	14	.989
Girardi,Joe	Col	84	707.2	479	45	6	7	2	.989
Kreuter,Chad	Det	112	897.0	518	67	7	10	4	.988
Fletcher,Darrin	Mon	127	918.1	620	40	8	3	4	.988
Hundley,Todd	NYN	123	942.2	592	63	8	6	4	.988
Olson,Greg	Atl	81	641.0	445	35	6	6	6	.988
Harper,Brian	Min	134	1124.2	736	61	10	6	18	.988
Santiago,Benito	Fla	136	1095.0	741	63	11	4	23	.987
Borders,Pat	Tor	138	1182.0	868	80	13	11	6	.986
Myers,Greg	Cal	97	644.1	369	44	6	6	5	.986
Macfarlane,Mike	KC	114	917.1	647	65	11	11	8	.985
Nilsson,Dave	Mil	91	719.0	430	30	9	3	7	.981
Average	---	114	922.0	630	57	6	7	7	.991

Catchers - The Rest

Player	Tm	G	Inn	PO	A	E	DP	PB	Pct.
Allanson,Andy	SF	8	45.2	30	0	0	0	0	1.000
Alomar Jr,Sandy	Cle	64	520.0	342	25	6	4	3	.984
Ausmus,Brad	SD	49	402.1	273	34	8	4	2	.975
Blowers,Mike	Sea	1	1.0	1	0	0	0	0	1.000
Cabrera,Francisco	Atl	2	3.0	4	0	0	0	0	1.000
Clark,Phil	SD	11	27.1	23	4	1	1	0	.964
Colbert,Craig	SF	10	63.2	51	3	1	0	0	.982
Decker,Steve	Fla	5	33.1	28	2	1	0	0	.968
Delgado,Carlos	Tor	1	3.0	2	0	0	0	0	1.000
Dorsett,Brian	Cin	18	127.1	111	5	0	0	0	1.000
Fisk,Carlton	ChA	25	125.2	75	5	0	0	2	1.000
Flaherty,John	Bos	13	77.0	35	9	0	0	1	1.000
Geren,Bob	SD	49	360.0	251	26	2	6	4	.993
Goff,Jerry	Pit	14	105.0	53	6	1	0	2	.983
Gonzales,Larry	Cal	2	5.1	4	0	0	0	0	1.000
Haselman,Bill	Sea	49	306.1	236	17	2	1	5	.992
Helfand,Eric	Oak	5	25.0	25	5	0	1	0	1.000
Hernandez,Carlos	LA	43	229.1	181	14	7	0	1	.965
Higgins,Kevin	SD	59	413.1	308	31	6	1	10	.983
Howard,Chris	Sea	4	5.0	5	0	0	0	0	1.000
Kmak,Joe	Mil	50	316.1	172	23	0	4	4	1.000
Knorr,Randy	Tor	39	256.1	168	20	0	4	0	1.000

Catchers - The Rest

Player	Tm	G	Inn	PO	A	E	DP	PB	Pct.
Lake,Steve	ChN	41	303.1	169	26	3	1	2	.985
Laker,Tim	Mon	43	230.1	136	18	2	2	9	.987
Lampkin,Tom	Mil	60	400.0	242	23	6	3	1	.978
LaValliere,Mike	Pit	1	9.0	12	0	0	0	1	1.000
LaValliere,Mike	ChA	37	259.2	164	28	0	2	4	1.000
Levis,Jesse	Cle	29	155.2	108	8	1	3	1	.991
Leyritz,Jim	NYA	12	37.0	31	1	0	0	0	1.000
Lindsey,Doug	Phi	2	3.0	3	0	0	0	0	1.000
Lindsey,Doug	ChA	2	5.0	3	0	0	0	0	1.000
Lopez,Javy	Atl	7	37.0	37	2	1	0	1	.975
Lyden,Mitch	Fla	2	11.1	4	0	0	0	0	1.000
Lyons,Steve	Bos	1	1.0	0	0	0	0	0	.000
Mayne,Brent	KC	68	505.0	356	27	2	1	5	.995
McGriff,Terry	Fla	3	19.0	12	0	0	0	0	1.000
McIntosh,Tim	Mil	1	1.0	0	0	0	0	0	.000
McIntosh,Tim	Mon	5	9.1	5	1	0	0	0	1.000
McKnight,Jeff	NYN	1	1.0	0	0	0	0	0	.000
McNamara,Jim	SF	4	17.0	12	0	0	0	0	1.000
Melvin,Bob	Bos	76	459.0	304	17	2	4	5	.994
Mercedes,Henry	Oak	18	119.0	66	10	1	1	1	.987
Natal,Bob	Fla	38	281.2	196	18	0	1	6	1.000
Nokes,Matt	NYA	56	399.2	245	19	2	0	1	.992
O'Brien,Charlie	NYN	65	494.1	325	39	5	5	0	.986
Orton,John	Cal	35	268.0	184	17	4	4	1	.980
Owens,Jayhawk	Col	32	221.2	138	18	7	3	3	.957
Pappas,Erik	StL	63	489.2	294	32	6	5	3	.982
Parent,Mark	Bal	21	143.0	83	5	1	0	1	.989
Parks,Derek	Min	7	50.0	28	4	1	1	2	.970
Parrish,Lance	Cle	10	62.1	47	10	3	1	3	.950
Petralli,Geno	Tex	39	288.1	178	11	2	4	2	.990
Pratt,Todd	Phi	26	191.2	169	7	2	3	0	.989
Prince,Tom	Pit	59	457.0	270	32	5	6	6	.984
Reed,Jeff	SF	37	239.2	180	14	0	4	4	1.000
Ronan,Marc	StL	6	33.0	29	0	0	0	1	1.000
Rowland,Rich	Det	17	109.2	75	7	1	1	0	.988
Russell,John	Tex	11	33.0	21	0	0	0	2	1.000
Santovenia,Nelson	KC	4	23.0	14	1	0	0	2	1.000
Sasser,Mackey	Sea	4	10.0	8	1	0	0	0	1.000
Sheaffer,Danny	Col	65	493.0	331	28	2	5	6	.994
Siddall,Joe	Mon	15	57.0	33	5	0	0	1	1.000
Spehr,Tim	Mon	49	241.2	166	22	9	3	0	.954
Surhoff,B.J.	Mil	3	10.2	9	0	0	0	0	1.000
Tackett,Jeff	Bal	38	259.2	167	16	2	1	3	.989
Tettleton,Mickey	Det	56	430.0	267	20	1	1	4	.997
Tingley,Ron	Cal	58	318.2	200	20	1	3	3	.995
Tucker,Scooter	Hou	8	59.2	56	2	0	0	0	1.000
Turner,Chris	Cal	25	194.0	116	14	1	0	1	.992
Villanueva,Hector	StL	17	143.1	86	3	0	0	1	1.000
Walbeck,Matt	ChN	11	69.0	49	2	0	0	1	1.000
Walters,Dan	SD	27	243.2	141	23	5	0	4	.970
Webster,Lenny	Min	45	269.2	177	12	0	1	1	1.000
Wedge,Eric	Col	1	9.0	6	1	0	0	0	1.000
Wilson,Dan	Cin	35	204.0	146	9	1	2	1	.994
Wrona,Rick	ChA	4	25.0	12	0	0	0	0	1.000

Catchers - Regulars - Special

Player	Tm	G	Inn	SBA	CS	PCS	CS%	ER	CERA
Olson,Greg	Atl	81	641.0	79	23	9	.29	208	2.92
Fletcher,Darrin	Mon	127	918.1	125	26	12	.21	329	3.22
Servais,Scott	Hou	82	653.2	74	18	3	.24	238	3.28
Berryhill,Damon	Atl	105	774.0	90	28	3	.31	288	3.35
Piazza,Mike	LA	146	1243.1	167	59	1	.35	473	3.42
Karkovice,Ron	ChA	127	1038.2	104	56	8	.54	408	3.54
Taubensee,Eddie	Hou	90	727.2	73	22	2	.30	290	3.59
Manwaring,Kirt	SF	130	1090.2	111	51	7	.46	446	3.68
Pena,Tony	Bos	125	915.1	83	31	0	.37	381	3.75
Daulton,Darren	Phi	147	1287.0	134	45	5	.34	563	3.94
Pagnozzi,Tom	StL	92	787.0	88	30	5	.34	349	3.99
Macfarlane,Mike	KC	114	917.1	123	53	11	.43	407	3.99
Wilkins,Rick	ChN	133	1077.1	122	56	6	.46	483	4.03
Hoiles,Chris	Bal	124	1039.2	113	46	15	.41	472	4.09
Borders,Pat	Tor	138	1182.0	161	53	1	.33	537	4.09
Valle,Dave	Sea	135	1131.1	125	57	8	.46	518	4.12
Santiago,Benito	Fla	136	1095.0	129	39	10	.30	504	4.14
Rodriguez,Ivan	Tex	134	1116.2	115	51	11	.44	516	4.16
Hundley,Todd	NYN	123	942.2	134	33	5	.25	440	4.20
Ortiz,Junior	Cle	95	707.2	86	39	2	.45	336	4.27
Oliver,Joe	Cin	133	1102.2	150	50	7	.33	537	4.38
Hemond,Scott	Oak	75	600.0	77	27	1	.35	298	4.47
Harper,Brian	Min	134	1124.2	169	55	14	.33	562	4.50
Kreuter,Chad	Det	112	897.0	102	45	10	.44	449	4.51
Stanley,Mike	NYA	122	1001.1	94	29	7	.31	502	4.51
Myers,Greg	Cal	97	644.1	94	27	4	.29	339	4.74
Slaught,Don	Pit	105	874.2	116	30	10	.26	478	4.92
Nilsson,Dave	Mil	91	719.0	82	22	4	.27	395	4.94
Steinbach,Terry	Oak	86	707.2	96	34	4	.35	413	5.25
Girardi,Joe	Col	84	707.2	93	29	4	.31	413	5.25
Average	---	114	922.0	110	38	6	.35	419	4.09

Catchers - The Rest - Special

Player	Tm	G	Inn	SBA	CS	PCS	CS%	ER	CERA
Allanson,Andy	SF	8	45.2	3	1	1	.33	18	3.55
Alomar Jr,Sandy	Cle	64	520.0	57	16	1	.28	295	5.11
Ausmus,Brad	SD	49	402.1	50	19	1	.38	197	4.41
Blowers,Mike	Sea	1	1.0	0	0	0	0	0	0.00
Cabrera,Francisco	Atl	2	3.0	0	0	0	0	0	0.00
Clark,Phil	SD	11	27.1	3	1	0	.33	18	5.93
Colbert,Craig	SF	10	63.2	4	2	0	.50	23	3.25
Decker,Steve	Fla	5	33.1	5	1	0	.20	13	3.51
Delgado,Carlos	Tor	1	3.0	0	0	0	0	1	3.00
Dorsett,Brian	Cin	18	127.1	12	3	0	.25	63	4.45
Fisk,Carlton	ChA	25	125.2	24	2	1	.08	61	4.37
Flaherty,John	Bos	13	77.0	14	5	1	.36	41	4.79
Geren,Bob	SD	49	360.0	58	19	2	.33	142	3.55
Goff,Jerry	Pit	14	105.0	11	4	1	.36	35	3.00
Gonzales,Larry	Cal	2	5.1	0	0	0	0	10	16.88
Haselman,Bill	Sea	49	306.1	45	10	1	.22	151	4.44
Helfand,Eric	Oak	5	25.0	5	2	0	.40	16	5.76
Hernandez,Carlos	LA	43	229.1	28	7	0	.25	100	3.92
Higgins,Kevin	SD	59	413.1	59	16	0	.27	198	4.31
Howard,Chris	Sea	4	5.0	2	0	0	0	3	5.40
Kmak,Joe	Mil	50	316.1	42	15	2	.36	145	4.13
Knorr,Randy	Tor	39	256.1	39	11	3	.28	138	4.85

Catchers - The Rest - Special

Player	Tm	G	Inn	SBA	CS	PCS	CS%	ER	CERA
Lake,Steve	ChN	41	303.1	22	12	0	.55	164	4.87
Laker,Tim	Mon	43	230.1	34	6	0	.18	121	4.73
Lampkin,Tom	Mil	60	400.0	41	13	0	.32	173	3.89
LaValliere,Mike	Pit	1	9.0	1	0	0	0	3	3.00
LaValliere,Mike	ChA	37	259.2	32	24	3	.75	121	4.19
Levis,Jesse	Cle	29	155.2	20	7	0	.35	66	3.82
Leyritz,Jim	NYA	12	37.0	5	1	0	.20	20	4.86
Lindsey,Doug	Phi	2	3.0	0	0	0	0	3	9.00
Lindsey,Doug	ChA	2	5.0	0	0	0	0	1	1.80
Lopez,Javy	Atl	7	37.0	5	2	0	.40	11	2.68
Lyden,Mitch	Fla	2	11.1	1	0	0	0	10	7.94
Lyons,Steve	Bos	1	1.0	0	0	0	0	0	0.00
Mayne,Brent	KC	68	505.0	66	18	3	.27	230	4.10
McGriff,Terry	Fla	3	19.0	0	0	0	0	17	8.05
McIntosh,Tim	Mil	1	1.0	0	0	0	0	2	18.00
McIntosh,Tim	Mon	5	9.1	0	0	0	0	1	0.96
McKnight,Jeff	NYN	1	1.0	0	0	0	0	0	0.00
McNamara,Jim	SF	4	17.0	1	0	0	0	9	4.76
Melvin,Bob	Bos	76	459.0	39	8	0	.21	192	3.76
Mercedes,Henry	Oak	18	119.0	13	8	0	.62	64	4.84
Natal,Bob	Fla	38	281.2	34	11	3	.32	120	3.83
Nokes,Matt	NYA	56	399.2	63	17	3	.27	176	3.96
O'Brien,Charlie	NYN	65	494.1	65	23	1	.35	207	3.77
Orton,John	Cal	35	268.0	26	9	3	.35	97	3.26
Owens,Jayhawk	Col	32	221.2	29	11	1	.38	149	6.05
Pappas,Erik	StL	63	489.2	56	19	4	.34	261	4.80
Parent,Mark	Bal	21	143.0	8	1	0	.13	84	5.29
Parks,Derek	Min	7	50.0	4	0	0	0	33	5.94
Parrish,Lance	Cle	10	62.1	18	6	2	.33	38	5.49
Petralli,Geno	Tex	39	288.1	45	15	10	.33	155	4.84
Pratt,Todd	Phi	26	191.2	16	4	2	.25	86	4.04
Prince,Tom	Pit	59	457.0	71	17	5	.24	250	4.92
Reed,Jeff	SF	37	239.2	28	12	0	.43	91	3.42
Ronan,Marc	StL	6	33.0	0	0	0	0	5	1.36
Rowland,Rich	Det	17	109.2	12	3	0	.25	59	4.84
Russell,John	Tex	11	33.0	2	1	1	.50	13	3.55
Santovenia,Nelson	KC	4	23.0	1	0	0	0	12	4.70
Sasser,Mackey	Sea	4	10.0	1	1	0	1.00	7	6.30
Sheaffer,Danny	Col	65	493.0	51	15	2	.29	299	5.46
Siddall,Joe	Mon	15	57.0	9	3	1	.33	14	2.21
Spehr,Tim	Mon	49	241.2	55	16	5	.29	109	4.06
Surhoff,B.J.	Mil	3	10.2	1	1	1	1.00	3	2.53
Tackett,Jeff	Bal	38	259.2	39	17	4	.44	137	4.75
Tettleton,Mickey	Det	56	430.0	45	9	4	.20	243	5.09
Tingley,Ron	Cal	58	318.2	26	11	4	.42	156	4.41
Tucker,Scooter	Hou	8	59.2	5	2	0	.40	31	4.68
Turner,Chris	Cal	25	194.0	28	5	4	.18	91	4.22
Villanueva,Hector	StL	17	143.1	22	5	3	.23	47	2.95
Walbeck,Matt	ChN	11	69.0	9	1	0	.11	26	3.39
Walters,Dan	SD	27	243.2	41	14	1	.34	125	4.62
Webster,Lenny	Min	45	269.2	30	11	4	.37	164	5.47
Wedge,Eric	Col	1	9.0	2	1	0	.50	4	4.00
Wilson,Dan	Cin	35	204.0	28	3	1	.11	119	5.25
Wrona,Rick	ChA	4	25.0	4	0	0	0	10	3.60

Pitchers Hitting
and Hitters Pitching

After last year's Handbook came out, a number of readers asked us an obvious question: If you include pitchers hitting in the Handbook, why not include hitters pitching as well? Being that we couldn't think of a good reason not to, we now present the first-ever hitters pitching section of the Major League Handbook.

Both sections include data for all active players. Well, let's say all active "non-zero" players. Any active pitcher who ever hit and any active hitter who ever pitched is shown along with their 1993 and career stats.

Who said Steve Lyons and Ted Williams have nothing in common?

Pitchers Hitting, Fielding and Holding Runners

Pitcher	1993 Hitting						Career Hitting										1993 Fielding and Holding Runners										
	Avg	AB	H	HR	RBI	SH	Avg	AB	H	2B	3B	HR	RBI	BB	SO	SH	G	Inn	PO	A	E	DP	Pct.	SBA	CS	PCS	CS%
Abbott, Jim	.000	0	0	0	0	0	.000	0	0	0	0	0	0	0	0	0	32	214.0	4	42	1	4	.979	22	1	5	.27
Abbott, Paul	.000	0	0	0	0	0	.000	0	0	0	0	0	0	0	0	0	5	18.1	2	3	1	0	.833	3	0	0	.00
Agosto, Juan	.000	0	0	0	0	0	.100	20	2	0	0	0	0	1	7	1	6	6.0	0	0	0	0	.000	1	0	0	.00
Aguilera, Rick	.000	0	0	0	0	0	.203	138	28	3	0	3	11	6	37	16	65	72.1	12	7	0	0	1.000	4	0	0	.00
Aldred, Scott	.000	0	0	0	0	0	.000	0	0	0	0	0	0	0	0	0	8	12.0	0	2	0	0	1.000	3	1	0	.33
Alvarez, Wilson	.000	0	0	0	0	0	.000	0	0	0	0	0	0	0	0	0	31	207.2	5	28	1	2	.971	38	13	4	.45
Andersen, Larry	1.000	1	1	0	0	0	.132	38	5	0	0	0	0	2	15	4	64	61.2	3	4	1	1	.875	5	1	0	.20
Anderson, Brian	.000	0	0	0	0	0	.000	0	0	0	0	0	0	0	0	0	4	11.1	0	1	0	0	1.000	1	0	0	.00
Anderson, Mike	.000	1	0	0	0	0	.000	1	0	0	0	0	0	0	0	0	3	5.1	0	1	0	0	1.000	0	0	0	.00
Appier, Kevin	.000	0	0	0	0	0	.000	0	0	0	0	0	0	0	0	0	34	238.2	26	14	1	4	.976	19	8	0	.42
Aquino, Luis	.080	25	2	0	0	4	.080	25	2	0	0	0	0	0	7	4	37	110.2	10	29	1	5	.975	15	4	1	.33
Armstrong, Jack	.152	66	10	0	3	4	.114	185	21	2	0	0	8	2	83	26	36	196.1	13	28	2	1	.953	21	2	1	.14
Arocha, Rene	.103	58	6	0	3	7	.103	58	6	1	0	0	3	2	24	7	32	188.0	9	28	4	3	.902	22	8	0	.36
Ashby, Andy	.139	36	5	0	1	2	.119	59	7	2	0	0	2	2	25	5	32	123.0	14	21	0	1	1.000	12	1	0	.08
Assenmacher, Paul	.500	2	1	0	0	0	.083	36	3	1	0	0	0	5	12	7	72	56.0	1	4	1	2	.833	5	1	0	.20
Astacio, Pedro	.161	62	10	0	2	7	.151	86	13	0	0	0	3	0	40	12	31	186.1	24	17	2	2	.953	31	12	0	.39
Austin, James	.000	0	0	0	0	0	.000	0	0	0	0	0	0	0	0	0	30	33.0	0	5	0	0	1.000	1	1	0	1.00
Avery, Steve	.160	75	12	0	5	8	.177	260	46	7	2	0	11	9	79	24	35	223.1	4	46	0	2	1.000	46	4	10	.30
Ayala, Bobby	.095	21	2	0	1	2	.067	30	2	1	0	0	1	0	13	3	43	98.0	13	10	6	1	.793	10	1	0	.10
Ayrault, Bob	.000	2	0	0	0	0	.000	2	0	0	0	0	0	0	2	0	24	30.0	0	3	0	0	1.000	4	0	0	.00
Bailey, Cory	.000	0	0	0	0	0	.000	0	0	0	0	0	0	0	0	0	11	15.2	0	5	0	0	1.000	5	2	0	.40
Ballard, Jeff	.364	11	4	0	0	1	.364	11	4	1	0	0	0	0	4	1	25	53.2	4	12	1	3	.941	3	0	1	.33
Bankhead, Scott	.000	0	0	0	0	0	.222	9	2	0	0	0	0	0	7	2	40	64.1	1	4	1	0	.833	5	2	0	.40
Banks, Willie	.000	0	0	0	0	0	.000	0	0	0	0	0	0	0	0	0	31	171.1	13	15	6	1	.824	12	6	0	.50
Barnes, Brian	.150	20	3	0	2	2	.140	107	15	0	0	0	4	10	51	11	51	100.0	3	15	0	1	1.000	11	2	1	.27
Batchelor, Richard	.000	1	0	0	0	0	.000	1	0	0	0	0	0	0	0	0	9	10.0	1	1	0	0	1.000	2	0	0	.00
Bautista, Jose	.190	21	4	0	1	2	.190	21	4	0	0	0	1	0	4	2	58	111.2	14	18	2	2	.941	7	2	0	.29
Beck, Rod	.000	4	0	0	0	1	.250	8	2	0	0	0	0	0	4	1	76	79.1	0	8	1	1	.889	1	0	0	.00
Bedrosian, Steve	.000	2	0	0	0	0	.093	151	14	0	0	0	2	3	57	12	49	49.2	3	5	0	0	1.000	8	2	0	.25
Belcher, Tim	.200	50	10	0	7	3	.124	372	46	8	0	2	25	2	142	41	34	208.2	19	17	2	2	.947	19	8	0	.42
Belinda, Stan	.000	1	0	0	0	0	.125	16	2	1	0	0	3	2	9	3	63	69.2	4	5	0	1	1.000	19	2	0	.11
Bell, Eric	.000	0	0	0	0	0	.000	0	0	0	0	0	0	0	0	0	10	7.1	0	0	0	0	.000	2	0	0	.00
Benes, Andy	.125	72	9	1	4	14	.116	285	33	6	0	4	14	14	128	32	34	230.2	16	15	1	2	.969	28	7	0	.25
Bere, Jason	.000	0	0	0	0	0	.000	0	0	0	0	0	0	0	0	0	24	142.2	11	14	2	1	.926	17	8	0	.47
Bergman, Sean	.000	0	0	0	0	0	.000	0	0	0	0	0	0	0	0	0	9	39.2	3	6	0	1	1.000	4	0	0	.00
Bielecki, Mike	.000	0	0	0	0	0	.079	267	21	0	0	0	12	11	135	34	13	68.2	5	11	0	1	1.000	15	1	0	.07
Black, Bud	.243	37	9	0	3	3	.154	162	25	4	0	0	11	4	44	22	16	93.2	3	22	2	2	.926	17	3	5	.47
Blair, Willie	.111	36	4	0	4	3	.094	53	5	1	0	0	4	2	33	4	46	146.0	9	16	0	0	1.000	12	4	0	.33
Boddicker, Mike	.000	0	0	0	0	0	.000	0	0	0	0	0	0	0	0	0	10	54.0	5	9	2	1	.875	9	3	0	.33
Boever, Joe	.000	0	0	0	0	0	.125	16	2	0	0	0	0	0	3	0	61	102.1	9	12	1	1	.955	7	3	0	.43
Bohanon, Brian	.000	0	0	0	0	0	.000	0	0	0	0	0	0	0	0	0	36	92.2	5	18	0	4	1.000	15	3	4	.47
Bolton, Rodney	.000	0	0	0	0	0	.000	0	0	0	0	0	0	0	0	0	9	42.1	4	9	0	0	1.000	2	0	0	.00
Bolton, Tom	.000	0	0	0	0	0	.000	14	0	0	0	0	0	0	5	1	43	102.2	6	15	2	2	.913	12	3	2	.42
Bones, Ricky	.000	0	0	0	0	0	.077	13	1	0	0	0	1	2	5	4	34	203.2	25	22	1	2	.979	25	5	0	.20
Borbon, Pedro	.000	0	0	0	0	0	.000	0	0	0	0	0	0	0	0	0	3	1.2	0	0	0	0	.000	0	0	0	.00
Bosio, Chris	.000	0	0	0	0	0	.000	0	0	0	0	0	0	0	0	0	30	164.1	13	21	1	1	.971	14	6	0	.43
Boskie, Shawn	.273	11	3	0	0	0	.200	115	23	4	1	1	6	5	35	8	39	65.2	3	5	1	0	.889	5	1	0	.20
Bottenfield, Kent	.220	50	11	0	3	3	.241	58	14	0	0	0	3	1	18	4	37	159.2	9	32	2	6	.953	22	6	0	.27
Boucher, Denis	.167	6	1	0	0	2	.167	6	1	1	0	0	0	0	3	2	5	28.1	1	4	0	0	1.000	3	0	2	.67
Bowen, Ryan	.118	51	6	0	3	3	.134	82	11	2	1	0	3	4	29	4	27	156.2	7	24	2	0	.939	22	6	1	.32
Brantley, Jeff	.107	28	3	0	3	1	.131	61	8	1	0	0	5	1	21	9	53	113.2	6	9	2	0	.882	6	5	0	.83
Brennan, Bill	.000	1	0	0	0	1	.000	3	0	0	0	0	0	1	2	1	8	15.0	2	2	0	0	1.000	4	2	1	.75
Brewer, Billy	.000	0	0	0	0	0	.000	0	0	0	0	0	0	0	0	0	46	39.0	1	4	2	0	.714	7	2	0	.29
Brink, Brad	.000	1	0	0	0	0	.077	13	1	0	0	0	0	0	5	1	2	6.0	0	0	1	0	.000	0	0	0	.00
Briscoe, John	.000	0	0	0	0	0	.000	0	0	0	0	0	0	0	0	0	17	24.2	1	4	0	0	1.000	2	2	0	1.00
Brocail, Doug	.182	33	6	0	0	11	.184	38	7	0	0	0	0	0	8	11	24	128.1	8	20	2	1	.933	14	4	0	.29
Bronkey, Jeff	.000	1	0	0	0	0	.000	1	0	0	0	0	0	0	0	0	21	36.0	3	10	0	1	1.000	1	1	0	1.00
Bross, Terry	.000	0	0	0	0	0	.000	0	0	0	0	0	0	0	0	0	2	2.0	0	0	0	0	.000	0	0	0	.00
Brow, Scott	.000	0	0	0	0	0	.000	0	0	0	0	0	0	0	0	0	6	18.0	3	8	0	1	1.000	2	0	0	.00
Brown, Kevin	.000	0	0	0	0	0	.000	1	0	0	0	0	0	0	0	0	34	233.0	28	42	3	2	.959	20	10	0	.50
Browning, Tom	.216	37	8	1	4	4	.153	607	93	13	1	2	32	25	194	70	21	114.0	10	19	0	3	1.000	12	3	4	.58
Brummett, Greg	.000	15	0	0	0	2	.000	15	0	0	0	0	0	1	5	2	13	72.2	5	9	0	0	1.000	13	1	0	.08
Bullinger, Jim	.000	1	0	0	0	0	.238	21	5	0	0	0	1	2	7	1	15	16.2	1	1	0	0	1.000	2	1	0	.50
Burba, Dave	.294	17	5	0	2	3	.188	32	6	1	0	0	3	2	15	6	54	95.1	7	12	1	0	.950	13	3	0	.23
Burgos, Enrique	.000	0	0	0	0	0	.000	0	0	0	0	0	0	0	0	0	5	4.0	1	0	0	0	.000	0	0	0	.00
Burkett, John	.118	76	9	0	4	12	.072	250	18	2	0	0	10	17	117	37	34	231.2	20	35	0	3	1.000	28	13	1	.50
Burns, Todd	.000	3	0	0	0	1	.000	3	0	0	0	0	0	0	1	1	49	95.2	7	5	2	1	.857	6	3	0	.50
Bushing, Chris	.000	0	0	0	0	0	.000	0	0	0	0	0	0	0	0	0	6	4.1	0	0	0	0	.000	0	0	0	.00
Butcher, Mike	.000	0	0	0	0	0	.000	0	0	0	0	0	0	0	0	0	23	28.1	1	1	0	0	1.000	4	0	0	.00
Cadaret, Greg	.000	2	0	0	0	0	.000	2	0	0	0	0	0	0	1	0	47	48.0	4	6	0	0	1.000	6	1	2	.50
Campbell, Kevin	.000	0	0	0	0	0	.000	0	0	0	0	0	0	0	0	0	11	16.0	1	1	0	0	1.000	2	2	0	1.00
Candelaria, John	.000	0	0	0	0	0	.174	596	104	20	3	1	48	44	162	43	24	19.2	0	0	0	0	.000	2	1	0	.50

Pitcher	1993 Hitting						Career Hitting										1993 Fielding and Holding Runners										
	Avg	AB	H	HR	RBI	SH	Avg	AB	H	2B	3B	HR	RBI	BB	SO	SH	G	Inn	PO	A	E	DP	Pct.	SBA	CS	PCS	CS%
Candiotti, Tom	.133	60	8	0	2	9	.121	116	14	3	0	0	3	2	22	21	33	213.2	10	30	3	3	.930	31	6	0	.19
Carpenter, Cris	.000	0	0	0	0	1	.267	30	8	0	0	0	5	0	6	7	56	69.1	3	12	0	1	1.000	6	1	0	.17
Cary, Chuck	.000	0	0	0	0	0	.000	0	0	0	0	0	0	0	0	0	15	20.2	1	3	0	0	1.000	2	2	0	1.00
Casian, Larry	.000	0	0	0	0	0	.000	0	0	0	0	0	0	0	0	0	54	56.2	4	4	0	0	1.000	1	0	0	.00
Castillo, Frank	.163	43	7	0	3	8	.126	143	18	0	0	0	5	6	37	19	29	141.1	7	34	1	2	.976	19	11	1	.63
Castillo, Tony	.000	0	0	0	0	0	.063	12	1	0	0	0	0	1	6	4	51	50.2	3	9	1	1	.923	5	0	1	.20
Charlton, Norm	.000	0	0	0	0	0	.082	85	7	1	0	0	0	3	50	10	34	34.2	0	3	0	1	1.000	3	0	0	.00
Christopher, Mike	.000	0	0	0	0	0	.000	0	0	0	0	0	0	0	0	0	9	11.2	0	1	0	0	1.000	0	0	0	.00
Clark, Mark	.000	0	0	0	0	0	.116	43	5	0	0	0	1	0	20	5	26	109.1	4	10	2	0	.875	18	10	0	.56
Clemens, Roger	.000	0	0	0	0	0	.000	0	0	0	0	0	0	0	0	0	29	191.2	11	20	1	1	.969	23	7	0	.30
Cone, David	.000	0	0	0	0	0	.154	395	61	8	0	0	20	16	86	36	34	254.0	24	24	1	4	.980	45	11	2	.29
Converse, Jim	.000	0	0	0	0	0	.000	0	0	0	0	0	0	0	0	0	4	20.1	2	6	0	0	1.000	4	2	0	.50
Cook, Andy	.000	0	0	0	0	0	.000	0	0	0	0	0	0	0	0	0	4	5.1	0	1	0	0	1.000	0	0	0	.00
Cook, Dennis	.000	0	0	0	0	0	.250	96	24	2	1	1	7	3	12	8	25	54.0	3	7	2	1	.833	6	3	2	.83
Cook, Mike	.000	0	0	0	0	0	.000	0	0	0	0	0	0	0	0	0	2	3.0	0	0	0	0	.000	0	0	0	.00
Cooke, Steve	.155	71	11	0	5	6	.162	74	12	2	0	0	6	0	17	8	32	210.2	7	23	3	1	.909	31	5	4	.29
Cormier, Rheal	.234	47	11	0	4	6	.173	127	22	4	0	0	7	0	29	17	38	145.1	8	27	3	2	.921	5	2	0	.40
Corsi, Jim	.000	0	0	0	0	0	.000	1	0	0	0	0	0	0	1	0	15	20.1	1	4	0	0	1.000	2	0	0	.00
Cox, Danny	.000	0	0	0	0	0	.109	359	39	3	1	0	12	13	152	41	44	83.2	4	4	1	1	.889	10	3	0	.30
Crim, Chuck	.000	0	0	0	0	0	.000	0	0	0	0	0	0	0	0	0	11	15.1	0	5	0	0	1.000	3	0	0	.00
Cummings, John	.000	0	0	0	0	0	.000	0	0	0	0	0	0	0	0	0	10	46.1	3	6	2	0	.818	6	4	0	.67
Daal, Omar	.000	0	0	0	0	0	.000	0	0	0	0	0	0	1	0	0	47	35.1	5	6	0	0	1.000	2	0	1	.50
Darling, Ron	.000	0	0	0	0	0	.145	525	76	21	2	2	21	15	175	65	31	178.0	12	17	1	0	.967	25	11	0	.44
Darwin, Danny	.000	0	0	0	0	0	.124	193	24	5	2	1	16	5	103	8	34	229.1	14	31	2	2	.957	16	5	0	.31
Davis, Mark	.250	4	1	0	0	0	.156	167	26	3	4	1	9	8	54	24	60	69.2	3	8	2	1	.846	10	1	1	.09
Davis, Storm	.000	0	0	0	0	0	.063	16	1	0	0	0	0	0	10	1	43	98.0	5	14	1	1	.950	18	3	0	.17
Dayley, Ken	.000	0	0	0	0	0	.210	81	17	0	0	0	2	7	32	7	2	0.2	0	0	0	0	.000	0	0	0	.00
DeLeon, Jose	.000	6	0	0	0	0	.091	419	38	1	1	0	9	15	171	51	35	57.1	2	3	0	0	1.000	13	8	0	.62
DeLucia, Rich	.000	0	0	0	0	0	.000	0	0	0	0	0	0	0	0	0	30	42.2	2	7	0	0	1.000	4	2	0	.50
Deshaies, Jim	.000	5	0	0	0	0	.089	372	33	0	0	0	12	23	185	44	32	184.1	4	24	0	0	1.000	26	7	11	.69
DeSilva, John	.000	0	0	0	0	0	.000	0	0	0	0	0	0	0	0	0	3	6.1	0	0	0	0	.000	0	0	0	.00
Dewey, Mark	.000	0	0	0	0	0	.000	2	0	0	0	0	0	2	2	0	21	26.2	2	6	0	0	1.000	2	0	0	.00
Dibble, Rob	1.000	1	1	0	1	0	.120	25	3	0	0	0	2	0	5	6	45	41.2	5	5	0	2	1.000	15	2	0	.13
DiPino, Frank	.000	0	0	0	0	0	.125	72	9	2	0	0	2	1	34	5	11	15.2	0	3	0	0	1.000	0	0	0	.00
Dipoto, Jerry	.000	0	0	0	0	0	.000	0	0	0	0	0	0	0	0	0	46	56.1	4	9	2	1	.867	1	0	0	.00
Dixon, Ken	.000	0	0	0	0	0	.000	0	0	0	0	0	0	0	0	0	4	2.2	0	1	0	0	1.000	0	0	0	.00
Doherty, John	.000	0	0	0	0	0	.000	0	0	0	0	0	0	0	0	0	32	184.2	14	20	5	1	.872	19	12	0	.63
Dopson, John	.000	0	0	0	0	0	.055	55	3	1	0	0	1	3	34	4	34	155.2	17	21	0	0	1.000	16	5	0	.31
Downs, Kelly	.000	0	0	0	0	0	.123	211	26	3	1	0	11	7	76	21	42	119.2	4	10	0	2	1.000	17	4	0	.24
Drabek, Doug	.085	71	6	1	3	9	.150	540	81	13	2	2	29	15	166	46	34	237.2	20	33	0	2	1.000	35	7	0	.20
Drahman, Brian	.000	0	0	0	0	0	.000	0	0	0	0	0	0	0	0	0	5	5.1	0	1	0	0	1.000	0	0	0	.00
Draper, Mike	.667	3	2	0	0	0	.667	3	2	0	0	0	0	0	1	0	29	42.1	2	8	1	0	.909	8	1	0	.13
Dreyer, Steve	.000	0	0	0	0	0	.000	0	0	0	0	0	0	0	0	0	10	41.0	2	4	0	0	1.000	4	2	0	.50
Eckersley, Dennis	.000	0	0	0	0	0	.133	180	24	3	0	3	12	9	84	5	64	67.0	0	5	0	0	1.000	14	2	0	.14
Edens, Tom	.000	1	0	0	0	0	.000	4	0	0	0	0	0	0	4	0	38	49.0	3	10	1	0	.929	5	1	0	.20
Eichhorn, Mark	.000	0	0	0	0	0	.000	2	0	0	0	0	0	0	1	1	54	72.2	7	18	0	1	1.000	11	3	0	.27
Eiland, Dave	.083	12	1	0	0	3	.095	21	2	0	0	1	2	0	8	4	10	48.1	4	8	1	2	.923	11	3	0	.27
Eldred, Cal	.000	0	0	0	0	0	.000	0	0	0	0	0	0	0	0	0	36	258.0	25	27	2	4	.963	30	9	0	.30
Erickson, Scott	.000	0	0	0	0	0	.000	0	0	0	0	0	0	0	0	0	34	218.2	18	33	3	3	.944	32	4	0	.13
Ettles, Mark	.000	2	0	0	0	0	.000	2	0	0	0	0	0	0	0	0	14	18.0	0	4	0	0	1.000	0	0	0	.00
Fajardo, Hector	.000	0	0	0	0	0	.000	3	0	0	0	0	0	0	1	0	1	0.2	0	0	0	0	.000	0	0	0	.00
Farr, Steve	.000	0	0	0	0	0	.000	0	0	0	0	0	0	0	0	0	49	47.0	6	10	0	0	1.000	5	1	0	.20
Farrell, John	.000	0	0	0	0	0	.000	0	0	0	0	0	0	0	0	0	21	90.2	5	11	0	0	1.000	17	2	1	.18
Fassero, Jeff	.063	32	2	0	0	5	.071	42	3	2	0	0	0	2	28	8	56	149.2	5	22	3	0	.900	16	3	1	.25
Fernandez, Alex	.000	0	0	0	0	0	.000	0	0	0	0	0	0	0	0	0	34	247.1	18	38	0	2	1.000	16	11	0	.69
Fernandez, Sid	.094	32	3	0	2	8	.192	496	95	14	2	1	31	12	183	64	18	119.2	2	10	0	1	1.000	17	3	1	.24
Fetters, Mike	.000	0	0	0	0	0	.000	0	0	0	0	0	0	0	0	0	45	59.1	5	7	1	5	.923	13	6	1	.54
Finley, Chuck	.000	0	0	0	0	0	.000	0	0	0	0	0	0	0	0	0	35	251.1	10	26	5	0	.878	30	9	0	.30
Fleming, Dave	.000	0	0	0	0	0	.000	0	0	0	0	0	0	0	0	0	26	167.1	9	28	0	1	1.000	20	8	4	.60
Flener, Huck	.000	0	0	0	0	0	.000	0	0	0	0	0	0	0	0	0	6	6.2	2	2	0	0	1.000	1	0	0	.00
Fletcher, Paul	.000	0	0	0	0	0	.000	0	0	0	0	0	0	0	0	0	1	0.1	0	0	0	0	.000	0	0	0	.00
Fossas, Tony	.000	0	0	0	0	0	.000	0	0	0	0	0	0	0	0	0	71	40.0	1	6	1	0	.875	3	0	0	.00
Foster, Kevin	.000	2	0	0	0	0	.000	2	0	0	0	0	0	0	0	0	2	6.2	1	0	0	0	1.000	2	0	0	.00
Foster, Steve	.000	0	0	0	0	1	.200	5	1	0	0	0	0	0	1	1	17	25.2	0	2	0	0	1.000	0	0	0	.00
Franco, John	.000	1	0	0	0	0	.111	27	3	0	0	0	1	0	8	3	35	36.1	3	9	0	0	1.000	4	0	0	.00
Fredrickson, Scott	.000	3	0	0	0	0	.000	3	0	0	0	0	0	3	0	0	24	29.0	4	1	0	0	1.000	3	2	0	.67
Freeman, Marvin	.000	0	0	0	0	2	.125	40	5	0	0	0	0	0	25	6	21	23.2	1	0	0	0	1.000	6	3	0	.50
Frey, Steve	.000	0	0	0	0	0	.000	3	0	0	0	0	0	1	2	0	55	48.1	2	6	0	0	1.000	4	1	0	.25
Frohwirth, Todd	.000	0	0	0	0	0	.000	2	0	0	0	0	0	0	0	2	70	96.1	8	21	1	3	.967	20	3	1	.13
Garces, Rich	.000	0	0	0	0	0	.000	0	0	0	0	0	0	0	0	0	3	4.0	0	0	0	0	.000	0	0	0	.00
Gardiner, Mike	.000	4	0	0	0	0	.000	4	0	0	0	0	0	0	3	0	34	49.1	1	7	0	0	1.000	6	1	1	.33
Gardner, Mark	.000	0	0	0	0	0	.116	155	18	1	2	0	7	4	63	21	17	91.2	6	5	1	1	.917	19	11	0	.58
Gibson, Paul	.000	0	0	0	0	0	.000	6	0	0	0	0	0	1	3	1	28	44.0	3	5	0	1	1.000	0	0	0	.00
Glavine, Tom	.173	81	14	0	3	11	.183	437	80	6	2	0	30	30	119	54	36	239.1	17	36	2	4	.964	14	5	0	.36

Pitcher	1993 Hitting						Career Hitting										1993 Fielding and Holding Runners										
	Avg	AB	H	HR	RBI	SH	Avg	AB	H	2B	3B	HR	RBI	BB	SO	SH	G	Inn	PO	A	E	DP	Pct.	SBA	CS	PCS	CS%
Gohr, Greg	.000	0	0	0	0	0	.000	0	0	0	0	0	0	0	0	0	16	22.2	1	1	0	1	1.000	1	0	0	.00
Gomez, Pat	.000	5	0	0	0	0	.000	5	0	0	0	0	0	0	1	0	28	31.2	0	3	1	0	.750	3	3	0	1.00
Gooden, Dwight	.200	70	14	2	9	6	.198	718	142	15	5	7	63	13	130	81	29	208.2	19	24	2	1	.956	38	10	0	.26
Gordon, Tom	.000	0	0	0	0	0	.000	0	0	0	0	0	0	0	0	0	48	155.2	19	21	2	1	.952	24	8	1	.38
Gossage, Goose	.000	0	0	0	0	0	.106	85	9	1	0	0	2	4	37	4	38	47.2	5	3	1	0	.889	7	1	0	.14
Gott, Jim	.000	1	0	0	0	0	.181	72	13	2	0	4	5	1	40	5	62	77.2	7	8	0	1	1.000	6	2	0	.33
Gozzo, Mauro	.000	0	0	0	0	0	.000	0	0	0	0	0	0	0	0	0	10	14.0	0	0	0	0	.000	1	0	0	.00
Grahe, Joe	.000	0	0	0	0	0	.000	0	0	0	0	0	0	0	0	0	45	56.2	3	13	0	1	1.000	4	0	0	.00
Granger, Jeff	.000	0	0	0	0	0	.000	0	0	0	0	0	0	0	0	0	1	1.0	0	0	0	0	.000	0	0	0	.00
Grant, Mark	.000	0	0	0	0	0	.067	104	7	0	0	0	2	10	46	14	20	25.1	1	6	0	1	1.000	2	1	0	.50
Grater, Mark	.000	0	0	0	0	0	.000	0	0	0	0	0	0	0	0	0	6	5.0	0	0	0	0	.000	0	0	0	.00
Green, Tyler	.000	2	0	0	0	1	.000	2	0	0	0	0	0	0	2	1	3	7.1	0	0	1	0	.000	1	1	0	1.00
Greene, Tommy	.222	72	16	2	10	6	.217	189	41	5	0	4	17	9	51	12	31	200.0	5	22	1	2	.964	23	5	0	.22
Greer, Ken	.000	0	0	0	0	0	.000	0	0	0	0	0	0	0	0	0	1	1.0	0	0	0	0	.000	0	0	0	.00
Grimsley, Jason	.000	0	0	0	0	0	.105	38	4	0	0	0	2	3	10	5	10	42.1	4	4	0	0	1.000	8	1	0	.13
Groom, Buddy	.000	0	0	0	0	0	.000	0	0	0	0	0	0	0	0	0	19	36.2	1	6	1	0	.875	6	1	1	.33
Gross, Kevin	.203	64	13	1	7	8	.162	612	99	19	1	5	33	28	258	62	33	202.1	11	40	0	1	1.000	28	10	0	.36
Gross, Kip	.000	0	0	0	0	0	.167	24	4	0	0	0	2	0	6	4	10	15.0	0	3	0	0	1.000	3	1	0	.33
Guardado, Eddie	.000	0	0	0	0	0	.000	0	0	0	0	0	0	0	0	0	19	94.2	6	8	0	1	1.000	17	3	2	.29
Gubicza, Mark	.000	0	0	0	0	0	.000	0	0	0	0	0	0	0	0	0	49	104.1	11	7	1	0	.947	13	2	0	.15
Guetterman, Lee	.500	2	1	0	1	0	.250	4	1	1	0	0	1	0	2	0	40	46.0	1	4	2	0	.714	5	0	0	.00
Gullickson, Bill	.000	0	0	0	0	0	.141	576	81	16	0	3	27	20	152	63	28	159.1	11	24	0	1	1.000	18	5	0	.28
Guthrie, Mark	.000	0	0	0	0	0	.000	0	0	0	0	0	0	0	0	0	22	21.0	0	5	0	0	1.000	7	1	2	.43
Guzman, Jose	.111	63	7	0	2	9	.111	63	7	0	0	0	2	1	15	9	30	191.0	12	28	5	1	.889	29	10	0	.34
Guzman, Juan	.000	0	0	0	0	0	.000	0	0	0	0	0	0	0	0	0	33	221.0	11	16	1	0	.964	42	16	1	.40
Haas, Dave	.000	0	0	0	0	0	.000	0	0	0	0	0	0	0	0	0	20	28.0	2	5	0	1	1.000	1	0	0	.00
Habyan, John	.000	0	0	0	0	0	.000	0	0	0	0	0	0	0	0	0	48	56.1	5	7	0	0	1.000	6	0	0	.00
Hammond, Chris	.190	63	12	2	4	5	.208	144	30	4	1	3	9	17	57	9	32	191.0	8	34	4	1	.913	11	2	4	.55
Hampton, Mike	.000	0	0	0	0	0	.000	0	0	0	0	0	0	0	0	0	13	17.0	0	2	1	0	.667	4	0	0	.00
Haney, Chris	.000	0	0	0	0	0	.114	35	4	0	0	0	4	0	4	4	23	124.0	7	19	0	0	1.000	11	2	2	.36
Hanson, Erik	.000	0	0	0	0	0	.000	0	0	0	0	0	0	0	0	0	32	215.0	25	25	3	3	.943	28	13	0	.46
Harkey, Mike	.093	54	5	0	0	5	.184	141	26	5	0	0	4	3	42	15	28	157.1	9	20	5	2	.853	13	6	0	.46
Harnisch, Pete	.104	67	7	0	2	10	.122	196	24	8	0	0	14	8	52	22	33	217.2	3	15	2	0	.900	21	6	0	.29
Harris, Gene	.000	1	0	0	0	0	.200	5	1	0	0	0	0	0	2	1	59	59.1	5	10	0	1	1.000	10	0	0	.00
Harris, Greg	.000	0	0	0	0	0	.215	65	14	2	2	0	4	1	28	2	80	112.1	8	13	3	1	.875	9	4	0	.44
Harris, Greg W.	.137	73	10	0	4	5	.107	178	19	4	1	0	7	13	73	22	36	225.1	17	38	3	3	.948	32	9	1	.31
Hartley, Mike	.000	0	0	0	0	0	.043	23	1	0	0	0	0	0	10	3	52	81.0	7	2	1	0	.900	15	4	0	.27
Harvey, Bryan	.000	0	0	0	0	0	.000	0	0	0	0	0	0	0	0	0	59	69.0	3	5	0	0	1.000	15	0	0	.00
Hathaway, Hilly	.000	0	0	0	0	0	.000	0	0	0	0	0	0	0	0	0	11	57.1	4	10	0	4	1.000	10	3	0	.30
Heaton, Neal	.000	0	0	0	0	0	.171	187	32	3	0	0	12	6	51	15	18	27.0	1	6	0	0	1.000	2	0	0	.00
Henke, Tom	.000	0	0	0	0	0	.000	0	0	0	0	0	0	0	0	0	66	74.1	6	8	0	1	1.000	5	2	0	.40
Henneman, Mike	.000	0	0	0	0	0	.000	1	0	0	0	0	0	0	1	0	63	71.2	6	5	1	0	.917	0	0	0	.00
Henry, Butch	.083	24	2	0	2	3	.128	78	10	0	0	1	9	2	13	8	30	103.0	5	12	1	1	.944	13	3	1	.31
Henry, Doug	.000	0	0	0	0	0	.000	0	0	0	0	0	0	0	0	0	54	55.0	5	7	0	0	1.000	4	0	0	.00
Henry, Dwayne	.000	1	0	0	0	0	.167	6	1	0	0	0	0	0	5	0	34	58.2	2	1	0	0	1.000	5	2	0	.40
Hentgen, Pat	.000	0	0	0	0	0	.000	0	0	0	0	0	0	0	0	0	34	216.1	12	21	1	1	.971	22	6	0	.27
Heredia, Gil	.154	13	2	0	0	4	.207	29	6	1	0	0	0	1	5	5	20	57.1	4	11	0	1	1.000	7	0	0	.00
Hernandez, Jeremy	.000	1	0	0	0	0	.000	5	0	0	0	0	0	0	2	0	71	111.2	3	17	1	1	.952	10	6	0	.60
Hernandez, Roberto	.000	0	0	0	0	0	.000	0	0	0	0	0	0	0	0	0	70	78.2	2	11	1	1	.929	6	4	0	.67
Hernandez, Xavier	.000	5	0	0	0	2	.037	27	1	0	0	0	0	2	15	3	71	96.2	1	8	0	0	1.000	11	2	0	.18
Hershiser, Orel	.356	73	26	0	6	8	.215	628	135	26	2	0	42	21	135	86	34	215.2	20	43	3	1	.955	20	10	0	.50
Hesketh, Joe	.000	0	0	0	0	0	.070	86	6	0	0	0	2	10	58	9	28	53.1	2	7	1	1	.900	6	1	1	.33
Hibbard, Greg	.092	65	6	0	3	3	.092	65	6	1	0	0	3	2	17	3	31	191.0	6	26	0	2	1.000	12	8	2	.83
Hickerson, Bryan	.143	28	4	0	4	4	.091	44	4	0	0	0	4	1	22	5	47	120.1	4	12	1	0	.941	10	6	0	.60
Higuera, Teddy	.000	0	0	0	0	0	.000	0	0	0	0	0	0	0	0	0	8	30.0	3	0	0	0	1.000	3	1	0	.25
Hill, Ken	.115	52	6	0	3	14	.143	245	35	6	1	1	14	19	66	44	28	183.2	24	38	1	2	.984	29	7	1	.28
Hill, Milt	.000	2	0	0	0	0	.000	3	0	0	0	0	0	0	3	0	19	28.2	4	0	1	0	.800	4	2	0	.50
Hillegas, Shawn	.000	0	0	0	0	0	.069	29	2	0	0	0	0	3	16	3	18	60.2	1	7	1	0	.889	6	4	0	.67
Hillman, Eric	.159	44	7	0	0	6	.140	57	8	1	0	0	0	0	21	11	27	145.0	11	21	4	1	.889	19	6	2	.42
Hitchcock, Sterling	.000	0	0	0	0	0	.000	0	0	0	0	0	0	0	0	0	6	31.0	1	3	0	0	1.000	5	1	1	.40
Hoffman, Trevor	.143	7	1	0	0	0	.143	7	1	0	0	0	0	0	1	0	67	90.0	6	11	0	0	1.000	8	1	0	.13
Holman, Brad	.000	0	0	0	0	0	.000	0	0	0	0	0	0	0	0	0	19	36.1	1	3	0	0	1.000	1	0	0	.00
Holmes, Darren	.000	0	0	0	0	0	.000	0	0	0	0	0	0	0	0	0	62	66.2	7	6	1	1	.929	5	2	0	.40
Holzemer, Mark	.000	0	0	0	0	0	.000	0	0	0	0	0	0	0	0	0	5	23.1	0	1	0	0	1.000	4	0	1	.33
Honeycutt, Rick	.000	0	0	0	0	0	.133	181	24	3	0	0	8	16	43	28	52	41.2	2	5	1	0	.875	5	3	0	.60
Hope, John	.077	13	1	0	0	0	.077	13	1	0	0	0	0	0	7	0	7	38.0	1	10	1	0	.917	5	2	0	.40
Horsman, Vince	.000	0	0	0	0	0	.000	0	0	0	0	0	0	0	0	0	40	25.0	0	2	0	0	1.000	3	1	0	.33
Hough, Charlie	.032	63	2	0	1	4	.150	193	29	4	0	1	13	4	44	14	34	204.1	6	41	1	1	.979	33	11	3	.42
Howard, Chris	.000	0	0	0	0	0	.000	0	0	0	0	0	0	0	0	0	3	2.1	0	0	0	0	.000	1	1	0	1.00
Howe, Steve	.000	0	0	0	0	0	.074	27	2	0	0	0	0	2	10	1	51	50.2	3	13	1	0	.938	5	0	1	.50
Howell, Jay	.000	0	0	0	0	0	.000	9	0	0	0	0	0	1	1	2	54	58.1	4	7	0	0	1.000	10	4	1	.50
Hurst, Bruce	.000	1	0	0	0	1	.113	274	31	5	0	0	8	20	141	37	5	13.0	0	4	0	0	1.000	4	1	0	.25
Hutton, Mark	.000	0	0	0	0	0	.000	0	0	0	0	0	0	0	0	0	7	22.0	1	3	1	0	.800	5	1	0	.20
Ignasiak, Mike	.000	0	0	0	0	0	.000	0	0	0	0	0	0	0	0	0	27	37.0	0	3	0	0	1.000	4	3	0	.75

	1993 Hitting						Career Hitting										1993 Fielding and Holding Runners										
Pitcher	Avg	AB	H	HR	RBI	SH	Avg	AB	H	2B	3B	HR	RBI	BB	SO	SH	G	Inn	PO	A	E	DP	Pct.	SBA	CS	PCS	CS%
Innis, Jeff	.000	0	0	0	0	2	.000	9	0	0	0	0	0	0	2	3	67	76.2	6	13	0	1	1.000	12	3	0	.25
Jackson, Danny	.077	65	5	0	2	12	.113	311	35	6	1	0	15	6	170	39	32	210.1	7	26	4	3	.892	22	4	3	.32
Jackson, Mike	.667	3	2	0	1	0	.182	22	4	2	0	0	1	1	4	3	81	77.1	3	13	1	0	.941	2	1	0	.50
Jean, Domingo	.000	0	0	0	0	0	.000	0	0	0	0	0	0	0	0	0	10	40.1	1	6	0	0	1.000	2	0	0	.00
Jimenez, Miguel	.000	0	0	0	0	0	.000	0	0	0	0	0	0	0	0	0	5	27.0	0	0	0	0	.000	2	1	0	.50
Johnson, Dave	.000	0	0	0	0	0	.000	0	0	0	0	0	0	0	0	0	6	8.1	1	0	1	0	.500	0	0	0	.00
Johnson, Jeff	.000	0	0	0	0	0	.000	0	0	0	0	0	0	0	0	0	2	2.2	1	0	1	0	.500	0	1	0	.50
Johnson, Randy	.000	0	0	0	0	0	.125	16	2	0	0	0	0	0	9	2	37	255.1	9	27	0	2	1.000	40	8	4	.30
Johnston, Joel	.333	6	2	0	0	1	.333	6	2	1	0	0	0	0	2	1	33	53.1	4	5	0	0	1.000	3	1	0	.33
Johnstone, John	.000	0	0	0	0	0	.000	0	0	0	0	0	0	0	0	0	7	10.2	2	0	0	0	1.000	1	0	0	.00
Jones, Barry	.000	0	0	0	0	0	.063	16	1	0	0	0	1	1	5	2	6	7.1	1	0	0	0	1.000	2	1	0	.50
Jones, Bobby J.	.050	20	1	0	0	2	.050	20	1	0	0	0	0	0	7	2	9	61.2	5	8	0	0	1.000	5	2	0	.40
Jones, Doug	.000	0	0	0	0	0	.000	4	0	0	0	0	0	0	2	0	71	85.1	2	12	1	0	.933	2	0	0	.00
Jones, Jimmy	.111	9	1	0	0	3	.166	193	32	2	0	2	11	17	61	31	12	39.2	4	4	0	1	1.000	5	0	0	.00
Jones, Todd	.000	0	0	0	0	0	.000	0	0	0	0	0	0	0	0	0	27	37.1	4	2	0	0	1.000	5	3	0	.60
Juden, Jeff	.000	0	0	0	0	0	.000	5	0	0	0	0	0	0	4	0	2	5.0	0	0	0	0	.000	1	0	0	.00
Kaiser, Jeff	.000	0	0	0	0	0	.000	0	0	0	0	0	0	0	0	0	9	8.0	0	1	0	0	1.000	5	1	0	.20
Kamieniecki, Scott	.000	0	0	0	0	0	.000	0	0	0	0	0	0	0	0	0	30	154.1	17	24	0	0	1.000	17	10	0	.59
Karsay, Steve	.000	0	0	0	0	0	.000	0	0	0	0	0	0	0	0	0	8	49.0	2	3	0	0	1.000	7	2	0	.29
Key, Jimmy	.000	0	0	0	0	0	.000	0	0	0	0	0	0	0	0	0	34	236.2	14	33	4	1	.922	21	4	2	.29
Kiefer, Mark	.000	0	0	0	0	0	.000	0	0	0	0	0	0	0	0	0	6	9.1	1	1	0	0	1.000	1	0	0	.00
Kiely, John	.000	0	0	0	0	0	.000	0	0	0	0	0	0	0	0	0	8	11.2	1	0	5	0	1.000	0	0	0	.00
Kile, Darryl	.094	53	5	1	1	8	.081	123	10	1	0	1	4	9	58	17	32	171.2	9	15	3	0	.889	14	5	0	.36
Kilgus, Paul	.200	5	1	0	0	0	.087	46	4	0	0	0	2	1	11	4	22	28.2	4	3	0	0	1.000	6	1	1	.33
King, Kevin	.000	0	0	0	0	0	.000	0	0	0	0	0	0	0	0	0	13	11.2	0	1	1	0	.500	1	0	0	.00
Klink, Joe	.000	2	0	0	0	1	.000	2	0	0	0	0	0	0	0	1	59	37.2	3	2	0	0	1.000	8	3	0	.38
Knudsen, Kurt	.000	0	0	0	0	0	.000	0	0	0	0	0	0	0	0	0	30	37.2	4	3	0	0	1.000	5	3	0	.60
Knudson, Mark	.000	1	0	0	0	0	.000	13	0	0	0	0	0	2	10	3	4	5.2	0	1	0	0	.500	0	0	0	.00
Kramer, Tom	.000	0	0	0	0	0	.000	0	0	0	0	0	0	0	0	0	39	121.0	9	13	1	0	.957	13	7	0	.54
Krueger, Bill	.000	0	0	0	0	0	.000	3	0	0	0	0	0	0	2	1	32	82.0	2	9	0	1	1.000	15	1	3	.27
Lancaster, Les	.000	4	0	0	0	0	.098	132	13	4	0	0	5	5	64	11	50	61.1	3	6	0	0	1.000	6	3	0	.50
Landrum, Bill	.000	0	0	0	0	1	.080	25	2	1	0	0	0	1	9	3	18	21.2	1	6	0	1	1.000	5	1	0	.20
Langston, Mark	.000	0	0	0	0	0	.167	66	11	2	0	0	3	0	28	1	35	256.1	10	47	2	4	.966	22	5	7	.55
Layana, Tim	.000	0	0	0	0	1	.000	6	0	0	0	0	0	0	3	1	1	2.0	0	1	0	0	1.000	2	0	0	.00
Leach, Terry	.000	0	0	0	0	0	.097	72	7	2	0	0	3	5	39	6	14	16.0	1	0	0	0	1.000	0	0	0	.00
Leary, Tim	.000	0	0	0	0	0	.221	163	36	6	0	1	19	5	57	28	33	169.1	15	25	0	3	1.000	19	9	0	.47
Lefferts, Craig	.000	0	0	0	0	0	.121	132	16	2	0	1	3	1	64	14	52	83.1	6	11	1	0	.944	8	1	3	.50
Leftwich, Phillip	.000	0	0	0	0	0	.000	0	0	0	0	0	0	0	0	0	12	80.2	6	11	1	2	.944	8	4	0	.50
Leibrandt, Charlie	.000	0	0	0	0	2	.120	267	32	3	2	0	14	13	72	33	26	150.1	9	45	2	6	.964	24	0	5	.21
Leiter, Al	.000	0	0	0	0	0	.000	0	0	0	0	0	0	0	0	0	34	105.0	4	12	1	0	.941	12	3	2	.42
Leiter, Mark	.000	0	0	0	0	0	.000	0	0	0	0	0	0	0	0	0	27	106.2	5	11	2	1	.889	12	4	0	.33
Leskanic, Curt	.154	13	2	0	1	1	.154	13	2	1	0	0	1	1	6	1	18	57.0	5	5	1	2	.909	1	1	0	1.00
Lewis, Richie	.500	2	1	0	1	1	.500	2	1	0	0	0	1	0	1	1	57	77.1	3	13	1	1	.941	8	2	1	.38
Lewis, Scott	.000	0	0	0	0	0	.000	0	0	0	0	0	0	0	0	0	15	32.0	5	1	2	0	.750	2	1	0	.50
Lilliquist, Derek	.000	0	0	0	0	0	.213	108	23	1	0	2	8	1	20	5	56	64.0	1	9	1	0	.909	2	0	0	.00
Linton, Doug	.000	0	0	0	0	0	.000	0	0	0	0	0	0	0	0	0	23	36.2	2	3	0	0	1.000	5	1	1	.40
Lloyd, Graeme	.000	0	0	0	0	0	.000	0	0	0	0	0	0	0	0	0	55	63.2	3	13	1	1	.941	2	0	0	.00
Looney, Brian	.000	1	0	0	0	0	.000	1	0	0	0	0	0	0	1	0	3	6.0	0	1	0	0	1.000	0	0	0	.00
Lopez, Albie	.000	0	0	0	0	0	.000	0	0	0	0	0	0	0	0	0	9	49.2	5	7	2	0	.846	8	3	0	.38
Luebbers, Larry	.250	24	6	0	0	1	.250	24	6	1	0	0	0	0	8	1	14	77.1	4	8	2	1	.857	13	8	0	.62
MacDonald, Bob	.000	0	0	0	0	0	.000	0	0	0	0	0	0	0	0	0	67	65.2	3	11	1	0	.933	5	1	2	.60
Maddux, Greg	.165	91	15	0	4	10	.181	581	105	11	0	2	33	7	159	55	36	267.0	39	59	7	6	.933	33	6	0	.18
Maddux, Mike	.000	3	0	0	0	0	.071	85	6	1	0	0	4	6	29	14	58	75.0	6	15	1	1	.955	12	2	1	.25
Magnante, Mike	.000	0	0	0	0	0	.000	0	0	0	0	0	0	0	0	0	7	35.1	4	6	0	1	1.000	4	0	4	1.00
Magrane, Joe	.114	35	4	0	1	4	.139	280	39	9	0	4	13	13	99	36	30	164.0	11	35	2	3	.958	35	3	10	.37
Mahomes, Pat	.000	0	0	0	0	0	.000	0	0	0	0	0	0	0	0	0	12	37.1	4	2	0	1	1.000	8	1	2	.38
Maldonado, Carlos	.000	0	0	0	0	0	.000	0	0	0	0	0	0	0	0	0	29	37.1	3	5	1	1	.889	2	0	0	.00
Manzanillo, Josias	.000	1	0	0	0	0	.000	1	0	0	0	0	0	0	1	0	16	29.0	2	5	0	1	1.000	2	0	0	.00
Martinez, Dennis	.159	69	11	0	4	9	.143	509	73	11	0	0	30	14	161	64	34	224.2	16	44	1	1	.984	55	6	0	.11
Martinez, Pedro	.000	4	0	0	0	2	.000	6	0	0	0	0	0	0	3	2	66	107.0	4	4	0	1	1.000	10	4	0	.40
Martinez, Pedro a.	.000	4	0	0	1	2	.000	4	0	0	0	0	0	0	2	2	32	37.0	2	4	1	0	.857	5	1	1	.40
Martinez, Ramon	.129	70	9	0	2	7	.125	321	40	3	0	1	22	3	111	32	32	211.2	27	31	0	4	1.000	27	11	0	.41
Mason, Roger	.167	6	1	0	0	0	.071	56	4	0	0	0	0	3	28	2	68	99.2	2	8	0	0	1.000	10	5	0	.50
Mauser, Tim	.000	0	0	0	0	0	.000	9	0	0	0	0	0	1	5	0	36	54.0	6	11	1	2	.944	7	3	0	.43
Maysey, Matt	1.000	1	1	0	0	0	1.000	1	1	0	0	0	0	0	0	0	23	22.0	1	2	2	0	.600	3	0	0	.00
McCaskill, Kirk	.000	0	0	0	0	0	.000	0	0	0	0	0	0	0	0	0	30	113.2	7	23	2	4	.938	17	8	1	.53
McClure, Bob	.000	0	0	0	0	0	.222	9	2	0	0	0	0	0	1	0	14	6.1	0	0	0	0	.000	2	2	0	1.00
McDonald, Ben	.000	0	0	0	0	0	.000	0	0	0	0	0	0	0	0	0	34	220.1	15	42	2	2	.966	30	10	1	.37
McDowell, Jack	.000	0	0	0	0	0	.000	0	0	0	0	0	0	0	0	0	34	256.2	23	43	3	2	.957	25	8	7	.60
McDowell, Roger	.500	2	1	0	0	0	.225	71	16	5	0	0	6	5	27	5	54	68.0	11	24	3	3	.921	14	6	0	.43
McElroy, Chuck	.000	6	0	0	0	0	.318	22	7	3	1	0	3	0	6	0	49	47.1	3	5	0	1	1.000	6	2	0	.33
McGehee, Kevin	.000	0	0	0	0	0	.000	0	0	0	0	0	0	0	0	0	5	16.2	2	2	0	0	1.000	2	0	0	.00
McMichael, Greg	.000	4	0	0	0	0	.000	4	0	0	0	0	0	0	2	0	74	91.2	7	18	1	2	.962	7	2	0	.29
Meacham, Rusty	.000	0	0	0	0	0	.000	0	0	0	0	0	0	0	0	0	15	21.0	2	4	0	1	1.000	1	0	0	.00

	1993 Hitting						Career Hitting										1993 Fielding and Holding Runners										
Pitcher	Avg	AB	H	HR	RBI	SH	Avg	AB	H	2B	3B	HR	RBI	BB	SO	SH	G	Inn	PO	A	E	DP	Pct.	SBA	CS	PCS	CS%
Melendez, Jose	.000	0	0	0	0	0	.080	25	2	1	0	0	0	1	18	1	9	16.0	1	3	0	0	1.000	0	0	0	.00
Menendez, Tony	.000	1	0	0	0	0	.000	1	0	0	0	0	0	0	1	0	14	21.0	1	2	1	0	.750	1	1	0	1.00
Mercker, Kent	.000	13	0	0	0	0	.031	32	1	0	0	0	2	1	24	0	43	66.0	1	4	1	0	.833	8	2	0	.25
Merriman, Brett	.000	0	0	0	0	0	.000	0	0	0	0	0	0	0	0	0	19	27.0	1	4	0	0	1.000	1	1	0	1.00
Mesa, Jose	.000	0	0	0	0	0	.000	0	0	0	0	0	0	0	0	0	34	208.2	15	29	3	0	.936	26	13	1	.54
Miceli, Danny	.000	0	0	0	0	0	.000	0	0	0	0	0	0	0	0	0	9	5.1	0	0	0	0	.000	2	0	0	.00
Milacki, Bob	.000	0	0	0	0	0	.000	0	0	0	0	0	0	0	0	0	5	16.0	0	3	0	0	1.000	1	0	0	.00
Militello, Sam	.000	0	0	0	0	0	.000	0	0	0	0	0	0	0	0	0	3	9.1	2	1	0	0	1.000	1	0	0	.00
Miller, Paul	.000	2	0	0	0	0	.000	8	0	0	0	0	0	0	3	0	3	10.0	0	1	1	0	.500	1	0	0	.00
Mills, Alan	.000	0	0	0	0	0	.000	0	0	0	0	0	0	0	0	0	45	100.1	6	10	3	2	.842	9	3	0	.33
Minchey, Nate	.000	0	0	0	0	0	.000	0	0	0	0	0	0	0	0	0	5	33.0	1	3	1	0	.800	2	1	0	.50
Minor, Blas	.200	10	2	0	0	0	.200	10	2	1	0	0	0	0	7	0	65	94.1	8	15	0	1	1.000	9	2	2	.44
Minutelli, Gino	.000	4	0	0	0	0	.000	7	0	0	0	0	0	0	1	0	9	14.1	0	1	0	0	1.000	2	0	0	.00
Miranda, Angel	.000	0	0	0	0	0	.000	0	0	0	0	0	0	0	0	0	22	120.0	4	13	2	1	.895	10	1	2	.30
Mlicki, Dave	.000	0	0	0	0	0	.000	0	0	0	0	0	0	0	0	0	3	13.1	1	1	0	0	1.000	4	2	0	.50
Moeller, Dennis	.000	0	0	0	0	0	.000	0	0	0	0	0	0	0	0	0	10	16.1	2	2	0	0	1.000	3	0	1	.33
Mohler, Mike	.000	0	0	0	0	0	.000	0	0	0	0	0	0	0	0	0	42	64.1	2	9	1	2	.917	11	1	2	.27
Monteleone, Rich	.000	0	0	0	0	0	.000	0	0	0	0	0	0	0	0	0	42	85.2	9	11	1	0	.952	6	1	0	.17
Montgomery, Jeff	.000	0	0	0	0	0	.000	2	0	0	0	0	0	0	1	0	69	87.1	6	13	0	0	1.000	8	1	0	.13
Moore, Marcus	.000	1	0	0	0	0	.000	1	0	0	0	0	0	0	1	0	27	26.1	0	1	2	0	.333	2	0	0	.00
Moore, Mike	.000	0	0	0	0	0	.000	1	0	0	0	0	0	0	0	0	36	213.2	27	43	2	3	.972	31	8	0	.26
Morgan, Mike	.061	66	4	0	1	5	.093	323	30	2	0	0	12	8	86	32	32	207.2	11	33	1	3	.978	31	13	1	.45
Morris, Jack	.000	0	0	0	0	0	.000	1	0	0	0	0	0	0	0	0	27	152.2	11	9	2	1	.913	27	10	0	.37
Moyer, Jamie	.000	0	0	0	0	0	.139	151	21	2	0	0	4	14	51	19	25	152.0	14	25	1	1	.975	11	5	1	.55
Mulholland, Terry	.065	62	4	0	0	8	.079	356	28	3	0	0	6	8	158	27	29	191.0	5	27	2	2	.941	6	4	1	.83
Munoz, Bobby	.000	0	0	0	0	0	.000	0	0	0	0	0	0	0	0	0	38	45.2	1	6	0	1	1.000	6	0	0	.00
Munoz, Mike	.000	0	0	0	0	0	.000	1	0	0	0	0	0	0	1	0	28	21.0	1	5	0	0	1.000	2	1	0	.50
Murphy, Rob	.500	2	1	0	0	1	.182	11	2	0	0	0	0	0	4	3	73	64.2	3	8	1	1	.917	4	1	0	.25
Mussina, Mike	.000	0	0	0	0	0	.000	0	0	0	0	0	0	0	0	0	25	167.2	12	19	0	1	1.000	9	6	0	.67
Mutis, Jeff	.000	0	0	0	0	0	.000	0	0	0	0	0	0	0	0	0	17	81.0	3	17	0	1	1.000	9	3	0	.33
Myers, Randy	.500	2	1	0	2	1	.190	58	11	3	0	0	6	2	31	5	73	75.1	1	7	0	0	1.000	2	0	1	.50
Nabholz, Chris	.128	39	5	0	1	3	.107	177	19	3	0	0	4	6	44	15	26	116.2	6	17	0	2	1.000	24	2	7	.38
Nagy, Charles	.000	0	0	0	0	0	.000	0	0	0	0	0	0	0	0	0	9	48.2	8	14	1	2	.957	12	2	0	.17
Navarro, Jaime	.000	0	0	0	0	0	.000	0	0	0	0	0	0	0	0	0	35	214.1	14	21	2	2	.946	29	6	0	.21
Neagle, Denny	.000	14	0	0	0	2	.000	25	0	0	0	0	0	0	6	4	50	81.1	1	5	0	0	1.000	21	3	2	.24
Nelson, Gene	.000	0	0	0	0	0	.000	0	0	0	0	0	0	0	0	0	52	60.2	4	8	0	1	1.000	4	1	0	.25
Nelson, Jeff	.000	0	0	0	0	0	.000	0	0	0	0	0	0	0	0	0	73	60.0	3	12	0	2	1.000	11	1	0	.09
Nen, Robb	.000	4	0	0	0	0	.000	4	0	0	0	0	0	0	0	0	24	56.0	6	6	0	2	1.000	7	2	0	.29
Nichols, Rod	.000	0	0	0	0	0	.000	0	0	0	0	0	0	0	0	0	4	6.1	1	2	0	1	1.000	0	0	0	.00
Nied, Dave	.174	23	4	0	2	3	.200	30	6	0	0	0	2	3	10	3	16	87.0	4	16	0	0	1.000	18	2	0	.11
Nielsen, Jerry	.000	0	0	0	0	0	.000	0	0	0	0	0	0	0	0	0	10	12.1	1	0	0	0	1.000	1	0	0	.00
Novoa, Rafael	.000	0	0	0	0	0	.200	5	1	0	0	0	1	1	2	0	15	56.0	4	6	0	0	1.000	4	1	0	.25
Nunez, Edwin	.000	0	0	0	0	0	.000	0	0	0	0	0	0	0	0	0	56	75.2	7	8	1	1	.938	8	3	0	.38
O'Donoghue, John	.000	0	0	0	0	0	.000	0	0	0	0	0	0	0	0	0	11	19.2	1	1	1	0	.667	3	0	0	.00
Ojeda, Bobby	.000	0	0	0	0	0	.127	347	44	2	1	1	9	11	102	30	9	43.0	3	9	0	1	1.000	3	1	0	.33
Olivares, Omar	.269	26	7	0	2	3	.232	164	38	6	0	2	16	3	46	10	57	118.2	8	36	4	3	.917	17	4	1	.29
Oliver, Darren	.000	0	0	0	0	0	.000	0	0	0	0	0	0	0	0	0	2	3.1	0	1	1	0	.500	1	0	0	.00
Olson, Gregg	.000	1	0	0	0	0	.000	1	0	0	0	0	0	0	1	0	50	45.0	2	7	0	0	1.000	2	1	0	.50
Ontiveros, Steve	.000	0	0	0	0	0	.083	12	1	1	0	0	3	1	2	0	14	18.0	0	2	1	2	.667	1	0	0	.00
Oquist, Mike	.000	0	0	0	0	0	.000	0	0	0	0	0	0	0	0	0	5	11.2	1	0	0	0	1.000	1	1	0	1.00
Orosco, Jesse	.000	1	0	0	0	0	.169	59	10	0	0	0	4	6	25	7	57	56.2	1	18	0	0	1.000	7	1	4	.71
Osborne, Donovan	.204	49	10	0	3	7	.159	107	17	1	1	0	3	3	34	9	26	155.2	8	24	0	1	1.000	9	2	3	.56
Osuna, Al	.000	0	0	0	0	0	.000	2	0	0	0	0	0	1	0	1	44	25.1	0	2	1	0	.667	0	0	0	.00
Otto, Dave	.222	18	4	0	4	1	.222	18	4	1	1	0	4	0	5	1	28	68.0	4	13	0	1	1.000	10	2	0	.20
Painter, Lance	.300	10	3	0	1	3	.300	10	3	0	1	0	1	1	5	3	10	39.0	1	9	0	0	1.000	6	2	2	.67
Pall, Donn	.000	0	0	0	0	0	.000	0	0	0	0	0	0	0	0	0	47	76.1	5	13	1	0	.947	4	0	0	.00
Parrett, Jeff	.091	11	1	0	0	0	.088	34	3	0	0	0	1	2	11	2	40	73.2	3	9	1	0	.923	13	2	0	.15
Patterson, Bob	.000	0	0	0	0	0	.115	52	6	1	0	0	4	2	22	6	52	52.2	3	7	0	0	1.000	5	1	1	.40
Patterson, Ken	.000	0	0	0	0	0	.000	1	0	0	0	0	0	0	1	1	46	59.0	1	8	1	0	.900	10	2	1	.30
Pavlik, Roger	.000	0	0	0	0	0	.000	0	0	0	0	0	0	0	0	0	26	166.1	10	27	3	2	.925	21	5	1	.29
Pennington, Brad	.000	0	0	0	0	0	.000	0	0	0	0	0	0	0	0	0	29	33.0	1	2	0	0	1.000	4	1	0	.25
Perez, Melido	.000	0	0	0	0	0	.000	0	0	0	0	0	0	0	0	0	24	163.0	5	16	0	1	1.000	17	5	1	.35
Perez, Mike	.000	1	0	0	0	0	.000	6	0	0	0	0	0	1	2	2	65	72.2	2	12	0	2	1.000	10	2	0	.20
Petkovsek, Mark	.000	0	0	0	0	0	.000	0	0	0	0	0	0	0	0	0	26	32.1	0	10	0	0	1.000	7	0	0	.00
Pichardo, Hipolito	.000	0	0	0	0	0	.000	0	0	0	0	0	0	0	0	0	30	165.0	20	27	0	1	1.000	15	7	0	.47
Plantenberg, Erik	.000	0	0	0	0	0	.000	0	0	0	0	0	0	0	0	0	20	9.2	3	1	0	1	1.000	0	0	0	.00
Plesac, Dan	.000	1	0	0	0	0	.000	1	0	0	0	0	0	0	1	0	57	62.2	0	9	1	2	.900	5	2	0	.40
Plunk, Eric	.000	0	0	0	0	0	.000	0	0	0	0	0	0	0	0	0	70	71.0	5	2	1	0	.875	7	1	0	.14
Poole, Jim	.000	0	0	0	0	0	.000	0	0	0	0	0	0	0	0	0	55	50.1	4	7	1	0	.917	3	0	1	.33
Portugal, Mark	.231	65	15	1	8	10	.180	239	43	4	0	2	18	9	43	30	33	208.0	21	28	2	2	.961	18	4	0	.22
Powell, Dennis	.000	0	0	0	0	0	.176	17	3	0	0	0	0	0	8	2	32	47.2	3	5	0	0	1.000	7	2	1	.43
Powell, Ross	.000	1	0	0	0	0	.000	1	0	0	0	0	0	0	1	0	9	16.1	0	2	1	0	.667	3	0	1	.33
Power, Ted	.000	0	0	0	0	0	.089	157	14	3	0	1	7	10	93	20	45	45.1	0	5	0	0	1.000	2	1	0	.50
Pugh, Tim	.222	54	12	0	1	7	.194	67	13	1	0	0	1	1	24	8	31	164.1	9	23	1	1	.970	26	7	0	.27

267

	1993 Hitting						Career Hitting										1993 Fielding and Holding Runners										
Pitcher	Avg	AB	H	HR	RBI	SH	Avg	AB	H	2B	3B	HR	RBI	BB	SO	SH	G	Inn	PO	A	E	DP	Pct.	SBA	CS	PCS	CS%
Quantrill, Paul	.000	0	0	0	0	0	.000	0	0	0	0	0	0	0	0	0	49	138.0	4	18	1	3	.957	13	1	0	.08
Radinsky, Scott	.000	0	0	0	0	0	.000	0	0	0	0	0	0	0	0	0	73	54.2	1	9	2	0	.833	2	0	0	.00
Rapp, Pat	.194	31	6	0	2	2	.182	33	6	1	0	0	2	1	13	3	16	94.0	5	15	1	0	.952	9	4	2	.67
Rasmussen, Dennis	.000	0	0	0	0	0	.193	259	50	8	0	0	14	13	82	19	9	29.0	0	5	0	1	1.000	5	0	4	.80
Reardon, Jeff	.000	2	0	0	0	1	.088	57	5	1	0	0	2	1	38	7	58	61.2	4	6	2	0	.833	7	1	0	.14
Reed, Rick	.000	0	0	0	0	0	.171	35	6	1	0	0	3	3	12	0	3	7.2	3	1	0	0	1.000	1	1	0	1.00
Reed, Steve	.000	9	0	0	0	2	.000	9	0	0	0	0	0	0	3	2	64	84.1	3	14	1	1	.944	15	6	1	.47
Reynolds, Shane	.500	2	1	0	0	0	.500	6	3	1	0	0	0	0	6	0	5	11.0	0	1	0	0	1.000	0	0	0	.00
Reynoso, Armando	.127	63	8	2	4	6	.111	72	8	0	0	2	4	4	26	7	30	189.0	16	34	6	5	.893	16	5	0	.31
Rhodes, Arthur	.000	0	0	0	0	0	.000	0	0	0	0	0	0	0	0	0	17	85.2	2	9	1	0	.917	9	3	1	.44
Righetti, Dave	1.000	1	1	0	1	0	.182	11	2	0	0	0	1	0	6	5	51	47.1	2	5	0	0	1.000	5	4	0	.80
Rijo, Jose	.268	82	22	1	8	12	.196	358	70	8	0	2	23	8	84	43	36	257.1	27	35	0	8	1.000	32	10	0	.31
Risley, Bill	.000	0	0	0	0	0	.000	2	0	0	0	0	0	0	0	0	2	3.0	1	0	0	0	1.000	0	0	0	.00
Rivera, Ben	.098	51	5	0	0	13	.095	84	8	0	0	0	2	5	35	15	30	163.0	8	14	1	1	.957	18	3	0	.17
Robertson, Rich	.000	0	0	0	0	0	.000	0	0	0	0	0	0	0	0	0	9	9.0	0	0	0	0	.000	1	0	0	.00
Rodriguez, Rich	.000	2	0	0	0	0	.000	16	0	0	0	0	0	2	3	2	70	76.0	7	9	1	1	.941	7	2	0	.29
Rogers, Kenny	.000	0	0	0	0	0	.000	0	0	0	0	0	0	0	0	0	35	208.1	18	44	4	5	.939	15	3	8	.73
Rogers, Kevin	.000	3	0	0	0	0	.167	12	2	0	0	0	0	0	8	3	64	80.2	2	7	1	1	.900	8	2	0	.25
Rojas, Mel	.083	12	1	0	0	0	.059	34	2	0	0	0	0	0	21	4	66	88.1	7	9	0	1	1.000	9	1	0	.11
Roper, John	.179	28	5	0	2	1	.179	28	5	0	0	0	2	0	11	1	16	80.0	7	8	0	0	1.000	14	4	0	.29
Rueter, Kirk	.077	26	2	0	3	8	.077	26	2	0	0	0	3	3	10	8	14	85.2	7	19	1	4	.963	11	3	4	.64
Ruffcorn, Scott	.000	0	0	0	0	0	.000	0	0	0	0	0	0	0	0	0	3	10.0	0	3	0	0	.000	5	0	0	.00
Ruffin, Bruce	.080	25	2	0	0	3	.080	288	23	4	0	0	6	21	138	23	59	139.2	7	16	1	3	.958	23	5	4	.39
Ruffin, Johnny	.333	3	1	0	0	0	.333	3	1	0	0	0	0	0	1	0	21	37.2	4	5	0	0	1.000	4	0	0	.00
Ruskin, Scott	.000	0	0	0	0	0	.154	13	2	1	1	0	1	1	9	2	4	1.0	0	1	0	0	.000	0	0	0	.00
Russell, Jeff	.000	0	0	0	0	0	.139	79	11	3	0	1	10	5	33	7	51	46.2	2	10	0	0	1.000	2	1	0	.50
Ryan, Ken	.000	0	0	0	0	0	.000	0	0	0	0	0	0	0	0	0	47	50.0	3	7	1	0	.909	5	2	0	.40
Ryan, Nolan	.000	0	0	0	0	0	.110	852	94	10	2	2	36	38	371	65	13	66.1	1	4	3	0	.625	17	4	0	.24
Saberhagen, Bret	.111	45	5	0	0	8	.110	73	8	1	0	0	0	6	19	11	19	139.1	13	30	2	0	.956	16	7	0	.44
Salkeld, Roger	.000	0	0	0	0	0	.000	0	0	0	0	0	0	0	0	0	3	14.1	0	2	0	0	1.000	0	0	0	.00
Sampen, Bill	.000	0	0	0	0	0	.111	27	3	0	0	0	1	0	15	5	18	18.1	2	2	0	0	1.000	6	2	0	.33
Sanders, Scott	.063	16	1	0	1	4	.063	16	1	0	0	0	1	0	6	4	9	52.1	3	2	0	0	1.000	8	4	0	.50
Sanderson, Scott	.000	14	0	0	0	1	.097	474	46	13	0	2	26	26	224	66	32	184.0	13	23	2	1	.947	13	6	0	.46
Sanford, Mo	.000	8	0	0	0	0	.000	16	0	0	0	0	0	1	9	3	11	16.0	3	2	3	0	.625	9	1	0	.11
Scanlan, Bob	.500	2	1	0	2	1	.067	30	2	0	0	0	3	1	12	3	70	75.1	3	6	0	0	1.000	9	4	0	.44
Schilling, Curt	.147	75	11	0	2	13	.155	142	22	2	0	0	6	3	41	21	35	235.1	6	38	0	1	1.000	22	9	2	.50
Schooler, Mike	.000	0	0	0	0	0	.000	0	0	0	0	0	0	0	0	0	17	24.1	1	3	0	0	1.000	6	1	0	.17
Schourek, Pete	.219	32	7	0	4	3	.125	96	12	1	0	0	8	5	33	5	41	128.1	5	17	0	2	1.000	14	3	1	.29
Schwarz, Jeff	.000	0	0	0	0	0	.000	0	0	0	0	0	0	0	0	0	41	51.0	3	1	1	0	.800	13	5	0	.38
Scott, Darryl	.000	0	0	0	0	0	.000	0	0	0	0	0	0	0	0	0	16	20.0	0	0	0	0	.000	4	0	0	.00
Scott, Tim	.000	4	0	0	0	1	.000	4	0	0	0	0	0	0	4	1	57	71.2	3	8	1	1	.917	20	2	0	.10
Scudder, Scott	.000	0	0	0	0	0	.113	71	8	0	0	1	3	6	30	7	2	4.0	0	0	0	0	.000	3	1	0	.33
Seanez, Rudy	.000	0	0	0	0	0	.000	0	0	0	0	0	0	0	0	0	3	3.1	0	1	0	0	1.000	0	0	0	.00
Sele, Aaron	.000	0	0	0	0	0	.000	0	0	0	0	0	0	0	0	0	18	111.2	3	9	5	1	.706	9	1	0	.11
Seminara, Frank	.200	10	2	0	0	1	.136	44	6	0	0	0	0	1	10	3	18	46.1	8	6	2	0	.875	6	3	0	.50
Service, Scott	.143	7	1	0	1	0	.111	9	1	0	0	0	0	1	5	0	29	46.0	5	5	0	0	1.000	3	1	0	.33
Shaw, Jeff	.067	15	1	0	0	0	.067	15	1	0	0	0	0	0	6	0	55	95.2	8	16	0	1	1.000	7	2	0	.29
Shepherd, Keith	.000	2	0	0	0	0	.000	2	0	0	0	0	0	0	0	0	14	19.1	3	2	2	0	.714	2	2	0	1.00
Shinall, Zak	.000	0	0	0	0	0	.000	0	0	0	0	0	0	0	0	0	1	2.2	1	0	0	0	1.000	0	0	0	.00
Shouse, Brian	.000	0	0	0	0	0	.000	0	0	0	0	0	0	0	0	0	6	4.0	0	1	0	0	1.000	0	0	0	.00
Slocumb, Heathcliff	.000	1	0	0	0	0	.000	6	0	0	0	0	0	0	4	0	30	38.0	3	4	0	2	1.000	4	0	0	.00
Slusarski, Joe	.000	0	0	0	0	0	.000	0	0	0	0	0	0	0	0	0	2	8.2	1	2	0	1	1.000	0	0	0	.00
Smiley, John	.250	32	8	0	5	5	.126	286	36	7	0	0	20	13	99	28	18	105.2	7	16	0	1	1.000	17	2	2	.24
Smith, Bryn	.000	6	0	0	0	0	.153	496	76	12	0	3	37	29	140	77	11	29.2	2	8	0	1	1.000	5	1	0	.20
Smith, Lee	.000	2	0	0	0	0	.047	64	3	0	0	1	2	3	42	4	63	58.0	2	2	0	0	1.000	14	2	0	.14
Smith, Pete	.222	27	6	0	5	3	.114	193	22	2	1	0	10	10	49	25	20	90.2	7	14	0	0	1.000	16	8	0	.50
Smith, Zane	.080	25	2	0	0	4	.152	468	71	11	2	0	27	13	91	68	14	83.0	8	8	0	2	1.000	9	2	0	.22
Smithberg, Roger	.000	0	0	0	0	0	.000	0	0	0	0	0	0	0	0	0	13	19.2	2	6	0	0	1.000	1	0	0	.00
Smoltz, John	.183	71	13	0	4	11	.146	364	53	8	1	2	21	33	147	45	35	243.2	29	23	0	1	1.000	17	4	1	.29
Spradlin, Jerry	.000	2	0	0	0	0	.000	2	0	0	0	0	0	0	1	0	37	49.0	2	6	0	0	1.000	6	2	0	.33
Springer, Russ	.000	0	0	0	0	0	.000	0	0	0	0	0	0	0	0	0	14	60.0	3	2	1	0	1.000	12	1	0	.08
Stanton, Mike	.000	0	0	0	0	0	.500	8	4	1	0	0	1	1	1	0	63	52.0	1	9	1	1	.909	6	1	0	.17
Stewart, Dave	.000	0	0	0	0	0	.196	51	10	1	1	0	4	3	17	6	26	162.0	13	9	0	1	1.000	25	12	0	.48
Stieb, Dave	.000	0	0	0	0	0	.000	1	0	0	0	0	0	0	0	0	4	22.1	0	3	0	0	.667	4	1	0	.25
Stottlemyre, Todd	.000	0	0	0	0	0	.000	0	0	0	0	0	0	0	0	0	30	176.2	11	19	1	2	.968	31	7	0	.23
Sutcliffe, Rick	.000	0	0	0	0	0	.184	539	99	21	1	4	54	34	137	51	29	166.0	9	30	1	2	.975	25	2	6	.32
Swan, Russ	.000	0	0	0	0	0	.000	0	0	0	0	0	0	0	0	0	23	19.2	0	6	0	0	1.000	2	2	0	.50
Swift, Bill	.263	80	21	0	4	10	.221	131	29	4	0	0	7	6	37	15	34	232.2	17	44	6	3	.910	23	11	0	.48
Swindell, Greg	.183	60	11	0	4	10	.150	140	21	3	0	0	8	1	31	15	31	190.1	2	32	1	0	.971	27	6	5	.41
Swingle, Paul	.000	0	0	0	0	0	.000	0	0	0	0	0	0	0	0	0	9	22.0	1	0	0	0	1.000	3	0	0	.00
Tanana, Frank	.155	58	9	0	5	3	.153	59	9	1	1	0	5	2	12	3	32	202.2	11	23	2	1	.944	21	5	1	.29
Tapani, Kevin	.000	0	0	0	0	0	.000	2	0	0	0	0	0	0	1	0	36	225.2	17	31	0	2	1.000	55	13	0	.24
Tavarez, Julian	.000	0	0	0	0	0	.000	0	0	0	0	0	0	0	0	0	8	37.0	2	3	0	2	1.000	4	2	0	.50
Taylor, Kerry	.000	12	0	0	0	1	.000	12	0	0	0	0	0	0	8	1	36	68.1	4	7	0	0	1.000	16	2	1	.19

	1993 Hitting						Career Hitting										1993 Fielding and Holding Runners										
Pitcher	Avg	AB	H	HR	RBI	SH	Avg	AB	H	2B	3B	HR	RBI	BB	SO	SH	G	Inn	PO	A	E	DP	Pct.	SBA	CS	PCS	CS%
Taylor, Scott	.000	0	0	0	0	0	.000	0	0	0	0	0	0	0	0	0	16	11.0	0	1	0	0	1.000	0	0	0	.00
Telford, Anthony	.000	0	0	0	0	0	.000	0	0	0	0	0	0	0	0	0	3	7.1	1	2	0	0	1.000	1	0	0	.00
Telgheder, Dave	.067	15	1	0	0	4	.067	15	1	1	0	0	0	1	8	4	23	75.2	3	7	0	0	1.000	9	5	0	.56
Tewksbury, Bob	.203	69	14	0	5	7	.146	254	37	4	0	0	13	16	99	29	32	213.2	19	46	0	2	1.000	27	6	0	.22
Thigpen, Bobby	.000	1	0	0	0	0	.000	1	0	0	0	0	0	0	0	0	42	54.0	1	5	0	2	1.000	8	4	0	.50
Timlin, Mike	.000	0	0	0	0	0	.000	0	0	0	0	0	0	0	0	0	54	55.2	7	10	1	1	.944	9	0	0	.00
Toliver, Fred	.000	2	0	0	0	0	.111	18	2	0	0	0	0	1	5	3	12	21.2	1	1	0	0	1.000	2	0	0	.00
Tomlin, Randy	.182	33	6	0	1	2	.149	175	26	2	0	0	4	7	44	24	18	98.1	9	18	1	2	.964	11	0	4	.36
Torres, Salomon	.231	13	3	0	0	3	.231	13	3	0	0	0	0	0	4	3	8	44.2	4	8	0	0	1.000	8	3	0	.38
Trachsel, Steve	.167	6	1	0	0	0	.167	6	1	0	0	0	0	1	2	0	3	19.2	1	5	0	0	1.000	2	0	0	.00
Trlicek, Ricky	.250	4	1	0	0	0	.250	4	1	0	0	0	0	0	3	0	41	64.0	7	12	0	2	1.000	7	1	0	.14
Trombley, Mike	.000	0	0	0	0	0	.000	0	0	0	0	0	0	0	0	0	44	114.1	6	19	0	2	1.000	13	6	0	.46
Tsamis, George	.000	0	0	0	0	0	.000	0	0	0	0	0	0	0	0	0	41	86.1	7	14	0	2	1.000	4	2	2	1.00
Turner, Matt	.000	2	0	0	0	0	.000	2	0	0	0	0	0	0	2	0	55	68.0	3	10	0	0	1.000	3	2	0	.67
Urbani, Tom	.188	16	3	0	0	2	.188	16	3	0	0	0	0	2	6	2	18	62.0	2	11	1	0	.929	7	6	0	.86
Valdez, Sergio	.000	0	0	0	0	0	.167	12	2	0	0	0	0	0	5	0	4	3.0	0	0	0	0	.000	2	1	0	.50
Valenzuela, Fern'ndo	.000	0	0	0	0	0	.202	807	163	22	1	8	72	8	119	77	32	178.2	11	36	4	2	.922	24	6	8	.58
Valera, Julio	.000	0	0	0	0	0	.200	5	1	0	0	0	2	0	1	0	19	53.0	4	4	1	1	.889	3	1	0	.33
Van Poppel, Todd	.000	0	0	0	0	0	.000	0	0	0	0	0	0	0	0	0	16	84.0	6	4	0	1	1.000	10	5	0	.50
Viola, Frank	.000	0	0	0	0	0	.140	179	25	2	0	0	6	3	40	22	29	183.2	10	29	4	1	.907	22	11	0	.50
Wagner, Paul	.190	42	8	0	1	4	.200	45	9	0	0	0	1	1	15	4	44	141.1	9	13	0	3	1.000	25	5	2	.28
Wainhouse, David	.000	0	0	0	0	0	.000	0	0	0	0	0	0	0	0	0	3	2.1	0	0	0	0	.000	2	0	0	.00
Wakefield, Tim	.163	43	7	1	3	4	.127	71	9	2	0	1	3	1	20	8	24	128.1	8	15	4	3	.852	13	5	0	.38
Walk, Bob	.121	58	7	0	2	7	.145	510	74	11	2	1	48	16	167	50	32	187.0	12	23	2	3	.946	25	6	0	.24
Walton, Bruce	.000	1	0	0	0	0	.000	1	0	0	0	0	0	0	0	0	4	5.2	1	1	0	0	1.000	0	0	0	.00
Ward, Duane	.000	0	0	0	0	0	.000	1	0	0	0	0	0	0	0	0	71	71.2	1	5	0	0	1.000	3	0	0	.00
Watson, Allen	.231	26	6	0	2	1	.231	26	6	3	0	0	2	1	2	1	16	86.0	3	10	1	1	.929	15	3	1	.27
Wayne, Gary	1.000	1	1	0	2	0	1.000	1	1	0	0	0	2	0	0	0	65	62.1	0	8	1	1	1.000	4	1	0	.25
Weathers, Dave	.100	10	1	0	0	3	.100	10	1	0	0	0	0	0	7	3	14	45.2	5	3	0	0	1.000	7	0	0	.00
Wegman, Bill	.000	0	0	0	0	0	.000	0	0	0	0	0	0	0	0	0	20	120.2	12	21	2	4	.943	17	7	0	.41
Welch, Bob	.000	0	0	0	0	0	.151	581	88	7	1	2	30	22	171	59	30	166.2	16	25	0	2	1.000	20	11	1	.60
Wells, David	.000	0	0	0	0	0	.000	0	0	0	0	0	0	0	0	0	32	187.0	10	22	1	0	.970	24	4	6	.42
Wendell, Turk	.143	7	1	0	0	0	.143	7	1	0	0	0	0	0	3	0	7	22.2	7	1	0	0	1.000	1	0	0	.00
Wertz, Bill	.000	0	0	0	0	0	.000	0	0	0	0	0	0	0	0	0	34	59.2	4	0	1	0	.800	1	0	0	.00
West, David	.400	5	2	0	2	0	.417	12	5	2	0	0	2	0	4	0	76	86.1	2	4	2	1	.750	8	3	0	.38
Weston, Mickey	.000	0	0	0	0	0	.000	2	0	0	0	0	0	0	2	0	4	5.2	0	0	0	0	.000	1	0	0	.00
Wetteland, John	.000	4	0	0	0	1	.135	37	5	1	0	1	6	0	18	8	70	85.1	1	5	3	0	.667	15	2	0	.13
Whitehurst, Wally	.083	24	2	0	0	10	.159	88	14	2	0	0	3	4	23	18	21	105.2	3	18	2	2	.913	10	7	0	.70
Whiteside, Matt	.000	0	0	0	0	0	.000	0	0	0	0	0	0	0	0	0	60	73.0	5	7	2	3	.857	10	6	0	.60
Wickander, Kevin	.000	2	0	0	0	0	.000	2	0	0	0	0	0	0	1	0	44	34.0	0	3	0	0	1.000	4	1	0	.25
Wickman, Bob	.000	0	0	0	0	0	.000	0	0	0	0	0	0	0	0	0	41	140.0	7	19	2	1	.929	29	9	0	.31
Williams, Brian	.200	10	2	0	0	3	.140	43	6	2	0	0	4	0	17	10	42	82.0	7	20	1	0	.964	8	2	0	.25
Williams, Mike	.083	12	1	0	0	3	.227	22	5	0	0	0	2	0	7	4	17	51.0	2	6	0	1	1.000	9	2	1	.33
Williams, Mitch	1.000	1	1	0	1	0	.188	16	3	0	0	1	4	1	4	0	66	62.0	2	3	2	0	.714	9	0	0	.00
Williams, Woody	.000	0	0	0	0	0	.000	0	0	0	0	0	0	0	0	0	30	37.0	5	6	0	1	1.000	0	0	0	.00
Williamson, Mark	.000	0	0	0	0	0	.000	0	0	0	0	0	0	0	0	0	48	88.0	8	11	0	0	1.000	7	4	0	.57
Willis, Carl	.000	0	0	0	0	0	.250	4	1	0	0	0	0	1	0	2	53	58.0	2	6	0	0	1.000	5	1	0	.20
Wilson, Steve	.000	2	0	0	0	0	.133	60	8	1	0	0	3	4	17	6	25	25.2	2	4	0	0	.857	6	1	0	.17
Wilson, Trevor	.138	29	4	1	2	8	.166	163	27	2	0	2	11	11	59	29	22	110.0	3	13	0	2	1.000	8	3	1	.50
Witt, Bobby	.000	0	0	0	0	0	.000	1	0	0	0	0	0	0	1	0	35	220.0	12	39	3	5	.944	28	8	1	.32
Witt, Mike	.000	0	0	0	0	0	.000	0	0	0	0	0	0	0	0	0	9	41.0	1	6	0	0	1.000	6	3	0	.50
Wohlers, Mark	.000	0	0	0	0	0	.000	3	0	0	0	0	0	0	3	0	46	48.0	6	6	0	1	1.000	3	0	0	.00
Worrell, Tim	.032	31	1	0	1	2	.032	31	1	1	0	0	1	0	15	2	21	100.2	6	11	1	0	.944	19	9	0	.47
Worrell, Todd	.000	0	0	0	0	0	.080	25	2	0	1	0	0	1	18	2	35	38.2	1	4	0	0	1.000	10	1	0	.10
Young, Anthony	.143	14	2	0	0	2	.127	55	7	1	0	0	0	2	20	5	39	100.1	9	14	3	1	.885	17	2	0	.12
Young, Cliff	.000	0	0	0	0	0	.000	0	0	0	0	0	0	0	0	0	21	60.1	4	5	0	1	1.000	8	3	1	.50
Young, Curt	.000	0	0	0	0	0	.000	1	0	0	0	0	0	0	0	0	3	14.2	1	3	0	0	1.000	3	0	1	.33
Young, Matt	.000	0	0	0	0	0	.000	3	0	0	0	0	0	0	2	0	22	74.1	4	10	1	0	.933	16	6	1	.44
Young, Pete	.000	1	0	0	0	0	.000	1	0	0	0	0	0	0	0	0	4	5.1	0	1	0	0	1.000	0	0	0	.00

Hitters Pitching

Player	1993 Pitching											Career Pitching										
	G	W	L	Sv	IP	H	R	ER	BB	SO	ERA	G	W	L	Sv	IP	H	R	ER	BB	SO	ERA
Brewer, Rod	1	0	0	0	1.0	3	5	5	2	1	45.00	1	0	0	0	1.0	3	5	5	2	1	45.00
Canseco, Jose	1	0	0	0	1.0	2	3	3	3	0	27.00	1	0	0	0	1.0	2	3	3	3	0	27.00
Dascenzo, Doug	0	0	0	0	0.0	0	0	0	0	0	0.00	4	0	0	0	5.0	3	0	0	2	2	0.00
Davis, Chili	1	0	0	0	2.0	0	0	0	0	0	0.00	1	0	0	0	2.0	0	0	0	0	0	0.00
Espinoza, Alvaro	0	0	0	0	0.0	0	0	0	0	0	0.00	1	0	0	0	0.2	0	0	0	0	0	0.00
Foley, Tom	0	0	0	0	0.0	0	0	0	0	0	0.00	1	0	0	0	0.1	1	1	1	0	0	27.00
Gladden, Dan	0	0	0	0	0.0	0	0	0	0	0	0.00	2	0	0	0	2.0	2	1	1	1	0	4.50
Gonzales, Rene	1	0	0	0	1.0	0	0	0	0	0	0.00	1	0	0	0	1.0	0	0	0	0	0	0.00
Jackson, Darrin	0	0	0	0	0.0	0	0	0	0	0	0.00	1	0	0	0	2.0	3	2	2	2	0	9.00
Jones, Tim	0	0	0	0	0.0	0	0	0	0	0	0.00	1	0	0	0	1.1	1	2	1	2	0	6.75
Litton, Greg	0	0	0	0	0.0	0	0	0	0	0	0.00	1	0	0	0	1.0	1	1	1	3	0	9.00
Lyons, Steve	0	0	0	0	0.0	0	0	0	0	0	0.00	2	0	0	0	3.0	4	1	1	4	2	3.00
Martinez, Dave	0	0	0	0	0.0	0	0	0	0	0	0.00	1	0	0	0	0.1	2	2	2	2	0	54.00
O'Neill, Paul	0	0	0	0	0.0	0	0	0	0	0	0.00	1	0	0	0	2.0	2	3	3	4	2	13.50
Oquendo, Jose	0	0	0	0	0.0	0	0	0	0	0	0.00	3	0	1	0	6.0	10	8	8	9	2	12.00
Pecota, Bill	0	0	0	0	0.0	0	0	0	0	0	0.00	2	0	0	0	3.0	5	2	2	0	0	6.00
Russell, John	0	0	0	0	0.0	0	0	0	0	0	0.00	1	0	0	0	0.1	0	0	0	0	0	0.00
Seitzer, Kevin	1	0	0	0	0.1	0	0	0	0	1	0.00	1	0	0	0	0.1	0	0	0	0	1	0.00
Tackett, Jeff	1	0	0	0	1.0	1	0	0	1	0	0.00	1	0	0	0	1.0	1	0	0	1	0	0.00
Wallach, Tim	0	0	0	0	0.0	0	0	0	0	0	0.00	2	0	0	0	2.0	3	1	1	0	0	4.50
Wilson, Glenn	0	0	0	0	0.0	0	0	0	0	0	0.00	1	0	0	0	1.0	0	0	0	0	1	0.00

Park Data

Two new parks later, we present another year's worth of park data. Surely, there has not been so much discussion of a park's effect on offense in a long time as that of Mile High Stadium in Denver. Although analysts like ourselves anticipated pepped up run production there, even we were surprised at just how much of a pitcher's nightmare the park turned out to be. Take a long look at our diagrams of both Municipal and Arlington Stadiums, because this will be the last time you'll find them here. Since this is only the second year we've done these and because our explanations were so good last year and because we're about out of original things to say in these intros, we'll pretty much leave what was in the book last year from here on alone. Read on.

In the charts that follow, the first block of columns shows how much the featured team totalled at home, how much opponents totalled against the featured team at home and the grand totals of both. The second block of columns shows how much the featured team totalled in away games, how much opponents totalled in away games and the grand totals of both. By combining both the featured team's and opponent totals, most team variance is negated and only the park variance is left. For example, if the featured team has a big home run hitter who hit 20 homers at home and 20 on the road, his numbers won't affect the park factor for homers one iota. However, if this guy hit 39 dingers at home and only one on the road, the park factor will be affected tremendously, and rightly so.

Now for the Index. In a nutshell, the Index tells you whether the park favors the stat you happen to be looking at. For example, how much of an advantage do Tiger right-handed power hitters (Fielder, Fryman, half-time Tettleton, and now Eric Davis) have hitting in Tiger Stadium? To determine the Index, you need to determine the frequency of the stat — in this case home runs — at Home vs. the frequency of the stat on the Road. Since 1991, right-handed batters have hit 358 home runs in 9,825 at-bats at Tiger Stadium, a frequency of .0364 HR per AB; in Tigers' road games, the frequency is .0312 HR per AB (315/10,109). Dividing the Home frequency by the Road Frequency gives us a figure of 1.17. This number is multiplied by 100 to make it more recognizable: 117. What does an Index of 117 mean? In this case it means it's 17% easier for righties to hit home runs in Tiger Stadium than it is in other American League parks.

271

The greater the Index is over 100, the more favorable the park is for that statistic. The lower the Index is under 100, the less favorable the park is for that statistic. A park that was neutral in a category will have an Index of 100. The only question left to answer is, what is **E-Infield**? This is infield **fielding** errors. Obviously, a ballpark itself doesn't have any effect on throwing errors, although there can be some official scoring bias that can affect the number of throwing errors charged.

For those of you who can stand even further technicalities: The index for the following categories are determined on a per at-bat basis: 2B, 3B, HR, SO, LHB-HR and RHB-HR. The index for AB, R, H, E and E-Infield are determined using per game ratios. All the other indices are based on the raw figures shown in the chart.

Finally, for most parks you'll notice that we include 1993 data as well as three-year totals (1991-1993). However, for parks where there have been changes over the last three years, we never combine data. For example, for Camden Yards, we show you 1993 data as well as 1992-1993 combined. On the other hand, for San Francisco, where they moved the right field fence in between the 1992 and 1993 seasons, 1993 data is shown, but is not combined with previous years. Instead, 1991-1992 combined is shown for comparison purposes.

Atlanta Braves

	1993 Season							1991-1993						
	Home Games			Away Games			Index	Home Games			Away Games			Index
	Braves	Opp	Total	Braves	Opp	Total		Braves	Opp	Total	Braves	Opp	Total	
G	81	81	162	81	81	162	--	243	243	486	243	243	486	--
Avg	.262	.246	.254	.262	.234	.249	102	.264	.249	.256	.252	.232	.242	106
AB	2693	2798	5491	2822	2596	5418	101	8038	8379	16417	8413	7911	16324	101
R	366	291	657	401	268	669	98	1127	949	2076	1071	823	1894	110
H	705	689	1394	739	608	1347	103	2125	2084	4209	2117	1838	3955	106
2B	116	130	246	123	110	233	104	349	375	724	368	336	704	102
3B	15	8	23	14	13	27	84	46	36	82	61	56	117	70
HR	78	52	130	91	49	140	92	233	170	403	215	138	353	114
SO	432	505	937	514	531	1045	88	1293	1436	2729	1483	1517	3000	90
E	80	88	168	49	100	149	113	231	242	473	145	233	378	125
E-Infield	50	64	114	37	74	111	103	174	193	367	109	193	302	122
LHB-Avg	.266	.255	.261	.250	.225	.241	109	.267	.267	.267	.256	.238	.249	108
LHB-HR	49	23	72	48	9	57	124	120	65	185	104	40	144	128
RHB-Avg	.257	.241	.247	.276	.239	.255	97	.261	.238	.248	.248	.229	.238	104
RHB-HR	29	29	58	43	40	83	69	113	105	218	111	98	209	103

ATLANTA

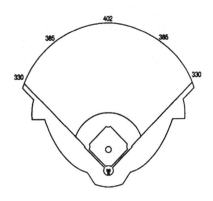

BALTIMORE

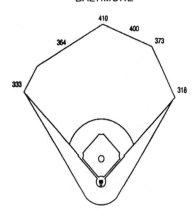

Baltimore Orioles

	1993 Season							1992-1993						
	Home Games			Away Games			Index	Home Games			Away Games			Index
	Orioles	Opp	Total	Orioles	Opp	Total		Orioles	Opp	Total	Orioles	Opp	Total	
G	81	81	162	81	81	162	--	162	162	324	162	162	324	--
Avg	.278	.260	.269	.256	.261	.259	104	.266	.254	.260	.260	.263	.262	99
AB	2722	2832	5554	2786	2641	5427	102	5401	5661	11062	5592	5343	10935	101
R	434	371	805	352	374	726	111	773	704	1477	718	697	1415	104
H	757	737	1494	713	690	1403	106	1438	1439	2877	1455	1407	2862	101
2B	148	140	288	139	144	283	99	256	259	515	274	275	549	93
3B	11	14	25	13	16	29	84	30	29	59	30	32	62	94
HR	87	81	168	70	72	142	116	162	150	312	143	127	270	114
SO	469	457	926	461	443	904	100	861	879	1740	896	867	1763	98
E	59	54	113	57	53	110	103	99	94	193	110	104	214	90
E-Infield	43	46	89	41	39	80	111	74	79	153	81	77	158	97
LHB-Avg	.300	.272	.286	.269	.252	.261	110	.285	.253	.268	.268	.257	.262	102
LHB-HR	23	21	44	29	23	52	83	45	47	92	43	41	84	109
RHB-Avg	.264	.253	.258	.247	.267	.257	101	.256	.255	.256	.256	.268	.261	98
RHB-HR	64	60	124	41	49	90	134	117	103	220	100	86	186	116

Boston Red Sox

	1993 Season							1991-1993						
	Home Games			Away Games				Home Games			Away Games			
	Red Sox	Opp	Total	Red Sox	Opp	Total	Index	Red Sox	Opp	Total	Red Sox	Opp	Total	Index
G	81	81	162	81	81	162	--	243	243	486	243	243	486	--
Avg	.281	.260	.270	.247	.243	.245	110	.273	.263	.268	.247	.245	.246	109
AB	2743	2847	5590	2753	2636	5389	104	8176	8572	16748	8311	7884	16195	103
R	393	363	756	293	335	628	120	1099	1078	2177	917	1001	1918	114
H	770	739	1509	681	640	1321	114	2228	2257	4485	2052	1930	3982	113
2B	193	163	356	126	118	244	141	525	455	980	358	372	730	130
3B	14	18	32	15	15	30	103	37	45	82	38	50	88	90
HR	54	53	107	60	74	134	77	168	175	343	156	206	362	92
SO	432	516	948	439	481	920	99	1223	1526	2749	1333	1413	2746	97
E	83	66	149	52	57	109	137	226	189	415	164	165	329	126
E-Infield	69	48	117	40	41	81	144	192	150	342	134	126	260	132
LHB-Avg	.315	.268	.287	.253	.242	.247	116	.293	.264	.277	.258	.238	.248	112
LHB-HR	24	23	47	32	32	64	74	64	51	115	63	67	130	86
RHB-Avg	.265	.252	.259	.244	.243	.244	106	.262	.263	.262	.241	.249	.245	107
RHB-HR	30	30	60	28	42	70	81	104	124	228	93	139	232	95

BOSTON

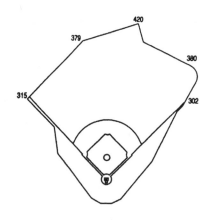

CALIFORNIA

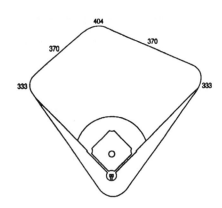

California Angels

	1993 Season							1991-1993						
	Home Games			Away Games				Home Games			Away Games			
	Angels	Opp	Total	Angels	Opp	Total	Index	Angels	Opp	Total	Angels	Opp	Total	Index
G	81	81	162	81	81	162	--	243	243	486	243	243	486	--
Avg	.264	.268	.266	.255	.272	.264	101	.252	.257	.255	.253	.266	.260	98
AB	2654	2841	5495	2737	2647	5384	102	7941	8415	16356	8284	7956	16240	101
R	363	398	761	321	372	693	110	965	1041	2006	951	1049	2000	100
H	701	761	1462	698	721	1419	103	2004	2163	4167	2097	2119	4216	99
2B	118	134	252	141	134	275	90	312	360	672	394	379	773	86
3B	12	4	16	12	11	23	68	35	16	51	38	37	75	68
HR	64	84	148	50	69	119	122	167	218	385	150	206	356	107
SO	437	464	901	493	379	872	101	1290	1431	2721	1450	1290	2740	99
E	84	81	165	60	66	126	131	206	220	426	173	195	368	116
E-Infield	48	53	101	48	48	96	105	153	171	324	141	164	305	106
LHB-Avg	.254	.274	.263	.254	.287	.268	98	.248	.263	.255	.268	.285	.275	92
LHB-HR	26	29	55	23	19	42	133	54	59	113	55	58	113	102
RHB-Avg	.271	.265	.268	.256	.266	.261	103	.255	.254	.255	.243	.258	.251	102
RHB-HR	38	55	93	27	50	77	116	113	159	272	95	148	243	109

Chicago Cubs

	1993 Season							1991-1993						
	Home Games			Away Games				Home Games			Away Games			
	Cubs	Opp	Total	Cubs	Opp	Total	Index	Cubs	Opp	Total	Cubs	Opp	Total	Index
G	82	82	164	81	81	162	--	246	246	492	239	239	478	--
Avg	.283	.266	.275	.258	.280	.269	102	.266	.255	.260	.252	.263	.257	101
AB	2769	2857	5626	2858	2688	5546	100	8366	8605	16971	8373	7879	16252	101
R	381	382	763	357	357	714	106	1082	1075	2157	944	1022	1966	107
H	784	761	1545	737	753	1490	102	2226	2193	4419	2110	2073	4183	103
2B	131	155	286	128	130	258	109	377	401	778	335	391	726	103
3B	16	23	39	16	15	31	124	51	71	122	48	52	100	117
HR	76	94	170	85	59	144	116	228	218	446	196	159	355	120
SO	453	472	925	470	433	903	101	1289	1452	2741	1329	1281	2610	101
E	80	77	157	71	76	147	106	208	215	423	170	195	365	113
E-Infield	44	49	93	35	54	89	103	149	168	317	111	157	268	115
LHB-Avg	.313	.256	.286	.268	.275	.271	106	.282	.263	.271	.266	.260	.263	103
LHB-HR	31	40	71	52	32	84	83	62	106	168	82	88	170	92
RHB-Avg	.255	.274	.265	.249	.284	.267	99	.256	.248	.252	.243	.266	.253	99
RHB-HR	45	54	99	33	27	60	162	166	112	278	114	71	185	147

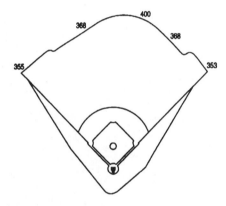

CHICAGO CUBS

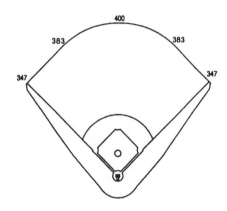

WHITE SOX

Chicago White Sox

	1993 Season							1991-1993						
	Home Games			Away Games				Home Games			Away Games			
	White Sox	Opp	Total	White Sox	Opp	Total	Index	White Sox	Opp	Total	White Sox	Opp	Total	Index
G	81	81	162	81	81	162	--	244	244	488	242	242	484	--
Avg	.270	.255	.262	.260	.256	.259	101	.266	.246	.256	.259	.252	.255	100
AB	2657	2770	5427	2826	2702	5528	98	8064	8385	16449	8511	8086	16597	98
R	384	333	717	392	331	723	99	1130	984	2114	1142	1051	2193	96
H	718	705	1423	736	693	1429	100	2148	2064	4212	2204	2036	4240	99
2B	109	93	202	119	124	243	85	346	293	639	377	363	740	87
3B	20	12	32	24	10	34	96	59	38	97	60	48	108	91
HR	82	70	152	80	55	135	115	210	211	421	201	191	392	108
SO	385	492	877	449	482	931	96	1159	1376	2535	1355	1331	2686	95
E	70	66	136	59	74	133	102	191	175	366	183	203	386	94
E-Infield	50	48	98	45	46	91	108	154	133	287	154	150	304	94
LHB-Avg	.276	.261	.269	.274	.267	.271	99	.272	.251	.262	.267	.251	.260	101
LHB-HR	25	25	50	23	24	47	111	72	76	148	67	66	133	112
RHB-Avg	.265	.250	.257	.247	.249	.248	104	.261	.242	.251	.252	.253	.252	100
RHB-HR	57	45	102	57	31	88	116	138	135	273	134	125	259	107

275

Cincinnati Reds

	1993 Season							1991-1993						
	Home Games			Away Games				Home Games			Away Games			
	Reds	Opp	Total	Reds	Opp	Total	Index	Reds	Opp	Total	Reds	Opp	Total	Index
G	81	81	162	81	81	162	--	243	243	486	243	243	486	--
Avg	.265	.267	.266	.263	.277	.270	99	.267	.254	.260	.255	.264	.260	100
AB	2659	2797	5456	2858	2752	5610	97	7988	8308	16296	8490	8080	16570	98
R	363	383	746	359	402	761	98	1091	1048	2139	980	1037	2017	106
H	705	747	1452	752	763	1515	96	2129	2109	4238	2165	2135	4300	99
2B	134	113	247	127	126	253	100	431	346	777	361	373	734	108
3B	10	20	30	18	34	52	59	43	60	103	56	77	133	79
HR	69	81	150	68	77	145	106	233	218	451	167	176	343	134
SO	494	497	991	531	499	1030	99	1392	1544	2936	1527	1509	3036	98
E	76	81	157	76	98	174	90	170	190	360	203	223	426	85
E-Infield	42	51	93	48	64	112	83	121	139	260	152	173	325	80
LHB-Avg	.257	.276	.269	.265	.279	.274	98	.271	.267	.269	.255	.261	.258	104
LHB-HR	13	42	55	10	24	34	158	69	88	157	42	63	105	148
RHB-Avg	.268	.260	.264	.263	.276	.268	99	.264	.244	.254	.255	.267	.260	98
RHB-HR	56	39	95	58	53	111	91	164	130	294	125	113	238	128

CINCINNATI

CLEVELAND

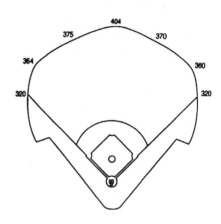

Cleveland Indians

	1993 Season							1992-1993						
	Home Games			Away Games				Home Games			Away Games			
	Indians	Opp	Total	Indians	Opp	Total	Index	Indians	Opp	Total	Indians	Opp	Total	Index
G	81	81	162	81	81	162	--	162	162	324	162	162	324	--
Avg	.272	.266	.269	.278	.295	.287	94	.278	.269	.273	.264	.280	.272	100
AB	2667	2838	5505	2952	2826	5778	95	5448	5758	11206	5791	5521	11312	99
R	387	351	738	403	462	865	85	753	748	1501	711	811	1522	99
H	726	756	1482	821	835	1656	89	1512	1550	3062	1530	1548	3078	99
2B	106	123	229	158	155	313	77	223	258	481	268	265	533	91
3B	19	5	24	12	16	28	90	34	15	49	21	33	54	92
HR	69	83	152	72	99	171	93	131	177	308	137	164	301	103
SO	384	435	819	459	453	912	94	813	910	1723	915	868	1783	98
E	74	66	140	100	77	177	79	159	124	283	156	124	280	101
E-Infield	54	40	94	68	53	121	78	122	87	209	114	89	203	103
LHB-Avg	.288	.266	.278	.290	.300	.295	94	.284	.269	.277	.276	.287	.281	99
LHB-HR	32	34	66	32	31	63	105	60	58	118	53	53	106	108
RHB-Avg	.256	.266	.262	.267	.292	.280	93	.272	.269	.270	.255	.276	.266	102
RHB-HR	37	49	86	40	68	108	87	71	119	190	84	111	195	101

Colorado Rockies

	1993 Season							1993 Season						
	Home Games			Away Games				Home Games			Away Games			
	Rockies	Opp	Total	Rockies	Opp	Total	Index	Rockies	Opp	Total	Rockies	Opp	Total	Index
G	81	81	162	81	81	162	--	81	81	162	81	81	162	--
Avg	.306	.308	.307	.240	.279	.260	118	.306	.308	.307	.240	.279	.260	118
AB	2754	2948	5702	2763	2712	5475	104	2754	2948	5702	2763	2712	5475	104
R	489	551	1040	269	416	685	152	489	551	1040	269	416	685	152
H	843	907	1750	664	757	1421	123	843	907	1750	664	757	1421	123
2B	158	142	300	120	138	258	112	158	142	300	120	138	258	112
3B	48	37	85	11	17	28	291	48	37	85	11	17	28	291
HR	77	107	184	65	74	139	127	77	107	184	65	74	139	127
SO	410	483	893	534	430	964	89	410	483	893	534	430	964	89
E	126	114	240	70	60	130	185	126	114	240	70	60	130	185
E-Infield	84	80	164	54	38	92	178	84	80	164	54	38	92	178
LHB-Avg	.261	.313	.300	.244	.278	.269	112	.261	.313	.300	.244	.278	.269	112
LHB-HR	4	36	40	15	30	45	87	4	36	40	15	30	45	87
RHB-Avg	.315	.303	.310	.240	.280	.255	121	.315	.303	.310	.240	.280	.255	121
RHB-HR	73	71	144	50	44	94	146	73	71	144	50	44	94	146

COLORADO

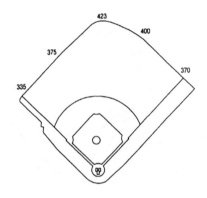

423
400
375
370
335
370

DETROIT

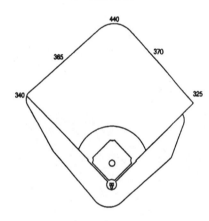

440
365
370
340
325

Detroit Tigers

	1993 Season							1991-1993						
	Home Games			Away Games				Home Games			Away Games			
	Tigers	Opp	Total	Tigers	Opp	Total	Index	Tigers	Opp	Total	Tigers	Opp	Total	Index
G	81	81	162	81	81	162	--	242	242	484	244	244	488	--
Avg	.273	.269	.271	.277	.284	.280	97	.260	.274	.267	.259	.282	.270	99
AB	2728	2837	5565	2892	2768	5660	98	8048	8547	16595	8634	8200	16834	99
R	457	408	865	442	429	871	99	1283	1209	2492	1224	1216	2440	103
H	746	762	1508	800	785	1585	95	2090	2338	4428	2239	2313	4552	98
2B	137	116	253	145	147	292	88	373	370	743	424	404	828	91
3B	20	14	34	18	21	39	89	42	39	81	38	67	105	78
HR	103	99	202	75	89	164	125	303	278	581	266	213	479	123
SO	526	443	969	596	385	981	100	1603	1211	2814	1759	1049	2808	102
E	88	61	149	74	77	151	99	190	182	372	192	205	397	94
E-Infield	52	45	97	50	51	101	96	130	149	279	142	159	301	93
LHB-Avg	.270	.296	.283	.288	.284	.286	99	.264	.288	.276	.258	.277	.267	103
LHB-HR	32	51	83	33	32	65	128	105	118	223	88	76	164	135
RHB-Avg	.276	.251	.263	.269	.283	.276	95	.257	.264	.261	.260	.285	.273	96
RHB-HR	71	48	119	42	57	99	124	198	160	358	178	137	315	117

Florida Marlins

	1993 Season							1993 Season						
	Home Games			Away Games				Home Games			Away Games			
	Marlins	Opp	Total	Marlins	Opp	Total	Index	Marlins	Opp	Total	Marlins	Opp	Total	Index
G	81	81	162	81	81	162	--	81	81	162	81	81	162	--
Avg	.251	.261	.257	.244	.261	.252	102	.251	.261	.257	.244	.261	.252	102
AB	2706	2861	5567	2769	2640	5409	103	2706	2861	5567	2769	2640	5409	103
R	299	369	668	282	355	637	105	299	369	668	282	355	637	105
H	680	748	1428	676	689	1365	105	680	748	1428	676	689	1365	105
2B	98	137	235	99	127	226	101	98	137	235	99	127	226	101
3B	16	15	31	15	18	33	91	16	15	31	15	18	33	91
HR	44	72	116	50	63	113	100	44	72	116	50	63	113	100
SO	544	525	1069	510	420	930	112	544	525	1069	510	420	930	112
E	77	88	165	71	76	147	112	77	88	165	71	76	147	112
E-Infield	55	60	115	47	46	93	124	55	60	115	47	46	93	124
LHB-Avg	.258	.261	.259	.234	.257	.245	106	.258	.261	.259	.234	.257	.245	106
LHB-HR	20	33	53	16	32	48	106	20	33	53	16	32	48	106
RHB-Avg	.246	.262	.254	.252	.264	.258	98	.246	.262	.254	.252	.264	.258	98
RHB-HR	24	39	63	34	31	65	95	24	39	63	34	31	65	95

FLORIDA

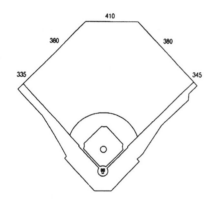

HOUSTON

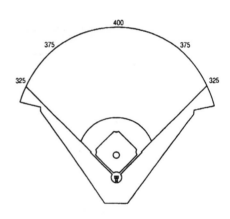

Houston Astros

	1993 Season							1992-1993						
	Home Games			Away Games				Home Games			Away Games			
	Astros	Opp	Total	Astros	Opp	Total	Index	Astros	Opp	Total	Astros	Opp	Total	Index
G	81	81	162	81	81	162	--	162	162	324	162	162	324	--
Avg	.267	.241	.254	.267	.260	.264	96	.258	.239	.249	.255	.264	.259	96
AB	2625	2751	5376	2839	2689	5528	97	5358	5594	10952	5586	5348	10934	100
R	363	285	648	353	345	698	93	665	578	1243	659	720	1379	90
H	700	664	1364	759	699	1458	94	1385	1337	2722	1424	1412	2836	96
2B	142	110	252	146	116	262	99	287	216	503	256	265	521	96
3B	19	12	31	18	13	31	103	41	32	73	34	42	76	96
HR	62	56	118	76	61	137	89	111	97	208	123	134	257	81
SO	436	570	1006	475	486	961	108	976	1109	2085	960	925	1885	110
E	61	63	124	85	74	159	78	111	110	221	149	126	275	80
E-Infield	41	45	86	65	54	119	72	82	82	164	118	102	220	75
LHB-Avg	.256	.238	.247	.280	.270	.275	90	.252	.240	.246	.265	.274	.269	91
LHB-HR	21	23	44	37	33	70	67	44	41	85	61	64	125	71
RHB-Avg	.276	.244	.260	.255	.251	.253	102	.264	.238	.251	.246	.254	.250	100
RHB-HR	41	33	74	39	28	67	110	67	56	123	62	70	132	90

Kansas City Royals

	1993 Season							1991-1993						
	Home Games			Away Games			Index	Home Games			Away Games			Index
	Royals	Opp	Total	Royals	Opp	Total		Royals	Opp	Total	Royals	Opp	Total	
G	81	81	162	81	81	162	---	243	243	486	243	243	486	---
Avg	.283	.257	.270	.244	.250	.247	109	.269	.257	.263	.254	.259	.257	102
AB	2785	2833	5618	2737	2603	5340	105	8208	8605	16813	8399	7973	16372	103
R	370	354	724	305	340	645	112	1028	1068	2096	984	1015	1999	105
H	788	728	1516	667	651	1318	115	2204	2212	4416	2137	2066	4203	105
2B	183	172	355	111	120	231	146	460	470	930	408	358	766	118
3B	23	19	42	12	9	21	190	77	65	142	41	33	74	187
HR	50	49	99	75	56	131	72	121	130	251	196	186	382	64
SO	401	471	872	535	514	1049	79	1165	1400	2565	1481	1423	2904	86
E	65	75	140	52	66	118	119	200	190	390	164	172	336	116
E-Infield	47	45	92	30	46	76	121	161	138	299	124	136	260	115
LHB-Avg	.290	.266	.278	.256	.267	.261	106	.270	.260	.265	.261	.272	.266	100
LHB-HR	17	23	40	36	24	60	67	41	48	89	89	86	175	50
RHB-Avg	.278	.250	.263	.232	.236	.234	112	.267	.255	.260	.248	.248	.248	105
RHB-HR	33	26	59	39	32	71	75	80	82	162	107	100	207	76

KANSAS CITY

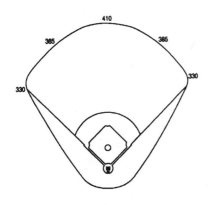

LOS ANGELES

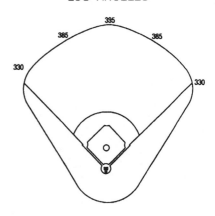

Los Angeles Dodgers

	1993 Season							1991-1993						
	Home Games			Away Games			Index	Home Games			Away Games			Index
	Dodgers	Opp	Total	Dodgers	Opp	Total		Dodgers	Opp	Total	Dodgers	Opp	Total	
G	81	81	162	81	81	162	---	243	243	486	243	243	486	---
Avg	.275	.250	.262	.248	.257	.252	104	.261	.248	.254	.248	.253	.250	101
AB	2716	2811	5527	2872	2733	5605	99	7968	8387	16355	8396	8062	16458	99
R	330	318	648	345	344	689	94	949	879	1828	939	984	1923	95
H	747	703	1450	711	703	1414	103	2078	2076	4154	2079	2043	4122	101
2B	104	107	211	130	116	246	87	282	302	584	344	349	693	85
3B	7	11	18	21	22	43	42	34	35	69	57	59	116	60
HR	66	48	114	64	55	119	97	149	127	276	161	154	315	88
SO	437	530	967	500	513	1013	97	1305	1604	2909	1488	1448	2936	100
E	81	69	150	70	82	152	99	224	223	447	224	188	412	108
E-Infield	63	53	116	52	52	104	112	194	180	374	182	139	321	117
LHB-Avg	.305	.258	.275	.227	.247	.239	115	.269	.254	.261	.243	.258	.250	104
LHB-HR	11	25	36	11	27	38	97	65	67	132	66	73	139	94
RHB-Avg	.262	.242	.254	.257	.269	.262	97	.253	.241	.247	.252	.249	.251	99
RHB-HR	55	23	78	53	28	81	97	84	60	144	95	81	176	83

Milwaukee Brewers

| | 1993 Season | | | | | | | 1991-1993 | | | | | | |
| | Home Games | | | Away Games | | | | Home Games | | | Away Games | | | |
	Brewers	Opp	Total	Brewers	Opp	Total	Index	Brewers	Opp	Total	Brewers	Opp	Total	Index
G	81	81	162	81	81	162	--	242	242	484	244	244	488	--
Avg	.268	.268	.268	.249	.274	.261	103	.266	.256	.261	.266	.266	.266	98
AB	2704	2852	5556	2821	2725	5546	100	7982	8465	16447	8658	8203	16861	98
R	371	381	752	362	411	773	97	1108	1033	2141	1164	1107	2271	95
H	724	764	1488	702	747	1449	103	2124	2170	4294	2302	2183	4485	97
2B	112	148	260	128	142	270	96	359	386	745	400	408	808	95
3B	17	22	39	8	26	34	114	61	36	97	52	60	112	89
HR	53	65	118	72	88	160	74	150	189	339	173	238	411	85
SO	442	425	867	490	385	875	99	1197	1275	2472	1316	1187	2503	101
E	82	74	156	67	72	139	112	194	202	396	162	205	367	109
E-Infield	68	50	118	45	44	89	133	166	151	317	133	157	290	110
LHB-Avg	.268	.268	.268	.247	.296	.269	100	.268	.253	.260	.260	.274	.267	98
LHB-HR	27	30	57	19	30	49	113	52	76	128	50	96	146	90
RHB-Avg	.268	.268	.268	.251	.258	.255	105	.265	.259	.262	.271	.260	.265	99
RHB-HR	26	35	61	53	58	111	56	98	113	211	123	142	265	81

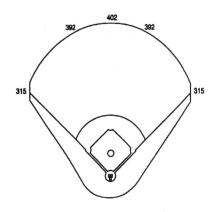

MILWAUKEE

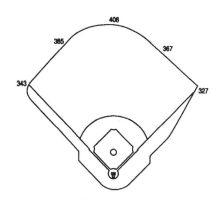

MINNESOTA

Minnesota Twins

| | 1993 Season | | | | | | | 1991-1993 | | | | | | |
| | Home Games | | | Away Games | | | | Home Games | | | Away Games | | | |
	Twins	Opp	Total	Twins	Opp	Total	Index	Twins	Opp	Total	Twins	Opp	Total	Index
G	81	81	162	81	81	162	--	243	243	486	243	243	486	--
Avg	.270	.277	.273	.259	.290	.274	100	.285	.264	.274	.263	.265	.264	104
AB	2768	2900	5668	2833	2718	5551	102	8255	8547	16802	8484	8034	16518	102
R	360	433	793	333	397	730	109	1139	1101	2240	1077	1034	2111	106
H	746	804	1550	734	787	1521	102	2349	2253	4602	2232	2131	4363	105
2B	141	196	337	120	153	273	121	412	502	914	394	392	786	114
3B	17	17	34	10	22	32	104	64	56	120	32	47	79	149
HR	56	70	126	65	78	143	86	174	201	375	191	207	398	93
SO	423	480	903	427	421	848	104	1185	1464	2649	1246	1236	2482	105
E	58	56	114	61	69	130	88	144	176	320	165	201	366	87
E-Infield	42	36	78	39	49	88	89	112	137	249	125	157	282	88
LHB-Avg	.265	.291	.283	.252	.304	.287	99	.270	.274	.273	.255	.278	.269	102
LHB-HR	16	32	48	16	32	48	95	62	74	136	56	73	129	103
RHB-Avg	.271	.266	.269	.261	.278	.268	100	.289	.256	.274	.266	.256	.262	105
RHB-HR	40	38	78	49	46	95	82	112	127	239	135	134	269	88

Montreal Expos

	1993 Season							1991-1993						
	Home Games			Away Games			Index	Home Games			Away Games			Index
	Expos	Opp	Total	Expos	Opp	Total		Expos	Opp	Total	Expos	Opp	Total	
G	81	81	162	82	82	164	---	230	230	460	256	256	512	---
Avg	.261	.237	.249	.253	.261	.257	97	.254	.236	.245	.250	.251	.250	98
AB	2640	2796	5436	2853	2705	5558	99	7481	7872	15353	8901	8426	17327	99
R	367	315	682	365	367	732	94	914	882	1796	1045	1036	2081	96
H	689	662	1351	721	707	1428	96	1898	1857	3755	2222	2112	4334	96
2B	139	159	298	131	128	259	118	370	401	771	399	371	770	113
3B	13	17	30	23	13	36	85	43	59	102	72	44	116	99
HR	62	50	112	60	69	129	89	147	131	278	172	191	363	86
SO	403	463	866	457	471	928	95	1277	1409	2686	1615	1448	3063	99
E	80	60	140	98	110	208	68	194	177	371	241	239	480	86
E-Infield	64	46	110	76	82	158	70	163	149	312	195	196	391	89
LHB-Avg	.274	.253	.262	.226	.263	.244	108	.259	.251	.254	.248	.248	.248	103
LHB-HR	23	26	49	20	27	47	102	53	64	117	69	77	146	90
RHB-Avg	.253	.225	.239	.270	.260	.265	90	.250	.225	.237	.251	.253	.252	94
RHB-HR	39	24	63	40	42	82	81	94	67	161	103	114	217	84

MONTREAL

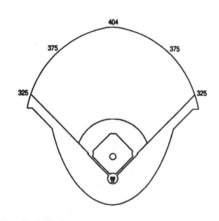

NEW YORK METS

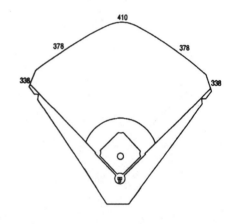

New York Mets

	1993 Season							1991-1993						
	Home Games			Away Games			Index	Home Games			Away Games			Index
	Mets	Opp	Total	Mets	Opp	Total		Mets	Opp	Total	Mets	Opp	Total	
G	81	81	162	81	81	162	---	244	244	488	241	241	482	---
Avg	.245	.264	.255	.251	.274	.262	97	.241	.259	.250	.243	.262	.252	99
AB	2668	2829	5497	2780	2693	5473	100	7923	8535	16458	8224	7927	16151	101
R	317	376	693	355	368	723	96	937	1029	1966	974	1014	1988	98
H	653	746	1399	697	737	1434	98	1909	2213	4122	2000	2077	4077	100
2B	102	129	231	126	146	272	85	348	379	727	389	389	778	92
3B	17	14	31	20	15	35	88	39	69	108	39	62	101	105
HR	75	72	147	83	67	150	98	174	176	350	194	169	363	95
SO	424	454	878	455	413	868	101	1279	1536	2815	1345	1384	2729	101
E	95	50	145	82	73	155	94	218	174	392	218	171	389	100
E-Infield	75	32	107	60	43	103	104	181	132	313	180	124	304	102
LHB-Avg	.249	.245	.247	.248	.293	.266	93	.242	.258	.250	.243	.267	.254	99
LHB-HR	44	20	64	45	21	66	96	94	62	156	103	55	158	98
RHB-Avg	.240	.275	.260	.254	.263	.259	101	.240	.260	.251	.243	.259	.251	100
RHB-HR	31	52	83	38	46	84	99	80	114	194	91	114	205	92

New York Yankees

	1993 Season							1991-1993						
	Home Games			Away Games				Home Games			Away Games			
	Yankees	Opp	Total	Yankees	Opp	Total	Index	Yankees	Opp	Total	Yankees	Opp	Total	Index
G	81	81	162	81	81	162	—	243	243	486	243	243	486	—
Avg	.280	.246	.263	.278	.285	.281	94	.267	.260	.263	.264	.273	.269	98
AB	2674	2743	5417	2941	2779	5720	95	8094	8437	16531	8655	8176	16831	98
R	389	342	731	432	419	851	86	1130	1109	2239	1098	1175	2273	99
H	750	676	1426	818	791	1609	89	2159	2195	4354	2289	2235	4524	96
2B	139	89	228	155	173	328	73	403	363	766	421	464	885	88
3B	10	10	20	14	20	34	62	25	37	62	36	68	104	61
HR	88	85	173	90	85	175	104	258	239	497	230	212	442	114
SO	395	474	869	515	425	940	98	1211	1376	2587	1463	1310	2773	95
E	68	62	130	57	59	116	112	173	176	349	198	169	367	95
E-Infield	44	40	84	41	45	86	98	135	138	273	161	137	298	92
LHB-Avg	.291	.251	.275	.274	.280	.276	99	.276	.263	.270	.264	.278	.270	100
LHB-HR	34	30	64	37	24	61	109	120	99	219	100	69	169	136
RHB-Avg	.269	.244	.255	.282	.287	.285	89	.259	.258	.259	.265	.270	.268	97
RHB-HR	54	55	109	53	61	114	102	138	140	278	130	143	273	101

NY YANKEES

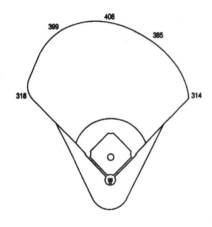

OAKLAND

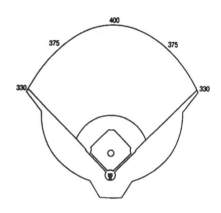

Oakland Athletics

	1993 Season							1991-1993						
	Home Games			Away Games				Home Games			Away Games			
	Athletics	Opp	Total	Athletics	Opp	Total	Index	Athletics	Opp	Total	Athletics	Opp	Total	Index
G	81	81	162	81	81	162	—	243	243	486	243	243	486	—
Avg	.252	.265	.259	.256	.287	.271	95	.248	.252	.250	.258	.276	.267	94
AB	2675	2835	5510	2868	2788	5656	97	7876	8371	16247	8464	8179	16643	98
R	333	387	720	382	459	841	86	1055	1064	2119	1165	1230	2395	88
H	674	752	1426	734	799	1533	93	1952	2112	4064	2187	2260	4447	91
2B	105	137	242	155	146	301	83	323	357	680	402	414	816	85
3B	5	15	20	16	20	36	57	26	44	70	38	60	98	73
HR	78	78	156	80	79	159	101	230	218	448	229	223	452	102
SO	533	479	1012	515	385	900	115	1404	1415	2819	1456	1184	2640	109
E	73	66	139	60	66	126	110	183	195	378	182	182	364	104
E-Infield	43	48	91	46	50	96	95	132	155	287	144	144	288	100
LHB-Avg	.260	.275	.269	.268	.303	.288	93	.254	.262	.259	.259	.286	.275	94
LHB-HR	25	32	57	26	31	57	106	54	77	131	53	89	142	95
RHB-Avg	.248	.257	.252	.250	.271	.259	97	.245	.243	.244	.258	.267	.262	93
RHB-HR	53	46	99	54	48	102	97	176	141	317	176	134	310	105

Philadelphia Phillies

	1993 Season							1991-1993						
	Home Games			Away Games				Home Games			Away Games			
	Phillies	Opp	Total	Phillies	Opp	Total	Index	Phillies	Opp	Total	Phillies	Opp	Total	Index
G	81	81	162	81	81	162	--	245	245	490	241	241	482	--
Avg	.276	.248	.262	.271	.255	.263	99	.261	.247	.254	.251	.256	.254	100
AB	2793	2920	5713	2892	2722	5614	102	8260	8549	16809	8446	7974	16420	101
R	441	371	812	436	369	805	101	1151	1036	2187	1041	1101	2142	100
H	771	725	1496	784	694	1478	101	2156	2112	4268	2123	2040	4163	101
2B	143	140	283	154	107	261	107	409	400	809	391	371	762	104
3B	26	20	46	25	19	44	103	61	60	121	59	57	116	102
HR	80	57	137	76	72	148	91	208	159	367	177	194	371	97
SO	499	629	1128	550	488	1038	107	1534	1639	3173	1600	1317	2917	106
E	83	88	171	77	74	151	113	200	200	400	210	212	422	93
E-Infield	69	58	127	53	56	109	117	166	152	318	167	172	339	92
LHB-Avg	.282	.256	.272	.278	.265	.274	99	.269	.252	.262	.264	.264	.264	99
LHB-HR	43	23	66	40	28	68	99	109	65	174	83	70	153	117
RHB-Avg	.267	.243	.253	.260	.249	.253	100	.253	.244	.248	.238	.250	.244	101
RHB-HR	37	34	71	36	44	80	84	99	94	193	94	124	218	83

PHILADELPHIA

PITTSBURGH

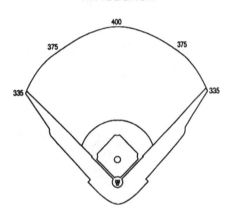

Pittsburgh Pirates

	1993 Season							1991-1993						
	Home Games			Away Games				Home Games			Away Games			
	Pirates	Opp	Total	Pirates	Opp	Total	Index	Pirates	Opp	Total	Pirates	Opp	Total	Index
G	81	81	162	81	81	162	--	246	246	492	240	240	480	--
Avg	.260	.276	.268	.273	.284	.279	96	.261	.261	.261	.262	.265	.264	99
AB	2719	2869	5588	2830	2698	5528	101	8097	8573	16670	8428	8065	16493	99
R	372	388	760	335	418	753	101	1117	979	2096	1051	1054	2105	97
H	708	791	1499	774	766	1540	97	2112	2238	4350	2212	2140	4352	98
2B	131	166	297	136	151	287	102	403	431	834	395	386	781	106
3B	25	28	53	25	22	47	112	82	65	147	72	51	123	118
HR	64	67	131	46	86	132	98	176	159	335	166	212	378	88
SO	485	419	904	487	413	900	99	1343	1386	2729	1402	1209	2611	103
E	68	80	148	67	69	136	109	175	190	365	181	173	354	101
E-Infield	42	48	90	33	47	80	113	137	142	279	127	129	256	106
LHB-Avg	.263	.277	.270	.287	.290	.289	94	.270	.263	.267	.274	.264	.270	99
LHB-HR	34	25	59	17	27	44	132	98	53	151	83	74	157	96
RHB-Avg	.259	.275	.267	.266	.280	.273	98	.254	.260	.257	.254	.266	.260	99
RHB-HR	30	42	72	29	59	88	81	78	106	184	83	138	221	82

San Diego Padres

	1993 Season							1991-1993						
	Home Games			Away Games				Home Games			Away Games			
	Padres	Opp	Total	Padres	Opp	Total	Index	Padres	Opp	Total	Padres	Opp	Total	Index
G	81	81	162	81	81	162	--	243	243	486	243	243	486	--
Avg	.255	.253	.254	.249	.280	.264	96	.257	.254	.256	.244	.265	.254	101
AB	2748	2860	5608	2755	2660	5415	104	8077	8501	16578	8310	8053	16363	101
R	345	376	721	334	396	730	99	999	1030	2029	933	1024	1957	104
H	701	725	1426	685	745	1430	100	2077	2163	4240	2026	2136	4162	102
2B	105	110	215	134	128	262	79	328	306	634	370	348	718	87
3B	14	23	37	14	17	31	115	42	47	89	52	52	104	84
HR	87	79	166	66	69	135	119	239	215	454	170	183	353	127
SO	526	527	1053	520	430	950	107	1432	1525	2957	1547	1324	2871	102
E	90	76	166	94	76	170	98	208	197	405	204	204	408	99
E-Infield	68	54	122	68	46	114	107	170	145	315	161	152	313	101
LHB-Avg	.261	.258	.259	.269	.284	.277	94	.260	.258	.259	.263	.269	.266	97
LHB-HR	35	44	79	35	29	64	119	91	105	196	74	81	155	126
RHB-Avg	.251	.249	.250	.233	.277	.253	99	.255	.252	.253	.228	.263	.245	103
RHB-HR	52	35	87	31	40	71	118	148	110	258	96	102	198	128

SAN DIEGO

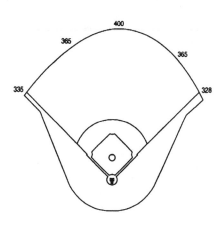

SAN FRANCISCO

San Francisco Giants

	1993 Season							1991-1992						
	Home Games			Away Games				Home Games			Away Games			
	Giants	Opp	Total	Giants	Opp	Total	Index	Giants	Opp	Total	Giants	Opp	Total	Index
G	81	81	162	81	81	162	--	162	162	324	162	162	324	--
Avg	.266	.243	.254	.285	.263	.275	93	.248	.239	.243	.242	.272	.257	95
AB	2663	2764	5427	2894	2708	5602	97	5329	5533	10862	5590	5369	10959	99
R	362	293	655	446	343	789	83	613	599	1212	610	745	1355	89
H	708	673	1381	826	712	1538	90	1322	1321	2643	1353	1461	2814	94
2B	127	92	219	142	93	235	96	238	208	446	197	268	465	97
3B	13	8	21	20	15	35	62	46	29	75	38	38	76	100
HR	82	81	163	86	87	173	97	126	122	248	120	149	269	93
SO	433	526	959	497	456	953	104	921	945	1866	1119	887	2006	94
E	51	84	135	64	93	157	86	118	116	234	104	136	240	98
E-Infield	35	70	105	52	71	123	85	98	104	202	87	113	200	101
LHB-Avg	.262	.246	.253	.303	.279	.291	87	.255	.250	.252	.260	.278	.270	94
LHB-HR	33	36	69	48	35	83	85	42	47	89	29	62	91	98
RHB-Avg	.268	.242	.255	.276	.251	.265	97	.244	.230	.237	.232	.268	.248	96
RHB-HR	49	45	94	38	52	90	109	84	75	159	91	87	178	90

Seattle Mariners

	1993 Season							1992-1993						
	Home Games			Away Games				Home Games			Away Games			
	Mariners	Opp	Total	Mariners	Opp	Total	Index	Mariners	Opp	Total	Mariners	Opp	Total	Index
G	81	81	162	81	81	162	---	162	162	324	162	162	324	---
Avg	.259	.251	.255	.261	.268	.265	96	.264	.261	.262	.260	.264	.262	100
AB	2698	2829	5527	2796	2654	5450	101	5440	5692	11132	5618	5310	10928	102
R	380	350	730	354	381	735	99	735	748	1483	678	782	1460	102
H	699	709	1408	730	712	1442	98	1435	1484	2919	1460	1404	2864	102
2B	141	151	292	131	125	256	112	314	316	630	236	263	499	124
3B	10	13	23	14	18	32	71	23	24	47	25	32	57	81
HR	74	66	140	87	69	156	88	152	129	281	158	135	293	94
SO	445	607	1052	456	476	932	111	862	1092	1954	880	885	1765	109
E	40	60	100	67	79	146	68	95	120	215	124	127	251	86
E-Infield	34	48	82	39	55	94	87	87	97	184	89	98	187	98
LHB-Avg	.261	.259	.260	.261	.273	.266	98	.268	.273	.270	.262	.266	.264	102
LHB-HR	33	26	59	44	16	60	99	69	43	112	75	34	109	103
RHB-Avg	.258	.246	.251	.261	.266	.263	95	.260	.254	.257	.258	.263	.261	99
RHB-HR	41	40	81	43	53	96	82	83	86	169	83	101	184	89

SEATTLE

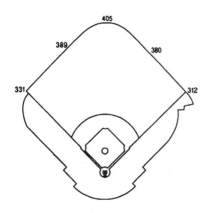

St. LOUIS

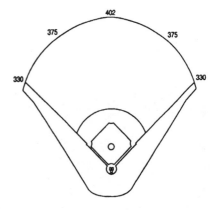

St. Louis Cardinals

	1993 Season							1992-1993						
	Home Games			Away Games				Home Games			Away Games			
	Cardinals	Opp	Total	Cardinals	Opp	Total	Index	Cardinals	Opp	Total	Cardinals	Opp	Total	Index
G	81	81	162	81	81	162	---	162	162	324	162	162	324	---
Avg	.279	.267	.273	.265	.285	.275	99	.273	.255	.264	.261	.273	.267	99
AB	2660	2815	5475	2891	2817	5708	96	5446	5692	11138	5699	5525	11224	99
R	376	321	697	382	423	805	87	704	618	1322	685	730	1415	93
H	741	751	1492	767	802	1569	95	1487	1449	2936	1485	1509	2994	98
2B	125	143	268	137	139	276	101	244	277	521	280	257	537	98
3B	18	20	38	16	24	40	99	44	34	78	34	44	78	101
HR	59	59	118	59	93	152	81	114	111	225	98	159	257	88
SO	394	388	782	488	387	875	93	883	821	1704	995	796	1791	96
E	83	64	147	108	70	178	83	134	111	245	151	120	271	90
E-Infield	49	48	97	78	54	132	73	88	87	175	115	94	209	84
LHB-Avg	.275	.262	.269	.262	.288	.273	99	.273	.250	.262	.258	.276	.266	98
LHB-HR	18	22	40	24	25	49	87	45	45	90	37	57	94	96
RHB-Avg	.281	.270	.275	.268	.283	.276	99	.273	.257	.265	.263	.271	.267	99
RHB-HR	41	37	78	35	68	103	78	69	66	135	61	102	163	84

Texas Rangers

	1993 Season							1991-1993						
	Home Games			Away Games				Home Games			Away Games			
	Rangers	Opp	Total	Rangers	Opp	Total	Index	Rangers	Opp	Total	Rangers	Opp	Total	Index
G	81	81	162	81	81	162	--	243	243	486	243	243	486	--
Avg	.273	.251	.262	.261	.282	.272	96	.265	.256	.260	.260	.273	.266	98
AB	2685	2798	5483	2825	2737	5562	99	8146	8499	16645	8604	8273	16877	99
R	414	341	755	421	410	831	91	1135	1117	2252	1211	1201	2412	93
H	734	703	1437	738	773	1511	95	2161	2173	4334	2237	2260	4497	96
2B	141	127	268	143	151	294	92	415	403	818	423	440	863	96
3B	22	15	37	17	14	31	121	58	42	100	35	47	82	124
HR	90	72	162	91	72	163	101	240	212	452	277	196	473	97
SO	473	521	994	511	436	947	106	1522	1638	3160	1537	1375	2912	110
E	75	71	146	81	80	161	91	230	174	404	214	200	414	98
E-Infield	51	45	96	57	54	111	86	170	132	302	159	144	303	100
LHB-Avg	.275	.233	.254	.257	.286	.271	94	.264	.242	.252	.260	.271	.265	95
LHB-HR	30	16	46	22	23	45	95	87	66	153	88	62	150	103
RHB-Avg	.272	.262	.267	.263	.281	.272	98	.266	.265	.266	.260	.275	.267	99
RHB-HR	60	56	116	69	49	118	105	153	146	299	189	134	323	94

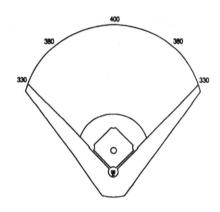

TEXAS

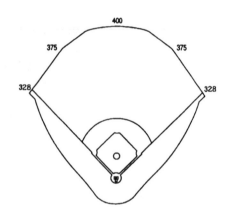

TORONTO

Toronto Blue Jays

	1993 Season							1991-1993						
	Home Games			Away Games				Home Games			Away Games			
	Blue Jays	Opp	Total	Blue Jays	Opp	Total	Index	Blue Jays	Opp	Total	Blue Jays	Opp	Total	Index
G	81	81	162	81	81	162	--	243	243	486	243	243	486	--
Avg	.285	.264	.274	.273	.257	.266	103	.271	.252	.262	.262	.245	.254	103
AB	2734	2857	5591	2845	2670	5515	101	8070	8449	16519	8534	7980	16514	100
R	437	390	827	410	352	762	109	1186	1068	2254	1125	978	2103	107
H	778	754	1532	778	687	1465	105	2190	2133	4323	2236	1955	4191	103
2B	161	138	299	156	102	258	114	452	396	848	425	321	746	114
3B	30	19	49	12	12	24	201	81	37	118	46	34	80	147
HR	90	81	171	69	53	122	138	244	213	457	211	166	377	121
SO	404	539	943	457	484	941	99	1347	1531	2878	1490	1417	2907	99
E	50	65	115	76	74	150	77	154	177	331	192	202	394	84
E-Infield	36	49	85	52	60	112	76	124	139	263	144	168	312	84
LHB-Avg	.314	.274	.289	.313	.280	.295	98	.287	.256	.271	.276	.258	.267	101
LHB-HR	24	32	56	32	27	59	92	57	66	123	79	72	151	79
RHB-Avg	.270	.255	.263	.252	.238	.246	107	.262	.250	.256	.253	.236	.245	104
RHB-HR	66	49	115	37	26	63	182	187	147	334	132	94	226	151

1993 Lefty-Righty Stats

Many of our customers would probably pay the cover price of this book for this next bunch of pages alone. It must be nice to get the rest of the book as an added bonus. However, it's probably a bit of a shame for those who discovered this book years ago and were able to beat the pants off their table or computer game league buddies for a few years on the strength of this "secret weapon." Unfortunately for you, lefty-righty numbers are now pretty common knowledge. But here's what to do. There's a green book we know about called the **STATS 1994 Minor League Handbook** that now has lefty-righty at-bats, hits, and batting averages for triple-A players. Does Chipper Jones eat lefties for lunch? You betcha' (51-124, .411). But that's enough free information. You already got the rest of this book.

Batters vs. Left-Handed and Right-Handed Pitchers

Batter	vs	Avg	AB	H	2B	3B	HR	BI	BB	SO	OBP	SLG	Batter	vs	Avg	AB	H	2B	3B	HR	BI	BB	SO	OBP	SLG
Abbott,Kurt	L	.231	26	6	0	0	2	3	1	9	.259	.462	Bass,Kevin	L	.225	80	18	9	0	2	15	9	13	.303	.413
Bats Right	R	.257	35	9	1	0	1	6	2	11	.297	.371	Bats Both	R	.315	149	47	9	0	1	22	17	18	.389	.396
Aldrete,Mike	L	.138	29	4	0	0	2	4	5	6	.265	.345	Batiste,Kim	L	.349	43	15	1	1	4	11	1	9	.356	.698
Bats Left	R	.283	226	64	13	1	8	29	29	39	.365	.456	Bats Right	R	.257	113	29	6	0	1	18	2	20	.276	.336
Alexander,M	L	.000	0	0	0	0	0	0	0	0	.000	.000	Bautista,D	L	.167	18	3	0	0	1	2	0	2	.167	.333
Bats Right	R	.000	0	0	0	0	0	0	0	0	.000	.000	Bats Right	R	.372	43	16	3	0	0	7	1	8	.378	.442
Alicea,Luis	L	.367	79	29	5	0	1	9	9	4	.432	.468	Bean,Billy	L	.200	15	3	1	0	0	2	0	2	.188	.267
Bats Both	R	.254	283	72	14	3	2	37	38	50	.343	.346	Bats Left	R	.265	162	43	8	0	5	30	6	27	.293	.407
Allanson,Andy	L	.167	12	2	0	0	0	0	1	0	.231	.167	Becker,Rich	L	.333	3	1	1	0	0	0	1	2	.500	.667
Bats Right	R	.167	12	2	1	0	0	2	0	2	.167	.250	Bats Both	R	.250	4	1	1	0	0	0	4	2	.625	.500
Alomar,R	L	.241	166	40	8	1	4	24	12	29	.297	.373	Bell,Derek	L	.299	177	53	6	0	11	30	10	31	.342	.520
Bats Both	R	.359	423	152	27	5	13	69	68	38	.449	.539	Bats Right	R	.244	365	89	13	1	10	42	13	91	.284	.367
Alomar Jr,S	L	.283	60	17	1	1	1	9	3	9	.318	.383	Bell,George	L	.193	109	21	4	0	3	12	4	17	.217	.312
Bats Right	R	.265	155	41	6	0	5	23	8	19	.318	.400	Bats Right	R	.226	301	68	13	2	10	52	9	32	.252	.382
Alou,Moises	L	.268	164	44	10	2	5	24	11	10	.320	.445	Bell,Jay	L	.342	190	65	14	2	3	21	33	30	.449	.484
Bats Right	R	.296	318	94	19	4	13	61	27	43	.350	.503	Bats Right	R	.295	414	122	18	7	6	30	44	92	.364	.415
Amaral,Rich	L	.372	148	55	14	1	0	21	10	12	.411	.480	Bell,Juan	L	.271	144	39	6	0	3	13	14	28	.344	.375
Bats Right	R	.236	225	53	10	0	1	23	23	42	.307	.293	Bats Both	R	.198	207	41	6	3	2	23	27	48	.289	.285
Amaro,Ruben	L	.500	28	14	2	2	1	5	4	1	.563	.821	Belle,Albert	L	.327	162	53	11	0	12	39	26	25	.412	.617
Bats Both	R	.100	20	2	0	0	0	1	2	4	.174	.100	Bats Right	R	.275	432	119	25	3	26	90	50	71	.353	.528
Anderson,B	L	.259	170	44	10	0	2	17	32	38	.390	.353	Belliard,R	L	.118	17	2	0	0	0	2	1	3	.167	.118
Bats Left	R	.264	390	103	26	8	11	49	50	61	.350	.456	Bats Right	R	.258	62	16	5	0	0	4	3	10	.324	.339
Anthony,Eric	L	.247	158	39	4	1	5	25	16	38	.314	.380	Benavides,F	L	.356	59	21	3	1	1	5	1	4	.367	.492
Bats Left	R	.250	328	82	15	3	10	41	33	50	.321	.405	Bats Right	R	.260	154	40	7	2	2	21	5	23	.281	.370
Arias,Alex	L	.284	81	23	2	0	0	8	9	4	.366	.309	Benjamin,Mike	L	.316	38	12	4	0	3	8	1	2	.333	.658
Bats Right	R	.262	168	44	3	1	2	12	18	14	.333	.327	Bats Right	R	.157	108	17	3	0	1	8	8	21	.242	.213
Armas,Marcos	L	.235	17	4	1	0	1	1	0	7	.278	.471	Benzinger,T	L	.486	37	18	1	1	2	11	4	5	.512	.730
Bats Right	R	.143	14	2	1	0	0	0	1	5	.200	.214	Bats Both	R	.236	140	33	6	1	4	15	9	30	.280	.379
Ashley,Billy	L	.200	10	2	0	0	0	0	1	4	.273	.200	Berroa,G	L	.188	16	3	0	0	0	0	2	5	.278	.188
Bats Right	R	.259	27	7	0	0	0	0	1	7	.286	.259	Bats Right	R	.056	18	1	1	0	0	0	0	2	.056	.111
Aude,Rich	L	.214	14	3	1	0	0	4	0	3	.214	.286	Berry,Sean	L	.232	95	22	3	1	3	9	17	15	.348	.379
Bats Right	R	.000	12	0	0	0	0	0	1	4	.077	.000	Bats Right	R	.275	204	56	12	1	11	40	24	55	.347	.505
Ausmus,Brad	L	.295	44	13	3	1	1	4	3	7	.340	.477	Berryhill,D	L	.272	81	22	5	1	2	14	6	13	.315	.432
Bats Right	R	.241	116	28	5	0	4	8	3	21	.261	.388	Bats Both	R	.236	254	60	13	1	6	29	15	51	.283	.366
Backman,Wally	L	.000	0	0	0	0	0	0	0	0	.000	.000	Bichette,D	L	.286	119	34	11	1	4	18	10	22	.346	.496
Bats Left	R	.138	29	4	0	0	0	0	1	8	.167	.138	Bats Right	R	.317	419	133	32	4	17	71	18	77	.348	.535
Baerga,Carlos	L	.315	219	69	5	3	6	33	7	25	.345	.447	Biggio,Craig	L	.295	183	54	11	2	8	19	32	22	.408	.508
Bats Both	R	.323	405	131	23	3	15	81	27	43	.360	.506	Bats Right	R	.283	427	121	30	3	13	45	45	71	.357	.459
Baez,Kevin	L	.180	50	9	5	0	0	4	3	8	.226	.280	Blankenship,L	L	.145	83	12	3	0	0	5	24	28	.336	.181
Bats Right	R	.184	76	14	4	0	0	3	10	9	.279	.237	Bats Right	R	.213	169	36	5	1	2	18	43	36	.377	.290
Bagwell,Jeff	L	.318	179	57	17	1	10	36	30	20	.408	.592	Blauser,Jeff	L	.283	145	41	8	2	5	16	22	25	.374	.469
Bats Right	R	.320	356	114	20	3	10	52	32	53	.376	.478	Bats Right	R	.312	452	141	21	0	10	57	63	84	.410	.425
Baines,Harold	L	.260	96	25	4	0	4	18	10	16	.330	.427	Blosser,Greg	L	.000	0	0	0	0	0	0	0	0	.000	.000
Bats Left	R	.328	320	105	18	0	16	60	47	36	.408	.534	Bats Left	R	.071	28	2	1	0	0	1	2	7	.133	.107
Balboni,Steve	L	.000	0	0	0	0	0	0	0	0	.000	.000	Blowers,Mike	L	.357	154	55	14	2	10	34	17	24	.424	.669
Bats Right	R	.600	5	3	0	0	0	0	0	2	.600	.600	Bats Right	R	.227	225	51	9	1	5	23	27	74	.311	.342
Barberie,Bret	L	.312	109	34	6	0	2	3	9	15	.370	.422	Bogar,Tim	L	.243	70	17	5	0	1	7	5	9	.293	.357
Bats Both	R	.263	266	70	10	2	3	30	24	43	.334	.350	Bats Right	R	.244	135	33	8	0	2	18	9	20	.304	.348
Barnes,S	L	.278	97	27	6	1	1	19	8	14	.327	.392	Boggs,Wade	L	.262	168	44	8	1	1	25	18	18	.323	.339
Bats Right	R	.286	63	18	2	0	1	8	3	5	.304	.365	Bats Left	R	.319	392	125	18	0	1	34	56	31	.401	.372

Batters vs. Left-Handed and Right-Handed Pitchers

Batter	vs	Avg	AB	H	2B	3B	HR	BI	BB	SO	OBP	SLG
Bolick,Frank	L	.237	59	14	3	0	2	8	8	8	.333	.390
Bats Both	R	.201	154	31	10	0	2	16	15	29	.283	.305
Bonds,Barry	L	.326	218	71	15	2	15	45	39	29	.423	.619
Bats Left	R	.343	321	110	23	2	31	78	87	50	.481	.717
Bonilla,Bobby	L	.277	155	43	5	1	10	32	12	15	.325	.516
Bats Both	R	.259	347	90	16	2	24	55	60	81	.363	.524
Boone,Bret	L	.266	79	21	4	1	4	11	9	19	.337	.494
Bats Right	R	.245	192	47	8	1	8	27	8	33	.285	.422
Borders,Pat	L	.244	119	29	8	0	2	16	6	15	.278	.361
Bats Right	R	.257	369	95	22	0	7	39	14	51	.287	.374
Bordick,Mike	L	.265	162	43	10	0	1	11	19	20	.351	.346
Bats Right	R	.242	384	93	11	2	2	37	41	38	.324	.297
Boston,Daryl	L	.231	13	3	0	0	1	4	0	4	.286	.462
Bats Left	R	.263	278	73	15	1	13	36	26	53	.327	.464
Bournigal,R	L	.500	4	2	0	0	0	0	0	0	.500	.500
Bats Right	R	.500	14	7	1	0	0	3	0	2	.500	.571
Branson,Jeff	L	.253	91	23	5	0	1	3	4	22	.281	.341
Bats Left	R	.238	290	69	10	1	2	19	15	51	.273	.300
Bream,Sid	L	.276	29	8	3	0	0	5	1	7	.290	.379
Bats Left	R	.258	248	64	11	1	9	30	30	36	.337	.419
Brett,George	L	.209	187	39	7	2	2	19	7	18	.246	.299
Bats Left	R	.295	373	110	24	1	17	56	32	49	.344	.501
Brewer,Rod	L	.267	15	4	1	0	0	0	2	3	.353	.333
Bats Left	R	.288	132	38	7	0	2	20	15	23	.360	.386
Briley,Greg	L	.214	14	3	0	0	1	3	0	4	.214	.429
Bats Left	R	.192	156	30	6	0	2	9	12	38	.253	.269
Brito,B	L	.333	33	11	2	0	4	9	1	9	.353	.758
Bats Right	R	.095	21	2	0	0	0	0	0	11	.095	.095
Brooks,Hubie	L	.327	110	36	10	0	1	13	7	12	.368	.445
Bats Right	R	.207	58	12	2	0	0	11	4	15	.266	.241
Brooks,Jerry	L	.000	3	0	0	0	0	0	0	1	.000	.000
Bats Right	R	.333	6	2	1	0	1	1	0	1	.333	1.000
Brosius,Scott	L	.210	81	17	4	0	3	11	5	14	.261	.370
Bats Right	R	.273	132	36	6	1	3	14	9	23	.317	.402
Brown,Jarvis	L	.263	38	10	3	1	0	1	5	9	.349	.395
Bats Right	R	.221	95	21	6	1	0	7	10	17	.330	.305
Browne,Jerry	L	.267	60	16	2	0	1	3	3	4	.302	.350
Bats Both	R	.245	200	49	11	0	1	16	19	13	.308	.315
Bruett,J.T.	L	.000	2	0	0	0	0	0	0	1	.000	.000
Bats Left	R	.278	18	5	2	0	0	1	1	3	.350	.389
Brumfield,J	L	.303	89	27	7	0	2	5	5	9	.340	.449
Bats Right	R	.251	183	46	10	3	4	18	16	38	.312	.404
Brumley,Mike	L	.000	2	0	0	0	0	0	0	1	.000	.000
Bats Both	R	.375	8	3	0	0	0	2	1	2	.444	.375
Brunansky,Tom	L	.178	101	18	4	2	3	14	15	23	.284	.347
Bats Right	R	.187	123	23	3	1	3	15	10	36	.248	.301
Buechele,S	L	.281	128	36	9	0	5	14	19	18	.378	.469
Bats Right	R	.268	332	89	18	2	10	51	29	69	.332	.425
Buford,Damon	L	.217	23	5	3	0	0	1	0	8	.250	.348
Bats Right	R	.232	56	13	2	0	2	8	9	11	.338	.375

Batter	vs	Avg	AB	H	2B	3B	HR	BI	BB	SO	OBP	SLG
Buhner,Jay	L	.320	172	55	10	0	9	32	35	44	.435	.535
Bats Right	R	.251	391	98	18	3	18	66	65	100	.353	.450
Bullett,Scott	L	.100	10	1	0	0	0	0	1	2	.182	.100
Bats Left	R	.222	45	10	0	2	0	4	2	13	.250	.311
Burks,Ellis	L	.281	153	43	4	1	8	28	25	24	.380	.477
Bats Right	R	.272	346	94	20	3	9	46	35	73	.339	.425
Burnitz,J	L	.242	33	8	1	2	1	3	4	6	.324	.485
Bats Left	R	.243	230	56	9	4	12	35	34	60	.341	.474
Bush,Randy	L	.000	1	0	0	0	0	0	0	0	.000	.000
Bats Left	R	.159	44	7	2	0	0	3	7	13	.275	.205
Butler,Brett	L	.330	206	68	5	2	0	17	28	18	.407	.374
Bats Left	R	.282	401	113	16	8	1	25	58	51	.378	.369
Butler,Rob	L	.294	17	5	2	0	0	1	2	4	.400	.412
Bats Left	R	.258	31	8	2	0	0	1	5	8	.361	.323
Byrd,Jim	L	.000	0	0	0	0	0	0	0	0	.000	.000
Bats Right	R	.000	0	0	0	0	0	0	0	0	.000	.000
Cabrera,F	L	.280	50	14	3	0	4	10	7	13	.368	.580
Bats Right	R	.182	33	6	0	0	0	1	1	8	.206	.182
Calderon,Ivan	L	.127	63	8	2	0	0	2	5	8	.188	.159
Bats Right	R	.239	176	42	8	2	1	20	16	25	.304	.324
Caminiti,Ken	L	.246	187	46	14	0	5	36	21	22	.319	.401
Bats Both	R	.270	356	96	17	0	8	39	28	66	.322	.385
Canate,Willie	L	.222	18	4	0	0	0	1	1	9	.250	.222
Bats Right	R	.207	29	6	0	0	1	2	5	6	.343	.310
Candaele,C	L	.268	41	11	1	0	1	2	4	4	.333	.366
Bats Both	R	.225	80	18	7	0	0	5	6	10	.279	.313
Canseco,Jose	L	.237	38	9	0	0	3	9	4	9	.302	.474
Bats Right	R	.259	193	50	14	1	7	37	12	53	.310	.451
Canseco,Ozzie	L	.222	9	2	0	0	0	0	0	2	.222	.222
Bats Right	R	.125	8	1	0	0	0	0	1	1	.222	.125
Caraballo,R	L	.000	0	0	0	0	0	0	0	0	.000	.000
Bats Both	R	.000	0	0	0	0	0	0	0	0	.000	.000
Carey,Paul	L	.000	2	0	0	0	0	0	0	1	.000	.000
Bats Right	R	.222	45	10	1	0	0	3	5	13	.300	.244
Carr,Chuck	L	.254	173	44	9	1	2	15	13	33	.309	.353
Bats Both	R	.272	378	103	10	1	2	26	36	41	.335	.320
Carreon,Mark	L	.350	100	35	8	0	6	25	11	14	.409	.610
Bats Right	R	.280	50	14	1	1	1	8	2		.296	.400
Carrillo,M	L	.400	5	2	0	0	0	0	1	1	.500	.400
Bats Left	R	.240	50	12	6	0	0	3	0	6	.255	.360
Carter,Joe	L	.296	162	48	6	1	10	34	12	28	.341	.531
Bats Right	R	.238	441	105	27	4	23	87	35	85	.302	.474
Castellano,P	L	.333	9	3	0	0	0	1	2	3	.455	.333
Bats Right	R	.161	62	10	2	0	3	6	6	13	.235	.339
Castilla,V	L	.333	87	29	4	2	3	8	5	11	.370	.529
Bats Right	R	.228	250	57	5	5	6	22	8	34	.253	.360
Cedeno,A	L	.341	164	56	7	2	4	18	14	21	.400	.482
Bats Right	R	.255	341	87	17	2	7	38	34	76	.320	.378
Cedeno,D	L	.273	11	3	0	0	0	1	0	3	.273	.273
Bats Both	R	.143	35	5	0	0	0	6	1	7	.162	.143

Batters vs. Left-Handed and Right-Handed Pitchers

Batter	vs	Avg	AB	H	2B	3B	HR	BI	BB	SO	OBP	SLG	Batter	vs	Avg	AB	H	2B	3B	HR	BI	BB	SO	OBP	SLG
Chamberlain,W	L	.328	134	44	9	1	9	25	10	23	.374	.612	Daulton,D	L	.213	188	40	10	1	8	29	38	45	.346	.404
Bats Right	R	.240	150	36	11	1	3	20	7	28	.270	.387	Bats Left	R	.283	322	91	25	3	16	76	79	66	.418	.528
Cianfrocco,A	L	.282	78	22	5	0	2	15	5	16	.310	.423	Davis,Butch	L	.255	55	14	2	2	2	8	3	11	.305	.473
Bats Right	R	.229	218	50	6	2	10	33	12	53	.278	.413	Bats Right	R	.240	104	25	8	2	1	12	2	17	.255	.385
Clark,Dave	L	.250	16	4	0	0	2	4	4	8	.400	.625	Davis,Chili	L	.260	131	34	7	0	8	31	13	32	.326	.496
Bats Left	R	.272	261	71	11	2	9	42	34	50	.356	.433	Bats Both	R	.238	442	105	25	0	19	81	58	103	.327	.423
Clark,Jerald	L	.276	116	32	9	1	2	15	5	15	.323	.422	Davis,Eric	L	.219	137	30	6	0	4	19	22	26	.323	.350
Bats Right	R	.285	362	103	17	5	11	52	15	45	.325	.450	Bats Right	R	.245	314	77	12	1	16	49	33	80	.317	.443
Clark,Phil	L	.323	133	43	11	0	4	17	8	14	.368	.496	Davis,Glenn	L	.222	36	8	0	0	0	1	3	10	.282	.222
Bats Right	R	.299	107	32	6	0	5	16	0	17	.315	.495	Bats Right	R	.156	77	12	3	0	1	8	4	19	.205	.234
Clark,Will	L	.269	182	49	6	1	1	28	17	22	.335	.330	Dawson,Andre	L	.317	126	40	9	1	7	22	5	14	.353	.571
Bats Left	R	.291	309	90	21	1	13	45	46	46	.386	.492	Bats Right	R	.257	335	86	20	0	6	45	12	35	.298	.370
Clayton,Royce	L	.247	170	42	10	0	2	16	9	29	.283	.341	Decker,Steve	L	.000	7	0	0	0	0	1	3	1	.273	.000
Bats Right	R	.298	379	113	11	5	4	54	29	62	.352	.385	Bats Right	R	.000	8	0	0	0	0	0	0	2	.000	.000
Colbert,Craig	L	.136	22	3	2	0	0	2	1	6	.174	.227	Deer,Rob	L	.281	121	34	7	1	9	21	22	40	.397	.579
Bats Right	R	.200	15	3	0	0	1	3	2	7	.294	.400	Bats Right	R	.186	345	64	10	0	12	34	36	129	.267	.319
Colbrunn,Greg	L	.324	74	24	4	0	4	17	2	14	.333	.541	Delgado,C	L	.000	0	0	0	0	0	0	0	0	.000	.000
Bats Right	R	.190	79	15	5	0	0	6	4	19	.235	.253	Bats Left	R	.000	1	0	0	0	0	0	1	0	.500	.000
Cole,Alex	L	.143	21	3	1	1	0	3	1	9	.182	.286	Denson,Drew	L	.000	2	0	0	0	0	0	0	0	.000	.000
Bats Left	R	.263	327	86	8	3	0	21	42	49	.349	.306	Bats Right	R	.333	3	1	0	0	0	0	0	1	.333	.333
Coleman,Vince	L	.290	100	29	5	3	1	6	7	17	.333	.430	DeShields,D	L	.311	161	50	8	3	2	13	24	22	.407	.435
Bats Both	R	.275	273	75	9	5	1	19	14	41	.309	.355	Bats Left	R	.288	320	92	9	4	0	16	48	42	.379	.341
Coles,Darnell	L	.213	61	13	1	0	0	5	8	9	.310	.230	Destrade,O	L	.294	177	52	5	3	6	28	13	39	.344	.458
Bats Right	R	.271	133	36	8	1	4	21	8	20	.324	.436	Bats Both	R	.237	392	93	15	0	14	59	45	91	.315	.383
Conine,Jeff	L	.299	167	50	7	2	5	28	20	36	.366	.455	Devereaux,M	L	.276	156	43	9	1	5	23	19	29	.352	.442
Bats Right	R	.290	428	124	17	1	7	51	32	99	.345	.383	Bats Right	R	.240	371	89	22	2	9	52	24	70	.286	.383
Cooper,Scott	L	.257	144	37	5	2	2	17	10	25	.321	.361	Diaz,Alex	L	.382	34	13	2	0	0	0	0	6	.382	.441
Bats Left	R	.288	382	110	24	1	7	46	48	56	.367	.411	Bats Both	R	.257	35	9	0	0	0	1	0	6	.257	.257
Cora,Joey	L	.255	161	41	4	1	0	8	19	19	.337	.292	Diaz,Mario	L	.333	51	17	4	0	1	6	4	4	.375	.471
Bats Both	R	.273	418	114	11	12	2	43	48	44	.356	.371	Bats Right	R	.253	154	39	6	1	1	18	4	9	.270	.325
Cordero,Wil	L	.243	148	36	11	2	1	14	14	18	.315	.365	DiSarcina,G	L	.210	119	25	4	0	0	7	3	10	.234	.244
Bats Right	R	.251	327	82	21	0	9	44	20	42	.304	.398	Bats Right	R	.249	297	74	16	1	3	38	12	28	.288	.340
Correia,Rod	L	.326	43	14	3	0	0	0	4	4	.396	.395	Donnels,Chris	L	.242	33	8	2	1	0	1	5	3	.342	.364
Bats Right	R	.235	85	20	2	0	0	9	2	16	.278	.259	Bats Left	R	.260	146	38	12	1	2	23	14	30	.323	.397
Costo,Tim	L	.316	38	12	2	0	2	7	1	1	.333	.526	Doran,Billy	L	.200	40	8	3	0	0	5	4	1	.267	.275
Bats Right	R	.167	60	10	3	0	1	5	3	16	.200	.267	Bats Both	R	.250	20	5	1	0	0	1	2	2	.318	.300
Cotto,Henry	L	.282	149	42	5	0	2	12	5	27	.301	.356	Dorsett,Brian	L	.333	24	8	2	0	1	4	2	6	.385	.542
Bats Right	R	.198	91	18	3	0	3	9	0	13	.215	.330	Bats Right	R	.205	39	8	2	0	1	8	1	8	.225	.333
Cromer,Tripp	L	.182	11	2	0	0	0	0	1	1	.250	.182	Ducey,Rob	L	.182	11	2	0	1	0	1	0	4	.167	.364
Bats Right	R	.000	12	0	0	0	0	0	0	5	.000	.000	Bats Left	R	.297	74	22	6	2	2	8	10	13	.376	.514
Cummings,M	L	.077	13	1	0	0	0	0	0	4	.077	.077	Duncan,M	L	.273	198	54	11	1	6	24	5	29	.291	.429
Bats Left	R	.130	23	3	1	0	0	3	4	5	.250	.174	Bats Right	R	.289	298	86	15	3	5	49	7	59	.312	.409
Curtis,Chad	L	.324	148	48	8	2	2	11	21	19	.408	.446	Dunston,S	L	.429	7	3	2	0	0	2	0	0	.429	.714
Bats Right	R	.271	435	118	17	1	4	48	49	70	.345	.343	Bats Right	R	.333	3	1	0	0	0	0	0	1	.333	.333
Cuyler,Milt	L	.182	77	14	2	1	0	8	6	14	.241	.234	Dykstra,Lenny	L	.281	217	61	14	2	2	18	48	29	.414	.392
Bats Both	R	.227	172	39	9	6	0	11	13	39	.291	.349	Bats Left	R	.317	420	133	30	4	17	48	81	35	.424	.529
Dascenzo,Doug	L	.237	59	14	3	0	0	5	0	7	.233	.288	Easley,Damion	L	.361	72	26	7	0	1	3	5	9	.418	.500
Bats Both	R	.172	87	15	2	1	2	5	8	15	.242	.287	Bats Right	R	.291	158	46	6	2	1	19	23	26	.380	.373
Daugherty,J	L	.600	5	3	0	0	0	1	0	1	.600	.600	Edmonds,Jim	L	.222	9	2	0	0	0	0	1	4	.300	.222
Bats Both	R	.193	57	11	2	0	2	8	11	14	.319	.333	Bats Left	R	.250	52	13	4	1	0	4	1	12	.264	.365

Batters vs. Left-Handed and Right-Handed Pitchers

Batter	vs	Avg	AB	H	2B	3B	HR	BI	BB	SO	OBP	SLG	Batter	vs	Avg	AB	H	2B	3B	HR	BI	BB	SO	OBP	SLG
Eisenreich,J	L	.293	58	17	2	1	1	11	6	11	.354	.414	Gainer,Jay	L	.000	3	0	0	0	0	0	1	1	.250	.000
Bats Left	R	.322	304	98	15	3	6	43	20	25	.365	.451	Bats Left	R	.184	38	7	0	0	3	6	3	11	.244	.421
Espinoza,A	L	.345	113	39	9	0	2	12	4	13	.364	.478	Galarraga,A	L	.350	117	41	6	1	6	25	6	16	.383	.573
Bats Right	R	.227	150	34	6	0	2	15	4	23	.248	.307	Bats Right	R	.377	353	133	29	3	16	73	18	57	.410	.612
Espy,Cecil	L	.231	13	3	0	0	0	1	1	2	.267	.231	Gallagher,D	L	.259	143	37	7	2	4	15	11	13	.312	.420
Bats Both	R	.234	47	11	2	0	0	4	13	11	.393	.277	Bats Right	R	.310	58	18	5	0	2	13	9	5	.397	.500
Everett,Carl	L	.000	5	0	0	0	0	0	0	1	.000	.000	Gallego,Mike	L	.305	151	46	9	0	5	17	17	13	.376	.464
Bats Both	R	.143	14	2	0	0	0	0	1	8	.200	.143	Bats Right	R	.270	252	68	11	1	5	37	33	52	.356	.381
Faneyte,R	L	.222	9	2	0	0	0	0	0	2	.222	.222	Gant,Ron	L	.295	149	44	6	1	8	34	23	13	.385	.510
Bats Right	R	.000	6	0	0	0	0	0	2	2	.250	.000	Bats Right	R	.267	457	122	21	3	28	83	44	104	.331	.510
Faries,Paul	L	.154	13	2	1	0	0	0	1	0	.214	.231	Garcia,Carlos	L	.304	191	58	15	2	4	15	10	17	.337	.466
Bats Right	R	.261	23	6	1	1	0	4	0	4	.250	.391	Bats Right	R	.251	355	89	10	3	8	32	21	50	.306	.363
Fariss,Monty	L	.158	19	3	1	1	0	2	4	9	.304	.316	Gardner,Jeff	L	.174	23	4	1	0	0	0	6	7	.345	.217
Bats Right	R	.200	10	2	1	0	0	0	1	4	.273	.300	Bats Left	R	.268	381	102	20	7	1	24	39	62	.336	.365
Felder,Mike	L	.190	63	12	1	1	0	2	5	6	.271	.238	Gates,Brent	L	.256	172	44	9	0	2	18	20	24	.337	.343
Bats Both	R	.215	279	60	6	4	1	18	17	28	.259	.276	Bats Both	R	.306	363	111	20	2	5	51	36	51	.366	.413
Felix,Junior	L	.250	68	17	4	0	4	11	2	11	.271	.485	Geren,Bob	L	.280	75	21	5	0	3	5	5	10	.325	.467
Bats Both	R	.233	146	34	7	1	3	11	8	39	.277	.356	Bats Right	R	.143	70	10	1	0	0	1	8	18	.231	.157
Fermin,Felix	L	.293	157	46	9	2	1	15	6	2	.323	.395	Gibson,Kirk	L	.275	40	11	2	0	0	8	1	12	.326	.325
Bats Right	R	.248	323	80	7	0	1	30	18	12	.293	.279	Bats Left	R	.259	363	94	16	6	13	54	43	75	.338	.444
Fernandez,T	L	.248	165	41	8	2	0	14	23	7	.339	.321	Gil,Benji	L	.222	9	2	0	0	0	0	1	4	.300	.222
Bats Both	R	.294	361	106	15	9	5	50	33	38	.353	.427	Bats Right	R	.104	48	5	0	0	0	2	4	18	.173	.104
Fielder,Cecil	L	.324	142	46	11	0	8	35	38	25	.462	.570	Gilkey,B	L	.343	137	47	8	2	4	22	11	15	.396	.518
Bats Right	R	.248	431	107	12	0	22	82	52	100	.333	.429	Bats Right	R	.293	420	123	32	3	12	48	45	51	.362	.469
Finley,Steve	L	.268	164	44	6	3	2	16	5	16	.297	.378	Girardi,Joe	L	.295	78	23	5	2	1	5	7	7	.349	.449
Bats Left	R	.265	381	101	9	10	6	28	23	49	.307	.388	Bats Right	R	.289	232	67	9	3	2	26	17	34	.345	.379
Fisk,Carlton	L	.290	31	9	0	0	1	3	0	3	.290	.387	Gladden,Dan	L	.261	138	36	6	0	8	20	8	13	.304	.478
Bats Right	R	.045	22	1	0	0	0	1	2	8	.154	.045	Bats Right	R	.271	218	59	10	2	5	36	13	37	.316	.404
Flaherty,John	L	.286	7	2	2	0	0	2	1	2	.375	.571	Goff,Jerry	L	.333	3	1	0	0	0	1	0	2	.333	.333
Bats Right	R	.056	18	1	0	0	0	0	1	4	.150	.056	Bats Left	R	.294	34	10	2	0	2	5	8	7	.429	.529
Fletcher,D	L	.260	77	20	3	0	2	11	11	11	.356	.377	Gomez,Chris	L	.154	52	8	1	0	0	3	4	5	.214	.212
Bats Left	R	.254	319	81	17	1	7	49	23	29	.311	.379	Bats Right	R	.316	76	24	6	0	0	8	5	12	.366	.395
Fletcher,S	L	.268	123	33	8	1	3	17	4	8	.292	.423	Gomez,Leo	L	.224	67	15	3	0	2	6	7	16	.303	.358
Bats Right	R	.291	357	104	23	4	2	28	33	27	.357	.395	Bats Right	R	.186	177	33	4	0	8	19	25	44	.293	.345
Floyd,Cliff	L	.000	2	0	0	0	0	0	0	0	.000	.000	Gonzales,L	L	.500	2	1	0	0	0	1	1	0	.667	.500
Bats Left	R	.241	29	7	0	0	1	2	0	9	.241	.345	Bats Right	R	.000	0	0	0	0	0	0	0	0	.000	.000
Foley,Tom	L	.417	12	5	1	0	0	1	0	1	.417	.500	Gonzales,Rene	L	.295	112	33	9	0	1	8	16	14	.388	.402
Bats Left	R	.242	182	44	10	1	3	21	11	25	.279	.357	Bats Right	R	.229	223	51	8	0	1	23	33	31	.326	.278
Fox,Eric	L	.125	16	2	0	0	1	4	1	3	.176	.313	Gonzalez,Juan	L	.333	108	36	8	0	9	20	7	20	.374	.657
Bats Both	R	.150	40	6	1	0	0	1	1	4	.171	.175	Bats Right	R	.304	428	130	25	1	37	98	30	79	.367	.626
Franco,Julio	L	.265	102	27	5	1	3	18	10	21	.330	.422	Gonzalez,Luis	L	.302	172	52	10	0	3	21	13	28	.369	.413
Bats Right	R	.295	430	127	26	2	11	66	52	74	.368	.442	Bats Left	R	.299	368	110	24	3	12	51	34	55	.357	.478
Frazier,Lou	L	.295	61	18	2	0	1	4	4	9	.338	.377	Goodwin,Tom	L	.000	1	0	0	0	0	0	0	0	.000	.000
Bats Both	R	.281	128	36	5	1	0	12	12	15	.340	.336	Bats Left	R	.313	16	5	1	0	0	1	1	4	.353	.375
Fryman,Travis	L	.265	166	44	7	1	9	29	23	32	.349	.482	Gordon,Keith	L	.000	1	0	0	0	0	0	0	0	.000	.000
Bats Right	R	.313	441	138	30	4	13	68	54	96	.390	.488	Bats Right	R	.200	5	1	0	0	0	0	0	2	.200	.200
Gaetti,Gary	L	.278	97	27	7	0	7	20	13	27	.365	.567	Grace,Mark	L	.352	193	68	14	1	6	41	21	12	.412	.528
Bats Right	R	.231	234	54	13	1	7	30	8	60	.270	.385	Bats Left	R	.312	401	125	25	3	8	57	50	20	.383	.449
Gagne,Greg	L	.314	137	43	12	0	2	20	12	26	.364	.445	Grebeck,Craig	L	.222	117	26	3	0	0	6	11	16	.289	.248
Bats Right	R	.268	403	108	20	3	8	37	21	67	.303	.392	Bats Right	R	.233	73	17	2	0	1	6	15	10	.364	.301

Batters vs. Left-Handed and Right-Handed Pitchers

Batter	vs	Avg	AB	H	2B	3B	HR	BI	BB	SO	OBP	SLG	Batter	vs	Avg	AB	H	2B	3B	HR	BI	BB	SO	OBP	SLG
Green,Shawn	L	.000	1	0	0	0	0	0	0	0	.000	.000	Henderson,D	L	.225	142	32	6	0	11	29	14	36	.291	.500
Bats Left	R	.000	5	0	0	0	0	0	0	1	.000	.000	Bats Right	R	.217	240	52	13	0	9	24	18	77	.265	.383
Greene,Willie	L	.063	16	1	0	0	1	2	0	10	.059	.250	Henderson,R	L	.315	130	41	4	0	12	16	35	23	.461	.623
Bats Left	R	.206	34	7	1	1	1	3	2	9	.250	.382	Bats Right	R	.279	351	98	18	2	9	43	85	42	.421	.419
Greenwell,M	L	.304	161	49	7	2	5	26	11	14	.362	.466	Hernandez,Ca	L	.267	30	8	1	0	1	1	1	3	.290	.400
Bats Left	R	.319	379	121	31	4	8	46	43	32	.387	.485	Bats Right	R	.246	69	17	4	0	1	6	1	8	.257	.348
Gregg,Tommy	L	.000	0	0	0	0	0	0	0	0	.000	.000	Hernandez,Ce	L	.000	10	0	0	0	0	0	1	4	.091	.000
Bats Left	R	.167	12	2	0	0	0	1	0	0	.154	.167	Bats Right	R	.143	14	2	0	0	0	1	0	4	.143	.143
Griffey Jr,K	L	.318	211	67	14	0	13	36	24	38	.394	.569	Hiatt,Phil	L	.250	80	20	5	0	2	12	7	28	.307	.388
Bats Left	R	.305	371	113	24	3	32	73	72	53	.416	.644	Bats Right	R	.203	158	32	7	1	5	24	9	54	.274	.354
Griffin,A	L	.148	27	4	0	0	0	1	0	6	.148	.148	Higgins,Kevin	L	.250	16	4	0	0	0	2	0	2	.250	.250
Bats Both	R	.235	68	16	3	0	0	2	3	7	.268	.279	Bats Left	R	.218	165	36	4	1	0	11	16	15	.297	.255
Grissom,M	L	.307	192	59	13	1	7	28	16	24	.362	.495	Hill,G	L	.275	153	42	6	1	12	33	11	36	.317	.562
Bats Right	R	.295	438	129	14	1	12	67	36	52	.346	.413	Bats Right	R	.250	108	27	8	1	3	14	6	35	.293	.426
Gruber,Kelly	L	.304	23	7	1	0	1	5	0	4	.304	.478	Hocking,Denny	L	.167	6	1	0	0	0	0	1	0	.286	.167
Bats Right	R	.262	42	11	2	0	2	4	2	7	.311	.452	Bats Both	R	.133	30	4	1	0	0	0	5	8	.257	.167
Guillen,Ozzie	L	.231	130	30	4	2	0	6	2	11	.241	.292	Hoiles,Chris	L	.318	110	35	9	0	8	25	25	22	.442	.618
Bats Left	R	.300	327	98	19	2	4	44	8	30	.312	.407	Bats Right	R	.307	309	95	19	0	21	57	44	72	.406	.573
Gutierrez,R	L	.277	159	44	3	1	3	12	22	32	.365	.365	Hollins,Dave	L	.323	195	63	14	3	8	34	13	33	.369	.549
Bats Right	R	.237	279	66	7	4	2	14	28	65	.316	.312	Bats Both	R	.244	348	85	16	1	10	59	72	76	.373	.382
Gwynn,Chris	L	.176	17	3	1	0	0	2	0	2	.176	.235	Horn,Sam	L	.000	4	0	0	0	0	0	1	1	.200	.000
Bats Left	R	.307	270	83	13	4	1	23	24	32	.364	.396	Bats Left	R	.517	29	15	1	0	4	8	0	4	.516	.966
Gwynn,Tony	L	.359	192	69	14	1	3	20	11	6	.393	.490	Hosey,Steve	L	.500	2	1	1	0	0	1	1	1	.667	1.000
Bats Left	R	.357	297	106	27	2	4	39	25	13	.401	.502	Bats Right	R	.000	0	0	0	0	0	0	0	0	.000	.000
Hale,Chip	L	.143	7	1	0	0	0	1	1	2	.333	.143	Housie,Wayne	L	.250	4	1	0	0	0	1	0	0	.250	.250
Bats Left	R	.341	179	61	6	1	3	26	17	15	.411	.436	Bats Both	R	.167	12	2	1	0	0	0	1	1	.231	.250
Hamelin,Bob	L	.400	5	2	0	0	0	2	0	2	.400	.400	Howard,Chris	L	.000	0	0	0	0	0	0	0	0	.000	.000
Bats Left	R	.205	44	9	3	0	2	3	6	13	.300	.409	Bats Right	R	.000	1	0	0	0	0	0	0	0	.000	.000
Hamilton,D	L	.264	182	48	3	1	1	10	13	25	.316	.308	Howard,Dave	L	.000	0	0	0	0	0	0	0	0	.000	.000
Bats Left	R	.334	338	113	18	0	8	38	32	37	.394	.459	Bats Both	R	.333	24	8	0	1	0	2	2	5	.370	.417
Hammonds,J	L	.279	43	12	3	0	2	7	0	7	.273	.488	Howard,Thomas	L	.156	109	17	1	0	1	8	9	34	.213	.193
Bats Right	R	.323	62	20	5	0	1	12	2	9	.338	.452	Bats Both	R	.305	210	64	14	3	6	28	15	29	.350	.486
Hansen,Dave	L	.000	2	0	0	0	0	0	0	1	.000	.000	Howitt,Dann	L	.000	3	0	0	0	0	0	0	2	.000	.000
Bats Left	R	.369	103	38	3	0	4	30	21	12	.472	.515	Bats Left	R	.219	73	16	3	1	2	8	4	16	.260	.370
Harper,Brian	L	.333	123	41	9	1	5	25	8	9	.373	.545	Hrbek,Kent	L	.224	58	13	1	0	3	14	12	12	.352	.397
Bats Right	R	.295	407	120	17	0	7	48	21	20	.339	.388	Bats Left	R	.246	334	82	10	1	22	69	59	45	.358	.479
Harris,Donald	L	.225	40	9	0	0	0	4	3	7	.295	.225	Huff,Michael	L	.188	16	3	1	0	1	1	2	5	.278	.438
Bats Right	R	.167	36	6	2	0	1	4	2	11	.205	.306	Bats Right	R	.179	28	5	1	0	0	5	7	10	.342	.214
Harris,Lenny	L	.333	15	5	1	0	0	1	0	1	.333	.400	Hughes,Keith	L	.000	0	0	0	0	0	0	0	0	.000	.000
Bats Left	R	.228	145	33	5	1	2	10	15	14	.300	.317	Bats Left	R	.000	4	0	0	0	0	0	0	0	.000	.000
Haselman,Bill	L	.280	50	14	4	0	1	8	2	3	.302	.420	Hulett,Tim	L	.288	104	30	6	0	0	7	6	18	.324	.346
Bats Right	R	.241	87	21	4	0	4	8	10	16	.323	.425	Bats Right	R	.308	156	48	9	0	2	16	17	38	.384	.404
Hatcher,Billy	L	.232	138	32	7	0	1	14	7	11	.269	.304	Hulse,David	L	.257	35	9	1	1	0	5	4	7	.350	.343
Bats Right	R	.308	370	114	17	3	8	43	21	35	.360	.435	Bats Left	R	.293	372	109	8	9	1	24	22	50	.331	.371
Hayes,Charlie	L	.338	142	48	14	0	5	21	6	21	.367	.542	Humphreys,M	L	.115	26	3	2	1	0	2	4	10	.226	.269
Bats Right	R	.295	431	127	31	2	20	77	37	61	.351	.515	Bats Right	R	.333	9	3	0	0	1	4	0	1	.333	.667
Helfand,Eric	L	1.000	1	1	0	0	0	0	0	0	1.000	1.000	Hundley,Todd	L	.259	54	14	2	0	0	5	5	14	.344	.296
Bats Left	R	.167	12	2	0	0	0	1	0	1	.167	.167	Bats Both	R	.223	363	81	15	2	11	48	18	48	.257	.366
Hemond,Scott	L	.299	77	23	7	0	2	7	15	25	.409	.468	Hunter,Brian	L	.161	56	9	3	1	0	6	2	11	.183	.250
Bats Right	R	.232	138	32	9	0	4	19	17	30	.321	.384	Bats Right	R	.083	24	2	0	0	0	2	0	4	.080	.083

Batters vs. Left-Handed and Right-Handed Pitchers

Batter	vs	Avg	AB	H	2B	3B	HR	BI	BB	SO	OBP	SLG	Batter	vs	Avg	AB	H	2B	3B	HR	BI	BB	SO	OBP	SLG
Huskey,Butch	L	.067	15	1	0	0	0	0	0	4	.067	.067	Karros,Eric	L	.312	170	53	14	1	5	27	8	20	.343	.494
Bats Right	R	.192	26	5	1	0	0	3	1	9	.207	.231	Bats Right	R	.223	449	100	13	1	18	53	26	62	.267	.376
Huson,Jeff	L	.222	9	2	1	1	0	1	0	2	.222	.556	Kelly,Bobby	L	.250	96	24	6	1	3	8	3	12	.280	.427
Bats Left	R	.111	36	4	0	0	0	1	0	8	.111	.111	Bats Right	R	.348	224	78	11	2	6	27	14	31	.384	.496
Incaviglia,P	L	.278	162	45	7	2	13	42	9	34	.318	.586	Kelly,Pat	L	.283	145	41	8	0	3	17	9	20	.333	.400
Bats Right	R	.272	206	56	9	1	11	47	12	48	.319	.485	Bats Right	R	.268	261	70	16	1	4	34	15	48	.309	.383
Jackson,Bo	L	.203	133	27	1	0	9	22	11	50	.264	.414	Kent,Jeff	L	.230	148	34	9	0	0	11	10	22	.277	.291
Bats Right	R	.258	151	39	8	0	7	23	12	56	.311	.450	Bats Right	R	.287	348	100	15	0	21	69	20	66	.338	.511
Jackson,D	L	.250	84	21	3	0	2	8	3	20	.273	.357	Kessinger,K	L	.600	5	3	1	0	0	0	0	1	.600	.800
Bats Right	R	.190	179	34	6	0	4	18	7	55	.220	.291	Bats Both	R	.182	22	4	0	0	1	3	4	3	.296	.318
Jaha,John	L	.233	172	40	6	0	6	26	15	36	.296	.372	King,Jeff	L	.324	188	61	12	1	4	34	18	13	.383	.463
Bats Right	R	.280	343	96	15	0	13	44	36	73	.357	.437	Bats Right	R	.281	423	119	23	2	5	64	41	41	.345	.381
James,Chris	L	.246	118	29	10	1	8	19	13	27	.316	.551	Kirby,Wayne	L	.231	108	25	3	1	0	9	12	21	.320	.278
Bats Right	R	.357	42	15	1	0	1	7	5	13	.438	.452	Bats Left	R	.280	350	98	16	4	6	51	25	37	.325	.400
James,Dion	L	.231	26	6	1	0	0	4	3	2	.310	.269	Klesko,Ryan	L	.000	1	0	0	0	0	0	1	1	.500	.000
Bats Left	R	.341	317	108	20	2	7	32	28	29	.397	.483	Bats Left	R	.375	16	6	1	0	2	5	2	3	.444	.813
Javier,Stan	L	.271	85	23	4	1	1	8	12	10	.357	.376	Kmak,Joe	L	.221	68	15	2	0	0	3	7	8	.303	.250
Bats Both	R	.303	152	46	6	3	2	20	15	23	.365	.421	Bats Right	R	.214	42	9	3	0	0	4	7	5	.340	.286
Jefferies,G	L	.351	148	52	8	0	8	29	9	6	.394	.568	Knoblauch,C	L	.269	156	42	9	0	0	10	10	13	.321	.327
Bats Both	R	.338	396	134	16	3	8	54	53	26	.414	.455	Bats Right	R	.280	446	125	18	4	2	31	55	31	.365	.352
Jefferson,R	L	.196	107	21	4	0	1	9	9	26	.283	.262	Knorr,Randy	L	.229	35	8	1	1	1	7	4	10	.308	.400
Bats Both	R	.270	259	70	7	2	9	25	19	52	.321	.417	Bats Right	R	.258	66	17	2	1	3	13	5	19	.310	.455
Jennings,Doug	L	.250	4	1	0	0	0	1	0	0	.250	.250	Koelling,B	L	.125	8	1	0	0	0	0	0	0	.125	.125
Bats Left	R	.250	48	12	3	1	2	7	3	10	.321	.479	Bats Right	R	.000	7	0	0	0	0	0	0	0	.125	.000
Johnson,Erik	L	.500	2	1	1	0	0	0	0	0	.500	1.000	Koslofski,K	L	.250	4	1	0	0	0	0	0	2	.250	.250
Bats Right	R	.333	3	1	1	0	0	0	0	1	.333	.667	Bats Left	R	.273	22	6	0	0	1	2	4	3	.407	.409
Johnson,H	L	.162	68	11	3	0	0	2	10	12	.269	.206	Kreuter,Chad	L	.209	110	23	4	0	5	17	17	32	.313	.382
Bats Both	R	.269	167	45	5	2	7	24	33	31	.386	.449	Bats Both	R	.318	264	84	19	3	10	34	32	60	.395	.527
Johnson,Lance	L	.272	147	40	5	2	0	9	10	16	.318	.333	Kruk,John	L	.292	185	54	6	1	5	30	27	39	.377	.416
Bats Left	R	.326	393	128	13	12	0	38	26	17	.368	.420	Bats Left	R	.329	350	115	27	4	9	55	84	48	.456	.506
Jones,Chipper	L	1.000	1	1	0	0	0	0	1	0	1.000	1.000	Lake,Steve	L	.192	78	15	4	0	3	6	3	10	.222	.359
Bats Both	R	.500	2	1	1	0	0	0	0	1	.500	1.000	Bats Right	R	.286	42	12	2	0	2	7	1	9	.302	.476
Jones,Chris	L	.299	97	29	7	2	2	13	2	22	.313	.474	Laker,Tim	L	.227	44	10	1	0	0	6	0	7	.222	.250
Bats Right	R	.250	112	28	4	2	4	18	8	26	.298	.429	Bats Right	R	.167	42	7	1	1	0	1	2	9	.222	.238
Jones,Tim	L	.143	7	1	0	0	0	0	0	1	.143	.143	Lampkin,Tom	L	.114	35	4	2	0	1	5	4	6	.205	.257
Bats Left	R	.278	54	15	6	0	0	1	9	7	.391	.389	Bats Left	R	.220	127	28	6	0	3	20	16	20	.299	.339
Jordan,Brian	L	.365	63	23	4	2	7	18	5	7	.412	.825	Landrum,Ced	L	.000	0	0	0	0	0	0	0	0	.000	.000
Bats Right	R	.288	160	46	6	4	3	26	7	28	.328	.431	Bats Left	R	.263	19	5	1	0	0	1	0	5	.263	.316
Jordan,Ricky	L	.275	69	19	0	1	2	7	6	13	.329	.391	Lankford,Ray	L	.207	116	24	1	1	0	7	26	38	.357	.233
Bats Right	R	.300	90	27	4	0	3	11	2	19	.319	.444	Bats Left	R	.251	291	73	16	2	7	38	55	73	.370	.392
Jorgensen,T	L	.273	66	18	3	0	1	6	7	7	.342	.364	Lansing,Mike	L	.247	150	37	6	0	1	12	15	20	.315	.307
Bats Right	R	.186	86	16	4	0	0	6	3	14	.211	.233	Bats Right	R	.305	341	104	23	1	2	33	31	36	.369	.396
Jose,Felix	L	.094	64	6	1	0	0	4	3	15	.134	.109	Larkin,Barry	L	.358	95	34	9	0	4	21	17	7	.448	.579
Bats Both	R	.276	435	120	23	3	6	39	33	80	.327	.384	Bats Right	R	.301	289	87	11	3	4	30	34	26	.375	.401
Joyner,Wally	L	.259	166	43	12	0	2	20	18	21	.340	.367	Larkin,Gene	L	.263	38	10	2	0	0	3	2	1	.310	.316
Bats Left	R	.308	331	102	24	3	13	45	48	46	.392	.517	Bats Both	R	.264	106	28	5	1	1	16	19	15	.372	.358
Justice,Dave	L	.294	177	52	5	0	11	36	18	27	.362	.508	LaValliere,M	L	.357	14	5	1	0	0	2	0	2	.357	.429
Bats Left	R	.260	408	106	10	4	29	84	60	63	.354	.517	Bats Left	R	.239	88	21	1	0	0	6	4	12	.266	.250
Karkovice,Ron	L	.198	121	24	5	0	7	18	12	39	.281	.413	Lee,Derek	L	.000	0	0	0	0	0	0	0	0	.000	.000
Bats Right	R	.241	282	68	12	1	13	36	17	87	.290	.429	Bats Left	R	.152	33	5	1	0	0	4	1	4	.176	.182

Batters vs. Left-Handed and Right-Handed Pitchers

Batter	vs	Avg	AB	H	2B	3B	HR	BI	BB	SO	OBP	SLG	Batter	vs	Avg	AB	H	2B	3B	HR	BI	BB	SO	OBP	SLG
Lee,Manuel	L	.233	43	10	1	0	0	1	3	8	.298	.256	Mack,Shane	L	.288	118	34	8	1	2	16	4	11	.317	.424
Bats Both	R	.216	162	35	2	1	1	11	19	31	.301	.259	Bats Right	R	.273	385	105	22	3	8	45	37	65	.340	.408
Leius,Scott	L	.000	1	0	0	0	0	0	0	0	.000	.000	Maclin,Lonnie	L	.000	0	0	0	0	0	0	0	0	.000	.000
Bats Right	R	.176	17	3	0	0	0	2	2	4	.238	.176	Bats Left	R	.077	13	1	0	0	0	1	0	5	.071	.077
Lemke,Mark	L	.309	139	43	5	2	5	14	17	6	.382	.482	Magadan,Dave	L	.237	118	28	7	0	0	18	19	22	.333	.297
Bats Both	R	.229	354	81	14	0	2	35	48	44	.317	.285	Bats Left	R	.285	337	96	16	0	5	32	61	41	.394	.377
Leonard,Mark	L	.000	0	0	0	0	0	0	0	0	.000	.000	Maksudian,M	L	.000	0	0	0	0	0	0	0	0	.000	.000
Bats Left	R	.067	15	1	1	0	0	3	3	7	.190	.133	Bats Left	R	.167	12	2	1	0	0	2	4	2	.353	.250
Levis,Jesse	L	.125	8	1	0	0	0	0	1	2	.222	.125	Maldonado,C	L	.257	105	27	5	0	5	20	12	24	.333	.448
Bats Left	R	.182	55	10	2	0	0	4	1	8	.193	.218	Bats Right	R	.164	116	19	2	0	3	15	12	34	.246	.259
Lewis,Darren	L	.267	172	46	7	3	0	15	13	16	.321	.343	Manto,Jeff	L	.125	8	1	0	0	0	0	0	1	.125	.125
Bats Right	R	.246	350	86	10	4	2	33	17	24	.292	.314	Bats Right	R	.000	10	0	0	0	0	0	0	2	.091	.000
Lewis,Mark	L	.235	17	4	2	0	0	3	0	3	.235	.353	Manwaring,K	L	.315	146	46	5	0	2	18	14	32	.379	.390
Bats Right	R	.257	35	9	0	0	1	2	0	4	.257	.343	Bats Right	R	.255	286	73	10	1	3	31	27	44	.328	.329
Leyritz,Jim	L	.289	149	43	9	0	6	22	25	35	.398	.470	Marrero,O	L	.300	10	3	0	0	0	0	1	4	.364	.300
Bats Right	R	.336	110	37	5	0	8	31	12	24	.426	.600	Bats Left	R	.197	71	14	5	1	1	4	13	12	.321	.338
Lind,Jose	L	.257	105	27	6	1	0	8	2	10	.270	.333	Martin,Al	L	.191	89	17	5	1	1	8	11	27	.277	.303
Bats Right	R	.245	326	80	7	1	0	29	11	26	.271	.273	Bats Left	R	.302	391	118	21	7	17	56	31	95	.353	.522
Lindeman,Jim	L	.222	9	2	0	0	0	0	0	3	.222	.222	Martin,N	L	.000	1	0	0	0	0	0	0	0	.000	.000
Bats Right	R	.429	14	6	3	0	0	0	2	4	.429	.643	Bats Right	R	.385	13	5	0	0	0	2	1	1	.429	.385
Lindsey,Doug	L	.000	0	0	0	0	0	0	0	0	.000	.000	Martinez,Ca	L	.276	116	32	5	0	2	12	12	14	.336	.371
Bats Right	R	.333	3	1	0	0	0	0	0	1	.333	.333	Bats Right	R	.219	146	32	5	0	3	19	8	15	.260	.315
Liriano,N	L	.212	33	7	1	0	0	4	2	8	.257	.242	Martinez,Ch	L	.000	2	0	0	0	0	0	0	0	.000	.000
Bats Both	R	.331	118	39	5	3	2	11	16	14	.407	.475	Bats Left	R	.000	13	0	0	0	0	0	4	4	.235	.000
Listach,Pat	L	.279	129	36	7	1	2	14	12	21	.343	.395	Martinez,Dave	L	.259	27	7	2	1	0	1	6	5	.394	.407
Bats Both	R	.225	227	51	8	0	1	16	25	49	.306	.273	Bats Left	R	.238	214	51	10	0	5	26	21	34	.306	.355
Litton,Greg	L	.308	104	32	12	0	2	15	12	14	.379	.481	Martinez,D	L	.500	6	3	0	0	1	3	0	2	.500	1.000
Bats Right	R	.286	70	20	5	0	1	10	6	16	.346	.400	Bats Right	R	.125	8	1	0	0	0	0	1	5	.222	.125
Livingstone,S	L	.261	23	6	0	0	0	3	2	2	.320	.261	Martinez,E	L	.111	36	4	1	0	0	3	10	3	.298	.139
Bats Left	R	.295	281	83	10	2	2	36	17	30	.329	.367	Bats Right	R	.283	99	28	6	0	4	10	18	16	.393	.465
Lofton,Kenny	L	.292	195	57	9	1	0	15	30	36	.388	.349	Martinez,Tino	L	.250	132	33	8	1	5	17	10	22	.322	.439
Bats Left	R	.342	374	128	19	7	1	27	51	47	.418	.439	Bats Left	R	.272	276	75	17	0	12	43	35	34	.352	.464
Longmire,Tony	L	.000	0	0	0	0	0	0	0	0	.000	.000	Mattingly,Don	L	.264	201	53	10	0	5	34	23	19	.344	.388
Bats Left	R	.231	13	3	0	0	0	1	0	1	.231	.231	Bats Left	R	.307	329	101	17	2	12	52	38	23	.377	.480
Lopez,Javy	L	.500	2	1	0	0	0	0	0	0	.500	.500	May,Derrick	L	.247	89	22	3	1	4	22	2	13	.266	.438
Bats Right	R	.357	14	5	1	1	1	2	0	2	.400	.786	Bats Left	R	.306	376	115	22	1	6	55	29	28	.352	.418
Lopez,Luis	L	.111	9	1	0	0	0	1	0	2	.100	.111	Mayne,Brent	L	.211	19	4	0	0	0	1	1	6	.250	.211
Bats Both	R	.118	34	4	1	0	0	0	0	6	.118	.147	Bats Left	R	.258	186	48	9	1	2	21	17	25	.324	.349
Lovullo,Torey	L	.286	63	18	2	0	1	7	6	3	.352	.365	McCarty,Dave	L	.206	107	22	3	1	0	3	5	22	.248	.252
Bats Both	R	.243	304	74	18	0	5	23	30	46	.310	.352	Bats Right	R	.218	243	53	12	1	2	18	14	58	.261	.300
Lyden,Mitch	L	.500	4	2	0	0	0	0	0	2	.500	.500	McClendon,L	L	.254	142	36	10	0	0	14	18	12	.335	.338
Bats Right	R	.167	6	1	0	0	1	1	0	1	.167	.667	Bats Right	R	.103	39	4	1	0	2	5	5	5	.200	.282
Lydy,Scott	L	.213	47	10	2	0	0	2	2	20	.260	.255	McGee,Willie	L	.319	144	46	9	0	1	13	7	21	.349	.403
Bats Right	R	.236	55	13	3	0	2	5	6	19	.311	.400	Bats Both	R	.293	331	97	19	1	3	33	31	46	.354	.384
Lyons,Steve	L	.111	9	1	0	0	0	0	1	1	.200	.111	McGriff,Fred	L	.274	201	55	9	1	8	30	25	38	.354	.448
Bats Left	R	.143	14	2	1	0	0	0	1	4	.200	.214	Bats Left	R	.301	356	107	20	1	29	71	51	68	.386	.607
Maas,Kevin	L	.300	20	6	1	0	0	0	1	3	.333	.350	McGriff,Terry	L	.000	6	0	0	0	0	0	1	1	.143	.000
Bats Left	R	.191	131	25	3	0	9	25	23	29	.314	.420	Bats Right	R	.000	1	0	0	0	0	0	0	1	.000	.000
Macfarlane,M	L	.233	150	35	9	0	4	19	21	34	.341	.373	McGwire,Mark	L	.455	22	10	3	0	3	12	4	3	.556	1.000
Bats Right	R	.298	238	71	18	0	16	48	19	49	.373	.576	Bats Right	R	.290	62	18	3	0	6	12	17	16	.438	.629

Batters vs. Left-Handed and Right-Handed Pitchers

Batter	vs	Avg	AB	H	2B	3B	HR	BI	BB	SO	OBP	SLG	Batter	vs	Avg	AB	H	2B	3B	HR	BI	BB	SO	OBP	SLG
McIntosh,Tim	L	.154	13	2	1	0	0	2	0	6	.154	.231	Munoz,Pedro	L	.255	102	26	3	0	6	19	9	26	.321	.461
Bats Right	R	.000	8	0	0	0	0	0	0	1	.000	.000	Bats Right	R	.223	224	50	8	1	7	19	16	71	.281	.362
McKnight,Jeff	L	.171	35	6	0	0	0	1	2	7	.237	.171	Murphy,Dale	L	.143	28	4	1	0	0	6	4	8	.235	.179
Bats Both	R	.279	129	36	3	1	2	12	11	24	.331	.364	Bats Right	R	.143	14	2	0	0	0	1	1	7	.200	.143
McLemore,Mark	L	.216	162	35	4	1	0	12	12	24	.270	.253	Murray,Eddie	L	.311	183	57	10	0	8	25	12	17	.352	.497
Bats Both	R	.310	419	130	23	4	4	60	52	68	.383	.413	Bats Both	R	.274	427	117	18	1	19	75	28	44	.313	.454
McNamara,Jim	L	.500	2	1	0	0	0	1	0	1	.500	.500	Myers,Greg	L	.375	24	9	3	0	0	4	0	4	.400	.500
Bats Left	R	.000	5	0	0	0	0	0	0	0	.000	.000	Bats Left	R	.244	266	65	7	0	7	36	17	43	.289	.350
McNeely,Jeff	L	.200	10	2	0	0	0	1	1	1	.273	.200	Naehring,Tim	L	.395	43	17	4	0	0	4	4	6	.447	.488
Bats Right	R	.333	27	9	1	1	0	0	6	8	.455	.444	Bats Right	R	.298	84	25	6	0	1	13	6	20	.341	.405
McRae,Brian	L	.322	199	64	8	4	5	26	3	23	.340	.477	Natal,Bob	L	.219	32	7	1	0	0	1	2	5	.265	.250
Bats Both	R	.264	428	113	20	5	7	43	34	82	.318	.383	Bats Right	R	.212	85	18	3	1	1	5	4	17	.277	.306
McReynolds,K	L	.222	126	28	8	1	2	12	22	18	.333	.349	Navarro,Tito	L	.000	4	0	0	0	0	0	0	0	.000	.000
Bats Right	R	.258	225	58	14	3	9	30	15	38	.306	.467	Bats Both	R	.077	13	1	0	0	0	1	0	4	.077	.077
Meares,Pat	L	.242	95	23	1	0	0	4	4	15	.267	.253	Neel,Troy	L	.357	98	35	6	0	4	15	10	22	.427	.541
Bats Right	R	.255	251	64	13	3	0	29	3	37	.266	.331	Bats Left	R	.271	329	89	15	0	15	48	39	79	.349	.453
Mejia,Roberto	L	.306	49	15	4	3	2	9	4	10	.352	.633	Newfield,Marc	L	.259	27	7	2	0	1	5	2	4	.300	.444
Bats Right	R	.211	180	38	10	2	3	11	9	53	.253	.339	Bats Right	R	.205	39	8	1	0	0	2	0	4	.225	.231
Melvin,Bob	L	.244	41	10	2	0	1	4	3	8	.295	.366	Newson,Warren	L	.667	3	2	0	0	0	0	2	0	.800	.667
Bats Right	R	.215	135	29	5	0	2	19	4	36	.238	.296	Bats Left	R	.270	37	10	0	0	2	6	7	12	.386	.432
Merced,O	L	.297	111	33	6	3	0	14	16	17	.386	.405	Nieves,Melvin	L	.167	6	1	0	0	1	1	0	4	.167	.667
Bats Left	R	.318	336	107	20	1	8	56	61	47	.423	.455	Bats Both	R	.195	41	8	0	0	1	2	3	17	.267	.268
Mercedes,H	L	.304	23	7	1	0	0	0	0	6	.304	.348	Nilsson,Dave	L	.272	81	22	5	2	2	19	12	15	.358	.457
Bats Right	R	.125	24	3	1	0	0	3	2	9	.222	.167	Bats Left	R	.251	215	54	5	0	5	21	25	21	.328	.344
Mercedes,Luis	L	.241	29	7	2	0	0	0	3	4	.313	.310	Nixon,Otis	L	.263	152	40	1	2	1	6	18	21	.339	.316
Bats Right	R	.200	20	4	0	1	0	3	3	3	.360	.300	Bats Both	R	.272	309	84	11	1	0	18	43	42	.357	.314
Merullo,Matt	L	.000	0	0	0	0	0	0	0	0	.000	.000	Nokes,Matt	L	.100	30	3	0	0	2	3	0	6	.129	.300
Bats Left	R	.050	20	1	0	0	0	0	0	1	.050	.050	Bats Left	R	.273	187	51	8	0	8	32	16	25	.329	.444
Meulens,H	L	.159	44	7	1	0	1	1	7	16	.275	.250	O'Brien,C	L	.271	118	32	8	0	1	13	7	5	.310	.364
Bats Right	R	.222	9	2	0	1	1	4	1	3	.300	.778	Bats Right	R	.229	70	16	3	0	3	10	7	9	.316	.400
Mieske,Matt	L	.261	23	6	0	0	2	4	2	4	.320	.522	O'Brien,Pete	L	.200	25	5	0	0	0	0	3	4	.286	.200
Bats Right	R	.229	35	8	0	0	1	3	2	10	.270	.314	Bats Left	R	.265	185	49	7	0	7	27	23	17	.341	.416
Miller,Keith	L	.071	28	2	0	0	0	0	5	8	.212	.071	O'Leary,Troy	L	.111	9	1	0	0	0	0	2	2	.273	.111
Bats Right	R	.200	80	16	3	0	0	3	3	11	.235	.238	Bats Left	R	.344	32	11	3	0	0	3	3	7	.400	.438
Millette,Joe	L	.000	5	0	0	0	0	0	0	0	.000	.000	O'Neill,Paul	L	.230	135	31	6	0	2	15	9	29	.279	.319
Bats Right	R	.400	5	2	0	0	0	2	1	2	.500	.400	Bats Left	R	.342	363	124	28	1	18	60	35	40	.400	.573
Milligan,R	L	.383	133	51	13	1	4	21	26	17	.484	.586	Obando,S	L	.295	44	13	2	0	2	10	3	11	.340	.477
Bats Right	R	.223	148	33	5	0	2	15	34	36	.370	.297	Bats Right	R	.250	48	12	0	0	1	5	1	15	.280	.313
Mitchell,K	L	.394	94	37	7	1	8	16	5	7	.424	.745	Offerman,Jose	L	.250	184	46	7	2	1	19	21	18	.327	.326
Bats Right	R	.319	229	73	14	2	11	48	20	41	.370	.541	Bats Both	R	.278	406	113	14	4	0	43	50	57	.354	.333
Molitor,Paul	L	.363	171	62	13	2	7	32	26	23	.446	.585	Olerud,John	L	.291	172	50	11	0	4	28	34	23	.413	.424
Bats Right	R	.320	465	149	24	3	16	79	51	48	.385	.482	Bats Left	R	.396	379	150	43	2	20	79	80	42	.500	.678
Mondesi,Raul	L	.315	54	17	3	1	2	5	2	7	.339	.519	Oliver,Joe	L	.291	134	39	11	0	6	25	10	17	.338	.507
Bats Right	R	.250	32	8	0	0	2	5	2	9	.294	.438	Bats Right	R	.218	348	76	17	0	8	50	17	74	.251	.336
Montoyo,C	L	.500	4	2	1	0	0	3	0	0	.500	.750	Olson,Greg	L	.237	97	23	3	0	3	15	6	5	.282	.361
Bats Right	R	.000	1	0	0	0	0	0	0	0	.000	.000	Bats Right	R	.218	165	36	7	0	1	9	23	22	.316	.279
Morandini,M	L	.212	99	21	2	2	1	6	9	10	.284	.303	Oquendo,Jose	L	.125	24	3	0	0	0	0	1	2	.160	.125
Bats Left	R	.258	326	84	17	7	2	27	25	63	.317	.371	Bats Both	R	.245	49	12	0	0	0	4	11	6	.377	.245
Morris,Hal	L	.244	86	21	4	0	0	8	7	20	.305	.291	Orsulak,Joe	L	.357	42	15	1	1	0	7	1	5	.364	.429
Bats Left	R	.338	293	99	14	0	7	41	27	31	.390	.457	Bats Left	R	.275	367	101	14	3	8	28	27	20	.327	.395

Batters vs. Left-Handed and Right-Handed Pitchers

Batter	vs	Avg	AB	H	2B	3B	HR	BI	BB	SO	OBP	SLG	Batter	vs	Avg	AB	H	2B	3B	HR	BI	BB	SO	OBP	SLG
Ortiz,Junior	L	.192	99	19	7	0	0	10	3	12	.231	.263	Petralli,Geno	L	.267	15	4	1	0	0	0	2	1	.353	.333
Bats Right	R	.240	150	36	6	0	0	10	8	14	.290	.280	Bats Both	R	.237	118	28	4	0	1	13	20	16	.348	.297
Ortiz,Luis	L	.500	6	3	0	0	0	1	0	1	.500	.500	Phillips,J.R.	L	.000	2	0	0	0	0	0	0	1	.000	.000
Bats Right	R	.000	6	0	0	0	0	0	0	1	.000	.000	Bats Left	R	.357	14	5	1	1	1	4	0	4	.357	.786
Orton,John	L	.054	37	2	0	0	0	0	4	9	.146	.054	Phillips,Tony	L	.316	171	54	8	0	1	10	40	28	.444	.380
Bats Right	R	.276	58	16	5	0	1	4	3	15	.323	.414	Bats Both	R	.311	395	123	19	0	6	47	92	74	.443	.405
Owen,Spike	L	.248	137	34	6	1	1	8	8	14	.290	.328	Piazza,Mike	L	.324	142	46	8	0	13	36	13	19	.377	.655
Bats Both	R	.223	197	44	10	1	1	12	21	16	.297	.299	Bats Right	R	.316	405	128	16	2	22	76	33	67	.368	.528
Owens,Jayhawk	L	.217	23	5	1	0	1	2	2	4	.280	.391	Pirkl,Greg	L	.214	14	3	0	0	1	4	0	1	.214	.429
Bats Right	R	.206	63	13	4	0	2	4	4	26	.275	.365	Bats Right	R	.111	9	1	0	0	0	0	0	3	.111	.111
Pagliarulo,M	L	.417	36	15	2	0	0	2	2	4	.462	.472	Plantier,Phil	L	.185	119	22	2	0	7	21	13	39	.277	.378
Bats Left	R	.290	334	97	23	4	9	42	24	45	.346	.464	Bats Left	R	.259	343	89	18	1	27	79	48	85	.354	.554
Pagnozzi,Tom	L	.280	75	21	2	0	2	12	5	4	.313	.387	Polidor,Gus	L	.500	2	1	1	0	0	0	0	0	.500	1.000
Bats Right	R	.251	255	64	13	1	5	29	14	26	.290	.369	Bats Right	R	.000	4	0	0	0	0	0	0	2	.000	.000
Palmeiro,R	L	.268	149	40	7	0	2	18	12	24	.323	.356	Polonia,Luis	L	.232	112	26	1	0	0	7	3	10	.248	.241
Bats Left	R	.304	448	136	33	2	35	87	61	61	.387	.621	Bats Left	R	.280	464	130	16	6	1	25	45	43	.346	.347
Palmer,Dean	L	.257	101	26	4	0	6	17	16	32	.372	.475	Pose,Scott	L	.167	6	1	0	0	0	0	0	0	.167	.167
Bats Right	R	.242	418	101	27	2	27	79	37	122	.308	.510	Bats Left	R	.200	35	7	2	0	0	3	2	4	.243	.257
Pappas,Erik	L	.319	69	22	3	0	1	9	14	13	.434	.406	Pratt,Todd	L	.400	25	10	4	0	4	9	2	4	.464	1.040
Bats Right	R	.258	159	41	9	0	0	19	21	22	.339	.314	Bats Right	R	.242	62	15	2	0	1	4	3	15	.273	.323
Paquette,C	L	.228	136	31	4	2	5	15	9	43	.276	.397	Pride,Curtis	L	.000	0	0	0	0	0	0	0	0	.000	.000
Bats Right	R	.214	257	55	16	2	7	31	5	65	.228	.374	Bats Left	R	.444	9	4	1	1	1	5	0	3	.444	1.111
Parent,Mark	L	.364	22	8	1	0	2	6	1	4	.391	.682	Prince,Tom	L	.229	70	16	0	0	4	4	4	9	.280	.343
Bats Right	R	.188	32	6	1	0	2	6	2	10	.229	.406	Bats Right	R	.174	109	19	6	0	2	20	9	29	.268	.284
Parker,Rick	L	.375	32	12	3	0	0	4	3	4	.429	.469	Puckett,Kirby	L	.295	139	41	8	1	7	20	18	19	.371	.518
Bats Right	R	.231	13	3	0	0	0	0	0	4	.231	.231	Bats Right	R	.296	483	143	31	2	15	69	29	74	.343	.462
Parks,Derek	L	.143	7	1	0	0	0	1	1	1	.250	.143	Pulliam,H	L	.333	45	15	5	0	1	6	1	9	.362	.511
Bats Right	R	.231	13	3	0	0	0	0	0	1	.231	.231	Bats Right	R	.059	17	1	0	0	0	0	1	5	.111	.059
Parrish,Lance	L	.000	5	0	0	0	0	0	0	2	.000	.000	Quintana,C	L	.250	104	26	1	0	0	9	15	18	.342	.260
Bats Right	R	.267	15	4	1	0	1	2	4	3	.421	.533	Bats Right	R	.241	199	48	4	0	1	10	16	34	.303	.276
Pasqua,Dan	L	.400	10	4	1	0	2	4	2	4	.500	1.100	Raines,Tim	L	.348	112	39	5	0	3	18	19	9	.439	.473
Bats Left	R	.193	166	32	9	1	3	16	24	47	.290	.313	Bats Both	R	.290	303	88	11	4	13	36	45	26	.386	.482
Patterson,J	L	.200	5	1	0	0	0	1	0	1	.200	.200	Ramirez,Manny	L	.115	26	3	0	0	1	1	0	5	.115	.231
Bats Both	R	.182	11	2	0	0	1	1	0	4	.182	.455	Bats Right	R	.222	27	6	1	0	1	4	2	3	.276	.370
Pecota,Bill	L	.412	34	14	2	1	0	5	1	1	.429	.529	Ready,Randy	L	.186	43	8	1	0	0	4	4	2	.255	.209
Bats Right	R	.214	28	6	0	0	0	0	1	4	.241	.214	Bats Right	R	.286	91	26	7	1	1	6	19	6	.414	.418
Peltier,Dan	L	.125	8	1	0	0	0	1	1	1	.222	.125	Reboulet,Jeff	L	.290	93	27	5	0	0	5	13	13	.380	.344
Bats Left	R	.276	152	42	7	1	1	16	19	26	.358	.355	Bats Right	R	.238	147	35	3	0	1	10	22	24	.341	.279
Pena,Geronimo	L	.333	93	31	9	0	3	14	9	19	.385	.527	Redus,Gary	L	.302	86	26	7	2	2	10	8	12	.358	.500
Bats Both	R	.211	161	34	10	2	2	16	16	52	.298	.335	Bats Right	R	.279	136	38	5	2	4	21	15	23	.346	.434
Pena,Tony	L	.253	83	21	4	0	2	6	2	10	.264	.373	Reed,Jeff	L	.375	8	3	0	0	2	2	2	2	.500	1.125
Bats Right	R	.154	221	34	7	0	2	13	23	36	.239	.213	Bats Left	R	.252	111	28	3	0	4	10	14	20	.333	.387
Pendleton,T	L	.297	175	52	9	1	4	27	9	20	.326	.429	Reed,Jody	L	.325	123	40	8	0	0	7	11	9	.381	.390
Bats Both	R	.262	458	120	24	0	13	57	27	77	.305	.400	Bats Right	R	.258	322	83	13	2	2	24	27	31	.314	.329
Pennyfeather,W	L	.150	20	3	1	0	0	1	0	2	.150	.200	Reimer,Kevin	L	.208	106	22	5	0	1	15	8	18	.277	.283
Bats Right	R	.286	14	4	0	0	0	1	0	4	.286	.286	Bats Left	R	.263	331	87	17	1	12	45	22	54	.311	.429
Perez,Eduardo	L	.268	41	11	2	1	0	9	2	8	.318	.366	Renteria,Rich	L	.211	95	20	3	1	1	12	6	13	.255	.295
Bats Right	R	.245	139	34	4	1	4	21	7	31	.284	.374	Bats Right	R	.280	168	47	6	1	1	18	15	18	.346	.345
Perry,Gerald	L	.250	8	2	0	0	0	0	2	1	.400	.250	Reynolds,H	L	.179	134	24	4	0	0	12	6	17	.213	.209
Bats Left	R	.344	90	31	5	0	4	16	16	22	.443	.533	Bats Both	R	.279	351	98	16	4	4	35	60	30	.387	.382

Batters vs. Left-Handed and Right-Handed Pitchers

Batter	vs	Avg	AB	H	2B	3B	HR	BI	BB	SO	OBP	SLG	Batter	vs	Avg	AB	H	2B	3B	HR	BI	BB	SO	OBP	SLG
Rhodes,Karl	L	.250	8	2	0	0	2	3	4	3	.500	1.000	Saunders,Doug	L	.217	23	5	1	0	0	0	1	0	.250	.261
Bats Left	R	.283	46	13	2	1	1	4	7	6	.377	.435	Bats Right	R	.205	44	9	1	0	0	0	2	4	.239	.227
Richardson,J	L	.000	1	0	0	0	0	0	0	0	.000	.000	Sax,Steve	L	.239	67	16	4	0	0	5	4	3	.282	.299
Bats Right	R	.217	23	5	2	0	0	2	1	3	.250	.304	Bats Right	R	.231	52	12	1	0	1	3	4	3	.286	.308
Riles,Ernest	L	.143	7	1	0	0	1	2	2	3	.300	.571	Scarsone,S	L	.256	39	10	4	0	0	3	2	11	.286	.359
Bats Left	R	.191	136	26	8	0	4	18	18	37	.291	.338	Bats Right	R	.250	64	16	5	0	2	12	2	21	.273	.422
Ripken,Billy	L	.222	45	10	2	0	0	3	4	7	.280	.267	Schofield,D	L	.171	35	6	0	0	0	1	6	8	.293	.171
Bats Right	R	.172	87	15	2	0	0	8	7	12	.265	.195	Bats Right	R	.200	75	15	1	2	0	4	10	17	.294	.267
Ripken,Cal	L	.282	177	50	7	0	7	31	21	18	.355	.441	Segui,David	L	.292	144	42	7	0	5	15	17	18	.364	.444
Bats Right	R	.248	464	115	19	3	17	59	44	40	.318	.412	Bats Both	R	.265	306	81	20	0	5	45	41	35	.345	.379
Rivera,Luis	L	.239	46	11	3	0	0	0	3	12	.286	.304	Seitzer,Kevin	L	.280	143	40	5	0	4	25	17	12	.356	.399
Bats Right	R	.190	84	16	5	1	1	7	8	24	.266	.310	Bats Right	R	.263	274	72	11	2	7	32	27	36	.328	.394
Roberson,K	L	.156	64	10	1	0	2	6	1	14	.169	.266	Servais,Scott	L	.297	138	41	10	0	7	24	12	21	.357	.522
Bats Both	R	.207	116	24	3	1	7	21	11	34	.292	.431	Bats Right	R	.183	120	22	1	0	4	8	10	24	.261	.292
Roberts,Bip	L	.179	84	15	5	0	0	5	8	10	.258	.238	Sharperson,M	L	.253	79	20	4	0	2	9	2	15	.277	.380
Bats Both	R	.264	208	55	8	0	1	13	30	36	.358	.317	Bats Right	R	.273	11	3	0	0	0	1	3	2	.429	.273
Rodriguez,H	L	.000	6	0	0	0	0	0	0	3	.000	.000	Shave,Jon	L	.545	11	6	1	0	0	3	0	1	.545	.636
Bats Left	R	.229	170	39	10	0	8	23	11	36	.275	.429	Bats Right	R	.250	36	9	1	0	0	4	0	7	.237	.278
Rodriguez,I	L	.278	108	30	6	0	2	16	9	18	.325	.389	Sheaffer,D	L	.396	48	19	2	0	1	7	.1	1	.400	.500
Bats Right	R	.271	365	99	22	4	8	50	20	52	.312	.419	Bats Right	R	.244	168	41	7	1	3	25	7	14	.271	.351
Ronan,Marc	L	.000	1	0	0	0	0	0	0	1	.000	.000	Sheets,Larry	L	.000	0	0	0	0	0	0	0	0	.000	.000
Bats Left	R	.091	11	1	0	0	0	0	0	4	.091	.091	Bats Left	R	.118	17	2	1	0	0	1	2	1	.250	.176
Rossy,Rico	L	.333	27	9	3	0	2	6	2	3	.400	.667	Sheffield,G	L	.326	135	44	4	0	4	23	16	10	.400	.444
Bats Right	R	.169	59	10	1	0	0	6	7	8	.258	.186	Bats Right	R	.281	359	101	16	5	16	50	31	54	.346	.487
Rowland,Rich	L	.229	35	8	3	0	0	4	3	10	.289	.314	Shelton,Ben	L	.200	10	2	1	0	0	3	2	1	.333	.300
Bats Right	R	.182	11	2	0	0	0	0	2	6	.308	.182	Bats Right	R	.286	14	4	0	0	2	4	1	2	.333	.714
Royer,Stan	L	.294	17	5	0	0	0	3	2	7	.368	.294	Sherman,D	L	.091	11	1	0	0	0	0	1	1	.167	.091
Bats Right	R	.310	29	9	2	0	1	5	0	7	.310	.483	Bats Left	R	.250	52	13	1	0	0	2	5	7	.344	.269
Russell,John	L	.300	10	3	1	0	0	2	1	3	.364	.400	Shields,Tommy	L	.188	16	3	0	0	0	0	1	6	.235	.188
Bats Right	R	.167	12	2	0	0	1	1	1	7	.231	.417	Bats Right	R	.167	18	3	1	0	0	1	1	4	.211	.222
Sabo,Chris	L	.252	135	34	9	0	4	20	16	21	.333	.407	Shipley,Craig	L	.229	96	22	3	0	1	7	7	10	.282	.292
Bats Right	R	.261	417	109	24	2	17	62	27	84	.309	.451	Bats Right	R	.239	134	32	6	0	3	15	3	21	.270	.351
Salmon,Tim	L	.230	122	28	2	1	7	24	25	31	.368	.434	Shumpert,T	L	.000	1	0	0	0	0	0	0	0	.000	.000
Bats Right	R	.300	393	118	33	0	24	71	57	104	.386	.567	Bats Right	R	.111	9	1	0	0	0	0	2	2	.273	.111
Samuel,Juan	L	.265	98	26	4	4	1	9	10	21	.339	.418	Siddall,Joe	L	.143	7	1	0	0	0	0	0	3	.143	.143
Bats Right	R	.209	163	34	6	0	3	17	13	32	.272	.301	Bats Left	R	.077	13	1	1	0	0	1	1	2	.143	.154
Sanchez,Rey	L	.297	118	35	1	0	0	8	3	5	.314	.305	Sierra,Ruben	L	.231	199	46	8	0	8	32	20	29	.297	.392
Bats Right	R	.274	226	62	10	2	0	20	12	17	.317	.336	Bats Both	R	.234	431	101	15	5	14	69	32	68	.283	.390
Sandberg,Ryne	L	.385	109	42	5	0	1	7	8	11	.427	.459	Silvestri,D	L	.444	9	4	0	0	1	3	3	1	.583	.778
Bats Right	R	.285	347	99	15	0	8	38	29	51	.339	.398	Bats Right	R	.167	12	2	1	0	0	1	2	2	.286	.250
Sanders,Deion	L	.143	35	5	0	0	0	2	0	8	.167	.143	Slaught,Don	L	.333	120	40	5	2	2	13	6	14	.374	.458
Bats Left	R	.295	237	70	18	6	6	26	16	34	.342	.498	Bats Right	R	.284	257	73	14	0	8	42	23	42	.347	.432
Sanders,R	L	.310	129	40	6	0	6	22	12	24	.366	.496	Smith,Dwight	L	.364	11	4	3	0	0	3	0	3	.462	.636
Bats Right	R	.262	367	96	10	4	14	61	39	94	.335	.425	Bats Left	R	.298	299	89	14	5	11	32	25	48	.351	.488
Santiago,B	L	.276	123	34	8	3	4	15	15	15	.355	.488	Smith,Lonnie	L	.303	132	40	3	1	5	20	28	30	.426	.455
Bats Right	R	.214	346	74	11	3	9	35	22	73	.268	.341	Bats Right	R	.242	91	22	3	3	3	7	23	22	.412	.440
Santovenia,N	L	.000	1	0	0	0	0	0	1	0	.500	.000	Smith,Ozzie	L	.320	150	48	9	1	1	16	9	4	.354	.413
Bats Right	R	.143	7	1	0	0	0	0	0	2	.143	.143	Bats Both	R	.276	395	109	13	5	0	37	34	14	.331	.334
Sasser,Mackey	L	.286	7	2	0	0	0	1	0	0	.286	.286	Snow,J.T.	L	.218	87	19	3	1	2	10	10	18	.306	.345
Bats Left	R	.215	181	39	10	2	1	20	15	30	.274	.309	Bats Both	R	.247	332	82	15	1	14	47	45	70	.333	.425

Batters vs. Left-Handed and Right-Handed Pitchers

Batter	vs	Avg	AB	H	2B	3B	HR	BI	BB	SO	OBP	SLG
Snyder,Cory	L	.265	151	40	11	0	3	13	15	36	.333	.397
Bats Right	R	.266	365	97	22	1	8	43	32	111	.330	.397
Sojo,Luis	L	.071	14	1	1	0	0	2	3	0	.235	.143
Bats Right	R	.212	33	7	1	0	0	4	1	2	.229	.242
Sorrento,Paul	L	.241	87	21	2	0	2	11	7	31	.305	.333
Bats Left	R	.261	376	98	24	1	16	54	51	90	.347	.457
Sosa,Sammy	L	.287	150	43	8	2	10	33	13	33	.344	.567
Bats Right	R	.252	448	113	17	3	23	60	25	102	.297	.458
Spehr,Tim	L	.245	53	13	5	0	1	5	4	7	.310	.396
Bats Right	R	.206	34	7	1	0	1	5	2	13	.237	.324
Spiers,Bill	L	.176	68	12	2	1	0	4	7	17	.273	.235
Bats Left	R	.254	272	69	6	3	2	32	22	34	.310	.320
Sprague,Ed	L	.247	146	36	11	0	2	11	12	20	.304	.363
Bats Right	R	.265	400	106	20	1	10	62	20	65	.312	.395
Stahoviak,S	L	.333	3	1	1	0	0	0	0	1	.333	.667
Bats Left	R	.185	54	10	3	0	0	1	3	21	.228	.241
Stairs,Matt	L	.500	2	1	1	0	0	1	0	1	.500	1.000
Bats Left	R	.333	6	2	0	0	0	1	0	0	.333	.333
Stankiewicz,A	L	.000	5	0	0	0	0	0	1	0	.167	.000
Bats Right	R	.000	4	0	0	0	0	0	0	1	.000	.000
Stanley,Mike	L	.307	166	51	6	0	14	38	30	27	.415	.596
Bats Right	R	.304	257	78	11	1	12	46	27	58	.371	.494
Staton,Dave	L	.286	7	2	1	0	0	0	0	3	.286	.429
Bats Right	R	.257	35	9	2	0	5	9	3	9	.333	.743
Steinbach,T	L	.296	108	32	4	0	6	13	9	19	.350	.500
Bats Right	R	.281	281	79	15	1	4	30	16	46	.326	.384
Stillwell,K	L	.160	25	4	0	0	0	0	3	5	.276	.160
Bats Both	R	.242	157	38	6	2	1	14	12	28	.292	.325
Stocker,Kevin	L	.395	81	32	5	0	0	7	13	9	.479	.457
Bats Both	R	.292	178	52	7	3	2	24	17	34	.377	.399
Strange,Doug	L	.248	109	27	6	0	0	13	6	19	.282	.303
Bats Both	R	.259	375	97	23	0	7	47	37	50	.329	.376
Strawberry,D	L	.143	21	3	1	0	0	1	8	5	.367	.190
Bats Left	R	.139	79	11	1	0	5	11	8	14	.233	.342
Suero,William	L	.364	11	4	0	0	0	0	1	1	.417	.364
Bats Right	R	.000	3	0	0	0	0	0	0	2	.000	.000
Surhoff,B.J.	L	.274	186	51	13	1	3	33	14	15	.328	.403
Bats Left	R	.273	366	100	25	2	4	46	22	32	.312	.385
Sveum,Dale	L	.133	15	2	0	0	0	1	3	5	.278	.133
Bats Both	R	.188	64	12	1	2	5	13	16			
Tackett,Jeff	L	.263	19	5	0	0	0	2	3	6	.364	.263
Bats Right	R	.147	68	10	3	0	0	7	10	22	.253	.191
Tarasco,Tony	L	.500	6	3	1	0	0	1	0	0	.500	.667
Bats Left	R	.172	29	5	1	0	0	1	0	5	.194	.207
Tartabull,D	L	.200	175	35	11	1	7	23	38	50	.341	.394
Bats Right	R	.275	338	93	22	1	24	79	54	106	.375	.559
Tatum,Jimmy	L	.250	32	8	2	0	1	5	1	8	.294	.406
Bats Right	R	.182	66	12	3	0	0	7	4	19	.222	.227
Taubensee,E	L	.200	50	10	1	0	1	6	1	9	.216	.280
Bats Left	R	.261	238	62	10	1	8	36	20	35	.315	.412
Tettleton,M	L	.260	123	32	9	1	7	28	32	28	.408	.520
Bats Both	R	.241	399	96	16	3	25	82	77	111	.360	.484
Teufel,Tim	L	.286	133	38	9	2	6	23	21	22	.381	.519
Bats Right	R	.179	67	12	2	0	1	8	6	17	.247	.254
Thomas,Frank	L	.311	151	47	9	0	14	38	33	14	.419	.649
Bats Right	R	.319	398	127	27	0	27	90	79	40	.429	.590
Thome,Jim	L	.302	43	13	5	0	2	11	11	4	.456	.558
Bats Left	R	.252	111	28	6	0	5	11	18	32	.356	.441
Thompson,Milt	L	.175	57	10	0	0	0	2	6	9	.250	.175
Bats Left	R	.279	283	79	14	2	4	42	34	48	.359	.385
Thompson,R	L	.352	145	51	12	0	5	20	14	21	.409	.538
Bats Right	R	.295	349	103	18	2	14	45	31	76	.361	.479
Thompson,Ryan	L	.217	92	20	4	0	1	2	3	28	.258	.293
Bats Right	R	.265	196	52	15	2	10	24	16	53	.322	.515
Thon,Dickie	L	.270	122	33	3	0	1	15	13	21	.336	.320
Bats Right	R	.268	123	33	7	1	0	18	9	18	.311	.341
Thurman,Gary	L	.276	58	16	2	1	0	8	5	15	.328	.345
Bats Right	R	.097	31	3	0	1	0	5	6	15	.243	.161
Tingley,Ron	L	.167	54	9	2	0	0	7	5	14	.233	.204
Bats Right	R	.250	36	9	5	0	0	5	4	8	.341	.389
Tinsley,Lee	L	.000	5	0	0	0	0	0	1	2	.167	.000
Bats Both	R	.214	14	3	1	0	1	2	1	7	.267	.500
Tomberlin,A	L	.167	6	1	0	0	0	0	0	4	.167	.167
Bats Left	R	.306	36	11	0	1	1	5	2	10	.359	.444
Trammell,Alan	L	.289	135	39	8	0	7	21	21	13	.386	.504
Bats Right	R	.350	266	93	17	3	5	39	17	25	.389	.492
Treadway,Jeff	L	.105	19	2	0	0	0	0	2	2	.227	.105
Bats Left	R	.322	202	65	14	1	2	27	12	19	.359	.431
Tubbs,Greg	L	.048	21	1	0	0	0	0	2	5	.130	.048
Bats Right	R	.263	38	10	0	0	1	2	12	5	.451	.342
Tucker,S	L	.250	8	2	0	0	0	1	1	2	.333	.250
Bats Right	R	.167	18	3	1	0	0	2	1	1	.211	.222
Turang,Brian	L	.302	63	19	6	0	0	5	7	3	.371	.397
Bats Right	R	.208	77	16	5	1	0	2	10	17	.315	.299
Turner,Chris	L	.500	12	6	2	0	0	2	5	3	.647	.667
Bats Right	R	.238	63	15	3	0	1	11	4	13	.290	.333
Uribe,Jose	L	.294	17	5	1	0	0	2	2	1	.400	.353
Bats Both	R	.222	36	8	0	0	0	1	6	4	.333	.222
Valentin,John	L	.248	129	32	11	1	3	10	13	20	.319	.419
Bats Right	R	.289	339	98	29	2	8	56	36	57	.356	.457
Valentin,Jose	L	.263	19	5	0	1	0	1	1	6	.333	.368
Bats Both	R	.235	34	8	1	0	0	6	6	10	.350	.412
Valle,Dave	L	.280	118	33	6	0	5	17	13	12	.370	.458
Bats Right	R	.249	305	76	13	0	8	46	35	44	.347	.370
Van Burkleo,T	L	.333	3	1	1	0	0	0	0	1	.333	.667
Bats Left	R	.133	30	4	2	0	1	1	6	8	.278	.300
Van Slyke,A	L	.308	117	36	3	1	1	14	7	14	.347	.376
Bats Left	R	.311	206	64	10	3	7	36	17	26	.362	.490
VanderWal,J	L	.118	17	2	1	0	0	0	4	1	.286	.176
Bats Left	R	.242	198	48	6	4	5	30	23	29	.323	.389

Batters vs. Left-Handed and Right-Handed Pitchers

Batter	vs	Avg	AB	H	2B	3B	HR	BI	BB	SO	OBP	SLG	Batter	vs	Avg	AB	H	2B	3B	HR	BI	BB	SO	OBP	SLG
Varsho,Gary	L	.400	5	2	0	0	0	0	0	2	.400	.400	White,Derrick	L	.348	23	8	2	0	2	3	1	6	.400	.696
Bats Left	R	.222	90	20	6	0	2	11	9	17	.297	.356	Bats Right	R	.115	26	3	1	0	0	1	1	6	.148	.154
Vaughn,Greg	L	.319	166	53	10	1	7	22	37	29	.443	.518	White,Devon	L	.254	185	47	15	1	3	16	15	37	.324	.395
Bats Right	R	.246	403	99	18	1	23	75	52	89	.336	.467	Bats Both	R	.281	413	116	27	5	12	36	42	90	.349	.458
Vaughn,Mo	L	.268	164	44	9	0	12	39	16	48	.351	.543	White,Rondell	L	.296	27	8	1	0	2	8	2	6	.345	.556
Bats Left	R	.309	375	116	25	1	17	62	63	82	.407	.517	Bats Right	R	.239	46	11	2	1	0	7	5	10	.308	.326
Velarde,Randy	L	.345	116	40	7	2	6	13	10	15	.402	.595	Whiten,Mark	L	.231	160	37	2	0	8	26	15	22	.296	.394
Bats Right	R	.255	110	28	6	0	1	11	8	24	.317	.336	Bats Both	R	.261	402	105	11	4	17	73	43	88	.333	.435
Velasquez,G	L	.143	14	2	0	0	1	2	0	8	.143	.357	Whitmore,D	L	.128	39	5	3	0	0	2	1	16	.209	.205
Bats Left	R	.217	129	28	2	0	2	18	13	27	.287	.279	Bats Left	R	.218	211	46	5	2	4	17	9	56	.257	.318
Ventura,Robin	L	.267	176	47	12	0	5	29	26	42	.361	.420	Wilkerson,C	L	.000	7	0	0	0	0	0	0	1	.000	.000
Bats Left	R	.259	378	98	15	1	17	65	79	40	.387	.439	Bats Both	R	.190	21	4	0	0	0	1	1	5	.227	.190
Villanueva,H	L	.167	12	2	0	0	2	5	0	4	.167	.667	Wilkins,Rick	L	.224	67	15	3	0	3	10	8	22	.325	.403
Bats Right	R	.140	43	6	1	0	1	4	4	13	.213	.233	Bats Left	R	.317	379	120	20	1	27	63	42	77	.385	.588
Vina,Fernando	L	.000	2	0	0	0	0	0	0	0	.000	.000	Williams,B	L	.325	191	62	13	0	7	29	26	33	.402	.503
Bats Left	R	.233	43	10	2	0	0	2	4	3	.340	.279	Bats Both	R	.239	376	90	18	4	5	39	27	73	.297	.348
Vizcaino,Jose	L	.297	128	38	4	0	0	8	14	15	.364	.328	Williams,G	L	.139	36	5	0	1	0	2	1	6	.179	.194
Bats Both	R	.284	423	120	15	4	4	46	32	56	.333	.366	Bats Right	R	.161	31	5	2	2	0	4	0	8	.188	.355
Vizquel,Omar	L	.197	132	26	6	0	0	6	11	16	.264	.242	Williams,M	L	.328	186	61	11	2	17	42	11	19	.363	.683
Bats Both	R	.273	428	117	8	2	2	25	39	55	.336	.315	Bats Right	R	.277	393	109	22	2	21	68	16	61	.306	.504
Voigt,Jack	L	.352	91	32	8	0	6	19	9	15	.410	.637	Wilson,Craig	L	.250	12	3	0	0	1	2	2	1	.357	.500
Bats Right	R	.213	61	13	3	1	0	4	16	18	.377	.295	Bats Right	R	.270	37	10	1	0	0	1	5	5	.357	.297
Walbeck,Matt	L	.091	11	1	0	0	0	2	1	0	.167	.091	Wilson,Dan	L	.167	18	3	0	0	0	1	1	3	.211	.167
Bats Both	R	.263	19	5	2	0	1	4	0	6	.263	.526	Bats Right	R	.241	58	14	3	0	0	7	8	13	.328	.293
Walewander,J	L	.500	2	1	0	0	0	2	1	0	.500	.500	Wilson,Glenn	L	.167	12	2	0	0	0	0	0	7	.167	.167
Bats Both	R	.000	6	0	0	0	0	1	4	1	.400	.000	Bats Right	R	.000	2	0	0	0	0	0	0	2	.000	.000
Walker,Chico	L	.319	72	23	6	1	2	11	3	4	.347	.514	Wilson,Nigel	L	.000	2	0	0	0	0	0	0	2	.000	.000
Bats Both	R	.177	141	25	1	0	3	8	11	25	.234	.248	Bats Left	R	.000	14	0	0	0	0	0	0	9	.000	.000
Walker,Larry	L	.238	185	44	5	2	7	27	24	28	.336	.400	Wilson,Willie	L	.235	102	24	4	0	0	4	3	12	.257	.275
Bats Left	R	.282	305	86	19	3	15	59	56	48	.391	.511	Bats Both	R	.277	119	33	7	3	1	7	8	28	.336	.412
Wallach,Tim	L	.194	139	27	5	0	5	21	6	23	.223	.338	Winfield,Dave	L	.292	137	40	9	1	4	19	11	21	.345	.460
Bats Right	R	.234	338	79	14	1	7	41	26	47	.290	.343	Bats Right	R	.263	410	108	18	1	17	57	34	85	.318	.437
Walters,Dan	L	.324	37	12	3	0	0	5	4	2	.390	.405	Womack,Tony	L	.000	5	0	0	0	0	0	0	1	.000	.000
Bats Right	R	.123	57	7	0	0	1	5	3	11	.164	.175	Bats Left	R	.105	19	2	0	0	0	0	3	2	.227	.105
Walton,Jerome	L	.000	1	0	0	0	0	0	1	1	.500	.000	Wood,Ted	L	.000	1	0	0	0	0	0	1	0	.500	.000
Bats Right	R	.000	1	0	0	0	0	0	0	1	.000	.000	Bats Left	R	.200	25	5	1	0	0	3	2	3	.259	.240
Ward,Turner	L	.367	30	11	2	1	1	6	3	5	.424	.600	Woodson,Tracy	L	.208	53	11	2	0	0	2	1	10	.218	.245
Bats Both	R	.153	137	21	2	1	3	22	20	21	.259	.248	Bats Right	R	.208	24	5	0	0	0	0	0	4	.208	.208
Webster,Lenny	L	.267	30	8	1	0	0	4	4	2	.353	.300	Wrona,Rick	L	.333	3	1	0	0	0	0	0	1	.333	.333
Bats Right	R	.171	76	13	1	0	1	4	7	6	.241	.224	Bats Right	R	.000	5	0	0	0	0	1	0	0	.000	.000
Webster,Mitch	L	.275	69	19	4	2	0	6	2	8	.292	.391	Yelding,Eric	L	.313	32	10	2	0	0	3	3	3	.371	.375
Bats Both	R	.223	103	23	2	0	2	8	9	16	.293	.301	Bats Right	R	.158	76	12	3	1	1	9	8	19	.238	.263
Wedge,Eric	L	.000	2	0	0	0	0	0	0	2	.000	.000	Young,Eric	L	.289	128	37	5	3	0	13	16	12	.372	.375
Bats Right	R	.222	9	2	0	0	0	1	0	2	.222	.222	Bats Right	R	.262	362	95	11	5	3	29	47	29	.349	.345
Wehner,John	L	.050	20	1	0	0	0	0	5	6	.240	.050	Young,Gerald	L	.000	3	0	0	0	0	0	0	0	.000	.000
Bats Right	R	.267	15	4	0	0	0	0	1	4	.313	.267	Bats Both	R	.063	16	1	0	0	0	1	4	1	.250	.063
Weiss,Walt	L	.234	128	30	6	0	0	11	23	19	.353	.281	Young,Kevin	L	.237	169	40	11	0	3	14	16	31	.303	.355
Bats Both	R	.277	372	103	8	2	1	28	56	54	.372	.317	Bats Right	R	.236	280	66	13	3	3	33	20	51	.298	.336
Whitaker,Lou	L	.122	49	6	1	0	0	8	7	10	.254	.143	Yount,Robin	L	.262	122	32	5	1	2	14	19	23	.362	.369
Bats Left	R	.314	334	105	31	1	9	59	71	36	.434	.494	Bats Right	R	.256	332	85	20	2	6	37	25	70	.313	.383

Batters vs. Left-Handed and Right-Handed Pitchers

Batter	vs	Avg	AB	H	2B	3B	HR	BI	BB	SO	OBP	SLG
Zambrano,E	L	.167	6	1	0	0	0	0	0	0	.167	.167
Bats Right	R	.364	11	4	0	0	0	2	1	3	.417	.364
Zeile,Todd	L	.271	133	36	7	1	4	24	18	19	.355	.429
Bats Right	R	.279	438	122	29	0	13	79	52	57	.352	.434
Zupcic,Bob	L	.216	97	21	6	2	2	6	11	14	.303	.381
Bats Right	R	.254	189	48	18	0	0	20	16	40	.311	.349
AL	L	.264	--	--	--	--	--	--	--	--	.336	.404
	R	.267	--	--	--	--	--	--	--	--	.338	.409
NL	L	.272	--	--	--	--	--	--	--	--	.333	.413
	R	.260	--	--	--	--	--	--	--	--	.325	.393
MLB	L	.268	--	--	--	--	--	--	--	--	.335	.409
	R	.264	--	--	--	--	--	--	--	--	.331	.401

Pitchers vs. Left-Handed and Right-Handed Batters

Pitcher	vs	Avg	AB	H	2B	3B	HR	BI	BB	SO	OBP	SLG	Pitcher	vs	Avg	AB	H	2B	3B	HR	BI	BB	SO	OBP	SLG
Abbott,Jim	L	.283	106	30	7	0	0	7	12	8	.364	.349	Batchelor,R	L	.368	19	7	1	0	1	5	1	2	.381	.579
Throws Left	R	.270	708	191	32	0	22	97	61	87	.327	.408	Throws Right	R	.350	20	7	1	0	0	1	2	2	.391	.400
Abbott,Paul	L	.244	41	10	2	1	1	5	8	5	.367	.415	Bautista,Jose	L	.232	185	43	8	0	3	19	19	25	.311	.324
Throws Right	R	.281	32	9	3	0	4	8	3	2	.343	.750	Throws Right	R	.264	235	62	11	2	8	28	8	38	.293	.430
Agosto,Juan	L	.333	12	4	1	0	1	3	0	1	.333	.667	Beck,Rod	L	.180	161	29	2	0	6	13	11	56	.231	.304
Throws Left	R	.286	14	4	0	0	0	3	0	2	.286	.286	Throws Right	R	.228	123	28	3	0	5	13	2	30	.254	.374
Aguilera,Rick	L	.200	145	29	5	2	3	13	8	30	.247	.324	Bedrosian,S	L	.203	74	15	2	0	2	12	5	16	.256	.311
Throws Right	R	.250	124	31	6	0	6	18	6	29	.282	.444	Throws Right	R	.188	101	19	5	0	2	12	9	17	.257	.297
Aldred,Scott	L	.429	7	3	0	0	1	4	2	2	.556	.857	Belcher,Tim	L	.259	394	102	18	3	8	50	48	52	.342	.381
Throws Left	R	.356	45	16	5	0	1	10	8	7	.463	.533	Throws Right	R	.241	398	96	15	4	11	40	26	83	.295	.382
Alvarez,W	L	.258	89	23	2	0	1	9	25	20	.432	.315	Belinda,Stan	L	.303	119	36	5	2	5	18	10	21	.362	.504
Throws Left	R	.227	640	145	26	1	13	57	97	135	.330	.331	Throws Right	R	.201	144	29	6	0	1	21	7	34	.240	.264
Andersen,L	L	.291	86	25	1	1	2	14	4	23	.330	.395	Bell,Eric	L	.500	8	4	0	0	0	0	1	1	.556	.500
Throws Right	R	.199	146	29	4	2	2	12	17	44	.282	.295	Throws Left	R	.250	24	6	1	0	0	5	1	1	.280	.292
Anderson,B	L	.167	6	1	0	0	0	1	0	0	.167	.167	Benes,Andy	L	.242	433	105	17	5	10	39	52	69	.327	.374
Throws Left	R	.270	37	10	3	1	1	5	2	4	.308	.486	Throws Right	R	.221	429	95	20	2	13	51	34	110	.278	.368
Anderson,Mike	L	.500	14	7	0	0	3	9	2	3	.563	1.143	Bere,Jason	L	.212	264	56	7	0	2	18	54	51	.348	.261
Throws Right	R	.385	13	5	0	0	0	1	1	1	.429	.385	Throws Right	R	.209	254	53	7	1	10	32	27	78	.293	.362
Appier,Kevin	L	.240	438	105	19	1	5	37	47	82	.311	.322	Bergman,Sean	L	.297	64	19	0	2	4	14	10	6	.395	.547
Throws Right	R	.184	425	78	20	2	3	26	34	104	.245	.261	Throws Right	R	.292	96	28	3	0	2	13	13	13	.373	.385
Aquino,Luis	L	.257	237	61	10	1	5	16	21	34	.320	.371	Bielecki,Mike	L	.312	141	44	7	0	4	20	14	22	.372	.447
Throws Right	R	.300	180	54	13	1	1	21	19	33	.376	.400	Throws Right	R	.309	149	46	11	0	4	16	9	16	.354	.463
Armstrong,J	L	.288	416	120	23	2	22	60	57	55	.373	.512	Black,Bud	L	.294	51	15	2	0	1	4	3	2	.333	.392
Throws Right	R	.250	360	90	12	4	7	38	21	63	.296	.364	Throws Left	R	.250	296	74	8	2	12	32	30	43	.319	.412
Arocha,Rene	L	.313	352	110	16	5	9	44	19	35	.348	.463	Blair,Willie	L	.282	308	87	17	4	8	47	26	44	.336	.442
Throws Right	R	.232	375	87	20	2	11	39	12	61	.258	.384	Throws Right	R	.331	293	97	13	2	12	43	16	40	.365	.512
Ashby,Andy	L	.307	274	84	7	2	7	41	31	35	.380	.423	Boddicker,M	L	.392	130	51	6	1	6	20	7	9	.429	.592
Throws Right	R	.365	230	84	22	1	12	49	25	42	.422	.626	Throws Right	R	.265	98	26	4	1	0	13	8	15	.333	.327
Assenmacher,P	L	.239	92	22	1	0	4	14	9	25	.314	.380	Boever,Joe	L	.291	172	50	12	1	4	30	21	20	.365	.442
Throws Left	R	.271	118	32	8	0	1	12	13	20	.344	.364	Throws Right	R	.235	217	51	10	2	5	25	23	43	.312	.369
Astacio,Pedro	L	.240	391	94	18	0	9	40	36	67	.303	.355	Bohanon,Brian	L	.319	91	29	3	0	2	19	15	12	.426	.418
Throws Right	R	.238	298	71	14	2	5	23	32	55	.317	.349	Throws Left	R	.289	270	78	19	1	6	34	31	33	.360	.433
Austin,James	L	.297	37	11	2	0	1	4	1	3	.316	.432	Bolton,Rodney	L	.337	92	31	4	2	1	19	8	8	.386	.457
Throws Right	R	.200	85	17	2	0	2	9	12	12	.306	.294	Throws Right	R	.289	83	24	2	0	3	13	8	9	.347	.422
Avery,Steve	L	.231	143	33	6	0	2	12	11	32	.286	.315	Bolton,Tom	L	.266	94	25	5	0	2	13	12	20	.361	.383
Throws Left	R	.268	684	183	29	3	12	62	32	93	.297	.371	Throws Left	R	.287	307	88	17	2	3	42	33	46	.363	.384
Ayala,Bobby	L	.270	185	50	8	1	6	21	26	36	.367	.422	Bones,Ricky	L	.256	390	100	21	6	12	46	27	12	.303	.433
Throws Right	R	.277	202	56	7	1	10	45	19	29	.350	.470	Throws Right	R	.298	410	122	20	5	16	54	36	51	.363	.488
Ayrault,Bob	L	.317	41	13	3	0	0	4	8	2	.420	.390	Borbon,Pedro	L	.000	2	0	0	0	0	0	3	1	.600	.000
Throws Right	R	.295	78	23	4	2	2	22	8	13	.364	.474	Throws Right	R	.600	5	3	1	0	0	1	0	1	.600	.800
Bailey,Cory	L	.333	18	6	1	1	0	4	7	3	.520	.500	Bosio,Chris	L	.258	299	77	10	4	8	33	35	51	.336	.398
Throws Right	R	.176	34	6	0	0	0	4	5	8	.275	.176	Throws Right	R	.201	303	61	14	0	6	26	24	68	.269	.307
Ballard,Jeff	L	.328	61	20	3	0	0	6	6	8	.382	.377	Boskie,Shawn	L	.218	110	24	4	0	3	9	12	18	.306	.336
Throws Left	R	.333	150	50	9	2	3	19	9	8	.379	.480	Throws Right	R	.291	134	39	7	2	4	19	9	21	.356	.463
Bankhead,S	L	.264	106	28	6	0	2	13	15	19	.352	.377	Bottenfield,K	L	.325	286	93	19	1	11	33	38	22	.405	.514
Throws Right	R	.238	130	31	5	0	5	19	14	28	.306	.392	Throws Right	R	.267	322	86	16	2	13	57	33	41	.341	.450
Banks,Willie	L	.290	393	114	21	1	10	37	43	80	.358	.425	Boucher,Denis	L	.263	19	5	2	1	0	4	1	4	.273	.474
Throws Right	R	.265	272	72	17	0	7	33	35	58	.353	.404	Throws Left	R	.221	86	19	2	1	1	3	2	10	.236	.302
Barnes,Brian	L	.352	88	31	8	1	2	16	17	12	.453	.534	Bowen,Ryan	L	.278	302	84	13	1	5	35	46	46	.372	.377
Throws Left	R	.251	295	74	15	2	7	41	31	48	.320	.386	Throws Right	R	.247	292	72	15	2	6	31	41	52	.342	.373

Pitchers vs. Left-Handed and Right-Handed Batters

Pitcher	vs	Avg	AB	H	2B	3B	HR	BI	BB	SO	OBP	SLG
Brantley,Jeff	L	.285	221	63	13	2	11	26	33	30	.374	.511
Throws Right	R	.231	212	49	2	1	8	23	13	46	.295	.363
Brennan,Bill	L	.333	30	10	1	0	2	5	7	7	.459	.567
Throws Right	R	.240	25	6	1	0	0	5	1	4	.286	.280
Brewer,Billy	L	.183	60	11	0	0	3	11	9	14	.286	.333
Throws Left	R	.267	75	20	4	1	3	5	11	14	.360	.467
Brink,Brad	L	.133	15	2	1	0	0	1	2	5	.235	.200
Throws Right	R	.167	6	1	0	0	1	1	1	3	.286	.667
Briscoe,John	L	.405	42	17	4	0	0	9	13	9	.536	.500
Throws Right	R	.173	52	9	2	0	2	7	13	15	.333	.327
Brocail,Doug	L	.292	243	71	11	2	8	35	30	30	.367	.453
Throws Right	R	.274	263	72	14	2	8	30	12	40	.309	.433
Bronkey,Jeff	L	.283	46	13	1	0	1	7	3	7	.320	.370
Throws Right	R	.286	91	26	7	0	3	15	8	11	.347	.462
Bross,Terry	L	.333	3	1	0	0	0	1	1	1	.500	.333
Throws Right	R	.333	6	2	0	0	1	5	0	0	.333	.833
Brow,Scott	L	.205	39	8	1	0	0	5	7	5	.319	.231
Throws Right	R	.367	30	11	1	0	2	7	3	2	.429	.600
Brown,Kevin	L	.254	512	130	22	2	9	52	50	75	.324	.357
Throws Right	R	.251	391	98	19	2	5	35	24	67	.311	.348
Browning,Tom	L	.250	76	19	4	0	2	6	7	9	.310	.382
Throws Left	R	.348	402	140	28	3	13	52	13	44	.369	.530
Brummett,Greg	L	.348	132	46	5	1	6	24	21	11	.427	.538
Throws Right	R	.250	144	36	4	1	6	16	7	19	.283	.417
Bullinger,Jim	L	.360	25	9	3	0	1	6	7	3	.485	.600
Throws Right	R	.225	40	9	2	1	0	2	2	7	.262	.325
Burba,Dave	L	.320	150	48	4	0	6	24	14	25	.381	.467
Throws Right	R	.225	209	47	8	1	8	29	23	63	.303	.388
Burgos,E	L	.000	0	0	0	0	0	0	1	0	1.000	.000
Throws Left	R	.238	21	5	1	0	0	1	5	6	.407	.286
Burkett,John	L	.282	464	131	16	4	8	50	22	71	.318	.386
Throws Right	R	.224	415	93	14	3	10	40	18	74	.269	.345
Burns,Todd	L	.230	139	32	10	1	4	19	14	16	.305	.403
Throws Right	R	.278	227	63	10	4	10	41	27	29	.350	.489
Bushing,Chris	L	.333	6	2	1	0	1	2	2	0	.444	1.000
Throws Right	R	.500	14	7	2	1	0	4	2	3	.563	.786
Butcher,Mike	L	.182	44	8	2	0	1	3	5	13	.294	.295
Throws Right	R	.220	59	13	0	0	1	12	10	11	.319	.305
Cadaret,Greg	L	.333	63	21	2	0	0	8	7	6	.408	.365
Throws Left	R	.273	121	33	6	0	3	22	23	19	.393	.397
Campbell,K	L	.417	24	10	1	0	0	3	5	4	.517	.458
Throws Right	R	.250	40	10	4	0	1	9	6	5	.354	.425
Candelaria,J	L	.290	31	9	2	0	0	4	1	12	.333	.355
Throws Left	R	.327	49	16	3	2	2	14	8	5	.414	.592
Candiotti,Tom	L	.231	415	96	15	2	5	39	46	75	.305	.313
Throws Right	R	.251	382	96	18	2	7	36	25	80	.304	.364
Carpenter,C	L	.327	110	36	11	1	3	20	14	13	.395	.527
Throws Right	R	.189	148	28	2	1	2	14	11	40	.259	.257
Cary,Chuck	L	.250	32	8	3	0	0	6	4	4	.375	.344
Throws Left	R	.311	45	14	3	1	1	11	7	6	.382	.489

Pitcher	vs	Avg	AB	H	2B	3B	HR	BI	BB	SO	OBP	SLG
Casian,Larry	L	.289	76	22	4	0	1	13	1	12	.296	.382
Throws Left	R	.257	144	37	8	0	0	11	13	19	.318	.313
Castillo,F	L	.287	268	77	13	2	14	45	25	37	.350	.507
Throws Right	R	.298	285	85	15	4	6	30	14	47	.345	.442
Castillo,Tony	L	.213	61	13	1	1	1	9	1	7	.222	.311
Throws Left	R	.256	121	31	3	1	3	14	21	21	.364	.372
Charlton,Norm	L	.095	21	2	0	0	0	3	5	9	.269	.095
Throws Left	R	.196	102	20	3	0	4	17	12	39	.278	.343
Christopher,M	L	.391	23	9	1	0	2	2	1	3	.417	.696
Throws Right	R	.192	26	5	0	0	1	4	1	5	.222	.308
Clark,Mark	L	.320	200	64	10	1	8	24	8	24	.349	.500
Throws Right	R	.243	226	55	11	2	10	29	17	33	.295	.442
Clemens,Roger	L	.260	404	105	19	3	8	44	51	84	.346	.381
Throws Right	R	.223	314	70	12	2	9	47	16	76	.273	.360
Cone,David	L	.226	500	113	16	3	14	52	66	81	.319	.354
Throws Right	R	.219	420	92	27	1	6	37	48	110	.304	.331
Converse,Jim	L	.326	46	15	5	0	0	5	9	5	.436	.435
Throws Right	R	.250	32	8	2	0	0	7	5	5	.342	.313
Cook,Andy	L	.125	8	1	0	0	0	0	5	1	.462	.125
Throws Right	R	.250	12	3	1	0	1	2	2	3	.357	.583
Cook,Dennis	L	.259	54	14	4	0	2	10	2	10	.276	.444
Throws Left	R	.308	156	48	13	4	7	23	14	24	.372	.577
Cook,Mike	L	.200	5	1	0	0	0	0	1	1	.333	.200
Throws Right	R	.000	6	0	0	0	0	2	1	2	.143	.000
Cooke,Steve	L	.265	136	36	7	3	2	20	12	25	.325	.404
Throws Left	R	.257	665	171	51	3	20	74	47	107	.306	.433
Cormier,Rheal	L	.207	145	30	3	0	3	10	8	23	.248	.290
Throws Left	R	.310	429	133	36	3	15	60	19	52	.342	.513
Corsi,Jim	L	.354	48	17	2	1	0	7	5	3	.415	.438
Throws Right	R	.314	35	11	0	0	1	6	5	4	.390	.400
Cox,Danny	L	.254	138	35	9	0	5	19	19	35	.342	.428
Throws Right	R	.211	180	38	3	0	3	13	10	49	.253	.278
Crim,Chuck	L	.308	26	8	0	0	1	4	1	4	.379	.423
Throws Right	R	.290	31	9	2	0	1	6	4	6	.361	.452
Cummings,John	L	.244	41	10	1	0	2	8	5	1	.340	.415
Throws Left	R	.336	146	49	6	0	4	22	11	18	.381	.459
Daal,Omar	L	.230	74	17	2	0	2	16	11	12	.326	.338
Throws Left	R	.339	56	19	2	1	3	11	10	7	.433	.571
Darling,Ron	L	.276	352	97	16	3	12	48	40	41	.349	.440
Throws Right	R	.286	353	101	23	1	10	49	32	54	.349	.442
Darwin,Danny	L	.251	475	119	28	3	19	52	32	52	.295	.404
Throws Right	R	.204	377	77	17	0	12	31	17	78	.242	.345
Davis,Mark	L	.255	94	24	3	1	5	15	13	28	.346	.468
Throws Left	R	.301	183	55	9	2	5	29	31	42	.403	.454
Davis,Storm	L	.232	177	41	8	0	3	26	32	39	.346	.328
Throws Right	R	.267	195	52	10	3	6	27	16	34	.330	.441
Dayley,Ken	L	.000	2	0	0	0	0	0	1	2	.333	.000
Throws Left	R	1.000	1	1	1	0	0	0	3	0	1.000	2.000
DeLeon,Jose	L	.264	91	24	6	1	3	10	15	16	.382	.451
Throws Right	R	.180	111	20	1	0	4	13	15	24	.292	.297

Pitchers vs. Left-Handed and Right-Handed Batters

Pitcher	vs	Avg	AB	H	2B	3B	HR	BI	BB	SO	OBP	SLG
DeLucia,Rich	L	.333	75	25	5	1	3	16	12	15	.420	.547
Throws Right	R	.223	94	21	1	0	2	13	11	33	.311	.298
Deshaies,Jim	L	.230	122	28	4	1	3	6	10	13	.309	.352
Throws Left	R	.271	572	155	35	3	23	75	47	72	.326	.463
DeSilva,John	L	.222	9	2	0	0	0	1	1	1	.273	.222
Throws Right	R	.375	16	6	3	0	0	4	0	5	.375	.563
Dewey,Mark	L	.194	36	7	2	0	0	7	6	5	.295	.250
Throws Right	R	.132	53	7	3	1	0	5	4	9	.230	.226
Dibble,Rob	L	.247	73	18	2	0	5	15	31	20	.476	.479
Throws Right	R	.205	78	16	0	2	3	18	11	29	.311	.372
DiPino,Frank	L	.333	12	4	3	0	0	3	2	1	.467	.583
Throws Left	R	.327	52	17	5	1	2	9	4	4	.373	.577
DiPoto,Jerry	L	.271	85	23	0	0	0	5	18	12	.394	.271
Throws Right	R	.270	126	34	7	0	0	18	12	29	.336	.325
Dixon,Steve	L	.400	5	2	1	0	0	5	3	1	.625	.600
Throws Left	R	.625	8	5	1	0	1	2	2	1	.700	1.125
Doherty,John	L	.308	389	120	19	3	12	42	24	36	.347	.465
Throws Right	R	.258	329	85	15	1	7	46	24	27	.317	.374
Dopson,John	L	.302	308	93	16	5	9	45	31	37	.365	.474
Throws Right	R	.260	296	77	18	1	7	32	28	52	.320	.399
Downs,Kelly	L	.320	225	72	7	0	7	32	38	20	.417	.444
Throws Right	R	.257	245	63	13	0	7	37	22	46	.320	.396
Drabek,Doug	L	.288	459	132	25	3	11	59	35	60	.337	.427
Throws Right	R	.246	447	110	16	1	7	38	25	97	.287	.333
Drahman,Brian	L	.333	9	3	0	0	0	0	1	0	.400	.333
Throws Right	R	.333	12	4	1	0	0	1	1	3	.385	.417
Draper,Mike	L	.384	73	28	9	0	0	8	10	6	.447	.507
Throws Right	R	.281	89	25	4	1	2	18	4	10	.302	.416
Dreyer,Steve	L	.266	79	21	4	0	3	8	16	10	.389	.430
Throws Right	R	.314	86	27	6	0	4	11	4	13	.352	.523
Eckersley,D	L	.323	130	42	7	3	5	34	9	25	.364	.538
Throws Right	R	.197	127	25	1	1	2	9	4	55	.231	.268
Edens,Tom	L	.267	75	20	3	1	1	8	13	10	.375	.373
Throws Right	R	.260	104	27	3	0	3	18	6	11	.297	.375
Eichhorn,Mark	L	.326	132	43	4	1	2	19	10	17	.382	.417
Throws Right	R	.224	147	33	11	1	1	26	12	30	.284	.333
Eiland,Dave	L	.314	102	32	6	0	0	15	13	5	.385	.373
Throws Right	R	.280	93	26	5	0	5	13	4	9	.316	.495
Eldred,Cal	L	.245	507	124	27	6	12	53	52	75	.320	.393
Throws Right	R	.234	462	108	20	1	20	57	39	105	.294	.411
Erickson,S	L	.342	474	162	31	7	7	57	44	55	.392	.481
Throws Right	R	.261	398	104	12	1	10	62	27	61	.320	.372
Ettles,Mark	L	.448	29	13	1	0	3	11	3	1	.485	.793
Throws Right	R	.217	46	10	2	0	1	10	1	8	.229	.326
Fajardo,H	L	.000	0	0	0	0	0	0	0	0	.000	.000
Throws Right	R	.000	2	0	0	0	0	0	0	1	.000	.000
Farr,Steve	L	.293	75	22	4	2	3	12	11	9	.391	.520
Throws Right	R	.222	99	22	6	0	5	24	17	30	.331	.434
Farrell,John	L	.323	189	61	16	1	10	34	28	22	.412	.577
Throws Right	R	.278	176	49	7	1	12	36	16	23	.355	.534
Fassero,Jeff	L	.183	115	21	4	0	1	14	15	29	.273	.243
Throws Left	R	.225	436	98	14	1	6	35	39	111	.287	.303
Fernandez,A	L	.260	442	115	27	1	15	43	34	82	.312	.428
Throws Right	R	.222	477	106	13	3	12	42	33	87	.280	.338
Fernandez,Sid	L	.185	81	15	2	0	2	5	12	16	.298	.284
Throws Left	R	.194	345	67	9	0	15	33	24	65	.250	.351
Fetters,Mike	L	.233	90	21	0	3	2	16	12	10	.317	.367
Throws Right	R	.311	122	38	6	0	2	26	10	13	.365	.410
Finley,Chuck	L	.313	128	40	7	0	2	10	14	22	.381	.414
Throws Left	R	.244	831	203	31	1	20	83	68	165	.303	.356
Fleming,Dave	L	.258	128	33	6	2	4	19	5	14	.297	.430
Throws Left	R	.298	524	156	29	0	11	56	62	61	.371	.416
Flener,Huck	L	.267	15	4	2	0	0	2	0	1	.267	.400
Throws Left	R	.273	11	3	0	1	0	1	4	1	.467	.455
Fletcher,Paul	L	.000	0	0	0	0	0	0	0	0	.000	.000
Throws Right	R	.000	1	0	0	0	0	0	0	0	.000	.000
Fossas,Tony	L	.129	70	9	2	0	0	7	6	22	.215	.157
Throws Left	R	.333	87	29	5	0	4	13	9	17	.396	.529
Foster,Kevin	L	.458	24	11	2	0	3	10	6	4	.567	.917
Throws Right	R	.222	9	2	1	0	0	0	1	2	.300	.333
Foster,Steve	L	.209	43	9	2	0	1	3	3	12	.261	.326
Throws Right	R	.255	55	14	1	1	0	7	2	4	.293	.309
Franco,John	L	.317	41	13	1	0	2	9	4	10	.378	.488
Throws Left	R	.311	106	33	3	0	4	19	15	19	.398	.453
Fredrickson,S	L	.212	52	11	0	1	0	5	10	8	.339	.250
Throws Right	R	.349	63	22	4	0	3	15	7	12	.411	.556
Freeman,M	L	.286	28	8	1	1	1	7	7	3	.429	.500
Throws Right	R	.250	64	16	4	0	0	9	3	22	.294	.313
Frey,Steve	L	.208	53	11	4	1	0	6	13	8	.386	.321
Throws Left	R	.240	125	30	4	0	1	20	13	14	.312	.296
Frohwirth,T	L	.267	116	31	3	1	4	18	18	9	.370	.414
Throws Right	R	.251	239	60	7	0	3	28	26	41	.327	.318
Garces,Rich	L	.500	8	4	0	0	0	1	1	1	.556	.500
Throws Right	R	.000	8	0	0	0	0	0	1	2	.111	.000
Gardiner,Mike	L	.261	92	24	5	1	2	14	11	14	.343	.402
Throws Right	R	.280	100	28	5	1	1	14	15	11	.368	.380
Gardner,Mark	L	.311	164	51	10	1	7	24	18	20	.376	.512
Throws Right	R	.236	174	41	16	1	10	34	18	34	.312	.511
Gibson,Paul	L	.224	67	15	5	0	1	11	5	14	.270	.343
Throws Left	R	.291	103	30	4	1	4	19	6	23	.327	.466
Glavine,Tom	L	.275	167	46	10	0	1	14	20	28	.353	.353
Throws Left	R	.256	743	190	40	4	15	63	70	92	.321	.381
Gohr,Greg	L	.324	37	12	1	2	0	5	6	11	.419	.459
Throws Right	R	.264	53	14	3	0	1	10	8	12	.375	.377
Gomez,Pat	L	.268	41	11	1	0	0	5	0	8	.256	.293
Throws Left	R	.308	78	24	5	1	2	14	19	18	.434	.474
Gooden,Dwight	L	.247	396	98	18	1	9	37	34	70	.307	.366
Throws Right	R	.236	382	90	16	3	7	44	27	79	.296	.348
Gordon,Tom	L	.228	294	67	11	2	6	30	41	72	.319	.340
Throws Right	R	.217	267	58	16	1	5	34	36	71	.310	.341

Pitchers vs. Left-Handed and Right-Handed Batters

Pitcher	vs	Avg	AB	H	2B	3B	HR	BI	BB	SO	OBP	SLG
Gossage,Goose	L	.246	69	17	5	0	0	9	15	14	.384	.319
Throws Right	R	.278	115	32	4	3	6	25	11	26	.339	.522
Gott,Jim	L	.222	153	34	4	0	5	18	9	41	.264	.346
Throws Right	R	.278	133	37	4	0	1	12	8	26	.322	.331
Gozzo,Mauro	L	.300	30	9	1	0	1	4	4	2	.382	.433
Throws Right	R	.091	22	2	0	0	0	0	1	4	.130	.091
Grahe,Joe	L	.317	82	26	6	0	1	5	10	10	.391	.427
Throws Right	R	.211	133	28	2	1	4	28	15	21	.294	.331
Granger,Jeff	L	1.000	1	1	0	0	0	0	0	0	1.000	1.000
Throws Left	R	.400	5	2	0	0	0	3	2	1	.571	.400
Grant,Mark	L	.395	38	15	2	0	0	6	4	6	.442	.447
Throws Right	R	.302	63	19	6	0	4	16	7	8	.366	.587
Grater,Mark	L	.429	7	3	0	0	0	2	1	0	.500	.429
Throws Right	R	.214	14	3	0	0	0	4	3	4	.353	.214
Green,Tyler	L	.462	13	6	0	0	1	4	2	4	.533	.692
Throws Right	R	.435	23	10	2	0	2	2	3	3	.500	.522
Greene,Tommy	L	.235	358	84	16	1	5	34	42	75	.314	.327
Throws Right	R	.232	393	91	20	3	7	36	20	92	.269	.351
Greer,Ken	L	.000	1	0	0	0	0	0	0	1	.000	.000
Throws Right	R	.000	2	0	0	0	0	0	0	1	.000	.000
Grimsley,J	L	.281	64	18	3	0	1	6	8	10	.361	.375
Throws Right	R	.315	108	34	3	0	2	12	12	17	.388	.398
Groom,Buddy	L	.279	43	12	3	0	2	5	3	5	.319	.488
Throws Left	R	.340	106	36	9	0	2	18	10	10	.397	.481
Gross,Kevin	L	.277	394	109	10	1	7	45	54	74	.363	.360
Throws Right	R	.287	401	115	16	2	8	50	20	76	.325	.397
Gross,Kip	L	.208	24	5	0	0	0	1	2	8	.269	.208
Throws Right	R	.258	31	8	2	0	0	1	2	4	.303	.323
Guardado,E	L	.318	88	28	6	3	2	15	4	12	.348	.523
Throws Left	R	.320	297	95	28	2	11	49	32	34	.384	.539
Gubicza,Mark	L	.311	190	59	12	2	1	33	23	33	.382	.411
Throws Right	R	.304	227	69	12	1	1	29	20	47	.359	.379
Guetterman,L	L	.234	47	11	0	0	1	4	7	7	.345	.298
Throws Left	R	.242	124	30	4	4	0	21	9	12	.294	.339
Gullickson,B	L	.329	316	104	24	4	13	52	23	25	.373	.554
Throws Right	R	.254	323	82	13	1	15	39	21	45	.300	.440
Guthrie,Mark	L	.148	27	4	1	0	0	2	3	6	.233	.185
Throws Left	R	.333	48	16	3	0	2	13	13	9	.460	.521
Guzman,Jose	L	.271	395	107	24	4	16	48	44	77	.343	.473
Throws Right	R	.243	334	81	15	1	9	35	30	86	.307	.374
Guzman,Juan	L	.280	428	120	18	1	7	41	65	73	.371	.376
Throws Right	R	.223	408	91	17	0	10	44	45	121	.302	.338
Haas,Dave	L	.426	47	20	1	0	2	6	4	7	.471	.574
Throws Right	R	.342	73	25	3	0	7	16	4	10	.372	.671
Habyan,John	L	.241	79	19	4	2	3	13	6	11	.287	.456
Throws Right	R	.290	138	40	8	0	3	19	14	28	.355	.413
Hammond,Chris	L	.266	128	34	6	2	3	10	22	23	.377	.414
Throws Left	R	.279	619	173	24	4	15	82	44	85	.326	.404
Hampton,Mike	L	.345	29	10	1	1	2	6	1	2	.367	.655
Throws Left	R	.383	47	18	5	0	1	11	16	6	.531	.553

Pitcher	vs	Avg	AB	H	2B	3B	HR	BI	BB	SO	OBP	SLG
Haney,Chris	L	.277	83	23	3	0	1	14	10	5	.362	.349
Throws Left	R	.288	410	118	22	2	12	62	43	60	.355	.439
Hanson,Erik	L	.229	428	98	23	3	4	33	33	95	.283	.325
Throws Right	R	.299	391	117	26	4	13	46	27	68	.351	.486
Harkey,Mike	L	.279	305	85	10	3	9	46	27	37	.337	.420
Throws Right	R	.330	309	102	13	5	8	40	16	30	.361	.482
Harnisch,Pete	L	.238	428	102	12	4	13	38	55	87	.328	.376
Throws Right	R	.186	370	69	20	0	7	37	24	98	.241	.297
Harris,Gene	L	.265	113	30	3	0	1	10	18	18	.371	.319
Throws Right	R	.245	110	27	1	1	2	16	19	21	.351	.327
Harris,Greg A	L	.253	198	50	9	2	2	29	31	44	.353	.348
Throws Right	R	.212	212	45	6	0	5	25	29	59	.329	.311
Harris,Greg W	L	.272	463	126	19	4	16	60	40	63	.331	.434
Throws Right	R	.270	418	113	26	5	17	56	29	60	.324	.478
Hartley,Mike	L	.246	138	34	9	0	2	16	18	22	.327	.355
Throws Right	R	.310	168	52	14	0	2	28	18	35	.393	.429
Harvey,Bryan	L	.132	121	16	1	0	0	5	9	43	.191	.140
Throws Right	R	.240	121	29	0	0	4	16	4	30	.254	.339
Hathaway,H	L	.250	44	11	3	0	0	4	4	2	.340	.318
Throws Left	R	.345	174	60	8	0	6	28	22	9	.421	.494
Heaton,Neal	L	.250	32	8	1	0	0	6	4	6	.385	.281
Throws Left	R	.321	81	26	4	0	6	22	7	9	.371	.593
Henke,Tom	L	.205	132	27	4	0	3	14	16	36	.289	.303
Throws Right	R	.206	136	28	2	0	4	16	11	43	.267	.309
Henneman,Mike	L	.285	130	37	7	2	3	21	20	20	.377	.438
Throws Right	R	.221	145	32	4	1	1	10	12	38	.288	.283
Henry,Butch	L	.343	99	34	11	1	2	16	7	10	.383	.535
Throws Left	R	.309	327	101	14	1	13	53	21	37	.347	.477
Henry,Doug	L	.314	102	32	4	1	2	13	13	20	.393	.431
Throws Right	R	.289	121	35	9	1	5	25	12	18	.355	.504
Henry,Dwayne	L	.281	89	25	6	4	2	21	21	12	.420	.506
Throws Right	R	.268	138	37	10	0	4	25	18	25	.350	.428
Hentgen,Pat	L	.284	426	121	20	4	11	45	33	49	.339	.427
Throws Right	R	.230	408	94	15	3	16	46	41	73	.304	.400
Heredia,Gil	L	.244	123	30	5	1	2	14	11	19	.304	.350
Throws Right	R	.353	102	36	4	0	2	8	3	21	.383	.451
Hernandez,J	L	.276	192	53	7	0	8	25	20	27	.340	.438
Throws Right	R	.273	231	63	8	4	6	33	14	43	.310	.420
Hernandez,R	L	.231	117	27	3	0	2	13	14	33	.311	.308
Throws Right	R	.225	173	39	3	2	4	20	6	38	.250	.335
Hernandez,X	L	.220	168	37	7	1	6	22	17	52	.293	.381
Throws Right	R	.204	186	38	12	0	0	21	11	49	.247	.269
Hershiser,O	L	.242	434	105	25	4	5	44	51	68	.320	.353
Throws Right	R	.251	383	96	17	2	12	51	21	73	.300	.399
Hesketh,Joe	L	.203	69	14	3	0	1	8	6	13	.263	.290
Throws Left	R	.338	142	48	12	0	3	25	23	21	.428	.486
Hibbard,Greg	L	.274	117	32	4	0	5	18	10	17	.338	.436
Throws Left	R	.288	614	177	50	3	14	66	37	65	.325	.448
Hickerson,B	L	.241	108	26	1	0	1	10	6	16	.274	.278
Throws Left	R	.307	362	111	20	1	13	41	33	53	.365	.475

Pitchers vs. Left-Handed and Right-Handed Batters

Pitcher	vs	Avg	AB	H	2B	3B	HR	BI	BB	SO	OBP	SLG	Pitcher	vs	Avg	AB	H	2B	3B	HR	BI	BB	SO	OBP	SLG
Higuera,Teddy	L	.154	13	2	1	0	0	1	1	5	.200	.231	Johnson,Dave	L	.421	19	8	0	0	3	10	5	3	.520	.895
Throws Left	R	.353	116	41	15	2	4	22	15	22	.432	.621	Throws Right	R	.263	19	5	1	0	0	3	0	4	.333	.316
Hill,Ken	L	.234	376	88	26	2	4	35	49	43	.322	.346	Johnson,Jeff	L	.250	4	1	1	0	0	0	1	0	.400	.500
Throws Right	R	.244	308	75	16	0	3	33	25	47	.307	.325	Throws Left	R	.688	16	11	2	0	1	9	1	0	.706	1.000
Hill,Milt	L	.250	48	12	1	1	2	7	4	8	.302	.438	Johnson,Randy	L	.183	71	13	4	0	0	6	4	27	.256	.239
Throws Right	R	.338	65	22	6	0	3	14	5	15	.375	.569	Throws Left	R	.204	842	172	33	3	22	82	95	281	.293	.329
Hillegas,S	L	.326	138	45	10	3	5	23	15	10	.391	.551	Johnston,Joel	L	.227	75	17	5	0	4	10	10	9	.318	.453
Throws Right	R	.306	108	33	4	1	3	20	18	19	.419	.444	Throws Right	R	.188	112	21	5	1	3	8	9	22	.248	.330
Hillman,Eric	L	.280	125	35	3	2	1	16	8	18	.326	.360	Johnstone,J	L	.348	23	8	2	0	1	5	5	1	.464	.565
Throws Left	R	.304	454	138	25	3	11	56	16	42	.326	.445	Throws Right	R	.333	24	8	2	0	0	2	2	4	.385	.417
Hitchcock,S	L	.286	21	6	0	0	0	3	5	2	.407	.286	Jones,Barry	L	.636	11	7	0	0	2	5	1	2	.667	1.182
Throws Left	R	.268	97	26	7	0	4	14	9	24	.333	.464	Throws Right	R	.304	23	7	1	0	0	4	2	5	.360	.348
Hoffman,T	L	.222	158	35	3	3	6	23	27	38	.332	.392	Jones,B	L	.224	125	28	7	1	1	7	17	21	.317	.320
Throws Right	R	.245	184	45	13	1	4	17	12	41	.290	.391	Throws Right	R	.306	108	33	11	0	5	20	5	14	.339	.546
Holman,Brad	L	.208	53	11	1	0	1	5	6	6	.288	.283	Jones,Doug	L	.273	165	45	5	0	2	21	12	25	.335	.339
Throws Right	R	.208	77	16	5	0	0	7	10	11	.337	.273	Throws Right	R	.322	177	57	6	0	5	29	9	41	.353	.441
Holmes,Darren	L	.228	136	31	5	2	1	13	13	22	.305	.316	Jones,Jimmy	L	.321	78	25	7	0	4	15	7	6	.376	.564
Throws Right	R	.216	116	25	4	0	5	17	7	38	.260	.379	Throws Right	R	.253	87	22	5	0	2	12	2	15	.270	.379
Holzemer,Mark	L	.296	27	8	1	0	0	4	6	2	.457	.333	Jones,Todd	L	.194	62	12	2	0	0	2	7	11	.282	.226
Throws Left	R	.356	73	26	7	0	2	19	7	8	.420	.534	Throws Right	R	.232	69	16	2	0	4	8	8	14	.312	.435
Honeycutt,R	L	.255	55	14	1	1	1	8	6	6	.328	.364	Juden,Jeff	L	.400	10	4	1	0	1	2	3	4	.538	.800
Throws Left	R	.184	87	16	3	0	1	6	14	15	.291	.253	Throws Right	R	.000	8	0	0	0	0	1	1	3	.100	.000
Hope,John	L	.303	66	20	2	0	0	7	7	3	.370	.333	Kaiser,Jeff	L	.357	14	5	2	0	1	3	1	4	.400	.714
Throws Right	R	.321	84	27	9	2	2	12	1	5	.341	.548	Throws Left	R	.294	17	5	2	0	0	3	4	5	.409	.412
Horsman,Vince	L	.304	46	14	1	0	0	4	8	7	.418	.326	Kamieniecki,S	L	.284	285	81	14	3	9	33	28	38	.348	.449
Throws Left	R	.212	52	11	1	0	2	12	7	10	.328	.346	Throws Right	R	.270	304	82	11	2	8	38	31	34	.338	.398
Hough,Charlie	L	.248	383	95	17	1	11	43	35	56	.310	.384	Karsay,Steve	L	.262	103	27	4	2	1	14	11	17	.330	.369
Throws Right	R	.270	396	107	25	1	9	48	36	70	.339	.407	Throws Right	R	.253	87	22	4	0	3	8	5	16	.305	.402
Howard,Chris	L	.250	4	1	0	0	0	0	2	0	.500	.250	Key,Jimmy	L	.260	131	34	3	0	6	13	6	26	.292	.420
Throws Left	R	.333	3	1	0	0	0	1	1	1	.500	.333	Throws Left	R	.244	758	185	32	4	20	68	37	147	.277	.376
Howe,Steve	L	.242	62	15	1	0	1	6	3	9	.288	.306	Kiefer,Mark	L	.083	12	1	0	0	0	0	1	2	.214	.083
Throws Left	R	.323	133	43	10	0	6	25	7	10	.361	.534	Throws Right	R	.105	19	2	0	0	0	3	4	5	.261	.105
Howell,Jay	L	.233	90	21	2	0	0	6	4	16	.263	.256	Kiely,John	L	.154	13	2	0	0	1	3	4	0	.353	.385
Throws Right	R	.225	120	27	4	0	3	17	12	21	.289	.333	Throws Right	R	.355	31	11	3	0	1	8	9	5	.512	.548
Hurst,Bruce	L	.200	5	1	0	0	0	2	1	1	.333	.200	Kile,Darryl	L	.236	330	78	8	2	8	36	44	59	.326	.345
Throws Left	R	.292	48	14	1	0	1	9	5	8	.358	.375	Throws Right	R	.241	307	74	13	2	4	30	25	82	.322	.336
Hutton,Mark	L	.292	48	14	3	0	1	6	7	5	.382	.417	Kilgus,Paul	L	.160	25	4	2	0	1	1	3	8	.276	.360
Throws Right	R	.294	34	10	2	0	1	9	10	7	.447	.441	Throws Left	R	.187	75	14	1	0	0	1	5	13	.238	.200
Ignasiak,Mike	L	.318	44	14	2	0	1	9	11	4	.456	.432	King,Kevin	L	.286	14	4	2	0	1	4	2	3	.412	.643
Throws Right	R	.202	89	18	2	1	1	11	10	24	.290	.281	Throws Left	R	.200	25	5	1	0	2	6	2	5	.241	.480
Innis,Jeff	L	.296	115	34	4	0	1	12	19	11	.409	.357	Klink,Joe	L	.216	74	16	2	0	0	6	13	12	.333	.243
Throws Right	R	.267	176	47	12	1	4	24	19	25	.347	.415	Throws Left	R	.323	65	21	6	1	0	16	11	10	.405	.446
Jackson,Danny	L	.294	143	42	5	0	4	19	16	24	.377	.413	Knudsen,Kurt	L	.392	51	20	2	0	5	15	8	6	.475	.725
Throws Left	R	.257	670	172	34	6	8	68	64	96	.319	.361	Throws Right	R	.221	95	21	3	0	4	13	8	23	.296	.379
Jackson,Mike	L	.246	126	31	4	1	3	21	13	23	.317	.365	Knudson,Mark	L	.364	11	4	0	1	1	4	3	2	.500	.818
Throws Right	R	.171	158	27	4	0	4	18	11	47	.236	.272	Throws Right	R	.522	23	12	1	0	3	11	2	1	.560	.957
Jean,Domingo	L	.243	74	18	4	2	2	10	7	11	.305	.432	Kramer,Tom	L	.234	235	55	8	0	10	32	32	29	.328	.396
Throws Right	R	.232	82	19	3	0	5	9	12	9	.330	.451	Throws Right	R	.303	234	71	16	2	9	29	27	42	.375	.504
Jimenez,M	L	.304	56	17	2	0	2	6	8	4	.391	.446	Krueger,Bill	L	.296	71	21	3	0	3	14	4	8	.333	.465
Throws Right	R	.213	47	10	2	0	3	6	8	9	.339	.447	Throws Left	R	.282	245	69	11	1	3	24	26	52	.356	.371

305

Pitchers vs. Left-Handed and Right-Handed Batters

Pitcher	vs	Avg	AB	H	2B	3B	HR	BI	BB	SO	OBP	SLG	Pitcher	vs	Avg	AB	H	2B	3B	HR	BI	BB	SO	OBP	SLG
Lancaster,Les	L	.237	97	23	7	1	1	7	12	16	.321	.361	Mahomes,Pat	L	.309	81	25	5	2	4	17	8	10	.374	.568
Throws Right	R	.246	134	33	7	0	4	28	9	20	.297	.388	Throws Right	R	.310	71	22	5	2	4	14	8	13	.370	.606
Landrum,Bill	L	.225	40	9	4	1	0	2	5	8	.311	.375	Maldonado,C	L	.327	52	17	1	0	2	12	8	6	.397	.462
Throws Right	R	.237	38	9	2	0	1	8	1	6	.256	.368	Throws Right	R	.256	90	23	7	1	0	8	9	12	.320	.356
Langston,Mark	L	.176	136	24	3	0	2	11	11	29	.238	.243	Manzanillo,J	L	.277	47	13	3	0	0	11	11	9	.400	.340
Throws Left	R	.243	806	196	36	1	20	78	74	167	.305	.365	Throws Right	R	.258	66	17	7	0	2	17	8	12	.351	.455
Layana,Tim	L	.800	5	4	1	0	1	4	0	0	.800	1.600	Martinez,D	L	.249	434	108	18	5	13	45	38	61	.312	.403
Throws Right	R	.375	8	3	1	0	0	1	1	1	.444	.500	Throws Right	R	.244	422	103	20	4	14	47	26	77	.300	.410
Leach,Terry	L	.227	22	5	0	0	0	1	0	2	.227	.227	Martinez,P J	L	.229	218	50	3	3	3	18	25	62	.308	.312
Throws Right	R	.263	38	10	3	0	0	3	2	1	.310	.342	Throws Right	R	.163	160	26	3	2	2	11	32	57	.310	.244
Leary,Tim	L	.331	347	115	29	3	9	38	33	34	.392	.510	Martinez,P A	L	.224	49	11	1	0	3	7	4	9	.296	.429
Throws Right	R	.266	327	87	9	4	12	48	25	34	.330	.428	Throws Left	R	.141	85	12	4	0	1	4	9	23	.223	.224
Lefferts,C	L	.253	87	22	3	0	2	11	6	17	.309	.356	Martinez,R	L	.246	414	102	19	3	9	41	76	68	.362	.372
Throws Left	R	.323	248	80	7	2	15	48	22	41	.374	.548	Throws Right	R	.264	379	100	12	3	6	36	28	59	.319	.359
Leftwich,P	L	.242	161	39	4	1	2	19	17	12	.315	.317	Mason,Roger	L	.284	148	42	5	0	3	19	17	30	.351	.378
Throws Right	R	.284	148	42	11	0	3	14	10	19	.340	.419	Throws Right	R	.217	221	48	8	1	7	32	17	41	.277	.357
Leibrandt,C	L	.384	86	33	9	1	2	12	4	10	.418	.581	Mauser,Tim	L	.202	104	21	4	0	3	13	10	26	.270	.327
Throws Left	R	.267	509	136	31	3	13	61	41	79	.323	.417	Throws Right	R	.288	104	30	7	1	3	20	14	20	.378	.462
Leiter,Al	L	.235	102	24	0	0	3	14	12	14	.313	.324	Maysey,Matt	L	.306	36	11	2	0	1	9	6	5	.395	.444
Throws Left	R	.241	286	69	5	0	5	30	44	52	.348	.311	Throws Right	R	.333	51	17	3	0	3	11	7	5	.417	.569
Leiter,Mark	L	.264	216	57	5	2	9	27	28	29	.348	.431	McCaskill,K	L	.350	200	70	14	2	7	35	21	19	.410	.545
Throws Right	R	.270	200	54	7	0	8	29	16	41	.326	.425	Throws Right	R	.285	260	74	12	0	5	37	15	46	.324	.388
Leskanic,Curt	L	.305	118	36	6	0	4	20	14	14	.381	.458	McClure,Bob	L	.450	20	9	2	0	1	5	3	3	.522	.700
Throws Right	R	.221	104	23	3	0	3	17	13	16	.306	.337	Throws Left	R	.364	11	4	0	0	1	3	2	3	.462	.636
Lewis,Richie	L	.258	132	34	8	1	4	28	23	28	.367	.424	McDonald,Ben	L	.230	439	101	17	5	5	37	49	92	.308	.326
Throws Right	R	.222	153	34	7	2	3	16	20	37	.309	.353	Throws Right	R	.225	373	84	15	0	12	39	37	79	.300	.362
Lewis,Scott	L	.317	60	19	1	1	2	8	4	4	.343	.467	McDowell,Jack	L	.258	493	127	21	1	8	41	33	82	.302	.353
Throws Right	R	.305	59	18	4	0	1	9	8	6	.384	.424	Throws Right	R	.275	488	134	22	3	12	52	36	76	.326	.406
Lilliquist,D	L	.270	63	17	0	1	0	6	2	13	.299	.302	McDowell,R	L	.315	124	39	6	1	1	20	17	11	.401	.403
Throws Left	R	.263	179	47	12	0	5	16	17	27	.325	.413	Throws Right	R	.264	140	37	3	1	1	12	13	16	.329	.321
Linton,Doug	L	.370	54	20	4	1	4	19	12	5	.471	.704	McElroy,Chuck	L	.303	66	20	2	0	2	9	12	10	.405	.424
Throws Right	R	.268	97	26	5	1	4	14	11	18	.345	.464	Throws Left	R	.267	116	31	7	0	2	14	13	21	.346	.379
Lloyd,Graeme	L	.192	78	15	2	0	2	11	1	12	.213	.295	McGehee,Kevin	L	.150	20	3	1	0	1	2	4	2	.320	.350
Throws Left	R	.285	172	49	6	1	3	23	12	19	.335	.384	Throws Right	R	.341	44	15	4	1	4	11	3	5	.388	.750
Looney,Brian	L	.250	4	1	1	0	0	0	0	1	.250	.500	McMichael,G	L	.194	155	30	4	1	1	12	16	37	.269	.252
Throws Left	R	.318	22	7	1	0	0	2	2	6	.375	.364	Throws Right	R	.217	175	38	3	0	2	11	13	52	.268	.269
Lopez,Albie	L	.271	96	26	2	0	3	11	22	11	.412	.385	Meacham,Rusty	L	.400	40	16	4	1	1	10	2	3	.432	.625
Throws Right	R	.253	91	23	5	0	4	19	10	14	.324	.440	Throws Right	R	.273	55	15	2	0	1	9	3	10	.333	.364
Luebbers,L	L	.267	146	39	5	0	5	24	21	16	.351	.404	Melendez,Jose	L	.190	21	4	0	2	0	3	5	3	.333	.381
Throws Right	R	.254	138	35	7	0	2	16	17	22	.338	.348	Throws Right	R	.171	35	6	2	0	2	8	0	11	.167	.400
MacDonald,Bob	L	.222	90	20	4	2	3	12	12	21	.314	.411	Menendez,Tony	L	.250	20	5	1	0	3	6	1	4	.273	.750
Throws Left	R	.294	160	47	12	0	5	36	21	18	.369	.463	Throws Right	R	.259	58	15	3	0	1	2	3	9	.306	.362
Maddux,Greg	L	.235	520	122	19	1	5	36	33	97	.280	.304	Mercker,Kent	L	.200	70	14	4	0	0	6	15	21	.341	.257
Throws Right	R	.228	464	106	19	1	9	39	19	100	.264	.332	Throws Left	R	.220	173	38	7	1	2	16	21	38	.311	.306
Maddux,Mike	L	.264	125	33	8	1	2	21	17	24	.351	.392	Merriman,B	L	.426	47	20	5	0	2	14	13	2	.548	.660
Throws Right	R	.225	151	34	5	2	1	17	10	33	.279	.305	Throws Right	R	.276	58	16	5	1	1	13	10	12	.394	.448
Magnante,Mike	L	.360	25	9	1	1	0	3	2	2	.407	.480	Mesa,Jose	L	.302	378	114	12	0	7	42	34	44	.360	.389
Throws Left	R	.264	106	28	4	1	3	12	9	14	.325	.406	Throws Right	R	.273	432	118	22	3	14	54	28	74	.320	.435
Magrane,Joe	L	.277	94	26	2	1	3	10	15	11	.387	.415	Miceli,Danny	L	.500	6	3	0	0	0	0	2	1	.625	.500
Throws Left	R	.281	531	149	34	1	16	73	43	51	.332	.439	Throws Right	R	.188	16	3	2	0	0	3	1	3	.235	.313

Pitchers vs. Left-Handed and Right-Handed Batters

Pitcher	vs	Avg	AB	H	2B	3B	HR	BI	BB	SO	OBP	SLG
Milacki,Bob	L	.324	34	11	1	1	2	4	8	5	.452	.588
Throws Right	R	.276	29	8	1	0	1	3	3	2	.344	.414
Militello,Sam	L	.333	21	7	2	0	1	3	1	2	.364	.571
Throws Right	R	.188	16	3	1	0	0	3	6	3	.458	.250
Miller,Paul	L	.278	18	5	1	0	1	1	0	2	.278	.500
Throws Right	R	.400	25	10	2	0	1	5	2	0	.444	.600
Mills,Alan	L	.285	137	39	2	1	5	19	20	16	.377	.423
Throws Right	R	.187	219	41	9	2	9	30	31	52	.291	.370
Minchey,Nate	L	.238	63	15	1	1	3	7	7	3	.314	.429
Throws Right	R	.290	69	20	7	0	2	7	1	15	.300	.478
Minor,Blas	L	.286	140	40	5	2	5	23	15	25	.350	.457
Throws Right	R	.248	218	54	7	2	3	20	11	59	.294	.339
Minutelli,G	L	.091	11	1	0	0	0	0	2	3	.231	.091
Throws Left	R	.171	35	6	1	1	2	7	13	7	.380	.429
Miranda,Angel	L	.210	81	17	7	0	0	6	15	16	.330	.296
Throws Left	R	.230	361	83	16	3	12	38	37	72	.303	.391
Mlicki,Dave	L	.182	33	6	1	0	1	3	4	4	.308	.303
Throws Right	R	.294	17	5	2	0	1	2	2	3	.368	.588
Moeller,D	L	.348	23	8	0	0	1	7	3	2	.444	.478
Throws Left	R	.360	50	18	4	0	1	12	4	11	.407	.500
Mohler,Mike	L	.192	73	14	4	0	0	12	13	16	.314	.247
Throws Left	R	.262	164	43	7	0	10	31	31	26	.382	.488
Monteleone,R	L	.273	139	38	4	3	10	25	21	26	.364	.561
Throws Right	R	.253	186	47	9	3	4	24	14	24	.300	.398
Montgomery,J	L	.234	158	37	8	2	1	17	13	24	.297	.329
Throws Right	R	.177	158	28	6	0	2	12	10	42	.229	.253
Moore,Marcus	L	.265	49	13	1	1	2	12	12	9	.394	.449
Throws Right	R	.315	54	17	4	1	2	11	8	4	.403	.537
Moore,Mike	L	.271	432	117	20	4	15	54	49	35	.346	.440
Throws Right	R	.271	406	110	20	0	20	65	40	54	.334	.468
Morgan,Mike	L	.245	424	104	16	4	7	41	51	63	.330	.351
Throws Right	R	.282	362	102	15	1	8	46	23	48	.328	.395
Morris,Jack	L	.318	321	102	17	4	9	50	37	41	.385	.480
Throws Right	R	.286	304	87	14	2	9	48	28	62	.350	.434
Moyer,Jamie	L	.304	102	31	8	0	3	9	10	13	.377	.471
Throws Left	R	.256	480	123	22	1	8	44	28	77	.302	.356
Mulholland,T	L	.216	134	29	7	1	3	16	10	15	.271	.351
Throws Left	R	.247	600	148	31	1	17	57	30	101	.284	.387
Munoz,Bobby	L	.203	59	12	3	0	0	4	10	10	.314	.254
Throws Right	R	.303	119	36	6	0	1	15	16	23	.380	.378
Munoz,Mike	L	.316	38	12	3	0	2	7	3	8	.357	.553
Throws Left	R	.302	43	13	3	2	0	12	12	9	.446	.465
Murphy,Rob	L	.293	82	24	3	0	2	10	4	14	.326	.402
Throws Left	R	.288	170	49	4	2	6	18	16	27	.349	.441
Mussina,Mike	L	.256	285	73	13	1	4	32	21	56	.307	.351
Throws Right	R	.256	351	90	21	1	16	46	23	61	.304	.459
Mutis,Jeff	L	.320	75	24	1	1	5	17	4	5	.363	.560
Throws Left	R	.279	247	69	15	0	9	35	29	24	.366	.449
Myers,Randy	L	.178	45	8	0	1	1	2	8	17	.302	.289
Throws Left	R	.239	238	57	15	0	6	26	18	69	.293	.378
Nabholz,Chris	L	.243	70	17	2	1	1	3	10	17	.354	.343
Throws Left	R	.235	353	83	16	0	8	44	53	57	.341	.348
Nagy,Charles	L	.288	104	30	4	0	2	14	6	14	.324	.385
Throws Right	R	.356	101	36	7	0	4	19	7	16	.409	.545
Navarro,Jaime	L	.317	448	142	20	9	11	66	38	60	.367	.475
Throws Right	R	.280	400	112	18	0	10	55	35	54	.344	.400
Neagle,Denny	L	.223	94	21	4	1	3	18	10	29	.305	.383
Throws Left	R	.272	224	61	14	1	7	36	27	44	.354	.438
Nelson,Gene	L	.320	75	24	8	1	1	13	18	5	.442	.493
Throws Right	R	.229	157	36	4	0	2	18	6	30	.263	.293
Nelson,Jeff	L	.354	48	17	4	0	3	17	10	12	.484	.625
Throws Right	R	.231	173	40	4	0	2	32	24	49	.337	.289
Nen,Robb	L	.216	97	21	3	2	0	9	18	17	.339	.289
Throws Right	R	.333	126	42	14	0	6	30	28	22	.449	.587
Nichols,Rod	L	.417	12	5	2	0	1	6	1	0	.462	.833
Throws Right	R	.308	13	4	0	0	0	1	1	3	.357	.308
Nied,Dave	L	.314	169	53	11	0	5	21	25	19	.394	.467
Throws Right	R	.277	166	46	8	1	3	31	17	27	.342	.392
Nielsen,Jerry	L	.261	23	6	2	0	0	4	0	3	.261	.348
Throws Left	R	.400	30	12	0	0	1	7	4	5	.447	.500
Novoa,Rafael	L	.227	44	10	2	0	2	9	0	3	.271	.409
Throws Left	R	.277	173	48	12	0	5	24	22	14	.360	.434
Nunez,Edwin	L	.270	137	37	9	1	0	15	12	28	.325	.350
Throws Right	R	.321	162	52	8	2	2	28	17	30	.405	.432
O'Donoghue,J	L	.217	23	5	1	0	0	2	5	4	.379	.261
Throws Left	R	.304	56	17	6	0	4	11	5	12	.361	.625
Ojeda,Bobby	L	.278	36	10	2	1	1	5	4	7	.341	.472
Throws Left	R	.292	130	38	11	0	4	17	17	20	.369	.469
Olivares,Omar	L	.276	232	64	18	2	6	42	28	35	.361	.448
Throws Right	R	.299	234	70	11	0	4	24	26	28	.378	.397
Oliver,Darren	L	.167	6	1	0	0	0	0	1	3	.286	.167
Throws Left	R	.143	7	1	0	0	1	1	0	1	.143	.571
Olson,Gregg	L	.212	85	18	4	0	1	13	9	24	.281	.294
Throws Right	R	.235	81	19	5	0	0	10	9	20	.311	.296
Ontiveros,S	L	.226	31	7	1	0	0	0	3	9	.294	.258
Throws Right	R	.324	34	11	3	0	0	7	3	4	.378	.412
Oquist,Mike	L	.267	15	4	0	0	0	2	2	0	.353	.267
Throws Right	R	.258	31	8	3	0	0	1	2	8	.303	.355
Orosco,Jesse	L	.313	64	20	5	0	1	8	3	15	.353	.438
Throws Left	R	.185	146	27	4	1	1	16	14	52	.262	.247
Osborne,D	L	.207	116	24	5	0	2	10	9	15	.264	.302
Throws Left	R	.269	479	129	22	5	16	51	38	68	.331	.436
Osuna,Al	L	.222	36	8	1	0	2	5	11	8	.400	.417
Throws Left	R	.184	49	9	0	0	1	5	2	13	.208	.245
Otto,Dave	L	.348	69	24	3	0	1	10	6	7	.416	.435
Throws Left	R	.307	199	61	11	2	8	24	22	23	.377	.503
Painter,Lance	L	.226	31	7	0	2	1	6	5	4	.333	.452
Throws Left	R	.360	125	45	10	1	4	18	4	12	.380	.552
Pall,Donn	L	.263	152	40	8	0	3	19	8	18	.300	.375
Throws Right	R	.257	144	37	3	0	3	18	6	22	.294	.340

Pitchers vs. Left-Handed and Right-Handed Batters

Pitcher	vs	Avg	AB	H	2B	3B	HR	BI	BB	SO	OBP	SLG	Pitcher	vs	Avg	AB	H	2B	3B	HR	BI	BB	SO	OBP	SLG
Parrett,Jeff	L	.295	149	44	7	0	1	28	21	35	.383	.362	Reynolds,S	L	.292	24	7	0	0	0	2	4	5	.393	.292
Throws Right	R	.250	136	34	6	1	5	23	24	31	.358	.419	Throws Right	R	.211	19	4	1	0	0	2	2	5	.286	.263
Patterson,Bob	L	.247	73	18	4	0	1	9	2	18	.263	.342	Reynoso,A	L	.277	379	105	23	7	10	47	32	64	.342	.454
Throws Left	R	.301	136	41	5	1	7	24	9	28	.347	.507	Throws Right	R	.276	366	101	12	3	12	44	31	53	.332	.423
Patterson,Ken	L	.276	76	21	4	0	3	13	14	10	.389	.447	Rhodes,Arthur	L	.300	40	12	4	0	1	5	7	2	.404	.475
Throws Left	R	.234	141	33	5	0	4	15	21	26	.331	.355	Throws Left	R	.271	292	79	16	5	15	50	42	47	.361	.514
Pavlik,Roger	L	.228	329	75	13	2	8	23	46	71	.324	.353	Righetti,Dave	L	.288	59	17	3	1	4	12	2	11	.311	.576
Throws Right	R	.264	288	76	12	1	10	33	34	60	.347	.417	Throws Left	R	.313	131	41	3	1	7	19	15	20	.388	.511
Pennington,B	L	.342	38	13	1	0	1	9	4	5	.419	.447	Rijo,Jose	L	.242	520	126	20	6	10	48	40	110	.297	.362
Throws Left	R	.233	90	21	3	1	6	26	21	34	.381	.489	Throws Right	R	.214	429	92	12	3	9	25	22	117	.253	.319
Perez,Melido	L	.281	342	96	15	1	9	38	40	81	.354	.409	Risley,Bill	L	.333	6	2	0	0	1	2	2	2	.500	.833
Throws Right	R	.252	305	77	19	2	13	48	24	67	.309	.456	Throws Right	R	.000	4	0	0	0	0	0	0	0	.200	.000
Perez,Mike	L	.272	114	31	4	1	2	13	10	21	.328	.377	Rivera,Ben	L	.301	316	95	13	6	7	45	43	52	.384	.446
Throws Right	R	.224	152	34	4	2	2	14	10	37	.269	.316	Throws Right	R	.246	325	80	6	4	9	38	42	71	.339	.372
Petkovsek,M	L	.409	44	18	3	2	2	8	3	6	.447	.705	Robertson,R	L	.333	15	5	0	0	0	2	3	4	.444	.333
Throws Right	R	.287	87	25	4	2	5	23	6	8	.330	.552	Throws Left	R	.417	24	10	3	0	0	2	1	1	.440	.542
Pichardo,H	L	.303	333	101	22	0	5	44	30	24	.358	.414	Rodriguez,R	L	.263	99	26	3	1	3	13	12	7	.348	.404
Throws Right	R	.259	317	82	24	0	5	32	23	46	.316	.382	Throws Left	R	.245	192	47	7	0	7	27	21	36	.322	.391
Plantenberg,E	L	.211	19	4	1	0	0	3	5	2	.400	.263	Rogers,Kenny	L	.222	90	20	6	2	0	6	5	20	.271	.333
Throws Left	R	.350	20	7	1	0	0	2	7	1	.519	.400	Throws Left	R	.268	708	190	40	5	18	85	66	120	.331	.415
Plesac,Dan	L	.258	89	23	4	1	2	12	6	29	.305	.393	Rogers,Kevin	L	.230	87	20	2	0	0	7	9	26	.323	.253
Throws Left	R	.321	159	51	5	1	8	32	15	18	.373	.516	Throws Left	R	.238	214	51	8	0	3	18	19	36	.302	.318
Plunk,Eric	L	.238	105	25	8	1	2	9	15	26	.333	.390	Rojas,Mel	L	.270	185	50	13	2	4	28	21	26	.338	.427
Throws Right	R	.218	165	36	9	0	3	23	15	51	.280	.327	Throws Right	R	.207	145	30	11	0	2	21	9	22	.269	.324
Poole,Jim	L	.177	79	14	3	0	0	9	6	15	.233	.215	Roper,John	L	.362	149	54	6	4	5	22	18	24	.435	.557
Throws Left	R	.174	92	16	2	0	2	11	15	14	.287	.261	Throws Right	R	.233	163	38	8	0	5	22	18	30	.314	.374
Portugal,Mark	L	.234	411	96	11	1	4	30	42	71	.305	.294	Rueter,Kirk	L	.250	48	12	1	0	0	4	2	5	.280	.271
Throws Right	R	.265	370	98	15	0	6	33	35	60	.332	.354	Throws Left	R	.266	274	73	19	0	5	26	16	26	.307	.391
Powell,Dennis	L	.159	63	10	2	0	1	7	5	17	.217	.238	Ruffcorn,S	L	.250	16	4	0	0	1	4	6	0	.455	.438
Throws Left	R	.314	102	32	5	0	6	16	19	15	.423	.539	Throws Right	R	.278	18	5	2	0	1	6	4	2	.391	.556
Powell,Ross	L	.154	13	2	0	0	0	0	2	3	.267	.154	Ruffin,Bruce	L	.233	120	28	5	0	3	13	25	28	.360	.350
Throws Left	R	.244	45	11	1	1	1	4	4	14	.306	.378	Throws Left	R	.279	419	117	19	3	7	52	44	98	.347	.389
Power,Ted	L	.314	70	22	3	1	2	11	9	11	.392	.471	Ruffin,Johnny	L	.295	78	23	3	4	1	9	5	15	.337	.474
Throws Right	R	.307	114	35	8	0	1	18	8	16	.347	.404	Throws Right	R	.191	68	13	4	0	3	11	6	15	.267	.382
Pugh,Tim	L	.348	325	113	15	4	12	55	35	40	.410	.529	Ruskin,Scott	L	.500	2	1	0	0	1	1	0	0	.500	2.000
Throws Right	R	.259	336	87	5	2	7	37	24	54	.317	.348	Throws Right	R	.500	4	2	1	0	0	3	2	0	.667	.750
Quantrill,P	L	.271	247	67	15	3	7	24	28	29	.350	.441	Russell,Jeff	L	.269	93	25	9	0	0	12	5	20	.307	.366
Throws Right	R	.285	295	84	14	3	6	38	16	37	.319	.414	Throws Right	R	.184	76	14	2	0	1	11	9	25	.264	.250
Radinsky,S	L	.239	88	21	2	0	0	7	6	29	.287	.261	Ryan,Ken	L	.232	82	19	6	0	0	11	18	29	.366	.305
Throws Left	R	.286	140	40	4	0	3	20	13	15	.351	.379	Throws Right	R	.238	101	24	4	1	2	18	11	20	.322	.356
Rapp,Pat	L	.269	175	47	11	2	3	20	26	17	.363	.406	Ryan,Nolan	L	.188	133	25	4	1	2	20	30	22	.339	.278
Throws Right	R	.293	184	54	10	2	4	24	13	40	.340	.435	Throws Right	R	.257	113	29	9	0	3	19	10	24	.315	.416
Rasmussen,D	L	.316	19	6	1	0	0	3	1	2	.333	.368	Saberhagen,B	L	.264	250	66	8	4	7	29	11	49	.298	.412
Throws Left	R	.330	103	34	6	2	4	19	13	10	.410	.544	Throws Right	R	.237	274	65	12	0	4	21	6	44	.253	.325
Reardon,Jeff	L	.297	118	35	9	1	0	11	8	10	.351	.390	Salkeld,Roger	L	.300	30	9	3	1	0	2	1	5	.323	.467
Throws Right	R	.246	126	31	6	1	4	18	2	25	.265	.405	Throws Right	R	.154	26	4	2	0	0	1	3	8	.267	.231
Reed,Rick	L	.222	9	2	1	0	0	2	1	1	.364	.333	Sampen,Bill	L	.514	37	19	2	0	1	9	3	4	.571	.649
Throws Right	R	.435	23	10	2	0	1	2	1	4	.480	.652	Throws Right	R	.162	37	6	1	1	0	5	6	5	.311	.243
Reed,Steve	L	.336	122	41	8	2	7	21	13	16	.410	.607	Sanders,Scott	L	.333	93	31	4	0	3	15	18	10	.446	.473
Throws Right	R	.209	187	39	5	0	6	22	17	35	.272	.332	Throws Right	R	.207	111	23	2	1	1	14	5	27	.237	.270

Pitchers vs. Left-Handed and Right-Handed Batters

Pitcher	vs	Avg	AB	H	2B	3B	HR	BI	BB	SO	OBP	SLG	Pitcher	vs	Avg	AB	H	2B	3B	HR	BI	BB	SO	OBP	SLG
Sanderson,S	L	.271	354	96	14	1	17	47	24	55	.317	.460	Smithberg,R	L	.231	26	6	0	0	2	4	3	1	.310	.462
Throws Right	R	.288	364	105	20	2	10	42	10	47	.311	.437	Throws Right	R	.175	40	7	3	0	0	5	4	3	.267	.250
Sanford,Mo	L	.349	63	22	4	2	2	14	17	13	.481	.571	Smoltz,John	L	.260	458	119	29	5	10	51	55	72	.345	.410
Throws Right	R	.214	70	15	2	1	2	9	10	23	.309	.357	Throws Right	R	.199	447	89	16	1	13	42	45	136	.272	.327
Scanlan,Bob	L	.305	118	36	11	1	2	23	13	22	.368	.466	Spradlin,J	L	.261	69	18	2	3	4	14	4	10	.297	.551
Throws Right	R	.259	166	43	14	1	4	25	15	22	.324	.428	Throws Right	R	.241	108	26	5	1	0	12	5	14	.267	.306
Schilling,C	L	.259	490	127	23	4	13	59	37	105	.310	.402	Springer,Russ	L	.301	123	37	4	0	5	16	15	20	.386	.455
Throws Right	R	.258	415	107	17	2	10	41	20	81	.295	.381	Throws Right	R	.305	118	36	6	0	6	25	17	11	.394	.508
Schooler,Mike	L	.382	34	13	1	1	1	8	5	4	.462	.559	Stanton,Mike	L	.218	55	12	2	0	1	9	13	15	.357	.309
Throws Right	R	.262	65	17	6	0	2	9	5	12	.314	.446	Throws Left	R	.269	145	39	9	0	3	24	16	28	.342	.393
Schourek,Pete	L	.315	124	39	6	2	1	15	11	17	.368	.419	Stewart,Dave	L	.245	269	66	16	2	8	36	36	44	.332	.409
Throws Left	R	.320	403	129	35	2	12	68	34	55	.371	.506	Throws Right	R	.239	335	80	14	2	15	46	36	52	.318	.427
Schwarz,Jeff	L	.216	74	16	4	1	1	9	20	19	.385	.338	Stieb,Dave	L	.222	45	10	1	0	0	6	10	5	.357	.244
Throws Right	R	.190	100	19	5	1	0	9	18	22	.320	.260	Throws Right	R	.378	45	17	0	1	1	9	4	6	.429	.489
Scott,Darryl	L	.171	35	6	3	0	0	5	4	6	.256	.257	Stottlemyre,T	L	.305	374	114	28	3	7	50	45	48	.375	.452
Throws Right	R	.317	41	13	3	0	1	13	7	7	.412	.463	Throws Right	R	.278	324	90	17	4	4	42	24	50	.328	.392
Scott,Tim	L	.180	128	23	2	0	1	13	20	39	.291	.219	Sutcliffe,R	L	.307	342	105	19	3	11	43	42	35	.386	.477
Throws Right	R	.317	145	46	11	2	3	22	14	26	.388	.483	Throws Right	R	.320	334	107	25	2	12	59	32	45	.384	.515
Scudder,Scott	L	.250	8	2	2	0	0	2	2	0	.400	.500	Swan,Russ	L	.231	26	6	1	0	0	5	7	3	.412	.269
Throws Right	R	.429	7	3	1	0	0	2	2	1	.600	.571	Throws Left	R	.358	53	19	2	0	2	9	11	7	.477	.509
Seanez,Rudy	L	.500	8	4	1	0	0	3	1	0	.556	.625	Swift,Bill	L	.268	471	126	20	0	12	47	42	64	.331	.386
Throws Right	R	.444	9	4	0	0	1	3	1	1	.500	.778	Throws Right	R	.177	390	69	10	1	6	25	13	93	.209	.254
Sele,Aaron	L	.229	218	50	12	0	2	16	33	44	.328	.312	Swindell,Greg	L	.318	129	41	11	3	3	11	8	20	.355	.519
Throws Right	R	.245	204	50	12	1	3	21	15	49	.314	.358	Throws Left	R	.275	632	174	32	5	21	79	32	104	.310	.441
Seminara,F	L	.287	101	29	5	1	3	21	13	13	.368	.446	Swingle,Paul	L	.286	14	4	0	0	2	2	0	3	.286	.714
Throws Right	R	.304	79	24	2	2	2	6	8	9	.382	.456	Throws Right	R	.393	28	11	4	0	0	5	6	3	.486	.536
Service,Scott	L	.231	65	15	2	4	1	10	13	9	.357	.431	Tanana,Frank	L	.245	159	39	8	0	4	11	10	35	.292	.371
Throws Right	R	.269	108	29	5	0	5	13	3	34	.288	.454	Throws Left	R	.280	633	177	33	4	24	84	45	81	.334	.458
Shaw,Jeff	L	.312	173	54	11	0	7	23	20	18	.383	.497	Tapani,Kevin	L	.280	528	148	34	5	13	65	34	93	.322	.438
Throws Right	R	.200	185	37	11	1	5	23	12	32	.271	.351	Throws Right	R	.260	365	95	22	1	8	41	23	57	.313	.392
Shepherd,K	L	.286	35	10	0	0	0	2	1	3	.306	.286	Tavarez,J	L	.343	70	24	3	0	2	11	6	7	.397	.471
Throws Right	R	.372	43	16	4	0	4	13	3	4	.417	.744	Throws Right	R	.337	86	29	5	0	5	15	7	12	.394	.570
Shinall,Zak	L	.250	4	1	0	1	0	0	1	0	.400	.750	Taylor,Kerry	L	.308	117	36	6	1	3	20	23	15	.418	.453
Throws Right	R	.375	8	3	1	0	1	1	1	0	.444	.875	Throws Right	R	.252	143	36	5	0	2	25	26	30	.377	.329
Shouse,Brian	L	.556	9	5	1	0	1	3	0	2	.500	1.000	Taylor,Scott	L	.313	16	5	2	0	1	5	4	3	.450	.625
Throws Left	R	.200	10	2	0	0	0	0	2	1	.333	.200	Throws Left	R	.310	29	9	4	0	0	8	8	5	.474	.448
Slocumb,H	L	.239	46	11	0	0	1	9	10	5	.368	.304	Telford,A	L	.353	17	6	0	0	1	2	1	3	.389	.529
Throws Right	R	.255	94	24	3	0	2	16	10	17	.321	.351	Throws Right	R	.333	15	5	1	0	2	6	0	3	.375	.800
Slusarski,Joe	L	.375	16	6	1	0	1	4	5	0	.524	.625	Telgheder,D	L	.281	153	43	12	1	4	17	12	19	.335	.451
Throws Right	R	.214	14	3	0	0	0	1	6	1	.450	.214	Throws Right	R	.271	144	39	7	1	6	22	9	16	.327	.458
Smiley,John	L	.275	51	14	2	1	1	7	9	5	.383	.412	Tewksbury,Bob	L	.313	431	135	19	4	6	41	10	47	.326	.418
Throws Left	R	.288	358	103	15	2	14	56	22	55	.330	.458	Throws Right	R	.289	426	123	23	0	9	46	10	50	.311	.406
Smith,Bryn	L	.371	70	26	2	1	1	14	5	4	.392	.471	Thigpen,Bobby	L	.333	108	36	7	1	4	22	13	15	.403	.528
Throws Right	R	.350	60	21	2	0	1	8	6	5	.435	.433	Throws Right	R	.336	113	38	5	0	3	23	8	14	.398	.460
Smith,Lee	L	.225	120	27	3	1	6	14	9	31	.275	.417	Timlin,Mike	L	.275	102	28	5	0	4	16	15	19	.361	.441
Throws Right	R	.255	102	26	6	2	5	15	5	29	.287	.500	Throws Right	R	.292	120	35	1	0	3	20	12	30	.358	.375
Smith,Pete	L	.275	178	49	5	2	8	22	21	25	.348	.461	Toliver,Fred	L	.286	42	12	1	0	1	7	1	9	.311	.381
Throws Right	R	.264	163	43	12	1	7	17	15	28	.328	.479	Throws Right	R	.242	33	8	1	0	1	6	7	5	.372	.364
Smith,Zane	L	.222	54	12	2	0	0	4	4	8	.276	.259	Tomlin,Randy	L	.315	73	23	7	2	1	13	2	10	.338	.507
Throws Left	R	.314	271	85	16	8	5	38	18	24	.356	.487	Throws Left	R	.285	302	86	23	3	10	39	13	34	.316	.480

Pitchers vs. Left-Handed and Right-Handed Batters

Pitcher	vs	Avg	AB	H	2B	3B	HR	BI	BB	SO	OBP	SLG	Pitcher	vs	Avg	AB	H	2B	3B	HR	BI	BB	SO	OBP	SLG
Torres,S	L	.169	83	14	2	0	4	11	17	12	.307	.337	Wertz,Bill	L	.214	103	22	5	0	2	13	15	21	.314	.320
Throws Right	R	.299	77	23	5	0	1	7	10	11	.386	.403	Throws Right	R	.258	124	32	4	0	3	15	17	32	.350	.363
Trachsel,S	L	.150	40	6	1	0	1	2	2	8	.190	.250	West,David	L	.193	83	16	2	1	2	12	23	25	.385	.313
Throws Right	R	.303	33	10	2	1	3	6	1	6	.314	.697	Throws Left	R	.195	226	44	9	0	4	33	28	62	.287	.288
Trlicek,Ricky	L	.308	117	36	9	1	1	20	9	14	.362	.427	Weston,Mickey	L	.273	11	3	1	0	0	2	1	2	.333	.364
Throws Right	R	.184	125	23	4	2	2	15	12	27	.261	.296	Throws Right	R	.471	17	8	0	0	0	3	0	0	.500	.471
Trombley,Mike	L	.320	222	71	18	3	9	40	31	40	.396	.550	Wetteland,J	L	.175	177	31	5	1	3	15	18	69	.254	.266
Throws Right	R	.262	229	60	15	3	6	33	10	45	.298	.432	Throws Right	R	.206	131	27	5	3	0	8	10	44	.268	.290
Tsamis,George	L	.348	89	31	5	0	4	22	6	9	.408	.539	Whitehurst,W	L	.278	187	52	8	2	6	23	22	23	.347	.439
Throws Left	R	.302	182	55	12	1	5	29	21	21	.364	.462	Throws Right	R	.274	208	57	12	1	5	21	8	34	.305	.413
Turner,Matt	L	.254	114	29	7	1	3	16	16	23	.344	.412	Whiteside,M	L	.298	84	25	5	0	0	6	7	9	.355	.357
Throws Right	R	.203	128	26	3	0	4	17	10	36	.261	.320	Throws Right	R	.273	194	53	5	1	7	27	16	30	.329	.418
Urbani,Tom	L	.175	40	7	0	0	1	8	6	8	.277	.250	Wickander,K	L	.263	57	15	1	0	2	11	13	13	.408	.386
Throws Left	R	.319	207	66	16	3	3	27	20	25	.371	.469	Throws Left	R	.364	88	32	5	2	6	22	9	10	.429	.670
Valdez,Sergio	L	.429	7	3	1	0	0	2	1	0	.500	.571	Wickman,Bob	L	.283	247	70	19	0	6	34	37	30	.379	.433
Throws Right	R	.167	6	1	0	0	1	2	0	2	.167	.667	Throws Right	R	.284	303	86	12	4	7	42	32	40	.359	.419
Valenzuela,F	L	.283	120	34	10	1	4	19	19	22	.379	.483	Williams,B	L	.241	133	32	5	0	4	15	19	32	.344	.368
Throws Left	R	.262	554	145	34	5	14	68	60	56	.335	.417	Throws Right	R	.253	174	44	9	2	3	24	19	24	.328	.379
Valera,Julio	L	.396	106	42	6	1	4	20	12	8	.458	.585	Williams,Mike	L	.234	94	22	5	1	4	13	14	12	.333	.436
Throws Right	R	.297	118	35	8	0	4	17	3	20	.320	.466	Throws Right	R	.269	104	28	7	1	1	16	8	21	.321	.385
Van Poppel,T	L	.241	166	40	8	2	5	29	39	25	.386	.404	Williams,M	L	.231	39	9	0	0	0	4	5	12	.326	.231
Throws Right	R	.245	147	36	9	0	5	16	23	22	.349	.408	Throws Left	R	.247	190	47	9	0	3	25	39	48	.377	.342
Viola,Frank	L	.272	114	31	8	2	1	8	13	11	.341	.404	Williams,W	L	.246	57	14	2	0	0	4	12	7	.377	.281
Throws Left	R	.257	580	149	24	3	11	55	59	80	.329	.366	Throws Right	R	.292	89	26	5	0	2	15	10	17	.366	.416
Wagner,Paul	L	.301	266	80	13	2	7	35	25	48	.356	.444	Williamson,M	L	.255	141	36	7	0	3	16	12	22	.314	.369
Throws Right	R	.227	277	63	8	0	8	30	17	66	.272	.343	Throws Right	R	.337	208	70	18	0	2	31	13	23	.366	.452
Wainhouse,D	L	.500	6	3	0	0	1	5	1	2	.571	1.000	Willis,Carl	L	.292	89	26	8	0	2	16	10	15	.364	.449
Throws Right	R	.500	8	4	1	0	0	4	4	0	.692	.625	Throws Right	R	.236	127	30	12	1	0	23	7	29	.274	.346
Wakefield,Tim	L	.270	211	57	14	2	5	35	46	26	.413	.427	Wilson,Steve	L	.311	45	14	2	1	0	4	6	9	.404	.400
Throws Right	R	.307	287	88	20	1	9	40	29	33	.372	.477	Throws Left	R	.271	59	16	3	0	2	10	8	14	.358	.424
Walk,Bob	L	.276	384	106	25	3	12	56	45	44	.349	.451	Wilson,Trevor	L	.179	84	15	4	0	1	6	4	12	.231	.262
Throws Right	R	.314	344	108	11	2	11	52	25	36	.364	.453	Throws Left	R	.301	316	95	10	2	7	35	36	45	.377	.411
Walton,Bruce	L	.308	13	4	0	0	1	2	0	0	.308	.538	Witt,Bobby	L	.280	428	120	32	3	7	48	45	56	.351	.418
Throws Right	R	.500	14	7	1	0	0	3	3	0	.588	.571	Throws Right	R	.258	411	106	15	1	9	48	46	75	.329	.365
Ward,Duane	L	.211	123	26	3	0	2	11	18	47	.310	.285	Witt,Mike	L	.213	75	16	2	0	2	11	16	10	.359	.320
Throws Right	R	.176	131	23	3	0	2	13	7	50	.221	.244	Throws Right	R	.280	82	23	3	0	5	11	6	20	.344	.500
Watson,Allen	L	.240	50	12	1	0	1	5	8	7	.345	.320	Wohlers,Mark	L	.225	71	16	1	0	1	9	12	18	.337	.282
Throws Left	R	.277	282	78	17	3	10	37	20	42	.327	.465	Throws Right	R	.212	99	21	6	0	1	15	10	27	.288	.303
Wayne,Gary	L	.277	101	28	4	5	3	22	7	23	.319	.505	Worrell,Tim	L	.270	189	51	5	1	5	26	27	19	.356	.386
Throws Left	R	.276	145	40	10	1	5	24	19	26	.353	.462	Throws Right	R	.268	198	53	11	1	6	32	16	33	.319	.424
Weathers,Dave	L	.309	97	30	10	1	1	7	7	15	.356	.464	Worrell,Todd	L	.313	80	25	6	0	4	18	8	19	.359	.538
Throws Right	R	.303	89	27	4	0	2	16	6	19	.354	.416	Throws Right	R	.313	67	21	2	0	2	10	3	12	.333	.433
Wegman,Bill	L	.326	221	72	14	4	5	28	13	18	.358	.493	Young,Anthony	L	.263	186	49	9	0	5	31	27	33	.353	.392
Throws Right	R	.259	243	63	21	1	8	33	21	32	.313	.453	Throws Right	R	.267	202	54	3	1	3	29	15	29	.320	.337
Welch,Bob	L	.307	371	114	23	3	11	50	30	35	.360	.474	Young,Cliff	L	.316	57	18	2	0	0	8	1	5	.339	.351
Throws Right	R	.314	299	94	13	2	14	41	26	28	.378	.512	Throws Left	R	.293	191	56	10	0	9	30	17	26	.355	.487
Wells,David	L	.250	108	27	4	1	2	7	9	20	.328	.361	Young,Curt	L	.333	12	4	1	0	0	0	1	2	.385	.417
Throws Left	R	.254	613	156	29	2	24	71	33	119	.295	.426	Throws Left	R	.217	46	10	0	0	5	6	5	2	.294	.543
Wendell,Turk	L	.372	43	16	4	0	0	5	4	7	.426	.465	Young,Matt	L	.236	55	13	0	0	1	6	10	17	.364	.291
Throws Right	R	.178	45	8	0	0	0	2	4	8	.245	.178	Throws Left	R	.273	227	62	11	0	7	29	47	48	.401	.414

Pitchers vs. Left-Handed and Right-Handed Batters

Pitcher	vs	Avg	AB	H	2B	3B	HR	BI	BB	SO	OBP	SLG
Young,Pete	L	.333	6	2	0	0	1	1	0	2	.333	.833
Throws Right	R	.154	13	2	1	0	0	1	0	1	.154	.231
AL	L	.274	--	--	--	--	--	--	--	--	.349	.412
	R	.261	--	--	--	--	--	--	--	--	.329	.405
NL	L	.266	--	--	--	--	--	--	--	--	.340	.399
	R	.262	--	--	--	--	--	--	--	--	.318	.399
MLB	L	.270	--	--	--	--	--	--	--	--	.344	.406
	R	.262	--	--	--	--	--	--	--	--	.324	.402

Leader Boards

You can tell a lot about the 1993 baseball season by looking at the Leader Boards on the following fourteen pages. (Trust us, you really can.) What kind of stuff?

First, it was fun year if you like offense: five players walloped 40 or more home runs this season, the most to reach that mark since 1970, when six players made it; John Olerud threatened .400 and smashed 54 doubles; a gang of players (11, to be exact) drew 100 or more walks — again, the most to reach that plateau since 1970; Lenny Dykstra scored 143 runs; three players hit higher than .355 (Galarraga .370, Gwynn .368, and Olerud .360), the first time that's happened since 1948, when Ted Williams (.369), Lou Boudreau (.355), and Stan Musial (.376) turned the trick.

Oh, you wanted pitching, too? Well, we watched Randy Johnson baffle hitters all year long, 301 of them for strikeouts; nine pitchers racked up 40 or more saves, bringing the total number of pitchers in history to reach the 40 mark in one season to 29; and just when you thought there were no more good **starting** pitchers, 12 of them hit the 18-win mark, only the 4th time since 1978 that a dozen or more pitchers reached that plateau.

In the Special Batting and Pitching Leaders section, you'll find some great clutch hitting — and pitching — performances (Runners in Scoring Position), some feats of derring-do (Steals of Third), and some thief-busting catchers (Caught Stealing by Catchers).

You may want to buy another copy of this Handbook, shrink-wrap it, and store it for posterity's sake: this year's career section will mark the final appearances of some of baseball's greatest stars: Nolan Ryan, George Brett, Carlton Fisk. Plus, you'll dig up some interesting stuff: Dennis Eckersley is only 15 wins away from 200; that would make him the only pitcher in major league history to win 200 games and save 200 games. Hey, Tony, why not put him back in the rotation for 1994?

In the Bill James Leader Boards, you get a little bit of everything: the best pitching games of the season (Game Scores), a list of the games most exciting players (Power/Speed Number), this season's tough-luck pitchers (Tough Losses), and glimpses of managerial extremes (Slow Hooks and Quick Hooks).

All of this, by the way, is brought to you by STATS' own board-certified members of the Baseball Statisticians Association. Have fun!

1993 American League Batting Leaders

Batting Average

Player, Team	AB	H	AVG
J OLERUD, Tor	551	200	.363
P Molitor, Tor	636	211	.332
R Alomar, Tor	589	192	.326
K Lofton, Cle	569	185	.325
C Baerga, Cle	624	200	.320
F Thomas, ChA	549	174	.317
M Greenwell, Bos	540	170	.315
T Phillips, Det	566	177	.313
P O'Neill, NYA	498	155	.311
L Johnson, ChA	540	168	.311

On-Base Percentage

Player, Team	PA	OB	OBP
J OLERUD, Tor	679	321	.473
T Phillips, Det	706	313	.443
R Henderson, Tor	609	263	.432
F Thomas, ChA	676	288	.426
C Hoiles, Bal	500	208	.416
K Griffey Jr, Sea	691	282	.408
R Alomar, Tor	679	277	.408
K Lofton, Cle	655	267	.408
P Molitor, Tor	724	291	.402
M Vaughn, Bos	633	247	.390

Slugging Percentage

Player, Team	AB	TB	SLG
J GONZALEZ, Tex	536	339	.632
K Griffey Jr, Sea	582	359	.617
F Thomas, ChA	549	333	.607
J Olerud, Tor	551	330	.599
C Hoiles, Bal	419	245	.585
R Palmeiro, Tex	597	331	.554
A Belle, Cle	594	328	.552
T Salmon, Cal	515	276	.536
M Vaughn, Bos	539	283	.525
P Molitor, Tor	636	324	.509

Games

C RIPKEN, Bal	162
R Palmeiro, Tex	160
P Molitor, Tor	160
M Bordick, Oak	159
G Gagne, KC	159
A Belle, Cle	159

Plate Appearances

P MOLITOR, Tor	725
C Ripken, Bal	718
T Phillips, Det	707
T Fryman, Det	695
A Belle, Cle	693

At Bats

C RIPKEN, Bal	641
P Molitor, Tor	636
R Sierra, Oak	630
B McRae, KC	627
C Baerga, Cle	624

Hits

P MOLITOR, Tor	211
J Olerud, Tor	200
C Baerga, Cle	200
R Alomar, Tor	192
K Lofton, Cle	185

Singles

K LOFTON, Cle	148
P Molitor, Tor	147
C Baerga, Cle	145
T Phillips, Det	143
W Boggs, NYA	140

Doubles

J OLERUD, Tor	54
D White, Tor	42
J Valentin, Bos	40
R Palmeiro, Tex	40
K Puckett, Min	39

Triples

L JOHNSON, ChA	14
J Cora, ChA	13
D Hulse, Tex	10
B McRae, KC	9
T Fernandez, Tor	9

Home Runs

J GONZALEZ, Tex	46
K Griffey Jr, Sea	45
F Thomas, ChA	41
A Belle, Cle	38
R Palmeiro, Tex	37

Total Bases

K GRIFFEY JR, Sea	359
J Gonzalez, Tex	339
F Thomas, ChA	333
R Palmeiro, Tex	331
J Olerud, Tor	330

Runs Scored

R PALMEIRO, Tex	124
P Molitor, Tor	121
D White, Tor	116
K Lofton, Cle	116
R Henderson, Tor	114

Runs Batted In

A BELLE, Cle	129
F Thomas, ChA	128
J Carter, Tor	121
J Gonzalez, Tex	118
C Fielder, Det	117

Ground Double Play

E SPRAGUE, Tor	23
C Fielder, Det	22
M McLemore, Bal	21
G Brett, KC	20
D Mattingly, NYA	19

Sacrifice Hits

J CORA, ChA	19
J Valentin, Bos	16
B McRae, KC	14
4 Players tied with	13

Sacrifice Flies

A BELLE, Cle	14
C Baerga, Cle	13
F Thomas, ChA	13
3 Players tied with	10

Stolen Bases

K LOFTON, Cle	70
L Polonia, Cal	55
R Alomar, Tor	55
R Henderson, Tor	53
C Curtis, Cal	48

Caught Stealing

L POLONIA, Cal	24
C CURTIS, Cal	24
M McLemore, Bal	15
R Alomar, Tor	15
3 Players tied with	14

Walks

T PHILLIPS, Det	132
R Henderson, Tor	120
J Olerud, Tor	114
F Thomas, ChA	112
M Tettleton, Det	109

Intentional Walks

J OLERUD, Tor	33
K Griffey Jr, Sea	25
F Thomas, ChA	23
M Vaughn, Bos	23
R Palmeiro, Tex	22

Hit by Pitch

D VALLE, Sea	17
M Macfarlane, KC	16
A Dawson, Bos	13
J Gonzalez, Tex	13
2 Players tied with	11

Strikeouts

R DEER, Bos	169
D Tartabull, NYA	156
D Palmer, Tex	154
J Buhner, Sea	144
M Tettleton, Det	139

1993 National League Batting Leaders

Batting Average

Player, Team	AB	H	AVG
A GALARRAGA, Col	470	174	.370
T Gwynn, SD	489	175	.358
G Jefferies, StL	544	186	.342
B Bonds, SF	539	181	.336
M Grace, ChN	594	193	.325
J Bagwell, Hou	535	171	.320
M Piazza, LA	547	174	.318
J Kruk, Phi	535	169	.316
O Merced, Pit	447	140	.313
R Thompson, SF	494	154	.312

On-Base Percentage

Player, Team	PA	OB	OBP
B BONDS, SF	674	309	.458
J Kruk, Phi	651	280	.430
L Dykstra, Phi	773	325	.420
O Merced, Pit	527	218	.414
G Jefferies, StL	612	250	.408
A Galarraga, Col	506	204	.403
J Blauser, Atl	705	283	.401
T Gwynn, SD	533	212	.398
M Grace, ChN	675	265	.393
J Bell, Pit	688	270	.392

Slugging Percentage

Player, Team	AB	TB	SLG
B BONDS, SF	539	365	.677
A Galarraga, Col	470	283	.602
M Williams, SF	579	325	.561
M Piazza, LA	547	307	.561
F McGriff, Atl	557	306	.549
D Bichette, Col	538	283	.526
B Bonilla, NYN	502	262	.522
C Hayes, Col	573	299	.522
J Bagwell, Hou	535	276	.516
D Justice, Atl	585	301	.515

Games

J CONINE, Fla	162
L Dykstra, Phi	161
T Pendleton, Atl	161
J Blauser, Atl	161
2 Players tied with	159

Plate Appearances

L DYKSTRA, Phi	773
B Butler, LA	716
J Blauser, Atl	710
C Biggio, Hou	707
J Bell, Pit	701

At Bats

L DYKSTRA, Phi	637
T Pendleton, Atl	633
M Grissom, Mon	630
E Karros, LA	619
J King, Pit	611

Hits

L DYKSTRA, Phi	194
M Grace, ChN	193
M Grissom, Mon	188
J Bell, Pit	187
G Jefferies, StL	186

Singles

B BUTLER, LA	149
G Jefferies, StL	143
M Grissom, Mon	140
J Bell, Pit	137
2 Players tied with	136

Doubles

C HAYES, Col	45
L Dykstra, Phi	44
D Bichette, Col	43
C Biggio, Hou	41
T Gwynn, SD	41

Triples

S FINLEY, Hou	13
B Butler, LA	10
J Bell, Pit	9
M Morandini, Phi	9
A Martin, Pit	8
E Young, Col	8
V Coleman, NYN	8

Home Runs

B BONDS, SF	46
D Justice, Atl	40
M Williams, SF	38
F McGriff, Atl	37
R Gant, Atl	36

Total Bases

B BONDS, SF	365
M Williams, SF	325
R Gant, Atl	309
M Piazza, LA	307
L Dykstra, Phi	307

Runs Scored

L DYKSTRA, Phi	143
B Bonds, SF	129
R Gant, Atl	113
F McGriff, Atl	111
J Blauser, Atl	110

Runs Batted In

B BONDS, SF	123
D Justice, Atl	120
R Gant, Atl	117
M Piazza, LA	112
M Williams, SF	110

Ground Double Play

C HAYES, Col	25
M GRACE, ChN	25
E Murray, NYN	24
J Bagwell, Hou	21
M Lemke, Atl	20

Sacrifice Hits

J OFFERMAN, LA	25
J Reed, LA	17
B Butler, LA	14
K Hill, Mon	14
A Benes, SD	14

Sacrifice Flies

L GONZALEZ, Hou	10
8 Players tied with	9

Intentional Walks

B BONDS, SF	43
L Walker, Mon	20
M Grace, ChN	14
R Wilkins, ChN	13
M Lemke, Atl	13
K Manwaring, SF	13
W Weiss, Fla	13

Stolen Bases

C CARR, Fla	58
M Grissom, Mon	53
O Nixon, Atl	47
G Jefferies, StL	46
D Lewis, SF	46

Caught Stealing

C CARR, Fla	22
B Butler, LA	19
E Young, Col	19
C Biggio, Hou	17
D Lewis, SF	15

Hit by Pitch

J BLAUSER, Atl	16
D Bell, SD	12
3 Players tied with	10

Walks

L DYKSTRA, Phi	129
B Bonds, SF	126
D Daulton, Phi	117
J Kruk, Phi	111
B Butler, LA	86

Strikeouts

C SNYDER, LA	147
J Conine, Fla	135
S Sosa, ChN	135
O Destrade, Fla	130
P Plantier, SD	124

1993 American League Pitching Leaders

Earned Run Average

Pitcher, Team	IP	ER	ERA
K APPIER, KC	238.2	68	**2.56**
W Alvarez, ChA	207.2	68	2.95
J Key, NYA	236.2	79	3.00
A Fernandez, ChA	247.1	86	3.13
F Viola, Bos	183.2	64	3.14
C Finley, Cal	251.1	88	3.15
M Langston, Cal	256.1	91	3.20
R Johnson, Sea	255.1	92	3.24
D Darwin, Bos	229.1	83	3.26
D Cone, KC	254.0	94	3.33

Won-Lost Percentage

Pitcher, Team	W	L	WL%
J GUZMAN, Tor	14	3	**.824**
B Wickman, NYA	14	4	.778
J Key, NYA	18	6	.750
R Johnson, Sea	19	8	.704
M Mussina, Bal	14	6	.700
D Fleming, Sea	12	5	.706
J Bere, ChA	12	5	.706
K Appier, KC	18	8	.692
J McDowell, ChA	22	10	.688
P Hentgen, Tor	19	9	.679

Opposition Average

Pitcher, Team	AB	H	AVG
R JOHNSON, Sea	913	185	**.203**
K Appier, KC	863	183	.212
D Cone, KC	920	205	.223
B McDonald, Bal	812	185	.228
C Bosio, Sea	602	138	.229
D Darwin, Bos	852	196	.230
W Alvarez, ChA	729	168	.230
M Langston, Cal	942	220	.234
C Eldred, Mil	969	232	.239
A Fernandez, ChA	919	221	.241

Games

G HARRIS, Bos	**80**
S Radinsky, ChA	73
T Fossas, Bos	71
D Ward, Tor	71
J Nelson, Sea	71

Games Started

C ELDRED, Mil	**36**
M MOORE, Det	**36**
M Langston, Cal	35
K Tapani, Min	35
C Finley, Cal	35

Complete Games

C FINLEY, Cal	**13**
K Brown, Tex	12
J McDowell, ChA	10
R Johnson, Sea	10
C Eldred, Mil	8

Games Finished

D WARD, Tor	**70**
R Hernandez, ChA	67
J Montgomery, KC	63
R Aguilera, Min	61
T Henke, Tex	60

Wins

J MCDOWELL, ChA	**22**
R Johnson, Sea	19
P Hentgen, Tor	19
K Appier, KC	18
J Key, NYA	18
A Fernandez, ChA	18

Losses

S ERICKSON, Min	**19**
C Eldred, Mil	16
K Tapani, Min	15
7 Pitchers tied with	14

Saves

J MONTGOMERY, KC	**45**
D WARD, Tor	**45**
T Henke, Tex	40
R Hernandez, ChA	38
D Eckersley, Oak	36

Shutouts

J MCDOWELL, ChA	**4**
M Moore, Det	3
R Johnson, Sea	3
K Brown, Tex	3
5 Pitchers tied with	2

Hits Allowed

S ERICKSON, Min	**266**
J McDowell, ChA	261
J Navarro, Mil	254
2 Pitchers tied with	243

Doubles Allowed

K TAPANI, Min	**56**
E Hanson, Sea	49
B Witt, Oak	47
C Eldred, Mil	47
H Pichardo, KC	46
K Rogers, Tex	46

Triples Allowed

R BONES, Mil	**11**
J Navarro, Mil	9
S Erickson, Min	8
6 Pitchers tied with	7

Home Runs Allowed

M MOORE, Det	**35**
C Eldred, Mil	32
D Darwin, Bos	31
R Bones, Mil	28
B Gullickson, Det	28

Batters Faced

C ELDRED, Mil	**1087**
J McDowell, ChA	1067
C Finley, Cal	1065
D Cone, KC	1060
R Johnson, Sea	1043

Innings Pitched

C ELDRED, Mil	**258.0**
J McDowell, ChA	256.2
M Langston, Cal	256.1
R Johnson, Sea	255.1
D Cone, KC	254.0

Runs Allowed

S ERICKSON, Min	**138**
J Navarro, Mil	135
M Moore, Det	135
K Tapani, Min	123
J Mesa, Cle	122
R Bones, Mil	122

Strikeouts

R JOHNSON, Sea	**308**
M Langston, Cal	196
J Guzman, Tor	194
D Cone, KC	191
C Finley, Cal	187

Walks Allowed

W ALVAREZ, ChA	**122**
D Cone, KC	114
J Guzman, Tor	110
R Johnson, Sea	99
2 Pitchers tied with	91

Hit Batters

R JOHNSON, Sea	**16**
K Brown, Tex	15
R Clemens, Bos	11
J Navarro, Mil	11
4 Pitchers tied with	10

Wild Pitches

J GUZMAN, Tor	**26**
T Gordon, KC	17
J Morris, Tor	14
D Cone, KC	14
D Wells, Det	13

Balks

W BANKS, Min	**5**
K ROGERS, Tex	**5**
J Deshaies, Min	4
S Radinsky, ChA	4
4 Pitchers tied with	3

1993 National League Pitching Leaders

Earned Run Average

Pitcher, Team	IP	ER	ERA
G MADDUX, Atl	267.0	70	2.36
J Rijo, Cin	257.1	71	2.48
M Portugal, Hou	208.0	64	2.77
B Swift, SF	232.2	73	2.82
S Avery, Atl	223.1	73	2.94
P Harnisch, Hou	217.2	72	2.98
T Candiotti, LA	213.2	74	3.12
T Glavine, Atl	239.1	85	3.20
K Hill, Mon	183.2	66	3.23
T Mulholland, Phi	191.0	69	3.25

Won-Lost Percentage

Pitcher, Team	W	L	WL%
M PORTUGAL, Hou	18	4	.818
T Greene, Phi	16	4	.800
T Glavine, Atl	22	6	.786
J Burkett, SF	22	7	.759
S Avery, Atl	18	6	.750
B Swift, SF	21	8	.724
J Fassero, Mon	12	5	.706
C Schilling, Phi	16	7	.696
G Maddux, Atl	20	10	.667
P Martinez, LA	10	5	.667

Opposition Average

Pitcher, Team	AB	H	AVG
P HARNISCH, Hou	798	171	.214
B Swift, SF	861	195	.227
J Rijo, Cin	949	218	.230
J Smoltz, Atl	905	208	.230
G Maddux, Atl	984	228	.232
A Benes, SD	862	200	.232
T Greene, Phi	751	175	.233
K Hill, Mon	684	163	.238
D Kile, Hou	637	152	.239
P Astacio, LA	689	165	.240

Games

M JACKSON, SF	81
R Beck, SF	76
D West, Phi	76
G McMichael, Atl	74
2 Pitchers tied with	73

Wins

T GLAVINE, Atl	22
J BURKETT, SF	22
B Swift, SF	21
G Maddux, Atl	20
2 Pitchers tied with	18

Hits Allowed

B TEWKSBURY, StL	258
D Drabek, Hou	242
G Harris, Col	239
T Glavine, Atl	236
C Schilling, Phi	234

Batters Faced

G MADDUX, Atl	1064
J Rijo, Cin	1029
J Smoltz, Atl	1028
T Glavine, Atl	1014
D Drabek, Hou	991

Walks Allowed

R MARTINEZ, LA	104
J Smoltz, Atl	100
T Glavine, Atl	90
R Bowen, Fla	87
A Benes, SD	86

Games Started

T GLAVINE, Atl	36
G MADDUX, Atl	36
J RIJO, Cin	36
S Avery, Atl	35
J Smoltz, Atl	35
G Harris, Col	35

Losses

D DRABEK, Hou	18
J Armstrong, Fla	17
G Harris, Col	17
A Young, NYN	16
C Hough, Fla	16

Doubles Allowed

S COOKE, Pit	58
G Hibbard, ChN	54
T Glavine, Atl	50
G Harris, Col	45
J Smoltz, Atl	45

Innings Pitched

G MADDUX, Atl	267.0
J Rijo, Cin	257.1
J Smoltz, Atl	243.2
T Glavine, Atl	239.1
D Drabek, Hou	237.2

Hit Batters

D KILE, Hou	15
J Burkett, SF	11
D Martinez, Mon	11
6 Pitchers tied with	9

Complete Games

G MADDUX, Atl	8
D Gooden, NYN	7
D Drabek, Hou	7
T Mulholland, Phi	7
C Schilling, Phi	7
T Greene, Phi	7

Saves

R MYERS, ChN	53
R Beck, SF	48
B Harvey, Fla	45
L Smith, StL	43
J Wetteland, Mon	43
M Williams, Phi	43

Triples Allowed

A REYNOSO, Col	10
B RIVERA, Phi	10
3 Pitchers tied with	9

Runs Allowed

G HARRIS, Col	127
B Walk, Pit	121
C Schilling, Phi	114
A Benes, SD	111
2 Pitchers tied with	110

Wild Pitches

T GREENE, Phi	15
A Benes, SD	14
B Rivera, Phi	13
J Smoltz, Atl	13
2 Pitchers tied with	12

Games Finished

R BECK, SF	71
R Myers, ChN	69
D Jones, Hou	60
J Wetteland, Mon	58
M Williams, Phi	57

Shutouts

P HARNISCH, Hou	4
R Martinez, LA	3
11 Pitchers tied with	3

Home Runs Allowed

G HARRIS, Col	33
J Armstrong, Fla	29
D Martinez, Mon	27
F Tanana, NYA	26
J Guzman, ChN	25

Strikeouts

J RIJO, Cin	227
J Smoltz, Atl	208
G Maddux, Atl	197
C Schilling, Phi	186
P Harnisch, Hou	185

Balks

P ASTACIO, LA	9
A Reynoso, Col	6
G Harris, Col	6
C Hammond, Fla	5
K Gross, LA	5
J Guzman, ChN	5

1993 American League Special Batting Leaders

Scoring Position

Player, Team	AB	H	AVG
P MOLITOR, Tor	190	73	.384
J Olerud, Tor	140	52	.371
D Mattingly, NYA	125	46	.368
L Johnson, ChA	118	43	.364
T Fernandez, Tor	105	38	.362
B Harper, Min	134	48	.358
M Greenwell, Bos	121	43	.355
M Vaughn, Bos	134	47	.351
C Baerga, Cle	167	57	.341
B Surhoff, Mil	130	44	.338

Leadoff On-Base%

Player, Team	PA	OB	OBP
T PHILLIPS, Det	698	309	.443
R Henderson, Tor	586	253	.432
R Amaral, Sea	174	71	.408
K Lofton, Cle	652	266	.408
T Raines, ChA	480	192	.400
W Boggs, NYA	290	115	.396
D Hamilton, Mil	336	130	.387
B Anderson, Bal	638	233	.365
C Knoblauch, Min	366	131	.358
J Cora, ChA	177	61	.345

Cleanup Slugging%

Player, Team	AB	TB	SLG
J GONZALEZ, Tex	535	338	.632
A Belle, Cle	591	328	.555
W Joyner, KC	178	96	.539
H Baines, Bal	385	201	.522
K Hrbek, Min	335	170	.507
D Tartabull, NYA	513	258	.503
G Vaughn, Mil	418	209	.500
T Neel, Oak	256	128	.500
J Carter, Tor	577	288	.499
M Vaughn, Bos	204	101	.495

Vs LHP

R AMARAL, Sea	.372
P Molitor, Tor	.363
M Blowers, Sea	.357
T Raines, ChA	.348
R Velarde, NYA	.345

Vs RHP

J OLERUD, Tor	.396
R Alomar, Tor	.359
K Lofton, Cle	.342
P O'Neill, NYA	.342
L Johnson, ChA	.326

Late & Close

P MOLITOR, Tor	.411
M Blowers, Sea	.392
S Alomar Jr, Cle	.391
M Greenwell, Bos	.386
P Meares, Min	.373

Bases Loaded

E BURKS, ChA	.636
D Thon, Mil	.625
R Alomar, Tor	.600
B Anderson, Bal	.571
C Hoiles, Bal	.571

OBP vs LHP

C FIELDER, Det	.461
R Henderson, Tor	.461
P Molitor, Tor	.445
T Phillips, Det	.444
G Vaughn, Mil	.443

OBP vs RHP

J OLERUD, Tor	.500
R Alomar, Tor	.449
T Phillips, Det	.443
L Whitaker, Det	.434
F Thomas, ChA	.429

BA at Home

P MOLITOR, Tor	.364
J Olerud, Tor	.346
K Griffey Jr, Sea	.332
M Vaughn, Bos	.332
M Greenwell, Bos	.332

BA on the Road

J OLERUD, Tor	.379
K Lofton, Cle	.337
R Alomar, Tor	.327
T Raines, ChA	.320
T Phillips, Det	.316

SLG vs LHP

M BLOWERS, Sea	.669
F Thomas, ChA	.649
R Henderson, Tor	.623
C Hoiles, Bal	.618
A Belle, Cle	.617

SLG vs RHP

J OLERUD, Tor	.678
K Griffey Jr, Sea	.644
J Gonzalez, Tex	.626
R Palmeiro, Tex	.621
F Thomas, ChA	.590

SB Success %

D WHITE, Tor	89.5
R Palmeiro, Tex	88.0
R Henderson, Tor	86.9
P Molitor, Tor	84.6
K Lofton, Cle	83.3

Times on Base

J OLERUD, Tor	321
T Phillips, Det	313
P Molitor, Tor	291
F Thomas, ChA	288
K Griffey Jr, Sea	282

AB per HR

J GONZALEZ, Tex	11.6
K Griffey Jr, Sea	12.9
F Thomas, ChA	13.4
C Hoiles, Bal	14.4
A Belle, Cle	15.6

Ground/Fly Ratio

L JOHNSON, ChA	2.41
T Phillips, Det	2.38
K Lofton, Cle	2.35
F Fermin, Cle	2.27
L Polonia, Cal	2.03

GDP/GDP Opp

D HENDERSON, Oak	1.1
K Gibson, Det	2.1
M Felder, Sea	2.4
D White, Tor	2.9
H Reynolds, Bal	3.2

% CS by Catchers

R KARKOVICE, ChA	53.9
D Valle, Sea	45.6
J Ortiz, Cle	45.4
I Rodriguez, Tex	44.4
C Kreuter, Det	44.1

Pitches Seen

T PHILLIPS, Det	2938
B Anderson, Bal	2816
R Ventura, ChA	2772
T Fryman, Det	2735
M Tettleton, Det	2733

Pitches per PA

R HENDERSON, Tor	4.31
M Tettleton, Det	4.29
B Anderson, Bal	4.24
C Hoiles, Bal	4.23
W Boggs, NYA	4.20

% Pitches Taken

R HENDERSON, Tor	69.8
M Tettleton, Det	65.1
K Lofton, Cle	63.8
R Ventura, ChA	63.8
B Anderson, Bal	63.7

Steals of Third

R HENDERSON, Tor	15
R ALOMAR, Tor	15
C Curtis, Cal	9
L Polonia, Cal	9
K Lofton, Cle	9

1993 National League Special Batting Leaders

Scoring Position

Player, Team	AB	H	AVG
A GALARRAGA, Col	128	54	.422
G Jefferies, StL	146	56	.384
T Gwynn, SD	87	32	.368
B Bonds, SF	123	44	.358
D Slaught, Pit	101	35	.347
A Van Slyke, Pit	85	29	.341
L Alicea, StL	77	26	.338
M Grace, ChN	152	51	.336
K Mitchell, Cin	103	34	.330
D May, ChN	134	44	.328

Leadoff On-Base%

Player, Team	PA	OB	OBP
L DYKSTRA, Phi	773	325	.420
M Grissom, Mon	151	62	.411
D DeShields, Mon	485	188	.388
B Butler, LA	670	258	.385
B Gilkey, StL	442	168	.380
C Biggio, Hou	702	262	.373
J Gardner, SD	183	67	.366
O Nixon, Atl	513	183	.357
D Smith, ChN	269	94	.349
R Gutierrez, SD	162	56	.346

Cleanup Slugging%

Player, Team	AB	TB	SLG
A GALARRAGA, Col	392	248	.633
K Mitchell, Cin	311	185	.595
M Williams, SF	566	315	.557
F McGriff, Atl	535	297	.555
P Plantier, SD	186	102	.548
B Bonilla, NYN	481	253	.526
T Zeile, StL	367	180	.491
D Justice, Atl	202	99	.490
O Merced, Pit	133	65	.489
L Walker, Mon	488	230	.471

Vs LHP

T GWYNN, SD	.359
M Grace, ChN	.352
R Thompson, SF	.352
G Jefferies, StL	.351
A Galarraga, Col	.350

Vs RHP

A GALARRAGA, Col	.377
B Bonds, SF	.343
G Jefferies, StL	.338
J Kruk, Phi	.329
J Bagwell, Hou	.320

Late & Close

M GRACE, ChN	.454
G Jefferies, StL	.402
W McGee, SF	.400
T Gwynn, SD	.371
B Bonds, SF	.370

Bases Loaded

L WALKER, Mon	.625
B Bonds, SF	.500
D Justice, Atl	.467
C Hayes, Col	.461
L Alicea, StL	.454

OBP vs LHP

J BELL, Pit	.449
B Bonds, SF	.423
L Smith, Atl	.414
L Dykstra, Phi	.414
M Grace, ChN	.412

OBP vs RHP

B BONDS, SF	.481
J Kruk, Phi	.456
L Dykstra, Phi	.424
O Merced, Pit	.423
D Daulton, Phi	.418

BA at Home

A GALARRAGA, Col	.402
T Gwynn, SD	.382
D Bichette, Col	.373
M Grace, ChN	.353
B Butler, LA	.347

BA on the Road

B BONDS, SF	.359
G Jefferies, StL	.342
T Gwynn, SD	.332
J Blauser, Atl	.330
O Merced, Pit	.326

SLG vs LHP

M WILLIAMS, SF	.683
M Piazza, LA	.655
B Bonds, SF	.619
W Chamberlain, Phi	.612
J Bagwell, Hou	.592

SLG vs RHP

B BONDS, SF	.716
A Galarraga, Col	.612
F McGriff, Atl	.607
R Wilkins, ChN	.588
P Plantier, SD	.554

SB Success %

E DAVIS, LA	86.8
M Grissom, Mon	84.1
D Bell, SD	83.9
G Jefferies, StL	83.6
M Lansing, Mon	82.1

Times on Base

L DYKSTRA, Phi	325
B Bonds, SF	309
J Blauser, Atl	283
J Kruk, Phi	280
B Butler, LA	272

AB per HR

B BONDS, SF	11.7
P Plantier, SD	13.6
D Justice, Atl	14.6
B Bonilla, NYN	14.8
F McGriff, Atl	15.1

Ground/Fly Ratio

W MCGEE, SF	3.47
B Butler, LA	2.63
O Nixon, Atl	2.55
M Duncan, Phi	2.34
D Lewis, SF	2.23

GDP/GDP Opp

D DAULTON, Phi	1.5
J Burnitz, NYN	3.2
P Plantier, SD	3.9
W Weiss, Fla	4.8
H Johnson, NYN	5.0

% CS by Catchers

K MANWARING, SF	46.0
R Wilkins, ChN	45.9
M Piazza, LA	35.3
T Pagnozzi, StL	34.1
D Daulton, Phi	33.6

Pitches Seen

L DYKSTRA, Phi	3027
B Butler, LA	2836
J Blauser, Atl	2831
J Bell, Pit	2786
C Biggio, Hou	2630

Pitches per PA

D DeSHIELDS, Mon	4.05
D Daulton, Phi	4.01
J Blauser, Atl	3.99
P Plantier, SD	3.99
J Bell, Pit	3.97

% Pitches Taken

D DeSHIELDS, Mon	65.3
E Young, Col	63.5
L Dykstra, Phi	63.1
D Daulton, Phi	62.6
B Butler, LA	61.9

Steals of Third

D LEWIS, SF	11
M GRISSOM, Mon	11
B Kelly, Cin	9
B Butler, LA	9
3 Players tied with	8

1993 American League Special Pitching Leaders

Baserunners Per 9 IP

Player, Team	IP	BR	BR/9
D DARWIN, Bos	229.1	248	9.73
K Appier, KC	238.2	265	9.99
J Key, NYA	236.2	263	10.00
R Johnson, Sea	255.1	300	10.57
A Fernandez, ChA	247.1	294	10.70
M Langston, Cal	256.1	306	10.74
C Bosio, Sea	164.1	203	11.12
D Wells, Det	187.0	232	11.17
M Mussina, Bal	167.2	210	11.27
B McDonald, Bal	220.1	276	11.27

Run Support Per 9 IP

Player, Team	IP	R	R/9
M MOORE, Det	213.2	150	6.32
J Guzman, Tor	221.0	152	6.19
M Mussina, Bal	167.2	114	6.12
K Rogers, Tex	208.1	141	6.09
P Hentgen, Tor	216.1	146	6.07
J Key, NYA	236.2	158	6.01
T Leary, Sea	169.1	112	5.95
J Doherty, Det	184.2	120	5.85
D Stewart, Tor	162.0	105	5.83
R Bones, Mil	203.2	131	5.79

Save Percentage

Player, Team	OP	SV	SV%
J RUSSELL, Bos	37	33	.892
J Montgomery, KC	51	45	.882
D Ward, Tor	51	45	.882
R Hernandez, ChA	44	38	.864
N Charlton, Sea	21	18	.857
T Henke, Tex	47	40	.851
R Aguilera, Min	40	34	.850
G Olson, Bal	35	29	.829
M Henneman, Det	29	24	.828
S Farr, NYA	31	25	.807

Hits per 9 IP

R JOHNSON, Sea	6.52
K Appier, KC	6.90
D Cone, KC	7.26
W Alvarez, ChA	7.28
B McDonald, Bal	7.56

Home Runs per 9 IP

K APPIER, KC	0.30
K Brown, Tex	0.54
H Pichardo, KC	0.55
T Stottlemyre, Tor	0.56
F Viola, Bos	0.59

Strikeouts per 9 IP

R JOHNSON, Sea	10.9
M Perez, NYA	8.2
J Guzman, Tor	7.9
R Clemens, Bos	7.5
W Banks, Min	7.2

GDP per 9 IP

J ABBOTT, NYA	1.2
J Doherty, Det	1.2
T Leary, Sea	1.1
R Sutcliffe, Bal	1.1
S Erickson, Min	1.1

Vs LHB

M LANGSTON, Cal	.176
N Ryan, Tex	.188
R Aguilera, Min	.200
T Henke, Tex	.205
D Ward, Tor	.211

Vs RHB

K APPIER, KC	.184
R Johnson, Sea	.204
D Darwin, Bos	.204
D Cone, KC	.219
A Fernandez, ChA	.222

OBP Leadoff Inning

K APPIER, KC	.235
J Moyer, Bal	.245
K Brown, Tex	.268
J Key, NYA	.279
E Hanson, Sea	.291

BA Allowed ScPos

D CONE, KC	.178
W Alvarez, ChA	.201
F Viola, Bos	.209
C Eldred, Mil	.212
K Appier, KC	.213

SLG Allowed

K APPIER, KC	.292
R Johnson, Sea	.322
W Alvarez, ChA	.329
B McDonald, Bal	.342
D Cone, KC	.343

OBP Allowed

D DARWIN, Bos	.272
K Appier, KC	.279
J Key, NYA	.279
R Johnson, Sea	.290
M Langston, Cal	.295

PkOf Throw/Runner

D CONE, KC	1.81
M Langston, Cal	1.70
R Clemens, Bos	1.56
M Perez, NYA	1.46
W Alvarez, ChA	1.46

SB% Allowed

K ROGERS, Tex	26.7
A Fernandez, ChA	31.3
M Mussina, Bal	33.3
J Deshaies, SF	34.8
J Doherty, Det	36.8

Pitches per Batter

T LEARY, Sea	3.33
D Darwin, Bos	3.37
J Abbott, NYA	3.40
J Doherty, Det	3.45
R Bones, Mil	3.46

Grd/Fly Ratio Off

J DOHERTY, Det	2.63
H Pichardo, KC	2.22
K Brown, Tex	2.17
S Erickson, Min	2.14
J Abbott, NYA	2.13

K/BB Ratio

J KEY, NYA	4.02
D Wells, Det	3.31
R Johnson, Sea	3.11
E Hanson, Sea	2.72
M Mussina, Bal	2.66

Wins in Relief

S RADINSKY, ChA	8
5 Pitchers tied with	7

Holds

R HONEYCUTT, Oak	20
G Harris, Bos	17
J Nelson, Sea	17
3 Pitchers with	16

Blown Saves

G HARRIS, Bos	10
J NELSON, Sea	10
D ECKERSLEY, Oak	10
T Henke, Tex	7
D Henry, Mil	7

% Inherited Scored

B BREWER, KC	10.3
P Quantrill, Bos	13.9
B Munoz, NYA	18.2
T Fossas, Bos	18.3
K Patterson, Cal	18.9

1st Batter OBP

D COX, Tor	.140
B MacDonald, Det	.158
L Casian, Min	.167
K Ryan, Bos	.175
R Aguilera, Min	.177

1993 National League Special Pitching Leaders

Baserunners Per 9 IP

Player, Team	IP	BR	BR/9
G MADDUX, Atl	267.0	286	9.64
J Rijo, Cin	257.1	282	9.86
B Swift, SF	232.2	256	9.90
T Mulholland, Phi	191.0	220	10.37
S Avery, Atl	223.1	259	10.44
P Harnisch, Hou	217.2	256	10.59
J Burkett, SF	231.2	275	10.68
T Greene, Phi	200.0	240	10.80
R Arocha, StL	188.0	231	11.06
D Gooden, NYN	208.2	258	11.13

Run Support Per 9 IP

Player, Team	IP	R	R/9
B RIVERA, Phi	163.0	125	6.90
T Greene, Phi	200.0	153	6.89
D Kile, Hou	171.2	123	6.45
B Swift, SF	232.2	152	5.88
K Gross, LA	202.1	132	5.87
B Tewksbury, StL	213.2	139	5.85
T Glavine, Atl	239.1	152	5.72
D Jackson, Phi	210.1	129	5.52
J Burkett, SF	231.2	142	5.52
J Smoltz, Atl	243.2	143	5.28

Save Percentage

Player, Team	OP	SV	SV%
R BECK, SF	52	48	.923
B Harvey, Fla	49	45	.918
G McMichael, Atl	21	19	.905
R Myers, ChN	59	53	.898
M Williams, Phi	49	43	.878
J Wetteland, Mon	49	43	.878
S Belinda, KC	22	19	.864
D Holmes, Col	29	25	.862
J Gott, LA	29	25	.862
L Smith, NYA	50	43	.860

Hits per 9 IP

P HARNISCH, Hou	7.07
B Swift, SF	7.54
J Rijo, Cin	7.62
J Smoltz, Atl	7.68
G Maddux, Atl	7.69

Home Runs per 9 IP

K HILL, Mon	0.34
M Portugal, Hou	0.43
G Maddux, Atl	0.47
T Candiotti, LA	0.51
D Jackson, Phi	0.51

Strikeouts per 9 IP

J RIJO, Cin	7.9
J Smoltz, Atl	7.7
J Guzman, ChN	7.7
P Harnisch, Hou	7.6
T Greene, Phi	7.5

GDP per 9 IP

B WALK, Pit	1.2
G Hibbard, ChN	1.1
S Avery, Atl	1.0
B Swift, SF	1.0
R Arocha, StL	1.0

Vs LHB

B HARVEY, Fla	.132
J Wetteland, Mon	.175
T Scott, Mon	.180
R Beck, SF	.180
J Fassero, Mon	.183

Vs RHB

B SWIFT, SF	.177
P Harnisch, Hou	.186
J Smoltz, Atl	.199
J Rijo, Cin	.214
A Benes, SD	.221

OBP Leadoff Inning

B SWIFT, SF	.241
J Fassero, Mon	.248
F Tanana, NYA	.263
T Candiotti, LA	.266
P Harnisch, Hou	.273

BA Allowed ScPos

D MARTINEZ, Mon	.174
R Martinez, LA	.183
J Rijo, Cin	.188
G Maddux, Atl	.210
D Brocail, SD	.213

SLG Allowed

G MADDUX, Atl	.317
M Portugal, Hou	.323
B Swift, SF	.326
K Hill, Mon	.336
T Candiotti, LA	.338

OBP Allowed

G MADDUX, Atl	.273
B Swift, SF	.277
J Rijo, Cin	.278
T Mulholland, Phi	.282
P Harnisch, Hou	.289

PkOf Throw/Runner

C HOUGH, Fla	1.77
A Reynoso, Col	1.70
J Armstrong, Fla	1.65
J Burkett, SF	1.51
K Hill, Mon	1.42

SB% Allowed

T MULHOL'ND, Phi	16.7
G HIBBARD, ChN	16.7
C Hammond, Fla	45.5
C Schilling, Phi	50.0
J Burkett, SF	50.0

Pitches per Batter

B TEWKSBURY, StL	3.20
G Hibbard, ChN	3.26
O Hershiser, LA	3.35
B Swift, SF	3.35
D Drabek, Hou	3.37

Grd/Fly Ratio Off

B SWIFT, SF	3.12
G Maddux, Atl	2.64
D Martinez, Mon	2.25
M Morgan, ChN	2.25
G Hibbard, ChN	2.17

K/BB Ratio

B TEWKSBURY, StL	4.85
G Maddux, Atl	3.79
J Rijo, Cin	3.66
J Burkett, SF	3.63
C Schilling, Phi	3.26

Wins in Relief

P MARTINEZ, LA	10
J Wetteland, Mon	9
S Reed, Col	9
B Minor, Pit	8
3 Pitchers tied with	7

Holds

M JACKSON, SF	34
B Scanlan, ChN	25
L Andersen, Phi	25
R Murphy, StL	24
X Hernandez, Hou	22

Blown Saves

R DIBBLE, Cin	9
M ROJAS, Mon	9
X Hernandez, Hou	8
D Jones, Hou	8
G Harris, SD	8

% Inherited Scored

A OSUNA, Hou	11.4
R Murphy, StL	12.1
T Hoffman, SD	13.3
J Wetteland, Mon	18.2
R Beck, SF	20.0

1st Batter OBP

J SHAW, Mon	.103
L Andersen, Phi	.121
M Wohlers, Atl	.125
J Brantley, SF	.143

1993 Active Career Batting Leaders

Batting Average

Player, Team	AB	H	AVG
W BOGGS	6773	2267	.335
T Gwynn	6190	2039	.329
F Thomas	1872	600	.321
K Puckett	6267	1996	.318
D Mattingly	6173	1908	.309
M Greenwell	3520	1082	.307
H Morris	1599	491	.307
E Martinez	1940	593	.306
P Molitor	8156	2492	.306
G Brett	10349	3154	.305
M Grace	3401	1033	.304
K Griffey Jr	2747	832	.303
C Baerga	2186	657	.301
J Franco	5948	1784	.300
J Kruk	3483	1044	.300
W Clark	4269	1278	.299
K Lofton	1219	364	.299
W McGee	6144	1832	.298
B Larkin	3506	1045	.298
T Raines	6880	2050	.298
D Hamilton	1654	492	.297
J Olerud	1829	544	.297
R Alomar	3551	1054	.297
B Harper	2893	858	.297
R Palmeiro	3867	1144	.296

On-Base Percentage

Player, Team	PA	OB	OBP
F THOMAS	2327	1026	.441
W Boggs	7943	3367	.424
R Henderson	8865	3599	.406
J Olerud	2181	868	.398
J Kruk	4102	1627	.397
R Milligan	2496	980	.393
E Martinez	2241	877	.391
B Bonds	4926	1924	.391
F McGriff	4234	1646	.389
D Magadan	3009	1169	.389
T Raines	7967	3086	.387
T Gwynn	6786	2594	.382
J Bagwell	1953	743	.380
K Lofton	1381	521	.377
M Grace	3865	1458	.377
B Butler	7793	2935	.377
K Griffey Jr	3108	1166	.375
D Tartabull	4490	1684	.375
M Greenwell	3946	1479	.375
W Clark	4865	1816	.373
L Dykstra	4416	1647	.373
O Merced	1493	556	.372
L Smith	5859	2179	.372
P Molitor	9094	3361	.370
G Brett	11598	4283	.369

Slugging Percentage

Player, Team	AB	TB	SLG
F THOMAS	1872	1050	.561
J Gonzalez	1815	971	.535
F McGriff	3560	1892	.531
B Bonds	4123	2169	.526
K Griffey Jr	2747	1428	.520
K Mitchell	3432	1768	.515
D Tartabull	3853	1964	.510
M McGwire	3207	1631	.509
D Strawberry	4664	2367	.508
J Canseco	3886	1971	.507
A Belle	1881	949	.505
C Fielder	2870	1436	.500
W Clark	4269	2129	.499
D Justice	1955	969	.496
J Olerud	1829	892	.488
G Brett	10349	5044	.487
A Dawson	9351	4529	.484
C Hoiles	1142	553	.484
K Hrbek	5918	2861	.483
E Davis	3575	1726	.483
E Murray	9734	4699	.483
D Mattingly	6173	2959	.479
D Winfield	10594	5063	.478
B Bonilla	4234	2005	.474
R Palmeiro	3867	1824	.472

Games

R YOUNT	2856
D Winfield	2850
G Brett	2707
E Murray	2598
C Fisk	2499
A Dawson	2431
O Smith	2349
L Whitaker	2214
D Murphy	2180
W Wilson	2137
A Trammell	2077
P Molitor	2016
R Henderson	1993
A Griffin	1962
H Baines	1962
C Ripken	1962

Runs Scored

R YOUNT	1632
D Winfield	1623
R Henderson	1586
G Brett	1583
E Murray	1420
P Molitor	1396
A Dawson	1303
L Whitaker	1283
C Fisk	1276
T Raines	1213
D Murphy	1197
W Wilson	1165
O Smith	1154
W Boggs	1150
A Trammell	1149

Runs Batted In

D WINFIELD	1786
E Murray	1662
G Brett	1595
A Dawson	1492
R Yount	1406
C Fisk	1330
D Murphy	1266
H Baines	1144
C Ripken	1104
K Hrbek	1033
L Parrish	1032
G Bell	1002
D Mattingly	999
L Whitaker	997
J Carter	994

Stolen Bases

R HENDERSON	1095
T Raines	751
W Wilson	667
V Coleman	648
O Smith	563
B Butler	476
S Sax	444
P Molitor	434
L Smith	369
J Samuel	358
O Nixon	352
R Sandberg	323
G Redus	322
W McGee	317
A Dawson	312

322

Hits

G BRETT	3154
R Yount	3142
D Winfield	3014
E Murray	2820
A Dawson	2630
P Molitor	2492
C Fisk	2356
W Boggs	2267
O Smith	2265
W Wilson	2202
L Whitaker	2199
A Trammell	2182
R Henderson	2139
D Murphy	2111
C Ripken	2087

Home Runs

D WINFIELD	453
E Murray	441
A Dawson	412
D Murphy	398
C Fisk	376
G Brett	317
L Parrish	317
C Ripken	297
D Strawberry	290
K Hrbek	283
J Carter	275
G Bell	265
H Baines	261
T Brunansky	261
R Yount	251

Strikeouts

D MURPHY	1748
D Winfield	1609
L Parrish	1447
A Dawson	1398
C Fisk	1386
R Deer	1379
R Yount	1350
E Murray	1285
J Samuel	1261
C Davis	1222
K Gibson	1155
G Gaetti	1147
W Wilson	1138
D Strawberry	1138
T Brunansky	1130

AB per HR

M McGWIRE	14.0
J Gonzalez	15.0
C Fielder	15.0
F McGriff	15.6
J Canseco	15.9
D Strawberry	16.1
S Horn	16.6
R Deer	17.0
B Jackson	17.1
S Balboni	17.2
A Belle	17.4
D Justice	17.6
E Davis	17.7
F Thomas	18.0
K Mitchell	18.1

Doubles

G BRETT	665
R Yount	583
D Winfield	520
E Murray	490
A Dawson	473
W Boggs	448
P Molitor	442
C Fisk	421
C Ripken	395
D Mattingly	390
L Whitaker	385
A Trammell	381
T Wallach	379
O Smith	369
H Baines	356

Walks

R HENDERSON	1406
E Murray	1187
D Winfield	1171
L Whitaker	1125
G Brett	1096
W Boggs	1078
T Raines	1003
O Smith	992
D Murphy	986
R Yount	966
B Butler	943
C Fisk	849
P Molitor	832
C Ripken	817
K Hrbek	801

K/BB Ratio

W BOGGS	0.48
O Smith	0.55
T Gwynn	0.57
M Grace	0.63
C Knoblauch	0.68
R Henderson	0.70
T Raines	0.71
D Magadan	0.73
M LaValliere	0.73
F Thomas	0.74
J Reed	0.75
M Greenwell	0.75
B Butler	0.79
D Mattingly	0.79
L Dykstra	0.79

GDP/GDP Opp

C QUINTANA	25.5
D Valle	25.8
S Horn	27.9
R Gonzales	28.1
T Pena	28.1
J Franco	28.3
I Rodriguez	28.6
A Belle	28.9
B Harper	29.2
L Sheets	29.7
T Steinbach	29.9
G Petralli	30.2
P Borders	30.3
D Clark	30.7
R Milligan	30.8

Triples

W WILSON	145
G Brett	137
R Yount	126
B Butler	109
T Raines	100
A Dawson	95
P Molitor	91
J Samuel	89
A Van Slyke	86
D Winfield	85
W McGee	84
T Fernandez	81
A Griffin	78
T Gwynn	78
V Coleman	70

Intentional Walks

G BRETT	229
E Murray	205
D Winfield	165
D Murphy	159
B Bonds	156
W Boggs	154
A Dawson	139
T Gwynn	139
H Baines	136
T Raines	135
C Davis	130
D Mattingly	122
D Strawberry	117
W Clark	112
C Fisk	105

SB Success %

E DAVIS	87.0
T Raines	84.9
M Grissom	84.6
S Javier	84.1
K Lofton	83.6
H Cotto	83.3
W Wilson	83.3
B Larkin	82.7
R Henderson	81.5
V Coleman	81.1
L Dykstra	80.6
O Smith	80.4
G Jefferies	80.0
A Van Slyke	79.7
G Redus	79.5

AB per RBI

C FIELDER	4.9
F Thomas	4.9
J Canseco	5.0
A Belle	5.0
M McGwire	5.1
J Gonzalez	5.2
D Tartabull	5.3
D Strawberry	5.4
D Justice	5.4
K Mitchell	5.6
E Davis	5.7
K Hrbek	5.7
S Horn	5.8
F McGriff	5.8
J Carter	5.8

1993 Active Career Pitching Leaders

Wins		Losses		Saves		Shutouts	
N RYAN	324	N RYAN	292	L SMITH	401	N RYAN	61
J Morris	244	F Tanana	236	J Reardon	365	R Clemens	35
F Tanana	240	C Hough	207	G Gossage	309	F Tanana	34
C Hough	211	J Morris	180	D Eckersley	275	F Valenzuela	31
B Welch	208	D Martinez	165	T Henke	260	D Stieb	30
D Martinez	208	M Moore	151	D Righetti	252	B Welch	28
D Eckersley	183	D Eckersley	149	J Franco	236	J Morris	28
J Candelaria	177	F Viola	145	B Thigpen	201	O Hershiser	24
D Stieb	175	B Welch	140	D Jones	190	D Gooden	23
F Viola	174	R Honeycutt	139	M Williams	186	B Hurst	23
R Sutcliffe	165	R Sutcliffe	135	S Bedrosian	184	D Martinez	23
R Clemens	163	D Stieb	135	R Myers	184	D Eckersley	20
B Gullickson	158	D Darwin	135	B Harvey	171	C Leibrandt	18
D Stewart	158	S Sanderson	134	J Montgomery	160	R Sutcliffe	18
S Sanderson	154	B Gullickson	131	G Olson	160	D Drabek	18
D Gooden	154					8 Pitchers tied with	16

Games		Games Started		CG Freq		Innings Pitched	
G GOSSAGE	966	N RYAN	773	J MORRIS	0.35	N RYAN	5386.2
J Reardon	869	F Tanana	616	F Valenzuela	0.32	F Tanana	4186.2
L Smith	850	J Morris	504	R Clemens	0.30	C Hough	3686.2
C Hough	837	D Martinez	476	N Ryan	0.29	J Morris	3683.1
N Ryan	807	B Welch	454	D Eckersley	0.28	D Martinez	3384.1
D Eckersley	804	C Hough	419	B Saberhagen	0.27	D Eckersley	3038.1
J Orosco	714	D Stieb	409	T Higuera	0.26	B Welch	3022.2
B McClure	698	F Viola	405	J McDowell	0.26	D Stieb	2845.1
D Righetti	688	M Moore	390	C Hough	0.25	F Viola	2760.2
L Andersen	670	S Sanderson	382	D Stieb	0.25	R Sutcliffe	2630.1
C Lefferts	666	R Sutcliffe	378	M Witt	0.24	M Moore	2544.2
S Bedrosian	657	B Gullickson	371	T Mulholland	0.24	F Valenzuela	2534.0
R Honeycutt	640	D Eckersley	361	B Hurst	0.24	J Candelaria	2526.1
F Tanana	638	J Candelaria	356	F Tanana	0.23	B Gullickson	2444.1
GA Harris	620	F Valenzuela	353	D Martinez	0.23	D Stewart	2415.0

Batters Faced		Home Runs Allowed		Walks Allowed		Strikeouts	
N RYAN	22575	F TANANA	448	N RYAN	2795	N RYAN	5714
F Tanana	17641	J Morris	375	C Hough	1613	F Tanana	2773
C Hough	15655	C Hough	366	J Morris	1323	J Morris	2378
J Morris	15484	N Ryan	321	F Tanana	1255	C Hough	2297
D Martinez	14135	D Eckersley	314	R Sutcliffe	1049	D Eckersley	2198
B Welch	12631	D Martinez	313	M Langston	1027	R Clemens	2033
D Eckersley	12489	F Viola	283	D Stieb	1017	M Langston	2001
D Stieb	11844	S Sanderson	266	M Moore	999	B Welch	1925
F Viola	11583	B Gullickson	258	F Valenzuela	997	F Valenzuela	1842
R Sutcliffe	11229	B Welch	257	B Welch	991	D Gooden	1835
M Moore	10892	B Hurst	250	D Martinez	990	D Martinez	1831
F Valenzuela	10661	J Candelaria	245	D Stewart	933	F Viola	1813
J Candelaria	10366	M Moore	240	B Witt	887	J Candelaria	1673
D Stewart	10268	D Stewart	227	F Viola	823	B Hurst	1665
B Gullickson	10223	T Browning	226	R Darling	801	R Sutcliffe	1653

Earned Run Average

Player, Team	IP	ER	ERA
J OROSCO	932.1	296	2.86
L Smith	1125.1	364	2.91
R Clemens	2222.2	726	2.94
O Hershiser	2020.2	662	2.95
K Appier	862.0	283	2.95
G Gossage	1762.0	583	2.98
M Eichhorn	784.1	261	2.99
D Gooden	2128.1	718	3.04
R McDowell	864.1	295	3.07
L Andersen	963.1	332	3.10
J Reardon	1122.2	388	3.11
J Rijo	1544.2	537	3.13
D Cone	1521.0	531	3.14
S Fernandez	1590.2	557	3.15
S Farr	796.0	280	3.17

Winning Percentage

Player, Team	W	L	W%
D GOODEN	154	81	.655
R Clemens	163	86	.655
J McDowell	81	49	.623
T Higuera	93	59	.612
J Key	134	87	.606
B Welch	208	140	.598
D Cone	95	65	.594
J Candelaria	177	122	.592
T Glavine	95	66	.590
D Stewart	158	114	.581
T Browning	120	87	.580
J Morris	244	180	.575
G Maddux	115	85	.575
O Hershiser	128	96	.571
B Saberhagen	120	90	.571

Opposition Batting

Player, Team	AB	H	AVG
N RYAN	19271	3923	.204
S Fernandez	5744	1174	.204
R Johnson	3871	834	.215
J Orosco	3411	765	.224
J DeLeon	6420	1441	.224
D Cone	5605	1264	.226
R Clemens	8255	1878	.227
G Gossage	6379	1453	.228
S Bedrosian	4134	945	.229
C Hough	13650	3165	.232
P Harnisch	3537	821	.232
J Smoltz	4549	1060	.233
L Smith	4164	972	.233
R Martinez	3548	830	.234
T Belcher	4612	1079	.234

Hits Per 9 Innings

Player, Team	IP	H	H/9
N RYAN	5386.2	3923	6.55
S Fernandez	1590.2	1174	6.64
R Johnson	1073.1	834	6.99
J Orosco	932.1	765	7.38
J DeLeon	1754.1	1441	7.39
G Gossage	1762.0	1453	7.42
D Cone	1521.0	1264	7.48
R Clemens	2222.2	1878	7.60
S Bedrosian	1116.2	945	7.62
C Hough	3686.2	3165	7.73
L Smith	1125.1	972	7.77
J Smoltz	1223.1	1060	7.80
P Harnisch	946.0	821	7.81
T Belcher	1242.1	1079	7.82
T Gordon	805.1	700	7.82

Homeruns Per 9 Innings

Player, Team	IP	HR	HR/9
R MCDOWELL	864.1	35	0.36
J Magrane	969.0	51	0.47
B Swift	1156.1	61	0.47
D Gooden	2128.1	114	0.48
K Appier	862.0	47	0.49
O Hershiser	2020.2	111	0.49
G Maddux	1709.0	96	0.51
M Gubicza	1756.0	99	0.51
D Jackson	1688.2	96	0.51
M Eichhorn	784.1	45	0.52
Z Smith	1568.1	90	0.52
L Andersen	963.1	56	0.52
K Hill	872.1	51	0.53
J Howell	801.0	47	0.53
N Ryan	5386.2	321	0.54

Baserunners Per 9 Innings

Player, Team	IP	BR	BR/9
S FERNANDEZ	1590.2	1814	10.26
B Saberhagen	1897.1	2175	10.32
R Clemens	2222.2	2561	10.37
D Eckersley	3038.1	3571	10.58
D Gooden	2128.1	2528	10.69
D Drabek	1732.0	2069	10.75
J Key	1932.1	2315	10.78
J Candelaria	2526.1	3028	10.79
J Smiley	1200.2	1454	10.90
O Hershiser	2020.2	2451	10.92
J Reardon	1122.2	1365	10.94
T Belcher	1242.1	1518	11.00
K Appier	862.0	1055	11.02
T Higuera	1321.1	1618	11.02
B Smith	1791.1	2205	11.08

Strikeouts per 9 Innings

Player, Team	IP	H	K/9
N RYAN	5386.2	5714	9.55
R Johnson	1073.1	1126	9.44
L Smith	1125.1	1110	8.88
T Gordon	805.1	754	8.43
D Cone	1521.0	1418	8.39
S Fernandez	1590.2	1458	8.25
R Clemens	2222.2	2033	8.23
J Orosco	932.1	826	7.97
M Davis	1112.1	978	7.91
B Witt	1393.0	1207	7.80
D Gooden	2128.1	1835	7.76
M Langston	2329.0	2001	7.73
J Rijo	1544.2	1323	7.71
G Gossage	1762.0	1473	7.52
J DeLeon	1754.1	1462	7.50

Walks per 9 Innings

Player, Team	IP	BB	BB/9
B TEWKSBURY	998.0	156	1.41
B Saberhagen	1897.1	375	1.78
K Tapani	889.0	186	1.88
G Swindell	1447.0	307	1.91
D Eckersley	3038.1	692	2.05
J Key	1932.1	447	2.08
J Candelaria	2526.1	592	2.11
B Wegman	1296.1	305	2.12
B Smith	1791.1	432	2.17
T Mulholland	1048.2	255	2.19
B Gullickson	2444.1	597	2.20
J Burkett	838.0	209	2.24
S Sanderson	2411.2	605	2.26
C Bosio	1354.1	348	2.31
D Drabek	1732.0	447	2.32

Strikeout to Walk Ratio

Player, Team	K	BB	K/BB
B SABERHAGEN	1267	375	3.38
G Swindell	1018	307	3.32
R Clemens	2033	619	3.28
D Eckersley	2198	692	3.18
K Tapani	547	186	2.94
D Gooden	1835	636	2.89
J Candelaria	1673	592	2.83
R Aguilera	641	234	2.74
L Smith	1110	416	2.67
E Hanson	740	285	2.60
B Tewksbury	402	156	2.58
T Higuera	1046	407	2.57
S Sanderson	1545	605	2.55
J Key	1117	447	2.50
C Bosio	868	348	2.49

1993 American League Bill James Leaders

Top Game Scores of the Year

Pitcher	Date	Opp	IP	H	R	ER	BB	K	SC
Johnson Randy, Sea	5/16	Oak	9.0	1	0	0	3	14	96
Key, NYA	4/27	Cal	9.0	1	0	0	1	8	92
Finley C, Cal	4/22	Cle	9.0	2	0	0	2	10	91
Alvarez W, ChA	6/15	Oak	9.0	3	0	0	1	11	91
McDonald, Bal	7/20	KC	9.0	1	0	0	3	9	91
Appier, KC	7/27	Tex	9.0	1	1	1	1	11	91

Top Game Scores of the Year

Pitcher	Date	Opp	IP	H	R	ER	BB	K	SC
Bere, ChA	9/8	Bos	8.0	2	0	0	0	13	91
Johnson Randy, Sea	9/21	Tex	9.0	3	0	0	1	11	91
McDowell J, ChA	8/1	Sea	9.0	2	0	0	2	9	90
Moore M, Det	8/23	Oak	9.0	1	0	0	0	5	90
Stottlemyre T, Tor	9/21	Bos	9.0	3	0	0	1	10	90

Offensive Winning%

J OLERUD, Tor	.861
F Thomas, ChA	.821
C Hoiles, Bal	.794
K Griffey Jr, Sea	.791
J Gonzalez, Tex	.771
R Henderson, Tor	.770
P Molitor, Tor	.749
R Palmeiro, Tex	.734
R Alomar, Tor	.733
T Salmon, Cal	.725

Power/Speed Number

R HENDERSON, Tor	30.1
A Belle, Cle	28.7
R Palmeiro, Tex	27.6
R Alomar, Tor	26.0
K Griffey Jr, Sea	24.7
R Sierra, Oak	23.4
P Molitor, Tor	22.0
D White, Tor	20.8
T Raines, ChA	18.2
C Baerga, Cle	17.5

Tough Losses

D CONE	10
C Finley	8
J Deshaies	7
J McDowell	6
J Abbott	6
B McDonald	6
S Sanderson	5
D Darwin	5
C Bosio	5
B Wegman	5
K Tapani	5
W Banks	5

Runs Created

J OLERUD, Tor	161
F Thomas, ChA	149
K Griffey Jr, Sea	146
P Molitor, Tor	135
R Palmeiro, Tex	128
R Alomar, Tor	125
J Gonzalez, Tex	122
A Belle, Cle	119
T Fryman, Det	117
R Henderson, Tor	116

Secondary Average

R HENDERSON, Tor	.528
F Thomas, ChA	.497
K Griffey Jr, Sea	.486
M Tettleton, Det	.448
J Olerud, Tor	.439
C Hoiles, Bal	.439
D Tartabull, NYA	.433
R Palmeiro, Tex	.414
T Salmon, Cal	.410
A Belle, Cle	.409

Slow Hooks

Blue Jays	25
Brewers	21
Angels	20
Athletics	17
Orioles	16
Mariners	14
Twins	13
Indians	12
Tigers	11
Royals	10
Yankees	10
Rangers	10
White Sox	6
Red Sox	4

Isolated Power

J GONZALEZ, Tex	.323
K Griffey Jr, Sea	.308
F Thomas, ChA	.290
C Hoiles, Bal	.275
A Belle, Cle	.263
R Palmeiro, Tex	.260
D Palmer, Tex	.258
D Tartabull, NYA	.253
T Salmon, Cal	.252
M Tettleton, Det	.247

Cheap Wins

J MCDOWELL	9
B Gullickson	5
R Sutcliffe	5
P Hentgen	5
M Moore	4
J Mesa	4
T Stottlemyre	4
S Erickson	4
M Mussina	4
H Pichardo	4
J Morris	3
J Key	3
C Finley	3

Quick Hooks

Indians	35
Athletics	31
Twins	22
Rangers	20
Orioles	18
Red Sox	15
Tigers	15
Royals	15
Brewers	14
Yankees	14
Mariners	14
Angels	12
Blue Jays	11
White Sox	8

1993 National League Bill James Leaders

Top Game Scores of the Year

Pitcher	Date	Opp	IP	H	R	ER	BB	K	SC
Kile, Hou	9/8	NYN	9.0	0	1	0	1	9	93
Rijo, Cin	9/25	Col	9.0	1	0	0	0	8	93
Belcher T, Cin	5/26	Atl	9.0	1	0	0	3	10	92
Harnisch, Hou	7/10	ChN	9.0	1	0	0	3	10	92
Harnisch, Hou	8/14	Col	9.0	3	0	0	2	12	91
Harnisch, Hou	9/17	SD	9.0	1	0	0	1	7	91

Top Game Scores of the Year

Pitcher	Date	Opp	IP	H	R	ER	BB	K	SC
Guzman Jos, ChN	4/6	Atl	9.0	1	0	0	2	7	90
Belcher T, Cin	4/20	Pit	9.0	3	0	0	1	9	89
Saberhagen, NYN	5/10	Fla	9.0	3	0	0	1	8	88
Jones B, NYN	9/29	StL	10.0	4	0	0	5	9	88
Kile, Hou	8/17	Fla	9.0	3	0	0	2	8	87

Offensive Winning %

B BONDS, SF	.877
A Galarraga, Col	.816
J Kruk, Phi	.774
L Dykstra, Phi	.769
G Jefferies, StL	.754
M Piazza, LA	.746
D Daulton, Phi	.740
T Gwynn, SD	.735
F McGriff, Atl	.733
O Merced, Pit	.719

Power/Speed Number

B BONDS, SF	35.6
S Sosa, ChN	34.4
R Gant, Atl	30.2
M Grissom, Mon	28.0
L Dykstra, Phi	25.1
L Walker, Mon	25.0
G Jefferies, StL	23.7
D Bell, SD	23.2
R Sanders, Cin	23.0
E Davis, LA	19.7

Tough Losses

C HOUGH	7
D GOODEN	7
F TANANA	7
J RIJO	7
D DRABEK	7
J ARMSTRONG	7
J Smoltz	6
A Benes	6
S Sanderson	5
S Fernandez	5
O Hershiser	5
B Saberhagen	5
G Maddux	5

Runs Created

B BONDS, SF	172
L Dykstra, Phi	142
J Kruk, Phi	117
F McGriff, Atl	114
G Jefferies, StL	112
M Piazza, LA	112
J Blauser, Atl	111
A Galarraga, Col	110
D Daulton, Phi	109
C Biggio, Hou	107
D Justice, Atl	107

Secondary Average

B BONDS, SF	.607
D Daulton, Phi	.465
L Dykstra, Phi	.419
L Walker, Mon	.412
B Bonilla, NYN	.400
F McGriff, Atl	.399
P Plantier, SD	.398
R Gant, Atl	.375
D Justice, Atl	.374
J Kruk, Phi	.374

Slow Hooks

Mets	14
Rockies	14
Pirates	11
Reds	10
Cubs	9
Phillies	9
Padres	9
Astros	8
Dodgers	6
Expos	6
Cardinals	5
Marlins	4
Braves	3
Giants	3

Cheap Wins

J BURKETT	6
B RIVERA	6
K Gross	5
B Tewksbury	5
T Belcher	5
B Walk	4
J Guzman	4
G Swindell	4
M Harkey	4
G Hibbard	4
C Hammond	4
A Reynoso	4
P Astacio	4

Quick Hooks

Expos	34
Rockies	29
Giants	27
Padres	26
Pirates	20
Reds	14
Phillies	14
Braves	13
Cubs	13
Astros	13
Dodgers	13
Cardinals	13
Marlins	13

Isolated Power

B BONDS, SF	.341
P Plantier, SD	.268
M Williams, SF	.268
F McGriff, Atl	.259
B Bonilla, NYN	.257
D Justice, Atl	.244
M Piazza, LA	.243
R Gant, Atl	.236
A Galarraga, Col	.232
D Daulton, Phi	.226

Player Profiles

As is our custom each year, we include in the Major League Handbook statistical profiles of several among the elite in professional baseball, and this year is no exception. Juan Gonzalez just turned 24 the day the World Series started and has already won more home run titles than Frank Robinson. Greg Maddux may become the first NL pitcher to win two consecutive Cy Young Awards since Sandy Koufax, and Bryan Harvey came back from the disabled list to save an amazing 70% of Florida's wins.

We have another custom of compiling these profiles into book form. It's called the **STATS 1994 Player Profiles** and has statistical breakdowns like these for every player who played in the majors this past season. That's over 500,000 statistics in just one book! If you would like to order a copy, just head to the back of this book and make use of the handy order form. All these stats for less than the price of a box seat ticket!

Juan Gonzalez — Rangers

	Avg	G	AB	R	H	2B	3B	HR	RBI	BB	SO	HBP	GDP	SB	CS	OBP	SLG	IBB	SH	SF	#Pit	#P/PA	GB	FB	G/F
1993 Season	.310	140	536	105	166	33	1	46	118	37	99	13	11	4	1	.368	.632	7	0	1	1981	3.37	170	164	1.04
Career (1989-1993)	.274	486	1815	277	497	101	5	121	348	122	395	25	43	8	7	.326	.535	15	2	13	7019	3.55	546	608	0.90

1993 Season

	Avg	AB	H	2B	3B	HR	RBI	BB	SO	OBP	SLG		Avg	AB	H	2B	3B	HR	RBI	BB	SO	OBP	SLG
vs. Left	.333	108	36	8	0	9	20	7	20	.374	.657	Scoring Posn	.308	159	49	9	0	16	76	17	33	.383	.667
vs. Right	.304	428	130	25	1	37	98	30	79	.367	.626	Close & Late	.324	74	24	6	0	6	18	3	17	.359	.649
Groundball	.346	104	36	10	0	7	24	5	19	.376	.644	None on/out	.369	141	52	12	1	9	9	7	21	.426	.660
Flyball	.306	108	33	4	1	13	32	8	15	.377	.722	Batting #4	.308	535	165	33	1	46	117	37	99	.367	.632
Home	.330	273	90	17	0	24	58	19	54	.386	.656	Batting #9	1.000	1	1	0	0	0	1	0	0	1.000	1.000
Away	.289	263	76	16	1	22	60	18	45	.349	.608	Other	.000	0	0	0	0	0	0	0	0	.000	.000
Day	.282	117	33	7	1	8	27	9	24	.361	.564	April	.321	78	25	4	0	7	12	6	17	.391	.641
Night	.317	419	133	26	0	38	91	28	75	.370	.652	May	.348	66	23	7	0	7	17	7	8	.434	.773
Grass	.307	460	141	25	1	37	102	34	85	.366	.607	June	.313	96	30	6	0	6	22	6	15	.353	.563
Turf	.329	76	25	8	0	9	16	3	14	.378	.789	July	.349	106	37	6	1	10	29	9	17	.402	.708
First Pitch	.398	88	35	11	0	9	25	5	0	.436	.830	August	.252	111	28	3	0	10	22	5	24	.314	.550
Ahead in Count	.357	129	46	10	0	14	42	17	0	.432	.760	September/October	.291	79	23	7	0	6	16	4	18	.333	.608
Behind in Count	.252	234	59	9	1	17	37	0	82	.280	.517	Pre-All Star	.320	284	91	19	1	23	60	24	46	.386	.637
Two Strikes	.213	216	46	5	0	14	31	15	99	.283	.431	Post-All Star	.298	252	75	14	0	23	58	13	53	.347	.627

1993 By Position

Position	Avg	AB	H	2B	3B	HR	RBI	BB	SO	OBP	SLG	G	GS	Innings	PO	A	E	DP	Fld Pct	Rng Fctr	In Zone	Outs	Zone Rtg	MLB Zone
As Designated Hitter	.220	41	9	2	0	2	5	2	9	.256	.415	10	10	---	---	---	---	---	---	---	---	---	---	---
As lf	.316	494	156	31	1	44	112	35	90	.376	.650	129	129	1100.0	265	5	4	0	.985	2.21	302	245	.811	.818

Career (1989-1993)

	Avg	AB	H	2B	3B	HR	RBI	BB	SO	OBP	SLG		Avg	AB	H	2B	3B	HR	RBI	BB	SO	OBP	SLG
vs. Left	.282	461	130	24	0	27	80	38	104	.334	.510	Scoring Posn	.272	544	148	24	1	33	223	53	129	.336	.502
vs. Right	.271	1354	367	77	5	94	268	84	291	.323	.544	Close & Late	.259	286	74	17	0	20	52	21	72	.320	.528
Groundball	.317	448	142	29	0	31	92	25	92	.355	.589	None on/out	.277	411	114	28	2	21	21	19	79	.325	.509
Flyball	.253	427	108	21	2	35	105	28	100	.308	.557	Batting #4	.284	835	237	46	1	66	164	56	176	.341	.578
Home	.284	913	259	55	3	54	161	57	218	.334	.528	Batting #5	.276	453	125	25	1	28	91	24	102	.314	.521
Away	.264	902	238	46	2	67	187	65	177	.318	.542	Other	.256	527	135	30	3	27	93	42	117	.313	.478
Day	.282	323	91	19	2	21	73	22	69	.345	.548	April	.302	182	55	9	0	12	32	12	38	.352	.549
Night	.272	1492	406	82	3	100	275	100	326	.322	.532	May	.304	273	83	23	1	15	55	25	49	.368	.560
Grass	.275	1515	417	79	4	100	288	104	333	.327	.531	June	.286	294	84	11	1	21	63	29	66	.347	.544
Turf	.267	300	80	22	1	21	60	18	62	.319	.557	July	.282	291	82	15	1	25	70	17	68	.324	.598
First Pitch	.359	209	75	17	0	20	49	12	0	.412	.727	August	.270	344	93	16	1	31	71	19	78	.319	.593
Ahead in Count	.357	412	147	34	1	41	117	61	0	.440	.743	September/October	.232	431	100	27	1	17	57	20	96	.278	.418
Behind in Count	.222	873	194	34	3	36	123	0	331	.229	.392	Pre-All Star	.295	854	252	49	3	54	171	74	173	.355	.549
Two Strikes	.186	833	155	27	3	31	96	49	395	.235	.337	Post-All Star	.255	961	245	52	2	67	177	48	222	.299	.522

Batter vs. Pitcher (career)

Hits Best Against	Avg	AB	H	2B	3B	HR	RBI	BB	SO	OBP	SLG	Hits Worst Against	Avg	AB	H	2B	3B	HR	RBI	BB	SO	OBP	SLG
Matt Young	.500	12	6	3	0	1	1	0	3	.500	1.000	Arthur Rhodes	.000	12	0	0	0	0	0	1	6	.000	.000
Mark Gubicza	.462	13	6	2	0	1	5	0	2	.462	.846	Chris Bosio	.053	19	1	0	0	0	0	1	7	.100	.053
Ron Darling	.429	14	6	1	0	2	5	2	3	.500	.929	Greg Harris	.077	13	1	0	0	0	1	1	3	.143	.077
David Wells	.385	13	5	0	0	2	6	2	1	.467	.846	Danny Darwin	.077	13	1	0	0	0	0	1	2	.143	.077
Charlie Hough	.333	12	4	1	0	2	4	1	2	.385	.917	Rich Monteleone	.077	13	1	1	0	0	0	0	3	.077	.154

Bryan Harvey — Marlins

	ERA	W	L	Sv	G	GS	IP	BB	SO	Avg	H	2B	3B	HR	RBI	OBP	SLG	GF	IR	IRS	Hld	SvOp	SB	CS	GB	FB	G/F
1993 Season	1.70	1	5	45	59	0	69.0	13	73	.186	45	1	0	4	21	.222	.240	54	28	9	0	49	15	0	72	70	1.03
Last Five Years	2.44	10	20	154	256	0	295.2	117	368	.189	199	22	1	24	110	.266	.280	186	188	49	1	180	38	3	300	263	1.14

1993 Season

	ERA	W	L	Sv	G	GS	IP	H	HR	BB	SO		Avg	AB	H	2B	3B	HR	RBI	BB	SO	OBP	SLG
Home	1.11	1	1	24	32	0	40.2	23	3	9	43	vs. Left	.132	121	16	1	0	0	5	9	43	.191	.140
Away	2.54	0	4	21	27	0	28.1	22	1	4	30	vs. Right	.240	121	29	0	0	4	16	4	30	.254	.339
Starter	0.00	0	0	0	0	0	0.0	0	0	0	0	Scoring Posn	.169	59	10	0	0	1	16	4	18	.203	.220
Reliever	1.70	1	5	45	59	0	69.0	45	4	13	73	Close & Late	.174	207	36	1	0	3	19	12	64	.213	.222
0 Days rest	0.00	0	0	11	11	0	10.2	4	0	2	13	None on/out	.281	57	16	0	0	1	1	2	13	.305	.333
1 or 2 Days rest	1.62	1	3	21	27	0	33.1	19	1	8	37	First Pitch	.406	32	13	1	0	2	6	2	0	.441	.625
3+ Days rest	2.52	0	2	13	21	0	25.0	22	3	3	23	Behind in Count	.134	142	19	0	0	1	5	0	64	.133	.155
Pre-All Star	1.63	1	2	25	33	0	38.2	26	3	7	47	Ahead in Count	.167	36	6	0	0	1	7	8	0	.292	.250
Post-All Star	1.78	0	3	20	26	0	30.1	19	1	6	26	Two Strikes	.124	145	18	0	0	1	7	3	73	.141	.145

Last Five Years

	ERA	W	L	Sv	G	GS	IP	H	HR	BB	SO		Avg	AB	H	2B	3B	HR	RBI	BB	SO	OBP	SLG
Home	2.44	8	7	78	134	0	162.1	119	15	61	193	vs. Left	.171	549	94	15	1	10	56	66	200	.257	.257
Away	2.43	2	13	76	122	0	133.1	80	9	56	175	vs. Right	.208	506	105	7	0	14	54	51	168	.276	.304
Day	1.49	1	2	42	65	0	78.1	48	5	26	99	Inning 1-6	.000	0	0	0	0	0	0	0	0	.000	.000
Night	2.77	9	18	112	191	0	217.1	151	19	91	269	Inning 7+	.189	1055	199	22	1	24	110	117	368	.266	.280
Grass	2.63	9	17	132	221	0	256.2	170	22	107	320	None on	.200	539	108	8	0	16	16	45	182	.262	.304
Turf	1.15	1	3	22	35	0	39.0	29	2	10	48	Runners on	.176	516	91	14	1	8	94	72	186	.271	.254
April	2.27	2	3	23	42	0	47.2	39	4	18	58	Scoring Posn	.157	312	49	6	1	6	87	59	117	.280	.240
May	2.73	3	4	26	50	0	62.2	50	5	21	70	Close & Late	.192	714	137	15	0	14	83	76	251	.266	.272
June	1.74	0	2	26	41	0	46.2	25	4	21	63	None on/out	.202	223	45	5	0	6	6	20	70	.267	.305
July	3.40	4	6	20	38	0	39.2	32	4	18	51	vs. 1st Batr (relief)	.233	227	53	7	0	7	21	26	70	.311	.357
August	0.71	0	1	28	38	0	50.2	19	3	14	65	First Inning Pitched	.192	847	163	18	1	17	96	98	288	.273	.276
September/October	3.91	1	4	31	47	0	48.1	34	4	25	61	First 15 Pitches	.204	732	149	13	1	18	72	68	239	.268	.298
Starter	0.00	0	0	0	0	0	0.0	0	0	0	0	First 15 Pitches	.152	282	43	8	0	5	28	41	112	.258	.234
Reliever	2.44	10	20	154	256	0	295.2	199	24	117	368	Pitch 31-45	.179	39	7	1	0	1	10	8	17	.306	.282
0 Days rest	0.57	2	0	40	45	0	47.1	22	2	12	43	Pitch 46+	.000	2	0	0	0	0	0	0	0	.000	.000
1 or 2 Days rest	3.11	5	15	72	115	0	136.0	98	9	65	190	First Pitch	.302	116	35	4	0	4	15	11	0	.359	.440
3+ Days rest	2.40	3	5	42	96	0	112.1	79	13	40	135	Ahead in Count	.130	629	82	8	0	6	38	0	324	.129	.172
Pre-All Star	2.18	5	10	83	144	0	169.0	119	13	64	206	Behind in Count	.321	140	45	5	0	10	40	54	0	.490	.571
Post-All Star	2.77	5	10	71	112	0	126.2	80	11	53	162	Two Strikes	.116	637	74	7	0	5	37	52	368	.182	.151

Pitcher vs. Batter (career)

Pitches Best Vs.	Avg	AB	H	2B	3B	HR	RBI	BB	SO	OBP	SLG	Pitches Worst Vs.	Avg	AB	H	2B	3B	HR	RBI	BB	SO	OBP	SLG
Kent Hrbek	.000	10	0	0	0	0	0	1	3	.091	.000	Tony Fernandez	.333	9	3	2	0	0	0	2	0	.455	.556
Mike Greenwell	.091	11	1	0	0	0	1	0	2	.083	.091												
Carlton Fisk	.100	10	1	0	0	0	0	2	5	.250	.100												
Kirby Puckett	.100	10	1	0	0	0	0	1	4	.182	.100												
Harold Reynolds	.182	11	2	0	0	0	0	0	6	.182	.182												

	ERA	W	L	Sv	G	GS	IP	BB	SO	Avg	H	2B	3B	HR	RBI	OBP	SLG	CG	ShO	Sup	QS	#P/S	SB	CS	GB	FB	G/F
1993 Season	2.36	20	10	0	36	36	267.0	52	197	.232	228	38	2	14	75	.273	.317	8	1	4.28	29	100	27	6	460	174	2.64
Last Five Years	2.84	89	59	0	178	178	1273.1	341	873	.238	1125	186	23	63	409	.293	.327	39	10	4.29	125	100	102	42	2192	877	2.50

1993 Season

	ERA	W	L	Sv	G	GS	IP	H	HR	BB	SO
Home	2.19	8	4	0	16	16	123.1	97	5	27	93
Away	2.51	12	6	0	20	20	143.2	131	9	25	104
Day	1.91	5	2	0	9	9	66.0	61	1	17	48
Night	2.51	15	8	0	27	27	201.0	167	13	35	149
Grass	2.41	16	6	0	27	27	202.0	168	12	41	148
Turf	2.22	4	4	0	9	9	65.0	60	2	11	49
April	3.09	2	2	0	6	6	43.2	40	5	9	31
May	2.35	3	2	0	6	6	46.0	33	2	11	40
June	2.70	2	2	0	5	5	36.2	35	2	7	21
July	3.17	5	2	0	7	7	48.1	48	3	8	37
August	1.53	4	1	0	6	6	47.0	36	1	6	29
September/October	1.39	4	1	0	6	6	45.1	36	1	11	39
Starter	2.36	20	10	0	36	36	267.0	228	14	52	197
Reliever	0.00	0	0	0	0	0	0.0	0	0	0	0
0-3 Days Rest	0.78	3	0	0	3	3	23.0	14	1	4	21
4 Days Rest	2.66	13	9	0	26	26	186.1	165	11	38	144
5+ Days Rest	2.03	4	1	0	7	7	57.2	49	2	10	32
Pre-All Star	2.83	8	8	0	20	20	146.1	129	10	32	113
Post-All Star	1.79	12	2	0	16	16	120.2	99	4	20	84

	Avg	AB	H	2B	3B	HR	RBI	BB	SO	OBP	SLG
vs. Left	.235	520	122	19	1	5	36	33	97	.280	.304
vs. Right	.228	464	106	19	1	9	39	19	100	.264	.332
Inning 1-6	.237	781	185	28	2	9	62	38	157	.275	.312
Inning 7+	.212	203	43	10	0	5	13	14	40	.265	.335
None on	.240	592	142	26	2	11	11	29	124	.280	.346
Runners on	.219	392	86	12	0	3	64	23	73	.262	.273
Scoring Posn	.210	233	49	6	0	2	57	20	42	.271	.262
Close & Late	.207	135	28	6	0	4	10	11	33	.270	.341
None on/out	.290	262	76	12	1	5	5	13	48	.331	.401
vs. 1st Batr (relief)	.000	0	0	0	0	0	0	0	0	.000	.000
First Inning Pitched	.255	137	35	7	0	2	15	7	35	.295	.350
First 75 Pitches	.229	729	167	23	2	9	53	35	144	.267	.303
Pitch 76-90	.265	132	35	9	0	1	12	5	30	.292	.356
Pitch 91-105	.167	84	14	3	0	3	6	6	19	.228	.310
Pitch 106+	.308	39	12	3	0	1	4	6	4	.400	.462
First Pitch	.275	171	47	9	0	0	19	4	0	.292	.327
Ahead in Count	.177	429	76	15	0	7	21	0	161	.185	.261
Behind in Count	.292	202	59	7	1	3	16	25	0	.368	.381
Two Strikes	.141	411	58	12	0	5	19	23	197	.190	.207

Last Five Years

	ERA	W	L	Sv	G	GS	IP	H	HR	BB	SO
Home	2.80	45	24	0	83	83	616.2	536	29	175	431
Away	2.88	44	35	0	95	95	656.2	589	34	166	442
Day	3.03	37	25	0	75	75	526.0	503	27	165	363
Night	2.71	52	34	0	103	103	747.1	622	36	176	510
Grass	2.91	67	41	0	128	128	916.1	804	51	258	631
Turf	2.67	22	18	0	50	50	357.0	321	12	83	242
April	3.16	11	8	0	23	23	156.2	140	9	37	99
May	2.92	11	13	0	29	29	212.2	173	11	60	146
June	3.27	10	13	0	30	30	200.2	170	10	64	142
July	3.06	19	5	0	30	30	212.0	204	12	58	141
August	2.28	19	9	0	33	33	253.0	213	11	71	166
September/October	2.61	19	11	0	33	33	238.1	225	10	51	179
Starter	2.84	89	59	0	178	178	1273.1	1125	63	341	873
Reliever	0.00	0	0	0	0	0	0.0	0	0	0	0
0-3 Days Rest	2.67	13	5	0	22	22	162.0	141	7	37	109
4 Days Rest	2.84	57	44	0	120	120	849.0	745	42	234	616
5+ Days Rest	2.95	19	10	0	36	36	262.1	239	14	70	148
Pre-All Star	3.20	36	37	0	92	92	633.1	553	34	179	440
Post-All Star	2.49	53	22	0	86	86	640.0	572	29	162	433

	Avg	AB	H	2B	3B	HR	RBI	BB	SO	OBP	SLG
vs. Left	.258	2733	704	111	17	35	248	237	472	.319	.349
vs. Right	.211	1992	421	75	6	28	161	104	401	.256	.297
Inning 1-6	.235	3795	891	154	20	48	337	269	715	.290	.324
Inning 7+	.252	930	234	32	3	15	72	72	158	.307	.341
None on	.229	2847	652	101	8	36	36	183	550	.280	.308
Runners on	.252	1878	473	85	15	27	373	158	323	.312	.356
Scoring Posn	.235	1066	251	42	11	11	319	124	202	.316	.326
Close & Late	.244	529	129	16	2	7	45	51	101	.313	.321
None on/out	.254	1238	315	41	4	19	19	85	218	.309	.340
vs. 1st Batr (relief)	.000	0	0	0	0	0	0	0	0	.000	.000
First Inning Pitched	.245	669	164	33	3	7	63	60	148	.313	.335
First 75 Pitches	.233	3439	800	132	19	42	273	240	643	.287	.319
Pitch 76-90	.244	636	155	27	0	8	64	39	120	.291	.324
Pitch 91-105	.257	412	106	14	1	9	49	33	71	.313	.362
Pitch 106+	.269	238	64	13	3	4	23	29	39	.353	.399
First Pitch	.287	792	227	38	5	13	95	33	0	.319	.396
Ahead in Count	.167	2043	341	43	7	16	108	0	729	.176	.218
Behind in Count	.329	1053	346	66	5	19	122	178	0	.425	.455
Two Strikes	.146	1915	279	38	8	11	98	129	873	.204	.191

Pitcher vs. Batter (career)

Pitches Best Vs.	Avg	AB	H	2B	3B	HR	RBI	BB	SO	OBP	SLG
Felix Jose	.000	16	0	0	0	0	0	1	7	.059	.000
Eric Karros	.000	13	0	0	0	0	1	1	3	.071	.000
Bob Melvin	.000	11	0	0	0	0	0	1	4	.083	.000
Dale Murphy	.059	34	2	0	0	0	0	1	12	.086	.059
Jeff Kent	.071	14	1	0	0	0	0	0	6	.071	.071

Pitches Worst Vs.	Avg	AB	H	2B	3B	HR	RBI	BB	SO	OBP	SLG
Hal Morris	.520	25	13	3	0	0	2	1	1	.538	.640
Bip Roberts	.480	25	12	3	0	0	3	7	4	.594	.600
Luis Gonzalez	.371	35	13	4	0	3	9	3	4	.421	.743
Andy Van Slyke	.362	58	21	6	0	4	11	10	12	.456	.672
Dion James	.333	12	4	1	1	1	5	2	2	.429	.833

Manager Tendencies

Baseball managers have tough jobs. They need to be experts in public relations and psychology, as well as knowing when to call for a pitchout. They are the first to get the blame when something goes wrong and often the last to get credit for winning. Now, on top of all that, STATS Inc. is analyzing their moves.

This year's Handbook takes an objective look at how managers use strategy. The Skippers are compared based on offense, defense, lineups, and pitching use. Ranking the managers is not attempted; there is plenty of room for argument on whether certain moves are good or bad. We are simply providing fodder for the discussion.

Offensively, managers have control over bunting, stealing and the timing of hit-and-runs. The Handbook looks at the quantity, timing and success of these moves. Defensively, the Handbook looks at the success of pitchouts, the frequency of intentional walks, and the pattern of defensive substitutions.

Making out the starting lineup is one of the most important tasks a manager has each day. The Handbook shows the number of lineups used, as well as the platoon percentage. The use of pinch-hitters and pinch-runners is also explored.

Finally, how does the manager use pitchers? For starters, the Handbook shows slow and quick hooks, along with the number of times a starter was allowed to throw more than 120 pitches. For relievers, it shows the number of relief appearances, and how often a pitcher gets a save going more than one inning (a dying breed).

Some explanation of the categories:

Stolen Base Success Percentage: SB/Attempts

Favorite count: The most common ball-strike count for the event.

Favorite outs: The most common number of outs when the event occurred.

Favorite score difference: The most common score difference when an event occurred. A negative number indicates that the manager's team was trailing. Interestingly, all the managers in this study like to steal the most when the score is tied.

Sacrifice Bunt Attempts: A bunt is considered a sac attempt if no runner is on third, there are 0 outs, or the pitcher attempts a bunt.

Sacrifice Bunt Success%: A bunt that results in a sacrifice or a hit, divided by the number of attempts.

Favorite inning: The most common inning in which an event occurred.

Hit and Run Success: The hit and run results in base runner advancement with no double play.

Pitchouts: The Total is simply the number of pitchouts called for by the manager during the year. Runners Moving indicates the number of times he "guessed right." CS% is percentage of runners caught stealing when he guessed right.

Intentional Walk Situation: Runners on base, first base open, and anyone but the pitcher up with the score difference no more than 2 or the tying run on base, at bat or on deck. "Percent of Situations" is the percentage of time the manager called for an intentional walk in an intentional walk situation.

Defensive Substitution: A straight substitution of one fielder for another, while the defensive team is 1 to 4 runs ahead.

Number of Lineups: Based on batting order, 1-8 for National Leaguers, 1-9 for American Leaguers.

Percent LHB vs. RHSP and RHB vs. LHSP: A measure of platooning. A batter is considered to always have the platoon advantage if he is a switch hitter.

Percent PH platoon: Frequency the manager gets his pinch-hitter the platoon advantage. Switch hitters always have the advantage.

Slow and Quick hooks: See the glossary for complete information. This measures how often a pitcher is left in too long, or pulled out too fast.

Offense

	Stolen Bases					Sacrifice Bunts				Hit and Run		
	Attempts	SB%	Favorite Count	Favorite Outs	Favorite Score Diff.	Attempts	Success%	Favorite Inning	Squeezes	Attempts	Success%	Favorite Count
AL												
Anderson, Sparky, Det	167	62.3	0-0	1	0	47	74.5	7	4	118	26.3	0-0
Garner, Phil, Mil	231	59.7	0-0	2	0	74	86.5	7	7	153	37.3	2-1
Gaston, Cito, Tor	219	77.6	0-0	2	0	61	85.2	7	3	84	25.0	2-2
Hargrove, Mike, Cle	214	74.3	0-0	1	0	56	78.6	7	6	138	47.1	3-1
Hobson, Butch, Bos	111	65.8	0-0	2	0	97	89.7	5	2	88	26.1	1-0
Kelly, Tom, Min	142	58.5	0-0	2	0	39	79.5	8	2	115	29.6	0-1
Kennedy, Kevin, Tex	180	62.8	2-2	2	0	95	80.0	7	4	140	35.0	2-2
La Russa, Tony, Oak	190	68.9	0-0	2	0	59	81.4	7	4	186	40.9	0-0
Lamont, Gene, ChA	163	65.0	0-0	2	0	93	84.9	7	17	110	26.4	1-1
McRae, Hal, KC	175	57.1	0-0	1	0	76	75.0	7	4	153	38.6	0-0
Oates, Johnny, Bal	127	57.5	0-0	2	0	65	84.6	8	0	90	38.9	0-0
Piniella, Lou, Sea	159	57.2	0-0	1	0	86	77.9	7	2	152	40.1	0-0
Rodgers, Buck, Cal	269	62.8	0-0	2	0	65	87.7	6	5	174	37.4	2-1
Showalter, Buck, NYA	74	52.7	0-0	2	0	35	74.3	8	2	51	31.4	1-0
NL												
Alou, Felipe, Mon	284	80.3	0-0	1	0	120	85.0	3	14	156	42.3	1-0
Baker, Dusty, SF	185	64.9	0-0	1	0	128	84.4	3	6	155	37.4	0-0
Baylor, Don, Col	236	61.9	0-0	1	0	88	86.4	7	11	166	39.2	0-0
Cox, Bobby, Atl	173	72.3	0-0	2	0	103	76.7	7	7	101	44.6	2-2
Fregosi, Jim, Phi	123	74.0	0-0	1	0	116	79.3	5	2	56	39.3	2-1
Green, Dallas, NYN	83	55.4	0-0	2	0	91	81.3	6	4	86	43.0	2-0
Howe, Art, Hou	163	63.2	0-0	1	0	107	83.2	3	4	106	37.7	2-1
Johnson, Davy, Cin	145	69.7	0-0	2	0	63	84.1	3	1	83	38.6	2-1
Lachemann, Rene, Fla	173	67.6	0-0	1	0	77	77.9	5	5	105	45.7	0-0
Lasorda, Tom, LA	187	67.4	0-0	1	0	137	83.2	3	7	161	40.4	1-0
Lefebvre, Jim, ChN	143	69.9	1-0	1	0	85	82.4	3	5	160	43.8	2-1
Leyland, Jim, Pit	147	62.6	0-0	2	0	100	84.0	5	6	126	36.5	1-0
Riggleman, Jim, SD	133	69.2	0-0	2	0	110	77.3	3	4	104	34.6	0-0
Torre, Joe, StL	225	68.0	0-0	2	0	81	81.5	3	3	162	38.9	2-2

Defense

	Pitchout			Runners			Defensive Subs				
	Total	Runners Moving	CS%	IBB	Percent of Situations	Score Diff.	Total	Favorite Inning	Pos. 1	Pos. 2	Pos. 3
AL											
Anderson, Sparky, Det	78	18	55.6	92	14.5	0	37	9	rf	cf	c
Garner, Phil, Mil	30	6	50.0	58	8.0	0	38	9	rf	3b	1b
Gaston, Cito, Tor	67	16	37.5	38	5.9	0	42	9	lf	rf	3b
Hargrove, Mike, Cle	77	9	77.8	53	7.6	0	80	9	3b	lf	1b
Hobson, Butch, Bos	99	19	57.9	87	12.9	0	51	9	lf	1b	cf
Kelly, Tom, Min	37	17	35.3	34	4.3	0	29	8	lf	rf	3b
Kennedy, Kevin, Tex	26	11	54.5	42	6.4	0	66	8	rf	cf	lf
La Russa, Tony, Oak	61	17	64.7	59	8.6	0	38	9	1b	3b	cf
Lamont, Gene, ChA	82	22	54.5	36	6.0	0	57	7	lf	cf	rf
McRae, Hal, KC	82	19	47.4	36	4.7	-1	79	8	rf	3b	ss
Oates, Johnny, Bal	30	4	75.0	50	7.7	0	36	9	1b	3b	ss
Piniella, Lou, Sea	83	22	77.3	56	8.5	0	32	8	lf	3b	1b
Rodgers, Buck, Cal	68	11	27.3	35	5.3	0	41	8	1b	c	rf
Showalter, Buck, NYA	24	6	50.0	58	9.8	0	38	9	lf	cf	rf
NL											
Alou, Felipe, Mon	44	15	26.7	38	4.5	0	58	7	1b	lf	3b
Baker, Dusty, SF	79	20	70.0	46	8.9	0	34	8	cf	c	1b
Baylor, Don, Col	75	10	60.0	66	9.9	0	38	9	3b	1b	cf
Cox, Bobby, Atl	66	20	50.0	59	8.7	0	65	9	ss	1b	c
Fregosi, Jim, Phi	30	17	35.3	33	5.1	0	73	9	rf	3b	ss
Green, Dallas, NYN	38	14	35.7	48	9.1	0	30	8	3b	cf	rf
Howe, Art, Hou	57	17	64.7	52	8.1	0	29	9	1b	cf	3b
Johnson, Davy, Cin	53	20	55.0	27	5.7	0	42	8	lf	c	3b
Lachemann, Rene, Fla	35	10	20.0	58	7.9	0	47	8	lf	rf	c
Lasorda, Tom, LA	39	10	70.0	68	10.3	-1	39	9	lf	3b	c
Lefebvre, Jim, ChN	96	23	91.3	61	9.2	-1	48	7	cf	c	1b
Leyland, Jim, Pit	39	8	37.5	43	5.5	0	44	8	cf	1b	lf
Riggleman, Jim, SD	67	20	60.0	72	10.3	0	51	8	3b	lf	2b
Torre, Joe, StL	52	14	50.0	50	7.2	0	52	9	1b	2b	3b

Lineups

	Starting Lineup			Substitutes			
	Lineups Used	% LHB Vs. RHSP	%RHB Vs. LHSP	#PH	#PR	Percent PH Platoon	PH BA
AL							
Anderson, Sparky, Det	112	60.1	99.8	116	59	83.6	0.316
Garner, Phil, Mil	134	62.4	71.8	126	25	69.0	0.193
Gaston, Cito, Tor	72	44.5	89.4	30	33	73.3	0.185
Hargrove, Mike, Cle	92	60.4	82.1	184	22	89.7	0.209
Hobson, Butch, Bos	132	34.0	72.5	153	73	69.9	0.179
Kelly, Tom, Min	138	26.3	96.5	162	32	82.1	0.222
Kennedy, Kevin, Tex	118	44.4	86.8	129	42	69.0	0.309
La Russa, Tony, Oak	149	44.3	94.8	117	36	80.3	0.250
Lamont, Gene, ChA	92	59.9	77.1	87	46	82.8	0.187
McRae, Hal, KC	121	56.7	83.8	150	27	59.3	0.260
Oates, Johnny, Bal	103	51.9	86.7	70	51	57.1	0.182
Piniella, Lou, Sea	117	56.2	80.9	168	41	79.8	0.265
Rodgers, Buck, Cal	120	51.7	94.1	125	36	81.6	0.272
Showalter, Buck, NYA	99	64.9	80.3	150	40	82.0	0.272
NL							
Alou, Felipe, Mon	137	46.7	74.9	254	30	83.5	0.249
Baker, Dusty, SF	83	42.5	75.8	247	20	76.5	0.179
Baylor, Don, Col	136	20.7	97.3	301	32	58.1	0.233
Cox, Bobby, Atl	47	66.3	78.5	250	58	73.2	0.261
Fregosi, Jim, Phi	73	70.5	66.7	231	20	63.2	0.253
Green, Dallas, NYN	75	68.2	92.1	238	14	91.2	0.270
Howe, Art, Hou	92	55.0	75.1	254	26	88.6	0.244
Johnson, Davy, Cin	93	33.2	84.3	182	33	82.4	0.197
Lachemann, Rene, Fla	102	56.6	91.2	242	15	68.6	0.132
Lasorda, Tom, LA	96	36.1	86.0	298	48	84.6	0.233
Lefebvre, Jim, ChN	99	55.4	81.4	265	22	75.1	0.246
Leyland, Jim, Pit	107	44.3	81.8	296	16	67.2	0.252
Riggleman, Jim, SD	114	51.6	75.2	317	36	74.4	0.220
Torre, Joe, StL	118	57.6	85.7	264	33	85.6	0.278

Pitching

	Starting Lineup			Relief	
	Slow Hooks	Quick Hooks	> 120 Pitches	Relief Apperance	Save > 1 IP
AL					
Anderson, Sparky, Det	11	15	14	375	14
Garner, Phil, Mil	21	14	25	353	4
Gaston, Cito, Tor	25	11	25	344	8
Hargrove, Mike, Cle	12	35	5	410	14
Hobson, Butch, Bos	4	15	19	389	12
Kelly, Tom, Min	13	22	11	356	16
Kennedy, Kevin, Tex	10	20	21	359	16
La Russa, Tony, Oak	17	31	17	424	9
Lamont, Gene, ChA	6	8	35	322	17
McRae, Hal, KC	10	15	40	303	20
Oates, Johnny, Bal	16	18	25	329	9
Piniella, Lou, Sea	14	14	38	353	7
Rodgers, Buck, Cal	20	12	28	320	24
Showalter, Buck, NYA	10	14	17	332	10
NL					
Alou, Felipe, Mon	6	34	5	385	30
Baker, Dusty, SF	3	27	0	414	9
Baylor, Don, Col	14	29	10	453	12
Cox, Bobby, Atl	3	13	18	353	6
Fregosi, Jim, Phi	9	14	32	350	1
Green, Dallas, NYN	12	8	12	223	9
Howe, Art, Hou	8	13	16	324	14
Johnson, Davy, Cin	8	11	13	279	9
Lachemann, Rene, Fla	4	13	12	409	13
Lasorda, Tom, LA	6	13	30	346	14
Lefebvre, Jim, ChN	9	13	7	422	11
Leyland, Jim, Pit	11	20	17	384	12
Riggleman, Jim, SD	9	26	2	397	11
Torre, Joe, StL	5	13	5	423	7

1994 Player Projections

Hello, and welcome to our fifth annual player projections. In this section of the book, we try to project what all major league players will do next year. This is the portion of the book where we told you, last year, that Andres Gallaraga would hit .250 with 9 homers and 38 RBI, that Mike Stanley would hit .249 with 4 homers and 23 runs, that Dante Bichette would hit .240 with 51 RBI, that George Bell would drive in 98 runs and Jose Canseco 101, that Andujar Cedeno would hit .236 and Damion Easley .226, that Gregg Jefferies would hit .284 and steal 19 bases, that Leo Gomez would hit 22 longballs, that Willie Greene would hit 20 homers and drive in 80 runs, that Brian McRae would struggle along under the .250 mark, that Brian Hunter would hit 20 homers (we only missed by 20), that Brian Jordan would hit .233 (maybe we should just avoid guys named "Brian"), that Jeff King would hit .237, that Jesse Levis would play 110 games and hit .284, that Jim Leyritz would hit .244, that Al Martin would hit .245 with five homers, that Chito Martinez would hit 24 homers for the Orioles.

All of these projections were. . .well, check out for yourself how these players did in '93, and if you don't want to bother, take our word for it: we really hit the nail on the head. Not that all of our projections were great ones. We did have some trouble with Charlie Hayes:

	G	AB	R	H	2B	3B	HR	RBI	BB	SO	SB	Avg
Projected	147	514	49	129	23	1	13	60	25	89	4	.251
Actual	157	573	89	175	45	2	25	98	43	82	11	.305

Oddly enough, Hayes hit almost exactly twice as many doubles, triples and homers as we had said he would. Of course, we have a handy excuse there (I won't use it), but what about Orlando Merced? We also missed the mark on Orlando:

	G	AB	R	H	2B	3B	HR	RBI	BB	SO	SB	Avg
Projected	127	398	59	101	19	4	7	50	52	71	8	.254
Actual	137	447	68	140	26	4	8	70	77	64	3	.313

Even when we got the playing time right, we still occasionally had problems getting anything else where it should be. Chris Hoiles, for example:

	G	AB	R	H	2B	3B	HR	RBI	BB	SO	SB	Avg
Projected	129	418	57	106	19	1	17	51	56	81	2	.254
Actual	126	419	80	130	28	0	29	82	69	94	1	.310

By dumb luck, we guessed almost exactly how many games and at bats he would have. Otherwise, we were out in left field. Another one of those is Alan Trammell; we got his playing time right, but we said he'd hit .269. Missed it by 60 points. We missed Hayes' batting average by only 54 points, Merced's by only 59 and Hoiles' by 56. We did almost that well on Paul O'Neill:

	G	AB	R	H	2B	3B	HR	RBI	BB	SO	SB	Avg
Projected	151	517	63	129	28	1	18	75	72	100	11	.250
Actual	141	498	71	155	34	1	20	75	44	69	2	.311

Which is closer than we came on Mike Pagliarulo:

	G	AB	R	H	2B	3B	HR	RBI	BB	SO	SB	Avg
Projected	106	299	26	72	16	1	8	30	21	49	1	.241
Actual	116	370	55	112	25	4	9	44	26	49	6	.303

Which is pretty good compared to how we did on John Olerud:

	G	AB	R	H	2B	3B	HR	RBI	BB	SO	SB	Avg
Projected	149	531	75	147	29	1	21	78	86	84	1	.277
Actual	158	551	109	200	54	2	24	107	114	65	0	.363

Everything's relative. We did relatively well on John Olerud, compared to how we did on Galarraga:

	G	AB	R	H	2B	3B	HR	RBI	BB	SO	SB	Avg
Projected	87	292	32	73	16	1	9	38	17	74	4	.250
Actual	120	470	71	174	35	4	22	98	24	73	2	.370

Look at it this way: we missed by only one strikeout! Actually, that may be the worst projection we have ever made, in several years of doing this stuff.

But there are lots of candidates. We missed Tony Phillips' batting average by 59 points, had him hitting .254. But on the average, we did pretty well there, because while we were 59 points too low on Tony Phillips, we were 56 points too high on Bip Roberts; we had him hitting .296. And if you read my other books, I remember one time I described Bip Roberts as a National League Tony Phillips, so you see, we just had them turned around; what we meant to say was that Tony Phillips would hit .296 and Bip Roberts .254.

Randy Velarde—we missed him by 54 points. We must have confused him with Kevin Young; we had said that Kevin Young would hit .291. Missed it by that much—55 points. We had Mike Piazza projected for 12 homers and 51 RBI:

	G	AB	R	H	2B	3B	HR	RBI	BB	SO	SB	Avg
Projected	140	415	42	116	22	2	12	51	28	76	0	.280
Actual	149	547	81	174	24	2	35	112	46	86	3	.318

Actually, we thought we had presented a strong, positive projection for Piazza. We thought we were going out on a limb here, since we were projecting him to be probably the best-hitting catcher in the National League except maybe Darren Daulton, which (we thought) was asking a lot from a rookie. We thought we had presented a strong projection for the other rookie of the year, too, Tim Salmon:

	G	AB	R	H	2B	3B	HR	RBI	BB	SO	SB	Avg
Projected	143	538	78	139	24	1	20	74	67	175	7	.258
Actual	142	515	93	146	35	1	31	95	82	135	5	.283

Twenty homers, 74 RBI; we thought we were coming out pretty aggressively. And who could blame us for misjudging Mark McLemore?

	G	AB	R	H	2B	3B	HR	RBI	BB	SO	SB	Avg
Projected	87	239	33	53	8	1	1	22	24	37	8	.222
Actual	148	581	81	165	27	5	4	72	64	92	21	.284

Sometimes we just had a blind spot. For example, we had a pretty reasonable projection for Rafael Palmeiro, except that we overlooked 17 home runs and 19 stolen bases:

	G	AB	R	H	2B	3B	HR	RBI	BB	SO	SB	Avg
Projected	160	621	90	183	36	4	20	86	64	72	3	.295
Actual	160	597	124	176	40	2	37	105	73	85	22	.295

And we did real well on Ruben Sierra, except that we missed his batting average by 56 points:

	G	AB	R	H	2B	3B	HR	RBI	BB	SO	SB	Avg
Projected	156	620	89	179	35	6	23	102	52	81	13	.289
Actual	158	630	77	147	23	5	22	101	52	97	25	.233

We named my new baby Reuben, by the way. The pitcher projections are John Dewan's baby, and he had some things to brag about of his own. His projections last year told you that only one major league pitcher would win twenty games: Roger Clemens. That looks pretty good compared to his projection for John Smiley, but that's John's problem; I guess I'll let him 'fess up to his own mistakes, if he takes a notion.

Steve Buechele was like Sierra: we had projected the rest of his stats almost perfectly—15 homers, 66 RBI, 57 runs scored—but we missed his batting average by 34 points.

We did get one thing right last year, though: we predicted last year that we would have an off year. This is part of what I wrote in this article a year ago:

Expansion is a real riddle for us, and will no doubt cause a number of erroneous projections for 1993. What a player hits is colored to a very significant extent by where he plays, what park he is in. A guy who hits .290 in one park might hit .260 in another. The differences can be greater than that.

So we can project Brian Hunter in Atlanta, but he could wind up playing every day in Miami, where (it is assumed) the ball will not travel, so rather than hitting twenty home runs he might hit eight. Or Brent Mayne; we project him to hit five home runs, playing in Kansas City, but if he winds up in Denver he might hit 15. . .

So we're not looking to improve our average similarity score next year.

Gee, it's great to get to quote something without having to ask permission. Why I said we had Brent Mayne projected to hit five home runs, I can't tell you; we actually had projected that he would hit two, which he did. Anyway, we predicted here last year that the prediction system was in for rough sledding, and it was. The basic problem was that there were so many players hopping teams last year, because of free agency and expansion, that we were dealing with a large unknown factor in many, many cases. There were two brand-new ballparks, in

Florida and Colorado. We knew that the Colorado park would be a hitter's haven, which isn't a hell of a lot of use if you don't know who is going to be playing there, and we didn't know anything about Joe Robbie Stadium.

In 1994 we'll have new stadiums to deal with in Texas and Cleveland. In 1995 Kansas City is replacing the turf with grass and may pull in their fences. None of that is on the same level as our problems of last year. We expect to have a good year in '94.

I've overstated the situation; 1993 wasn't that atypical. We always have a certain number of projections which are very, very good, a certain number which are terrible, and a slightly larger number which are in between. It's like 30-40-30; 30 percent of the predictions are great, 30 percent are poor, and 40 percent are OK. Last year it was maybe 28-40-32 (I dated that girl one time. . .)

When we first started this we were flying blind, really had no idea whether we could project what a player would hit with any accuracy. In the first years I was shocked to discover that we were very close a good percentage of the time, so I would normally start out this article by writing about those (to me) surprisingly good projections. Eventually, later in the article, I would have to own up to the bad projections; I just decided to turn things around this year, talk more about the bad ones.

Fundamentally, John Dewan and I make no pretense of being able to foresee the future. We essentially predict that a player will continue to do in the future about what he has done in the past, with minor modifications . . . as he matures, he will gain power; as he gets older, he will slow down, etc. The only real "edge" we have is that we know how to read minor league statistics, and know what kind of a major league hitter somebody is going to be based on his minor league hitting numbers—most of the time.

But if a player's career takes a sudden turn for the worse, we're not going to predict that. If a player suddenly begins hitting dramatically better than he has in the past, our prediction is going to look bad in retrospect.

Well, let me say a few thousand words about some of our good projections from last year. We had 38 projections last year which scored at 950 or better (down from 43 in 1992), and 159 which scored at 900 or better (down from 174). This is a "950" projection:

Pat Borders

	G	AB	R	H	2B	3B	HR	RBI	BB	SO	SB	Avg
Projected	136	409	38	103	22	2	11	49	24	65	1	.252
Actual	138	488	38	124	30	0	9	55	20	66	2	.254

Or this:

Mike Bordick

	G	AB	R	H	2B	3B	HR	RBI	BB	SO	SB	Avg
Projected	155	550	60	132	14	1	3	46	51	72	8	.240
Actual	159	546	60	136	21	2	3	48	60	58	10	.249

A 950 projection, as a rule, is a projected record which looks so much like the player's actual record that you wouldn't really know which was which, unless this was a player that you had followed closely. For example, which of these is Jose Lind's actual 1993 statistical line, and which was our projection?

	G	AB	R	H	2B	3B	HR	RBI	BB	SO	SB	Avg
Lind 1993?	136	431	33	107	13	2	0	37	13	36	3	.248
Lind 1993?	124	418	39	105	18	3	2	40	27	39	5	.251

That scores at 945. I'm a Royals' fan; hell, I don't know which one is the actual line. Fred McGriff scores at 944:

	G	AB	R	H	2B	3B	HR	RBI	BB	SO	SB	Avg
Projected	155	550	88	156	26	2	34	100	105	119	6	.284
Actual	151	557	111	162	29	2	37	101	76	106	5	.291

And Larry Walker at 949:

	G	AB	R	H	2B	3B	HR	RBI	BB	SO	SB	Avg
Projected	146	506	72	142	26	3	20	72	49	106	20	.281
Actual	138	490	85	130	24	5	22	86	80	76	29	.265

Normally, when the system completely misses on a player one year, it will nail him pretty good the next year. Gary Sheffield, for example—in the 1992 book he made us look like idiots, hitting .330 with 33 home runs after we had said he should hit .269 with 13 homers. But last year, we did alright on Sheffield:

	G	AB	R	H	2B	3B	HR	RBI	BB	SO	SB	Avg
Projected	157	568	83	167	31	2	22	86	54	43	17	.294
Actual	140	494	67	145	20	5	20	73	47	64	17	.294

Better than alright. One thing the projection system does well, apparently, is to combine the player's most recent performance with his numbers from earlier years, to make an estimate of where the player's skills are right now. Brady Anderson was another player we were apologizing for last year, but we got even on him in 1993:

	G	AB	R	H	2B	3B	HR	RBI	BB	SO	SB	Avg
Projected	161	611	86	154	18	5	12	64	97	103	46	.252
Actual	142	560	87	147	36	8	13	66	82	99	24	.262

Mike Bordick was another; a year ago we had egg on our face after projecting him to hit .214 as a part-time player. He hit .300 as a regular—so we projected him in '93 to play regularly and hit .240, and the projection was very good.

Bret Barberie, after hitting .353 in 57 games in '91 and skidding to .232 in '92, settled in the middle right where we said he would:

	G	AB	R	H	2B	3B	HR	RBI	BB	SO	SB	Avg
Projected	122	353	44	94	16	2	5	42	57	63	10	.266
Actual	99	375	45	104	16	2	5	33	33	58	2	.277

We hit his doubles, triples and homers right on the nose; we usually do that with one player a year. We came close to that with Rob Deer (936):

	G	AB	R	H	2B	3B	HR	RBI	BB	SO	SB	Avg
Projected	131	439	62	94	17	1	25	64	71	155	3	.214
Actual	128	466	66	98	17	1	21	55	58	169	5	.210

Ellis Burks has been way up and way down; we projected him right in the middle, and were pretty much right:

	G	AB	R	H	2B	3B	HR	RBI	BB	SO	SB	Avg
Projected	122	407	59	112	27	4	14	57	37	66	7	.275
Actual	146	499	75	137	24	4	17	74	60	97	6	.275

We hit his batting average on the nose, got the power basically right, got the playing time fairly close. But we didn't do as well with him as we did with his one-time teammate, Mike Greenwell, whose career was in a similar position a year ago:

	G	AB	R	H	2B	3B	HR	RBI	BB	SO	SB	Avg
Projected	146	543	71	162	30	4	13	77	54	39	10	.298
Actual	146	540	77	170	38	6	13	72	54	46	5	.315

It scores at only 930 (don't ask me why) but that's probably my favorite projection of 1993. We took a player who had been up and down, a player about whom almost everybody was saying "Who knows what to expect of this guy", and we made a projection for him that was virtually perfect. I don't know how we could have done any better.

Don Mattingly had a comeback season; we had him pegged pretty well, too:

	G	AB	R	H	2B	3B	HR	RBI	BB	SO	SB	Avg
Projected	136	532	67	155	34	1	14	73	38	34	1	.291
Actual	134	530	78	154	27	2	17	86	61	42	0	.291

Sometimes we're just lucky. We didn't have any idea whether Julio Franco could play, or not, but the computer said he might hit .289, and he did:

	G	AB	R	H	2B	3B	HR	RBI	BB	SO	SB	Avg
Projected	120	470	76	136	21	2	8	52	61	65	24	.289
Actual	144	532	85	154	31	3	14	84	62	95	9	.289

That scores at 905. A 900 projection is still a good projection. Jeff Bagwell, for example, scores at only 910, but we feel good about it:

	G	AB	R	H	2B	3B	HR	RBI	BB	SO	SB	Avg
Projected	161	567	80	169	32	5	18	90	78	89	8	.298
Actual	142	535	76	171	37	4	20	88	62	73	13	.320

Jay Buhner scores at only 914:

	G	AB	R	H	2B	3B	HR	RBI	BB	SO	SB	Avg
Projected	151	550	74	135	22	2	27	88	73	156	2	.245
Actual	158	563	91	153	28	3	27	98	100	144	2	.272

The highest-scoring projection of last year (don't ask me why) is for Alex Cole, at 979:

	G	AB	R	H	2B	3B	HR	RBI	BB	SO	SB	Avg
Projected	105	334	48	87	7	3	1	20	40	58	28	.260
Actual	126	348	50	89	9	4	0	24	43	58	30	.256

Eric Anthony's projection scores at 971:

	G	AB	R	H	2B	3B	HR	RBI	BB	SO	SB	Avg
Projected	142	487	56	119	20	1	18	71	44	124	10	.244
Actual	145	486	70	121	19	4	15	66	49	88	3	.249

Some of the other players we had projected well were Alex Arias (950), Juan Bell (960), Damon Berryhill (948), Jeff Branson (940), Bernardo Brito (955), Sid Bream (965), Scott Brosius (964), Ken Caminiti (946), Darnell Coles (947), Henry Cotto (968), Chad Curtis (944), Andre Dawson (950), Mike Devereaux (957), Gary DiSarcina (961), Steve Finley (941), Rene Gonzales (942), Brian Harper (944), Thomas Howard (944), Todd Hundley (949), Mark Lemke (965), Scott Livingstone (943), Dave Magadan (949), Brent Mayne (941), Willie McGee (950), Mickey Morandini (964), Greg Myers (955), Otis Nixon (960), Pete O'Brien (961), Joe Oliver (956), John Orton (960), Spike Owen (952), Terry Pendleton (963), Geno Petralli (957), Kirby Puckett (942), Randy Ready (956), Harold Reynolds (974), Cal Ripken (944), Ivan Rodriguez (957), Chris Sabo (960), Reggie Sanders (944), Paul Sorrento (953), Eddie Taubensee (946), Milt Thompson (957), Dickie Thon (948), Ron Tingley (971), John VanderWal (959), Gary Varsho (965), Omar Vizquel (946), Chico Walker (970), Willie Wilson (970), and Robin Yount (969).

We take a particular pride in our ability to project the batting stats of young players, playing regularly for the first or second time (please forget about all of Tommie Lasorda's relatives.) Among the first-year regulars that we projected with a fair degree of accuracy were Wilfredo Cordero, Carlos Garcia, Jeff Gardner and Bernie Williams:

	G	AB	R	H	2B	3B	HR	RBI	BB	SO	SB	Avg
				Wilfredo Cordero								
Projected	151	516	61	135	20	2	9	50	40	135	8	.262
Actual	138	475	56	118	32	2	10	58	34	60	12	.248
				Carlos Garcia								
Projected	141	461	56	119	20	5	8	50	24	78	17	.258
Actual	141	546	77	147	25	5	12	47	31	67	18	.269
				Jeff Gardner								
Projected	114	373	40	92	12	1	0	28	49	40	3	.247
Actual	140	404	53	106	21	7	1	24	45	69	2	.262
				Bernie Williams								
Projected	153	632	95	166	29	5	13	67	86	112	26	.263
Actual	139	567	67	152	31	4	12	68	53	106	9	.268

John Jaha had had an interesting minor league career, and there was some controversy about what kind of a major league hitter he really was. We didn't miss by much:

	G	AB	R	H	2B	3B	HR	RBI	BB	SO	SB	Avg
Projected	130	497	84	141	25	1	20	85	57	107	13	.284
Actual	153	515	78	136	21	0	19	70	51	109	13	.264

And he'll hit better than .264 in some future years. Chris Donnels wasn't a regular and we didn't expect him to be, but we feel we had assessed him pretty accurately despite his .195 batting average in 82 games before 1993:

	G	AB	R	H	2B	3B	HR	RBI	BB	SO	SB	Avg
Projected	69	201	22	50	9	0	3	22	35	37	3	.249
Actual	88	179	18	46	14	2	2	24	19	33	2	.257

We had projected that Bret Boone would hit .251, exactly what he did hit, although we had expected him to play fulltime.

Bob Zupcic had misleading stats in 1992, his first shot at the majors, but by factoring in his minor league record we were able to project accurately what kind of player he would be:

	G	AB	R	H	2B	3B	HR	RBI	BB	SO	SB	Avg
Projected	107	335	36	83	18	0	5	35	26	50	4	.248
Actual	141	286	40	69	24	2	2	26	27	54	5	.241

In the case of Deion Sanders, we had projected that he would bat 272 times, hit six triples and hit six homers, all matching exactly what he did; we missed by one RBI on him, also.

So let me summarize the claims we make for these projections:

1) Sometimes we're right.

2) Sometimes we're wrong.

— *Bill James*

1994 Pitcher Projections

Our first year of pitcher projections is now under our belts. What can we say about them? The main thing I can say is that I'm very happy we did them. I manage four teams in four different leagues in Bill James Fantasy Baseball and I won my division in all of them. I felt that my pitching staffs were better because of these pitching projections.

Here are a couple of our most successful projections:

	ERA	W	L	Sv	G	GS	IP	H	HR	BB	SO	BB/9
					Jeff Montgomery							
Projected	2.54	6	3	44	66	0	85	69	5	28	76	10.3
Actual	2.27	7	5	45	69	0	87	65	3	23	66	9.1
					Erik Hanson							
Projected	3.49	12	9	0	30	29	183	180	13	56	129	11.6
Actual	3.47	11	12	0	31	30	215	215	17	60	163	11.5

We projected Jeff Montgomery to save more games than he ever did in his career . . . he even beat our projection. We thought Erik Hanson would bounce back after a terrible season in 1992; he did.

Nevertheless, these projections are far from perfect. We had a lot of "dog" projections. Like John Smiley, Mike Mussina and Dennis Eckersley. I don't think that's because our system is bad. There's plenty of room for improvement, but it's not a bad system. It's just that you can't predict a pitcher finding control all of a sudden. You can't predict those common injuries (much more common than position players) which will disable a pitcher for major parts of campaigns. You can't predict a pitcher's fastball all of a sudden having an inch-and-a-half less movement than a year before. Mister Dependable himself, Roger Clemens, fell off my long list (of two) of consistently good starting pitchers. Greg Maddux is currently a list of one, though Jose Rijo is bucking for a spot.

With the caveat that I stated last year that "it's impossible to project pitching statistics," we are trying to improve on the system. Last year we projected winning percentages that were way too high. That was a clear-cut "bug" in our program. We fixed that this year. In addition we think we made strides in some additional areas: improved ERA accuracy, improved save totals and better estimates on playing time. One area that we felt real good about last year was in projecting home runs allowed. Despite the hitter's year that we had, we were within one home run allowed for 25% of the pitchers for whom we did projections.

Finally, let me give credit to my partner in developing these projections, Mike Canter. Mike combined his baseball knowledge with his computer programming skills (along with a background in mathematical/statistical techniques) to help analyze, develop and re-develop the pitcher projection system.

— John Dewan

Projections for 1994 Batters

Batter	Age	Avg	G	AB	R	H	2B	3B	HR	RBI	BB	SO	SB	CS	OBP	SLG
Abbott,Kurt	25	.246	90	207	25	51	8	1	3	22	12	47	6	3	.288	.338
Aldrete,Mike	33	.247	85	223	24	55	12	1	4	25	30	53	1	1	.336	.363
Alicea,Luis	28	.253	119	332	40	84	16	5	3	34	42	48	6	4	.337	.358
Alomar,Roberto	26	.312	155	597	100	186	31	6	15	82	78	66	56	14	.391	.459
Alomar Jr,Sandy	28	.266	95	312	28	83	17	1	5	35	16	34	3	3	.302	.375
Alou,Moises	27	.280	146	529	75	148	27	5	15	81	43	58	22	8	.334	.435
Amaral,Rich	32	.275	78	244	34	67	15	1	1	19	25	39	15	7	.342	.357
Anderson,Brady	30	.266	151	563	85	150	25	7	12	62	91	94	37	15	.369	.400
Anthony,Eric	26	.256	144	480	61	123	20	2	17	71	43	101	6	5	.317	.413
Arias,Alex	26	.263	97	312	35	82	13	1	3	26	27	24	6	3	.322	.340
Ashley,Billy	23	.214	35	112	13	24	5	0	4	14	5	35	2	1	.248	.366
Aude,Rich	22	.267	30	101	14	27	5	0	3	15	9	20	1	1	.327	.406
Ausmus,Brad	25	.237	101	300	34	71	11	1	7	34	25	47	11	5	.295	.350
Baerga,Carlos	25	.308	158	624	93	192	29	3	17	95	41	70	9	4	.350	.446
Baez,Kevin	27	.204	77	201	16	41	8	0	1	15	12	29	0	1	.249	.259
Bagwell,Jeff	26	.301	152	552	82	166	33	5	18	88	77	91	10	5	.386	.476
Baines,Harold	35	.277	132	451	63	125	23	2	15	76	62	61	1	1	.365	.437
Barberie,Bret	26	.278	130	490	58	136	23	2	7	57	70	85	9	6	.368	.376
Barnes,Skeeter	37	.267	58	105	16	28	7	0	2	14	8	14	5	3	.319	.390
Bass,Kevin	35	.251	110	227	25	57	11	1	5	25	19	37	6	3	.309	.374
Batiste,Kim	26	.265	91	279	27	74	12	2	3	28	7	44	5	5	.283	.355
Bautista,Danny	22	.259	81	212	23	55	9	0	3	21	10	38	10	4	.293	.344
Bean,Billy	30	.245	55	102	10	25	4	0	1	12	7	13	2	2	.294	.314
Becker,Rich	22	.270	140	507	77	137	28	7	12	53	70	128	21	8	.359	.424
Bell,Derek	25	.275	140	510	76	140	20	6	15	70	42	98	25	9	.330	.425
Bell,George	34	.258	106	364	40	94	18	1	13	60	18	49	2	2	.293	.420
Bell,Jay	28	.273	157	616	93	168	30	6	12	58	65	108	12	8	.342	.399
Bell,Juan	26	.229	108	301	39	69	11	3	3	28	28	70	5	4	.295	.316
Belle,Albert	27	.276	158	595	84	164	30	2	35	118	57	116	12	7	.339	.509
Benavides,Freddie	28	.230	96	269	21	62	11	1	2	22	10	45	3	3	.258	.301
Benjamin,Mike	28	.192	64	151	17	29	7	1	2	14	9	35	2	1	.238	.291
Benzinger,Todd	31	.253	86	170	16	43	8	1	3	20	11	30	2	2	.298	.365
Berry,Sean	28	.242	108	310	40	75	16	2	9	38	30	70	6	4	.309	.394
Berryhill,Damon	30	.227	123	357	28	81	18	1	10	43	23	79	1	1	.274	.367
Bichette,Dante	30	.272	139	489	61	133	26	2	14	63	25	100	17	9	.307	.419
Biggio,Craig	28	.280	159	601	92	168	30	3	11	52	80	88	26	14	.364	.394
Blankenship,Lance	30	.218	100	257	43	56	11	1	2	24	56	56	15	6	.358	.292
Blauser,Jeff	28	.275	152	585	98	161	25	3	17	75	88	113	13	8	.370	.415
Blowers,Mike	29	.254	112	342	44	87	22	2	8	45	38	86	2	2	.329	.401
Bogar,Tim	27	.243	80	255	25	62	12	1	2	22	13	38	4	4	.280	.322
Boggs,Wade	36	.313	140	530	78	166	34	2	7	57	79	40	1	1	.402	.425
Bolick,Frank	28	.235	48	132	16	31	7	0	4	18	17	28	1	1	.322	.379
Bonds,Barry	29	.293	155	550	116	161	35	5	33	111	137	80	41	14	.434	.555
Bonilla,Bobby	31	.268	144	511	80	137	30	3	21	83	78	80	4	3	.365	.462
Boone,Bret	25	.259	137	528	65	137	25	2	16	72	48	120	9	11	.321	.405
Borders,Pat	31	.249	130	462	39	115	26	1	10	54	24	68	1	1	.286	.374
Bordick,Mike	28	.245	151	530	57	130	18	2	3	47	52	64	10	8	.313	.304
Boston,Daryl	31	.242	135	285	40	69	17	2	8	30	33	54	9	7	.321	.400
Branson,Jeff	27	.247	116	328	32	81	14	1	3	26	20	55	4	5	.290	.323
Bream,Sid	33	.251	100	175	18	44	10	0	5	26	20	25	2	1	.328	.394

Projections for 1994 Batters

Batter	Age	Avg	G	AB	R	H	2B	3B	HR	RBI	BB	SO	SB	CS	OBP	SLG
Brewer,Rod	28	.239	103	272	26	65	13	1	5	35	25	41	1	1	.303	.349
Briley,Greg	29	.250	82	168	18	42	10	1	3	14	10	28	8	4	.292	.375
Brooks,Hubie	37	.251	76	223	24	56	13	1	5	32	18	39	2	1	.307	.386
Brosius,Scott	27	.235	85	255	30	60	14	1	7	30	17	48	7	4	.283	.380
Brown,Jarvis	27	.251	73	215	28	54	9	3	2	16	17	36	10	4	.306	.349
Browne,Jerry	28	.267	110	382	45	102	16	3	3	42	40	38	4	3	.336	.348
Brumfield,Jacob	29	.253	98	293	40	74	14	2	4	26	23	44	23	8	.307	.355
Buechele,Steve	32	.245	144	503	54	123	20	2	14	65	51	96	2	2	.314	.376
Buford,Damon	24	.233	103	210	31	49	10	1	1	16	16	34	16	7	.288	.305
Buhner,Jay	29	.252	158	552	83	139	25	2	27	89	86	149	2	3	.353	.451
Burks,Ellis	29	.265	155	550	78	146	32	5	18	75	59	103	9	10	.337	.440
Burnitz,Jeromy	25	.224	139	450	63	101	18	5	17	58	53	103	19	11	.306	.400
Butler,Brett	37	.273	146	546	78	149	18	5	3	34	91	72	33	19	.377	.341
Butler,Rob	24	.267	129	382	50	102	21	2	0	21	29	64	11	11	.319	.332
Cabrera,Francisco	27	.248	72	101	10	25	4	0	3	13	6	17	0	0	.290	.376
Calderon,Ivan	32	.268	64	190	25	51	13	1	5	27	19	26	8	4	.335	.426
Caminiti,Ken	31	.259	145	545	65	141	26	1	11	67	48	81	8	5	.319	.371
Candaele,Casey	33	.237	61	131	11	31	6	1	1	11	11	15	2	1	.296	.321
Canseco,Jose	29	.261	118	436	78	114	21	1	27	86	58	120	14	8	.348	.500
Carr,Chuck	25	.266	151	527	72	140	18	3	3	36	42	75	55	20	.320	.328
Carreon,Mark	30	.264	105	265	27	70	10	0	8	34	18	32	2	1	.311	.392
Carter,Joe	34	.248	157	612	83	152	31	3	27	101	44	114	13	6	.299	.441
Castilla,Vinny	26	.237	100	300	28	71	12	2	6	30	11	40	1	1	.264	.350
Cedeno,Andujar	24	.251	155	550	57	138	26	5	13	64	34	126	8	6	.295	.387
Chamberlain,Wes	28	.258	108	368	41	95	20	2	11	52	24	63	7	3	.304	.413
Cianfrocco,Archi	27	.252	109	345	38	87	15	3	8	46	18	87	4	1	.289	.383
Clark,Dave	31	.257	115	288	34	74	13	1	9	43	31	56	3	3	.329	.403
Clark,Jerald	30	.253	147	487	49	123	22	3	14	62	28	90	5	3	.293	.396
Clark,Phil	26	.276	97	275	32	76	14	1	7	35	15	35	3	2	.314	.411
Clark,Will	30	.297	143	525	79	156	30	4	21	88	66	81	6	4	.376	.490
Clayton,Royce	24	.257	154	540	65	139	19	5	7	61	44	93	20	11	.313	.350
Colbrunn,Greg	24	.270	58	159	16	43	11	0	4	23	5	30	2	1	.293	.415
Cole,Alex	28	.265	124	362	53	96	9	4	1	24	47	59	26	15	.350	.320
Coleman,Vince	32	.258	82	287	45	74	10	3	2	19	29	48	32	13	.326	.334
Coles,Darnell	32	.244	65	197	23	48	9	1	5	22	12	27	1	1	.287	.376
Conine,Jeff	28	.280	158	583	74	163	29	4	13	75	59	115	3	4	.346	.410
Cooper,Scott	26	.278	155	550	59	153	26	2	11	63	57	69	3	2	.346	.393
Cora,Joey	29	.254	143	528	91	134	17	6	2	46	65	55	24	11	.336	.320
Cordero,Wil	22	.253	144	501	59	127	25	2	10	55	37	82	10	6	.305	.371
Correia,Rod	26	.241	65	195	22	47	7	0	2	17	10	29	4	3	.278	.308
Cotto,Henry	33	.250	120	320	43	80	12	1	6	30	13	54	22	6	.279	.350
Cummings,Midre	22	.241	112	403	48	97	22	1	8	33	24	68	5	3	.283	.360
Curtis,Chad	25	.277	151	571	84	158	23	3	10	61	64	80	51	24	.350	.380
Cuyler,Milt	25	.244	86	258	42	63	8	4	2	22	22	51	16	5	.304	.329
Dascenzo,Doug	30	.232	78	181	22	42	7	1	1	13	14	19	5	4	.287	.298
Daulton,Darren	32	.233	132	438	64	102	21	1	17	74	85	95	7	2	.358	.402
Davis,Chili	34	.249	151	562	73	140	27	2	19	86	88	124	5	4	.351	.406
Davis,Eric	32	.245	120	420	57	103	17	2	18	61	59	113	28	6	.338	.424
Dawson,Andre	39	.265	107	392	40	104	18	2	14	61	18	54	3	2	.298	.429
Deer,Rob	33	.205	106	361	51	74	13	1	18	46	56	137	3	2	.312	.396

Projections for 1994 Batters

Batter	Age	Avg	G	AB	R	H	2B	3B	HR	RBI	BB	SO	SB	CS	OBP	SLG
Delgado,Carlos	22	.283	29	120	19	34	7	0	6	22	19	27	2	1	.381	.492
DeShields,Delino	25	.281	136	519	82	146	19	6	6	48	77	103	51	18	.374	.376
Destrade,Orestes	32	.256	145	540	56	138	18	2	17	79	56	112	1	1	.326	.391
Devereaux,Mike	31	.253	147	598	71	151	25	4	17	73	46	103	10	7	.306	.393
Diaz,Mario	32	.268	84	209	23	56	10	0	2	21	8	17	1	1	.295	.344
DiSarcina,Gary	26	.243	132	423	42	103	16	1	3	40	18	38	8	6	.274	.307
Donnels,Chris	28	.258	96	260	28	67	14	1	4	30	44	46	4	2	.365	.365
Ducey,Rob	29	.238	112	281	38	67	13	2	6	27	31	75	7	7	.314	.363
Duncan,Mariano	31	.255	129	490	59	125	21	3	10	52	15	88	12	5	.277	.371
Dunston,Shawon	31	.263	120	410	48	108	19	3	9	37	19	56	16	8	.296	.390
Dykstra,Lenny	31	.284	145	570	107	162	34	3	12	51	98	54	41	11	.389	.418
Easley,Damion	24	.253	89	293	34	74	12	1	3	26	22	39	11	6	.305	.331
Edmonds,Jim	24	.279	94	233	31	65	14	1	5	31	20	64	3	4	.336	.412
Eisenreich,Jim	35	.279	132	355	41	99	21	3	4	41	23	36	6	3	.323	.389
Espinoza,Alvaro	32	.252	100	286	28	72	13	1	3	25	9	36	2	2	.275	.336
Everett,Carl	24	.245	28	106	14	26	7	1	3	8	10	40	6	1	.310	.415
Felder,Mike	31	.245	95	233	27	57	6	2	2	13	17	22	11	5	.296	.313
Fermin,Felix	30	.254	127	406	37	103	10	2	1	32	26	18	4	3	.299	.296
Fernandez,Tony	32	.270	146	563	74	152	27	5	5	45	56	60	21	13	.336	.362
Fielder,Cecil	30	.256	156	593	87	152	21	0	36	120	84	141	0	0	.349	.474
Finley,Steve	29	.272	152	573	75	156	21	8	7	49	44	63	33	12	.324	.373
Fletcher,Darrin	27	.245	128	380	29	93	18	1	7	48	26	43	1	1	.293	.353
Fletcher,Scott	35	.255	117	380	47	97	17	2	3	39	29	33	11	6	.308	.334
Floyd,Cliff	21	.272	155	530	81	144	18	3	22	99	51	124	24	9	.336	.442
Foley,Tom	34	.223	89	157	13	35	10	1	2	15	11	26	1	1	.274	.338
Franco,Julio	32	.281	118	438	69	123	21	2	8	54	52	68	15	5	.357	.393
Frazier,Lou	29	.224	90	170	25	38	3	0	1	12	24	37	14	5	.320	.259
Frye,Jeff	27	.283	140	508	82	144	30	6	4	42	58	67	11	10	.357	.390
Fryman,Travis	25	.276	156	617	85	170	35	3	22	95	58	138	10	5	.338	.449
Gaetti,Gary	35	.233	121	425	42	99	21	1	13	50	24	87	3	2	.274	.379
Gagne,Greg	32	.252	148	511	60	129	28	3	10	50	29	91	10	10	.293	.378
Galarraga,Andres	33	.288	135	500	58	144	27	2	17	70	25	102	6	5	.322	.452
Gallagher,Dave	33	.262	108	233	29	61	13	1	2	27	23	29	3	3	.328	.352
Gallego,Mike	33	.238	118	370	48	88	11	1	6	35	49	62	4	4	.327	.322
Gant,Ron	29	.256	157	579	97	148	29	4	27	98	65	109	32	13	.331	.459
Garcia,Carlos	26	.260	140	530	68	138	23	5	10	56	29	82	21	10	.299	.379
Gardner,Jeff	30	.258	135	400	49	103	15	2	1	31	51	54	4	3	.341	.313
Gates,Brent	24	.296	145	547	68	162	34	2	9	74	59	73	7	4	.365	.415
Gibson,Kirk	37	.246	86	281	43	69	13	2	9	36	36	67	10	4	.331	.402
Gil,Benji	21	.232	65	190	19	44	4	0	6	24	14	57	7	3	.284	.347
Gilkey,Bernard	27	.294	142	489	73	144	27	4	10	53	57	63	19	13	.368	.427
Girardi,Joe	29	.280	106	329	30	92	13	2	2	29	26	42	4	3	.332	.350
Gladden,Dan	36	.253	102	312	41	79	13	2	5	36	22	49	7	4	.302	.356
Gomez,Chris	23	.239	97	284	26	68	13	1	1	24	22	39	3	3	.294	.303
Gomez,Leo	27	.244	130	386	48	94	17	1	15	49	50	77	1	1	.330	.409
Gonzales,Rene	32	.237	98	249	28	59	8	0	3	22	33	36	4	3	.326	.305
Gonzalez,Juan	24	.279	149	567	89	158	32	2	37	109	41	119	3	2	.327	.538
Gonzalez,Luis	26	.275	155	550	69	151	30	5	17	78	46	90	16	10	.331	.440
Grace,Mark	30	.298	158	604	81	180	32	3	11	77	74	40	6	3	.375	.416
Grebeck,Craig	29	.257	90	226	28	58	12	1	3	25	32	29	2	2	.349	.358

Projections for 1994 Batters

Batter	Age	Avg	G	AB	R	H	2B	3B	HR	RBI	BB	SO	SB	CS	OBP	SLG
Greene,Willie	22	.260	138	496	66	129	25	2	24	74	56	121	6	8	.335	.464
Greenwell,Mike	30	.297	146	538	74	160	31	4	13	76	51	43	9	6	.358	.442
Griffey Jr,Ken	24	.315	154	577	93	182	37	3	32	105	75	79	16	8	.394	.556
Grissom,Marquis	27	.278	159	629	93	175	29	5	13	68	46	84	74	16	.327	.402
Guillen,Ozzie	30	.263	136	471	45	124	18	5	3	47	11	39	13	9	.280	.342
Gutierrez,Ricky	24	.244	140	472	66	115	10	3	3	37	57	86	9	6	.325	.297
Gwynn,Chris	29	.280	115	318	39	89	14	3	5	35	24	38	1	1	.330	.390
Gwynn,Tony	34	.319	130	514	67	164	25	4	5	50	40	19	8	5	.368	.412
Hale,Chip	29	.256	95	344	41	88	16	3	1	32	38	29	2	2	.330	.328
Hamelin,Bob	26	.237	109	321	37	76	13	2	11	44	42	62	2	1	.325	.393
Hamilton,Darryl	29	.298	140	506	72	151	20	3	5	57	47	52	28	13	.358	.379
Hammonds,Jeffrey	23	.279	137	531	61	148	27	0	14	71	17	96	16	9	.301	.409
Hansen,Dave	25	.255	116	247	25	63	10	1	4	28	30	35	2	2	.336	.352
Harper,Brian	34	.291	136	484	50	141	24	1	9	67	23	25	1	1	.323	.401
Harris,Lenny	29	.267	122	191	22	51	7	1	1	17	16	14	7	3	.324	.330
Haselman,Bill	28	.237	72	211	25	50	13	0	7	28	22	53	2	2	.309	.398
Hatcher,Billy	33	.257	133	456	52	117	22	2	5	42	26	53	10	8	.297	.346
Hayes,Charlie	29	.267	155	562	62	150	29	1	18	74	33	94	7	5	.308	.418
Hemond,Scott	28	.237	92	232	31	55	13	1	3	21	26	52	9	6	.314	.341
Henderson,Dave	35	.236	90	313	35	74	16	1	11	39	28	78	2	2	.299	.399
Henderson,Rickey	35	.270	129	444	94	120	22	2	13	50	105	67	51	13	.410	.417
Hernandez,Carlos	27	.276	55	105	9	29	4	0	2	10	5	12	1	1	.309	.371
Hiatt,Phil	25	.227	102	331	41	75	13	2	11	46	15	105	5	4	.260	.378
Higgins,Kevin	27	.239	75	201	19	48	6	0	1	17	17	17	1	1	.298	.284
Hill,Glenallen	29	.255	115	353	42	90	18	4	15	50	27	83	10	6	.308	.456
Hoiles,Chris	29	.271	138	450	69	122	23	0	22	62	67	91	1	1	.366	.469
Hollins,Dave	28	.262	151	530	89	139	26	3	19	78	79	103	5	4	.358	.430
Horn,Sam	30	.234	94	231	27	54	10	0	14	36	29	77	0	0	.319	.459
Hosey,Steve	25	.261	35	115	15	30	6	1	3	15	10	27	4	3	.320	.409
Howard,Dave	27	.217	76	138	12	30	3	1	1	11	9	22	2	1	.265	.275
Howard,Thomas	29	.262	111	313	41	82	17	2	4	32	23	58	13	8	.313	.367
Hrbek,Kent	34	.264	126	421	63	111	22	1	18	78	72	56	4	3	.371	.449
Hulett,Tim	34	.235	91	234	28	55	12	1	4	22	18	55	1	1	.290	.346
Hulse,David	26	.284	129	472	69	134	14	6	3	34	24	85	26	14	.319	.358
Hundley,Todd	25	.231	131	424	44	98	19	2	9	48	31	82	1	1	.284	.349
Hunter,Brian	26	.230	80	200	23	46	8	1	8	30	13	36	1	1	.277	.400
Huskey,Butch	22	.219	80	288	31	63	11	0	10	43	18	64	4	1	.265	.361
Huson,Jeff	29	.234	72	205	28	48	8	1	2	18	27	28	8	4	.323	.312
Incaviglia,Pete	30	.257	96	358	45	92	17	2	16	57	29	93	2	2	.313	.450
Jackson,Bo	31	.232	86	285	32	66	9	0	16	45	23	106	0	2	.289	.432
Jackson,Darrin	30	.236	77	254	29	60	8	1	8	29	14	52	4	2	.276	.370
Jaha,John	28	.280	151	514	88	144	27	1	21	85	58	106	14	8	.353	.459
James,Chris	31	.248	72	157	15	39	7	1	4	18	9	27	1	1	.289	.382
James,Dion	31	.289	112	291	48	84	18	2	5	30	32	27	0	0	.359	.416
Javier,Stan	30	.244	119	254	33	62	11	3	2	24	29	42	12	3	.322	.335
Jefferies,Gregg	26	.302	150	567	77	171	31	3	15	80	55	33	32	9	.363	.446
Jefferson,Reggie	25	.269	110	350	43	94	15	2	10	43	26	71	1	1	.319	.409
Johnson,Howard	33	.238	118	403	63	96	20	1	16	61	63	88	21	10	.341	.412
Johnson,Lance	30	.279	153	559	69	156	16	10	1	47	33	41	34	12	.319	.349
Jones,Chipper	22	.310	118	407	58	126	23	5	11	55	27	49	12	4	.353	.472

348

Projections for 1994 Batters

Batter	Age	Avg	G	AB	R	H	2B	3B	HR	RBI	BB	SO	SB	CS	OBP	SLG
Jones,Chris	28	.224	97	245	28	55	10	2	5	26	15	68	7	3	.269	.343
Jordan,Brian	27	.267	88	292	36	78	13	4	8	39	18	47	12	6	.310	.421
Jordan,Ricky	29	.270	87	178	20	48	9	1	4	22	7	30	1	1	.297	.399
Jorgensen,Terry	27	.263	69	224	27	59	14	1	4	25	19	27	1	0	.321	.388
Jose,Felix	29	.272	153	529	64	144	28	3	10	63	44	103	27	13	.328	.393
Joyner,Wally	32	.275	144	538	71	148	31	1	16	72	59	61	6	5	.347	.426
Justice,Dave	28	.264	155	553	90	146	25	3	29	100	88	97	6	6	.365	.477
Karkovice,Ron	30	.227	125	401	53	91	18	1	18	57	34	113	5	3	.287	.411
Karros,Eric	26	.264	151	549	68	145	31	2	20	81	38	90	2	2	.312	.437
Kelly,Bobby	29	.285	118	452	63	129	21	2	12	55	35	70	28	8	.337	.420
Kelly,Pat	26	.263	131	407	53	107	22	3	7	44	27	69	15	8	.309	.383
Kent,Jeff	26	.257	145	525	75	135	32	1	19	78	49	107	11	7	.321	.430
King,Jeff	29	.254	152	560	70	142	24	3	13	78	50	59	7	6	.315	.377
Kirby,Wayne	30	.264	95	288	42	76	10	3	3	30	20	29	16	7	.312	.351
Klesko,Ryan	23	.250	80	200	25	50	9	0	8	27	20	33	3	4	.318	.415
Knoblauch,Chuck	25	.287	156	599	92	172	26	6	3	54	75	47	31	11	.366	.366
Knorr,Randy	25	.256	62	195	18	50	8	0	6	23	14	36	0	0	.306	.390
Koslofski,Kevin	27	.266	76	244	26	65	9	2	3	24	20	43	6	5	.322	.357
Kreuter,Chad	29	.248	117	343	50	85	15	1	8	37	52	70	1	1	.347	.367
Kruk,John	33	.293	146	515	81	151	23	3	13	72	90	93	5	3	.398	.425
Lampkin,Tom	30	.237	79	198	22	47	8	1	2	20	22	21	6	4	.314	.318
Lankford,Ray	27	.260	142	516	77	134	27	7	12	65	67	122	35	20	.345	.409
Lansing,Mike	26	.276	111	388	49	107	19	2	4	39	35	46	23	8	.336	.366
Larkin,Barry	30	.290	126	473	72	137	23	4	11	62	61	53	18	5	.371	.425
Larkin,Gene	31	.261	75	184	22	48	12	1	2	21	20	20	2	1	.333	.370
LaValliere,Mike	33	.261	77	176	12	46	7	0	1	18	20	16	1	1	.337	.318
Lee,Manuel	29	.244	115	386	46	94	12	3	3	32	37	81	6	3	.310	.313
Leius,Scott	28	.260	96	346	51	90	15	2	4	34	38	50	7	6	.333	.350
Lemke,Mark	28	.235	145	480	52	113	18	3	6	41	61	47	2	2	.322	.323
Levis,Jesse	26	.260	45	100	8	26	5	0	1	11	8	10	1	1	.315	.340
Lewis,Darren	26	.252	140	515	77	130	14	5	3	43	46	56	41	17	.314	.317
Lewis,Mark	24	.260	99	281	34	73	14	1	5	28	16	43	3	3	.300	.370
Leyritz,Jim	30	.258	104	279	40	72	16	0	9	41	38	55	1	1	.347	.412
Lind,Jose	30	.249	122	402	37	100	16	3	1	39	21	35	4	2	.286	.311
Liriano,Nelson	30	.263	65	198	28	52	9	3	2	20	19	28	6	6	.327	.369
Listach,Pat	26	.263	135	520	81	137	18	4	2	44	54	110	39	15	.333	.325
Litton,Greg	29	.244	94	225	26	55	12	1	4	27	22	44	1	1	.312	.360
Livingstone,Scott	28	.268	119	370	48	99	16	1	5	49	31	49	2	2	.324	.357
Lofton,Kenny	27	.294	152	588	100	173	21	8	3	45	68	79	59	15	.367	.372
Lopez,Javy	23	.302	83	262	31	79	15	1	10	35	8	30	2	2	.322	.481
Lovullo,Torey	28	.243	99	321	41	78	19	1	8	41	38	46	4	4	.323	.383
Lydy,Scott	25	.266	49	143	22	38	7	1	3	17	17	39	4	2	.344	.392
Maas,Kevin	29	.238	76	227	31	54	10	0	10	31	34	54	2	1	.337	.414
Macfarlane,Mike	30	.247	131	417	52	103	26	2	15	55	36	88	3	3	.307	.427
Mack,Shane	30	.292	144	517	78	151	22	4	13	65	49	87	20	11	.353	.426
Magadan,Dave	31	.273	128	418	49	114	20	1	4	47	78	55	1	1	.387	.354
Maldonado,Candy	33	.229	75	214	24	49	11	1	7	29	26	55	1	1	.313	.388
Manwaring,Kirt	28	.240	125	400	35	96	13	2	4	39	34	60	2	2	.300	.313
Martin,Al	26	.257	141	482	71	124	21	6	14	56	36	123	19	10	.309	.413
Martinez,Carlos	28	.275	73	218	24	60	10	1	5	31	11	31	3	2	.310	.399

349

Projections for 1994 Batters

Batter	Age	Avg	G	AB	R	H	2B	3B	HR	RBI	BB	SO	SB	CS	OBP	SLG
Martinez,Dave	29	.269	120	349	42	94	14	4	6	36	31	49	12	7	.329	.384
Martinez,Edgar	31	.304	140	527	90	160	35	1	14	57	74	66	6	3	.389	.454
Martinez,Tino	26	.260	129	442	56	115	24	1	15	60	51	63	2	2	.337	.421
Mattingly,Don	33	.289	145	574	76	166	35	1	16	82	49	43	1	1	.345	.437
May,Derrick	25	.284	140	482	58	137	24	2	9	68	27	50	9	6	.322	.398
Mayne,Brent	26	.251	97	255	25	64	11	1	2	28	21	35	3	3	.308	.325
McCarty,Dave	24	.264	103	329	48	87	14	1	8	40	29	65	4	4	.324	.386
McGee,Willie	35	.282	129	461	53	130	23	4	4	39	33	76	12	7	.330	.375
McGriff,Fred	30	.281	154	545	92	153	26	2	33	101	98	118	6	4	.390	.517
McGwire,Mark	30	.240	141	521	83	125	22	1	34	94	108	121	2	1	.370	.482
McKnight,Jeff	31	.254	65	142	16	36	7	0	2	15	14	22	1	1	.321	.345
McLemore,Mark	29	.257	109	350	47	90	12	2	2	36	38	51	13	8	.330	.320
McNeely,Jeff	24	.236	109	351	40	83	11	2	2	22	27	83	18	8	.291	.296
McRae,Brian	26	.257	154	607	78	156	26	9	8	64	37	96	21	11	.300	.369
McReynolds,Kevin	34	.252	113	305	36	77	15	1	10	39	38	38	4	2	.335	.407
Meares,Pat	25	.252	120	417	44	105	22	2	3	37	10	68	5	5	.269	.336
Mejia,Roberto	22	.236	140	478	58	113	23	5	12	45	22	116	11	6	.270	.381
Melvin,Bob	32	.225	90	240	14	54	10	0	3	26	12	52	0	0	.262	.304
Merced,Orlando	27	.271	143	458	71	124	22	4	8	61	73	76	6	5	.371	.389
Mieske,Matt	26	.234	93	261	33	61	12	2	8	28	19	48	5	5	.286	.387
Miller,Keith	31	.258	88	233	29	60	11	1	2	17	18	31	9	4	.311	.339
Milligan,Randy	32	.256	102	285	38	73	14	1	8	37	59	56	1	1	.384	.396
Mitchell,Kevin	32	.283	113	381	54	108	21	2	19	70	38	55	2	1	.348	.499
Molitor,Paul	37	.293	147	587	92	172	31	4	13	74	71	67	20	6	.369	.426
Mondesi,Raul	23	.246	143	516	58	127	18	5	11	54	15	115	13	12	.267	.364
Morandini,Mickey	28	.255	132	447	55	114	18	6	3	36	36	69	12	4	.311	.342
Morris,Hal	29	.297	120	421	54	125	23	1	9	54	44	56	6	5	.363	.420
Munoz,Pedro	25	.271	107	336	37	91	17	2	10	48	21	79	5	4	.314	.423
Murray,Eddie	38	.269	142	531	60	143	24	1	18	86	50	70	5	2	.332	.420
Myers,Greg	28	.249	112	325	26	81	17	0	7	40	22	45	2	1	.297	.366
Naehring,Tim	27	.260	131	480	51	125	26	0	10	55	56	78	1	1	.338	.377
Natal,Bob	28	.238	58	172	17	41	8	0	4	19	14	33	0	0	.296	.355
Neel,Troy	28	.269	149	547	73	147	29	1	20	77	73	131	4	5	.355	.435
Newfield,Marc	21	.257	40	140	14	36	8	0	5	17	8	20	1	1	.297	.421
Nieves,Melvin	22	.266	151	538	69	143	25	2	23	73	46	150	5	4	.324	.448
Nilsson,Dave	24	.284	131	419	53	119	25	2	7	61	42	40	6	6	.349	.403
Nixon,Otis	35	.260	122	420	68	109	8	1	1	20	48	52	48	17	.335	.290
Nokes,Matt	30	.247	109	340	38	84	12	0	16	52	26	46	1	1	.301	.424
O'Brien,Charlie	33	.211	84	194	17	41	11	0	3	19	18	20	1	1	.278	.314
O'Brien,Pete	36	.248	71	206	22	51	9	0	6	29	20	21	0	0	.314	.379
O'Leary,Troy	24	.287	50	115	17	33	7	1	1	15	11	19	3	2	.349	.391
O'Neill,Paul	31	.261	148	509	64	133	28	1	19	73	66	87	7	5	.346	.432
Obando,Sherman	24	.257	70	202	29	52	7	0	7	27	13	39	1	1	.302	.396
Offerman,Jose	25	.261	155	575	73	150	16	5	2	46	73	98	31	17	.344	.317
Olerud,John	25	.309	154	550	92	170	36	1	24	92	99	77	1	1	.414	.509
Oliver,Joe	28	.245	129	432	36	106	23	0	12	58	29	77	1	1	.293	.382
Olson,Greg	33	.235	60	162	15	38	7	0	2	15	18	16	1	0	.311	.315
Orsulak,Joe	32	.272	118	305	37	83	13	2	4	27	20	25	4	2	.317	.367
Ortiz,Junior	34	.244	74	172	14	42	7	0	1	16	11	17	1	1	.290	.302
Owen,Spike	33	.235	118	362	39	85	16	3	3	25	39	40	5	4	.309	.320

350

Projections for 1994 Batters

Batter	Age	Avg	G	AB	R	H	2B	3B	HR	RBI	BB	SO	SB	CS	OBP	SLG
Pagliarulo,Mike	34	.251	95	243	27	61	12	1	6	25	14	36	2	2	.292	.383
Pagnozzi,Tom	31	.252	116	377	29	95	19	1	4	39	25	46	4	5	.299	.340
Palmeiro,Rafael	29	.286	160	615	106	176	37	3	25	88	75	80	9	4	.364	.478
Palmer,Dean	25	.240	153	550	86	132	27	2	31	89	60	162	9	8	.315	.465
Pappas,Erik	28	.247	82	227	28	56	13	0	5	28	32	39	3	2	.340	.370
Paquette,Craig	25	.234	111	415	46	97	19	2	11	54	19	108	6	6	.267	.369
Pasqua,Dan	32	.236	53	123	17	29	7	1	4	17	18	28	1	1	.333	.407
Peltier,Dan	26	.256	76	238	27	61	12	2	3	25	25	40	2	3	.327	.361
Pena,Geronimo	27	.265	93	249	40	66	16	3	6	30	26	54	15	8	.335	.426
Pena,Tony	37	.238	98	273	25	65	14	1	3	27	20	40	3	2	.290	.330
Pendleton,Terry	33	.269	153	598	76	161	28	2	14	75	38	78	6	2	.313	.393
Perez,Eduardo	24	.250	142	515	59	129	21	3	11	67	30	111	21	12	.292	.367
Perry,Gerald	33	.245	94	102	12	25	4	0	2	13	12	18	4	3	.325	.343
Petralli,Geno	34	.245	57	102	9	25	5	0	1	11	12	15	1	0	.325	.324
Phillips,Tony	35	.261	145	551	102	144	21	2	8	53	105	96	12	8	.380	.350
Piazza,Mike	25	.311	155	550	71	171	26	2	27	94	45	84	3	3	.363	.513
Plantier,Phil	25	.274	152	562	90	154	29	2	32	100	83	135	5	4	.367	.504
Polonia,Luis	29	.288	133	514	75	148	17	6	2	38	45	56	48	22	.345	.356
Pride,Curtis	25	.261	70	153	25	40	5	1	5	18	13	38	10	5	.319	.405
Prince,Tom	29	.192	65	177	16	34	9	0	3	18	18	27	2	2	.267	.294
Puckett,Kirby	33	.301	151	604	86	182	33	4	16	87	40	90	11	6	.345	.449
Pulliam,Harvey	26	.245	82	208	22	51	10	1	4	23	14	38	1	1	.293	.361
Quintana,Carlos	28	.274	76	226	30	62	10	0	4	27	28	34	0	0	.354	.372
Raines,Tim	34	.283	137	516	91	146	24	5	8	51	76	51	37	10	.375	.395
Ramirez,Manny	22	.289	147	515	87	149	35	0	26	94	51	115	1	3	.353	.509
Ready,Randy	34	.241	55	133	19	32	7	1	2	16	24	18	1	1	.357	.353
Reboulet,Jeff	30	.223	113	278	30	62	13	1	2	23	41	41	4	3	.323	.299
Redus,Gary	37	.251	95	231	33	58	14	3	5	23	25	38	10	4	.324	.403
Reed,Jeff	31	.226	51	93	6	21	5	0	1	9	9	15	0	0	.294	.312
Reed,Jody	31	.269	145	543	67	146	34	1	5	46	55	46	5	5	.336	.363
Reimer,Kevin	30	.251	110	351	40	88	21	1	11	47	29	71	2	3	.308	.410
Renteria,Rich	32	.234	106	273	25	64	16	1	2	28	21	31	1	1	.289	.322
Reynolds,Harold	33	.246	142	500	66	123	23	4	3	42	59	50	18	10	.326	.326
Rhodes,Karl	25	.247	96	259	35	64	13	2	8	35	26	50	5	5	.316	.405
Ripken,Cal	33	.271	162	635	82	172	32	2	23	88	61	53	4	3	.335	.436
Rivera,Luis	30	.222	75	203	23	45	11	1	2	19	18	43	2	2	.285	.315
Roberson,Kevin	26	.254	67	228	29	58	11	1	10	30	12	55	2	1	.292	.443
Roberts,Bip	30	.283	137	492	81	139	24	4	4	41	57	67	38	14	.357	.372
Rodriguez,Henry	26	.235	66	200	20	47	9	1	5	23	10	36	1	2	.271	.365
Rodriguez,Ivan	22	.272	140	470	49	128	24	2	9	57	23	68	3	3	.306	.389
Sabo,Chris	32	.258	136	500	71	129	33	2	17	67	40	80	9	5	.313	.434
Salmon,Tim	25	.268	151	548	94	147	31	1	28	92	81	157	8	8	.362	.482
Samuel,Juan	33	.251	104	327	39	82	18	4	6	34	27	74	11	5	.308	.385
Sanchez,Rey	26	.262	112	355	35	93	11	2	1	28	19	21	5	3	.299	.313
Sandberg,Ryne	34	.279	141	535	81	149	26	3	16	68	64	75	14	6	.356	.428
Sanders,Deion	26	.270	112	307	49	83	11	7	8	32	22	48	26	10	.319	.430
Sanders,Reggie	26	.286	139	479	82	137	23	6	17	67	54	106	23	9	.358	.466
Santiago,Benito	29	.255	130	440	45	112	19	2	12	55	26	78	7	7	.296	.389
Sax,Steve	34	.273	78	150	19	41	6	1	1	12	11	10	8	3	.323	.347
Scarsone,Steve	28	.248	66	202	24	50	8	1	4	20	11	45	4	3	.286	.356

Projections for 1994 Batters

Batter	Age	Avg	G	AB	R	H	2B	3B	HR	RBI	BB	SO	SB	CS	OBP	SLG
Schofield,Dick	31	.216	41	97	11	21	4	1	1	8	13	18	2	1	.309	.309
Segui,David	27	.278	148	485	52	135	27	0	7	56	55	52	2	2	.352	.377
Seitzer,Kevin	32	.280	125	415	52	116	22	2	6	55	46	39	9	7	.351	.386
Servais,Scott	27	.241	102	294	23	71	11	0	5	29	20	37	1	1	.290	.330
Shave,Jon	26	.255	88	188	21	48	8	1	1	16	9	26	2	3	.289	.324
Sheaffer,Danny	32	.256	79	242	24	62	11	1	2	26	11	20	2	2	.289	.335
Sheffield,Gary	25	.293	147	535	77	157	29	3	20	80	52	50	13	8	.356	.471
Shipley,Craig	31	.240	80	179	14	43	6	0	2	15	6	25	4	2	.265	.307
Shumpert,Terry	27	.227	94	238	27	54	14	1	3	23	17	43	11	6	.278	.332
Sierra,Ruben	28	.276	148	594	87	164	31	5	22	97	50	80	17	5	.332	.456
Slaught,Don	35	.277	115	375	31	104	22	2	6	48	30	51	2	1	.331	.395
Smith,Dwight	30	.272	133	371	50	101	19	4	8	43	28	66	11	9	.323	.410
Smith,Lonnie	38	.251	107	243	39	61	16	2	5	32	40	55	6	3	.357	.395
Smith,Ozzie	39	.252	130	515	67	130	20	2	1	37	60	31	27	8	.330	.305
Snow,J.T.	26	.271	148	528	78	143	28	2	18	77	66	84	3	2	.352	.434
Snyder,Cory	31	.237	122	384	42	91	21	1	12	48	28	108	3	2	.289	.391
Sorrento,Paul	28	.262	155	550	72	144	29	1	21	79	68	117	2	1	.343	.433
Sosa,Sammy	25	.253	159	586	86	148	22	5	24	77	39	144	35	14	.299	.430
Spiers,Bill	28	.259	87	251	38	65	8	2	3	29	22	36	8	6	.319	.343
Sprague,Ed	26	.262	142	519	58	136	26	2	16	70	45	98	1	1	.321	.412
Stanley,Mike	31	.263	125	419	59	110	17	1	15	64	68	94	1	0	.366	.415
Staton,Dave	26	.246	84	260	29	64	12	0	13	39	20	67	0	0	.300	.442
Steinbach,Terry	32	.267	127	445	47	119	20	1	10	54	33	67	3	3	.318	.384
Stillwell,Kurt	29	.243	75	210	21	51	10	2	2	21	17	33	3	2	.300	.338
Stocker,Kevin	24	.263	140	520	82	137	23	3	4	43	48	81	19	7	.326	.342
Strange,Doug	30	.248	126	412	45	102	21	1	6	39	32	63	5	3	.302	.347
Strawberry,Darryl	32	.250	122	420	65	105	20	2	21	76	61	99	8	5	.345	.457
Surhoff,B.J.	29	.265	155	550	66	146	25	3	6	72	41	43	12	9	.316	.355
Tackett,Jeff	28	.208	42	101	11	21	3	0	1	9	11	16	0	0	.286	.267
Tarasco,Tony	23	.286	81	140	20	40	5	1	4	15	7	21	6	3	.320	.421
Tartabull,Danny	31	.269	136	487	77	131	28	2	26	92	91	135	3	2	.384	.495
Taubensee,Eddie	25	.249	102	313	30	78	15	1	7	35	27	65	1	1	.309	.371
Tettleton,Mickey	33	.237	152	523	78	124	22	1	26	85	114	143	3	5	.374	.432
Teufel,Tim	35	.226	102	230	26	52	13	1	6	28	32	49	4	2	.321	.370
Thomas,Frank	26	.330	157	560	110	185	37	2	35	121	130	82	4	3	.457	.591
Thome,Jim	23	.292	140	521	73	152	29	3	16	80	66	115	4	4	.371	.451
Thompson,Milt	35	.268	110	291	39	78	12	2	4	29	30	52	14	7	.336	.364
Thompson,Robby	32	.265	136	483	67	128	25	3	14	50	52	90	10	7	.336	.416
Thompson,Ryan	26	.246	140	505	65	124	22	4	15	50	36	132	11	10	.296	.394
Thon,Dickie	36	.244	86	246	21	60	10	1	3	25	16	41	6	3	.290	.329
Trammell,Alan	36	.270	94	326	46	88	16	2	7	42	34	33	9	5	.339	.396
Treadway,Jeff	31	.280	104	246	25	69	15	1	3	24	18	21	2	1	.330	.386
Turang,Brian	27	.246	56	183	24	45	9	1	3	17	14	26	6	3	.299	.355
Turner,Chris	25	.244	104	349	45	85	14	0	4	54	44	63	4	2	.328	.318
Valentin,John	27	.257	151	538	60	138	37	1	12	60	64	81	2	2	.336	.396
Valle,Dave	33	.225	133	374	41	84	16	1	9	41	37	57	1	0	.294	.345
Van Slyke,Andy	33	.277	129	484	71	134	22	5	13	67	53	80	10	4	.348	.424
VanderWal,John	28	.244	100	250	33	61	15	2	5	29	31	55	3	1	.327	.380
Vaughn,Greg	28	.243	153	559	89	136	25	3	27	91	77	127	10	9	.335	.444
Vaughn,Mo	26	.275	155	550	71	151	29	1	27	98	82	116	4	3	.369	.478

Projections for 1994 Batters

Batter	Age	Avg	G	AB	R	H	2B	3B	HR	RBI	BB	SO	SB	CS	OBP	SLG
Velarde,Randy	31	.259	110	305	36	79	16	1	6	30	28	59	4	2	.321	.377
Velasquez,Guillermo	26	.262	50	145	14	38	7	0	4	21	10	25	0	0	.310	.393
Ventura,Robin	26	.276	158	588	88	162	28	1	19	91	98	72	3	4	.379	.423
Vizcaino,Jose	26	.264	155	550	58	145	13	3	3	46	38	67	10	6	.311	.315
Vizquel,Omar	27	.253	150	506	53	128	14	3	2	34	45	51	12	10	.314	.304
Voigt,Jack	28	.259	83	259	40	67	12	1	7	30	33	54	4	2	.342	.394
Walker,Chico	35	.241	71	162	17	39	5	0	3	16	15	27	6	2	.305	.327
Walker,Larry	27	.282	145	521	78	147	26	3	21	81	59	95	22	9	.355	.464
Wallach,Tim	36	.234	66	239	23	56	12	1	5	31	20	43	1	1	.293	.356
Ward,Turner	29	.255	41	106	15	27	5	1	2	12	16	14	2	2	.352	.377
Webster,Lenny	29	.237	60	152	17	36	10	0	2	15	12	15	1	1	.293	.342
Webster,Mitch	35	.233	65	103	14	24	7	2	2	12	10	23	2	2	.301	.398
Weiss,Walt	30	.241	130	410	45	99	14	2	2	35	60	54	8	4	.338	.300
Whitaker,Lou	37	.262	126	420	69	110	21	2	11	60	82	48	4	3	.382	.400
White,Devon	31	.253	151	624	98	158	28	5	16	52	54	131	35	8	.313	.391
White,Rondell	22	.307	138	475	79	146	23	6	12	66	27	84	19	7	.345	.457
Whiten,Mark	27	.254	154	551	76	140	18	4	16	70	63	111	14	9	.331	.388
Whitmore,Darrell	25	.261	77	253	31	66	14	2	5	32	13	64	6	5	.297	.391
Wilkins,Rick	27	.258	135	445	54	115	19	1	19	56	48	105	3	2	.331	.434
Williams,Bernie	25	.269	152	579	82	156	30	5	13	67	69	96	16	12	.347	.406
Williams,Matt D.	28	.261	157	567	78	148	25	3	31	90	35	106	5	5	.304	.480
Wilson,Nigel	24	.264	107	239	33	63	15	2	10	31	11	67	4	3	.296	.469
Winfield,Dave	42	.250	123	456	55	114	20	2	14	61	50	89	3	2	.324	.395
Yelding,Eric	29	.242	57	153	14	37	4	1	1	12	9	27	8	5	.284	.301
Young,Eric	27	.264	125	413	57	109	12	3	3	34	42	29	35	15	.332	.329
Young,Kevin	25	.279	135	430	52	120	24	4	6	49	38	64	8	7	.338	.395
Yount,Robin	38	.245	122	444	53	109	22	3	7	57	45	81	8	4	.315	.356
Zeile,Todd	28	.266	151	560	74	149	29	3	14	80	74	86	11	9	.352	.404
Zupcic,Bob	27	.233	129	347	43	81	23	1	5	37	32	57	4	3	.298	.349

These Guys Can Play Too and Might Get A Shot

Batter	Age	Avg	G	AB	R	H	2B	3B	HR	RBI	BB	SO	SB	CS	OBP	SLG
Bowie,Jim	29	.304	138	480	62	146	31	0	11	81	38	57	5	2	.355	.438
Brooks,Jerry	27	.281	116	384	40	108	19	1	6	42	12	46	1	4	.303	.383
Busch,Mike	25	.226	122	399	52	90	22	1	12	41	32	93	0	2	.283	.376
Dodson,Bo	23	.282	101	316	46	89	24	2	7	47	28	73	0	6	.340	.437
Eenhoorn,Robert	26	.252	82	302	38	76	21	1	4	37	14	41	2	4	.285	.368
Franco,Matt	24	.279	130	420	42	117	32	2	8	49	30	63	3	5	.327	.421
Gonzalez,Alex	21	.267	142	544	75	145	27	5	14	55	26	117	27	10	.300	.412
Hall,Billy	25	.243	124	469	64	114	21	4	3	37	25	94	20	7	.281	.324
Masse,Billy	27	.288	117	386	66	111	31	1	15	75	67	70	12	7	.393	.490
McCoy,Trey	27	.262	133	431	62	113	24	2	25	84	47	89	2	2	.335	.501
McDavid,Ray	22	.244	126	426	52	104	15	3	9	44	48	111	22	8	.321	.357
Mouton,James	25	.259	134	505	79	131	33	6	9	57	45	90	26	9	.320	.402
Nevin,Phil	23	.234	123	418	42	98	16	1	5	58	32	109	5	0	.289	.313
Oliva,Jose	23	.218	125	403	54	88	18	4	18	56	30	140	0	5	.273	.417
Petagine,Roberto	23	.302	128	417	59	126	32	1	10	72	57	100	4	4	.386	.456
Timmons,Ozzie	23	.268	107	351	52	94	20	1	17	46	42	85	3	10	.346	.476
Veras,Quilvio	23	.279	128	427	70	119	16	5	1	41	62	67	38	16	.370	.347

Projections for 1994 Pitchers

Pitcher	Age	ERA	W	L	Sv	G	GS	IP	H	HR	BB	SO	BR/9
Abbott,Jim	26	3.93	13	11	0	31	31	213	217	15	73	113	12.3
Aguilera,Rick	32	2.70	6	3	43	65	0	70	56	6	21	58	9.9
Andersen,Larry	41	2.72	4	2	0	54	0	53	44	3	16	56	10.2
Appier,Kevin	26	3.07	15	11	0	33	33	229	200	12	78	172	10.9
Aquino,Luis	29	3.56	3	4	0	30	13	96	97	6	31	45	12.0
Armstrong,Jack	29	4.69	8	14	0	36	30	186	194	24	74	119	13.0
Assenmacher,Paul	33	3.45	5	3	1	71	0	60	55	6	21	61	11.4
Avery,Steve	24	3.17	16	10	0	35	35	227	220	17	44	126	10.5
Ballard,Jeff	30	4.83	2	3	0	25	5	54	65	7	13	16	13.0
Bankhead,Scott	30	4.09	3	4	0	45	0	66	66	7	27	43	12.7
Beck,Rod	25	2.36	7	3	46	72	0	84	67	7	15	79	8.8
Bedrosian,Steve	36	3.42	4	3	0	49	0	50	41	6	19	30	10.8
Belcher,Tim	32	3.52	15	10	0	34	33	215	195	17	76	140	11.3
Belinda,Stan	27	3.09	5	4	2	62	0	70	56	7	26	58	10.5
Benes,Andy	26	3.66	13	14	0	34	34	231	211	21	86	174	11.6
Bielecki,Mike	34	4.32	4	5	0	15	13	73	78	6	24	49	12.6
Black,Bud	37	4.31	6	8	0	20	20	121	120	16	43	57	12.1
Boever,Joe	33	3.60	6	5	4	68	0	105	97	7	48	74	12.4
Bolton,Tom	32	4.60	4	4	0	41	8	94	102	8	43	58	13.9
Bosio,Chris	31	3.71	12	9	0	30	27	187	173	17	67	113	11.6
Brantley,Jeff	30	3.65	5	5	0	54	9	106	92	10	51	86	12.1
Brown,Kevin	29	3.73	15	13	0	34	34	244	246	15	77	154	11.9
Browning,Tom	34	4.20	6	7	0	19	19	105	118	12	18	45	11.7
Burkett,John	29	3.39	14	11	0	33	33	218	220	18	38	130	10.7
Burns,Todd	30	3.95	4	5	0	44	7	98	95	11	37	48	12.1
Cadaret,Greg	32	4.30	3	4	0	47	4	67	65	5	40	49	14.1
Candiotti,Tom	36	3.09	14	10	0	33	31	210	183	12	70	155	10.8
Carpenter,Cris	29	3.08	5	3	0	62	0	76	62	8	24	49	10.2
Castillo,Tony	31	4.41	3	3	0	51	0	51	56	4	20	28	13.4
Charlton,Norm	31	3.00	2	1	9	25	0	30	26	2	10	29	10.8
Clemens,Roger	31	2.96	15	10	0	33	33	210	177	11	73	176	10.7
Cone,David	31	3.42	14	14	0	34	34	253	210	18	113	227	11.5
Cook,Dennis	31	4.25	3	3	0	27	12	89	89	13	28	53	11.8
Cox,Danny	34	3.86	4	3	2	38	0	77	73	8	29	55	11.9
Crim,Chuck	32	4.38	2	2	0	26	0	39	45	4	12	16	13.2
Darling,Ron	33	4.48	10	13	0	32	30	187	190	21	76	95	12.8
Darwin,Danny	38	3.26	14	11	0	33	33	207	188	22	44	135	10.1
Davis,Mark	33	5.34	2	5	2	49	2	64	68	9	43	52	15.6
Davis,Storm	32	4.26	4	4	2	45	6	95	101	8	41	56	13.5
DeLeon,Jose	33	3.51	4	3	0	34	8	77	69	7	32	54	11.8
Deshaies,Jim	34	3.77	9	9	0	26	26	155	147	17	48	72	11.3
Dibble,Rob	30	2.82	4	2	30	51	0	51	37	3	26	74	11.1
Dopson,John	30	4.71	7	12	0	31	27	151	164	17	57	73	13.2
Downs,Kelly	33	4.01	5	5	0	40	15	128	124	10	62	68	13.1
Drabek,Doug	31	3.17	16	12	0	34	34	244	227	17	62	165	10.7
Eckersley,Dennis	39	2.66	6	3	31	66	0	71	63	6	12	84	9.5
Eichhorn,Mark	33	3.00	6	3	0	58	0	78	77	2	19	50	11.1
Erickson,Scott	26	3.92	13	12	0	33	33	216	220	17	70	109	12.1
Farr,Steve	37	3.31	4	2	4	49	0	49	39	5	23	38	11.4
Farrell,John	31	5.92	2	6	0	16	12	73	85	12	35	36	14.8

355

Projections for 1994 Pitchers

Pitcher	Age	ERA	W	L	Sv	G	GS	IP	H	HR	BB	SO	BR/9
Fassero,Jeff	31	2.90	8	5	0	30	30	205	179	6	76	173	11.2
Fernandez,Alex	24	3.69	15	11	0	32	32	227	221	22	62	138	11.2
Fernandez,Sid	31	2.88	12	9	0	28	28	181	138	17	55	148	9.6
Finley,Chuck	31	3.70	13	13	0	34	34	236	223	22	77	161	11.4
Fossas,Tony	36	3.65	3	3	0	67	0	37	34	2	16	25	12.2
Franco,John	33	3.86	2	2	14	34	0	35	36	2	13	26	12.6
Freeman,Marvin	31	3.41	3	2	0	33	0	37	33	3	14	27	11.4
Frey,Steve	30	3.64	3	3	12	54	0	47	42	4	25	24	12.8
Frohwirth,Todd	31	2.88	7	4	1	68	0	100	85	4	38	62	11.1
Gardner,Mark	32	3.87	7	8	0	22	21	121	110	13	48	83	11.8
Gibson,Paul	34	4.50	2	3	0	33	0	50	54	5	21	34	13.5
Glavine,Tom	28	3.56	15	12	0	35	35	235	220	14	88	126	11.8
Gooden,Dwight	29	3.33	12	12	0	30	30	208	198	12	61	147	11.2
Gordon,Tom	26	3.78	6	7	0	28	28	193	173	16	98	183	12.6
Gossage,Goose	42	4.30	2	3	0	36	0	44	42	6	23	34	13.3
Gott,Jim	34	3.11	5	4	6	64	0	81	71	5	30	72	11.2
Grant,Mark	30	4.70	1	3	0	21	3	44	54	4	14	23	13.9
Greene,Tommy	27	3.39	12	10	0	28	28	186	170	16	58	145	11.0
Gross,Kevin	33	3.99	10	13	0	33	31	203	207	13	74	154	12.5
Gubicza,Mark	31	4.21	3	5	0	39	10	107	122	6	37	76	13.4
Guetterman,Lee	35	4.25	3	4	0	46	0	53	59	4	18	19	13.1
Gullickson,Bill	35	4.65	9	12	0	30	30	180	199	25	50	63	12.4
Guthrie,Mark	28	4.15	2	2	0	33	0	39	40	3	16	33	12.9
Guzman,Jose	31	4.01	10	13	0	31	31	202	197	18	78	166	12.3
Guzman,Juan	27	3.42	15	9	0	31	31	208	171	11	103	186	11.9
Habyan,John	30	3.34	4	3	2	51	0	62	62	4	17	43	11.5
Hanson,Erik	29	3.67	13	10	0	31	30	206	205	16	57	141	11.4
Harnisch,Pete	27	3.32	14	11	0	33	33	214	183	18	78	176	11.0
Harris,Greg	38	3.24	7	5	2	77	1	111	89	7	61	89	12.2
Harris,Greg W.	30	4.31	7	15	0	30	30	190	202	22	63	104	12.6
Hartley,Mike	32	3.75	4	4	0	51	0	72	66	7	35	57	12.6
Harvey,Bryan	31	1.93	5	2	44	48	0	56	38	4	13	66	8.2
Heaton,Neal	34	4.22	2	2	0	23	0	32	33	4	13	19	12.9
Henke,Tom	36	2.51	6	2	40	63	0	68	48	6	23	67	9.4
Henneman,Mike	32	3.41	5	3	25	62	0	74	71	4	27	56	11.9
Henry,Doug	30	3.72	4	4	9	59	0	58	55	5	23	44	12.1
Henry,Dwayne	32	3.76	4	3	0	43	1	67	57	5	39	51	12.9
Hernandez,Xavier	28	3.12	6	5	21	74	0	101	86	8	38	94	11.0
Hershiser,Orel	35	3.62	12	13	0	33	33	214	208	14	71	136	11.7
Hesketh,Joe	35	4.24	3	4	0	29	12	85	88	9	34	58	12.9
Hibbard,Greg	29	3.77	10	12	0	31	30	186	191	17	46	77	11.5
Higuera,Teddy	35	5.66	3	7	0	13	13	89	107	8	47	80	15.6
Hill,Ken	28	3.37	13	10	0	30	30	195	170	12	79	117	11.5
Hillegas,Shawn	29	5.27	2	3	0	16	5	41	43	5	22	22	14.3
Holmes,Darren	28	3.97	2	5	25	55	0	59	62	4	20	47	12.5
Honeycutt,Rick	40	3.07	4	2	2	53	0	41	36	2	15	27	11.2
Hough,Charlie	46	3.88	10	13	0	32	32	195	185	20	68	103	11.7
Howe,Steve	36	2.63	4	1	0	41	0	41	36	3	7	22	9.4
Howell,Jay	38	2.67	4	2	0	50	0	54	46	3	18	38	10.7
Hurst,Bruce	36	4.24	5	9	0	20	20	123	119	11	57	75	12.9

356

Projections for 1994 Pitchers

Pitcher	Age	ERA	W	L	Sv	G	GS	IP	H	HR	BB	SO	BR/9
Innis,Jeff	31	3.26	5	5	0	70	0	80	73	4	31	39	11.7
Jackson,Danny	32	4.17	11	14	0	33	33	207	219	13	79	109	13.0
Jackson,Mike	29	2.96	6	4	0	76	0	79	64	7	29	71	10.6
Johnson,Randy	30	2.93	18	9	0	34	33	240	180	21	93	283	10.2
Jones,Doug	37	3.73	5	5	13	74	0	94	94	6	18	76	10.7
Jones,Jimmy	30	4.19	2	3	0	16	12	73	79	7	23	41	12.6
Key,Jimmy	33	3.40	16	10	0	34	34	230	225	23	42	147	10.4
Klink,Joe	32	3.32	3	3	0	59	0	38	35	1	17	21	12.3
Krueger,Bill	36	4.18	4	4	0	33	14	114	124	10	37	66	12.7
Lancaster,Les	32	4.24	3	4	0	47	0	70	72	7	28	40	12.9
Langston,Mark	33	3.28	15	12	0	34	34	247	215	20	82	188	10.8
Leach,Terry	40	2.06	3	1	0	26	0	35	28	1	9	10	9.5
Leary,Tim	35	4.84	8	11	0	31	26	160	179	20	55	59	13.2
Lefferts,Craig	36	4.31	4	5	0	45	16	121	135	14	29	73	12.2
Leibrandt,Charlie	37	3.93	10	10	0	28	28	165	173	12	49	93	12.1
Lilliquist,Derek	28	3.86	4	4	0	61	1	63	64	7	19	42	11.9
Maddux,Greg	28	2.53	21	9	0	36	36	267	233	13	52	198	9.6
Maddux,Mike	32	2.81	5	3	4	55	0	77	67	3	24	53	10.6
Magrane,Joe	29	4.10	8	10	0	27	25	145	150	11	51	61	12.5
Martinez,Dennis	39	3.24	15	11	0	34	33	225	206	19	69	142	11.0
Martinez,Ramon	26	3.91	10	12	0	30	30	191	170	15	94	120	12.4
Mason,Roger	35	3.38	4	3	0	51	0	72	63	8	24	49	10.9
McCaskill,Kirk	33	4.00	4	4	7	52	1	72	74	5	28	35	12.8
McDonald,Ben	26	3.75	14	12	0	34	34	223	197	24	87	164	11.5
McDowell,Jack	28	3.35	18	11	0	34	34	258	240	21	69	168	10.8
McDowell,Roger	33	4.19	3	5	0	58	0	73	80	2	35	37	14.2
McElroy,Chuck	26	3.81	3	4	0	57	0	59	53	4	34	53	13.3
Mercker,Kent	26	3.09	4	3	0	46	4	67	53	4	34	55	11.7
Mesa,Jose	28	4.24	11	12	0	32	31	193	210	17	57	94	12.5
Milacki,Bob	29	4.22	2	2	0	11	8	49	52	6	17	26	12.7
Monteleone,Rich	31	3.78	5	4	0	44	0	88	82	10	32	57	11.7
Montgomery,Jeff	32	2.62	6	3	43	68	0	86	70	5	26	70	10.0
Moore,Mike	34	4.23	13	13	0	36	36	217	214	20	90	102	12.6
Morgan,Mike	34	3.47	13	12	0	33	33	218	201	15	78	114	11.5
Morris,Jack	39	4.50	10	11	0	29	29	182	190	17	77	109	13.2
Moyer,Jamie	31	3.91	9	9	0	25	25	152	163	12	38	90	11.9
Mulholland,Terry	31	3.26	13	10	0	30	29	204	197	16	43	117	10.6
Murphy,Rob	34	4.65	3	5	0	68	0	62	71	7	22	43	13.5
Myers,Randy	31	3.51	5	4	49	71	0	77	67	6	38	70	12.3
Nabholz,Chris	27	3.71	9	9	0	28	25	143	121	8	77	93	12.5
Nagy,Charles	27	3.88	12	10	0	28	28	197	211	14	53	130	12.1
Navarro,Jaime	26	4.12	12	14	0	35	34	225	238	17	77	105	12.6
Nelson,Gene	33	4.34	3	3	4	44	1	58	59	6	25	29	13.0
Nunez,Edwin	31	3.99	4	4	0	54	0	70	71	5	28	57	12.7
Ojeda,Bobby	36	4.33	10	11	0	30	30	181	181	13	88	105	13.4
Olivares,Omar	26	3.72	6	6	0	49	16	145	140	12	53	83	12.0
Olson,Gregg	27	2.70	5	2	33	59	0	60	50	2	24	58	11.1
Orosco,Jesse	37	2.82	4	2	9	58	0	51	43	4	16	57	10.4
Osuna,Al	28	3.41	3	3	0	51	0	37	29	4	22	28	12.4
Pall,Donn	32	3.36	4	3	0	44	0	75	71	7	21	37	11.0

Projections for 1994 Pitchers

Pitcher	Age	ERA	W	L	Sv	G	GS	IP	H	HR	BB	SO	BR/9
Parrett,Jeff	32	4.39	3	5	0	49	4	82	84	7	42	67	13.8
Patterson,Bob	35	3.95	4	3	0	55	0	57	57	7	15	45	11.4
Patterson,Ken	29	4.08	3	3	0	41	0	53	46	6	31	29	13.1
Perez,Melido	28	3.72	13	9	0	28	28	191	173	17	75	170	11.7
Perez,Mike	29	2.73	6	3	26	69	0	79	67	4	26	48	10.6
Plesac,Dan	32	3.97	3	4	0	53	1	68	67	7	28	47	12.6
Plunk,Eric	30	4.18	4	4	10	66	0	71	67	7	36	64	13.1
Portugal,Mark	31	3.66	10	10	0	28	27	172	159	15	64	108	11.7
Powell,Dennis	30	4.41	3	3	0	38	1	51	54	4	26	33	14.1
Power,Ted	39	3.71	4	3	22	51	0	63	63	4	23	34	12.3
Radinsky,Scott	26	3.21	5	3	5	71	0	56	51	3	23	43	11.9
Rasmussen,Dennis	35	3.97	1	1	0	9	5	34	35	3	11	15	12.2
Reardon,Jeff	38	3.75	4	4	4	59	0	60	67	5	10	37	11.6
Righetti,Dave	35	4.19	3	4	0	52	1	58	59	6	24	38	12.9
Rijo,Jose	29	2.57	19	8	0	35	35	242	200	14	58	206	9.6
Rodriguez,Rich	31	3.56	4	5	3	67	0	81	74	7	35	48	12.1
Rogers,Kenny	29	4.07	10	11	0	26	26	190	194	17	65	139	12.3
Rojas,Mel	27	2.74	7	3	3	67	0	92	75	6	30	60	10.3
Ruffin,Bruce	30	4.58	3	6	0	48	10	112	124	9	52	91	14.1
Russell,Jeff	32	3.06	4	3	41	54	0	53	46	4	18	40	10.9
Saberhagen,Bret	30	3.09	12	11	0	29	29	204	204	14	28	150	10.2
Sampen,Bill	31	4.28	2	3	0	29	1	40	42	4	18	20	13.5
Sanderson,Scott	37	4.46	6	8	0	22	20	121	135	18	22	66	11.7
Scanlan,Bob	27	3.65	4	5	0	70	0	79	78	4	28	38	12.1
Schilling,Curt	27	2.87	17	10	0	34	34	232	205	15	56	167	10.1
Schooler,Mike	31	3.82	2	2	0	29	0	33	32	3	13	24	12.3
Smiley,John	29	3.63	14	12	0	32	32	223	215	20	65	143	11.3
Smith,Lee	36	3.23	5	3	39	65	0	64	57	6	16	58	10.3
Smith,Pete	28	4.14	5	5	0	17	13	87	82	10	34	49	12.0
Smith,Zane	33	3.53	6	6	0	17	17	102	102	7	27	40	11.4
Smoltz,John	27	3.53	15	12	0	35	35	245	212	20	100	211	11.5
Stanton,Mike	27	3.54	4	3	4	64	0	56	52	5	20	41	11.6
Stewart,Dave	37	4.19	11	10	0	28	28	174	155	23	78	109	12.1
Stottlemyre,Todd	29	4.24	11	10	0	29	28	176	179	16	69	98	12.7
Sutcliffe,Rick	38	5.23	5	9	0	25	15	136	156	14	61	64	14.4
Swan,Russ	30	4.13	2	2	0	34	3	48	49	4	22	21	13.3
Swift,Bill	32	2.79	16	8	0	33	30	210	187	11	50	124	10.2
Swindell,Greg	29	3.91	11	12	0	31	30	198	211	20	42	128	11.5
Tanana,Frank	40	4.25	12	11	0	32	32	197	205	25	54	105	11.8
Tapani,Kevin	30	3.70	14	12	0	35	35	224	226	19	57	145	11.4
Tewksbury,Bob	33	3.35	13	12	0	32	32	220	239	14	21	93	10.6
Thigpen,Bobby	30	4.17	3	3	0	46	0	54	52	5	28	37	13.3
Tomlin,Randy	28	3.40	8	8	0	24	23	135	140	9	22	59	10.8
Valenzuela,Fernando	33	4.78	9	13	0	32	31	179	191	18	79	78	13.6
Viola,Frank	34	3.92	11	12	0	31	31	202	197	15	79	101	12.3
Walk,Bob	37	4.59	7	12	0	33	29	153	164	16	57	67	13.0
Ward,Duane	30	2.41	7	2	47	74	0	82	62	4	28	97	9.9
Wayne,Gary	31	4.03	3	4	0	57	0	58	58	6	23	40	12.6
Wegman,Bill	31	3.86	9	10	0	25	24	168	166	17	47	78	11.4
Welch,Bob	37	4.80	7	11	0	27	25	152	169	20	51	58	13.0

Projections for 1994 Pitchers

Pitcher	Age	ERA	W	L	Sv	G	GS	IP	H	HR	BB	SO	BR/9
Wells,David	31	3.65	11	8	0	35	25	165	160	19	37	108	10.7
West,David	29	4.26	4	5	5	62	0	76	69	10	40	65	12.9
Wetteland,John	27	2.75	6	3	52	69	0	85	66	6	32	106	10.4
Williams,Mitch	29	3.71	4	4	38	65	0	68	55	3	50	64	13.9
Williamson,Mark	34	3.88	3	3	0	36	1	65	65	5	24	39	12.3
Willis,Carl	33	2.63	5	2	2	55	0	65	59	3	13	41	10.0
Wilson,Steve	29	4.38	2	3	0	37	0	39	40	4	18	32	13.4
Wilson,Trevor	28	3.60	8	7	0	23	21	125	113	11	45	68	11.4
Witt,Bobby	30	3.84	13	12	0	34	32	211	201	14	87	131	12.3
Witt,Mike	33	4.61	3	3	0	9	9	41	38	4	22	30	13.2
Worrell,Todd	34	3.45	3	3	24	46	0	47	42	5	17	44	11.3
Young,Curt	34	4.78	1	2	0	10	4	32	34	4	13	9	13.2

About STATS, Inc.

READ THIS. REALLY. It's new this year. Those of you who've been buying our books faithfully for more than one season know that this little description of our company never changes. At least you think it never changes. Anyway, since that first About STATS, Inc. was written four years ago, unlike the article, the company has changed quite a bit.

Back then, we were the hotshot new kids on the baseball block, with three reporters tracking all kinds of interesting, new data on every major league game. That data took us a long way. We found that baseball fans were very interested in that data. We worked with major league teams. We worked with the media. (We revolutionized the boxscore business, both in timeliness and accuracy. Everything from boxscores to same day pitching matchup details to feature articles led to interaction with television, newspaper, and magazine accounts.) We worked with the individual baseball fan. (Our Major League Handbook allowed fans to begin reviewing the past season in November, and not have to wait for the Spring. Our Bill James Fantasy Baseball game became undoubtedly the most realistic, intense fantasy baseball game available. Our STATS On-Line allowed baseball fanatics not only access to boxscores, but In-Progress boxscores, half-inning by half- inning. Our year-end reports on·disk let fans do their own number crunching, without the hassle of data entry.)

But it's time to move on to new horizons. Let's face it, knowing that Bryan Harvey rarely blows a save and that Mile High Stadium outrageously favors hitters isn't exactly ground-breaking information anymore.

Where do we go from here? Well, in case you haven't noticed there are three other major professional sports out there which could use a bit of revolutionary data analysis. For example, what gets Steve Young most of his passing yards, his arm or his receivers' legs? I bet you'd have a guess, but do you really know? Or how about the NBA? All the games are basically decided in the last two minutes, right? But what makes you so sure? Perhaps the last three games you watched on TV? We're well into the answers already. Although a couple years worth of data may not be definitive, it makes for good hypotheses and two years turns into five years in three years (revolutionary!). In fact, you can phone us or walk over to your nearest bookstore and purchase a new product we're extremely proud of: the *STATS*

Basketball Scoreboard 1993-1994, our first non-baseball book. You'll find the answer above in there (a first quarter lead has held up 57 percent of the time over the last two seasons) and the customary "many, many more." In football there's no book yet, but we have football data on STATS On-Line, which, for computer users, is far better, since the data is always current. If you're not an On-Line customer already, you have twice as many reasons to sign up now. As for hockey, we'll be gathering data for the first time this year, so by next Handbook, we'll be able to tell you about hockey also.

Do we need help collecting all this data? You bet we do. For baseball, although we're fairly stocked in some cities at this point, we're always looking for new reporters. For football, we have numerous openings. We have no reporter network yet in basketball or hockey, but things could change in the near future. You won't be able to quit your job reporting for STATS, but you'll have some fun and learn lots about the sports you love.

For more information write to:

STATS, Inc.
7366 North Lincoln Ave.
Lincolnwood, IL 60646-1708

. . .or call us at 1-708-676-3322. We can send you a STATS brochure, a free information kit on Bill James Fantasy Baseball, the BJFB Winter Game, STATS Fantasy Football, or info on our brand new game, STATS Fantasy Hoops.

And, by the way, we haven't forgotten baseball (as if you thought we ever could). You'll definitely want a copy of our brand new *Batter versus Pitcher MATCH-UPS!* book which will give you the scoop on how every active pitcher has done against every active batter. The perfect ballpark or TV companion, it will be pocket-sized (another STATS first) and will be out in February.

Turn to the last pages in this book to find a handy order form and additional information about the fine products from STATS.

Glossary

% Inherited Scored

A Relief Pitching statistic indicating the percentage of runners on base at the time a relief pitcher enters a game that he allows to score.

1st Batter OBP

The On-Base Percentage allowed by a relief pitcher to the first batter he faces in a game.

Active Career Batting Leaders

Minimum of 1,000 At Bats required for Batting Average, On-Base Percentage, Slugging Percentage, At Bats Per HR, At Bats Per GDP, At Bats Per RBI, and K/BB Ratio. One hundred (100) Stolen Base Attempts required for Stolen Base Success %. Any player who appeared in 1993 is eligible for inclusion provided he meets the category's minimum requirements.

Active Career Pitching Leaders

Minimum of 750 Innings Pitched required for Earned Run Average, Opponent Batting Average, all of the "Per 9 Innings" categories, and Strikeout to Walk Ratio. Two hundred fifty (250) Games Started required for Complete Game Frequency. One hundred (100) decisions required for Win-Loss Percentage. Any player who appeared in 1993 is eligible for inclusion provided he meets the category's minimum requirements.

BA ScPos Allowed

Batting Average Allowed with Runners in Scoring Position.

Batting Average

Hits divided by At Bats.

Catcher's ERA

The Earned Run Average of a catcher. To figure this for a catcher, multiply the Earned Runs Allowed by the pitchers while he was catching times nine and divide that by his number of Innings Caught.

Cheap Wins/Tough Losses/Top Game Scores

First determine the starting pitcher's Game Score as follows: (1)Start with 50. (2)Add 1 point for each out recorded by the starting pitcher. (3)Add 2 points for each inning the pitcher completes after the fourth inning. (4)Add 1 point for each strikeout. (5)Subtract 2 points for each hit allowed. (6)Subtract 4 points for each earned run allowed. (7)Subtract 2 points for an unearned run. (8)Subtract 1 point for each walk.

If the starting pitcher scores over 50 and loses, it's a Tough Loss. If he wins with a game score under 50, it's a Cheap Win. The top Game Scores of 1993 are listed.

Cleanup Slugging%

The Slugging Percentage of a player when batting fourth in the batting order.

Complete Game Frequency

Complete Games divided by Games Started.

Earned Run Average

(Earned Runs times 9) divided by Innings Pitched.

Fielding Percentage

(Putouts plus Assists) divided by (Putouts plus Assists plus Errors).

Hold

A Hold is credited anytime a relief pitcher enters a game in a Save Situation (see definition below), records at least one out, and leaves the game never having relinquished the lead. Note: a pitcher cannot finish the game and receive credit for a Hold, nor can he earn a hold and a save.

Isolated Power

Slugging Percentage minus Batting Average.

K/BB Ratio

Strikeouts divided by Walks.

Late & Close

A Late & Close situation meets the following requirements: (1)the game is in the seventh inning or later, and (2)the batting team is either leading by one run, tied, or has the potential tying run on base, at bat, or on deck. Note: this situation is very similar to the characteristics of a Save Situation.

Leadoff On Base%

The On-Base Percentage of a player when batting first in the batting order.

Offensive Winning Percentage

The Winning Percentage a team of nine John Oleruds (or anybody) would compile against average pitching and defense. The formula: (Runs Created per 27 outs) divided by the League average of runs scored per game. Square the result and divide it by (1+itself).

On Base Percentage

(Hits plus Walks plus Hit by Pitcher) divided by (At Bats plus Walks plus Hit by Pitcher plus Sacrifice Flies).

Opponent Batting Average

Hits Allowed divided by (Batters Faced minus Walks minus Hit Batsmen minus Sacrifice Hits minus Sacrifice Flies minus Catcher's Interference).

PA*

The divisor for On Base Percentage: At Bats plus Walks plus Hit By Pitcher plus Sacrifice Flies; or Plate Appearances minus Sacrifice Hits and Times Reached Base on Defensive Interference.

PCS (Pitchers' Caught Stealing)

The number of runners officially counted as Caught Stealing where the initiator of the fielding play was the pitcher, not the catcher. Note: such plays are often referred to as "pickoffs", but appear in official records as Caught Stealings. The most common "pitcher caught stealing scenario" is a 1-3-6 fielding play, where the runner is officially charged a Caught Stealing because he broke for second base. "Pickoff" (fielding play 1-3 being the most common) is not an official statistical category.

PkOf Throw/Runner

The number of pickoff throws made by a pitcher divided by the number of runners on first base.

Plate Appearances

At Bats plus Total Walks plus Hit By Pitcher plus Sacrifice Hits plus Sacrifice Flies plus Times Reached on Defensive Interference.

Power/Speed Number

A way to look at power and speed in one number. A player must score high in both areas to earn a high Power/Speed Number. The formula: (HR x SB x 2) divided by (HR + SB).

Quick Hooks and Slow Hooks

A Quick Hook is the removal of a pitcher who has pitched less than 6 innings and given up 3 runs or less. A Slow Hook goes to a pitcher who pitches more than 9 innings, or allows 7 or more runs, or whose combined innings pitched and runs allowed totals 13 or more.

Range Factor

The number of Chances (Putouts plus Assists) times nine divided by the number of Defensive Innings Played. The average for a Regular Player at each position in 1993:

Second Base: 5.14   Left Field: 2.14
Third Base: 2.68   Center Field: 2.78
Shortstop: 4.68   Right Field: 2.23

Run Support Per 9 IP

The number of runs scored by a pitcher's team while he was still in the game times nine divided by his Innings Pitched.

Runs Created

A way to combine a batter's total offensive contributions into one number. The formula: (H + BB + HBP - CS - GIDP) times (Total Bases + .26(TBB - IBB + HBP) + .52(SH + SF + SB)) divided by (AB + TBB + HBP + SH + SF).

Save Percentage

Saves (SV) divided by Save Opportunities (OP).

Save Situation

A Relief Pitcher is in a Save Situation when:

upon entering the game with his club leading, he has the opportunity to be the finishing pitcher (and is not the winning pitcher of record at the time), and meets any one of the three following conditions:

(1) he has a lead of no more than three runs and has the opportunity to pitch for at least one inning, or

(2) he enters the game, regardless of the count, with the potential tying run either on base, at bat, or on deck; or

(3) he pitches three or more innings regardless of the lead and the official scorer credits him with a save..

SB Success%

Stolen Bases divided by (Stolen Bases plus Caught Stealing).

Secondary Average

A way to look at a player's extra bases gained, independent of Batting Average. The formula: (Total Bases - Hits + TBB + SB) divided by At Bats.

Slugging Percentage

Total Bases divided by At Bats.

Total Bases

Hits plus Doubles plus (2 times Triples) plus (3 times Homeruns).

Win-Loss Percentage or Winning Percentage

Wins divided by (Wins plus Losses).

Bill James and STATS, Inc.
Present a Star-Studded Line-up
Six Essential Books Perfect for Any Baseball Fan!

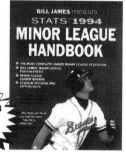

Complete 1993 Statistics in Each Book

Available November 1st

- Best Seller–the earliest and most complete stats
- Exclusive **Bill James** 1994 projections
- **Career** data for every active major leaguer
- Exclusive 1994 pitcher projections
- **Lefty/Righty** stats for every hitter and pitcher
- Available Nov 1, 1993

- **All minor leaguers**, AAA through rookie leagues
- Careeer stats for AAA and AA minor leaguers
- **Bill James'** exclusive **major league equivalencies**
- Team batting and pitching
- First time in print–**AAA lefty/righty data**
- Available Nov 1, 1993

- The most complete player breakdowns ever printed, over 27 in all, includes:
- Against lefty/righty pitchers
- Ahead/behind in the count
- Month by month breakdown
- NEW for 1994 – Team and League Profiles!
- Includes 1993 and last 5 years
- Available Nov 1, 1993

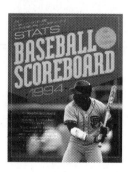

NEW!

- The unique STATS analysis used by teams, networks and now YOU!
- Find out the answers to questions like:
  "Why play for one run?"
  "Who are baseballs tablesetters?"
  "What makes for an efficient defense?"
- Available Mar 15, 1994

- Includes all 1993 Major Leaguers
- Complete stats for batters vs. pitchers
- Most and least dominating match-ups
- Available Feb 1, 1994

- The most in-depth, easy-to-use, professional quality scouting reports ever made available to the public.
- Complete scouting reports on over 700 players
- Essential information on each teams hottest prospects
- Available Feb 1, 1994

To Order, Fill Out the Order Form in This Book
Or Call 1-800-63-STATS.

Bill James FANTASY BASEBALL

If You Like Fantasy Baseball, You'll Love Bill James Fantasy Baseball...

"Hi, This is Bill James. A few years ago I designed a set of rules for a new fantasy baseball league, which has been updated with the benefit of experience and the input of a few thousand owners.

The idea of a fantasy league, of course, is that it forges a link between you and your ballplayers; YOU win or lose based on how the players that you picked have performed. My goal was to develop a fantasy league based on the simplest and yet most realistic principles possible — a league in which the values are as nearly as possible what they ought to be, without being distorted by artificial category values or rankings, but which at the same time are so simple that you can keep track of how you've done just by checking the boxscores. There are a lot of different rules around for fantasy leagues, but none of them before this provided exactly what I was looking for. Here's what we want:

1) We want it to be realistic. We don't want the rules to make Randy Johnson the MVP just because of his strikeouts. We don't want Chuck Carr to be worth more than Fred McGriff because he steals lots of bases. We want good ballplayers to be good ballplayers.

2) We prefer it simple. We want you to be able to look up your players in the morning paper, and know how you've done.

3) We want you to have to develop a real team. We don't want somebody to win by stacking up starting pitchers and leadoff men. We don't want somebody to corner the market on home run hitters.

I made up the rules and I'll be playing the game with you. STATS, Inc. is running the leagues. They'll run the draft, man the computers, keep the rosters straight and provide you with weekly updates. Of course you can make trades, pick up free agents and move players on and off the inactive list; that not my department, but there are rules for that, too. It all starts with a draft . . ."

- Draft Your Own Team and Play vs. Other Owners! Play by Mail or With a Computer On-Line!

- Manage Your Roster All Season With Daily Transactions! Live Fantasy Phone Lines Every Day of the Baseball Season!

- Realistic Team and Individual Player Totals That Even Take Fielding Into Account!

- The Best Weekly Reports in the Business!

- Play Against Bill James' Own Drafted Teams!

- Get Discounted Prices by Forming Your Own Private League of 11 or 12 owners! (Call or write for more information)

- Money-Back Guarantee! Play one month, and if not satisfied, we'll return your franchise fee!

All This, All Summer Long — For Less Than An Average of $5 per week.

Reserve your BJFB team now! Sign up with the STATS Order Form in this book, or send for additional Free Information.

Bill James Fantasy Baseball: The Winter Game

Are you out in the cold about how to manage a ballclub while snowflakes cover the playing field? Using players from all eras of Major League Baseball, Bill James Fantasy Baseball: *The Winter Game* allows you to manage a team in an entirely new way.

"With Bill James Fantasy Baseball there is no off-season!"

The Winter Game is not about numbers, but abilities. Babe Ruth may or may not hit 60 home runs, but he will hit for terrific average and power and walk like crazy, and if you need him to pitch, he can do it, though it will cut into his hitting. And Ed Walsh will be durable, can start or relieve, and will strike out many hitters without too many walks.

To determine players' abilities in the most accurate manner, Bill James got together with John Dewan and Dick Cramer of STATS, Inc., and Tom Tippett, one of the nation's top computer game designers. These men and many others brought vast knowledge of historical players to the discussion.

In The Winter Game you'll compete against 11 other owners in a head-to-head format covering a 154-game season. You set your lineups (versus right- and left-handed pitchers), set your pitching rotation (and relievers), decide how often to hit-and-run, bunt, steal, etc.

LEAGUES START YEAR-ROUND — BEGINNING 11/1/93!

STATS On-Line

STATS On-Line is your link to the most accurate, up-to-the-minute baseball information available anywhere! The STATS database covers everything you'd ever want to know about the national pasttime and other sports! All you need is a computer and a modem. STATS will provide the rest!

ALL NEW — STATS On-Line now provides in-depth football data!

STATS On-Line allows you to share in the same information that STATS provides for such clients as ESPN, the Associated Press and USA Today, and many Major League teams.

IN-PROGRESS BOXSCORES

Watch each game as it happens around the country — LIVE — updated each half inning. You'll get a full baseball boxscore seconds after completion of each half inning.

FANTASY GAMES

You can play any of STATS' fantasy games on-line including **Bill James Fantasy Baseball, Bill James Fantasy Baseball: The Winter Game, STATS Fantasy Football** and **STATS Fantasy Hoops.**

BASEBALL LIVE

Baseball Live allows you to track the players you want to know about. You set up your teams (as many as you want) through STATS On-Line. Then you can see at a glance how all your players are performing — LIVE!

To order STATS On-Line or to reserve a Winter Game team, fill out the enclosed order form in this book or call 1-800-63-STATS.

Product (Date Available)	Quantity	Your Price	Total
Bill James/STATS 1994 Major League Handbook (11/1/93)		$17.95	
Player Projections Update (3/1/94)		9.95	
Bill James/STATS 1994 Minor League Handbook (11/1/93)		17.95	
STATS 1994 Player Profiles (11/1/93)		17.95	
Bill James/STATS 1994 BVSP Match-Ups! (2/1/94)		6.99	
STATS 1994 Baseball Scoreboard (3/1/94)		15.00	
The Scouting Report: 1994 (3/1/94)		16.00	
STATS Basketball Scoreboard 1993-1994 (10/1/93)		15.00	
Discounts on previous editions while supplies last:			
Major League Handbook 1990 (#) 1991 (#) 1992 (#) 1993 (#)		9.95	
Minor League Handbook 1992 (#) 1993 (#)		9.95	
Player Profiles 1993		9.95	
Baseball Scoreboard 1991 (#) 1992 (#) 1993 (#)		9.95	
The Scouting Report 1992 (#) 1993 (#)		9.95	
U.S.—For first class mailing—add $2.50 per book		2.50	
Canada—all orders—add $3.50 per book		3.50	
Order 2 or more books—subtract $1 per book		−1.00	
SUBTOTAL			
Illinois Residents Include 7.75% Sales Tax			
TOTAL			

☐ Yes, I can't wait! Sign me up to play **Bill James Fantasy Baseball** in 1994. Enclosed is my deposit of $25.00 on the franchise fee of $89.00. A processing fee of $1.00 per player is charged during the season for roster moves.

☐ Yes, I can't wait! Sign me up to play **BJFB: The Winter Game** in 1994. Enclosed is my deposit of $50.00 on the franchise fee of $129.00. A processing fee between 50 cents to $1.00 per player is charged during the season for roster moves and changes to manager profiles.

Team Nickname:_____ _____ (example: San Francisco Crab)

Would you like to play in a league with a team drafted by Bill James? Yes No (circle one)
Would you like to receive information on playing fantasy games on-line by computer? Yes No (circle one)

Please Rush Me These Free Informational Brochures: ☐ Pro-Line Brochure
☐ **Bill James Fantasy Baseball Info Kit**   ☐ **STATS Fantasy Hoops Info Kit (NEW!)**
☐ **STATS Fantasy Football Info Kit**   ☐ **BJFB: The Wnter Game Info Kit**
☐ **STATS Baseball Reporter Brochure**   ☐ **STATSfax Brochure (sent via fax)**
☐ **STATS Football Reporter Brochure**   ☐ **STATS On-Line Brochure**
☐ **STATS Product Guide (Including Year-End-Reports information)**

Return this form (don't tear your book; copy this page) to:

STATS, Inc.
7366 N. Lincoln Ave.
Lincolnwood, IL
60646-1708

Please Print:

Name_____   Phone_____

Address_____   Fax_____

City_____State_____   Zip_____

Method of Payment (U.S. Funds only):   **Credit Card Information:**

☐ Check (no Canadian checks)   Cardholder Name_____

☐ Money Order   Visa/MasterCard No._____

☐ Visa   Exp. Date_____

☐ MasterCard   Signature_____

For faster credit card service: call 1-800-63-STATS (1-800-637-8287) to place your order,
or fax this form to 1-708-676-0821.

HB94